Fundamentals of Business Law

Fundamentals

PRENTICE-HALL, INC.
Englewood Cliffs, New Jersey 07632

# of Business Law

THIRD EDITION

ROBERT N. CORLEY
Distinguished Professor of Legal Studies
The University of Georgia

ERIC M. HOLMES
Professor of Law
The University of Georgia

WILLIAM J. ROBERT
Professor of Business Law
University of Oregon

Library of Congress Cataloging in Publication Data

Corley, Robert Neil.
Fundamentals of business law.

"A Special projects book."
Includes index.
1. Commercial law—United States. I. Holmes, Eric M.
II. Robert, William J. III. Title.
KF889.C64 1982 346.73′07 81-5951
ISBN 0-13-332189-4 347.3067 AACR2

10 9 8 7 6 5 4 3 2

This is a Special Projects book,
designed, edited, and supervised by
Maurine Lewis, *director*
Doug Thompson, *acquisitions editor*
Ray Keating, *manufacturing buyer*
Don Martinetti, *cover designer*

Prentice-Hall International, Inc., *London*
Prentice-Hall of Australia Pty. Limited, *Sydney*
Prentice-Hall of Canada, Ltd., *Toronto*
Prentice-Hall of India Private Limited, *New Delhi*
Prentice-Hall of Japan, Inc., *Tokyo*
Prentice-Hall of Southeast Asia Pte. Ltd., *Singapore*
Whitehall Books Limited, Wellington, *New Zealand*

Preface

Most students in business law are not headed for careers in law but, rather, careers that require a knowledge of fundamental principles of law. To these students, at every level of higher education, *Fundamentals of Business Law* is directed.

In the 1980s, a business law course must be concerned with traditional legal topics and with the legal environment in which business is conducted. It must include not only the legal principles of contracts and the Uniform Commercial Code, but also topics such as the court system and government regulation of business. This third edition continues our effort to modernize business law by combining the traditional and legal environment topics.

To satisfy the needs of today's students and to facilitate learning we use several techniques. Numerous section headings readily identify the subject matter. Cases within the text save the students valuable time, and carefully prepared briefs illustrate the material. Each chapter has approximately six case briefs—252 in this third edition, of which 153 are new. We believe that all the advantages of studying actual cases will result from this format; moreover, cases presented in this manner are more easily understood. Review questions and problems at the end of each chapter are almost all new to this edition.

Throughout the text, we illustrate that the law is in a state of constant change and that the dynamic quality of the law is its ability to adapt to changing conditions. One of the important chapters in contracts deals with public policy contract defenses. The trend toward greater government regulation of business decisions is evidenced by four chapters dealing with government and business.

Recognizing that people in business have educational needs different from those of lawyers, we try to meet the requirements of businesspeople by stressing aspects of law that are essential to the decision-making process. We believe the material will make a valuable contribution to the education of tomorrow's business leaders, who must be familiar with the legal aspects of business problems.

The text is divided into eight parts, so that instructors may select subjects with which they wish to deal, in any order of their choosing. Sufficiently flexible for either the quarter-system school or the semester-system school, the book has adequate material for at least two courses.

Part I introduces students to the various sources of law and the judicial system. It traces a lawsuit from the pleadings through the appellate process and discusses arbitration in detail as an alternative to litigation. There is a separate chapter on criminal law because of the increasing importance of white-collar crime and the problems business managers face as a result of the high crime rate. The chapter on torts places special emphasis on the various tort theories used to impose tort liability, especially on the business community. Problems related to malpractice by professional persons such as accountants are highlighted.

"Contracts" (Part II) is naturally designed to give the student an understanding of the basic and traditional concepts of contracts as well as recent developments of the closely related law of "sales" under the Uniform Commercial Code. Since the UCC and traditional contract law totally intersect at the offer and acceptance stage, they are treated as a "unified" body of law in chapter 7, to avoid duplication. The Uniform Commercial Code, including Revised Article 9, is attached to the text as an appendix, and appropriate sections are referred to in brackets within the text, for easy reference. Part II is organized in a logical sequence, as typical contract disputes arise; that is, starting with forming the contract (offer and acceptance), to validating the contract (consideration), to attacking the contract (defenses), to performing it (performance and breach). We believe this approach to be unique and, from our experience in the classroom, logically and practically helpful to students. In this and other parts, we introduce some important concepts and information about economic regulation generally.

Part III is devoted to the Uniform Commercial Code. Without repeating those points emphasized under the law of contracts, it covers the traditional sales, commercial paper, and secured transactions. Recognizing the major importance of products liability to all businesses, we have accorded it a separate chapter. The discussion of commercial paper places increased emphasis on the liability of parties (especially banks) in transactions involving commercial paper. It also recognizes the decreased importance of the "holder in due course" concept, now that the 1976 FTC regulation significantly protects consumer defenses against finance companies and other transferees. Because of the recent proliferation of security problems for creditors and sellers of goods, three chapters now cover secured transactions. Emphasis is placed upon priority disputes between the secured party under Article 9 and other claimants, including the bankruptcy trustee. Since the Revised Article 9 of the Code has been enacted in over 25 states, with passage in the remaining states likely in the near future, the revision receives special attention along with the original version.

Part IV contains four important chapters that deal with the law as it relates to creditors and debtor consumers. Chapter 24 is a logical extension of secured transactions under the Code. It covers the use of real property as security for debts. Chapter 25 deals with other methods of protecting creditors such as suretys and guarantors. Chapter 26, the special chapter on the laws assisting debtors and consumers, gathers in one place much of the recent legislation aimed at protecting consumers. It points to the trend from "let the buyer beware" to "let the seller beware." Chapter 27, "Bankruptcy," is written to give students a thorough understanding of bankruptcy law in practice as well as in theory, to make students aware that bankruptcy is an uncomplicated, common proceeding in which the debtor is able to keep a substantial amount of his property while ridding himself of his debts. It also gives an important place to adjustment and reorganization proceedings.

Part V discusses property, including personal property, bailments, real estate transactions, wills, estates, and trusts, with special attention to transactions involving property. Studying property law from a transactional approach is of immediate practical value.

Part VI, "Agency," covers the subject in three chapters. Chapter 32 deals with terminology, creation, and termination of relationships. The other two deal with agency and the law of contracts and the law of torts. Chapter 34 points out the important role that *respondeat superior* plays in our legal system.

Part VII discusses business organizations in three stages. In addition to the factors used in selecting the form of organization, these stages are (1) the method of creation of the various forms of organization, (2) the legal aspects of operating the various forms of organization, and (3) the law as it relates to dissolution of business organization. Special types of business organizations, such as the Sub-Chapter S corporation and the professional service association, are explained.

Part VIII deals with government regulation of business and provides essential background for courses in other areas. The antitrust law chapter, for example, is background material for courses in marketing.

Corley and Robert find that their new co-author is the most significant change in this third edition. Professor Eric M. Holmes of the University of Georgia has brought many new ideas and insights to the study of contracts and the Uniform Commercial Code, areas in which he is nationally recognized as a leader in legal education. He lectures throughout the country and writes extensively on these subjects. Professor Holmes received his J.D. from the University of North Carolina at Chapel Hill in 1969, his L.L.M. from Columbia in 1975, and his S.J.D. from Columbia in 1981.

Barbara George has written a student workbook to accompany the text. We know that many students will benefit from its use, and we want to express our appreciation to her for its preparation. We want to thank Professor Peter Shedd of the University of Georgia for assisting in the preparation of the test bank. He brought valuable expertise based on a successful teaching career.

The authors would also like to acknowledge the assistance of the following professors who reviewed the manuscript and provided many helpful suggestions: Jonathan G. Butler, Curtis Clarke, James Elliott, John Gubbay, Ann W. Lake, and Richard E. Vizard. We also wish to thank Doug Thompson, Business Law Editor at Prentice-Hall, and Maurine Lewis, director of Special Projects, for her valuable assistance. She was truly a co-author. Finally, we want to thank Pam Sherwood of Athens, Georgia, for her valuable assistance in the preparation of the manuscript.

RNC

EMH

WJR

Contents

II CONTRACTS

III UNIFORM COMMERCIAL CODE

IV CREDITORS, DEBTORS, AND CONSUMERS

VI AGENCY

VII BUSINESS ORGANIZATIONS

Stan Wakefield

I

Introduction to the Law

1

Law

Before beginning the study of business law, one should have an understanding of our legal system—where our laws come from, how they are applied, and how they may be changed. The early chapters of this text will discuss the legal system, and the later chapters will consider the law as it relates to business.

Now more than ever before in our nation's history, the direct relationship between law and the problems facing our society has a direct and substantial impact upon business and its decision-making processes. Solutions to many of society's problems are found in laws regulating business activity. The basic approach to solving the problems of air and water pollution is found in the law. To provide equal employment opportunity, the law now has a significant impact on all hiring, promoting, and firing. In the field of consumer protection, laws regulate the debtor-creditor relationship and other matters of consumer interest. The law thus serves as a scheme of social control of the business community.

Our view of the law will be a broad one, and our first consideration will be the question: What is law? In everyday conversation, people use the word *law* in many different ways, but it is a word that is very difficult to define. In its broad context it expresses a variety of concepts. Law has been defined as rules and regulations established by government and applied to people in order for civilization to exist. Law and legal theory, however, are far too complex for such a simple definition.

In attempting to define *law,* it is helpful to look at its purposes or functions. A basic purpose of law in a civilized society is to maintain order. This is the prime function of that body of law known as the *criminal law.* Another role of law is to resolve disputes that arise between individuals and to impose responsibility if one person has a valid, legal claim against another, as in a suit for breach of contract. It is important that one bear in mind that the law is not simply a statement of rules of conduct but is also the means whereby remedies are afforded when one person has wronged another.

In one sense, all issues and disputes in our society—political, social, religious, economic, or otherwise—ultimately become legal issues to be resolved by the courts. Thus it can be said that law is simply what the courts determine it to be as an expression of the public will in resolving these issues and disputes.

Another view of law is that it is a method of social control—an instrument of social, political, and economic change. Law is both an instrument of change and a result of changes that take place in our society. The law brings about changes in our society; society brings about changes in the law. The law—responding to the goals, desires, needs, and aspirations of society—is in a constant state of change. Sometimes the law changes more rapidly than does the attitude of the majority of society. In this event, the law and our legal system provide leadership in bringing about changes. At other times our society is ahead of the law in moving in new directions, and changes in the law are brought about by the people. In the field of ecology, for example, various groups have put pressure on legislators to clean up the air and water. As a result, laws have been enacted, requiring devices installed to control pollution. Here the public pressure resulted in the enactment of laws, and the law was a follower rather than a leader. It is important to note that the law is not static—that it is constantly changing and that the impetus for the changes may come from many different sources.

In still another sense, *law* has been defined as the rules and principles applied by the courts to decide controversies. These rules and principles fall into three categories.

1. Laws, including the federal Constitution and state constitutions, that have been passed by legislative bodies.
2. Common law, or case law, derived from cases decided by the courts.
3. Procedural rules, which determine how lawsuits are handled in the courts and include matters such as the rules of evidence and related issues.

The first two elements provide the rules of substantive law that the courts apply, to decide controversies. The third provides the machinery whereby these rules of substantive law are given effect and applied, to resolve controversies.

The sexes

While we are on the subject of definitions, we should point out that the pronoun *he* can mean "he or she," and we intend that inclusive meaning in almost every instance. In order to save the reader from tiresome repetition of the phrase "he or she," we use the common gender *he.*

Classifications of law

As noted above, laws are sometimes classified as *substantive* or *procedural.* The law that is used to decide disputes may be classified as *substantive* law. On the other hand, the legal procedures that determine how a lawsuit is begun, how the trial is conducted, how appeals are taken, and how a judgment is enforced are called *procedural* law. Substantive law is the part of the law that defines rights; procedural law establishes the procedures whereby rights are enforced and protected. For example, A and B have entered into an agreement, and A claims that B has breached the agreement. The rules that provide for bringing B into court and for the conduct of the trial are rather mechanical, and they constitute procedural law. Whether the agreement was enforceable and whether A is entitled to damages are matters of substance and would be determined on the basis of the substantive law of contracts.

Law is also frequently classified into areas of *public* and *private* law. Public law includes those bodies of law that affect the public generally; private law includes the areas of the law concerned with relationship between individuals.

Public law may be divided into three general categories.

1. *Constitutional law* concerns itself with the rights, powers, and duties of federal and state governments under the U.S. Constitution and the constitutions of the various states.
2. *Administrative law* is concerned with the multitude of administrative agencies, such as the Federal Trade Commission and the National Labor Relations Board.
3. *Criminal law* consists of statutes that forbid certain conduct as being detrimental to the welfare of the state or the people generally and provides punishment for their violation.

Private law is that body of law that pertains to the relationships between individuals in an organized society. Private law encompasses the subjects of contracts, torts, and property. Each of these subjects includes several bodies of law. The law of contracts, for example, may be subdivided into the subjects of sales, commercial paper, agency, and business organizations. The major portion of this text covers these subjects, which constitute the body of law usually referred to as business law.

The law of torts is the primary source of litigation in this country and is also a part of the total body of law in areas such as agency and sales. A *tort* is a wrong committed by one person against another or against his property. The law of torts is predicated upon the premise that in a civilized society people who injure other persons or their property should compensate them for their loss.

The law of property may be thought of as a branch of the law of contracts, but in many ways our concept of private property contains much more than the contract characteristics. Property is the basic ingredient in our economic system, and the subject matter may be subdivided into several areas, such as wills, trusts, estates in land, personal property, bailments, and many more.

Sources of Law

The unique characteristic of American law is that a very substantial part of it is not to be found in statutes enacted by legislatures but rather in cases decided by our courts. This concept of decided cases as a source of law comes to us from England. It is generally referred to as the *common law.* Our common law system of heavy reliance on case precedent as a source of law must be constrasted with civil law systems, which developed on the European continent. The civil law countries have codified their laws—reduced them to statutes—so that the main source of law in those countries is to be found in the statutes rather than in the cases. Under the common law system, of course, we have a large number of statutes and ordinances, but these are only a part of our law.

In our system, statutes must be in keeping with the constitutions—federal and state—and the courts can declare void a statute that is found to violate constitutional provisions. Statutes and constitutions are sometimes classified as *written law.* Also included under this heading are treaties that by the federal constitution are also a part of the supreme law of the land. Case law, as opposed to written law, is not set forth formally but is derived from an analysis of each case that uncovers what legal propositions the case stands for. It is not proper to call this *unwritten law,* because it is, in fact, in writing. Case law, however, must be distinguished from statutory law in that it is not the product of the legislature but is rather the product of the courts. When a court decides a case, particularly upon an appeal from a lower-court decision, the court writes an opinion setting forth, among other things, the reasons for its decision. From these written opinions, rules of law can be deduced, and these make up the body of what is called case law or common law. The basic characteristic of the common law is that a case, once it is decided, establishes a precedent that will be followed by the courts when similar controversies arise later.

A third source of law is administrative law. Federal, state, and local administrative agencies make law by promulgating rules and regulations as well as by making decisions concerning matters under their jurisdiction.

In summary, our law comes from written laws such as constitutions, statutes, ordinances and treaties; from case law, which is based on judicial decisions; and from the rules and decisions of administrative agencies.

Constitutions

The Constitution of the United States and the constitutions of the various states are the fundamental written law in this country. A federal law must not violate the U.S. Constitution. All state laws must conform to, or be in harmony with, the federal Constitution as well as with the constitution of the appropriate state.

Two very important principles of constitutional law are basic to our judicial system. They are closely related to each other and are known as the *doctrine of separation of powers* and the *doctrine of judicial review.*

The doctrine of separation of powers results from the fact that both state and federal constitutions provide for a scheme of government consisting of three branches—legislative, executive, and judicial. Separation of powers ascribes to each branch a separate function and a check and balance of the functions of the other branches. The doctrine of separation of powers implies that each separate branch will not perform the function of the other and that each branch has limited powers. The system of checks and balances may be briefly summarized as follows:

SENATE: approves key executive and judicial appointments.

BOTH HOUSES: exercise control through power to appropriate funds and to limit or expand authority of the executive branch or the jurisdiction of the judicial branch in most cases.

EXECUTIVE: may veto legislation and appoint judges. (In some states, the judiciary is elected.)

JUDICIARY: reviews actions of the executive and has power to review laws, to determine whether or not they are constitutional.

The doctrine of judicial review is the heart of the concept of separation of powers. This doctrine and the doctrine of supremacy of the Constitution were established at an early date in our country's history in the celebrated case of *Marbury* v. *Madison.*[1] In this case, Chief Justice Marshall literally created for the court a power that the founding fathers had refused to include in the Constitution. This was the power of the judiciary to review the actions of the other branches of government and to set them aside as null and void if in violation of the Constitution. In creating this power to declare laws unconstitutional, Chief Justice Marshall stated:

> Certainly, all those who have framed written constitutions contemplated them as forming the fundamental and paramount law of the nation, and consequently, the theory of every such government must be that an act of the legislature, repugnant to the constitution, is void. This theory is essentially attached to a written constitution and is, consequently, to be considered by this court as one of the fundamental principles of our society.

Justice Marshall then decided that courts have the power to review the action of the legislative and executive branches of government to determine if they are constitutional. This doctrine of judicial review has, to some extent, made the courts the overseers of government and of all aspects of our daily lives.

Statutes

The power of courts over legislation is not limited to the doctrine of judicial review. Courts also interpret legislation by resolving ambiguities and filling the gaps in the statutes. By its very nature, most legislation is general, and courts must apply general statutes to specific facts. Interpretation is necessary to find the intent of the legislature.

One technique of statutory interpretation is to examine the legislative history of an act, to determine the purpose of the legislation or the evil it was designed to correct. Legislative history includes the committee hearings, the debates, and any statement made by the executive in requesting the legislation. Legislative history does not always give a clear understanding of the legislative intent, because the legislature did not consider many questions of interpretation that confront courts. The real problem often is to determine what the legislature *would have* intended, had it considered the question.

Judges use several generally accepted rules of statutory interpretation in determining the legislative intent. One rule is that criminal statutes and taxing laws should be strictly or narrowly construed. As a result, doubts as to the applicability of criminal and taxing laws will be resolved in favor of the accused or the taxpayer, as the case may be. Another rule of statutory construction is that remedial statutes (those creating a judicial remedy on behalf of one person at the expense of another) are to be liberally construed, in order that the statute will be effective in correcting the condition sought to be remedied. The power

[1]U.S.(Cranch) 137 (1803).

of courts to interpret legislation means that in the final analysis it is what the court says a statute means that determines its effect.

Uniform state laws

Since each state has its own constitution, statutes, and body of case law, there are substantial differences in the law among the various states. It is important to recognize that ours is a federal system wherein each state has a substantial degree of autonomy; thus it can be said that there are really fifty-one legal systems—a system for each state plus the federal legal structure. In many legal situations it does not matter that the legal principles are not uniform throughout the country. This is true when the parties to a dispute are citizens of the same state; then the controversy is strictly *intrastate* as opposed to one having *interstate* implications. But when citizens of different states are involved in a transaction (perhaps a buyer in one state contracts with a seller in another), many difficult questions can arise from the lack of uniformity in the law. Assume that a contract is valid in one state but not in the other. Which state's law controls? Although a body of law called conflict of laws (see page 10) has been developed to cover such cases, uniformity is still more desirable.

Two methods of achieving uniformity in business law are possible: (1) federal legislation governing business law and (2) the same laws concerning at least certain phases of business transactions could be adopted by legislatures of all states. The latter method has been attempted by a legislative drafting group known as the National Conference of Commissioners on Uniform State Laws. This group of commissioners appointed by the governors of the states endeavors to promote uniformity in state laws on all subjects for which uniformity is desirable and practical. Their goal is accomplished by drafting model acts.

The most significant development for business in the field of uniform state legislation has been the Uniform Commercial Code, prepared for the stated purpose of collecting in one body the law that "deals with all the phases which may ordinarily arise in the handling of a commercial transaction from start to finish. . . ." The detailed aspects of the Code, as it is often called, constitute a significant portion of this text, and sections of the Code are referred to, in brackets, where appropriate.

The field of commercial law is not the only area of new uniform statutes. Many states are adopting modern procedures and concepts in criminal codes and other uniform laws dealing with social problems. In addition, the past few years have seen dynamic changes in both state and federal statutes setting forth civil procedures and revising court systems. The future will undoubtedly bring many further developments to improve the administration of justice. The trend, despite some objection, is to cover more areas of the law with statutes and to rely less on precedent in judicial decisions, or common law, as a source of law. Many of these new statutes tend to be uniform throughout the country.

Case Law

Stare decisis

Notwithstanding the trend toward reducing law to statutory form, a substantial portion of our law has its source in decided cases. This case law, or common law, is based on the concept of precedent and the doctrine of *stare decisis,* which means "to stand by decisions and not to disturb what is settled." This means that the case has established a precedent. The doctrine of *stare decisis* must be contrasted with the concept of *res adjudicata,* which means that "the thing has been decided." *Res adjudicata* applies when, between the parties themselves, the matter is closed at the conclusion of the lawsuit. The losing party cannot again ask a court to decide the dispute. *Stare decisis* means that a court of competent jurisdiction has decided a controversy and has, in a written opinion, set forth the rule or principle that formed the basis for its decision, so that rule or principle will be followed by the court in deciding subsequent cases. Likewise, subordinate courts in the same jurisdiction will be bound by the rule of law set forth in the decision. *Stare decisis,* then, affects persons who are not parties to the lawsuit, but *res adjudicata* applies only to the parties involved.

Stare decisis provides both certainty and predictability to the law. It is also expedient. Through reliance upon precedent established in prior cases, the common law has resolved many legal issues and brought stability into many areas of the law, such as the law of contracts. The doctrine of *stare decisis* provides a system wherein businesspeople may act in a certain way, confident that their actions will have certain legal effects. People can rely on prior decisions and, knowing the legal significance of their action, can act accordingly. There is reasonable certainty as to the results of conduct. Courts usually hesitate to renounce precedent. They generally assume that if a principle or rule of law announced in a former judicial decision is unfair or contrary to public policy, it will be changed by legislation. It is important to note that an unpopular court ruling can usually be changed or overruled by statute. Precedent has more force on trial courts than on courts of review; the latter have the power to make precedent in the first instance.

Inherent problems

The common-law system as used in the United States has several inherent difficulties. First of all, the unbelievably large volume of judicial decisions, each possibly creating precedent, places "the law" beyond the actual knowledge of lawyers, let alone laypersons. Large law firms employ lawyers whose major task is to search case reports for "the law" to be used in lawsuits and in advising their clients. Today, computers are being used to assist in the search for precedent, because legal research involves examination of cases in hundreds of volumes. Because the total body of ruling case law is beyond the grasp of lawyers, it is obvious that laypersons who are supposed to know the law and govern their conduct accordingly *do not* know the law and cannot always follow it, even with the advice of legal counsel.

Another major problem involving case law arises because conflicting precedents are frequently presented by opposing lawyers. One of the major tasks of the court in such cases is to determine which precedent is applicable to the present case. In addition, even today, many questions of law arise on which there has been no prior decision or in areas where the only authority is by implication. In such situations the judicial process is "legislative" in character and involves the creation of law, not merely its discovery.

It should also be noted that there is a distinction between precedent and mere dictum. As authority for future cases, a judicial decision is coextensive only with the facts upon which it is founded and the rules of law upon which the decision is actually predicated. Frequently, courts make comments on matters not necessary to the decision reached. Such expressions, called dicta, lack the force of an adjudication and, strictly speaking, are not precedent that the court will be required to follow within the rule of *stare decisis.* Dictum or implication in prior cases may be followed if sound and just, however, and dicta that have been repeated frequently are often given the force of precedent.

Finally, our system of each state having its own body of case law creates serious legal problems in matters that have legal implications in more than one state. The problem is discussed in more detail under the heading "Conflict of laws," which follows the next heading.

Rejection of stare decisis

The doctrine of *stare decisis* has not been applied in a fashion that renders the law rigid and inflexible. If a court, especially a reviewing court, finds that the prior decision was "palpably wrong," it may overrule and change it. By the same token, if the court finds that a rule of law established by a prior decision is no longer sound because of changing conditions, it may reverse the precedent. The strength and genius of the common law is that no decision is *stare decisis* when it has lost its usefulness or the reasons for it no longer exist. The doctrine does not require courts to multiply their errors by using former mistakes as authority and support for new errors. Thus, just as legislatures change the law by new legislation, so do courts change the law, from time to time, by reversing former precedents. Judges, like legislators, are subject to social forces and changing circumstances. As personnel of courts change, each new generation of judges deems it a responsibility to reexamine precedents and adapt them to the present.

It should be noted, also, that in many cases a precedent created by a decision will not be a popular one and may be out of step with the times. When that happens, the precedent can be nullified by passage of a statute providing results different from those obtainable through the judicial decision.

Stare decisis may not be ignored by mere whim or caprice. It must have more impact on trial courts than on reviewing courts. It must be followed rather rigidly in daily affairs. In the whole area of private law, uniformity and continuity are necessary. It is obvious that the same rules of tort and contract law must be applied from day to day. *Stare decisis* must serve to take the capricious element out of law and to give stability to a society and to business.

In the area of public law, however, especially constitutional law, the doctrine is frequently ignored. The Supreme Court recognizes that "it is a constitution which we are expounding, not the gloss which previous courts may have put on it."[2] Constitutional principles are often considered in relation to the times and circumstances in which they are raised. Public law issues are relative to the times, and precedent often is ignored so that we are not governed by the dead.

Conflict of laws

Certain basic facts about our legal system must be recognized. First of all, statutes and precedents, in all legal areas, vary from state to state. In many states the plaintiff in an automobile accident case must be completely free of fault in order to recover judgment; but in other states the doctrine of comparative negligence is used, so that a plaintiff found to be 20 percent at fault could recover 80 percent of injuries received. Second, the doctrine of *stare decisis* does not require that one state recognize the precedent or rules of law of other states. Each state is free to decide for itself questions concerning its common law and interpretation of its own constitution and statutes. (However, courts will often follow decisions of other states if they are found to be sound. They are considered persuasive authority. This is particularly true in cases involving uniform acts, when each state has adopted the same statute.) Third, many legal issues arise out of acts or transactions that have contact with more than one state. A contract may be executed in one

[2]Chief Justice John Marshall in *McCullough* v. *Maryland,* 4 Wheat 316, 407.

state, performed in another, and the parties may live in still others; or an automobile accident may occur in one state involving citizens of different states.

These hypothetical situations illustrate the following fundamental question: Which state's *substantive* laws are applicable in a multiple-jurisdiction case in which the law or jurisdictions differ from one state to the other?

The body of law known as conflict of laws or choice of laws answers this question. It provides the court or forum with the applicable substantive law in the multistate transaction or occurrence. The law applicable to a tort is generally said to be the law of the state of place of injury. Thus, a court sitting in state X would follow its own rules of procedure, but it would use the tort law of state Y if the injury occurred in Y. Several rules are used by courts on issues involving the law of contracts.

1. The law of the state where the contract was made.
2. The law of the place of performance.
3. "Grouping of contacts" or "center of gravity" theory, which uses the law of the state most involved with the contract.

Many contracts designate the applicable substantive law. A contract that provides "This contract shall be governed by the law of the State of New York" will be enforced if New York has at least minimal connection with the contract.

It is not the purpose of this text to teach conflict of laws, but the reader should be aware that such a body of law exists and should recognize those situations in which conflict of law principles will be used. The trend toward uniform statutes and codes has tended to decrease these conflicts, but many of them still exist. So long as we have a federal system and fifty separate state bodies of substantive law, the area of conflicts of law will continue to be of substantial importance in the application of the doctrine of *stare decisis* and statutory law.

The law in the federal courts

Our dual system of federal and state courts creates a unique problem in "conflicts." The federal courts use their own body of procedural law and their own body of substantive law in cases involving federal law. Decisions of the U.S. Supreme Court on questions involving the U.S. Constitution, treaties, and federal statutes are binding on state courts. Federal courts also have jurisdiction of cases involving citizens of different states, even though no federal law is involved. The jurisdiction of federal courts is discussed more fully in chapter 2. Since there is no body of federal common law, suits based on diversity of citizenship (suits between citizens of different states), federal courts use the substantive law, including conflict-of-law principles, of the state in which they are sitting. As in all cases, the federal courts do use their own rules of procedure, however. Thus, just as the state courts are bound by federal precedent in cases involving federal law and federally protected rights, federal courts are bound by state precedent in others.

Full faith and credit

One further aspect of the scope of precedent must be noted. Article IV, Section 1, of the U.S. Constitution provides: "Full Faith and Credit shall be given in each State to the Public Acts, Records, and judicial Proceedings of every other State. . . ." This does not mean that the precedent in one state is binding in other states, but only that the final decisions or judgments rendered in any given state by a court with jurisdiction shall be enforced between the original parties in other states. "Full Faith and Credit" is applicable to the result of a specific decision as it affects the rights of the parties and not to the reasons or principles upon which it was based. Full faith and credit requires that a suit be brought on the judgment in the other state.

The nature of the judicial process

In this chapter we have briefly examined the great powers of the judiciary that result from the doctrine of judicial review, from the role of courts in interpreting and applying statutes, and from the very nature of the concept of *stare decisis.* We now turn to an examination of the processes by which these powers are exercised. Recognizing that a court may declare a law unconstitutional, we may ask when and why will it do so? Why does a court announce one rule of law or follow one precedent rather than another? What type of reasoning is used by courts? What factors influence the courts in their decisions? Of course, no absolute answers can be given to these questions, but a consideration of them is essential to an understanding of the legal process and the role of courts.

The judicial system has a rather obvious priority of sources. Constitutions prevail over statutes; statutes prevail over case law; precedent would prevail over dicta; dicta would usually be persuasive over mere argument. Admittedly, however, in spite of our more than two hundred years as a nation, many legal issues are not directly covered by a statute or case precedent. Litigation is frequently brought to challenge a statute or its meaning or to seek to change a precedent. Frequently the decided cases are in conflict, or the case involves issues of conflicting social policies.

Thus the law is not a system of known rules applied by judges. When many legal issues are presented to a court, the law applicable to those issues is made by the court, not merely found in some statute or case. In the sense that the law is made, not found, the role of the courts is legislative in character. When the applicable law is not known or clearly established, the court must examine the rationale, or *ratio decidendi,* of existing statutes and cases and then extend or contract this *ratio* in deciding the case before it.

In describing the nature of the judicial process, Justice Cardozo[3] indicated that logic, history, custom, and utility influence judges in the application of the *ratio decidendi.* The use of logic or analogy has been evident in our common law system and is ordinarily considered to be the chief method employed by courts. Using logic satisfies our desire for certainty and predictability in the law. History and custom have played a major role in the development of business law. Throughout this text, there will be references to the historical development of various concepts and statutes. Statutory changes in the law frequently come about because the law recognizes the customary practices of businesspeople. It is interesting to speculate, for example, whether checks not bearing a signature might someday be legal. The fourth force, utility, refers to the elements of justice, morals, and social welfare. This factor, which Cardozo called the method of sociology, has become the major influence in many areas of the law in recent years. As public policy considerations have played an everincreasing role in the development of our law, utility can be recognized as the dominant influence in areas such as civil rights and government regulation of business.

The forces discussed by Cardozo can also be seen in the various kinds of reasoning used by courts in determining a rule of law or its applicability. A court may base its determination upon the literal meaning of words appearing in the rule, upon the purpose of the rule, upon similarities between the facts of the case to be decided and the facts of

[3]Benjamin Cardozo, *The Nature of the Judicial Process* (New Haven, Conn.: Yale University Press, 1921).

decided cases, or upon considerations of social policy. Thus, reasoning may be literal, purposive, precedent oriented, or policy oriented.

It is obvious that there is no set formula followed by courts in deciding cases. Those forces that dictate the end product vary not only from case to case but from time to time. It is not possible for anyone to "know the law" or to predict with absolute certainty the outcome of any case in the courts. Each case is peculiar in facts and circumstances. In almost all legal disputes, victory or defeat may depend on either the facts or the law. Judicial discretion, however, is not an arbitrary power of the individual judge, to be exercised when and as that judge's caprice or passion or partiality dictates. A judge may not simply disagree with a certain accepted rule of law and therefore not use it in court. There must be a deep commitment to the judicial system and to the rule of law.

REVIEW QUESTIONS AND PROBLEMS

1. What are two basic purposes of law?
2. Determine whether the following areas of law are categorized as private or public law: (a) criminal law, (b) property law, (c) tort law, (d) labor law, (e) contract law.
3. To what extent is the judiciary the overseer of the government? Explain.
4. Why is there a trend toward uniform state laws?
5. The basic characteristic of the common law is that a case once decided establishes a precedent that will be followed by the courts when similar issues arise later. Do courts always follow precedent? Explain.
6. *Stare decisis* is less likely to be followed in the area of public law than in the area of private law. Explain.
7. What is the function of the body of law known as conflict of laws?
8. What are the four forces that Cardozo said shaped the law?
9. What is meant by the term *full faith and credit?*
10. What is the distinction between a tort and a crime?

2

The Resolution of Disputes

In our society, a variety of methods can be used to resolve conflicts and disputes. The most common is a compromise or settlement agreement between the parties to the dispute. Conflicts and disputes that are not settled by agreement between the parties may be resolved by litigation. A second important method for resolving unsettled conflicts and disputes is known as *arbitration,* submission of a controversy to a nonjudicial body for a binding decision. Litigation has been the traditional method of resolving disputes, but today more and more disputes are being submitted to arbitration because litigation consumes much time and money. A third method leads many issues to a governmental agency for decision. Some disputes submitted to these agencies are between whole segments of society, and thus the decision is of general application in a manner similar to a statute. The basic legal principles applicable to litigation and arbitration will be discussed in this chapter. The role of administrative agencies will be discussed in chapter 43.

Compromises and settlements

Most disputes are resolved by the parties involved, without resort to litigation or arbitration. Only a small fraction of disputes end up in court or even in a lawyer's office. Among the multitude of reasons why compromise is so prevalent a technique for settling disputes, some may be described as personal, others as economic.

The desire to compromise is almost instinctive. Most of us dislike trouble, and many fear going to court. Our moral and ethical values encourage compromise and settlement. Opinions of persons other than the parties to the dispute are often an influential, motivating force in many compromises, adding external forces to the internal ones that encourage people to settle their differences amicably.

Compromise and settlement of disputes is also encouraged by the economics of many situations. Lawsuits are expensive to both parties. As a general rule, both parties must pay their own attorney's fees, and the losing party must pay court costs. As a matter of practical economics, the winning party in a lawsuit is a loser to the extent of the attorney's fees—often quite substantial.

At least two additional facts of economic life encourage business to settle disputes out of court. First, business must be concerned with its public image and the goodwill of its customers. Although the motto "The customer is always right" is not universally applicable today, the influence of the philosophy it represents cannot be underestimated. It often is simply not good business to sue a customer. Second, juries are frequently sympathetic to individuals who have suits against large corporations or defendants who are covered by insurance. Close questions of liability, as well as the size of verdicts, are more often than not resolved against business concerns because of their presumed ability to pay. As a result, business seeks to settle many disputes rather than submit them to a jury for decision.

The duty of lawyers to seek and achieve compromise whenever possible is not usually understood by laypersons. In providing services, lawyers will devote a substantial amount of their time, energy, and talent to seeking a compromise solution of the disputes of their clients. Attempts to compromise will be made before resort to the courts in most cases. Of all the disputes that are the subject of legal advice, the great majority are settled without resort to litigation. Of those that do result in litigation, the great majority are settled before the case goes to trial or even during the trial. Literally, the attempt of the lawyers to resolve the dispute never ends. It occurs before suit, before and during the trial, after verdict, during appeal, and even after appeal. As long as there is a controversy, it is the function of lawyers to attempt to resolve it.

Lawyers on both sides of a controversy seek compromise for a variety of reasons. A lawyer may view the client's case as weak, either on the law or on the facts. The amount of money involved, the necessity for a speedy decision, the nature of the contest, the uncertainty of legal remedy, the unfavorable publicity, and the expense entailed are some other reasons for avoiding a court trial. Each attorney must evaluate the client's cause and seek a satisfactory—though not necessarily the most desirable—settlement of the controversy. The settlement of disputes is perhaps the most significant contribution of lawyers to our society.

Mediation

The term *mediation* describes the process by which a third party assists the parties to a controversy when they seek a compromise. Although a mediator cannot impose a binding solution on the parties, a disinterested and objective mediator is often able to bring about a compromise that is satisfactory to them.

The mediation of labor disputes is the function of the National Mediation and Conciliation Service. This government agency, staffed with skilled negotiators, has assisted in the settlement of countless labor disputes. Mediation is playing an expanding role in the relationship between the business community and the consuming public. Better Business Bureaus and others are serving as mediators of consumer complaints and, on occasion, as arbitrators under arbitration agreements. Their efforts have resolved thousands of consumer complaints, in part because they provide some third parties to whom a consumer can turn.

An amendment to the Federal Trade Commission Act has given added impetus to mediation as a means of resolving consumer complaints. This law provides that if a business adopts an informal dispute-resolution system to handle complaints about its product warranties, then a customer cannot sue the manufacturer or seller for breach of warranty without first going through the informal procedures. This law does not deny consumers the right to sue, nor does it compel a compromise solution. It simply favors mediation by requiring an attempt at settlement before litigation.

Arbitration

Arbitration is a procedure whereby a controversy is submitted to a person or persons other than the courts for a final, binding decision. Arbitration may be required by statute in certain cases; however, such cases are rare, and the right to arbitrate usually arises from a contract. Since the right is based on a contract, the parties are obligated to arbitrate only those issues that they have agreed to arbitrate.

There are several advantages to using arbitration as a substitute for litigation. For one thing, it is much quicker and far less expensive. An issue can be submitted to arbitration and decided in less time than it takes to complete the pleading phase of a lawsuit. Then, too, arbitration creates less hostility than does litigation, and it allows the parties to continue their business relationship while the dispute is being decided somewhat more peacefully. Finally, under the arbitration process, complex issues can be submitted to an expert for decision. If an issue arises concerning construction of a building, in arbitration it can be submitted to an architect for decision. Besides lawyers, other specialists frequently serve as arbitrators: physicians decide issues relating to physical disabilities, certified public accountants resolve disputes on the book value of stock, and engineers make decisions relating to industrial production. Of course, a substantial amount of arbitration is also conducted by the academic community, especially in the area of labor relations.

The process

The first step in the arbitration process is known as the *submission,* a term used to describe the act of referring an issue or issues to arbitration process. The submitted issues may be factual, legal, or both; they may include questions concerning the interpretation of the arbitration agreement. The scope of the arbitrator's powers is controlled by the language of the submission. All doubts concerning the arbitrability of the subject matter of a dispute are resolved in favor of arbitration.

After the submission, the arbitrator will hold a hearing at which testimony is received. The hearings are usually informal, and the strict rules of evidence are frequently not followed. The arbitrator then makes a decision called an *award* but often does not give reasons for it.

An award is binding on all issues submitted and may be judicially enforced. In court, every presumption is in favor of the validity of an arbitration award, and doubts are resolved in its favor. Arbitrators are not bound by principles of substantive law or the rules of evidence, unless the submission so provides. As a result, errors of law or fact do not justify a court in setting aside the decision of the arbitration process. The arbitrator is the sole and final judge of the evidence and the weight to be given it. The scope of judicial review is whether or not the issues contained in the submission have been decided.

Once an issue is submitted for arbitration, the arbitrator is responsible for questions of law. They are no longer open to judicial intervention or to judicial review. Unless the submission is to the contrary, the means by which arbitrators reach their decision is superfluous, although they have an obligation to act fairly and impartially and to decide on the basis of the evidence before them. It is therefore misconduct for arbitrators to seek outside evidence by independent investigation without the consent of the parties.

Litigation

The function of courts

Many controversies cannot be settled by the parties or by arbitration. When other methods for resolving conflicts and controversies have not succeeded, there must be an ultimate method for accomplishing this goal. Our system of government has selected courts to settle controversies between persons and between persons and the state.

The rule of law applied by the court to the facts as found by the jury or court produces a decision that settles the controversy. Although there are obviously other agencies of government that resolve controversies, it is peculiar to our system that for final decision all controversies may ultimately end up in court. Whether the issue is the busing of schoolchildren, the legality of abortions, the enforceability of a contract, or the liability of a wrongdoer, the dispute, if not otherwise resolved, goes to the courts for a final decision.

State court systems

The judicial system of the United States is a dual system consisting of state courts and federal courts. The courts of the states, although not subject to uniform classification, may be grouped as follows: supreme courts, intermediate courts of review (in the more populous states), and trial courts. Some trial courts have general jurisdiction; others have limited jurisdiction. A justice of the peace or a magistrate has power to hear civil cases only if the amount in controversy does not exceed a certain sum, and they hear only those cases covering certain specified minor criminal matters.

Lawsuits are instituted in one of the trial courts. Even a court of general jurisdiction has geographical limitations. In many states the trial court of general jurisdiction is called a circuit court, because in early times a single judge sitting as a court traveled the circuit from one county to another. In other states the trial court is called the superior court or the district court. Each area has a trial court of general jurisdiction.

Most states also have trial courts of limited jurisdiction. They may be limited as to subject matter, amount in controversy, or area in which the parties live. Courts with jurisdiction limited to a city are often called municipal courts.

Courts may also be named according to the subject matter with which they deal. Probate courts deal with wills and the estates of deceased persons; family courts, with divorces, family relations, juveniles, and dependent children; criminal and police courts, with violators of state laws and municipal ordinances; and traffic courts, with traffic violations. For an accurate classification of the courts of any state, the statutes of that state should be examined. Figure 2•1 illustrates the jurisdiction and organization of reviewing and trial courts in a typical state.

The small-claims court is a court of growing importance. It is an attempt to provide a prompt and inexpensive means of settling thousands of minor disputes that often include suits by consumers against merchants for lost or damaged goods or for services poorly

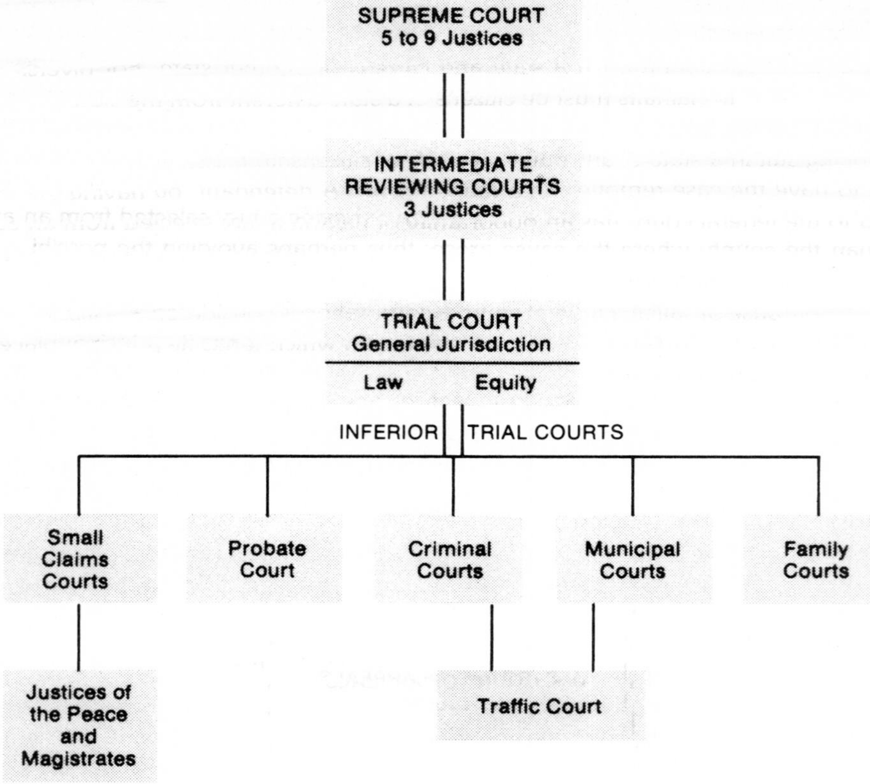

Fig. 2·1 A typical state judicial system.

performed. Landlord-tenant disputes and collection suits are also quite common in small-claims courts. In these courts, the usual court costs are greatly reduced. The procedures are simplified, so that the services of a lawyer are usually not required. Most of the states have authorized small-claims courts and have imposed a limit on their jurisdiction. Some states keep the amount as low as $500; others exceed $2,500, but $1,000 is a typical limit.

The federal court system

Congress creates our courts, but the Constitution limits the courts' jurisdiction. The Constitution created the Supreme Court and authorizes Congress to establish inferior courts from time to time. Congress has created eleven United States courts of appeal, the United States district courts (at least one in each state), and others to handle special subject matter, such as the Court of Customs and Patent Appeals, the Court of Claims, and the Tax Court. Figure 2·2 illustrates the federal court system.

The district courts are the trial courts of the federal judicial system. They have original jurisdiction, exclusive of the courts of the states, over all federal crimes; that is, all offenses against the laws of the United States. The accused is entitled to a trial by jury in the state and district where the crime was committed.

In civil actions, the district courts have jurisdiction only when the matter in controversy is based on either diversity of citizenship or a federal question. Diversity of citizenship exists in suits between (1) citizens of different states, (2) a citizen of a state and a citizen of a foreign country, (3) a state and citizens of another state. For diversity of citizenship to exist, all plaintiffs must be citizens of a state different from the state in which any one of the defendants is a citizen. Diversity of citizenship does not prevent the plaintiff from bringing suit in a state court, but if diversity of citizenship exists, the defendant has the right to have the case removed to a federal court. A defendant, by having the case removed to the federal court, has an opportunity of having a jury selected from an area larger than the county where the cause arose, thus perhaps avoiding the possibility of jurors prejudicial to the plaintiff.

For the purpose of suit in a federal court, a corporation is considered a "citizen" both of the state where it is incorporated and of the state in which it has its principal place of business. As a result, there is no federal jurisdiction in many cases in which one of the parties is a corporation. If any one of the parties on the other side of the case is a citizen

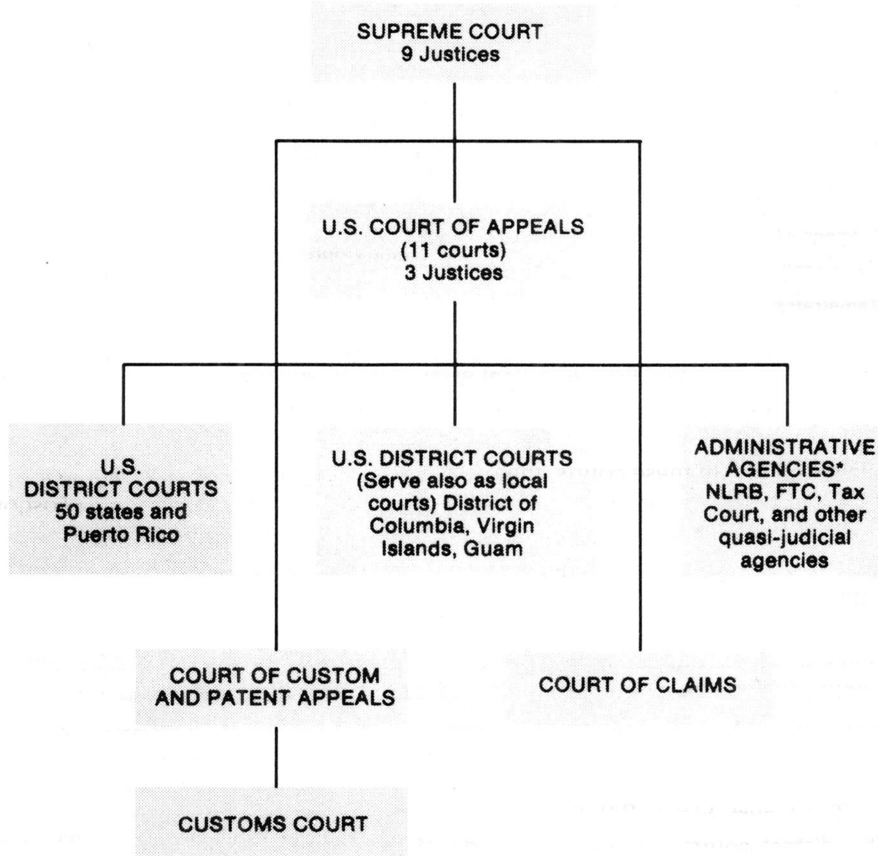

* The federal administrative agencies are not officially part of the federal court system but are included in this chart because their rulings can be appealed to a federal court.

Fig. 2·2 Federal court system.

either of the state in which the corporation is chartered or is doing its principal business, there is no diversity of citizenship and thus no federal jurisdiction.

Federal jurisdiction based on a federal question exists if the lawsuit arises out of rights granted by the Constitution, laws, or treaties of the United States.

In addition to requiring either a federal question or diversity of citizenship as a basis of jurisdiction, the federal courts also have a jurisdictional amount in diversity of citizenship cases. This jurisdictional amount is $10,000. If a case involves multiple plaintiffs with separate and distinct claims, each claim must satisfy the jurisdictional amount. Thus, in a class action suit, the claim of each plaintiff must meet the $10,000 minimum, unless changed by statute.

Direct appeals from the decisions of the district courts to the United States Supreme Court may be made in several situations, such as (1) in criminal cases when the decision of the lower court is based upon the invalidity or construction of a statute upon which the indictment or information was founded, (2) when the lower court has held an act of Congress unconstitutional in a case in which an agency of the government is a party; and (3) when the lower court consisting of three judges has either granted or denied after notice an interlocutory or permanent injunction. However, in most cases an appeal is taken from a U.S. district court to the court of appeals.

The intermediate courts of appeal from the U.S. district courts are called the United States Courts of Appeals. The federal judicial districts are divided into eleven circuits, and a court of appeals has been established for each circuit. These courts are not trial courts and are limited to appellate jurisdiction.

In most cases the decisions of the courts of appeals are final. Cases in the courts of appeals may be reviewed by the Supreme Court by a *writ of certiorari* granted upon a petition of any party before or after a decision in the courts of appeals. The writ of certiorari to review a judgment of the courts of appeals is within the discretion of the Supreme Court. The writ will be issued when necessary to secure uniformity of decision or to bring cases of grave public concern to the court of last resort for decision.

Courts of appeals decisions may also be reviewed by the Supreme Court in cases in which a state statute has been held unconstitutional and a federal question is presented. In addition, the courts of appeals may by certification seek instructions from the Supreme Court on any question of law in any civil or criminal case.

The U.S. district courts and the courts of appeals cannot review, retry, or correct the judicial errors charged against a state court. Final judgments or decrees rendered by the highest court of a state are reviewed only by the Supreme Court of the United States. State cases appealed to the U.S. Supreme Court must concern the validity of a treaty or statute of the United States or must present a question involving the validity of a state statute on the grounds that the statute is repugnant to the Constitution, treaties, or laws of the United States and that the state decision is in favor of the statute's validity. When a case involves the constitutionality of a state statute or treaty or when a citizen's rights, privileges, or immunities under the constitution or laws are impaired, the case may be brought to the Supreme Court by writ of certiorari. In all other cases the decision of the highest state court is not subject to review.

Law and equity

Historically, trial courts in the United States have been divided into two parts—a court of law and a court of equity or chancery. The term *equity* arose in England because the failure of the law courts to provide adequate remedies often made it impossible to obtain justice in the king's courts of law. The only remedy at law was a suit for money damages.

In order that justice might be done, the person seeking a remedy sought redress from the king in person. Because the appeal was to the king's conscience, he referred such matters to his spiritual adviser, the chancellor, who was usually a church official and, in giving a remedy, usually favored the ecclesiastical law.

By such method, there developed a separate system of procedure and different rules for deciding matters presented to the chancellor. Suits involving these rules were said to be brought "in chancery" or "in equity," in contradistinction to suits "at law" in the king's courts. Courts of equity were courts of conscience and recognized many rights that were not recognized by common law courts. For example, trusts in lands were recognized; rescission was allowed on contracts created through fraud; injunction and specific performance were developed.

In a few states, courts of equity are still separate and distinct from courts of law. In most states, the equity and law courts are organized under a single court with two dockets—one at law, the other in equity. Whether the case is in equity or at law is determined by the remedy desired. Modern civil procedure laws usually have abolished distinction between actions at law and in equity. However, pleadings usually must denote whether the action is legal or equitable because, as a general rule, there is no right to a jury trial of an equitable action. The constitutional guarantee to a trial by jury applies only to actions at law.

Courts of equity use maxims instead of strict rules of law. There are no *legal* rights in equity, for the decision is based on moral rights and natural justice. Some of the typical maxims of equity are:

- Equity will not suffer a right to exist without a remedy.
- Equity regards as done that which ought to be done.
- Where there is equal equity, the law must prevail.
- He who comes into equity must do so with clean hands.
- He who seeks equity must do equity.
- Equity aids the vigilant.
- Equality is equity.

These maxims guide the chancellor in exercising his discretion. The clean-hands doctrine prohibits a party who is guilty of misconduct in the matter in litigation from receiving the aid of the court.

The decision of the court in equity is called a decree. A judgment in a court of law is measured in damages, whereas a decree of a court of equity is said to be *in personam;* that is, it is directed to the defendant, who is to do or not to do some specific thing.

Decrees are either final or interlocutory. A decree is final when it disposes of the issues in the case, reserving no question to be decided in the future. A decree quieting title to real estate, granting a divorce, or ordering specific performance is usually final. A decree is interlocutory when it reserves some question to be determined in the future. A decree granting a temporary injunction, appointing a receiver, and ordering property to be delivered to such a receiver would be interlocutory.

Failure upon the part of the defendant to obey a decree of a court of equity is contempt of court because the decree is directed not against his property but against his person. Any person in contempt of court may be placed in jail or fined by order of the court.

Equity jurisprudence plays an ever-increasing role in our legal system. The movement toward social justice requires more reliance on the equitable maxims and less reliance on rigid rules of law.

Operating the System

Highly technical, the court system must be operated by numerous persons with special training and skills: judges, attorneys, bailiffs, court reporters, and clerks. It also requires responsible citizens to serve as jurors if justice is to be achieved.

Judges and justices

The judge, by virtue of the office, owes very high duties to the state, its people, the litigants, the law, the witnesses, and the jury. Since the court is the protector of constitutional limitations and guarantees, a judge should be temperate, attentive, patient, impartial, studious, diligent, and prompt in ascertaining the facts and applying the law. Judges should be courteous and considerate of jurors, witnesses, and others in attendance upon the court, but they should criticize and correct unprofessional conduct of attorneys.

The trial judge renders decisions at the people's level. It is in the trial courts that the law is made alive and its words are given meaning. Since a trial judge is the only contact that most people have with the law, the ability of that judge is largely responsible for the effective function of the law. Members of reviewing courts are usually called *justices,* to distinguish them from trial court judges, whose role is substantially different. The trial judge has direct contact with the litigation and the litigants, whereas the justice rarely has any contact with litigants. Justices must do much more than simply decide a case; they are required to write reasons for their decision, so that anyone may examine them and comment on their merits. Each decision becomes precedent to some degree, a part of our body of law. Thus, the legal opinion of the justice—unlike that of the trial judge, whose decision has direct effect only upon the litigants—affects society as a whole. The justice, in deciding a case, must consider not only the result between the parties involved but the total effect of the decision on the law. In this sense, the justice is a legislator.

The jury

The court ascertains the law applicable to a case; the jury ascertains facts if they are in dispute, and its fact finding results in a verdict. In cases tried without a jury, the court is the fact finder.

The Sixth and Seventh Amendments to the United States Constitution guarantee the right of trial by jury both in criminal and civil cases. The Fifth Amendment provides for indictment by a grand jury for capital offenses and infamous crimes. (*Indictment* is a word used to describe the decision of the grand jury.) A grand jury differs from a petit jury in that the grand jury determines whether evidence of guilt is sufficient to warrant a trial; the petit jury determines guilt or innocence in criminal cases and decides the winner in civil cases. In civil cases, the right to trial by a jury is preserved in suits at common law when the amount in controversy exceeds $20. State constitutions have like provisions guaranteeing the right of trial by jury in state courts.

Historically, the jury consisted of twelve persons, but many states and some federal courts now have rules of procedure that provide for smaller juries both in criminal and civil cases. Historically, too, a jury's verdict was required to be unanimous. Today, some states authorize less than unanimous verdicts. If fewer than twelve persons serve on the jury, however, the verdict must be unanimous.

The jury system is much criticized by those who contend that many jurors are unqualified to distinguish fact from fiction, prejudiced, and easily swayed by skillful trial lawyers. However, the "right to be tried by a jury of his peers" in criminal cases is felt by most members of the bench and bar to be as fair and effective a method as has been devised for ascertaining the truth and giving an accused his or her "day in court."

The persons who are selected to serve on trial juries are drawn at random from lists of qualified voters in the county or city where the trial court sits. Most states, by statute, exempt from jury duty those who are in certain occupations and professions, such as doctors, dentists, pharmacists, embalmers, the police, firemen, lawyers, newspaper people. Many others attempt to avoid serving because it involves a loss of money or time away from a job; but because of the importance of jury duty, most judges are reluctant to excuse citizens.

Jury duty in long, complex cases creates a very difficult situation. Because few people can afford to serve for many months, juries in such cases frequently consist of the less informed or alert among the unemployed and retired, often those who cannot understand the issues in cases such as the antitrust case to break up IBM. It has therefore been proposed to take long and complex matters out of the jury system.

Lawyers

A discussion of the court system would not be complete without some references to the trial lawyers who represent participants in litigation. A lawyer, as an officer of the court, owes a duty to the court as well as to the client, a duty to aid in the search for truth and the administration of justice. Counselors as well as advocates, lawyers seek to compromise disputes and to settle lawsuits. They are advocates not only in court and before the jury, but also in any dealing with the opposing counsel.

It is obvious that a lawyer must be fully advised of a client's problems and all matters affecting them. To encourage clients' cooperation, the rules of evidence provide that confidential communications to a lawyer are privileged. The law does not permit a lawyer to reveal such facts and testify against a client, even if called to the stand to do so at a trial. This is called the attorney-client privilege, and it may extend to communications made to employees of the lawyer in certain cases. The privilege extends to corporations as well as to individuals.

The competency of lawyers, especially to try lawsuits, is a subject of frequent criticism. Chief Justice Burger commented that at least half of the lawyers in the country are not qualified to try a case in court. He believes that higher qualifications must be required for the trial bar and that lawyers who are not qualified should not be allowed to engage in trial practice. Justice Burger argues that significant experience at the state court level should be a prerequisite to practice in the federal courts. While there are those who disagree with the Chief Justice, nevertheless one should be careful in choosing a lawyer, especially for litigation.

REVIEW QUESTIONS AND PROBLEMS

1. A business woman is involved in a dispute related to her business. Certain that she is right, she is considering legal action. List the reasons why it may be financially advantageous to her business to avoid court and make a compromise and settlement at less money than she claims is owed to her.

2. What is the difference between *arbitration* and *mediation?*

3. What are the advantages of arbitration over a judicial decision?

4. Define the terms *submission* and *award* as used in arbitration.

5. What is the advantage of having a small-claims court?

6. If a citizen of Illinois sues a citizen of Indiana and a citizen of Illinois for $20,000, does a federal court have jurisdiction if the subject matter of the suit is not a federal question? Why?

7. A citizen of Alabama sues a citizen of Mississippi for $7,500 in the Alabama State Court. Jurisdiction is obtained by service of process in Mississippi. Can the Mississippi defendant have the case removed to the federal courts? Why?

8. A citizen of Georgia, crossing the street in New Orleans, was struck by a car. The driver was a citizen of Texas, but the car was owned by his employer, a Pennsylvania corporation with its principal place of business in Atlanta, Georgia. The pedestrian sues both the driver and his company in the federal district court in New Orleans, claiming damages in the amount of $100,000. Does the court have jurisdiction? Why?

9. Describe three major duties or functions of lawyers.

10. What is a petition for a writ of certiorari?

11. Describe three controversies that would be decided in a court of equity or chancery in states that still distinguish between courts of law and courts of equity.

3

Lawsuits

We have previously noted that law may be classified as *substantive law* or *procedural law.* Substantive law defines the rights and duties of citizens and is the result of legislative action or judicial action. Procedural law specifies the method and means by which the substantive law is made, enforced, and administered. Procedural rules prescribe the methods by which courts apply substantive law to resolve conflicts. Substantive rights have no value unless there are procedures that provide a means for establishing and enforcing them.

Judicial procedure is concerned with rules by which a lawsuit is conducted. One common method of classifying judicial procedure is to divide it into two parts—*criminal* and *civil.* Criminal procedure prescribes the rules of law for apprehension, prosecution, and punishment of persons who have committed crimes. Civil procedure prescribes rules by which parties to civil lawsuits use the courts to settle their disputes.

In most cases there are three basic questions to be answered: (1) What are the facts? (2) What evidence is relevant and proper to prove the facts? (3) What rules of law apply to the facts? The jury answers the first question; the court answers the second. The court also provides the answer to the third by instructing the jury as to the law applicable to the facts found by the jury.

The parties to litigation

In a criminal case, *the people* bring the action against the named defendant. Most civil cases use the term *plaintiff* to describe the party bringing the lawsuit, and *defendant* describes the party against whom it is brought; but in some cases, especially in courts of equity, the parties are described as the *petitioner* and the *respondent.*

When the result at the trial court level is appealed, the party appealing is usually referred to as *appellant,* and the successful party in the trial court is called the *appellee.* Many jurisdictions, in publishing the decisions of reviewing courts, list the appellant first and the appellee second, even though the appellant may have been the defendant in the trial court.

In most states and in the federal courts, all persons may join in one lawsuit as plaintiffs if the causes of action arise out of the same transaction or series of transactions and involve common questions of law or fact. In addition, the plaintiffs may join as defendants all persons who are necessary to a complete determination or settlement of the questions. In addition, if a defendant alleges that a complete determination of a controversy cannot be made without other parties, that defendant may bring in new third parties as third-party defendants. This procedure is usually followed when someone is liable to a defendant who, in turn, is liable to the plaintiff.

Two problem areas or issues relating to the parties to a lawsuit frequently arise in litigation. The first of these issues is generally described as "standing to sue." The second is class-action suits. These special problems are discussed more fully below.

Standing to sue

The question of standing to sue is whether the litigant is entitled to have the court decide the dispute. The issue arises because of the limited role of courts in our society. The Constitution requires that a plaintiff must allege a case or controversy between himself and the defendant if the court is to hear the case. A plaintiff must have a personal stake in the outcome of the controversy, and this stake must be based on some threatened or actual injury resulting from the defendant's action. Without the requirement of "standing," courts would be called upon to decide abstract questions of wide public significance. Such questions are best resolved by the political process.

When the asserted harm is a generalized grievance shared in substantially equal measure by all or a large class of citizens, that harm alone normally does not grant standing to sue. For example, a taxpayer filed suit challenging the budget of the CIA. The court held that the taxpayer lacked standing to sue. Likewise, a plaintiff must assert his own legal rights and not those of some third party. A citizen objected to the army's surveillance of civilians, but the case was dismissed without a showing that the plaintiff was one of the civilians under surveillance.

Standing to sue is in no way dependent upon the merits of the plaintiff's contention that particular conduct is illegal. The presence of standing is determined by the nature and source of the plaintiff's claim. As a general rule, "standing" requires that a complaining party have a personal stake in the outcome of the controversy, a stake that would result in adversity from all aspects of the issues being presented for decision. A complainant must present facts sufficient to show that his or her individual needs require the remedy being sought in suits directed at government. A plaintiff must show that he or she has sustained or is immediately in danger of sustaining a direct injury as a result of some governmental action included in the lawsuit. In civil rights cases and in cases involving threats to the environment, the courts have been rather liberal in finding a personal stake in a plaintiff bringing an action relating to those subjects.

Class-action suits

A class-action suit is one in which a person files suit on his own behalf and on behalf of all other persons who may have a similar claim. A class-action suit may be brought on behalf of all purchasers of a defective product. The number of people who comprise a class is frequently quite large. Class-action suits are popular because they often involve matters in which no one member of the class would have a sufficient financial interest to warrant filing suit. The combined interest of all members of the class not only makes litigation feasible, but often makes it very profitable for the lawyer who handles the suit.

Because many defendants consider class-action suits a form of harassment, courts have tended to discourage the suits. For example, cases have held that all members of the class be given actual notice of the lawsuit. They must be given individual notice, not merely public notice. In addition, plaintiffs who bring the class-action suit must pay all court costs of the action, including the cost of compiling names and addresses of members of the class.

If a class-action suit is in federal court because of diversity of citizenship, the claim of each member of the class must meet the jurisdictional amount of $10,000. This requirement, together with the requirement of notice to each member of the class, has greatly reduced the number of class-action suits in the federal courts. However, the practice of plaintiffs' lawyers combining a single grievance into a lawsuit on behalf of every possible litigant is quite common in state courts. There are numerous state class-action statutes that allow consumers and others to file suit in state courts on behalf of all citizens of that state.

Jurisdiction

The first requirement in any lawsuit is that it must be brought before a court that has the power to hear the case. This power to hear the case is known as *jurisdiction,* and it has two aspects: jurisdiction over the subject matter and jurisdiction over the parties. Jurisdiction over the subject matter means that the lawsuit is of the type that the court was created to decide. A probate court would not have jurisdiction to determine questions of law involving a civil suit for damages. A criminal court would have no jurisdiction in a divorce matter. Courts may also be limited by the amounts of money involved in the case. For example, federal courts hear suits for damages only if they involve at least $10,000.

A court must also have jurisdiction over the parties—the plaintiff and the defendant. A plaintiff voluntarily submits to the jurisdiction of the court when the suit is filed.

Jurisdiction over the defendant is accomplished by the service of a summons issued by the court. It is delivered to a sheriff or other person, to be served upon the defendant. Jurisdiction over a defendant in a limited number of cases may be obtained by publishing a notice in a newspaper. This method is possible in a suit for divorce or one concerning real estate, something important enough to be written up in a public notice that would be deemed adequate to notify the defendant. Publication may also be accompanied by proper attachment proceedings. In such cases, service by publication brings under the court's jurisdiction all attached property of a nonresident defendant if it lies within the territorial limits of the court. When this technique is employed, the attached property may be used to satisfy any judgment. Most cases, however, require the actual service of a summons on the defendant in order to give him notice of the suit.

Many states allow a summons to be served upon any member of the family above a specified age, such as ten years, at the defendant's home. In such cases, a copy is also mailed to the defendant.

Long-arm statutes

Historically, the jurisdiction of courts to enter judgment against a person required actual personal service of the summons on the defendant in the state in which the suit was brought. This was necessary in order to give the defendant notice of the suit and an opportunity to defend. Because the jurisdiction of courts was limited to geographical areas such as a state or a county, power to issue and serve a summons beyond the borders of the state or county did not exist.

Limiting the jurisdiction of courts to persons physically present in the state is no longer accepted. Personal jurisdiction over nonresidents has been expanded because modern transportation and communication facilities have minimized the inconveniences to a nonresident defendant who must defend himself in courts beyond his home state. There is no longer any logical reason to deny a local citizen a remedy in local courts for an injury caused by a nonresident temporarily present in the state. The first extension of jurisdiction over nonresidents occurred in auto accident cases. This extension was made by creating a legal "fiction" that resulted in the summons being served within the state whose court issued the summons. This legal fiction was created by the enactment of statutes providing that a nonresident, by using the state highways, automatically appointed a designated state official, usually the secretary of state, as his agent to accept service of process. The summons would be served on the secretary of state, who would notify the defendant of the suit, and the defendant was then subject to the power of the court.

These nonresident motorist statutes opened the door for adoption of other statutes, called long-arm statutes, which further extend the jurisdiction of courts over nonresidents, whether individuals or corporations. Long-arm statutes typically extend the jurisdiction of courts to cases in which a tort injury has been caused by a nonresident "doing business" in the state.

They also usually extend jurisdiction to cases arising out of the ownership of property located within the state. Of course, the conduct of business such as entering into contracts confers jurisdiction. Thus, a nonresident individual or a corporation may be subject to a suit for injuries if either has certain "minimal contacts" within the state, so long as the maintenance of the suit does not offend traditional notions of fair play and substantial justice.

What "minimal contacts" and activities are necessary to bring the defendant into a state is a fact question depending upon each particular case. Whatever the basis for the action may be, either in contract or in tort, the court can acquire jurisdiction over the defendant if these minimal contacts are present.

Venue

As previously discussed, the term *jurisdiction* defines the power of the court to hear and adjudicate the case. Jurisdiction includes the court's power to inquire into the facts, apply the law to the facts, make a decision, and declare and enforce a judgment. *Venue* relates to, and defines, the particular territorial area within the state, county, or district in which the civil case should be brought and tried. Matters of venue are usually determined by statute. In a few states, the subject of venue is covered in the state constitution.

Venue statutes usually provide that actions concerning interests in land must be commenced and tried in the county or district in which the land is located. Actions for the recovery of penalties imposed by statute against public officers must be commenced and tried in the county or district in which the cause of action arose. Suits for divorce must be commenced and tried in the county in which one of the parties resides. All other suits or actions must be commenced and tried in the county in which one or all of the defendants reside or in the county in which the transaction took place or where the wrong was committed. A tort action may be commenced and tried either in the county or district where the tort was committed or where the defendant resides or may be found. If the defendants are nonresidents, and assuming that proper service can be made upon them under a long-arm statute, the suit may be commenced and tried in any county the plaintiff designates in his complaint.

The judge may change the place of trial at the request of either party when it appears from an affidavit of either party that the action was not commenced in the proper venue. A change of venue may also be requested on the ground that the judge has an interest in the suit or is related to any parties to the action or has manifested a prejudice so that he cannot be expected to conduct a fair and impartial trial. A change of venue is often requested in criminal trials when the inhabitants of the county allegedly are so prejudiced against the defendant that a fair trial is not possible. The convenience of witnesses and the parties may also justify a change of venue.

Proceedings Prior to Trial

Pleadings

A *pleading* is a legal document filed with the court that sets forth the position and contentions of a party. The purpose of pleadings in civil actions is to define the issues of the lawsuit. This is accomplished by each party making allegations of fact and the other party either admitting the allegations or denying them. The procedure begins when the plaintiff files with the clerk of the court a pleading usually called a *complaint.* In some types of cases this initial pleading is called a *declaration* or a *petition.* The clerk then issues a summons that, together with a copy of the complaint, is served on the defendant. The summons notifies the defendant of the date by which he is required to file a pleading in answer to the allegations of the complaint or to file some other pleading attacking the complaint.

If the defendant has no legal basis to attack the sufficiency of the complaint, an answer will be filed in which the defendant admits or denies each material allegation of the complaint. This answer will put in issue all allegations of the complaint that are denied.

In addition to admissions and denials, an answer may contain affirmative defenses, which if proved will defeat the plaintiff's claim. The answer may also contain *counterclaims,* causes of action the defendant has against the plaintiff. Upon receipt of the defendant's answer, the plaintiff will, unless the applicable rules of procedure do not so require, file a reply that specifically admits or denies each new allegation in the defendant's answer. These new allegations are those found in the affirmative defenses and counterclaims. Thus the allegations of each party are admitted or denied in the pleadings. Allegations of fact claimed by either party and denied by the other become the issues to be decided at the trial.

Motions attacking pleadings

The first pleading (complaint), in order to be legally sufficient, must allege facts sufficient to set forth a right of action or the plaintiff's right to legal relief. The defendant's attorney, after studying the complaint, may (instead of answering) choose one of several different ways to challenge its legal sufficiency. For example, by motion to the court, the defendant may object to the complaint, pointing out specifically its defects. The defendant, through such motion, admits for purposes of argument all the facts alleged in the complaint. His position is that those facts are not legally sufficient to give the plaintiff the right to what is sought in the complaint. Such motion, called a *demurrer* at common law, raises questions of law, not questions of fact. If the court finds that the complaint does set forth facts sufficient to give the plaintiff what is sought, it will deny the motion. The defendant will then be granted time to answer the complaint. Should he fail to do so within the time limit set by the court, a judgment by default may be entered for the plaintiff. If the court finds, however, that the complaint fails to state facts sufficient to give the plaintiff the relief sought, the court will allow the motion and dismiss the suit but will give to the plaintiff permission to file an amended complaint. The plaintiff will thus be given an opportunity to restate the allegations so that he may be able to set forth a right to recover from the defendant.

In addition to a motion to dismiss for failure to allege a valid cause of action, a defendant may also move to dismiss the suit for reasons that as a matter of law would prevent the plaintiff from winning his suit. Such matters as a discharge in bankruptcy, a lack of jurisdiction of the court to hear the suit, or an expiration of the time limit during which the defendant is subject to suit may be raised by such a motion. These are technical matters that raise questions of law for the court's decision.

Decisions based on pleadings

Most states and the federal courts have procedures known as *motions for summary judgment* or *motions for judgment on the pleadings,* by which either party may seek a final decision without a trial. In hearings on these motions, the court examines all papers on file in the case, including affidavits that may have been filed with the motion or in opposition to it, to see if a genuine material issue of fact remains. If there is no such question of fact, the court will then decide the legal question raised by the facts and find for one party or the other. This is possible only when there are no facts in dispute. In such cases there is no reason for a trial, and the issues between the parties are pure questions of law.

A defendant that fails to answer the allegations of the plaintiff is in default, and a court of law may enter a default judgment against him. In effect, the defendant has admitted the allegations of the plaintiff. A court of equity would enter a similar order known as a decree *pro confesso.* A plaintiff who fails to reply to new matter such as a counterclaim is also subject to a judgment or decree by default.

Discovery procedures

During the pleading stage and in the interval before the trial, the law provides for procedures called *discovery* procedures. Discovery is designed to take surprise out of litigation and to ensure that the results of lawsuits are based on the merits of the controversy rather than on the ability, skill, or cunning of counsel. Discovery procedures prevent a party or a witness from remaining silent about material facts. They ensure that all potential testimony and other evidence is equally available to both parties. With each side fully aware of the strengths and weaknesses of both sides, the second of the avowed purposes of discovery—to encourage settlement of suits and to avoid actual trial—is facilitated. Modern discovery procedures result in the compromise and settlement of a large majority of all civil suits.

Discovery practices include the deposing (questioning under oath) of other parties and witnesses; written questions answered under oath by the opposite party; compulsory physical examinations by doctors chosen by the other party in personal injury cases; orders requiring the production of statements, exhibits, documents, maps, photographs, and so on; and serving of demands by one party on the other to admit facts under oath.

These procedures allow a party to learn not only about matters that may be used as evidence but also about matters that may lead to the discovery of evidence.

Just prior to the trial, a pretrial conference between the lawyers and the judge will be held in states with modern rules of procedure. At this conference the pleadings, results of the discovery process, and probable evidence are reviewed in an attempt to settle the suit. The issues may be further narrowed, and the judge may even predict the outcome in order to encourage settlement.

The Trial

Jury selection

Not every case can be settled, even under modern procedures. Some must go to trial on the issues of fact raised by pleadings that remain after the pretrial conference. If the only issues are questions of law, the court will decide the case without a trial by a ruling on one of the motions previously mentioned. If the case is at law and either party has demanded a jury trial, the case will be set for trial and a jury empaneled. If the case is in equity or if no jury demand has been made, it will be set down for trial before the court. For purposes of the following discussion, we shall assume a trial before a jury.

The first step of the trial is to select the jury. Prior to calling the case, the clerk of the court will have summoned potential jurors known as the *venire.* They will be selected at random from lists of eligible citizens, and the appropriate number (usually twelve) will be called into the jury box for the conduct of *voir dire* examination.

In *voir dire,* the court and attorneys for each party question prospective jurors to determine their fairness and impartiality. Jurors are sworn to answer truthfully and may be challenged or excused for cause, such as bias or relation to one of the parties. A certain number of *peremptory challenges,* for which no cause need be given, may also be exercised to reject jurors.

Introduction of evidence

After selecting the jurors, the attorneys make opening statements. An opening statement is not evidence. Its purpose is to familiarize the jury with essential facts that each side expects to prove, in order that the jury may understand the overall picture of the case and the relevancy of each piece of evidence. After the opening statements, the plaintiff presents his evidence.

Evidence is presented in open court by means of examination of witnesses and the production of documents and other exhibits. The party calling a witness questions him to establish the facts about the case. As a general rule, a party calling a witness is not permitted to ask *leading questions,* questions in which the desired answer is indicated by the form of the question. After the party calling the witness has completed his direct examination, the other party is given the opportunity to cross-examine the witness. Matters inquired into on cross-examination are limited to those matters that were raised on direct examination. After cross-examination, the party calling the witness again has the opportunity of examining the witness, and this examination is called redirect examination. It is limited to the scope of those matters covered on cross-examination and is used to clarify matters raised on cross-examination. After redirect examination, the opposing party is allowed recross-examination, with the corresponding limitation on scope of the questions. Witnesses may be asked to identify exhibits. Expert witnesses may be asked to give their opinion, within certain limitations, about the case, and sometimes experts are allowed to answer hypothetical questions.

In the conduct of a trial, rules of evidence govern admissibility of testimony and exhibits and establish which facts may be presented to the jury. Each rule of evidence is based on some policy consideration and the desire to give each party an opportunity to present his evidence and contentions without unduly taking advantage of the other party. Rules of evidence were not created to serve as a stumbling block to meritorious litigants or to create unwarranted roadblocks to justice. On the contrary, rules of evidence were created and should be applied to ensure fair play and to aid in the goal of having controversies determined on their merits. Modern rules of evidence are liberal in the sense that they allow the introduction of most evidence that may contribute to the search for truth.

Motions during the trial

A basic rule of evidence is that a party cannot introduce evidence unless it is competent and relevant to the issues raised by the pleadings. A connection between the pleadings and the trial stage of the lawsuit is also present in certain motions made during the trial. After the plaintiff has presented his evidence, for example, the defendant will usually make a motion for a directed verdict. This motion asks the court to rule as a matter of law that the plaintiff has failed to establish the case against the defendant and that a verdict should be entered for the defendant as a matter of law. The court can direct a verdict for the defendant only if the evidence taken in the light most favorable to the plaintiff establishes as a matter of law that the defendant is entitled to a verdict. The defendant argues that the plaintiff has failed to prove each allegation of his complaint. Just as a plaintiff must allege certain facts or have his complaint dismissed by motion to dismiss, he must also have some proof of each essential allegation or lose his case on a motion for a directed verdict. If he has some proof of each allegation, the motion will be denied.

In cases tried without a jury, either party may move for a finding in his favor. Such a motion will be allowed during the course of the trial if the result is not in doubt. The judge in ruling on such motions weighs the evidence, but he may end the trial before all the evidence is presented only if there is no room for a fair difference of opinion as to the result.

If the defendant's motion for directed verdict is overruled, the defendant then presents his evidence. After the defendant has presented all his evidence, the plaintiff may bring in rebuttal evidence. When neither party has any additional evidence, the attorneys and the judge retire for a conference to consider the instructions of law to be given the jury.

Jury instructions

The purpose of jury instructions is to acquaint the jury with the law applicable to the case. Because the function of the jury is to find the facts, and the function of the court is to determine the applicable law, there must be a method to bring them together in an orderly manner that will result in a decision. At the conference, each attorney submits to the court the instructions he feels should be given to the jury. The court examines these instructions and confers with the attorneys about any objections to proposed instructions. A party that fails to submit an instruction on a point of law cannot later object to the failure to instruct on that point. Similarly, the failure to object to an instruction is a waiver of the objection. The court then decides which instructions will be given to the jury.

A jury instruction tells the jury that if they find certain facts, then their verdict should be for the plaintiff. If they fail to find these facts, then the verdict should be for the defendant.

Burden of proof

The term *burden of proof* has two meanings. It may describe the person with the burden of coming forward with evidence on a particular issue. The party alleging the existence of a certain fact usually has the burden of coming forward with evidence to establish that fact. The more common usage of the term, however, is to identify the party with the burden of persuasion. The party with this burden must convince the trier (judge or jury) of the facts in the issue. If a party with the burden of persuasion fails to do so, that party loses the issue.

The extent of proof required to satisfy the burden of persuasion varies, depending upon the issue and the type of case. There are three distinct levels of proof recognized by the law: (1) beyond a reasonable doubt standard, (2) manifest weight standard, and (3) clear and convincing proof standard. For criminal cases, the burden of proof is described as "beyond a reasonable doubt." This means that the prosecution in a criminal case has the burden of convincing the trier, usually a jury, of fact that the defendant is guilty of the crime charged and that the jury has no reasonable doubt about guilt. This burden of proof does not require evidence beyond any doubt, but only beyond a reasonable doubt. A reasonable doubt is one that a reasonable person viewing the evidence might reasonably entertain.

In civil cases the party with the burden of proof will be subject to one of two standards: the manifest weight of the evidence standard or the clear and convincing proof standard. Manifest weight standard is used most frequently. It requires that a party convince the jury by a preponderance of evidence that the facts are as contended. By *preponderance of evidence* we mean that there is greater weight of evidence in support of the proposition than there is against it.

The clear and convincing proof requirement is used in certain situations in which the law requires more than a simple preponderance of evidence but less than proof beyond a reasonable doubt. In a securities law case, proof of fraud usually requires clear and convincing evidence if a plaintiff is to succeed. A slight preponderance of evidence in favor of the party asserting the truth of a proposition is not enough. Unless the evidence clearly establishes the proposition, the party with the burden of proof fails to sustain it and loses the lawsuit.

Verdicts and judgments

After the conference on jury instructions, the attorneys argue the case before the jury. The party with the burden of proof, usually the plaintiff, is given an opportunity to open the argument and to close it. The defendant's attorney is allowed to argue only after the plaintiff's argument and is allowed to argue only once. After the arguments are completed, the court reads instructions to the jury. The jury then retires to deliberate.

Upon reaching a verdict, the jury returns from the jury room, announces its verdict, and judgment is entered. Judgments are either *in rem* or *in personam.* A judgment *in rem* is an adjudication entered against a thing—property, real or personal. The judgment is a determination of the status of the subject matter. Thus a judgment of forfeiture of goods for the violation of a revenue law is a judgment *in rem.* Although a judgment *in rem* is limited to the subject matter, it nevertheless affects the rights and duties of persons. Although a decree dissolving a marriage seriously affects persons, it is nevertheless a judgment *in rem* because it affects a status, the marriage relation. A judgment *in rem* is binding not only on the persons previously concerned with the status or thing but on all other persons.

A judgment against a particular person is a judgment *in personam,* limited in its application to such person only, whereas a judgment *in rem* is conclusive on all persons.

Proceedings after the Trial

Post-trial motions

After judgment is entered, the losing party starts the procedure of post-trial motions, which raise questions of law concerning the conduct of the lawsuit. These motions seek relief such as a new trial or a judgment, notwithstanding the verdict of the jury. A motion seeking a new trial may be granted if the judge feels that the verdict of the jury is contrary to the manifest weight of the evidence. The court may enter a judgment opposite to that of the verdict of the jury if the judge finds that the verdict is, as a matter of law, erroneous. To reach such a conclusion, the court must find that reasonable men viewing the evidence could not reach the verdict returned. For example, a verdict for the plaintiff based on sympathy instead of evidence could be set aside.

After the judge rules on the post-trial motion, the losing party may appeal. It should be noted that lawsuits usually end by a ruling on a motion, either before trial, during the trial, or after the trial. Motions raise questions of law that are decided by the court. The right to appeal is absolute if perfected within the prescribed time. All litigants are entitled to a trial and a review, providing the proper procedures are followed.

Appeals

A dissatisfied party—plaintiff or defendant—has a right to appeal the decision of the trial court to a higher court, provided that he proceeds promptly and properly. Appellate procedures are not uniform among the states, and the appellant must comply with the appropriate statute and rules of the particular court. Appeals are usually perfected by the appellant's giving *notice of appeal* to the trial court and opposing parties.

Most states require that within at least ten days after giving notice of appeal, the appellant must file an appeal bond, in effect guaranteeing to pay costs that may be charged against him on the appeal. This bond permits the appellee to collect costs if the appellant loses an appeal.

The statutes usually require that within a specified time after an appeal is perfected, the appellant shall file with the clerk of the appellate court a *transcript,* consisting of a copy of the judgment, decree, or order appealed from, and other papers required by rules of the court.

The transcript alone, however, is not enough to present the case to the appellate court. The appellant must prepare and file a "brief" that contains a statement of the case, a list of the assignment of errors upon which the appellant has based his appeal, his legal authorities and argument. The brief contains the arguments on both fact and law by which the attorney attempts to show how the lower court committed the errors alleged.

The appellee (respondent) files a brief of like character, setting out his side of the case with points, authorities, and arguments. By such procedure, the case on the issues raised goes to the appellate court for decision.

The appellate court, upon receipt of the appeal, will place it on the calendar for hearing. Attorneys will be notified of the time and will be given an opportunity for oral argument. After the oral argument, the court prepares a written opinion stating the applicable law involved and giving the reasons for its decision. The court, by its decision, may affirm or reverse the court below, or the court may send the case back for a new trial. At the end of each published opinion found in the reports, a word or a few words will express the court's decision: "affirmed," "reversed," "reversed and remanded," or whatever the case requires.

Enforcement of judgments and decrees

A decision of a court becomes final when the time provided for a review of the decision has expired. In the trial court, decision is final at the expiration of time for appeal. In a reviewing court, it is expiration of the time to request a rehearing or to request a futher review of the case. After the decision has become final, judicial action may be required to enforce the decision. In most cases the losing party will voluntarily comply with the decision and satisfy the judgment or otherwise do what the decree requires, but the assistance of the court is sometimes required to enforce its final decision.

If a judgment for dollar damages is not paid, the judgment creditor may apply for a *writ of execution.* This writ directs the sheriff to seize personal property of the judgment debtor and to sell enough thereof to satisfy the judgment and to cover the costs and expenses of the sale. The writ authorizes the sheriff to seize both tangible and intangible personal property, such as bank accounts. If the judgment debtor's personal property seized and sold by the sheriff does not produce sufficient funds to pay the judgment, the writ of execution is returned to the court with a statement of the extent to which the judgment is unsatisfied. If an execution is returned unsatisfied in whole or in part, the judgment becomes a lien on any real estate owned by the debtor if it is within the jurisdiction of the court that issued the writ of execution. An unpaid judgment creditor is entitled to have the real estate sold at a judicial sale and to have the net proceeds of the sale applied on the judgment. A judgment creditor with an unsatisfied writ of execution has not only a lien on real property owned by the judgment debtor at the time the judgment becomes final, but also a judicial lien on any real property acquired by the judgment debtor during the life of judgment.

Garnishment is another important method used by judgment creditors to collect a judgment. A judgment creditor can "garnish" the wages of the judgment debtor or his bank account or any other obligation owing to him from a third party. In the process of garnishment, the person owing the money to a judgment debtor—the employer, bank of deposit, third party—will be directed to pay the money into court rather than to the judgment debtor, and such money will be applied against the judgment debt.

In connection with writs of execution and garnishment proceedings, it is extremely significant that the laws of the various states have statutory provisions that exempt certain property from writs of execution and garnishment. The state laws limit the amount of wages that can be garnished and usually provide for both real-property and personal-property exemptions. This will be discussed with the materials on bankruptcy.

In recent years many states have adopted a *citation proceeding,* which greatly assists the creditor in collecting a judgment. The citation procedure begins with the service of a "citation" on the judgment debtor to appear in court at a stated time for examination under oath about his financial affairs. It also prohibits the judgment debtor from making any transfer of property until after the examination in court. At the hearing, the judgment creditor or his attorney questions the judgment debtor about his income, property, and affairs. Any nonexempt property that is discovered during the questioning may be ordered sold by the judge, with the proceeds applied to the judgment. The court may also order that weekly or monthly payments be made by the judgment debtor. In states that have adopted the citation proceeding, the difficulties in collecting a judgment have been substantially reduced.

One important method of collecting a judgment is also relevant to the procedures that may be used to commence a lawsuit. The procedure with these dual purposes is known as *attachment.* Attachment is a method of acquiring *in rem* jurisiction of a nonresident defendant who is not subject to the service of process. The court may "attach" property of the nonresident defendant, and in so doing the court acquires jurisdiction over the defendant to the extent of the value of the property attached. Attachment as a means of obtaining *in rem* jurisdiction is used in cases involving the status of a person, such as divorce, or the status of property, such as in eminent domain (acquisition of private property for public use) proceedings.

Attachment as a method of ensuring collection of a judgment is used by a plaintiff who fears that the defentant will dispose of his property before the court is able to enter a final decision. The plaintiff has the property of the defendant seized, pending the outcome of the lawsuit.

Attachment and the procedures controlling its use are governed by statutes that vary among the states. The attaching plaintiff-creditor must put up a bond with the court for the protection of the defendant, and the statutes provide methods whereby the attachment may be vacated by the defendant. If the plaintiff receives a judgment against the defendant, the attached property will be sold to satisfy the judgment.

In spite of the remedies the creditor may use, it frequently develops that the judgment is of little value because of the lack of assets that can be reached or because of other judgments. It must be remembered that a judgment standing alone has little value. In many cases, the debtor may file a voluntary petition in bankruptcy, which will extinguish the judgment debt. In other cases, the creditor recognizes the futility of attempting to use additional legal process to collect, and the matter simply lies dormant until it dies a natural death by the expiration of the time allowed to collect the claim or judgment. Everyone should be aware that some people are judgment-proof and that in such cases the law has no means of collecting a judgment. Debtors are not sent to prison simply because of their inability to pay debts or judgments.

REVIEW QUESTIONS AND PROBLEMS

1. Who is an appellant? An appellee?
2. Give an example of a factual situation in which a case would be dismissed because the plaintiff lacked "standing to sue."
3. Give an example of a factual situation that might result in a class-action suit.
4. Distinguish *venue* from *jurisdiction.*
5. X was riding in a camper box attached to a truck, when the truck collided with a bus. The impact caused X to be thrown against the camper-box's door, which opened and allowed X to fall, resulting in his death. X's widow brought suit in West Virginia state court against Y, a West Virginia company that manufactured the camper box. Z is a New Jersey corporation with its principal place of business in New Jersey. Process has been served on Z under West Virginia's long-arm statute. Z's contact with West Virginia occurred when its product came into the state as a component part of Y's product. Does the court have jurisdiction over Z Company? Why?
6. What function do the pleadings serve?
7. What are the purposes of discovery procedures? Explain.
8. When is a motion for summary judgment proper?
9. What are the purposes of discovery procedures?
10. What is a *voir dire* examination, and what is its purpose?
11. What are jury instructions, and what purpose do they serve? Explain.
12. The burden of persuasion in litigation is described by three different terms, depending upon the extent of proof required. Name these three terms.
13. What is a writ of execution?

4

Torts

A tort is an omission (failure to act) or a wrongful act (other than a breach of contract) against a person or his property. The term is somewhat difficult to define, but the word *wrongful* in the definition means a violation of one person's legal duty to another. The victim of a tort may recover damages for the injuries received, usually because the other party was "at fault" in causing the injury.

Acts or omissions, to be tortious, need not involve moral turpitude or bad motive or maliciousness. Moreover, an act or an omission that does not invade another's rights is not tortious, even though the actor's motive is bad or malicious.

Torts as private wrongs must be contrasted with crimes, which are public wrongs. The purpose of the criminal law is to punish the wrongdoer, while the purpose of the law of torts is to compensate the victim of wrongful conduct. To deter intentional torts, however, the law may impose punitive in addition to actual damages.

The same act may be both a crime and a tort: an assault and battery is both a wrong against society and a wrong against the victim. Society may punish the guilty party, and the victim may sue in tort to recover damages. It must be recognized that the criminal action does not benefit the victim of the crime or compensate him for his injury. Such compensation is left to the civil law of torts.

Theories of tort liability

Tort liability is predicated on two premises: (1) in a civilized society one person should not intentionally injure another or his property, and (2) all persons should exercise reasonable care and caution in the conduct of their affairs. The first premise has resulted in a group of torts labeled *intentional torts.* The second premise is the basis for the general field of tort liability known as *negligence.* Liability based on negligence is liability based on fault, just as it is in an intentional tort. However, because the wrong in negligence is of a lesser degree than it is in torts, the theory of damages in negligence cases does not include punishment. For simple negligence, a person is entitled to collect only actual damages from the wrongdoer; that is, enough money to make the injured party whole. He is not entitled to collect punitive damages to discourage the wrongdoer from repeating his negligence.

A third theory of tort liability, called strict liability, is not based on wrongful conduct in the usual sense, although the party committing the tort usually does something intentionally or negligently. Strict liability is based on the peculiar factual situations and the relationship of the parties. To the extent that an activity by one party causes injury, there is liability because of the injury, not because the defendant was at fault in the traditional sense of wrongdoing. Although there is no fault in the sense of wrongdoing, there is fault in that actions caused the injuries. Strict liability is imposed when harm is caused by dangerous or trespassing animals, blasting operations, or fire.

Every person legally responsible is liable for his or her own torts. It is no defense that the wrongdoer is working under the direction of another. That fact may create liability on the part of the other person, but it is no defense to the wrongdoer. The theory of liability by which one person is liable for the torts of another is known as *respondeat superior.* This theory imposes liability on principals or masters for the torts of their agents or servants if the agent or servant is acting within the scope of employment when the tort was committed. This subject is discussed more fully in chapter 34.

If two or more persons jointly commit a tort, all may be held liable for the total injury. The liability is said to be joint and several. All are liable, and each is liable for the entire damage.

Intentional Torts

There are several intentional torts that often involve the business community as either plaintiffs or defendants. The imposition of liability for these torts provides protection to basic, individual interests of people and their property. The torts may involve (1) interference with the personal freedom of an individual, (2) interference with property rights, (3) interference with economic relations, and (4) wrongful communications. Table 4·1 briefly describes each.

Interference with personal freedom

Assault and battery and false imprisonment involve business more commonly than they should. If an employee of a business engages in a fight with a customer, a lawsuit on the theory of assault and battery is likely to follow. Similarly, if an employee wrongfully physically restrains a customer, there may be a tort action for false imprisonment. Assume that P is suspected of shoplifting and D physically restrains him. If D is wrong, and P is not a shoplifter, a tort has been committed.

Inflicting mental distress is a tort very important to the business community. It is an invasion of a person's peace of mind by insults or other indignities or by outrageous conduct. If someone without a privilege to do so, by extreme and outrageous conduct, intentionally causes another person severe emotional distress with bodily harm resulting

Table 4·1 Intentional torts common to business

Theory of liability	Description
Interference with personal freedom	
Battery	Intentional and unpermitted physical contact with a person's body.
Assault	Causing the apprehension of a harmful or offensive contact with a person's body.
Assault and battery	A combination of assault and battery (some hits and some misses).
False imprisonment	A wrongful restraint of a person's freedom of movement.
Mental distress	Wrongful interference with a person's peace of mind by insults, indignities, or outrageous conduct.
Interference with property	
Trespass to land	An unauthorized entry upon the land of another.
Trespass to chattels	A direct intentional interference with a chattel in possession of another person, such as taking it or damaging it.
Conversion	Interference with a person's chattels to the extent that the wrongdoer ought to pay for the chattel.
Nuisance	An intentional invasion or disturbance of a person's rights in land or the conduct of an abnormally dangerous activity.
Interference with economic relations	
Disparagement	Injurious falsehoods about a person's business or property, damaging prospective advantage.
Contracts	Inducing a party to a contract to breach it, or interfering with its performance.
Prospective advantage	Interfering with an expectancy such as employment or an opportunity to contract.
Wrongful communications	
Slander	Oral defamation. Holding a person's name or reputation up to hatred, contempt, or ridicule, or causing others to shun him.
Libel	Written defamation.
Invasion of privacy	Interfering with one's right to be let alone by (1) appropriating the name or picture of a person, (2) intruding upon a person's physical solitude, (3) the public disclosure of private facts, and (4) publicity that places a person in a false light in the public eye.
Fraud	An intentional misstatement of a material existing fact relied upon by another, to his injury.

from that distress, the offender is subject to liability for the other's emotional distress and bodily harm. Liability does not exist for every case of hurt feelings or bad manners—only where conduct is so outrageous in character and so extreme in degree that it goes beyond all possible bounds of decency. For liability, the conduct must be regarded as atrocious, utterly intolerable in a civilized community. Liability exists in cases in which the facts, if told to an average person, would lead him to exclaim "Outrageous!" High-pressure tactics of collection agencies, including violent cursing and accusations of dishonesty, have often been held to be outrageous.

Interference with property

The tort of trespass is a common one and is applied both to real and personal property. Trespass to land occurs when there is an unauthorized entry upon the land of another. The person in exclusive possession of land is entitled to enjoy the use of that land free from interference of others. Entry upon the land of another is a trespass even if the one who enters is under the mistaken belief that he is the owner or has a right, license, or privilege to enter.

Trespass to land may be *innocent* or *willful.* An innocent trespass would occur when one goes on another's land by mistake or under the impression that he has a right to be there. It is still an intentional wrong because persons intend the natural and probable consequences of their acts. A trespass is willful if the trespasser knowingly goes on another's land, aware that he or she has no right to do so. In a trespass case, if the trespass is willful, the plaintiff is entitled to exemplary or punitive damages, which may include attorney's fees. It should be kept in mind that except for tort cases involving punitive damages, every litigant pays his or her own attorney's fees in tort cases.

A trespass to personal property—goods and the like—is unlawful interference with the control and possession of the goods of another. One is entitled to have exclusive possession and control of his personal property and may recover for any physical harm to his goods by reason of the wrongful conduct of another. The intent need not be wrongful. If a person mistakenly interferes with the goods of another, a trespass has occurred. A trespass to goods may occur by theft of the goods or by damage to the goods. In such cases, the owner recovers the property and is entitled to be paid for the damage to the property and for its loss of use during the period that the owner lost possession of the property.

The action of conversion is quite similar to trespass. It differs in that a suit for conversion of goods is used when the interference is so significant that the wrongdoer is compelled to pay the full value of the goods as damages. Conversion, in theory, is a judicial sale of the chattel to the wrongdoer. Using someone else's lumber for building purposes would be a conversion. Among the factors used to determine if the interference is relatively minor (trespass) or serious (conversion) are (1) the extent and duration of the interference, (2) the defendant's motives, (3) the amount of actual damage to the goods, and (4) the inconvenience and other harm suffered by the plaintiff. Conversion results from conduct intended to affect the chattel. The intent required is not conscious wrongdoing but an intent to exercise control over the goods. For example, a purchaser of stolen goods is guilty of conversion even though he does not know the goods are stolen. An act of interference with the rights of the true owner establishes the conversion.

Conversion frequently occurs even though the defendant's original possession of the goods is lawful. It may result from several actions, such as a transfer of the goods to another person or to another location. A laundry that delivers shirts to the wrong person is guilty of a conversion. If the laundry refuses to deliver the shirts to the owner, a conversion has occurred. Destruction, alteration, or misuse of a chattel may also constitute a conversion.

Tort liability may also be predicated upon the unreasonable use by a person of his own property. Any improper or indecent activity that causes harm to another person, to his property, or to the public generally is tortious. Such conduct is usually described as a *nuisance,* either private or public. A private nuisance disturbs only the interest of some private individual, whereas the public nuisance disturbs or interferes with the public in general. The legal theory supporting tort liability in these areas is that an owner of property, although conducting a lawful business thereon, is subject to reasonable limitations and must use his property in a way that will not unreasonably interfere with the health and comfort of his neighbors or with their *right to the enjoyment of their property.* The ownership of land includes the right to reasonable comfort and convenience in its occupation. In addition to tort liability, the remedy of an injunction is used to abate a nuisance.

A nuisance may result from intentional conduct or from negligence. Although malice may be involved, most nuisances are intentional in the sense that the party creating the nuisance did so with the knowledge that harm to the interests of others would follow. A nuisance requires a substantial and unreasonable interference with the rights of others and not a mere annoyance or inconvenience.

A nuisance may exist because of the type of business activity being conducted. Operation of a drag strip or a massage parlor has been held to constitute a private nuisance to the neighbors. Many nuisances result from the manner in which business is conducted. Pollution of the air or water by a business frequently results in tort liability based on the nuisance theory. Most tort litigation dealing with private nuisances is resolved by weighing the conflicting interests of adjoining landowners. If one party is seriously injuring the other, the activity may be enjoined and dollar damages awarded. Even if the courts are unwilling to enjoin an activity, dollar damages may still be awarded because of a nuisance.

Interference with economic relations

Interference with commercial or economic relations includes three business torts: (1) disparagement (2) interference with contractual relations, and (3) interference with prospective advantage. Disparagement is a communication of an injurious falsehood about a person's property, quality of product, or character and conduct of business in general. Such false statements are regarded as "unfair" competition and are not privileged. The basis of the tort is the false communications that result in interference with the prospect of sale or some other advantageous business relation. The falsehood must be communicated to a third party and must result in specific pecuniary loss. The loss of specific customers, sales, or business transactions must be demonstrated. Although closely related, slander or personal defamation of one's reputation is another tort, which will be discussed with other wrongful communications.

Interference with contractual relations usually takes the form of inducing a breach of contract. In order to hold someone liable for interference with a contract, a direct causal relation and improper motive must be shown. Mere loss suffered from a broken contract is insufficient. Crucial to the question of liability is the balancing of the conflicing interests of the parties involved. For example, assume that a depositor tells the bank's president that she believes one of the cashiers is dishonest. She suggests that the cashier be discharged. Has the depositor committed a tort? The policy of protecting employees from wrongful interference with the employment contracts must be weighed against the desirability of ensuring that bank employees are honest. The trend of cases is to allow recovery for all wrongful interferences with the rights of others. Any intentional invasion or interference with the property or contractual rights of others without just cause is a tort. The economic harm due to the breach of an existing contract is weighed against the motive and the reasonableness of the action. The courts tend to favor the sanctity of existing contracts over other interests such as unrestricted competition.

Interference with prospective or potential advantage is considered a tort, in order to protect the expectancies of future contractual relations, including the prospect of obtaining employment, employees, or customers. It is no tort to use fair business practices to beat a business rival to prospective customers; however, the competitor's motive and means of accomplishment determine liability. Fraud, violence, intimidation, and threats that drive away potential customers from one's market result in liability. As in suits for lost profits, obtaining sufficient proof that losses were actually suffered is sometimes difficult.

Another interference with economic relations tort is the wrongful appropriation of another's good will or business value. It is a tort to infringe on another's patent, trademark, or copyright. In addition, a trade name such as Holiday Inn or Coca-Cola is entitled to protection from theft or appropriation by another. Many cases involving the appropriation of another's business values involve words or actions that are deceptively similar to those of another. It is a tort to use a name or take an action that is deceptively similar to the protected interests of another. But what degree of similarity may exist before a wrong is committed? In general, it can be said that whenever the casual observer, as distinct from the careful buyer, tends to be misled into purchasing the wrong article, an injunction as well as a tort action is available to the injured party.

The remedy of injunction is perhaps more important than the tort action where there is infringement of a patent, copyright, or trademark. The injunction that prohibits the continued appropriation protects not only the owner of the right but the consuming public as well.

Trade secrets are also protected by the law of torts and courts of equity. Information about one's trade, customers, processes, or manufacture is confidential; but if it is not patented or copyrighted, another firm may make the same discoveries fairly—through research, study, or observation—and may use them freely. If the second firm bribes or hires an employee of the first company, however, in order to obtain secrets, the second firm may be enjoined from using them.

Wrongful communications

Defamation consists of the twin torts of libel and slander. Libel is generally written; slander is oral. A defamatory communication is one that holds a person up to hatred, contempt, or ridicule or causes a person to be shunned by others. Tort liability for defamation exists in order to protect a person's name and reputation.

As a general rule, a charge of slander requires proof of actual damage; however, four categories of statements justify the awarding of damages without actual proof of damage. These are statements (1) imputing the commission of a crime of moral turpitude; (2) imputing the presence of a loathsome disease; (3) relating to the conduct of a business, trade, profession, or office; and (4) accusing a female of unchastity. All other slanders require proof of special damage.

The law of libel is complicated by the written aspect of defamation. Freedom of the press, for example, is guaranteed by the First Amendment, which the law must adhere to. Furthermore, application of the law of libel depends upon whether or not the person defamed is a public figure, subject to a set of standards different from those governing the rest of society. Celebrities must prove malice in order to collect damages.

If a statement is libelous on its face, it is actionable without proof of special damages. If additional facts are necessary to establish that a writing is defamatory, the law for libel is the same as for slander, and—unless the statement falls into one of the four categories previously noted—proof of actual damage is required.

Some defamatory statements are absolutely privileged. Statements made as a part of a judicial proceeding cannot constitute a tort because of the need for all witnesses to be able to testify freely, without fear of a subsequent lawsuit. Legislative proceedings and many executive communications are also absolutely privileged.

Some defamatory statements are subject to a qualified or limited privilege. For example, many communications to public officials are privileged in order to encourage citizens to report matters to officials. In addition, fair comment on matters of public concern cannot result in tort liability.

In recent years, the law has developed a tort known as *invasion of the right of privacy*. The right of privacy is the right to be let alone, but it may be invaded in numerous ways, as set forth in Table 4•1. Many cases involve newspaper or magazine stories about one's private life. A detective magazine that publishes a picture of a family at the funeral of a loved one may be guilty of an invasion of privacy. But this tort must be distinguished from libel and slander. Invasion of privacy does not involve defamation. It involves wrongful intrusion into one's private life in such a manner as to outrage or to cause mental suffering, shame, or humiliation to a person of ordinary sensibilities. The protection is for a mental condition, not a financial one. Invasion of privacy is the equivalent of a battery to one's integrity; actual damage need not be proven. Unjustified invasion of privacy entitles the victim to damages. Punitive damages may be collected if malice is shown.

The intentional tort of fraudulent misrepresentation is the subject of more litigation than any other of the intentional torts. It is used not only as the basis of suits for dollar damages, but to avoid contract liability and as a basis to rescind or cancel otherwise valid contracts. It will be discussed more fully with the materials on contracts.

Negligence

By most definitions, negligence has four basic elements: (1) a duty imposed upon a person in favor of others, (2) an act or omission that constitutes a breach of this duty, (3) proximate cause, and (4) an injury to another. In a few states, negligence actions also require proof of freedom from contributory negligence.

The concept of a legal duty means that a person must meet certain standards of conduct in order to protect others against unreasonable risks. These standards of conduct may vary, depending upon the relationship of the parties. An owner of property would owe a higher duty to a business visitor than to a trespasser. The duty owed to a trespasser is only to warn of known dangers, while the duty to business visitors is to protect them against known dangers and dangers that, with reasonable care, he might discover. Therefore, conduct that might be considered negligent to a business visitor might not be so to a trespasser.

Whenever the law imposes a duty upon a person, another person has a right, and there exists a right-duty relationship. This relationship exists because the law recognizes it.

Moral obligation does not impose a duty or create a right. The duty must be owed to the person claiming injury. An airline owes a duty to its passengers, and the passengers have the right to safe transportation. Assume that this duty is breached and the plane crashes, killing all on board. Assume also that one of the passengers was a key employee of a large company. The company has no claim or tort action against the airline, because the right-duty relationship did not exist between the airline and the company.

To determine if a person's conduct is negligent, it is generally judged against the standard of a "reasonable man." This nonexistent person is used by juries and courts in determining if a person has been subjected to an unreasonable risk. The concept of the reasonable man is discussed further in the next section.

Negligence is sometimes defined as a failure to exercise due care. People are required to exercise due care and caution for the safety of others when the risk of injury to another is present. Failure to do so is negligence. In determining if a person has exercised due care and caution, the law recognizes that some injuries are caused by unavoidable accidents. There is no tort liability for injuries received in unavoidable accidents. It is only when a person is guilty of unreasonble conduct that tort liability is imposed. Some conduct is declared to be unreasonable by statute, while most conduct is judged by case law standards and the reasonable-man concept.

Proximate cause is the element of negligence perhaps most difficult to understand. *Proximate cause* means that the act or the omission complained of is the cause of injury. There must be a causal connection between the breach of the duty and the injury or damage. Problems in applying the rule of proximate cause arise because events sometimes break the direct sequence between an act and injury. In other words, the chain of events sometimes establishes that the injury is remote from the wrongful act. Assume that a customer slips on the floor of a store and breaks a leg. While en route to the hospital in an ambulance, there is a collision in which the customer is killed. The store would not be liable for the wrongful death because its negligence was not the proximate cause of the death, although it was one event in the chain of causation of death.

The issue of proximate cause must be decided on a case-by-case basis. Proximate cause requires that the injury be the natural and probable consequence of the wrong. Proximate cause means that the injury was foreseeable from the wrong; and without the wrong, the injury would not have occurred. Issues of foreseeability are often difficult.

Assume that a plaintiff suffered a heart attack when informed that her daughter and granddaughter were killed in an auto accident. The plaintiff could not collect from the party at fault in the auto accident, because her injury was not foreseeable and predictable. There was no proximate cause.

Proximate cause need not be the sole cause nor the one nearest in time. Where several causes contribute together to an injury, they each may constitute proximate cause. If two autos, each with a negligent driver, collide and injure some third party, both drivers are liable. The negligence of each is a proximate cause of the injury.

The reasonable man

Negligence presumes a uniform standard of behavior. As previously noted, this standard is that of a reasonable, prudent man using ordinary care and skill. The reasonable man (meaning, or course, man or woman) is a community ideal of reasonable behavior that varies from situation to situation. Therefore, the standard is applied by asking the question: what would the reasonable man do under these circumstances?

The reasonable man's physical characteristics are those of the actor in the case being tried. If a person is disabled, so is the reasonable man. On the other hand, the actual mental capacity of the actor may be very different from that of a reasonable man. The law cannot allow a person who has bad judgment or a violent temper to injure others without liability simply because of these mental defects. While the mental capacity required ignores temperament, intellect, and education, it does take age into account. Children may be liable for negligence. In judging the conduct of a child, the standard is what to expect of children of like age, intelligence, and experience. Some courts have held that children below the age of 7 are, as a matter of law, incapable of negligence; from 7 to 14 they are presumed to be incapable, but this presumption may be rebutted; and from 14 to majority they are capable, but this may also be rebutted. It is clear that a minor driving a car is held to the same standard as an adult.

The reasonable-man test implies that everyone has a minimum level of knowledge. A reasonable man is presumed to know that gasoline will burn; that ice is slippery; and that the greater the speed of an automobile, the greater the danger of injury. In addition, if the person in question has knowledge superior to most people, the law requires that he conduct himself according to his actual skill and knowledge. A skilled orthopedic surgeon is held to a higher degree of care than a general practitioner of medicine.

Among the factors that affect the application of the reasonable-man standard are community customs, emergencies, and the conduct of others. If a person conducts himself in the manner customary to the community, then such conduct probably is not negligent. If everyone does it, then it probably is not unreasonable behavior. Custom, however, does not as a matter of law establish due care, because everybody may in fact be negligent. It has been held that following generally accepted accounting principles may still constitute negligence. The effect of emergencies is obvious. A person in an emergency situation is usually not held to as high a standard as a person who is not confronted with an emergency. The actual effect of the emergency is not to lower the standard but to qualify it by asking: is this conduct reasonable under the circumstances?

Negligence actions often involve the conduct of others. An operator of a business may be negligent in the selection of employees. If a tavern employs a bartender with violent tendencies, liability based on a theory of negligence may be imposed for injuries to customers caused by the bartender. Likewise, entrusting an automobile to one incapable of driving would be a negligent act.

Degrees of negligence

Courts sometimes talk about degrees of negligence. These have been created for several reasons, such as the extent of the risk involved and the legal relationship of the parties. As a general rule, the greater the risk, the higher the duty owed to others. In addition, the fact that a person is being paid to be careful usually increases the duty owed. A common carrier is an insurer of the goods carried and is liable except for Acts of God and the public enemy if the goods are damaged.

The degrees of negligence are sometimes described as slight negligence, which is the failure to exercise great care; ordinary negligence, which is the failure to use ordinary care; and gross negligence, which is the failure to exercise even slight care. Such distinctions are of special importance when personal property is entrusted by one person to another. The duty owed depends upon the legal relationship. If the duty is to exercise great care, there is liability for slight negligence; and if the duty is to exercise only slight care, there is liability only for gross negligence. Gross negligence is sometimes known as wilful and wanton misconduct or a conscious disregard for the safety of others.

Negligence by professional persons—malpractice

Among the more significant trends in the law of negligence is the substantial increase in malpractice suits by patients and clients against professional persons such as doctors or accountants. A malpractice suit may be predicated on a theory of breach of contract; but the usual theory is negligence, failure to exercise the degree of care and caution that the professional calling requires. Negligence by professional persons is not subject to the reasonable-man standard. Their standard is stated in terms of the knowledge, skill, and judgment usually possessed by members of the profession, because a professional person holds himself out to the public as having the degree of skill common to others in the same profession. However, professional persons do not guarantee infallibility. Although malpractice suits involve standards of professional conduct, the issue of negligence is submitted to a jury as a question of fact for a decision. In many cases, juries find that liability exists, even though members of the profession contend and testify that the services performed were all that could reasonably be expected under the circumstances.

Malpractice suits against doctors and hospitals have multiplied so rapidly that they have significantly affected the practice of medicine and the cost of malpractice insurance. They have also been a significant cause of spiraling medical costs, a major factor in inflation. Not only has the number of malpractice suits more than doubled in recent years, but the size of the verdicts has frequently reached astronomical proportions.

Many doctors and some hospitals have been unable to obtain adequate malpractice insurance coverage. More significantly, many doctors have been reluctant to attempt difficult medical procedures that could result in a malpractice suit. Because of the trends in malpractice litigation, most doctors are practicing defensive medicine: prescribing tests that are probably not indicated, requiring longer hospital stays, and consulting with other doctors as a matter of routine. Defensive medicine obviously is more costly.

Malpractice cases against lawyers have also increased significantly; and although their impact on the cost of legal services is not as significant as it is in medical services, their importance is growing. Malpractice litigation against accountants is another area of great significance. Several aspects of this type of negligence action are discussed in the next section.

The liability of accountants

An accountant is liable to a client for breach of contract if the services are not performed as agreed upon. There is liability to the client also if the services are negligently performed. Negligence is present if the accountant fails to exercise the degree of care and caution that the professional calling requires.

Accountants may have liability also to third parties, because the services are frequently performed for the benefits of others as well as the client. When third parties sue an accountant on a theory of negligence, it is necessary to distinguish between third parties that the accountant knew would rely on his work and third parties that may be described as unforeseen. While there is some conflict between various jurisdictions, the majority and better-reasoned rule is that an accountant is liable for negligence in the performance of his services to those persons whose reliance on the financial representations was actually foreseen by the accountant. The Restatement of Torts (second), a legal treatise, extends the liability of the accountant to persons who he knows will receive the product of his services, transmitted by his client. If an accountant knows that his financial statements are to be furnished to banks as a part of the process of obtaining a loan, the negligent accountant has liability to a lending bank for negligence in the preparation of the financial statements relied upon by the bank.

The liability of the accountant for negligence is limited to the class of third persons who come within the description "actually foreseen." It is the law in most jurisdictions that an accountant is not liable on a theory of general negligence to "unforeseen" third persons, because there is no contractual connection with the third party. Third persons without a contractual connection can sue for fraudulent acts of accountants but not for mere negligence. There is no liability to unforeseen third parties for mere negligence, even though the accountant recognizes that some third party may rely on his work.

It should be noted that an accountant may also be liable to third persons under the federal securities laws. This statutory liability, which will be discussed later with the materials on corporations, may involve issues of negligence. Under the Securities Act of 1933, an accountant is liable to any purchaser of a security upon proof that the portion of a registration statement attributable to the accountant contains an untrue statement of a material fact or omits to state a material fact necessary to prevent the statements made from being misleading.

The accountant's defense, however, may be that he had, after reasonable investigation, reasonable grounds to believe—and did believe—that the statements contained in the registration statement were true and that there was no omission to state a material fact required or necessary to make the statements not misleading. In other words, "due diligence" or "lack of negligence" is a defense to an allegation of a 1933 Securities Law violation. In determining whether or not an accountant has made a reasonable investigation, the law provides that the standard of reasonableness is that required of a prudent man in the management of his own property.

Problems of the fault system

In recent years the fault system has been widely criticized, primarily in automobile accident litigation, and major changes have been suggested. Among the system's inherent problems are (1) court congestion and delays, (2) overcompensation of minor claims and undercompensation of major claims, (3) the high cost of liability insurance, (4) inaccurate testimony and unreliable evidence, (5) inconsistency of juries, and (6) the high cost of operating the system.

Of the criticisms directed at automobile accident litigation, perhaps none is more significant than the high cost of operating under the fault theory, an expense that is readily apparent in automobile insurance premiums. There are also substantial additional costs to the victim of the automobile accident, to the alleged wrongdoer, and to society as a whole.

To collect damages, most victims must hire an attorney, whose fee is usually contingent on the total amount collected. The contingent fee system means that the attorney is paid a percentage of the recovery, but nothing if the case is lost. Usual contingent fees are 33-1/3 percent if a trial is held, and 40 to 50 percent if the case is appealed. Contingent fees make the legal system and the best lawyers available to all, irrespective of ability to pay; however, if the injuries are very substantial and liability is easily established, the fees of the attorney may be unfair and unreasonable. Assume a $1,500,000 verdict is given for the loss of two legs. If is difficult to see how the attorney's $500,000 could have been earned if the liability is clear. The chance of earning similarly large fees has encouraged "ambulance chasing" of potentially big cases, especially in large cities.

The alleged wrongdoer in most tort litigation is usually defended by an insurance company. A substantial portion of the insurance premium dollar is spent on investigations and in trying to prevent payment to the person seeking the damages. Thus, both parties to the occurrence are spending considerable sums attempting to determine what, if anything, one must pay the other. Moreover, society must operate an extensive court system and pay judges, court personnel, and jurors to try these cases and to settle these controversies. Obviously, the fault system is a very expensive system to operate.

Studies have been conducted attempting to show that the great majority of automobile accident victims are not appropriately compensated. The theory of damages tells us that the victim of a tort should receive a sum of money that will compensate him for the damage he has sustained. The damages paid should make him "whole." In other words, dollar damages are supposed to place the victim of the tort in as good a position as he would have been in had the tort not been committed. This, of course, is impossible, because no amount of money can replace an arm, a leg, or an eye, let alone a life. Therefore, in very serious cases, especially those that involve substantial pain and suffering, any money damages are probably inadequate.

In very minor cases, however, many plaintiffs are overcompensated. A person with little or no personal injury who brings suit will frequently be overcompensated for injuries because of the nuisance value of the case. Because it will cost money to investigate and defend the case and because the amount of jury verdicts are highly unpredictable, insurance companies frequently pay some amount to obtain a settlement of a claim, even though the claimant is probably not entitled to the amount paid.

The theory of fault was developed long before there were automobiles. Now, in many auto accident cases the litigation is quite unrealistic. Witnesses usually do not remember exactly what happened, so they testify to what they thought (sometimes hoped) happened. Witnesses with faulty memories have their memories refreshed and tend not to testify about what actually happened but about what somebody said happened.

Many factors influence verdicts in these negligence cases. One very important factor is sympathy for the plaintiff or animosity toward the defendant. A very seriously injured person or the next of kin of a deceased is frequently the obvious beneficiary of sympathy. When the testimony is conflicting and the memory of witnesses questionable, sympathy may play a major role. Animosity is frequently just as important. If a teenager runs a stop sign and kills an innocent bystander, a jury is likely to award high damages, especially if the jury believes an insurance company for the teenager will pay.

Finally, the fault system in auto accident litigation has traditionally proceeded on the premise that the accident was the defendant's fault and that negligence on the part of the plaintiff did not contribute to the plaintiff's injuries. In other words, the plaintiff has been required to be free from *contributory negligence*. The law has required that the defendant be 100 percent at fault and the plaintiff 0 percent at fault. This all-or-nothing requirement, of course, built an element into any case that encouraged settlement. Today the legislature in some states and the courts in others are abandoning the doctrine of contributory negligence and substituting for it a doctrine known as *comparative negligence*. Under the doctrine of comparative negligence, liability is assessed in proportion to the fault of each party. In some states using comparative negligence, a plaintiff can collect even if equally at fault or more at fault than the other party, but in other states, when the degree of fault reaches 50 percent, a plaintiff is barred from recovery. Thus the fault system varies greatly from state to state in its theories and their application.

The trend toward no-fault

In recent years there have been numerous proposals to eliminate the fault system in auto accident cases. These proposals have taken various forms. Some have recommended that auto accident cases be turned over to an administrative agency for decision. Others have recommended that the fault system be replaced by a no-fault system, or a system of first-party insurance.

Although the approaches to no-fault vary from state to state, most have elements in common. First of all, a party injured in an auto accident collects from his own insurance company just as he would if he were collecting on his own health insurance. Payment is made irrespective of fault. Just as health insurance would pay the hospital bill of a person attempting suicide, so would no-fault insurance pay the hospital bill of a person injured in an automobile accident even if he were at fault. Second, claimants are entitled to collect their medical bills, lost earnings, and out-of-pocket expenses up to a stated amount. Third, most no-fault laws contain a formula for computing the amount to be paid for pain and suffering, which may be an amount equal to a patient's medical bills. If the total medical bill is $500, an additional $500 would be paid for pain and suffering. Fourth, tort claims may still be filed in very serious cases. The approach of no-fault has been to keep the fault system for serious cases, such as permanent disability, disfigurement, and death. Only the minor cases are usually covered by no-fault legislation. This is accomplished by the law's setting a threshold above which the fault system is retained. Finally, claimants cannot collect their medical bills under no-fault if the medical bills are paid by any other form of health insurance or by workmen's compensation. This eliminates duplicate payment of medical expenses.

Critics of no-fault have been able to delay its enactment in many states, have obtained repeal in a few, and have kept the threshold quite low in others. Among the most often cited objections are (1) the victims of automobile accidents are receiving substantially less for their injuries under no-fault than they would receive under the fault system, and (2) the elimination of the jury system from auto accident litigation deprives a plaintiff of the very important fundamental right to trial by jury. No-fault has not been universally accepted.

REVIEW QUESTIONS AND PROBLEMS

1. May the same act be both a crime and a tort? Explain.
2. List 3 theories of tort liability.
3. Give two examples of conduct that constitutes each of the following: (1) Interference with the personal freedom of an individual (2) Interference with property rights (3) Interference with economic relations (4) Wrongful communications.
4. The CAT collection agency, trying to collect fees owed to a physician, called the ex-patient 10 to 20 times daily for several days, using obscene, threatening language. CAT also wrote several threatening letters. The former patient sued CAT for damages, alleging severe emotional distress. Was CAT's conduct tortious? Explain.
5. Contrast these torts: (1) trespass to goods (2) conversion.
6. Ninety-eight homeowners sued a ready-mix concrete company to enjoin operation of a ready-mix concrete plant. The homeowners lived in a residential neighborhood boardering an industrial area. The concrete plant was noisy, and dust from the concrete accumulated on the houses and cars parked outside. Are the homeowners entitled to an injunction? Explain.
7. A law firm sued several of its former members for damages and to enjoin them from soliciting the firm's clients. The former associates encouraged the older firm's clients to terminate that relationship and become clients of the new group. Was the new firm guilty of tortious conduct? Explain.
8. A physician photographed a dying patient in his hospital room. When the doctor lifted his patient's head to place a blue towel under it for color contrast, the dying man raised a clenched fist in protest and turned away from the camera. The patient's wife told the doctor before he entered the room that her husband did not wish to be photographed. As his widow, she is suing the doctor for invading her late husband's privacy. Is the doctor liable? Why?
9. Compare the duty an owner of premises owes to a *business visitor* with that owed to a *trespasser.*
10. A hardware store sought financing from a local bank. To evaluate the store's financial condition, the bank required it to submit certified financial statements, and the store's owner hired an accountant for that purpose. The statements represented the store as quite solvent; so the bank, relying on these statements, made the loan. In fact, however, the store was insolvent, and the bank lost a substantial sum of money. May the bank recover its losses from the accountant? Why?
11. On a rainy day, Nancy entered a grocery store to shop. When she stepped off a cloth mat at the entrance and onto the terrazzo floor, she slipped and fell. Water had accumulated on the floor from other customers' feet and from grocery carts coming back into the store. The store had been mopped and cleaned periodically throughout the morning, and the area in which Nancy fell had been mopped and cleaned ten minutes prior to the accident. Is the grocery liable to Nancy for her injuries? Why?
12. List five areas of auto accident litigation that are being used to support the demand for a change in the system.
13. Explain in general terms the approach of most no-fault systems for automobile accident cases.

5

Criminal Law

Much of the law is concerned with wrongful conduct; if it is wrongful against society, it is a crime. Of course, criminal conduct usually affects individual persons, but this effect is, by definition, tortious. In this chapter, we shall briefly discuss some of the general principles of the criminal law.

Criminal law and business

The criminal law is of great significance to the business community, which must cope with a soaring crime wave. Cash and inventory are being stolen at the rate of at least $40 billion per year. This amounts to 17 percent of total business income before taxes. White-collar crimes, such as kickbacks, theft by computer, embezzlement, and fraud, are increasing at an alarming rate. Arson and the fire insurance losses that result from it are also a billion-dollar problem.

Theft from business is both an internal and an external problem. Employees, from the lowest-paid to those in the executive suites, are stealing from their employers. It is estimated that 9 to 10 percent of all employees steal from their employers, on a regular basis. Many of these crimes go undetected, and many that are discovered go unreported. It has been estimated that 30 percent of all business failures are the result of internal theft and that many retail outlets lose at least 50 percent of their profits to unaccountable "inventory shrinkage." Many stores mark up goods an extra 15 percent to cover such losses, which means that the consuming public actually pays the bill for theft.

Bribery, kickbacks, and payoffs have become so common that the Securities and Exchange Commission demands that the amounts paid be included in the reports filed by major corporations. One reason for the massive amount of white-collar crime is that, in the past, the risk of being caught and sent to prison was slight. White-collar crime has often been considered a legitimate cost of doing business, especially overseas. A business is usually hesitant to prosecute its employees, because disclosure would have an adverse effect on the image of the business. Even when there have been successful prosecutions, sentences have been minimal in the light of the economic consequences of the crimes.

Now that the relation of crime to business has reached crisis proportions, many people are advocating new approaches, in an attempt to alter criminal conduct. Perhaps the most common suggestion is to impose stiff penalties, especially for white-collar crime. Another is greatly to improve the internal controls of businesses, so that internal theft and wrongdoing are more likely to be discovered. Finally, there is a trend toward punishing corporate officials who commit crimes in behalf of their corporations. A corporate official who fixes prices with competitiors in violation of the Sherman Antitrust Act is more likely to go to jail now than he was in the past, and the fine for such conduct has been greatly increased. Knowledge about the criminal law, its enforcement, and crime prevention are key elements in business decision making. This chapter will introduce the student to some of the problems involved in the criminal law and its enforcement.

Classes of crimes

Since a crime is a public wrong against society, criminal actions are prosecuted by the government on behalf of the people. Historically, upon a person's conviction of a crime, one of the following punishments has been imposed by society: (1) death, (2) imprisonment, (3) fine, (4) removal from office, or (5) disqualification to hold and enjoy any office or to vote. Among the purposes of punishment and of the criminal law are the protection of the public and the deterrence of crime. Punishment is also imposed simply for the sake of punishment, as well as the isolation and suppression of the criminal element of society.

Crimes are traditionally classified as treason, felonies, and misdemeanors. *Treason* against the United States consists of levying war against it or in adhering to its enemies, giving them aid and comfort. *Felonies* are offenses usually defined by statute to include all crimes punishable by incarceration in a penitentiary. Examples are murder, grand larceny, arson, and rape. Crimes of lesser importance than felonies—such as petty larceny, trespass, and disorderly conduct—are called *misdemeanors,* usually defined as any crimes not punishable by long imprisonment but punishable by fine or confinement in the local jail.

Violation of traffic ordinances, building codes, and similar municipal ordinances, prosecuted before a city magistrate, are sometimes termed *petty offenses* or *public torts* instead of crimes. The distinction is insignificant; because whether they are called crimes or public torts, the result is the same—the party charged may be fined or put in jail or both.

Terminology

The criminal law has developed some terminology separate and distinct from that of civil-law cases. The word *prosecution* is used to describe criminal proceedings, and *prosecutor* is the name usually given to the attorney who represents the people. Although the proceedings are brought on behalf of the people of a given state or of the United States, the people are generally not called the plaintiff, as in a civil case. Rather, the case is titled *U.S.* v. *John Doe,* or *State of Ohio* v. *John Doe.*

In felony cases, the usual procedure is for a court to conduct a preliminary hearing to determine if there is sufficient evidence that the accused committed the crime charged to justify submission of the case to the grand jury. If the court finds this probable cause, the accused is *bound over* to the grand jury. The grand jury examines evidence against the accused and determines if it is sufficient to cause a reasonable person to believe that the accused probably committed the offense. If this *probable cause* exists, the grand jury *indicts* the accused by returning to the court what is called a *true bill.* If it is the opinion of the grand jury that the evidence is insufficient to indict, then a *no true bill* is returned to the court. Indictment by the grand jury will be discussed with the Fifth Amendment, later in this chapter.

If the crime involved is a misdemeanor or if the accused waives the presentment of the case to the grand jury, the prosecution may proceed by filing the charges in a document known as an *information.* Both an indictment and an information serve to notify and to inform the accused of the nature of the charges, so that a defense may be prepared.

The technical aspects of the various crimes are beyond the scope of this text; however, it should be recognized that every crime has elements that distinguish it from other crimes. Larceny, robbery, and burglary are crimes with many common characteristics, yet they are legally distinct. Robbery is theft with force; larceny implies no force. Burglary is breaking and entering with intent to commit a felony (usually larceny). One act may be more than one crime, and it is possible to be convicted of more than one crime for any particular act. Many crimes are actually a part of another crime and are known as *lesser included offenses.* An assault would be a lesser included offense of forcible rape.

Criminal cases differ from civil cases in the amount of proof required to convict. In a civil case, the plaintiff is entitled to a verdict if the evidence preponderates in his favor. In other words, if, when weighing the evidence, the scales tip ever so slightly in favor of a plaintiff, the plaintiff wins. In a criminal case, however, the people or prosecution must prove the defendant's guilt beyond a reasonable doubt. Note that the law does not require proof "beyond the shadow of a doubt" or proof that is susceptible of only one conclusion. It does require such a quantity of proof that a reasonable man viewing the evidence would have no reasonable doubt about the guilt of the defendant.

Act and intent

As a general rule, a crime involves a combination of *act* and *criminal intent.* Criminal intent without an overt act to carry it out is not criminal. If Joe says to himself, "I am going to rob the First National Bank," no crime has been committed. Some act toward carrying out this intent is necessary. But if Joe communicates his desire to Frank, who agrees to assist him, then a crime has been committed. This crime is known as *conspiracy.* The criminal act was the communication between Joe and Frank.

Just as a crime requires an act, most crimes also require criminal intent. A legislature may declare an act to be a crime without intent, but crimes that do not require intent are rare. A wrongful act committed without the requisite criminal intent is not a crime. Criminal intent may be supplied by negligence to the degree that it equals intent. For example, if a person drives a car so recklessly that another is killed, his criminal intent may be supplied by the negligent act.

Criminal intent is not synonymous with motive. Motive is not an element of a crime. Proof of motive may help in establishing guilt, but it is not an essential element of a prosecution.

Some crimes are known as *specific intent* crimes. When a crime has a specific intent as a part of its definition, that specific intent must be proved beyond a reasonable doubt. In a burglary prosecution, there must be proof of intent to commit some felony, such as larceny, rape, or murder. Also, if a crime is defined in part "with intent to defraud," this specific intent must be proved, as any other element of the crime must be.

There is a presumption of intent in crimes that do not require a specific intent. The intent in such crimes may be implied by the facts. In other words, the doing of the criminal act implies the criminal intent. The accused may rebut this presumption, however. The accused is presumed to intend the natural and probable consequences of his acts. Thus, if one performs an act that causes a result that the criminal law is designed to prevent, he is legally responsible, even though the actual result was not intended. If a robber dynamites a safe and a passerby is killed in the explosion, the robber is guilty of homicide even though he did not actually intend to kill the passerby; the robber intended the natural and probable consequences of his act.

Defenses to criminal prosecutions

A defendant in a criminal case may avail himself of a variety of defenses. He may contend that he did not commit the act of which he is accused. He may present an alibi—proof that he was at another place when the crime was committed. He may also contend that if he did the act, it was not done with the requisite intent. There are also many technical defenses used on behalf of persons accused of crimes. Some of them are described in the following paragraphs.

Entrapment. This is a defense commonly raised in certain crimes, such as the illegal sale of drugs. Entrapment means that the criminal intent originated with the police. When a criminal act is committed at the instigation of the police, fundamental fairness seems to dictate that the people should not be able to contend that the accused is guilty of a crime. Assume that a police officer asked Bill to obtain some marijuana. Bill could not be found guilty of illegal possession, because the criminal intent originated with the police officer. Entrapment is sometimes described as a positive defense, because the accused must, as a basis for the defense, admit that the act was committed.

Immunity from prosecution. This is another technical defense. The prosecution may grant immunity in order to obtain a "state's witness." When immunity is granted, the person receiving it can no longer be prosecuted, and thus he no longer has the privilege against compulsory self-incrimination. When several persons have committed a crime together, it is common practice for one to be given immunity so that evidence is available against the others. The one granted immunity has a complete defense.

Insanity. A person cannot be guilty of a crime if he or she lacks the mental capacity to have the required criminal intent. Likewise, a person who is insane cannot properly defend the suit, so insanity at the time of trial is also a defense. This was used in the famous "Son of Sam" murder case in New York.

The defense of insanity poses many difficult problems for courts and for juries. Many criminal acts are committed in fits of anger or passion. Others, by their very nature, are committed by persons whose mental state is other than normal. Therefore, a major difficulty exists in defining insanity. In the early criminal law, the usually accepted test of insanity was the "right-from-wrong" test. If the accused understood the nature and consequences of the act and had the ability to distinguish right from wrong at the time of the act involved, the accused was sane. If he or she did not know right from wrong or did not understand the consequences of the act, insanity was a defense.

Subsequently, the courts of some states, feeling that the right-and-wrong test did not go far enough, adopted a test known as "irresistible impulse." Under this test, it was not enough that the accused knew right from wrong. If the accused was possessed of an irresistible impulse to do what was wrong, and this impulse was so strong that it compelled him or her to do what was wrong, insanity was a defense.

As psychiatry and psychology began to play a greater role in the criminal law and in the rehabilitation of criminals, many courts became dissatisfied with both the "right-and-wrong" and "irresistible-impulse" tests of insanity. A new test known as the "Durham rule" was developed. Under the Durham rule, an accused is not criminally responsible if his act was the product of a mental disease or defect. This new test has not received universal acceptance. Perpetrators of some crimes almost always have some mental abnormality, and the Durham rule makes their conduct unpunishable. Sexual assault on a child is probably committed only by one with some mental depravity, but the Durham rule makes prosecution of such cases more difficult and might result in freeing many who are guilty. Today there is a wide disparity among the states as to which test of insanity will be followed. All three tests have had significant acceptance. In the years ahead, additional developments in the law of insanity are likely.

Intoxication. This defense is quite similar to insanity, but its application is much more restricted. Voluntarily becoming intoxicated is generally no defense to a crime. It is simply no excuse for wrongful conduct. However, if the crime charged is one of specific intent and the accused was so intoxicated that he could not form the specific intent required, then intoxication is a defense of sorts. It can be used to establish lack of the required specific intent. In a prosecution for an assault with intent to rape, intoxication sufficient to negate the intent would be a defense.

Other defenses. Return of property stolen, payment for damages caused, and forgiveness by the victim of a crime are not defenses. If a person shoplifts and is caught, it is no defense that the goods were returned or that the store owner has forgiven him. Since the wrong is against society as a whole, the attitude of the actual victim is technically immaterial. As a practical matter, however, many prosecutors do not prosecute cases that the victims are willing to abandon.

Ignorance of the law is not a defense to a criminal prosecution. Everyone is presumed to know the law and to follow it. No other system would be workable. The various constitutional protections and guarantees available to a defendant may prohibit or impede prosecution of a case. They may make it impossible for the prosecution to obtain a conviction. If evidence of the crime is illegally obtained, that evidence is inadmissible; and by preventing its admission, the accused may obtain an acquittal. These constitutional and procedural aspects of the cirminal law are discussed in the sections that follow.

Criminal Law and the Constitution

The Constitution of the United States is a major source of the law as it relates to crimes. Constitutional protections and guarantees govern the procedural aspects of criminal cases. The Bill of Rights—especially the Fourth, Fifth, Sixth, and Eighth Amendments—contains these constitutional guarantees. The Fourteenth Amendment "picks up" the constitutional protections of the Bill of Rights and makes them applicable to the states.

As these constitutional guarantees are studied, two aspects of constitutional law should be kept in mind. First, constitutional guarantees are not absolutes. Every one of them is limited in its application. Just as freedom of speech under the First Amendment does not allow one to cry "Fire!" in a crowded theater, the Fourth Amendment constitutional protection against illegal search and seizure is not absolute. Both are limited protections. Second, in determining the extent of limitations on constitutional guarantees, the courts are balancing the constitutional protections against some other legitimate legal or social policy of society. For example, a state enacted a so-called hit-and-run statute requiring the driver of a motor vehicle involved in an accident to stop at the scene and give his name and address. Such action may obviously be self-incriminating, in that the person is admitting the identity of the driver of the vehicle involved. Thus, the law created a conflict between the state's demand for disclosures and the protection of the right against self-incrimination. The Supreme Court, in resolving this conflict, noted that the mere possibility of incrimination is insufficient to defeat the strong policies in favor of a disclosure, and it held that the law did not violate the Constitution.

The Fourth Amendment

Several procedural issues may arise as a result of the Fourth Amendment's protection against illegal search and seizure. Among the more common Fourth Amendment issues in criminal cases are (1) the validity of searches incident to an arrest without a warrant, (2) the validity of search warrants—the presence of probable cause, (3) the validity of consents to searches by persons other than the suspect, and (4) the extent of the protection afforded.

To illustrate the first issue, assume that a student is arrested for speeding. Is it a violation of the Fourth Amendment if the police officer searches the trunk of the car without a search warrant and finds heroin? The answer is yes, and the student could not be convicted of illegal possession of drugs, because the evidence was unconstitutionally obtained.

A search may be illegal even if it is conducted pursuant to a search warrant. The Constitution provides that a search warrant may be issued only if probable cause for its issue is presented to the court.

The validity of a consent to search premises without a search warrant is frequently an issue in a criminal case. A parent may consent to a police search of a child's room in the family home. Is this a valid waiver of the constitutional protection of the Fourth Amendment? The decision depends on many factors, including the age of the child, the extent of emancipation, and the amount of control the parents have over the total premises. Similar issues are raised when a landlord consents to the search of premises leased to a tenant. As a general rule, such consents are not sufficient to eliminate the need for a search warrant.

The protection afforded by the Fourth Amendment is not limited to premises. It prohibits the use of electronic surveillance equipment to obtain information. In one case, evidence of gambling, obtained by listening in on telephone conversations, was inadmissible, since it was illegally obtained.

Fourth Amendment issues frequently have an effect on civil law as well as criminal law. The protection has been extended to prohibit activities such as inspection of premises by a fire inspector without a search warrant. Criminal charges for violating building codes cannot be based on a warrantless inspection of the premises if the owner objects. The Supreme Court, however, has held that it is not a violation of the Fourth Amendment when a caseworker searches the premises of a welfare recipient. The need of government to know how its welfare funds for a child were being spent by its mother exceeded the need to give additional protection to the Fourth Amendment guarantees.

In recent years, the protection of the Fourth Amendment has been narrowed somewhat by court decisions. In order to protect police officers, it has been held that officers may search someone being arrested and the immediate area around the person for weapons. In addition, police officers have been allowed to take paint samples and tire impressions from autos parked on a public street. Officers searching an automobile are given far more latitude than police who are searching a person, a home, or a building. Today, persons lawfully arrested may be convicted of other crimes with evidence obtained as the result of such searches.

The Fifth Amendment

Almost eveyone understands that a person "pleading the Fifth Amendment" is exercising the right against compulsory self-incrimination. The Fifth Amendment also (1) contains a due process clause, which requires that all court procedures in criminal cases be fundamentally fair; (2) requires indictment by a grand jury for a capital offense or infamous crime; and (3) prohibits double jeopardy.

A grand jury decides if there is sufficient evidence of guilt to justify the accused's standing trial. It is contrasted with a petit jury, which decides guilt or innocence. Grand juries are usually made up of twenty-three persons, and it takes a majority vote to indict a defendant. It takes less proof to indict a person and to require him to stand trial than it does to convict. The grand-jury provision contains an exception for court-martial proceedings.

The grand-jury provision is limited to capital offenses and infamous crimes. *Infamous crimes* are those that involve moral turpitude. The term indicates that one convicted of such a crime will suffer infamy. Most felonies are infamous crimes.

The prohibition against double jeopardy means that a person cannot be tried twice for the same offense. A defendant who is acquitted in a criminal case cannot be retried on the same offense; however, a defendant who, on appeal, obtains a reversal of a conviction may be tried again. The reversal, in effect, means that the defendant was not in jeopardy.

Notwithstanding the foregoing provisions of the Fifth Amendment, the protection against compulsory self-incrimination is still its most important constitutional protection. The prohibition against being compelled to be a witness against oneself extends both to oral testimony of an accused before and during his trial, to documents, and to statements before grand juries, legislative investigation committees, and judicial bodies in civil and criminal proceedings.

A statement or a document does not have to be a confession of crime in order to qualify under the privilege. Both are protected if they might serve as a "link in the chain of evidence" that could lead to prosecution. The protection of the Fifth Amendment is the right to remain silent and to suffer no penalty for silence.

To illustrate the extent of the protection provided by the Fifth Amendment, the Supreme Court has held that (1) a prosecutor may not comment on the failure of a defendant to explain evidence within his knowledge, (2) a court may not tell the jury that silence may be evidence of guilt, (3) an attorney may not be disbarred for claiming his privilege at a judicial inquiry into his activities, just as a policeman may not be fired for claiming the privilege before the grand jury, and (4) the privilege protects a state witness against incrimination under federal as well as state law, and a federal witness against incrimination under state law as well as federal law. To illustrate this latter concept, assume that a person is granted immunity from state prosecution in order to compel him to testify. He cannot be compelled to testify if it is possible that his testimony will lead to a conviction under federal law. The granting of immunity must be complete.

Limitations on the protections afforded by the Fifth Amendment are also readily apparent. The hit-and-run-driver law case previously discussed is one example. In another situation, it was held that the prosecution can use as evidence in a drunken-driving case the analysis of a blood sample taken without consent of the accused. Such evidence is admissible even though the accused, on the advice of counsel, objected to the extraction of blood. The Fifth Amendment reaches an accused's communications, whatever form they might take, but compulsion that makes a suspect the source of "real or physical evidence" does not violate it. For example, compulsory fingerprinting or taking voice samples for evidence does not violate the Fifth Amendment. In addition, the protection is personal and does not prevent the production of incriminating evidence by others. Tax records of a potential defendant were in the hands of an accountant, and the IRS sought to subpoena them. The defendant could not use the Fifth Amendment to prevent the accountant from complying with the subpoena.

The Sixth Amendment

The Sixth Amendment contains several provisions relating to criminal cases. It guarantees to a defendant the right (1) to a speedy and public trial, (2) to a trial by jury, (3) to be informed of the charge against him, (4) to confront his accuser, (5) to subpoena witnesses in his favor, and (6) to have the assistance of an attorney.

The right to a speedy trial is of great concern today. Most states require that a defendant in jail be tried within a minimum period of time—such as four months. This limits the punishment of those not convicted of a crime.

The right to a jury trial does not extend to state juvenile-court delinquency proceedings, as they are not criminal prosecutions; however, juveniles do have the right to counsel, to confront the witnesses against them, and to cross-examine them. Thus it can be seen that there are many technical aspects to the Sixth Amendment.

Perhaps no provision of the Sixth Amendment has been given a broader interpretation in recent years than the right to counsel. During this period, the Supreme Court, in a series of decisions, has been confronted with two fundamental questions: (1) At what stage of the proceedings does the right to counsel attach? and (2) To what types of cases is it applicable?

For many years, it was thought that the right to counsel existed only during the trial and that it did not exist during the investigation of the crime. During the 1960s, the Supreme Court extended the right to counsel to events before the trial.

In *Massiah* v. *United States,* 377 U.S. 201, the Court observed that "a Constitution which guarantees a defendant the aid of counsel at . . . trial could surely vouchsafe no less to an indicated defendant under interrogation by the police in a completely extrajudicial proceeding. Anything less . . . might deny a defendant 'effective representation by counsel at the only stage when legal aid and advice would help him.'" In *Escobedo* v. *Illinois,* 378 U.S. 478, the Court extended the right to an accused under arrest but not under indictment at the time he asked for a lawyer. The Court in that case said that the "guiding hand of counsel was essential when the police were seeking to obtain a confession from the accused." This was the stage when legal aid and advice were most critical. What happened at the interrogation could certainly affect the whole trial, since rights "may be irretrievably lost, if not then and there asserted, as they are when an accused represented by counsel waives a right for strategic purposes."

Subsequent to *Escobedo,* other decisions expanded and clarified the Sixth Amendment protection. Perhaps the best known of these cases is *Miranda* v. *State of Arizona,* 86 S.Ct. 1602, which resulted in the development of what has become known as the "*Miranda* warning." This warning notifies the accused that he has the right to remain silent, that anything he says may be used against him in court, that he has the right to the presence of an attorney and to have an attorney appointed before questioning if he cannot afford one. The *Miranda* case recognized that a defendant may waive the right to counsel, provided the waiver is made voluntarily, knowingly, and intelligently.

Other decisions have required that the *Miranda* warning be given to an accused who was not in custody at a police station but on whom the investigation was centering, if the accused was being deprived of his freedom of action in any significant way. Today the right to counsel has been extended to postindictment lineups, because the Sixth Amendment protection extends the right to counsel whenever necessary to ensure a meaningful defense. An accused is guaranteed that he need not stand alone against the state at any stage of the prosecution, formal or informal, in court or out, where counsel's absence might detract from the accused's right to a fair trial.

In the 1970s, the Supreme Court in a series of decisions tended to limit the effect of the *Miranda* decision. It held that a confession obtained without the requisite warning being given could nevertheless be used to impeach a defendant who denied under oath committing the crime. The law relative to the *Miranda* warning is still developing, and more limitations may be imposed.

The courts have also extended the types of cases to which the right to counsel attaches. Historically, the right existed only in felony cases. Today, it extends to any case, felony or misdemeanor, in which the accused may be incarcerated. In addition, the right to counsel extends to juveniles in juvenile proceedings. It also extends to investigations by the Internal Revenue Service. Thus, any person charged with any crime for which he may be put in jail or prison has the right to counsel at all stages of the proceedings, from the time the investigations center upon him as the accused, through his last appeal.

The Eighth Amendment

The Eighth Amendment provides that "excessive bail shall not be required, nor excessive fines imposed, nor cruel and unusual punishments inflicted." Bail is excessive if greater than necessary to guarantee the presence of the accused in court at the appointed time. The function of bail is not to restrict the freedom of the accused prior to trial, because of the presumption of innocence. Most states today require that only a small percentage of the actual bail be posted. The law may require that 10 percent of the total bail be deposited with the court. If the defendant fails to appear, the persons signing the bail bond then owe the other 90 percent.

At one time, the Eighth Amendment was used as the basis for declaring the death penalty to be unconstitutional; however, many legislative bodies reinstated the death penalty, and some of these laws were later held to be constitutional.

The Fourteenth Amendment

The Fourteenth Amendment is quite general in its language. To the extent relevant here, it provides, "No State shall make or enforce any law which shall abridge the privileges or immunities of citizens of the United States; nor shall any State deprive any person of life, liberty, or property, without due process of law; nor deny to any person within its jurisdiction the equal protection of the laws." The three major provisions are known as the "privileges and immunities" clause, the "due process" clause and the "equal protection" clause. Although all three clauses play a significant role in constitutional law, the due-process clause and the equal-protection clause have been involved in more significant criminal law litigation than has the privileges-and-immunities clause.

The term *due process of law* cannot be narrowly defined. It describes fundamental principles of liberty and justice. Simply stated, due process means "fundamental fairness and decency." It means that government may not act in a manner that is arbitrary, capricious, or unreasonable.

The issues in due process cases are usually divided into questions of *procedural* due process and *substantive* due process. Substantive due process issues arise when property or other rights are directly affected by governmental action. Procedural due process cases are often concerned with whether proper notice has been given and a proper hearing has been conducted. Such cases frequently involve procedures established by state statute. Due process has been used in criminal cases to strike down varied state action such as forced pleas and trials held with excess publicity. Many of the cases decided by the Supreme Court relating to the Fourteenth Amendment have simply ruled that the federal standard on a given issue was to be the minimum state standard. These cases use the due process clause to "pick up" or to "incorporate" the federal standards of criminal jurisprudence and to make them applicable to the states.

The equal protection clause is used more often in civil litigation, such as school desegregation cases. It is used to prevent all types of invidious discrimination, such as discrimination based on race, creed, color, sex, or national origin. It has been used in the criminal law where discriminating laws or practices were involved.

Contemporary problems

The criminal law system has failed generally to deter crime or to accomplish most of its other assumed goals. An ever-increasing crime rate, especially in larger communities, puts crimes of violence as well as the so-called white-collar crimes constantly in the news. Because our penal system has not found the means to rehabilitate the convicted, a significant portion of all crimes are committed by repeat offenders.

Many people believe that the inadequacy of criminal law results from its failure to provide swift and sure punishment for those committing wrongs against society. Delays in all steps of criminal procedure are quite common, most of them probably the result of defense tactics, as time favors the accused. But court congestion also contributes to delay, and vice versa. Recent decisions such as those expanding the right to counsel have contributed to court congestion too.

One of the more controversial procedures in the criminal law is commonly referred to as *plea bargaining,* by which an accused pleads guilty to a lesser offense than that which is charged, or there is an agreement to less than normal punishment in return for a plea of guilty. Plea bargaining is essential, because the case load is too great to try all cases; however, plea bargaining has many adverse side effects. It allows persons who have committed serious crimes to go almost immediately back on the streets to commit more crimes after only paying a fine or serving a much shorter sentence than would have been imposed if they had been convicted of the crime originally charged.

The increased criminal law case load has had a great impact on the work of reviewing courts. Today, approximately 75 percent of those convicted of crimes appeal their convictions. This increase is largely due to the fact that the indigent defendant is now entitled to a free appeal. We do not have enough judges to handle this case load properly, and delay is inevitable.

Another inherent problem in our criminal law system arises from the fact that many recent law-school graduates join the staff of either the prosecutor or the public defender. Criminal cases are thus frequently tried by lawyers with little experience and a minimum of training. After gaining experience, they leave for private practice. The criminal law has, to a significant degree, become an internship for training lawyers for private practice.

The free legal services provided to indigents also create some problems. Many people close to the situation believe that the free public defender, who is frequently underpaid by the state and overworked because of the volume of cases, often does not do an adequate job in defending clients. In addition, these attorneys are to all intents and purposes on the court payroll, which may affect the vigor of their representation of defendants. As a result, an adequate legal defense is a goal that is yet to be achieved for many defendants.

Many other problems arise as a result of the failures of our criminal-law system. Overcrowded jails, unworkable probation systems, unequal sentences, plea bargaining that tends to favor the wealthy, and the failure of sentencing laws to deter crime are but a few of the obvious ills. Most legal scholars agree that the criminal law system needs a drastic overhaul. In fact, the Supreme Court, in its process of reviewing convictions, is bringing about many changes. It is requiring prompt trials or the dismissal of charges. Other decisions have reduced the number of appeals that are available to a convicted defendant. Finally, the Court is reconsidering many of the highly technical aspects of the Bill of Rights as they affect criminal prosecutions. In many of these cases, the Court is balancing the competing and conflicting policies more heavily in favor of the police and the victims of crimes than in favor of the accused.

REVIEW QUESTIONS AND PROBLEMS

1. What is the basic distinction between a *felony* and a *misdemeanor?*
2. What is the purpose of the grand jury? Petit jury?
3. What is the difference between a *general intent crime* and a *specific intent crime?*
4. Dan Ho was suspected by immigration officers of having information concerning the smuggling into the United States of other Chinese. The immigration officers went to Dan and suggested that he bring certain Chinese into the United States illegally. Dan refused at first but later agreed. After doing so, Dan was arrested. Does Dan have a valid defense to the charges? Why?
5. Compare the three tests of insanity currently used by the courts in criminal cases.
6. When police entered her room without a warrant, Suzy swallowed two "uppers." Portions of the capsules were recovered by the police with the use of a stomach pump. Was the evidence lawfully obtained? Why?
7. Devin was arrested and tried for burglary. The jury deliberated for three days and then informed the judge that it was hopelessly deadlocked and could not return a verdict. A new trial was scheduled, but Devin objected, contending that a second trial constituted double jeopardy. Is he correct? Why?
8. Jimmie, who had previously been convicted of gambling, was called to testify before a state investigation of gambling activities. He refused to answer any questions on the ground that it might tend to incriminate him. The state court held that the privilege of refusing self-incrimination is not available to a witness in a state proceeding and sentenced Jimmie to jail for contempt. Upon appeal, should the conviction be reversed? Why?
9. List three protections afforded by the Fifth Amendment other than the protection against compulsory self-incrimination. Give an example of each.
10. What statements must be contained in the Miranda warning given to an accused in a criminal case?
11. What are some of the problems inherent in the criminal law system?

II

Contracts

6

Introduction to Contracts

Among the various meanings of the word *contract* is its technical definition: a promise or several promises under which the law recognizes a duty to perform and for which, if breached, the law gives the aggrieved party a remedy. Realistically, a contract is a legal device to control the future through promises. By definition, a promise is a present commitment, however expressed, that something will or will not be done. Parties are allowed to create rights and duties between themselves, and the state will enforce them through legal machinery. When people execute a contract, by their mutual assent they create the law of their contract, which sets up the bounds of their liability. It is important, then, that you keep two points in mind: (1) a contract contains a present undertaking or commitment concerning future conduct of the parties, and (2) the law sanctions the commitment by putting its legal machinery behind it.

Elements of a contract

There are four basic elements to the formation of a contract:

1. An agreement that is a manifestation of the parties' mutual assent as found in two legal concepts called offer and acceptance.

2. Bargained-for consideration or other validation device, which the law uses to validate and make the mutual assent legally operative.
3. Two or more parties who are legally competent; that is, they have the legal capacity to contract (be of legal age and sane).
4. The transaction must be legal, which means that it must have a legal purpose consistent with law and sound public policy.

These elements of a contract will be considered in detail in the chapters that follow. For the moment, the four elements are useful in giving us a way to think about contract law.

How to approach and solve contract law problems

Problems in contract law fall into three groupings: (1) preformation, (2) contract formation, and (3) contract performance. The initial approach to any contract problem is to decide at which of the three stages it arises. We are now at the preformation stage and are concerned with definitions, elements and classification of contracts, and sources of contract law. Subsequent chapters are organized around the three stages and follow a logical progression from forming to performing a contract. This organization will cause you to ask and answer the following progressive questions:

1. Where do I find contract law, and which legal rules do I apply to the problem before me?
2. Has an offer been made?
3. Has there been an acceptance?
4. If there has been an offer and acceptance (mutual assent), is there a validation device like consideration to make the offer-acceptance legally operative?
5. Assuming a valid contract has been formed, are there any legal defenses—illegality, statute of frauds, incapacity, mistake, and the like—to nullify the contract?
6. Assuming a valid, formed contract with no defenses to its formation, how is the contract to be performed? (This question concerns performance problems under the general heading of the law of conditions.)
7. Do third parties have rights or duties that may be legally recognized under the contract?

At this juncture, you are not equipped to answer any of the questions; however, when you have finished the chapters on contracts, come back and consider them. The law of contracts will then attain a sharper focus.

Classification of contracts

Before attempting to solve formation and performance problems, it is desirable to classify contracts according to their characteristics:

1. Form: bilateral and unilateral.
2. Expressions: express, implied-in-fact, and implied-in-law.
3. Performance: void, voidable, enforceable, unenforceable, executed, executory.

Bilateral and unilateral contracts

An initial classification, this one based on form, must be made before resolving any contract issue. Is the contract *bilateral* or *unilateral?* The usual contract is bilateral, based on an exchange of mutual promises. Virgil promises to sell his truck to Jimmy Hicks for $2,000, and Hicks promises to buy Virgil's truck for $2,000. The bilateral contract is formed as soon as the promises are exchanged. It is immaterial that neither has rendered any performance, because the law recognizes that each party has a legal duty to carry out the terms of the agreement. Since each party has a duty and a right to the other's performance, the contract is bilateral, or two sided.

BILATERAL CONTRACT

Fig. 6·1

Whereas a bilateral contract is characterized by a promise for a promise, a unilateral contract is characterized by a promise for an act. The offeror (person who makes the offer) promises the offeree (person to whom the offer is addressed) a benefit if the offeree does some act, such as painting a house, mowing the grass, fixing a car, climbing a flagpole, or eating a goldfish. A unilateral contract therefore is a one-sided contract with one promiser and one promisee.

UNILATERAL CONTRACT

Fig. 6·2

The classic example of a unilateral contract occurs when I say to you: "If you will walk across the Brooklyn Bridge, I will pay you $250." There is no unilateral contract as yet. Legally, I have made an *offer* for a unilateral contract, which will become a contract only when you complete the act that I requested. At the moment you complete the act (walk across the bridge), the unilateral contract is formed with one promise, one duty, and one right. Prior to completing the act, we only have an offer for a unilateral contract. Many people fail to remember this distinction, which causes later mistakes. You won't, will you?

Express and implied contracts

The second classification is based on how the parties express their agreement. An *express* contract is the most obvious and occurs when the parties state their agreement orally or in writing. When the parties manifest their agreement by conduct rather than by words, it is said to be *implied-in-fact.* This distinction is totally unimportant, since all true contracts are express, whether express by words or by conduct. You drive up to a full-service gas station and say, "Fill it up." The station attendant fills it up. Although you've said nothing about paying, it is an implied-in-fact term. The contract then is partly express and partly implied. You're walking down Lexington Avenue and come upon a grocery stand filled with apples under a sign stating 35 cents per apple. You pick one up and take a bite. At that moment, an implied-in-fact contract expressed totally by conduct is formed. It is sometimes difficult, however, to distinguish express contracts (whether true express or implied-in-fact) from implied-in-law contracts.

Quasi contracts

Implied-in-law contracts, sometimes referred to as quasi contracts, are not true contracts. Rather, they are legal fictions that courts use to prevent wrongdoing and the unjust enrichment of one person at the expense of another. When one party confers a benefit upon another, the party receiving the benefit may be unjustly enriched if he were not required to pay for the benefit received. Suppose that you mistakenly thought you owned a tract of land. You paid taxes and made improvements on the land. Certainly, the true owner should legally have to reimburse you for the taxes. Regarding the improvements, the true owner likewise should have to pay for the value of those improvements, which were benefits to the owner. To avoid any unjust enrichment, courts permit the party who conferred the benefit to recover the reasonable value of that benefit. At common law, this legal action was brought in the form of a contract action—hence the name quasi contract. Nonetheless, there is no real promise, and none of the other elements of a true contract are present.

The dividing line between implied-in-fact and implied-in-law contracts is often blurred. In both instances, the plaintiff who has given a benefit (such as delivering goods or performing services) expects to be paid. Whereas a defendant in an implied-in-fact contract knows or should know of the expectation of payment, the defendant in the case of a quasi contract is not required to know of any expectation but only to be unjustly enriched. The following two cases may aid your understanding of these distinctions.

CASE

P (plaintiff) presented to his employer (Stardust Hotel in Las Vegas) his idea that a recreational vehicle park constructed and operated by the hotel would be very profitable. P indicated that he wanted to be paid for his idea, either in money or by participation in the venture. D (defendant, the employer) said the hotel was *not* interested; but two years later, D opened a recreational vehicle park adjacent to the hotel. P sued, asserting that D had implemented his idea.

ISSUE Can P recover damages based on either breach of an express or implied-in-fact contract or based on a quasi contract?

DECISION No.

REASONS

1. The terms of an express contract are stated in words, while those of an implied-in-fact contract are manifested by conduct. There is no evidence that the parties orally or in writing contracted for the purchase and sale of P's idea. P alleged only that he expected compensation, not that he was promised compensation.
2. There is no evidence of conduct by D suggesting that it intended to contract with P nor any evidence from which it might be implied-in-fact that D promised to compensate P.
3. Since P's idea was entirely unsolicited, no recovery can be made on the theory of quasi contract. Not only must P prove that he expected to be paid and that D was unjustly enriched, but it must be shown that P was not a volunteer or officious intermeddler. One who officiously confers a benefit on another is not entitled to recover on an implied-in-law contract.

Smith v. Rection Corp., 541 P.2d 663 (Nev.) 1975.

Compare and distinguish the above case with the next one.

CASE

P, an employee of D, has a novel idea for a safety device to be used on elevator chairs manufactured by D. P made a drawing and a model of his idea and showed it to D. D used the safety device on its defective elevator chairs already sold thereby saving money in not having to replace the chairs. D refused to pay P anything, claiming that it had a shop right to use the idea under the rule that inventions made by employees using company tools on company time can be freely used by the employer. P was not employed by D to do any engineering or design concept work.

ISSUE Can P recover for D's unjust appropriation of his novel idea?

DECISION Yes. Recovery allowed in quasi contract for the reasonable value of D's unjust enrichment.

REASON P had a property right in the safety device developed on his own time. D did not have a right under the shop right doctrine since the device was orginated and developed by P at home. P is entitled to $30,000 damages for unjust enrichment based on cost savings to D in using the idea.

Dewey v. American Stair Glide Corp., 557 S.W.2d 643 (Mo.) 1977.

One final point should be noted. For some time, sellers would ship goods to persons who had not requested them. This technique was used to sell items like religious bookmarks, neckties, records, books, and the like. The seller would then make a contract claim based either on acceptance by conduct in keeping the goods (implied-in-fact) or unjust enrichment when buyer retained and used the goods (implied-in-law). To stop this unfair method of selling goods, the U.S. Postal Services Act, 39 U.S.C. §3009 (1970), was enacted. It allows the recipient of unsolicited goods to treat them as a gift and retain, use, discard, or dispose of the goods in any manner without obligation. There are also state statutes relieving the recipient of any duty to pay for unsolicited goods when the goods have been received through the mail or otherwise.

Classification in relation to performance

The third way to classify contracts is according to performance. To do so, you must understand the following terms: valid, void, voidable, executed, enforceable, and unenforceable. A *valid* contract is one that is in all respects in accordance with legal requirements and will be enforced by the courts. A *void* contract is a contract that in the eyes of the law never existed. The only contract that is void is an illegal one. An illegal contract is void in the sense that there is no legal machinery to protect the bargain of the parties. A *voidable* contract is one in which one or more parties have the power to end the contract. A voidable contract will be enforced unless one of those parties elects to disaffirm it. A contract executed by one who is under legal age is voidable and can be disaffirmed (set aside) by the underage party.

When one party is entitled to a money judgment or to specific performance because of breach, the contract is *enforceable.* Although legally there may be a contract, a defense to that contract may deny any party any remedy under the contract. Later chapters discuss these defenses to contract formation. Such a contract is said to be *unenforceable.* For example, the law requires that a contract for the sale of land be in writing; if it is oral, then it is unenforceable. An *executed* contract is one that has been fully performed by the contracting parties. An *executory* contract is one that is yet to be performed. The traditional definition of contract, in terms of promises that are commitments regarding the future, stresses the executory nature of most contracts. When Martha offers to sell Walter a beer for $1.00, and Walter promises to buy, the contract is bilateral and executory. If Martha (rather than promising) hands Walter a beer, and he simultaneously gives her $1.00, then the contract is executed. Although there is nothing to perform under an executed contract, modern definitions of contract include executed in addition to executory contracts. Note also that an agreement may be mixed; that is, executed by one party and executory on the part of the other.

Sources of contract law

Before attempting to solve any contract question, you must ask: What law do I apply? That question seems simple, but it can at times be one of the most perplexing you will confront. While contract law is a fusion of case and statutory law in relation to some contracts, it may be totally case or solely codified law regarding other types of contracts. Thus, the first step is to identify the subject matter of the contract. It may, for instance, be a real property contract, an employment contract, construction contract, and so on. In most cases, you will have to know only two bodies of contract law that in theory attempt to provide the same rules. Let's back up a moment to see how this happened.

The bulk of contract law is judgemade, case law and is, for the most part, uncodified. The basic rules are found primarily in the written opinions of courts. Specialized areas of contract law such as labor law and insurance law have been partially codified; but in most instances, the problem solver's task is to gather a number of similar contract cases, distill them, and pull out a general rule in summary style. That task is greatly helped by a project called the Restatements of Law, which started, in 1920, to state the basic principles of common law cases in a simple, uniform style. The first area chosen was contracts, and in 1932 the Restatement (First) of Contracts was published. It reflects the *classical* theory of contract law, which sought certainty, predictability, and stability through the formulation of strict, rigid rules of contract formation and performance. Since the Restatements were not intended to be enacted by the states, they are not law but only persuasive authority that a court may (or may not) follow. Nonetheless, since the 1950s there has been a retreat from the classical theory and consequently from the Restatement (First) of Contracts.

Two reasons can explain this rejection of classical theory. First, the Uniform Commercial Code (hereinafter called the Code) was initially enacted in 1952 in Pennsylvania and then by every state and territory except Louisiana and Puerto Rico. The Code has a very flexible approach to contract formation and performance. The second reason stems from the influence of the Code. In 1950 it was decided that the Restatement had to be restated not only to bring general-law contracts into conformity with the philosophy of the Code but to correct past errors. The first Restatement was criticized as unduly simplistic by fostering the illusory notion that all the common law governing myriad contracts could be reduced to an algebraic set of simple rules. Sometime in the 1980s the Restatement (Second) of Contracts will be completed.

Let's return to the original question: What law do I apply? Most contracts (employment, construction, real property, general business, and the like) will follow general common law rules as stated in cases and the second Restatement.

If the contract concerns a sale of goods (personal property), then it is governed by the Code. Whereas the Restatement is only persuasive authority, which courts are free to ignore, the Code is legislatively enacted law. When the Code applies to a transaction in goods, then the court must apply Code rules. Although the Code has 10 articles, most of them do not affect basic contract rules; however, Article Two–Sales does have many contract rules that are relevant to any consideration of contract law. These rules concern contract formation and performance and will be dealt with in the materials on contracts,

Part II. Article Two-Sales also has special rules concerning matters like risk-of-loss or product liability, not directly related to general-law contracts. Those other matters will be considered in Part III, "Uniform Commercial Code." A brief introduction to the Code at this juncture will sharpen these divisions in your mind.

Introduction to the Uniform Commercial Code

The rules and principles of commercial law are of ancient origin. Throughout the centuries, merchants engaged in trade and commerce have recognized many customs and usages that regulate and control their conduct and relationships. Gradually over the years, a body of law developed, based upon the practices of merchants and called the law merchant. For centuries the law relating to commercial transactions was based on case law rather than statutes until, starting in 1896, a number of statutes were drafted in relation to certain aspects of business transactions. Today most of these statutes have been replaced by one law known as the Uniform Commercial Code. This Code relates to all aspects of a business transaction involving the sale and transfer of, and payment for, goods.

When there are references to the Code in the text, they will be placed in brackets. These references pertain to sections of the law, which is set forth in its entirety as an Appendix at the end of the book. For example, the purposes of the Code are to simplify, clarify, and modernize the law governing commercial transactions, to permit the continued expansion of commercial practices, and to make uniform law among the various states [1-102]. Section 1-102 may be referred to for the exact language of the law.

Although the Code provides definite rules that govern commercial transactions, the parties may, by mutual agreement, provide for a different result. To a large degree, the Code gap-fills those situations that have not been covered by the parties in their contract. Accordingly, the parties to a transaction can, within limits, tailor their agreement to suit their needs. The Code supplies the rules and principles that will apply if the parties have not otherwise agreed.

To accomplish these purposes, the concept of the Code is that a "commercial transaction" is a single subject of the law, notwithstanding its many legal relations. Any transaction could (at various points in time) involve an executory contract for sale, an executed sale, the giving of a check for a part of the purchase price, and the acceptance of security (collateral) for the balance. The check may be negotiated by the seller to some other person, and at the same time it will pass through a bank for collection. If the goods are shipped or stored, a bill of lading or warehouse receipt or both will likely be involved. Especially in international sales, a letter of credit may be used in connection with the sale and its financing. Thus, at the base of a commercial transaction is a sale accompanied by a method of payment for the goods purchased. The Code deals with all the phases that may ordinarily arise in the handling of a commercial transaction, from start to finish.

It is important to note that the Code does not cover every legal problem that may arise in a commercial transaction. The title Uniform Commercial Code is somewhat misleading. First, it is not uniform, since many states, in enacting the Code, added nonuniform amendments. Article 9—Secured Transactions has at least 954 nonuniform amendments. Second, it does not cover all commercial transactions. Employment, construction, insurance, and real property contracts, for example, are not within the coverage of the Code. The Code is restricted to transactions involving various aspects of the sale, financing, and security in respect to *personal property*. Finally, the Code is not a true code. In theory, a code is a legislative enactment that entirely preempts the field and has within it all the answers to all possible questions. In contrast, a *statute* must be interpreted by courts. The meaning of the statute thus becomes the text of the statute and the cases decided under it. A code, however, is exhaustive, and cases decided under it are irrelevant. The meaning of any code lies solely in its text. The drafters of the U.C.C. (Code) decided that it would be more like a statute that can be explained or supplemented by case law. In fact, the Code explicitly states that it shall be supplemented by extra-code law unless the provision or section states otherwise [1-103]. Thus, since Article 2-Sales has very few provisions on contract formation, the cases and Restatement that are discussed in the contracts chapters of this text will directly supplement the Code. Do you understand now that the Code is really a case-law "code"?

Although the Code provisions are law, the drafters of the Code prepared "official comments" for each of its provisions. The official comments are not law, but they have been looked upon favorably by courts in order to determine what a particular section means or how it is to be interpreted and applied. The official comments are explanatory, often telling what the drafters were seeking to accomplish. They are significant and have had considerable impact on the law of the Code.

This text places special emphasis on Article 2-Sales, Article 3-Commercial Paper, Article 4-Bank Deposits and collections, and Article 9-Secured Transactions. Other articles are also mentioned in appropriate sections. From the beginning of the study, it must be recognized and firmly kept in mind that Article 2-Sales is restricted to transactions involving the sale of goods generally defined as "movable" physical property. This definition excludes intangible items of property such as contract claims and contracts for the sale of investment securities — stocks and bonds—which are covered by Article 8.

Since most rules concerning contract formation and performance are the same as common law and under the Code, these rules will be considered, whenever possible, at the same time. When the Code has special rules different from the common law, these will be set out carefully either in the text or at the end of the chapter. Rules for sale-of-goods transactions that have nothing to do with the general law of contracts will be discussed with the Code in Part III.

Judicial Remedies for Breach of Contract

Any breach of contract or a threat to breach defeats the reasonable expectations of the parties and may affect third parties who are not parties to the contract. An actual or potential breach causes all interested parties to attempt resolution of their problems as expeditiously as possible.

Three primary methods are used to obtain a resolution: negotiation and compromise, arbitration, and legal action. The third method is one of last resort, used less frequently than the first. Most differences that arise over breaches of contracts are settled by the parties without litigation. The threat of court action often has a salutary effect on a person who has either breached or threatened to breach a contract and often produces cooperation in effecting an out-of-court settlement.

Many contract cases do reach the courts, and remedies are provided for the purpose of granting appropriate relief to the injured party. Three basic remedies are afforded for breach of contract: dollar damages, specific performance, and rescission. In general, these remedies are exclusive—a party must elect one to the exclusion of the others.

Money damages are recoverable in a court of law; specific performance and rescission are equitable remedies. Although damages are always recoverable for loss sustained as the result of a breach of contract, the equitable remedies are not so readily available. They will be allowed less often—usually only if the remedy at law (damages) is not adequate under the circumstances of the case. If a person can be adequately compensated by receipt of money damages, he will not be allowed the equitable remedies.

Damages—generally

The purpose and the theory of damages is to make the injured party whole. As a result of the payment of money, the injured party is in the same position he would have occupied had the breach of contract not occurred. Damages give just compensation for the losses that flowed from the breach. In other words, a person is entitled to the benefits of his bargain. If a purchaser receives less than he bargained for, the difference between the actual value and the contract price constitutes the damages. Unusual and unexpected damages resulting from peculiar facts unknown to either party at the time the agreement was entered into are generally not recoverable.

The question as to the amount of damages is usually one of fact for the jury. A jury may not speculate about or guess the amount of damage. Damages that are uncertain, contingent, remote, or speculative cannot be recovered. Loss of profits may be included as an element of recoverable damages if they can be computed with reasonable certainty from tangible and competent evidence.

A party suing for breach of contract is not entitled to recover the amount expended for attorney's fees unless the contract so provides or special legislation permits it. Litigation is expensive, even for the winner, since the legal expenses will usually substantially reduce the net recovery. Court costs, however, which include witness fees and filing costs, are usually assessed against the losing party.

Rules concerning damages

The injured party is duty bound to mitigate the damages, to take reasonable steps to reduce to a minimum the actual loss resulting from the breach. He cannot add to his loss or permit the damages to be enhanced when it is reasonably within his power to prevent such occurrence.

When a contract is willfully and substantially breached after part performance has occurred, there may be some benefit conferred on the nonbreaching party. Furthermore, the benefit may be of such character that the nonbreaching party cannot surrender it to the other. In construction contracts, the benefit received from partial performance cannot be returned. Under these circumstances, the law does not require the innocent person to pay for the benefit conferred. As a result, the party who has refused to complete the job is penalized because of the failure to perform.

A different result obtains when the breach is unintentional, resulting from a mistake or a misunderstanding. In this situation, the party may be required to pay for the net benefit received on a theory of quasi contract. The court may award damages in the amount necessary to complete the performance, in which event the defaulting party is automatically credited for the partial performance.

When partial performance of a contract confers benefits of such a nature that they can be returned, the recipient must either return the benefits or pay for their reasonable value. This rule is applied to willful breaches as well as unintentional breaches.

Specific performance

The legal remedy of dollar damages or the equitable remedy of rescission may not be adequate to provide a proper remedy to a party injured by a breach of contract. The only adequate remedy may be to require the party in breach to perform the contract.

Specific performance is granted in cases when the court in the exercise of its discretion determines that dollar damages would not be an adequate remedy. Specific performance is not a matter of right but rests in the sound discretion of the court. To warrant specific performance, the contract must be clear, definite, complete, and free from any suspicion of fraud or unfairness. Dollar damages are considered inadequate and specific performance the proper remedy when the subject matter of the contract is unique. Since each parcel of real estate differs from every other parcel of real estate, all land is unique, and courts of equity will therefore specifically enforce contracts to sell real estate. Examples of unique personal property are antiques, racehorses, heirlooms, and the stock of a closely held corporation. Such stock is unique because each share has significance in the power to control the corporation.

CASE

P and D entered into an agreement whereby P was to receive one-third of the stock in a closely held corporation upon payment of $45,000 to D. D refused to transfer the stock, and P sought specific performance.

ISSUE Is P entitled to specific performance?

DECISION Yes.

REASON Closely held stock is not available in the market, so that it is really a unique commodity. As a result, P had no adequate remedy at law, and specific performance was the only remedy.

Peters v. Wallach, 321 N.E.2d 806 (Mass.) 1975.

If the subject matter of a contract is goods, specific performance will be ordered whenever commercial needs and considerations make it equitable to do so. The remedy is liberally granted as a matter of policy. Contracts that involve personal services or relationships will not be specifically enforced, however; the only remedy in such cases is money damages. Thus, courts will not usually order specific performance of employment contracts.

Rescission

The other equitable remedy is rescission of a contract, which is disaffirmance of a contract and the return of the parties to the status quo (the position each occupied prior to entering into the contract). Rescission is afforded, for example, when a contract has been induced by fraud or misrepresentation.

A party who discovers facts that warrant rescission of a contract has a duty to act promptly. If he elects to rescind, he must notify the other party within a reasonable time, so that rescission may be accomplished at a time when parties may still be restored, as nearly as possible, to their original positions. A party entitled to rescission may either avoid the contract or affirm it. Once he makes his choice, he may not change it. Failure to rescind within a reasonable time is tantamount to affirming the contract

CASE

After buying a home and lot from D, P later discovered that the home site had not been approved by the health board because it lacked enough topsoil to sustain a septic tank and overflow field for sewage disposal. P charged that D knew of this condition and that there was no practical means of correcting it. P sues for rescission, incidental and punitive damages.

ISSUE Is P entitled to rescind the realty sale contract and deed? If so, can punitive damage also be awarded in a case in which equitable rescission is decreed?

DECISION Yes to both issues.

REASONS 1. D's failure to inform P of the sewage problem amounted to fraud and deceit, so that rescission is proper.

2. Incidental damages concerning the purchase, moving costs, and attorney's fees are also allowable, provided they are reduced by the reasonable rental value of the property for the period of P's occupancy.

3. Punitive or exemplary damages are awarded to punish a D and to deter others from similar conduct in the future. An award of punitive damages is permissible in equity, and fraud is the type of conduct on which to base such an award. Since both are based on a consistent theory of redress, rescission and punitive damages are not inconsistent under the doctrine of election for inconsistent and irreconcilable remedies.

Hutchison v. Pyburn, 567 S.W.2d 762 (Tn.) 1977.

The party who seeks rescission must return what he has received in substantially the same condition in which he received it. Because this remedy is an equitable one, it is subject to the usual maxims of equity courts.

Damages—terminology

Several terms are used to describe certain types of damages. *Nominal* damages are awarded if no measurable actual loss is established. In such cases, one dollar is awarded to the plaintiff, to show that a technical breach has occurred.

The term *liquidated damages* or *liquidated damage clause* is used to describe the situation in which the parties provide in their contract for the amount of damages to be awarded in the event of a breach. These provisions will be enforced unless the court considers the stipulation to be a penalty for failure to perform, rather than compensation for damages. Should the court find that the term was inserted primarily to force actual performance and not to compensate for probable injury, it will be considered to be a penalty and will not be enforced. In order to be valid and not a penalty, the amount of recovery agreed upon must bear a reasonable relation to the probable damage to be sustained by the breach. Recovery is allowed for the amount agreed upon by the parties, although the damages acutally suffered may vary somewhat from those agreed upon in the contract.

CASE

After 8 years of doing business as a film-producing partnership, the two partners decided to incorporate. Two years later D wanted to go his separate way, and the corporation agreed to buy his stock for $50,000, payable at the rate of $5,000 per year for 10 years. The stock purchase agreement had a covenant that D would not compete with the corporation by performing any film-producing services for anyone that the corporation had dealt with previously. If the covenant were breached, then the outstanding balance of the stock purchase price would be cancelled. A year later D did violate the agreement but received only $1,650 from P's former customer. The debt at that time was $40,000.

ISSUE Is the forfeiture provision a valid liquidated damages clause, so that the balance of $40,000 is cancelled?

DECISION No. The provision is a penalty rather than a liquidated damages clause, and P is therefore entitled to recover only the actual damages resulting from the breach of the covenant not to compete.

REASONS 1. The parties are bound by a stipulation for liquidated damages. If the stipulated sum is a penalty, it is not enforceable. The distinction between a penalty and a valid liquidated damages clause is that a penalty is a security for performance rather than a sum to be paid in lieu of performance. A penalty is designed to punish for breach of contract, whereas liquidated damages are intended as fair compensation for breach. A penalty is designed to prevent breach by the threat of punishment.

2. One factor to consider is whether the stipulated sum is a constant or whether it is based upon, and varies with, the nature and extent of breach. In this case the forfeiture did decrease with each annual payment, reducing the balance due on the original $50,000 note. However, it was not based on, nor did it vary with, the nature and extent of the breach.

Aztec Film Productions, Inc. v. Quinn, 569 P.2d 1366 (Ariz.) 1977.

The term *punitive* or *exemplary* damages refers to damages awarded to one party to punish the other's conduct as well as to deter others from such conduct in the future. Punitive damages are the last of the three broad types of damages available in contract actions. The three are: *compensatory,* which makes the aggrieved party whole; *nominal,* which recognizes a technical injury; and *punitive,* which makes an example out of the wrongdoer and is a windfall to the plaintiff. While it is not the purpose of a civil proceeding to punish a party, punitive damages are nonetheless frequently awarded in tort actions. While punitive damages under the classical theory could not be given in contract actions, the modern trend is to allow them when the contract breach is fraudulent, oppressive, malicious, or otherwise shows an intent by the breaching party to harm the other's justifiable expectations under the contract.

CASE

P severed his right foot while working for his landlord. P made a claim under his hospitalization policy with D but D denied payment relying on a clause stating that it did not have to pay if P received workers' compensation benefits. P was not an employee but his landlord had submitted a questionable claim for workers' benefits. At the time of the accident, P was 39 years old, had two minor children, and earned $500 per month. He needed 5 separate operations to restore his foot. Since D refused to pay any medical bills, P had to resort to ruses to be admitted to hospitals and had to use different doctors. His unpaid medical bills made him a poor credit risk; he could not borrow money, and his business failed. He had to move 5 times for nonpayment of rent. His utilities were shut off for nonpayment. His wheelchair was repossessed. Several times he was unable to afford medicine for his constant pain. He had two nervous breakdowns. P finally sued for policy benefits and punitive damages.

ISSUE Is P entitled to punitive damages in a breach of contract action?

DECISION Yes.

REASON Since D knew that workers' compensation coverage was doubtful, its refusal to pay was unreasonable and in bad faith as a matter of law. However, to recover punitive damages, bad faith is not sufficient. Intent to do harm must be shown. The contract-breaker must act with "intent to vex, injure or annoy, or with a conscious disregard of the plaintiff's rights." D's conduct was held to be sufficiently oppressive and malicious to justify an award of punitive damages. The trial court had awarded $75,000 compensatory and $500,000 punitive damages.

Silberg v. California Life Insurance Co., 521 P.2d 1103 (Cal.) 1974.

Special rules under the Code

The Code specifically provides that a contract clause calling for unreasonably large liquidated damages is void. To be valid under the Code, a liquidated damage clause must be reasonable in light of the anticipated or actual harm caused by the breach, the difficulties of proof of loss, and the inconvenience or nonfeasibility of otherwise obtaining an adequate remedy [2-718(1)].

Another form of liquidation of damages is the forfeiture of goods when a buyer defaults after paying part of the price or making a deposit as security. The Code provides that, in the absence of a liquidated damage clause, a buyer who defaults and does not receive the goods is entitled to recover from the seller any amount (1) by which his payments exceed 20 percent of the price or (2) $500, whichever is smaller [2-718(2)]. Thus, if the buyer had made a deposit of $500 on the purchase of appliances for $1,500, he would (after his breach and return of the goods) be entitled to recover $200 from the seller. If the sale contract contained a liquidated damage clause, the buyer would be entitled to recover the amount by which his deposit exceeds the amount provided for in such clause. Thus, a buyer who has made a part payment will not be unduly penalized by his breach, and the seller will not receive a windfall.

There is a Code provision relating to the obligation of buyers when there has been a breach by the seller after part of the goods has been delivered. The buyer may, on notifying the seller of his intention to do so, deduct from the price still due under the contract the damages suffered because of the seller's breach [2-717].

Construction and interpretation of contracts

Courts are often called upon to construe or interpret contracts. Although there is a technical distinction between *construction* (courts construe a contract's legal effect) and *interpretation* (juries interpret the parties' intentions), these words are generally interchangeable. The basic purpose of construing a contract is to determine the intention of the parties. If the language is clear and unambiguous, construction is not required, and the intent expressed in the agreement will be followed. When the language of a contract is ambiguous or obscure, courts apply certain established rules of construction in order to ascertain the supposed intent of the parties. These rules will not be used to make a new contract for the parties or to rewrite the old one, however, even if the contract is inequitable or harsh. They are applied by the court merely to resolve doubts and ambiguities within the framework of the agreement.

The general standard of interpretation is to use the meaning that the contract language would convey to a reasonably intelligent person who is familiar with the circumstances in which the language was used. Thus, language is judged objectively, rather than subjectively, and is given a reasonable meaning. What one party says he meant or thought he was saying or writing is immaterial, since words are given effect in accordance with their meaning to a reasonable person in the circumstances of the parties. In determining the intention of the parties, it is the expressed intention that controls, and this will be given effect unless it conflicts with some rule of law, good morals, or public policy.

The language is judged with reference to the subject matter of the contract, its nature, objects, and purposes. Language is usually given its ordinary meaning, but technical words are given their technical meaning. Words with an established legal meaning are given that legal meaning. The law of the place where the contract was made is considered a part of the contract. Isolated words or clauses are not considered; instead, the contract is considered as a whole to ascertain the intent of the parties. If one party has prepared the agreement, an ambiguity in the contract language will be construed against him, since he had the chance to eliminate the ambiguity. As an aid to the court in determining the intention of the parties, business custom, usage, and prior dealings between the parties are considered.

In the interpretation of contracts, the construction that the parties have themselves placed on the agreement is often the most significant source of the intention of the parties. The parties themselves know best what they have meant by their words of agreement, and their action under that agreement is the best indication of what that meaning was.

CASE

P, a construction company, had a contract with D, the state of New Mexico, to construct a highway for an agreed price. The contract, consisting of 400 pages, was drafted by P, heavily loaded in favor of the state, and ambiguous with regard to payment for extra work. D's key employees believed that P was entitled to payment for extras under the contract.

ISSUE In case of ambiguity, will a contract be construed against the party preparing it?

DECISION Yes.

REASONS
1. The law requires the construction of ambiguities and uncertainties in a contract most strongly against the party who drafted the contract. The construction principle is called *contra proferentem;* that is, construe the language strongly against the profferor or author of the language.
2. It is logical to assume that the parties to a contract know best what is meant by its terms. Consequently, the construction of a contract adopted by the parties, as evidenced by their conduct and practices, is entitled to great weight, if not the controlling weight, in ascertaining their intention and their understanding of the contract.

Schultz & Lindsay Construction Co. v. State, 494 P.2d 612 (N.M.) 1972.

REVIEW QUESTIONS AND PROBLEMS

1. What are the basic elements of a contract?
2. How is a bilateral offer accepted? How is a unilateral offer accepted?
3. What is the difference between an implied-in-fact contract and an implied-in-law contract? Now answer the following three problems:
   a) Pierre leased a restaurant and lounge from Scott. Pierre, with Scott's knowledge and consent, extensively remodeled the premises. One year later Pierre failed to pay the rent and was evicted. He sued for the amount spent in remodeling. Scott claims he is not liable because he had never agreed to pay for the work. Should Pierre succeed? Why or why not?
   b) Nursing Company assumed the operation of a nursing home. The previous owner had a contract with Linen Supply. Linen Supply continued to furnish services after Nursing Company assumed ownership. Nursing Company argues that it does not have to pay for the linen services because it had no express contract with Linen Supply. Can Linen Supply recover based on breach of an express contract? Why or why not?
   c) Architect was retained by Builder to design a motel and draft final working plans. His fee was 4 percent of the construction costs. After Architect drafted the preliminary plans, Builder decided not to build, since the land was not large enough to accommodate the motel. Builder knew the size of the lot; Architect did not. Builder claims that Architect's services were of no value to him. In Architect's lawsuit the court found for him. Did Architect recover on a contract? What kind? How much should Architect recover?
4. What are the various classifications of contracts?
5. How does the first and second *Restatement of Contracts* differ from the *Uniform Commercial Code?*
6. Fay and Ray were sole shareholders of the Empire State Building Company. They signed an agreement that at either's death the other will have the option to purchase the deceased's shares for $1 per share. Fay died. Ray sought specific performance from Fay's widower, who contended that the shares were worth more than $1 and refused to sell. Did Ray or Fay's widower win? Why?
7. Kong was fired from his job with the Empire State Building Company for "no good reason." Although his employment contract was not for a definite term, Kong sues to be reinstated in his job. Did he win? Why or why not?
8. After driving your new car for a few weeks, you discover that it was actually used. Its odometer had been set back. Are you entitled to punitive damages from the dealership? Why or why not?
9. Suppose you have made reservations through American Express with the Plaza Hotel. Your reservations were confirmed by the hotel and guaranteed by American Express. Upon your arrival, the Plaza refused you a room, stating there were none available. In addition to your out-of-pocket expenses for contract breach, are you entitled to recover punitive damages? Why or why not?
10. Insured had an automobile insurance policy that provided theft coverage and included equipment that was "part of the vehicle." Insured's CB radio was stolen from his car. The insurance company refused to pay the theft claim because the radio was not part of the vehicle. Is the CB radio covered by the policy? Discuss.
11. The following is from an actual case. Pratt, an inventor, invented a device and fuel that allows a car to go 400 miles to the gallon. It would cost 1 cent per gallon to manufacture the fuel. Pratt promised to transfer a 49 percent interest in the process and marketing control to Weeks for a price of $50,000. Experts testified that the process was worth from $200,000 to $1 billion. Should Weeks be entitled to a decree of specific performance? Explain. Note: Anyone having information about this process or its whereabouts, please call the authors of this textbook!

7

The Agreement: Offer and Acceptance

The first requirement of a valid, enforceable contract is an agreement between the parties. Generally, an agreement is reached when one party, the offeror, makes an offer and the other party, the offeree, accepts it.

Mutual assent

Offer and acceptance are the acts by which the parties have a "meeting of the minds." They reach an accord on the terms of their agreement. This accord is also referred to as manifestation of mutual assent. Frequently, parties may have had a discussion regarding a contract but have not yet indicated their willingness to be bound by any contract.

Objective theory of contracts

Mutual assent, then, is the first ingredient of a contract. Classical common-law rules required that the assent of both parties exactly match at the same point in time; that is, that there be a subjective meeting of the minds. Since nobody can actually know the inner thoughts of another, this requirement proved unworkable. Subsequently, the issue was framed in terms of whether one party had the right to rely on the assent as expressed by the other party. If so, then it was the manifestation of the assent that became the basic contract element. Rather than dealing with subjective thoughts, modern contract law follows an objective theory based on the manifestation of mutual assent. Assent to the formation of a contract is legally operative only if it is objectively manifested.

Meeting of the minds

Unless there is an objective "meeting of the minds" of the parties on the subject matter and terms of the agreement, no contract is formed. To determine whether the minds have met, both the offer and acceptance must be analyzed. The offeror may have had something in mind quite different from that of the offeree. Notwithstanding, the intention of the parties is determined not by what they think but by their outward conduct; that is, by what each leads the other reasonably to believe.

CASE

P sued D, an insurance company, for specific performance of an alleged oral contract to settle a claim for personal injuries arising out of an automobile accident. D's adjuster had offered P $7,500 to settle the claim. The insurance company had paid $2,400 in advance payments. The insurance adjuster intended to deduct the advance payments to P from the $7,500 and to pay P $5,100 net. P believed that the $7,500 would be in addition to the payment already received.

ISSUE Is there a contract to settle the claim?

DECISION No.

REASONS

1. It is elementary in contract law that mutual assent must be expressed by the parties to the agreement. When the minds of the parties have not met on any part or provision of a proposed contract, all of its portions are a nullity.
2. The meeting of the minds must be found in the objective manifestation of the parties. The apparent mutual assent, essential to the formation of a contract, must be gathered from the language employed by them, or manifested by their words or acts, and it may be manifested wholly or partly by written or spoken words or by other acts or conduct.
3. The parties to the alleged oral contract in the instant case used the same language, but the overt manifestations reveal that they attached different meanings to their words (a latent ambiguity), and there was, in fact, never a mutual assent.
4. When one party meant one thing and the other party meant another, the difference going to the essence of the supposed contract, the court finds no contract in law or equity unless it should find that one party knew or had reason to know what the other party meant or understood.

Trujillo v. Glen Falls Insurance Company, 540 P.2d 209 (N.M.) 1975.

Definition of offer

An offer is a conditional promise made by the offeror to the offeree. It is conditional because the offeror will not be bound by his promise unless the offeree responds to it in the proper fashion. The response sought by the offeror is expressed in his offer and will be that the offeree: (1) do something (perform an act), (2) refrain from doing something (forbearance), or (3) promise to do something or to refrain from doing something. If the offeree complies with the terms of the offer within the proper time, there is an agreement. The main idea, however, is that the offeror's manifestation must create a reasonable expectation in the offeree that the offeror is willing to contract. This expectation arises when the offeror's promise demonstrates a *present commitment* to do or refrain from doing some specified thing in the future in exchange for one of the three responses by the offeree listed above. So your first task will be to determine if an offer has been made.

Test for offer

The test for determining if an offer has been made is as follows: What would a reasonable person in the position of the offeree think the manifestation from the offeror meant? In our legal system, the reasonable person is the jury; the test asks the jury to make that factual determination. For purposes of this course, you should take the position of the reasonable person and ask yourself the basic question. You should look at all the surrounding circumstances, to determine what the offeree *ought* to have understood. It makes no difference what the offeror actually intended, because the test looks to the presumed intent of the offeror. In making the analysis of the offeror's presumed intent, juries (as well as you) weigh the answers to these three questions:

1. Did the offeror's manifestation demonstrate a present commitment or only an intent to bargain? (Language of present commitment is necessary for an offer.)
2. How definite were the terms as communicated? (The more definite, the more likely it was an offer.)
3. To whom was the manifestation addressed? (If addressed to a specific person rather than the public generally, then probably it was an offer.)

Language used

To decide if an offer was made, the first step is to evaluate the language used. If there are no words of present commitment or undertaking, then probably the manifestation was only a preliminary negotiation or an invitation to the other party to make an offer. The following is preliminary negotiation language: "I am asking," "I would consider," "I am going to sell," etc. Such language is generally construed as inviting offers, because there is no present commitment. Answer the following:

PROBLEM: In reply to Ronald McDonald's inquiry if Griese would sell his business for $30,000 (Bob Griese Fried Chicken), Griese said: "It would not be possible for me to sell unless I got $45,000 in cash." Ronald hands Griese $45,000. Was there an offer? No. Griese was only saying that he would consider offers that were at least $45,000. He made no commitment to sell.

PROBLEM: "I quote you $20.00 per hockey puck for immediate acceptance." Is this communication an offer? Probably. In general, price quotations are not considered offers, because there is no present commitment. Here there is promissory language "for immediate acceptance," which would lead a reasonable person in the offeree's position to think an offer was made.

Definiteness of offer

Many transactions involve lengthy negotiations between the parties, often with an exchange of numerous letters, proposals, and conversations. It is frequently difficult to establish the point at which the parties have concluded the negotiation stage and have entered into a binding contract. The key question in such situations is whether a definite offer was made and accepted or whether the letters, communications, and proposals were simply part of continuing negotiations. The courts must examine the facts of each case, and to those facts they must apply the basic contract rules concerning the requirements of an offer. An offer must be definite and must be made under such circumstances that the person receiving it has reason to believe that the other party (offeror) is willing to deal on the terms indicated.

One of the reasons for the requirement of definiteness is that courts may have to determine at a later date whether or not the performance is in compliance with the terms. Consequently, if the terms are vague or impossible to measure with some precision, of if major terms are absent, no contract results. Therefore, before a proposal can ripen into a contract, the offer must be sufficiently definite (when coupled with the acceptance) so a court can be reasonably certain regarding both the *nature* and *extent* of the assumed duties. Otherwise, a court has no basis for adjudicating liability. The more certain and definite the communications, the more reasonable it is for you to conclude that an offer is intended. But the issue remains: How definite must an offer be? The law has progressed through three stages.

Doctrine of indefiniteness

Classical contract theory adopted rules that struck down many contracts because of indefiniteness. Courts often pushed this approach to such extreme limits that complete definiteness of *all* terms was required, whether material or not. Modern contract law has undercut (if not destroyed) the doctrine of indefiniteness. If parties have intended to make a contract, uncertainty concerning incidental or collateral matters is now not fatal to the contract's existence.

The second Restatement (Sec. 32) requires that the terms of the contract be *reasonably certain.* The test for determining reasonable certainty is: Do the stated terms provide a basis for determining the extent of breach and for giving a suitable remedy? If the essential terms are so uncertain that there is no way to decide if the agreement has been duly kept or broken, there is no contract. The Restatement then requires reasonable certainty as to all material terms.

Code approach

Favoring contract formation, the Code rejects the rule that the offer must contain all material terms. It provides that a contract may leave out one or more material terms so long as "the parties intended to make a contract and there is a reasonably certain basis for giving an appropriate remedy" [2-204(3)]. The Code makes three fundamental rules. First, the parties must intend (under the objective theory) to make a contract—the most basic rule. Second, one or more material terms can be omitted without the contract failing for indefiniteness. Finally, the contract must contain enough terms so a court can fashion an appropriate remedy. If there is no reasonably certain basis for providing an appropriate remedy, then a court will conclude that the parties did not adequately manifest their intentions.

Gap-filling

Courts should be willing to fill gaps or missing terms under an agreement, especially if the parties intent to contract but are silent regarding some terms. Although there is an alleged split between the Code and Restatement over material terms, the trend of the Code and modern case law is to supply reasonable terms—even material terms. Time for performance and the price to be paid, for example, are important terms and usually are included in the contract. If no time clause is included, a court in most contracts will supply a reasonable time for performance [2-309 (1)]. If no price is specified, a court will rule that a reasonable price was intended [2-305]. Gap-filling the price term also applies when the parties have agreed that the price is to be fixed by a market or other standard and that standard fails. In a non-Code case, however, if the contract is totally executory (neither party has performed), the contract with an unspecified price term may not be enforced. NOTE: A court can gap-fill a missing term but cannot rewrite the contract. There can be no gap-filling if the parties state they do not intend to be bound unless, for example, the price is agreed upon. Courts follow the presumption that the parties intend reasonable terms; that presumption applies only to omitted terms. If a term is vague, for instance, the parties have manifested an intention that cannot be presumed. Gap-filling is not allowed. Thus, when parties express their intention on a matter now claimed indefinite or missing, the court cannot supply an external, reasonable term. To do so would be inconsistent with the express intention of the parties.

The Code also has special rules for particulars of performance. It is permissible for the contract to grant a party the right to specify particulars of performance, such as specifications relating to assortment of the goods. Specification of such particulars must be made in good faith and within limits set by commercial reasonableness [2-311]. Unless otherwise agreed, specifications concerning the assortment of the goods are at the buyer's option, and those relating to method and mode of shipment are at the seller's option [2-311(2)]. Older common-law cases held such a contract to be vague and indefinite.

Fashioning a remedy

Although the Code allows material terms to be supplied by the court, the contract must contain sufficient terms so that the court can fashion an appropriate remedy [2-204(3)]. Quite naturally, the question arises: What term or terms are absolutely necessary before a court can state a proper remedy? The quintessential term that must be in every contract is the *quantity* term. Without it, a court has no basis to figure damages. It is easy to overlook this basic requirement. Consider the following:

PROBLEM: Cey Cheese writes to you: "Cey Cheese quotes you Eatum cheese at $1.10 per pound in carload lots only and subject to sight draft with bill of lading attached, F.O.B. Marietta, Georgia." Is this letter an offer? No. It has no quantity term. Carload lots is not a quantity term. If it were an offer, you would know how many carload lots were available, that is, it would have a quantity term. Suppose a court erroneously said it was an offer, then you could accept by ordering 1 carload or 100 carloads or 1 million carloads. Do you see why it is absolutely necessary to have a quantity term?

Note that so long as a quantity term is present, the written contract can omit most material terms. Figure 7·1 would not fail for indefiniteness under the Code. In fact, it complies with other rules we will discuss later, like the Statute of Frauds [2-201], which require a written contract.

MEMO

CEY CHEESE
25 Model Lane
Marietta, Georgia

Sold today 5 carloads of Grade A
Eatum cheese to B. A. Stewart.

Fig. 7·1

This writing contains a subject matter (Grade A Eatum cheese), a quantity term (5 carloads), and the signature of the seller (Cey Cheese). Under the Code, a signature can be printed, stamped, or written, an initial, a thumbprint, or (as in the above example) a billhead or letterhead [1-201(39)].

Offeree addressed

In addition to the language used and the definiteness of the communication, the last factor to consider is the person addressed by the manifestation. Since an offer creates in someone the power of acceptance, it is required that the communication sufficiently identify the offeree or the class from whom the offeree may emerge. If the expression definitely identifies the party or parties addressed, it is likely to be deemed an offer. Offers of rewards are illustrative: the addressee is indefinite, but the expression is deemed an offer. Although the offeree is unidentified and unknown at the time the reward offer is made, the performance of the act requested in the reward is not only an acceptance but also identifies the offeree. The usual rule, however, is that if the addressee is an indefinite group, as in the case of advertisements, then it probably will not be considered an offer.

In general, advertisements, estimates, quotes, catalogs, circulars, proposals, and the like are not offers, for several reasons. There is no quantity term or language of present commitment; the goods are seldom adequately described. Practically speaking, advertisers do not intend the communication to be an offer that can ripen into a contract on the basis of the terms expressed. But a legal rule is not like a mathematical principle. Rather, it contains a lot of grey areas. It is possible for an ad or quote to constitute an offer, depending on all the surrounding circumstances.

CASE

In preparing its bid for a highway building project, D requested several suppliers of sectional steel plate to submit quotations for 3,468 lineal feet of steel plate. P's quotation was the lowest and D used it in its bid for the highway project. After D was awarded the highway project, P requested D to issue a purchase order for the steel. D sent P a proper purchase order. Later a dispute arose, and D claimed that its purchase order was the only offer; therefore, the terms of the purchase order control.

ISSUE Was P's quote an offer that was accepted by D when it issued the purchase order or was the purchase order the offer that P accepted by shipping the steel?

DECISION P's quotation was an offer.

REASONS Whether a quotation constitutes an offer or merely an invitation to make an offer depends on its terms and the facts surrounding its issuance. Four facts demonstrate that the quote is an offer.

1. The quote sets forth all the terms necessary to constitute a binding contract upon acceptance.
2. The course of dealing between the parties shows an intention to treat the quote as an offer.
3. P asked for a purchase order because it was anticipating a price rise and wanted to fix the price by having D accept the price quoted.
4. The terms of the quotation were tailored to allow D to meet the specifications of the highway project.

Earl M. Jorgensen Co. v. Mark Construction Inc., 540 P.2d 978 (Hawaii) 1975.

Auctions—special offer situation

Auctions are either with reserve or without reserve. An auction is considered to be "with reserve" unless it is specifically announced to be "without reserve." In a "with reserve" auction, the bidders are the offerors, and the acceptance occurs with the fall of the hammer. Thus, the auctioneer may withdraw the goods at any time, and the owner or his agents may bid. In a "without reserve" auction, the auctioneer makes the offer, and each bid is an acceptance subject to there being no higher bid. In either auction, the bidder can withdraw her bid freely before the fall of the hammer.

The Code has a separate section that covers sales of goods by auction [2-328]. In an auction sale, the sale is completed when the auctioneer strikes his hammer. At the point when the hammer falls, the person making the highest bid is entitled to the article and must pay for it. It sometimes happens that while the auctioneer's hammer is falling, but before it has struck the table, another bid is made. In this case, the Code provides that the auctioneer can either reopen the bidding or declare the goods sold under the bid on which the hammer was falling [2-328(2)]. One who is selling goods at auction cannot bid at his own sale unless notice has been given that he retains this privilege. The Code provides that if the auctioneer knowingly receives a bid that has been made by the seller or on his behalf, and no notice has been given that the seller has the privilege of bidding at his own sale, the buyer has a choice of remedies. If the seller's wrongful bidding has bid up the price, the bidder can refuse to be bound by the sale. If he wishes to do so, he could demand that the goods be sold to him at the price of the last good-faith bid prior to the completion of the sale [2-328(4)]. The Code provisions are designed to protect people who bid at auction sales and to prevent them from being defrauded or otherwise ripped off.

An offer must be communicated

An offer is not effective until it has been communicated to the offeree by the offeror. It can be effectively communicated only by the offeror or his duly authorized agent. If the offeree learns of the offeror's intention to make an offer from some outside source, no offer results. Also, to be effective, the offer must be communicated through the medium or channel selected by the offeror. Thus, if Terry was in Margaret's office and noticed on the desk a letter directed to Terry and containing an offer, the offer would not have been communicated to Terry. She would not be in a position to accept the offer.

An offer to the public may be made through newspapers or posted notices. As far as a particular individual is concerned, it is not effective until he learns that the offer has been made. As a result, a person without actual knowledge cannot accept the offer. If a reward is offered for the arrest of a fugitive, and a person makes the arrest wthout actual knowledge of the offer of the reward, there is no contract.

An offer is effective even though it is delayed in reaching the offeree. Because the delay normally results from the negligence of the offeror or his chosen means of communication (for example, a telegraph company), he should bear the loss resulting from the delay. If the delay is apparent to the offeree, the acceptance will be effective only if it is communicated to the offeror within a reasonable time after the offer would normally have been received. If the offeree knows that there has been a delay in communicating the offer, he cannot take advantage of the delay.

It should be noted that printed material often found on the back of contract forms and occasionally on letterheads, unless embodied in the contract by reference to it, is not generally considered part of any contract set forth on the form or letterhead. It is not a part of the contract because it has not been communicated to the offeree by the offeror.

Duration of Offers

Revocable and irrevocable offers

Assuming that an offer has been made, you must consider the next legal issue, the duration of that offer; that is, how long does the offeree have the power to accept? This issue turns on a determination of whether the offer is revocable or irrevocable. Some simple legal rules can aid that determination. The offeror is legally recognized as the master of the offer. The offeror creates the power to accept in the offeree and retains the power to revoke. If the offer is revoked, the power to accept terminates.

Likewise, if the offeree accepts, the offer is merged into the contract, so there is no longer any offer to revoke. Since most offers are revocable, they will be discussed first; then we shall consider irrevocable offers and the law of acceptances.

Revocable Offers

How might a revocable offer be revoked? An offer that has been properly communicated continues in existence until it (1) lapses or expires, (2) is terminated by operation of law (illegality and incapacity), (3) is rejected by the offeree, or (4) is revoked (directly or indirectly) by the offeror.

Lapse of time

An offer does not remain open indefinitely, even though the offeror fails to revoke it. If an offer does not stipulate the period during which it is to continue, it remains open for a reasonable time, a period that a reasonable person might conclude was intended. Whether an offer has lapsed because of the passage of time is usually a question of fact for the jury after it has given proper weight to all related circumstances, one of which is the nature of the property. An offer involving property that is constantly fluctuating in price remains open a relatively short time in comparison with property that has a more stable price. Other facts that should be considered are the circumstances under which the offer is made, the relation of the parties, and the means used in transmitting the offer. An offer made orally usually lapses when the conversation ends, unless the offeror clearly indicates that the proposal may be considered further by the offeree.

If the offer stipulates the period during which it may be accepted, it automatically lapses at the end of that period. This rule raises two issues. First, how do you measure the time period? Assume the offer is in a letter that states it will remain open for 5 days. The letter is dated May 1st and received by the offeree on May 7th. One might argue that the offer lapsed on May 6th, since the letter is dated May 1st. Since an offer is not an offer until communicated, however, and if there is no contrary intent, the time will be measured from the time the offeree *receives* the offer. The rationale is to protect the offeree unless he has some reason to know that time should be measured from some earlier date. The second issue is this: If the offer stipulates that it will remain open for 5 days, can the offeror nevertheless revoke it anytime during the 5-day period? The answer is YES, which may seem somewhat perplexing, but remember that the offeror is the master and still has the power to revoke. It is possible that the offer with a stated time period may have become irrevocable, but that will be discussed later.

Rejection by offerees

Rejection by the offeree causes an offer to terminate. An offeree who rejects cannot later bind the offeror by tendering an acceptance. A rejection terminates an offer even though the offeror had promised to keep the offer open for a specified time. An attempted acceptance that departs from the terms of the offer is a rejection of the offer. It is a counteroffer, because it implies that the terms set forth in the offer are not acceptable. To Lyle's offer to sell a house for $95,000, Wood responded, "I accept your offer, provided that a new roof is put on the house." Here the acceptance varies from the offer and is therefore not effective as an acceptance. Rather, it is a counteroffer and a rejection.

It is often difficult to determine whether a communication by an offeree is a rejection or merely an expression of a desire to negotiate further on the terms of the agreement. Thus, it is possible to suggest a counterproposal in a way that clearly indicates the offer is still being considered and is not being rejected. The offeree wishes a reaction from the offeror to the suggested changes. Also, the offeree may, in his acceptance, set forth terms not included in the offer, but only those that would be implied as normally included in such an agreement. The inclusion of such terms will not prevent formation of a contract.

CASE

P leased property from D. The lease contained an option to purchase the premises for $25,000 at any time during the term of the lease. P decided to exercise the option and to purchase the property, and he so notified D in writing. In the writing, P stated that he would pay the purchase price as soon as D furnished him proof of title to the property and furnished him with a deed warranting that the title was good. D refused to sell to P. D contended that P had added conditions to the option with regard to proof of good title, and therefore the purported acceptance was actually a rejection.

ISSUE Did P properly accept the offer contained in the option?

DECISION Yes.

REASONS

1. An option is defined as a right acquired by contract to accept or reject a present offer within the time limited. If the person who holds the option does signify acceptance of the offer within the time limited and upon the terms stated, the obligations become mutual and are capable of enforcement at the instance of either party.
2. Nothing was said expressly in the option regarding the kind of deed or proof of title, but in a real estate transaction a buyer is entitled to both of these. The addition of these in the acceptance did not go beyond what the seller would have had to have furnished in any event.
3. While the lessor did not promise in so many words that he would give a deed or furnish proof of title, the obligation to do so could be fairly implied. The lessee's so-called counterconditions are in reality only suggested ways and means by which his purchase of the premises can be appropriately effected by the lessor.

Department of Public Works v. Halls, 210 N.E.2d 226 (Ill.)1965.

A request for further information by an offeree who indicates that he still has the offer under consideration will not constitute a rejection of the offer.

Rejection of an offer is not effective in terminating it until the rejection has been received by the offeror or his agent or is available to him at his usual place of business. Consequently, a rejection that has been sent may be withdrawn at any time prior to delivery to the offeror. Such action does not bar a later acceptance.

Termination of an offer by operation of law

Several events will terminate an offer as a matter of law. Notice of their occurrence need not be given or communicated to the offeree or the offeror, as the offer ends instantaneously upon the occurrence of the event. Such events include the death or insanity of either party or the destruction of the subject matter of the offer or illegality that occurs after the offer is made. The occurrence of any one of these events eliminates one of the requisites for a contract, thereby destroying the effectiveness of the acceptance of the offer to create a contract. Thus, if the offeror dies before the offeree has communicated acceptance to him, the offer is terminated, and the acceptance would have no effect. The usual rule is that an offer is not revoked until the revocation is actually received. Note that death or incapacity is an exception (so watch out). In either instance, the offer is terminated at the moment of death or on the date a legal guardian is appointed. Another event is the promulgation by a law-making body of a statute or ordinance making illegal the performance of any contract that would result from acceptance of the offer. Supervening illegality of the proposed contract legally terminates the offer.

There is a distinct difference between the termination of an offer and the termination of a contract. It should be emphasized that death, for example, terminates an offer but not a contract. As a general rule, death of either party does not excuse performance of contracts, although it would excuse performance in contracts for personal service. To illustrate the effect of the death of one of the parties to an offer, assume that Jeffrey offers to sell to Clint a certain electronic computer for $15,000. After Jeffrey's death, Clint, without knowledge of the demise, mails his acceptance to Jeffrey and immediately enters into a contract to resell the computer to West for $17,000. Jeffrey's estate has no duty to deliver the machine, even though West may have a claim against Clint for breach of contract if the latter failed to deliver the computer to him. Had Clint's acceptance become effective before Jeffrey's death, the executor of the estate would have been obligated to deliver the computer.

Actual revocation by offeror

If the offer is not irrevocable, an offeror may revoke at any time before it is accepted by the offeree. As stated, the offeror may revoke even though he has promised to hold the offer open for a definite period. So long as it remains a revocable offer, it can be legally withdrawn, although morally or ethically such action may be unjustified. Because of ethical considerations, as you will see, the law may stop the offeror from revoking. The next section discusses the three ways the law may recognize that an offer is irrevocable.

The offeror, possessing the power to revoke, can terminate the offer by communicating the revocation to the offeree. This communication can be direct or indirect. A directly communicated revocation to the offeree is effective only when received. Merely sending a notice of revocation is insufficient. It must be received by the offeree or reach a destination where it would be available to him. Nonetheless, the communication of the revocation is effective when actually received, regardless of how or by whom it is conveyed. Just as the offer is not an offer until received, a revocation is not effective until receipt. Why? Since the offeror is the master of the offer and can protect his interests, the law's policy is to protect the offeree.

Although most revocations are directly made, the law recognizes that the revocation can occur indirectly through some third party not associated with the offeror. Indirect revocation occurs when the offeree secures reliable information from a third party that the offeror has engaged in conduct that indicates to a reasonable person that the offeror no longer wishes to make the offer. An effective indirect revocation requires that (1) the third party give correct information, (2) the offeror's conduct would indicate to a reasonable person that the offeror no longer recognizes the offer, and (3) the third party is a reliable source.

Revocation of an offer for a unilateral contract

In the case of a bilateral contract (promise for a promise), it is rather easy to pinpoint acceptance by when the offeree's promise occurs. Thus, it is also easy to decide if an offeror's revocation is communicated before the attempted acceptance. In a unilateral contract (promise for an act), difficult issues arise, which will be discussed under the section on the law of acceptances. For the moment, let's note two legal rules that control the timing of revocation in the unilateral contract situation. (1) The older common law view was that since acceptance consists of performing an act (such as building a ship or mowing the lawn), the offeror could revoke at any time prior to *complete* performance. You can readily see the unfairness in this position. Suppose that you had mowed almost the entire yard when the offeror told you that he revoked. No contract is formed, so you have no contractual theory (except possibly quasi-contract) on which to sue. (2) The modern position is that once the offeree begins to perform, the offer becomes irrevocable.

Irrevocable Offers

The offeror, as master of the offer, retains the power to revoke his offer. Although most offers are thus revocable, the law acknowledges that an offer may be irrevocable. The issue is: How may the offeror lose the power to revoke, so that the offer is legally irrevocable?

When offer is irrevocable

The answer is that power to revoke may be lost by: (1) contract (2) legislation, and (3) conduct of the offeree. We shall see that all three ways are based on option contract principles.

Option contract

The offeror can sell away his power to revoke. Recall that an offeror can revoke the offer even if he says he will not or that the offer will remain open for a specified time. For a consideration, however, the offeror can give away his power to revoke, thereby creating an option contract.

An option is a contract based upon some consideration, whereby the offeror binds himself to hold an offer open for an agreed period of time. It gives the holder of the option the right to accept the continuing offer within the specified time. Quite often the offeree pays or promises to pay money in order to have the option (the continuing offer) remain open. The consideration need not be money. It may be anything that the law recognizes as legal value. The significant fact is that the offer has been transformed into a contract of option because of consideration supplied by the offeree. The offer becomes irrevocable for the period of the option. Of course, the offeree in an option contract is under no obligation to accept the offer; he simply has the right to do so.

Frequently, an option is part of another contract. A lease may contain a clause that gives to the tenant the right to purchase the property within a given period at a stated price; a sale of merchandise may include a provision that obligates the seller to supply an additional amount at the same price if ordered by the purchaser within a specified time. Such options are enforceable because the initial promise to pay rent serves as consideration for both the lease and the right to buy. The original purchase price of goods serves as consideration for the goods purchased and the option to buy additional goods.

Legislation: firm offers

Several states have statutes that make certain types of offers irrevocable. The most significant statute is found in the Code [Sec. 2-205], which operates to make a merchant's offer irrevocable *without consideration*. Remember the Code [Art. 2] applies only to the sale of goods. The requisites of this so-called "firm offer" under the Code are: (1) assurance given in a signed writing that the offer will be held open, (2) offeror is a merchant, and (3) the transaction involves the sale of goods. The offer is then irrevocable for the time stated in the offer (but no longer than 3 months) or for a reasonable time not to exceed 3 months if the offer has no stated time period. If the writing, assuring the offer will remain open, is on a form supplied by the offeree, it must be separately signed by the offeror. The offeree in a firm offer can rely upon the continuing legal obligation of the offeror and make other commitments on the strength of it. In effect, the firm offer by a merchant is the equivalent of an option without consideration.

Offeree's conduct: performance or reliance

Note that the irrevocable offers discussed so far are either true options or legislatively created option contracts. The third irrevocable offer springs from a situation analogous to an option contract. When the offeree starts to perform or relies on the offer, the law protects the offeree by holding that the offeror has lost the power to revoke. Analytically, the offeree has done something that the law sees as legal value. This legal value buys away the power to revoke, just as actual consideration does in a true option contract. The legal value consists of either part performance in the unilateral contract situation or reliance (substantial change of position) by the offeree.

Irrevocable offer for a unilateral contract

Suppose Lucy says to Shirley: "I will pay you $50.00 to sew the letter L on four of my sweaters." When Shirley finishes sewing the L's (the act requested), that is acceptance. At that moment, a contract springs into existence. It is a unilateral contract with only one duty—to pay $50.00; however, problems can arise prior to complete performance. After Shirley starts to perform, can Lucy revoke her offer for a unilateral contract? The classical position is that the offer could be revoked anytime prior to *complete* performance. The offeree who had partly performed is relegated to a quasi-contract action for the reasonable value of the services bestowed upon the offeror. Since this action could cause unfair results, modern law favors the proposition that the offeree should be given a reasonable time to perform fully, once she starts to perform. The majority of courts hold that the offer is irrevocable for that reasonable time. These courts follow either the first or second Restatement of Contracts rule. The first Restatement (Sec. 45) provides that part performance creates a contract. The offeror is protected, however, in that she owes no duty under the contract until the act requested is fully performed. The second Restatement (Sec. 45) provides that "an option contract is created when the offeree tenders or begins the invited performance." The consideration for the option contract is the part performance by the offeree. Thus, the start of performance by the offeree creates the option contract that makes the offer in the principal contract irrevocable. Analytically, however, there is little difference between the two Restatements except for the use of the label "option contract."

CASE

D, a utility company, offered a promotional allowance to any homeowner who uses electricity as the primary method of heating. The allowance was conditioned on the installation meeting the D's approval standards. P, a home builder, changed the construction plans on his homes to provide for an electrical, rather than an oil, heating system. After the homes were 90 percent completed with all electrical systems completely installed, P, to avoid taxes, sold the homes. At the time of sale, P had not fully complied with D's approval standards, although the homes were completed in full compliance with the standards.

ISSUE Since D's promotional allowance is a standing offer to enter into a unilateral contract, was a contract formed prior to P's selling the homes to a third party?

DECISION Yes. P is entitled to the promotional allowance.

REASONS 1. The trial court erred in ruling that "if an act is required in return for a promise, that act and only that act and the whole of that act must be performed or there is no contract."

2. When the offeree enters upon the performance of the specified act, the offer is thus accepted and forms a binding contract by part performance. When P undertook to install the heating system, P accepted D's offer.
3. When P changed construction plans and built homes with electricity as the primary method of heating, in order to obtain the promotional allowance as advertised by D (the utility company), a unilateral contract was formed. D is liable for the allowance, even though P transferred ownership of the homes before the electrical system was fully installed in compliance with D's requirements.

Motel Services v. Central Maine Power Co., 394 A.2d 786 (Maine) 1978.

Reliance and irrevocability

Just as part performance by the offeree can create an option contract, reliance by the offeree upon the offer can likewise take away the offeror's power to revoke. A father promised his daughter $20,000 so she could buy a home. Relying upon the promise, she executed a contract to purchase a home and put down $3,500. The father died (recall that death revokes an offer), and his executor refused to pay the $20,000. Could she recover anything? The court held that she was entitled to a recovery based upon the promissory estoppel theory. *In re Estate of Bucci,* 488 P.2d 216 (Colo.) 1971. The doctrine of *promissory estoppel* will be discussed in detail in the next chapter. For now, simply note that reliance (substantial change of position) by the offeree on the offer can make the offer irrevocable. Drawing an analogy to an option contract, promissory estoppel makes the offer legally enforceable, regardless of any further action by the offeree.

The Law of Acceptances

Definition

A contract consists of an offer by one party (offeror) and its acceptance by the person (offeree) to whom it is made. Figuratively speaking, an offer hangs like a suspended question. The acceptance must be a positive answer to that question. The offeror says: "I will sell you this article for $200. Will you buy it?" The offeree now has the legal power to accept this offer, and if she does so in proper fashion, a contract will result. A contract therefore results when the offeree (promisee) answers the question in the affirmative. An acceptance is an indication by the offeree of her willingness to be bound by the terms of the offer. Acceptance may, if the offer permits, take the form of an act (unilateral offer), an oral return promise communicated to the offeror (bilateral offer), or the signing and delivery of a written instrument. The last-named method is the most common in transactions of considerable importance and in those that are more formal. If a written contract is the agreed method of consummating the transaction, the contract is formed only when it has been signed by both parties and has been delivered.

Indifferent offeror

All contract theories (classical, Restatement, and Code) recognize that the offeror is the master of the offer. As such, the offeror has the power to control both the *manner* (bilateral or unilateral) and the *medium* (phone, letter, telegram, carrier pigeon, etc.) of acceptance. If the offeror specifically seeks only a promise, then the offeree can accept only by promising (bilateral contract). Likewise, the offeror may want only an act as acceptance (unilateral contract). Modern law recognizes the more realistic proposition that the offeror usually is indifferent to how the offeree accepts. Given this indifference, the general rule is that the offeree may accept in any *reasonable manner* (promising or acting) and by any *reasonable medium* of communication. The Code states: "Unless otherwise unambiguously indicated by the language [of the offer], an offer to make a contract shall be construed as inviting acceptance in any manner and by any medium reasonable in the circumstances" [2-206(1) (a)]. The second Restatement has similar language (Rest. 2d Sec. 29). Note that the Code rule starts by recognizing that the offeror as master may unambiguously indicate what he wants in the acceptance. Such an unambiguous declaration by the offeror is rare. Note in the following case the disastrous effect of the offeree's failure to follow the offeror's dictates.

CASE

P, a utility, needed steel to support 758 steel towers covering 180 miles. Bids were requested from 5 companies. D's bid was the lowest. P was worried about not only steel prices but also delivery schedules. D's bid had the delivery schedule P required. Additionally, D's bid had a standard acceptance clause as follows: "ACCEPTANCE: Should you desire to enter into a contract on the terms set herein, please so indicate by signing and returning to us within 7 [typewritten insertion] days from the date hereof. This bid shall become a contract upon, but not before, acceptance by our Home Office." Since this clause was buried in the fine print of the bid, it was apparently overlooked by P. P awarded D the contract to supply steel, first by letter and then by sending out purchase orders. Later, when the steel was not delivered according to the schedule set out in D's bid, P sued D to recover $7 million as damages for breach of contract.

ISSUE Did P accept D's bid (offer) which contained a set delivery schedule for the steel?

DECISION No. P neither signed the bid form nor returned it to D within 7 days.

REASONS

1. An acceptance clause is a valid contractual provision. In effect, it causes the offeree, by signing, to make an offer back to D. Since P never complied with the acceptance clause, the numerous letters, forms, and other written communications did not form a contract.
2. Because the steel was shipped by D and used by P, a contract was formed. The contract is an implied-in-fact contract based on the conduct of the parties. Since their contract did not contain a delivery schedule, the court properly gap-filled a reasonable time for delivery [2-309 (1)].
3. Although D did not deliver the steel as set forth in its bid, it nonetheless did deliver the steel within a reasonable time.

West Penn Power Co. v. Bethlehem Steel Corp., 348 A.2d 144 (Pa.) 1975.

Acceptance by offeree

Only the person to whom the offer is made can accept the offer. Offers to the public may be accepted by any member of the public who is aware of the offer. An offeree cannot assign the offer to a third party. Option contracts, however, although a form of offer, are usually assignable and may be accepted by the assignee (the person to whom the option is transferred).

If goods are ordered from a firm that has discontinued business, and the goods are shipped by its successor, the offeror (the purchaser) is under no duty to accept the goods. If he does accept them, knowing that they were shipped by the successor, then by implication he agrees to pay the new concern for the goods at the contract price. If he does not know of the change of ownership when he accepts the goods, he is not liable for the contract price. His only liability is in quasi contract for the reasonable value of the goods, and of course he could return them to the seller if he so elected.

Acceptance of a Bilateral Contract

An offer for a bilateral contract is accepted by a promise from the offeree, given in response to the promise of the offeror. The offeree's promise is to perform in the manner required by the offer. The promise of the offeree (acceptance) must be communicated to

Manner of accepting bilateral contracts

the offeror or his agent and may consist of any conduct on the part of the offeree that clearly shows an intention to be bound by the conditions prescribed in the offer. In construing the language of a purported acceptance, the usual rules of construction are applied, including the principle that ambiguous language is to be construed against the person using it.

The acceptance may take the form of a signature to a written agreement—even a nod of the head or any other indication of a willingness to perform as required by the offer. No formal procedure is generally required. If the offer is made to two or more persons, the acceptance is not complete until each of the parties has indicated acceptance. Until all have responded and accepted, the offeror is at liberty to withdraw the offer.

When it is understood that the agreement will be set forth in a written instrument, the acceptance is effective only when the document has been signed and delivered (unless it was clearly the intention of the parties that the earlier verbal agreement be binding and that the writing act merely as a memorandum or evidence of the oral contract that was already effective and binding upon the parties).

Counter-offers under the mirror image rule

In forming a bilateral contract, an acceptance may have terms new or different from those stated in the offer. This variance between the offer and acceptance has engendered two legal positions. The first is the *mirror image* or *matching acceptance* rule. It requires that the acceptance be absolute and unconditional. To be effective, an acceptance must conform exactly to the terms of the offer. *Any* deviation from the terms of the offer and the acceptance will be held to be a counteroffer, which constitutes a rejection terminating the original offer. NOTE: Once a counteroffer is made (that is, the acceptance is not a mirror image of the offer), then the attempted acceptance becomes a *new* offer and the original offer terminates. This rule (counteroffer = rejection = new offer) was discussed previously in this chapter under duration of offers. You may want to reread that section. As stated there, it may be difficult to decide if the acceptance is a counteroffer or merely a counterinquiry. The original offer does not terminate if the offeree merely suggests or requests new or different terms or makes a counterinquiry. Monty offers to sell one antique cabinet to Brian for $3,500. Brian replies, "Will you take $3,000?" This is only a counterinquiry. Suppose Brian wires, "Please send lowest cash price for cabinet." This is not a counteroffer but only a request for different terms. But in the usual case, Brian would say, "I'll pay only $2,500." This is a counteroffer under the mirror image rule. The modern approach is demonstrated by the Code.

Variance under the Code

The Code rejects the mirror image rule of the classical law of contracts. Under the Code, a definite expression of acceptance of a written confirmation operates as an acceptance. This is true even though the acceptance states terms additional to, or different from, those offered or agreed upon, unless acceptance is made conditional upon agreement to the additional or different terms [2-207(1)]. This means that the additional or different terms do not prevent the formation of a contract, unless they are expressed in the form of a counterproposal. The terms in question will otherwise be treated simply as new proposals.

When the contract is *between merchants,* such terms become part of the contract unless "(a) the offer expressly limits acceptance to the terms of the offer; (b) they materially alter it; or (c) notification of objection to them has already been given or is given within a reasonable time after notice of them is received" [2-207(2)].

The problem of variance arises in three similar situations: (1) an acceptance states terms additional to, or different from, those offered, (2) a written confirmation of an informal or oral agreement sets forth terms additional to, or different from, those previously agreed upon, and (3) the printed forms used by the parties are in conflict, especially in the "fine print." The Code takes the position that in all three situations "a proposed deal which in commercial understanding has in fact been closed is recognized as a contract" [2-207].

"Battle of the forms"

To illustrate the variance in offer and acceptance and the Code approach, a typical "battle of the forms" will be used. Businesspeople constantly confront this battle of forms (involving forms such as purchase orders, acknowledgments, invoices) when goods are bought at a distance. In the typical situation below, carefully follow each step in the Code analysis.

1. Buyer orders goods from Seller and sends Seller a purchase order form that contains no mention of warranties. (Warranties will be explained later in Part III, "Uniform Commercial Code.") When the form is received by Seller, an acknowledgment form is sent to Buyer. It accepts Buyer's order; and on the front, in bold, large print, provides:

This acknowledgment is subject to all of the terms and conditions on the reverse side of this document, and the parties are bound thereby.

2. On the reverse side, the following appears:

Seller hereby warrants the goods described on the reverse side hereof to be free from defects due to faulty materials or workmanship for a period of 90 days from the date of acceptance of the goods. This warranty is in lieu of any other warranty, express or implied, *including the implied warranty of merchantability.*

3. The goods are shipped and used by Buyer. An invoice expressed in the same words as those in the acknowledgment is enclosed with the shipment. Later, when the goods fail to operate, Buyer wants to claim breach of implied warranty against Seller. What results?

4. At common law, Seller's acceptance did not match Buyer's offer in that it added a different term, the disclaimer of implied warranties. Thus, Seller made a counteroffer (that is, a *new* offer) that was accepted by Buyer when Buyer used the goods. Seller's form controls and its terms become the contract terms. The Code (and Restatement) rules can provide a different answer.

5. The first part of 2-207(1) states a two-part rule. [1] "A definite and seasonable expression of acceptance or a written confirmation which is sent within a reasonable time *operates* as an acceptance *even though* it states terms additional to, or different from, those offered or agreed upon, [2] unless acceptance is expressly made conditional on assent to the additional or different terms" [2-207(1)].

6. The first part of the rule provides that the acceptance can *operate* as an acceptance, even though it is not a mirror image of the offer. The word *operate* shows that the Code recognizes that this result is a fiction. Operate means "let's pretend it's an acceptance." At common law, if the offeree injects new or different terms, then it would be a counteroffer. Under the Code, it is deemed an acceptance. The second part of the rule does allow for true counteroffers. It recognizes that the offeror is the master of the offer. If

an offeree says that his acceptance is *expressly* conditioned on "my terms," then he makes a true counteroffer and the mirror image rule applies. The counteroffer is now a new offer. But in the typical case, the offeree does not make an *express* counteroffer; so the first rule generally applies. Steps 7 and 8 show how the Code deals with new or different terms.

7. Merchant and nonmerchant rules are in section 2-207(2).
   a) Between merchants, the additional and different terms automatically become part of the contract terms *unless*
      (1) The offer expressly limits acceptance to the terms of the offer.
      (2) They *materially alter* it.
      (3) Notification of objection to them has already been given or is given within a reasonable time after notice of them is received.

Therefore, continuing the above example, the disclaimer of warranties is a different term that *materially alters* the contract and is hence expunged. The usual issue concerns terms that *materially alter* the contract. Examples of such terms include the disclaimer of warranties and limitation of remedies clauses, arbitration clauses, a clause requiring that complaints be made in a time materially shorter than customary, and a clause requiring a guaranty of 90 percent or 100 percent deliveries (as a contract by a cannery, in which the usage of trade allows greater quantity leeways).

   b) The nonmerchant rule is simpler. Different terms are automatically rejected. Additional terms are construed as proposals for additions to the contract.

8. There is one final rule [Section 2-207(3)], allows a contract to be made by the conduct of the parties even though the forms exchanged clearly show that no contract is created by those forms. In such cases, the terms are those matters which both parties agreed to, as well as other terms "gap-filled" by other Code sections.

CASE

P and D are merchants in the textile business. P sold yarn to D in the following way. D made an oral offer; P then sent a written acknowledgment; then D sent a written purchase order. P's acknowledgment form contained this language: "The acceptance of this order is conditional on the assent by the buyer to all of the conditions and terms on the reverse side hereof." On the reverse side was an arbitration provision stating that all controversies shall be settled by arbitration. D's purchase order made no objection to any terms in P's acknowledgment form. Later, D refused to pay for the shipment of yarn, claiming it did not include "dyeable yarn." P sues to compel arbitration.

ISSUE Was there an agreement to arbitrate or was the arbitration provision a "material alteration" of the contract within Code section 2-207(2)(b)?

DECISION There was an agreement to arbitrate. P's form controls.

REASONS
1. D's claim that the arbitration clause in P's form was a material alteration of the contract is negated by the rule that arbitration is common in the textile industry. In these circumstances, the arbitration clause cannot be considered a material alteration [2-207(2)(b)].
2. D's failure to notify P of its objection to the arbitration clause within a reasonable time after receipt of the acknowledgment gave the clause binding effect [2-207 (2)(c)]. P's acknowledgment also had this language: "Your assent will be assumed unless you notify us to the contrary immediately upon receipt of this acknowledgment."

In re Arbitration Between Gaynor-Stafford Industries, Inc. v. Mafco Textured Fibers, 384 N.Y.S.2d 788 (N.Y.) 1976.

Based upon the policy of protecting the offeree, the law renders offers, revocations, and counteroffers effective only when received by the offeree. Now consider the rule that a bilateral offer is not accepted until the offeree *communicates* his acceptance to the offeror. A conflict has long existed regarding when the communication takes effect: (1) upon receipt by the offeror or (2) upon dispatch of the communication by the offeree. Since the offeror is the master and can protect himself, the law again seeks to protect the offeree by following the dispatch rule. The acceptance is effective when deposited in the medium of communication, such as a mailbox. The moment a letter of acceptance is mailed, the contract is formed, even if the offeror never receives the letter. Note that the offeror as master can provide that acceptance is effective only when the communication is received by the offeror. But few offerors so provide, and the dispatch rule generally applies.

Mode of accepting bilateral contracts: dispatch rule

CASE

P leased restaurant property to D. The lease provided for an initial term of five years and contained option provisions providing for extensions of two successive five-year periods. In order to exercise the option to renew, D was required to give P written notice six months before the expiration of the initial term. More than six months before the initial term expired, D prepared, signed, properly stamped and addressed, and deposited a letter notifying P of his intent to exercise the option. P never received the letter.

ISSUE Did the exercise of the option require actual receipt of the letter?

DECISION No. The option was an offer, and it was accepted as soon as the letter was deposited in the mail.

REASONS
1. The option contract is an irrevocable offer, the acceptance of which creates a binding bilateral contract.
2. It is well established that the acceptance of an offer to enter into a bilateral contract is effective and deemed communicated as soon as deposited in the regular course of mail.

Palo Alto Town & County Village, Inc. v. BBTC Co., 110 Cal. Rptr. 93 (1973).

The dispatch or deposited acceptance rule has the effect of placing on the offeror any possible loss resulting from failure by the communicating agency to deliver the acceptance. Thus, even though a letter of acceptance is lost in the mail, a contract may exist. The offeror, in such cases, is duty bound to perform, even though he may have entered into other contracts as a result of his failure to receive a reply from the offeree. He can avoid this result by stating in his offer that the acceptance shall not be effective until it is actually received by him.

As indicated previously, an offer may be either unilateral or bilateral. Most offers are bilateral; but when there is doubt as to whether they are unilateral or bilateral, the courts tend to construe them as bilateral. When an offer is unilateral, the offeror does not desire a *promise* of performance; he insists on substantial completion of the act or forbearance requested. As a general rule, substantial performance of the act requested constitutes an acceptance of a unilateral offer. If the offeree ceases performance short of substantial performance, there is no acceptance and no contract.

Accepting a unilateral offer

A difficult question arises when an offeror seeks to withdraw a unilateral offer during the course of the offeree's attempted performance of the act requested. Today, the generally accepted view is that an offeror of a unilateral offer cannot withdraw during the performance by the offeree. The offeror becomes bound when performance is commenced or tendered, and the offeree has a duty to complete performance. It is part performance by the offeree that legally "buys away" the offeror's power to revoke. One final issue regarding unilateral offers has not been discussed: what is part performance?

Sometimes it is difficult to decide if an offeree is partly performing or merely preparing to perform. Let's take the classic example. I offer to pay you $100 if you walk across the Brooklyn Bridge. You start to walk and get about halfway across the bridge, and I run up beside you and shout: "I revoke." You respond, "You cannot revoke, because my part performance has made your offer irrevocable, like an option contract." You're legally correct. But decide if any of the following are part performances or merely preparing to perform. (1) You buy a pair of running shoes to use in crossing the bridge. (2) You start on a daily exercise routine to get in shape for the walk. (3) You catch a cab that delivers you to the Brooklyn Bridge. These are only preparatory acts that do not constitute part performance. Note, however, that these acts were done in *reliance* on the offer to pay $100 for crossing the bridge. The theory of promissory estoppel (discussed in next chapter) may protect these preparatory acts by making the offer irrevocable. Can you think of situations that would constitute only reliance on an offer (that is, preparatory acts) and not part performance?

Unilateral offers and the Code

The Code makes some changes in the law of acceptance of unilateral offers. Basically, the Code provides that an order for goods may be accepted either by a shipment of the goods or by a prompt promise to ship the goods [2-206(1)(b)]. To illustrate: A merchant who desparately needs several items of merchandise mails a letter to a manufacturer asking for immediate shipment of the articles listed. This unilateral offer could be accepted by the act of shipment, even though the offeror (the buyer) had no actual knowledge of the acceptance. The buyer, however, could withdraw her offer at any time before the seller's delivery to the carrier. This revocation could harm a seller who has incurred expense by procuring, assembling, or packing the goods for shipment. Under the Code, such an offer may be treated either as a unilateral offer and accepted by shipment or it may be treated as a bilateral offer and accepted by a promise to ship. The seller, under the Code, is thus afforded an opportunity to bind the bargain prior to the time of shipment if he wants to do so.

Silence as assent

As a general rule, the offeror cannot force the offeree to speak. Therefore, mere silence by the offeree does *not* amount to acceptance, even though the offeror in his offer may have stated that a failure to reply would constitute an acceptance. However, a previous course of dealing between the parties, the receipt of goods by the offeree under certain circumstances, or the solicitation of an offer could impose a duty on the offeree to speak in order to avoid a contractual relationship.

Silence of itself does not constitute an acceptance, but silence with intent to accept may do so. If you receive a renewal on your fire insurance policy, and you intend to keep and pay for it, that constitutes acceptance of the offer to insure you for the new period. Mailing out the renewal policy constituted the offer to insure, and the retention of the policy was the acceptance if you intended to avail yourself of the insurance protection. Obviously, the requisite intent will often be difficult to determine.

CASE

P construction company entered into a contract to build an apartment building for D and to have it completed by a certain date. Owing to extremely bad weather and other circumstances, P asked for extensions of time. These were submitted to D's architect on a printed form. D's architect agreed to some extensions but ignored the request for others. D sought damages because the building was not completed on schedule.

ISSUE Was the silence or lack of disapproval a grant of the request for extensions?

DESICION Yes.

REASON When relations between the parties justify the offeror's expectation of a reply or where a duty exists to communicate either an acceptance or rejection, silence will be regarded as an acceptance.

Brooke Towers Corp. v. Hunkin-Corkey Construction Co., 454 F.2d 1203 (1972) (applying Colo. law).

REVIEW QUESTIONS AND PROBLEMS

1. Andy and Barney were drinking at their favorite watering hole. During their conversation, the subject of Andy's farm came up. Barney said, "I bet you wouldn't take $50,000 cash for that farm of yours." Andy said he would. Barney replied, "I bet you won't put that in writing." Andy did. Barney later sued to enforce the contract. Andy's defense is that it was all a joke: "I was as high as a Georgia pine. We were just two doggoned drunks bluffing to see who could talk the biggest and say the most." Is Barney entitled to specific performance? Why or why not?
2. Suppose I invite you over next Saturday to a catfish and hush puppy dinner, and you agree to come. You arrive next Saturday, only to find I've left town. (a) Do you have a contract action against me? (b) Would it make any difference if we signed a contract stating, "We intend to make this a binding obligation."? (c) Would it make any difference if you had to drive 325 miles to my house?
3. Seller and Buyer execute a contract for 500 jogging shoes. The contract has all the basic terms, except the parties "agree to agree" on the price per shoe at a later date. (a) Is there a contract? Consult Code 2-305(1). (b) If so, what happens if they later fail to agree? (c) Would your answer change if Seller says, "I need *at least* $10.00 per set of shoes," and Buyer accepts? Explain.
4. Seller wires Buyer that she will sell between 5,000 and 7,000 tons of steel at $80 per ton. Buyer replies that he agrees to buy 6,000 tons. Is a contract formed? Why or why not?
5. Seller wrote a general circular to 10 buyers asking, "Do you want to buy 240 good 1,000-pound cattle at $8.25? Must be sold by Friday. Phone me at Wichita, Kans." One buyer telegraphs an immediate acceptance for all 240 cattle. Is there a contract? Why or why not?
6. The following ad appeared in your local newspaper: "1 black lapin stole, beautiful, worth $139.50. $1.00. FIRST COME, FIRST SERVED." You are the first to appear at the store and tender $1.00. Is a contract formed? Why or why not?
7. Seller offers to sell Buyer a boat for $500. Buyer replies, "I think I want the boat, but let me have a week to consider." Seller replies, "O.K. I won't sell the boat to anyone until after one week from today." The next day, Seller sells the boat to Popeye for $600. The day after that, Buyer tenders $500, and then Seller says he has already sold the boat. (a) Is Seller contractually liable to Buyer? (b) Would your answer change if, before Buyer tendered the $500, Officious Intermeddler, a third party, told Buyer that the boat was sold to Popeye? (c) Would your answer to b change if Seller were a merchant and his promise not to sell for a week were in writing?
8. Having lost her driver's license, Wanda says to you, "If you will drive me to Maryjane, New Mexico, I promise to pay you $200." You promise to drive her. Is there a contract? Why or why not?
9. Dairy mails Retailer an offer to sell 100 gallons of milk at a stated price. Retailer promptly replies, "Please send immediately 100 gallons of milk in

one-gallon plastic containers." Dairy ignores Retailer's reply. If the milk is not sent, has Dairy breached a contract? Explain.

10. Dairy makes the same offer as in the previous question, and Retailer simply replies, "Accept your offer for 100 gallons of milk at stated price. Prompt acknowledgment must be made of receipt of this letter." Is there a contract? Why or why not?

11. Offeror mails Offeree an offer. Offeree writes an acceptance but then decides not to accept. Later, Offeree accidently mails the letter of acceptance with various other letters. (a) Is there a contract? (b) Would your answer change if Offeree mailed the letter of acceptance while sleepwalking? (c) Would your answer change if Offeree accidentally dropped the letter on the sidewalk and a passerby later saw and mailed the letter?

12. A salesperson for Company solicited an order from Farmer for a seeding machine. The order was sent to Company's home office for approval. Farmer did not hear anything more from Company. Several months later, Farmer sues Company for failure to deliver the seeding machine. What results?

8

Consideration and Its Alternatives

To have a *valid* contract, the union of offer and acceptance (mutual assent) must be validated by bargained-for consideration or its equivalent. Not every agreement (offer and acceptance) will be legally enforced. In the validation process, promises that ought to be enforced are separated from those that should not. If an agreement is based upon a *bargain* or consists of some *detriment* to the promisee or *benefit* to the promisor, then the promises ought to be legally enforceable. (Legal detriment will be explained in the third paragraph following.) In other words, the validation devices help courts determine whether they should recognize a particular type of exchange as creating legal obligations that are described as contractual duties. After analyzing the situation, if you find an offer and acceptance, you must determine if that union is valid. The presence of a validation device is basic in making that determination.

Validation devices

At early common law, a valid contract was one under seal. A seal could be a waxed impression made by a signet ring, an impression on the paper, the word *Seal,* the letters L.S. (*locus sigilli* "the place of the seal"), or just a pen scratch. Eventually, the ceremony of sealing was abandoned, and the word *Seal* or *L.S.* was universally used so much that the distinction between sealed and unsealed instruments was lost. Since the seal was no longer a true validation device, most states made it wholly inoperative or allowed it only presumptive evidence of consideration. The Code has completely wiped out the effect of a seal. In abandoning the seal, courts then turned to other devices to validate contracts. That process of finding and defining validation devices continues today. Although the process is not complete, one can definitely find at least three validation devices that most states recognize. The predominant one is bargained-for consideration that involves either a detriment to the promisee (one receiving the promise) or a benefit to the promisor. The other two devices are spinoffs from a bargained-for consideration and actually split consideration into two parts. They eliminate the bargain element and use either the detriment to the promisee (*promisory estoppel*) or the benefit to the promisor (moral obligation) to validate the promise. Because bargained-for consideration is by far the most important and most frequently used of the three validation devices, it will be given primary emphasis in this chapter.

The Three Elements of Bargained-for Consideration

If the following three elements are present, then the agreement was based on a true bargain: (1) the promisee incurs legal detriment, (2) a promise induced that detriment, and (3) the detriment induced the making of that promise. In effect, these three elements define the word *bargain,* which gives a court sufficient justification to validate (that is, enforce) the agreement.

Promisee must suffer legal detriment

Legal detriment occurs when the promisee does or promises to do an act that he is not legally obligated to do, or refrains from doing or promises to refrain from doing an act that he has the legal right to do. Legal detriment is not necessarily synonymous with real detriment or loss. For example, Uncle tells Niece that if she stops smoking for one month, then Uncle will give her $500. If Niece refrains from smoking for a month, she incurs legal detriment. Since quitting smoking may actually be a benefit, no real detriment may be present. But because she has a legal right to smoke, she incurs legal detriment by giving up that right. On the other hand, a debtor who has successfully avoided paying a creditor may suffer real detriment if he decides to pay. The act of paying, however, is not legal detriment, since he was doing only what he was already legally obligated to do.

The promise must induce the detriment

The promisee must know of the promise and intend to accept it when he or she incurs or promises to incur the legal detriment. You will generally find that the promise causes the detriment, so this element should not raise any problems.

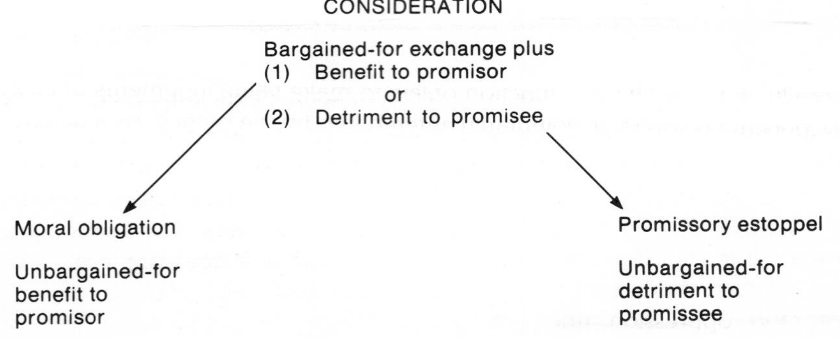

Fig. 8·1

The detriment must induce the promise

The promisor must have made the promise at least in part to exchange it for the detriment incurred by the promisee. This element raises the most problems. The issue is whether the legal detriment proximately caused the promise to be made. Generally, most factual patterns require one to decide if the detriment was merely a condition to a gift or was bargained for, in that it induced the promise. One way to respond is to see if the detriment will be of some benefit to the promisor. Accordingly, analyze the following examples. You say to a tramp, "If you go around the corner to the clothing store, you may purchase an overcoat on my credit." It is a legal detriment to the tramp to make the walk, but the walk is not consideration, because (on a reasonable construction) the walk was not requested as the price of the promise. It was merely a condition to a gratuitous promise. An aid (though not a conclusive test) is to ask whether the happening of the condition will be a benefit to the promisor. Dotty writes to her sister-in-law: "If you will come down to see me, I promise you a place to raise your family." If the sister-in-law moves, is that consideration? Although moving is a legal detriment, it was simply a condition to a gift, since Dotty was promising to make a gift. The moving was therefore not bargained for as a trade for the promise. NOTE: If you conclude that the legal detriment did not induce the promise, then you are concluding that the legal detriment was not bargained for. You should at that point consider using promissory estoppel (unbargained-for detriment), which is subsequently discussed.

CASE

P was employed by D company and was injured on her job. D promised P that she would be paid the same benefits as those provided under the state's Workmen's Compensation Act, although the company did not participate in the compensation program. Companies that chose not to participate were subject to tort suits by injured employees. D paid compensation for some time but then discontinued payments. P brought suit to enforce the promise, but D contended that the promise was not enforceable and that P's only remedy was in tort.

ISSUE Is there consideration to support D's promise to pay an amount equal to workmen's compensation?

DECISION Yes

REASONS

1. By agreeing to accept benefits measured by provisions of the workmen's compensation law, P gave up her acknowledged right to sue in tort for her full damage. This is detriment to the promisee.
2. D also received a benefit. In consideration of limiting its liability to the equivalent of benefits that might accrue under the Workmen's Compensation Act, D escaped liability in tort for P's full disability.

Tigrett v. Heritage Building Co., 533 S.W.2d 65 (Tex.) 1976.

Adequacy of consideration

Historically, it has not been a function of law to make value judgments or economic judgments concerning contracts voluntarily entered into by the parties. As a general rule, courts have not attempted to weigh the consideration received by each party to determine if it is fair in the light of that which the other party gave. It has been sufficient in law if a party received something of legal value for which he bargained. The law is concerned only with the existence of consideration, not with its value. It does not inquire into the question of whether the bargain was a good one or bad one for either party. In the absence of fraud, oppression, undue influence, illegality, or statutory limitation, parties have been free to make any contract they please. The fact that it is onerous or burdensome for one or the other has been immaterial.

Today, this philosophy is changed to a substantial degree. The Code provides that contracts that are so one-sided as to be unconscionable are unforceable [2-302]. Courts as well as legislative bodies have attempted to protect consumers by changing the historical view of consideration. These matters will be discussed further in subsequent chapters dealing with consumer protection.

There has always been one exception to the general rule of adequacy of consideration. In contracts that call for the exchange of money between the parties, the adequacy of consideration is scrutinized. A promise to pay $1,000 in one year for an immediate $100 loan is not only usurious and illegal but also unenforceable because of the inadequacy of consideration. Since money has an ascertainable fixed value, there is no basis for holding that the payment of $100 is sufficient consideration to support the promise to pay $1,000. Although it could be argued that the borrower may have needed the $100 so badly that it was worth it for him to promise to pay the larger sum, such has not been an acceptable argument to the courts. It is one thing to indulge in the presumption that in ordinary contracts the parties have provided for a reasonable relationship between the detriment to the promisee and the benefit to the promisor, but the basis for the presumption fails when money alone is involved on both sides. Note, however, that if something in addition to money is provided by the promisee, adequacy of consideration is no longer an issue. Thus, if Huyler pays $100 to Lang and in addition promises to attend a political meeting in return for Lang's promise to pay him $1,000 later, the promise would be supported by consideration.

Recitals of consideration

Most written contracts have a provision reciting that there is consideration. The contract may state: "For, and in consideration of, the mutual promises exchanged, the parties agree as follows." If the recital takes this form, "For, and in consideration of, $1.00 in hand paid," etc., it raises an issue related to adequacy of consideration. Nominal consideration will generally validate a promise, but *sham* consideration will not. Although consideration does not have to be the sole inducement, it must be one inducement to making a promise. If out of friendship I sell you my valuable horse for $30.00, my promise is supported by consideration. Your detriment (paying $30) need not be the sole inducement, but it must at least be some inducement to my promise to sell. This requirement establishes the bargain. Obviously, the recital of $1.00, even if it is paid, is a sham (pretense). What is considered a sham is a recital of fact contrary to fact. The recital is a sham—not because $1.00 is economically inadequate—but because it is not a material inducing factor. On the other hand, a promise is never considered a sham.

There is an exception for option contracts, because the business community customarily expects them to be valid. Consequently, the Second Restatement of Contracts does accept sham consideration (e.g., recital of $1.00) if there is a signed writing in a business context involving either an option contract or a guarantee of credit.

Major Problem Area—Mutuality of Obligation

This doctrine applies only to bilateral contracts. In a bilateral contract, each party must be bound, or neither party is bound. Although this is a simple rule, its application can be rather difficult. The problem of mutuality arises when one party tries to show that a promise is defective in that it does not promise anything. Since it is defective, it cannot provide consideration to support the other promise. When a promise is not supported by consideration, one party is not legally bound. Thus, since one party is not bound, no one is contractually bound. The moving party tries to show that a promise is defective because it fails under one of the following:

The promise is *illusory*.

The promisor is already bound (*pre-existing duty*) to do what he promises to do.

The promise is to forbear from suing, but the promisor has an *invalid claim* (no right to sue).

The promise is void for *illegality* or is voidable and unenforceable because of *incapacity to contract*. (These two invalidating devices are discussed later. Illegality is in chapter 10; incapacity is in chapter 11.)

Illusory promises

There must be a true restriction on the promisor's ability to renege; otherwise, the promise cannot be construed as providing consideration. Courts require that there be a *possibility* that the promisor will incur legal detriment, otherwise the promisor's promise is illusory. In a typical illusory promise, the promisor's promise is conditional. The first step is to analyze the nature of the condition and determine if the condition is based on something beyond the promisor's control or within his control.

When the promise is conditioned on a fortuitous event (something beyond either party's control), the promise is not illusory. Example: I promise to buy your car for $2,500 if it rains tomorrow or if I am hired by the TNT Corporation or if the Atlanta Braves win the next World Series. Since it is possible that it will rain or that I will get the job or Atlanta may win, there is a possibility that I will have to buy your car (legal detriment).

If the condition is within the control of the promisor, then the promise may be illusory. Example: "If I decide to buy a car, I'll buy yours" or "I'll buy your car if I am fully satisfied with its performance" or "I'll buy your car, but I can cancel at anytime" or "If I get a loan, then I'll buy your car." Since the condition in each example is within the promisor's control, arguably the promise is illusory. Nonetheless, courts attempt to validate these conditional promises by implying duties on the promisor.

CASE

P contracted to deliver trap rock to an airport project "as required" by D and in accordance with D's delivery instructions. D refused to request any trap rock, which deprived P of $10,000 in profits. The contract had this provision: "Cancellation by the United States may be effected at any time." D thereby had the right to cancel at any time.

ISSUE Was D's promise illusory, since D had an unrestricted power of cancellation?

DECISION No.

REASONS

1. The reservation of a power to effect cancellation at any time did not mean that D did not promise to order and pay for the rock. D could not actually cancel at any time (such as a moment after the contract was made) because D had to give notice of cancellation within a reasonable time.
2. A promise is not made illusory by the fact that the promisor has an option between two alternative performances if each constitutes detriment. D's alternative performances were either to order trap rock or to give notice of its intent to cancel within a reasonable time. The implied duty to give notice constitutes legal detriment.

Sylvan Crest Sand & Gravel Co. v. United States, 150 F.2d 642 (2d Cir.) 1945.

Implying promises

If the condition is one of personal satisfaction, for instance, courts will usually restrict the promisor's free will by imposing a promise that any dissatisfaction must be in good faith. Thus, a promise to buy goods if satisfied is not illusory since the promisor cannot refuse the goods unless actually dissatisfied. Another example is the implied promise to use best efforts regarding the condition. In my promise to buy your car only if I get a bank loan, courts will imply that I promised to use reasonable diligence to get a loan. I must take affirmative action (detriment).

Requirement and output contracts

Requirement contracts ("I'll buy all the widgits I need from you this year") and output contracts ("I'll sell you all the widgits I manufacture") were formerly invalidated as illusory; but today, these contracts are upheld. Courts find them enforceable because the seller of output or buyer of requirements has incurred legal detriment in that he has given up the right to sell to, or buy from, others. The Code explicitly enforces these contracts with a rule against unreasonably disproportionate quantities [2-306]. Both parties must act in good faith in their outputs or requirements. Moreover, the fact that a party to either contract might go out of business does not make the contract illusory. The Code provides protection by requiring "that no quantity unreasonably disproportionate to any stated estimate or in the absence of a stated estimate to any normal or otherwise comparable prior output or requirements may be tendered or demanded" [2-306(1)]. Some courts have invalidated these contracts when the promisor had no previously established business and therefore could not reasonably estimate *quantity*. The Code, however, uses the good faith requirement to uphold such contracts by new businesses. Therefore, the promisor must conduct his business in good faith and pursuant to commercially reasonable standards, so that his output or requirements will approximate a reasonably foreseeable figure.

Preexisting duty

The preexisting duty rule is a second way in which a party may claim no mutuality of obligation. When one promises to do what he is already legally obligated to do or promises to refrain from what he legally cannot do, then the promisor incurs no legal detriment. Therefore, it is traditionally stated that a promise to perform or the perfor-

CASE

D offered a $25,000 reward for information leading to the arrest and conviction of the person or persons who shot a Wells Fargo agent. P, a licensed polygraph operator, is employed by the government to interrogate persons assigned by law enforcement agencies. On the second day of questioning, during a polygraph exam on an *unrelated* matter, a suspect admitted to P that he had shot and killed the Wells Fargo guard. P sues to recover the $25,000 reward.

ISSUE Did P provide consideration to validate the reward offer?

DECISION No. P is not entitled to the reward offered.

REASONS P was under a preexisting contractual duty to furnish law enforcement agencies with all useful information revealed to him through interrogations. When P "accepted" the reward offer by giving the information to the authorities, he was doing only what he was bound to do as part of his employment. The performance of a preexisting duty does not constitute consideration necessary to support a contract.

Slattery v. Wells Fargo Armored Service Corp., 366 So.2d 157 (Fla.) 1979.

mance of an existing duty is not consideration. The preexisting duty may be either a legal duty or a contractual duty.

The problem of preexisting obligations has arisen in various circumstances. It is possible to categorize these cases under three headings: (1) Modifications of Code and non-Code contracts, (2) Promise by a stranger for additional compensation, and (3) Discharge of debts.

Modifications of non-Code contracts

The typical situation occurs when one party to the contract refuses to continue performance unless and until the terms of the contract are modified. To ensure performance, the other party may assent to the demands and agree to terms that are more burdensome than those provided in the agreement. He may agree to pay more or accept less, but his promise in many cases is not supported by consideration. An employee may seek more money for the work he is already contractually bound to do, or a contractor may want more pay for the same work and materials specified in the original contract. In either case, the employee and contractor do not incur legal detriment to support the promise to modify.

Although some modifications are in bad faith or even extortionate, many are in good faith and should be validated. Assuming good-faith dealings, courts will find exceptions to the preexisting duty rule by using any of these rationales: (1) new or different duties, (2) unforeseeable difficulties, and (3) rescission.

New or different duties

If the promisor agrees to assume a new duty, give something in addition, or vary the preexisting duty (e.g., accelerating performance) the promise supplies consideration to support the promised modification. Usually an owner who promises a contractor an additional sum to complete a job under contract is not legally bound to pay the additional sum. If, however, the promisee (contractor) agrees to do anything other than, or different from, that which the original contract required, consideration is provided. The contractor who agrees to complete his work at an earlier date or in a different manner may recover on a promise by the owner to pay an additional amount.

Unforeseen difficulties

The parties to a contract often make provisions for contingencies that may arise during the course of the performance of the contract. Wisely, they recognize that problems may arise and make performance more difficult. Frequently, however, they do not make any provisions at all, or they make some that do not encompass all the difficulties that may render performance by either party more burdensome than anticipated. In the absence of an appropriate contract clause, two questions are raised when unanticipated difficulties arise during the course of performance: (1) Will the party whose performance is rendered more difficult be required to complete performance without any adjustment in compensation? (2) Will a promise to pay an additional sum because of the difficulty be enforceable?

Excuses for breach of contract are discussed in chapter 12. For purposes of this discussion, it must be recognized that additional hardship is not an excuse for breach of contract as a general rule. Thus, the answer to the first question is usually yes.

The second question assumes that a promisor, although not required to do so, has promised to pay an additional sum because of the difficulty. Courts have held that where a truly unforeseen difficulty arises, and because of it a promise is made to pay an additional sum, the promise will be enforced.

CASE

D entered into a contract with a city to collect all the trash in the city for five years for an agreed-upon compensation. The number of required collections increased substantially, and the city agreed to pay an additional $10,000 per year because of the increased amount of trash. P, a group of citizens of the city, objected to the increased payments and sought to recover $20,000 paid over a two-year period.

ISSUE Was the promise to pay an additional sum enforceable?

DECISION Yes

REASONS
1. The general rule is that a promise to pay more for work already required to be performed is not enforceable. There is an exception to this general rule for unforeseen difficulties.
2. The modern trend of cases recognizes that courts should enforce agreements modifying contracts when unexpected or unanticipated difficulties arise during the course of the performance of a contract, as long as the parties agree voluntarily to the modification.
3. The city was not required to promise to pay an additional sum; but when it did so, the promise was enforceable.

Angel v. Murray, 322 A.2d 630 (R.I.) 1974.

Unforeseen difficulties are those that seldom occur and are extraordinary in nature. Price changes, strikes, inclement weather, and shortage of material occur frequently and are not considered to fall into this category. Thus it may be that a person who has contracted to build a building finds that the cost of materials has risen since he entered the contract, or he may be faced with a carpenters' strike. Nevertheless, he must perform at the original price unless he has made provisions in the contract that some relief shall be given when such things occur.

Rescission

If the contract is rescinded (the existing duty is destroyed), then there is no preexisting duty. The parties are now free to make a new contract on whatever terms they desire. Note that there are three contracts involved: (1) the original contract, (2) the rescission contract (yes, it is a contract), and (3) the new contract. Further, note that rescission is generally not presumed, so the facts must show an actual rescission such as tearing up the original contract.

Modifications of Code contracts

The Code has made substantial inroads into the validation element of a contract, especially regarding alteration or modification of contracts by not requiring consideration to support the changes. Under the Code, parties to a binding contract for the sale of goods may change the terms; and if the change is mutually agreeable, no consideration is required to make it binding [2-209(1)]. This means that if a buyer agrees with the seller to pay more than the contract price for goods purchased, he will be held to the higher price. To illustrate: A car manufacturer entered into a contract with a tire dealer to purchase a certain number of tires at a stated price. Thereafter, the dealer told the manufacturer that because of higher production and labor costs, he would need to be paid $5 more per tire in order to carry on with the contract. If the auto maker agrees to pay the additional sum, his promise to do so will be binding even though there is no consideration present.

The Code section that sustains modifications of a contract without any additional consideration could, if not limited in some way, permit a party with a superior bargaining position to take advantage of the other party to a contract. Accordingly, the Code provides that the parties must act in good faith, and the exercise of bad faith in order to escape the duty to perform under the original terms is not permitted. The "extortion" of a modification without a legitimate reason therefore is ineffective, because it violates the good-faith requirement.

To safeguard against false allegations that oral modifications have been made, it is permissible to include in the contract a provision that modifications are not effective unless they are set forth in a signed writing [2-209(2)]. If a consumer enters into such a contract, in addition to signing the contract he must sign the restrictive provision, to assure that he is aware of the limitation. Otherwise, it is not effective. If the restrictive provision is not signed, a consumer is entitled to rely upon oral modifications. The provision is apparently designed to protect the unwary consumer against reliance upon statements made to him that certain provisions of the contract do not apply to him or that others are subject to oral change. He is entitled to be forewarned not to rely upon anything but the printed word, and it is expected that the double signing will bring this message to his attention.

The Code allows necessary and desirable modifications of sales contracts without regard to technicalities that hamper such adjustments under traditional contract law. The safeguards against improper and unfair use of this freedom are found in the requirements of good faith and the "observance of reasonable commercial standards of fair dealing in the trade." There is recognition of the fact that changes and adjustments in sales contracts are daily occurrences and that the parties do not cancel their old contract and execute an entirely new one each time a change or modification is required.

Promises by a stranger for additional compensation

The typical case involves a third-party, a stranger to an existing contract, who promises additional compensation in order to encourage one party to perform. Jockey executes a bilateral contract with Horse Owner to ride the horse in a specific race. A stranger promises Jockey an additional $600 to fulfill his contract to ride. Older law held that Jockey could not enforce the stranger's promise because Jockey was only doing what he is contractually obligated to do. The Restatement is contrawise and uses this rationale: "In third-party cases, there is less likelihood of economic coercion or other unfair pressure than there is if the duty is owed to the promisee." If the facts show no coercion, then the better approach is to allow recovery.

Discharge of liquidated debts and claims

As previously noted, if the consideration on each side of an agreement involves money, the consideration must be equal. Because of this rule, a debtor and creditor cannot make an enforceable agreement to have a liquidated debt of a fixed amount discharged upon payment of less than the amount agreed to be owing. In other words, there is no consideration for the agreement to accept less than the full amount owed. In most states the unpaid portion is collectible even though the lesser sum has been paid. If there is no dispute as to the amount owed, a debtor who sends in a check for less than the amount of the indebtedness and marks on the check "paid in full" will still be liable for the balance due.

The payment of the lesser sum is the performance of an existing obligation and cannot serve as consideration for a release of the balance. If there is evidence that the creditor made a gift of the balance to the debtor, then the creditor cannot recover that balance. A paid-in-full receipt given to the debtor by the creditor is usually regarded as evidence that a gift was intended. Likewise, where the debt is evidenced by a note, the cancellation and return of the note upon receipt of part payment is judged as a gift of the balance due.

CASE

P sold lumber to D, who agreed to pay $2,447.61. Later, D offered to pay P 35 percent of the sum in full satisfaction. D paid the 35 percent in two checks, which P cashed. On the second and last check, D marked "Final installment." P now sues to recover the 65 percent of the original amount due.

ISSUE Was P's promise to accept 35 percent of the debt as full payment enforceable?

DECISION No.

REASONS

1. A check that purports to be payment in full does not preclude the creditor who cashes it from showing that, in fact, it was not in full so long as the account is not disputed.
2. The two checks were in payment of a liquidated and undisputed debt. By paying only part of the debt, D suffers no detriment. By these partial payments, P has received no more than it was entitled to receive for the lumber sold. No consideration exists for the discharge of the balance due P for its lumber.

Baillie Lumber Co. v. Kincaid Carolina Corp., 167 S.E.2d 85 (N.C.) 1969.

Just as a promise to pay an additional sum for the completion of an existing contract is enforceable if the promise does something other than, or in addition to, the required performance, a debtor may obtain a discharge of the debt by paying a lesser sum than the amount owing if he gives the creditor something in addition to the money. The settlement at the lower figure will then be binding on the creditor. Since the value of consideration is ordinarily unimportant, the added consideration may take any form. Payment in advance of the due date, payment at a place other than that agreed upon, surrender of the privilege of bankruptcy, and presentment of a secured note for less than the face of the debt have all been found sufficient to discharge a larger amount than that paid. The mere giving of an unsecured note for a lesser sum than the entire debt will not release the debtor of his duty to pay the balance. The note is only a promise to pay; consequently, the promise to pay less than is due will not discharge the debt.

Discharge of unliquidated debts and claims

A promise to forbear from suing to collect a debt or a claim is sufficient consideration to support a promise to pay for a release, and the compromise results in a binding settlement. The parties are surrendering their rights to litigate the dispute, and this detriment serves as consideration. As a result, when one party has a claim against another party and the amount due is disputed or unliquidated (uncertain in amount), a compromise settlement at a figure between the amount claimed or demanded and the amount admitted to be owing is binding on the parties. Payment of money that one claims is not owing is consideration for the loss of the right to litigate the dispute.

It does not matter whether the claim is one arising from a dispute that is contractual in nature, such as one involving damaged merchandise, or is tortious in character, such as one rising from an automobile accident. The compromise figure agreed to by both parties operates as a contract to discharge the claim. This kind of settlement contract is known legally as an accord and satisfaction. The dispute over the amount owed by the debtor must be in good faith or the rules for liquidated debts are applicable. If the dispute is not in good faith, the creditor could pursue the debtor for the difference, even though the creditor had agreed to settle for a lesser amount.

Accord and satisfaction

An accord and satisfaction is a fully executed contract between a debtor and a creditor to settle a disputed claim. The accord consists of an agreement whereby one of the parties is to do something different by way of performance than that called for by the contract. This accord is satisfied when the substituted performance is completed and accepted by the other party. Both must be established. The cashing of a check marked "paid in full" when it is tendered to settle a *disputed* claim is a typical example of an accord and satisfaction.

CASE

P had entered into a contract to furnish material and labor for plumbing modifications in D's house. A dispute developed over the amount that D owed P, and D made out a check on which he wrote "payment of account in full." When P received the check, he crossed out the words "payment in full," wrote in "paid on account," and deposited it.

ISSUE Was there an accord and satisfaction when P deposited the check?

DECISION Yes.

REASONS
1. It is well settled that when an account is made the subject of bona fide dispute between the parties as to its correctness, and the debtor tenders his check to the creditor upon condition that it be accepted in full payment, the creditor must either refuse to receive the check or accept the same burdened by its attached condition.
2. If the creditor accepts the check and cashes it, he impliedly agrees to the condition.

Burgamy v. Davis, 313 S.W.2d 365 (Tex.) 1958.

An accord may be either oral or written. For an accord and satisfaction to discharge a claim, the claim must be disputed between the parties. If the creditor is not aware of the dispute, the cashing of a check tendered in the usual course of business with a "full payment" notation will not operate as an accord and satisfaction. An accord, like any other agreement, requires a meeting of the minds. An accord will not be implied from ambiguous language. The intent to settle the dispute must be clear.

Composition of creditors

An additional method of satisfying a debt by payment of a sum less than the amount claimed or admitted is a "composition of creditors." This is a procedure whereby a person's creditors agree to accept a certain sum of money or property or both in full and complete settlement of the debtor's obligations to them. The creditors prorate the debtor's assets, which are made available to them, and agree with one another and the debtor to accept a percentage of their claims in full satisfaction. The composition is a type of insolvency proceeding enabling a person in debt to satisfy his debts by making most, if not all, of his assets available for distribution to his creditors. Of course, this raises a legal question about the consideration to support full satisfaction in acceptance of a sum less than the amount admittedly due. The consideration for which each of the assenting creditors bargains may be any one of the following: (1) the promise of each of the other creditors to forgo a portion of his claim; (2) the action of the debtor in securing the acquiescence of the other creditors; (3) the debtor's forbearance or a promise to forbear paying the assenting creditors more than the stipulated proportion. Thus the law encourages mutual agreements between a debtor and his creditors to the extent of precluding the participating creditors from thereafter collecting the difference between their pro rata share and the amount of the debt.

Forbearance

Consideration, which usually takes the form of a promise or an action, may take the opposite form: forbearance from acting or a promise to forbear from taking some action.

CASE

P entered into a contract to purchase stock from D corporation. Thereafter, P brought an action against D to rescind the contract and to recover money from the corporation. At the time of the suit, P attached the corporate bank account. He agreed to release the bank account and not to make any further attachments if the corporation would maintain a special trust bank account of $28,000 to take care of any judgment P might obtain. D sought to avoid its obligation to maintain a trust account.

ISSUE Was there consideration to support D corporation's promise?

DECISION Yes.

REASON The relinquishment of a legal right constitutes sufficient consideration for a contract. Here P relinquished his right to make any further attachments—a forbearance.

Lefton v. Superior Court for Los Angeles, 100 Cal. Rptr. 598 (1972).

The law also considers the waiver of a right or the forbearance to exercise a right to be sufficient consideration for a contract. The right that is waived or not exercised may be one that exists either at law or in equity. It may be a waiver of a right that one has against someone other than the promisor who bargains for such a waiver.

There are numerous other examples of forbearances that may constitute consideration. Relinquishment of alleged rights in an estate will furnish consideration to support a return promise to pay money. An agreement by the seller of a business not to compete with the person who has bought a business from him is another example of forbearance. Mutual promises to forbear are sufficient to support each other. They are commonly used as a part of a settlement of a dispute.

Forbearance to sue

Although forbearances generally constitute consideration, a problem can arise when the forbearance is a promise not to bring a lawsuit. Clearly, a promise to forbear from suing is a legal detriment and, if bargained-for (as in a release or covenant not to sue), is valid. The problem arises when the underlying claim is invalid. Arguably, a promise not to sue on an invalid claim really promises nothing, since the promisor has no claim on which to sue. Thus, older cases held that the promise regarding the invalid claim was not legal detriment. Modern courts hold that a promise to surrender or forbear from suing on an invalid claim is consideration provided two matters are proven: (1) the promisor thought the claim was valid (subjective honesty), and (2) the claim had some reasonable basis in law and in fact (objective test). The general rule now is that surrender of or forbearance to assert an invalid claim is detriment if the claim is asserted in good faith and is not palpably unreasonable.

Alternative Validation Devices

Promissory estoppel

When bargained-for consideration is not present, a court may nonetheless validate a promise based on promissory estoppel. Promissory estoppel (as well as moral obligation) is a relatively new validation device and is sparingly used. A good way to view promissory estoppel (sometimes called detrimental reliance) is to see it as unbargained-for detriment. When a promisor's promise induces a promisee's detriment, this validation device estops the promisor from denying contractual duties because of a lack of consideration. Promissory estoppel forces the promisor to live up to his promise. Eric promises his friend Grayson $5,000 to buy a car. In reliance on that promise, Grayson buys a car for $5,000. Clearly, there is no benefit to Eric, so there is no bargained-for consideration. There is detrimental reliance, however, which a court will use to make Eric fulfill his promise to pay $5,000. The court will use the phrase promissory estoppel (that is, unbargained-for detriment) in validating Eric's promise.

The doctrine of promissory estoppel is an equitable doctrine used where there is, in fact, no consideration. It allows enforcement of a promise made by someone who reasonably expects the promisee, relying on the promise, to exercise forbearance or take some substantial action. Moreover, if the promise is not enforced by the court, injustice would be inevitable. The promise without consideration becomes enforceable because of the reliance upon it. Reliance must have been foreseeable by the promisor, and there must be a change of position. When Mrs. Westervelt promises her church $1,000 to be used to construct a new building, the church, relying on her promise and on promises and pledges by others, undertakes the construction project. Mrs. Westervelt's promise may be binding because she induced the church materially to change its position, in reliance on her promise. If the $1,000 pledge were to be used to discharge an existing mortgage, however, the promise would likely be unenforceable for lack of consideration. The church did not change its position, in reliance on the promise. The doctrine of promissory estoppel is limited in its application and provides only a limited means of enforcing promises that fail to pass the test of consideration. Although the modern tendency is to apply the doctrine to a wide variety of situations, it has been used frequently in the following situations:

1. Bidding on construction projects. The cases hold that a subcontractor's bid is irrevocable if used by the general contractor in submitting his bid for the primary contract.
2. Promised pensions and other employee benefits. Notwithstanding the fact that the employee continues to work (preexisting duty and hence no consideration), courts validate employer promises of benefits by using promissory estoppel.
3. Promises of dealer franchises. The doctrine of promissory estoppel has been used to permit recovery when there has been justifiable reliance upon preliminary negotiations, wherein a franchise was promised.

Moral obligation

Moral obligation, a third validation device, may be seen as unbargained-for benefit; that is, the past benefit induces the later promise. Past consideration (that is, past benefit) is said to be insufficient to support a present promise to pay for that benefit. Yet, at early common law, cases held that a promise was enforceable if made in recognition of a moral obligation arising out of a benefit previously received. Although not widely accepted, this holding has been recognized today in at least two instances: (1) promises relating to an earlier legal obligation that the law now will not enforce and (2) promises to pay for benefits received.

Obligations discharged by law

A new promise to pay a debt is enforceable without consideration even though it has been discharged in bankruptcy or barred by a statute of limitations (a statute that cuts off a claim if no suit is brought within a stated time period) or otherwise discharged by law. Some courts state that the past debt, together with the moral obligation to pay, is sufficient to validate the new promise to pay the debt. The rule is simply an application of an older view that an antecedent debt was sufficient consideration to support a later promise to pay it. Courts do have some different rules for debts discharged in bankruptcy and debts barred by a statute of limitations. A court can infer a promise from part payment of a debt barred by the statute of limitations, but an express, written promise is required for debts discharged in bankruptcy. There appears to be no good rationale for this and other distinctions between the two ways of discharging obligations.

Promises for benefits received

In discussing quasi contracts, in chapter 6, we said that there is (in circumstances of unjust enrichment) a right of action to recover the value of benefits bestowed upon another person without his request. When such a right exists, a subsequent promise to pay for the benefits received is validated by the doctrine of moral obligation. Examples of benefits conferred: someone rescues and repairs another's boat; medical services are rendered to an unconscious person; one is injured in saving another's life. Then there is a subsequent promise by the other to pay the person who gave the benefit. This minority validation device, usually applied only when the past benefit is a material one, validates that subsequent promise.

Material benefit rule

The material benefit rule applies to a circumstance in which a reasonable promisee would expect compensation. Someone has received something of value in the form of money or other material benefits that created a moral obligation to pay for what was received. Later, the recipient promises something. That promise is validated by the material benefit rule. The Restatement (Second) §89-A provides: "A promise made in recognition of a benefit previously received by the promisor from the promisee is binding to the extent necessary to prevent injustice."

REVIEW QUESTIONS AND PROBLEMS

1. What are the three elements of bargained-for consideration? How do promissory estoppel and moral obligation differ from consideration?
2. Burt pays 25 cents in return for a 30-day option to purchase real estate from Reynold for $100,000. The next day Reynold tries to revoke the option. Can Reynold revoke? Why or why not?
3. Humphrey pays Doug $250 for a 60-day option to buy Doug's farm. Near the end of the option period, Humphrey asks for and gets a 15-day extension. No money was paid for the extension. After the original 60-day period but within the 15-day extension, Doug withdraws the offer. Can Doug legally revoke the offer? Why or why not?
4. Buyer agreed with Seller that Buyer would buy 1,500,000 gallons of a particular grade of oil. The agreement stated: "Seller may cancel any unshipped portion of this order if for any reason it should discontinue making this grade of oil." Was this a valid agreement? Why or why not?
5. Widgit, a manufacturer of widgits, agreed to supply Midgit all the widgits that Midgit needed in his gidgit business. For several years prior to this agreement, Midgit used between 2,500 to 3,000 Widgit widgits per month. On the sixth month, Midgit ordered 10,000 widgits. Widgit said it would not honor the order. (*a*) Is this a valid agreement? (*b*) Is Widgit liable to Midgit for breach of contract? Why or why not?
6. Captain Ahab agreed to sell Charlie tunas for $1.50 each. Ten sailors agreed to work for Ahab for 5 cents for each tuna caught during a particular voyage. Midway through the voyage, the sailors demanded that they be paid 10 cents for each tuna caught. Captain Ahab agreed to so increase their wages. Ahab in turn wrote to Charlie: "Owing to increased costs, I will have to charge you $2.00 per tuna." (*a*) How much does Ahab legally have to pay the sailors? (*b*) How much does Charlie legally have to pay Ahab for tunas?
7. F. R. Atkins buys a used car on credit from J. P. Richmann. The debt is $2,000. Atkins later discovers that the car has a cracked valve and demands that Richmann correct it. When J. P. refuses, F. R. sends J. P. a check for $1,500 marked "debt paid in full." Should Richmann cash the check? Why or why not?
8. Oxford Construction Company constructs a building for Bob Hudson and sends a final bill for $100,000. Bob questions the amount of the bill and sends Oxford a check for $25,000 marked "paid in full." Oxford cashes the check, then sends another bill for $75,000. Does Bob have to pay? Why or why not?
9. Hoffman wanted to acquire a franchise from Red Owl Stores. Red Owl told Hoffman that if he would sell his bakery and buy a certain tract of land, he would be given a franchise. Hoffman did these things but was not given the promised franchise. Hoffman sued and Red Owl defended on the ground that there is no consideration to support the contract. Who won? Why?
10. Harpo employs Zeppo to repair a vacant house. By mistake, Zeppo repairs the house next door, which belongs to Groucho. Groucho later promises to pay Zeppo the value of the repairs. Is Groucho's promise binding? What results if the reasonable value of the repairs is $400 and Groucho promises to pay $600 but later refuses to pay anything? Explain.
11. Employer, returning from a vacation, discovers that Employee has done some work not required by the employment contract. Employer says, "Since you did this extra work, I will pay you an additional $200 next payday." Is Employer legally obligated to pay the $200? Explain.

9 Contract Defenses: Form of the Agreement

Assuming that an agreement (offer-acceptance) has been legally validated, it may still not be "operative"; that is, not legally enforceable. This chapter and the two that follow consider the policing process whereby courts decide which expressions of assent are "operative" and which are "inoperative." In making that determination, courts allow certain defenses to invalidate otherwise valid contracts. Typically, courts must answer questions like these: (1) Should oral promises be enforceable? If a contract must be in writing, then oral contracts are legally inoperative. Certain oral expressions of assent are inoperative under a law known as the statute of frauds. (2) Is the written contract the exclusive evidence of the parties' agreement, or may other evidence be considered? Certain statements or understandings that occur *prior* to the written contract may be inoperative because of a law called the parol evidence rule. (3) If a contract suggests a lack of good faith or unfairness, is contrary to public policy, or is unconscionable, should that contract be inoperative? Probably, but the answer in many cases is not so simple.

Although many defenses may cause a

court to refuse to enforce an otherwise valid contract, they can generally be classified under one of three headings:

1. Form of the agreement: statute of frauds and the parol evidence rule
2. Public policy: illegality and unconscionability
3. Avoidance and reformation: incapacity, mistake, fraud, misrepresentation, duress, and undue influence

This chapter will discuss the first of these classifications; the next two chapters will cover the others.

As a general rule, an oral contract is just as valid and enforceable as a written contract, although written contracts have obvious advantages. First, it is much easier to establish the existence and terms of a written contract, since the writing in itself proves the contract terms. The terms of an oral agreement must be established by testimony, and the testimony is often conflicting. Second, the terms of a written contract cannot ordinarily be varied by oral evidence. This parol evidence rule is discussed below.

The statute of frauds recognizes that some contracts are susceptible to fraudulent proofs and perjured testimony; therefore, it requires that these contracts, to be enforceable, must be written. The various contracts covered by the statute of frauds are exceptions to the general rule on the validity of oral contracts.

A few states have statutes that require some contracts to be executed with special formalities, such as signing before a notary public. Some statutes, such as those relating to wage assignments by an employee, require that a contract of assignment be on a sheet of paper separate from other contracts to which the assignment is related. The purpose of this statute is to protect a wage earner against a blanket assignment of his wages without his being fully aware of the import of his action.

Another issue relating to the form of the agreement involves an oral agreement reached with the understanding that the parties will subsequently execute and sign a formal instrument. The question is whether the informal agreement is binding until the document is prepared and signed. The mere fact that a subsequent formal writing was contemplated does not prevent the informal agreement from being enforceable if the parties have actually reached an agreement. The oral contract will be enforced unless there is clear evidence that the parties intended not to be bound until the written contract was signed and delivered. As a result, if the written contract does not accurately express the agreement, a party may refuse to sign it and may enforce the actual oral agreement. If the parties expressly stipulate that there shall be no binding contract until it is reduced to writing and signed, such a stipulation is obviously a condition precedent to a binding contract.

The Parol Evidence Rule

The parol evidence rule prevents the introduction of evidence of prior oral or written agreements that might vary or contradict the present written contract. When parties to a contract embody the terms of their agreement in a writing intended to be the final and complete expression of their agreement, then the written contract cannot be contradicted, explained, or supplemented by previous oral or written agreements. Everything that transpires prior to the execution of the written contract is assumed to be integrated into it. The written contract is deemed the only permissible evidence of the agreement. All earlier negotiations, understandings, representations, and agreements are said to have merged in the written contract. Therefore, parol (extrinsic) evidence is not admissible to supplement, subtract from, alter, vary, or contradict the agreement as written.

Exceptions

But most legal rules have exceptions based on notions of equity, good conscience, and common sense. The parol evidence rule has several such exceptions. First, since the rule presumes all prior negotiations are merged into the written contract, it obviously cannot apply to agreements made after the written contract. Thus, the rule does not prevent the use of oral evidence to establish modifications agreed upon subsequent to the execution of the written contract. Likewise, the rule is inapplicable to evidence of a cancellation of the agreement. Other exceptions include evidence of fraudulent misrepresentations, lack of delivery of an instrument when delivery is required to give it effect, and errors in drafting or reducing the contract to writing. Moreover, oral evidence is always allowed to clarify the terms of an ambiguous contract.

Perhaps the most important exception is the partial integration rule. This exception requires the judge to determine if the written contract is totally or merely partially integrated. A total integration occurs when the parties intend the written contract to be the *final and complete* statement of their agreement. If they do, evidence of prior agreements is not permitted for any reason. A partial integration occurs when the parties intend the writing to be final on the terms as written but not necessarily complete on all terms of their agreement. Although the contract cannot be *contradicted* under the partial integration rule, it can be *supplemented* or *explained* by prior agreements between the parties.

CASE

P's (a father and 2 sons) own 50 percent of a wholesale liquor distributorship. With the owners of the other 50 percent, P's offered to sell the business to D. In the negotiations, P's got D to agree orally that D would relocate P's in a new distributorship in another city. Later, all parties signed a written buy-sell contract. D's oral promise was not included in the written agreement. P's sue D for breach of the oral agreement.

ISSUE Is the written contract a total integration or is the oral promise one that the parties would not necessarily have included in the written contract?

DECISION The contract is a partial integration.

REASONS
1. There are several reasons why it would not be expected that the oral promise would be integrated into the sales contract. First, it is expectable such an agreement, as one to obtain a new distributorship for only a few of the persons who are parties to the contract, would not normally be integrated into an instrument for the sale of corporate assets. Second, P (father) was a lifelong friend of D, executive vice-president. "It is not surprising that a handshake would have been thought sufficient." Finally, although the written agreement has numerous boilerplate clauses, it does not contain the customary merger clause stating that the agreement is a total integration.
2. The oral promise supplements and does not contradict the written sales agreement. The written agreement concerns the sale of corporate assets; the oral agreement concerns the relocation of P's.

Lee v. Joseph E. Seagram & Sons, Inc., 552 F.2d 447 (2d Cir. 1977) (N.Y. law).

To decide if the contract is a total or partial integration, the judge uses a reasonable person test. He looks to the evidence of the prior agreement. If reasonable persons would have *normally* and *naturally* included the prior agreement in the written contract, then the writing is totally integrated. If they would not, then the contract is partially integrated, and the evidence is allowed in to explain or supplement the written contract. In most cases, the written contract will be viewed as totally integrated unless the additional terms are the kind that might naturally be agreed upon and not included in the writing by reasonable persons situated as were the original parties. In that event, consistent additional terms are admissible.

Parol evidence and the Code

The Code recognizes that the parol evidence rule prevents the use of oral evidence to contradict or vary the terms of a written memorandum or of a contract that is intended to be the final expression of the parties. The impact of the rule is greatly reduced, however, by the Code's provision that a written contract may be explained or supplemented by a prior course of dealing between buyer and seller, by usage of trade, or by the course of performance. The Code also allows evidence of consistent additional terms to be introduced, based on the partial integration rule [2-202]. The provisions allowing such evidence are designed to ascertain the true understanding of the parties concerning the agreement and to place the agreement in its proper perspective. The assumption is that prior dealings between the parties and the usages of the trade were taken for granted when the contract was worded. Often a contract for sale involves repetitive performance by both parties over a period of time. The course of performance is indicative of the meaning that the parties, by practical construction, have given to their agreement. It is relevant to interpretation of the agreement and thus is admissible evidence.

When oral evidence of a course of dealing, trade usage, or course of performance is introduced under the Code's exceptions to the parol evidence rule, the law recognizes an order of preference in the event of inconsistencies. Express terms will prevail over an interpretation based on the course of performance, and the course of performance will prevail over an interpretation predicated upon either the course of dealing or the usage of trade [2-208].

The Statute of Frauds

Of ancient English origin, the statute of frauds was enacted because of a mistrust of juries and because of the notion that some contracts seemed to require written form. The statute of frauds makes some contracts voidable and unenforceable unless evidenced by a writing signed by the party sought to be bound. The statute has an evidentiary rather than a substantive function as it attempts to obviate perjury by requiring written evidence in proving contracts. It also places restraints on the jury, which might not perceive that a party is lying about an oral contract. Yet the statute, rather than deterring fraud, has often promoted fraud or injustice by voiding socially useful contracts, thereby frustrating the parties' legitimate expectations. Consequently, courts have recognized numerous exceptions and have narrowly construed the language of the statute.

Generally, the statute may be used as a defense, even though there is no factual dispute over the existence of the contract or its terms. A contract that requires a writing may come into existence at the time of the oral agreement, but it is not enforceable until written evidence of the agreement is available. The agreement is valid in every respect except for the lack of proper evidence of its existence. The statute creates a defense in suits for the breach of executory oral contracts if they are covered by its provisions.

The statute of frauds has always required a writing in connection with (1) contracts to be liable for another person's debts; (2) contracts involving real property; (3) agreements that cannot be performed within one year from the date of making; and (4) contracts for the sale of goods priced $500 or more. States have enacted special statute of frauds provisions, such as requiring a writing for all life insurance contracts, real estate listing agreements, and promises to pay debts that have been discharged in bankruptcy. Many statutes provide that any agreement required to be in writing may be modified only by a writing. Such a provision does not bar all oral modifications, but it does bar any modification of an essential element necessary to satisfy the statute of frauds. If the contract as orally modified would violate the statute, the statute is a defense. The sections that follow discuss the contracts under the general statute of frauds.

Promise to answer for the debt of another

For the statute to be defense, a promise to answer for the debt of another must be a secondary promise. A primary promise is not within the statute and is enforceable even though oral. For example, a promise ("Sell goods to Billy Bob, and I will pay for them") is a primary or original promise and enforceable even though oral. An oral promise to pay one's own obligation is not within the statute of frauds.

On the other hand, a promise ("Sell goods to Billy Bob; if he doesn't pay you for them, I will") is a secondary promise and must be in writing to be enforceable. Note that in the second situation the primary responsibility to pay is Billy Bob's, and the other party has agreed to pay only if Billy Bob doesn't pay.

An original or primary promise can be distinguished from a secondary promise by analyzing the leading object or main purpose of the promisor in making the promise. When the leading object is to become a guarantor of another's debt, the promise is collateral, and it is covered by the statute. When the leading object of the promisor is to subserve some interest or purpose of his own, even though it involves the debt of another, the promise is original, and it is not within the statute. When the issue arises, the court must determine whether the promisor primarily intended to benefit himself.

CASE

P's engineering firm used D (an attorney) to recover for professional services rendered the X corporation, a land developer. D owned 18 percent of the stock of X corporation and was its legal counsel. X corporation also owed D $14,000 in legal fees. In order to encourage P to finish its survey work for X, D had orally promised to pay P's bill.

ISSUE Is D liable for the oral promise to pay for the services rendered to X corporation?

DECISION Yes.

REASONS

1. The promise was not within the statute of frauds as a special promise to answer for the debt of another, since the consideration (continued professional services) was mainly desired for D's personal benefit, in that D's corporation owed him $14,000 for legal services. Continued engineering and surveying services were necessary to secure additional financing. If the corporation was eventually successful, the amount that D would receive would be substantial.
2. Where the consideration for which a new promise is given is beneficial both to the promisor and to the original debtor, the factor that is determinative of whether the statute of frauds applies is whether such consideration is desired mainly for the promisor's benefit or for benefit of the original debtor. In applying the rule, the jury must examine all circumstances bearing on the transaction and the relationship of the parties to one another. It must endeavor to discern the intent, purpose, and object of the promisor. In such examination, the nature of the consideration will be of great, if not paramount, importance.
3. Under the "original v. collateral promise" test, where the leading object or main purpose of the promise is to become surety for another's debt, the promise is a collateral one and within the statute of frauds. On the other hand, where the principal purpose is to subserve or promote some

interest personal to the promisor, then the promise will be deemed an original one and not controlled by the statute.

Howard M. Schoor Assoc., Inc. v. Holmdel Hts. Con. Co., 343 A.2d 401 (N.J.) 1975.

Contracts involving real property

Since the law has always placed importance on contracts involving land, it is logical that the statute of frauds should require a writing for a contract creating or transferring any interest in land. In addition to contracts involving a sale of an entire interest, the statute is applicable to contracts involving interests for a person's lifetime (called life estates), to mortgages, to easements, and to leases for a period in excess of one year.

One problem under the statute is to determine what is real property. Generally, it is land and all things affixed to the land. What is the status of things such as standing timber, minerals, and growing crops? Is an oral contract to sell oil and gas a contract involving real estate? The general rule is that these items are real property if the title to them is to pass to the buyer before they are severed from the land; they are personal property if title to them passes subsequently. The Code provides that a contract to sell minerals, oil, and the like, or a contract for a structure or its materials to be removed from realty is a contract for the sale of goods if they are to be severed by the seller [2-107]. If the buyer is to sever them, the contract affects and involves land and is subject to the real estate provisions of the statute of frauds. The Code also provides that a contract for the sale apart from the land of growing crops or of timber is a contract for the sale of goods, whether they are to be severed by the buyer or by the seller [2-107(2)].

The statute of frauds is not applicable to executed contracts. A party who has purchased or sold land under an oral contract cannot obtain a refund of his money or cannot obtain a return deed to his land. The statute of frauds does not allow rescission. It serves only as a defense to a suit for breach of an executory contract. This principle creates a special problem in real estate contracts because many oral contracts involving real estate become partially executed as a result of part payment by the buyer or surrender of possession to the buyer by the seller or both. Since the statute of frauds is a complete defense to an executory oral contract involving real estate and it is no defense to a fully executed contract, what is the status if the contract is partially performed?

The problem of part performance to satisfy the statute of frauds provisions on real estate has two aspects. First, the part performance must establish and point unmistakably and exclusively to the existence of the alleged oral agreement. Part performance eliminates the statute of frauds as a defense in such cases because it eliminates any doubt that the contract was made, and thus the reason for the defense does not exist.

Second, the part performance must be substantial enough to warrant specific performance of the oral agreement. In other words, it must be such that returning the parties to the status quo is not reasonably possible. To illustrate the foregoing, assume that a buyer under an oral contract has paid part of the purchase price. The money can be returned, and the statute of frauds would be a defense because even if it were admitted that the oral contract was entered into, there would be no equitable reason to enforce the oral agreement. However, when the seller under an oral contract also delivers possession to the buyer, the defense of the statute of frauds becomes more tenuous, because returning the parties to the status quo becomes somewhat difficult. When improvements are made by one in possession, a return to the status quo becomes quite difficult, if not impossible.

From the foregoing, it is clear that the transaction is taken out of the statute if the buyer has taken possession, paid all or part of the price, and made valuable improvements. Less part performance may also take the contract out of the statute if the buyer takes possession and pays part of the price, giving good evidence of a contract. If he also pays taxes and mortgage payments, specific performance may be warranted. Payment of the price, standing alone, is not a basis for specific performance and will not satisfy the statute; but if the buyer enters into possession and makes valuable improvements, there is sufficient part performance to make the contract enforceable and to satisfy the statute.

CASE

P entered into an oral contract to purchase a farm from D. P went into possession on the farm, made several improvements, tore down an old farmhouse, paid taxes, and made payments on the purchase price. D thereafter refused to deed the farm to P. P sought specific performance of the contract.

ISSUE Is the oral contract to sell real property enforceable under these circumstances?

DECISION Yes.

REASONS
1. The statute of frauds requires a transfer of real property to be in writing, but the statute does not apply when there has been partial or complete performance. Here, virtually all the terms of the contract had been performed.
2. Here the contract was established from the fact of the buyer's possession, payments, and improvements to the premises.

Brown v. Burnside, 487 P.2d 957 (Idaho) 1972.

Contracts not to be performed within one year

A contract is within the statute if, by its terms, it cannot be performed within one year from the time it is made. The period is measured from the time an oral contract is made to the time when the promised performance is to be completed. Thus, an oral agreement to hire a person for two years or to form and carry on a partnership for ten years would not be enforceable.

The decisive factor in determining whether a long-term contract comes within the statute is whether performance is possible within a year from the date of making. If a contract, according to the intentions of the parties as shown by its terms, may be fully performed within a year from the time it is made, it is not within the statute of frauds, even though the time of its performance is uncertain and may probably extend—and in fact does extend—beyond the year.

CASE

In May, 1969, P received $1,500 from D. P seeks a declaratory judgment that the money was a gift and not a loan. D wants to introduce evidence that P made the following promise: "I will pay you back in January of 1970 or later in 1970 when I receive my income tax refund for taxable year 1969." P objects to this evidence in that it violates the statute of frauds applicable to contracts that cannot be performed in one year.

ISSUE Could the oral promise possibly be performed within one year from May, 1969?

DECISION Yes. Oral promise is not within the statute of frauds.

REASON By its terms, the oral agreement was capable of being performed within a year. Repayment in January of 1970, one alternative promised, would have been such performance. Also, the income tax refund for 1969 could have been received in less than a year from May, 1969. Both alternative promises of payment could possibly occur within the one-year period. Moreover, the rule is that either alternative, standing alone, is sufficient to take the oral promise out of the statute.

Frigon v. Whipple, 360 A.2d 69 (Vt.) 1976.

Even though it is most unlikely that performance could be rendered within one year, the statute does not apply if there is even a remote possibility that it could. Thus, a promise to pay $10,000 "when cars are no longer polluting the air" would be enforceable even though given orally. Moreover, if a contract, otherwise to continue for more than a year, is by its own terms subject to termination within a year, it is not within the prohibition of the statute of frauds.

Thus, the question is not how long performance will *probably run* but can the contract *possibly be performed* within one year from the making of the contract. This rule requires you to distinguish possible performance from probable performance. To put the matter in sharper focus, the rule should be stated: An oral contract that by its terms has no possibility of being performed within one year from the date of formation must be evidenced by a writing.

Contracts for the sale of goods—generally

The Code contains several provisions regarding the statute of frauds. The provision applicable to the sale of goods stipulates that a contract for the sale of goods for the price of $500 or more is not enforceable unless there is some writing sufficient to indicate that a contract for sale has been made. The writing must be signed by the defendant or his authorized agent or broker [2-201].

The liberal approach of the Code is seen in its provisions that the writing need not contain all material terms of the contract, and that errors in stating a term will not affect the fact that the statute of frauds is not a defense. The writing need not indicate which party is the buyer or which is the seller or include the price or time of payment. The only term that must appear is the quantity term, which need not be accurately stated, but a contract will not be enforceable beyond the quantity stated in the writing. Since the requirement is that the contract be signed by the party to be charged, it need not be signed by a plaintiff who is seeking to enforce it.

Confirmation between merchants exception

The Code provisions relating to the sale of goods contain four exceptions to the rule that requires a writing if the contract involves $500 or more. One exception is limited to transactions between "merchants." It arises from the business practice of negotiating contracts orally, often by telephone. A merchant who contracts orally with another merchant can satisfy the statute of frauds requirement by sending a confirming writing to the other merchant [2-201(2)]. This confirmation will satisfy the statute, *even though it is not signed by the party to be charged,* unless written notice of objection to its contents is given within ten days after it is received. This means that a merchant who has dealt orally with another merchant will have an enforceable contract unless the merchant receiving the writing objects within the ten-day period.

Specially manufactured goods exception

A second exception to the writing requirement under the Code relates to conduct that clearly shows a contract has been made. The Code explicitly excludes from the statute transactions that involve goods to be specially manufactured. To fit within this exception, three requirements must be met [2-201(3)(a)].

1. The goods are to be specially manufactured for the particular buyer and are not suitable for sale to others.
2. The seller has made a substantial beginning to manufacture or obtain the goods.
3. The circumstances reasonably indicate that the goods are for the buyer [2-201(3)(a)].

CASE

P, a printer, sues D corporation to recover the price of printing services. After some negotiations on the phone and checking D's credit, P printed business cards, letterheads and envelopes, invoices, and order forms and prepared an etching and rubber stamp with D's corporate name.

ISSUE Is the oral contract within the Code's statute of frauds provision?

DECISION No.

REASON The statute of frauds is no defense in the lawsuit to recover on the oral contract for printing special materials not suitable for sale to others.

Associated Lithographers v. Stay Wood Products, Inc., 279 N.W.2d 787 (Minn.) 1979.

Judicial admissions exception

Another substitute for a writing is based upon recognition that the required writing is simply a formality and that a contract may very well exist. The extant contract is unenforceable without proof of its existence; but when proof is available, its effect becomes retroactive. If the party who is resisting the contract admits its existence in the proper circumstances and surroundings, such admission will substitute for a writing. Thus, the Code provides that an oral contract for the sale of goods is enforceable if (when legal action is brought to enforce it) the defendant admits in the court proceedings that a contract for sale was made. It is quite possible that the admission will be made in the pleadings or testimony. That judicial admission satisfies the statutory requirement [2-201(3)(b)].

CASE

P sued D to enforce an oral contract for the sale of a mobile home. D defended on the ground that the contract was unenforceable under the statute of frauds. At the trial, D took the stand and on cross-examination admitted to facts which, as a matter of law, established that a contract was formed.

ISSUE Is the contract enforceable?

DECISION Yes.

REASONS
1. Section 2-201(3)(b) of the Uniform Commercial Code provides that a contract that does not satisfy the requirements of 2-201(1) (written evidence) but is valid in other respects is enforceable if the party against whom enforcement is sought admits in his pleading, testimony, or otherwise in court that a contract for sale was formed.
2. Involuntary admissions in open court are sufficient to obtain enforcement of an otherwise unenforceable contract under the statute of frauds.

Lewis v. Hughes, 346 A.2d 231 (Md.) 1975.

Performance exception

The final exception is the part-performance exception that was earlier explained regarding real property contracts. The Code excepts oral contracts for the sale of goods that have been paid for or received and accepted [2-201(3)(c)]. At common law, part performance would take the entire contract out of the statute of frauds. You will recall that the statute did not apply, either, to possession of land that had been improved and partially paid for. In the sale of goods, the Code changes that basic rule and takes the contract out of the statute only to the extent of the part performance; that is, to the extent either of payment or goods shipped and received. Any unperformed part of the contract is still within the statute, and some writing is still required.

Contracts involving personal property other than goods

The Code has several additional sections that require a writing. A contract for the sale of securities such as stocks and bonds is not enforceable unless (1) there is a signed writing setting forth a stated quantity of described securities at a defined or stated price, (2) delivery of the security has been accepted or payment has been made, (3) within a reasonable time a writing in confirmation of the sale or purchase has been sent and received and the party receiving it has failed to object to it within ten days after receipt, or (4) the party against whom enforcement is sought admits in court that such a contract was made. Note that this relates only to contracts for the sale of securities [8-319].

Another section concerns contracts for the sale of personal property other than goods or securities. For these contracts, which involve matters such as royalty rights, patent rights, and rights under a bilateral contract, a writing is required if the amount involved exceeds $5,000 [1-206].

In the article on secured transactions, discussed later in chapter 21, the Code usually requires a signed security agreement. Therefore, when a person borrows money and gives the lender an interest in his property as security, the debtor (borrower) must sign a security agreement [9-203].

Promissory estoppel exception

In the preceding chapter, concerning the validation process, you were introduced to the promissory estoppel validation device. The estoppel concept is sometimes used by courts to prevent a party to an oral contract from using the statute of frauds as a defense. Estoppel requires that a party, to his or her detriment, rely on the oral promise. It is this detrimental reliance that will cause hardship and loss if the statute is allowed as a defense.

CASE

P, a contractor, sues D for lost profits incurred when D repudiated the contract for P to construct an addition to a nursing home. P and D made two oral contracts: one to build the addition; another to enter into a written contract to build. Shortly after these oral agreements were reached, D refused to execute a written contract. P had orally promised to remedy any defect in construction up to one year from the date of substantial completion of the addition. D claims the oral promises could not be performed within one year from the date the contract was made in violation of the statute of frauds.

ISSUE Are the oral contracts within the one-year provision of the statute of frauds?

DECISION Yes, but promissory estoppel precludes application of the statute.

REASON Though there has been no satisfaction of the statute of frauds, an estoppel may preclude D's use of the statute as a defense. A promise to execute a written contract, if detrimentally relied on, may give rise to an effective promissory estoppel if the statute would otherwise operate to defraud.

Retama Manor Nursing Centers, Inc. v. Lee Roy Cole, 582 S.W.2d 196 (Tex.) 1979.

In fact, the part performance exception is an earlier concept that courts used for achieving fairness and preventing an unfair result. There is now a trend in a few jurisdictions to depart from narrower doctrines like part performance and to predicate decisions on estoppel. Estoppel is used whenever the plaintiff's equities are so great that any contrary decision would be unconscionable. The term *unconscionable* is significant. In most cases, parties will rely on oral promises. But the doctrine of estoppel is inapplicable unless equity and justice absolutely require it. In such cases, the statute of frauds (if allowed to be used) would itself constitute a fraud on the relying party.

The writing requirement

The statute of frauds does not require a formal written contract signed by both parties. All that is required is a note or memorandum that provides written evidence of the transaction. It must be signed by the party sought to be bound by the agreement (the defendant). The memorandum need contain only the names of the parties, a description of the subject matter, the price, and the general terms of the agreement. A memorandum of sale of real property must describe the real estate with such certainty that a court may order its conveyance.

Under the statute, one party may be bound by an agreement even though the other party is not. Only the party who resists performance need have signed. Such a result is predicated on the theory that the agreement is legal in all respects, but proper evidence of such an agreement is lacking. This is furnished when the person sought to be charged with the contract has signed a writing.

The note or memorandum may consist of several writings, even though the writing containing the requisite terms is unsigned. However, it must appear from an examination of all the writings that the writing signed by the party to be charged was signed with the intention that it refer to the unsigned writing. In effect, the writings must be connected by internal reference in the signed memorandum to the unsigned one, so that they may be said to constitute one paper relating to the contract. If the signed memorandum makes no reference to the unsigned memorandum, they may not be read together. Parol evidence is inadmissible to connect them.

As to the signature of the party sought to be charged, it may be quite informal and need not necessarily be placed at the close of the document. It may be in the body of the writing or elsewhere, as long as it identifies the writing with the signature of the person sought to be held.

REVIEW QUESTIONS AND PROBLEMS

1. Sloane bought a mobile home from Up-Side-Down Charlie's. The written contract of sale disclaimed any warranty obligation of the seller. Sloane experienced numerous problems with the mobile home, which Charlie refused to repair. Sloane sued and contended that Charlie (the seller) orally promised that if problems did arise he would "take care of them." Is this oral promise admissible in court? Why or why not?
2. Johnny entered into a written installment sale contract to sell certain property to June. When she failed to make the installment payments on time, they executed a new long-term contract. Just before June signed, she orally promised to pay interest on all past and future late payments. Is her oral promise admissible in court? Why or why not?
3. A butcher sold hamburger meat on credit to the Goods Eats Restaurant. When the restaurant was late in paying its bills, the butcher contacted Jim, who orally promised to pay any bill that the restaurant failed to pay. Is this oral promise admissible in court? Why or why not? Would your answer change if Jim said: "The restaurant is on hard times. Send the bills to me, and I'll pay." In the original case, would it make any difference if Jim had some financial interest in the restaurant? Why or why not?
4. Chisholm had a written option to purchase 1.862 acres of land out of a 10-acre tract owned by the Cartwrights. The exact piece of property covered by the option was not specified. If Chisholm sues for specific performance of the option, will the statute of frauds be a valid defense?
5. Suppose that the Cartwrights orally agreed to sell their ranch to Chisholm. Chisholm then paid for a title search and preparation of a mortgage deed and $2,860 for a preliminary survey and design of a subdivision on the land. If Chisholm now sues for specific performance, will the oral promise be enforced? Why or why not? Would your answer change if Chisholm additionally hauled fertilizer to the farm, piped water to the feedlots, made cement platforms for feeding livestock, and fed the Cartwrights' dogs? Why or why not?
6. A rental car company hired Owens as a sales representative. To safeguard its list of customers, the company and Owens orally agreed that Owens would be employed for one year and, upon termination of employment, Owens would not compete in the same capacity in a similar business for two years. Five months later, Owens resigned and began work for a competitor. The company sues Owens for damages and to enjoin his employment with their competitor. Who should win? Explain.
7. Suppose the rental car company orally hired Owens to work for one year from the date he moves from California to Buffalo. When sued for breach of contract, Owens pleads the statute of frauds as a defense. Is the statute a valid defense? Why or why not?
8. Suppose Owens was orally given an exclusive right to do the company's commercials for as long as he wished. Is the statute a valid defense to that oral promise? Why or why not?
9. Farmer made an oral contract with Grain Operator for the sale of soybeans for future delivery. Five days later, in confirmation of the oral contract, Grain Operator sent Farmer a written contract for his signature. Farmer refused to sign. When sued, Farmer claimed that he was not liable for breach of contract, since the contract was not in writing. At the trial it was proven that Farmer had been farming for 34 years, had 150 acres of soybeans, and had sold his crop to grain operators in "cash sales" and "future contracts" for at least five years. Is Farmer liable? Why or why not?
10. Alex signed an order form to purchase a car from Baker's Better Cars Company for $2,500. Neither Baker nor anyone else from his company signed the form. Alex made a $50 down payment. Later, Baker tells Alex that there was a mistake; the price is $2,675. Alex sues, and Baker defends on the ground that the company had not signed the form. Is the defense valid? Why or why not? Would your answer change if Alex had bought two cars rather than one? Explain.
11. Barney made an oral contract to buy land from Fred. In reliance upon the oral contract, Barney passed up an opportunity to buy other land that would have been suitable for his needs. Fred later refuses to sell, and Barney sues. Who should win? Why?

10

Contract Defenses: Public Policy

If either the consideration or the subject matter of a contract is contrary to public policy, the agreement may be illegal or unconscionable. A contract provision is contrary to public policy if it is injurious to the interests of the public, contravenes some established interest of society, violates the policy or purpose of some statute, or tends to interfere with the public health, safety, morals, or general welfare. Although all agreements are subject to the paramount power of the government and to the judicial power to declare contracts illegal, contracts are not to be lightly set aside on the grounds of public policy. Doubts will usually be resolved in favor of legality.

The term *public policy* is vague and variable, changing as our social, economic, and political climates change. As society becomes more complex, courts turn more and more to statutory enactments in search of current public policy. A court's own concept of right and wrong as well as its total philosophy will frequently come into play in answering complex questions of public policy.

An endless variety of other contracts may be against public policy: wagering agreements, contracts to affect the administration of justice (concealing evidence or suppressing a criminal investigation), contracts to influence legislative or executive action, and contracts to interfere with, or injure, public service. Such contracts

CASE

P, an insured, injured his right lower leg. Doctors worked unsuccessfully for 118 days to save his foot. The insurance policy provided that D insurance company would pay disability benefits if an insured lost a foot through "dismemberment by severance" within 90 days after an accident. D denied liability because severance of P's foot was not within the 90-day limitation. P sued, but the court dismissed, stating: "The policy is a contract, and we cannot rewrite it. Nor do we feel that we can declare it void as against public policy. The limb was not severed within the specified ninety days, and the loss is therefore not covered." P appealed.

ISSUE Is the 90-day limitation provision against public policy?

DECISION Probably.

REASON The court on appeal sent the case back down to the trial court and instructed the trial court to hear evidence on the question if this provision complies with public policy.

Strickland v. Gulf Life Insurance Company, 242 S.E.2d 148 (Ga.) 1978.

are frequently declared illegal by statute; others are held to be illegal because they are contrary to public policy. Of course, lobbying is legal as long as it does not amount to bribery or undue influence.

Illegality

An additional requirement for a valid contract is that it have a lawful purpose or object. Contracts that do not have a lawful object are illegal and therefore *unenforceable.*

Basic effect

As a general rule, the status of an illegal contract is that a court will not entertain a lawsuit involving it. If the illegal contract is executory, neither party may enforce performance by the other. If the contract is executed, the court will not allow recovery of what was given in performance. An illegal contract cannot be ratified by either party; and the parties can do nothing to make it enforceable. Stated simply, when there is an illegal contract, the court literally "leaves the parties where it finds them."

A party to an illegal contract cannot recover damages for breach of that contract. If one party has performed, he cannot, generally, recover either the value of his performance or any property or goods transferred to the other. As a result of the rule, one wrongdoer may be enriched at the expense of the other wrongdoer, but the courts will not intercede to rectify this, because the purpose is to deter illegal bargains.

Although there are numerous examples of illegal contracts, we shall consider only the following: violations of license requirements, agreements in restraint of trade, agreements not to compete, restrictive covenants in real estate transactions, and usury.

Violations of license requirements

A contract that calls for performance of an act or a service may be illegal for one of two reasons. The act or service itself may be illegal; thus, any contract involving it is illegal. Prostitution is an illegal activity in most states; therefore, contracts to engage in prostitution are illegal per se in those states. Other personal service contracts are not illegal per se but may be illegal if the party performing or contracting to perform the service is not legally entitled to do so. For example, doctors, dentists, pharmacists, architects, lawyers, surveyors, real estate brokers, and others rendering specialized professional services must be licensed by the appropriate body before entering into contracts with the general public.

As a general rule, if the service rendered requires a license, the party receiving the benefit of the service can successfully refuse to pay an unlicensed plaintiff on the ground that the contract is illegal. This is true even if the person is licensed in another jurisdiction but not the one in which the services were rendered. A real estate broker licensed in one state cannot perform services in another state. If he does so, he cannot collect for the services.

The practice of law by unauthorized persons is a significant problem. A person who practices law without a license is not only denied the right to a fee but also subject to criminal prosecution in many states, and such activity may also be enjoined. Since the practice of law primarily entails giving advice, difficult questions are presented when advice is given by business specialists such as certified public accountants, insurance brokers, bankers, and real estate brokers. Although the line between permissible and impermissible activities of these business specialists is often difficult to draw, some activities and services performed by various business specialists clearly constitute unauthorized practice of law. An accountant's handling of a complicated tax case has been held to constitute unauthorized practice of law, and a real estate broker's preparation of a real estate contract of sale is illegal in most states. Business specialists should be aware that giving legal advice and preparing legal documents are illegal performances by one not licensed to practice law. A major danger in doing these things is the loss of the right to compensation.

Agreements in restraint of trade

Several federal laws declare that agreements in restraint of trade are illegal. These laws are discussed in chapter 44 with other aspects of government regulation of business. In the meantime, it should be recognized that price fixing and other agreements tending to eliminate competition are generally illegal. An agreement among lawyers that they will not represent one another's clients for five years is illegal; however, agreements such as those between a franchiser and its franchisees are usually found to be legal. They are legal because their effect on competition is minimal compared with the interests of the franchiser in having similarity in all of its franchised operations. Thus, certain exclusive dealing contracts are legal.

Another form of agreement that may be legal even though it is in partial restraint of trade is an agreement not to compete. An agreement by one person not to compete with another is frequently contained in a contract for the sale of a going business. The seller, by such a provision, agrees not to compete with the buyer. Agreements not to compete are also commonly found in contracts creating a business or a professional practice. Each partner or shareholder in the closely held corporation agrees not to compete with the firm or practice, should he leave the business or professional activity. In addition, as a part of their employment contract, many employees agree that they will not compete with their employer upon termination of their employment.

Agreements not to compete

Agreements not to compete must be a part of another contract, to be legal. A bare agreement by one party not to compete with another is against public policy. If Lori threatens to open a business to compete with Elaine, and Elaine offers Lori $1,000 to agree not to do so, the contract is illegal. A covenant ancillary to an agreement will be enforced if it is reasonably necessary for the protection of a purchaser, the remaining members of a business, or an employer, provided the covenant (1) is reasonable in point of time, (2) is reasonable in the area of restraint, (3) is necessary to protect goodwill, (4) does not place an undue burden on the covenator, and (5) does not violate the public interest. Each covenant is examined by the court to see if it is reasonable to both parties and to the general public. Factors such as uniqueness of product, patents, trade secrets, type of service, employee's contact with customers, and other goodwill factors are significant on the reasonableness issue. In the employment situation, whether or not the employee will become a burden on society and whether or not the public is being deprived of his skill and so forth are factors.

The law will look with more favor on these covenants if they involve the sale of a business interest rather than employment. In fact, an agreement not to compete may even be presumed in the case of a sale of business and its goodwill, and the seller must not thereafter directly or by circular solicit business from his old customers, although he may advertise generally. Agreements between a buyer and seller or between partners are more likely to be held valid than are employer-employee contracts, because there is more equality of bargaining power in the first two situations than in the last named. A seller or a former partner could readily refuse to sign an agreement not to compete, whereas an employee seeking a job might feel obligated to sign almost anything in order to gain employment.

Good will is a factor in the sale of almost any going business, and a court will protect that asset. Since a company's good will refers to the entire company, not to any single employee, upon termination an employee seldom takes away the good will. But he may take trade secrets or customers; and when an employer legitimately seeks protection from either possibility, courts may uphold the covenant not to compete.

CASE

In 1969, after a federal law was enacted requiring all newly constructed sewage treatment plants to have an operations and maintenance manual (O&M manual), P was one of the first companies to develop and market an O&M manual. P had D's (3 key employees) sign an employment agreement that required them never to use or disclose any confidential information, prohibited them from taking such information when their employment terminated, and restricted their right to compete with P for 2 years. When D's quit and competed with P in violation of the employment contract, P sued for a permanent injunction and damages.

ISSUE Is the covenant not to compete legal?

DECISION Yes.

REASONS
1. Evidence supported the finding that the customer list was confidential: P was the first entrant in the O&M manual market; it compiled a customer list at considerable expense, and it did not reveal names on the list.
2. Although restrictive covenants are usually strictly construed, they will be enforced to the extent that they are reasonable.
3. Contractual prohibitions against competing with P by soliciting P's customers for a 2-year period after termination of employment were reasonable.

Cherne Industrial, Inc. v. Grounds & Associates, 278 N.W.2d 81 (Minn.) 1979.

Restrictive covenants in real estate transactions

Comparable to the employee's agreement not to compete is a restrictive provision in a contract for the sale or lease of real property. The landowner may wish to prevent the use of his land for any purpose that would be competitive with his own business. In a lease, the landowner may provide that the lessee cannot operate an appliance store on the leased property. In that case, the landowner (who owns an appliance store) wants to avoid competition, and he does so by the restrictive provision. Although on its face the provision does restrict trade, it is binding because other property in the community can be used for competitive purposes. Nonetheless, the restriction may be unenforceable as an illegal restraint under the Sherman Antitrust Act. It may also be illegal if the Federal Trade Commission rules that the restriction is an unfair method of competition. These matters are discussed further in chapter 44.

Usury

State statutes limit the amount of interest that may be charged upon borrowed money. Any contract by which the lender is to receive more than the maximum interest allowed by the statute is usurious and illegal. In most states, the civil penalty for usury is that the lender is denied the right to collect any interest. Of course, there are also criminal penalties for charging illegal interest.

The law against usury is generally not violated if the seller sets a cash price different from a credit price, but he cannot disguise interest by calling it something else. If the buyer is charged for making a loan, it is interest, regardless of the terminology used in many states.

The laws on usury are not violated by collection of the legal maximum interest in advance or by adding a service fee that is no larger than reasonably necessary to cover the incidental costs of making the loan (inspection, legal, and recording fees). A seller can also add a finance or carrying charge on long-term credit transactions. Some statutes allow special lenders such as pawnshops, small loan companies, or credit unions to charge in excess of the otherwise legal limit. In fact, the exceptions to the maximum interest rate in most states far exceed the situations in which the general rule is applicable. The laws relating to usury were designed to protect debtors from excessive interest. This goal has been thwarted by these exceptions, so only modest protection is actually available.

The purchase of a note at a discount greater than the maximum interest is not usurious unless the maker of the note is the person who is discounting it. A note is considered the same as any other personal property and may be sold for whatever it will bring upon the market.

As long as one lends the money of others, he may charge a commission in addition to the maximum rate. A commission may not be legally charged when one is lending his own funds, even though he has to borrow the money with which to make the loan and expects to sell the paper shortly thereafter.

Interest rates have increased substantially over the past few years, prompting many states to raise the legal maximum to 12 or more percent for consumer loans. Additional statutory exceptions have also been created which may allow businesses to be charged as much as 20 percent or more. Today, in most states, there is no maximum legal rate of interest when the borrower is a business, whether or not it is incorporated. Some states limit this exception to a fixed sum, such as $10,000, but little protection is afforded by such laws. Loans to corporations have long been exempt in most states; the extension to all business loans is a recognition of the demands of the money market.

Another new trend in the law of usury is that of federal laws superseding state laws with regard to federally guaranteed loans, such as FHA mortgage loans. As a result, interest on federally guaranteed loans can exceed the maximum allowed by the states.

Exceptions to illegality

There are three basic exceptions to the rule that a person who is a party to an illegal contract will not be granted any relief. First, if a person is within the category of those for whose protection the contract was made illegal, he may obtain back what he has paid or may even be able to enforce the illegal agreement. For example, both federal and state statutes require that a corporation follow certain procedures before securities (stocks and bonds) may be offered for sale to the public. It is illegal to sell securities without having complied with the legal requirements. One who purchases securities from a corporation that has failed to follow the necessary procedures is allowed to obtain a refund of the purchase price if he desires to do so. The act of one party (the seller) is more illegal than that of the other party (the buyer). Many other statutes are designed to protect one party in an illegal transaction, and the protected party is allowed a legal remedy.

A second exception applies when a person is induced by fraud or duress to enter into an illegal agreement. In such cases, the courts do not regard the defrauded or coerced party as being an actual participant in the wrong, and they will, therefore, allow restitution of what he has rendered by way of performance. It has been suggested that the same result would obtain if the party were induced by strong economic pressure to enter into an illegal agreement.

Third, there is a doctrine called *locus poenitentiae,* which may provide the remedy of restitution to one who has become a party to an illegal contract. Literally, the phrase means "a place for repentance"; that is, "an opportunity for changing one's mind." As applied to an illegal contract, it means that within very strict limits, a person who repents before actually having performed any illegal part of the contract may rescind it and obtain restitution of his part performance.

Unconscionability

Many contracts today are mass-standardized form contracts entered into by parties who are unequal in knowledge and unequal in bargaining power. Early common law ignored the inequality and applied a doctrine of caveat emptor. Modern law, in contrast, uses the concept of unconscionability to police against contractual abuses by the superior party. Unconscionability comes from equity and is used by courts in varied situations. It is codified in the Code [2-302]. Unconscionability is an exciser device that allows a judge to strike offensive terms from written contracts. It is a question of law for the judge. Although no precise meaning is given, its avowed purpose is to prevent *oppression* and *unfair surprise.*

For a contract to be conscionable, its material terms need to be conspicuous, to be understandable by an ordinary person, and to result from a true bargain. It cannot be a contract of bargain but is one of adhesion where one party imposes terms on another party. Thus, a party must be able to *find* and to *understand* all material terms, as well as have the right to *bargain* over them. The contract cannot be oppressively imposed.

Unconscionability has been used to excise substantially offensive provisions like disclaimer-of-warranties and limitation-of-remedies clauses, exculpatory clauses, and confession of judgment clauses. The doctrine allows a judge to strike any portion of the contract or to strike the entire contract or to limit the application of a clause, in order to avoid any unconscionable result [2-302].

Generally, courts will not enforce an unconscionable bargain. Many bargains are so harsh, severe, and unfair that one party may be unduly oppressed. This doctrine allows the court to protect that party.

CASE

P, an oil company, sued D, one of its dealers, to recover possession of a leased service station. The lease and the dealer agreement gave P the power to cancel on ten days' written notice if P believed that D was indulging in practices that tended to impair the quality, good name, good will, or reputation of P's product. The same agreements gave D, the dealer, the right to terminate only by notice not less than sixty days prior to the expiration of any yearly period. Failure to give the notice resulted in automatic renewal of the lease.

ISSUE Are the contract terms on termination unconscionable?

DECISION Yes.

REASONS
1. Termination provisions of an agreement involving the sale of goods which, if applied strictly, are so one-sided that they lead to absurd results, will be declared unconscionable.
2. There is imposed on both parties an obligation of good faith and the observance of reasonable commercial standards of fair dealing in the trade.
3. The parties need not be in business forever, and the trial court must decide what kind of notice is required under all the circumstances between the parties.

Ashland Oil, Inc. v. Donahue, 223 S.E.2d 433 (W.Va.) 1976.

Contracts of adhesion

The term *contract of adhesion* was developed in the French civil law. It has been widely used in international law, and in recent years the term has become important in our law of contracts. An adhesion contract is a standardized contract entirely prepared by one party. As a result of the disparity or inequality of bargaining power between the draftsman and the second party, the terms are submitted on a take-it-or-leave-it basis. The standardized provisions are such that they are merely "adhered to," with little choice as a practical matter on the part of the "adherer." If the terms are viewed as unsatisfactory, the party cannot obtain the desired service or product.

Contracts of adhesion are strictly construed against the drafting party. Courts carefully police these contracts to ensure that they are conscionable, and the courts will excise clauses that are oppressive or cause unfair surprise. Employment contracts, insurance policies, and leases are frequently held to be contracts of adhesion.

Tickets disclaiming liability

Tickets purchased for entrance into places of amusement, for evidence of a contract for transportation, or for a service often contain provisions that attempt to limit or to define the rights of the holder of the ticket. It is generally held that the printed matter on the ticket is a part of an offer that is accepted by the holder of the ticket if he is aware of the printed matter, even though he does not read it. Some cases hold that the purchaser is presumed to know about the printed matter, even though his attention is not called to it at the time the ticket is delivered.

If a ticket is received merely as evidence of ownership and is to be presented later as a means of identification, the provisions on the ticket are not a part of the contract unless the recipient is aware of them or his attention is specifically directed to them. Tickets given at checkrooms or repair shops are usually received as a means of identifying the article to be returned, rather than as setting forth the terms of a contract. Thus, the fine print on such tickets is usually not a part of the offer and acceptance unless communicated.

Many terms on tickets may be unconscionable and will not be enforced in any event. The terms are unconscionable when public policy, as previously noted, would declare such a provision in a formal contract to be unconscionable. The equality of the bargaining power of the parties and the nature of the product or service are major factors to be considered in determining unconscionableness.

Contracts disclaiming liability

A party to a contract may include a provision that states that the party has no tort liability even if the party is at fault. Such a clause is commonly called an *exculpatory clause.* These disclaimers of liability are not favored by the law and are strictly construed against the party relying on them. Courts frequently declare these clauses, because contrary to public policy, to be unconscionable. Some states by statute provide that exculpatory clauses in certain contracts like leases are unconscionable per se and thus unenforceable.

REVIEW QUESTIONS AND PROBLEMS

1. A landlord brought an action to evict a tenant who had refused to pay rent for several months, claiming that the premises were uninhabitable and in violation of the Housing Code regulations. Was the tenant right? Explain.
2. A real estate broker prepared a contract for the sale of land for a seller and a buyer. A state statute makes it illegal for brokers to prepare such agreements. What two legal dangers does the broker face?
3. Assume that you want to open a retail wine and cheese specialty shop in a shopping mall that is being developed. How might you reduce competition by the terms of your lease with the mall? Explain fully.
4. An experienced veterinarian with an established practice engaged the services of an associate veterinarian. The contract provided that if the associate left, she could not practice her profession for a period of 5 years within the radius of 30 miles from the town where the two had their practice. The agreement is later terminated, and the associate claims that the provision is unenforceable. Is she right? Why or why not?
5. Ketchum sold his plant, which manufactures window frames, to Cheatham. As part of the sales contract, Ketchum agreed to refrain from manufacturing or selling window frames within a 150-mile radius of Cheatham's plant for as long as Cheatham was engaged in that business. Thereafter, Ketchum does manufacture window frames, and Cheatham sues for an injunction. Does Cheatham carry the day and romp home? Why or why not?
6. Greene worked for Company as a welder of precision titanium castings. Titanium is a reactive metal difficult to weld. Greene became certified after 20 hours of training. Later, she went to work for a competitor of Company. Company sues to enforce a "noncompetition" provision in the employment contract, which states that Greene will not go to work for a competitor of Company for a stated period. Assuming the area and time of the restraint are reasonable, should a court uphold the provision? Why or why not?
7. An action is brought against a department store because it charges a 1½ percent service charge per month on all revolving charge accounts. The usury law allows a maximum of 7½ percent per year. Is the charge usurious? Explain.
8. The Fourth of July Company agreed to ship a quantity of fireworks to Behan. After Behan pays in full, he learns that state law prohibits this type of sale. Before the fireworks are sent, Behan calls to cancel this contract and to demand his money back. May he recover his money in court? Why or why not?
9. Clifford bought a refrigerator on an installment basis from the Golden Rule Appliance Company. The contract had this clause: "In the event of default by the buyer, Golden Rule shall have the right to repossess all merchandise previously delivered to the buyer, regardless of whether payment has been made for any item." When Clifford could not pay for the refrigerator, Golden Rule repossessed the refrigerator and a washing machine that had been previously delivered and paid for. Was Golden Rule's action legal? Why or why not?
10. Mack leased a service station from Rodney Oil Company. Rodney's employee was repairing the gas pump when he negligently sprayed gasoline on Mack. The gas ignited and injured Mack. The

lease stated that Rodney was not liable for its negligence and that Mack would pay Rodney for any damages or loss caused by the oil company on the leased premises. Does Mack have to pay the oil company? Explain.

11. Mack's brother Hollis rented a trailer and hitch from the oil company. The same fellow that sprayed gas on Mack improperly attached the trailer to Hollis's car. As a result, the car overturned and Hollis was injured. The oil company denies liability because the rental agreement has a clause that relieves it from any liability in case of accident. Is the company liable to Hollis? Why or why not?

11

Contract Avoidance and Reformation

A valid contract may be rendered inoperative through the equitable remedy of *rescission.* When a party has the right to disaffirm or rescind a contract, that contract is said to be *voidable.* A party that avoids a contract will be returned to the same position that he occupied before he entered into the contract. If he has paid money and received goods or other benefit, he is entitled to return the goods or benefit and get his money back. The typical grounds for exercising the right to rescind a contract are (1) incapacity, (2) mistake, (3) fraud and misrepresentation, and (4) duress and undue influence. In some instances, a court may equitably reform rather than rescind the contract. Reformation generally is applicable when all parties to the contract are laboring under the same mistake (that is, a mutual mistake). We shall now undertake a careful study of these various ways to rescind or reform a valid contract.

Incapacity

Incapacity refers to the mental state of a party to a contract. A party lacks capacity to contract if he fails to have a full understanding of his rights and fails to have sufficient mental capacity to understand the nature, purpose, and legal effect of the contract. Capacity-to-contract issues generally involve infants, mental incompetents, and intoxicated persons. Temporary incapacity due to some phenomenon like shock may make a contract voidable.

A party without mental capacity to contract (if he has not been adjudicated insane) can avoid the contract or defend on lack of mental capacity. The contract is voidable but not void unless the incapacitated party chooses to avoid it. No other party may raise the issue. If a person has been judged insane or is totally without understanding, then the contract is void, not merely voidable. If a contract is disaffirmed by an insane person, he must return all the consideration or benefit received, assuming the other party has treated him in good faith. But if the contract is unconscionable or the other party has unfairly overreached, the incapacitated party can rescind by returning whatever he has left of the consideration received.

Minors and insane persons are presumed to lack the requisite capacity to contract. The test of insanity for avoiding a contract is different from the test of insanity for matters involving criminal intent, making a will, commitment to a mental institution, or other purposes. In contract law, the test is whether the person has sufficient mental capacity to understand the nature of the transaction. Insanity may be of a temporary nature, such as that caused by intoxication or drug addiction.

Minors' contracts

The age of majority and capacity to contract has been lowered to eighteen in most states; however, the statutory law of each state must be examined to determine the age of majority for contracts.

A person below the age of capacity is called *an infant* or *a minor*. Minors have the right to avoid contracts. The law grants minors this right in order to promote justice and to protect them from their presumed immaturity, lack of judgment and experience, limited will power, and imprudence. An adult deals with a minor at his own peril. A contract between an infant and an adult is voidable only by the infant. The right to disaffirm exists, irrespective of the fairness of the contract and whether or not the adult knew he was dealing with a minor. It even extends to contracts involving two minors.

Legislation in many states has, in a limited way, altered the right of minors to avoid their contracts. Purchase of life insurance or contracts with colleges or universities are binding, and some statutes take away the minor's right to avoid contracts after marriage. A few give the courts the right to approve contracts made by emancipated minors.

Avoiding contracts by minors

A minor has the right to disaffirm contracts; but until steps are taken to avoid the contract, the minor remains liable. A minor can disaffirm a purely executory contract by directly informing the adult of the disaffirmance or by any conduct that clearly indicates an intent to disaffirm. If the contract has been fully or partially performed, the infant also can avoid it and obtain a return of his consideration. If the infant is in possession of consideration that is passed to him, he must return it to the other party. He cannot disaffirm the contract and at the same time retain the benefits.

The courts of various states are in conflict when an infant cannot return the property he purchased in its original condition. The majority of the states hold that the infant may disaffirm the contract and demand the return of the consideration with which he has parted. A few courts, however, hold that if the contract is advantageous to the infant and if the adult has been fair in every respect, the contract cannot be disaffirmed unless the infant returns all the consideration received. These courts take into account the depreciation of the property while in the possession of the infant.

The minor may avoid both executed and executory contracts at any time during the minority and for a reasonable period of time after majority. What constitutes a reasonable time depends on the nature of the property involved and the specific circumstances. Many states establish a maximum period, such as two years, by statute.

Ratification

Ratification means "to approve and sanction, to make valid, or to confirm." It applies to the approval of a voidable transaction by one who previously had the right to disaffirm. Applied to contracts entered into by infants, it refers to conduct of a former minor after majority, conduct that indicates approval of, or satisfaction with, a contract. It eliminates the right to disaffirm.

Generally, an executed contract is ratified if the consideration is retained for an unreasonable time after majority. Ratification also results from acceptance of the benefits incidental to ownership, such as rents, dividends, or interest. A sale of the property received or any other act that clearly indicates satisfaction with the bargain made during minority will constitute a ratification. In general, a contract that is fully executory is disaffirmed by continued silence or inaction after reaching legal age. Ratification is not possible until the infant reaches legal age, because prior to that date the contract can always be avoided.

Liability for necessaries

The law recognizes that certain transactions are clearly for the benefit of minors and hence are binding upon them. The term *necessaries* is used to describe the subject matter of such contracts. A minor is not liable in contract for necessaries; the liability is in quasi contract. The fact that the liability is quasi contractual has two significant features: (1) the liability is not for the contract price of necessaries furnished, but rather for the reasonable value of the necessaries; (2) there is no liability on executory contracts, but only for necessaries actually furnished.

What are necessaries? In general, the term includes whatever is needed for a minor's subsistence as measured by his age, station in life, and all his surrounding circumstances. Food and lodging, medical services, education, and clothing are the general classifications of necessaries. It is often a close question as to whether a particular item or service is to be regarded as a necessary.

CASE

D, an infant, went to P employment agency to seek aid in finding work. D agreed to pay a fee if a job were found for him. P obtained a job for D and presented a bill for $295. D refused to pay.

ISSUE Is a contract with an employment agency a necessary?

DECISION No.

REASONS
1. The services of a professional employment agency may not be considered "necessary," so that a minor may disaffirm a contract for such services.
2. It makes no difference that D has profited by the efforts of P. P's services were advantageous to D, who clearly was in need of a job when they were rendered; however, it does not appear that they were necessary for him to earn a livelihood.

Gastonia Personnel Corp. v. Rogers, 168 S.E.2d 31 (N.C.) 1969.

Third-party rights

If an infant sells goods to an adult, the latter obtains only a voidable title to the goods. The infant can disaffirm and recover possession from the adult buyer. At common law, even a good-faith purchaser of property formerly belonging to a minor could not retain the property if the minor elected to rescind. This rule has been changed under the Code. It provides that a person with voidable title has "power to transfer a good title to a good-faith purchaser for value" [2-403]. The common-law rule, however, is still applicable to sales of real property by minors. If Minor sells his farm to Major, who in turn sells the farm to Good Faith Purchaser, Minor may avoid against Good Faith Purchaser and regain the farm. You may think that's unfair, but remember that Minor's name appears in the record books and is in the chain of title. Minor must, of course, return all consideration to Major. Major, in turn, is liable on the warranty deed to Good Faith for failing to convey clear title.

Mental incapacity

A contract is voidable by a mental incompetent or an alcoholic (or a guardian appointed for such person). An adjudicated incompetent's contracts, however, are void. The general test for determining mental competency is whether the party was capable of understanding the nature, purpose, and consequences of his acts at the time of contract formation. The Restatement (Second) of Contracts provides that a party is incompetent if he is unable to act in a reasonable manner in relation to the transaction, and the other party has reason to know of this condition. The incompetent can ratify the contract during a lucid interval or upon complete recovery even without formal restoration by judicial action.

Mistake

A mistake is a state of mind that is not in accord with the facts. A variety of mistakes may occur at various stages of a commercial transaction. They may involve errors in arithmetic or in setting forth the terms of the contract; the mistake may be bilateral (both parties are mistaken) or unilateral (only one party is laboring under a mistake).

In order that a mistake by one or both of the parties may warrant relief to either of them, the mistake must be a material one. The relief afforded by virtue of the mistake will depend upon a number of factors, including the point of time at which the mistake is discovered, the extent to which performance has already progressed, the extent to which one or the other of the parties has changed his position in reliance on the contract before the mistake was discovered, and the extent to which the parties can be restored to the status quo.

Bilateral mistake

The word *bilateral* in the law of mistakes means a two-sided or mutual mistake. All parties to the contract have made a factual assumption that is false. To have a bilateral mistake, all parties must be laboring under the same (identical) mistake. If a bilateral mistake is present, courts will first try to reform the contract so that it will reflect the true intentions and expectations of all parties. If the contract cannot be reformed, then the court will give either party the right to avoid the contract and thereby return to the state existing before the contract. Avoidance may be denied if the other party, relying on the contract, has changed his position to the extent that he cannot be restored to his former position. Two people enter into a buy-sell contract for a racehorse named Stewball, which both parties believe to be stabled in the next town. Both parties are unaware that the horse has perished in a fire. Since the contract cannot be reformed, the court will find that no contract exists unless one party was at fault in causing the horse's death. Thus, when the subject matter of the contract has been destroyed prior to the date of the agreement, no contract results, because there is no meeting of the minds.

The usual case for mutual mistake involves an agreement made more burdensome by the mistake. The agreement then may be voidable. There are also cases in which the language used in the contract is clearly subject to two interpretations, and each party construes it differently. Assume that floor covering for certain rooms is sold for a lump sum on the assumption by both parties that only a certain number of square feet is involved. If the area is substantially greater than both parties thought to be true, the contract is voidable at instance of the seller.

In the transaction of business, it is customary in many situations to dispose of property about which the contracting parties willingly admit that all the facts are not known. In such instances, the property is sold without regard to its quality or characteristics. Such agreements may not be rescinded if later the property appears to have characteristics that neither of the parties had reason to suspect or if it otherwise differs from their expectations. Under such conditions the property forms the subject matter of the agreement, regardless of its nature. If shortly after a farm is sold, a valuable deposit of ore is discovered on it, the agreement could not be rescinded by the seller on the grounds of mutual mistake.

Unilateral mistake

When only one party is laboring under a mistake, it is said to be a unilateral (one-sided) mistake. Generally, a contract entered into because of some mistake or error by only one party affords no relief to that party. The majority of such mistakes result from carelessness or lack of diligence by the mistaken party and therefore should not affect the rights of the other party. If the nonmistaken party knows that the other party is mistaken but ignorant of his mistake, then courts may allow the mistaken party to avoid the contract. NOTE: only the avoidance remedy is available. As will be later explained, reformation is not an available remedy, since it can be used only to correct the written contract to reflect the actual intentions of both parties. Reformation is available only for a case of mutual mistake. The general rule for unilateral mistake is that the contract is generally not avoidable. But if the nonmistaken party knows about the mistake, then the party who is unaware of his mistake has a right to avoid the contract. The contract is said to be voidable at the will of the mistaken party when the other party is the only one of the two who knows of the mistake.

As the discussion of both bilateral and unilateral mistakes suggests, the court will deny relief to a party who negligently causes his mistake or will grant relief when the nonmistaken party unfairly has knowledge while the other is ignorant of his mistake. In mistake cases, courts thus make decisions on notions of risk analysis; that is, who *ought* to bear the risk-of-loss caused by the mistake. In allocating the risk to one or both parties,courts are influenced by the negligence, conscious ignorance, and unequal knowledge of the mistake by any party. Two classic examples will help show you this process of risk allocation.

Mistake in value

Since it is difficult to know the true value of any item, the law presumes that parties bargain over price, and their agreement establishes the value of the item. You are well aware of the saying that value is "whatever the market will bear." Consequently, no relief is granted for either a mutual or unilateral mistake in value. If you buy 100 shares of stock with the assumption that they will increase in value, and the stock later declines, this unilateral mistake in value goes unremedied. That's a risk you assumed.

PROBLEM: A woman finds a yellow stone about the size of a bird's egg and thinks it might be a gem. She takes it to a jeweler who honestly states that he is not sure what the stone is. Nonetheless, he offers her $15 for the stone, and she sells it. The stone is later discovered to be an uncut diamond worth $3,000. *RESULT:* No relief will be granted. There was no mistake of fact, only of value. Both parties bargained on the basis of conscious ignorance, both thereby assuming the risk that the stone might be worth nothing or might be a valuable gem. *RULE:* When parties are uncertain or consciously ignorant of the qualities of the thing sold, there is no right of avoidance for mistake.

Mistake in quality

In contrast to the rule on mistakes in value, courts do allow rescission (or possibly reformation) for mutual mistakes concerning the quality of the thing sold. Again, it is a matter of risk allocation. *PROBLEM:* Buyer and seller both mistakenly believed a cow of excellent breeding stock to be sterile. The cow was sold for beef at a price far below what she would otherwise have brought for breeding purposes. *RESULT:* When the mistake became apparent, the seller wanted to rescind. The parties were not negligent in being mistaken, nor were they consciously ignorant. Both parties thought they knew what they were buying and selling. But what they bought and sold was in fact not what they contemplated buying and selling. A sterile cow is substantially different from a breeding cow. There is as much difference between them as between an ox and a cow. Since there is no good basis to place the risk of the mistake on either party, the contract is voidable for mutual mistake. *RULE:* A mutual mistake regarding the quality of the item sold, a quality that goes to its very essence, is grounds for avoiding a contract.

CASE

P, a coin dealer, sues to rescind a purchase by D, who paid $500 for a dime both parties thought was minted in 1916 at Denver. P asserts a mutual mistake of fact as to the genuineness of the coin as Denver-minted. D contends the mistake is to value only.

ISSUE Is this a mutual mistake in value for which no relief is granted or is the mistake a mutual one regarding the qualities of the subject matter?

DECISION Rescission for mutual mistake of fact granted.

REASONS

1. It is undisputed that both parties believed the coin was a genuine one from the Denver Mint. The mistake was mutual, since both parties were laboring under the same misapprehension regarding the material fact of genuineness.
2. It is well established that a party to a contract can assume the risk of being mistaken regarding the value of the thing sold. For that rule to apply, both parties must be conscious that the material fact may not be true, and they must base their contract on that possibility. The risk of the existence of the doubtful fact is then assumed as one of the elements of the bargain. In this case, however, both parties were certain that the coin was genuine. Rescission is allowed. A different case would be presented if either party were uncertain regarding genuineness of coin or of its value as genuine.

Beachcomber Coins, Inc. v. Boskett, 400 A.2d 78 (N.J.) 1979.

Reformation of written contracts

In most instances a written contract is preceded by negotiations between the parties who agree orally upon the terms to be set forth in the final written contract. This is certainly the case when the parties contemplate a written statement signed by both as necessary to a binding agreement; that is, the oral agreement was not itself to have binding effect. Of course, the parties could intend otherwise. They could regard the oral agreement as binding without any writing, or they could regard the writing as simply a subsequent memorial of their oral agreement.

Suppose the written agreement that is finally executed by the parties contains a mistake. The signed writing does not conform to what the parties agreed to orally. Frequently, the draftsman or typist may make an error that is not discovered prior to the signing of the contract, and the party benefiting from the error seeks to hold the other party to the agreement as written. For such situations, courts of equity provide a remedy known as reformation.

CASE

P (seller) seeks to reform a sales contract in which D (buyer) promised to buy a 1975 tractor for $34,756. D was to receive a $12,000 trade-in allowance for his 1973 tractor. Both parties knew that there was a $15,000 lien on D's 1973 tractor. By mutual mistake, the amount of the lien was incorrectly stated as only $3,000 instead of $15,000. The contract then gave D credit for his trade-in in the amount of $9,000 instead of minus $3,000. P sues to reform the contract to correct the error on the trade-in credit.

ISSUE Is P entitled to reformation?

DECISION Yes.

REASONS P alleged facts from which it appeared that the contract did not conform to the parties' intentions and agreement, and thus an action for reformation is proper. Courts will reform contracts and deeds in accordance with the true intention of the parties when their intentions have been frustrated by mutual mistake in reducing their agreement to writing.

All Brake and Drive Unit Service, Inc. v. Peterson, 388 N.E.2d 93 (Ill.) 1979.

Fraud and Misrepresentation

A contract is voidable if one party has been induced and injured by reliance on the other's misrepresentation of a material fact. The misrepresentation may be intentional, in which case the law considers the misrepresentation to be *fraudulent.* It may be unintentional, in which case there has been no fraud but only innocent misrepresentation. In both cases, the victim of the misrepresentation may rescind the contract. In the case of fraudulent misrepresentation, the victim is given the choice of the additional remedy of a suit for dollar damages.

While the elements of actionable fraud are stated differently from state to state, the following are those generally required:

1. *Scienter,* or intention to mislead. *Scienter* means knowledge of the falsity, or statements made with such utter recklessness and disregard for the truth that knowledge is inferred.
2. A false representation or the concealment of a material fact.
3. Justifiable reliance on the false statement or concealment.
4. Injury as a consequence of the reliance.

Innocent misrepresentation does not require proof of *scienter* but does require proof of all the other elements of fraud. The absence of *scienter* is the reason that a suit for dollar damages cannot be based on an innocent misrepresentation.

Rescission is permitted only in case the defrauded party acts with reasonable promptness after he learns of the falsity of the representation. Undue delay on his part waives his right to rescind, thus limiting the defrauded party to an action for recovery of damages. A victim of fraud loses his right to rescind if, after having acquired knowledge of the fraud, he indicates an intention to affirm the contract. These principles result from the fact that rescission is an equitable remedy.

Scienter

The requirement of intent to mislead is often referred to as *scienter,* a Latin word meaning "knowingly." *Scienter* may be present in circumstances other than the typical false statement made with actual intent to deceive. *Scienter* may be found when there has been a concealment of a material fact. Moreover, a statement that is partially or even literally true may be fraudulent in law if it is made in order to create a substantially false impression. Intention to mislead may also be established by showing that a statement was made with reckless disregard of truth. An accountant who certifies that financial statements accurately reflect the financial condition of a company may be guilty of fraud if he has no basis for the statement. Perhaps he does not intend to mislead, but his statement is so reckless that the intention is inferred from the lack of actual knowledge.

CASE

Four oral surgeons appeal an order suspending their licenses to practice because they submitted false claims to Blue Shield. The surgeons argued that the clerical staff is responsible for filing claims and that there is no evidence that any of them knowingly or with fraudulent intent made a false claim.

ISSUE Is the *scienter* requirement met in this case?

DECISION Yes.

REASONS

1. There is no evidence that the submission of false claims was the responsibility of the clerical staff. Moreover, this argument is ludicrous, since the dentists assumed full responsibility for all claims submitted over their signature to Blue Shield.
2. The dentists are responsible for the submission of false claims by reason of their reckless ignorance or because of their special circumstances.
3. The practice at their clinic indicates a reckless ignorance of the falsity of the claim. Fraud may be proven by showing false representations made knowingly or recklessly.
4. Fraud may also be proven where a duty to know of the false representations is imposed by special circumstances. Dentists who sign claims for compensation for oral surgery, thereby giving their approval, are acting in special circumstances.

Miller, D.D.S. et al. v. Pa. State Dental Council and Examining Bd., 396 A.2d 83 (Pa.) 1979.

False representation

To establish fraud, there must be an actual or implied misrepresentation of a fact. The misstatement of fact must be material or significant to the extent that it has a moving influence upon a contracting party, but it need not be the sole inducing cause for entering into the contract.

False statements in matters of opinion, such as the value of property, are not factual and are usually not considered actionable. An intentional misstatement even with regard to value may be fraudulent if the person making the statement has another opinion and knowingly states a false opinion. This concept is sometimes used when the person who is allegedly fraudulent is an expert, such as a physician, or when the parties stand in a fiduciary relationship (a position of trust) to each other. Assume that a doctor, after examining a patient for an insurance company physical, states that he is of the opinion that the person has no physical disability. If his actual opinion is that the patient has cancer, the doctor is guilty of fraud. He has misstated a fact (his professional opinion). The same is true if a partner sells property to the firm of which he is a member. His false statement of opinion concerning the value of the property will supply the misstatement-of-fact element. Each partner is a fiduciary toward his fellow partners and the firm, and he must give honest opinions.

The misstatement may be oral and may in fact be partly true. A half-truth (or partial truth) that has the net effect of misleading may form the basis of fraud, just as if it were entirely false. A partial truth in response to a request for information becomes an untruth whenever it creates a false impression and is designed to do so.

An intentional misrepresentation of existing local or state law affords no basis for rescission, because it is not a statement of fact in the technical sense. Statements of law are traditionally seen as assertions of opinion. The present tendency is strongly in favor of recognizing that a statement of law, like most statements, may be intended and understood (according to the circumstances) as one of fact or one of opinion.

A misrepresentation may be made by conduct as well as by language. Any physical act that attempts to hide vital facts relating to property involved in the contract is, in effect, a misstatement. One who turns back the odometer on a car, fills a motor with heavy grease to keep it from knocking, or paints over an apparent defect asserts an untruth as effectively as if he were speaking. Such conduct, if it misleads the other party, amounts to fraud and makes rescission or an action for damages possible.

CASE

P sued D to recover actual and punitive damages for fraud in the sale of a used car. The mileage on the odometer at the time of sale was 34,676 miles. The previous owner testified that the car had 74,624 miles when it was traded in.

ISSUE Was D's conduct fraudulent and was P entitled to punitive damages?

DECISION Yes to both questions.

REASONS
1. A representation is not confined to words or positive assertions; it may consist of deeds, acts, or artifices calculated to mislead another and to allow the fraudulent party to obtain an undue advantage over him.
2. The term *fraud* embraces all multifarious means employed by one individual to take advantage of another by false suggestions or suppression of truth, including all surprises, tricks, cunning, disassembling, mechanical alterations, and unfair ways by which another is cheated.
3. P was entitled to $200 actual damages and $7,000 punitive damages.

Cates v. Darland, 537 P.2d 336 (Okl.) 1975.

Silence as fraud

Historically, the law of contracts has followed caveat emptor, especially in real estate transactions. The parties to a contract are required to exercise ordinary business sense in their dealings. As a result, the general rule is that silence in the absence of a duty to speak does not constitute fraud.

In at least three situations there is a duty to speak the truth, and failure to do so will constitute actionable fraud. First of all, there is a duty to speak when the parties stand in a fiduciary relationship (the trust that should exist among partners in a partnership, between a director and a corporation, or between an agent and a principal). Because such parties do not deal "at arm's length," there is the duty to speak and to make a full disclosure of all facts.

The second duty is based on justice, equity, and fair dealing. This duty occurs when a vital fact is known by one party but not the other; had it been known, there would have been no contract. While this concept is difficult to define or describe, it is not difficult to apply on a case-by-case basis, especially when the suit is in equity for rescission. When there is a latent defect in property (one not apparent upon inspection), the vendor has a duty to inform the purchaser of the defect. Failure to do so is fraudulent.

CASE

P's (home buyers) sue D (real estate broker) for intentional concealment of termites on the property bought by P's. D represented to P's that the property was "a good sound house" and was a good investment. Later and prior to the actual sale, D learned that the house had considerable termite infestation but failed to disclose that fact to P's. Within a few days after they signed the contract of sale, P's discovered the termites and paid $5,980 to correct the damage.

ISSUE Does D's failure to inform P's of the termites constitute a fraud?

DECISION Yes.

REASONS
1. A party is under a duty to speak and is liable for concealment if he fails to disclose a material fact that justifiably induces the other party to act, and the nondisclosing party knows that the concealment will render a prior statement untrue or misleading.
2. When informed of the termites, D's nondisclosure made the earlier representation subject to a material qualification. This nondisclosure, coupled with the hidden nature of the termites, entitled P's to rely on D's earlier representation regarding the soundness of the property and imposed a duty on D to disclose.

Miles v. Perpetual Savings & Loan Co., 388 N.E.2d 1367 (Ohio) 1979.

The third duty is that of a person who has misstated an important fact on some previous occasion and is obligated to correct the statement when negotiations are renewed or as soon as he learns about his misstatement. This is not a true exception to the silence rule, because there is in fact a positive misstatement.

The gist of these exceptions is that one of the parties has the erroneous impression that certain things are true, whereas the other party is aware that they are not true and also knows of the misunderstanding. It therefore becomes his duty to disclose the truth. Unless he does so, most courts would hold that fraud exists. This does not mean that a potential seller or buyer has to disclose all the facts about the value of property he is selling or buying. It is only when he knows that the other party to the agreement is harboring a misunderstanding on some vital matter that the duty to speak arises.

Before a false statement can be considered fraudulent, the party to whom it has been made must reasonably believe it to be true and must act on it, to his damage. If he investigates before he acts upon it, and the falsity is revealed, no action can be brought for fraud. The cases are in conflict concerning the need to investigate. Some courts have indicated that if all the information is readily available for ascertaining the truth of the statements, blind reliance upon the misrepresentation is not justified. In such a case, the party is said to be negligent in not taking advantage of the facilities available for confirming the statement.

Justifiable reliance

CASE

P bought a newspaper and printing business from D. Thereafter, P sought to rescind the contract on the grounds that D had misrepresented the financial condition of the business. P was in possession of certain financial documents that were inconsistent, on their face, pertaining to the financial affairs of the business.

ISSUE Was P entitled to rely upon D's statements about the financial condition of the business?

DECISION No.

REASON P could tell from the inconsistencies in the documents that something was wrong. He should therefore have investigated. Since he did not, he was not entitled to rely on the accuracy of the statements.

Jahraus v. Bergquist, 494 P.2d 110 (Colo.) 1972.

If a party inspects property or has an opportunity to do so, and if a reasonable investigation would have revealed that the property was not as it had been represented, he cannot be considered misled. On the other hand, some courts deny that there is any need to investigate. They hold that one who has misrepresented facts cannot avoid the legal consequences by saying in effect: "You should not have believed me. You should have checked as to whether or not what I told you was true." Generally, reliance is justified when substantial effort or expense is required to determine the actual facts. The standard of justified reliance is not whether a reasonably prudent man would be justified in relying but whether the particular individual involved had a right to rely. In any case, the issue of whether or not the reliance is justified is for the jury.

In order to prevail, the party relying upon the misstatement must offer proof of resulting damage. Normally, resulting damage is proved by evidence that the property in question would have been more valuable had the statements been true. Injury results when the party is not in as good a position as he would have been had the statements been true.

Injury or damage

In an action for damages for fraud, the plaintiff may seek to recover damages on either of two theories. He may use the "benefit of the bargain" theory and seek the difference between the actual market value of what he received and the value if he had received what was represented. A plaintiff may also use the "out-of-pocket" theory and collect the difference between the actual value of what was received and its purchase price.

Perhaps the most significant aspect of a suit for dollar damages is that the victim of fraud is entitled to punitive damages in addition to compensatory damages. If the fraudulent representations are made maliciously, willfully, wantonly, or so recklessly that they imply a disregard of social obligations, punitive damages as determined by a jury may be awarded. (Refer to *Cates v. Darland,* the third case back.)

Duress and undue influence

Equity allows a party to rescind an agreement that was not entered into voluntarily. The lack of free will may take the form of duress or undue influence. A person who has obtained property under such circumstances should not in good conscience be allowed to keep it. A person may lose his free will because of duress (some threat to his person, family, or property). Or with more subtle pressure, one person may overpower the will of another by moral or social force rather than by physical or economic force. Cases of undue influence frequently arise in situations involving the elderly. In cases in which free will is lacking, some courts hold that the minds of the parties did not meet. If a person has free choice, there is no duress, even though some pressure may have been exerted upon him. A threat of a lawsuit is not duress that will allow rescission. Under certain circumstances, economic pressure may constitute duress.

CASE

P corporation was awarded a $6 million contract by the navy for the production of radar sets. It was a very severe contract that imposed substantial penalties for late deliveries and gave the navy the right to cancel in case of default by P corporation. P corporation entered into a contract with D corporation, whereby the latter agreed to furnish many of the components. After making some deliveries, D corporation refused to deliver any more unless the price was increased. Being unable to get the components elsewhere, P corporation acceded to the demand. Later P sued to have the increased price set aside.

ISSUE Did the facts warrant a finding of duress, so that the contract was voidable?

DECISION Yes.

REASONS

1. A contract is voidable for duress when it is established that the party making the claim was forced to agree to it by means of a wrongful threat precluding the exercise of free will.
2. The existence of economic duress or business compulsion is demonstrated by proof that immediate possession of needful goods is threatened. It should be noted that a mere threat by one party to breach the contract by not delivering the required items, though wrongful, does not in itself constitute economic duress.
3. It must appear that (1) the threatened party could not obtain the goods from another source of supply and (2) the ordinary remedy of an action for breach of contract would not be adequate.

Austin Instrument, Inc. v. Loral Corporation, 272 N.E.2d 533 (N.Y.) 1971.

REVIEW QUESTIONS AND PROBLEMS

1. Ian, age 17, lied about his age so that he could charge a full-fare plane ticket. The airline offered a half-fare flight to anyone under 18, but that required cash; Ian needed credit, which was available to adults only. When Ian arrived at his destination, his grandfather reimbursed him for the ticket. That surprise led Ian to disaffirm the loan contract. The airline sued. What was the result? Explain.

2. A minor sold a painting for $200. Upon reaching majority, he discovered that the painting he sold was worth $2,000. He sued to recover the painting. What was the result? Explain. Would the result change if he waited 2 months after reaching majority? Two years?

3. Leon, an infant, signed a contract with Step-Up Employment Agency, in which Leon promised to pay a fee if Step-Up secured him a job as a pianist. Step-Up did find suitable employment, but Leon refused to pay the $500 fee, since he was a minor. Can Step-Up recover the fee? Why or why not?

4. Slick, to no avail, had long sought Plenty's Stradivarius violin. One night Slick plied Plenty with food and drink and persuaded him to agree to sell the violin for a reasonable price. Sober now, Plenty wants to disaffirm. Can he? Explain.

5. After making a visual inspection, Buyer bought property from Seller and proceeded to build a home. When the possibility of soil slippage soon became apparent, construction was halted. Buyer sued Seller to rescind the sale. Soil Expert testified that the property was not suitable for the construction of a residence. Seller was unaware of the stability hazard of the soil when the sale was transacted. Could Buyer rescind? Why or why not?

6. Sarah Jane bought a used car from Tricky Dick. The bill of sale showed that the car was a 1972 Oldsmobile, when, in fact, the car was really a 1971 Oldsmobile. Tricky was aware that the car was a 1971 model. Can Sarah Jane rescind this transaction? Why or why not?

7. A representative for a data-processing company bought a computer after the computer salesperson assured her that the machine would be adequate for her purposes. The data-processing representative was aware of the specifications of the computer, but she later discovered that its printout was too slow for her company's needs. She seeks to rescind the contract on the basis of misrepresentation. With what result? Explain.

8. Brad purchased a residential lot from Hubert. Subsequently, Brad learned that the lot had been filled. The existence of the fill was not mentioned during the negotiations nor did Brad make any inquiry. May Brad successfully sue to rescind the contract? Why or why not?

9. Big Electric Power Company formulated a plan to acquire a large area of land for a hydroelectric project. Harion owned 138 acres of land in the area. Burroughs, an undisclosed agent of the power company, offered to buy Harion's land. To Harion's inquiry about why Burroughs wanted the land, Burroughs falsely replied he had just come into a large sum of money that he wanted to invest in land. They then executed a buy-sale contract with a purchase price of $4,100. Alleging that he would have asked $27,000 if he had known the power company to be the real buyer, Harion sues to rescind. Does he win? Explain.

10. Jimmy borrowed money from the Core Credit Corporation and signed a security agreement as collateral. When the loan was not repaid on the due date, Core told Jimmy that it would enforce its rights under the security agreement unless a renewal note giving additional collateral was signed. If Jimmy refused, he would be in default. Core could foreclose, which would bankrupt Jimmy. Jimmy signed. Later, he was unable to meet either the original or renewal obligation. If Core sues, can Jimmy successfully raise the defense that the renewal note was voidable for duress? Why or why not?

12

Contract Performance and Breach

We have now encountered most of the basic issues in contract law. First, there has to be an agreement consisting of offer and acceptance. Second, the agreement must be validated by a device like bargained-for consideration. Finally, the valid agreement should not be legally unenforceable owing to defenses based on form, public policy, fair dealing, and the like. Assuming a valid contract exists without any defense to its formation, the next grouping of contract issues concerns performance under that contract. Whereas courts might apply strict rules of law to offer, acceptance, and consideration issues, they are more flexible in adjudicating disputes concerning contract breach at the performance stage. The point to remember is that courts as a matter of policy adopt rules that encourage contract performance and are more tolerant of "faulty" performances. Courts use a number of excuses to allow a defaulting party to recover for whatever performance has occurred.

The most basic issue at the performance stage that a court must resolve is whether or not there has been a *breach* (material or immaterial) of the contract. Obviously, if there is no breach, then the contract has been performed, and no party can claim any damage. To resolve the issue of contract breach, courts confront two questions. (1) Does any party owe a current duty to perform? The answer to that question involves the law of *conditions.* If no one has a duty to perform, obviously there is no issue of breach of contract. Moreover, if someone has a duty to perform and does so, then there is no issue other than damages to be recovered. But if someone has a present duty to perform and does not do so or performs in an unworkmanlike manner, the issue then is: (2) What are the rights of a defaulting party?

To avoid hardship to the party in default or to prevent unjust enrichment of the other party who has received some performance, courts may allow some relief to a party who fails fully to perform. That relief comes in either of two ways. First, the unconditional duty to perform may be said to have been satisfied either by the doctrine of substantial performance or by the doctrine of divisibility. Second, the unconditional duty may be legally excused. Courts may use six devices to excuse the defaulting party: (1) hindrance, prevention, or noncooperation; (2) waiver, estoppel, or election; (3) anticipatory repudiation; (4) impossibility; (5) commercial impracticability under the Code; and (6) frustration of purpose.

Although the ultimate issue at the performance stage is one of material breach, the real issues lie in other legal concepts. The thrust of this chapter concerns the subsidiary issues that determine whether a material or immaterial breach has occurred. Thus, the focus will be on the law of conditions and on ways courts might protect a defaulting party. Again, the two subsidiary issues are: (1) Does any party owe a duty to perform? (2) What are the rights of a defaulting party?

Conditions

A condition is an act or event (other than a lapse of time) that, unless excused, must occur before performance under a contract becomes due. A legislator promises to pay a constituent $150 next year on July 4th. Since the only event that must occur before she is obligated to pay $150 is a lapse of time, her promise is unconditional. If the legislator promises to pay the constituent $150 on July 4th of next year only if it rains on that date, then the promise is conditional. The duty to pay arises only if the condition (rain) happens on the stated date.

Conditions distinguished from promises

Liability for breach of contract cannot be imposed upon a party unless he makes a promise and breaches it. Furthermore, liability cannot be imposed on a party for the failure of a condition to occur unless the party has promised to cause the condition to occur. There is no exclusive or conclusive test to determine whether a particular contractual provision is a promise or a condition. Although no particular words are necessary for the existence of a condition, terms such as *if, provided that, on condition that,* and others that condition a party's performance usually connote an intent for a condition rather than a promise. In the absence of a clause expressly creating a condition, whether a certain contractual provision is a condition rather than a promise must be gathered from the contract as a whole and from the intent of the parties.

Conditions determine when a party has to perform. Many promises are unconditional and absolute, so the party has an immediate duty to perform. Where the promise is unconditional, the failure to perform pursuant to its terms will be a breach of contract unless the duty is excused. Where a promise is conditional, the duty is dormant or unactivated until the condition occurs. A duty to perform is conditional if something other than the passage of time must occur before the duty becomes absolute; that is, becomes activated. The promise becomes absolute by the occurrence of the condition. Example: I promise to pay you $100 on October 1st. Since the only event that must occur before I am obligated to pay is the passage of time, my promise is unconditional; that is, absolute and dependent. Example: I promise to pay you $100 on October 1st if the Atlanta Braves win the pennant. My promise is conditional and dependent. My duty to perform is activated and becomes absolute only if the Braves win the pennant.

Classification of conditions

Conditions are classified in two ways: (1) by time—*when* the conditioning event must occur in relation to the promise. Under this division, conditions are labeled as *conditions precedent, concurrent conditions,* and *conditions subsequent;* (2) by manner of creation—whether the parties create the condition (*express condition*) or whether the court creates the condition based on equitable considerations of adjusting the rights and duties of the parties (*constructive conditions*).

Conditions Precedent, Concurrent, and Subsequent

Conditions precedent

A condition precedent is a fact that, unless excused, must exist or occur before a duty of immediate performance of a promise arises. It usually takes the form of performance by the other party. Contracts often expressly provide that one party must perform before there is a right to performance by the other party. The first party's performance is a *condition precedent* to the duty of the other party to perform. Since one party must perform before the other is under a duty to do so, the failure of the first party to perform permits the other to refuse to perform and to cancel the contract and sue for damages.

Not all the terms that impose a duty of performance on a person are of sufficient importance to constitute conditions precedent. As a general rule, if a provision is relatively insignificant, its performance is not required before recovery may be obtained from the other party. In such cases, the party who was to receive performance merely deducts the damages caused by the breach. Determining whether the breach of a particular provision is so material that it justifies rescission is a construction problem. If the damage caused by the breach can be readily measured in money, or if the nature of the contract has not been so altered that it defeats the justifiable expectations of the party entitled to performance, the clause breached is generally not considered a condition precedent.

CASE

P sought to rescind a contract for the construction of a house to be built by D. D failed to follow certain specifications: (1) bathroom fixtures were white rather than colored, (2) sealdown shingles were used instead of T-lock shingles, (3) only the front was brick instead of an all-brick exterior, and (4) there was a two-inch bow in the foundation.

ISSUE Does D's deviation from the specifications justify rescission by P?

DECISION Yes.

REASONS
1. Not every breach gives rise to the right to rescind a contract. In order to warrant rescission of a contract the breach must be material and the failure to perform so substantial that it defeats the object of the parties in making the agreement. Obviously, the variance in the appearance of the bathroom fixtures is not so substantial that it would constitute a material breach of contract.
2. The variance in the shingles and the brick veneer are entirely different matters. We are inclined to agree with plaintiffs that there was a material breach of the contract. Substantial variations such as shown here entitle the purchaser to rescind the contract.

Whiteley v. O'Dell, 548 P.2d 798 (Kan.) 1976.

If, in the foregoing case, the contractor had substantially followed all of the specifications but had completed the work ten days late, rescission would not have been justified. Such a breach is of minor importance. The purchaser would have been required to pay the contract price less any damages sustained because of the delay. It is often difficult to judge whether the breach of a particular provision is so material that it justifies rescission. If the damage caused by the breach can be readily measured in money, and if the other party receives basically what he was entitled to under the contract, the clause breached is not considered a condition precedent.

Concurrent conditions

If parties are to exchange performances at the same time, their performances are concurrently conditioned. "I promise to sell you my car for $700 on April 1st." Payment of $700 and tender of the car are concurrent conditions of exchange. Since a contract seldom states that performances are simultaneously conditioned on one another, courts will generally find constructive concurrent conditions if both parties can perform simultaneously. Suppose, in the example above, no date for performance was set. In that case, nobody could demand that the other perform until he or she has performed or tendered performance. Each party's performance is constructively conditioned on concurrent performance by the other party. Conceptually, you may think of concurrent conditions as making each party's duty to perform as a condition precedent to the other.

The condition subsequent

A condition subsequent stated in the contract is an event that discharges a duty of performance that has become absolute. In an insurance contract you might find the following example: "In the event of accident or loss, written notice containing all particulars shall be given by the insured to the Insurer as soon as practicable. No action shall be brought after the expiration of 12 months from the occurrence of any loss." The insurance company's duty to pay under the policy does not arise (become absolute) until the insured gives notice. The requirement of notice is an express condition precedent. Failure to bring suit within 12 months will discharge the absolute duty. This requirement is an express condition subsequent. Note that conditions subsequent are rare.

Express and Constructive Conditions

Conditions can be classified also according to the way they are created. This method of classification recognizes three types of conditions: (1) express conditions specifically set out in the contract as activating or discharging duties; (2) implied-in-fact conditions, which a reasonable person understands to be implied by the parties in their contract; (3) constructive conditions (or implied-in-law conditions), which the parties purportedly did not consider but the court imposes by construction, to achieve fundamental fairness between the parties.

Constructive conditions are created by courts; express and implied-in-fact conditions are created by the parties, either expressly or by implication in the written contract. Therefore, it might be easier to think in terms of two types of conditions: (1) court-created (constructive) and (2) party-created (express or implied). When the parties create the condition, courts ordinarily will tolerate less deviation in the occurrence of the event than if the condition is constructive. Hence, the traditional rule is that strict compliance with an express condition is required, but only substantial compliance is required with a constructive condition.

Interpretation of promises and conditions

The form of relief available to the nonbreaching party depends on the interpretation of a contract provision. For that reason, it is of great importance to determine if a provision is a condition, promise, or promise and condition. An action for postive relief (breach of contract) is available for breach of a promise. But the failure of an express condition excuses only performance; it provides no legal action for damages. Suppose you agree to buy and I agree to sell fireworks for $500. The contract states: "The goods to be shipped by U.P.S. on or before July 1st." The goods are shipped on July 5th, which is a material delay. How could a court interpret the quoted phrase? There are at least three possible interpretations. (1) *Express condition* (i.e., an implied-in-fact condition in this example): Since the condition did not occur to activate your duty to pay, you have no such duty. Therefore, I cannot sue you for not accepting and paying for the fireworks. But you cannot sue me, since I made no promise to ship on July 1st. (2) *Promise only:* This interpretation allows you to sue for breach of promise to ship on July 1st. But you must also pay for the goods, since your duty is not conditioned on shipment by July 1st. (3) *Both condition and promise:* Now you can sue me, but you cannot be sued, since your promise to pay is conditional. Assuming no special facts, most courts adopt the last interpretation.

Express conditions

An express condition is included in a contract and designated as a condition that must be strictly performed before the other party's duty to perform arises. The penalty for failure to perform an express condition properly may be the loss of the right to receive payment or otherwise to obtain the return performance. The parties may stipulate that something is a condition precedent, even though it would not ordinarily be considered so. If that stipulation is made, failure to perform exactly as specified affords ground for rescission, unless the court construes the clause to be a penalty provision and therefore unenforceable.

A contract may provide that "time is of the essence of this agreement." This means that performance on or before the date specified is a condition precedent to the duty of the other party to pay or to perform. Another common express condition precedent, found in many construction contracts, provides that the duty of the owner to make the final payment on completion of the building is conditioned upon the builder's securing an architect's certificate. This is certification by the owner's architect that the construction is satisfactory and in accordance with the plans and specifications. Thus, the condition is, to a large degree, outside the control of both parties and within the exclusive control of a third party, the architect.

Conditions of personal satisfaction

A common provision in many contracts expressly conditions a party's performance on his personal satisfaction with the other party's performance. Suppose that Wyeth agrees to paint your portrait to your personal satisfaction for $20,000. When he is finished, you say that you are not satisfied with it and refuse to pay the $20,000. The condition precedent of your personal satisfaction, you argue, has not happened, to activate your duty to pay. Do you think it would make any difference if 50 art experts state that the portrait is a masterpiece? To answer that question and to avoid unfair forfeitures, the law has adopted rules involving two categories of satisfaction cases: (1) situations involving personal taste, fancy, or judgment (subjective dissatisfaction) and (2) situations involving mechanical fitness, utility, or marketability (objective dissatisfaction).

When the satisfaction condition concerns your individual taste or judgment, as in the case of Wyeth's painting, the law requires that you be genuinely dissatisfied. Your dissatisfaction must be honest and in good faith, which is a subjective fact question. If you are dissatisfied with the bargain (paying $20,000), however, then you are refusing to pay in bad faith. The condition in that case is excused. The testimony of the art experts can therefore be used as circumstantial evidence of bad faith. This fact issue is given to the jury to determine.

When the satisfaction condition concerns something like construction or repair that can be measured objectively, the law requires reasonable rather than personal satisfaction. If the average person would be satisfied (reasonable, objective satisfaction), then you must pay, despite the fact that you might be personally dissatisfied. Thus, performance that is objectively satisfactory must be paid for, notwithstanding personal (subjective) dissatisfaction.

Implied-in-fact conditions

An implied-in-fact condition is not stated expressly in the agreement but nonetheless is understood by the average person to be implied by the parties in their contract. Even though the contract does not expressly provide that "time is of the essence" in an agreement, one might fairly conclude that the parties implied that time of performance was very material. Failure to perform on time in such cases may be a material breach.

CASE

On May 14, 1973, P entered into a contract to purchase a motor vehicle from D, an auto dealer, and paid $1,000 down. P informed D that he intended to use the vehicle for camping during the summer. The vehicle was to be delivered in June, but no delivery was made through August. P seeks to cancel the contract and to obtain a refund of the $1,000.

ISSUE Is time of the essence in this agreement (an implied-in-fact condition precedent)?

DECISION Yes.

REASON Plaintiff's known intent to use the vehicle for camping during the summer made timely performance necessary, and failure to make delivery was a material breach of contract.

Hedrick v. Goodwin Brothers, Inc., 325 N.E.2d 73 (Ill. App.) 1975.

Constructive conditions

In a bilateral contract, one party can perform, regardless of what the other party does, although, in many cases it would be very inequitable to require one party to perform without requiring the other to perform. Thus, in the interest of fairness, to assure that all parties will get what they bargained for, courts make performances of promises constructively conditional on one another. In an employment contract, one must work before getting paid. Thus, working is a constructive condition precedent, which must occur to activate the duty to pay an employee. The following indicate typical instances in which the rule applies.

Constructive condition precedent

When the contract provides that one performance must occur before the other (or such is understood by custom), the former is a constructive condition precedent to the latter. Also, when one performance can be performed in an instant, but the other will take time, the performance of the one that will take time is a constructive condition precedent to the other. When a contractor promises to build a house for an owner, who will pay him $75,000, a court will construe the contractor's performance as a condition that must happen in order to activate the owner's duty to pay.

Constructive condition concurrent

If both performances can be simultaneously performed (or the contract fixes the same time for performance of the promises), the promises are constructively concurrent. Each is a constructive condition precedent to the other. To activate the other's duty to perform, a party must tender his performance. Most contracts for the sale of goods under the Code are examples of constructive concurrent conditions of exchange. NOTE: The express contract terms or custom, usage of trade, course of dealing, and the like can change the rule. A passenger, by custom, pays for an airline ticket before the airline's duty to provide transportation is activated.

Tender and the constructive condition

A tender in the law of contracts is an offer to perform. When a person makes a tender, it means that he is ready, willing, and able to perform. The tender is especially significant in contracts requiring both parties to perform at the same time. One party can place the other party in default by making a tender of performance without having actually rendered the performance.

The concept of tender is applied not only to concurrent condition situations but also to contract performance in general. In most contracts, one party or the other is required to tender payment. Such a tender requires that there be a bona fide, unconditional offer of payment of the amount of money due, coupled with an actual production of the money or its equivalent. A tender of payment by check is not a valid tender when an objection is made to this medium of payment. When a tender is refused for other reasons, one may not later complain about the use of a check as the medium of tender. A person to whom a tender is made must specify any objection to it or waive it, so that the debtor may know and comply with the creditor's demands.

Tenders of payment are often refused for one reason or another. A party may contend that the tender was too late. The creditor may refuse to accept the offer to pay because he believes that the amount tendered is less than the amount of the debt. If it turns out that the tender was proper, the valid tender will have three important legal effects.

1. It stops interest from accruing after the date of the tender.
2. In case the creditor later brings legal action recovering no more than the amount tendered, he must pay the legal costs.
3. If the debt were secured by a security interest in property belonging to the debtor, this security interest would be extinguished.

Thus a tender of payment, although it does not discharge the debt, has important advantages to the person making it.

Tender under the Code

The Code article that deals with the sale of goods has two provisions relating to tender. Unless the buyer and the seller have otherwise agreed, *tender of payment* by the buyer is a condition to the seller's duty to deliver the goods sold [2–511(1)]. Unless the seller demands payment in legal tender, the buyer is authorized to make payment by check [2–511(2)]. The Code also provides for the manner of a seller's tender of delivery of the goods involved in the contract. The Code requires that the seller make the goods available to the buyer and that he give the buyer reasonable notification that the goods are available for him [2–503(1)]. If the seller gives notice that the goods are available for the buyer and the buyer does not tender payment, then the buyer would be placed in default. Tender of delivery is a condition to the buyer's duty to accept the goods [2–507(1)].

Recovery by a party in default

The law of conditions is used by courts to determine if a party has an absolute or a conditional duty to perform. A party who has an absolute performance but fails to perform according to the letter of the agreement generally cannot recover. His duty is a constructive condition precedent to activate the duty of the other party. In an employment contract, the duty to work and the duty to pay are constructively conditioned on each other. Suppose an employee is hired for a salary of $24,000 per year. According to the usual interpretation, work for a month by the employee is a constructive condition precedent to activate the employer's duty to pay $2,000 at the end of the month. Payment of the $2,000 is a constructive condition precedent to the employee's duty to work the next month. As you can see, working must occur to activate the duty to pay; payment activates the duty to work; working activates the duty to pay, and so on until the end of the year. As you can see, the duties of working and paying are *alternating constructive conditions precedent.*

When a party fails to perform a duty that is a constructive condition to another's duty of performance, two legal effects occur. First, the party has breached. Second, the other party's duty to perform has not been activated. Nonetheless, there are instances when the defaulting party may recover or at least have his breach excused. Such a holding happens when a court states that the constructive condition precedent has either been *satisfied* or *excused.* The remainder of this chapter explores doctrines that either satisfy or excuse constructive conditions.

Satisfaction of Constructive Conditions

There are two ways a constructive condition may be satisfied: (1) substantial performance or (2) divisibility. Divisibility will be discussed subsequently.

Substantial performance or immaterial breach

Whereas the usual rule is that express conditions must be strictly met, constructive conditions need be only substantially performed. Because constructive conditions are imposed in the interest of good faith and fair dealing, it naturally follows that substantial performance of a constructive condition satisfies the condition. Thus, the other party's duty to perform is activated. Note that substantial performance is not complete performance, so there has been an immaterial breach. In fact, there are several legal ways to say the same thing. Substantial performance and immaterial breach are equivalents; material breach and insubstantial performance are also equivalents.

Effect of material and immaterial breach

If a party substantially but not completely performs, a technical or immaterial breach occurs. Although the nonbreaching party can sue for damages for this technical breach, the suing party must still perform, because the constructive condition precedent has been satisfied. Thus, an immaterial breach does not excuse the nonbreaching party of his duty of performance under the contract.

The consequences of a material breach can be more severe. Normally, a material breach gives the nonbreaching party an option (or election right). He can opt to treat the contract at an end (total breach) or choose to continue under the contract (partial breach). A partial breach, in effect, reinstates the contract. If a partial breach is elected, all parties must continue to perform under the contract, and the nonbreaching party can sue for damages that accrued from the breach. If a total breach is elected, the contract is at an end (the nonbreaching party's duty to perform is discharged), and there is an immediate right to all remedies for breach of the entire contract. Now we know at least three ways of saying the same thing:

Material breach = Insubstantial performance = Total breach (unless aggrieved party elects a partial breach)

Immaterial breach = Substantial performance = Partial breach (no election allowed; entitled only to damages)

Divisibility

In some contracts, total performance may be the constructive condition to the other's duty to perform. If the contract is legally divisible, performance of the divisible portion may fulfill the constructive condition precedent to activate the other's corresponding divisible performance. A defaulting plaintiff will still be liable for the part breached, but he can sue for the divisible portion already performed. A contractor promises to build 20 houses for $400,000 at $20,000 per house for developer. Since building takes time and payment is an instant act, building is a constructive condition precedent to the duty to pay. If the contractor builds 15 houses and then goes bankrupt, no recovery is allowed under the doctrine of substantial performance. If the contract is divisible, the contractor would be allowed to recover $300,000, the prorated price per house completed.

Performance of a contract may take place in portions rather than all at one time, giving rise to several questions: (1) Is the contract divisible on both sides, so that the second party is under a duty to perform in part after the first party performs an installment? (2) Does a material breach of any installment justify a rescission of the balance of the agreement? (3) If one party is in default, may he nevertheless recover for the performance rendered prior to default?

The concept of divisibility is applicable to a variety of contracts including insurance, employment, construction, and sales contracts. As a general proposition, employment contracts are interpreted to be divisible, but construction contracts are usually deemed to be entire. The divisibility of contracts for the sale of goods is the subject of several Code provisions discussed in the third paragraph below.

There have been numerous cases involving the question of whether or not a contract is divisible. No general test can be derived from these cases, and parties seldom provide specifically for division in their contract. Courts are called upon to determine in any given case whether the parties intended that (1) each would accept part performance of the other in return for his own without regard to subsequent events or (2) the divisions of the contract were made merely for the purpose of requiring periodic payments as the work progresses. In any event, the party who breaches is liable for damages resulting from his breach.

The parties may specify whether a contract is divisible or entire. Thus, a contract may contain a clause stipulating that each delivery is a separate contract, or other language may be used to show the intention of the parties that their agreement is to be treated as if it were a series of contracts.

Under the Code, unless the parties have otherwise agreed, a sales contract is entire;

all the goods called for by the contract must be tendered in a single delivery, and payment in full is due upon such tender [2-307]. If the contract permits installment deliveries, the seller can demand a proportionate share of the price for each delivery as it is made, provided the price can be apportioned, as for goods sold at a certain price per item. If there is a substantial default on an installment (the goods tendered or delivered may not conform to the contract), the buyer may reject the installment [2−612(2)]. When an installment breached indicates that the seller will not satisfactorily perform the balance of the contract or that he is unreliable, the buyer can rescind the entire contract. [2−612(3)]. Should the buyer accept a nonconforming installment without giving notice of cancellation or demanding that the seller deliver goods that conform, he may not use the breach as a basis for rescission.

Excuses for Nonperformance

A party to a contract may be relieved from the duty to perform or from his liability for breach if he is legally excused from contract performance. Moreover, a duty under a conditional promise may be activated not only by performance of the condition but also if the condition is excused. Actual failure of an express or a constructive condition may be legally excused in any of the following six ways: (1) hindrance, prevention or noncooperation; (2) waiver, estoppel, or election; (3) anticipatory repudiation; (4) impossibility; (5) commercial impracticability, and (6) frustration of purpose.

Hindrance, prevention, and noncooperation

In every contract there is an implied duty of good faith and fair dealing requiring each party not to prevent or substantially hinder the other party's performance. If a party whose promise is conditional wrongfully prevents the condition from occurring, then the condition is excused. The dependent duty is immediately activated. Although the cases vary, the wrongful conduct can be characterized as either wrongful prevention, hindrance, or noncooperation.

The conduct must be wrongful, which usually means that no party reasonably contemplated or assumed the risk of the kind of conduct that occurred. Seller agrees to sell Buyer 3,000 tons of railroad rails for $50 per ton. The rails are in short supply. Seller fails to deliver, because Buyer has been buying rails from Seller's only sources. A court held that although Buyer did substantially hinder Seller's performance, it was not wrongful. Seller assumed the risk of such market conditions.

The wrongful prevention of performance by one party to a contract will excuse nonperformance by the other party. It is obvious that a person may not recover for nonperformance of a contract if he is responsible for the nonperformance. If a party creates a situation that makes it impossible for the other party to perform, the other party is excused. To illustrate: Barrow had leased a building to Calhoun for the operation of an ice cream store. The rent was to be a percentage of the gross income. Thereafter, Calhoun established another ice cream store a block away and did very little business in the building rented to her by Barrow. Calhoun has prevented the normal performance of the contract by carrying on another business that detracted from the profits. Barrow may cancel the lease without liability because Calhoun has prevented the performance of the contract.

Waiver, estoppel, or election

When one party whose promise is subject to an express or a constructive condition indicates by conduct or words that he will not insist on it, courts will excuse the condition. Although we generally call this excuse a waiver, courts may say that one has waived the condition or is estopped to assert the condition or has elected one right, thereby excusing the condition. Technically, the excuse can be used in three ways: (1) true waiver, (2) estoppel waiver, and (3) election waiver.

True waiver

A true waiver occurs only when there is a voluntary and intentional relinquishment of a known right. If a condition is not a material part of the bargain, it can be voluntarily waived, but the waiver can be withdrawn prior to any detrimental reliance on the waiver by the other party. One cannot waive a material part of the bargain. Contractor agrees to build a house for Buyer before June 1st for $75,000. Time is made of the essence. Buyer says, "Forget about the June 1st deadline. I won't insist on it." The condition is excused, since it is not a material part of the bargain. The time limitation (although waived) may be reimposed, provided no reliance has occurred. Buyer says, "Even though you have not substantially built the house, I'll pay you $75,000 anyway." The constructive condition of building is not waived, since it is a material part of the bargain. The attempted waiver is little more than a disguised gift. Of course, new consideration would support such a waiver. If no consideration is given, however, a waiver will be effective if the condition is not a material part of the bargain.

Estoppel

A true waiver can be revoked any time before the other party has substantially and justifiably changed his position in reliance upon the waiver. Thus, when the other party relies, the waiver becomes irrevocable, and the nonoccurrence of the condition is excused under the doctrine of equitable estoppel (estoppel in pais). Suppose in the preceding example that Contractor was having difficulty raising money for the construction. Buyer said he would not insist on the June 1st completion date. This true waiver could be withdrawn. But if Contractor, relying to his detriment on Buyer's statement, ceased diligent efforts to raise construction capital, the express condition is excused. The waiver is binding (estoppel waiver).

Election

The true waiver and estoppel waiver are used to excuse conditions before they are due to occur; a waiver after failure of a condition is an election waiver. The condition that failed can be either an express or a constructive condition. A waiver merely excuses a condition; it does not renounce a right to damages or discharge a contract. The election waiver occurs when a party chooses to treat the failure of the condition as a partial breach. When a condition has failed, the other party can elect to terminate the contract (total breach) or to continue under the contract (partial breach). If partial breach is chosen, the condition that failed to occur is deemed waived. Contractor agrees to build Buyer a house. Contractor falls so far behind that there is a material breach. There is a failure of a constructive condition, which gives Buyer the right to elect to continue with the contract and sue for partial breach or to terminate the contract and sue for total breach.

Anticipatory repudiation

Before the time specified for performance, there can be no actual breach, but there may be a breach by anticipatory repudiation. The expression explains itself: repudiation occurs before performance is due; one of the parties to a bilateral contract repudiates the contract. The repudiation may be express or implied. An express repudiation is a clear, positive, unequivocal refusal to perform. An implied repudiation results from conduct in which the promisor puts it out of his power to perform, making substantial performance of his promise impossible. In either case, the repudiation must be positive and unequivocal.

CASE

P had entered into a contract to purchase two campers from D and had made a deposit of $1,000 as partial payment. P then wired D not to ship the campers. By letter, P later explained the reason for delaying the shipment. Subsequently, P decided not to buy the campers and demanded a return of his $1,000. D refused, and P instituted legal action. D contended that the claim was barred by the statute of limitations (three years), since the action was not commenced within three years from the date of the telegram. The suit was within three years from the demand for the return of the down payment.

ISSUE Was the instruction not to ship an anticipatory repudiation?

DECISION No.

REASON The telegram was simply an implication that plaintiff would not perform his part of the contract at that time. Such action is "not the equivalent of a positive and unequivocal refusal to perform" at any time.

McMahon v. Fiberglass Fabricators, Inc., 496 P.2d 616 (Ariz.) 1972.

When a promisor repudiates his prospective duty to perform, the nonrepudiating party has an election of remedies. He can treat the repudiation as an anticipatory breach and immediately seek damages for breach of contract, rather than having to wait until the time set for the repudiating party's performance. Thus, the doctrine excuses any express or constructive conditions to the repudiating party's duty and thereby permits an immediate lawsuit. Rather than suing, the injured party can treat the repudiation as an empty threat, wait until the time for performance arrives, and exercise his remedies for actual breach if a breach does, in fact, occur. If the injured party disregards the repudiation and treats the contract as still in force, then the repudiation is nullified, and the injured party is left with his remedies, if any, invocable at the time of performance.

The doctrine of anticipatory breach does not apply to promises to pay money on or before a specified date. If a promissory note matures on June 1, 1985, and in 1981 the maker states that he will not pay it when the maturity date arrives, that would not give rise to a present cause of action by the holder.

The Code provides that after a breach including anticipatory repudiation, the buyer may "cover" by making in good faith and without unreasonable delay any reasonable purchase of, or contract to purchase, goods in substitution for those due from the seller [2-712]. The difference between the cost of cover and the contract price, together with any incidental or consequential damages, may be recovered by the buyer from the seller. Failure of the buyer to effect cover does not bar him from recovering damages for nondelivery, but damages will be limited to those that could not have been obviated by proper cover.

A party may retract his repudiation, provided he does so prior to any material change of position by the other party in reliance upon it. The retraction would simply be a notice that he will perform the contract, after all. The Code allows a retraction of anticipatory repudiation until the repudiating party's next performance is due, unless the aggrieved party has, since the repudiation, canceled or materially changed his position or otherwise indicated that he considers the repudiation final [2-611]. Retraction may be by any method that clearly indicates to the aggrieved party that the repudiating party intends to perform, but it must include adequate assurance that he will in fact perform if the other party demands it [2-609]. Retraction reinstates the repudiating party's rights under the contract, with due excuse and allowance to the aggrieved party for any delay occasioned by the repudiation.

Impossibility of performance

Actual impossibility of performance is a valid excuse for breach of contract and releases a party from his duty to perform. Impossibility is much more than mere "additional hardship." As a general rule, in the absence of an appropriate contract provision, circumstances that impose additional hardship on one party do not constitute an excuse for breach of contract. The fact that the promised performance of a contractual obligation may be more difficult than expected at the time the promise was made does not discharge the promisor from his duty to perform. Therefore, most contracts provide that manufacturers, suppliers, or builders shall be relieved from performance in case of fire, strikes, difficulty in obtaining raw materials, or other incidents imposing hardship over which they have no control. Without such a provision there would be no excuse, as they do not constitute impossibility of performance.

To have the effect of releasing a party from his duty to perform, the impossibility must render performance "physically and objectively impossible." If objective impossibility is present, the discharge is mutual; that is, the promisor is discharged, and the promisee is also discharged from his corresponding obligation. Many cases state that in order for impossibility to exist, there must be a fortuitous or unavoidable occurrence that was not reasonably foreseeable. The fact that an act of God is involved does not necessarily create an excuse. If a house under construction is destroyed by fire, the contractor is not excused from his obligation to complete the house. The contractor takes the risk of fire unless he protects himself by expressly contracting that he shall not be held liable for an act of God or other untoward circumstance against which he is not willing to be bound.

CASE

D agreed to loan P $3,850,000 to build a shopping center. The agreement required P to deposit $77,000, which would be retained by D as liquidated damages if the loan was not closed according to the commitment. Later, P found it needed at least another million dollars to construct the shopping center. When D refused to loan this additional amount, P financed the entire project through another lender. P sues to get the $77,000 deposit.

ISSUE Did D's refusal to increase the loan create an impossibility of performance, entitling P to a refund of the $77,000 deposit?

DECISION No.

REASON The impossibility of performance must be objective in that no one can perform the duty. It cannot exist merely because of the inability of the promisor to perform. Any impossibility in this case exists by reason of P's inability to complete the construction project at a cost within the loan commitment.

White Lakes Shopping Ctr. v. Jefferson Standard Life Ins. Co., 490 P.2d 609 (Kan.) 1971.

Likewise, if the situation is caused by the promisor or by developments that he could have prevented, avoided, or remedied by corrective measures, there is no excuse. For this reason, the failure of a third party, such as a supplier, to make proper delivery does not create impossibility. Impossibility will not be allowed as a defense when the obstacle was created by promisor or was within his power to eliminate. It must not exist merely because of the inability or incapacity of the promisor to do it; that is, subjective impossibility is no excuse.

Specific cases of impossibility

There are four basic situations in which impossibility of performance is frequently offered as an excuse for nonperformance. In the first of these, performance becomes illegal because of the enactment of some law or governmental action. A manufacturer or supplier may be prevented from making delivery of merchandise because of government allocations, as in the mandatory allocation of fuel oil and gasoline. Government action that merely makes an agreement more burdensome than was anticipated does not afford a basis for relief.

The second situation is the death or incapacitating illness of one of the contracting parties. This is not deemed to be a form of impossibility unless the contract demands the personal services of the disabled or deceased person. Ordinary contracts of production, processing, and sale of property are unaffected by the death or illness of one or both of the parties. In the event of death, it is assumed that the contract will be carried out by the estate of the deceased. If a contract is for personal services or it clearly implies that the continued services of the contracting party are essential to performance, death or illness will excuse nonperformance. In contracts for personal services, the death of the employer also terminates the relation. The estate of the employer in prematurely terminating the contract is not liable for damages to the employee.

Many agreements involve the continued existence of certain subject matter essential to completion of the contract. The third rule is that destruction of any subject matter essential to the completion of the contract will operate to relieve the parties of the obligations assumed by their agreement. A different situation arises where property that only one of the parties expected to use in his performance is destroyed. If a factory from which the owner expected to deliver certain shoes is destroyed by fire, performance is not excused, inasmuch as performance is still possible, even though an undue hardship may result. The shoes needed to fill the order can be obtained from another source. Had the contract stipulated that the shoes were to be delivered from this particular factory, however, its destruction would have operated to excuse a failure to perform. In recent years, there has been a trend toward holding that where both parties understood that delivery was to be made from a certain source, even though it was not expressly agreed, destruction of the source of supply will relieve the obligor from performing.

The last form of impossibility arises when there is an essential element lacking. This situation has never been satisfactorily defined; but apparently, the agreement may be rescinded when some element or property is lacking, although the parties assumed it existed or would exist. Some courts would hold that no contract, in fact, existed, because of mutual mistake. This is said to be a form of impossibility at the time of making the contract, and courts have tended to act as if there had been no meeting of the minds. It must be definitely proved that performance is substantially impossible because of the missing element. Davis contracts to build an office building at a certain location. Because of the nature of the soil, it is utterly impossible to build the type of building provided for in the agreement; the agreement must therefore be terminated. The missing element is the proper condition of the soil. In other words, from the very beginning, the contract terms could not possibly have been complied with, and in such cases the courts are prone to excuse the parties if nobody is at fault.

Commercial impracticability

The Code recognizes that without the fault of either party, unexpected developments or government action may cause the promised performance to become impracticable. In some cases, the Code authorizes substituted performance. If the loading or unloading facilities fail on the agreed-upon carrier, making it unusable, a commercially reasonable substitute must be tendered and accepted if it is available [2–614].

The Code also provides that commercial impracticability is often an excuse for a seller who fails to deliver goods or is delayed in making the delivery. The excuse is limited to cases in which unforeseen supervening circumstances not within the contemplation of the parties arise [2–615(a)]. The law does not specify all the contingencies that may justify the application of the doctrine of commercial impracticability. Increased costs will not excuse the seller unless they are due to some unforeseen contingency that alters the basic nature of the contract.

CASE

D agreed to supply P with a petroleum product for three years. The contract had a complicated pricing formula that allowed D to adjust prices as its costs increased, but there was a fixed ceiling on the amount of any increase. When the Arabs dramatically increased oil prices following the 1973 Middle East war, D's costs more than doubled. Since the ceiling on price increases in the contract would not allow D to raise its prices in proportion to the Arab increase, D refused to perform unless P renegotiated the ceiling provision. P sued, and D contended that its duty under the contract was excused because of commercial impracticability.

ISSUE Had D's performance under the contract become impracticable because its costs nearly doubled, allegedly owing to unforeseeable events arising out of the 1973 Middle East war?

DECISION No.

REASONS

1. The contract contemplated that foreseeable cost increases would be passed on to P. However, the existence of the ceiling provision impels the conclusion that the parties intended that the risk of a substantial and unforeseen rise in cost would be borne by D. Moreover, impracticability cannot be based on added expense alone.
2. Although not necessary to the decision, the Arab oil price rises were not a "contingency, the non-occurrence of which was a basic assumption on which the contract was made" [2–615(a)].

Publicker Industries Inc. v. Union Carbide Corp., 17 UCC Rep. Serv. (Pa.) 1975.

Neither increased costs nor a rise in the market excuse performance. But a severe shortage of raw materials or of supplies due to a contingency such as war, an unforeseen shutdown of major sources of supply, a local crop failure, or the like, which increases costs or prevents a seller from securing necessary supplies, does constitute commercial impracticability.

In order to use the excuse, the seller is required to notify his customers seasonably of the delay or nondelivery. This notification is to allow the buyers to take prompt action to find another source of supply. The notice must include an estimate of the buyer's allocation when the seller is able to perform partially [2–615(c)] and is subject to the Code's allocation requirement [2–615(b)].

Upon receipt of a notice of a substantial or indefinite delay in delivery or of an allocation, the buyer has two alternative courses of action. The buyer may terminate the contract insofar as that delivery is concerned. He may also terminate and discharge the whole contract if the deficiency substantially impairs the value of the whole contract [2–616(1)]. The buyer may also modify the contract by agreeing to take his available quota in substitution. If the buyer fails to modify the contract within a reasonable time not exceeding 30 days, the contract lapses with respect to the deliveries covered by the seller's notice [2–616(2)].

Frustration

Since performance is possible, there is no actual impossibility in frustration, but something happens to prevent achievement of the object or purpose of the contract. In such cases the courts may find an implied condition that certain developments will excuse performance.

Frustration has the effect of excusing nonperformance. It arises whenever there is an intervening event or change of circumstances that is so fundamental it is entirely beyond that which was contemplated by the parties. Frustration is not impossibility, but it is more than mere hardship. It is an excuse created by law to eliminate liability when a fortuitous occurrence has defeated the reasonable expectations of the parties. It will not be used when the supervening event was foreseeable or assumed as a part of the agreement.

CASE

P, a contractor, agreed with D, a city, to construct a golf course for $230, 329.88. After P had completed all of the clearing and dirt work, a torrential rainfall of 12.47 inches occurred in a 10-hour period. It will cost $60,000 to restore the golf course to its condition prior to the rain. P seeks to be relieved from the contract. The contract contained provisions that implied that the contractor was to assume all risks relative to ground conditions and weather.

ISSUE Is the contractor relieved of liability by the doctrine of commercial frustration?

DECISION No.

REASONS

1. The commercial frustration doctrine is set forth in Restatement of Contracts §288 (1932), as follows: where the assumed possibility of a desired object or effect to be attained by either party to a contract forms the basis on which both parties enter into it, and this object or effect is or surely will be frustrated, a promisor who is without fault in causing the frustration, and who is harmed thereby, is discharged from the duty of performing his promise unless a contrary intention appears.
2. A partial frustration by subsequent events is less likely to be held to discharge a contractor from a duty than is total frustration.
3. Thus it follows that P is not entitled to relief under the commercial frustration doctrine because the contract expressed a contrary intent and the doctrine is not applicable in the event of only a partial frustration that only increases the cost of performance.

Pete Smith Co., Inc. v. City of El Dorado, 529 S.W.2d 147 (Ark.) 1975.

REVIEW QUESTIONS AND PROBLEMS

1. Wardell listed his property for sale with Hamilton, a real estate broker. Hamilton arranged for Arnold to buy the house, provided that Arnold sold some antiques for Hamilton by October 1st. Arnold failed to sell the antiques and thus failed to buy the house. Wardell's exclusive listing with Hamilton Realty expired in November. In June of the next year, Arnold bought the house from Wardell without the services of Hamilton Realty. Contending that he found Arnold first, Hamilton sues Wardell for his broker's commission. Should Hamilton succeed? Why or why not?

2. Husband and Wife were lost at sea when the Lusitania was sunk. Husband had a life insurance policy which provided: "$5,000 to his wife, if living, if not, then to the Husband's executors." Should the money be paid to the executor of Husband or Wife? Explain.

3. Dawson contracts to sell and Evans to buy 500 barrels of apples "of such quality to be satisfactory in buyer's honest judgment," delivery to be in installments. After 100 barrels are delivered and paid for, may Evans cancel the remaining 400 barrels by simply saying that she is not satisfied and refuses to take any more? Why or why not?

4. Harte contracted with Connolly to install a new roof on Connolly's house. It was agreed that the roofing shingles were to be "Russet glow," a shade of brown. The roof was installed, and many of the shingles were discolored, showing streaks of yellow. Harte replaced some of the shingles, but the new shingles did not match the others. The overall appearance of the roof is that it has been patched with nonblending colors. The roof is functional and is guaranteed to last 15 years. Must Connolly pay? Why or why not? Would your answer change if Harte were building a house for Connolly and on the scheduled completion date had done everything required by the contract except grading and paving? Why or why not?

5. Johnson agreed to erect 6 signs on a highway near Clark's Place. Four small signs are to read: "4 miles to Clark's Place, 3 miles to Clark's Place," etc. One large sign is to read: "STOP! You're at Clark's Place." The sixth sign reads: "Turn around, You've just missed Clark's Place." Clark agreed to pay $30 each for the 5 small signs and $50 for the large sign. Johnson erected only 3 small signs and sues for $90. May he recover? Why or why not?

6. Wells contracted with the state to erect a building according to the state's specifications and to lease it to the state. Time was made of the essence in the contract. Wells completed the building two months late. The state cancelled the contract and leased space elsewhere. Wells sued and proved at trial that the delay was caused by the state's failure to indicate locations for electrical fixtures, outlets, and other details as required by the contract. Did Wells win? Why or why not?

7. A real estate broker contracted to sell a piece of land to Marilyn Curry. At her request, the contract stated: "This contract is contingent upon the buyer obtaining a rezoning for a mobile home park and campground. This contract is to be void if the rezoning is not obtained within 120 days." After 65 days, Curry notifies the broker that she would buy the property, irrespective of a zoning change. The zoning change was not obtained during the 120-day period. The broker now refuses to convey, and Curry sues. Who wins? Why?

8. Stacey, a pro football quarterback, signed a 7-year contract with the Professional Football League for $875,000. Stacey was to receive $50,000 upon signing and another $50,000 at the end of the first year. Although he received the $50,000 upon signing, the league could pay but $20,000 at the end of the year. At that time, the league was in financial difficulties to the tune of $1,600,000 indebtedness and an overdraft at the bank for $67,000. Should Stacey treat the contract as rescinded? Why or why not?

9. Grace agreed to take dancing lessons from Fred for a specified period at a predetermined price. After only part of the lessons were completed, Grace became disabled and could not fulfill the rest of the contract. Should she be released from the contract? Why or why not?

10. John Henry Mining Company was hired to drill a coal mine. The mine failed because tunneling became too difficult. Is John Henry excused for discontinuing? Why or why not?

13

Contract Rights of Third Parties

The discussion of contracts up to this point has dealt with the law of contracts as applied to the contracting parties. Frequently, persons who are not parties may have rights and even duties under the contract. In two basic situations, the rights and duties of third parties (persons not involved in the original contract) may come into play: (1) when there is an assignment of the contract—a party to a contract (assignor) transfers to a third party (assignee) his rights under the contract; or (2) when there is a third-party beneficiary contract, one in which a party contracts with another party for the purpose of conferring a benefit upon a third party (beneficiary). In both situations, a primary question that frequently arises is whether the third party (assignee or beneficiary) can enforce the contract.

Often these two categories of third parties are confused. That confusion can be dispelled if you remember that a third-party beneficiary's rights are created by the *formation* of the contract. By contrast, the rights of an assignee arise *after* contract formation, when one party under the existing contract assigns rights to the assignee.

Assignments

Terminology and requirements

A bilateral contract creates *rights* for each party and imposes on each corresponding *duties.* Each party is an obligor (has an obligation to perform the duties), and each is an obligee (is entitled to receive the performance of the other). Either party may desire to transfer to another his rights or both his rights and duties. A party *assigns* rights and *delegates* duties. The term *assignment* may mean a transfer of one's rights under a contract, or it may mean a transfer both of rights and duties. The person making the transfer is called the *assignor,* and the one receiving the transfer is called the *assignee.*

A person who has duties under a contract cannot relieve himself of those duties by transferring the contract or delegating the duties to another person. An obligor that delegates duties as well as assigning rights is not thereby relieved of liability for proper performance if the assignee fails to perform. An assignor continues to be responsible for the ultimate performance.

No particular formality is essential to an assignment. Consideration, although usually present, is not required. As a general proposition, an assignment may be either oral or written, although it is of course desirable to have a written assignment. Some statutes require a writing in certain assignment situations. For example, an assignment of an interest in real property must be in writing in most states.

Assignment construct

The typical assignment may also include a delegation of duties, as it does when a business is sold. The seller not only assigns all contract rights but also delegates all current contract duties. Thus, the basic assignment construct looks like Fig. 13.1.

Consent—generally

Although public policy prevents the assignment of some contract rights, the rights under most contracts can be freely assigned by either party without consent from the nonassigning party. However, many states, by statute, prohibit or severely limit the assignment of wages under an employment contract; and most prohibit assignment of rights created by the law, such as the right to collect for personal injuries.

As a general rule, contract rights may be assigned by one party without the consent of the other. In most contracts, it is immaterial to the party performing who receives the performance. A party has no right to object to most assignments.

Nonassignable rights

Of the several classes of contracts that are exceptions to the general rules and may not be transferred without the consent of the other party, the most important pertain to personal rights or personal duties. A personal right or duty is one in which personal trust and confidences are involved, or one in which skill, knowledge, or experience of one of

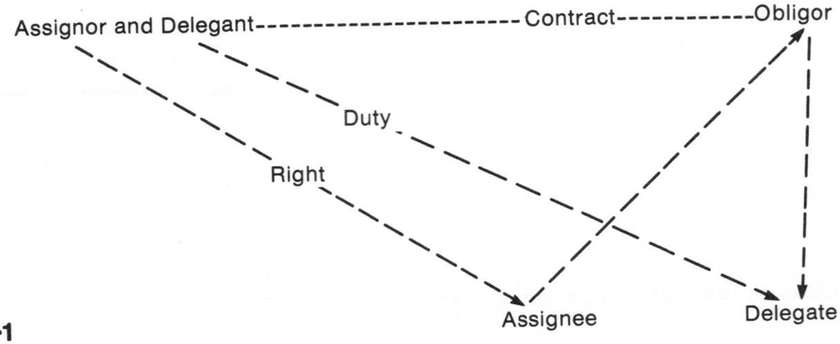

Fig. 13·1

the parties is significant. The personal acts and qualities of one or both of the parties form a material and integral part of the contract. A lease contract with rent being a percentage of sales is based on the ability of the lessee and would be unassignable without the consent of the lessor. Likewise, an exclusive agency contract would be unassignable.

Some duties that might appear to be personal in nature are not considered so by the courts. Unless the contract provides to the contrary, a building contractor without consent may delegate responsibility to a subcontractor for certain portions of the structure. Since construction is usually to be done according to specifications, the agreement is assignable. It is presumed that all contractors are able to follow specifications. Of course, the assignee must substantially complete the building according to the plans and specifications. The obligator will not be obligated to pay for it if it is not, and the assignor will be liable in event of default by the assignee.

CASE

D, owner of 6 pizza restaurants, contracted with Virginia Coffee Service to install cold drink vending machines in each restaurant. A year later, P purchased the assets of Virginia Coffee Service, and the 6 contracts with D were assigned to P. D contends that when it contracted with Virginia, it relied on Virginia's skill, judgment, and reputation. Thus, D argues that Virginia's duties under the vending machine contract could not be delegated.

ISSUE Are the original 6 agreements personal service contracts that cannot be assigned?

DECISION No.

REASONS
1. The agreements were either a license or concession granted Virginia and were assignable, since they did not impose on Virginia duties of a personal or unique character, which could not be delegated.
2. All painters do not paint portraits like those of Sir Joshua Reynolds, nor landscapes like Claude Lorraine's, nor do all writers create dramas like Shakespeare's or fiction like the work of Dickens. Rare genius and extraordinary skill are not transferable, and contracts for their employment are therefore personal and cannot be assigned. But rare genius and extraordinary skill are not necessary to workmanlike digging or to the servicing of cold drink machines; therefore, contracts for such work are not personal and may be assigned.

Macke Co. v. Pizza of Gaithersburg, Inc., 270 A.2d 645 (Md.) 1970

Another example of a contract that is unassignable without consent is one in which an assignment would place upon a party an additional burden or risk not contemplated at the time of the agreement. An assignment of the right to purchase merchandise on credit is an example. Most states hold that one who has agreed to purchase goods on credit, and has been given the right to do so, may not assign his right to a third party (assignee), since the assignee's credit may not be as good as that of the original contracting party (assignor).

CASE

P, a seller of real property, sues to have D's claim as an assignee of the original buyer (Greer) declared void. The original contract of sale (earnest money contract) provided for an extension of credit by P to Greer and did not require a total cash payment at the time of closing.

ISSUE Is a contract for the sale of real estate assignable by the buyer if it provides for credit from the seller to the buyer?

DECISION No.

REASON Rights are not assignable without consent if they arise out of a contract involving an extension of credit between the parties. Because a relationship of personal trust and confidence is created between the parties, without consent the law will not allow any substitution of parties.

Lancaster v. Greer, 572 S.W.2d 787 (Tex.) 1978.

This reasoning may be questionable, because the seller could hold both the assignor and the assignee responsible; however, the inconvenience to the seller in collecting has influenced most courts to disallow any assignment. But in contracts giving the seller substantial security for payment—such as retention of title to the goods, a mortgage on the goods, or a security interest in the goods—the courts have held that the right to purchase on credit is assignable.

Consent under the Code

The Code contains provisions that generally approve the assignment of rights and delegation of duties by buyers and sellers of goods. The duties of either party may be delegated *unless* the parties have agreed otherwise or the nondelegating party ". . . has a substantial interest in having his original promisor perform or control the acts required by the contract" [2–210(1)]. Accordingly, a seller can ordinarily delegate his obligations under the contract if there is no substantial reason why the delegated performance would be less satisfactory than the personal performance of the assignor.

The Code does provide that rights cannot be assigned if the assignment would materially change the duty of the other party, increase materially the burden or risk imposed on him by his contract, or impair materially his chance of obtaining return performance [2–210(2)]. These Code provisions, in effect, incorporate the personal rights and duties exception previously discussed.

Anti-assignment clauses: prohibition vs. invalidation

Some contracts contain a clause stating that the contract cannot be assigned without the consent of the other party. Older cases held these clauses to be against public policy and unenforceable, an unlawful restraint on alienation (right to sell one's property). Recognizing freedom of contract, modern courts uphold the clause prohibiting assignment and find it legally operative. Nonetheless, looking to the *language* of the clause in non-Code cases, courts have reached three different results. (1) The clause *prohibits* assignment; for example, "This contract cannot be assigned without the other party's consent." Courts hold that this creates a promise (*duty* in the assignor) not to assign, but the assignor still has the *power* to assign. Thus, the assignment is effective, but the obligor has a legal claim against the assignor for breach of his *promise* (duty) not to assign. (2) The clause *invalidates* the contract; for example, "In the event of an assignment, this contract is void." Although the assignment is still effective, courts give the obligor an option to avoid the contract for breach of the condition. (3) The only way to prohibit an assignment is to *make it void;* for example, "Any purported assignment is void." Unless the nonassigning party (obligor) consents, courts hold that such a clear stipulation obviously contemplates that the assignment itself is ineffective. Rather than merely creating a *duty* (promise) not to assign, this invalidation clause deprives any party of the power to assign. Thus, the outcome in a given case depends on whether the clause (1) prohibits assignment, (2) invalidates the contract if assigned, or (3) invalidates an assignment.

CASE

Parties to a franchise contract seek a declaratory judgment to adjudicate their rights and duties when the contract contains this clause: "Any assignment is subject to the approval of the franchisor." The trial court held that the clause was unenforceable, being against public policy.

ISSUES Is the anti-assignment clause an unlawful restraint on alienation? If the clause is lawful, does it make an assignment ineffective?

DECISION The contract limitation against assignment, unless approved, is proper and valid. The clause, however, is a mere promise not to assign; any assignment would therefore be effective.

REASONS
1. It is a fundamental principle that one of the primary incidents of property ownership is the right of disposition or alienation. The right is not limitless; it can be defeated by a clear provision to that effect.
2. A restriction on assignment does not leave the assignor entirely powerless. Although a contract contains a promise not to assign, as in this case, the assignment is effective. The promise creates a *duty* in the assignor not to assign. It does not deprive the assignor of the *power* to assign. If the power is exercised, the assignor is liable for breach of his duty, but the assignment would be effective.

Hanigan v. Wheeler, 504 P.2d 972 (Ariz.) 1972.

Free assignability under the Code

The Code has effected significant changes regarding anti-assignment clauses. First, in Article 2 it notes the progressive undermining of the original rule validating these clauses, as shown by the preceding discussion. The Code observes that the courts have already construed the heart out of anti-assignment clauses. Second, in Article 9 it acknowledges the economic need of freedom of contract rights in modern commercial society. Thus an anti-assignment clause is ineffective to prohibit the assignment of an account or contract right [9–318(4)]. In a sale of business, typically both the rights are assigned and the duties are delegated. Lacking a release, the delegating party is still liable on the duties delegated. Consequently, Article 2 of the Code provides that in a sales situation, a clause prohibiting assignment should be construed as barring only the delegation of duties [2–210(3)]. Therefore, a generally phrased anti-assignment clause is to be read as allowing an assignment but forbidding any delegation of duties. Despite the use of the word *anti-assignment,* the drafters of the Code took notice that in a sales situation the parties were usually more concerned with delegation than with assignment. Moreover, they saw great commercial need for free assignability of rights and struck the compromise of allowing assignment but prohibiting delegation when confronted with an anti-assignment clause.

Claims for money

As a general rule, claims for money due or to become due under existing contracts may be assigned. An automobile dealer may assign to a bank the right to receive money due under contracts for the sale of automobiles on installment contracts. Although the law tends toward greatly reducing or eliminating the right of employees to assign wages, an employee may assign a portion of his pay to a creditor, in order to obtain credit or to satisfy an obligation. The Uniform Consumer Credit Code (adopted in several states) provides that a seller cannot take an assignment of earnings for payment of a debt arising out of a consumer credit sale. Lenders are not allowed to take an assignment of earnings for payment of a debt arising out of a consumer loan. The Consumer Credit Code is a part of the trend toward greater consumer and debtor protection.

When a claim for money is assigned, an issue that frequently arises is the liability of the assignor in case the assignee is unable to collect from the debtor-obligor. If the assignee takes the assignment merely as *security* for a debt owed to him by the assignor, it is clear that if the claim is not collected the assignor still has to pay the debt to the assignee. But if someone *purchases* a claim against a third party, generally he has no recourse against the seller (assignor) if the third party (debtor-obligor) defaults. If the claim is *invalid* or sold expressly "with recourse," the assignor would be required to reimburse the assignee if the debtor-obligor did not pay.

In all cases, an assignor *warrants* that the claim he assigns is a valid, legal claim, that the debtor-obligor is really obligated to pay, and that there are no valid defenses to the assigned claim. If this warranty is breached (that is, if there are valid defenses or the claim is otherwise invalid) the assignee has recourse against the assignor.

Rights of the assignee

An assignment is more than a mere authorization or request to pay or to perform for the assignee rather than the assignor. The obligor-debtor *must* pay or perform for the assignee, who now, in effect, owns the rights under the contract. If there is a valid assignment, the assignee owns the rights and is entitled to receive them. Performance for the original party will not discharge the contract. Unless the contract provides otherwise, the assignee receives the identical rights of the assignor. Since the rights of the assignee are neither better nor worse than those of the assignor, any defense that the third party (obligor) has against the assignor is available against the assignee. Part payment, fraud, duress, or incapacity can be used as a defense by the third party (obligor) if an action is brought against him by the assignee, just as the same defense could have been asserted against the assignor, had he been the plaintiff. A common expression defining the status of the assignee is that he "stands in the shoes" of the assignor.

CASE

D, Hudson Supply, owed an open account to Eastern Brick & Tile Co. These accounts were sold and assigned to P. When P sought to collect on the assigned accounts, D refused to pay on the ground that Eastern owed more money to D than D owed Eastern.

ISSUE Can a defensive setoff be asserted against P, the assignee of a money claim?

DECISION Yes.

REASONS
1. An assignee of a money claim takes only the rights of the assignor. Thus, setoffs available against the assignor may also be asserted against the assignee.
2. Any defense an obligor like D has against an assignor like Eastern can be asserted against an assignee such as P.

Hudson Supply & Equipment Company v. Home Factors Corp., 210 A.2d 837 (D.C.) 1965.

Some contracts contain a provision to the effect that "if the seller assigns the contract to a finance company or bank, the buyer agrees that he will not assert against such assignee any defense that he has against the seller-assignor." This "waiver of defense" clause is an attempt to give the contract a quality usually described as negotiability. Although the concept of negotiability will be discussed in detail in chapter 19, it is a legal rule that cuts off defenses by giving one party a protected status. If a negotiable instrument is properly negotiated to a party, then that party has the protected status called a holder in due course. Thus most defenses of the original party (the buyer above) cannot be asserted against the holder in due course (the finance company or bank above). The purpose of the concept of negotiability is to encourage the free flow of commercial paper. Adding a provision to a contract that gives it the same effect obviously places the assignee in a favored position and makes contracts with such clauses quite marketable.

As a part of the growing movement toward greater consumer protection, the Federal Trade Commission has ruled that such clauses cutting off defenses of consumers against delinquent sellers when a contract is assigned constitute an unfair method of competition. They are therefore illegal. The commission has also prohibited the use of the holder-in-due-course concept against consumers. This 1976 action by the Federal Trade Commission will be discussed further in chapter 19.

Duties of the parties

As previously noted, an assignor is not relieved of his obligations by a delegation of them to the assignee. The assignor is still liable if the assignee fails to perform as agreed, in which case the assignor would have a cause of action against the assignee. If a party who transfers a contract to a third person wishes to be released of liability, a legal arrangement known as a *novation* is required. The requirements for a valid novation are discussed in chapter 20.

The liability of the assignee to a third person is a complicated issue determined by careful examination of the transaction to see whether it is an assignment of only the rights under the agreement or whether the duty has also been delegated. This is often difficult to determine when the language used refers only to an "assignment of the contract."

As a general rule, the *mere assignment* of a contract calling for the performance of affirmative duties by the assignor, with nothing more, does not impose those duties upon the assignee. There is a decided trend in such cases to hold that an assignment of an entire contract carries an implied assumption of the liabilities. When the assignee undertakes and agrees to perform the duties as a condition precedent to enforcement of the rights or has assumed the obligation to perform as part of the contract of assignment, he has liability for failure to perform.

A lease between a landlord and tenant is illustrative. First, if a tenant merely assigns a lease, the assignee who accepts the benefits of the contract becomes obligated to perform the duties. Thus, the assignee must pay rent as long as he takes the benefit of a tenant. If the assignee vacates the property prior to the end of the lease, he is not liable for future rents. But if the assignee expressly assumes the burdens of the lease, then a sublease is created, and the new tenant must pay rent until the end of the sublease. Note that in the sublease, the prior tenant is not excused from the delegated duty to pay rent unless the landlord consents to recognize the sublessee as the only tenant. If the landlord consents, a novation occurs which discharges the first tenant.

Under the Code, an assignment of "the contract" or of "all my rights under the contract" or an assignment in similar general terms is an assignment of rights. Unless the language or the circumstances (as in an assignment for security) indicate the contrary, it is also a delegation of performance of the duties of the assignor and an assumption of these duties by the assignee. Its acceptance by the assignee constitutes a promise to perform these duties. This promise is enforceable by either the assignor or the other party to the original contract [2–210(4)].

When the assignor delegates his duties, although the assignor remains liable, the obligee may feel insecure about the ability of the assignee to perform the delegated duties. The obligee may demand that the assignor supply adequate assurance that the assignee will, in fact, render proper performance [2–210(5)].

Notice

Immediately after the assignment, the assignee should notify the third party obligor or debtor of his newly acquired right. This notification is essential for two reasons.

1. In the absence of any notice of the assignment, the third party is at liberty to perform (pay the debt or do whatever else the contract demands) for the original contracting party, the assignor. In fact, he would not know that anyone else had the right to require performance or payment. Thus, the right of the assignee to demand performance can be defeated by his failure to give this notice. The assignor who receives performance under such circumstances becomes a trustee of funds or property received from the obligor and can be compelled to turn them over to the assignee. Upon receipt of notice of assignment, the third party *must perform* for the assignee, and his payment or performance to the assignor would not relieve him of his obligation to the assignee.

2. The notice of assignment is also for the protection of innocent third parties. The assignor has the *power*, although not the *right*, to make a second assignment of the same subject matter. If notice of the assignment has been given to the obligor, it has much the same effect as the recording of a mortgage. It furnishes protection for a party who may later consider taking an assignment of the same right. A person considering an assignment should, therefore, always communicate with the debtor to confirm that the right has not previously been assigned. If the debtor has not been notified of a previous assignment, and if the prospective assignee is aware of none, in many states the latter can feel free to take the assignment. He should immediately give notice to the debtor. In other words, the first assignee to give notice to the debtor, provided such assignee has no knowledge of a prior assignment, will prevail over a prior assignee in most states.

CASE

In order to get a construction job, a contractor was required to put up a performance bond. The purpose of the bond was to assure that the contractor would perform properly and pay all bills. D, a bonding company, agreed to write the bond provided that the contractor would assign (as security) payments under the construction contract. The contractor agreed. Thereafter, the contractor borrowed money from P bank and assigned the right to the same payments to the bank. P was the first to notify the owner of its assignment.

ISSUE Does P have priority over D?

DECISION Yes.

REASON The first assignee to give notice will prevail over the first-in-time assignee.

Boulevard National Bank of Miami v. Air Metals Industry, 176 So.2d 94 (Fla.) 1965.

In some states, it is held that the first party to receive an assignment has a prior claim, regardless of which assignee gave notice first. In these states, the courts act on the theory that the assignor has parted with all his interest by virtue of the original assignment and has nothing left to transfer to the second assignee. In all states, however, the party who is injured by reason of the second assignment has a cause of action against the assignor, to recover the damages he has sustained. The assignor has committed a wrongful and dishonest act by making a double assignment.

Third-party Beneficiary Contracts

The basic third-party beneficiary situation occurs when two parties make a valid contract in which the performance of one party (let's call her Farley) is to benefit a third party. The third-party beneficiary contract looks like Fig. 13.2. A third-party beneficiary does not always have a right to sue on the contract. Only an *intended,* as contrasted with an *incidental,* third-party beneficiary can sue. Generally, an intended beneficiary is either a creditor or a donee beneficiary.

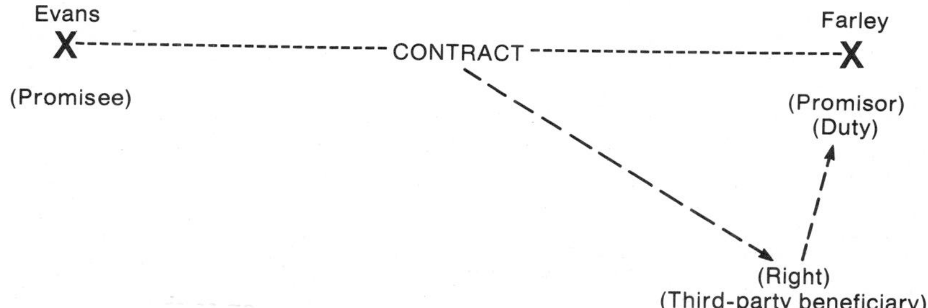

Fig. 13·2

Donee and creditor beneficiaries

Contracts are often made for the express purpose of benefiting some third party. These *third-party beneficiary contracts* are of two types: *donee-beneficiary* and *creditor-beneficiary.* Both types of third-party beneficiary contracts are entitled to enforce a contract made in their behalf because the promisee has provided that the performance shall go to the beneficiary rather than to himself.

If the promisee purchased a promise in order to make a gift to a third party, that party is a donee beneficiary. The most common example of such an agreement is the contract for life insurance, in which the beneficiary is someone other than the insured. The insured has made a contract with the life insurance company for the purpose of conferring a benefit upon a third party—namely, the beneficiary named on the policy.

If the promisee has contracted for a promise to pay a debt that he owes to a third party, the third party is a creditor beneficiary. The debtor has arranged to pay the debt by purchasing the promise of the other contracting party to satisfy his obligation. The promisee obtains a benefit because his obligation to the creditor will presumably be satisfied.

CASE

D corporation agreed with its four resigning directors to pay each of their legal expenses arising out of an SEC investigation into prior activities of the corporation. One of the directors hired P (law firm) to represent him in the SEC matter. After D corporation refused to pay P for the legal expenses in representing the director, P sued D as a third-party beneficiary to the agreement between D and its directors.

ISSUE Is P a creditor beneficiary entitled to sue the promisor D, or is P no more than an incidental beneficiary without a right to sue on the contract?

DECISION P is a third-party creditor beneficiary.

REASON To be a creditor beneficiary, the performance promised must be one that in fact discharges another party's obligation to the third party; if it will not do this, the third person may be a creditor of the promisee, but he is not a creditor beneficiary of the contract. Here, D agreed that payments for legal expenses would be made directly to the directors' legal counsel.

Choate, Hall & Stewart v. SCA Services, Inc., 392 N.E.2d 1045 (Mass.) 1979.

How to determine if intended or incidental

A third-party beneficiary is not entitled to enforce a contract unless he can establish that the parties actually intended to make the contract for his benefit. The third party need not be named as a beneficiary in the contract if he can show that he is a member of a group for whose benefit the contract was made.

CASE

A university athletic department leased an airplane to fly its football team. The lease provided that the university would furnish liability insurance to cover any deaths or injuries resulting from the operation of the plane. No such insurance was purchased, and the plane crashed, killing all on board. (The crash resulted when the plane was 2900 pounds in excess of allowable takeoff weight.) The estates of the deceased players sued the university, claiming to be third-party beneficiaries of the contract.

ISSUE Were the estates of the passengers entitled to sue on the contract?

DECISION Yes.

REASONS
1. A person may avail himself of a promise made by a second party to a third party for the benefit of the first party, even though the first party had no knowledge of the contract when it was made.
2. Here the contract provision requiring insurance was for the benefit of the passengers. They could sue for its breach.

Brown v. Wichita State University, 540 P.2d 66 (Kan.) 1975.

If the benefit to the third party is only incidental, the beneficiary cannot sue. An orphanage lost a suit that was based on an agreement between several merchants to close their places of business on Sunday, with a provision that anyone remaining open was to pay $100 to the orphanage. The court stated that the contract was entered into primarily to benefit the contracting parties and that the orphanage was only indirectly to be a beneficiary. Contracts of guarantee, assuring the property owner that contractors performing construction contracts for him will properly complete the project and pay all bills have been held in many states to benefit the person supplying material and the laborers. Thus, if the supplier of lumber and building materials were not paid by the contractor, he could bring legal action against the person who gave the guarantee.

Vesting of rights

In most states, a contract made for the express purpose of benefiting a third party may not be rescinded without the consent of the beneficiary after its terms have been accepted by the beneficiary. The latter has a vested interest in the agreement from the moment it is made and accepted. An insurance company cannot accept a change of the named beneficiary in a life insurance policy without the consent of the beneficiary, unless the life insurance contract gives the insured the right to make this change. Until the third-party beneficiary has either accepted or acted upon provisions of a contract for his benefit, the parties to the contract may abrogate the provisions for the third party's benefit and divest him of the benefits that would otherwise have accrued to him under the contract. Infants, however, are *presumed* to accept a favorable contract upon its execution, and it may not be changed to deprive an infant of his benefits.

One who seeks to take advantage of a contract made for his benefit takes it subject to all legal defenses arising out of contract. Thus, if the obligee has not performed or satisfied the conditions precedent to the other party's obligation, the third party would be denied recovery.

REVIEW QUESTIONS AND PROBLEMS

1. How does an assignment differ from a delegation?
2. Athens Lie Detector company, for good consideration, gave Yarbrough an exclusive license to operate certain lie detector machines as part of the agreement. The company agreed to tell him how the manufacturing process works. Athens assigned its rights and delegated its duties under the contract to Travers. Are the rights assignable? Are the duties delegable? Explain.
3. Simpson agreed with Van Cleef's Truck City to supply a coin-operated phonograph in Van's place of business, the income to be shared by both parties. Simpson assigned his rights and delegated his duties to Rogers and Westley. Van now refuses to perform and Rogers and Westley sue. Who wins? Why?
4. Andrews entered into a five-year employment contract with Arnold as president of its subsidiary. Then Andrews decided to sell the subsidiary to Long, Inc. The contract of sale provided for assignment of Arnold's contract of employment, but Arnold was unaware of the assignment and sale. Is he obligated to work for Long, Inc.?
5. Suppose a contract for the sale of goods contains this clause: "Under no circumstances may any rights under this contract be assigned." After the seller delivers goods to the buyer, may the seller assign the buyer's unpaid account to a third party? Explain.
6. Debtor owed money to Worker for work performed. Worker assigned his claim to Bank and notified Debtor of the assignment. Bank then demanded payment from Debtor, but Debtor refused and paid Worker instead. Can Bank now collect from Debtor? Why or why not? Suppose Debtor was not notified of the assignment to Bank. Subsequently, Worker assigned his claim to Dewey and Debtor was informed of this assignment. To whom should Debtor make payment? Explain.
7. Brown purchased a car from Morgan, who falsely told him that the car was in good condition when she knew that it needed extensive repairs. Morgan assigned the installment sale contract to Friendly Finance Company, which then sued Brown for nonpayment. Brown claims the right to set aside the contract for fraud. Can he use that defense against the finance company? Explain.
8. Gaither entered into a contract with a nonprofit corporation whereby Gaither would receive $700 per month while in medical school, provided that he return to his small home town, Chester, to practice medicine for ten years after becoming a licensed physician. The residents of Chester voted approval of bonds to construct a medical clinic. Gaither practiced medicine in Chester for about five weeks but then left for Mt. Clement. Do the representatives of the medical clinic and the citizens of Chester have a right to sue Gaither? Explain.
9. General Greer had an insurance policy with the Good Insurance Company. Upon being injured in a car accident, he was treated, free of personal cost, at a governmental medical facility. The policy required Good to pay all reasonable medical expenses and provided that it would pay any person or organization rendering the services for the insured. Should the government sue for reimbursement of the reasonable medical expenses rendered to Greer? Explain.
10. Hunt, an employee of the Marie Reading School, was injured when the elevator he was operating fell. The school had a contract with Shaft Elevator Inc., whereby Shaft was to inspect and service the elevator on a regular basis. Hunt contended that Shaft had not properly inspected the elevator and that its omission caused the accident. Can Hunt maintain an action against Shaft? Why or why not?

The Port Authority of N.Y. and N.J.

III

Uniform Commercial Code

14

Introduction to Sales Contracts

As we learned in the chapters on contracts, the Code has changed many older, classical contract rules to conform with business realities and the reasonable expectations of the contracting parties. Many common-law contract rules also have been changed or modified by Article 2 of the Code, to achieve a more commercially desirable result, since some basic contract rules concerning employment, construction, and real property contracts are simply inappropriate in a sale-of-goods context. The important Code modifications or changes are listed in Table 14.1. These new Code rules have already been discussed in the chapters on contracts and will not be discussed further in this book. Rather, our concern will be with more specialized rules dealing with sales of goods.

The next three chapters (concerning Article 2 of the Code) will consider the terms of a sales contract, the rights and duties of delivering and accepting goods, remedies available to buyers and sellers, and warranties in the context of products liability law. This chapter explores the basic terms of a sales contract; the transfer of, and title to, goods; payment and delivery obligations; and risk-of-loss when the goods are lost or damaged.

Don't memorize the sections of the code.

Table 14·1 Special rules for contracts for the sale of goods

Code Section 2	*Rule*
	Offer and Acceptance
204	All terms need not be included in negotiations in order for a contract to result.
205	Firm, written offers by merchants are irrevocable for a maximum of three months.
206(1)(a)	An acceptance may be made by any reasonable means of communication and is effective when deposited.
206(1)(b)	Unilateral offers may be accepted either by a promise to ship or by shipment.
206(1)(b)	Failure to reject may constitute an acceptance.
206(2)	Acceptance by performance requires notice within a reasonable time, or the offer may be treated as lapsed.
207	Variance in terms between offer and acceptance may not be a rejection and may be an acceptance.
305	The price need not be included in a contract.
311(1)	Particulars of performance may be left open.
	Consideration
203	Adding a seal is of no effect.
209(1)	Consideration is not required to support a modification of a contract for the sale of goods.
	Voidable Contracts
403	A minor may not disaffirm against an innocent third party.
721	Rescission is not a bar to a suit for dollar damages.
	Illegality
302	Unconscionable bargains will not be enforced.

Definitions

Article 2 of the Code is applicable to transactions in "goods" [2–102]. It is not applicable to sales of other types of property or to other types of contracts. The term *goods* encompasses things that are movable; that is, items of personal property (chattels) that are of a tangible, physical nature [2–105(1)]. Although broadly interpreted to include even electricity, the definition of goods excludes investment securities (covered by Article 8 of the Code) and negotiable instruments (covered by Article 3 of the Code).

Being limited to *goods,* Article 2 necessarily excludes contracts for personal service, construction, intangible personal property, and the sale of real estate. Goods "associated" with real estate *may* be within Article 2 in sales of "structures," "minerals," and the "like" *if severance is to be made by the seller.* If severance is to be made by the buyer, then the contract involves a sale of an interest in land. Growing crops (including timber under a 1972 amendment) fall within Article 2, regardless of who severs them.

A sale consists of the passing of title to goods from the seller to the buyer for a price [2–106(1)]. The seller is obligated to transfer and deliver or tender delivery of the goods, and the buyer is obligated to accept and pay in accordance with the contract [2–301]. In general, the parties to a contract for sale can agree upon any terms and conditions that are mutually acceptable.

Table 14·1 *(cont.)*

Code Section 2	*Rule*
	Form of the Agreement
201	Statute of frauds • $500 price for goods. • Written confirmation between merchants. • Memorandum need not include all terms of agreement. • Payment, acceptance, and receipt limited to quantity specified in writing. • Specially manufactured goods. • Admission pleadings or court proceedings that a contract for sale was made.
	Rights of Third Parties
210(4)	An assignment of "the contract" or of "rights under the contract" includes a delegation of duties.
	Performance of Contracts
209	Claims and rights may be waived without consideration.
307, 612	Rules on divisible contracts.
511	Tender of payment is a condition precedent (rather than a condition concurrent) to a tender of delivery.
610, 611	Anticipatory breach may not be withdrawn if the other party gives notice that it is final.
614	Impracticability of performance in certain cases is an excuse for nonperformance.
	Discharge
725	The statute of limitations is four years, but parties can reduce it by mutual agreement to not less than one year.

Special provisions of Article 2 relate to transactions involving a merchant, a professional businessperson who "holds himself out as having knowledge or skill peculiar to the practices or goods involved in the transaction" [2–104(1)]. This designation is of great importance and is recognition of a professional status for a businessperson, justifying standards of conduct different from those of "nonprofessionals." The courts of some states have held that farmers are merchants when selling grain and other items raised by them. Other courts have held that farmers are not merchants, so from state to state there is variation in whether or not Code provisions relating to merchants apply also to farmers.

Another term used in Article 2 is *future goods,* goods that are not in existence at the time of the agreement or that have not been "identified"; that is, designated as the specific goods that will be utilized in the transaction [2–105(2)].

The Code provisions on the sale of goods are based on two additional assumptions: (1) that the parties should be given the maximum latitude in fixing their own terms and (2) that the parties will act in "good faith." Good faith means honesty in fact in the conduct or transaction [1–201(19)]. In the case of a merchant, "good faith" also includes the observance of reasonable commercial standards of fair dealing in the trade [2–103(1)(b)].

Terms of the Sales Contract

The terms of a sales contract are supplied by three sources: (1) the express agreement of the parties; (2) course of dealing, usage of trade, course of performance; and (3) the Code and other applicable statutes.

Express agreement of parties

The general rule in sales law is that the parties are free to make their own contract. The parties are privileged to contract expressly regarding most basic terms—quality, quantity, price, delivery, payment, and the like. In general, their agreement is sufficient to displace any otherwise applicable Code section. For example, all the Code gap-filling provisions can be displaced. But the principle of freedom of contract under the Code is not without exceptions. Section 1-102(3), for instance, states that the parties cannot "disclaim" their Code obligations of "good faith, diligence, and care." Other provisions explicitly state that they cannot be varied by the parties' agreement. Parties may provide a liquidated damages clause, but it cannot be a penalty [2-718(1)]. Consequential damages may be limited, but the limitation cannot be unconscionable [2-719(3)]. Still other sections state that they can be varied. Code provisions on the price term [2-309], place of delivery [2–503], time provision [2–309], manner of seller's delivery [2–503] can be varied. Most Code sections do not state whether they are or are not variable, but it is clear that some cannot be varied by a contrary agreement. An obvious example is the statute of frauds [2–201] or the doctrine of unconscionability [2–303]. So the Code affects the parties' agreement in a variety of ways.

Course of dealing, usage of trade, course of performance

The agreement of the parties includes in their bargain any previous course of dealing between the parties, general trade custom and usage, and any past course of performance on the present agreement. These three sources are not only relevant in interpreting express contract terms but also may constitute contract terms. A *course of dealing* is a sequence of prior conduct between the parties, which gives a firm basis for interpreting their communications and conduct between themselves [1-205(1)]. A *usage of trade* is a practice or custom in the particular trade, used so frequently it justifies the expectation that it will be followed in the transaction in question [1-205(2)]. *Course of performance* concerns a contract that requires repeated performances. When an earlier performance has been accepted by the other party, then that performance can be used to give meaning to the agreement regarding future performance [2-208(1)]. When any of these sources is conflicting, the Code [2–208(2)] adopts the following initial hierarchy of presumed probative values:

1. Express terms
2. Course of performance
3. Course of dealing
4. Usage of trade

But the last three do more than interpret the first. They may supplement, cut down, even subtract whole terms from the express agreement of the parties. More importantly, course of performance, course of dealing, and usage of trade may directly override express terms, so that an express contract term like "7 white goods" is changed to "10 black goods."

CASE

D (buyer) agreed to buy at least 31,000 tons of phosphate for three years from P (seller). When market conditions changed, D ordered only a fraction of the minimum and sought to renegotiate the deal. P refused and sued. At trial, D wanted to introduce two forms of proof: (1) a usage of trade that express price and quantity terms in such contracts were never considered in trade as more than mere projections, to be adjusted according to market forces; (2) course of dealing over a six-year period, which showed repeated and substantial deviations from the stated quantities or prices in other written contracts between P and D. The trial judge refused to admit such evidence.

ISSUE Was the trial judge in error in refusing to admit evidence of course of dealing and usage of trade purportedly showing that the express price and quantity terms were mere projections to be adjusted according to market forces?

DECISION Yes. Evidence should have been admitted.

REASONS

1. The test of admissibility is not whether the contract appears on its face to be complete in every detail, but whether the proffered evidence of course of dealing and usage of trade reasonably can be construed as consistent with the express terms of the agreement.
2. The contract is silent about adjusting prices and quantities to reflect a declining market. It does not prohibit or permit adjustment; it is neutral on the subject of adjustment. Moreover, the contract is silent on the use of such evidence to explain or supplement the written contract. Thus, this neutrality allows the court to use prior dealing and trade usage to supplement the contract and explain its terms.

Columbia Nitrogen Corp. v. Royster Co., 451 F.2d 3 (Va. law) 1971.

Gap-filling under the Code

Written contracts have gaps in them when the parties either intentionally or inadvertently leave out basic terms. Article 2 of the Code has a number of gap-filler provisions which, taken together, comprise a type of standardized statutory contract. As stated earlier, the parties can expressly vary the effect of these provisions by their agreement (including course of dealing, trade usage, and course of performance). The most important gap-filler provisions involve price, quantity, quality, delivery, and payment.

Price

The price term of the contract can be left open, with the price to be fixed by later agreement of the parties, or some agreed market standard or other standard may be designated for fixing the price [2–305]. It may even be agreed that the buyer or the seller shall fix the price, in which event he is obligated to exercise good faith in doing so. If the contract is silent on price, or if for some reason the price is not set in accordance with the method agreed upon, it will be determined as a reasonable price at the time of delivery. Thus, if it appears that it is their intention to do so, parties can bind themselves even though the price is not actually agreed upon.

CASE

P sued D, an oil company, to recover personal property obtained by D under an alleged option contract. The purported contract gave D the right to purchase the property at P's cost less depreciation to be mutually agreed upon. The parties failed to agree on the amount of depreciation and P claimed that as a result, there was no valid agreement.

ISSUE Is the contract binding?

DECISION Yes.

REASONS 1. The contract was valid even though the price was yet to be determined.

2. Under the circumstances it was the function of the court to determine the method and the amount of reasonable depreciation.

Schmieder v. Standard Oil Co. of Indiana, 230 N.W.2d 732 (Wis.) 1975.

Quantity

The Code also allows flexibility in the quantity term of a sales contract. There may be an agreement to purchase the entire output of the seller, or the quantity may be specified as all that is required by the buyer. To ensure fair dealing between the parties in "output" and "requirements" contracts, the Code provides that if parties estimate the quantity involved, no quantity that is unreasonably disproportionate to the estimate will be enforced [2-306]. If the parties have not agreed upon an estimate, a quantity that is in keeping with normal or other comparable prior output or requirements is implied.

Delivery

The term *delivery* signifies a transfer of possession of the goods from the seller to the buyer. A seller makes delivery when he physically transfers into the possession of the buyer the actual goods that conform to the requirements of the contract. He satisfies the requirement that he "transfer and deliver" when he "tenders delivery" [2–507].

A proper tender of delivery requires the seller to make available conforming goods at the buyer's disposition and to give the buyer any notification reasonably necessary to take delivery [2–503(1)]. The seller's tender must be at a reasonable hour, and he must keep the goods available for a reasonable time to enable the buyer to take possession.

Unless the contract provides to the contrary, the place for delivery is the seller's place of business. If the seller has no place of business, it is his residence [2-308(a)]. In a contract for the sale of identified goods that are known to both parties to be at some other place, that place is the place for their delivery [2-308(a)(b)].

Goods are frequently in the possession of a bailee such as a warehouseman. In this event, in order to make delivery, the seller is obligated to either (1) tender a negotiable document of title (warehouse receipt) representing the goods or (2) procure acknowledgment by the bailee (warehouseman) that the buyer is entitled to the goods [2-503(4)(a)].

Unless otherwise agreed, the seller is required to tender the goods in a single delivery rather than in installments over a period of time. The buyer's obligation to pay is not due until such a tender is made [2-307]. In some situations, the seller may not be able to deliver all the goods at once, or the buyer may not be able to receive the entire quantity at one time, in which event more than a single delivery is allowed.

Time of performance

If the time for performance has not been agreed upon by the parties, the time for shipment or delivery or any other action under a contract shall be a *reasonable* time [2-309(1)]. What a reasonable time is depends upon what constitutes acceptable commercial conduct under all of the circumstances, including the obligation of good faith and reasonable commercial standards of fair dealing in the trade.

A definite time for performance may be found to exist, even though the contract did not express it. Such definite time may be implied from a usage of the trade or course of dealing or performance or from the circumstances of the contract.

Payment is due at the time when, and place where, the buyer is to receive the goods [2–310]. *Receipt of goods* means taking physical possession of them. The buyer is given the opportunity to inspect the goods before paying for them [2–513(1)]. Preliminary inspection by the buyer does not require that the seller surrender possession of the goods; however, when the shipment is C.O.D., the buyer is not entitled to inspect the goods before payment of the price [2–513(3)(a)].

The parties may enter into an open-ended contract that calls for successive performances, such as one thousand barrels of flour per week. If the contract does not state the duration, it will be valid for a reasonable time. Unless otherwise agreed, either party can terminate it any time.

Abbreviations

As a matter of convenience, a number of contract terms are generally expressed as abbreviations. *F.O.B.* (free on board) is the most commonly used. *F.O.B. the place of shipment* means that the seller is obligated to place the goods in possession of a carrier, so that they may be shipped to the buyer. *F.O.B. the place of destination* means that the seller is obligated to cause the goods to be delivered to the buyer [2–319(1)(c)]. Thus, if Athens, Georgia is the seller's place of business, "F.O.B. Athens, Georgia" is a *shipment contract.* "F.O.B. Champaign, Illinois," Champaign being the place where the buyer is to receive the goods, is a *destination contract,* and the seller must provide transportation to that place at his own risk and expense. He is responsible for seeing to it that the goods are made available to the buyer at the designated place [2–319(1)(b)].

If the terms of the contract also specify *F.O.B. vessel, car, or other vehicle,* the seller must at his own expense and risk load the goods on board. *F.A.S. vessel* (free alongside) at a named port requires the seller at his own expense and risk to deliver the goods alongside the vessel in the manner usual in the port or on a dock designated and provided by the buyer [2–319(2)].

C.I.F. means that the price includes, in a lump sum, the cost of the goods and of the insurance and freight to the named destination [2–320]. The seller's obligation is to load the goods, to make provision for payment of the freight, and to obtain an insurance policy in favor of the buyer. Generally, *C.I.F.* means that the parties will deal in terms of the documents that represent the goods; the seller performs his obligation by tendering to the buyer the proper documents, including a negotiable bill of lading and an invoice of the goods. The buyer is required to make payment against the tender of the required documents [2–320(4)].

Returned goods

The buyer and seller may agree that the buyer has the privilege of returning the goods that have been delivered to him. If the goods are delivered primarily for use, as in a consumer purchase, the transaction is called a *sale on approval.* If the goods are delivered primarily for resale, it is called a *sale or return* [2–326(1)]. The distinction is an important one, because goods delivered "on approval" are not subject to the claims of the buyer's creditors until the buyer has indicated his acceptance of the goods; goods delivered on "sale or return," however, are subject to the claims of the buyer's creditors while they are in his possession [2–326(2)]. Delivery of goods on consignment, such as a transaction in which a manufacturer or a wholesaler delivers goods to a retailer who has the privilege of returning any unsold goods, is a "sale or return." The goods in possession of the buyer-consignee are subject to the claims of the buyer's creditors, unless the seller complies with the filing provisions of Article 9 dealing with secured transactions [2-326(3)].

A characteristic of the sale on approval is that risk of loss in the event of theft or destruction of the goods does not pass to the buyer until he accepts the goods. Failure seasonably to notify the seller of his decision to return the goods will be treated as an acceptance. After notification of election to return, the seller must pay the expenses of the return and bear the risk of loss. In contrast, the buyer in a sale or return transaction has the risk of loss in the event of theft or destruction of the goods [2-327(2)].

CASE

P company delivered stereo tapes, cartridges, and stereo equipment to D, a service station operator, for resale. P company's salesman had written on the invoice, "Terms 30-60-90. This equipment will be picked up if not sold in 90 days." D's service station was burglarized about two weeks later, and the stereo equipment was stolen.

ISSUE Who must bear the loss resulting from the burglary?

DECISION D.

REASONS
1. The transaction was a "sale or return."
2. Unless otherwise agreed, a transaction whereby goods delivered for resale may be returned to the seller is a sale or return. When a transaction is a sale or return agreement, the risk of loss is on the buyer.

Collier v. B & B Parts Sales, Inc., 471 S.W.2d 151 (Tex.) 1971.

Adequate assurance

A concept applicable to both parties in a sales transaction is known as adequate assurance. Under certain circumstances, either party may be concerned about the other's future performance. If a buyer is in arrears on other payments, the seller will naturally be concerned about making further deliveries. Or a buyer may discover that the seller has been delivering faulty goods to other customers and will be fearful that the goods that he is to receive may also be defective. The law recognizes that no one wants to buy a lawsuit and that merely having the right to sue for breach of contract is a somewhat "hollow" remedy. There is a need to protect the party whose reasonable expectation of due performance is jeopardized.

The Code grants this protection by providing that the contract for sale imposes an obligation on each party that the other's expectation of receiving due performances will not be impaired [2-609]. A party who has reasonable grounds for insecurity about the other's performance can demand in writing that the other offer convincing proof that he will, in fact, perform. Having made the demand, he may then suspend his own performance until he receives assurance. If none is forthcoming within a reasonable time, not to exceed thirty days, he may treat the contract as repudiated [2-609(2)].

Two factual problems are presented. What are reasonable grounds for insecurity? What constitutes an adequate assurance of performance? The Code does not particularize but does provide that between merchants, commercial standards shall be applied to answer these questions [2-609(2)].

Transfer of Title to Goods

The concept of title to goods is somewhat nebulous, but it is generally equated with ownership. Issues related to the passage of title are important in the field of taxation and in areas of the law such as wills, trusts, and estates. The Code has deemphasized the importance of title, and the location of title at any given time is usually not the controlling factor in determining the rights of the parties on a contract of sale. As a general rule, the rights, obligations, and remedies of the seller, the buyer, and the third parties are determined without regard to title [2–401]. However, the concept of title is still basic to the sales transaction, since, by definition, a sale involves the passing of title from the seller to the buyer.

The parties can, with few restrictions, determine by their contract the manner in which title to goods passes from the seller to the buyer. They can specify any conditions that must be fulfilled in order for title to pass. Since they seldom specify, however, the Code sets forth specific provisions as to when title shall pass, if the location of title becomes an issue. As a general rule, it provides that title passes to the buyer at the time and place at which the seller completes his performance with reference to the physical delivery of the goods.

Identification to the contract

Title to goods cannot pass until the goods have been *identified* to the contract [2–401(1)]. Identification requires that the seller specify the particular goods involved in the transaction [2–501(1)]. Carson may contract with Boyd to purchase 100 mahogany desks of a certain style. Boyd may have several hundred of these desks in the warehouse. Identification takes place when Carson or Boyd specifies the particular hundred desks that will be sold to Carson. There could not, of course, be a present identification of future goods (those not yet in existence or not owned by the seller).

Although identification can be made at any time and in any manner "explicitly agreed to" by the parties [2–501(1)], they usually do not make provision for identification—in which event the Code rules determine when it has occurred. If goods that are the subject of a contract are in existence and identified at the time the parties enter into the contract, identification occurs and title passes at the time and place of contracting [2–501(1)(a)]. If the goods are in a warehouse and the seller delivers the warehouse receipt to the buyer, identification occurs and title passes at the time and place the document of title (warehouse receipt) is delivered [2–401(3)(a)].

Contracts to sell future goods and agricultural items raise more difficult identification problems. For future goods, the seller provides identification when he ships the goods or marks them as the goods to which the contract refers [2–501(1)(b)]. The requirement is that the seller make an appropriate designation of the specific goods.

CASE

Ds were package liquor store operators. They were in the practice of paying for large quantities of liquor in advance, in order to take advantage of quantity discounts. Ds would then order out the liquor as they needed it. When Ds learned that a supplier was having financial difficulties, Ds seized a good deal of the undelivered liquor. The supplier then went into bankruptcy. P, the trustee in bankruptcy, claimed that under the arrangement, Ds were simply creditors and that Ds did not have title to the liquor.

ISSUE Did Ds have title to the liquor, so that P could not reclaim it?

DECISION No.

REASON Title to goods does not pass to the buyer until the goods have been identified to the contract. When the contract calls for the sale of goods from a larger stock, title does not pass to the buyer until the specific goods are separated and set apart for the buyer. The retailers must, therefore, return the liquor to the trustee in bankruptcy.

In re Colonial Distributing Company, 291 F.Supp. 154 (1968) (S.C. law).

There are special provisions for agricultural items—crops and animals—because of their nature. When there is a sale of a crop to be grown, identification occurs when the crop is planted. If the sale is of the unborn young of animals, identification takes place when they are conceived [2–501(c)].

Identification occurs, and title passes insofar as the specific goods are concerned, when the seller completes his performance with respect to the physical delivery of the goods. When a shipment contract specifies that a seller is to send the goods to the buyer but is not required to deliver them at the destination, title passes at the time and place of shipment [2–401(2)]. If the contract requires that the seller deliver at the destination, title will not pass until the seller has tendered the goods to the buyer at that point.

If the buyer rejects the goods when tendered to him, title will be revested in the seller. Upon the buyer's refusal to receive or retain the goods, the title automatically returns to the seller, whether or not the buyer was justified in his action. The same result obtains if the buyer has accepted the goods but subsequently revokes his acceptance for a justifiable reason [2–401(4)].

As a means of assurance that the price will be paid before the buyer can obtain title to the goods, a seller may ship or deliver goods to the buyer and reserve title in himself. Under the Code, such an attempted reservation of title does not prevent the title from passing to the buyer. It is limited to the reservation of a security interest in the goods. [2–401(1)]. To give protection to the seller, the security interest must be perfected under the provisions of Article 9. This will be discussed in chapters 21 and 22. Accordingly, a seller who simply reserves a security interest will not have availed himself of protection against the claims of third parties against the property sold unless the seller complies with the law relating to secured transactions.

The title of good-faith purchasers

A purchaser of goods usually acquires at least as good a title as the seller possessed. Moreover, a good-faith purchaser for value may acquire a better title than the seller had if the seller's title was voidable [2–403]. Assume that Spenser obtains goods by fraud or pays for them with a check that is later dishonored. Spenser has voidable title to the goods. If he should sell the goods to Jackson who does not know that Spenser's title was voidable, Jackson has clear title to the goods. Thus a good-faith purchaser for value has better title than did the seller.

Title issues frequently arise when the same goods are sold to more than one buyer. Franklin sells goods to Talmadge, who leaves them at Franklin's store, with the intention of picking them up later. Before Talmadge takes possession, Franklin sells them to Bell, a good-faith purchaser. Bell has title to the goods; because if possession of goods is entrusted to a merchant who deals in goods of that kind, the merchant has the power to transfer all rights of the entrusting owner to a buyer in the ordinary course of business [2–403(2)(3)]. A good-faith purchaser buying from a merchant in the ordinary course of business acquires good title. This rule is applicable to any delivery of possession to a merchant with the understanding that the merchant is to have possession. Thus the rule applies to consignments and bailments as well as to cash sale, but the facts of each case must be examined to ensure that the buyer qualified as a good-faith purchaser for value.

CASE

P and D were automobile dealers. Both had been using the services of X company for the purpose of selling used cars at auction. P delivered two cars to X company for sale in December. Shortly thereafter D, who was holding uncollected checks from X company in the sum of $30,000, went to X company and exchanged two of the checks totaling $7,460 for the two cars that had been delivered by P. P sought to recover the cars from D. P argued that D did not obtain clear title to the cars.

ISSUE Was P entitled to recover the cars from D?

DECISION Yes.

REASONS
1. D was not a good-faith purchaser for value of the cars.
2. A preexisting debt is not sufficient consideration; therefore, D was not a bona fide purchaser for value.
3. D knew or should have known that X company was not the true owner of the automobiles in question.

National Car Rental v. Fox, 500 P.2d 1148 (Ariz.) 1972.

Payment and Delivery Obligations

The sales transaction involves an exchange: goods for price. The basic obligation of the seller is to tender the goods, while that of the buyer is to accept the goods and pay the price. Both responsibilities are measured by the contract [2–301].

Concurrent conditions

In the absence of a contrary agreement, payment is due at the time and place at which the buyer is to receive the goods [2–310(a)]. The basic obligations are concurrent conditions of exchange. Accordingly, a buyer who wants credit (to get the goods before he pays in full) must specifically negotiate for it in the contract. Between merchants, most domestic sales transactions are handled on "open account" (i.e., the seller ships the goods on the buyer's simple promise to pay for them in 30, 60, or 90 days). The buyer is not required to sign a note evidencing his obligation to pay or to grant the seller a security interest in the goods to cover his obligation.

Documentary transactions

When the parties are separated by distance and the seller is unwilling to extend credit to the buyer, they may employ a documentary exchange. As the procedure is sometimes called, the buyer is to pay "cash against documents." In this procedure, the seller utilizes documents of title to control the goods until he is paid. The document of title may be a bill of lading issued by a railroad or steamship company or a warehouse receipt or "any other document which in the regular course of business or finance is treated as adequately evidencing that the person in possession of it is entitled to receive, hold, and dispose of the document and the goods it covers" [1–201(15)]. Documents of title are multipurpose commercial instruments. They not only act as a receipt for the goods but also state the terms of the shipment or storage contract between the seller and the transit or warehouse company.

Shipment under reservation

In a typical documentary exchange, the seller may ship the goods by rail to the buyer and receive from the railroad a negotiable bill of lading made to the order of the seller. The railroad thereby obligates itself to deliver the goods to the holder of the bill of lading [7–403(4)] and will be liable to the seller for misdelivery.

At this point, the seller has shipped "under reservation." His procurement of the negotiable bill reserves a security interest in the goods for their price, which the buyer owes him [2–205]. This security interest arises under Article 2. Neither a security agreement nor a filing under the law of secured transactions in Article 9 is required so long as the buyer has not lawfully obtained possession of the goods [9–113]. Chapters 21, 22, and 23 discuss security interests and security agreements under Article 9.

The seller will endorse the bill of lading and send it to his bank. He will attach to it a sight draft or demand for immediate payment of the purchase price by the buyer. The seller's bank will forward the documents to a bank in the city of the buyer. It is the obligation of that bank to release the bill of lading to the buyer only after he has paid the draft for the purchase price [4–503(a)]. Without the bill of lading, the buyer will not be able to get the goods from the railroad; only when he is in possession under a regular chain of endorsements is the buyer the holder to whom the carrier is obligated to deliver. On the other hand, the buyer is not obligated to pay until he has some assurance that the goods are on the way to him as evidenced by the bill of lading.

Other types of documentary transactions

The foregoing outlines only one common type of documentary transaction. There are many variations. Similar protections can be obtained if the seller ships under a nonnegotiable bill of lading, taking care to consign the goods to himself or his agent. The railroad is now obligated to deliver to the consignee or to the person specified by his written instructions [7–403(4)]. The seller will withhold any instructions to deliver to the buyer until he has been paid. Under this procedure, possession of the document of title is not required to take delivery from the carrier. But note that the seller cannot name the buyer as consignee in the bill of lading; if he does, control over the shipment is lost.

Risk of Loss

In breach of contract cases

The Code sets forth a number of rules for determining which party to a sales contract must bear the risk of loss in the event of theft, destruction, or damage to the goods during the period of the performance of the contract. The approach is contractual rather than title oriented and covers two basic situations: (1) no breach of contract cases and (2) cases in which one of the parties is in breach. Of course, the provisions are applicable only if the contract has not allocated the risk of loss [2–303].

If the contract has been breached, the loss will be borne by the party who has breached [2–510(1)]. Thus, if the seller has tendered or delivered goods that are "nonconforming," the seller bears the risk of loss. He remains responsible until he rectifies the nonconformity or the buyer accepts the goods despite their defects.

CASE

D, engaged in the business of installing underground telephone lines, ordered 3 reels of underground cable from P to be delivered at D's place. P delivered reels of aerial rather than underground cable. When D informs P of the mistake, P tells D to return the cable. D tries but was unable to return the cable because of a trucking strike. The cable was stolen 3 months later from D's regular storage space, where P had delivered it. P sues for the purchase price.

ISSUE Is P entitled to recover the purchase price from D?

DECISION No.

REASONS 1. The Code provides that if the goods delivered give the buyer a right to reject, the risk of loss remains on the seller until the seller corrects the situation or the goods are accepted. Here, D had a valid right to reject. If D takes possession of the goods, responsibility expires after a reasonable time in which the seller can repossess.

2. D attempted in good faith to return the reels. P—with full notice of the place of storage, which was at the place of delivery—did "nothing but sleep on its rights for more than three months."

Graybar Electric Co. v. Shook, 195 S.E.2d 514 (N.C.) 1973

A buyer has the privilege of revoking his acceptance of the goods under proper circumstances (discussed in the next chapter). If the buyer rightfully revokes his acceptance, the risk of loss is back on the seller to the extent that the buyer's insurance does not cover the loss. In this situation, the seller has the benefit of any insurance carried by the buyer (the party most likely to have applicable insurance), but any uninsured loss is on the breaching seller.

Loss may occur while goods are in the seller's control, before the risk of loss has passed to the buyer. If the buyer repudiates the sale (breaches the contract) at a time when the seller has identified proper goods to the contract, the seller can impose the risk of loss upon the buyer for a reasonable time. The basic concept of the Code is that the burden of losses should be that of the party who has failed to perform as required by contract.

If no breach exists

In three distinct situations in risk of loss cases, neither party is in breach: (1) the contract may call for shipment of the goods; (2) goods may be the subject of a bailment; (3) the contract may be silent on shipment, and no bailment exists.

Shipment. A shipment contract requires only that the seller make necessary arrangements for transport; a destination contract imposes upon the seller the obligation to deliver at a destination. If a contract between buyer and seller provides for shipment by carrier under a shipment contract (F.O.B. shipping point), the risk of loss passes to the buyer when the goods are delivered to the carrier. If shipment is made under a destination contract (F.O.B. destination), risk of loss does not pass to the buyer until goods arrive at the destination and are available to the buyer for delivery [2-509(1)]. When the parties do not use symbols such as C.I.F., F.A.S., or F.O.B. or otherwise make provision for risk of loss, it is necessary to determine whether a contract does or does not require the seller to deliver at a destination. The presumption is that a contract is one of shipment, not destination, and that the buyer should bear the risk of loss until arrival, unless the seller has either specifically agreed to do so or the circumstances indicate such an obligation.

CASE

P, a seller of goods, sued D, the buyer, for their purchase price. The contract contained no F.O.B. terms. After the goods were delivered to the carrier for shipment, they were destroyed. The contract was silent on the risk of loss.

ISSUE Who has the risk of loss?

DECISION The buyer.

REASONS 1. The parties may, by their agreement, control who has the risk of loss.

2. Under Article 2 of the Code, the "shipment" contract is regarded as the normal one and the "destination" contract as the variant type. The seller is not obligated to deliver at a named destination and bear the concurrent risk of loss until arrival unless he has specifically agreed so to deliver, or the commercial understanding of the terms used by the parties contemplates such delivery.

3. Thus, a contract that contains neither an F.O.B. term nor any other term explicitly allocating loss is a shipment contract, and the buyer has the risk of loss during shipment.

4. The court rejects D's argument that because the contract provided that goods be "shipped to" the buyer, it is a destination contract. Regarding risk of loss, a "ship to" term has no significance in determining whether a contract is a shipment or destination contract.

Eberhard Manufacturing Company v. Brown, 232 N.W.2d 378 (Mich.) 1975.

Bailments. Often, the goods will be in the possession of a bailee, such as a warehouse, and the arrangement is for the buyer to take delivery at the warehouse. If the goods are represented by a negotiable document of title—a warehouse receipt, for instance—when the seller tenders the document to the buyer, the risk of loss passes to the buyer. Likewise, risk passes to the buyer upon acknowledgment by the bailee that the buyer is entitled to the goods [2-509(2)]. In this situation, it is proper that the buyer assume the risk, as the seller has done all that could be expected to make the goods available to the buyer. It should be noted that if a nonnegotiable document of title is tendered to the buyer, risk of loss does not pass until the buyer has had a reasonable time to present the document to the bailee [2–503(4)(b)]. A refusal by the bailee to honor the document defeats the tender, and the risk of loss remains with the seller.

Other cases. In all cases other than shipment and bailment as mentioned above, the passage of risk to the buyer depends upon the status of the seller. If the seller is a merchant, risk of loss will not pass to the buyer until he receives the goods, which means "takes physical possession of them" [2-509(3)].

A nonmerchant seller transfers the risk by *tendering* the goods [2-509(3)]. A tender of delivery requires that the seller make conforming goods available to the buyer and give him reasonable notice, so that he may take delivery. The risk of loss remains with the merchant seller even though the buyer has paid for the goods in full and has been notified that the goods are at his disposal. Continuation of the risk in this case is justified on the basis that the merchant would be likely to carry insurance on goods within his control, whereas a buyer would not likely do so until he had actually received the goods.

CASE

P, a seller of a mobile home, sued D, the buyer, for the price of the home. After P and D had executed the contract of sale, the mobile home was stolen from P's lot.

ISSUE Did the seller retain the risk of loss after the contract was signed?

DECISION Yes.

REASONS 1. While a contract of sale may transfer the risk of loss to the buyer before delivery of the goods, such a provision is so unusual that a seller who desires to achieve this result must clearly communicate this intent to the buyer. It must be done in clear, unequivocal language.

2. A seller of a mobile home is a merchant. In a sale by a merchant, the risk of loss passes to the buyer on his receipt of the goods. Receipt of the goods means taking physical possession of them.
3. The risk of loss is determined not by title to the goods but by contract principles. The party who has control of the goods generally bears the loss.

Caudle v. Sherrard Motor Company, 525 S.W.2d 238 (Tex.) 1975.

REVIEW QUESTIONS AND PROBLEMS

1. In determining whether Article 2 applies to any transaction involving the sale of goods, you must consider both the *type* of transaction and the *subject matter* of the transaction. Does Article 2 apply or not apply to the following transactions:
   a) Nullen rents a car from Best Rentals, Inc.
   b) Roberts buys a house from Landers.
   c) Farmer John sells growing corn to Oliver.
   d) Dr. Dracula provides a blood transfusion.
   e) Marc Spitz installs a swimming pool.
   f) Gerber repairs a car.
   g) The Valley Electric Company supplies electricity to the public.
   h) Harry sells a used hearse to a reporter.
   i) A mother buys a piano from Justin Piano, Inc., for her daughter and son.
2. Easy Mark buys jade carvings from Sly for $83,000. Easy Mark is totally unfamiliar with the quality and value of jade carvings. Sly knew that Easy Mark had no knowledge of jade carvings. Later, Easy Mark learns that he could have bought similar carvings for $20,000. Does Code section 2-305 give Easy Mark any rights against Sly? Explain.
3. A fruit grower entered into a contract to sell oranges to a fruit processor. The contract did not contain a specified price. Is the contract enforceable? Why or why not?
4. A sporting goods manufacturer contracts to sell 200 leather basketballs to a pro team. The contract does not contain any terms regarding delivery. What are the manufacturer's delivery obligations?
5. The Macon Whoopies, a newly-formed hockey club, contracts to buy 150 hockey pucks from a wholesaler in Youngstown, Ohio. What are the wholesaler's delivery obligations if the agreement states: (a) F.O.B. Macon? (b) F.O.B. Youngstown? (c) C.I.F. Macon? (d) Ship to the Macon Whoopies, Macon, Georgia?
6. A distributor of mobile homes had a contract with Mobiles, Inc., by which Mobiles would supply the distributor's needs for a stated period. The contract provided for termination upon 30 days' notice. Upon learning that Mobiles intended to terminate, the distributor placed an order for mobile homes that amounted to nine times the usual monthly order. Mobiles refused to fill the order, and the distributor sued. Who won and why?
7. Locke, a car dealer, sold a new car to Mercer, another car dealer. To protect himself until Mercer paid for the car, Locke retained possession of the certificate of origin (issued by the manufacturer) and the bill of sale. Before paying Locke, Mercer sold the car to a third party, who was unaware of arrangements between the two dealers. Can Locke recover the car from the third party? Why or why not?
8. A grocer in New Ulm, Minnesota, ordered coffee from a New Jersey roaster. Although the coffee was shipped in the very best containers, rats gnawed into them while the coffee was in transit. Who has the risk of loss if the coffee was shipped F.O.B. New Ulm? Explain.
9. Brown Burgers contracted to sell one of its used stoves to Palma Pizza. After the contract was executed but before the stove was to be picked up, it was damaged by vandals who broke into Brown Burger's storeroom. When Palma refused to accept the stove, Brown sued to recover the purchase price. Who won and why if (a) the contract provided "F.O.B. buyer's truck"? (b) the contract stated that the stove was to be thoroughly cleaned before being placed in the store room, but it had not been cleaned?

15

Breach and Remedies

The law recognizes that each party to a contract for the sale of goods has certain rights and obligations unless the contract legally eliminates them. In addition, the Code has several provisions relating to the remedies of the buyer and the seller in the event of a breach of the contract by the other party.

As a general rule, a seller is obligated to deliver or tender delivery of goods that measure up to the requirements of the contract and to do so at the proper time and at the proper place. The goods and other performance of the seller must "conform" to the contract [2-106(2)].

The seller is required to tender delivery as a condition to the buyer's duty to accept the goods and pay for them [2-507(1)]. Thus, the seller has performed when he has made the goods available to the buyer. The buyer, in turn, must render his performance, which means he must accept the goods and pay for them.

The parties may, in their agreement, limit or modify the remedies available to each other. The measure of damages may be limited or altered. The agreement may limit the buyer's remedies to return of the goods for refund or replacement of the goods or parts.

The parties may limit or exclude consequential damages, and such limitations and exclusions will be enforced if they are not unconscionable [2–719(3)]. A limitation of consequential damages for injury to the person in the case of *consumer goods* is prima facie unconscionable, but limitations where the loss is commercial are not.

These rights and remedies are examined in the sections that follow. Keep in mind that these sections cover sales contracts that are silent on the matter under discussion.

Checklist of Code remedies

Two sections of the Code [2–703 and 2–711] *list* the remedies of the seller and the remedies of the buyer. The word *list* is italicized because that is the sole function of these two sections. Each section provides both parties with four remedies, which are exact counterparts. Table 15.1 shows their significant correlation.

Table 15·1 Comparison of Code remedies

Seller's remedies [2-703]	*Buyer's remedies* [2-711]
1. Resell the goods and recover damages [2-706].	1. Cover (buy same goods elsewhere) and recover damages [2-712].
2. Cancel the contract.	2. Reject the contract.
3. Recover damages for nonacceptance [2-708].	3. Recover damages for nondelivery [2-713].
4. Sue for the actual price of the goods [2-709].	4. Sue to get the goods (specific performance or replevy) [2-716].

The four remedies are listed in the Code not only as equivalent actions but also as equivalent in order of importance. The Code drafters, for instance, considered that *upon breach* the seller would resell the goods and sue the buyer for any difference between the resale price and the original contract price, and the buyer would cover by buying substitute goods and sue the seller for any difference between the cover price and the original contract price.

Obviously, before either party has one of the four remedies, one of the parties must have breached the contract. There are at least four possible situations in which either party can be in breach of contract:

1. *Anticipatory repudiation* by the buyer or by the seller.
2. *Failure of performance* (buyer fails to pay or seller fails to deliver).
3. A rightful or wrongful *rejection* by the buyer.
4. A rightful or wrongful *revocation of acceptance* by the buyer.

Anticipatory repudiation and failure to perform have been discussed in Part II, "Contracts." This chapter will consider the buyer's right to reject and right to revoke acceptance. Before proceeding to discuss the Code remedies, however, it might be helpful to get a visual overview in Figs. 15.1, 15.2, and 15.3 (see pp. 194, 197, 199).

Buyer's Remedies

Buyer's right to inspect and to reject

The buyer has a right before payment or acceptance to inspect the goods at any reasonable time and place and in any reasonable manner [2–513(1)]. The place for the inspection is determined by the nature of the contract. If the seller is to send the goods to the buyer, the inspection may be postponed until after arrival of the goods.

If the contract provides for delivery C.O.D., the buyer must pay prior to inspection. Likewise, payment must be made prior to inspection if the contract calls for payment

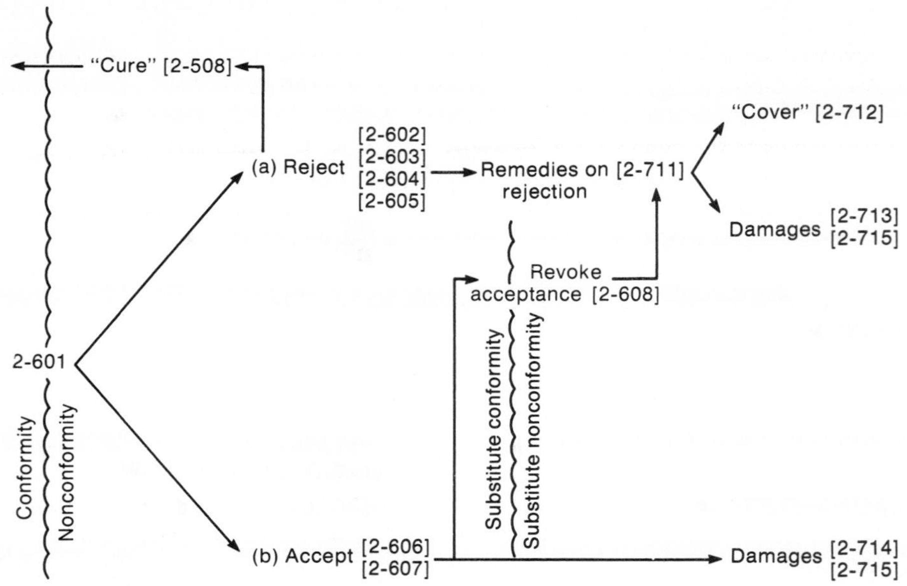

Fig. 15·1 Buyer's remedies on tender of defective goods.

against documents of title [2–513(3)]. When the buyer is required to make payment prior to inspection, the payment does not impair his right to pursue remedies if subsequent inspection reveals defects [2–512].

The buyer must pay the expenses of inspection, but he can recover his expenses from the seller if the inspection reveals that the goods are nonconforming and he therefore rejects them [2–513(2)].

If the goods or the tender of delivery fails to conform to the contract, the buyer has the right to reject them. Several options are available. The buyer may reject the whole, or he may accept either the whole or any commercial unit or units and reject the rest [2–601]. A *commercial unit* is one that is generally regarded as a single whole for purposes of sale, one that would be impaired in value if divided [2–105(6)]. When the buyer accepts nonconforming goods, he does not impair his right of recourse against the seller. Provided he notifies the seller of the breach within a reasonable time, he may still pursue his remedy for damages for breach of contract, even though he accepts the goods.

The right to reject defective or nonconforming goods is dependent on the buyer's taking action within a reasonable time after the goods are tendered or delivered to him. If the buyer rejects, he must seasonably notify the seller of this fact. Failing to do so would render the rejection ineffective and constitute an acceptance [2–602(1)]. If the buyer continues in possession of defective goods for an unreasonable time, he forfeits his right to reject them.

A buyer who rejects the goods after taking physical possession of them is required to hold the goods with reasonable care, at the seller's disposition, long enough for the seller to remove them [2–602(2)(b)]. Somewhat greater obligations are imposed upon a merchant buyer who rejects goods that have been delivered to him [2–603]. The merchant is under a duty to follow the seller's reasonable instructions as to the disposition of the goods. If the seller does not furnish instructions as to the disposition of the rejected goods, the merchant buyer must make reasonable efforts to sell them for the seller's account if they are perishable or if they threaten to decline in value speedily. If not the latter, the buyer has three options. He may store the rejected goods for the seller's account, reship them to the seller, or resell them for the seller's account [2-604].

CASE

D bought a mobile home from P. The mobile home was delivered from Texas to Columbia, S.C. When it was set up, numerous defects were discovered; and 17 days after delivery, D sent a rejection notice. At the time of rejection, D was paying rent on a trailer space, storage on his furniture, and rent on another place to live. When P refused to return D's down payments, D moved into the mobile home to minimize expenses. He lived in it for a year, then had it taken back to El Paso, where he had purchased it. P sued for the purchase price, but the trial court held that D had properly rejected and awarded him $2,000 in damages.

ISSUE Did D correctly reject the mobile home?

DECISION No.

REASONS

1. Initially, D did properly reject by giving the P (seller) notice of the defects within a reasonable time after delivery [2-602]. D's subsequent conduct, however, legally destroyed the rejection.
2. Under 2-604, if the buyer notifies the seller of his rejection within the time required, and if the seller does not remit instructions to the buyer within a reasonable time, then the buyer may either store, reship, or resell the goods. These are optional alternatives; but, obviously, the buyer is going to have to do one of these three things.
3. Because D did not do one of the three things when he moved into the mobile home, he accepted it [2-606] and became liable for the contract price [2-607].

Bowen v. Young, 507 S.W.2d 600 (Tex.) 1974.

Code section 2–711(3) gives a buyer a security interest in the goods in his possession and the right to resell them. The buyer should have resold the mobile home, deducted all expenses regarding care, custody, resale, and other matters (such as the down payment), and then have remitted any money left over to the seller in Texas [2–604 and 2–711(3)].

The requirement of seasonable notice of rejection is very important. Without such notice, the rejection is ineffective [2-602(1)]. As a general rule, a notice of rejection may simply state that the goods are not conforming, without particular specification of the defects relied upon by the buyer. If, however, the defect could have been corrected by the seller had he been given particularized notice, then the failure to particularize will take away from the buyer the right to rely upon that defect as a breach justifying a rejection [2–605(1)(a)]. Therefore, a buyer should always give detailed information relative to the reason for the rejection.

In transactions between merchants, the merchant seller is entitled to demand a full and final written statement of all the defects. If the statement is not forthcoming after a written request for it, the buyer may not rely upon these defects to justify his rejection or to establish that a breach has occurred [2-605(1)(b)].

Buyer's right to revoke an acceptance

The buyer has *accepted* goods if (1) after a reasonable opportunity to inspect them, he indicates to the seller that the goods are conforming or that he will take or retain them in spite of their nonconformity, (2) he has failed to make an effective rejection of the goods, or (3) he does any act inconsistent with the seller's ownership [2-606].

The buyer may revoke his acceptance under certain circumstances. In many instances, the buyer will have accepted nonconforming goods because the defects were not immediately discoverable or he reasonably assumed that the seller would correct by substituting goods that did conform. In either of these events, the buyer has the privilege of "revoking his acceptance" by notifying the seller of this fact [2–608(1)]. Revocation must take place within a reasonable time after the buyer has discovered, or should have discovered, the reason for revocation [2–608(2)]. If a buyer revokes his acceptance, he is then placed in the same position with reference to the goods as if he had rejected them in the first instance [2–608(3)]. He has a security interest in the goods for the payments made and is entitled to damages, as if no acceptance had occurred.

CASE

P, a cash buyer of a mobile home, sued D, the seller, for damages for breach of contract. The home was delivered on June 7, 1973, but P was not given the keys for three weeks. When P finally gained access, he found that the windows and doors would not shut tightly, the floors were buckled, and the rafters were warped. When it rained, the floors flooded, and the water caused an electrical failure. P occupied the mobile home for three months before moving out. D claimed that the right to cure the defects still existed.

ISSUE Is P entitled to revoke the acceptance?

DECISION Yes.

REASONS

1. A buyer, including those who pay cash, is entitled to a reasonable time after the goods are delivered to inspect them and to reject them if they do not comply with the contract. Cash payment does not waive this right.
2. The fact that P stayed in the home for three months does not eliminate his right to revoke the acceptance. P could assume that D would cure the defects and the revocation could be based on the failure to cure the defects.
3. A buyer who revokes an acceptance has the same rights as if the goods had been originally rejected. These rights include as much of the price as has been paid plus incidental and consequential damages.
4. D originally had a right to cure the defects; however, when D's employee told P that he did not know how long it would take, this right was lost. The right to cure defects requires a conforming tender within a reasonable time.

Davis v. Colonial Mobile Homes, 220 S.E.2d 802 (N.C.) 1975.

Damages when the buyer covers

The buyer who has not received the goods he bargained for may cover—arrange to purchase the goods he needs from some other source in substitution for those due from the seller [2–712]. This is a practical remedy, as the buyer must often proceed without delay in order to obtain goods needed for his own use or for resale. The only limitation is that the buyer must act reasonably and in good faith in arranging for the cover [2–712(1)].

A buyer may recover from a seller the difference between what he paid for the substitute goods and the contract price [2–712(2)]. He may also recover incidental and consequential damages sustained. Incidental damages are defined as those that are reasonably incurred in connection with handling rejected goods and "commercially reasonable charges, expenses or commissions in connection with effecting cover and any other reasonable expense incident to the delay or other breach" [2–715(1)]. Consequential damages include "any loss resulting from general or particular requirements and needs of which the seller at the time of contracting had reason to know and which could not reasonably be prevented by cover or otherwise" [2-715(2)]. The buyer is obligated to keep his damages to a minimum by making an appropriate cover insofar as his right to any consequential damages is concerned.

The cover remedy has the advantage of providing certainty as to the amount of the buyer's damages. The difference between the contract price and the price paid by the buyer for substitute goods can be readily determined. Although the buyer must act reasonably and in good faith, he need not prove that he obtained the goods at the cheapest price available.

Damages for nondelivery

The aggrieved buyer who did not receive any goods from the seller or who received nonconforming goods is not required to cover; instead, he may bring an action for damages [2-712(3)]. The measure of damages for nondelivery or repudiation is the difference between the contract price and the market price when the buyer learned of the breach [2-713]. The buyer is also entitled to any incidental or consequential damages sustained. Damages to which a buyer is entitled consist of "the loss resulting in the ordinary course of events from the seller's breach as determined in any manner which is reasonable" [2-714(1)]. In a purchase for resale, it would be appropriate to measure the buyer's damage upon nondelivery as the difference between the contract price and the price at which the goods were to be resold. In other words, the damages equal the difference between the contract price and the fair market value of the goods.

Another recourse open to the buyer is the right to deduct damages from any part of the price still due under the same contract [2-717]. The buyer determines what his damages are and withholds this amount when he pays the seller. He is required to give notice to the seller of his intention to deduct. When the buyer's damages are established by the cover price, the amount is clear-cut. In other instances, the seller might question the amount of the deduction, and this dispute would have to be resolved between the parties or by a court.

Damages may be deducted only from the price due under the same contract. A buyer could not deduct damages for goods under one contract from the price due under other contracts from the same seller.

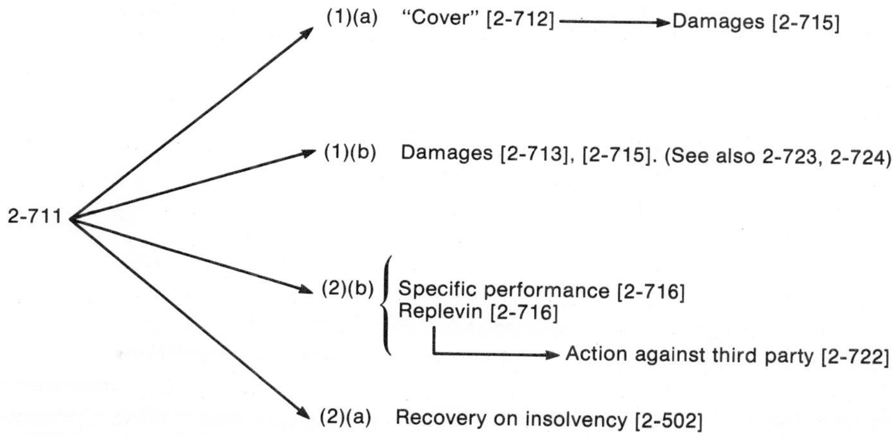

Fig. 15·2 Buyer's remedies on nondelivery (or rejection or revocation of acceptance).

Buyer's right to the goods

Under proper circumstances, the buyer has rights in, and to, the goods. The remedy of specific performance is available (1) when the goods are unique and (2) when other circumstances make it equitable that the seller render the required performance [2-716(1)]. To obtain specific performance, the buyer must have been unable to cover. The Code does not define "unique," but it is fair to assume that it would encompass output and requirement contracts in which the goods were not readily or practically available from other sources.

CASE

P entered into a contract to purchase 4,000 tons of cryolite, a chemical used in the production of aluminum, from D. When D did not deliver the chemical, P brought a suit for specific performance. P contended that cryolite was not readily available from any other source.

ISSUE Is P entitled to the remedy of specific performance?

DECISION Yes.

REASON One of the factors to be taken into account in determining whether specific performance will be allowed is the ability of the plaintiff to "cover." Here P has demonstrated that he would not be able to cover, and he is therefore entitled to specific performance.

Kaiser Trading Company v. Associated Metals and Minerals Corp., 321 F.Supp. 923 (1970) (Cal. law).

Another remedy that enables the buyer to reach the goods in the hands of the seller is the statutory remedy of replevin. *Replevin* is an action to recover the goods that one person wrongfully withholds from another. A buyer has the right to replevin goods from the seller if the goods have been *identified* to the contract and the buyer is unable to effect cover after making a reasonable effort to do so [2–716(3)].

A related remedy that also reaches the goods in the hands of the seller is the buyer's right to recover them if the seller becomes insolvent [2–502]. The right exists only if (1) the buyer has a "special property" in the goods (that is, existing goods have been identified to the contract), and (2) the seller becomes insolvent within ten days after he received the first installment payment from the buyer. Without these circumstances, the buyer is relegated to the position of a general creditor of the seller. It is apparent that if the buyer can recover the goods, he is in a much better position than he would be as a general creditor, particularly if he had paid a substantial amount of the purchase price. To exercise this remedy, the buyer must make and keep good a tender of any unpaid portion of the price.

Seller's Rights and Remedies

The Code establishes certain rights and remedies for sellers just as it does for buyers. One of the most significant rights is to "cure" a defective performance. A seller has several alternative courses of action when a buyer breaches the contract. The seller may cancel the contract if the buyer's breach is material. Under certain circumstances, a seller may withhold delivery or stop delivery if the goods are in transit. A seller also has the right to resell the goods and recover damages or simply to recover damages for the buyer's failure to accept the goods. Finally, the seller may, under certain circumstances, file suit to recover the price of the goods. The remedies of the seller are cumulative and not exclusive. The technical aspects of "cure" and of these remedies are discussed in the sections that follow.

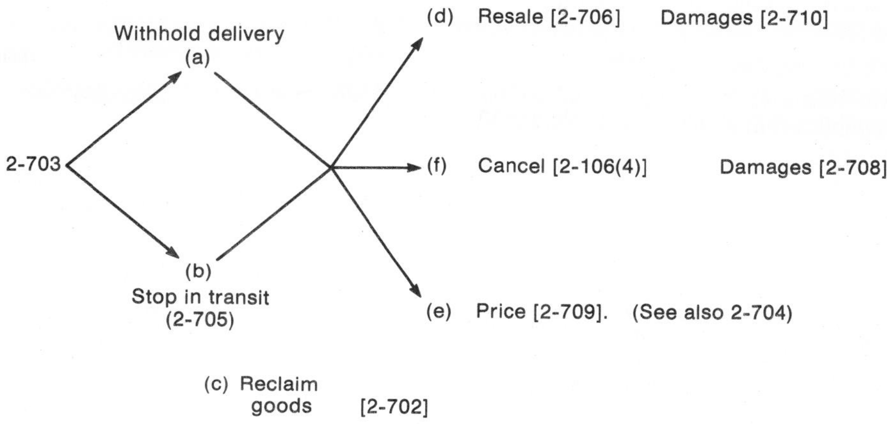

Fig. 15·3 Seller's remedies.

Cure

Upon inspecting the goods, if the buyer finds that they do not conform to the contract, he may reject them, providing he acts fairly in doing so. If the rejection is for a relatively minor deviation from the contract requirements, the seller must be given an opportunity to correct the defective performance. This is called cure. The seller may accomplish this by notifying the buyer of his intention to cure, then tendering proper or conforming goods if the time for performance has not expired. If the time for performance has expired, the seller—if he has reasonable grounds to believe that the goods will be acceptable in spite of the nonconformity—will be granted further time to substitute goods that are in accordance with the contract. The main purpose of this rule allowing cure is to protect the seller from being forced into a breach by a surprise rejection at the last moment by the buyer. The seller, in order to take advantage of this privilege, must notify the buyer of his intention to cure.

Right to reclaim goods on buyer's insolvency

If a seller discovers that a buyer on credit is insolvent, the seller will want to withhold delivery or stop it before it is completed. A buyer is insolvent "who either has ceased to pay his debts in the ordinary course of business or cannot pay his debts as they become due or is insolvent within the meaning of the federal bankruptcy law" [1-201(23)].

A seller, upon discovering that a buyer is insolvent, may refuse to make any further deliveries except for cash, and he may demand that payment be made for all goods theretofore delivered under the contract [2–702(1)]. If goods are en route to the buyer, they may be stopped in transit and recovered from the carrier [2–705]. If they are in a warehouse or other place of storage awaiting delivery to the buyer, the seller may stop delivery by the bailee. Thus, the seller can protect his interests by retaining or reclaiming the goods prior to the time they come into the possession of the insolvent buyer.

This right to reclaim the goods on the buyer's insolvency includes situations in which the goods have come into the buyer's possession. If the buyer has received goods on credit while he is insolvent, the seller can reclaim the goods by making a demand for them within ten days after their receipt by the buyer [2–702(2)]. By receiving the goods, the buyer has, in effect, made a representation that he is solvent and able to pay for them. If the buyer has made a written misrepresentation of solvency within the three-months' period before the goods were delivered to him, and the seller has justifiably relied on the writing, the ten-day limitation period during which the seller can reclaim the goods from the insolvent buyer does not apply [2–702(2)].

CASE

D submitted to P a year-old financial statement that was inaccurate. On the basis of that statement, P, a carpet company, sold carpeting to D on credit. Six weeks later, P discovered that D was insolvent, and P reclaimed the carpeting. Thereafter D filed a petition in bankruptcy. D's trustee contended that P had not acted within the time limits in reclaiming the goods from the insolvent buyer.

ISSUE Did P act within the time limits of the Code in reclaiming the goods?

DECISION Yes.

REASONS
1. A seller has a three-months' period within which to recover goods from an insolvent buyer if the buyer has made false statements in writing about his financial condition.
2. The three-months' time begins on the date that the financial statement is presented to the seller, not on the date it is originally written. Although the written statement was prepared one year before credit was extended, the seller reclaimed the carpeting six weeks after the statement was presented.

In re Bel Air Carpets, 452 F.2d 1210 (1971) (Cal. law).

The importance to a seller of the privilege of reclaiming goods or stopping them in transit should be obvious. If the insolvent buyer is adjudicated a bankrupt, the goods will become a part of the bankrupt estate and will be sold by the trustee in bankruptcy for the benefit of *all* the creditors of the buyer. If the seller is able to reclaim the goods, his loss will be kept to a minimum.

Right to reclaim goods from a solvent buyer

The right to stop goods in transit or to withhold delivery is not restricted to the insolvency situation. If the buyer has (1) wrongfully rejected a tender of goods, (2) revoked his acceptance, (3) failed to make a payment due on or before delivery, or (4) repudiated with respect to either a part of the goods or the whole contract, the seller can also reclaim the goods. This right extends to any goods directly affected by the breach.

To stop delivery by a carrier, the seller must give proper and timely notice to the carrier, so that there is reasonable time to follow the instructions [2–705(3)]. Once the goods have been received by the buyer, or a bailee has acknowledged that he holds the goods for the buyer, the right of stoppage is at an end. Only in the case of insolvency [2–705(2)] can the seller reclaim the goods after they are in the buyer's possession.

The right to stop delivery to a solvent buyer is restricted to carload, truckload, planeload, or larger shipments. This restriction is designed to ease the burden on carriers that could develop if the right to stop for reasons other than insolvency applied to all small shipments. The seller who is shipping to a buyer of doubtful credit can always send the goods C.O.D., and thus preclude the necessity for stopping in transit. Of course, the seller must exercise care in availing himself of this remedy, as improper stoppage is a breach by the seller and would subject him to an action for damages by the buyer.

Right to resell goods

The seller who is in possession of goods at the time of the buyer's breach has the right to resell the goods [2–706]. If part of the goods has been delivered, he can resell the undelivered portion. In this way the seller can quickly realize at least some of the amount due from the buyer. He also has a claim against the buyer for the difference between the resale price and the price that the buyer had agreed to pay. The resale remedy thus affords a practical method and course of action for the seller who has possession of goods that were intended for a breaching buyer.

Frequently, a buyer will breach or repudiate the contract prior to the time that goods have been identified to the contract. This does not defeat the seller's right to resell the goods. The seller may proceed to identify goods to the contract [2–704(1)(a)] and then use his remedy of resale. If the goods are unfinished, the seller may use his remedy of resale if he can show that the unfinished goods were intended for the particular contract [2–704(1)(b)].

The seller is also given other choices of action when the goods are in process at the time he learns of the breach. He may (1) complete the manufacture and identify the goods to the contract, or (2) resell the unfinished goods for scrap or salvage value, or (3) take any other reasonable action in connection with the goods [2–704(2)]. The only requirement is that the seller use reasonable commercial judgment in determining which course of action he will take in order to mitigate his damages. Presumably he would take into consideration factors such as the extent to which the manufacture had been completed and the resalability of the goods if he elected to complete the manufacture. Thus, the law allows the seller to proceed in a commercially reasonable manner in order to protect his interests.

When the seller elects to use his remedy of resale, the resale may be either a private sale or a public (auction) sale [2–706(2)]. It must be identified as one relating to the broken contract. If the resale is private, the seller must give the buyer reasonable notification of his intention to resell [2–706(3)]. If the resale is public, the seller must give the buyer reasonable notice of the time and place, so that he can bid or can obtain the attendance of other bidders. With goods that are perishable or threaten to decline speedily in value, the notice is not required. The seller is permitted to buy at a public sale or resale. The prime requirement is that the sale be conducted in a commercially reasonable manner [2–706(2)].

If the resale brings a higher price than that provided for in the contract, the seller is not accountable to the buyer for any profit [2–706(6)].

CASE

P and her husband operated a laundry and dry cleaning business in Charlotte, N.C. When her husband died, P contracted to sell the business to D for $20,100. After D's check bounced and D refused to deposit sufficient funds so the check might be honored, P told D that she would "look to the remedies available at law." Later, P sold the business for $10,700 and sued D for the difference. The trial court awarded her $9,300, the difference between the contract price and the resale price pursuant to 2–706.

ISSUE Is P entitled to the resale-contract price differential?

DECISION No.

REASONS
1. This is a case of first impression. Article 2 of the Code applies to "transactions in goods" (2–105). The sale of a laundry and dry cleaning business involves such a transaction and therefore comes within Article 2.
2. Code section 2–706 requires P to give the buyer reasonable notification of her intention to resell at private sale. Since she failed to give notice, she is relegated to damages based on the difference between the market price and contract price plus any incidental damages, but minus expenses saved as a result of the buyer's breach [2–708].

Miller v. Belk, 207 S.E.2d 792 (N.C.) 1974.

Right to collect damages for nonpayment

In many situations, resale would not be an appropriate or satisfactory remedy. The seller may elect to bring an action for damages if the buyer refuses to accept the goods or repudiates the contract [2–708]. The measure of damages is the difference between the market price at the place for tender and the unpaid contract price, plus incidental damages [2–708]. Incidental damages include expenses reasonably incurred as a result of the buyer's breach [2–710].

Usually, this measure of damages will not put the seller in as good a position as he would have had if the buyer had performed and the seller had not lost the sale. Under such circumstances, the measure of damages includes the profit the seller would have made from full performance by the buyer [2–708(2)] as well as incidental damages. In computing profit, the reasonable overhead of the seller may be taken into account. The measure of damages recognizes that a seller suffers a loss, even though he may ultimately resell for the same amount that he would have received from the buyer. He has lost a sale and the profit on the sale.

Right to collect the purchase price

When the buyer fails to pay the price as it becomes due, the seller may sue for the contract price of the goods if the goods were (1) accepted by the buyer, (2) lost or damaged within a commercially reasonable time after the risk of loss passed to the buyer, or (3) identified to the contract, and the seller was unable to sell them at a reasonable price, or the circumstances indicated that the effort to do so would be unavailing [2–709]. Thus, an action for the price is generally limited to situations in which the buyer has accepted the goods, the goods were destroyed after risk of loss passed to the buyer, or the resale remedy is not practicable. In other cases, the suit for dollar damages would be used [2–709(3)].

If the seller sues for the price, the goods are, of course, held by the seller on behalf of the buyer; they become, in effect, the buyer's goods. After the seller obtains a judgment against the buyer, the seller may still resell the goods at any time prior to collection of the judgment, but he must apply the proceeds toward satisfaction of the judgment. Payment of the balance due on the judgment entitles the buyer to any goods not resold [2–709(2)].

CASE

D, city of Louisville, executed a requirements contract with P, whereby P would provide D with all its requirements of parking meters for seven months at $54.20 per meter. Two days later, a new mayor took office and repudiated the contract. D contracted with Duncan to supply meters at $46.92. P sues for the price of 1,000 meters manufactured pursuant to D's order and for lost profits of $27.95 per meter based on the number of meters D bought from Duncan the first year ($27.95 × 4,250 meters = $118,787.50).

ISSUE Is P entitled to the purchase price under 2–709(1)(b) and for lost profits on the requirements contract pursuant to 2–708(2)?

DECISION Yes.

REASONS

1. The 1,000 parking meters are unsold and unsalable. P, under 2–709(1)(b), can recover the price of the meters identified to the contract, since P is unable after reasonable effort to resell them.
2. P is also entitled to the profits lost on meters that would have been sold under the requirements contract. Code section 2–708(2) permits recovery of the profit, including a reasonable overhead, which P would have made from a full performance by the buyer. Although it is proper to look to the orders under the Duncan contract to establish D's requirements, P can do so for only seven months, not for one year. Since D purchased a total of 3,450 meters during the first seven months under the Duncan contract, P's loss profits would be $96,427.50 ($27.95 × 3,450 meters).

City of Louisville v. Rockwell Mfg. Co., 482 F.2d 159 (Ky.) 1973.

REVIEW QUESTIONS AND PROBLEMS

1. Amy orders 3 white slips from a department store. They arrive C.O.D., and Amy pays the delivery person. At what point in time is Amy deemed to have accepted the goods? Explain.
2. In the prior question, assume that Amy opens the box and discovers black slips were sent. If she does not want these slips, what must she now do? Explain.
3. Slacks, Inc. sells tank tops to a fashionable boutique. Upon receipt, the store inspects them, discovers defects, and seasonably rejects them. Slacks instructs the store either to sell the tank tops or return them. The boutique does neither. Is it liable for anything? Explain.
4. Maria buys a new stove from Stove Store. After using it several times, she discovers that its temperature readings are not quite correct. These slight deviations would be significant only to a gourmet cook, which Maria is. May she reject? May she revoke acceptance? Explain.
5. A country music festival promoter contracted to buy 2,000 kegs of beer at $50 per keg. When the beer that arrived was found to be flat, the promoter rejected it. He could not buy that brand from any other source in time for the festival, so he bought 2,000 kegs of another beer at $55 per keg. What are the promoter's Article 2 damages? Explain.
6. An office manager ordered dictating equipment from Office Aids. After her order was booked, the manufacturer improved the equipment by adding an erasure prevention device. Believing that the manager would want this new feature, Office Aids delivered the newer device. Assuming that the manager made an effective rejection, what rights does Article 2 give to Office Aids? Explain.
7. Ray ordered a color TV from a local store. When it was delivered, he saw that the picture had a reddish tint. The man who installed the set offered to take it back to the shop to repair it, but Ray objected. "I don't want a repaired TV. I want a refund." The store maintained it would repair the set but not refund Ray's money. Later, Ray sued to recover his payments. Did he win? Why or why not?
8. A progressive country band contracted to buy a bus, to be delivered on May 15th. On May 1st, the band anticipatorily repudiated the contract. Fourteen months following the breach, the seller sold the bus at a private sale, then sued the band to recover the difference between the resale price and the contract price. Should this recovery be allowed by the court? Why or Why not?
9. In the previous question, would it make a difference if the private sale took place on May 16th but the seller failed to give the band (buyer) notice of the resale? Why or why not?
10. Xenon Corporation entered into a contract to manufacture goods for a construction company. Xenon requested delivery instructions but the construction company did not furnish them. As a result, the goods were never delivered. Is Xenon entitled to recover the price of the goods? Why or Why not?

16

Products Liability

In the law of sales of goods the word *warranty* describes the obligation of the seller with respect to goods that have been sold. As a general rule, a seller is responsible for transferring to the buyer a good title and goods that are of the proper quality, free from defects. He may also be responsible for the proper functioning of the article sold and for its suitability to the needs of the buyer. Thus, a warranty may extend not only to the present condition of goods but also to the performance that is to be expected of them.

A seller may make a variety of statements about the goods. It is necessary to evaluate these to determine which statements are warranties and which do not impose legal responsibility because they are merely sales talk.

A warranty made by a seller is an integral part of the contract. If the warranty is breached and the buyer notifies the seller of the breach within a reasonable time, the buyer may bring an action for breach of warranty. A breach of warranty may also result in injuries to the buyer or to third persons. Thus, the law relating to warranties has tort aspects also.

The obligation of a seller of goods to the buyer has been subject to reevaluation in recent years. In early law, the parties were usually in fairly equal bargaining positions, and the law did not regard the seller as having any substantial obligation to the buyer. *Caveat emptor* ("let the buyer beware") was the philosophy of the early law of sales.

As the nature of the sales transaction changed, the need for more protection to the buyer was recognized. *Caveat emptor* was gradually replaced by *caveat venditor* ("let the seller beware"). The law took the position that if the goods were defective, the seller should be held responsible. As the law changed to *caveat venditor,* various tort and contract theories developed, imposing liability on manufacturers, packers, producers, and sellers for injuries caused by defective products. These theories are discussed in this chapter.

The Code has several provisions relating to warranties. It draws a distinction between express warranties made by a seller and those implied from the transaction. The seller may guarantee the product directly, in which case it is an *express* warranty, or the warranty may be *implied* from the transaction and the circumstances. The Code classifies warranties as (1) express warranties, (2) implied warranties, and (3) warranties of title. When the seller is a merchant, special treatment is sometimes afforded to the warranty. This is also true with respect to modifications or exclusions of warranties. A recent federal law on warranties is discussed in chapter 26 with other aspects of consumer protection.

Warranties

Express warranties

An express warranty is one that is made as a part of the contract for sale and becomes a part of the basis of the bargain between the buyer and the seller [2-313(1)(a)]. An express warranty, as distinguished from an implied warranty, is part of the contract because it has been included as part of the individual bargain. To create an express warranty, the seller does not have to use formal words such as "warrant" or "guarantee," nor must he have the specific intention to make a warranty [2-313(3)]. A label on a bag of insecticide stated that it was developed especially to control rootworms. This was an express warranty that the insecticide was effective to control the rootworm. The word *guarantee* is often used, however. A contract of sale of automobile tires stated that the tires were guaranteed for 36,000 miles against all road hazards, including blowouts. This constituted an express warranty that the tires would not blow out during the first 36,000 miles of use.

CASE

P sued D, manufacturer, to recover for injuries. P was hit on the head by a golf ball following a practice swing with a golf-training device. D's catalog stated that the device was a "completely equipped backyard driving range." The label on the shipping carton and on the cover of the instruction booklet urged players to "drive the ball with full power." They also stated: "Completely safe—Ball will not hit player."

ISSUE Is D liable for breach of an express warranty?

DECISION Yes.

REASONS 1. A seller's statements, whether of fact or opinion, that become a part of the basis of the bargain constitute express warranties. The buyer need not prove reliance on the statement.

2. The statements here were more than mere puffing. They were factual descriptions of the characteristics of the product and express warranties.

Hauter v. Zogarts, 534 P.2d 377 (Cal.) 1975.

When any *affirmation of fact or promise* is made by the seller to the buyer (the affirmation or promise relating to the goods and becoming part of the basis of their bargain), an express warranty is created [2–313(1)(a)]. These statements by the seller create an express warranty that the goods will conform to his affirmation or promise. Any statement of fact or even of opinion, if it becomes a part of the basis of the bargain, is an express warranty.

Most statements of opinion, such as those concerning the value of the goods, do not give rise to an express warranty. As a general rule, a buyer is not justified in relying upon mere opinions, and they are not usually a part of the basis of the bargain, although they might be in some situations. The opinion of an expert with regard to the value of a gem might be considered as justifying the reliance of the buyer, and thus the opinion becomes part of the basis of the bargain.

Statements are warranties if they can properly be considered as terms of the agreement ultimately reached by the parties. The seller makes warranties in order to induce the sale of goods; and for this reason, warranties are regarded as essential parts of the contract. It should be remembered that warranties made after the sale of goods has been consummated are binding without any new consideration (2–209).

An express warranty may be made in a variety of ways. The seller may specifically make a factual statement about the goods, such as "this engine will produce 500 horsepower" or "this fabric is 100 percent nylon." These factual statements may be on labels or in a catalog or other sales promotion material. A direct promise may state "This grass seed is free from weeds." Generally, words that are descriptive of the product are warranties that the goods will conform to the description [2–313(1)(b)]. Descriptions may also be in the form of diagrams, pictures, blueprints, and the like. Technical specifications of the product would constitute warranties if they were part of the basis for the bargain. An express warranty can also be based on the instructions of the seller regarding use of the product.

Just as the seller may describe the goods, he may inform the buyer by showing him a model or a sample of what is being sold. Fabrics or clothing might be purchased on the basis of samples shown to the buyer, or a seller might display a working model of an engine. In either event, there would be an express warranty that the goods will conform to the sample or model if the parties have made this a part of their bargain [2–313(1)(c)].

The implied warranty of merchantability

Express warranties come into existence by virtue of the bargaining of the parties; implied warranties come into being as a matter of law, without any bargaining, and as an integral part of the normal sales transaction. Express warranties are negotiated aspects of the bargain between seller and buyer; implied warranties are legally present, unless clearly disclaimed or negated. Implied warranties exist even if a seller is unable to discover the defect involved or unable to cure it if it can be ascertained. Liability for breach of warranty is not based on fault but on the public policy of protecting the buyer of goods.

A warranty that the goods shall be merchantable is implied in a contract for sale if the seller is a merchant who deals in goods of the kind involved in the contract. It is not enough that the defendant sold the goods. The seller defendant must have been a merchant of goods. A person making an isolated sale is not a merchant.

A bank selling a repossessed car is not a merchant, and there is no implied warranty of merchantability in such a sale. This important warranty imposes a very substantial obligation upon the merchant seller. For goods to be merchantable, they must at least be the kind of goods that

a) pass without objection in the trade under the contract description; and

b) in the case of fungible goods, are of fair average quality within the description; and

c) are fit for the ordinary purposes for which such goods are used; and

d) run, within the variations permitted by the agreement, of even kind, quality, and quantity within each unit and among all units involved; and

e) are adequately contained, packaged, and labeled as the agreement may require; and

f) conform to the promises or affirmations of fact made on the container or label if any [2-314].

The foregoing standards provide the basic acceptable standards of merchantability. Fungible goods (b) are those usually sold by weight or measure, such as grain or flour. The term "fair average quality" generally relates to agricultural bulk commodities and means that they are within the middle range of quality under the description. Fitness for ordinary purposes (c) is not limited to use by the immediate buyer. If a person is buying for resale, the buyer is entitled to protection, and the goods must be honestly resalable by him. They must be acceptable in the ordinary market without objection. Subsection e is applicable only if the nature of the goods and of the transaction require a certain type of container, package, or label. Where there is a container or label and a representation thereon, the buyer is entitled to protection under subsection f, so that he will not be in the position of reselling or using goods delivered under false representations appearing on the package or container. He obtains this protection even though the contract did not require either the labeling or the representation.

CASE

P bought a glass jar of mixed nuts with this label: "Planters Dry Roasted MIXED NUTS no oils or sugar used in processing." P broke his tooth when he bit down on an unshelled nut found among the mixed nuts. He sued D, seller, for breach of express and implied warranty of merchantability. He claimed the clear glass jar showing unshelled nuts created an express warranty and that the nuts were not merchantable since they contained a foreign object.

ISSUE Is D, seller, liable for breach of either express or implied warranty?

DECISION No.

REASONS 1. The clear glass showing unshelled nuts was not an affirmative representation that all the mixed nuts were shelled. The use of the jar, while revealing shelled nuts, was a mere passive marketing tool.

2. In assessing the merchantability of goods, state regulations are pertinent. Pursuant to such legislation and regulation, the presence of an unshelled filbert is acceptable, since the presence of limited quantities of unshelled nuts is permissible. Moreover, since shells are a natural incident of the original food, P cannot use the foreign substance doctrine, which might make the product unmerchantable owing to the foreign impurity. An unshelled filbert is not a foreign substance but a natural part of the original food.

Coffer v. Standard Brands, Inc., 226 S.E.2d 534 (N.C.) 1976.

The implied warranty of merchantability imposes a very broad responsibility upon the merchant seller to furnish goods that are at least of average quality. In any line of business, the word *merchantable* may have a meaning somewhat different from the Code definition, and the parties by their course of dealing may indicate a special meaning for the term.

One purpose of this warranty is to require sellers to provide goods that are reasonably safe for their ordinary intended use. Although the law does not require accident-proof products, it does require products that are reasonably safe for the purposes for which they were intended when they are placed in the stream of commerce.

Liability for breach of the warranty of merchantability extends to direct economic loss as well as to personal injuries and to property damage. (Product liability based on this theory is discussed more fully later in this chapter.) Direct economic loss includes damages based on insufficient product value. In other words, the buyer is entitled to collect the difference in value between what was received and what the product would have had if it had been of merchantable quality. Direct economic loss also includes the cost of replacements and the cost of repairs. These damages need not be established with mathematical certainty, but reasonable degrees of certainty and accuracy are required so that the damages are not based on speculation.

The warranty of fitness for a particular purpose

Under the warranty of merchantability, the goods must be fit for the *ordinary purposes* for which such goods are used. An implied warranty of fitness for a *particular purpose* is created if, at the time of contracting, the seller has reason to know any particular purpose for which the buyer requires the goods and is relying on the seller's skill or judgment to select or furnish suitable goods [2–315]. In these circumstances, the seller must select goods that will accomplish the purpose for which they are being purchased.

CASE

P purchased a farm tractor from D. Claiming that the tractor could not handle heavy-duty plowing and that the engine failed earlier than it should have, P sued. He alleged that these problems constituted breaches of the warranties of merchantability and fitness for particular purpose.

ISSUE Was either implied warranty breached in this case?

DECISION No.

REASONS
1. The implied warranty of fitness is not involved in this case. First, there is no evidence whatever that the buyer relied on the seller's skill in selecting this particular tractor. Second and more important, when goods are put to ordinary use (plowing), the concept of merchantability—not fitness for particular purpose—applies. A particular purpose differs from the ordinary purpose for which the goods are used. Shoes are made for walking (general purpose), but the buyer may want shoes to go skiing or mountain climbing. Ordinary farm work includes heavy-duty plowing.
2. Although the tractor may not have been merchantable, the court does not rule on that issue, since the case was not brought within four years after sale, as required by the Code.

Wilson v. Massey-Ferguson, Inc., 315 N.E.2d 580 (Ill.) 1974.

The implied warranty of fitness applies both to merchants and nonmerchants but normally pertains only to merchants, since a nonmerchant does not ordinarily possess the required skill or judgment. The buyer need not specifically state that he has a particular purpose in mind or that he is placing reliance upon the seller's judgment if the circumstances are such that the seller has reason to realize the purpose intended or that the buyer is relying on him. For the warranty to apply, however, the buyer must actually rely upon the seller's skill or judgment in selecting or furnishing suitable goods. Both issues are questions of fact for a jury.

There is a difference between merchantability and fitness for a particular purpose, although both may be included in the same contract. Particular purpose involves a specific use by the buyer; ordinary use, as expressed in the concept of merchantability, means the customary function of the goods. Thus, a dishwasher could be of merchantable quality because it could ordinarily be used to wash dishes; but it might not be fit for a particular purpose because it would not be suited to the dishwashing needs of a restaurant.

Breach of the warranty of fitness for a particular purpose may result in disaffirmance of the contract. If the product causes an injury including economic loss, it may also result in a suit for dollar damages. This also will be discussed further as a part of products liability, later in this chapter.

The warranty of title

The *warranty of title* is treated as a separate implied warranty under the Code. Since the concept of title is intangible and is often overlooked by the buyer, the law ensures such a warranty by including it in the sale as a matter of law.

A seller warrants that he is conveying good title to the buyer and that he has the right to sell the goods. He further warrants that there are no encumbrances or liens against the property sold and that no other person can claim a security interest in them [2–312]. In effect, the seller implicitly guarantees to the buyer that he will be able to enjoy the use of the goods free from the claims of any third party. Of course, property may be sold to a buyer who has full knowledge of liens or encumbrances, and he may buy the property subject to these claims. In this event, there would not be a breach of warranty of title. The purchase price would, however, reflect that he was obtaining less than complete title.

Warranty of title can be excluded or modified only by specific language or by circumstances making clear that the seller is not vouching for the title [2–312(2)]. Judicial sales and sales by executors of estates would not imply that the seller guarantees the title. Also a seller could directly inform the buyer that he is selling only the interest that he has and that the buyer takes it subject to all encumbrances.

A seller who is a merchant, regularly dealing in goods of the kind that are the subject of the sale, makes an additional warranty. He warrants that the goods are free of the rightful claim of any third person by way of infringement of the third person's interests—that the goods sold do not, for example, infringe upon a patent. But a buyer may furnish to the seller specifications for the construction of an article, and this may result in the infringement of a patent. Not only does the seller not warrant against such infringement, but the buyer must also protect the seller from any claims arising out of such infringement [2–312(3)].

Disclaimers of warranties

A seller will often seek to avoid or restrict warranty liability. The Code provisions on exclusion or modification of warranties are designed to protect the buyer from unexpected and unfair disclaimers.

During the course of the dealings between buyer and seller, there may be both statements or conduct relating to the creation of an express warranty and statements or conduct tending to negate or limit such warranties. To the extent that it is reasonable, the two different kinds of statements or conduct shall be construed as consistent with each other [2–316(1)]. Negation or limitation is inoperative to the extent that such construction is unreasonable. In other words, if the express warranty and the attempt to negate warranties cannot be construed as consistent, the warranty predominates. The seller may have given the buyer an express warranty and may then have included in the contract a provision that purports to exclude "all warranties express or implied." That disclaimer will not be given effect, and the express warranty will be enforceable.

Implied warranties can be excluded if the seller makes it clear that the buyer is not to have the benefit of them. To exclude or modify the implied warranty of merchantability, the word *merchantability* must be used [2–316(2)]. If the disclaimer is included in a written contract, it must be set forth in a conspicuous manner. The disclaimer clause of the contract should be in larger type or a different color of ink or indented, so that it will be brought to the buyer's attention. It has been held that a disclaimer will not be effective if it is set forth in the same type and color as the rest of the contract.

To exclude or modify any implied warranty of fitness for a particular purpose, the exclusion must be conspicuously written. The statement, "there are no warranties which extend beyond the description on the face hereof" is sufficient to exclude the implied warranty of fitness for a particular purpose [2–316(2)]. An exclusionary clause should be printed in type that will set it apart from the balance of the contract.

CASE

P, the buyer of a tractor and backhoe, sued D, the seller, for breach of express warranties and for breach of the implied warranties of merchantability and of fitness for a particular purpose. The sales contract above the buyer's signature contained the following:

The equipment covered hereby is sold subject only to the applicable manufacturer's standard printed warranty, if any, in effect at the date hereof, receipt of a copy of which is hereby acknowledged, and no other warranties, express or implied, including without limitation, the implied warranties of merchantability and fitness for a particular purpose shall apply.

The type size of the foregoing was slightly larger than the rest of the contract, but it was not boldface.

ISSUE Was the disclaimer effective to negate the express and implied warranties?

DECISION No.

REASONS

1. The exclusion of the implied warranty of merchantability, if in writing, must be conspicuous.
2. The exclusion of the implied warranty of fitness for a particular purpose must be in writing and conspicuous.
3. The word *conspicuous* means that a reasonable person ought to have noticed it.
4. The Code provisions on exclusion of warranties were intended to protect the buyer from the situation where a salesperson's "pitch," advertising brochure, or large print in the contract giveth, and the disclaimer clause, in fine print, taketh away.
5. A valid disclaimer must be prominently set forth in large, bold print in a position that will compel notice. This one did not.

Dorman v. International Harvester Company, 120 Cal. Rptr. 516 (1975).

The Code also provides for other circumstances in which implied warranties may be wholly or partially excluded. The seller may inform the buyer that he is selling goods "as is," "with all faults." Or other language may call the buyer's attention to the exclusion and make it plain that the sale involves no implied warranty [2–316(3)(a)]. The implied warranty of merchantability may be excluded by oral agreement or by the *parties'* course of performance. The Code does not guarantee every buyer a good deal.

The buyer's examination of the goods or a sample or a model is also significant in determining the existence of implied warranties. If, before entering into the contract, the buyer has examined the goods, sample, or model as fully as he desired, there is no implied warranty on defects that an examination ought to have revealed to him [2–316(3)(b)]. If the seller demands that the buyer examine the goods fully, but the buyer refuses to do so, there is no implied warranty on those defects that a careful examination would have revealed. By making the demand, the seller is giving notice to the buyer that the buyer is assuming the risk with regard to defects that an examination ought to reveal. If the buyer simply fails to make an examination when the goods are available to him for this purpose, the seller will not be protected if a demand has not been made [2–316(3)(a)].

A course of dealing between the parties, course of performance, or usage of trade can also be the basis for exclusion or modification of implied warranties. These factors can be important in determining the nature and extent of implied warranties in any given transaction [2–316(3)(c)].

The Code also allows the parties to limit the remedies available in the event of a breach of warranty [2–719]. The agreement may provide for remedies in addition to, or in substitution of, those provided by the Code. The parties may also limit or alter the measure of damages. These provisions usually limit a buyer's damages to the repayment of the price upon return of the goods. Contracts often allow a seller to repair defective goods or replace nonconforming parts, without further liability. These provisions in effect eliminate a seller's liability for consequential damages and allow a seller to "cure" a defect or cancel a transaction by refunding the purchase price, without further liability.

Clauses limiting the liability of a seller are subject to the Code requirement on unconscionability [2–719]. Limitations of consequential damages for personal injury related to consumer goods are prima facie unconscionable. Limitations of damages for commercial loss are presumed to be valid.

Disclaimers of implied warranties are greatly limited by federal law today. As a part of the law relating to consumer protection, Congress passed the Magnuson-Moss warranty law. This law and the Federal Trade Commission rules adopted to carry out its purposes prohibit the disclaimer of implied warranties where an express warranty is given. This law is discussed further in chapter 26.

Third-party beneficiaries of warranties

Historically, suits for breach of warranty required "privity of contract," a contractual connection between the parties. Lack of privity of contract was a complete defense to the suit. Two aspects of privity-of-contract requirements are sometimes described as *horizontal* and *vertical*. The *horizontal* privity issue is: to whom does the warranty extend? Does it run only in favor of the purchaser, or does it extend to others who may use or be affected by the product? The *vertical* privity issue is: against whom can action be brought for breach of warranty? Can the party sue only the seller, or will direct action lie against wholesalers, manufacturers, producers, and growers?

When privity of contract is required, only the buyer can collect for breach of warranty, and he can collect only from the seller. A seller who is liable may recover from the person who sold to him. Thus the requirement of privity of contract not only prevented many suits for breach of warranty where privity did not exist but also encouraged multiple lawsuits over the same product.

It is not surprising that the law has generally abandoned strict privity of contract requirements. It has done so by statute and also case by case.

The drafters of the Code provisions on horizontal privity recognized that there was a great deal of divergence of opinion on the privity issue. Accordingly, the Code contains three alternative provisions that states may adopt [2–318]. Alternative A has been adopted by thirty jurisdictions. It provides that a warranty extends to any person in the family or household of the buyer or a guest in the home—if it is reasonable to expect that such person may consume, or be affected by, the goods and is injured by them.

Alternative B has been adopted in eight jurisdictions, and alternative C is the law in four states. The remaining states have either omitted the section entirely or have drafted their own version on the extent of the warranties. Alternatives B and C extend warranties to any natural person who may be reasonably expected to use, consume, or be affected by the goods and who is injured by them.

These Code provisions on horizontal privity do not attempt to deal with the vertical privity issue. The Code is neutral on it and leaves the development of the law to the courts, case by case. The courts of most states have abandoned the privity of contract requirement, and persons injured by products are allowed to sue all businesses in the chain of distribution without regard to the presence of privity of contract.

The trend of the law on product liability is clearly in the direction of extending greater protection to consumers and to the demise of privity of contract as a defense. In fact, many states have abolished the defense of lack of privity of contract.

CASE

P purchased a contaminated cheeseburger from a vending machine where he worked. P suffered acute food poisoning when he ate the cheeseburger. P sued D, the baking company that baked the bun, for breach of the warranty of merchantability. D moved to dismiss for lack of privity of contract.

ISSUE Is lack of privity of contract a defense to a breach of implied warranty?

DECISION No.

REASONS
1. For many years, West Virginians suffering injuries as the result of defective products have been unable to recover against defendant manufacturers, wholesalers, or retailers for breach of warranty unless they stood in privity of contract with the defendant. At the same time, West Virginia manufacturers, wholesalers, and retailers selling products nationally have been exposed to extensive liability for defective products manufactured in this state and sold elsewhere because the majority of American jurisdictions have abolished privity as a requirement in warranty actions.
2. In order to correct the situation referred to in 1, above, and to bring the state in line with the rest of the country, the requirement of privity is abolished.

Dawson v. Canteen Corp., 212 S.E.2d 82 (W.Va.) 1975.

Products Liability

One of the consequences of manufacturing or selling a product is *products liability,* the responsibility to a consumer or user if the product is defective and causes injury to a person or property. The subject of products liability involves several legal theories. A suit for dollar damages for injuries caused by a product may be predicated on the theory of (1) negligence, (2) misrepresentation, (3) breach of warranty, either express or implied, or (4) strict liability.

Products liability cases may be brought against manufacturers, sellers, or anyone in the chain of sale. They may be brought by the buyer, by another user of the product, or by some third party whose only connection with the product is an injury caused by it. The sections that follow discuss all four theories listed in the preceding paragraph, but the theory of strict liability has become the dominant one in most cases.

The trend of the law on products liability is clearly in the direction of extending greater protection to consumers. A manufacturer has an obligation to the public to market a safe product, free from defects. A producer is presumed to know of defects in its products and is therefore in bad faith in selling defective products. The consumer is entitled to protection from injuries.

The potential liability under all theories of products liability is usually covered by products liability insurance. In recent years, the cost of this insurance has skyrocketed. It has become a significant cost item in many products with a high exposure to products liability suits.

Negligence

In order to recover on a negligence theory, a plaintiff has to establish the negligence of the defendant, its failure to exercise reasonable care. Contributory negligence on the part of the plaintiff is a bar to a recovery. The mere fact that an injury occurs from the consumption or use of a product does not ordinarily raise a presumption that the manufacturer was negligent.

In a negligence action, privity of contract is not required, since it is not a contract action. A negligence suit can be brought not only by the person who purchased the defective product but also by any person who suffered an injury on account of a defect in the product if the defect was the proximate cause of his injury.

The Restatement of Torts (Second), Section 395, states the rule as follows:

> A manufacturer who fails to exercise reasonable care in the manufacture of a chattel which, unless carefully made, he should recognize as involving an unreasonable risk of causing physical harm to those who use it for a purpose for which the manufacturer should expect it to be used and to those whom he should expect to be endangered by its probable use, is subject to liability for physical harm caused to them by its lawful use in a manner and for a purpose for which it is supplied.

The plaintiff, of course, must by appropriate evidence prove that the manufacturer was negligent—failed to exercise reasonable care. He may be able to rely on the doctrine of *res ipsa loquitur,* "the thing speaks for itself," if (1) the instrumentality involved was within the exclusive control of the defendant at the time of the act of negligence, both as to operation and inspection; (2) the injury was not the result of any voluntary action or contribution on the part of the plaintiff; and (3) the accident ordinarily would not have occurred had the defendant used due care. If an elevator falls, killing an occupant, the manufacturer has liability, because the very happening of the accident creates a presumption of negligence.

Another method of establishing negligence is to prove that the manufacturer violated some statutory regulation in the production and distribution of his product. Some industries are subject to regulation under state or federal laws on product quality, testing, advertising, and other aspects of production and distribution. Proof of a violation of a statute may be sufficient to establish negligence of a manufacturer in such industries. Negligence established by proof of violation of a statute is called *negligence per se.*

Negligence is frequently based on failure of a manufacturer to warn of a known danger related to the product. A manufacturer who knows, or should know, his product to be dangerous has a duty to exercise reasonable care and foresight in preventing it from injuring or endangering people. Reasonable care includes the duty to warn of the danger. Negligence is often based on a design defect, also. In determining whether a manufacturer exercised reasonable skill and knowledge concerning the design of its product, factors include the cost of safety devices, their use by competitors, their effect on function, and the extent to which the manufacturer conducted tests and kept abreast of scientific development. A manufacturer is not an insurer, nor is he required to supply accident-proof merchandise; nontheless, the responsibilities for injuries often rest with whoever is in the best position to eliminate the danger inherent in the use of the product. A manufacturer of a rotary power lawnmower may be liable for negligent design if a user is able to put his hands or feet in contact with the moving blades of the mower.

Misrepresentation

If the seller has advertised the product through newspapers, magazines, television, or otherwise and has made misrepresentations with regard to the character or quality of the product, tort liability for personal injury may be imposed on him. The Restatement of Torts (Second), Section 402B, summarizes the liability of a seller for personal injuries resulting from misrepresentation:

> One engaged in the business of selling chattels who, by advertising, labels, or otherwise, makes to the public a misrepresentation of a material fact concerning the character or quality of a chattel sold by him is subject to liability for physical harm to a consumer of the chattel caused by justifiable reliance upon the misrepresentation, even though
>
> (a) it is not made fraudulently or negligently, and
>
> (b) the consumer has not bought the chattel from or entered into any contractual relation with the seller.

The rationale of the Restatement position is that a great deal of what the consumer knows about a product comes to him through the various media, and sellers should be held responsible for injuries caused by misrepresentations made to the public. A manufacturer may advertise that a certain shampoo contains no harmful ingredients and is perfectly safe to use even by people with tender skin. If someone uses the shampoo and suffers a skin ailment as a result thereof, he would be entitled to recover.

Breach of warranty

An action for personal injuries based upon a defective product can be predicated on a breach of either an express warranty or an implied warranty. The implied warranty may be either the implied warranty of merchantability or the implied warranty of fitness for a particular purpose. Most cases involve the warranty of merchantability, however.

As previously noted, there has been a gradual elimination of the privity requirement in cases of personal injuries caused by defective products. The early cases that abandoned the privity requirement involved personal injury and sickness caused by food and drugs. The law took the position that as a matter of social policy a packer, grower, or manufacturer of a product consumed by human beings should be liable if that product caused injury. Liability would be a deterrent to the sale of dangerous foods and drug products, and the loss would be on the party best able to afford it. Privity of contract had never been required for a negligence action, and the elimination of the requirement in breach of warranty actions was a recognition of the similarity of the two theories and of the difficulty of proving negligence of the seller of products such as canned goods. The breach of warranty theory eliminated the need to prove fault, and the elimination of privity of contract made the new theory realistically available and workable. It also avoided multiplicity of suits.

Various courts have used different justifications to eliminate the privity requirement in cases involving products other than food and drugs. Some have employed the dangerous instrumentality theory in nonfood cases. These courts said that privity was not required in such cases because food was inherently dangerous; therefore, if another product was inherently dangerous, the same rationale would be applied, and privity of contract would not be required. The law in effect fed on itself and expanded. Other courts stated that "warranties run with goods" in much the same way that a warranty involving the title to land runs with the land. A warranty is an invisible appendage that is a part of the goods; and as such, it belongs to anyone who is affected by the goods.

Today, in almost every state, the requirement of privity of contract has been relaxed or abolished, and an action can be maintained for breach of implied warranty without privity of contract. An action based upon such breach, being a contract action, does not require proof of negligence on the part of the manufacturer or seller. This is a great advantage to the injured plaintiff, who must prove only that the product was defective and that such defect was the proximate cause of his injury.

CASE

P, a farmer, had contracted to grow sweet corn for processing and freezing for the A canning company. Before planting, he consulted with D, who sold herbicides. D recommended a product manufactured by X chemical company. Following this recommendation, P applied the product. Thereafter, his corn crop was stunted, twisted, and infested with parasites.

ISSUE 1. Was the seller (D) liable in damages to P?

2. Was the manufacturer (X chemical company) liable in damages to P?

DECISION Yes to both questions.

REASONS 1. D is responsible because there was an implied warranty of fitness for a particular purpose. P had communicated to D his need for a herbicide to control weeds on his farmland.

2. X chemical company is liable, in spite of disclaimers, because it had represented that the product was compatible with corn, even though it had no real knowledge about corn in the area where P farmed.

Dobias v. Western Farmers Association, 491 P.2d 1346 (Wash.) 1971.

An express warranty may also be the basis of a claim for injuries without privity. It has been held that advertising constitutes an express warranty by the seller and that the affirmations and promises made to the consumer through radio, television, or the printed media can be relied upon by him and can be the basis for a suit by an injured party against the advertiser.

Strict Liability

The latest development in products liability is known as the theory of *strict liability.* This development imposes liability wherever damage or injury is caused by a defective product that is unreasonably dangerous to the user or consumer. It is the logical result of the elimination of the need to prove negligence and of the demise of the privity requirement in breach of warranty actions. In states that have adopted the strict liability theory, the theories of negligence and breach of warranty are becoming less significant.

The theory of strict liability was developed by legal scholars as a part of the Restatement of the Law of Torts. Section 402A of the Restatement (Second) provides the following:

> 402A. Special Liability of Seller of Product for Physical Harm to User or Consumer.
>
> (1) One who sells any product in a defective condition unreasonably dangerous to the user or consumer, or to his property, is subject to liability for physical harm thereby caused to the ultimate user or consumer, or to his property, if
>
> (a) the seller is engaged in the business of selling such a product, and
>
> (b) it is expected to and does reach the user or consumer without substantial change in the condition in which it is sold.
>
> (2) The rule stated in Subsection (1) applies although
>
> (a) the seller has exercised all possible care in the preparation and sale of his product, and
>
> (b) the user or consumer has not bought the product from or entered into any contractual relation with the seller.

The courts have relied heavily upon the foregoing in developing the law of strict liability. Today, it is the law in most states.

Theory of strict liability

The law of products liability based on the theory of strict liability has developed in response to changing societal concerns over the relationship between the consumer and the seller of a product. The increasing complexity of the manufacturing and distributional processes places upon injured parties a nearly impossible burden of proving negligence where, for policy reasons, it is felt that a seller should be responsible for injuries caused by defects in products. Therefore, the strict liability theory holds that a seller of a product is responsible for injury caused by his defective product, even if he had exercised all possible care in its design, manufacture, and distribution. The theory in effect imposes liability without fault, and a seller is effectively the guarantor of his product's safety.

Strict liability is based on the proposition that a manufacturer, by marketing and advertising his product, impliedly represents that it is safe for its intended use. No current societal interest is served by permitting the manufacturer to place a defective article in the stream of commerce and then to avoid responsibility for damages caused by the defect.

Strict liability is limited to products that are unreasonably dangerous. A product may be defective and unreasonably dangerous as a result of its manufacture, or the defect may be a result of design; however, a "defective condition" is not limited to defects in design or manufacture. The seller must provide with the product every element necessary to make it safe for use. One such element may be warnings or instructions concerning use of the product. A seller must give any warning and instructions required to inform the user or consumer of possible risks and inherent limitations of his product. If the product is defective, without warnings, and the defect is a proximate cause of the plaintiff's injury, the seller is liable.

CASE

P suffered a stroke allegedly caused by an oral contraceptive pill, Ovulen, manufactured by D drug company. The lower court in P's personal injury suit would not instruct the jury on the theory of strict liability because failure to warn of the dangers of the drug related solely to the theory of negligence.

ISSUE Is the D's failure to warn of dangers, adverse reactions, and side effects which may result from Ovulen a basis for the imposition of strict liability pursuant to §402A of the Restatement (Second) of Torts?

DECISION Yes.

REASONS

1. Apparently, the trial court perceived no difference between a negligence claim and a strict liability claim based on a failure to warn. But there is a difference.
2. Under a negligence theory, the issue is whether D was negligent in marketing Ovulen without using reasonable care to warn of its hazards and side effects, such as thrombosis.
3. Under a strict liability theory, the test is whether D's failure to warn of the potential dangers makes its product unreasonably dangerous. The defect is not the dangerous side effect but the failure to warn without regard to the reasonableness of the D's action in selling the drug without an adequate warning. On remand, the jury ought to be instructed on the theory of strict liability.

Hamilton v. Hardy, 549 P.2d 1099 (Colo.) 1976.

The theory of strict liability has been applied to leases of goods as well as to sales. The potential liability extends to all commercial suppliers of goods. Strict liability has been applied both to personal injuries and to damage to the property of the user or consumer. Some courts have refused to extend it to property damage, and most courts have refused to extend it to economic loss.

Strict liability may be imposed upon a seller of goods manufactured by a *third person* if the seller fails to give proper warning that a product is or is likely to be dangerous or if the seller fails to exercise reasonable care to inform buyers of the danger or otherwise to protect them against it. A similar duty to give warning applies to the manufacturer. A warning must be placed on a container or label if a product is explosive, poisonous, or otherwise injurious. Some cases extend the liability to the manufacturer of a component part of a product that fails. The manufacturer of an engine as well as the manufacturer of an airplane may be liable to victims of a plane that crashes because of mechanical failure of the engine.

The theory imposes liability on manufacturers and designers as well as on the seller of the goods; but in most states, it is not applicable to the sale of used goods. In almost every state, the liability extends not only to users and consumers but also to bystanders, such as pedestrians.

CASE

P, while shopping in a grocery store, was injured when a bottle of pop exploded. P sued D, the bottler, for her personal injuries. D contended that it had no liability because the doctrine of strict liability does not extend to bystanders.

ISSUE Is D liable?

DECISION Yes.

REASONS
1. The rule of strict products liability in tort applies to any person engaged in the business of supplying products for use or consumption, including any manufacturer of such product and any wholesaler, retail dealer, distributor, or other middleman.
2. The rule of strict products liability in tort extends not only to users and consumers but also to bystanders whose injury from the defective product is reasonably foreseeable.
3. The risk of personal injury and property damage will be minimized by charging the costs of injuries against the manufacturer who can procure liability insurance and distribute its expense among the public as a cost of doing business. Since the risk of harm from defective products exists for mere bystanders and passersby as well as for the purchaser or user, there is no substantial reason for protecting one class of persons but not the other.
4. The result does not give the bystander a "free ride." When products and consumers are considered in the aggregate, bystanders, as a class, purchase most of the same products to which they are exposed as bystanders. Thus, as a class, they indirectly subsidize the liability of the manufacturer, middleman, and retailer and in this sense do pay for the insurance policy tied to the product.

Embs v. Pepsi-Cola Bot. Co. of Lexington, 528 S.W.2d 703 (Ky.) 1975.

Proof required

A cause of action in strict liability requires proof that the defendant sold the product in a defective condition unreasonably dangerous to the user or consumer, that it reached the plaintiff without a change of condition, and that the product caused an injury to the plaintiff. The test as to whether or not a defect is unreasonably dangerous depends upon the reasonable expectations of the ordinary consumer. If the average consumer would reasonably anticipate the hazards of a product and fully appreciate the risk, it is not unreasonably dangerous. In strict liability cases, there are no issues on disclaimer of warranties, there is no problem of inconsistency with express warranties, and knowledge of the seller of the defect need not be proved. Of course, privity of contract is not required, and neither is reliance on the warranty by the injured party.

Strict liability requires only two elements of proof: that the product was defective, and that the defect was a proximate cause of the plaintiff's injuries. Even if a plaintiff proves injury from a product, he cannot recover without proving a defect. There is no liability, for instance, simply because someone becomes ill from drinking whiskey. If the plaintiff proves the defect, then he must prove causation between that defect and the injury. Finally, the defect must have existed when the product left the seller's hands. A seller is not liable if a safe product is made unsafe by subsequent changes. All of a plaintiff's proof may be made by circumstantial evidence.

Strict liability is not synonymous with *absolute liability*. There must be proof that some dangerous defect caused the injury despite the fact that the product was being used in the manner reasonably anticipated by the seller or manufacturer.

CASE

ISSUE The following question was certified to be answered by the New Hampshire supreme court: "Where a five-year-old child who was playing with matches is seriously burned when his pajama top ignited; where the fabric was not treated with an effective fire-retardant material, but was 100 percent cotton . . . ; and where the question for the jury is whether such fabric is 'unreasonably dangerous to the user or consumer' as provided by Restatement of Torts 2d §402A(1), should the definition of 'unreasonably dangerous' be framed in terms of the five-year-old child who uses the pajamas or in terms of the child's parent who purchases them?"

DECISION The answer to the certified question is that the definition of "unreasonably dangerous" should be framed in terms of the parent who bought the pajamas for the child.

REASONS

1. The test for determining "unreasonably dangerous" is in Comment i to §402A; the product "must be dangerous to an extent beyond that which would be contemplated by the ordinary consumer."
2. Five-year-old children do not contemplate the unavoidable dangers of cotton pajamas and their flammable characteristics. There would be no basis from which to ascertain unreasonableness. Therefore, the seller would become an insurer of its product.

Bellotte v. Zayre Corp., 352 A.2d 723 (N.H.) 1976.

The crucial difference between strict liability and negligence is that the existence of due care, whether on the part of seller or consumer, is irrelevant to the former. The seller is responsible for injury caused by his defective product, even if he has exercised all possible care in the preparation and sale of the product.

In most products liability cases, the injured party sues all those in the channel of distribution, including the manufacturer, the wholesaler, the distributor, and the retailer.

In products liability cases involving multiple defendants, the onus of tracing the defect is on the defendant dealers and manufacturer, so that a plaintiff may be compensated while leaving it to the defendants to fight out the question of responsibility among themselves. Anyone who had a hand in putting the defective product in the stream of commerce, whether technically innocent or not, has liability to the injured party.

It is generally held that contributory negligence is not a defense to a suit based on the theory of strict liability. This is somewhat of an oversimplification, however, because misuse of a product is a defense. Moreover, a person who voluntarily encounters a known unreasonable danger is not entitled to recover.

Failure to heed a warning with regard to a product will bar a recovery. This, in effect, means that "assumption of the risk" is a defense to a strict liability action. Misuse and abnormal use of a product is a defense because the manufacturer or seller could not have reasonably foreseen the misuse. If a backwoodsman uses a sharp hunting and fishing knife to shave and he cuts his throat, it is highly conceivable that the manufacturer would be entitled to a defense of misuse of the instrument.

REVIEW QUESTIONS AND PROBLEMS

1. It is often very difficult to determine whether a seller's statement is merely a permissible puff (sales talk) or an express warranty. The cases, as a consequence, produce different results. Now it's your turn. Which of the following are puffing and which are express warranties? Assume the *seller makes the following statement* about the goods sold *to the buyer:*
   a) The jukebox is a good machine and will probably not get out of order.
   b) October is not too late to plant this grass seed.
   c) This car is supposed to last a lifetime. It's in perfect condition.
   d) This dredge pipe has expandable ends that will seal upon the spill going through.
   e) This feed additive will increase your milk production and will not harm your dairy herd.
   f) These filter tanks should be able to remove iron and manganese from the water.
   g) This used car has never been wrecked.
2. Now try it again. In which of the following circumstances was the implied warranty of merchantability breached?
   a) In defendant's restaurant, plaintiff bought a martini with an unpitted olive. Plaintiff broke a tooth when he attempted to eat the olive, thinking it had been pitted.
   b) Plaintiff bought a bowl of fish chowder at defendant's restaurant. The soup contained a fish bone, which lodged in plaintiff's throat. Plaintiff had to undergo two esophagoscopies before the bone was removed.
   c) Plaintiff sues American Tobacco Company, alleging that the company's cigarettes are not merchantable because they cause or contribute to lung cancer.
   d) Plaintiff is bitten by a spider concealed in a pair of blue jeans sold by defendant's store.
   e) Seller sold cattle feed that contained the female hormone stilbestrol, which causes cattle to grow more rapidly than normal. Although stilbestrol may help fatten cattle more quickly, it causes abortions in pregnant cows and sterility in bulls. The plaintiff farmer raises cattle for breeding rather than for slaughter, so he sues. The label on the cattle feed package did not mention the fact that it contained stilbestrol.
   f) Drain cleaner is advertised as "safe." But it contains a 30 percent concentration of sodium hydroxide, a caustic substance proven destructive to human tissue.
   g) Plaintiff bought and used a lawnmower for approximately one year. One day while the plaintiff was mowing, an unknown object was hurled out of the grass chute and penetrated the eye of plaintiff's five-year-old son. Plaintiff sued on behalf of his son for breach of the implied warranty of merchantability.
   h) Plaintiff's Ford Pinto's gas tank exploded on impact.
   i) Plaintiff bought a cookbook from defendant retail book dealer. Four days later, while following a recipe in the book, plaintiff ate a small slice of one of the ingredients, a plant commonly known as elephant's ear, and became violently ill. Plaintiff sued for breach of the implied warranty of merchantability.
   j) Plaintiff bought a product that caused her to have an allergic reaction.
3. A business student went to an exclusive campus clothing store to buy a pair of shoes. He told the salesperson that he needed shoes to wear to interviews with large Wall Street firms. The salesperson recommended white patent leather loafers, which he bought. The Wall Street firms took one look at the shoes and terminated the interviews. Did the campus store breach any implied warranty? Explain.
4. The purchase agreement for a mobile home stated: "Standard Manufacturer Warranty—OTHERWISE SOLD AS IS." The buyer subsequently discovered defects and sued for breach of the implied warranty of merchantability. He contended that the disclaimer was ineffective because it did not contain the word *merchantability* and was not conspicuous. Was the buyer correct? Why or why not?
5. During training exercises, a soldier in the Marines was injured by a defective grenade. He sued the grenade manufacturer for breach of the implied warranty of merchantability. What result? Explain.
6. A forklift truck operator was injured when the equipment failed to function properly. The truck had been leased by his employer from State Trucking Lines, the manufacturer. The operator sued State, claiming that it be charged with strict liability. Did the operator win? Why or why not?

17

Introduction to Commercial Paper

The term *commercial paper* describes two basic types of negotiable instruments: the *note* (a promise to pay, other than a certificate of deposit) and the *draft* (an order to some other entity to pay). A *check* is a typical draft, an order from the drawer, directing the drawee (bank) to pay money to the payee of the check.

Negotiable means that the written contract can move freely as a substitute for money. That is one of the functions of commercial paper. The other is its use as a credit device. If an appliance dealer buys an air conditioner from a manufacturer and pays by check, the check substitutes for money. If the dealer pays with a 60-day note, the note is a credit device. The manufacturer may sell the note and receive money for it.

The concept of negotiability

Negotiable instruments developed because of the commercial need for something that would be readily acceptable in lieu of money and would accordingly be readily transferable in trade or commerce. Substantial protection and assurance of payment must be given to any person to whom the paper might be transferred. To accomplish this protection, it is necessary to insulate the transferee from most of the defenses that a primary party, such as the maker of a note, might have against the payee. The purpose of the negotiability trait is to prevent the primary party from asserting defenses to the instrument against the person to whom the paper was transferred.

To accomplish the foregoing, Article 3 of the Code provides that a person to whom commercial paper is negotiated takes it free of personal defenses of the maker or drawer. This basic theory of negotiability can be further explained by noting the difference between the *assignment* of a contract and the negotiation of a negotiable instrument. Assume that the dealer owes the manufacturer $100, but he has a counterclaim because the air conditioner was defective. If a third party purchased a right from the manufacturer, it would be subject to the dealer's defense of failure of consideration. The third party, the assignee, would secure no better right against the dealer than the original right held by the manufacturer, the assignor. The third party therefore could not collect $100 from the dealer.

In this example, if the evidence of the debt is not a simple contract for money but a negotiable promissory note given by the dealer to the manufacturer, and it is properly negotiated to a third party, the third party is in a position superior to that which he occupied when he was an assignee. Assuming that he is a "holder in due course," he has a better title because he is free of the personal defenses that are available against the manufacturer, the original party to the paper. The dealer, therefore, cannot use the defense of failure of consideration against the third party, and the third party can collect the $100.

Transfer of the instrument free of personal defenses is the very essence of negotiability. Three requirements must be met before a holder is free from personal defenses. First, the instrument must be negotiable; that is, it must comply with the statutory formalities and language requirements. An instrument that does not qualify is nonnegotiable, and any transfer is an assignment subject to defenses. Second, the instrument must be properly *negotiated* to the transferee. Third, the party to whom negotiable commercial paper is negotiated must be a *holder in due course* or have the rights of a holder in due course. Each of these concepts is discussed in the next chapters.

The defenses that cannot be asserted against a holder in due course are called *personal defenses. Real defenses,* on the other hand, may be asserted against anyone, including a holder in due course. Real defenses are matters that go to the very existence of the instruments. Personal defenses such as failure of consideration involve less serious matters and usually relate to the transaction out of which they arose.

Kinds of commercial paper

Article 3 of the Code, Commercial Paper, is restricted in its coverage to the draft, the check, the certificate of deposit, and the note. A *certificate of deposit* is a type of savings account wherein the bank agrees to repay the sum with interest at a specified time [3–104(2)].

A note is two-party paper, as is a certificate of deposit. The parties to a note are the *maker,* who promises to pay, and the *payee,* to whom the promise is made. The draft and the check are three-party instruments. A draft presupposes a debtor-creditor relationship between the *drawer* and the *drawee* or some other obligation on the part of the drawee in favor of the drawer. The drawee is the debtor; the drawer is the creditor. The drawer creditor orders the drawee debtor to pay money to a third party, who is the *payee.* The mere execution of the draft does not obligate the drawee on the paper. The drawee's liability on the paper arises when it formally *accepts* the obligation to pay in writing upon the draft itself. By accepting, the drawee becomes primarily liable on the paper [3–410(1)]. Thereafter, the drawee is called an *acceptor,* and its liability is similar to the liability of the maker of a promissory note.

A check drawn by a bank upon itself is a *cashier's check.* A *certified check* is a check that has been "accepted" by the drawee bank. Certification is discussed further in the next section. *Traveler's checks* are like cashier's checks in that the financial institution issuing them is both the drawer and the drawee. Traveler's checks are negotiable when they have been completed by the identifying signature. A *bank draft* is a banker's check; that is, it is a check drawn by one bank on another bank, payable on demand. Such drafts are often used in the check collection process and are called "remittance instruments" in this connection.

Ambiguous terms and rules of construction

In view of the millions of negotiable instruments that are made and drawn daily, it is to be expected that a certain number of them will be ambiguously worded. Accordingly, the Code provides a number of rules to be applied in interpreting negotiable instruments.

Some instruments are drawn in such a manner that it is doubtful whether the instrument is a draft or a note. It may be directed to a third person but contain a promise to pay, rather than an order to pay. The holder may treat it as either a draft or a note and present it for payment to either the person who signed it or the apparent drawee. Where a draft is drawn on the drawer, it is treated as a note [3–118(a)].

An instrument may contain handwritten terms, typewritten terms, or printed terms. Where there are discrepancies in the instrument, handwritten terms control typewritten and printed terms, and typewritten terms control printed terms [3–118(b)]. Thus, a printed note form may state that it is payable on demand, but there may be typed or written on the note "payable thirty days from date." Such an instrument would be payable in thirty days.

There may also be a conflict between the words and the figures of an instrument. Thus a check may have the words "fifty dollars" and the figures "$500." The words control, and the check would be for fifty dollars. If the words are ambiguous, the figures will control [3–118(c)]. In a check with the words "Five seventy five dollars" and the figures "$5.75," the figures will control. In some cases, the ambiguity may arise from the context of the words.

If an instrument provides for the payment of interest but does not state the rate, the rate will be at the judgment rate at the place of payment. An unsatisfied money judgment bears interest at a rate specified by statute, and whatever this judgment rate is in a particular state will thus be applicable in this situation. Interest will run from the date of the instrument or, if it is undated, from the date of issue [3–118(d)].

If two or more persons sign an instrument as maker, acceptor, drawer, or indorser as part of the same transaction, they are jointly and severally liable unless the instrument otherwise specifies. This means that the full amount of the obligation could be collected from any one of them or that all of them might be joined in a single action. Joint and several liability is imposed even though the instrument contains such words as "I promise to pay" [3–118(e)].

Banking Transactions

The check is the most common form of commercial paper. Article 4 of the Code—Bank Deposits and Collections—provides uniform rules to govern the collection of checks and other instruments for the payment of money. These rules govern the relationship of banks with one another and with depositors in the collection and payment of *items*.

Terminology

The following terminology of Article 4 [105] is significant, especially with regard to the designation of the various banks in the collection process:

a) "Depositary bank" means the first bank to which an item is transferred for collection even though it is also the payor bank;

b) "Payor bank" means a bank by which an item is payable as drawn or accepted;

c) "Intermediary bank" means any bank to which an item is transferred in course of collection except the depositary or payor bank;

d) "Collecting bank" means any bank handling the item for collection except the payor bank;

e) "Presenting bank" means any bank presenting an item except a payor bank;

f) "Remitting bank" means any payor or intermediary bank remitting for an item.

Timing is important in the check collection process. Many of the technical rules of law refer to a *banking day,* which is defined as "that part of any day on which a bank is open to the public for carrying on substantially all of its banking functions" [4–104(1)(c)]. A bank is permitted to establish a cutoff hour of 2 P.M. or later, so that the bank may have an opportunity to process items, prove balances, and make the necessary entries to determine its position for the day. If an item is received after the cutoff hour or after the close of the banking day, it may be treated as having been received at the opening of the next banking day [4–107]. The term *midnight deadline* with respect to a bank means midnight on its banking day following the banking day on which it receives a check or a notice regarding the check [4–104(1)(h)].

Another important term is *clearinghouse,* an association of banks engaged in clearing or settling accounts between banks in connection with checks [4–104(1)(d)].

Checks are sometimes payable "through" a bank, rather than by the bank. This is often true of settlement checks issued by insurance companies and dividends paid by corporations.

The words "payable through" do not make the bank the drawee; they do not authorize or order the bank to pay the instrument out of funds in the account of the drawee; nor do they order or require the bank to take the paper for collection [3–120]. The bank's authority in this situation is extremely limited; it is merely a funnel through which the paper is to be presented properly to the drawee or maker.

A related situation is that in which a note or an acceptance of a draft contains the language "payable at" a designated bank. In recognition of varying banking practices in different sections of the country, the Code provides two alternatives, either of which could be adopted by a state in enacting the Code; namely, that (1) a note or an acceptance of a draft "payable at a bank" is like a draft on the bank; and upon its due date the bank is authorized, without consultation, to make the payment out of any available funds of the maker or acceptor; or (2) such words *are not* an order or authorization, but a mere direction to the bank to request instructions from the maker or acceptor [3–121].

Certified checks

Either the drawer or the holder of a check may present it to the drawee bank for certification. The bank will stamp "certified" on the check, and an official of the bank will sign it and date it. By certifying, the bank assumes responsibility for payment and sets aside funds from its customer's account to cover the check.

Certification may or may not change the legal liability of the parties upon the instrument. When the *drawer* has a check certified, such a certification merely acts as additional security and does not relieve the drawer of any liability. On the other hand, when the *holder* of a check secures certification by the drawee bank, he thereby accepts the bank as the only party liable thereon. Such an act discharges the drawer and all prior indorsers from liability [3–411(1)]. The effect of such certification is similar to a payment by the bank and redeposit by the holder.

The refusal of a bank to certify a check at the request of a holder is not a dishonor of the instrument. The bank owes the depositor a duty to pay but not necessarily the duty to certify checks that are drawn on it, unless there is a previous agreement to certify [3–411(2)]. A drawer cannot stop payment on a check after the bank has certified it.

Principles of Bank Collection

Terminology

If a check is deposited in a bank other than the bank on which it is drawn, it must be sent to the drawee bank for payment. This collection process may involve routing the item through a number of banks that typically credit or debit accounts they maintain with one another. In particular, the regional Federal Reserve Banks, with which most banks have accounts, play a major role in this process. An example may help you understand the terminology used in the collection process.

Suppose Holmes in Athens, Georgia, mails his check drawn on the First Athens Bank to Exxon in Houston, Texas, in payment of an obligation. Exxon deposits the check in the First National Bank of Houston, which forwards it to the Federal Reserve Bank of Houston, which sends it to the Federal Reserve Bank of Atlanta, which presents it to the First Athens Bank for payment. The relationship of these parties is depicted in Fig. 17.1.

The collection process

As Fig. 17.1 indicates, the collection process begins when the customer (Exxon) deposits a check to its account. The account is provisionally credited by the bank. The check then passes through the collecting banks, each of which provisionally credits the account of the prior bank. When the check finally reaches the payor-drawee bank (First Athens Bank), that bank debits the drawer's (Holmes's) account.

The payor bank then credits the account of the presenting bank, remits to it or, if both belong to the same clearinghouse, includes the check in its balance there. If the payor bank honors the check, the settlement is final. Transactions prior to this final settlement by the payor bank are called "provisional settlements," because it is not known until final settlement whether the check is "good." If the payor bank dishonors the check, each provisional settlement is *revoked*, and the depositary bank which had given its provisional credit to the customer for the deposit cancels it. The dishonored check is then returned to the customer.

When a bank has received a check for collection, it has the duty to use ordinary care in performing its collection operations. These operations include presenting the check to the drawee or forwarding it for presentment, sending notice of nonpayment if it occurs and returning the check after learning that it has not been paid, and settling for the check when it receives final payment. Failure of the collecting bank to use ordinary care in handling a check subjects the bank to liability to the depositor for any loss or damage sustained. And depositary banks have additional responsibilities.

To act seasonably, a bank is generally required to take proper action before the

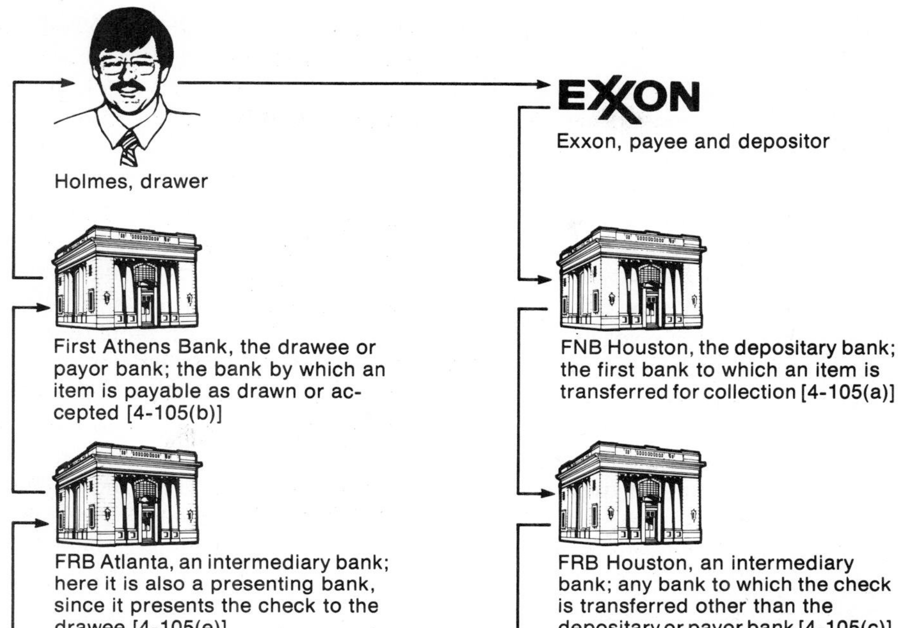

Fig. 17·1

midnight deadline following the receipt of a check, a notice, or a payment. Thus, if a collecting bank receives a check on Monday and presents it or forwards it to the next collecting bank any time prior to midnight Tuesday, it has acted seasonably.

If a check has been dishonored, as in the case of an "N.S.F." (not sufficient funds) check, the presenting bank will revoke its provisional settlement and charge the item back to the account of the next prior collecting bank. Likewise, other banks in the chain of collection will charge back. The final step is a charge-back to the customer's account by the depositary bank. Each of the collecting banks must return the item or send notification of the facts by its midnight deadline. The right to charge back by the depositary bank is not affected by the fact that the depositor may have drawn against the provisional credit.

A depositor does not have the right to draw against uncollected funds. Accordingly, he is not entitled to draw against an item payable by another bank until the provisional settlement his depositary bank has received becomes final [4–213(4)(a)]. Many banks allow their customers this privilege, even though they have no legal right to do so.

If the deposit is an item *on which the depositary bank is itself the payor* ("on us" items) the credit becomes final on the opening of the second banking day following receipt of the item [4–213(4)(b)].

A customer who deposits an item for collection should indorse it, but quite frequently a customer forgets that signature. The depositary bank may supply the missing indorsement. If the bank states on the item that it was deposited by a customer or credited to his account, such a statement is as effective as the customer's indorsement. This is a practical rule intended to speed up the collection process by making it unnecessary to return to the depositor any items he may have failed to indorse [4–205].

Collection from the payor bank

Most items in the collection process are presented through a clearinghouse or by mail. Collecting banks are agents of the payee-depositor, and all credits are initially provisional. If the item is dishonored, the collecting bank that has given credit for it may charge back against the account or obtain reimbursement from its customer if it returns the item or sends notice of dishonor within the midnight deadline or a longer reasonable time after it learns of the dishonor [4–212(1)]. In this situation, the midnight deadline would be midnight one or two banking days after the bank learns of the dishonor.

Final payment is the process by which the payor bank substitutes its own obligation for that of the drawer. Final payment usually occurs whenever the payor bank makes a provisional settlement for the item (a credit) and then fails to revoke its credit within its midnight deadline after receipt of the item. If the payor bank makes a provisional settlement for an item on the banking day it is received, that bank has until final payment of the check—but not later than the midnight deadline on the following day—to decide whether or not the item is good. Within this time the bank may revoke the settlement and return the item or, if this is not possible, send written notice of nonpayment. This enables the bank to defer posting until the next day. When a check drawn by one customer of a bank is *deposited by another customer of the same bank* for credit on its books, the bank may return the item and revoke any credit given at any time on the following day.

Failure of the payor-drawee bank to take action within the prescribed time limits may make it accountable to the person who deposited the check if the check is not paid. This liability is imposed if the bank (1) retains a check presented to it by another bank without settling for it by midnight of the banking day of receipt or (2) does not pay or return the check or send notice of dishonor within the period of its midnight deadline. If the payor bank is also the depositary bank (that is, if the check deposited by the customer is one that is drawn on his bank) settlement on the day of receipt is not required, but the bank must return the check or send notice of dishonor before its midnight deadline [4–212(3)].

An item is finally paid by a payor bank when the bank (1) pays the item in cash, (2) settles for the item without reserving the right to revoke the settlement, (3) completes the process of posting the item, or (4) makes a provisional settlement and fails to revoke it within the time prescribed [4–213(1)]. Upon final payment, the payor bank is accountable for the item.

Another problem relates to the *order of payment of checks.* There is no priority among checks drawn on a particular account and presented to a bank on any particular day. The checks and other items may be accepted, paid, certified, or charged to the indicated account of its customer in any order convenient to the bank [4–303(2)].

An item does not always proceed through the clearinghouse. It may be presented directly to the payor bank for payment over the counter. If the payor bank pays the item, it may not later collect back the payments if its customer has insufficient funds on deposit [4–213].

CASE

Several checks were drawn on an account at D, the payor bank. The checks had been given to P, who deposited them in his account, also at D bank. The bank discovered that the checks were forged but did not charge back P's account until two to ten days after the checks were deposited.

ISSUE Was it an error to give judgment to D, payor bank?

DECISION Yes.

REASON Final payment normally occurs when the payor bank that gives provisional credit fails to revoke its credit within its midnight deadline after receipt of the item [4–213(1)(d)]. This final payment rule applies to payor banks like D who are also the depositary banks. It was an error to grant judgment for D since it appeared to make final payment of the checks.

Trading Associates, Inc. v. Trust Co. Bank, 235 S.E.2d 661 (Ga.) 1977.

Stop payments

A customer has the right to stop payment on checks drawn on his account. Only the drawer has this right; it does not extend to holders—payees or indorsees. To be effective, a stop-payment order must be received at a time and in a manner that will afford the bank a reasonable opportunity to stop payment before it has taken other action on the item [4–403]. If a check has been certified, the depositor cannot stop payment, whether he or the payee procured the certification. An oral stop order is binding on the bank for only fourteen days unless confirmed in writing within that period. Unless renewed in writing, a written stop order is effective for only six months [4–404].

A bank that honors a check upon which payment has been stopped is liable to the drawer of the check for any loss he has suffered because of the failure to obey the stop order. The burden is on the customer to establish the amount of his loss. It may be that the customer cannot establish any loss. Thus, if the drawer did not have a valid reason to stop payment, he cannot collect from a bank that fails to obey the stop-payment order [4–403(3)]. The bank cannot by agreement disclaim its responsibility for its failure to obey stop-payment orders [4–103(1)]. Thus, a form signed by a customer agreeing not to hold the bank responsible for failure to pay could not be enforced.

Because of the concept of negotiability previously noted, a stop order on a check gives the drawer only limited protection. If the check is negotiated by the payee to a holder in due course, that holder can require payment of the amount of the check, notwithstanding the stop order.

CASE

D equipment company bought equipment from X and gave him a check drawn upon Y bank in payment. It was understood that the equipment would be delivered the following day. When it was not delivered, D stopped payment on the check. X attempted to cash the check at Y bank, but payment was refused. X then took the check to his own bank, P bank, which cashed it. When the check was sent to Y bank, that bank refused to honor it because of the stop order. P bank seeks to collect the amount of the check from D equipment company.

ISSUE Does the stop order protect D equipment company against the claim of the bank?

DECISION No.

REASONS 1. The bank was a holder in due course and had no reason to know of the stop order.

2. If a check gets into the hands of a holder in due course, the drawer will be liable to that person, notwithstanding the stop payment order.

Suit & Wells Equipment Co., Inc. v. Citizens National Bank of Southern Maryland, 282 A.2d 109 (Md.) 1971.

Relationship between a Bank and Its Customers

The legal relationship between a bank and its depositors is that of debtor and creditor. If the depositor is a borrower of the bank, the reverse relationship (creditor-debtor) also exists between the bank and its customers. The dual relationship provides the bank with a prompt and easy method of protecting itself in the event of a depositor's default or pending insolvency. A bank can "seize" bank deposits under its right of set-off (an independent right to deduct debts from customers' accounts) if such action becomes necessary to protect its account receivable.

CASE

P, a grain elevator, sued D bank for wrongful dishonor of its checks. P owed D $272,000 on certain promissory notes; $190,000 was owed on short-term notes, and the balance was due on long-term notes. These notes were secured by mortgage and security agreements. P, in negotiating a new loan, told D's officers that it lost $22,000 during the last year and that its checking account had been overdrawn by $35,000. It sought to borrow $50,000. The loan was turned down, and P's elevator closed for two days. D bank then set off P's $71,000 checking account balance against its loans and returned all of P's checks when presented for payment.

ISSUE Is D liable for not honoring P's checks and for seizing the checking account?

DECISION No.

REASONS

1. A bank may set off a general deposit account against a depositor's matured debts. Here the notes allowed acceleration of the due dates if the bank in good faith felt insecure.
2. Since the bank in good faith believed itself insecure, acceleration of the notes was proper.

Farmers Co-op El., Inc., Duncombe v. State Bank, 236 N.W.2d 674 (Iowa) 1975.

Rights and duties of banks

A bank is under a duty to honor checks drawn by its customer when there are sufficient funds in his account to cover the checks. If there are insufficient funds, the bank may honor the checks, even though this action creates an overdraft. The customer is indebted to the bank for the overdraft and implicitly promises to reimburse the bank [4–401(1)].

CASE

After giving a creditor her check for $800, D called her bank, P, about the possibility of a stop-payment order. The bank employee told D that the order could not be issued until the next business day. D then asked what would happen if she deliberately created an overdraft by withdrawing most of her money from her checking account. The bank employee stated that according to P's internal policies, the check would not be honored. D withdrew money from her account to create an overdraft on the $800 check. P nevertheless paid the $800 in question and now sues D to recover the amount of the overdraft.

ISSUE Did P bank correctly pay the $800, giving it the right to recover the overdraft from D?

DECISION Yes.

REASONS

1. D's conversations with the bank employee did not constitute an agreement that the check would be dishonored. The employee stated only an opinion regarding what might happen.
2. Notwithstanding the bank's own internal policies, it can lawfully pay the check and seek recourse from D. Section 4–401 clearly gives the bank the option to pay an overdraft and to charge the customer's account for that overdraft when the check is otherwise properly payable.

Continental Bank v. Fitting, 559 P.2d 218 (Ariz.) 1977.

If a bank wrongfully dishonors a check, it is liable to its customer for damages proximately caused by the wrongful dishonor. When the dishonor occurs by mistake, as distinguished from a malicious or willful dishonor, liability is limited to the *actual damages proved* [4–402]. Provision is also made for *consequential damages* proximately caused by the wrongful dishonor and may include damages for arrest or prosecution of the customer. The Code rejects early common law decisions holding that, if the dishonored item were drawn by a merchant, he was defamed in his business because of the reflection on his credit. Consequently, a merchant cannot recover damages on the basis of defamation, and he is limited to actual damages.

If a bank in good faith pays an altered check, it can charge the account of its customer only according to the original tenor of the check. Thus, if a check is raised, the bank can charge its customer's account only with the original amount of the check [4–401(2)(a)]. If a person signs his name to an incomplete check and it is thereafter completed and presented to the drawee bank that pays it, the bank can charge the customer's account for the full amount if it pays in good faith and does not know that the completion was improper [4–401(2)(b)].

A bank is entitled, but not *obligated,* to pay a check that is over six months old and it may charge the check to the customer's account [4–404]. Certified checks do not fall within the six months' rule; they are the primary obligation of the certifying bank, and the obligation runs directly to the holder of the check.

As a general proposition, the death or incompetency of a person terminates the authority of others to act on his behalf. If this principle were applied to banks, a tremendous burden would be imposed upon them to verify the continued life and competency of drawers. A bank's authority to pay checks therefore continues until it knows that a customer has died or has been judged incompetent and the bank has had a reasonable opportunity to act [4–405].

Rights and duties of depositors

Banks make available to their customers a statement of account and canceled checks. Within a reasonable time after they are received by the customer, he is under a duty to examine them for forgeries and for raised checks. The bank does not have the right to charge an account with forged checks, but the customer's failure to examine and to notify will prevent him from asserting the forgery (or alteration) against the bank if the bank can establish that it suffered a loss because of this failure. The bank may be able to prove that prompt notification would have enabled it to recover from the forger [4–406(2)].

CASE

A and B were partners who maintained a bank account in D bank. One of their employees, without their knowledge or consent, wrote checks on the partnership bank account and forged the names of A and B. D bank honored these checks and charged the partnership account. Sometime later, A and B discovered the forgeries and sought to recover from the bank. The bank claimed that A and B were negligent, in that they received most of the canceled checks and did not discover the forgeries for several months.

ISSUE Can A and B recover from the bank?

DECISION No.

REASON Under the Code, a customer of a bank is precluded from asserting a forgery against a bank when he has failed to exercise reasonable care.

Terry v. Puget Sound National Bank, 492 P.2d 534 (Wash.) 1972.

The Code does not specify the period of time within which the customer must report forgeries or alterations. It does specify that if the same wrongdoer commits successive forgeries or alterations, the customer must examine and notify the bank within fourteen days after the first item and statement were available to him. Otherwise, he cannot assert the same person's forgeries or alterations paid in good faith by the bank [4–406(2)(b)]. This rule is intended to prevent the wrongdoer from having the opportunity to repeat his misdeeds. If the customer can establish that the bank itself was negligent in paying a forged or altered item, the bank cannot avail itself of a defense based upon the customer's tardiness in examining and reporting [4–406(3)]. The same result occurs when a bank processes an item that has been materially altered or contains an unauthorized indorsement. If a person's negligence contributes to the alteration or unauthorized signature, the bank is not liable for the item paid unless the bank failed to observe reasonable commercial standards. Thus, if both parties are "at fault," the bank is liable, because its fault prevents it from asserting the fault of the other party.

A customer is precluded from asserting a forged signature or alteration on a check after one year from the time the check and statement were made available to him, even though the bank was negligent. Forged indorsements must be reported within three years [4–406(4)]. If a payor bank, as a matter of policy or public relations, waives its defense of tardy notification by its customer, it cannot thereafter hold the collecting bank or any prior party for the forgery [4–406(5)].

REVIEW QUESTIONS AND PROBLEMS

1. To acquire a sound understanding of the legal principles governing commercial paper, you must be able to recognize various forms. Give the *name* of each of the following four *forms* and the *parties* to the form.

John E. Murray, Jr.
School of Law
Pittsburgh, PA
NO. 157
8-26
430
January 4, 19 82
PAY TO THE ORDER OF Eric M. Holmes $ 70.00
Seventy and no/100 DOLLARS
Pleasant Hills Office
MELLON BANK
John E. Murray Jr.
:0430--0026: 243--7716: 0157 :0000000007000:

(a)

FIRST CITY BANK OF NEW YORK
New York, New York
No. 4762 May 1, 1982
THIS CERTIFIES THAT THERE HAS BEEN DEPOSITED with the undersigned the sum of $400,000.00
four hundred thousand DOLLARS
Payable to the order of Sara Oil Company on July 27, 1989, with interest only to maturity at the rate of TWELVE per cent (12%) per annum upon surrender of this certificate properly indorsed.
FIRST CITY BANK OF NEW YORK BY;
M. Hopkins, Vice President
Authorized Signature

(b)

Moscow, Idaho June 7, 19 82
One year from date pay to the order of Betty Stein
Four thousand Dollars
Andre Pellier
To: Robert Shaw
47 Peachtree Street
Atlanta, Georgia 30303

(c)

$2,000.00 October 3, 19 82
Upon acceptance Pay to Paula Payee
Two thousand and no/100 DOLLARS
Value Received and Charge Same to Account of Hanover Insurance Co., payable through Case Bank.
George Perkins
George Perkins, Vice-President
Hanover Insurance Company

(d)

2. Merriam signed a promissory note payable to the order of Coburn. The printed figures in note stated $27,000 as the principal, but in the body of the note the principal was typed as "Two Hundred

Twenty-Five Dollars." Merriam made no payments, and Coburn sued for $27,000 plus interest. During the trial, evidence was introduced that the note was payable in monthly installments of $225. Is Merriam liable to pay $27,000 or $225? Explain.

3. Kilpatrick made a check payable to the order of Shaefer, who then had the check certified. Kilpatrick made a stop-payment order to the bank before the check was presented for payment. Should the bank pay the check to Shaefer if Kilpatrick has a valid defense to an action on the instrument? Explain.

4. Dodge does her banking with the First State Bank of Los Angeles. Sanford banks with the Middle National Bank of Chicago. Dodge sent Sanford a check drawn on her Los Angeles bank. Sanford deposited the check in the Chicago bank and received a provisional credit. The Chicago bank sent the check to the Western State Bank of Denver for collection. The Denver bank received the check but misplaced it. Is the Chicago bank liable for the negligence of the Denver bank? Why or why not?

5. Pearl is the holder of a check drawn by Sharpe on Washington State Bank. Pearl also maintains an account at Washington State Bank. The check is deposited at the bank on Monday. On that same day, Sharpe's account is overdrawn, but she promises to make a substantial deposit, so the bank holds the check until Thursday. Sharpe does not make the deposit, and the bank, on Friday, returns the check to Pearl marked "Insufficient Funds." Can Pearl require the bank to make good on the check? Why or why not?

6. Men's Wear drew a check payable to Zino & Co. When Zino did not receive it in the mail, Men's Wear placed a stop-payment order in writing with the Drawee Bank. Approximately one year later, Drawee Bank paid on the check to a collecting bank and charged Men's Wear's account. Men's Wear had not renewed its stop-payment order. Is Drawee Bank liable to Men's Wear for failing to honor the stop-payment order? Why or why not?

7. An attorney had a bank account labeled "Special Account" for holding his client's money in escrow. If the attorney makes a withdrawal from this escrow account for his own personal use, does his client have grounds for a legal claim against the bank? Why or why not?

8. Dolly's bank wrongfully dishonored two small checks that she had drawn. She brought an action against the bank and recovered a judgment of $831.50 for the following: $1.50 for a telephone call to one of the payees; $330.00 for two weeks' lost wages; and $500.00 for illness, embarrassment, and inconvenience. Should a court uphold this judgment on appeal? Why or why not?

9. Lucas was a depositor in the Bank of the Potomac. Certain indorsements on checks drawn by Lucas were forged, but he did not inform the bank of the forgeries for over three years. Lucas claims that he was excused from giving earlier notice. Is the bank liable for honoring these checks with forged indorsements? Why or why not?

10. Forest Products, Inc., a manufacturer of wooden handles, employed Mimms as its general office manager. Mimms had a personal checking account with the State Bank, but Forest did not have an account there. Mimms forged the signature of the president of the company on a letter addressed to State Bank, authorizing Mimms to cash and deposit checks made payable to Forest. Checks deposited were to be credited to Mimms's account. During the next two years, Mimms either cashed or deposited $18,000 worth of checks that belonged to Forest. Forest sued the State Bank. At trial, it was determined that the bank had not acted in accordance with reasonable commercial standards, and Forest Products was negligent in not making a timely inspection of its books. Should the bank be held liable? Why or why not?

18

The Creation and Transfer of Commercial Paper

Chapter 16 introduced the concept of negotiability. There, we learned that a holder in due course of a negotiable instrument is not subject to personal defenses asserted by prior parties to the instrument. This chapter and the next one examine in detail this legal principle. The negotiability principle is our primary concern in this chapter, which will answer two basic questions:

1. What legal requirements must be met if an instrument is to qualify for the special treatment afforded negotiable instruments?
2. How is a transfer by assignment distinguished from a transfer by negotiation?

The next chapter primarily concerns the concept of holder in due course and will answer these two basic questions:

1. What requirements must be met for a holder to qualify as a holder in due course?
2. Which defenses are personal defenses and which are real defenses?

Requirements of Negotiability

The negotiability of an instrument is determined by the terms written on the face of the instrument. In order to be negotiable, it must satisfy four basic requirements: it must (1) be signed by the maker or drawer; (2) contain an unconditional promise or order to pay a sum certain in money; (3) be payable on demand or at a definite time; and (4) be payable to order or to bearer [3–104(1)].

The first requirement is simply that there be a writing signed by the maker or drawer [3–104(1)(a)]. It is not required that any particular type or kind of writing be used, nor is it necessary that the signature be at any particular place upon the instrument. The instrument may be in any form that includes "printing, typewriting, or any other intentional reduction to tangible form" [1–201(46)]. A symbol is a sufficient signature if "executed or adopted by a party with present intention to authenticate a writing" [1–201(39)]. The use of the word *authenticate* in the definition of *signed* makes it clear that a complete signature is not required. The authentication may be printed or written and may be placed on the instrument by stamp.

The necessity of a promise or order

A negotiable note must contain a *promise* to pay. Although the word *promise* is used in almost all notes, a word or words expressing an undertaking to pay may be substituted. The promise must be derived from the language of the instrument, not from the fact that a debt exists. A mere acknowledgment of a debt in writing (an IOU) does not contain a promise. Even though a written memorandum is sufficient evidence and creates a valid enforceable instrument upon which recovery may be had, it is not negotiable.

A draft must contain an *order* to pay. The purpose of the instrument is to order the drawee to pay money to the payee or his order. The drawer must use plain language to show an intention to make an order and to signify more than an authorization or request. It must be a direction to pay. Thus, an instrument in the following form would not be negotiable: "To John Doe. I wish you would pay $1,000 to the order of Richard Roe. [Signed] Robert Lee." This would nevertheless be a valid authorization for John Doe to make payment to Richard Roe.

The promise or order must be unconditional

Negotiable instruments serve as a substitute for money and as a basis for short-term credit. If these purposes are to be served, it is essential that the instruments be readily received in lieu of money and freely transferable. Conditional promises or orders would defeat these purposes, for it would be necessary that every transferee determine whether or not the condition had been performed prior to his taking the instrument. The instruments would not freely circulate. In recognition of these facts, the law requires that the promise or order be unconditional.

The question of whether or not the promise or order is conditional arises when the instrument contains language in addition to the promise or order to pay money. The promise or order is conditional if the language of the instrument provides that payment is controlled by, or is subject to, the terms of some other agreement [3–105(2)(a)]. Clearly, a promise or order is conditional if reference to some other agreement is *required* and if payment is *subject to* the terms of another contract.

CASE

D executed a note and purchase-money mortgage to X. X negotiated the note to P. The note contained the following stipulation: This note with interest is secured by a mortgage on real estate, of even date herewith, made by the maker hereof in favor of the said payee. . . . The terms of said mortgage are by this reference made a part hereof. When P sued D to collect the note and to foreclose the mortgage, D alleged that X was guilty of fraud. P claimed to be a holder in due course and not subject to the defense.

ISSUE Is the note negotiable, so that P is a holder in due course?

DECISION No.

REASONS 1. The note, incorporating by reference the terms of the mortgage, did not contain an unconditional promise to pay. It was therefore not negotiable, and P could not be a holder in due course.

2. Mere reference to a note being secured by mortgage is a common commercial practice and in itself does not impede the negotiability of the note. There is, however, a significant difference between a note stating that it is "secured by a mortgage" and one that provides, "the terms of said mortgage are by this reference made a part hereof." In the former instance, the note merely refers to a separate agreement that does not impede its negotiability; in the latter instance, the note is rendered nonnegotiable.

Holly Hill Acres, Ltd. v. Charter Bk. of Gainesville, 314 So.2d 209 (Fla.App.) 1975.

Negotiability is destroyed also if reference to another writing would be necessary to determine the exact nature of the promise or order. A mere reference to some other contract or document does not condition the promise or order, however, nor does it impair negotiability. A distinction, then, is to be drawn between additional language that imposes the terms of some other agreement and language that simply gives information about the transaction that gave rise to the instrument. Thus, the use of the words "subject to contract" conditions the promise or order, while the words "as per contract" would not render the promise or order conditional. The latter is informative rather than restrictive. Implied or constructive conditions, such as the implication that no obligation would arise until an executory promise has been performed, do not render a promise or order conditional [3–105(1)(a)].

Statements of the consideration for which the instrument was given and statements of the transaction out of which the instrument arose are simply informative [3–105(1)(b)]. A draft may have been drawn under a letter of credit, and a reference to this fact does not impose a condition [3–105(1)(d)]. Notes frequently contain a statement that some sort of security has been given, such as a mortgage on property, or that title to goods has been retained as security for the payment of the note. In either case, the purpose is to make clear to the holder that the promise to pay is secured by something in addition to the general credit of the maker; and as a consequence, a mere reference to the security does not destroy negotiability [3–105(1)(e)].

Notes given in payment for property purchased on installment often provide that title to the property shall not pass to the maker of the note until all necessary payments for have been made. A statement to this effect in a note does not condition the promise to pay.

The particular fund concept

A statement that an instrument is to be paid only out of a particular fund imposes a condition [3–105(2)(b)]. Such an instrument does not carry the general personal credit of the maker or drawer and is contingent upon the sufficiency of the fund on which it is drawn.

There are two exceptions to the foregoing rule with regard to a limitation to payment out of a particular fund. An instrument issued by a government or government agency may still be negotiable although payment is restricted to a particular fund [3–

105(1)(g)]. Second, an instrument issued by or on behalf of a partnership, unincorporated association, trust, or estate may be negotiable even though it is limited to payment out of their entire assets [3–105(1)(k)].

The preceding case demonstrates that mere references to some other contract or agreement do not impair negotiability. Likewise, a note is not considered conditional merely because it makes reference to a particular source or fund.

CASE

D executed a note with P bank to secure an uninterrupted line of credit. The note, in pertinent part, recited that it was "payable in installments or payable $80.00 per week from Jack and Jill contract." P bank sued D to recover the proceeds of the note.

ISSUE Is the promise to pay a conditional promise?

DECISION No.

REASONS
1. A note is not made conditional because it indicates a particular source or fund from which reimbursement is expected.
2. A promise to pay will be held unconditional whenever it is possible to do so without doing violence to the ordinary meaning of the language used.
3. Under the statute providing that an order is not unconditional if the instrument states that it is to be paid "only" out of a particular fund or source, the key word is "only."

Bank of Viola v. Nestrick, 390 N.E.2d 636 (Ill.) 1979.

Sum certain in money

To be negotiable an instrument must be payable in money. Instruments payable in chattels such as wheat or platinum are therefore not negotiable. *Money* means a medium of exchange that is authorized or adopted by a domestic or foreign government as a part of its currency [1–201(24)]. The amount payable may be stated in foreign as well as domestic money [3–107(2)]. If the sum payable is stated in foreign currency, payment may be made in the dollar equivalent unless it is specified in the instrument that the foreign currency is the only medium of payment.

The language used in creating commercial paper must be certain with respect to the amount of money promised or ordered to be paid. Otherwise, its value at any period could not be definitely determined. If the principal sum to be paid is definite, negotiability is not affected by the fact that it is to be paid with interest, in installments, with exchange at a fixed or current rate, or with cost of collection and attorney's fees in case payment shall not be made at maturity [3–106].

If at any time during the term of the paper its full value can be ascertained, the requirement that the sum must be certain is satisfied. The obligation to pay costs and attorney's fees is part of the security contract, separate and distinct from the primary promise to pay money, and does not therefore affect the required sum certain. The certainty of amount is not affected if the instrument specifies different rates of interest before and after default; nor is the certainty affected by a provision for a stated discount for early payment or an additional charge if payment is made after the date fixed [3–106(1)(c)]. The principal amount to be paid, however, must be certain in order for the note to be negotiable.

CASE

D, an employer, gave P (a pension fund company) a note stating that P promised to pay D "all current contributions as they become due under the collective bargaining agreement . . . in addition to the sum of $15,606.44 with interest."

ISSUE Does the note contain an unconditional promise to pay a sum certain?

DECISION No.

REASONS
1. To be certain on the amount to be paid, the language or figures must allow another holder to figure the sum.
2. The promise to pay in this note does not contain a "sum certain," since a further holder of the note could not determine how much is due without evidence beyond the note's language.

Central States, Southeast & Southwest Areas, Health and Welfare Fund v. Pitman, 338 N.E.2d 793 (Ill.) 1978.

Time of payment must be certain

As a substitute for money, negotiable instruments would be of little value if the holder were unable to determine when he could demand payment. A negotiable instrument, therefore, must be payable on demand or at a "definite time" [3–104(1)(c)].

An instrument is payable on demand when it so states, when payable at sight or on presentation, or *when no time of payment is stated* [3–108]. In general, the words "payable on demand" are used in notes and the words "at sight" in drafts. If nothing is said about the due date, the instrument is demand paper. A check is a good illustration of such an instrument. The characteristic of demand paper is that its holder can require payment at any time by making a demand upon the person who is obligated on the paper.

The requirement of a definite time is in keeping with the necessity for certainty in instruments. It is important that the value of an instrument can always be determined. This value will be dependent upon the ultimate maturity date of the instrument. If an instrument is payable only upon an act or event, the time of its occurrence being uncertain, the instrument is not payable at a definite time even though the act or event has occurred [3–109(2)]. Thus, an instrument payable "thirty days after my father's death" would not be negotiable.

The requirement of certainty as to the time of payment is satisfied if it is payable on or before a specified date [3–109(1)(a)]. Thus, an instrument payable "on or before" June 1, 1986, is negotiable. The obligor on the instrument has the privilege of making payment prior to June 1, 1986, but is not required to pay until the specified date. An instrument payable at a fixed period after a stated date, or at a fixed period after sight, is payable at a definite time [3–109(1)(b)]. The expressions "one year after date" or "sixty days after sight" are definite as to time.

CASE

P demanded payment from D on a $2,300 note. The note stated that it was due at request with 30 days' notice. D refused to pay the note, and P sued to collect the proceeds.

ISSUE Is the note payable on demand?

DECISION Yes.

REASONS
1. Instruments payable on demand include those in which no time for payment is stated.
2. The 30-day notice provision was meant to give the debtor a reasonable time of 30 days to pay the debt.
3. The creditor was free to demand payment at any time.

Shields v. Prendergast, 244 S.E.2d 475 (N.C.) 1978.

Acceleration and extension clauses

Two types of provisions appearing on the face of instruments may affect the definite time requirement. The first, an *acceleration clause,* hastens or accelerates the maturity date of an instrument. Accelerating provisions may be of many different kinds, but one provides that in case of default in payment, the entire note shall become due and payable. Another kind gives the holder an option to declare the instrument due and payable when he feels insecure about ultimate payment. An instrument payable at a definite time subject to any acceleration is negotiable [3–109(1)(c)]. If, however, the acceleration provision permits the holder to declare the instrument due when he feels insecure, the holder must act in good faith in the honest belief that the likelihood of payment is impaired. The presumption is that the holder has acted in good faith, placing the burden on the obligor-payor to show that such act was not in good faith [1–208].

The second type of provision affecting time is an *extension clause,* the converse of the acceleration provision. It lengthens time for payment beyond that specified in the instrument. A note payable in two years might provide that the maker has the right to extend the time of payment six months. An instrument is payable "at a definite time subject to extension at the option of the holder, or to extension to a further definite time at the option of the maker or acceptor or automatically upon or after a specified act or event" [3–109(1)(d)]. If an extension is at the option of the holder, no time limit is required. The holder always has a right to refrain from undertaking collection. An extension at the option of the maker or acceptor, however, or an automatic extension must specify a definite time for ultimate payment, or negotiability is destroyed.

The Magic Words of Negotiability

The *words of negotiability* express the intention to create negotiable paper. The usual words of negotiability are *order* and *bearer* [3–110], [3–111]. When these words are used, the maker or drawer has in effect stated that the instrument may be negotiated to another party. When the word *bearer* is used, it means that payment will be made to anyone who *bears* or possesses it. When the word *order* is used, it means that it will be paid to the designated payee or anyone to whom the payee orders it to be paid.

Other words of equivalent meaning may be used, but to ensure negotiability it is preferable to use the conventional words. If the instrument is not payable to "order" or to "bearer," it is not negotiable, and all defenses are available in suits on the instrument.

CASE

P sued D to recover on two promissory notes. The notes stated: "Buyer agrees to pay to Seller. . . ." D attempted to assert several personal defenses to the note. P claimed to be a holder in due course.

ISSUE Is P a holder in due course of a negotiable instrument?

DECISION No.

REASONS
1. To be a negotiable instrument, the writing must be payable to order or to bearer. The notes sued on were payable "to seller" and, therefore, were not negotiable instruments.
2. There can be no holder or holder in due course of an instrument that is not negotiable. The transferee of such an instrument is an assignee.
3. P is subject to all defenses.

Locke v. Aetna Acceptance Corporation, 309 So.2d 43 (Fla.App.) 1975.

Order paper

If the terms of an instrument provide that it is payable to the order or assigns of a person who is specified with reasonable certainty, the instrument is payable to order [3-110(1)]. The expressions "Pay to the order of John Doe" or "Pay to John Doe or order" or "Pay to John Doe or assigns" create order paper. The note in the previous case, *Locke v. Aetna Acceptance Corporation,* would have been negotiable had it been made payable to the order of the seller.

An instrument may be payable to the order of two or more payees together, such as A and B, or in the alternative, A or B. An instrument payable to A and B must be indorsed by both. One payable to the order of A or B may be negotiated by either [3-116].

CASE

A check in settlement of accounts was drawn payable to the order of X *and* the Y concrete company. The check, indorsed only by Y, was deposited in Y's bank. When the check was presented for payment to D bank, it refused payment because of the missing indorsement of X.

ISSUE Was D bank justified in refusing to honor the check?

DECISION Yes.

REASON Because the check was made payable to the order of two payees, the signatures of both payees were required for negotiation.

Clinger v. Continental National Bank, 503 P.2d 363 (Colo.) 1972.

An instrument may be payable to the order of an estate, a trust, or a fund. Such instruments are payable to the order of the representative of the estate, trust, or fund [3-110(1)(e)]. An instrument payable to the order of a partnership or an unincorporated association such as a labor union is payable to such partnership or association. It may be indorsed by any person authorized by the partnership or association. [3-110(1)(g)].

Bearer paper

The basic characteristic of bearer paper as distinguished from order paper is that it can be negotiated by delivery without indorsement. An instrument is payable to bearer when created if it is payable (1) to bearer, (2) to the order of bearer (as distinguished from the order of a specified person or bearer), (3) to a specified person or bearer (notice that it is not to *the order of* a specified person or bearer), or (4) to "cash" or "the order of

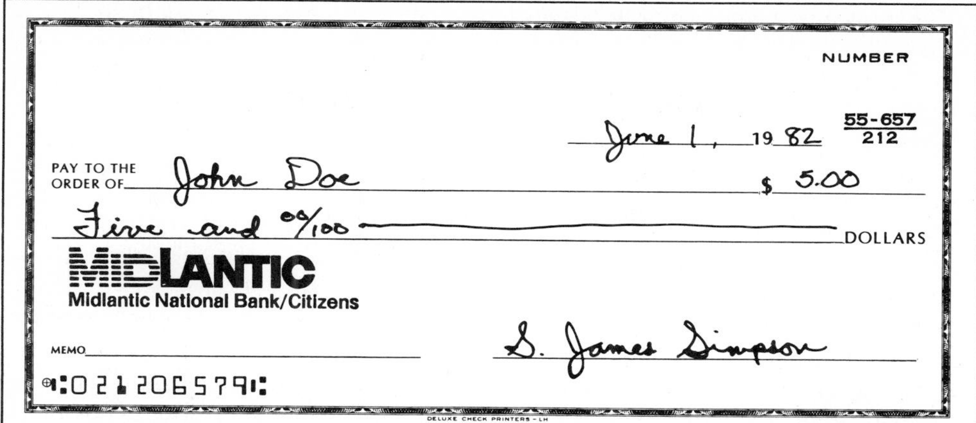

NUMBER

June 1, 19 82 55-657/212

PAY TO THE ORDER OF John Doe $ 5.00

Five and 00/100 DOLLARS

MIDLANTIC
Midlantic National Bank/Citizens

MEMO S. James Simpson

⑆0212065791⑆

DELUXE CHECK PRINTERS – LH

Fig. 18·1 Order paper payable to the order of John Doe [3-100(1)]. It requires John Doe's indorsement if it is to be negotiated.

cash," or any other indication that does not purport to designate any specific payee [3–111].

Although bearer paper can be negotiated without indorsement, the person to whom it is transferred will often require an indorsement. The reason for this is that an indorser has a greater liability than one who negotiates without indorsement. Also, if the instrument is dishonored, identification of the person who negotiated the paper becomes easier with an indorsement.

Terms and omissions not affecting negotiability

Some additional terms, usually for the benefit of the payee or other holder, may be included in commercial paper without impairing negotiability. Many instruments contain statements indicating that collateral has been given. These statements, including provisions relating to the rights of the payee or holder in the collateral, do not affect negotiability [3–112(1)(b)(c)].

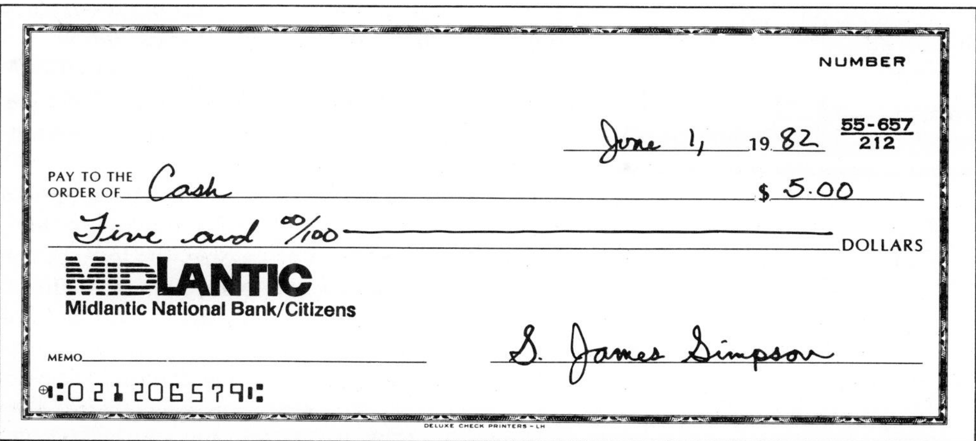

NUMBER

June 1, 19 82 55-657/212

PAY TO THE ORDER OF Cash $ 5.00

Five and 00/100 DOLLARS

MIDLANTIC
Midlantic National Bank/Citizens

MEMO S. James Simpson

⑆0212065791⑆

DELUXE CHECK PRINTERS – LH

Fig. 18·2 Bearer paper. Its negotiation is effective without an indorsement [3-111].

The drawer of a check or draft may include a provision that the payee, by indorsing or cashing it, acknowledges full satisfaction of an obligation of the drawer. The provision will not affect negotiability [3–112(f)]. Checks or drafts drawn by insurance companies in settlement of claims usually contain such a provision.

Often, the consideration for which an instrument was given is set forth in the instrument, and it is common to include words such as "for value received" or "in payment for services rendered." The omission of words stating the consideration for which an instrument was given will not affect its negotiability. Nor is the negotiable character of an instrument otherwise negotiable impaired by omission of a statement of the place where the instrument is drawn or payable [3–112(1)(a)].

Whether there is no date, a wrong date, an antedate, or a postdate is not important from the standpoint of negotiability [3–114(1)]. Any date that does appear on the instrument is presumed correct until evidence is introduced to establish a contrary date [3–114(3)]. Any fraud or illegality connected with the date of the instrument does not affect its negotiability but merely gives a defense.

Incomplete instruments

A person may sign an instrument that is incomplete in that it lacks one or more of the necessary elements of a complete instrument. Thus, a paper signed by the maker or drawer, in which the payee's name or the amount is omitted, is incomplete.

An incomplete instrument cannot be enforced until it is completed [3–115(1)]. If the blanks are subsequently filled in by any person in accordance with the authority or instructions given by the party who signed the incomplete instrument, it is then effective as completed. A person might leave blank, signed checks with an employee who must pay for goods to be delivered. When the employee fills in the amounts and names of the payees, the checks are perfectly valid.

A date is not required for an instrument to be negotiable; however, if a date is necessary to ascertain maturity ("payable sixty days from date"), an undated instrument is an incomplete instrument. The date may be inserted by the holder. If an instrument is payable on demand or at a fixed period after date, the date that is put on the instrument controls, even though it is antedated or postdated [3–114(2)].

Negotiation and assignment

The general rule governing the transfer of almost all types of property is that a person can transfer no greater interest than he owns. *Assignments* follow that general rule. The general law of assignments was discussed in chapter 13. When one attempts to transfer rights by assignment, it is generally stated that the assignee steps into the shoes of the assignor. Thus, the transfer of an instrument by assignment vests in the assignee only those rights that the assignor had.

By contrast, the key feature of negotiability is that a *negotiation* might confer upon a transferee greater rights than were held by the transferor. If the transfer is by negotiation, the transferee becomes a *holder* [3–202(1)]. A holder has, for example, the legal power to transfer the instrument by assignment or negotiation; he can usually enforce it in his own name [3–301]; he can discharge the liability of any party in several ways (as we shall later explain); and he enjoys several procedural advantages. Moreover, the holder has the opportunity to become a holder in due course which, as the next chapter demonstrates, gives him rights not granted by the instrument. Thus, in an *assignment,* only the rights of the transferor are passed to the transferee; but in a *negotiation,* there is the possibility of granting greater rights.

Transfer by negotiation

Two methods of negotiating an instrument make the transferee a holder. If the instrument is payable to bearer, it may be negotiated by delivery alone; if it is order paper, indorsement and delivery are required [3-202(1)]. The indorsement must be placed on the instrument itself or on a paper so firmly affixed to it that it becomes a part thereof. The indorsement paper that is annexed is called an *allonge.* The indorsement must be made by the holder or by someone who has the authority to do so on behalf of the holder [3-202(2)]. If the payee is a corporation, an officer will indorse on its behalf. The indorsement should include the corporate name, but this is not actually required.

The indorsement, to be effective as negotiation, must convey the entire instrument or any unpaid balance due on the instrument. If it purports to indorse less than the entire instrument it will be effective only as a partial assignment [3-202(3)]. An indorsement reading "Pay to A one-half of this instrument" would not be a negotiation, and A's position would be that of an assignee.

The indorser may add to his indorsement words of assignment, condition, waiver, guarantee, or limitation or disclaimer of liability, and the like. The indorsement is nevertheless effective to negotiate the instrument [3-202(4)]. Thus if A, the payee of a negotiable instrument, signs his name on the reverse side with the words, "I hereby assign this instrument to B," he has effectively indorsed the instrument, and a party to whom it is delivered is a holder.

If the name of the payee is misspelled, the payee may negotiate by indorsing either the name appearing on the instrument or in his true name, or both. A person who pays the instrument or gives value for it may require that both names be indorsed [3-203]. The desirable practice is to indorse in both names when the name of the payee is misspelled.

Indorsements

The ordinary indorsements used in negotiating paper are either special or blank. If added terms condition the indorsement, it is also a restrictive indorsement, which limits the indorsee's use of the paper. Also, the indorser may *limit* or qualify his liability as an indorser by adding words such as "without recourse." This qualified indorsement has the effect of relieving the indorser of his contractual liability as an indorser—that he will pay if the primary obligor refuses to do so. A qualified indorsement will also be a blank or a special indorsement. These indorsements are discussed in the sections that follow.

Blank indorsements

A blank indorsement consists of the indorser's name written on the instrument. If an instrument drawn payable to order is indorsed in blank, it becomes payable to bearer [3-204(2)]. After the blank indorsement, if it is indorsed specially, it reverts to its status as order paper, and indorsement is required for further negotiation [3-204(1)]. If a check, on its face payable to the order of Henry Smith, is indorsed "Henry Smith," it becomes bearer paper and can be negotiated by mere delivery. A thief or finder could pass title to the instrument.

Special indorsements

A special indorsement specifies the person to whom or to whose order it makes the instrument payable. When an instrument is specially indorsed, it becomes payable to the *order of* the special indorsee and requires his indorsement for further negotiation. Thus an indorsement "Pay to John Jones" or "Pay to the order of John Jones" is a special indorsement and requires the further indorsement by John Jones for negotiation. If a bearer instrument is indorsed specially, it requires further indorsement by the indorsee.

Fig. 18·3 Order paper, payable to the order of Henry Smith. With his bank indorsement, shown at right, the order paper becomes bearer paper, negotiable by mere delivery.

This is true if the instrument was originally bearer paper or if it became bearer paper as the result of a blank indorsement. In other words, the last indorsement determines whether the instrument is order paper or bearer paper [3–204].

The holder of an instrument may convert a blank indorsement into a special indorsement by writing above the blank indorser's signature any contract consistent with the character of the indorsement [3–204(3)]. Thus, Richard Roe, to whom an instrument has been indorsed in blank by John Doe, could write above Doe's signature, "Pay to Richard Roe." The paper would not require Roe's indorsement for further negotiation.

Restrictive indorsements

A person who indorses an instrument may impose certain restrictions upon his indorsement; that is, the indorser may protect or preserve certain rights in the paper and limit the rights of the indorsee. Of the four types of restrictive indorsement, one is conditional (for example, "Pay John Doe if Generator XK-711 arrives by June 1, 1982"). Or the indorsement may purport to prohibit further transfer of the instrument, such as, "Pay to John Doe only" [3–205(a)(b)]. When a check is deposited in a bank and will be processed through bank collection, the indorsements "For collection," "For deposit

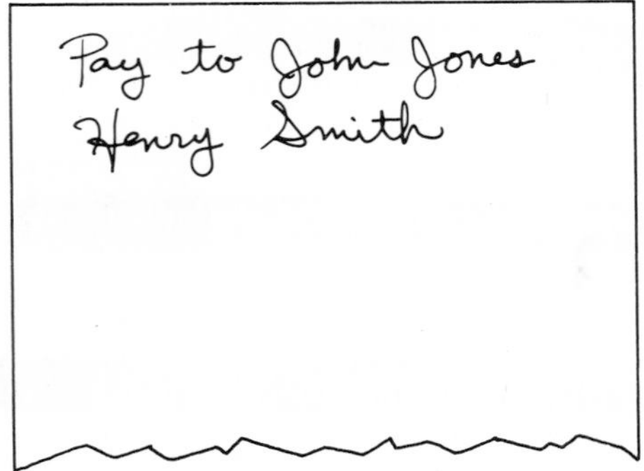

Fig. 18·4 A special indorsement by Henry Smith. For negotiation, it requires further indorsement by John Jones.

Fig. 18·5 A restrictive indorsement by Henry Smith. Subsequent holders should be only the banks in the collection process.

only," and "Pay any bank" are restrictive [3–205(c)]. In the fourth type, the indorser stipulates that it is for the benefit or use of the indorser or some other person, such as, "Pay John Doe in trust for Richard Roe" [3–205(d)].

A restrictive indorsement does not prevent further transfer or negotiation of the instrument [3–206(1)]. Thus, an instrument indorsed "Pay to John Doe only" could be negotiated by John Doe in the same manner as if it had been indorsed "Pay to John Doe."

The effect of restrictive indorsements is substantially limited when applied to banks. An intermediary bank or a payor bank that is not a depositary bank can disregard any restrictive indorsement except that of the bank's immediate transferor. This limitation does not affect whatever rights the restrictive indorser may have against the bank of deposit or his rights against parties outside the bank's collection process [3-206(2)]. Under a conditional indorsement or an indorsement for collection or deposit, a transferee (other than an intermediary bank) becomes a holder for value if it pays consistent with the indorsement [3-206(3)]. If it complies with the other requirements of section 3-302, it will be a holder in due course.

When the indorsement is for the benefit of the indorser or another person, such as "Pay to John Doe in trust for Richard Roe," only the first taker is required to act consistently with the restrictive indorsement [3-206(4)]. John Doe has the obligation to use the instrument or the proceeds from it for the benefit of Richard Roe. John Doe could negotiate the instrument to John Smith, who could qualify as a holder in due course and ignore the restriction. If the instrument is transferred in violation of Doe's fiduciary duty—if Doe transfers it to Roe in payment of a debt that he personally owes to Roe—Roe is not a holder in due course [3-304(2)].

REVIEW QUESTIONS AND PROBLEMS

1. What are the four requirements of a negotiable instrument?
2. Hodge wrote a letter to her attorney as follows: "I agree to pay your firm as attorneys' fees the sum of $2,760, payable at the rate of $230 per month for twelve (12) months beginning January 1, 1982." The letter was signed "Very truly yours, Barbara Hall Hodge." Is the letter a negotiable instrument? Why or why not?
3. Skyblast Freight executed a note which contained the following provisions: "This note is payable from the proceeds of the sale of the Skyblast Freight Building." Is the note negotiable? Why or why not?
4. When the Steins bought a new condominium, they executed a note that was secured by a mortgage to the Liverpool Bank. This note contained all the requirements of a negotiable instrument as well as the following: "This note is secured by a mortgage." Given that language, is the note negotiable? Why or why not?
5. An architect signed a note to the order of Bonnell to be paid from "jobs now under construction." Is the note negotiable? Explain.
6. Larkin signed a note containing the following notation: "with interest at bank rates." Is the note negotiable. Why or why not?
7. Midas executed a note payable to bearer in "ten ounces of gold." Is the note negotiable? Explain.
8. Standard Oil executed a note payable to Texas Oil Industries, which was due "as soon as Texas Oil Industries shall deliver to Standard Oil Company fifty thousand gallons of crude oil." Texas transferred the note to its principal shareholder. After delivery of the oil, could the shareholder claim the status of a holder of a negotiable instrument? Explain.
9. A note provides: "Payable on January 1, 1982, but payable at any time T&J Partnership dissolves." Is this note negotiable? Why or why not?
10. Bob issued a check payable to the order of Gary, who lost it without indorsing it. Can a finder of the check negotiate it? Why or why not?
11. Quincey signed a promissory note payable to the order of Unger, who indorsed the note in blank over to Pritchard. Pritchard then transferred the note to Truax by delivery. Is Truax a holder of the instrument?
12. Welch wrote a check to Clarence, who indorsed it and gave it to Malcolm Ward. Ward wrote "Pay to Malcolm Ward" above Clarence's blank indorsement. Is the paper now order or bearer paper? Explain.
13. A caterer, holder of a check, wishes to protect herself against its loss or theft. It has been indorsed to her in blank. How may she gain this protection? Explain.

If a person in possession of an instrument is the original party to whom the instrument was issued or drawn, he has the right to transfer the instrument to a third person. But a third party in possession may be a thief or finder whose rights and powers will be determined by whether the paper is order or bearer paper. A thief or finder may negotiate bearer paper, but neither has the right or power to negotiate order paper.

When an instrument is rightfully in possession of a third party, the third party may be an *assignee*, a *transferee*, a *holder*, or a *holder in due course*. An assignee has a simple contract, in contrast to a negotiable instrument. A transferee with the status of an assignee has a negotiable instrument, but it has not been properly negotiated. A holder is in possession of a negotiable instrument that has been properly negotiated. After certain special requirements are met, the holder may qualify as a holder in due course.

19

Holders in Due Course and Defenses

A *holder* is a person in possession of a negotiable instrument payable to him or to his order or to bearer [[1–201(20)]. Thus, either the original payee or a third party may qualify as a holder of an instrument and may transfer or negotiate it. A holder may legally discharge it or enforce payment in his own name [3–301]. A thief or finder may qualify as a holder of a bearer instrument. A holder who does not qualify as a holder in due course is in a position equivalent to that of an assignee of a simple contract in that he cannot enforce payment in the event that a defense to the instrument legally exists.

A *holder in due course* is a holder who, because he meets certain requirements, is given a special status and a preferred position in the event that there is a claim or a defense to the instrument [3–302]. If there is no claim or defense to the instrument, it is immaterial whether the party seeking to enforce it is a holder or a holder in due course. A holder in due course can enforce payment, notwithstanding the presence of a personal defense to the instrument. (Later in the chapter, we shall see that defenses fall into two categories: personal and real.) A holder in due course will not be able to enforce the instrument in the event that a real defense is asserted. The preferred status of a holder in due course exists only where the defense to the instrument is a personal defense.

Issues as to whether or not a party is a holder in due course usually arise when the party seeks to collect on the instrument. But occasionally a party is sued on a negligence theory for losses incurred in transactions involving an instrument. To avoid liability, the defendant must establish that he is or was a holder in due course. Thus, a holder in due course is free of claims and is not subject to defenses.

The Requirements to Be a Holder in Due Course

In order to qualify as a holder in due course, a holder must meet three basic requirements. He must take the instrument (1) for value, (2) in good faith, and (3) without notice that it is overdue, that it has been dishonored, or that any other person has a claim to it or defense against it [3–302(1)].

A payee may be a holder in due course if all of the requirements are met. Since a holder in due course is free of only personal defenses of parties with whom he has not dealt, any situation that allows a payee to be a holder in due course would be unusual.

When an instrument is acquired in a manner other than through the usual channels of negotiation or transfer, the holder will not be a holder in due course. Thus, if an instrument is obtained by an executor in taking over an estate, is purchased at a judicial sale, is obtained through legal process by an attaching creditor, or is acquired as a transaction not in the regular course of business, the party acquiring it is not a holder in due course [3–302(3)].

Value

A holder must have given value for an instrument in order to qualify as a holder in due course. A person to whom an instrument was transferred as a gift would not qualify as a holder in due course. *Value* does not have the same meaning as *consideration* in the law of contracts. A mere promise is consideration, but it is not value. As long as a promise is executory, the value requirement to be a holder in due course has not been met [3–303].

CASE

As a deposit on a contract to purchase F.I.B.'s restaurant, X made out a check for $7,000 payable to the order of "Robert Biscamp, Attorney for F.I.B." The D attorney deposited the check into its trust account for F.I.B. The plaintiff bank claims it erroneously paid the $7,000, since at the time of payment X had only $8.50 in his checking account. P seeks a court order to have D attorney return the money. D attorney claims that payment is final, since D is a holder in due course.

ISSUE Is D attorney a holder in due course?

DECISION No.

REASON To attain the status of a holder in due course, the holder must take the instrument "for value." A holder takes an instrument for value to the extent that the agreed consideration has been performed. But an executory contract, such as this one to buy the restaurant, is not value. If no value has been given, the D holder loses nothing if the P bank recovers the payment.

Maplewood Bank & Trust Company v. F.I.B., Inc., 362 A.2d 44 (N.J.) 1976.

While a mere promise is not value, if the promise to pay is negotiable in form, it does constitute value [3–303(c)]. A drawer who issues his check in payment for a negotiable note that he is purchasing from the holder becomes a holder for value even before his check is cashed.

A holder who takes an instrument in payment of an existing debt is a holder for value [3–303(b)]. Thus, if Ada owed Brenda $500 on a past-due account and transferred a negotiable instrument to Brenda in payment of such account, Brenda would qualify as a holder for value.

A purchaser of a limited interest in paper can be a holder in due course only to the extent of the interest purchased [3–302(4)]. If a negotiable instrument is transferred as collateral for a loan, the transferee may be a holder in due course, but only to the extent of the debt that is secured by the pledge of the instrument.

A person who purchases an instrument for less than its *face value* can be a holder in due course to the full amount of the instrument. Cora is the payee of a note for $1,000. She may discount the note and indorse it to Wick for $800. Wick has nevertheless paid value and is entitled to collect the full $1,000.

CASE

P, a bank, received a check to deposit to D's account. D subsequently wrote checks withdrawing most of the proceeds of the deposited check. P paid these checks before receiving notice that the deposited check was bad.

ISSUE By paying D's checks, did P give value, so that it can qualify as a holder in due course?

DECISION Yes.

REASON The bank credited a check to a customer's account. The customer withdrew most of the proceeds from that check before the bank had notice of any infirmity. The bank had thus given value, so it was a holder in due course.

Serve v. First National Bank of Atlanta, 237 S.E.2d 719 (Ga.) 1977.

Good faith

A holder must take the instrument in good faith in order to qualify as a holder in due course [3–304]. *Good faith* is defined as "honesty in fact in the conduct or transaction concerned." [1–201(19)]. If a person takes an instrument under circumstances that clearly establish the fact that there is a defense to the instrument, he does not take it in good faith. Failure to follow accepted business practices or to act reasonably by commercial standards, however, does not establish lack of good faith.

CASE

P bought equipment from a dealer who was to supply additional equipment to P weekly. These additional items would permit P to make tapes that the dealer was to purchase. P gave the dealer a note for the equipment; but the additional equipment was never delivered and the dealer went out of business. Before closing, the dealer discounted the note at a bank that had purchased other notes from the dealer. The bank had a very close relationship with the dealer and apparently knew of the dealer's shady business practices. The bank now sues P to collect the proceeds of the note.

ISSUE Did the bank take the note in "good faith," in order to become a holder in due course?

DECISION No.

REASON Sufficient facts existed to alert the bank that the original deal in which the note was generated was not a completely above-board transaction. Moreover, the bank knew that the dealer's business was inherently suspect; therefore, it could not take the note in good faith.

Security Central National Bank v. Williams, 368 N.E.2d 1264 (Ohio) 1976.

The good-faith requirement has often been challenged by consumers when consumer paper was immediately transferred by a seller to a bank. If the bank qualified as a holder in due course, the consumer would have to pay, even though the goods were defective. Consumers would contend that the close relationship between the seller and its bank constituted lack of good faith. This issue has been eliminated for all practical purposes today by a 1976 Federal Trade Commission ruling allowing consumers to use all defenses when sued on consumer paper. This FTC rule will be discussed in detail later in this chapter.

Without notice

Closely related to good faith is the requirement that the transferee must not have notice of any claim or defense to the instrument, that it is overdue or has been dishonored [3-304]. A person has notice of a fact if he has actual knowledge of it, has received notification of it, or (from the facts and circumstances known to him) has "reason to know" that it exists [1-201(25)]. The law generally provides that a person has reason to know a fact if his information would indicate its existence to a person of ordinary intelligence (or of the intelligence of the person involved, if that is above the ordinary). He also has reason to know the facts if they are so highly probable that a person exercising reasonable care will assume their existence.

Certain irregularities on the face of an instrument put a purchaser on notice that there may be a claim or defense to the instrument. If there is visible evidence of forgery or alteration, a purchaser is put on notice of a claim or defense [3-304(1)(a)].

CASE

P, an insurance company, brought an action as a legal substitute for a savings association. The savings association was the drawer of a subsequently altered check drawn on the savings association's checking account at D bank.

ISSUE If the alteration could be discovered by reasonable examination, could D bank qualify as a holder in due course?

DECISION No.

REASON If the instrument bears such visible evidence of alteration that its validity is questioned, a subsequent taker cannot be without notice. The D bank has such notice and thus cannot be a holder in due course.

New Hampshire Insurance Company v. Bank of Southwest, 548 S.W.2d 560 (Tex.) 1979.

The fact that a party "has notice" does not, standing alone, create a right to sue [3–304(1)(a)]. Code section 3–304(1)(a) is a notice section and is applicable only in helping to determine the status of a purchaser of an altered instrument if a dispute concerning the instrument arises. It does not give that purchaser any substantive legal right to sue.

If an instrument is incomplete in some important respect at the time it is purchased, notice is imparted [3–304(1)(a)]. Blanks in an instrument that do not relate to material terms do not impart notice. Knowledge that blanks in an instrument were completed after it was issued does not give notice of a claim or defense; but if the purchaser has notice that the completion was improper, he is not a holder in due course [3–304(4)(d)].

Knowledge that a defense exists or that it has been dishonored usually prohibits the status of a holder in due course. In some situations, knowledge of certain facts does *not,* of itself, give the purchaser notice of a defense or claim. Awareness that an instrument is antedated or postdated does not prevent a holder from taking in due course [3–304(4)(a)]. Knowledge of a separate contract is not notice. Although a defense will arise if the contract is not performed, such knowledge does not prevent one from becoming a holder in due course. Of course, if the purchaser is aware that the contract has been breached or repudiated, he will not qualify as a holder in due course.

Actual notice to prevent a party from being a holder in due course must be received at a time and in a way that will give a reasonable opportunity to act on it [3–304(6)]. A notice received by the president of a bank one minute before the bank's teller cashes a check is not effective in preventing the bank from becoming a holder in due course.

Before overdue

To be a holder in due course, a purchaser of an instrument must take it without notice that it is overdue [3–302(1)(c)]. A purchaser of overdue paper is charged with knowledge that some defense may exist.

A purchaser has notice that an instrument is overdue if he has reason to know that any part of the principal amount is overdue [3–304(3)(a)]. Past-due interest does not impart notice to the holder [3–304(4)(f)].

Demand paper poses a special problem, since it does not have a fixed date of maturity. A purchaser of demand paper cannot be a holder in due course if he has reason to know that he is taking it after a demand has been made, or if he takes it more than a reasonable length of time after its issue [3–304(3)(c)]. What is a reasonable or an unreasonable time is determined on the basis of a number of factors—the kind of instrument, the customs and usages of the trade or business, and the particular facts and circumstances involved. In the case of a check, a reasonable time is presumed to be thirty days [3–304(3)(c)]. The thirty-day period is a presumption rather than an absolute rule.

Holder from a holder in due course

A transferee may have the rights of a holder in due course, even though he personally does not meet all the requirements. Because a transferee obtains all the rights that the transferor had, a person who derives title through a holder in due course also has those rights. Code section 3–201(1) states this principle, the shelter provision, which advances the marketability of commercial paper.

The main significance of the shelter provision is that it permits one who is not a holder in due course to share the shelter from claims and defenses enjoyed by the holder in due course from whom he got the instrument. Example: Paul fraudulently induces Adrian to execute and deliver a note to him. Paul then negotiates the note to Tom, making Tom a holder in due course. When the note matures, Tom negotiates it to Harvey, although Harvey realizes that it is overdue and that his awareness prevents him from being, in his own right, a holder in due course. No matter. He has all the rights held by Tom, who was a holder in due course, so he is free of Adrian's defense and can recover the amount of the note.

The shelter provision is subject to a limitation. A person who formerly held the paper cannot improve his position by later reacquiring it from a holder in due course. If a former holder was himself a party to any fraud or illegality affecting the instrument, or if he had notice of a defense or claim against it as a prior holder, he cannot claim the rights of a holder in due course by taking from a later holder in due course.

Defenses

A holder in due course takes commercial paper free from the *personal* defenses of the parties to the paper. [3–305]. One who is not a holder in due course or who does not have the rights of one under the shelter provision is subject to such defenses. All transferees, including holders in due course, are subject to what are referred to as *real* defenses.

In general, real defenses relate to the existence of any obligation on the part of the person who asserts them. The most obvious real defense is forgery of the signature of a maker of a note or the drawer of a check. The person whose signature was forged has not

Table 19·1
Commercial paper: typical defenses

Personal defenses	*Real defenses*
Lack or failure of consideration	Unauthorized signature
Nonperformance of a condition precedent	Material alteration
Nondelivery, conditional delivery, or delivery for a special purpose	Infancy, if it is a defense to a simple contract
Payment	Lack of capacity
Slight duress	Extreme duress
Fraud in the inducement	Fraud in the inception
Theft by the holder or one through whom he holds	Illegality
Violation of a restrictive indorsement	Discharge in bankruptcy
Unauthorized completion	Discharge of which the holder has notice
Other defenses to a simple contract	
Any real defense where the party was negligent	

entered into any contract, and he has an absolute defense even against a holder in due course.

The Code generally specifies which defenses are real and which are personal. A few defenses—infancy being one—are real in some states and personal in others, but Table 19.1 groups them according to their usual status. The sections that follow discuss some of the defenses in detail, with special emphasis on the real defenses. The basic aspects of most personal defenses were discussed in the materials on contracts.

Real defenses

The real defense of unauthorized signature includes signatures by agents without authority and forgeries [3–404(1)]. It applies to indorsements as well as to the signature creating the instrument.

The most common example of a material alteration is the "raising" of a check [3–407]. A check drawn in the amount of $50 might be raised by alteration to $500, a real defense to the extent of the alteration. A subsequent holder in due course could enforce the check only in the amount of its original $50. In the next chapter, we shall see that a material alteration of an instrument operates to discharge it. A basic change in the contract without the permission of its creator will cancel it.

The defense of lack of capacity is a real defense if the state law so provides. If it is a defense to a simple contract, it is a real defense [3–305(2)(a)]. The same is true for all forms of illegality. If a contract is merely voidable, the defense is personal; if the contract is void or unenforceable, the defense is a real one. If state law provides that usurious contracts are null and void, usury is a real defense.

Personal defenses

A distinction exists between fraud in the *inducement* and fraud in the *inception* or *execution*. Inducement pertains to the consideration for which an instrument is given. The primary party intended to create an instrument but was fraudulently induced to do so. Such a defense is personal and is not available against a holder in due course. Fraud in the *inception* exists where a negotiable instrument is procured from a party when circumstances are such that the party does not know that he is giving a negotiable instrument. Fraud in the inception is a real defense [3–305(2)(c)]. The theory is that since the party primarily to be bound has no intention of creating an instrument, none is created. Such fraud is rare because persons are usually charged with knowledge of what they sign.

CASE

D executed a note to Home Improvements, Inc., in the amount of $3,283.20 for various improvements to be made on D's home. The company transferred the note to P bank. P sues D on the note. D inserts the personal defense that Home Improvements made material misrepresentations in inducing D to sign the note. The court gives judgment to P, since P is a holder in due course and is not subject to the personal defense.

ISSUE Does a defense of fraud in the inducement exist so that judgment for P is inappropriate?

DECISION Yes.

REASONS 1. The misrepresentation claimed as a fraud in the inducement defense need be no different from that of ordinary fraud, but, it must induce the party claiming fraud to sign the instrument. Additionally, the complaining party must have signed the instrument without knowledge, or without a reasonable opportunity to obtain knowledge, of the true facts. Finally, this lack of knowledge may relate either to the character of the instrument or its essential facts.

2. Regarding consumers, a court should liberally construe the absence of a reasonable opportunity to know.
3. Fraud in the inducement is viewed as so heinous that its victim should be allowed to escape even from a holder in due course.

Hidalgo v. Surety Savings and Loan Association, 502 S.W.2d 220 (Tex.) 1973.

Another personal defense, acquisition of title by or through a thief, is easily preventable. Conversion of bearer paper to order paper precludes its negotiation by a thief or finder.

A holder in due course is not subject to the defense of unauthorized completion of an instrument [3–407(3)]. The defense is personal. The person who left the blank space must bear the risk of wrongful completion.

Negligence of a party, frequently present in situations of fraud and material alteration, will reduce a real defense to a personal defense [3–406]. A check written with a wide, blank space preceding the amount offers a wrongdoer an easy place to raise that amount. The negligent check writer has reduced the defense to a personal one.

CASE

P, a husband whose wife (W) had signed a check, sued D, the bank on which it was drawn. X had repaired a lightning rod for W. She owed $1.26. W handed her checkbook to X to fill out the check in payment. He wrote it in such a way that the figures were to the far right-hand side, so that there was space to add 684 to the left. The words were written close to the printed word "dollars" on the check, so that there was space to add "Six thousand eight hundred forty" ahead of it. D honored the check for $6,841.26.

ISSUE Is the alteration a real or personal defense?

DECISION Personal.

REASONS
1. W was negligent in allowing the check to be prepared in a manner that could be easily raised.
2. The loss would not have occurred except for W's negligence.

Williams v. Montana National Bank of Bozeman, 534 P.2d 1247 (Mont.) 1975.

FTC rule protecting consumers from a holder in due course

The holder in due course concept was predicated on the need for commercial paper to move freely as "a courier without luggage" and the equivalent of money. Use of commercial paper was encouraged by freeing it of personal defenses if its holder is a holder in due course. Today, consumer advocates argue that protection of the consumer is more important than the reasons for the holder in due course concept and that all defenses should always be available to the consumer-debtor. They feel that the best protection for a consumer is the right to withhold payment if goods are defective or not delivered.

A number of states have enacted statutes prohibiting the use or enforcement of clauses that cut off defenses. Courts in many states have held that a holder was not a holder in due course when the finance company was closely connected with the seller. Courts have also strictly construed the application of the holder in due course rule.

Doubts about the negotiability of instruments have been resolved against negotiability. Several states have achieved this result by the enactment of the Uniform Consumer Credit Code, whose provisions are applicable to instruments other than checks. This code offers two alternative approaches to the problem. A state legislature can select the one it considers best suited to the needs of the state.

One alternative simply gives maximum protection to the consumer by allowing him to assert all claims and defenses against the assignee of any paper that he signed. The other alternative provides that the assignee can give written notice of the assignment to the debtor. The consumer is then given the right to assert defenses for three months. After the three-months' period, the assignee is free of any defense, and the debtor's only remedy is against the seller.

Since these state efforts were not universal, in 1976 the Federal Trade Commission, acting under its authority to prohibit unfair or deceptive methods of competition, adopted a rule that prohibits the use of the holder in due course concept against consumers. It also provides that a clause purporting to cut off defenses is an unfair method of competition and illegal.

The FTC rule is designed to eliminate substantial abuses often inflicted upon the purchaser of consumer goods. Under the holder in due course concept, consumers were often required to pay for defective merchandise and even for merchandise not received. Since consumer paper was usually sold to a bank or other financial institution, the purchaser of the paper would qualify as a holder in due course. As such, it would be able to collect, and the consumer was left to fight it out with the seller when a problem arose.

The FTC rule is applicable to any sale or lease of goods or services to consumers in commerce. In such a transaction, it is an unfair or deceptive act or practice for a seller to receive a credit contract that does not contain the following provision in at least 10-point bold type:

NOTICE

ANY HOLDER OF THIS CONSUMER CREDIT CONTRACT IS SUBJECT TO ALL CLAIMS AND DEFENSES WHICH THE DEBTOR COULD ASSERT AGAINST THE SELLER OF GOODS OR SERVICES OBTAINED PURSUANT HERETO OR WITH THE PROCEEDS HEREOF.

Thus the holder could not be a holder in due course, because the holder agrees to be subject to all defenses.

To prevent sellers from sending buyers directly to the lender and thus circumventing the law, the rule has a special provision relating to lending institutions. It declares that it is an unfair or deceptive practice for a seller to accept in payment the proceeds of a purchase-money loan unless the following is included in the loan agreement in 10-point bold type:

NOTICE

ANY HOLDER OF THIS CONSUMER CREDIT CONTRACT IS SUBJECT TO ALL CLAIMS AND DEFENSES WHICH THE DEBTOR COULD ASSERT AGAINST THE SELLER OF GOODS OR SERVICES OBTAINED WITH THE PROCEEDS HEREOF.

For the purpose of the foregoing rule, a purchase-money loan exists if the seller refers the consumer to the creditor or is affiliated with the creditor by common control, contract, or business arrangement. This means that if the lending institution regularly does business with the seller or has an understanding that its customers may obtain financing, the provision must be included in the loan contract. Again, it provides that all defenses are available to the consumer.

As a result of the FTC rule, if a consumer-purchaser or buyer has any defense against the seller, it may assert that defense against the bank or other financial institution that seeks to collect the debt. Thus, banks and other financial institutions must make sure that the seller stands behind the products sold. In addition, they must deal with only responsible parties on a recourse basis if losses are to be avoided.

The full effect of the FTC rule is not yet known. Sellers of defective merchandise about which customers constantly complain will probably lose their sources of credit. Financial institutions will be much more careful in buying consumer paper. Almost all transfers will be with recourse. Violators of the rule are subject to a $10,000-per-day fine, so compliance ought to be easily obtained.

REVIEW QUESTIONS AND PROBLEMS

1. What basic requirements must be met in order to qualify as a holder in due course?
2. Hadley drew a check to the order of Larsen, who indorsed it to Richards in payment of an existing indebtedness. Hadley stopped payment on the check before Richards deposited it. Hadley seeks to assert his defense of failure of consideration against Richards. Should Hadley succeed? Why or why not?
3. Evans wrote and delivered two promissory notes to Cey Cheese, Inc. Cey Cheese indorsed the two notes to a law firm for legal services to be performed. Cey Cheese had obtained the notes from Evans by fradulent representations but the law firm was unaware of this. When the firm tried to collect, Evans asserted the defense of fraud in the inducement. Is this defense effective against the law firm? Why or why not?
4. Dolan owed Luboff $3,046. Fiske gave Dolan her signed blank check with instructions to cash it for $800 and give the cash to Luboff as a partial payment. Instead, Dolan wrote out the check for $3,046 and delivered it to Luboff, who then negotiated the check to Weil. Fiske stopped payment on the check. Is Weil a holder in due course? Why or why not?
5. On September 28, 1981, Margaret bought a series of art lessons. As payment, she transferred two checks payable to the order of Margaret Kearney, one dated December 29, 1981, and the other dated January 14, 1982. On October 3, 1981, Sussex Enterprises acquired the checks and a week later transferred them for a discount (deduction from the gross sum of the checks) to Rennie's Retreat. On November 1, 1981, Margaret returned the lessons and stopped payment on the checks. She claims that Rennie's Retreat cannot sue, since it is not a holder in due course. Is she correct? Explain.
6. Nevers executed a note payable to the order of Young and dated as due on January 1, 1981. On March 1, 1981, Young negotiated the note to Glassen. Will Glassen be subject to the personal defenses of Nevers? Why or why not?
7. Pellato acquired a negotiable instrument as a gift from her friend, Gaines. Gaines was given the note for laundering services and was a holder in due course. Is Pellato a holder in due course? Explain.
8. DuBois was an officer and stockholder of a corporation. She executed a note payable to a local bank and had the proceeds placed in the corporation's account at the bank. When the corporation later failed, the bank brought an action against DuBois. She contends that there was a failure of consideration. Would this defense be good against the bank? Why or why not?
9. Merck gave a merchant a check in the amount of $500 in payment for some linoleum installed in Merck's home. When the check was dishonored, the merchant sued to recover on the check. Merck contends that the linoleum was not satisfactory. The trial judge ruled that the check was not subject to any defenses arising from claimed breaches of contract or failure of consideration. Was the judge correct? Why or why not?
10. In the previous question, assume that Merck signed a consumer credit contract instead of the $500 check. Would the FTC rule change the result if the consumer credit contract had been duly negotiated by the merchant to ABC Company, which became a holder in due course? Explain.

20

Liability of Parties to Commercial Paper

In our discussions of the rights of holders and holders in due course, we usually assumed that the party being sued had liability unless a valid defense could be asserted against the plaintiff. In this chapter, we go to the basic issue of the liability of a defendant in the absence of a defense.

In a transaction involving commercial paper, liability may be predicated on either the instrument itself or on the underlying contract. No person is liable on the instrument itself unless his signature appears thereon, but the signature may be affixed by a duly authorized agent [3-401(1)]. Persons whose signatures appear on instruments may have different types of liability, depending on their status. This chapter will discuss the liability of various parties to commercial paper transactions. Unless indicated otherwise, liability is predicated on the instrument itself and on the rules of the Code relating to commercial paper.

Liability based on signatures

A person's liability on commercial paper results from his signature on the instrument. The signature may be affixed as a maker or drawer on the face of the instrument, or it may be an indorsement on the back.

The general principles of the law of agency are applicable to commercial paper. A principal is bound by the duly authorized acts of his agent. If the agent is not authorized to sign, the principal is not bound unless he (1) ratifies it or (2) is estopped from asserting lack of authority. An agent who fails to bind his principal because of failure to name him or because of lack of authority will usually be personally liable to third parties.

An agent is also personally liable if he fails to show his representative capacity [3–403(2)(a)]. This occurs if the agent signs his own name without indicating either the name of his principal or the fact that he is signing in a representative capacity [3–403(2)(a)]. However, an agent can relieve himself of liability to the person to whom he issued the paper by proving that such party knew he was acting only as an agent for his principal [3–403(2)(b)].

CASE

P, a supplier for a corporation, sued D, the corporate president, to collect three checks drawn on the corporate account, which had insufficient funds. The checks bore the printed name of the corporation in the upper-left-hand corner. There were no words before, after, above, or below D's signature in the lower right-hand corner.

ISSUE Is D personally liable on the checks?

DECISION Yes.

REASONS

1. The drafts do not show prima facie that D signed in a representative capacity. Although the corporate name is on the checks, there is nothing preceding or following D's signature to show that he was signing in a representative capacity.
2. D is personally liable under 3–403(b)(2) of the Code unless there is a different agreement between the parties. No such agreement was proven here.

Griffin v. Ellinger, 530 S.W.2d 329 (Tex.) 1975.

For purposes of internal control, many businesses and other organizations require that instruments be signed by at least two persons or that they be countersigned. When the agreement requires two signatures, the drawee may not pay on only one signature, even if the one signing is authorized. The authority is limited or divided; both must sign.

CASE

P, a partnership, had an agreement with D, a bank, that checks on the partnership account must be signed by any two of the three general partners. For about a year, D, the bank, honored 37 checks totaling $235,012.02, drawn on the partnership account. All of these checks were signed by either Partner X or Partner Y. Partner Z, who is also a plaintiff in this action, signed only one check. The partnership and Plaintiff Z sued the bank for wrongfully honoring these 37 checks.

ISSUE May a depositor hold its bank accountable when the bank has honored checks bearing only one signature drawn on a two signature account?

DECISION Yes.

REASONS

1. The bank erroneously relied on Code section 4–406(1) and (4) which require a customer to examine statements received from the bank and report an unauthorized signature within one year from date of receipt. The signatures in this case were authorized.
2. The infirmity in this case is the failure to have a second authorized signature.

Wolfe v. University National Bank, 310 A.2d 558 (Md.) 1973.

Another issue concerning signatures relates to the capacity in which the signature is affixed. The liability of primary parties such as makers of notes is different from the liability of secondary parties such as indorsers. The capacity of a signature may be ambiguous because of its physical location or because of the language used.

The capacity in which a person signs is usually obvious because of the location of the signature. Makers and drawers usually sign in the lower right-hand corner of an instrument, and indorsers sign on the back of an instrument. A drawee normally places his signature of acceptance on the face of the instrument, but his signature on the back would clearly indicate that he was signing as an acceptor unless he could establish otherwise. When the signature does not reveal the obligation of the party who signs, the signature is an indorsement [3–402].

Liability of banks in cases of forgery

Banks have a special problem in connection with forgeries. Checks presented to drawee banks for payment may bear forged signatures of drawers or forged indorsements. If the drawer's signature was forged, the bank that honors the check has not followed the order of the drawer and cannot charge his account [3–418]. If charged, it must be recredited. Likewise, the bank will have to make restitution to the party whose name was forged on the check as an indorsement [3–419(1)(c)]. In either case, the loss initially is that of the bank that pays the instrument bearing the forgery.

In the case of a forged drawer's signature, the drawee bank as a general rule cannot collect payment from the party who received it. The bank has the signature of the drawer on file and is charged with knowledge of the forgery. This general rule is subject to the exception that if the party receiving payment is the forger or dealt with the forger and was negligent in doing so, the drawee may recover the payment. Thus, if a collecting bank was negligent, the drawee bank that paid on a forged drawer's signature could recover from the collecting bank.

A drawee who pays on a forged indorsement has greater rights in seeking to recover the payment than does the drawee who pays on a forged drawer's signature. In the case of a forged indorsement, the drawee has no way of knowing about the forgery, and thus it can collect from the person to whom payment was made, who in turn can collect from all prior parties back to the forger.

A bank sometimes cashes a check indorsed by an agent who lacks authority. When it does, the bank is held liable to the payee if the bank is charged with knowledge of the lack of authority. Just as in the case of forgery by a stranger, the drawer can insist that the drawee recredit his account with the amount of any unauthorized payment.

FORGED DRAWER

Facts: Forger signs drawer's name to a $5,000 check and issues it to payee. Payee indorses and delivers it to Nancy, who takes for value, in good faith and without notice of the forgery. Nancy presents the check to drawee for payment, and drawee pays.

Drawer vs. drawee: Drawer discovers the forgery and requests drawee to recredit his account for $5,000. Will drawer win? Yes. The check was not "properly payable" since drawee did not follow drawer's genuine order [4–401(1)].

Drawee vs. Nancy: May drawee now recover from Nancy? No. Payment is final in favor of a holder in due course such as Nancy, who had no knowledge of the forgery and thus breached no presentment warranty [3–418, 3–417(1)(b)].

Drawee vs. forger: May drawee now recover from forger? Yes. An unauthorized signature operates as the signature of the unauthorized signer [3–404(1)].

FORGED INDORSEMENT

Facts: Drawer issues a check "to the order of Payee" for $5,000. Forger steals the check from payee, forges payee's name on the check and sells the check to Nancy, who deposits it in her account with Depositary Bank. The check proceeds through the bank collection process, where it is ultimately paid by drawee.

Payee vs. drawer: Because the check was stolen, payee was not paid. May payee require drawer to issue another check? Yes, under 3-804, although a court might require payee to give some security to reimburse drawer, in the event drawer may have to pay twice.

Drawer vs. drawee: Can drawer now require drawee to recredit his account for the first check that was stolen and forged? Yes. The check was not "properly payable" since drawee did not follow drawer's genuine order to pay "to the order of Payee" [4–401(1)].

Payee vs. drawee: Assume that payee seeks recovery from drawee, rather than requiring drawer to issue a new check. Will payee win? Yes. An instrument is converted when it is paid by drawee on a forged indorsement [3–419(1)(c),(2)].

Drawee vs. Depositary Bank: If drawee has either recredited drawer's account or paid payee for conversion of the check, may drawee now recover from Depositary Bank? Yes. Depositary Bank breached a presentment warranty that it had good title to the check (that is, a warranty of no forged indorsements) [3–418, 4–207(1)(a)].

Depositary Bank vs. Nancy: Will Depositary Bank now be able to recover from Nancy? Yes. Nancy breached a transfer warranty that all signatures were genuine [4–207(2)(b)].

Nancy vs. forger: Can Nancy now recover from forger? Yes. She can recover either on breach of a transfer warranty or on the contract of indorsement, since the signature by forger operates as his signature [3–417(2)(b), 3–404(1)].

Impostors: fictitious payees

A situation similar to forgery arises when an instrument is made payable to a fictitious person or to an impostor. The drawer's signature is genuine, but the instrument is indorsed in the fictitious name or the name of the person who is being impersonated. In the impostor situation, one person poses as someone else and induces the drawer to issue a check payable to the order of the person being impersonated. The imposter then signs the name of the person being impersonated. The indorsement by the imposter is effective, and the loss falls on the drawer rather than on the person who took the check or the bank that honored it. [3–405(1)(a)].

The loss falls upon the drawer because the check was indorsed by the person whom the drawer intended to indorse it. If the check is intended for the party named but is diverted and forged by an employee, the "impostor rule" is not applicable.

A typical fictitious payee is a dishonest employee authorized to sign his employer's name to checks or one who draws checks that he presents to his employer for the latter's signature. Thus the employee may draw payroll checks or checks payable to persons with whom the employer would be expected to do business. He either signs the checks or obtains his employer's signature and then cashes the checks, indorsing the name of the payee. If he is in charge of the company's books, he is able to manipulate the books when the canceled checks are returned and may thus avoid detection. The Code imposes this loss on the employer; the dishonest employee can effectively indorse in the payee's name [3–405(1)(c)].

CASE

A was employed by P brokerage company. He devised a scheme to defraud his employer by issuing fraudulent orders to sell customers' securities. When P company issued a check to the customer whose stock had been sold, A would obtain the check, forge the customer's indorsement, and pocket the money. When the fraud was discovered, P sought to recover its losses from the D bank upon whom the checks were drawn.

ISSUE Is D liable for honoring the checks on a forged indorsement?

DECISION No.

REASONS 1. Although A did not deal directly with the person who wrote the check, he did initiate the transaction that a check be drawn, and he knew that the payee was not to have any interest in it.

2. The Code protects the drawee bank under these circumstances by providing that the indorsement by the employee is effective.

New Amsterdam Casualty Co. v. First Pennsylvania Banking and Trust Co., 451 F.2d 892 (1971) (Pa. law).

Liability Based on Status

Classifications: primary and secondary

For the purposes of liability, the Code divides the parties to commercial paper into two groups—primary parties and secondary parties. The *primary parties* are the makers of notes and the acceptors of drafts. These parties have incurred a definite obligation to pay and are the parties who, in the normal course of events, will *actually* pay the instrument.

The *secondary parties* are drawers of drafts, drawers of checks, and indorsers of any instrument. These parties do not expect to pay the instrument but assume, rather, that the primary parties will fulfill their obligations. The drawer and indorsers expect that the acceptor will pay the draft. The indorsers of a note expect that the maker will pay when the note matures. Drawers and indorsers have a responsibility to pay if the primary parties do not, *provided* that certain conditions precedent are satisfied. The drawer and the indorser are, in effect, saying that they will pay if the primary party (acceptor or maker) does not, but only if the party entitled to payment has made proper demand upon the primary party and due notice of the primary party's dishonor of the instrument has then been given to them [3–413(2)]; [3–414(1)].

Liability of primary parties

A primary party engages that he will pay the instrument according to its terms. The maker thus assumes an obligation to pay the note as it was worded at the time he executed it. The acceptor assumes responsibility for the draft as it was worded when he gave his acceptance [3–413(1)].

If a maker signs an incomplete note, when the note is completed—even though the completion is unauthorized—it can be enforced against him by a holder in due course. On the other hand, if an instrument is materially altered after it is made, the maker has a real defense in the absence of negligence. The maker confirms to all subsequent parties the existence of the payee and his capacity to indorse [3–413(3)].

The drawee of a check or draft is not liable on the instrument until acceptance. Upon acceptance, the acceptor is primarily liable. An acceptance must be in writing on the draft and signed by the drawee-acceptor [3–410(1)]. Acceptance is usually made by the drawee's writing or stamping the word *Accepted,* with his name and the date, across the face of the instrument. The usual means for accepting a check is to have it certified. The acceptance makes the drawee-acceptor the primary obligor; the drawer and all other parties become secondary parties.

A party presenting a draft for acceptance is entitled to an *unqualified acceptance* by the drawee. Thus, when the drawee offers an acceptance that in any manner varies or changes the direct order to pay or accept, the holder may refuse the acceptance [3-412(1)]. The paper is dishonored, and upon notice of dishonor or protest, the holder may hold responsible all prior parties on the paper—back to, and including, the drawer.

The Liability of Secondary Parties

Drawers

The drawer engages that upon *dishonor* of the draft and any necessary notice of dishonor or protest, he will pay the amount of the draft to the holder or to any indorser who takes it up [3-413(2)]. In effect, the drawer assumes a conditional liability on the instrument—that he will pay if the instrument is dishonored and he is properly notified of this fact. The party who draws a draft or check, like one who makes a note or accepts a draft, affirms to all subsequent parties the existence of the payee and his then capacity to indorse [3-413(3)]. In addition, most drawers have liability on the underlying contract or transaction in which they deliver the instrument as drawer.

Indorsers

Indorsers of checks, drafts, or notes have two kinds of liability. First, they are liable on their *contract of indorsement* [3-414(1)]. The indorsement contract can either be unqualified or qualified. The majority of transferors indorse without qualification. The unqualified indorser does not say "I will pay" but rather says "I will pay if the instrument is dishonored and any necessary notice of dishonor is given and any necessary protest is made." The unqualified indorser's liability, which runs to subsequent parties [3-414(1)] is discussed later in this chapter. A *qualified* indorser indorses with the words "without recourse." By indorsing "without recourse," the qualified indorser disclaims any liability. In effect, the qualified indorser says "I do not guarantee that the other party will pay. If he does not pay, I will not pay."

Second, an indorser has *unconditional* liability. This unconditional liability is based on breach of warranty. An indorser makes warranties with reference to the instrument that is transferred [3-417(2)]. He warrants that he has good title to the instrument, that all signatures are genuine or authorized, that the instrument has not been materially altered, and that no defense of any party is good against him. He also warrants that he does not know of any insolvency proceedings with respect to any of the parties involved [3-417(2)(e)].

The warranties are made whether the transfer is by delivery only, by qualified indorsement (without recourse), or by unqualified indorsement. It is important to note that liability is automatic if any of the warranties are breached. The indorser and transferor by delivery must make good without regard to the performance of any conditions precedent, such as presentment or notice of dishonor.

Transferors without indorsement

All secondary parties have unconditional liability because this liability is based on a theory of breach of warranty. Technically speaking, the party who presents an instrument for payment and signs it is not an indorser. The signature is a receipt for the payment; but in presenting the instrument, the person warrants that no indorsements are forged, that so far as he knows the signature of the maker or drawer is genuine, and that it has not been materially altered [3-417(1)]. The person who pays or accepts will thus have recourse against the presenting party if the warranties are breached. There is no warranty that the drawer has sufficient funds on deposit to cover a check. If a drawee pays a check when the drawer has insufficient funds on deposit, the party presenting the check is not liable for breach of warranty. The warranty with regard to the drawer's signature is not absolute; it assures only that the warrantor has no knowledge that such signature is forged or unauthorized.

A transferor without an indorsement (bearer paper) also makes warranties to the transferee, the same warranties a qualified indorser makes, but different from the warranties of an unqualified indorser in only one particular way. The qualified indorser's warranty about defenses is simply that he has no *knowledge* of any defense [3–417(3)]. In the delivery of bearer paper without indorsement, the warranties run only to the immediate transferee, whereas the indorser's warranties extend to subsequent holders [3–417(2)].

Accommodation parties and guarantors

One who signs an instrument for the purpose of lending his name and credit to another party to an instrument is an "accommodation" party [3–415(1)]. His function is that of a surety. He may sign as an indorser, maker, or acceptor or as a co-maker or co-acceptor. The accommodation party is liable in the capacity in which he signed [3–415(2)]. As an indorser, he does not indorse for the purpose of transferring the paper but rather to lend security to it.

CASE

D (as well as the president and secretary) signed a note on behalf of a corporation, stating, "the undersigned jointly and severally promise to pay. . . ." Although this signature clearly indicates a co-maker, D contends that she is an accommodation party (or surety under pre-Code law).

ISSUE Is D a surety?

DECISION Yes.

REASONS
1. Although D signed the note as a co-maker, she also signed her name for the purpose of lending her name to the corporation. Therefore, D is a co-maker as well as an accommodation party. One can be both a maker and an accommodation party.
2. Because D is an accommodation party, she is therefore a surety. Comment 1 to Section 3–415 clearly states: "Subsection (1) recognizes that an accommodation party is always a surety."
3. It is common practice for a surety to appear on a note either as a co-maker or as an indorser.

Philadelphia Bond & Mortgage Co. v. Highland Crest Homes, Inc., 340 A.2d 476 (Pa.) 1975.

There is some significance to the surety status of an accommodation party. In some situations he is entitled to be discharged under the general law and may exercise this right against one who is not a holder in due course [3–415(3)]. He is not liable to the party accommodated; and if he is required to pay, he can obtain reimbursement from the accommodated party [3–415(5)].

The liability of an accommodation party arises without express words. A guarantor's liability is based on words of guaranty. If the words "Payment guaranteed" or their equivalent are added to a signature, the signer engages that if the instrument is not paid when due, he will pay it *without previous resort by the holder to other parties on the paper* [3–416(1)]. If the words "Collection guaranteed" are added to a signature, the signer becomes liable only after the holder has reduced his claim against the maker or acceptor to judgment, and execution has been returned unsatisfied, or after the maker or acceptor has become insolvent or it is otherwise apparent that it is useless to proceed against him [3–416(2)].

A guarantor waives the conditions precedent of presentment, notice of dishonor, and protest. The words of guarantee do not affect the indorsement as a means of transferring the instrument but impose upon such indorser the liability of a co-maker [3–416(5)].

Conditional Liability

The term *conditional liability* is used to describe the secondary liability that results from the status of parties as drawers or unqualified indorsers. The adjective *conditional* refers to the fact that certain conditions precedent must be fulfilled to establish liability [3–501]. The conditions precedent are *presentment, dishonor, notice of dishonor,* and in some instances *protest.* Presentment is a demand for acceptance or payment, and such demand will be made by the holder upon the maker, acceptor, or drawee. [3–504(1)] There may be two or more makers, acceptors, or drawees, in which event the presentment can be made to any one of them [3–504(3)(a)].

The importance of exact compliance with the conditions precedent cannot be overemphasized. Failure to comply will result in the discharge of the secondary parties.

Presentment—generally

Presentment is a demand made upon a maker or drawee [3–504(1)]. In relation to a note, it is a demand for payment made by the holder upon the maker. In the case of a draft, it may be either a demand for acceptance or a demand for payment.

The drawee of a draft is not bound upon the instrument as a primary party until acceptance. The holder will usually wait until maturity and present his draft to the drawee for payment, but he may present it to the drawee for acceptance before maturity in order to give credit to the instrument during the period of its term. The drawee is under no legal duty to the holder to accept; but if he refuses, the draft is dishonored by nonacceptance. A right of recourse arises immediately against the drawer and the indorsers, and no presentment for payment is necessary.

In most instances, it is not necessary to present an instrument for *acceptance.* Presentment for *payment* alone is usually sufficient, but *presentment for acceptance must be made in order to charge the drawer and indorsers of a draft* in a few cases. If the date of payment depends upon presentment, as for a draft payable after sight, presentment is required in order to determine the maturity date of the instrument [3–501(1)(a)]. Failure to make a proper presentment for payment results in the complete discharge of an indorser [3–501(1)(b)]. A limited discharge is accorded to drawers and to the acceptor of a draft payable at a bank or to the maker of a note payable at a bank. Such parties are discharged to the extent that the failure to make a proper presentment caused them a loss.

Presentment—how and where

Presentment may be made by personally contacting the primary party and making a demand for acceptance or payment. Presentment may be made by mail or through a clearinghouse [3–504(2)(a)(b)]. Presentment by mail is effective when received. If the instrument specifies the place of acceptance or payment, presentment may be made there. If no place is specified, presentment may be made at the place of business of the party to accept or to pay. Presentment is excused if neither the party to accept or pay nor anyone authorized to act for him is present or accessible at such place [3–504(2)(c)]. A draft accepted or a note made payable at a bank in the United States must be presented at that bank [3-504(4)].

To balance the liberal attitude regarding what will suffice as a presentment, Section 3-505(1) gives the party on whom presentment is made the power to require

1. exhibition of the instrument
2. reasonable identification of the person making presentment
3. evidence of authority if presentment is made for another
4. production of the instrument at a place specified in it or (if none is specified) at any reasonable place
5. a signed receipt on the instrument for any partial or full payment and its surrender upon full payment

If the primary party does not avail himself of these rights, the presentment is perfectly valid, no matter how or where the presentment is made. If he does require proper presentment, a failure to comply invalidates the presentment, but the instrument is not dishonored. The requirement of identification of the presenting party applies to bearer paper as well as order paper [3-505].

Presentment—when

In general, an instrument must be presented for payment on the day of maturity. The presentment must be made at a reasonable hour and if at a bank, during banking hours.

When an instrument is payable on demand, it must be presented or negotiated within a reasonable time after such secondary party became liable; for example, after his indorsement [3-503(1)(e)]. Thus, in the case of a demand note, an indorser would be discharged if presentment were not made within a reasonable time after he indorsed the note.

Note that presentment within a "reasonable time" is required when a definite maturity date is not included in the instrument; that is, sight and demand instruments. A reasonable time for presentment is determined by the nature of the instrument, any usage of banking or trade, and the facts of the particular case [3-503(2)].

The drawer of a check is liable for it for a reasonable time, presumed to be thirty days after date or issue, whichever is later. In that time, a check must be presented for payment or to initiate bank collection [3-504(2)(a)]. The presumed reasonable time in which the indorser is liable is seven days after his indorsement [3-504(2)(b)].

Thus the drawer must back up a check for a longer period than an indorser; but the drawer, having issued the check, is not being imposed upon by the requirement to keep funds on hand for thirty days to cover it. After a thirty-day period, also, a purchaser should be notified that his uncashed check is stale. An indorser is in a different position and is entitled to prompt notice, so that he may take adequate steps to protect himself against his transferor and prior parties if the check is dishonored.

Dishonor

The party who presents an instrument is entitled to have the instrument paid or accepted. If the party to whom the instrument is presented refuses to pay or accept, the instrument is dishonored [3-507(1)]. The presenting party then has recourse against indorsers or other secondary parties, provided he gives proper notice of such dishonor.

When a draft is presented to the drawee for *acceptance,* the drawee may wish to ascertain some facts from the drawer before he assumes the obligation of an acceptor. As a result, the law allows the drawee to defer acceptance until the close of the next business day following presentment [3-506(1)]. If the drawee needs more time within which to obtain information, the holder can give him one additional business day within which to accept. The secondary parties are not discharged by the one-day postponement. The holder who presents the draft for *acceptance* is seeking the drawee's obligation on the paper and will not receive payment until a later date. For this reason, the Code permits a longer period of time within which to accept a draft than is allowed when the draft is presented for payment. When an instrument is presented for payment, the party to whom presentment is made is allowed a reasonable time to examine the instrument, to determine whether the instrument is properly payable, but payment must be made in any event on the same day that it is presented and before the close of business on that day [3-506(2)].

Notice of dishonor

When an instrument has been dishonored on proper presentment, the holder must give prompt notice of the dishonor, in order to have a right of recourse against unqualified indorsers [3-507(2)]. Failure to give prompt and proper notice of dishonor results in the discharge of indorsers. Notice of dishonor should also be given to the drawer. Failure to do so discharges the drawer only to the extent of a loss caused by the improper notice—the bank may have failed before he received notice of dishonor [3-502(1)].

Generally, notice is given to secondary parties by the holder or by an indorser who has received notice. Any party who may be compelled to pay the instrument may notify any party who may be liable on it [3-508(1)].

Except for banks, notice must be given before midnight of the third business day after dishonor [3-508(2)]. A person who has received notice of dishonor and wishes to notify other parties must do so before midnight of the third business day after receipt of the notice.

Banks must give any necessary notice before the bank's "midnight deadline"—before midnight of the next banking day following the day on which a bank receives the item or notice of dishonor [3-508(2)].

CASE

P was the payee on a check for $5,000 drawn on D bank. P deposited the check for collection in his own bank on June 18, 1973. The check reached D bank through normal banking channels on June 22, 1973. D did not pay or return the check or send notice of dishonor until after midnight of June 23, 1973. An indorser wants to intervene in the action to assert certain defenses. P objects on the ground that D bank is strictly liable for failure to send notice of dishonor before its midnight deadline, and therefore the indorser is not liable.

ISSUE Is D bank absolutely liable and are all indorsers excused from liability?

DECISION Yes.

REASONS
1. Unless excused, notice of dishonor is necessary to charge any indorser.
2. Whether a check is properly payable or not, a bank that retains a check beyond its midnight deadline without paying it, returning it, or sending notice of dishonor is accountable for the amount of the check [4-302].
3. Obviously, the D bank became accountable for the amount of the check when it retained it beyond midnight of June 23, 1973.

Templeton v. First Nat. Bank of Nashville, 362 N.E.2d 33 (Ill.) 1977.

Notice may be given in any reasonable manner, including oral notice, notice by telephone, and notice by mail. The notice must identify the dishonored instrument and state that it has been dishonored. Written notice is effective when sent, even though it is not received, if it bears proper address and postage [3–508(4)].

Proper notice preceded by any necessary presentment and dishonor imposes liability upon secondary parties to whom such notice of dishonor is given. Proper notice operates for the benefit of all parties who have rights on the instrument against the party notified [3–508(8)]. Thus it is necessary to notify a party only once for his liability to be fixed. Assume that A, B, C, and D are indorsers in that order.

Holder gives notice to A and C only.

C will not be required to give additional notice to A.

If C is compelled to pay, he would have recourse against A.

B and D are discharged if they are not notified by the holder or one of the indorsers.

This result follows because indorsers are in general liable in the order of their indorsement. An indorser who is required to pay can recover from an indorser prior to him. But each indorser is entitled to notice of dishonor, so that he can take appropriate steps to pass the responsibility on to those prior to him on the paper.

Protest

Protest is a certificate stating the following: an instrument was presented for payment or acceptance, it was dishonored, and the reasons, if any, given for refusal to accept or pay [3–509]. It is a formal method for satisfying the conditions precedent and is required only for drafts that are drawn or payable outside the United States. The protest requirement is in conformity with foreign law in this respect. In other cases, protest is optional with the holder. Protest serves as evidence both that presentment was made and that notice of dishonor was given. It creates a presumption that the conditions precedent were satisfied.

Excuses for failure to perform conditions precedent

An unexcused delay in making any *necessary* presentment or in giving notice of dishonor discharges parties who are entitled to performance of the conditions precedent. Indorsers are completely discharged by such delay; and drawers, makers of notes payable at a bank, and acceptors of drafts payable at a bank are discharged to the extent of any loss caused by the delay [3–502]. Delay in making presentment, in giving notice of dishonor, or in making protest is excused when the holder has acted with reasonable diligence and the delay is not due to any fault of the holder. He must, however, comply with these conditions or attempt to do so as soon as the cause of the delay ceases to exist [3–511(1)].

CASE

P bank forwarded two checks to D bank for collection. D bank failed to give notice of dishonor by its midnight deadline. D claims to be excused because of a computer breakdown. Section 4–108 of the Code excuses delays by banks if caused by "emergency conditions or other circumstances beyond the control of the bank provided it exercises such diligence as the circumstances require."

ISSUE Is D excused from giving proper notice of dishonor?

DECISION Yes.

REASONS 1. The computer malfunction constituted both an emergency condition and a circumstance beyond the control of the bank, and the bank acted with diligence.

2. A computer failure qualifies for the application of the section excusing delays.

Port City State Bank v. American Nat. Bank, Lawton, Okla., 486 F.2d 196 (1973).

The performance of the conditions precedent is entirely excused if the party to be charged has *waived* the condition. When such waiver is stated on the face of the instrument, it is binding on all parties; when it is written above the signature of the indorser, it binds him only [3-511(6)]. Most promissory notes contain such a waiver.

The performance of the conditions precedent is also excused if the party to be charged has himself dishonored the instrument or has countermanded payment or otherwise has no reason to expect or right to require that the instrument be accepted or paid [3-511(2)(b)]. If a drawer of a check has stopped payment on the check, the drawer is not in a position to complain about slow presentment or any lack of notice of dishonor.

Discharge

The liability of various parties may be discharged in a variety of ways, many of them previously noted [3-601]. Certification of a check at the request of a holder discharges all prior parties [3-411]. Any ground for discharging a simple contract also discharges commercial paper [3-601(2)].

Payment usually discharges a party's liability. This is true even if the payor has knowledge of the claim of another person. Payment does not operate to discharge liability if the payor acts in bad faith and pays one who acquired the instrument by theft. Payment is also no defense if paid in violation of a restrictive indorsement [3-603].

A holder may discharge any party by intentionally canceling the instrument or by striking out or otherwise eliminating a party's signature. The surrender of the instrument to a party will also discharge that party [3-605].

If a holder agrees not to sue one party or agrees to release collateral, then all parties with rights against such party or against the collateral are discharged from liability. This assumes that there is no express reservation of rights by the holder and that the party claiming discharge did not consent to the holder's actions [3-606].

When an instrument is reacquired by a prior party, he may cancel all intervening indorsements. In this event, all parties whose indorsements are canceled are discharged [3-208].

Fraudulent and material alteration of an instrument discharges any party whose liability is affected by the alteration. Of course, this is not true if the alteration is agreed to or if the party seeking to impose liability is a holder in due course [3-407]. In fact, no discharge is effective against a holder in due course unless he has notice of the discharge when he takes the instrument [3-602].

REVIEW QUESTIONS AND PROBLEMS

1. Bob Cratchit, an accountant and agent for Mr. Scrooge, signed one note like this: "Mr. Scrooge, Bob Cratchit," and another note like this: "Bob Cratchit, Agent." Is Cratchit individually liable on either note? Explain.

2. Is Scrooge liable when Cratchit signed "Mr. Scrooge, Bob Cratchit"? Explain. Is this the proper way for an agent to sign: "InterGalactic Transport Corp., by Flash Gordon, pres."? Explain.

3. H. M. Pease, president of Storey, Inc., was sued by the payee of a promissory note signed "Storey, Inc.," and immediately thereunder, "H. M. Pease." Is Pease personally liable on the note? Why or why not?

4. Crean, assistant comptroller of Thatcher Company, Inc., drew checks on the corporate bank account, payable to "Thatcher Company," omitting the "Inc." The checks were sent to Crean's accomplice, Andover, who deposited them in another bank and later drew checks on that account. Andover had previously opened the account under the name of Thatcher Company and had filled out an account card showing that Andover was the president and the authorized signatory. It was the duty of Crean to draw checks to be placed in another bank to cover payrolls of Thatcher Company, Inc. The company contends that the bank is liable for all funds drawn out of the account. Is the bank liable? Why or why not?

5. The superintendent of ABC, Inc., had the responsibility of verifying bills and approving them for payment. He picked up a number of checks and instead of delivering them to the payees, forged the indorsements and cashed the checks. ABC, Inc. demanded that the drawee bank reimburse ABC for the amount paid out on these checks. Is the drawee bank liable? Explain.

6. Litt was one of two signers of a note. The word "guarantor" followed Litt's signature. The holder of the note sued Litt, whose only defense was that the holder must first sue the other signer before suing him. Is Litt's defense illegal or is it binding on the other litigant? Explain.

7. A local bank lent money to a travel agency in exchange for its promissory note. The president of the agency indorsed the note on the back, guaranteeing payment if the company defaulted. The bank sued and got a judgment against the company, but the company did not pay anything. The bank now sues the president. Is she liable? Why or why not?

8. Hopkins, the holder of a note, transferred the note by a blank indorsement to Beggs. Beggs did not present the note to the maker for payment nor did he notify Hopkins of any dishonor. Can Beggs maintain an action against Hopkins as an indorser? Why or why not?

9. The defendant received a check drawn on the plaintiff's bank. The defendant indorsed the check and received payment from his bank. That bank sent the check for collection to the plaintiff bank, and the check was honored. Several days later, P discovered that the drawer of the check did not have an account and that it had mistakenly charged the check to another of its customers. P then sought to recover from D as an indorser. D contended that the check had not been dishonored within the time allowed by law. Is D liable as an indorser? Why or why not?

10. Sue indorsed a note. Above all indorsements was printed, "Notice of protest waived." The note was not paid when it became due. The holder sent notice to Sue's former address, and she did not receive it. Was she properly notified? Why or why not?

21 Introduction to the Secured Transaction

Now that we are familiar with contracts for the sale of goods (Article 2 of the Code) and payment by checks or drafts (Articles 3 and 4), we are going to look into another aspect of a commercial transaction that involves some type of security for the purchase price (Article 9, Secured Transactions).

Article 9 is not only the most novel article of the Code but also the most criticized and amended. It is novel because it substitutes a simple, unified body of law for the confusing, haphazard accretion of nineteenth-century personal property devices. Article 9 sweepingly removes the sundry pre-Code security devices, which are identified later in the chapter, and replaces them with one basic security device, the *security agreement*. Moreover, it revamps the numerous, almost chaotic filing requirements that developed separately over the years, fuses them into one basic filing form (the *financing statement*), and creates a more rational, accessible place to file that form.

Notwithstanding the novel attempt to unify a chaotic system of personal property security law, state legislatures, when enacting the 1962 uniform version of Article 9, amended it to solve individual state problems. As early as 1966, of the 54 sections of Article 9, 47 had been nonuniformly amended by at least 30 different state legislatures. Article 9 was fittingly described as the "Un-Uniform Commercial Code." Consequently, a review committee studied the article and recommended the 1972 Official Text, a new draft of the 1962 version. Twenty-five states have enacted the 1972 revision, and the other states will probably follow by the end of the 1980s.

Now, two versions of Article 9 do pose a problem for us: which one do we study? Although we need to know something about both Code versions (nobody promised you a rose garden), our emphasis will be on the 1972 Code. The 1972 version of Article 9 is included in the Code at the end of the book, and the text refers to it. When it is necessary to discuss the 1962 version, the reference will be described as the "1962 Code" or "1962 version." (Example: 9-103 of the 1962 Code.)

Article 9 of the Code

In a *secured transaction,* personal property is given as security that an obligation will be satisfied. A borrower or buyer gives security to a lender or seller; the obligation secured is usually the payment of money. Secured transactions occur at all levels of commerce. Manufacturers finance raw materials, retailers and wholesalers finance inventory, and consumers finance their purchases by giving their creditors security in the form of personal property. These transactions take many forms, but they are all secured transactions under Article 9 of the Code.

The simplest form of secured transaction is a *pledge.* In a pledge transaction, a borrower gives physical possession of his property (perhaps a watch) to a lender, as security for a loan. If the loan is not repaid, the lender can sell the watch to satisfy the debt. Stocks and bonds are frequently used as collateral in pledge transactions. In many transactions, the pledge is not satisfactory as a security arrangement because it requires that possession of the personal property be delivered to the creditor. Therefore, security devices that allow the debtor to retain and use the property have been developed. In the early law, these devices were covered by different statutes and separate rules of law. Among the common terms used to describe such security arrangements were chattel mortgages, conditional sales contracts, trust receipts, factor's liens, and assignment of accounts receivable. These terms continue to be used, even though they have been replaced by a single security device under the Code: the *security interest.* Whatever name is used, the purpose of the secured transaction is to give a creditor an interest in the debtor's personal property that the creditor can use to obtain satisfaction of the debt, in the event of nonpayment. Such personal property is called *collateral* [9-105 (1)(c)].

The nature of security

In a Platonic society, debts would not be incurred at all; in a less than Platonic system, debts are incurred. Not only is debt respectable in our society, without it our modern economy would come to a screeching halt. Literally billions of dollars in debt are incurred each month. The common denominator of all those who lend money (creditors) is that they want to be paid. Since most debtors repay their debts, the safeguard for lenders and for sellers of goods on credit is the likelihood that the debtor will *voluntarily* repay. But when a debtor does not repay, then it may be crucial that the creditor have some form of security for payment.

It is possible, however, to lend money or extend credit on an "open credit" basis (unsecured). Since the fact that an unsecured (open credit) commercial transaction is not unusual, you may wonder why security is important. To understand that, you need to know the difference between the rights of a creditor when he is unsecured (the open-credit situation) and when he has taken a *security interest* in certain property (*collateral*) of the debtor. Suppose Morley borrows $4,000 from a credit company and later buys $3,000 worth of equipment on open credit from a hardware store. Later, Morley defaults on the loan and fails to pay the $3,000 to the seller. Assume Morley's only property exempt from brankruptcy is the equipment. What are the rights of the two creditors in relation to the equipment?

If either creditor extended credit on an open basis (unsecured creditor), then that creditor could not seize the equipment. Rather, the unsecured creditor must first sue the debtor and obtain a judgment. Then, as a *judgment creditor,* it may pursue the enforcement procedures available to a judgment creditor that were discussed in chapter 3. The lawsuit to obtain the judgment and the enforcement procedures are costly in both time and money.

If the creditor were secured (having been granted a security interest in the equipment), then the secured creditor, upon default by the debtor, could seize the equipment. However, if the secured creditor could not seize the equipment peacefully, then it would have to institute formal foreclosure proceedings. The secured creditor's right to have the equipment (collateral) applied to the payment of the debt upon default is commonly referred to as *foreclosure* (the right to cut off debtor's rights in the collateral as well as junior third-party interests). The right of foreclosure is cheaper and less time-consuming than the procedure an unsecured creditor must follow. The rights of a secured creditor upon the debtor's default are further explained in chapter 23.

Unsecured creditors suffer another disadvantage when compared with secured creditors. Since many debtors are either insolvent or bankrupt, unable to pay all their debts, some creditors and some debts are either not paid in full or sometimes not paid at all. The unsecured creditor then suffers a loss, but the secured creditor has either someone else or some property to turn to for payment. Having property of the debtor (e.g., the equipment), the secured creditor is, in effect, given priority over unsecured creditors.

The right of the secured creditor to proceed against the collateral after the debtor's default (with the right of *priority* over claims of third parties) is of the very essence of a secured transaction. It is this right that distinguishes the secured from the unsecured creditor. The unsecured creditor has no rights against any specific property owned by the debtor. He must first get a judgment, then secure a writ of execution, and finally levy on the debtor's property. This levy may come too late in the game, since earlier secured claims usually have exhausted the debtor's property. Debts may be secured by personal property (a secured transaction under Article 9), real estate (mortgage or mechanic's lien), or another individual (suretyship). The last two forms of security are discussed in chapters 24 and 25.

The scope of Article 9

Although Article 9 deals primarily with secured transactions, it also covers outright sales of certain types of property, such as accounts receivable [9-102(1)(b)]. Thus, a sale of the accounts receivable of a business must comply with the Code requirements as if the accounts were security for a loan.

CASE

X, a contractor, sold his accounts receivable, including progress payments on a construction job, to D bank. The bank did not file a financing statement. Thereafter, the government filed a tax lien against X for unpaid payroll taxes. The government claims priority to the progress payments.

ISSUE Which claimant has priority?

DECISION The government.

REASON The Code requires that the assignee of accounts receivable record its interest to protect it from the claims of third parties. The Code subordinates the rights of a secured party to claims of creditors if there is not a proper filing.

United States v. Tigg, 465 F. 2d 1264 (Ark. Law) 1972.

Except for sales, such as those of accounts receivable, the main test to be applied in determining whether a given transaction falls within the purview of Article 9 is whether it was indended to have effect as security. Every transaction with such intent is covered [9-102(1)(a)]. A lease with option to buy may be considered a security transaction rather than a lease if the necessary intent is present.

Certain credit transactions are expressly excluded from Article 9 coverage [9–104]. The exclusions in general are transactions that are not basically of a commercial character, such as landlord's liens, a wage assignment, or a transfer of an insurance policy. One important exclusion is the lien given, by state law, for services and materials; for example, the artisan's lien given to a person who repairs a car.

Terminology

A *security interest* is an interest the creditor has in personal property or fixtures belonging to the debtor. It secures either payment of money or performance of an obligation [1-201(37)]. The reference to *fixtures* is included because personal property is often attached to real property, in which event it is called a fixture [9-102(1)].

The security interest comes into being when the debtor and the creditor enter into what is called a *security agreement* [9-105(h)]. The property in which a security interest is given is called *collateral* [9-105(c)]. The parties to the security agreement are the *debtor,* who owes the obligation and is giving the security, and the *secured party,* who is the lender, seller, or other person in whose favor there is a security interest [9-105(d)(i)]. Thus, the typical transaction involves an agreement (security agreement) between a debtor and a secured party, whereby the debtor agrees to give to the secured party a security interest in the debtor's collateral.

Before a security interest is effective between the parties, it must *attach* to the collateral [9-204]; and before it is effective to give priority over the rights of third parties, the security interest must be *perfected* [9–301]. Attachment is the means whereby the secured party acquires rights in the collateral; perfection is the method whereby the secured party is given priority over claims of third parties. Perfection usually occurs by filing a *financing statement.*

In sum, using Code terminology, you would say: "A *debtor,* pursuant to a *security agreement,* gives a *security interest* in certain *collateral* to secure a loan or a sale on credit. When the loan is granted or the goods are sold, a security interest *attaches* to the collateral. In order to *perfect* the security interest against the claims of third parties, a *financing statement* is *filed,* or the secured party takes physical possession of the collateral (*possessory security interest*)." Note, however, that many commercial people continue to use pre-Code terminology, which is permissible under the Code. You must be aware of these other terms. The Code, as Table 21.1 shows, simply retranslates the pre-Code terminology into Code vocabulary.

Table 21·1
Code terminology and its pre-Code equivalent

Code		Pre-Code								
Secured transaction	=	Chattel mortgage	=	Conditional sale	=	Assignment of accounts	=	Pledge	=	Trust receipt
Debtor	=	Mortgagor	=	Conditional sales vendee	=	Assignor	=	Pledgor	=	Trustee
Secured party	=	Mortgagee	=	Conditional sales vendor	=	Assignee	=	Pledgee	=	Entruster
Security interest	=	Lien	=	Title	=	Sale or security	=	Lien	=	Security interest
Security agreement	=	Chattel mortgage	=	Conditional sales contract	=	Assignment	=	Pledge contract	=	Trust receipt

Creation of an Article 9 Security Interest

The ultimate goal of the secured party is to have an enforceable, attached, and perfected security interest. The remainder of this chapter is devoted to these three concepts: *enforceability, attachment,* and *perfection.* There is a slight difference between the '62 Code and the '72 Code, in that the '62 Code has the requirement of enforceability in one section [9-203(1)(b)] and attachment in another section [9-204]. Thus, it is possible for a secured party to have a security interest (an attachment) that is not enforceable against anyone. For that reason, the '72 Code combines the two concepts (enforceability and attachment) in one section and makes the same requirements for both [9-203(1)]. With that exception, the '62 and '72 versions are virtually the same; and the following discussion, unless otherwise indicated, applies to both versions.

The steps a party must take to create an attached, enforceable security interest are set out in Section 9-203 of the '72 Code (9-203 and 9-204 of the '62 Code). If you take the steps as outlined in 9-203, then a security interest springs into existence. The Code drafters called this moment of creation "attachment." At the time of attachment, the security interest is also enforceable against the debtor and third parties [9-203(1), 9-201]; however, third parties might defeat the security interest if it is not perfected. Perfection will be discussed next, but first we must create the Article 9 security interest.

Attachment

Attachment is the event that creates a valid and enforceable Article 9 security interest. So, what must a secured party do to make this creation? Section 9-203 of the '72 Code requires the secured party to take these four apparently simple steps:

1. Make a security agreement with the debtor.
2. Make sure the debtor has "rights in the collateral."
3. Give value.
4. Make the security interest enforceable either by putting the security agreement in writing, which the debtor signs, or take possession of the collateral pursuant to the agreement.

The four steps can occur in any order. A security agreement may be executed and the secured party may give values (such as a loan) before the debtor acquires rights in the collateral. The following example will aid your understanding of attachment. Assume that Sewall, a small manufacturing company, is seeking a loan for $5,000 from a bank. Sewall intends to buy a model 711 Reaper sewing machine, which will be the collateral. The following progressive steps occur:

1. *A security agreement and financing statement are signed by Sewall but not by the bank. Sewall has yet to deal with Reaper.* Under the '72 Code, only the debtor is required to sign the two documents. The '62 Code requires that the secured party also sign the financing statement. Note also the illogical position under the '62 Code: the security interest is now enforceable (9-203), but it is not in existence because it has not attached (9-204). Remember that the '72 Code changes this result by combining the two concepts.
2. *The bank now signs the financing statement.* This is required by '62 Code; unnecessary under '72 Code [9-402(1)].
3. *The bank files the financing statement in the appropriate place.* We will discuss the financing statement in more detail later in this chapter. For now, note that a secured party can file it before the security interest attaches. In fact, it is wise for a secured party to file at the earliest possible moment. Nonetheless, the filing does not perfect the security interest until it attaches [9-303].
4. *Now Sewall contracts with Reaper to buy the Model 711 machine.* According to Article 2, we learned that a buyer does not have any rights in the goods until the goods are identified to the contract [2-501(1)(b)].
5. *Reaper removes a Model 711 machine from its inventory and marks it for delivery to Sewall.* Now the goods are identified to the contract. Therefore, the debtor, Sewall, has rights in the collateral [2-501].
6. *The bank, for the first time, makes a binding committment to loan Sewall the $5,000.* The requirement that the secured party give value is met. Agreeing to loan money, as well as actually making a loan, is the giving of value [1-201(44)].

Not until step 6 is an Article 9 security interest created; because until then, it has not attached. At Step 6, we find a *written* security agreement signed by the debtor; the debtor has rights in the collateral, and the secured party has given value. Thus, an attached and enforceable security interest comes into existence. Additionally, the security interest is perfected, since a proper financing statement has been filed. Let us now learn a few more rules about the elements of attachment.

Creation of the Security Interest

The security agreement

The basic instrument in a secured transaction is the security agreement [9-105(h)]. It must be in writing, unless the security arrangement is a possessory one and the secured party is in possession of the collateral [9-203(1)]. The only other formal requirements are that the agreement be signed by the debtor and describe the collateral so that it can be identified.

CASE

P sold office furniture to X real estate company. To secure the sale, the parties entered into a security agreement. The security agreement stated that the collateral is "furniture as per attached listing." No listing was attached, nor was any listing included in the financing statement. X real estate company sold the furniture to Y real estate company.

ISSUE Does P have security interest in the furniture?

DECISION No.

REASON The Code requires (1) that the security agreement contain a description of the collateral, and (2) that the description reasonably identifies what is described. The security agreement in question does not meet these criteria.

J. K. Gill Co. v. Fireside Realty, Inc., 499 P.2d 813 (Or.) 1972.

The security agreement will usually contain many other provisions. The forms in general use include a statement of the amount of the obligation and the terms of repayment, the debtor's duties in respect to the collateral, such as insuring it, and the rights of the secured party on default. In general, the parties can include such terms and provisions as they may deem appropriate to their particular transactions.

Value

For purposes of attachment, value is defined somewhat differently than it is in commercial paper (Article 3). Basically, *value* means that a secured party has furnished to the debtor any consideration sufficient to support a simple contract [1-201(44)]. When a bank loans money or makes a binding executory promise to extend credit to a merchant and takes a security interest in the merchant's inventory, value is given as soon as the secured party loans or agrees to loan. Value is also given when the secured party takes his security interest to secure a pre-existing claim against the debtor.

Rights in collateral

Another requirement for attachment is that the debtor have rights in the collateral. Under the 1962 Code, it was provided that the debtor has no rights in crops until planted; in fish until caught; in an account until it comes into existence; in oil, gas, and minerals until they are extracted; and in timber until it is cut [9-204(2)]. These special rules were eliminated in the 1972 Code as unnecessary and in many cases confusing.

It is clear that the debtor buyer gets rights in the collateral against his seller upon delivery of the goods. A number of recent cases have held that the buyer can acquire rights prior to shipment, the earliest time being when the seller identifies the goods to the contract. A frequently litigated issue is whether the buyer of goods acquires rights in delivered goods if the buyer's check in payment bounces. Most courts have held in the affirmative, so that the buyer's secured party prevails over the unpaid seller holding the bounced check. The outcome can change, however, if the buyer has misrepresented its solvency to the seller.

The security agreement may provide that property acquired by the debtor at any later time shall also secure some or all of the debtor's obligation under the security agreement. Many security agreements contain a clause called an *after-acquired property clause* such as the following:

> The security interest of the secured party under this security agreement extends to all collateral of the type that is the subject of this agreement and is acquired by the debtor at any time during the continuation of this agreement.

Under this clause, as soon as the debtor acquires rights in new property, a security interest in the new property vests in favor of the secured party [9-204(3)].

This clause obviously binds a debtor quite severely. The Code limits the effect of after-acquired property clauses in relation to consumer goods, since the clauses seem best suited to commercial transactions and might work undue hardship on a consumer. Unless a consumer obtains goods within ten days after the secured party gives value, a security interest usually cannot attach under an after-acquired property clause in consumer goods contracts. Accessions that are given as additional security—such as the offspring of farm animals—are exceptions [9-204(2)]. The original Code had a similar provision limiting the security interest in crops to one year. The revised Code eliminated this rule on crops because it did not accomplish its goal of limiting security interests in crops. Lenders avoided the rule by filing a financing statement and then executing a new security agreement each year.

The subject of after-acquired property interests is discussed in more detail in the next chapter. For now, remember that a security interest cannot attach until the debtor has rights in the collateral.

CASE

On May 14, 1974, seller received from manufacturer a mobile home, No. 1495, which seller sold to debtor on June 26, 1974. Debtor financed the purchase through a bank, which took and recorded its security interest in July of 1974. In the fall of 1974, seller began financing its sales of mobile homes through a loan company. On November 15, 1974, the loan company loaned seller $44,000 for 8 mobile homes. In return, the loan company received a manufacturer's statement of origin dated November 14, 1974, which (among the mobile homes listed) was No. 1495. When debtor refused to make further payments, the bank repossessed the mobile home No. 1495. The loan company claimed that its security interest in No. 1495 should prevail.

ISSUE Does the loan company have a security interest in mobile home No. 1495?

DECISION No.

REASONS
1. In order for the loan company to prevail, its security interest in No. 1495 must have attached. When seller conveyed the home to debtor on June 26, 1974, title vested in debtor.
2. The statement of origin issued to seller on November 14, 1974, was not effective to convey any title or interest to seller or from seller to loan company.
3. Since seller had no rights in the collateral after June 26, 1974, the loan company's security interest never attached.

C.I.T. Financial Service v. First National Bank, 344 So.2d 125 (Miss.) 1977.

Classifying the Collateral

Between the debtor and secured party, the security agreement protects the secured party's security interest. But the secured party also wants protection against third parties who may later make claims against the secured collateral. Perfection of the security interest will give this desired protection to the secured party. Before discussing perfection, however, we must learn how to classify the collateral. Why? Because basic questions involving perfection (how, when, and what to perfect) are answered by proper classification of the collateral. There are a wealth of cases concerning secured parties who misclassified collateral and thereby failed to perfect properly. Correct classification leads to perfect perfection.

Collateral may be classified according to its physical makeup into (1) tangible, physical property or goods, (2) documentary; property that has physical existence, such as a negotiable instrument, but is simply representative of a contractual obligation, and (3) purely intangible property, such as an account receivable. Each type of collateral presents its own peculiar problems, and the framework of Article 9 is structured on the peculiarities of each type. There may be a security interest not only in the collateral itself but also in the proceeds of the sale of collateral [9-306(1)]. Table 21.2 shows the tangible and intangible personal property that may be subject to a security interest.

Goods as collateral

Four classifications of goods are established: consumer goods, equipment, farm products, and inventory. In determining the classification of any particular item of goods, it is necessary to take into account not only the physical attributes but also the status of the debtor who is either buying the property or using it as security for a loan and the use the debtor will make of the goods. Keep in mind that the classification will determine the place of filing to perfect the security interest against third parties. It may also affect the rights of the debtor on default.

Consumer goods. Goods fall into this classification if they are used or bought primarily for personal, family, or household purposes [9-109(1)].

Equipment. Goods that are used or bought for use primarily in a business, in farming, in a profession, or by a nonprofit organization or government agency fall within this category [9-109(2)]. The category is something of a catchall, embracing goods that otherwise defy classification. Since equipment often is attached to realty and becomes a "fixture," the discussion of fixtures later is especially significant for the equipment classification.

Farm products. This category includes crops and livestock, supplies used or produced in farming operations, and the products of crops or livestock in their unmanufac-

Table 21·2
Collateral subject to a security interest

Tangible property ("goods")	*Documentary collateral*	*Intangible property*
Any personal property that is movable at the time the security interest attaches or that is a fixture [9-105 (1) (h)]. A fixture is a special type of Article 9 collateral [9-313]. Goods are classified as one of the following: Consumer goods [9-109 (1)] Equipment [9-109 (2)] Farm products [9-109 (3)] Inventory [9-109 (4)]	Involves some indispensable piece of paper and has both tangible and intangible aspects. Documentary collateral is classified into one of the following: Chattel paper [9-105 (1) (b)] Documents of title [9-105 (1) (f)] Instruments [9-105 (1) (i)]	Not evidenced by an indispensable writing, which distinguishes it from documentary collateral. Intangible property consists of one of the following: Account [9-106] Contract right [9-106 '62 Code]; deleted by '72 Code and definition of account, above, reworded to cover it General intangibles [9-106]

tured state (*e.g.*, ginned cotton, wool, milk, and eggs), provided that the items are in the possession of a debtor who is engaged in farming operations [9-109(3)]. Farm products are *not* equipment or inventory. Note that goods cease to be farm products and must therefore be reclassified when (1) they are no longer in the farmer's possession, or (2) they have been subjected to a manufacturing process. Thus, when the farmer delivers his farm products to a marketing agency for sale or to a frozen-food processor as raw materials, the products in the hands of the other party are inventory. Likewise, if the farmer maintained a canning operation, the canned product would be inventory, even though it remained in his possession.

Inventory. Inventory consists of goods that are held by a person for sale or lease or are to be furnished under a contract of service. They may be raw materials, work in process, completed goods, or material used or consumed in a business [9-109(4)]. The basic test to be applied in determining whether goods are inventory is whether they are held for immediate or ultimate sale or lease. The reason for the inclusion of materials used or consumed in a business (e.g., supplies of fuel, boxes, and other containers for packaging the goods) is that they will soon be used in making an end product for sale.

The proper classification of goods is determined on the basis of its nature and intended use by the debtor. A television set in a dealer's warehouse is inventory to the dealer. When the set is sold and delivered to a consumer customer, it becomes a consumer good. If an identical set were sold on the same terms to the owner of a tavern, to be used for entertaining customers, the set would be equipment in the hands of the tavern owner. The secured party cannot rely on the classification furnished by the debtor. All facts must be analyzed to ensure proper classification and proper filing.

Documentary collateral

Three types of property paper are included for convenience under this heading: chattel paper, documents of title, and instruments. They comprise various categories of paper used in commerce, paper that is either negotiable or to some extent dealt with as though negotiable. All are evidenced by an "indispensable writing" and are representative of obligations and rights.

Chattel paper. Chattel paper refers to a writing or writings that evidence both (1) an obligation to pay money, and (2) a security interest in, or a lease of, specific goods [9-105(1)(b)]. The chattel paper is *itself* a security agreement. A security agreement in the form of a conditional sales contract, for example, is often executed in connection with a negotiable note or a series of notes. The group of writings (the contract plus the note) taken together as a composite constitute "chattel paper." A typical situation involving chattel paper as collateral is one in which a secured party who has obtained it in a transaction with his customer may wish to borrow against it in his own financing. To illustrate: A dealer sells an electric generator to a customer in a conditional sales contract, and the customer signs a negotiable installment note. At this point, the contract is the security agreement; the dealer is the secured party; the customer is the debtor; and the generator is the collateral (equipment). The dealer, needing funds for working capital, transfers the contract and the note to a finance company as security for a loan. In the transaction between dealer and finance company, the contract and note are the collateral (chattel paper), the finance company is the secured party, the dealer is the debtor, and the customer is now designated as the "account debtor."

Documents of title. Included under this heading are bills of lading, warehouse receipts, and any other document that in the regular course of business or financing is treated as sufficient evidence that the person in possession of it is entitled to receive, hold, and dispose of the document and the goods it covers [1-201(15)].

Instrument. As distinguished from chattel paper, an *instrument* means (1) negotiable instrument, (2) an investment security such as stocks and bonds, or (3) any other writing that evidences a right to the payment of money and is not itself a security agreement or lease [9-105(i)]. To qualify as an instrument, the "other writing" must also be one that is in ordinary course of business transferred by endorsement or assignment. Thus, the classification includes, in addition to negotiable instruments, those that are recognized as having some negotiable attributes. Instruments are frequently used as collateral, and they present certain problems in this connection because of their negotiable character.

Intangible collateral

Under this heading are three items: (1) accounts, (2) contract rights, and (3) "general intangibles." They are distinguished from the "semi-intangibles" discussed in the preceding section by virtue of the fact that they are not represented by an indispensable writing.

Account. *Account* means any right to payment arising out of the sale of goods or the rendition of services, the right not being evidenced by either an instrument or chattel paper [9-106]. It is an account receivable and represents a right to payment earned by the seller's performance (the sale of goods or services actually rendered).

Contract right. This is a right to payment under a contract, a right not yet earned but, rather, to be earned by performance under an existing contract [9-106]. A contract does exist; and when the party performs his obligations under the contract, an account receivable arises. Contract right is deleted in the revised 1972 Code. The word "account" is redefined to include a contract right, which is thought of as an account before the right to payment becomes unconditional by the creditor's performance.

General intangibles. This heading includes miscellaneous intangible personal property that may be used as commercial security but does not fall within any of the preceding five classifications of intangible or semi-intangible property. Examples are goodwill, literary rights, patents, and copyrights [9-106].

Perfection of the Security Interest

Third-party claims against collateral arise in a variety of circumstances. The debtor's other creditors may wish to have the collateral sold to satisfy their claims. The debtor might give a security interest in the same collateral to another person, sell the collateral, or become bankrupt, and the bankruptcy trustee might seek to include the collateral as an asset of the bankrupt estate. An unperfected security interest is, in general, subordinate to the claims of others who acquire an interest in the collateral without knowledge of the unperfected security interest, even though it is subsequently perfected.

To have a valid security interest and priority over third persons claiming an interest in the property, the secured party must perfect the security interest [9-303) (1)]. Historically, security interests in personal property have been subject to challenge by parties (a judgment creditor, the trustee in bankruptcy, or the like) on the ground that the interest was secret and therefore fraudulent. Since 1601, a secret transfer is always held to be a "badge of fraud." To overcome this charge, Article 9 generally requires that security interests be perfected either by possession of the collateral by the secured party or by public filing of a financing statement. Both steps are designed to give notice to third parties that financing is occurring on the security of the assets involved. In certain cases, however, for practical reasons of commerce, a security interest may be automatically perfected when it attaches (for example, when a consumer buys a good on credit and gives the seller a security interest in the attaches). The Code provides various ways in which the security interest may be perfected.

Methods of perfection

A security interest may be perfected by (1) possession, (2) attachment, and (3) filing. Several factors must be taken into account in determining which of the three methods of perfection is appropriate in any given transaction: (1) the kind of collateral in which security interest was created, (2) the use the debtor intends to make of the collateral, and (3) the status of the debtor in relation to the secured party.

Before considering these three methods of perfection, we must keep in mind that even a perfected security interest is subordinate to some third-party rights. A person who repairs or improves the collateral may have an artisan's lien for his services and materials, and that is superior to the secured party's interest [9-310]. In the ordinary course of business, a buyer of inventory goods from a debtor will obtain title to the goods free of the perfected security interest. There is an exception to this general rule for farm products. A buyer of farm products in the ordinary course of business does not take them free of perfected security interest [9-307].

Perfection by possession

The simplest way to give notice of a security interest is for the secured party to take possession of the collateral [9-305]. The delivery of pledge property is the means of perfecting a security interest in it. A secured party's possession of the collateral gives notice of his security interest; hence, no public filing is required. As noted previously, the possessory security interest does not require a written security agreement. This is the simplest method of handling a secured transaction; but its use is quite limited because most debtors either need or want possession of the collateral.

Possession is the required method of perfection of a security interest in instruments. It is the optional method for collateral consisting of goods, negotiable documents of title, and chattel paper [9-305]. However, possession is the only method whereby complete protection in documents and chattel paper can be obtained, since (1) the rights of holders to whom a document has been negotiated by the debtor will prevail over the secured party, even though there has been a filing, and (2) the purchaser of chattel paper from the debtor is given such protection if he takes possession without *actual notice* of the security interest, gives new value, and takes possession in the ordinary course of his business [9-308]. The knowledge requirement is eliminated in '72 code.

For a variety of commercial reasons, it may be necessary or desirable that the secured party with a possessory security interest temporarily release possession of the collateral to the debtor. Since the release is of short duration, it would be cumbersome to require a filing. The Code therefore provides that a security interest *remains perfected* for a period of 21 days without filing when a secured party having a perfected security interest releases the collateral to the debtor. This grace period applies only to (1) instruments, (2) negotiable documents, and (3) goods in the hands of a bailee not covered by a negotiable document of title. The purposes for which the collateral may be released to the debtor, in the case of *goods* or *documents* representing the goods, are limited to making them available to the debtor for the purpose of (1) ultimate sale or exchange, or (2) loading, unloading, storing, shipping, transshipping, manufacturing, processing, or otherwise dealing with them in a manner preliminary to their sale or exchange [9-3024(5)].

If *instrument* is temporarily released to the debtor, the purpose must be to enable the debtor to make a presentation of it, collect it, renew it, obtain registration of a transfer, or make an ultimate sale or exchange. The risk attendant upon such a release (an improper or unauthorized negotiation to a holder or a sale to a bona fide purchaser by the debtor) is always present.

Perfection by attachment

The second method of perfection is by the attachment of the security interest without further action required. This method primarily concerns transactions involving installment sales to consumers and to sales of farm equipment that have a purchase price of $2,500 or less [9-302]. The provision on farm equipment is deleted in the Revised Article 9. The Revised Article 9 eliminates farm equipment from perfection by attachment because the effect of the law had been to make farm equipment unacceptable as collateral to many lenders. The transaction must be a purchase-money security interest, explained in the next chapter. In such transactions, the secured party obtains a perfected security interest without filing a financing statement.

CASE

Using a conditional sale contract designated a purchase-money security agreement, P sold a television set and tape player to a customer. On the day of the purchase, the customer pledged the items to D (a pawnbroker) as security for a loan. P did not file any financing statement.

ISSUE Which creditor has priority?

DECISION The seller.

REASONS
1. The property was consumer goods. Filing is not required to perfect a purchase-money security interest in consumer goods. P's security interest was perfected when the contract was signed and the goods were delivered [9-302(1)(d)].
2. P's security interest was automatically perfected when goods were sold to the consumer. Therefore, P's perfected interest prevails over D's subsequent possessory security interest [9-312(5)].

Kimbrell's Furniture Company, Inc. v. Friedman, 198 S.E.2d 803 (S.C.) 1973.

The protection afforded the secured party is limited in perfection by attachment. He is protected against the claims of creditors of the debtor and from others to whom the farmer or consumer debtor may give a security interest in the collateral, but he is *not* protected against the rights of a consumer or farmer good-faith purchaser from the debtor. If another consumer buys the collateral from the debtor consumer without knowledge of the security interest, the purchaser will take the collateral free of the security interest [9-307(2)]. The secured party can obtain protection against the risk by filing a financing statement if he wishes to do so. The exemption from the filing requirement does not apply if the collateral is a motor vehicle that is required to be licensed.

Perfection by Filing the Financing Statement

The most common method of perfecting a security interest is by filing a financing statement. This document, which is to be distinguished from the security agreement, is signed by the debtor and the secured party and includes their addresses. It contains a description of the collateral and indicates that debtor and secured party have entered into a security agreement. Simple forms are available with spaces for additional provisions as agreed upon by the parties, but this basic information is all that is required. If crops or fixtures constitute the collateral, then the financing statement must include a description of the real estate concerned [9-402].

A financing statement is not a substitute for a security agreement. A security agreement may be filed as a financing statement if it contains the required information and is signed by both parties, but a financing statement will usually not qualify as a security agreement. Most businesspeople use a separate financing statement, because filing a security agreement would make public some information that the parties might prefer to keep confidential.

CASE

P and debtor had dealings over a considerable period during which debtor would borrow money and sign a promissory note and financing statement, which P would file. The financing statement stated that the collateral was "All of debtor's contracts and accounts receivable presently owned or hereafter acquired." The contracts in question in this case were not actually assigned to P; P simply filed the usual statement.

ISSUE Can a financing statement qualify as a security agreement?

DECISION No.

REASONS

1. Section 9-105(h) states that a security agreement means an agreement that creates or provides for a security interest. The financing statement and promissory note fail to qualify as a security agreement because nowhere in either form is there any evidence of an agreement by the debtor to grant P a security interest.
2. The majority rule is that the financing statement cannot be a security agreement unless it contains further proper language that grants or creates a security interest.

Crete State Bank v. Lauhoff Grain Co., 239 N.W.2d 789 (Neb.) 1976.

The purpose of filing is to give notice that the secured party who filed it may have a security interest in the described collateral. Potential creditors are charged with the task of going to the recorder's office to check to see if the proposed collateral is already encumbered. A person searching the records finds only minimal information and must obtain more from the parties to the financing statement. A procedure is established for such disclosure by the secured party at the request of the debtor.

The financing statement may provide a maturity or expiration date, but more often it is silent on this point, since the statement usually will not mention the debt or obligation. In the absence of such data, the filing is effective for a period of five years, subject to being renewed by the filing of a continuation statement signed by the secured party [9-403(2)]. If renewed, it continues the effectiveness of the original statement for another five years.

The presence in the records of a financing statement constitutes a burden upon the debtor, since it reveals to all persons with whom he may be dealing that his property is or may be subject to the claims of others. The Code therefore provides for the filing of a *termination statement* to clear the record when the secured party is no longer entitled to a security interest. Failure of the secured party to send a termination statement within ten days after written demand by the debtor subjects him to a $100 penalty and also renders him liable for any loss occasioned to the debtor [9-404(1)].

Filing a financing statement is *required* in order to perfect a nonpossessory security interest in most secured transactions. As a general rule, filing is required in the case of an assignment of accounts receivable or contract rights. An exception exists for certain isolated transactions. If the assignment does not encompass a significant portion of the outstanding accounts or contract rights of the assignor, filing is not required [9-302(1)(e)].

The Code allows the states to file the financing statement in a central filing system, a local filing system, or a combination [9-401]. A central filing system means that all filing is in the state capital except for fixtures, which are filed locally. Local filing means that filing is at the county level. Most states have enacted dual filing systems. The usual system requires local filing for fixtures, local filing for farm-related collateral and consumer goods, and central filing for other collateral, such as inventory and equipment.

The Code makes special provisions for goods such as motor vehicles that have a certificate of title. The filing requirements of the Code do not apply, and the usual method of indicating a security interest is to have it noted on the certificate of title [9-302(3)]. If the security interest is properly perfected on the certificate of title, the security interest is valid even though a substitute certificate of title fails to disclose the interest of the secured party.

Optional and required filing

In most instances, the secured party has the option either to file a financing statement to perfect or to take a possessory security interest. Sometimes the secured party *must* file, and sometimes the secured party *cannot* file to perfect. Those instances depend on the classification of the collateral, which we previously considered. The secured party *cannot file* an *instrument* (for example, an Article 3 promissory note or an Article 8 stock certificate) but must take possession to perfect. The rule of mandatory possession is based on the idea that when collateral consists of instruments, it is the universal practice for the secured party to take possession of them in pledge. Thus, it would have been unwise for the Code drafters to provide the alternative of perfection by filing, since it would in no way correspond with the commercial practice and would serve no useful function.

As stated, for most types of collateral, filing or taking possession are alternative methods of perfection. Chattel paper, negotiable documents of title, and goods (consumer goods, equipment, farm products, and inventory) are subject to the option of filing or taking possession. But if the collateral has no tangible existence, common sense tells us that it cannot be physically possessed. A security interest in accounts (contract rights under '62 Code) and general intangibles may therefore under the Code be perfected *only by filing.*

CASE

P, an accountant, lent money to a company, which was already indebted to P for services rendered. As security for the loan and to secure payment for the services, the company assigned to P a portion of its expected recovery of a pending lawsuit. P did not file a financing statement with regard to the assignment. Subsequently, D Corp. was awarded a judgment against the company in another lawsuit. D, without knowledge of the assignment to P, had the sheriff levy against the company's property. Pursuant to the sheriff's execution sale, all of the company's rights in the pending lawsuit were sold to D. When the lawsuit was settled, P claimed rights to the proceeds.

ISSUE Is P entitled to the proceeds of the lawsuit pursuant to his security interest?

DECISION No.

REASON The assignment of a pending lawsuit is an assignment of a general intangible. The Code requires the filing of a financing statement to perfect a security interest in general intangibles [9-301(1)(b)(3)], [9-302(1)(e)].

Friedman, Lobe & Block v. C.L.W. Corp., 512 P.2d 769 (Wash.) 1973.

REVIEW QUESTIONS AND PROBLEMS

1. Diana owns a pleasure craft. In need of money, she telephones Shirley and asks for a $2,000 loan. Shirley says that she will lend the money if Diana will grant her a security interest in the pleasure craft to secure payment. Diana agrees. Immediately thereafter, Shirley files a financing statement in the appropriate place covering the craft. Later, Diana becomes insolvent and the marina, an unsecured creditor, has the sheriff levy on the craft pursuant to a judgment it obtained. Is Shirley's security interest enforceable under the 1972 Code? Under the 1962 Code? Explain.
2. A bank entered into a security agreement with Albright. The agreement provided that the bank was to have a security interest in all of Albright's inventory and proceeds. The financing statement described the collateral as "all inventory plus proceeds thereof." Does the bank's security interest include accounts receivable arising from the sale of inventory? Why or why not?
3. Suppose in the previous question, the security agreement listed the collateral as "all Albright's equipment, furniture, and fixtures"; and in spaces provided for classification of the collateral, the bank put a check mark by "inventory, accounts receivable, and contract rights." When Albright became bankrupt, the bankruptcy trustee contended that the bank was not a secured creditor regarding inventory, accounts receivable, and contract rights. Is the trustee correct? Why or why not? (Remember that the 1972 Code eliminates "contract right" and places it under the definition of "account.")
4. Two farmers obtained fertilizer and other supplies from Dyke Dealers and gave them a promissory note stating that the note was covered by a security agreement. In fact, no security agreement had been executed, but the parties had signed and filed a financing statement. Subsequently, the farmers sold their crop. Dyke claims the right to the crop by virtue of its security interest. Does Dyke have a security interest in the crop? Why or why not?
5. On October 1st Fenster Equipment Company delivers movie cameras to Hill Productions for a week's trial use. On October 3rd, Hill borrows $10,000 from Large Loan Company and signs a security agreement that grants Large Loan a security interest in the movie cameras. On October 7th, Hill agrees to buy the cameras. Fenster finances the entire purchase price and retains a security interest in the cameras. Does Fenster have a security interest in the cameras? Does Large Loan? When did the security interest(s) arise? Explain.
6. Classification of collateral may not be as easy as the text may indicate. See if you can correctly classify the following collateral. *a*). Burns Rentals leases and sells TVs and cars. Burns obtains financing from City Bank, enabling him to buy 25 new cars and 100 new TVs. Classify the cars and TVs. *b*). Burns has 50 cars on his lot for lease. Classify the cars. *c*). Burns sells a truck to Boyce and retains a security interest in the truck. Boyce uses the truck exclusively for week-end camping and fishing trips. Classify the truck. *d*). Burns assigns Boyce's promissory note and security agreement to City Bank as collateral for a loan. Classify the collateral. *e*). Burns Rentals buys 300 new Philco TVs for his annual summer sale. Classify the TVs in the hands of Philco; in Burns' possession. Virgil, owner of Virgil's Truck City and Bar, buys a TV during the sale. The set is delivered to Virgil in its original carton and put in the back of his sixteen wheeler. What type of goods did Virgil buy? *f*). When Philco sells TVs to Burns, it packages them in special shipping cartons, using packaging materials such as styrofoam and excelsior. Philco maintains a large supply of these materials. Classify them. *g*). Burns has a large supply of diesel fuel and oil for his fleet of trucks. Classify the diesel fuel and oil. Classify the trucks.
7. Podner manufactures western wear and keeps a ledger of its accounts receivable, as well as copies of all purchase orders and all invoices. Podner borrows $25,000 from the Bank of the Potomac and signs a security agreement granting the bank a

security interest in all Podner's accounts receivable. Rather than filing a financing statement, the bank stamps on Podner's ledger in bold print as follows: "Pledged to the Bank of the Potomac." The bank then takes all Podner's purchase orders and invoices into its possession. The bank later notifies all of the account debtors of Podner to pay the Bank of the Potomac directly. Does the bank have an enforceable and perfected security interest under the Code? Explain.

8. Vesey buys an accordion from Dean Company "on time" with Dean retaining a security interest in the accordion. The parties execute a purchase money security agreement. Must Dean file a financing statement to perfect his security interest? Why or why not?

9. Would your answer to the last question change given these new facts: The purchase-money security agreement states: "Vesey warrants and covenants that the collateral is bought or used primarily for household, consumer, or personal use." Vesey, a few days later, turns professional. Explain your answer.

10. By answering the following, check your knowledge of the business decisions involved in secured transactions. *a*). Assume you are a retailer with a large amount of outstanding accounts receivable and you are in need of cash to pay expenses. How might you raise the necessary cash? Explain. *b*). Assume that you are considering loaning money to Fred Tauber of Tauber & Sons and taking a security interest in certain property of Tauber & Sons. What should you do prior to lending the money? Explain. *c*). Assume you are arranging to finance another's business. It will be a secured financing plan that works on a continuing basis (in the next chapter, this plan is referred to as a floating lien.) What provisions should you require for inclusion in the security agreement and in the financing statement? Explain. *d*). Assume you are a secured party and are in doubt about whether you have to file and, if so, where to file. What do you do? Explain.

The dominant theme of this chapter is the consequence of perfection or nonperfection, which involves priorities among conflicting interests in the same collateral. The fundamental question is "When will a secured party's security interest be subordinate to a third party's rights?" Or to put it another way, "Upon the default of a debtor, what are the risks of third-party priority?" A major portion of Article 9 deals with priority, but it also has three important technical aspects, which we shall explain: (1) the "floating lien," (2) the purchase money security interest, and (3) problems associated with fixtures.

22 Priority between the Secured Party and Third-Party Claims

The rules of Article 9 are primarily concerned with the limits of the secured party's protection against those who *purchase* goods from the debtor and those who are *creditors* of the debtor. We know that the limits of protection are typically measured by whether or not the secured party has perfected. Although a perfected security may be or become subordinate to other interests, the general rule of Article 9 is that after perfection, the secured party is protected against those who purchase from, or are creditors of, the debtor and, in particular, against any representative of creditors in insolvency proceedings instituted by, or against, the debtor [9-303, comment 1]. Before detailing the priority rules, let us first identify the possible conflicting interests of third parties.

Conflicting third-party interests

Collateral is frequently the subject of conflicting claims. Two or more persons may claim a security interest in the same collateral, or a person may claim that he has a better right to the collateral than does the secured party. Among the many ways in which conflicting claims to collateral arise, the following are some of the more important situations.

1. A debtor gives more than one security interest in the same collateral.
2. A trustee in bankruptcy claims the collateral in connection with bankruptcy proceedings involving the debtor.
3. A debtor sells the collateral to a good-faith purchaser who is not aware of the security interest.
4. Collateral becomes attached to real property, so that it is a fixture.
5. Collateral becomes attached to personal property that belongs to another or in which another has security interest.
6. Collateral has been repaired or improved by the services or materials of another.
7. Collateral has been processed (e.g., raw material in which there is security interest is converted into a finished product).
8. The government or some other creditor claims a lien on the property.

In all the foregoing situations, as well as many others, it becomes necessary to sort out the conflicting interests and determine a priority among them.

The interests that can compete with the secured party roughly fall into two categories: (1) those who purchase from the debtor, and (2) creditors of the debtor. As Table 22.1 demonstrates, the list of potential third-party interests is rather long. (The table includes relevant Code priority sections.)

Secured Party v. Secured Party

Two or more creditors may obtain security interests covering the same collateral. If the value of the collateral is less than the total of the claims it secures, upon the debtor's default it will be necessary to determine the priority of competing security interests.

Regular security interest

Section 9-312 governs most secured party v. secured party priority contests. It contains special rules to be applied when the conflicting security interests are regular or when at least one of the interests is a purchase money security interest. The general rule governing priority between regular perfected security interests in the same collateral is found in 9-312(5)(a) of the Code.

Section 9-312(5)(a) has a first-in-time rule; that is, the first secured party either to file or to perfect will have priority. "Conflicting security interests rank according to priority in time of filing or perfection. Priority dates from the time a filing is first made covering the collateral or the time the security interest is first perfected, whichever is earlier" [9-312(5)(a)]. This rule underscores the special status of filing a financing statement. Filing can occur at any time, even prior to attachment. The following example will help illustrate this rule. SP-1 files against Debtor on November 1st. On December 1st, SP-2 gives value to Debtor who signs a written security agreement granting SP-2 a nonpurchase money security interest. SP-1 does the same on January 1st. Who has priority? SP-1. Although SP-2 was first to perfect and first to give value, SP-1 was first to file. Filing is authorized at any time, even before a security is created. This example shows that the Code adopts a pure "race type" statute; the first to file or perfect wins. Knowledge is unimportant. It

Table 22·1 Conflicting third-party interests

Other secured parties

Regular security interest [9-312 (5)]

Purchase money security interest [9-312 (3) & (4)]

Purchaser of collateral from debtor

Buyer in the ordinary course of business [9-307 (1)]

Farmer buyer of farm equipment with a purchase price not in excess of $2,500 if secured party has perfected without filing [9-307 (2) of the 1962 Code; the 1972 revision eliminates this provision]

Consumer buyer of consumer goods from another consumer [9-307 (2)]

Lien creditors

Judicial lien creditor [9-301 (1) (b)]

Federal tax lien [26 U.S.C. §§ 6321, 6322, 6323 (a)]

Laborer's, artisan's, or materialman's lien [9-310]

Bankruptcy trustee [11 U.S.C. § 544 (a) (1979)]

Special Priority rules

Fixtures [9-313 of 1962 and 1972 Code]

Accessions [9-314]

Commingled and processed goods [9-315]

Returned or repossessed goods [9-306 (5)]

The floating lien

makes no difference whether or not SP-1 knew of SP-2's interest at the time SP-1 makes his advance. The virtue of a race statute is certainty and predictability. Whoever wins the race (first in time) has priority.

The 1962 Code has a similar rule in 9-312 (a) and (b). Priority is ranked in the order of filing if both security interests are perfected by filing *or* in the order of perfection, unless both interests are perfected by filing.

CASE

P sued D to determine which of them had priority in the collateral of X, a debtor of both parties. P, who had financed X for a long time, obtained a financing statement covering X's inventory and equipment. This was filed on June 5, 1972. P gave no value at that time, and no security agreement was entered into. On March 5, 1973, P and X signed a security agreement, and P loaned X money.

On June 1, 1972, however, D had loaned X a sum of money and had entered into a security agreement covering the same collateral. D filed a financing statement on June 27, 1972.

ISSUE Which party has priority in the collateral?

DECISION P.

REASONS 1. Both parties have perfected security interests, which were perfected by filing.

2. If both interests are perfected by filing, the order of filing determines priority, and P filed first.

3. D's security interest was perfected first, because perfection required attachment to the collateral as well as filing. Attachment requires an agreement to that effect, and value must be given. D was perfected on June 27, 1972. P was perfected on March 5, 1973.
4. Notwithstanding that D was the first to perfect, P wins because the law gives priority to the first to file. It does so in order to protect the filing system.

Enterprises Now v. Citizens & So. Dev., 218 S.E.2d 309 (Ga.) 1975.

Future advances

Problems with future advances arose under the 1962 Code, but it had no specific provision concerning them. A future advance occurs when the original secured party makes a second loan to the debtor, and that secured party may or may not be committed by the security agreement to make the additonal loan(s). The main problem occurs in this context: SP-1 files, loans, and perfects his security interest. SP-2 later files, loans, and perfects. Under the rule above, SP-1 would win, since he was first to file. But what happens when SP-1 loans additional money (a future advance) after SP-2 has filed and perfected? SP-2 will argue that he had filed before the second loan. The 1962 Code had no answer, but the 1972 Code provides a simple solution in 9-312(7).

If the future advance is made while a security interest is perfected by filing or by taking possession, the security interest with priority under the "first to file or perfect" rule [9-312(5)(a)] has the same priority with respect to future advances. Likewise, if the secured party makes a commitment (at the time he is perfected) to lend money later, then the future advance has the same priority as the original loan. In all other situations, the future advance has priority from the date the advance is made [9-312(7) of the 1972 Code]. The rule is justified by the necessity of protecting the filing system; that is, allowing the secured party who files first to make later loans without each time, as a condition for perfection, having to check for filings later than his.

Purchase money security interests (PMSI)

There are two types of purchase money security interests (often referred to as PMSI): (1) seller's PMSI: a seller of goods retains a security interest in the goods as collateral to secure payment of the purchase price, and (2) lender's PMSI: a lender advances money to enable the debtor to acquire the collateral, and the money is, in fact, used to buy the collateral [9-107]. A secured party with a PMSI enjoys a preferred status in some situations. As we learned in the previous chapter, a seller's PMSI in consumer goods is automatically perfected upon attachment. The 1962 Code makes a seller's PMSI in farm equipment with a purchase price of less than $2,500 automatically perfected upon attachment. The 1972 revised Code eliminates this special treatment of farm equipment. In 9-312, there are two other important preferred status provisions for a PMSI: one in inventory collateral, the other in noninventory collateral.

PMSI in inventory

A security agreement usually will provide that the security interest in inventory continues into after-acquired inventory. If that security interest is perfected by filing, then it will defeat any later secured party under the first-in-time rule. But this rule effectively stops a debtor seller from subsequently financing a new line of inventory, since the seller cannot give the subsequent secured party (new lender) priority on the new inventory. Code 9-312(3) changes this rule and gives preferred status to a later PMSI in new inventory. Example: A bank loans a store money secured by all the store's inventory now owned or hereafter acquired. The bank properly files a financing statement. A year later, a loan company advances money to allow the store to acquire a new line of appliances. Before the new appliances arrive, the loan company properly files a financing statement covering the appliances. An officer of the loan company then telephones the loan officer of the bank and tells him that the loan company intends to finance the new appliances for the store on a PMSI. The loan company now has priority over the Bank but only in relation to the new appliances.

The requirements of 9-312(3) are rather simple. First, the PMSI secured party must perfect its PMSI and give the other secured party notice that it has (or expects to have) a PMSI in certain described inventory. Perfection and notice must occur prior to the debtor receiving the inventory. The purpose of the notice is to protect the other secured party so he will not make new loans based on the after-acquired inventory or otherwise rely on the new inventory as his collateral.

Although oral or written notification was permitted under the '62 Code, the '72 Code requires the notification to be in writing. Therefore, the loan company's notice via telephone in the above example was sufficient under the '62 Code but would not be under the '72 Code. There is one other major distinction between the two versions of the Code. Under the '62 Code the PMSI secured party had to give notice to all secured parties who had filed and to any other secured parties known to him. The '72 Code requires the PMSI secured party to give notice to all secured parties who have filed a financing statement covering the same types of inventory before the PMSI files. Courts strictly enforce the notice requirement.

CASE

P, a manufacturer of appliances, entered into a security agreement covering all of X's inventory in the fall of 1970. A financing statement was filed on November 27, 1970. On November 24, 1970, X entered into another security agreement with D bank covering all of X's inventory as collateral. D filed its financing statement on December 9, 1970.

X later became bankrupt. P's claim was for $23,682.30. X's inventory of P's products was only $12,974.96, and $10,707.34 of them had been sold by X without payment to P. D took over all of X's inventory and repaid P the $12,974.96. P sues for the $10,707.34, claiming an interest in *all* of the inventory, not only its own products.

ISSUE Is P entitled to priority in the other inventory items?

DECISION Yes.

REASONS
1. P was clearly the prior secured creditor. The security interest was the total inventory, not simply P's own manufactured products.
2. D could have protected itself by complying with the purchase money security interest procedures relating to inventory.

Borg-Warner Accep. Corp. v. First Nat. Bank, 238 N.W.2d 612 (Minn.) 1976.

PMSI in noninventory collateral

For collateral other than inventory, a purchase money security interest is superior to conflicting security interests in the same collateral, provided the purchase money security interest is perfected at the time the debtor receives the collateral or within ten days thereafter [9-312(4)]. Thus, prior notice to other secured parties is not required in cases of equipment if the security interest is perfected within ten days. The prior notice requirement is limited to a PMSI in new inventory under 9-312(3).

A secured party with a purchase money security interest is given a special status for ten days after the debtor receives the property. Of course, the secured party must file within the ten-day period. The protection during such period is limited. It gives priority over the rights of only (1) transferees in bulk (buyers of all or a substantial portion of a business) from the debtor and (2) lien creditors, to the extent that such rights arise between the time the purchase money security interest attaches and the time of filing [9-301(2)]. The secured party is not protected against (1) a sale by the debtor to another party or (2) a secured transaction wherein the collateral is given as security for a loan during the period prior to filing.

Secured Party v. Buyers of Collateral

We now turn our attention to the secured party's priority when the collateral is sold or transferred to a third party. In general, the secured party's security interest continues in any collateral sold or transferred unless the security agreement authorizes such a sale or transfer. Under Section 9-306(2), if the debtor makes an unauthorized sale or transfer, then the security interest usually, but not always, continues in the collateral in the hands of the buyer. Three classes of buyers take priority over the secured party, even though the sale was unauthorized (see Table 22.1). Let us now consider these buyers.

Buyer in the ordinary course of business

A buyer in the ordinary course of business "takes free of a security interest created by his seller even though the security interest is perfected and even though the buyer knows of its existence" [9-307(1)]. A buyer in the ordinary course of business is a buyer who buys goods from a seller (except a pawnbroker) who is in the business of selling goods of that kind [1-201(9)]. When you buy goods at the grocery store, department store, and gas station, you are a buyer in the ordinary course of business. The rule typically applies when a seller sells its inventory. The reason for this rule should be obvious: when you buy goods from a professional seller, you expect to get clear title to the goods and would never think that they might be subject to a security interest. This rule, then, simply codifies the customary expectations of buyers in our society. It has been applied to buyers of new cars from a dealership and to a dealer buyer who buys from another dealer. It would not apply to you if you bought a used car from a car repair garage, since the garage is not in the business of selling goods of that kind. One court held that a person who buys a used car from a car rental company (which sells its older rental cars from time to time) is not a buyer in the ordinary course of business.

CASE

In the textile industry, processors customarily buy more greige goods (unfinished fabric) than they will use, and they sell their surplus to other processors. Following industry practice, Mills Fabrics, a processor, sold its surplus to P, another processor. P then demanded that D, the manufacturer, deliver the cloth that Mills Fabrics had previously purchased. D refused, asserting a security interest in the goods, to insure payment.

ISSUE Was P's purchase of the unfinished textiles in the ordinary course of Mills Fabrics' business, so that P can take the cloth free of D's perfected security interest?

DECISION Yes.

REASONS 1. Mills Fabrics' sale to P was in the ordinary course of business, even though its predominant business purpose is, like P's, the processing of unfinished fabrics into finished goods.

2. All subdivision (1) of section 9-207 requires is that the sale be of the variety reasonably to be expected in the regular course of business.

3. Thus, since it is customary in the trade for processors to sell excess goods, Mills Fabrics' sale of excess goods to P was reasonably expected and is in the ordinary course of business.

Tanbro Fabrics Corp. v. Deering Milliken, 350 N.E.2d 590 (N.Y.) 1976.

Buyer of farm products

The buyer-in-ordinary-course-of-business rule does not apply to a person buying farm products from a person engaged in farming operations [9-307(1)]. Typically, farmers or ranchers get loans and grant security interests in their crops or cattle. This rule allows the secured party to follow its security interest into the hands of a cattle buyer or a grain elevator or food processor. To understand the reason for this exception, you need only ask who makes most of the loans to farmers and ranchers—the federal govenrment. If state law did not grant priority to the government's security interest over buyers of farm products, then the government might refuse to lend or might pass special legislation giving it a preferred status. Although the drafters of the '72 Code wanted to eliminate this exception, the threat of federal reaction caused them not to change the special rule for farm products.

CASE

A farmer gave the plaintiff a security interest in a cotton crop. Plaintiff, an agency of the United States government, properly perfected its security interest by filing a financing statement. The farmer ginned the cotton in his own ginning mill and then sold the product to D, buyer. The P, United States, claims that it has a security interest in the ginned cotton in the hands of D, buyer.

ISSUE Is D, buyer, a buyer in the ordinary course of business under 9-307(1)?

DECISION Yes.

REASON By definition, ginned cotton does not cease to be a farm product [9-109(3)] so long as the seller is engaged in farming operations. The facts show that the farmer here was both a *farmer* and *owner* of the Gin Co., which sold the ginned cotton. Therefore, the D, buyers, bought from the Gin Co., which was not engaged in farming operations. Therefore, these buyers are buyers in the ordinary course of business under 9-307(1).

United States v. Hext, 444 F.2d 804 (Tex. law) 1971.

Buyer of consumer goods

Earlier in this chapter, we learned that a PMSI in consumer goods is automatically perfected when it is created (that is, when it attaches). Section 9-302(1)(d) provides that a PMSI in consumer goods (except for motor vehicles, which must be registered) is perfected without filing. This exception is a practical one because it would be costly for a seller of consumer goods to file after each sale, and the flood of financing statements would inundate our courthouses. The automatic perfection rule also follows prior commercial customs of no required filing. Nonetheless, a seller with a PMSI in consumer goods might have to file to get priority over another consumer buyer.

Section 9-307(2) allows a consumer buyer of consumer goods from another consumer to take free of the PMSI "unless prior to the purchase the secured party has filed a financing statement covering such goods." Smith buys a sofa from Furniture Company and gives it a PMSI in the sofa for the unpaid purchase price. Furniture Company does not file a financing statement. A few months later, Smith sells the sofa to her next-door neighbor, Jones, who uses the sofa in his home. Although Furniture Company has an automatically perfected security interest in the sofa, the sale is free of that PMSI if Jones paid value, did not know of the PMSI, and uses the sofa for "consumer" purposes [9-307 (2)]. This example shows that 9-307(2) applies when a consumer (Smith) sells consumer goods (sofa) to another consumer (Jones). If Furniture Company had filed a financing statement, then Jones's purchase would be subject to the PMSI.

Secured Party v. Lien Creditor

In addition to other secured parties and buyers of the collateral, a secured party's security interest can conflict with parties holding liens arising from operation of law. Four types of liens created by law may come into conflict with an Article 9 security interest: (1) judicial lien, (2) federal lien, (3) artisan's or materialman's lien, and (4) the lien creditor rights of a bankruptcy trustee.

Judicial lien

Article 9 defines a lien creditor as either a creditor who acquired a lien on the debtor's property by a sheriff's levy based on the creditor's judgment or a trustee in bankruptcy [9-301(3)]. The first creditor is more generally called a judicial lien creditor and was discussed in the preceding chapter, under the concept of security. This creditor, having obtained a judgment in a lawsuit, seeks to collect that judgment by levy, attachment, execution, or the like on the debtor's property. Article 9 has some awkward language in section 9-301(1)(b) that covers conflicts between a lien creditor and an Article 9 security interest. It states in the negative that an unperfected security interest is subordinate to the rights of a person who becomes a lien creditor before the security interest is perfected. Stated positively, the Code provides a first-in-time rule: a secured party who perfects before the judicial lien creditor levies will prevail. To apply the rule, look to the time that the levy is made (for example, October 3). If the secured party has perfected at any time prior to that levy on October 3, then the secured party's security interest has priority over the judicial lien creditor. Stated in another affirmative way, priority goes to a person who becomes a lien creditor before the security interest is perfected. A person becomes a lien creditor at the time of attachment, levy, execution or the like under 9-301(3).

Federal tax lien

Throughout history the sovereign has insisted upon special deference. The United States government is no exception, especially when it comes to collecting taxes. Confronting a delinquent taxpayer, Uncle Sam comes armed with the most comprehensive lien that arises by operation of law, the federal tax lien. Section 6321 of the Internal Revenue Code accords the U.S. a lien on all property of the taxpayer. *All* means "all," including property subject to an Article 9 security interest. Priority disputes between Article 9 secured parties and federal tax liens are governed by the Internal Revenue Code, not by Article 9.

The rule affecting Article 9 secured parties is easy to find and to apply. The rule is the typical first-in-time priority rule. The federal tax lien is subordinate to the secured party's security interest until notice of the tax lien is filed. Filing of the tax lien can be made with the clerk of the local United States District Court unless state law provides a filing place for the property subject to the lien. Most states have statutes allowing filing of a federal tax lien in a particular state, county, or local office.

Just as with the judicial lien, the first-in-time rule is easy to apply. The secured party must be perfected. A federal tax lien that is filed after the date of perfection is inferior to the earlier perfected security interest.

Laborer's, artisan's, or materialman's lien

The *common-law lien* on goods, allowed for repair, improvement, storage, or transportation, is superior to a perfected security interest as long as the lien claimant retains possession of the property. *Statutory liens* also have such priority unless the statute expressly subordinates them. Even though a lien is second in point of time, it will be granted priority over a perfected security interest in the goods unless the statute creating the lien provides that it is subordinate [9-310]. The reason for giving superiority to a second-in-time lien is the presumption that the service rendered by the lienholder has added to or protected the value of the property.

CASE

X, the owner of a motor vehicle, left it with D for extensive repair. D's bill was $1,152.38. Earlier, X had entered into a security agreement with P bank to secure a loan. The unpaid balance of the loan was $2,846.29. The automobile was sold to satisfy these claims, but the sale price was insufficient to pay both.

ISSUE Which party has priority?

DECISION The possessory lienholder (repairman).

REASONS
1. Under the Code, a mechanic in possession of a motor vehicle is entitled to priority over a prior secured creditor.
2. When a person in the ordinary course of his business furnishes services or materials for goods subject to a security interest, and he has those goods in his possession, a lien given on them by statute or rule of law takes priority over a perfected security interest *unless the lien is statutory and the statute expressly provides otherwise.*

Krueger v. Texas State Bank, 328 S.W.2d 121 (Tex) 1975.

The bankruptcy trustee

The subject of bankruptcy will be thoroughly explained subsequently in chapter 27. Bankruptcy is a remedy granted not by the Code but by the federal Bankruptcy Reform Act of 1978. When a debtor (voluntarily or involuntarily) is put into bankruptcy, his nonexempt assets are required to be turned over to a trustee to be sold to satisfy the claims of unsecured creditors. If a secured party has a security interest in some of those assets, then the security interest is threatened. The bankruptcy trustee, created by federal law, is another third party who may defeat certain Article 9 secured parties. It is the trustee's job to gather and liquidate the debtor's estate, reduce it to cash, and make a prorata payment to the bankrupt's *unsecured* creditors.

The trustee will attempt to show that the Article 9 security interest is ineffective. If the attempt is successful, it will increase the available assets and, in turn, increase the prorata distribution to the unsecured creditors. The acid test for an Article 9 security interest is said to be its ability to survive the trustee's attack. Several sections of the 1978 Bankruptcy Act give the trustee powers to avoid an Article 9 security interest; many of them—such as the power to avoid the security interest as a *preference* under section 547—will be considered in Chapter 27, "Bankruptcy." The problem of the secured party's right to *proceeds* in bankruptcy will be discussed in connection with the floating lien later in this chapter. For now, we shall analyze one important right of the bankruptcy trustee in its quest to set aside a security interest.

Trustee's judgment lien creditor's rights

The most frequent clash between the secured party and the trustee occurs when the security interest is not perfected. The trustee will prevail over an unperfected security interest by using the bankruptcy act and the Code. Section 544(a) gives the trustee the rights under state law of a hypothetical lien creditor; that is, it allows the trustee to pretend it is a lien creditor. The relevant state law is section 9-301(1)(b). In essence, section 544 (a) provides that on the *date* the bankruptcy petition is filed, the trustee can assert the same rights that a lien creditor would have on that date under state law. This rule is easy to apply.

Assume that the bankruptcy petition was filed on October 10, and the secured party filed to perfect on October 11. Section 544 (a) gives the trustee the rights of a lien creditor under the Code section 9-301(1)(b). As we already know, when the lien creditor levies, thereafter it beats out an unperfected security interest but is inferior to a previously perfected security interest. Now, apply that reasoning to the time the bankruptcy petition is filed. If before that date (October 10 in our example) the security interest is perfected, then the trustee loses. But in our example perfection occurred on October 11. Since the security interest was unperfected on October 10, the trustee (as in the case of a lien creditor) will prevail.

There is one instance in which the secured party is unperfected on the date of bankruptcy but will nonetheless prevail under section 544(a). The Code has a 10-day grace period for filing a PMSI in 9-301(2). Assume a secured party makes a PMSI loan to the debtor on May 1 and that the secured party files to perfect on May 8. Since filing was within the 10-day period, the security interests relates back to May 1 under 9-301(2). Therefore, on the date of bankruptcy (May 3) the security interest is perfected and is superior to a lien creditor under section 9-301(1)(b). The trustee with the rights of that lien creditor would also lose in this situation.

Section 544 (a) can be dramatically summarized as follows: if the secured party (with the exception of a PMSI) perfects his security interest a second before the bankruptcy petition is filed, the trustee cannot use section 544 (a) to invalidate that secured interest.

Special Priority Rules

Fixtures—original Article 9 (1962)

Goods that are collateral for a security agreement may be attached to real property, making them fixtures [9-313(1)]. This situation raises a question of priority between the secured party and one who has a security interest in the real property (e.g., one who has a mortgage upon the real property). An example of a fixture is a heating system installed in a building. Article 9 does not determine the circumstances under which goods become fixtures, but it does provide rules for determining priorities when a fixture is involved.

A security interest that attaches to goods before they become fixtures has total priority if it is *perfected* before they becomes fixtures [9-313(2)]. Even if it is not perfected, it will have (based on *attachment*) priority over prior mortgages because of the value added to the real estate. It will be inferior to subsequent purchasers or mortgagees because they presumably bought or loaned on the value of the property including the fixtures [9-313(3)].

The secured party who has priority is entitled, upon default, to remove the fixtures. He is required to reimburse an encumbrancer or owner other than the debtor for the cost of repair of any physical damages caused by the removal [9-313(5)].

We have said that filing is required to perfect a security interest in fixtures, regardless of their classification as consumer goods, farm equipment, and so forth. The filing should be done in the office where real estate mortgages are filed or recorded.

Fixtures—revised Article 9 (1972)

No portion of the 1962 version of Article 9 has been more criticized than the provisions relating to fixtures. The original Code failed to recognize many principles of real estate law relating to competing interest in land and the relative priority of such interests. The Revised Code attempts to correct these errors in the following ways.

Building materials are clearly not classified as fixtures [***9-313(2)***]. The Revised Code recognizes three categories of goods: (1) those that retain their chattel character and are not part of the real estate, (2) building materials that lose their chattel character entirely and are a part of the real estate, and (3) an intermediate class that becomes a part of the real estate for some purposes but may be a part of a secured transaction. The third category is *fixtures.*

The term fixture filing is used to require filing where a mortgage on real estate would be filed. The financing statement for fixture filing must (1) show that it covers fixtures, (2) recite that it is to be filed in the real estate records, (3) describe the real estate, and (4) show the name of the record owner if the debtor does not own the real estate.

A mortgage may describe fixtures and thus be used as a financing statement. In such cases, the mortgage is exempt from the five-year limitation on financing statements.

Two basic priority rules are based on fixture filing. First, if fixture filing occurs before the goods become fixtures or within ten days thereafter, then the security interest is superior to any *earlier* realty interest, such as a prior recorded mortgage [9-313(4)(a)]. The second rule concerns subsequent realty interests and is another first-in-time rule. If the security interest is fixture-filed *before* a conflicting interest arises, then it prevails [9-313(4)(b)].

A special filing rule applies to soft fixtures (readily removable factory or office machines or readily removable replacements of domestic appliances). These fixtures can be perfected by any method allowed under Article 9, such as filing, taking possession, fixture filing, or automatic perfection. If you replace a stove (a fixture) in your house and give a PMSI to the seller, the PMSI in consumer goods (stove) would thus automatically be perfected [9-313(4)(c)].

A special priority provision for a construction loan gives it total priority [***9-313 (6)***]. Thus, a security interest in fixtures added as part of new construction is always subordinate to the construction mortgage or to a mortgage given to refinance a construction mortgage.

Accessions

In addition to being affixed to real estate, goods may be installed in, or affixed to, other goods and become *accessions.* In general, a perfected security interest that attaches to goods *before* they become accessions has priority over a security interest in the whole and subsequent purchasers of the whole [9-314(1)]. A security interest may attach to goods after they have become joined with other goods. The secured party has the same priority as stated above, but his security interest will prevail over another security interest in the whole only if the holder of the security interest in the whole has consented in writing to the security interest [9-314(2)]. As in the case of fixtures, the secured party can, upon default, remove his collateral from the whole; but he must make payment for the cost of repair of any physical damage caused by removal [9-314(4)].

Commingled and processed goods

In a manufacturing process, several items—including raw materials and components, each of which may be subject to different security interests—may combine to make a finished product. The security to which the financing party is entitled will ultimately be the product that results from the combination of the materials in which he has a security interest. If a security interest in the raw materials was perfected, the security interest continues in the product if the identity of the goods is lost *or* the orginial financing statement provided for a security interest that covered the "product" [9-315(1)]. In a situation in which component parts are assembled into a machine, the secured party would generally have a choice of claiming either (1) a security interest in the machine or (2) an interest in a component part as provided for security interests in accessions [9-314 (1)]. If he stipulates "product," he cannot claim an accession. When more than one security interest exists in the product, the secured parties share in the product in proportion to the costs of their materials used [9-315(2)].

Returned or repossessed goods

Conflicting claims to collateral may arise when a debtor who sells an item from inventory receives in return either chattel paper or an account receivable, and the goods are subsequently reacquired. The debtor may have reacquired the goods under several circumstances. The buyer may have returned them because of his dissatisfaction; the seller may have repossessed them because of a default by the buyer; or the seller may have stopped the goods in transit upon discovery of the buyer's insolvency. In any event, the goods are now again in the possession of the debtor. There may be a conflict between the inventory secured party and the transferee of the chattel paper or account receivable related to the returned goods.

The original security interest of the inventory secured party attaches to the returned or repossessed goods. The security interest in the goods continues to be perfected, provided it has not lapsed or terminated. The transferee of the chattel paper has priority over the inventory secured party unless an account receivable was transferred. Then, for returned or repossessed goods, the transferee of the account is subordinate to the party having a security interest in inventory with respect to goods that were returned or repossessed [9-306(5)].

The "floating lien"

The security agreement may provide that property acquired in the future by the debtor will also constitute collateral. The agreement may also provide that future advances to the debtor will be covered by the security agreement [9-204]. A secured party may have a security interest in the debtor's assets, even though the debtor has the freedom to use or to dispose of the collateral. A secured party financing a retailer can maintain a security interest in the debtor's constantly changing inventory. The secured party can also have a security interest in the proceeds of the sale of inventory in the debtor's ordinary course of business. The amount of credit may vary from time to time.

The secured party's security interest is protected against the claims of third parties by virtue of the public notice that such financing arrangement has been made. The amount of the debt and the actual collateral can be constantly changing if the security agreement is worded to include after-acquired property and future advances of money. This sort of arrangement allows the secured party to tie up most of the assets of a debtor, a possibility considered acceptable in business financing but restricted toward consumers. The Code limits after-acquired clauses on consumer goods to goods obtained within ten days after the secured party gives value [9-204(2)].

Proceeds

The passing of the security interest from goods to the proceeds of the sale is an important part of the "floating lien" concept. A debtor may sell or otherwise dispose of the collateral, but the secured party may have an interest in the "identifiable proceeds," whether "cash proceeds" or "noncash proceeds," such as an account receivable [9-306 (1)].

Two different factual situations may arise. A debtor may have the authority to dispose of the collateral, as in a sale of inventory. Or he may dispose of the collateral without authority to do so. In either situation, the secured party has an interest in the proceeds. In the former, he loses his security interest in the collateral that is sold in the ordinary course of business [9-307]. In the latter, he retains a security interest in the collateral and thus has a security interest both in the collateral and the proceeds [9-306].

Should the financing statement provide for a security interest in proceeds, under the '62 Code no further filing would be required [9-306(3)]. If (1) the financing statement did not cover proceeds or (2) the security interest was perfected by possession or attachment, a perfected security interest in proceeds continues for ten days. At the end of the ten-day period, the interest in the proceeds ends unless the secured party has filed a financing statement covering proceeds within the ten-day period. Under the '72 Code, the interest in the proceeds continues, in almost every instance, automatically perfected.

Proceeds in bankruptcy

Special provisions relate to the secured party's interest in proceeds if the debtor becomes involved in bankruptcy or other insolvency proceedings [9-306 (4)]. In general, the secured party is entitled to reclaim from the trustee in bankruptcy proceeds that can be identified as relating to the original collateral. If the proceeds are no longer identifiable because they have been commingled or deposited in an account, the secured party nonetheless has a perfected security interest in an amount up to the proceeds received by the debtor within ten days prior to the commencement of the bankruptcy proceedings.

REVIEW QUESTIONS AND PROBLEMS

In some of the following questions, certain abbreviations will be used. SP-1 means Secured Party Number One. SP-2 means Secured Party Number Two. D means debtor. LC means lien creditor, a creditor who has acquired a lien on the collateral by attachment, levy, or the like [9-301 (3)]. Non-Code law determines at what time and in what fashion the lien is acquired. We will assume that the lien arises when the sheriff levies. B means buyer of the collateral.

1. Using section 9-312(5) of the 1972 Code, determine which party, SP-1 or SP-2, has priority in the following situations:

   (*a*)

   Feb. 1: SP-1 files a financing statement in D's inventory.

   Feb. 10: SP-2 takes a security interest in D's inventory and files a financing statement.

Mar. 10: SP-1 takes a security interest in D's inventory.

(*b*)

Feb. 1: SP-1 takes a security interest in D's jewelry by pledge.
Mar. 1: SP-2 takes a security interest in D's jewelry and properly files a financing statement covering the jewelry.

(*c*)

Feb. 1: SP-1 files a financing statement covering D's jewelry.
Mar. 1: SP-2 takes a security interest in D's jewelry by pledge.
Apr. 1: SP-1 takes a security interest in D's jewelry.

2. On April 1, SP-1 loans $20,000 to D, a merchant who sells machinery, and takes a security interest in D's present inventory of machines and machines to be later acquired by D. SP-1 files his financing statement on April 2. SP-2, a manufacturer, wants to sell machines to D and retain a security interest in the machines. The machines are inventory under 9-10 9 (4). SP-2 does the following:

   May 1: SP-2 properly files a financing statement covering the machines to be sold.
   May 2: SP-2 sends notification to SP-1 of SP-2's forthcoming PMSI in the machines SP-2 is going to sell D.
   May 5: SP-2 delivers the machines to D.

   Does the security interest of SP-1 take priority over the security interest of SP-2? Explain.

3. Mayflower Light Company is a discount house with a full range of lighting equipment and fixtures for sale. To purchase its lighting inventory, Mayflower secures a loan from Downey Credit Corp. (DCC). DCC takes and perfects a security interest in the "inventory and proceeds" as well as the "after-acquired property" of Mayflower. DCC therefore has taken a "floating lien." To understand the risks of secured party with a "floating lien," solve the following problems:

   a) Amory Janes, a consumer, buys a lamp from Mayflower on an installment basis.

   Does Janes take the lamp subject to DCC's security interest? Explain.

   If Janes sells the lamp to his next-door neighbor, does she take it subject to DCC's security interest? Explain.

   Since Mayflower sold the lamp on an installment plan, it retained a security interest in the lamp. Must it file to perfect its security interest? See 9-302(1)(d).

   Assume that the lamp needs to be repaired and Janes takes it to the local lamp repairer. The repairperson asserts a possessory lien to secure payment of the repair charges. Does DCC's security interest have priority over this lien arising by operation of law? Explain.

4. On June 1, SP-1, a merchant seller of machines, sells and delivers to D a machine for his personal use. The machine then is consumer goods under 9-109(1). SP-1 retains a security interest in the machine to secure payment of the purchase price. SP-1 does not file a financing statement. Based on these facts, determine who has priority in the following situations:

   a) On June 5, SP-2 loans $750 to D and takes a security interest in the same machine. SP-2 properly files his financing statement on June 6th. Does SP-1 have priority over SP-2? Explain.

   b) On June 15, LC, a creditor of D, acquires a lien on the same machine by levy of the sheriff. Does SP-1 have priority over LC? Explain.

   c) On June 5, B buys the same machine from D and receives possession the same day. Does SP-1 have priority over B? Explain.

5. On June 1st, SP-1 obtains a security interest in D's equipment and perfects by filing on July 1st. On August 1, IRS files in the manner required by the Internal Revenue Code. In a priority dispute between SP-1 and IRS, who prevails? Explain. Would your answer change if SP-1 perfects its security interest on August 30? Explain.

6. SP-1 takes a security interest in D's inventory on February 1. D files a bankruptcy petition on February 5. SP-1 files a financing statement on February 9 to perfect its security interest in D's inventory. May the trustee use Section 544 (a) of the 1978 Bankruptcy Code to prevail over SP-1's security interest? Would your answer change if SP-1's security interest was a PMSI? Explain.

7. Acme Glass Company sells Welch four mirrors on credit and installs the mirrors in Welch's house. The glass company retains a security interest in the mirrors and immediately fixture files. Will the company's security interest be superior under the Revised Code to that of (*a*) First Bank, which has a mortgage on the house? (b) To a new owner who buys the house from Welch? Explain both answers.

23

Debtor's Default and Its Consequences

A debtor's default is the event that puts the Article 9 security interest to an acid test. Default and its consequences are primarily a legal rather than a business concern. When negotiating parties transact their business, they seldom discuss the possibility of default; but if it does occur, the situation becomes a legal one. Any creditor, secured or unsecured, may sue and get a judgment; but secured creditors may—and most of them do—invoke Part 5, Article 9, which defines their rights and remedies in default situations.

It is the secured party's rights in the collateral that distinguish secured from unsecured creditors, as we saw in chapter 21. The crunch provisions of Part 5 permit the secured party to take possession of the collateral and dispose of it to satisfy his claim. He may obtain the collateral by self-help (if this procedure does not breach the peace) or by court action [9-503]. Once the collateral is in hand, the secured party has two alternatives: *foreclosure sale,* its proceeds to be applied to the unpaid debt, or *strict foreclosure,* retention of the collateral in satisfaction of the debt. But at any time before either alternative regarding disposition becomes final, the debtor has the right to *redeem* the collateral by paying off the debt.

One other remedy is available to the secured party. When the security agreement covers both real and personal property, the secured party may proceed under Part 5 of

Article 9 with respect to the personal property or may proceed exclusively under real property law with respect to both the real and personal property [9-501(4)].

In the usual situation, the secured party will choose to satisfy the debt by means of resale of the collateral or strict foreclosure. Before he can make that choice, however, he must first repossess the collateral.

Self-help repossession

Generally, a secured party will attempt "peaceable" self-help repossession, since it is swift and inexpensive; but the main drawback is that self-help techniques must not result in a "breach of the peace." Countless judicial opinions have considered whether self-help repossession is peaceable or not under particular situations, and pre-Code cases are also relevant. Although it is not feasible to attempt an exhaustive list of all the circumstances in which the peace was or was not breached, a general list of recurrent factual patterns and rules is possible.

The following three sets of circumstances are usually deemed "peaceable" in connection with a repossession. First, the secured party removes the collateral (a car) from the street or parking lot without the knowledge or objection of the debtor. More than likely "jump-starting" the car without the use of the ignition key will be upheld. If the removal is from the debtor's open premises such as a driveway, it is not objectionable. Second, removal without the debtor's consent (or even if debtor knows but does not make an express objection) is not a breach of the peace. Finally, removal of the collateral from the premises of a third party (such as a garage, parking lot, neighbor's yard) is lawful so long as neither the debtor nor third person expressly objects.

In four other situations, however, repossession will usually involve a "breach of the peace." First, it is a breach to threaten or appear to threaten violence to the debtor or other person who is present, whether or not any violence occurs. Second, removal of the collateral over the express objection of the debtor (even if there is no violence) is a breach. Most courts also find a breach of the peace when the removal is over the express objection of a third party. Third, the use of trickery is a breach—posing as a policeman or obtaining the aid of a policeman or other law enforcement officer who acts beyond his official authority. Fourth and finally, unauthorized entry into the debtor's home, garage, or other building for the purpose of repossession is unlawful.

CASE

D, bank, hired a licensed "repossessor" to remove a Cadillac automobile from the defaulting debtor's premises. P, the debtor, sued for conversion because the repossessor got the car by breaking the lock on P's garage door. Conversion is an unauthorized assumption and exercise of the right of ownership over the personal property belonging to another and to the exclusion of the owner's rights. The trial court dismissed P's action, notwithstanding the fact that the jury decided for P.

ISSUE Where one is otherwise entitled to take possession of property, does repossession by means of an unlawful entry constitute a conversion?

DECISION Yes.

REASON Because D's hired repossessor gained possession of the car by breaking into P's garage, D is liable for compensatory damages for conversion. Knowledge or intent or bad faith of D is not an element of a conversion claim. However, since D neither authorized nor ratified the unlawful act of the repossessor, D is not liable for exemplary or punitive damages.

Henderson v. Security National Bank, 140 Cal. Rptr. 388 (Cal.) 1977.

Repossession by judicial action

Repossession by judicial action can be accomplished by several means. The secured party can bring a replevin action, which is a common-law action that is now largely codified. In some states, the action may be for claim and delivery or under a special personal property foreclosure act. Obviously, repossession by court action is more expensive than self-help; however, the Code does make the debtor liable for most court costs, including attorney's fees. The secured party is well-advised to use the courts when the debtor will not part with the goods without a fight. Under the typical judicial action, the plaintiff files a complaint, makes an affidavit, and posts a required bond. Then, the sheriff seizes the property. Unless the debtor objects within a specified time, the property is delivered to the secured party.

If the collateral is accounts, chattel paper, instruments, or general intangibles, repossession is not necessary. The secured party can simply proceed to collect whatever may become due on the collateral. He may give reasonable notice to the person who owes the account receivable, to make payment directly to the secured party [9-502(1)].

Constitutional problems

Repossession under the Code can give rise to two separate constitutional problems. One involves the constitutionality of repossession under a writ of attachment or replevin. The other concerns the possible unconstitutionality of Section 9-503 itself as permitting self-help repossession.

In some cases, state statutes allowing pre-judgment remedies by a creditor against a debtor have been struck down by the United States Supreme Court. In the important case of *Fuentes v. Shevin,* 407 U.S. 67 (1972), the Court held unconstitutional several state statutes permitting pre-judgment replevin of property, because the statutory procedures deprived debtors of their property without due process "insofar as they deny a right to a prior opportunity to be heard before chattels are taken from their possessors." The Court has indicated that replevin or a similar pre-judgment proceeding may be constitutional when the writ is issued by a judge rather than by a clerk. Given the impact of the *Fuentes* rule, most states amended their statutes by providing the debtor some opportunity to be heard before the property is seized, and their constitutionality is now seldom in doubt.

The 1970s were years of considerable litigation over the constitutionality of self-help repossession as permitted under Section 9-503. The constitutional requirements of no deprivation of property without due process of law and of the prohibition of unreasonable seizures allegedly were not being followed. The difficulty in these challenges, however, is that the constitutional limitations apply only to *state action.* Although *state action* occurs when a writ is issued under a replevin statute and the sheriff seizes the collateral, it is difficult to find any *state action* when the secured party privately and without court or other state assistance repossesses the collateral.

The Supreme Court of the early 1980s had not considered a direct constitutional attack on self-help repossession. Nonetheless, virtually all lower federal courts that entertained the question have ruled that Section 9-503 does not involve *state action.* Given the preponderance of favorable decisions to date, it appears that the self-help feature of Section 9-503 is constitutionally valid. One should also note that the 1972 Code Revision Committee thought it unnecessary to recommend any change in the self-help provision of Article 9.

Alternative to repossession

Rather than going out to pick up the collateral or taking court action, a secured party can tailor his default remedies by way of the security agreement to suit his particular needs. The security agreement can, for instance, put the debtor to work. It can provide that the debtor assemble the collateral and make it available to the secured party at a place reasonably convenient to both parties [9-503]. If the debtor refuses, then the secured party may use judicial help in requiring a debtor in possession of collateral spread out at a number of places to gather the collateral at one place.

CASE

P loaned D $1,800,000 secured by heavy road-building equipment used by D in five states. P put a clause in the security agreement that P could "require borrower to assemble the collateral and make it available . . . at a place to be designated . . . which is reasonably convenient to all parties." When D defaulted, P told D to assemble the equipment, but D refused and continued to work. D refused to close down its five-state operation.

ISSUE Is P entitled to an injunction compelling D to assemble and turn over the collateral?

DECISION Yes.

REASON The Code provides for the enforcement of the provision to assemble and make available to the creditor, but it does not attempt to specify what types of relief are available. Injunctive relief is not only within the court's jurisdiction but is also the only appropriate remedy for enforcement of the agreement's provision, in view of the location of the property in five different states.

Clark Equipment Company v. Armstrong Equipment Company, 434 F.2d 54 (5th Cir. Ala.) 1971.

In the case of collateral such as heavy equipment, the physical removal from the debtor's plant and storage elsewhere pending resale may be excessively expensive and, in some cases, impractical. Thus, the Code allows the secured party, without removal, to render equipment unusable and to dispose of the collateral on the debtor's premises [9-503]. Any such action must, of course, be "commerciably reasonable."

Duties when secured party has possession

The Code imposes certain duties on a secured party in possession of the collateral [9-207]. The most important duty is to exercise reasonable care in the custody and preservation of the collateral. If the collateral is chattel paper or instruments, reasonable care includes taking steps to preserve rights against prior parties unless otherwise agreed. Example: Debtor pledged its stock in ABC Corporation to Creditor to secure a loan. While Creditor was in possession, ABC issued rights to current stockholders to buy additional shares, which rights would expire if not exercised by a stated date. Knowing of this right, Creditor failed to notify Debtor about it before the expiration date. Creditor thus failed to exercise due care and would be liable to Debtor for any loss caused by the failure to notify.

The secured party also has certain rights against the debtor. First, any reasonable expenses incurred in connection with the collateral are chargeable to the debtor and are secured by the collateral [9-207(2)(a)]. Second, the risk of accidental loss or damage to the collateral is on the debtor to the extent that the loss is not covered by insurance

[9-207(2)(b)]. Finally, the secured party is entitled to hold as additional security any increase or profits received from the collateral [9-207(2)(c)].

Disposition of Collateral

Foreclosure by sale

After default, a secured party may sell, lease, or otherwise dispose of the collateral [9-504]. The usual disposition is by public or private sale.

Code provisions governing this disposition are extremely liberal and are based on the rationale that the prime concern is to get the best return possible on the resale, since that ostensibly benefits all parties. The higher the resale price, the greater likelihood of a surplus for the debtor and the less the likelihood of a deficiency. The resale can be private or public and by one or more contracts [9-504(3)]. A *public sale* is a sale by auction, possibly on the courthouse steps. A *private sale* is a sale through commercial channels such as a dealer who regularly sells goods of that kind.

Although the Code opts for very flexible rules for the resale, it does not leave the debtor unprotected, at the secured party's mercy. Indeed, the Code imposes definite restrictions on the secured party, who must adhere or risk the Code remedies for the debtor. Of these restrictions, two are the most important: (1) *every aspect* of the disposition must be *commercially reasonable,* and (2) the secured party must give the debtor *reasonable notification* of the resale.

Commercially reasonable resale

Resale may be as a unit or in parcels and at any time and place and on any terms; but every aspect of the resale, including the *method, manner, time, place,* and *terms* must be commercially reasonable. The term *commercially reasonable* is not defined in the Code, but case law has developed some rules to assist in making the determination in future cases. First, the fact that a better price could have been obtained at another time or by another method is not of itself sufficient to establish that the resale was unreasonable. However, recent case law indicates that a resale at a price substantially under what might well have been received is not commercially reasonable. In particular, if the sale is followed by a second sale at a substantially greater price, it is not reasonable. If the secured party has not exerted much effort (as in failing to contact a number of prospective buyers), the sale may be held not commercially reasonable.

The Code allows the secured party to buy the collateral at any public sale, but the right to buy-in at a private sale is restricted. Only if the collateral is of a type normally sold in a recognized market or is subject to universal price quotations can the secured party buy-in at a private sale [9-504(3)]. This prohibition against the creditor's buying at a private, nonjudicial sale acknowledges that creditors can overreach by conducting a sham sale, buying the collateral at a low price, and then holding the debtor liable for a substantial deficiency. The resale in that case is commercially unreasonable.

CASE

P, a furniture manufacturer, sold furniture to D on credit secured by a security agreement. When D did not pay as agreed, P repossessed the furniture. P approached one possible buyer for the items but failed to sell them. P then sold to himself at a private sale and sued D for a deficiency of $7,000. D contends that he is entitled to credit for the full value of the repossessed goods because the private sale was improper.

ISSUE Was the private sale a proper method for determining the deficiency?

DECISION No.

REASONS
1. Every aspect of the disposition of collateral at a private sale must be commercially reasonable.
2. A secured party may buy at a private sale only if the collateral is of a type commonly sold in a recognized market or subject to widely distributed price quotations.
3. For a private sale to the secured party, the value of the collateral must be readily ascertainable.

Luxurest Furn. Mfg. Co. v. Furniture, Etc., 209 S.E.2d 63 (Ga.) 1974.

A resale is recognized as commercially reasonable if the secured party either (1) sells the collateral in the customary manner in a recognized market or (2) sells at a price current in such market at the time of resale or (3) sells in conformity with reasonable commercial practices among dealers in the type of property sold.

Time for disposition

Unlike prior statutes, the Code does not set forth any *time* within which the resale or disposition must occur. An exception applies to consumer goods, which (if debtor has paid over 60 percent of the price or loan) must be sold within 90 days after the secured party has taken possession. The absence of any prescribed period for resale conforms to the Code philosophy of encouraging disposition by private sale through regular commercial channels. It may not be wise to dispose of goods if the market collapses or to sell a large inventory in parcels over time rather than in bulk; but the resale must be commercially reasonable, and the creditor is not allowed to delay when no reason exists for not making a prompt sale.

CASE

D, creditor, seized P's tractor and trailer (collateral) on default and then held the collateral for over a year without taking any steps for further disposition. In the interim, D sued P for the underlying debt, got a judgment and then used the collateral to satisfy that judgment. In effect, D was holding the collateral as added security. P had demanded an accounting, which D did not make. P claims he is entitled to damages.

ISSUE Must a secured party who has repossessed the collateral attempt either to resell the seized collateral or accept it in satisfaction of the debt (strict foreclosure)?

DECISION Yes.

REASONS The creditor had two options (to resell or keep the collateral) and it did neither. A creditor who takes possession under 9-503 must pursue his claim under one of these options, and failure to do so subjects him to damages.

Farmer State Bank of Parkston v. Otten, 204 N.W.2d 178 (S.D.) 1973.

Reasonable notification

Although the debtor returned the goods or knew that the secured party, upon repossession, intended to resell them, a secured party is not free to assume that the repossession itself serves as *notice* of a possible public or private resale within a reasonable time. The Code does require that the secured party give the debtor reasonable notification of the time and place of any *sale,* either public or private [9-504(3)]. This notice gives the debtor a deadline within which to protect himself in whatever manner he sees fit.

The notice must be *sent* to the debtor and (to be reasonable) must be sent in time for the debtor to take appropriate steps to protect his interests if he so desires. A provision in the 1972 Code states that the notice of resale need not be given if the debtor has signed *after default* a statement renouncing or modifying his right to notification of sale. There is no equivalent in the 1962 Code.

In the case of consumer goods, notice must be given only to the debtor. With the exception of consumer goods, the 1972 Code requires that notice be sent to any other secured party from whom the secured party has received written notice of an interest. The 1962 Code required that notice be sent to all secured parties who had filed financing statements or who were known by the secured party.

When notification is required by the Code, it must be reasonable in all situations, or the secured party is usually denied the right to sue the debtor for a deficiency judgment.

CASE

D, debtor, defaulted on his obligation to pay for an automobile and voluntarily surrendered it to P, the secured party. P sent D notice by registered mail stating that the present balance was $4,013.09; and if it were not paid in 8 days, the car would be sold. The car was placed on P's lot after repossession and was not sold until about 18 months later. D contends that the notice is not reasonable, since it did not include credits for unearned finance charges and insurance premiums.

ISSUE In P's suit to recover a deficiency judgment, is the suit barred if the secured party failed to account in the notice of disposition of the car for the rebate of unearned finance charges and insurance premiums?

DECISION Yes. P's suit for deficiency judgment was denied.

REASONS
1. The Code requires "reasonable notification" of the disposition to give the debtor an opportunity to protect its interests.
2. The notice in this case failed to reflect a refund credit of $654.61 for unearned finance charges and insurance premiums. Certainly, the insertion of an unduly inflated figure in the notice discourages and perhaps frustrates the debtor's attempts to find another buyer or to exercise his redemption rights.
3. The notice, stating a balance that was inflated above the amount actually owed, was not reasonable notification as required by the Code.

Wilmington Trust Company v. Conner, 415 A.2d 773 (Del.) 1980.

Notice not required

Notification of an impending disposition is not required if the collateral is (1) perishable or (2) threatens to decline speedily in value or (3) is of a type customarily sold on a recognized market [9-504(3)]. Examples of goods sold on a customary market include commodities or corporate stock sold on an exchange. Used cars are not considered items customarily sold in a recognized market.

Rights of parties following resale

The person who buys the collateral at a sale receives it free of the security interest under which the sale was made and free, also, of any subordinate security interest

[9-504(4)]. Thus, the good-faith purchaser at a disposition sale receives substantial assurance that he will be protected in his purchase. After the sale has been made, the proceeds of the sale will be distributed and applied as follows: (1) the expenses of the secured party in connection with the repossession and sale; (2) the satisfaction of the debt owing to the secured party; (3) satisfaction of the indebtedness owing to persons who have a subordinate security interest in the collateral; and (4) if any surplus remains after the satisfaction of all the above, the secured party shall account for it to the debtor [9-504 (1)]. If the sale is proper in all respects but does not produce enough to satisfy all the above charges, the debtor is liable for any deficiency [9-504(2)].

Strict foreclosure

The secured party who prefers to keep the collateral in satisfaction of the obligation, rather than dispose of it, is entitled to make that proposition in writing and send it to the debtor [9-505(2)]. Except in the case of consumer goods, the proposal must also be sent to all persons who have filed a financing statement covering the collateral or who are known to have a security interest in it. Within prescribed time limits, the debtor, a secured party entitled to receive notification, or any other secured party can object in writing to the proposal, in which event the collateral would have to be sold. If no such notice is forthcoming, the matter is closed, and the secured party can retain the collateral in satisfaction [9-504(2)].

Special provisions relate to consumer transactions. Disposition of the goods is *compulsory,* and a sale must be made within ninety days after possession is taken if, in the case of (1) a purchase money security interest in consumer goods, 60 percent of the cash price has been paid; or (2) a security interest based upon a loan against consumer goods, 60 percent of the loan has been repaid. The consumer can, however, waive this right by signing a statement to that effect after default [9-504(1)]. These rules exist because there will presumably be a surplus in the event of a sale, and the debtor is entitled to it promptly.

Debtor's remedies

Except for the ninety-day period for consumer goods, the secured party is not required to make disposition of the repossessed goods within any time limits. The debtor has the right to redeem the property until (1) the property has been sold or contracted to be sold, or (2) the obligation has been satisfied by the retention of the property. The debtor must, as a condition to redemption, tender the full amount of the obligation secured by the collateral plus expenses incurred by the secured party in connection with the collateral and (if so provided in the agreement) attorney's fees and legal expenses [9-506].

If the secured party fails to comply with the provisions of the Code relating to default, a court may order disposition or restrain disposition, as the situation requires. If the sale has already taken place, the secured party is liable for any loss resulting from his noncompliance, and he may lose his right to recover any deficiency. If the collateral is consumer goods, the consumer debtor is entitled to recover from the secured party an amount not less than (1) the credit service charge plus 10 percent of the principal amount of the debt or (2) the time-price differential plus 10 percent of the cash price [9-507(1)]. Thus, the secured party who forecloses a security interest in consumer goods must be very careful to comply with the law as it relates to their sale.

Note that if the creditor fails to follow the compulsory sale of consumer goods under the "60 percent-90 day" rule of Section 9-505(1), then the debtor may either recover in conversion or under the liability provisions of Section 9-507(1). Under the latter section, he may recover "any loss caused by the failure to comply" and, for consumer goods, the Code penalty.

CASE

D, secured party, repossessed P's pickup truck after P (debtor) had paid over 60 percent of the cash price. D failed to dispose of the truck within the 90-day period. P sued for the statutory penalty under Section 9-507(1).

ISSUE When the secured party fails to follow the compulsory sale of consumer goods for which 60 percent of the cash price has been paid, may the debtor elect between conversion and statutory damages?

DECISION Yes.

REASONS

1. Failing to follow the compulsory sale rules, D is liable for either conversion of the goods or damages under the penalty provisions of Section 9-507(1).
2. The conversion value of the truck was $231.20 and the statutory penalty was $236.32. P is awarded $236.32.

Crosby v. Basin Motor Company, 488 P.2d 127 (N.M.) 1971.

REVIEW QUESTIONS AND PROBLEMS

1. The following situations involve a debtor who was in arrears in his auto payments. When he failed to respond to requests for payment from the secured party, the secured party sent an agent to repossess the car. Is the agent's repossession of the car peaceful in the following instances?
   a) When the agent repossesses, the car is parked in front of the debtor's house.
   b) The agent at 11:00 P.M. tows away the car from the *parking lot* at the apartment house complex where the debtor had an assigned space.
   c) The car is parked in the debtor's driveway.
   d) The car is parked in the debtor's unlocked garage.
   e) The car is parked in the debtor's locked garage. The agent unlocked the garage door, removed the car, and locked the garage.
   f) The car is parked at a service station after a tune-up. The station owner permits the agent to remove the car.
   g) The car is parked on the road in front of the debtor's house. As the agent starts to enter the car, the debtor bursts from the door of his house, shouting epithets, and demanding that his car not be moved. But the agent is able to start the car and drive away before the debtor can get to the car.
   h) In the previous question (*g*), would it make any difference if the debtor jumped into the car, which the agent then towed away?
   i) The agent comes to the debtor's house and states that he is from the local police department. The debtor then allows the agent to take the car.
   j) The agent comes to the debtor's house and states that he is from the city water department and needs to check the debtor's pipe system. The agent then sneaks into the garage and drives the car away.
2. When the debtor defaulted in his car payments, the secured party repossessed the car by removing it from its parking place on the street. The debtor contends that the "self-help" repossession procedures under the Code are unconstitutional. Is the debtor correct? Why or why not?
3. Debtor bought a used car from Dealer at the price of $1,395. Dealer then assigned debtor's chattel paper (the sales contract and promissory note) to Finance Company, which thus became the secured party. Upon default, Finance Company repossessed the car and sold it back to Dealer for $348. Dealer made repairs costing $402 and then resold the car for $1,050. Did the sale from Finance Company comply with the requirements of a foreclosure sale under the Code? Why or why not?
4. Secured Party, intending to sell the repossessed collateral privately one week later, sent a certified letter to Debtor stating his intention to sell. Debtor, who lived on a rural mail route, received a notice that the letter was being held for him at the post office. Debtor did not pick up the letter for two weeks, at which time the collateral was already sold. Was the notice of the private sale in compliance with the Code requirements? Why or why not?
5. On June 6, Secured Party sent notice of public sale of the collateral to be held on June 8. The notice was not received by Debtor until June 10. Did this notice conform to the Code requirements? Why or why not?
6. What is strict foreclosure and when is it permitted? When is strict foreclosure not permitted? Explain.

Irene Springer

IV

Creditors, Debtors, and Consumers

24

Real Property as Security

The chapters on contracts and the Uniform Commercial Code dealt with many aspects of the law that are of substantial consequence to creditors. We saw basic legal procedures available to creditors—their right to sue for breach of contract and to use certain collection methods to enforce judgments obtained in such suits. The secured transaction, discussed in the preceding chapters, is a very significant method used by creditors to ensure payment of debts.

In this chapter and the next we shall be concerned with several additional aspects of the law that are important to creditors. Real estate mortages, mechanic's liens, suretyship, and various other forms of liens will be discussed. The remaining chapters of the book will discuss several of the laws, including bankruptcy proceedings, that are designed to protect debtors and consumers.

Mortgages

A real estate mortgage is an interest in real property, an interest created for the purpose of securing the performance of an obligation, usually the payment of a debt. A mortgage is not a debt—only security for a debt. The owner of the estate in land that is being used as security for the debt is called the *mortgagor;* the party to whom the security interest in the real estate is conveyed is called the *mortgagee.*

Three distinct legal theories relate to mortgages. The first of these, the *title theory,* was developed at common law. At common law and in those few states following the title theory, a mortgage on land is an absolute conveyance of the title of the land by the owner to the mortgagee, upon condition that the title will revert to the mortgagor when the obligation is performed or the money is repaid. If the mortgagor fails to repay the debt, the property will remain the property of the mortgagee.

The second theory about mortgages is usually known as the *lien theory,* although it is sometimes called the *equitable theory.* Under this theory, a mortgage is not a conveyance of title but only a method of creating a lien on the real estate. The lien or equitable theory avoids the harshness that often results on default in title-theory states when the mortgagee is allowed to keep the real property without any obligation to the former owner. Under the lien theory, a mortgagee does not have title when the mortgagor defaults; he simply has a lien that can be foreclosed. Upon foreclosure of the lien, any proceeds of the sale in excess of the debt and the costs of sale remain the property of the mortgagor. In addition, lien-theory states grant to the mortgagor a right to redeem his property after the default and foreclosure. This right to redeem is known as the mortgagor's *equity of redemption.* The time period during which a mortgagor may redeem is usually prescribed by statute. When it is not, it is fixed by the court in the foreclosure proceedings. If a mortgagor wishes to redeem, he pays the total debt plus the costs of sale. But if the property is not redeemed within the prescribed period, it becomes the absolute property of the purchaser at the foreclosure sale.

Many states do not follow the title theory or the lien theory; they have reached a compromise between the two theories, an *intermediate theory.* By the intermediate theory, a mortgage is a conveyance of title, but the equitable theories are applied to it. Mortgages must be foreclosed; and the mortgagor has an equity of redemption, even though the mortgagee has "title." The great majority of states are either lien-theory or intermediate-theory states; the title theory has little support.

Types of mortgages

A mortgage usually states that the property is conveyed to the mortgagee, subject to the conditions set forth in the mortgage. It is executed with all the formalities of a deed. The contract between the parties with respect to the loan need not be included in the mortgage but may be set forth in a separate document.

In order that the mortgagee may give notice to third parties that he has an interest in the real estate, it is necessary that the mortgage be recorded in the recording office of the county where the real estate is situated. Recording serves to notify subsequent parties of the lien or encumbrance of the mortgage.

An instrument known as a *deed of trust,* sometimes called a *trust deed,* may be used as a substitute for a mortgage for the purpose of securing debts. The property is conveyed by the borrower, who executes the deed of trust, to a trustee to hold in trust for the benefit of the noteholders. If the debt is paid at the time required by the contract, the trustee reconveys the property to the borrower or releases the lien. If there is a default in payment, the trustee forecloses the trust deed and applies the proceeds to the payment of the debt secured.

Deeds of trust are used instead of mortgages when the note is likely to be negotiated and when numerous notes are secured by the same property. A trust deed may also be used to secure bonds held by many different persons. An important feature of the deed of trust is that the note secured by it can be freely negotiated, separate and apart from the deed of trust. When the mortgagor pays the note, he surrenders it to the trustee under the trust deed, and the latter makes it a matter of record that the obligation has been satisfied.

Property that one does not own cannot be mortgaged, but a mortgage may be drawn to cover property to be acquired in the future. A mortgage of such property creates no lien at the time of its execution; a court of equity, however, will recognize that the lien exists at the time the property is acquired by the mortgagor. If the mortgage is properly recorded, the lien has priority over all rights of others that arise or are created after the recording of the mortgage.

A mortgage may also be given prior to the time when the money is advanced to the mortgagor. Such a mortgage is usually called a *mortgage to secure future advances.* When the mortgagee advances the money, the mortgage is a valid lien as of the date when the mortgage was recorded.

When a mortgage is given as a part or the whole of the purchase price of land, it is known as a *purchase money mortgage*. In some jurisdictions, a deficiency decree obtained upon the foreclosure of a purchase-money mortgage will not be enforced.

A deed absolute on its face (one which purports to be only a deed—no qualifications) may be shown by parol evidence to be a mortgage if such evidence indicates that the intention of the parties was to make the transfer security for a loan. The grantor of the deed must prove by clear, precise, and positive evidence that it was the intention of the parties to use the deed for the purpose of securing a loan.

CASE

P's initiated this action to recover the statutory penalty (three times the amount of interest paid) on an alleged loan transaction with D, wherein an alleged usurious rate of interest was exacted. D moved for summary judgment, which the trial court granted.

In July 1966, P's were in default on a mortgage on their home. The institutional mortgagee declined to refinance the obligation and referred P's to D, who proposed to refinance by means of a security agreement in the form of an absolute deed with an option to repurchase. P's contend that the parties intended from its inception that the transaction was a loan, secured by a mortgage on the home. D contends that the transaction was a conditional sale (a sale with an option to repurchase at an advanced price); therefore, there was no usury.

ISSUE Can a deed absolute on its face actually be a mortgage?

DECISION Yes.

REASONS

1. Whether a transaction in the form of a sale with an option to repurchase is, in fact, a sale or a loan disguised as a sale, to cover up a scheme to collect usurious interest, is an issue for the trier of fact. The controlling question is what was the intention of the parties at the time of the execution and delivery of the instrument?
2. A mortgage may exist, although the mortgagee has no right to compel payment. The law may imply a promise to repay a debt under particular circumstances of any case where it is clear that the lender had relied on the property for his security, being satisfied that he is protected by its high value in relation to the amount loaned.
3. A warranty deed, absolute in form, is presumed to convey a fee simple title, but where there is a written agreement between the parties, indicating that the deed has been given for security purposes, the court will look to the real transaction and treat it as a mortgage.
4. An instrument need not be in any particular form to be a mortgage, so long as the intention of the parties is shown. In equity, a deed, absolute upon its face, may be shown by parol

> evidence to have been given for security purposes only; and if such showing be made, equity will give effect to the intention of the parties.

Kjar v. Brimley, 407 P.2d 23 (Utah) 1972.

Rights and duties of the parties

The mortgagor is usually personally liable for the mortgage debt, not by reason of the mortgage but because he makes a note, a bond, or other contract that evidences the debt secured by the mortgage. When there is more than one mortgagor, not all of them need sign the note or be liable on the underlying obligation. In such a case, the property is given as security for the debt, but only those signing the note or incurring the obligation have personal liability.

Payment of the mortgage debt terminates the mortgage. Upon payment, the mortgagor is entitled to a release or satisfaction of the mortgage. This release should be recorded in order to clear the title to the land; otherwise, the unreleased mortgage will remain a cloud on the title. If the mortgagee refuses to give a release, he can be compelled to do so in a court of equity.

The mortgagor is entitled to retain possession of the real estate during the period of the mortgage unless a different arrangement is provided for in the mortgage. The mortgagor may not use the property in a manner that will reduce materially its value. Mining ore, pumping oil, or cutting timber are operations that cannot be conducted by the mortgagor during the period of the mortgage unless the right to do so is reserved in the mortgage agreement. The rights will be implied when they are being conducted at the time the mortgage is created.

Any parcel of real estate may be subject to more than one encumbrance—the owner may execute more than one mortgage. In addition, mortgaged land may be subject to a lien for property taxes. As a general rule, the first recorded mortgage has priority over any subsequently recorded mortgage. Taxes usually have priority over mortgages.

A mortgagee has a right to pay off any superior mortgage in order to protect his security, and he can charge the amount so paid to the mortgagor. Likewise, he may pay taxes or special assessments that are a lien on the land and recover the sum expended. The mortgagor is under a duty to protect the security; but should he fail to do so, the mortgagee has the right to make any reasonable expenditures necessary to protect the security for a debt.

Transfer of mortgaged property

The mortgagor may sell, will, or give away the mortgaged property, subject, however, to the rights of the mortgagee. A transferee from a mortgagor has no greater rights than the mortgagor. For example, a grantee of the mortgagor's interest may redeem the land by paying off the debt. A grantee of mortgaged property is not personally liable for the mortgage debt, unless he impliedly or expressly assumes and agrees to pay the mortgage. An assumption of a debt secured by a mortgage must be established by clear and convincing evidence. A purchase "subject to" a mortgage is usually considered not to be a legally enforceable assumption. If the grantee assumes the mortgage, he becomes personally liable for the debt, even when the land is worth less than the mortgage.

To illustrate the foregoing, assume that Berg purchases real estate worth $28,000, which is subject to a mortgage of $20,000. Berg pays the former owner $8,000 cash. If she assumes and agrees to pay the mortgage, she is personally liable for the $20,000. If the property is sold at a foreclosure sale, Berg is liable for any deficiency; however, if she merely purchased the property "subject to" the mortgage when she paid the $8,000, Berg would have no liability for any deficiency on foreclosure.

If the grantee of the mortgaged property assumes and agrees to pay the indebtedness, he thereby becomes the person primarily liable for the debt. Between the grantee and the mortgagor, by virtue of his promise to the mortgagor to pay the debt, he is the principal debtor, and the mortgagor is a surety. This assumption by the grantee, however, does not relieve the mortgagor of his obligation to the mortgagee, and the mortgagor continues to be liable unless he is released from his indebtedness by the mortgagee. Such a release must comply with all the requirements for a novation.

Mortgage Foreclosures

If the mortgagor fails to perform any of his obligations as agreed, the mortgagee may declare the whole debt due and payable, and he may foreclose for the purpose of collecting the indebtedness. The statutes of the various states specify the procedure by which mortgages are foreclosed. The common types of foreclosure proceedings are (1) strict foreclosure, (2) foreclosure by suit in equity, and (3) foreclosure by exercise of the power of sale.

Strict foreclosure gives the mortgagee clear title to the land. A decree of strict foreclosure provides that if the debt is not paid by a certain date, the mortgagor loses the realty and the mortgagee takes it free from the rights of junior mortgagees and lienholders. It is used only where it is clear that the mortgaged property is not worth the mortgage indebtedness, the mortgagor is insolvent, and the mortgagee accepts the property in full satisfaction of the indebtedness.

Foreclosure by suit in equity

The usual method of foreclosing a mortgage is a proceeding in a court of equity. If the mortgagor is in default, the court will authorize the sale of all the land at public auction. Following the sale, the purchaser receives a deed to the land. The funds received from the sale are used to pay court costs, the mortgage indebtedness, and inferior liens in the order of their priority. If any surplus remains, it is paid to the former owner of the property. Since foreclosure proceedings are in a court of equity, the validity of the proceedings is always subject to the usual equitable principles.

CASE

P, mortgagor, paid $72,000 down and signed a purchase money mortgage note for the $287,000 balance due on realty. When P defaulted, over $300,000 in principal and interest was still owing. At a public auction, D, the mortgagee, bid $25,000 for the property and agreed to forgive the balance of principal and interest due. D filed suit to enjoin the sale on the equitable ground that the price was "shockingly inadequate."

ISSUE May an inadequate purchase price be made adequate by the mortgagee's waiver of his right to claim a deficiency against the mortgagor?

DECISION Yes.

REASON Equity will enjoin a foreclosure sale for a "shockingly inadequate" auction price; but if the purchaser mortgagee is forgiving the entire outstanding debt, the price is not "shockingly inadequate."

Garland v. Hill, 357 A.2d 374 (Md.) 1976.

Foreclosure of a second mortgage (one that is second in time to another) is made subject to all superior liens; it does not affect a first mortgage. The buyer at the foreclosure sale takes title, and the first mortgage remains a lien on the property. All inferior liens are cut off by foreclosure. Foreclosure of a first mortgage eliminates the rights of the second.

The statutes in many states provide a period of time after the sale, within which the mortgagor or other persons having an interest are entitled to redeem the property. Where such statutes are in force, the purchaser is not entitled to a deed until after the expiration of the period within which redemption may be made. The purchaser may request that the court appoint a receiver and order the mortgagor to pay rent during the redemption period. The purchaser is entitled to the net rent during this period.

Foreclosure by exercise of power of sale

The mortgage often provides that upon default by the mortgagor, the mortgagee may sell the land without judicial process. This method of foreclosure can be made only in strict conformity with the terms of the mortgage. The power of sale makes the mortgagee the agent of the mortgagor to sell the land. In many states, however, a power of sale in the mortgage is expressly forbidden by statute, and foreclosures must be effected by judicial proceeding. A power of sale granted in a mortgage or a deed of trust is not revocable, since the agency is coupled with an interest; therefore, the death or insanity of the mortgagor will not revoke the power. In states where the exercise of power is regulated by statute, the sale must be public after the prescribed notice is given. In the absence of statute or mortgage agreement, however, the sale may be private. Since a mortgagee who sells land under a power of sale is acting as an agent for the mortgagor, he is not allowed to purchase at the sale, because an agent cannot himself purchase that which he has been given authority by his principal to sell. The purchaser at such a sale secures only the title that the mortgagor had when he made the mortgage.

The mortgagor's right to redeem

At any time after default, a mortgagor may exercise his *right to redeem* from the mortgage (the right to have the lien of the mortgage removed from the land). To do that, he must pay the entire mortgage debt with interest and all other sums, including costs to which the mortgagee may be entitled by reasons of the mortgage. In addition, there are statutory formalities to be substantially complied with. Strict compliance is not required, providing technical violations do not harm the purchase at the foreclosure sale.

CASE

P, mortgagee, foreclosed on D's, mortgagor's, business property for failure to make a loan payment. Utah law provides a six-months' redemption period whereby if tender is made and certain statutory formalities are complied with, the mortgagor may again have the right to the property. D assigned his right of redemption to Basic Investment, Inc., who tendered a check for the outstanding deficiency one day prior to the expiration of the redemption period. Several days later, P returned the check for failure to comply with the statutory requirement of providing a certified copy of the judgment, as the Utah law required.

ISSUE Where the mortgagor's redemption tender does not strictly comply with the statutory rule, but the mortgagee is not harmed thereby, may he nonetheless reject the tender?

DECISION No.

REASONS 1. Statutes dealing with redemption are regarded as remedial in character and should be given liberal construction and application, to permit a property owner who can pay his debts to do so and thus make his creditor whole and save his property.

2. A bona fide tender for the outstanding indebtedness will work a redemption, notwithstanding technical noncompliance with statutory formalities, providing that the mortgagee is not injured thereby.

United States v. Loosley, 551 P.2d 506 (Utah) 1976.

In most states, a mortgagor may also, within a specified period of time after a foreclosure sale, redeem the real estate. To do so, he must pay to the court, for the benefit of the purchaser at the foreclosure sale, the sum of money, with interest and costs, for which the premises were sold. The period of time allowed for redemption varies greatly from state to state, and a few states deny this right to redeem. Generally, the redeeming mortgagor is also required to pay, after the foreclosure sale, all costs incurred by the purchaser in protecting and preserving the property during the period from the sale of the redemption. During this period, the purchaser or someone appointed by the court will have possession of the real estate as well as title from the judicial sale. In some states, the redemption price includes the value of any improvements made by the purchaser during the period of his possession.

Deficiency judgments

A person who executes the note or bond secured by the mortgage is personally liable for the debt. If the property that is the security for the debt does not sell for a sum sufficient to pay the indebtedness, the debtor remains liable for the deficiency, and a judgment may be entered for this unpaid balance. This judgment may be collected from the debtor's other property or income.

In order not to impose too great a hardship on mortgagor debtors, different schemes have been devised to limit the amount of a debtor's liability for deficiencies. Some states have simply outlawed all deficiency judgments. Many other states have statutes that are applicable only to purchase money mortgages. Thus, when a mortgage is given to secure payment of the balance of the purchase price of real property, in these states the mortgagee is not entitled to a deficiency judgment. In these states, if the mortgage proceeds are not used to finance the purchase of the real property, deficiency judgments are allowed. The elimination of liability for deficiencies rests on several theories: that the mortgagee loaned his money on the security of the land and not the personal credit of the purchaser debtor; that a mortgagee creditor should share with the debtor the risk of declining land value; and that if the land is the limit of the security, sounder loans and fewer inflationary ones will be made.

Mechanic's Liens

Mechanic's lien laws provide for filing liens upon real estate that has been improved. Their purpose is to protect contractors, laborers, and materialmen in the event of nonpayment of their accounts. Because the state laws vary slightly in the protection accorded and the procedure required to obtain it, the laws of the state in which the property is located should be consulted.

The persons usually entitled to a lien include those who (1) deliver material, fixtures, apparatus, machinery, forms, or form work to be used in repairing, altering, or constructing a building upon the premises; (2) fill, sod, or do landscape work in connection with the premises; (3) act as architect, engineer, or superintendent during the construction of a building; or (4) furnish labor for repairing, altering, or constructing a building.

Persons who contract with the owner, whether they furnish labor or material or agree to construct the building, are known as *contractors.* Thus, virtually any contract between the owner and another that has for its purpose the improvement of real estate gives rise to a lien on the premises in favor of those responsible for the improvement. Improvements include fixtures.

CASE

D, CAP Interiors, had furnished carpeting for six new homes. The carpets were laid over concrete or rough unfinished plywood floors and were glued to the floors. The United Benefit Life Insurance Company had a mortgage upon the real property, which it claimed was superior to the lien of CAP for the carpeting.

ISSUE Was the carpeting a lienable item?

DECISION Yes.

REASONS
1. The test is whether the article or item is permanently affixed to the realty or permanently attached to what is thus permanent, as by means of cement, plaster, nails, bolts, or screws.
2. From the circumstances in this case, it is apparent that the owner intended that the carpets stay affixed to the realty, making them a lienable item, improvement upon the property.

United Benefit Life Ins. Co. v. Norman, 484 P.2d 527 (Okla.) 1971.

In addition to contractors, anyone who furnishes labor, materials, or apparatus to contractors, or anyone to whom a distinct part of the contract has been sublet, has a right to a lien. These parties are customarily referred to as *subcontractors.* Their rights differ slightly from those of contractors, and some of these differences will be considered in later sections.

Property that is subject to an existing mortgage is frequently improved. When this occurs, questions may arise about the priority between the mortgagee and the holder of a mechanic's lien. As a general rule, the mechanic's lien is superior to any mortgage, because presumably the value of the improvements has increased the value of the property to the extent of the liens. Consequently, the value of the property remaining as security under the mortgage after satisfying the mechanic's lien is as great as it was prior to the improvement that resulted in the lien. Some states, however, by statute provide that mechanic's liens are subject to prior recorded mortgages because the person furnishing the labor or materials was aware of the existing debt and mortgage.

Perfection of mechanic's liens

In some states, a contractor has a lien as soon as the contract to repair or to improve the real estate is entered into. In others, the lien attaches as soon as the work is commenced. A supplier of materials usually has a lien as soon as the materials are furnished. A laborer has a lien when the work is performed. The statutes relating to mechanic's liens provide for the method of perfecting these mechanic's liens and for the time period during which they may be perfected.

The usual procedure is that the party seeking to perfect a mechanic's lien files or records a notice of lien in the office of the county in which deeds to real estate are recorded. Some statutes provide for filing in the county of residence of the owner. A copy of the notice is sent to the owner of record and to the party contracting for the repair or improvement. This notice must be filed within the prescribed statutory period. The law then requires a suit to foreclose the lien and specifies that it be commenced within an additionally prescribed period. Anything less than strict observance of the filing requirements eliminates the mechanic's lien but not the debt.

CASE

D, a construction company, filed a $5,000 materialman's lien for construction work on P's home. The Arkansas statute required that the lien be filed in the debtor's county of residence. D filed the lien in the wrong county. P filed a petition to have the lien dismissed. D argued that dismissal was not an appropriate remedy because P had actual notice of the debt owing and of the lien.

ISSUE Will a materialman's lien be dismissed for failure to comply with the statutory requirement that it be filed in the debtor's county of residence within a stipulated time limit?

DECISION Yes.

REASONS

1. The materialman's lien is an extraordinary statutory remedy, which is not available to most merchants; therefore, there must be substantial compliance with the law for the remedy to be enforced.
2. A misfiled lien does not substantially comply because a third party searching the record would not be put on notice of the lien.
3. The lienor may still proceed against the debtor to collect the debt, using any remedy available to a general, unsecured creditor.

Cone v. Jurczyk, 547 S.W.2d 108 (1977).

Most mechanic's lien laws provide a relatively long period, such as two or three years, during which a contractor may file a mechanic's lien and proceed to enforce it against the property interest of the party with whom he contracted. This time period is relatively long because the obligation is known to the owner, and he is in no way prejudiced if the lien is not promptly filed.

A much shorter time period is set for subcontractors, laborers, and materialmen to file their mechanic's liens. The owner of the premises may not know the source of materials and may not know the names of all persons performing services on the premises. To this extent, the liens of subcontractors, materialmen, and workers may be secret, and the owner may pay the wrong person. Therefore, the time period in which the statutory procedures must be followed is relatively short, such as 60 to 90 days.

If the property is sold or mortgaged, the existence of any mechanic's lien often would be unknown to the purchaser or mortgagee. For this reason the statutes on mechanic's liens usually specify the same short period of time for the perfection of the mechanic's lien—whether by a contractor, subcontractor, materialman, or laborer, if it is to be effective against good-faith purchasers of the property or subsequent mortgagees. Under these statutory provisions, a mechanic's lien that could be enforced against the property interest of the original contracting owner cannot be enforced against the property interest of the new owner or mortgagee after the expiration of the prescribed statutory period. Thus, during the relatively short statutory period, a mechanic's lien is good against innocent third parties even though it has not been properly perfected. Consequently, a purchaser of real estate should always ascertain if any repairs or improvements have been made to the premises within the time period for filing mechanic's liens. If it is determined that repairs or improvements have been made, the procedures outlined in the next section should be followed.

If a contractor, subcontractor, supplier of material, or laborer fails to file his notice of lien within the appropriate prescribed time period or fails to commence suit within the additional period, the lien is lost.

Since a person entitled to a mechanic's lien has a prescribed period within which to file his lien, the date on which this time period starts to run is frequently quite important. Most statutes provide that in the case of a supplier, the time period starts to run from the date the materials are delivered; and in the case of a contractor or subcontractor performing services, the time for filing starts to run from the completion of the work. This latter concept requires further clarification, however.

Should a contractor or subcontractor be able to postpone the time for filing by performing additional services at a later date? Assume that a contractor has allowed the time for filing his lien to elapse. Should the time period start all over if he makes a minor repair, such as adjusting a doorknob or touching up a paint job? Common sense would say no, and most statutes provide that a contractor or subcontractor cannot extend the statutory period of time by performing minor trifling repairs after the work has been substantially completed. In other words, trivial work done or materials furnished after the contract has been substantially completed will not extend the time in which a lien claim can be filed.

CASE

P, a contractor, claimed a mechanic's lien on D's property and sought to foreclose it. On November 10, 1964, the architect signed a completion certificate, but the plaintiff continued to do finishing work until January 2, 1965. The lien was filed on March 11. The law required that liens be filed within 90 days of the completion of the work.

ISSUE Did P file his lien within the time limit?

DECISION No.

REASONS
1. The construction was substantially completed on November 10, 1964, when the architect certified substantial completion.
2. The trivial work done or materials furnished after the contract has been substantially completed will not extend the time in which a lien claim can be filed.
3. The lien was not filed within 90 days of completion of the work.

Mitchell v. Flandro, 506 P.2d 445 (Idaho) 1973.

Protecting against mechanic's liens

Mechanic's lien statutes usually provide that an owner is not liable for more than the contract price if he follows the procedures outlined in the law. These usually require that the owner, prior to payment, obtain from the contractor a sworn statement setting forth all the creditors and the amounts due, or to become due, to each of them. It is then the duty of the owner to retain sufficient funds at all times to pay the amounts indicated by the sworn statements. In addition, if any liens have been filed by the subcontractors, it is the owner's duty to retain sufficient money to pay them. He is at liberty to pay any balance to the contractor. If the amount owed is insufficient to pay all the creditors, they share proportionately.

An owner has a right to rely upon the truthfulness of the sworn statement of the contractor. If the contractor misstates the facts and obtains a sum greater than that to which he is entitled, the loss falls upon the subcontractors who dealt with him, rather than upon the owner. Under such circumstances, the subcontractors may look only to the contractor to make good their deficit. Payments made by the owner, without his first obtaining a sworn statement, may not be used to defeat the claims of subcontractors, materialmen, and laborers. Before making any payment, the owner has the duty to require the sworn statement and to withhold the amount necessary to pay the claims indicated.

The owner may also protect himself by obtaining waivers of the contractor's lien and of the liens of subcontractors, suppliers, and laborers. In a few states, a waiver of the lien by the contractor is also a waiver of the lien of the subcontractors, as they derive their rights through those of the contractor. However, in most states, lien waivers must be obtained from all persons furnishing labor or materials.

REVIEW QUESTIONS AND PROBLEMS

1. Pam executed a deed, absolute on its face, conveying 600 acres to Steve. Steve had loaned Pam $35,000; and the parties agreed that if Pam repaid the $35,000 with interest, Steve would reconvey the property to Pam. The property was worth approximately $2,000 per acre. Thirteen years later, Steve claimed to be the owner of the land, and Pam filed suit to have the deed declared a mortgage. What was the result? Why?
2. Able held a mortgage on Baker's property. Baker left the state and was in arrears in his payments on the mortgage. Able took possession of the property and sold it to Carter. Nineteen months later, Baker returned and brought an action against Carter for possession of the premises, and for a reasonable rental value during the time Carter occupied the premises. Should Baker win? Why?
3. Perry filed suit to foreclose a real estate mortgage. The mortgage was signed by Harry and Mary, the owners of the real estate; however, only Mary signed the note which the mortgage secured. Harry objected to the foreclosure. Is Perry entitled to foreclose? Why?
4. Pat purchased property from Mort and assured and agreed to pay Mort's mortgage to Dick. This mortgage was an open-end mortgage. Pat ascertained the balance of the debt at the date of purchase of the land from Dick, but Dick made a later loan to Mort which was in default. Pat sought to enjoin Dick from collecting the late debt of Mort by foreclosing the mortgage. Is P entitled to an injunction? Why?
5. Dave gave Pete an open-end mortgage on his property. The mortgage covered loans up to $25,000. At the time of the mortgage Pete owed Dave $3,860. This debt was later paid in full and Pete subsequently borrowed $16,245. Is this late debt secured by the mortgage? Explain.
6. Don gave Peter a mortgage to secure a debt of $2,400. The mortgage covered future advances from Peter to Don. Later, unknown to Don, Peter executed a second mortgage to Jon. Peter then loaned Don an additional $6,000. Upon foreclosure, the value of the property was insufficient to pay both mortgages. Peter claims priority over Jon for both loans. Is Peter correct? Explain.
7. Carver Lumber filed suit to foreclose a mechanic's lien. Commercial Bank, who held a purchase money on the property, claimed priority over Carver Lumber. Commercial Bank's mortgage was executed after Carver Lumber began work on the property. Is the bank correct? Explain.
8. A mortgagor redeemed his property, which had been sold at a foreclosure sale. Improvements made by the purchaser amounted to $3,000. Included in that sum was $350 for the value of the purchaser's personal services in supervising and helping in the repairs and improvements. Should the mortgagor be required to pay $3,000 to the purchaser for the value of improvements? Why?

9. Al's property was subject to two mortgages. The bank, holder of the first mortgage, foreclosed, and the property was sold for $41,000. On the date of the foreclosure sale, the amount owed on the first mortgage was $37,000. Al was also indebted to the bank for $10,000 on a promissory note not covered by the mortgage. Is the bank entitled to the surplus funds resulting from the sale of the property? Why?

10. Swann contracted with Diver Company for the construction of a house on his property. Upon completion, Swann made a substantial payment to Diver and instructed him to pay Materials Inc. for building material supplied for the house. Diver delivered a $3,400 check and a $3,400 promissory note to Materials in exchange for its waiver of lien. Both the check and the note proved to be worthless, and Materials informed Swann that the waiver was rescinded. Is Materials entitled to a mechanic's lien? Why?

11. A company began building a shopping center upon land it owned, and it entered into a contract with Paul to do the plumbing work. Paul performed the work but was not paid. Paul commenced mechanic's lien foreclosure. Dick had a prior recorded mortgage on the property and claimed priority over Paul. Is Dick correct? Why?

12. When Art financed a new home through the XYZ Company, he signed a note and a mortgage for $40,000. Several years later, Art sold the home to Carla, who agreed to pay the mortgage payments. Carla did not pay, and XYZ instituted a foreclosure action. Should Art be concerned? Why?

13. At the time Andy purchased a new home, his attorney examined the recorded documents affecting interests in the property. No mechanic's liens were revealed. A short time after Andy bought the home, Burt, a roofer, demanded payment for a roof installed prior to Andy's purchase. Could Burt have any rights against Andy's property? Why?

In discussing the use of real and personal property as security, we mentioned persons other than the debtor who guarantee or secure a debt. In early history, these people were hostages. Today, they are known as sureties or guarantors. This chapter will discuss the law of suretyship. It will also discuss some other laws that protect creditors—the law relating to artisan's liens and Article 6 of the Code dealing with transfers of inventory in bulk.

25 Additional Laws Assisting Creditors

Artisan's liens

An *artisan's lien* is a security interest in personal property in favor of one who has performed services on the personal property, usually in the form of a repair. From a very early date, the common law permitted one who expended labor or material upon the personal property of another to retain possession of the property as security for his compensation. The right arose when the task was completed; and it was not assignable, because it was personal. The lien did not arise if the creditor had agreed to extend credit. At common law, the lien also existed in favor of public warehousemen and common carriers of goods entrusted to their care; in almost every state, it has been extended by statute to cover all cases of storage or repair.

The artisan's lien is generally superior to prior liens of record or the claim of a party with a security interest in the goods. Because it is based on possession, voluntary surrender of possession terminates the lien, unless the surrender is only temporary, with an agreement that the property will be returned. If the artisan parts with possession, reacquisition will not recreate the lien.

CASE

P took his vehicle to D's garage for service repairs. After D performed the desired repairs, P offered payment. D refused to relinquish possession of the vehicle, however, until P paid for work previously performed on the same vehicle.

ISSUE Does D have a lien for the previous repairs, so that P may not regain possession of the car?

DECISION No.

REASONS By statute and under the common law, the validity of a repairman's lien is conditioned on his continuous possession of the article. When D parted with possession, the lien was lost. It does not reattach when possession is reacquired.

Welcome Home Center, Inc. v. Central Chevrolet Co., Inc., 249 S.E. 896 (1978).

A lienholder may temporarily surrender possession, with an agreement that the lien will continue; but if the rights of a third party arise while the lienholder is not in possession of the property, the lien is lost. Surrender of part of the goods will not affect the lien on the remaining goods. Surrender of possession will not terminate the lien if a notice of lien is recorded in accordance with state lien and recording statutes.

At common law, the lienholder retained the property until a judgment was obtained; then he levied execution on the property. Modern statutes permit the lienholder to foreclose, and the property is sold to satisfy the claim. These statutes usually require notice to the owner prior to the sale. Any surplus proceeds after the claim is satisfied are paid to the owner of the property.

Bulk transfers—generally

Article 6 of the Uniform Commercial Code is concerned with bulk transfers. A *bulk transfer* occurs when a major part of the materials, supplies, merchandise, or other inventory is transferred not in the ordinary course of business. The creditors had presumably extended credit on the strength of these assets, and the sale of them could jeopardize the ability of the creditor to collect the debt, since the debtor might fail to pay the debt after receiving the proceeds of the sale. The law attempted to remedy this situation by imposing certain requirements on debtors and those who purchase inventory from them, if the sale is to pass title to the property free of the claims of creditors. Between the parties, a contract of sale is valid without compliance; but if the statutory requirements are not met, the property in the hands of the purchaser is subject to the claim of the seller's creditors.

CASE

P misfiled a financing statement necessary to perfect its security interest in Frydlewicz's inventory and was therefore a general creditor. Before Frydlewicz went bankrupt, he sold all of the inventory to D in bulk. Frydlewicz and D did not comply with Article 6 of the Code on bulk transfers. Specifically, D did not demand that Frydlewicz provide him with a list of his existing creditors and the amounts owed to each. P filed suit to recover the inventory from D.

ISSUE Does a transferee in bulk who fails to comply with the Code requirements for the sale have priority over a general creditor?

DECISION No.

REASONS
1. Here the transfer was more than 50 percent of Frydlewicz's inventory not in the ordinary course of business, and it was therefore subject to the law.
2. Although a transferee in bulk is generally given priority over unsecured creditors, such priority is dependent upon the transferee's compliance with Article 6 of the Code.
3. The purpose of requiring such compliance is to prevent what happened here. The law attempts to protect a creditor from a merchant who owes debts, sells out his stock in trade to anyone for any price, pockets the proceeds, and disappears, leaving the creditors unpaid.

National Bank of Royal Oak v. Frydlewicz, 241 N.W.2d 471 (Mich.) 1976.

Article 6 covers sales of inventory if (1) the sale is in bulk and not in the ordinary course of business; (2) it is of the major part of the materials, supplies, merchandise, or other inventory; and (3) the seller's principal business is the sale of merchandise from stock. Ordinarily, a sale of a manufacturing concern is not subject to the law; it would be subject if the firm maintained a retail outlet that it was selling. Enterprises that manufacture what they sell—certain bakeries, for example—would be included. Enterprises whose principal business is the sale of services rather than merchandise are not covered.

Article 6 is applicable to transfers of a substantial part of the equipment of an enterprise if they are made in connection with bulk transfers of inventory. A sale of just the equipment of a business is not subject to the law.

Article 6 requirements

Basically, Article 6 imposes two requirements: (1) a schedule of the property and a list of the creditors of the seller and (2) notification of the proposed sale to the seller's creditors. An optional provision of Article 6 requires mandatory application of the proceeds of the transfer to the debts of the *transferor.* The states are free to adopt or not to adopt this provision, which gives additional protection to the seller's creditors. If it is not adopted, the proceeds of the sale need not be paid directly to the creditors.

It is the duty of the *transferee* to obtain from the transferor a schedule of the property transferred and a sworn list of the transferor's creditors, their addresses, and the amount owed to each. The transferee can rely on the accuracy of this listing and must keep it for six months, available to creditors, or file it at the designated public office.

The transferee must then give notice personally or by registered mail to all persons on the list of creditors and to all other persons known to the transferee to assert claims against the transferor. Notice must be given at least ten days before the transferee takes possession of the goods or pays for them (whichever happens first) and must contain the following information: (1) that a bulk transfer is about to be made; (2) names and business addresses of both transferor and transferee; and (3) whether the debts of the creditors are to be paid in full as a result of the transaction and, if so, the address to which the creditors should send their bills. If no provision is made for payment in full of the creditors, the notice must contain the following additional information: (1) estimated total of transferor's debts; (2) location and description of property to be transferred; (3)

the address where creditor list and property schedule may be inspected; (4) whether the transfer is in payment of, or security for, a debt owing to transferee and, if so, the amount of the debt; and (5) whether the transfer is a sale for new consideration and, if so, the amount of the consideration and the time and place of payment.

In states that have adopted the optional provision of Article 6, the transferee is obligated, in effect, to see that creditors are paid in full or pro rata from the "new consideration" paid by the transferee. Failure to do so creates personal liability for the value of the property.

If the required procedures have been followed, the transferor's creditors will have had ample opportunity to take any necessary steps to protect their interests. Their action might include the levying of execution against the property or obtaining a writ of attachment or a temporary injunction to stop the sale. If Code procedures have not been followed, the transfer is ineffective as to the creditors, and they may collect the debt from the property. The creditors must act within six months after the transferee took possession, unless the transfer was concealed, in which case they must act within six months after they learn of the transfer. A purchaser who buys for value and in good faith from the transferee obtains the property free of objection based on noncompliance with the Code.

Article 6 is applicable to bulk sales by auction. The auctioneer is required to obtain a list of creditors and of the property to be sold. (All persons who direct, control, or are responsible for the auction are collectively called the auctioneer.) The auctioneer is also required to give ten days' notice of sale to all persons on the list of creditors. Failure to do so makes the auctioneer liable to the creditors as a class for the proceeds of the auction, at most.

Suretyship

Suretyship, a method that does not involve an interest in property, provides security for a creditor. In suretyship, the security for the creditor is provided by a third person's promise to be responsible for the debtor's obligation.

In the law of suretyship, the person who borrows money or assumes direct responsibility to perform is called the *principal, principal debtor,* or *obligor.* The party who promises to be liable for the principal's obligation is called the *surety,* or *guarantor.* The party entitled to performance or payment is customarily called the *creditor* or *obligee.*

The term *surety* has both a broad and a narrow meaning. In the broad sense, it describes third persons who are liable for the debts or obligations of another person. In this sense, a surety may be primarily as well as secondarily liable. The term *surety* in this broad sense includes guarantors. A contract of guaranty is one in which a third party, the guarantor, promises the person who is the creditor that he will pay the debt or fulfill the obligation only *if the debtor does not.* The obligation of a guarantor is secondary to that of the principal debtor. There are two types of guaranty agreements—special and general. A special guaranty runs only to a named creditor and is generally not assignable.

CASE

H Co., an appliance store, purchased appliances from S. The appliances were financed by a floor plan arrangement with M. As additional security, S and M required D personally to guarantee the debts of H Co. The language of the guaranty agreement established that it was a special guaranty in favor of only S and M. Later, M assigned the guaranty to P, who now sues to enforce it. D claims that a special guarantee cannot be assigned.

ISSUE Can an assignee of a special guaranty collect from the obligor?

DECISION No.

REASONS 1. There are two types of guaranties. An instrument of guaranty addressed to all persons generally, or "to whom it may concern" may be enforced by anyone to whom it was presented and who acts upon it. This is a general guaranty. A guaranty which is special is addressed to a particular person, firm, or corporation, and only the promisee named in the instrument acquires any rights under it.

2. Generally, contract rights can be assigned unless they involve obligations of a personal nature or there is some public policy against the assignment. However, special rules govern the assignability of guaranties, and these rules involve the characterization of the guaranty as special or general. A special guaranty is usually not assignable.

3. The majority rule, and the rule to be applied here, is that once a guaranty is correctly categorized as special, it is not assignable without a specific assignability provision or other special circumstances.

Financeamerica, Etc. v. Harvey E. Hall, Inc., 380 A.2d 1377 (Del. Super.) 1977.

Guaranty agreements are sometimes classified as absolute or conditional. Under an absolute guaranty, a creditor can go directly to the guarantor to collect. In a conditional guaranty, the creditor must have made reasonable but unsuccessful attempts to collect from the principal before the guarantor can be held liable.

Surety in the narrow sense of the word does not include a guarantor but is limited to one who is primarily liable. The fundamental difference between a contract of guaranty and one of suretyship is that a guarantor's contract is collateral to, and independent of, the contract, the performance of which he guarantees; a surety is an original obligation. In modern law, the distinction between a surety and a guarantor is of little significance. The Restatement of Security treats suretyship and guaranty as synonymous. Unless otherwise noted, the legal principles of suretyship discussed in this chapter include guaranty contracts.

A contract of suretyship can be distinguished from a contract of indemnity. Both provide security for a promisee, but a surety makes a promise to a person who is *to receive* performance of an act or payment of a debt by another; whereas in a contract of indemnity, the promise is made to one who is promising *to do* an act or *to pay* a debt. Suretyship provides security to creditors; indemnity provides security to debtors. Indemnity is a promise to the debtor, or obligor, to save him harmless from any loss that he may incur as a result of the debt or promise.

Performance bonds and fidelity bonds are contracts of suretyship. A performance bond provides protection against losses that may result from the failure of a contracting party to perform the contract as agreed. The surety (bonding company) promises the party entitled to performance to pay losses caused by nonperformance by the principal in an amount not to exceed the face of the bond. Fidelity bonds give protection against the dishonest acts of a person. They protect employers from losses caused by embezzlement by an employee—the bonding company promises to repay the employer any loss caused by defalcation of the covered employees not to exceed a stated amount. Thus, bonding companies are sureties in the sense that the term *surety* includes security either for the payment of money or for the faithful performance of some other duty.

The suretyship contract

Suretyship usually results from an agreement of the parties, but it may also result by operation of law. Assume that Jones sells his retail lumber business to Smith, who assumes and agrees to pay, as part of the purchase price, all of Jones's outstanding liabilities. Between Smith and Jones, Smith has now become the primary debtor. Jones is a surety and secondarily liable. As soon as the creditors are notified of the sale, they are obligated to respect the new relationship but not to attempt to recover from Smith before looking to Jones.

Suretyship most often results from an express contract between the surety and the creditor, whereby the surety assumes responsibility for the principal's performance for the creditor. The surety agrees that he may be called upon to pay or to perform in case the principal defaults. The contract of suretyship requires consideration. In most instances, the consideration that supports the surety's promise is the same as that received by the principal.

Contracts of suretyship often require interpretation. If the promise to pay the debt of another does not contain a time or an amount limitation, the courts tend to limit the liability to one transaction and to construe the guaranty as for a single purchase rather than a continuing offer. If it is to be continuous, but no duration is specified, it will cease to be operative after the expiration of a reasonable length of time. Where there is a time limitation in the guaranty, the courts tend to construe the guaranty as continuous for the period stated, in a reasonable amount. When there is a limit on amount but not on time, the guaranty is likewise continuous, with the maximum liability being the amount stated.

Some sureties are paid for serving in that capacity; others are not. Those paid are described as compensated sureties and are usually bonding or insurance corporations. Many cases distinguish between the protection afforded an uncompensated surety and that afforded a compensated surety. The uncompensated sureties are favorites of the law, and it goes to great lengths to protect them. It is assumed that the compensated sureties can take care of themselves.

CASE

P sued D to collect on a surety bond. D was a compensated surety in the business of writing bonds. P had failed to notify D within the time period stated in the bond of the default of the principal obligor. D contends that P's failure to give prompt notice discharges its obligations.

ISSUE Does P's failure to give the notice discharge the compensated surety?

DECISION No.

REASONS
1. Actual damage resulting from failure to give notice must be pled and proved as a defense by a compensated surety.
2. The failure to give a compensated surety notice of a principal's default as required in the bond does not relieve the surety when the failure results in no loss to it.

Carnival Cruise Lines v. Financial Indem. Co., 347 So.2d 825 (Fla. App.) 1977.

Another major difference in the treatment afforded compensated as contrasted with uncompensated sureties is in the interpretation of the contract. Ambiguous provisions of surety agreements are construed in favor of the unpaid surety and against the creditor. Ambiguous provisions of surety agreements involving compensated sureties are resolved against the surety. This distinction results from the fact that ambiguous language is generally construed against the party using it. In the case of unpaid sureties, the language is usually framed by the creditor and signed by the surety. In the case of compensated sureties, the contract is usually prepared by the surety.

Fiduciary aspects

The suretyship relation is, within limits, fiduciary in character, involving special trust and confidence between the parties. For this reason, a creditor possessing information affecting the risk must communicate such information to the surety before the contract is made. This duty applies only to information that is significant to the risk.

Since the contract is between the surety and the creditor, any misconduct of the principal that induces the surety to become one does not permit the surety to avoid the contract. At the time of the contract, however, a creditor who is aware of the principal's misrepresentation is obligated to inform the surety of the misrepresentation. An employer may know of past defalcations of an employee whom he seeks to bond. When the contract is being formed, the employer must reveal that information to the surety. Similarly, a creditor who learns that the principal has misrepresented his financial condition to a prospective surety is obligated to warn the surety of the unanticipated risk. If the creditor fails to warn the surety, the surety's promise is not enforceable.

An employer who discovers that a bonded employee has been guilty of misappropriation of funds should immediately discharge the employee unless the surety assents to his continued employment. To continue the employee at his task subjects the surety to a risk not contemplated. Rehabilitation of the employee by giving him a second chance can be undertaken only with the consent of the surety. If the surety does not consent, and if the employee is guilty of misappropriation a second time, the surety is not liable on the surety bond.

Liability of Sureties

General principles

A surety is liable to the creditor as soon as the principal defaults. The creditor need not exhaust his remedies against the principal before looking to the surety. Unless a contract of surety requires a debtor to give the surety notice of default, a creditor may sue a surety who has not been notified.

CASE

D signed as guarantor of a promissory note signed by Akins and payable to P. D expressly inserted a provision into the note that if the principal debtor defaulted, D must be promptly notified if he was to be liable. After the maker defaulted, no notice was given of that fact by P to D. P sued D for the proceeds. D contended that the lack of notice discharged his liability.

ISSUE When a surety contract expressly requires notice of the default, is the surety liable on the note if the payee does not promptly notify the surety?

DECISION No.

REASONS

1. The law favors the guarantor or surety. A surety's contract of liability will be strictly construed, and the surety will not be held liable beyond the terms of his contract.
2. D was entitled to the notice upon which he insisted when he endorsed the note.

Lee v. Vaughn, 534 S.W.2d 221 (Ark.) 1976.

When there is more than one surety on an obligation, the liability of the sureties is described as "joint and several." This means that the creditor may sue them jointly for the debt or he may sue each surety separately for the total debt. If the sureties are sued jointly, the entire judgment against them can be collected from one debtor, just as if the debtor had been sued separately. The problem of allocating shares of the obligation between the sureties does not concern the creditor, and this matter is left exclusively to the sureties as a result of this joint and several liability.

Whenever two or more sureties become secondarily liable for the same obligation of the principal, they become cosureties, even if one surety does not know of the existence of the other. There is an implied contract between cosureties that they will share any loss equally unless they have agreed otherwise. As long as the balance of a claim remains outstanding and unpaid, a cosurety has no right to contribution (other sureties will help pay off the debt—they will contribute) unless he has paid more than his share of the claim, and then only to the extent of the excess. This he may recover from any cosurety unless it compels the latter to pay more than his full share.

The liability of a surety may be released and the surety discharged upon the happening of several events. Among these are changes in the contract terms, extension of the time of payment, payment of the obligation, and any other act that materially prejudices the rights of the surety. These matters are discussed in the sections that follow.

Effect of an extension of time of payment on liability

Debtors frequently seek an extension of time for payment from the creditor. For a debt secured by a promise of a surety, the creditor should be careful not to extend the time for performance without the surety's consent. As a general rule, a binding contract between the principal and creditor definitely extending the time within which performance may be demanded releases the unpaid surety absolutely. A similar contract will release the compensated surety only if the compensated surety can show actual injury as a result of the extension agreement. Injury is shown when the ability of the principal to perform has perceptibly weakened during the period of extension.

A contract of extension releases the unpaid surety because the surety's right to proceed against the principal has been postponed and the financial status of the principal may become less sound during the period of the extension. In addition, there is a new contract to which the surety has not agreed.

To release the surety, the extension agreement must be a binding, enforceable contract. As such, it must be for a definite time and must be supported by consideration. Consideration for an extension may take the form of an advance payment of interest or a note promising to pay it or an increase in the interest rate or treatment of the old note as paid in full in consideration of a new note. Merely promising to pay the original debt at a future date will not supply the consideration, because performance of a preexisting contract is not consideration.

The creditor's indulgence or passive permission to take more time than the contract calls for does not release the surety. The surety is in no sense injured by such conduct, because he is free at any time to perform and immediately start suit against the principal.

In an extension agreement that stipulates reservation of rights against the surety, only the creditor is bound to wait. The surety is free at any time to complete performance for the principal and immediately to sue him for damages suffered, since to him the arrangement is quite similar to mere indulgence.

CASE

P filed suit against D, a guarantor on a note. The original note was renewed by the maker with a new note. D did not consent to the renewal, and P did not specifically reserve its rights against D. D claims to be discharged from liability on the note.

ISSUE Did the extension of the time of payment release D?

DECISION Yes.

REASONS
1. It is immaterial whether the renewal note is treated as full payment of the original note or as an extension of the time of payment of the original note. If the note was paid, D has no liability. If renewed without D's consent, he has no liability.
2. Unless the creditor expressly reserves his rights against the guarantor, an uncompensated or noncommercial guarantor is discharged if the debtor and creditor, without the guarantor's consent, make a binding agreement to extend the time of payment by the principal.

Bank of Waynesboro v. Ghosh, 576 S.W.2d 759 (Tenn.) 1979.

Additional grounds for discharge

In addition to an extension of the time for payment, any other material change in terms of the contract between the principal and the creditor, without the consent of the surety, discharges him. Such a change in terms is a novation. A novation without the consent of the surety discharges the surety, regardless of whether the change in the contract was to his injury or benefit, because the new contract is no longer his contract. In some states, a change of interest rate when there is a continuing guaranty is an exception. Because interest rates are expected to change, that change upon renewal of a debt does not discharge the sureties. But a creditor's failure to comply with the terms of the contract of suretyship will discharge the surety.

A discharge of the principal debtor, unless assented to, also releases the surety. This rule is subject to those exceptions existing in the case of an extension of time; that is, the surety is not released if the principal debtor is discharged with reservation of rights against the surety or if the surety is protected by securities or is a paid surety and is not injured.

Payment of the principal obligation by the debtor or someone in his behalf discharges the surety. A valid tender of payment by either the principal or the surety, but rejected by the creditor, also releases the surety. It is not necessary that the tender be kept good or continuously available in order for the surety to be released. Since the creditor has had an opportunity to receive his money, the surety is no longer liable.

The surety's defenses

Numerous defenses enable a surety to avoid liability, in addition to discharge. Some of these defenses are available only to the surety; others belong to the principal but are also available to the surety. One important defense is that of lack of a principal obligation. In other words, the surety is not bound if the principal is not bound. This may occur when the principal fails to sign the contract although expected to do so. A similar defense arises when the signature of a person shown by contract to be a cosurety is missing. Since failure of a cosurety to sign affects the right of contribution, the signature is a condition precedent to liability.

The creditor has a duty to obtain the genuine signature of the principal, and failure to do so is an absolute defense for the surety. The same rule is not used when the cosurety's signature is forged and this fact is unknown to the creditor. The burden is on the surety to ascertain if the cosurety's signature is genuine. Many other defenses available to the principal may be asserted by the surety against the creditor, particularly when the principal is willing to have the defenses so used. Defenses such as mutual mistake, fraud, illegality, lack or failure of consideration, or undue influence, if available to the principal, may be used by the surety.

There are three important exceptions to the general rule that defenses available to the principal may be used by the surety to avoid liability to the creditor. These defenses are infancy, bankruptcy, and the statute of limitations. Infancy and bankruptcy are not available to the surety as a defense because the surety is employed in the first instance to protect the creditor against the inability of the debtor to perform. If a minor avoids a contract and, in so doing, fails to return all of the consideration that he has received, the surety is required to make up any deficiency between the value of the item returned and the amount of the indebtedness.

The statute of limitations available to the principal debtor may not be used by the surety. Each has his own period after which he is no longer liable to the creditor, and the period may be longer for one than for the other. Thus, the debtor may be liable on an oral contract, whereas the surety is liable on a written contract, or the debtor may have made a part payment that extends the period of his liability but has no effect upon the liability of the surety.

Setoffs and counterclaims of both the principal and the surety may be used as a defense by the surety under certain circumstances. The surety can set off any claim it has against the creditor and use the setoff to reduce or eliminate the liability. If the debtor is insolvent, if the principal and surety are sued jointly, or if the surety has taken an assignment of the claim of the debtor, the surety is entitled to use as a defense any setoff that could be used by the principal debtor in a suit by the creditor.

Rights of the Parties

Rights of the surety against the principal

One who becomes a surety at the request, or with the approval, of the principal is entitled to reimbursement for any loss caused by the principal's default. Normally, the surety is not permitted to add attorney's fees that he had to pay for his defense or fees paid to the creditor's attorney. All attorneys' fees can be avoided by performance of contract terms; when the principal fails to perform, it becomes the immediate duty of the surety to act. Attorneys' fees incurred in a bona fide attempt to reduce the amount of the recovery are an exception to this general rule.

The surety may recover only the amount paid by him. Thus, if he settles a claim for less than the full amount owing to the creditor, his right to recover is limited to the sum paid under the settlement. Furthermore, bankruptcy of the principal, even though it takes place before the surety is called upon to perform, releases the principal from further liability to the surety.

Subrogation rights

Literally, *subrogation* means the substitution of one person in place of another. A creditor has the right to step into the shoes of the surety and to enforce the surety's rights against the principal. Assume that the principal delivered corporate stock to the surety in order to protect the surety in the event of the principal's default. The creditor, to the extent of his claim, may substitute his position for that of the surety with reference to the stock. In the event of the return of the stock by the surety to the principal, the creditor is entitled to follow the stock into the hands of the debtor and subject it to a lien. The creditor may also secure an injunction against return of the stock to the principal, thus having it impounded by the court until the principal debt falls due, at which time the stock may be sold for the benefit of the creditor.

The surety who fully performs the obligation of his principal is subrogated to the creditor's rights against the principal. The surety who pays his principal's debt becomes entitled to any security that the principal has placed with the creditor to secure that particular debt. If the creditor has obtained a judgment against the principal, the surety receives the benefit of the judgment when he satisfies the principal's debt.

Because of the right of subrogation, a creditor in possession of collateral given to him by the principal is not at liberty to return it without the consent of the surety. Any surrender of security releases the surety to the extent of its value, his loss of subrogation damaging him to that extent. Failure of the creditor to make use of the security, however, does not release the surety, since the latter is free to pay the indebtedness and to obtain the security for his own protection. If the creditor loses the benefit of collateral by inactivity—failure to record a mortgage or notify an indorser—the surety is released to the extent that he is injured. In general, if the person who is entitled to protection under the contract of suretyship does anything that will materially prejudice the rights of the surety, the surety will, to that extent at least, be discharged.

REVIEW QUESTIONS AND PROBLEMS

1. Al's garage repaired Walker's automobile and installed a new engine. Al wished to retain a lien on the car for parts and labor. How can he accomplish this? Explain.
2. Bush held a perfected security interest in Unser's automobile. The automobile was in a bad state of repair, and Unser took it to Billy's garage for repairs. Unser defaults on the car payment to Bush and is unable to pay Billy's repair bill. Which party has priority to the proceeds of a sale of the automobile? Explain.
3. Brown owns a shoe store. He purchases his inventory from Kenny Shoe Company, to whom his payments are now delinquent. Both parties agree Kenny will buy out Brown by accepting Brown's assets as full payment of its account. What advice do you have for Brown and Kenny?
4. Discuss the different treatment given by law to a *compensated surety* as distinguished from an *uncompensated surety*.
5. Sam wrote a letter of guaranty to Carl on behalf of Rex, a retailer. The letter stated that Sam "does guarantee payment of any credit granted by you not to exceed ten thousand dollars ($10,000)." Rex was involved in a series of individual transactions with Carl, of which none exceeded $10,000, and the total amount did not exceed $10,000. Rex failed to pay, but Sam contends that his total liability is limited to one transaction. Is Sam correct? Why?
6. Howard's Markets operated a chain of grocery stores. D's, the corporate shareholders, personally guaranteed the debts of the corporation to P. The corporation went insolvent and filed a petition in bankruptcy. The trustee in bankruptcy entered into an agreement with P, by which P accepted the corporate inventory in satisfaction of the corporate debts. The inventory was worth $122,000 less than the debts. P sued D's for the $122,000. D's claimed the discharge of the company discharged D's. Are D's liable? Explain.
7. A husband and wife mortgaged their house for $30,000 and purchased life insurance on the husband's life in declining amounts equal to the debt. The insurance proceeds were payable to the mortgagee. Later the couple sold the house to a buyer who assumed and agreed to pay the balance of the mortgage debt as part of the purchase price. The husband died, and the insurance proceeds paid off the mortgage, but the buyer refused to pay the wife and she filed suit for the amount of the insurance. What was the result? Why?
8. Upshaw guaranteed payment of a $14,400 loan from a bank to Chaney. The guaranty was limited to this loan and renewals. Subsequently, the bank loaned Chaney an additional $4,000, and Chaney executed a new note for the total debt. Did execution of the new note discharge the guarantor? Explain.
9. What is the basic difference between an absolute and a conditional guaranty?
10. Give an example of a suretyship relation that arises by operation of law.
11. Name three exceptions to the general rule that defenses available to the principal are available to the surety.

26

Debtor and Consumer Protection

The preceding chapters discussed several laws designed to assist creditors in the collection of debts. Numerous laws also attempt to protect consumers and debtors from physical and financial harm. These laws seek to protect consumers in their contracts, especially those that involve credit, and from injury caused by products.

Historically, caveat emptor ("Let the buyer beware") was the fundamental principle applicable to most contracts entered into by the consuming public. Today, the fundamental principle is "Let the seller beware." This dramatic change was discussed as a part of the law of sales, especially in chapter 16, "Products Liability." The chapters on contracts (Part II) also contained several discussions of legal principles that directly benefit consumer debtors. Concepts such as unconscionability and fraud as grounds for rescission of contracts are typical of the legal remedies protecting the buying public. The law relating to usury is typical of laws extending financial protection to debtors.

Consumer protection is a goal of all branches of government. Many principles discussed in this chapter are based on statutes enacted by federal and state governments. Courts have also been active in extending protection to consumers. The demise of privity of contract in the breach-of-warranty cases is an example of judicial consumer protection. Finally, administrative agencies such as the Federal Trade Commission are active in the protection of consumer debtors. The FTC holder-in-due-course rule is typical of its active role as a consumer protection agency.

The law has been aiding the consumer debtor for several reasons. Consumers and debtors frequently have less bargaining power than sellers and creditors. Many are financially unsophisticated, easily deceived, and lack information needed to make intelligent decisions. Therefore, much of the consumer movement has been directed at providing all of the relevant information, so that borrowers and purchasers will be able to make reasonably intelligent decisions in the marketplace. Other laws are aimed at equalizing the bargaining power between buyer and seller. This equalization is often accomplished by declaring a provision illegal if it is one that would not be agreed to by a party with equal bargaining power.

Federal law on warranties

Lawyers customarily wrote warranties in language so technical and misleading that many so-called warranties on products were actually disclaimers of warranties. Prior to the adoption of the federal law on warranties and the FTC rules designed to accomplish its goals, a wide gap separated what the consumer was led to believe and what the manufacturer and seller would do under a warranty. To alleviate this problem, to provide consumers with adequate information about express warranties, and to prevent deceptive warranties, Congress enacted the Magnuson-Moss Warranty Act. This law and the Federal Trade Commission rules adopted under it are applicable to all products costing over $5.

The first requirement of the law is that a warrantor of a consumer product must, by means of a written warranty, fully and conspicuously disclose in simple and readily understood language the terms and conditions of the warranty. A consumer product is one normally used for personal, family, or household purposes. The law and the rules then specify what must be included in the written warranty. It must include, among other things, a statement of what the warrantor will do in the event of a defect or breach of warranty, at whose expense, and for what period of time. It must also tell the consumer what he must do and what expenses he must bear.

Any exceptions or exclusions from the warranty must be indicated. The warranty must set forth the step-by-step procedure the consumer is to follow in order to obtain performance of the warranty. The law does not require that a warranty be given or that, if given, it be in writing. If one is given, however, it must include the items provided by law and be in simple, readily understood language.

The law also requires that each warranty be labeled "full" or "limited" if the product sells for over $15. A full warranty must indicate its duration. Products covered by a full warranty must be repaired or replaced by the seller without charge and within a reasonable time in the event there is a defect, malfunction, or failure to conform to the written warranty. A purchaser of a limited warranty is put on notice to find out its limits.

To assist the consumer in making an intelligent purchase decision, sellers are required to make available all information about the warranties. Prior to the sale, this information must be clearly and conspicuously displayed in close connection with the warranted product.

A significant aspect of the federal law deals with informal mechanisms for the resolution of consumer disputes. The law does not require such mechanisms, but it strongly encourages sellers to use them. If a seller establishes a procedure for an independent or government entity to resolve disputes with its buyers, the consumer must resort to the procedure before filing suit against the seller. Consumers are given access to these informal dispute procedures free of charge.

Under the federal law, a warrantor may not impose any limitation on the duration of any implied warranty. Any warrantor may not exclude or limit consequential damages for breach of any warranty unless the exclusion or limitation appears conspicuously on the face of the warranty. No supplier may disclaim or modify any implied warranty if there is a written warranty or if, at the time of sale or within 90 days, the supplier enters into a service contract with the buyer. This latter restriction does not prevent a seller from limiting the time period of a written warranty. The time period of the warranty must also be set forth in clear and unmistakable language on the face of the warranty. A warrantor may not make a warranty conditional on the consumer's using any article or service that is identified by a brand, trade, or corporate name, unless this provision is waived by the Federal Trade Commission. The law also authorizes class-action suits for damages for breach of warranty if at least 100 persons are affected. This could be of substantial help to consumers.

Some persons question whether it is possible to write a warranty in simple and readily understandable language. It will take years of working with the new law before all its ramifications are known, but it has made warranties more detailed and changed their language substantially. Many sellers have opted for the limited warranty; and a few companies, rather than become involved with all the law's requirements, have taken away their warranty in its entirety.

Consumer Product Safety Act

In 1972 Congress enacted the Consumer Product Safety Act, creating the Consumer Product Safety Commission and a Product Safety Advisory Council. The commission has broad authority. It imposes safety standards on manufacturing and commercial operations relating to consumer products and, with a few exceptions, identifies and regulates almost all aspects of safety in all products sold to the public.

The implementation of the law started when the voluntary safety standards of several industries became mandatory. The Product Safety Advisory Council and staff technicians then developed new standards where they were found to be necessary. A major function of the commission has been to gather and disseminate information relating to product hazards and injuries caused by various products. In the development of product safety standards, consumers and consumer organizations, trade associations, the industries involved, and governmental officials are given an opportunity to participate.

The breadth of the law is apparent from its definition of a consumer product. The term includes any article produced or distributed for sale to, or use by, a consumer in or around a permanent or temporary household or residence, a school, in recreation or otherwise. Since there is no requirement that the goods be sold, the law covers free samples and products sold to others but used by consumers.

Manufacturers of products are required to furnish information about their products to the commission. This information may include technical data; it must include all information on new products. The law also requires manufacturers to notify (1) the commission whenever they learn that a product is defective or fails to meet applicable standards and (2) the general public and (3) known purchasers whenever it is found that a product is defective or in violation of a safety rule.

Once a product safety rule has been adopted, a variety of private and public enforcement procedures are available. Courts are authorized to issue injunctions, which may result in the removal of a product from the market. The law provides a penalty of $2,000 for each violation, up to a maximum of $500,000 for each product involved in a violation. A consumer is authorized to sue in federal courts for injuries caused by a product if the manufacturer is knowingly in violation of a product safety rule, provided the claim meets the jurisdictional amount ($10,000) of the federal courts. The law does not change the theories of common law liability previously discussed, but it does create a federal question for purposes of federal jurisdiction.

There is yet insufficient data to evaluate the effectiveness of the Consumer Product Safety Act. Its supporters contend that it has substantially reduced deaths and permanent disabling injuries. It has had a marked impact not only on manufacturers but on private labelers, distributors, and retailers. The retailers are required to permit inspection of their premises and to furnish to the commission information relating to the products they sell.

Unfair or deceptive business practices

By federal statute, the FTC is responsible for preventing unfair or deceptive acts or practices in commerce. As a result of this law, the FTC has a Bureau of Consumer Protection actively engaged in regulating advertising and the sale of goods. Advertising is unfair or deceptive if it has a tendency or capacity to mislead consumers.

The FTC has found numerous unfair and deceptive promotional devices and advertisements. One ad violated the law by comparing the seller's price to a higher "regular" price or a manufacturer's list price. It is deceptive to refer to a "regular price" unless the seller usually and recently sold the items at that price in the regular course of business. Also, it has been held deceptive to refer to the "manufacturer's list price" when that list price is not the ordinary and customary retail sales price of the item in the locality. "Bait and switch" promotions are another violation of the FTC act. In a "bait and switch" sales technique, a product is advertised at a low price that will bring in customers whom the advertiser then tries to switch to other products he prefers to sell.

Ads that are false or misleading about the quality of a product or its source are also unfair and deceptive. Disparaging the product of a competitor may be stopped by the FTC on the ground that such ads are unfair. Words that are technically not false may be held to be deceptive if they give the wrong impression to consumers. The words "guaranteed for life" were held to be deceptive when the seller intended the life to be the life of the product, and consumers thought that the guarantee was for the life of the purchaser of the product.

Many states have laws designed to aid and protect consumers in a multitude of transactions. These laws, which are enacted pursuant to the police power, are usually enforced by the state attorney general, but they may be enforced by consumers and class-action suits.

CASE

P filed suit against D's, a hospital and a collection agency, for a declaratory judgment that D's were guilty of unfair business practices. D's hospital contracts with its patients were signed upon admission to the hospital. They provided that the patients would pay a reasonable collection fee if the hospital bill was referred to a collection agency or to an attorney for collection. When the hospital turned bills over to the collection agency, one third of the bill was automatically added to it as the collection fee.

ISSUE Is this practice illegal?

DECISION Yes.

REASONS 1. By statute, California outlaws unlawful and unfair business practices.

2. The practice here is a violation because the charge is in excess of the actual costs of collection, and it is fixed and added before any costs are incurred. Contracts in which the damages are determined in advance are illegal unless it would be impractical or extremely difficult to fix the actual damages.

3. The contract is an adhesion contract. There is no relationship whatever between the charge assessed and the actual expenses required to collect an account.

Bondanza v. Peninsula Hospital & Med. Ctr., 590 P.2d 22 (Cal.) 1979.

The Uniform Deceptive Trade Practices Act has been adopted by seven states. This act removes restrictions on common law tort actions for deceptive business practices. It recognizes a cause of action for financial loss as a result of misleading identification of a business or goods or as a result of false or deceptive advertising. It also recognizes common law liability to a competitor because of false or deceptive advertising.

Among the types of conduct considered unfair and deceptive are the following: (1) advertising goods or services without intent to sell them as advertised; (2) misrepresenting the character, extent, volume, or nature of the business; (3) advertising secondhand, used, defective, blemished, or rejected merchandise without disclosure of those facts; (4) selling unassembled items without disclosure of that fact; (5) selling merchandise marked "Made in U.S.A." when it is manufactured elsewhere.

The Uniform Deceptive Trade Practices Act also attempts to prevent one person from passing off his goods or services as those of another. It includes within the concept of deceptive trade practice conduct that causes confusion or misunderstanding about the goods or the seller. In addition to allowing suits for dollar damages, this act authorizes courts to enjoin such conduct.

Home solicitation

Under its authority to prevent unfair and deceptive business practices, the Federal Trade Commission has regulated door-to-door selling. The FTC rule covers any sale, lease, or rental of consumer goods with a purchase price of $25 or more, at places of business other than the normal place of business of the seller. It does not cover mail-order or telephone sales or sales in which the buyer has requested the seller to visit his home.

The law requires the seller to furnish the buyer with a copy of the contract in the same language—e.g., Spanish—used in the oral presentation. The contract must, in 10-point type, notify the buyer that the transaction may be canceled at any time prior to midnight of the third business day after the date of the transaction. The seller is required to furnish the buyer with a form to be used to cancel, so that all the buyer is required to do is to sign the form and send it to the seller. The seller also must orally inform the buyer of the right to cancel.

The law requires the seller to honor the notice of cancellation within ten days, refund all payments made and all property traded in, and return any instruments signed by the buyer. If the purchase is canceled, all security arrangements are null and void. If the goods have been delivered to the buyer prior to cancellation, the seller must, within ten days, notify the buyer whether the seller intends to repossess or to abandon the goods.

Real estate settlements law

Since the purchase of a home is the most significant transaction ever entered into by most people, the law contains provisions aimed at assisting buyers with this transaction. At one time, the amount of settlement costs or closing costs in real estate transactions often came as a surprise, if not a shock, to many purchasers. To aid home buyers and borrowers, Congress in 1974 enacted a law requiring the disclosure of all costs to buyers and borrowers prior to the consummation of a real estate transaction. The law assumes that the disclosure of the total cost will allow buyers and borrowers to shop for credit and thus reduce the settlement costs in many cases. The disclosure statement also gives advance notice of the cash required at settlement.

The law requires the use of a standard form for advance disclosure of closing costs and for recording the actual charges incurred at settlement in all covered transactions. Some settlement costs are typically paid by sellers; others are the obligation of buyers. The form covers both categories of expenses. Among the common items disclosed are loan origination fees, loan discount points, appraisal fees, attorney's fees, inspection fees, title charges, and the cost of surveys.

The law also outlaws certain practices that are contrary to the interest of the home-buying public. Among these are giving kickbacks for referring a borrower to a lender, charging or accepting a fee for something other than services actually performed, and requiring that a home seller purchase title insurance from any particular title company. For the title insurance violation, there is a liability equal to three times the cost of the title insurance.

In addition to the foregoing, the law prevents a lender from requiring that more than one month's deposit for taxes and insurance be placed in an escrow account in advance. Finally, in order to discourage speculation in housing, the law gives a buyer the right to be informed of the previous purchase price of a house if it was purchased within two years and not used as a residence by the seller.

Debtor Protection

Exemptions

Typical of state laws protecting debtors are those exempting property from debts. In most states, the exemption statutes include both real and personal property. The real property exemption is usually called the homestead exemption. It provides that upon the sale of the family home to satisfy a judgment debt, a certain amount of the sale price shall be paid to the judgment debtor, to be his property free of the debt. Assume a homestead exemption of $15,000 and that the family home sold for $36,000 at public auction to satisfy a judgment for $10,000. The house was mortgaged for $16,000 prior to the judgment. The debtor would receive $15,000, the mortgagee $16,000, and the creditor $5,000, leaving the judgment unsatisfied to the extent of the $5,000. Of course, the judgment creditor could collect the balance from other nonexempt property, if any.

The reason for the homestead exemption is to provide sufficient funds to the debtor for another home. Public policy favors the debtor and his family's having a home rather than the creditor's being able to collect the entire debt. The homestead exemption is not everywhere available to debtors who do not have a family, thus evidencing the policy of protecting the family. In some states, the exemption is for the total value of the family home. The exemption is usually broadly construed and may extend to the proceeds of forced sales and to the proceeds of insurance claims.

CASE

P obtained a judgment for $72,000 against D. Later D's house burned down, and the insurance company advanced $10,000 of the fire insurance proceeds to D for the down payment on a new house. The company withheld part of the proceeds until the exact loss was determined. P sought to attach the balance of the proceeds to be applied to the judgment. D contended that the proceeds were exempt under the homestead exemption.

ISSUE Is the money exempt under the homestead exemption?

DECISION Yes.

REASONS
1. When the owner of a homestead voluntarily sells the property, the proceeds of the sale are not exempt. On the other hand, when the property is subjected to a forced sale, the debtor's share of the proceeds is exempt if he intends to use the money to acquire another homestead.
2. The recovery of fire insurance proceeds is a forced sale, and they are exempt.
3. Those proceeds are exempt from execution for a reasonable period of time, to allow a person to invest in another homestead.

Exchange Bank & Trust Co. v. Mathews, 591 S.W.2d 354 (Ark.) 1980.

Statutes in most states also exempt a certain amount of personal property, including wearing apparel, family pictures, books, Bibles, and other personal possessions, and a specified dollar value of other items. The new federal law on bankruptcy creates exemptions for debtors subject to its provisions. These quite liberal exemptions are discussed in chapter 27, on bankruptcy.

Limitations on garnishment

By statute, states and the federal government limit the amount that may be withheld from disposable earnings of an employee to pay judgment creditors (garnishment). The federal law, which is a part of the Consumer Credit Protection Act, provides that for an individual, the maximum part of the total disposable earnings subject to garnishment in any week *may not* exceed the *lesser* of

1. twenty-five percent of the disposable earnings for that week or
2. the amount by which the disposable earnings for that week exceed thirty times the federal minimum hourly wage prescribed by the Fair Labor Standards Act.

Disposable earnings means earnings after deductions for income taxes and Social Security taxes.

The federal law does not preempt the field of garnishment or affect any state law. Many state laws exempt larger amounts than does the federal law, and the net effect of the federal law is to exempt the larger amount that either provides. Both the state and the federal law illustrate a public policy against using a wage earner's income to pay judgment debts. In some states, the amount exempt is left to the courts, in order to avoid undue hardship on the debtor.

CASE

A state statute allows a debtor whose wages are subject to garnishment to petition the courts for a reduction of the amount subject to garnishment. A debtor seeking such a reduction must establish that undue hardship would result from the garnishment proceeding.

ISSUE May a debtor be restricted to all but the barest necessities by a garnishment proceeding?

DECISION No.

REASONS

1. After the deduction of the garnishment from a person's wages, enough money should remain to meet ordinary and necessary expenses with something left over for unforeseen expenses and some discretionary spending, so that incentive to work is not destroyed. The garnishment of a debtor's nonexempt income should not make it impossible for the debtor to provide for the family.
2. In large measure, what is ordinary and necessary depends on facts peculiar to each debtor's situation. Expenses for the family's clothing, education, recreation, dwelling, medical care, transportation, and food should be given foremost consideration. In appropriate situations, expenses for tools for the debtor's trade or occupation would be considered an ordinary and necessary expense.
3. There are other expenses that are not ordinary but may be necessary. These expenses should be considered in appropriate cases. Such items are expenses pursuant to other courts' orders; e.g., child support or alimony or expenses for support of other persons whom the debtor is legally or morally obligated to assist, such as children of a former marriage, a former wife, parents, or other relatives.
4. Trial courts should evaluate the reasonableness of obligations and expenses by comparison to similar families in the same locality and shopping area. Reasonableness should be determined mostly on comparable experience, but adjustments should be made for extraordinary or peculiar circumstances.
5. Courts should also consider the relationship between the debtor's total assets and liabilities.

Cottrell v. Public Finance Corp., 256 S.E.2d 575 (W.Va.) 1979.

Many employers in the past have discharged employees who were the subject of garnishment proceedings, but federal law now prohibits this practice in situations involving only one garnishment proceeding. The federal law covers all places of employment.

Truth in lending

In 1969, the federal Consumer Credit Protection Act was enacted. Its principal provisions were designed to assist debtors, and it is commonly known as the Truth-in-Lending Act (TILA). This law gives protection to people who buy property on credit and to people who borrow money for personal, family, household, or agricultural purposes. Its terms and provisions apply not only to those who lend money or sell on credit in the ordinary course of business but also to anyone who arranges for the extension of credit. It applies only to natural persons and is not applicable to business loans. If a purchaser or borrower is other than a natural person (for example, a corporation or partnership), or if the purchase or loan is for business rather than personal, family, household, or agricultural use, the law is not applicable. It covers real estate credit transactions as well as personal property transactions, but it is not applicable if the personal property loan or purchase exceeds $25,000. Nor is it applicable to agricultural credit transactions if the amount financed exceeds $25,000. If a transaction is both a personal and business one, the courts will look to the dominant portion of the transaction to determine if compliance is required. Doubts should be resolved in favor of compliance, however.

CASE

P sued D to foreclose a mortgage on D's family home. D sought to rescind the mortgage because P had failed to comply with the federal Truth-in-Lending Act. The debt secured by the mortgage totaled approximately $13,000, of which $1,000 was used to purchase a boat and $12,000 was used in D's business. It is undisputed that P did not furnish D any Truth-in-Lending disclosures.

ISSUE Is this mortgage subject to the federal Truth-in-Lending law?

DECISION No.

REASONS

1. The intent of Truth-in-Lending is to inform the debtor of credit terms and protect unwary consumers from overreaching practices of unscrupulous creditors. It covers only consumer loans to individuals, not business or commercial loans.
2. A consumer loan is primarily for personal, family, household, or agricultural purposes. It covers credit transactions in which a security interest is retained or acquired in a personal residence.
3. Not every loan transaction that results in a security interest in the debtor's residence is subject to this statutory right of rescission. The transaction must be otherwise subject to the act; i.e., it must be a consumer loan rather than a business or commercial one.
4. The boat loan is subject to the law, but the business loan is not. The decision to pledge the house as security for a business loan does not lose its quality as a business decision merely because the personal home was the collateral.
5. A transaction in which the ratio of private purpose funds to business purpose funds is only one-to-twelve is not primarily for personal purposes. Since the mortgage was not a consumer credit transaction, the Truth-in-Lending Act was inapplicable to it, and no such statutory right of rescission existed.

State v. DeWitt, 286 N.W.2d 379 (Iowa) 1979.

The law does not apply to a sale by one consumer to another consumer, since the sale is not in the seller's ordinary course of business. Typical of transactions covered are installment loans and sales, short-term notes, real estate loans, home improvement loans, and farm loans.

The Federal Reserve Board, having the responsibility of developing regulations to implement the purpose of the law, has adopted Regulation Z, containing detailed requirements for compliance. The purpose of the Truth-in-Lending Act is to disclose the cost of credit to a prospective purchaser or borrower, so that he may shop for credit. The theory is that he may then obtain disclosure statements from several dealers or financers, compare them, and determine whether or not he wishes to go ahead with his purchase or loan.

The goal of the Truth-in-Lending Act is accomplished by the use of disclosure statements. A copy of it is given to the borrower, and the original is retained by the lender for two years or until the debt is paid, whichever is longer. Separate disclosure statements are required for each transaction, including refinancing. These statements inform the borrower of the amount financed, the finance charge, and the annual percentage rate. They also disclose the amount of each payment and the number of payments. It is important to realize that the annual percentage rate generally will not be the same as the interest rate. One important reason for this difference is that the annual percentage rate is based upon the finance charge, and the finance charge includes all charges imposed by the creditor, only one of which is interest. The finance charge may include the cost of credit reports, credit life insurance, health insurance, appraisals, and so forth.

Any creditor subject to the law who fails to make the required disclosure may be sued by the debtor within one year from the date of the violation for *twice the amount of the finance charge.* This may not be less than $100 or more than $1,000. If the creditor has made an incorrect disclosure, he must, within fifteen days after discovering the error, notify the debtor and make whatever adjustments are necessary to ensure that the debtor will not be required to pay a finance charge in excess of the amount of the percentage rate actually disclosed. If the creditor is to avoid penalty, he must discover the error and give notice to the debtor before the debtor notifies or institutes action against him.

Disclosure statements must meet rigid technical requirements. If both sides of a sheet of paper are used for a contract, each must refer the signer to the other side by including a statement: "NOTICE: See other side for important information." The contract must not violate state laws relating to such transactions.

CASE

P sued to collect on a promissory note, which was in default. D counterclaimed for twice the finance charge, contending that P's security agreement and loan disclosure statement violated the federal Truth-in-Lending Act. The disclosure statement described the security interest as covering defendant's automobile and "All of the household consumer goods of every kind now owned or hereafter acquired by Debtors in replacement of said consumer goods (and proceeds) now or hereafter located in or about Debtors residence above set forth."

ISSUE Did P violate the federal Truth-in-Lending law by taking a security interest in after-acquired household goods?

DECISION Yes.

REASONS

1. This security interest is in direct conflict with the provisions of subdivision 2 of section 9-204 of the Uniform Commercial Code, which in no uncertain terms limits the security interest a creditor may take in consumer goods to those acquired within 10 days after the creditor gives value. Thus, it is illegal.
2. Regulation Z adopted pursuant to the provisions of the Truth-in-Lending Act also requires "a clear identification of the property to which the security interest relates"; and the Federal Reserve Board has called it a violation if a creditor represents that it has an interest in all after-acquired property of the debtor.
3. A security interest in after-acquired property without time limitation violates the Truth-in-Lending Act and Regulation Z.
4. Designed to prevent "unscrupulous and predatory creditor practices," the act is remedial in nature and must be liberally construed to effectuate the legislative intent. It reflects a transition in policy from a philosophy of let-the-buyer-beware to one of let-the-seller-disclose.

Public Loan Co., Inc. v. Hyde, 390 N.E.2d 1162 (N.Y.) 1979.

The law makes some distinctions between loans secured by first mortgages and those secured by second mortgages. If the mortgage is a first mortgage in connection with a purchase, the lender is required to state only the annual interest cost; he does not have to state the total interest cost over the life of the loan. If the mortgage is a second mortgage or is a first mortgage not connected with the purchase of the property, the lender must disclose the annual interest and the total interest ultimately to be paid. The law also gives a second mortgagor, and first mortgagors unconnected with a purchase, three days in which to cancel the loan without penalty or obligation. These provisions relating to second mortgages and to borrowing by homeowners are designed to eliminate credit abuses and instinctive borrowing using real estate as security. Prior to the law, people frequently gave second mortgages without realizing it, and the law therefore requires notice that a mortgage is involved. The law also requires that the creditor give the debtor notice of the fact that the transaction may be rescinded.

The Consumer Credit Protection Act also protects borrowers by prohibiting misleading advertising, such as representing lower down payments and lower installment payments than are actually available. If an advertisement contains any details of a credit plan, it must also include as disclosures substantial information on finance charges, rates, cash price, down payment, and other information that is included in the specific regulations used to enforce the law.

Uniform Consumer Credit Code

The Commissioners on Uniform State Laws have prepared a Uniform Consumer Credit Code designed for many of the purposes of the federal Truth-in-Lending Act. The Uniform Consumer Credit Code (UCCC) also attempts to protect consumers by utilizing the technique of full disclosure of all pertinent facts about the credit transaction to buyers. The UCCC is applicable to virtually every transaction involving credit: retail installment sales, consumer credit, small loans, and usury.

The UCCC does not fix rates of interest but, rather, sets maximums that may be charged. When the amount financed is $300 or less, the maximum is 36 percent per year; and when the amount is more than $300 but less than $1,000, it is 21 percent per year. The credit code has detailed provisions covering matters such as delinquency charges, deferral charges, service charges on refinancing or loan consolidation, and revolving charge accounts. It also prohibits most deficiency judgments when goods sold as a part of a consumer credit sale are repossessed.

CASE

P, a finance company, sued D to recover a deficiency judgment on a promissory note. P had previously repossessed and sold D's automobile, on which it held a security interest.

Kansas had enacted the Uniform Consumer Credit Code. This statute prohibits deficiency judgments when the buyer has a defense arising from the sale, the goods are repossessed, and the cash sale was less than $1,000 (conditions in this case). The law is applicable in any of these five situations:

1. The lender knows that for a commission, brokerage, or referral fee, the seller arranged for the extension of credit by the lender.
2. The lender is a person related to the seller.
3. The seller guarantees the loan or otherwise assumes the lender's risk of loss.
4. The lender directly supplies the seller with the contract document used by the consumer to evidence the loan, and the seller significantly participates in the preparation of the document.
5. The loan is conditioned upon the consumer's purchase of the goods or services from the particular seller.

ISSUE Is P entitled to a deficiency?

DECISION Yes.

REASONS

1. As to the first four criteria, the facts clearly establish that P had no contact or relationship of any kind whatsoever with Cox Motors. Cox Motors had not referred D to P, nor had Cox prepared or helped to prepare the contract document used by the D to evidence the loan.
2. As to the fifth criterion, there is no evidence in the stipulated facts to show that the loan from P to D was conditioned upon the consumer purchasing the goods from the particular seller, Cox Motors. The fact that P's check for the proceeds of the loan was made payable to Cox Motors as well as to D does not in itself establish that the loan was so conditioned.
3. In this case, P did not make an "all in the family" loan and is not precluded from recovering a deficiency judgment on the unpaid balance of the debt arising from the loan.

Central Finance Co., Inc. v. Stevens, 558 P.2d 122 (Kan.) 1976.

The UCCC requires a written disclosure that conspicuously sets forth the required facts prior to a sale or loan. Just as in the Truth-in-Lending Act, the annual percentage rate is the key fact that must be disclosed. The difference between the cash price and the credit price is also essential as a part of the disclosure. The provisions on advertising generally require that the ad include the rate of the credit service charge as well as the amount of the charge.

In addition to regulating the cost of credit, the UCCC prohibits certain types of agreements. It prohibits the use of the holder-in-due course concept and outlaws agreements cutting off defenses. It prohibits the use of multiple agreements to obtain higher interest. It also prohibits "balloon" payments. If any scheduled payment is more than twice as large as the average payment, the buyer has the right to refinance the balloon payment, without penalty, on terms no less favorable than the original terms. The balloon-payment provision is not applicable to a sale for agricultural purposes or one pursuant to a revolving charge account.

The UCCC prohibits debtors from assigning their earnings as part of a credit sale. It also prohibits referral sales schemes in which the buyer is given credit on a purchase for furnishing the names of other purchasers.

Violations of the UCCC may be punished criminally. In addition, debtors are relieved of their obligation to pay the finance charge, and they are entitled to recover, from creditors who violate the law, up to three times the finance charge actually paid. Of course, debtors are not obligated to pay charges in excess of those allowable by the act. If a debtor entitled to a refund is refused a refund, the debtor is entitled to recover the total amount of the credit service charge or ten times the excess charge, whichever is greater. If the excess charge was in deliberate violation of the act, the penalty may be recovered even if the excess has been repaid.

Credit card protection

Lost or stolen credit cards are often used for unauthorized purchases, resulting in a loss to either (1) the business that dealt with the wrong person, (2) the credit card company (which may be the same as number 1, as in the case of an oil company's gasoline credit card), or (3) the actual cardholder. The law seeks to limit the cardholder's loss and to impose most of the losses on the issuer of the card.

The Truth-in-Lending Law provides that a cardholder is liable only up to $50 for the unauthorized use of a credit card and only if (1) the credit card is an accepted card, one that the cardholder has requested, (2) the liability is incurred prior to notice to the issuer of the loss or theft, (3) within two years before the unauthorized use, the issuer warned the cardholder of his liability and (4) the card issuer has provided the cardholder with a preaddressed notice form that may be mailed in the event of loss or theft of the card. No cardholder is liable unless the issuer has provided a method whereby the user of the card can be identified as the person authorized to use it. Such identification may be by signature, photograph, or fingerprint on the card. It may be also by electronic or mechanical confirmation.

The law also prohibits the issuance of credit cards except upon application therefor or upon the renewal of an existing card. Thus, no liability for unauthorized purchases is present if the card was issued without being requested.

The warning to the cardholder, which the law requires, may be given by printing it on the card. The notice must state that liability in case of loss or theft shall not exceed $50 and that notice of loss or theft may be given orally or in writing. The notice may contain the name and address of the person to receive the notice.

Most credit card contracts provide that defenses against the seller cannot be asserted against the credit card company. Such contracts are valid even though the holder-in-due-course concept has been eliminated as applied to consumers. Firms such as American Express, Diner's Club, Carte Blanche, and the various banks with cards cannot operate effectively if subject to a variety of claims and defenses by their cardholders.

Debt collection

Because some debt collectors used harassment, deception, and personal abuse to collect debts, Congress in 1978 passed the Fair Debt Collection Practices Act (FDCPA), regulating consumer debt collection practices by collection agencies. Efforts by creditors are exempt from the act, since it is assumed that they will avoid using harassment in order to retain the debtor's good will.

The law permits a bill collector to communicate with third parties, such as neighbors or employers of the debtor, but it limits the contact. Third parties may not be informed that the consumer owes a debt. When an attorney represents the debtor, and the bill collector knows it, the collector may not get in touch with anyone else except the attorney, unless the attorney fails to respond to the collector's communication.

The act also restricts the methods that may be used in the collection process. The collector may not (1) physically threaten the debtor, (2) use obscene language, (3) pretend to be an attorney unless he is, (4) threaten the debtor with arrest or garnishment unless the collector or creditor is legally entitled to such action and intends to take it, or (5) telephone the debtor repeatedly with intent to annoy. In telephoning the debtor, the collector must make a meaningful disclosure of his identity and may not telephone collect or before 8:00 A.M. or after 9:00 P.M. In addition to these specific prohibitions, the act forbids the collector in general from using any "unfair or unconscionable" means to collect the debt.

If a debtor desires to stop repeated contacts, he need only notify the collector in writing of this wish. Any further contact by the collector following such notification violates the act. The collector's sole remedy in such cases is to sue the debtor. Violations of the law entitle the debtor to sue the collector for actual damages, including damages for invasion of privacy and infliction of mental distress, court costs, and attorney's fees. In the absence of actual damages, the court may still order the collector to pay the debtor up to $1,000 for violations.

Fair Credit Reporting Act

This law is not designed to prevent credit reporting. Its purpose is to prevent abuses in the system of credit reports that may result from inaccurate information in a report. It is also designed to prevent the undue invasion of individual privacy in the collection and dissemination of information about a person's credit record. The act is applicable to anyone who prepares or uses a credit report in connection with (1) extending credit, (2) selling insurance, or (3) hiring or discharging an employee. It covers credit reports on consumers but not on businesses. Violations of the act entitle an injured party to punitive damages as well as actual damages.

The law covers two situations. First of all, it covers cases in which an individual is rejected for credit, insurance, or employment because of an adverse credit report. When this occurs, the person has the right (1) to be told the name of the reporting agency, (2) to require the agency to reveal the information given in the report, and (3) to correct the information or at least give the person's own version of the facts in dispute.

This law has one important limitation. A report containing information solely about transactions or experiences between the consumer and the person making the report is not a "consumer report." Assume that a bank is asked for information about its credit experience with one of its customers. If it reports only the bank's experiences, the report is not covered by the act. The law covers only credit reporting agencies that obtain information from several sources, compile it, and furnish it to potential creditors.

Although businesses can often avoid giving credit information, most of them are subject to the "user" provisions of the act. The "user" provision requires that consumers seeking credit be informed if their application is denied because of an adverse credit report. They must be informed of the source of the report and of the fact that within 60 days they may make a written request to be told what information was received. They may then challenge the accuracy of the report.

The second situation covered by this law involves investigative consumer reports. A consumer is entitled to be informed when one of these reports is being made. Upon request, he is entitled to know (1) the nature and scope of the investigation, (2) the kind of information that has been placed in the credit reporting agency's file, and (3) the name of anyone to whom the report has been sent. He also has the right to require a consumer reporting agency to reinvestigate any material that he finds to be inaccurate in his file and the right to have removed from his file any inaccurate material or material that cannot be verified by the reporting agency. If there is a dispute over accuracy, the consumer has the right to place a 100-word statement in his file setting forth his position on the disputed matter. This statement must be included in all future agency reports that contain the material in dispute.

The consumer has a right to require that obsolete information included in the consumer report be removed from the file. Included are bankruptcies that occurred more than fourteen years prior to the report; lawsuits and judgments that antedate the report by more than seven years or until the statute of limitations has expired, whichever is longer; and, in general, adverse items of entered information that antedate the report by more than seven years.

Fair Credit Billing Act

This 1974 law requires that a creditor must take certain steps if a debtor, within 60 days of the receipt of a bill, complains that the billing is in error. First of all, the creditor is required to acknowledge the notice within 30 days. Second, the creditor, within two billing cycles and within not more than 90 days, must either (1) correct the error or (2) send a written statement of clarification to the debtor.

The act further provides that a creditor operating an open-end credit plan may not, until explanation of the complaint or its correction, curtail, restrict, or close the debtor's account. In addition, the law prohibits a creditor from reporting or threatening to report the debtor to a credit rating organization. Violation of either of these provisions results in a forfeiture of the right to collect the amount stated in the billing.

The law also contains several provisions relating to the accounting practices of creditors. Prompt posting of all payments is required, to prevent the application of additional finance charges. Creditors of revolving charge accounts cannot impose finance charges on a new purchase unless a statement including the finance charge is rendered at least fourteen days prior to the date the finance charge could be avoided by paying the original bill.

The law also contains some restrictions on credit card issuers and their business practices. Issuers of credit cards may not prohibit sellers who honor these cards from offering discounts for cash or immediate payment by check.

Equal Credit Opportunity Act

Congress enacted the Equal Credit Opportunity Act (ECOA) in 1975, to prevent discrimination in granting credit. The act prohibits discriminating against or discouraging credit seekers because of their sex, marital status, race, color, age, religion, national origin, or receipt of welfare.

The ECOA applies to all businesses that regularly extend credit, including financial institutions, retail stores, and credit card issuers. It also extends to anyone who steers consumers to lenders.

A female cannot be denied the right to open a credit account separate from her husband's or in her maiden name. Unless the husband will be using the account or the female consumer is relying on her husband's credit rating, it is illegal even to ask if she is married. It is also illegal to ask about birth-control practices or childbearing plans or, on a credit checklist, to assign negative values to the fact that a woman is of childbearing age.

The ECOA requires that specific reasons be given a consumer who is denied credit. In making the decision, businesses extending credit must consider alimony, child support, income from part-time jobs, and welfare payments as income. If both spouses use an account, credit reporting agencies must report on both parties, so that females will have a credit rating.

The law allows suits for dollar damages by victims of credit discrimination. Victims are entitled to recover actual damages, punitive damages up to $10,000, attorney's fees, and legal costs. Actual damages can include recovery for embarrassment and mental distress. Punitive damages can be recovered even in the absence of actual damages. In addition to private remedies, the government may bring suit to enjoin violations of the ECOA and to access civil penalties.

The future

The preceding sections have discussed several of the important new laws and legal principles that give substantial protection to consumers, especially to debtor consumers. There are other proposed laws or changes in existing laws that are designed to give even more protection. Some of these have been enacted in a few states; others are being developed by courts and legislatures at this time. There is a definite trend toward allowing class-action suits on behalf of consumers. Most consumers cannot afford to sue because their complaints do not involve a sufficient amount of money to warrant the retention of an attorney. Class-action suits, which allow one plaintiff to sue on behalf of all persons similarly situated, make such suits worthwhile. Legislation has been introduced in many states authorizing class-action suits on behalf of consumers, and consumer protection agencies are authorized to take legal action on behalf of consumers. The Truth-in-Lending Act allows class-action suits subject to a maximum recovery of $500,000 or 1 percent of the net worth of the creditor, whichever is less.

The 1980s have seen a slowing down of the consumer movement. Business objects to being overregulated and points to regulation as one of the causes of inflation. There is real doubt about whether the cost of many consumer protection techniques exceeds their benefit. Much of the consumer protection legislation does not fare well when it is subjected to cost-benefit analysis. Today, it is much more difficult than it was in the 1970s to enact consumer-debtor protection statutes.

REVIEW QUESTIONS AND PROBLEMS

1. What is the basic purpose of the Truth-in-Lending law?
2. The Charge It Company issued a credit card to Albert. Albert's card was stolen, and he immediately notified Charge It. The thief used Albert's card for motel and gasoline purchases for two months. Does Albert or the credit card company suffer the loss? Explain.
3. Alice was rejected for life insurance on the basis of a report from an independent credit agency. What are her rights concerning the report? Why?
4. Friendly Finance held a mortgage on Dandy's six-unit apartment building. Dandy fell behind on his payments and, to avoid foreclosure, agreed to execute a mortgage on his home in favor of Friendly. This second mortgage secured a note for the amount that Dandy was in arrears on his payments. When the second mortgage was entered, Friendly did not comply with the Truth-in-Lending law. Dandy now sues Friendly for his actual damages plus twice the amount of the finance charge. Should Dandy succeed? Why?
5. Irma Lard, a housewife, visited the ABC Figure Salon and signed a weight-reducing contract that provided for a program to be completed within 12 months at a cost of $300. When Irma returned home, she felt that she had been subjected to extreme sales pressure and, later that same day, sent a letter to ABC requesting that the contract be canceled. Should ABC be required to cancel the contract? Why?
6. Briefly describe the main purpose of each of the following laws:
   a) Fair Credit Reporting Act
   b) Equal Credit Opportunity Act
   c) Truth-in-Lending Act
   d) Magnuson-Moss Warranty Act
   e) Fair Debt Collection Practices Act
   f) Real Estate Settlements Law
7. Ed, a realtor, often extended credit to his clients when additional money was needed to close transactions. He did not comply with Truth-in-Lending and contended that he was not a creditor under the act. A client sued Ed for double the interest. What result? Why?
8. Harry, a wage earner, earned $200 per week. His employer withheld 20 percent for income and FICA taxes. A garnishment action was commenced against Harry and the employer to collect a judgment against Harry. Using the federal law as a standard, how much of Harry's wages may be garnisheed each week?
9. The No-Refill Ballpoint Pen Company provided full warranties on its pens. What is the significance of this full warranty?
10. The Perfect-Sound Stereo Company advertised a radio for $29.95 in the local campus daily. When students attempted to purchase the stereo, they were told that it was of poor quality but that they had a special deal on a good quality radio for $49.95. Several students wish to complain. Whom should they contact?

27 Bankruptcy

The law of bankruptcy provides possible solutions to problems that arise when a person, partnership, corporation, or municipality is unable, or finds it difficult, to satisfy obligations to creditors. Bankruptcy has its roots in the law of the Roman Empire and has been a part of English jurisprudence since 1542. The laws relating to bankruptcy have been periodically amended in the United States, the latest revision (1978) being effective October 1, 1979.

This latest revision contained significant changes, which have made "going bankrupt" a much more acceptable solution to financial problems. During the first year of the new law, the number of individual bankruptcies rose dramatically to an all-time high. Under the new law, filing for bankruptcy is not a socially unacceptable act or an admission of failure. It is generally considered to be an acceptable solution to financial distress both for individuals and businesses.

The federal bankruptcy laws have two distinct approaches to the problems of debtors. One approach is to liquidate debts and provide honest debtors with a fresh start. The liquidation approach recognizes that misfortune and poor judgment often create a situation in which a debtor will never be able to discharge his debts by his own efforts, or at least it will be very difficult to do so. Public policy dictates that such debtors should be able to obtain a fresh start not only in their personal lives but in business as well. Public policy also recognizes that if a person is to make a fresh start, minimum assets are required. Therefore, the new law increases the amount of property that the debtor is allowed to retain.

The second approach of the bankruptcy law is to postpone the time of payment of debts or to reduce some of them to levels that make repayment possible. This approach is found in the reorganization sections for businesses and in the adjustment of debts provisions for municipalities and individuals with regular incomes. The reorganization and adjustment provisions are aimed at rehabilitation of debtors. These procedures, if utilized, prevent harassment of debtors and spare them undue hardship, while enabling most creditors eventually to obtain some repayment.

Types of proceedings

There are four types of bankruptcy proceedings, each identified by a chapter of the statute: Chapter 7, Liquidation; Chapter 9, Adjustment of Debts of a Municipality; Chapter 11, Reorganization; Chapter 13; Adjustment of Debts of an Individual with Regular Income. Chapter 9 adjustment proceedings recognize the financial plight of many governmental units such as New York City and Cleveland, Ohio. A municipal governmental entity may be a debtor under Chapter 9 if state law or a public official authorized by state law permits it. The municipality must be unable to meet its debts as they mature, and it must desire to effect a plan to adjust its debts. Because of the special and limited use of these proceedings, they will not be discussed further in this text.

Liquidation proceedings are used to eliminate most of the debts of the debtor. Adjustment and reorganization proceedings cover cases in which debtors attempt to pay off creditors over an extended period of time under a court approved plan. The law allows a case filed under one chapter to be converted to another chapter, with the debtor's consent.

Bankruptcy proceedings also may be described as either voluntary or involuntary. Voluntary proceedings are at the instigation of the debtor; involuntary proceedings are at the instigation of creditors. All debtors covered by a chapter may voluntarily seek relief under it.

The statute specifies which debtors under each chapter are subject to involuntary proceedings. Farmers and not-for-profit corporations are not subject to involuntary proceedings under either Chapter 7 or Chapter 11. A *farmer* is defined as a person who receives more than 80 percent of gross income for the taxable year preceding the bankruptcy case from a farming operation he owns and operates. The term *farming operation* includes tillage of the soil; dairy farming; ranching; production or raising of crops, poultry, or livestock; and production of poultry or livestock products in an unmanufactured state.

Liquidation proceedings

Cases under Chapter 7 may involve individuals, partnerships, or corporations, but only individuals may receive a discharge from the court. A discharge voids any judgment against the debtor to the extent that it creates a personal liability. A discharge covers all debts that arose before the date of the order for relief. It is irrelevant whether or not a claim was filed or allowed. A discharge also operates as an injunction against all attempts to collect the debt—by judicial proceedings, telephone calls, letters, personal contacts, or other efforts. Under all types of proceedings, once they are commenced, creditors are prohibited from attempting to collect their debts.

The debts of partnerships and corporations that go through liquidation proceedings are not discharged. These businesses are still technically liable for their debts; however, the lack of discharge is immaterial unless the partnership or corporation acquires assets later. This lack of discharge stops people from using "shell" businesses after bankruptcy for other purposes.

Certain businesses are denied the right to liquidation proceedings. Railroads, insurance companies, banks, savings and loan associations, homestead associations, and credit unions may not be debtors under Chapter 7. Nor may domestic and foreign insurance companies and financial institutions. These organizations are subject to the jurisdiction of administrative agencies that handle all aspects of such organizations, including problems related to insolvency. Under this arrangement, there are alternative legal provisions for their liquidation.

Chapter 7 has special provisions relating to liquidation proceedings involving stockbrokers and commodities brokers. These special provisions are necessary to protect their customers, because bankruptcies of this kind usually involve large indebtedness and substantial assets. Stockbrokers and commodity brokers are subject only to Chapter 7. Chapter 11 and Chapter 13 proceedings are not possible for them.

Reorganization proceedings

As a general rule, any debtor subject to liquidation (Chapter 7) is also subject to reorganization (Chapter 11). An exception exists for railroads. The public interest in railroads prevents their liquidation, but the law recognizes that financial reorganization is not only possible but often desirable, and Chapter 11 reorganization is a common occurrence for railroads. Chapter 11 of the Bankruptcy Act contains detailed provisions on all aspects of the plan of reorganization and its execution. As soon as practicable after the order for relief, the court appoints a committee of creditors holding unsecured claims. The committee ordinarily consists of persons with the seven largest claims, and it may employ attorneys, accountants, or other agents to assist it. Working with the trustee and the debtor concerning the administration of the case, it represents the interests of the creditors. It may investigate the financial conditions of the debtor and will assist in the formulation of the reorganization plan.

The court in reorganization cases will usually appoint a trustee before approval of the plan of reorganization. If the court does not appoint a trustee, it will appoint an examiner who conducts an investigation into the affairs of the debtor, including any mismanagement or irregularities.

After the trustee or the examiner conducts the investigation of the acts, conduct, assets, liabilities, financial conditions, and other relevant aspects of the debtor, a written report of this investigation is filed with the court. The trustee may file a plan of reorganization if the debtor does not, or it may recommend conversion of the case to liquidation proceedings. The trustee will also file tax returns for the debtor, file reports with the court, and may even operate the debtor's business unless the court orders otherwise. The debtor may file a plan of reorganization with the voluntary petition or later, in an attempt to extricate the business from its financial difficulties and help it to survive. The plan will classify claims, and all claims within a class will be treated the same. All unsecured claims for less than a specified amount may be classified together. The plan will designate those classes of claims that are unimpaired under the plan and will specify the treatment to be given claims that are impaired.

The plan must provide a means for its execution. It may provide that the debtor will retain all or part of the property of the estate. It may also propose that property be sold or transferred to creditors or other entities. Mergers and consolidations may be proposed. In short, the plan will deal with all aspects of the organization of the debtor, its property, and its debts. Some debts will be paid in full, some will be partially paid over an extended period of time, and others may not be paid at all. The only limitation is that all claimants must receive as much as they would receive in liquidation proceedings.

Holders of claims or interests in the debtor's property are allowed to vote and to accept or reject the proposed plan of reorganization. A class of claims has accepted a plan if at least two-thirds in amount and more than half in number of claims vote yes. Acceptance by a class of interests such as equity holders requires a two-thirds yes vote.

A hearing is held on the confirmation of a plan, to determine if it is fair and equitable. The statute specifies several conditions, such as good faith, which must be met before the plan is approved. Also before approval, it must be established that each holder of a claim or interest has either accepted the plan or will receive as much under the reorganization plan as would be received in liquidation proceedings. For secured creditors, this means that they will receive the value of their security either by payment or by delivery of the property.

Confirmation of the plan makes it binding on the debtor, equity security holders, and creditors. Confirmation vests the property of the estate in the debtor and releases it from all claims. Debts that arose prior to the confirmation are discharged unless the plan provides otherwise. Of course, nondischargeable taxes remain as obligations.

Adjustment of individual debts

Chapter 13 proceedings are used to adjust the debts of individuals with regular income whose debts are small enough and whose income is significant enough that substantial repayment is feasible. Unsecured debts of individuals utilizing Chapter 13 proceedings cannot exceed \$100,000, and the secured debts cannot exceed \$350,000. Persons utilizing Chapter 13 will usually be employees earning a salary, but persons engaged in business also qualify. Self-employed persons who incur trade debts are considered to be engaged in business.

The debtor files a plan that provides for the use of all or of a portion of his future earnings or income for the payment of debts. The income is under the supervision and control of the trustee. Except as provided in the plan, the debtor keeps possession of his property. If the debtor is engaged in business, the debtor continues to operate the business. The plan must provide for the full payment of all claims entitled to priority unless the creditors with priority agree to a different treatment. The plan may divide unsecured claims into classes. If it does, all claims within a class must be given the same treatment.

Unsecured claims not entitled to priority may be repaid in full or reduced to a level not lower than the amount that would be paid upon liquidation. The secured creditors may be protected by allowing them to retain their lien, by payment of the secured claim in full, or by the surrender of the property to the secured claimant. The usual plan will provide for payments over three years, but the court may extend the payment period up to a total of five years.

The plan may modify the rights of holders of secured and unsecured claims, except that the rights of holders of real estate mortgages may not be modified. Claims arising after the filing of the petition may be included in the plan. This is a realistic approach, because all of the debts of the debtor must be taken into account if the plan is to accomplish its objectives.

A plan may provide for concurrent payments on secured and unsecured claims. It may reject executory leases and contracts, as if the case were in liquidation.

When the court conducts a hearing on the confirmation of the plan, if it is satisfied that the debtor will be able to make all payments to comply with it, the plan will be approved. Of course, the plan must be proposed in good faith, be in compliance with the law, and be in the best interest of the creditors.

As soon as the debtor completes all payments under the plan, the court grants the debtor a discharge of all debts, unless the debtor waives the discharge. Debts on which the final payment is due after the plan is completed are not discharged. Of course, debts for alimony and child support and debts incurred for willful and malicious conversion or for injury to property are not discharged.

Courts, after a hearing, may also grant a discharge, even though all payments have not been made, if the debtor's failure to complete the payments is due to circumstances for which the debtor should not justly be held accountable. In such cases, the payments under the plan must be not less than those which would have been paid on liquidation, and modification must not be practicable.

Remember that a debtor may convert a case under Chapter 13 to a liquidation proceeding under Chapter 7 at any time. Any waiver of this right is unenforceable.

Case Administration

Chapter 3 of the statute, concerned with case administration, is applicable to cases filed under any of the four types of proceedings. It covers the various aspects of the commencement of cases, the rules of law relating to the trustee and other officers of the court involved in bankruptcy, the principles governing the administration of bankruptcy estates, and the administrative powers of the courts and officers involved in the proceedings.

The sections dealing with the administration of bankrupt estates cover matters such as the meetings of creditors, investment of the money of the estate, and tax returns that must be filed by the trustee. The tax provision deals with matters such as loss carrybacks, investment credit carryovers, and capital gains.

The most technical portion of Chapter 3 is entitled "administrative powers." These sections grant the bankruptcy court and the trustee a wide range of powers to accomplish the statutory purposes of bankruptcy. The law recognizes that attempts by creditors to collect from the debtor must be stopped so that the bankruptcy proceeding may handle all aspects of the debtor's affairs. There is a provision for automatic stays of other litigation. In addition, the law grants the power to the trustee to use, sell, or lease the property of the debtor. The trustee is given the power to terminate executory contracts and leases. The sections that follow discuss aspects of case administration applicable to all four types of proceedings.

Voluntary cases—commencement

Voluntary cases are commenced by the filing of a petition with the bankruptcy court. The petition is filed by the debtor. In recognition of the fact that husbands and wives often owe the same debts, a joint case may be filed. A joint case is a voluntary case concerning a husband and wife, and it requires only one petition. The petition must be signed by both spouses, since one spouse cannot take the other into bankruptcy without the other's consent.

All petitioners must pay a filing fee of $60, in installments if they prefer. Only one filing fee is required in a joint case. A petition filed by a partnership as a firm is not a petition on behalf of the partners as individuals. If they intend to obtain individual discharges, separate petitions are required.

The voluntary petition in bankruptcy constitutes an *order for relief* of the debtor as a bankrupt. The petition contains lists of secured and unsecured creditors, all property owned by the debtor, property claimed by the debtor to be exempt, and a statement of affairs of the debtor. The statement of affairs of a debtor engaged in business is much more detailed than the one filed by a debtor not in business.

Involuntary cases—commencement

Involuntary cases are commenced by one or more creditors filing a petition. If there are twelve or more creditors, the petition must be signed by at least three creditors whose unsecured claims are not contingent and aggregate at least $5,000. If there are fewer than twelve creditors, only one need sign the petition, but the $5,000 amount must still be met. Employees, insiders, and transferees of voidable transfers are not counted in determining the number of creditors. Insiders are persons such as relatives, partners of the debtor, directors and officers of the corporation involved. The subject of voidable transfers is discussed later in this chapter.

Creditors may commence involuntary proceedings in order to harass the debtor. To protect the debtor, the court may require the petitioning creditors to file a bond to indemnify the debtor. This bond will cover the amounts for which the petitioning creditors may have liability to the debtor. The liability may include court costs, attorney's fees, and damages caused by taking the debtor's property.

Until the court enters an order for relief in an involuntary case, the debtor may continue to operate his business and to use, acquire, and dispose of his property. However, the court may order an interim trustee appointed to take possession of the property and to operate the business. If the case is a liquidation proceeding, the appointment of the interim trustee is mandatory unless the debtor posts a bond guaranteeing the value of the property in his estate.

Since some debtors against whom involuntary proceedings are commenced are, in fact, not bankrupt, the debtor has a right to file an answer to the petition of the creditors and to deny the allegations of the petition. If the debtor does not file an answer, the court orders relief against the debtor. If an answer is filed, the court conducts a trial on the issues raised by the petition and the answer. Courts will order relief in an involuntary proceeding against the debtor only if it finds that the debtor is generally not paying his debts as they become due. Relief may also be ordered if, within 120 days before the filing of the petition, a custodian, receiver, or agent has taken possession of property of the debtor for the purpose of enforcing a lien against the debtor.

The meeting of creditors

In a voluntary case, the debtor has filed the required schedules with the petition. In an involuntary case, if the court orders relief, the debtor will be required to complete the same schedules as the debtor in a voluntary proceeding. From this point, the proceedings are identical. All parties are given notice of the order for relief. If the debtor owns real property, notice is usually filed in the public records of the county where the land is situated. The notice to creditors will include the date by which all claims are to be filed, and the date of a meeting of the creditors with the debtor. This meeting of creditors must be within a reasonable time after the order for relief. The debtor appears at the meeting with the creditors, and the creditors are allowed to question the debtor under oath. The court may also order a meeting of any equity security holders of the debtor.

At the meeting of creditors, the debtor may be examined by the creditors to ascertain if property has been omitted from the list of assets, if property has been conveyed in defraud of creditors, and other matters that may affect the right of the debtor to have his obligations discharged.

In liquidation cases, the first meeting of creditors includes the important step of electing a permanent trustee. This trustee will replace the interim trustee appointed by the court at the time the order for relief was entered. The law designates those creditors entitled to vote and the requirements for election of the trustee.

The trustee's powers and duties

The trustee is the representative of the estate and has the capacity to sue and to be sued. Trustees are authorized to employ professional persons such as attorneys, accountants, appraisers, and auctioneers and to deposit or invest the money of the estate during the proceedings. In making deposits or investments, the trustee must seek the maximum reasonable net return, taking into account the safety of the deposit or investment.

The statute has detailed provisions on the responsibilities of the trustee under the tax laws. As a general rule, the trustee has responsibility for filing tax returns for the estate. After the order for relief, income received by the estate is taxable to it and not to an individual debtor. The estate of a partnership or a corporation debtor is not a separate entity for tax purposes. While the technical requirements of the tax laws are beyond the scope of this text, it should be remembered that the bankruptcy laws contain detailed rules complementary to the Internal Revenue Code in bankruptcy cases, and both must be followed by the trustee.

The statutory duties of the trustee in liquidation proceedings are to: (1) collect and reduce to money the property of the estate; (2) account for all property received; (3) investigate the financial affairs of the debtor; (4) examine proofs of claims and object to the allowance of any claim that is improper; (5) oppose the discharge of the debtor if advisable; (6) furnish information requested by a party in interest; (7) file appropriate reports with the court and the taxing authorities, if a business is operated; and (8) make a final report and account and file it with the court.

Bankruptcy cases operate to stay other judicial or administrative proceedings against the debtor, and these stays of proceedings may operate to the detriment of a creditor or third party. For example, a stay would prevent a utility company from shutting off service. When the trustee continues to operate the debtor's business, it is frequently necessary to use, sell, or lease property of the debtor. In order to prevent irreparable harm to creditors and other third parties as a result of stays and the use, sale, or lease of the debtor's property, a trustee may be required to provide "adequate protection" to third parties. In some cases, adequate protection requires that the trustee make periodic cash payments to creditors. In others, the trustee may be required to provide a lien to the creditor. When the sale, lease, or rental of the debtor's property may decrease the value of an entity's interest in property held by the trustee, a creditor may be entitled to a lien on the proceeds of any sale, lease, or rental. The court is empowered to determine if the trustee has furnished adequate protection; and when the issue is raised, the burden of proof is on the trustee.

A trustee that is authorized to operate the business of the debtor is authorized to obtain unsecured credit and to incur debts in the ordinary course of business. These debts are paid as administrative expenses.

Executory contracts and unexpired leases

Bankrupt debtors are frequently parties to contracts that have not been performed. Also, they are often lessees of real property, and the leases usually cover long periods of time. The liability for future rent is generally limited to one year's rent or 15 percent of the unpaid rent, not to exceed three years' rent, whichever is greater.

As a general rule, the trustee is authorized, subject to court approval, to assume or to reject an executory contract or unexpired lease. If the contract or lease is rejected, the other party has a claim subject to some statutory limitations. A rejection by the trustee creates a prepetition claim for the rejected contract or lease debt subject to these limitations.

If the contract or lease is assumed, the trustee will perform the contract or assign it to someone else, and the estate will presumably receive the benefits. If the trustee assumes a contract or lease, he must cure any default by the debtor and provide adequate assurance of future performance. In shopping-center leases, adequate assurance includes protection against declines in percentage rents and preservation of the tenant mix.

A trustee may not assume an executory contract that requires the other party to make a loan, deliver equipment, or issue a security to the debtor. A party to a contract based on the financial strength of the debtor is not required to extend new credit to a debtor in bankruptcy.

Contracts and leases often have clauses prohibiting assignment of them. The law also prohibits the assignment of certain contract rights, such as those which are personal in nature. The trustee in bankruptcy is allowed to assume contracts, notwithstanding a clause prohibiting the assumption or assignment of the contract or lease. The trustee is not allowed to assume a contract if applicable nonbankruptcy law excuses the other party from performance to someone other than the debtor, unless the other party consents to the assumption.

The statute invalidates contract clauses that automatically terminate contracts or leases upon filing of a petition in bankruptcy or upon the assignment of the lease or contract. The law also invalidates contract clauses that give a party other than the debtor the right to terminate the contract upon assumption by the trustee or assignment by the debtor. Such clauses hamper rehabilitation efforts and are against public policy. They are not needed, because the court can require the trustee to provide adequate protection and can insure that the other party receives the benefit of its bargain.

Debtors are sometimes lessors instead of lessees. If the trustee rejects an unexpired lease of a debtor lessor, the tenant may treat the lease as terminated but may remain in possession for the balance of the lease. There is a similar provision for contract purchasers of real estate. They may treat the rejection as a termination, or they may remain in possession and make the payments due under the contract. A purchaser that treats a contract as terminated has a lien on the property to the extent of the purchase price paid.

If the trustee assigns a contract to a third party and the third party later breaches the contract, the trustee has no liability. This is a change of the common law in which an assignor is not relieved of his liability by an assignment. An assignment by a trustee in bankruptcy is, in effect, a novation if the assignment is valid.

Chapter 5

Chapter 5 of the bankruptcy law contains three subsections. The first deals with creditors and claims. It provides for filing proof of claims and for priorities among them. The second subsection is concerned with the debtor's duties and the effect of a discharge on the obligations of the debtor. This subsection details the exemptions available to debtors and the grounds for denying a discharge. Finally, Chapter 5 has several provisions dealing with the property of the bankruptcy estate. Its sections dealing with preferences, fraudulent transfers, and set-offs are of great importance. The discussions in this chapter are based on Chapter 5 and are applicable to all four types of proceedings.

Creditors and claims

Creditors are required to file proof of their claims if they are to share in the debtor's estate. Filed claims are allowed unless a party in interest objects. If an objection is filed, the court conducts a hearing to determine the validity of the claim. A claim may be disallowed if it is: (1) unenforceable because of usury, unconscionability, or failure of consideration, (2) for unmatured interest, (3) an insider's or attorney's and exceeds the reasonable value of the services rendered, (4) for unmatured alimony or child support, and (5) for rent or breach of an employment contract, and it exceeds the statutory limitations for such claims.

Illegality can be raised, because any defense available to the debtor is available to the trustee. Postpetition interest is not collectible, because interest stops accruing at the date of filing the petition. Bankruptcy operates as an acceleration of the principal due. From the date of filing, the amount of the claim is the total principal plus interest to that date.

Unreasonable attorney's fees and claims of insiders are disallowed because they encourage concealing assets or returning them to the debtor. Since alimony claims are not dischargeable in bankruptcy, there is no reason to allow a claim for postpetition alimony and child support.

The amount of rent that may be included in a claim is limited. The law is designed to compensate the landlord for his loss, but not to allow the claim to be so large that other creditors will not share in the estate. A landlord's damages are limited to the rent for the greater of one year or 15 percent of the remaining lease term, not to exceed three years. In liquidation cases, the time is measured from the earlier of the date of filing the petition and the date of surrender of possession. In cases filed under Chapters 9, 11, and 13, the claim is limited to three years' rent. Of course, these limitations are not applicable to rent owed by the trustee, an administrative expense for which the estate is liable.

Landlords often have a security deposit for rent. To the extent that the security deposit exceeds the rent allowed as a claim, it must be paid over to the trustee to be a part of the bankruptcy estate. If the security deposit is less than the claim, the landlord keeps the security deposit, and it will be applied in satisfaction of the claim. The limitations on claims for rent are applicable to bona fide leases, not to leases of real property, which are financing or security leases.

The limitation for damages resulting from termination of employment contracts is similar to the one for rent. Damages are limited to compensation for the year following the earlier of the date of the petition and that of the termination of employment.

Claims are sometimes contingent or otherwise unliquidated and uncertain. The law authorizes the court to estimate and to fix the amount of such claims, if necessary, to avoid undue delay in closing the estate. The same is true for equitable remedies such as specific performance. Courts will convert such remedies to dollar amounts and proceed to close the estate.

If a secured claim is undersecured—that is, if the debt exceeds the value of the collateral—the claim is divided into two parts. The claim is secured to the extent of the value of the collateral. It is an unsecured claim for the balance.

Payment of claims

In liquidation cases, the property available is first distributed among the priority claimants in the order established. These priorities are discussed in the next section. Second, property is then distributed to general unsecured creditors who file their claims on time. Third, payment is made to unsecured creditors who tardily file their claims. Fourth, distribution is made to holders of penalty, forfeiture, or punitive damage claims. Punitive penalties, including tax penalties, are subordinated to the first three classes of claims, as a matter of policy. Regular creditors should be paid before windfalls to persons and entities collecting penalties. Fifth, postpetition interest on prepetition claims is paid if any property is available to do so. After the interest is paid, any surplus goes to the debtor. Claims within a particular class are paid pro rata if the trustee is unable to pay them in full.

Priorities

The law establishes certain priorities in the payment of claims. The general order of priority is as follows:

1. Administrative expenses
2. Involuntary GAP creditors
3. Wages, salaries, and commissions
4. Contributions to employee benefit plans
5. Consumer deposits
6. Claims of governmental units for certain taxes

Administrative expenses include all costs of administering the debtor's estate, including taxes incurred by the estate. Typical costs include attorney's fees, appraiser's fees, and wages paid to persons employed to help preserve the estate.

The term "involuntary GAP creditor" describes a person who extends credit to the estate after the date of filing a petition under Chapter 11 and before a trustee is appointed or before the order for relief. Such claims include taxes incurred as the result of the conduct of business in this period.

The third class of priority is limited to amounts earned by an individual within 90 days of the filing of the petition or the cessation of the debtor's business, whichever occurred first. The priority is limited to $2,000 for each individual, but it includes vacation, severance, and sick leave pay as well as regular earnings. The employee's share of employment taxes is included in the third priority category, provided the wages and the employee's share of taxes have been paid in full. The category does not include fees paid to independent contractors.

CASE

P's are claims adjustors and attorneys who had rendered professional services to bankrupt insurance companies. They seek priority in the distribution of the bankrupt estate, contending that their fees for services qualify as wage claims.

ISSUE Do the fees qualify as wages for priority purposes?

DECISION No.

REASONS 1. Amounts due independent contractors are not within the wage claim priority.

2. The professional services were rendered as independent contractors. Priority status is limited to employees.

White v. State Ex Rel. Block, 597 P.2d 172 (Alaska) 1979.

The fourth priority recognizes that fringe benefits are an important part of many labor-management contracts. The priority is limited to claims for contributions to employee benefit plans, arising from services rendered within 120 days before commencement of the case or cessation of the debtor's business, whichever occurs first. The priority is limited to $2,000 multiplied by the number of employees less the amount paid under priority 3. The net effect is to limit the total priority for wages and employee benefits to $2,000 per employee.

The fifth priority was added in 1978 as an additional method of consumer protection. It protects consumers who have deposited money in connection with the purchase, lease, or rental of property or the purchase of services for personal, family, or household use that were not delivered or provided. The priority is limited to $900.00.

The sixth priority is for certain taxes. Priority is given to income taxes for a taxable year that ended on or before the date of filing the petition. The last due date of the return must have occurred not more than three years before the filing. Employment taxes and transfer taxes such as gift, estate, sale, and excise taxes are also given sixth-class priority. Again the transaction or event that gave rise to the tax must precede the petition date, and the return must have been due within three years. The bankruptcy law has several very technical aspects relating to taxation, and they must be carefully reviewed for tax returns filed by the trustee and claims for taxes.

After priority claims are paid, all other unsecured claims are paid a proportional share out of remaining assets; but usually there are no assets at this stage of the proceedings.

Exemptions

To give debtors a fresh start with some property, the law grants certain exemptions. Technically, all property of the debtor becomes property of the bankruptcy estate, but the debtor is then permitted to claim some of it exempt from the proceedings. That property is then returned to the debtor. Exemptions are granted by both federal laws and state and local laws.

CASE

The state of Alaska allowed an exemption for pictures belonging to the debtor not to exceed $300 in value. P, a debtor, owned a picture worth more than $300 and sought to recover $300 of the sale price when it was sold by the court. The creditors contended that the debtor was not entitled to any exemption for paintings worth more than $300.

ISSUE Is P entitled to $300 of the sale price?

DECISION Yes.

REASONS 1. Exemption laws emerged from bankruptcy law policies concerned with maintaining basic economic vitality in individual debtors and reasonably protecting creditors' rights to satisfaction of legally incurred debts.

2. Personal and household exemptions are designed to ensure that debtors will have necessary items for living in reasonable comfort and for earning a living.
3. In addition to useful household items, the exemption statutes also commonly apply to more personalized, arguably less necessary items such as family pictures, Bibles, wedding rings and other jewelry, books, historical and scientific collections, guns, church pews, and cemetery lots. The states also allow debtors and members of their families to keep all of their clothing or whatever is necessary. Alaska's limited value exemption for pictures thus represents a legislative judgment that such items are among the amenities of life in which a debtor may preserve at least a limited investment.
4. Exemption laws are remedial in character and should be liberally construed in favor of the debtor. A debtor's exemption rights in an item of property are not completely eliminated because that item's value exceeds the statutory allowance.
5. The exemption extends to the proceeds of a sale, otherwise the exemption is meaningless.

Gutterman v. First Nat. Bank of Anchorage, 597 P.2d 969 (Alaska) 1979.

The Bankruptcy Act exempts the following property:

1. Real property used as a residence, up to $7,500.
2. The debtor's interest, not to exceed $1,200, in one motor vehicle.
3. The debtor's interest, not to exceed $200 in any particular item, in household furnishings, wearing apparel, appliances, books, animals, crops, or musical instruments that are held primarily for the personal family or household use of the debtor and his dependents.
4. The debtor's interest in jewelry, not to exceed $500.
5. The debtor's interest in other property, not to exceed $400, plus any unused real property exemption.
6. The debtor's interest, not to exceed $750, in any implements, professional books, or tools of the trade of the debtor, or the trade of his dependents.
7. Unmatured life insurance contracts.
8. The cash value of life insurance, not to exceed $4,000.
9. Professionally prescribed health aids.
10. The debtor's rights to receive benefits such as Social Security, Unemployment Compensation, Public Assistance, disability benefits, alimony, child support and separate maintenance reasonably necessary, and payments of pension, profit-sharing, annuity, or similar plans.
11. The debtor's right to receive payment traceable to the wrongful death of an individual on whom the debtor was dependent or to life insurance on the life of such a person or to payments for personal injury not to exceed $7,500.

Every state has enacted statutes granting exemptions to persons domiciled there, and the exemptions vary greatly from state to state. In Texas, the total value of the homestead is exempt. Other states have very large exemptions. Some people move to California prior to filing, so that they may benefit from that state's $20,000 exemption. Among the lower exemptions, one state's allowance is $750. Individuals may claim the larger exemptions offered by their states if it is to their advantage to do so. In order to encourage states to raise their exemptions, the law provides that the federal exemptions will be available to debtors of states unless a state specifically passes a law denying its residents the larger exemptions.

As a general rule, exempt property is not liable during or after the case for any debts that arise before the commencement of the case. Exceptions to the general rule apply to tax claims, alimony, child support, and separate maintenance. Exempt property can be used to collect such debts after the proceeding. The discharge in bankruptcy does not prevent enforcement of valid liens against exempt property; however, judicial liens and nonpossessory, nonpurchase money security interests in household goods, wearing apparel, professional books, tools, and professionally prescribed health aids may be avoided. A debtor may redeem such tangible personal property from a lien securing a dischargeable consumer debt by paying the lien holder the amount of the secured claim. Exempt property is free of such liens after the proceedings. Waivers of exemptions are unenforceable, to prevent creditors from attempting to deny debtors the necessary property to gain a fresh start.

Debts that are not discharged

Although the purpose of bankruptcy proceedings and especially those under Chapter 7 is to eliminate the debts of the debtor, not all debts are discharged. A discharge in bankruptcy does not discharge an individual debtor from the following debts:

1. Certain taxes and customs duties.
2. Debts for obtaining money, property, services, or credit by false pretenses, false representations, or actual fraud.
3. Unscheduled debts.
4. Debts for fraud or defalcation while acting in a fiduciary capacity and debts created by embezzlement or larceny.
5. Alimony, child support, and separate maintenance.
6. Liability for willful and malicious torts.
7. Tax penalties if the tax is not dischargeable.
8. Student loans less than five years old.
9. Debts owed before a previous bankruptcy to which discharge was denied for grounds other than the six-year rule.

The taxes that are not discharged are the same ones that receive priority under the second, third, and sixth categories discussed in the section on priorities. If the debtor failed to file a return, filed it beyond its last due date, or filed a fraudulent return, those taxes are not discharged. One of the most common tax liabilities that is not discharged in bankruptcy is the one for unpaid withholding and social security taxes.

CASE

According to the Internal Revenue Code, any person who is required to collect and turn over federal taxes must do so or be liable for an amount equal to the taxes. Sotelo was the principal officer and majority shareholder of a corporation. He failed to turn over taxes withheld from wages of employees of the corporation. The corporation and Sotelo were both adjudicated bankrupt. The bankruptcy court held that Sotelo was personally liable for the taxes and that the liability was not dischargeable in bankruptcy.

ISSUE Is the debt for unpaid withholding taxes on employees dischargeable?

DECISION No.

REASONS

1. The statute leaves no doubt about the nondischargeability of "taxes" that the bankrupt has collected or withheld from others as required by the laws of the United States or any state but has not paid over.
2. The liability was not imposed for a failure to collect taxes, but for failure to turn them over to the government.
3. The debt was a tax, not a penalty for failure to pay taxes.
4. The legislative history of the law indicates that a principal purpose of the legislation was to establish a three-year limitation on taxes that would be nondischargeable in bankruptcy. Under former law, there was no such time limitation. The new section ensured the discharge of most taxes. With regard to unpaid withholding taxes, however, the three-year limitation was made inapplicable.

United States v. Sotelo, 98 S.Ct. 1795 (1978).

For a debt to be denied discharge because of fraud, the creditor must have placed reasonable reliance on a false statement in writing. The denial to unscheduled debts means that the claim of any creditor who is not listed or who does not learn of the proceedings in time to file a claim is not discharged. The bankrupt, under such circumstances, remains liable for it unless he can prove that the creditor did have knowledge of the proceedings in time to file a claim. Proof of actual knowledge is required; and although such knowledge often exists, care should be taken to list all creditors, so that all claims will unquestionably be discharged.

Tort liability claims based on negligence are discharged. Tort liability claims arising from willful and malicious acts are not discharged. A judgment arising out of an assault and battery is not discharged.

The provision denying discharge to student loans is new. It seeks to give creditors and the government five years to collect student loans. There is an exception if the debtor is able to convince the court that undue hardship on him and his dependents will result if the student loan debt is not discharged.

Grounds for denying discharge

A discharge in bankruptcy is a privilege, not a right. Therefore, in addition to providing that certain debts are not discharged, the Bankruptcy Act specifies the following grounds for denying an individual debtor a discharge (remember that only individuals may be discharged):

1. Fraudulent transfers.
2. Inadequate records.
3. Commission of a bankruptcy crime.
4. Failure to explain a loss of assets or deficiency of assets.
5. Refusing to testify in the proceedings or to obey a court order.
6. Any of the above within one year in connection with another bankruptcy case of an insider.
7. Another discharge within six years.
8. Approval by the court of a waiver of discharge.

The first three grounds for denying discharge are predicated on wrongful conduct by the debtor in connection with the case. Fraudulent transfers involve acts such as removing, destroying, or concealing property with the intent to hinder, delay, or defraud creditors or the trustee. The conduct must occur within one year preceding the case, or it may occur after the case is commenced.

A debtor is also denied a discharge if he has concealed, destroyed, mutilated, falsified, or failed to keep or preserve any books and records relating to his financial condition. A debtor is required to keep records from which his financial condition may be ascertained, unless the act or failure is justified.

Bankruptcy crimes are generally related to the proceedings. They include a false oath, the use or presentation of a false claim, or bribery in connection with the proceedings and with the withholding of records.

The six-year rule, which allows a discharge only if another discharge has not been ordered within six years, extends to Chapter 11 and Chapter 13 proceedings, as well as to those under Chapter 7. Discharge under Chapter 11 will bar another discharge for six years, and confirmation of a plan under Chapter 13 generally has the same effect. It does not have that effect if all of the unsecured claims were paid in full, or if 70 percent of them were paid and the debtor has used his best efforts to pay the debts.

Either a creditor or the trustee may object to the discharge. The court may order the trustee to examine the facts to see if grounds exist for the denial of the discharge. Courts are also granted the authority to revoke a discharge within one year if it was obtained by fraud on the court.

The Estate

Property of the estate

The bankruptcy estate consists of all legal or equitable interests of the debtor in property, wherever located. The property may be tangible or intangible and includes causes of action. All property is included in the estate to begin with, but the debtor may exempt portions entitled to exemption, as we previously discussed.

The estate includes property that the trustee recovers by using his power to avoid prior transactions. It also includes property inherited by the debtor or received as a beneficiary of life insurance within 180 days of the petition. Proceeds, products, offspring, rents, and profits generated by or coming from property in the estate are also part of the estate.

Except as previously noted, property acquired by the debtor after commencement of the case—including earnings from employment—belongs to the debtor. Property held in trust for the benefit of the debtor under a spendthrift trust does not become a part of the estate. Other restrictions on the transfer of the property of the debtor are invalid, and property subject to such restrictions is a part of the bankruptcy estate.

The trustee and the estate

A trustee in bankruptcy has several rights and powers with respect to the property of the debtor. First of all, the trustee has a judicial lien on the property, just as if the trustee were a creditor. Second, the trustee has the rights and powers of a judgment creditor who obtained a judgment against the debtor on the date of the adjudication of bankruptcy and who had an execution issued that was returned unsatisfied.

Third, the trustee has the rights of a bona fide purchaser of the real property of the debtor as of the date of the petition. Finally, the trustee has the rights of an actual unsecured creditor to avoid any transfer of the debtor's property and to avoid any obligation incurred by the debtor that is voidable under any federal or state law. As a result of these rights, the trustee is able to set aside transfers of property and to eliminate the interests of other parties where creditors or the debtor could do so.

The trustee also has the power to avoid certain liens of others on the property of the debtor. Liens that first become effective on the bankruptcy or insolvency of the debtor are voidable. As a general rule, liens that are not perfected or enforceable on the date of the petition against a bona fide purchaser of the property are also voidable. Assume that a seller or creditor has an unperfected lien on goods in the hands of the debtor on the date the petition is filed. The lien is perfected later. That lien is voidable if it could not be asserted against a good-faith purchaser of the goods. Liens for rent and for distress for rent are also voidable.

The law imposes certain limitations on all these rights and powers of the trustee. A purchase money security interest under Article 9 of the code may be perfected after the petition is filed if it is perfected within ten days of delivery of the property. Such a security interest cannot be avoided by the trustee if properly perfected.

The rights and powers of the trustee, like those of a seller of goods in the ordinary course of business, allow him to reclaim goods if the debtor was insolvent when he received them. The seller must demand the goods back within 10 days, and the right to reclaim is subject to any superior rights of secured creditors. Courts may deny reclamation and protect the seller by giving him priority as an administrative expense.

Preferences

One of the goals of bankruptcy proceedings is to provide an equitable distribution of a debtor's property among his creditors. To achieve this goal, the trustee in bankruptcy is allowed to recover transfers that constitute a preference of one creditor over another. As one judge said, "A creditor who dips his hand in a pot which he knows will not go round must return what he receives, so that all may share." To constitute a recoverable preference the transfer must (1) have been made by an insolvent debtor; (2) have been made to a creditor for, or on account of, an antecedent debt owed by the debtor before the transfer; (3) have been made within 90 days of the filing of the bankruptcy petition; and (4) enable the creditor to receive a greater percentage of his claim than he would receive under a distribution from the bankruptcy estate in a liquidation proceeding.

Insofar as the time period is concerned, there is an exception when the transfer is to an insider. Then, the trustee may avoid the transfer if it occurred within one year of the date of filing the petition, provided the insider had reasonable cause to believe the debtor was insolvent at the time of the transfer.

A debtor is presumed to be insolvent during the 90-day period prior to the filing of the petition. Any person contending that the debtor was solvent has the burden of coming forward with evidence to prove solvency. Once credible evidence is introduced, the party with the benefit of the presumption of insolvency has the burden of persuasion on the issue.

Recoverable preferences include not only payments of money but also the transfer of property as payment of, or as security for, a prior indebtedness. Since the law is limited to debts, payments by the debtor of tax liabilities are exempt from the preference provision and are not recoverable. A mortgage or pledge may be set aside as readily as direct payments. A pledge or mortgage can be avoided if received within the immediate 90-day period prior to the filing of the petition in bankruptcy, provided it was obtained as security for a previous debt.

Payment of a fully secured claim does not constitute a preference and, therefore, may not be recovered. Transfers of property for a contemporaneous consideration may not be set aside, because there is a corresponding asset for the new liability. A mortgage given to secure a contemporaneous loan is valid even when the mortgagee took the security with knowledge of the debtor's insolvency. An insolvent debtor has a right to attempt to extricate himself, as far as possible, from his financial difficulty. If the new security is personal property, it must be perfected within ten days after the security interest attaches.

The law also creates an exception for transfers in the ordinary course of business or in the ordinary financial affairs of persons not in business. The payment of such debts within 45 days after they are incurred is not recoverable if the payment is made in the ordinary course of business. This exception covers ordinary debt payments such as utility bills. The law on preferences is directed at unusual transfers and payments and not to those occurring promptly in the ordinary course of the debtor's affairs.

Set-offs

Any person owing money to the debtor may set-off against the amount owed any sum that the debtor owes him, provided such amount would be allowable as a claim. To the extent of this set-off, he becomes a preferred creditor, but he is legally entitled to this preference. This, however, does not apply when the claim against the debtor has been purchased or created for the purpose of preferring the creditor. Assume that a bank has loaned a bankrupt $2,000 and that the bankrupt has $1,500 on deposit at the time of bankruptcy. The bank is a preferred creditor to the extent of the deposit. This set-off will be allowed unless the evidence discloses that the deposit was made for the purpose of preferring the bank. In that case, the deposit becomes a part of the bankrupt estate because of the collusion.

Since the filing of the petition in bankruptcy operates as a stay of all proceedings, the right of set-off operates at the time of final distribution of the estate. Since the law allows the trustee to use the funds of the debtor with court approval, parties who wish to exercise the right of set-off should seek "adequate protection."

The right of set-off will usually be exercised by a creditor against a deposit that has been made within 90 days of the filing of a petition in bankruptcy. Quite frequently, there are several such deposits, and there also may have been several payments on the debt during the 90-day period. As a result of these variables, the application of offset principles is sometimes difficult.

The law seeks to prohibit a creditor from improving his position during the 90-day period. It does so by limiting the amount that may be set-off. This amount is calculated by determining the amount by which, on the first day of the 90-day period, the claim against the debtor exceeds the amount on deposit. The insufficiency is the amount by which the debt owed exceeds the amount on deposit.

Assume that a petition in bankruptcy was filed on September 2. On June 1, the debtor owes $1,000 to the creditor, and the debtor deposits with the creditor a total of $500. On September 1, the debtor owes the same $1,000, but the deposit totals $1,000. The set-off is limited to $500, which was the amount of insufficiency on the first day of the 90-day period.

Fraudulent transfers and obligations

A transfer of property by a debtor may be fraudulent under federal or state law. The trustee may proceed under either to set aside a fraudulent conveyance. Under federal law, a fraudulent conveyance is a transfer within one year of the filing of the petition, with the intent to hinder, delay, or defraud creditors. Under state law, the period may be longer and is usually within the range of two to five years.

Fraudulent intent may be inferred from the fact that the consideration is unfair, inadequate, or nonexistent. Solvency or insolvency at the time of the transfer is significant, but it is not controlling. Fraudulent intent exists when the transfer makes it impossible for the creditors to be paid in full or for the creditors to use legal remedies that would otherwise be available.

The intent to hinder, delay, or defraud creditors may also be implied. Such is the case when the debtor is insolvent and makes a transfer for less than a full and adequate value. Fraudulent intent is present if the debtor was insolvent on the date of the transfer when the obligation was incurred, or if the debtor became insolvent as a result of the transfer or obligation.

CASE

An insolvent corporation sold its only asset to a director of the corporation for a price equal to approximately 50 percent of its fair market value. The sale was made to prevent the firm's creditors from attaching the asset, to obtain payment of their claims. The creditors filed suit to set aside the sale and to cause the asset to be sold at a judicial sale.

ISSUE Was the sale fraudulent under the Uniform Fraudulent Conveyances Act?

DECISION Yes.

REASONS

1. Under the Uniform Fraudulent Conveyances Act, certain conveyances are fraudulent regardless of the presence or absence of any intent to defraud.
2. Under the act, every conveyance made and every obligation incurred by a person who is or will be thereby rendered insolvent is fraudulent to creditors if the conveyance is made or the obligation incurred without fair consideration.
3. Fair consideration under the act is defined generally as consideration that fairly represents the value of the property transferred. And when it works against creditors, consideration that is merely good and valuable will not support a conveyance that will render the grantor insolvent.
4. Here the sale was not for fair consideration, and the debtor was insolvent; therefore, the conveyance to the purchaser director was fraudulent as a matter of law.

Montana Ass'n. of Credit Management v. Herbert, 593 P.2d 1059 (Mont.) 1979.

If the debtor is engaged in business or is about to become so, the fraudulent intent will be implied when the transfer leaves the businessperson with an unreasonably small amount of capital. The businessperson may be solvent; nevertheless, he has made a fraudulent transfer if the net result of the transfer leaves him with an unreasonably small amount of capital, provided the transfer was without fair consideration. Whether or not the remaining capital is unreasonably small is a question of fact.

The trustee may also avoid transfer or obligation when a debtor intends to incur obligations beyond the debtor's ability to repay as they mature. Assume that a woman is about to enter business and that she plans to incur debts in the business. Because of her concern that she may be unable to meet these potential obligations, she transfers all her property to her husband, without consideration. Such a transfer may be set aside as fraudulent. The requisite intent is supplied by the factual situation at the time of the transfer and the state of mind of the transferor. The actual financial condition of the debtor in such a case is not controlling but does shed some light on the intent factor and state of mind of the debtor.

The trustee of a partnership debtor may avoid transfers of partnership property to partners if the debtor was or thereby became insolvent. This rule was made to prevent a partnership's preferring partners who are also creditors over other partners. Such transfers may be avoided if they occurred within one year of the date of filing the petition.

If a transferee is liable to the trustee only because the transfer was in defraud of creditors, the law limits the transferee's liability. To the extent that the transferee does give value in good faith, the transferee has a lien on the property. For the purpose of defining value in the fraudulent transfer situation, the term includes property or the satisfaction or securing of a present or existing debt. It does not include an unperformed promise to support the debtor or a relative of a debtor.

REVIEW QUESTIONS AND PROBLEMS

1. What is the major purpose of the law of bankruptcy?
2. To what extent does a discharge in bankruptcy cause harm to the debtor's credit rating? Explain.
3. The bankruptcy law has two approaches to the problems of debtors and four types of proceedings. Describe these approaches and list the four types of proceedings.
4. Bankruptcy proceedings may be either voluntary or involuntary. Give an example of an individual that may not be subjected to involuntary proceedings.
5. Name three types of businesses that are not entitled to have liquidation proceedings.
6. A restaurant went through voluntary bankruptcy proceedings. Later, it resumed business and acquired assets. Are the creditors at the time of the bankruptcy proceedings entitled to collect the debts scheduled in the proceedings from these assets? Explain.
7. Is a bankruptcy estate required to file a tax return? If so, who must file it?
8. What is the amount of *unsecured* debts that a person may owe and still be entitled to follow the adjustment of individual debt procedures? *Secured* debts? What is the minimum amount that must be owed for involuntary proceedings?
9. What are the major purposes of the meeting of creditors?
10. The Popcorn Shop entered into a twenty-year lease at an annual rental of $4,000 per year. Two years later, the lessee commenced voluntary liquidation proceedings. Assuming that the rent was current to the date of filing, how much is the lessor entitled to claim in the proceedings? Explain. If there is a security deposit, may the lessor retain it?
11. Senator Klaghorn proved in court that CAN TV committed libel with malice against him. The case resulted in a judgment against CAN TV, which filed for bankruptcy. Will a discharge in bankruptcy relieve CAN TV from its debt to the senator? Why?
12. Heavily in debt, a woman's only assets were her residence, in which her equity was approximately $5,000, an automobile worth $300, and $500 in cash. If she goes through bankruptcy, which of the foregoing items will she be able to retain? Explain.
13. Tracy filed a petition in bankruptcy on November 2. The Conley Bank seeks to establish its right of set-off, based upon the following facts: On August 1, Tracy owed the bank $2,000; Tracy's deposits totaled $2,000. One month later, Tracy's debt was still $2,000, but his deposits had been reduced to $1,000. On September 10, Tracy's debt remained the same, but his deposits totaled only $400. On November 1, Tracy's debt was still $2,000, but he had increased his deposits to $2,000. What is the maximum amount of set-off to which the bank is entitled? Why?
14. On August 5, Barney made purchases at a store in the amount of $1,000. Receiving the bill while insolvent, he made payment in full. Three weeks later, Barney filed a petition in bankruptcy. The trustee sued to recover the $1,000, contending that the payment was a preferential transfer. Should the trustee succeed? Why?

Irene Springer

V

Property

28

General Principles of the Law of Property

The term *property* is meaningless unless it is associated with people or with legal entities that qualify as persons. Some of the terms frequently used in expressing this association are *ownership, title,* and *possession.* The word *owner* usually describes someone who possesses all of the rights or interests associated with the thing involved. The word *title* is often used synonymously with *ownership. Title* is also used to signify the method by which ownership is acquired, as by a transfer of title. It may also be used to indicate the evidence by which ownership is established—a written instrument called a title, as a car title. Thus the word *title* has a variety of meanings, depending upon the context.

The word *possession* is equally difficult to define accurately. Its meaning is also dependent somewhat on the context in which it is used. Possession implies the concept of physical control by a person over property and the personal and mental relationship to it. While it is physically possible to possess a watch or a ring, it is obviously physically impossible to possess one thousand acres of land in the same manner. Yet the word *possession* as a legal term is used in both instances. Possession describes not only physical control but the power to obtain physical control by legal sanctions, if necessary.

In the early law, property was thought of as a thing that could be touched, possessed, and delivered. As the law of property developed, courts began to recognize that property was more accurately described as the "bundle of rights" a person had in respect to a thing. Today, property is thought of as an object or a thing over which someone exercises legal rights.

Defining property as a "bundle of rights" enables courts and the law to develop a variety of interests in property. A person may possess all of the bundle of rights in relation to a thing, in which case he is the only owner. On the other hand, the bundle of rights may be divided among several people, in which case there is incomplete ownership by any one person. The owner of a tract of land authorizes the local public utility companies to install power and telephone lines through his land. The utility companies are granted what is called an *easement,* which is a property right. As a result, the owner has less than the full bundle of rights, and the title is subject to an *encumbrance.*

One other fact of life must be recognized when studying the law of property. There can be no property rights without a government and a legal system to create and enforce them. Private property rights cannot exist without some method of keeping the bundle of rights for the true owner and for restoring these rights to him if he is deprived of them. It should also be recognized that no one person has a complete bundle of rights, since the law limits private property rights and the use of private property to some extent in the public interest. The owner of land may not use it in violation of the local zoning ordinance. The owner of an automobile may not use it contrary to the law without penalty. Much of our legal system is designed to provide a means of creating, transferring, and limiting the bundle of rights that individuals possess in relation to land, movable objects, or things or intangibles—which we collectively call property.

Classifications

From the standpoint of its physical characteristics, property is classified as either personal property or real property. Land and things affixed to, or growing upon, the land come under the heading of *real property.* All other property is said to be *personal property.* In many ways, the law treats personal property differently from real property. Chapter 29 covers the special rules of law applicable to personal property, with emphasis on bailments. Chapter 30 discusses many of the legal concepts applicable to real estate, and chapter 31 covers real estate transactions. The material in this chapter is generally applicable both to personal and real property.

Personal property may be classified as either tangible or intangible. The term *tangible personal property* includes objects such as goods. The term *intangible personal property* refers to things such as accounts receivable, good will, patents, and trademarks. Intangible personal property has value, as tangible property has, and each can be transferred.

The term *chattel* is used to describe personal property generally, but chattels may also be classified as *chattels real* and *chattels personal.* Chattels real describes an interest in land, such as a leasehold; chattels personal is applied to movable personal property.

When the term *chattel* is used in connection with intangible personal property, the property is referred to as *chattels personal in action.* A chattel personal in action—or *chose in action,* as it is frequently called—is something to which one has a right to possession, but concerning which he may be required to bring some legal action in order ultimately to enjoy possession. A contract right may be said to be a chose in action because a lawsuit may be necessary to obtain the rights under the contract. A negotiable instrument is a common form of chose in action. Although the instrument itself may be said to be property, in reality it is simply evidence of a right to money, and it may be necessary to maintain an action to reduce the money to possession.

The distinction between real and personal property

The distinction between real and personal property, significant in a variety of situations, is important in determining the law applicable to a transaction that has contact with more than one state. Such issues are known as conflict-of-laws problems.

As a general rule, conflict of laws principles provide that the law of the situs—the law of the state where real property is located—determines all legal questions concerning real property. Legal issues concerning conflict of laws relating to personal property are not so easily resolved. Conflict of laws rules may refer to the law of the owner's domicile to resolve some questions and to the law of the state with the most significant contacts with the property to resolve others. The law of the situs of the property is also used to resolve some legal issues. Therefore, the description of property as real or personal has a significant impact on the determination of the body of substantive law that is used to decide legal issues concerning the property.

In most states, real and personal property are handled under different rules of law and procedures when their owner dies. Insofar as inheritance is concerned, however, many modern statutes abolish any distinction between the two.

During the lifetime of the owner, the distinction between real and personal property is significant, since the methods of transferring them are substantially different. Formal instruments such as deeds are required to transfer an interest in land, whereas few formalities are required in the case of personal property. A bill of sale may be used in selling personal property; but it is not generally required, and it does not, in any event, involve the technicalities of a deed. The transfer of personal property is, as a rule, quite simply accomplished (a motor vehicle transfer may require the delivery of a certificate of title) whereas formality is required to transfer real property.

Systems for taxing real estate are different from those for taxing personal property in many states. Property taxes on real estate are very significant in every state, while personal property taxes often are less significant. Typical of the issues that may arise are those relating to mobile homes. Is a mobile home that is placed on a foundation real estate and thus subject to real estate taxation, or is it personal property? Similar questions make it apparent that parties to various transactions and courts are frequently called upon to label property as either real or personal. If the issue is likely to arise, it should always be covered in agreements.

Fixtures

When property has characteristics of both personal and real property, it is commonly referred to as a fixture, an article of personal property that has become attached, annexed, or affixed to real property. It is personal property, such as a furnace or an air conditioner, that has become part of the real property. The question of whether or not an item is a fixture and thus part of the real estate arises in determining: (1) the value of real estate for tax purposes; (2) whether or not a sale of the real estate included the item of property in question; (3) whether or not the item of property is a part of the security given by a mortgagor of the real estate to a mortgagee; and (4) whether the item belongs to the owner of the building or to the tenant on termination of a lease. Fixture issues also arise under Article 9 of the Uniform Commercial Code in disputes between secured creditors and persons with an interest in the land. The UCC provides that no security interest exists in "goods incorporated into a structure in the manner of lumber, bricks, tile, cement, glass, metal work and the like." A party with a security interest in such goods loses it when the goods are incorporated into the real estate.

If property is a fixture: (1) it is included in the value of real estate for tax purposes; (2) it is sold, and title to it passes with the real estate; (3) it is a part of the security covered by a mortgage; and (4) it belongs to the landlord owner, not to the tenant on termination of a lease. Of course, the lease itself may govern the rights of the parties to the property, and the agreement may be contrary to these general rules.

CASE

The state of New Jersey sought to tax as real property cranes used in the loading and unloading of ships designed to carry freight in containers. These large cranes were mounted and movable on tracks at the pier. Each crane weighed 1,000,000 pounds and required special concrete piles for the base of the piers. Each crane was 50 feet wide and stood 170 feet above the rail. The boom could be raised to 245 feet. Complex electrical systems were required for operation of the cranes. The cranes were movable by barge.

ISSUE Were the cranes fixtures and thus taxable as part of the real estate?

DECISION No.

REASONS

1. The test is whether removal or severance of particular goods or chattels will result in material injury to the realty. The meaning of "material injury" is irreparable or serious physical damage. Serious physical damage to property occurs with the removal of something essential to its support.
2. Fixtures include only chattels that, if removed, would do irreparable or serious physical injury or damage to the freehold.
3. The cranes were taxable as machinery and equipment but not as real estate.

City of Bayonne v. Port Jersey Corp., 399 A.2d 649 (N.J.) 1979.

What is a fixture? Tests

Courts use several tests in deciding whether or not an item of personal property has become a part of the real estate, so that it is a fixture. These tests are usually described as the annexation, adaptation, and intention tests.

Annexation test

The common law required the chattel to be "let into" or "united" to the land. The test of annexation alone is inadequate, for many things attached to the soil or buildings are not fixtures, and many things not physically attached to the soil or buildings are considered fixtures. Articles of furniture substantially fastened but easily removed are not necessarily fixtures. Physical annexation may be only for the purpose of more convenient use. On the other hand, machinery that has been annexed but detached for repairs or other temporary reasons may still be considered a fixture, although severed.

Doors, windows, screens, storm windows, and the like, although readily detachable, are generally considered fixtures because they are an integral part of the building and pertain to its function. The mode and degree of attachment and whether the article can be removed without material injury to the article, building, or land are often important considerations in determining whether the article is a fixture. Electric ranges connected to a building by a plug or vent pipe are not fixtures, but the removal of wainscoting, wood siding, fireplace mantels, and water systems would cause a material injury to the building and land; therefore, these items are fixtures.

Adaptation test

Because the annexation test alone is inadequate to determine what is a fixture, the adaptation test has been developed. Adaptation means that the article is used in promoting the purpose for which the land is used. Thus, if an article is placed upon, or annexed to, land to improve it, make it more valuable, and extend its use, it is a fixture. Pipes, pumps, and electric motors for an irrigation system are chattels that may be adapted to become fixtures. This test alone is not adequate because rarely is an article attached or placed upon land except to advance the purpose for which the land is to be used.

Intention test

Annexation and adaptation as tests to determine whether a chattel has become realty are only part of the more inclusive test of intention. Annexation and adaptation are evidence of an intention to make a chattel a fixture; however, there may be a clear intent that chattels attached and adapted are not to become fixtures. If the intent of the parties is clear, property that would otherwise become a part of the real estate may remain the personal property of another.

CASE

P claims ownership of certain gasoline dispensing equipment—two gasoline pumps, one 3,000-gallon gasoline storage tank, one 1,000-gallon gasoline storage tank, and a one-half-horsepower air compressor—located on D's real property, consisting essentially of a grocery store and service station known as Marley's Store. D claims these items are fixtures, title to which passed to them when they purchased the realty on which the items are located. P claimed that it installed the equipment under an agreement that allowed P to remove it whenever P's gasoline was no longer sold on the premises.

ISSUE Is the equipment a fixture and part of the real estate?

DECISION No.

REASONS

1. As a general rule, whatever is attached to the land is understood to be a part of the realty; but as this depends to some extent upon circumstances, the rights involved must always be subject to explanation by evidence. Whether a thing attached to the land is a fixture or chattel personal depends upon the agreement of the parties, express or implied.
2. A building or other fixture that is ordinarily a part of the realty is held to be personal property when placed on the land of another by contract or consent of the owner.
3. A licensee is one who is given simple permission to erect buildings or make other improvements on the land of another but is not granted any estate or term of years in the land. Buildings or other improvements erected by licensees do not become part of the realty. They remain the personal property of the licensee.
4. Here, there was an agreement that the equipment was to remain P's personal property, notwithstanding affixation to the realty.

Lee-Moore Oil Co. v. Cleary. 245 S.E.2d 720 (N.C.) 1978.

In addition to annexation and adaptation as evidence of an intention, the following situations and circumstances also imply intention: (1) the kind and character of the article affixed; (2) purpose and use for which the annexation has been made; and (3) relation and situation of the parties making the annexation. The relation of landlord and tenant suggests that items such as showcases, acquired and used by the tenant, are not intended to become permanently part of the real property. Such property, called trade fixtures, is an exception to the general rule of fixtures because they are generally intended to be removed by the tenant at the end of the lease.

Multiple ownership

There are three distinct methods by which two or more people may own property at the same time.

1. Tenancy in common.
2. Joint tenancy or tenancy by the entireties. A tenancy by the entireties is a joint tenancy in real estate held between spouses. It is recognized in some states.
3. Community property. Limited to only a few states.

Several states have modified the common law characteristics of these forms of ownership, so it is essential that each state's law be consulted for the technicalities of these tenancies.

The main distinction between a tenancy in common and a joint tenancy is the effect of death on the tenancy. In the event of the death of a tenant in common, his or her share in the property passes to the executor named in the will or to the administrator of the deceased's estate. If property is held in joint tenancy, the interest of a deceased owner automatically passes to the surviving joint owner. Such property is not subject to probate or to the debts of the deceased joint tenant. Thus joint tenancy with the right of survivorship passes the title of the deceased by operation of law to the survivor or survivors, free of the claims of anyone else except for taxes that may be due.

Both joint tenancy and tenancy in common ownership may include two or more persons who may or may not be related. In tenancy in common, the share of the tenants may differ. One may own an undivided two-thirds; the other an undivided one-third. In joint tenancy, the interests must not only be equal, but they must be created at the same time. This requirement is sometimes described as the unities of title and possession.

In some states, property acquired by either spouse after the marriage is community property. While there are slight deviations in the approach to community property, such laws usually provide that the husband shall have the management and control of community personal property, just as if he were the sole owner. He may not transfer more than one-half of it by will; the other half automatically passes to his widow. Community property laws often provide additional limitations on the disposition of community property real estate. The usual requirement is that the wife must join in any conveyance of real estate, but not personal property.

Special aspects of joint tenancy

When there is a question about which form of ownership exists in any specific case, the law usually favors property passing by will or intestacy, rather than its passing by right of survivorship. Courts do not find that property is held in joint tenancy with the right of survivorship unless there is a contract between the two co-owners clearly stating that such is the case and that the right of survivorship is to apply. Bank signature cards and stock certificates that use the term *joint tenancy* or "with the right of survivorship" create such a contract, as does the language "as joint tenants and not as tenants in common." In most states the contract must be signed by both parties to be effective. Failure to use the proper language or have a properly executed contract results in a tenancy in common.

CASE

The deceased had purchased a certificate of deposit from a bank and had provided that ownership was in his and his nephew's name. The nephew did not know of the joint ownership of the certificate until after his uncle died, and the nephew admitted that he had not signed a signature card. The bank paid the proceeds of the certificate to the nephew, and the executor of the deceased's estate sought to recover the funds.

ISSUE Must a signature card be signed by all the parties in order to create a joint tenancy in a bank certificate of deposit?

DECISION Yes.

REASON Under the statute, a signed agreement is necessary to create rights of survivorship in the deposit.

In re estate of White, 282 N.E.2d 235 (Ill.) 1972.

Several additional aspects of holding property in joint tenancy frequently result in litigation. First of all, joint tenancy is often used as a substitute for a will. A party wishing to leave property to another on death sometimes puts the property in joint tenancy. Is a present gift intended? Does the new joint tenant have the right to share in the income of the property prior to the death of the original owner? Such issues are frequently litigated.

A similar issue arises when one person in ill health or incapacitated adds another person's name to a savings or a checking account in order to allow the latter to pay bills and handle the former's business transactions. The signature card often provides for a joint tenancy. Was a joint tenancy or mere agency intended? Joint tenancy arrangements are frequently challenged successfully on the ground that the right of survivorship was not intended.

Another difficulty involves describing the property held in joint tenancy. Frequently, a contract covering a safety deposit box will provide that it be held in joint tenancy. Does such a contract cover the contents of the box as well? If two people hold a safety deposit box in joint tenancy, and the box contains $20,000 in cash, most courts would hold that the cash was not held in joint tenancy.

Another disadvantage of the joint tenancy arrangement is the ease with which it may be severed or terminated. Each joint tenant has the power to terminate the right of survivorship by a simple transfer or conveyance of his interest to a third party. The severance of the unities of title and possession converts the joint tenancy to a tenancy in common.

CASE

A warranty deed dated November 6, 1958 conveyed 560 acres of farmland to P and D "as joint tenants and not as tenants in common with the right of survivorship." In 1973, P filed suit to partition the land equally between them. D objected, contending that partition would deny the right of survivorship to which he was entitled and that the right of survivorship was indestructible.

ISSUE Is property held in joint tenancy subject to partition?

DECISION Yes.

REASONS
1. Once joint title in real estate has been established, partition may be had as a matter of law.
2. Joint tenancy may be terminated or severed by any act that destroys one or more of its unities, and it may be severed also by the act of joint tenants in destroying unity of possession, as by partition. A joint tenant's act destroying one or more of the coexisting unities necessary to existence of joint tenancy operates as a severance of the joint tenancy and extinguishes the right of survivorship.

Yunghans v. O'Toole 258 N.W.2d 810 (NEB.) 1977.

Finally, joint tenancy property creates many gift and estate tax problems. The creation of a joint tenancy is generally a taxable gift, even if the joint tenants are husband and wife. The fact that a taxable gift has occurred may result in lower transfer taxes as well as higher ones.

Wills, Estates, and Trusts

Perhaps no problem associated with the ownership of property is of greater significance than the various methods available for disposing of that property on death. Although the methods and techniques for distributing property on death have always been of considerable importance, their significance is greatly increased today because of the very substantial death taxes imposed by both federal and state governments. As a result of these death taxes, associated income tax problems, and other related concerns, specialists are actively engaged in *estate planning.*

A person who dies without leaving a will is said to die *intestate.* When a person dies intestate, the property passes, according to the applicable statute, to the heirs at law or next of kin of the deceased. These statutes provide that property will, in effect, pass to the deceased's closest relatives, since the law presumes that this would be the intent of the deceased. A typical statute provides that property of a person dying and leaving a spouse and children will pass one-third to the spouse and two-thirds to the children.

A person making a will is said to die testate and is generally referred to as the *testator.* The personal representative of a deceased who dies without a will is an *administrator,* whereas the personal representative of a testator is an *executor.* A gift of real estate by will is usually called a *devise;* a gift of personal property is called a *bequest.*

Wills—execution

A *will* is a document that expresses a person's intention as to the disposition of his or her property on death. It also serves several additional functions. It designates the personal representative who is to be responsible for settling the affairs of the deceased. A will may make provisions for the appointment of guardians of the person and the estate of a minor child. Many wills provide for payment of taxes that may be due on the death of the deceased and for matters such as whether or not the personal representative should be required to have sureties on the official bond.

Legal provisions vary from state to state; but the law generally stipulates that to be valid, a will must be executed by a person possessing testamentary capacity and must be signed either by the testator or by someone in his presence and at his direction. In most states, a will must be attested to in the presence of the testator by two or more credible witnesses.

Testamentary capacity does not require a perfect mind or average intelligence. Testamentary capacity first of all requires a minimum age, such as 18 years. The person executing the will must have sufficient mental capacity to comprehend and remember who are the natural objects of his affection, to comprehend the kind and character of his property, and to understand that he or she is engaged in making a will. Less mental capacity is required to execute a will than is required to execute ordinary business transactions and contracts. Since many people at the time of making a will are in poor health, the law recognizes that many testators will not be of perfect mind, and all that is required is a minimum capacity to understand the nature and the plan involved in making the will.

The testator need not sign the will, since many people who are physically incapacitated will not be able to do so. It may be signed by someone else in the testator's presence and at his direction. It will not be set aside simply by proving that the signature on it is not that of the deceased.

In most states, the testator need not sign in the presence of witnesses if he acknowledges to them that the instrument is his own and that it bears his signature. The witnesses need not be informed that the document is a will, but only that it is the testator's instrument. The signature aspect of attestation is that the testator watch the witnesses sign, and in most states it is essential that the witnesses testify that the testator watched them sign as attesting witnesses.

A credible witness is one who is competent to testify in support of the will. If the witness is an interested party, he takes something under the will; then, in most states, the witness will not be allowed to receive any more property as a result of the will than he would have received had there been no will. In other words, a witness to the will cannot profit or gain any property as a result of the will. He will be required to testify and will lose whatever the will gives him in excess of his intestate share of the deceased's estate.

A will that on its face is properly executed may be challenged on several grounds. With the exception of lack of testamentary capacity, the most frequently cited ground for a will contest is undue influence. This ground for challenging a will is defined as influence that overpowers the mind of the testator and deprives him of his free agency in the execution of the will. It is the equivalent of saying, "This is not my wish, but I must do it." It is more than mere persuasion, for here there is an exercise of independent judgment and deliberation. A presumption of undue influence is often found to exist where there is a fiduciary relationship between a testator and a beneficiary who takes substantial benefits from the will. This is especially true if the beneficiary is a nonrelated dominant party and the testator a dependent party and the will is written, or its preparation procured, by the beneficiary.

CASE

An undertaker had served as confidential adviser to a now deceased woman eighty years of age. He managed all of her affairs. At a time when her mind was deteriorating, the undertaker called in his attorney to draw a will for her. The will left virtually all of the estate to the undertaker. The will was contested, and the probate court disallowed it on the ground of undue influence.

ISSUE Did the conduct of the undertaker constitute undue influence?

DECISION Yes.

REASONS

1. When a confidential or trust relationship exists between a testator and a beneficiary under a will, the law requires the closest scrutiny and most careful examination of all of the circumstances. Here, the facts clearly establish a relationship of trust and confidence and an elderly spinster with a weakened mind.
2. In connection with the execution of the will and operating at the time the will is made, undue influence means influence amounting to moral coercion, destroying free agency, or importunity that could not be resisted, so that the testator—unable to withstand the influence or too weak to resist it—was constrained to do that which was not her actual will but against it.

Barton v. Beck Estate, 195 A.2d 63 (Me.) 1963.

Wills—revocation, republication, revival, and renunciation

A will is said to be *ambulatory,* or not effective, until the death of the testator. It may be revoked at any time. Among the common methods of revoking a will are physical destruction, making a will declaring the revocation, a later will that is inconsistent with the prior will, marriage, and divorce. In many states, divorce revokes the will only to the extent of bequests or devises to the former spouse. Marriage revokes a will because it is presumed that the testator would want a different plan of distribution as the result of the marriage. It is therefore important that whenever there is a marriage or a divorce, the law of the state of the domicile be consulted to determine its effect on a prior will.

State laws usually prohibit partial revocation of a will except by a duly signed and attested instrument. Additions, alterations, substitutions, interlineations, and deletions on the face of a will are therefore ineffective, and the will stands as originally executed. The law prohibits partial revocation because of the ease with which such minor changes could be made by third parties even after the death of the person whose will is involved.

Unless a provision is made for a child born after the execution of the will, or unless the will by clear and convincing language indicates that after-born children are to be disinherited, the after-born child in most states takes from the estate whatever he or she would have received had there been no will. A legal adoption has the same effect. This stipulation is based on the assumption that the testator at the time of the execution of the original will would not have considered the after-born child and that a provision would have been intended had the child been considered.

In most states, a will that is in any manner totally revoked can be revived only by the reexecution of the will or by an instrument in writing declaring the revival and executed in the same manner as a new will. To illustrate, assume that a person during her lifetime has executed four wills, each specifically revoking the former. None of these wills had been destroyed until the testator, shortly before her death, physically destroyed will number 4. Is number 3 then valid? In most states, the answer is no. Wills are not stacked one on the other so that the revocation of the latest will revives the earlier will. In the situation described, the person would die without a will. A similar problem arises when a person executes a codicil or a minor change to a will. When a codicil is executed and it specifically refers to a former will, it has the effect of bringing the former will down to the date of the codicil, and the will is then construed as of the date of the codicil. A codicil can validate a previously invalid will. It can also validate a will that has been revoked by marriage or divorce.

The law in most states gives a spouse certain rights that cannot be denied by will. These rights include support during the period of administration, with a statutory minimum usually provided. The court will determine the exact amount, based on the size of the estate and the standard of living of the surviving spouse. A spouse may also *renounce* a will and take a statutory share in lieu of provisions made by the will. In other words, one spouse cannot completely prevent his or her property from passing to a surviving spouse by making different provisions in the will. In many states, a spouse receives one-half the estate upon renunciation, irrespective of the provisions of the will. It should be recognized that the right to renounce usually exists for spouses only—children can be completely disinherited.

Substitutes for wills

Numerous methods, legal devices, and techniques can serve as a valid substitute for a will. In one sense, the law of intestacy is a substitute for a will because it is, in effect, a state-made will for people who have not taken the trouble to execute one for themselves.

Among the more common substitutes for wills are contracts, including life insurance contracts, trusts, and joint tenancy property.

Life insurance policies name a beneficiary to receive the proceeds on the death of the insured. This beneficiary may be the estate of the insured, in which case the proceeds will pass under the will of the deceased; or if the insured dies without a will, the proceeds will go according to the laws of intestacy. The usual arrangement is to name an individual beneficiary and successive beneficiaries in the event the primary beneficiary predeceases the insured. In that case, the provisions of the will are immaterial, and the life insurance will be paid in accordance with the terms of the policy, even if the will purports to cover life insurance.

Individuals enter into numerous contracts that have the effect of disposing of property on death. Some contracts stipulate the terms of a will or surrender rights to renounce a will or to take an intestate share. Such contracts are known as *antenuptial agreements.*

In Part VII, "Business Organizations," reference will be made to *buy and sell* agreements between partners and between the shareholders of closely held corporations. These contracts, in effect, dispose of the interests of partners and shareholders on death. The contractual agreement will dispose of the property, irrespective of any provision in a will, in much the same manner as does life insurance. Other contracts, including employment contracts and leases, may have a similar effect.

A living trust is another substitute for a will when it contains provisions as to the disposition of property on the death of a life tenant. Since this device is so important and so commonly used, it is discussed more fully in the section that follows.

The use of joint tenancies as a means of common ownership was previously discussed. *Joint tenancy* is a substitute for a will because ownership passes to the surviving joint tenant on the death of one joint tenant.

Trusts

The word *trust* is generally used to describe an express private trust. An *express private trust* is a fiduciary relationship with respect to property, which subjects the person with legal title to property (the trustee) to equitable duties to deal with the property for the benefit of another (the beneficiary). In other words, a *trust* is a fiduciary relationship under which one person, the trustee, holds title to property and deals with it for the benefit of another person known as the *beneficiary.* The most important single aspect of the relationship is its fiduciary character. The trustee is under an absolute obligation to act solely for the benefit of the beneficiary in every aspect of the relationship. Both real and personal property may be held in trust.

A trust may be created by a transfer of property during one's lifetime (a *living,* or *inter vivos, trust*), or it may be created by a transfer on death (a *testamentary trust*). The person creating the trust is usually called the *settlor,* although he is sometimes referred to as the *creator* or the *trustor* in estate planning literature. The settlor may create the trust by a transfer of property to the trustee, or the settlor may declare himself to be trustee of described property for the benefit of designated beneficiaries.

Consideration is not required to create a trust, and of course, consideration is rarely present in a testamentary trust. Since the statute of frauds is applicable to the creation of a trust, to be valid, a trust involving real estate requires written evidence of the intention to create the trust and an exact description of the property held in trust. Personal property may be held in a trust that is created orally.

A trust may have several beneficiaries, and their rights may be dependent upon several variable factors. The trustee may be authorized to determine which beneficiaries shall receive the income of the trust and how much each shall receive. The right of a trustee to allocate the income of the trust among the beneficiaries is sometimes referred to as a "sprinkling trust" provision. It has the advantage of allowing the trustee with actual knowledge of the needs of the beneficiaries to take those needs into account in the distribution of income. A trust may also have successive beneficiaries. A trust could provide that the income would go to the deceased's spouse for life; and on the death of the spouse, to their children for life; on the children's death, to grandchildren.

A settlor may be a trustee as well as one of the beneficiaries of a trust. A trustee may be one of the beneficiaries of a trust, but the sole trustee cannot be the sole beneficiary. If the sole trustee is the sole beneficiary of a trust, there is a merger of the legal and equitable interests, causing a termination of the trust by operation of law.

When the settlor is also the trustee and life beneficiary, the trust operates in effect as a will. It is nevertheless valid in most states, even though it is not executed with the formality required of a will. In such case, it is used to avoid probate proceedings and to save the costs involved in such proceedings.

Other types of trusts

In addition to the express private trust, the law recognizes charitable trusts, resulting trusts, and constructive trusts, the last two being created by operation of law. A court of equity will create a constructive trust in order to prevent unjust enrichment, possibly when a transfer of property is procured by fraud or violation of some fiduciary duty. Courts of equity also create resulting trusts, or a trust results because the person with legal title is not intended to have it. If a child purchases property in the name of a parent, there is no presumption of a gift, and the child may establish that the parent holds title in trust for the child.

The charitable trust is a valuable estate planning tool, because it is not subject to death taxes. Living donors qualify for income tax deductions. The charitable trust differs from a private trust in that it can benefit an indefinite group and can have perpetual existence. Among typical charitable purposes for which a trust can be created are religion, education, health, public comfort, and aiding the poor.

Perhaps the single most important principle in the law of charitable trusts is a doctrine known as *cy pres*. The doctrine of cy pres provides that if a particular charitable purpose cannot be carried out in the manner directed by the settlor, the court may direct the application of the trust property to another charitable purpose consistent with the general charitable intention. The words *cy pres* mean "as nearly as," and the courts simply choose another charitable purpose that is as nearly as possible like the one designated by the settlor.

CASE

Clem Boyd provided in her will for a scholarship fund to be established in memory of her parents at Georgia Tech, Emory University, and Agnes Scott College. The will recited that the scholarship was "for benefit of deserving and qualified poor white boys and girls." It was clear that the racial restriction was unenforceable under the equal protection clause of the Fourteenth Amendment. Clem Boyd's executor commenced this action for a construction of the will and direction as to what to do with the amount set aside as a scholarship fund.

ISSUE Should the doctrine of cy pres be employed to exclude the discriminatory racial classification?

DECISION Yes. The scholarship funds could be used for the benefit of all students.

REASONS

1. When a charitable bequest cannot be performed in the exact manner provided by the testator, a court will try to carry out the testator's intentions "as nearly as possible." This is the cy pres doctrine.
2. When the specific intent of the testator may not legally or practically be carried into effect and the testator has exhibited a general charitable intent, a court will accomplish the general charitable intent as nearly as possible.
3. Here, there was a general charitable intent, and cy pres could be invoked to establish a charitable scholarship fund with the racial restrictions deleted.

Trammell v. Elliott, 230 Ga. 841 (1973).

REVIEW QUESTIONS AND PROBLEMS

1. What is the advantage of describing property as a "bundle of rights"?
2. Is it possible for one person to be the absolute owner of an item of property? Explain.
3. List three situations in which the distinction between real and personal property is important. Give an example of each.
4. Compare *tenancy in common, joint tenancy,* and *community property* insofar as the transfer of the property on the death of the owner is concerned.
5. List the three tests for determining if personal property has become a fixture.
6. Borg operated a ski lift on leased land. The lease stipulated that the lift might not be removed under any circumstances. The state attempted to tax the lift as personal property. Borg sought to have it taxed as real property. Who was correct? Explain.
7. Turner owned and operated a comprehensive cable television system that contained about 630 miles of feeder cable. The cable was annexed to telephone poles owned by the telephone company, under a lease that required removal if the telephone company should need the space for its own service needs. The county assessed the television cable system as real property, contending that the cable is a fixture under common law principles. Should the television cable be classified as a fixture? Why?
8. Tom died January 5, 1981. His widow presented for probate a will dated October 14, 1980. Betty, one of the witnesses to the will, testified that she did not see Tom sign the will dated October 14, 1980, that Tom was not present when she signed as a witness, nor did Tom acknowledge his signature to her. Was the will of October 14, 1980 properly executed? Explain.
9. A husband and wife owned real property in joint tenancy. When the husband died, his will gave a life estate in the property to his wife, with the remainder going to the children. What interest does the wife own in the real estate? Why?
10. Jud executed a will in his hospital room, where he was dying from acute alcoholism and cancer. He was under sedation and had been given two ounces of whiskey. The will provided that Jud's property was to be divided between his wife and daughter. When the will was challenged, witnesses testified that the will had been read to Jud, and he appeared to understand it. Is the will valid? Why?
11. Dan executed a will and left the original with his sister. Later, Dan wrote across his copy, "This will is hereby revoked." This was unattested. On Dan's death, the sister sought to admit the will to probate. What was the result? Why?
12. Marcia, a trustee, was given broad authority by the trust instrument in the administration of the trust. Using trust funds, she made a personal profit from a real estate investment. Valerie, a beneficiary to the trust, sued to recover the profits for the estate. What was the result? Explain.
13. A mother deposited $10,000 of her money in a joint account with her son in a savings and loan association. Both signatures were required for withdrawal, and the signature card contained the following: "Any funds placed in, or added to, the account by any one of the parties is and shall be conclusively intended to be a gift to the other party to the extent of his pro rata share." The mother retained possession of the passbook and subsequently brought suit, claiming that she is the sole owner of the funds. Is the mother correct? Why?

29

Personal Property and Bailments

Now that we are acquainted with some of the legal principles applicable to personal property, we should find out some of the methods of acquiring title to it. We'll also discuss the transfer of possession but not ownership of personal property and the legal problems that may arise from that transaction known as a bailment.

Acquiring Title to Personal Property

Methods

Title to personal property may be acquired through any of the following methods: *original possession, transfer, accession,* or *confusion.* Original possession is a method of extremely limited applicability. It may be used to obtain title over wild animals and fish or things that are available for appropriation by individuals. Property that is in its native state and over which no one as yet has taken full and complete control belongs to the first person who reduces such property to his exclusive possession. Property once reduced to ownership, but later abandoned, belongs to the first party next taking possession.

In addition to the above, it might be said that property created through mental or physical labor belongs to the creator unless he has agreed to create it for someone else for compensation. Books, inventions, and trademarks might be included under this heading. This kind of property is usually protected by the government through means of copyrights, patents, and trademarks.

Title by transfer

Personal property may be transferred by sale, operation of law, will, or gift. The law relating to transfer by sale was discussed in connection with the Uniform Commercial Code. Transfers by operation of law include judicial sales, mortgage foreclosures, and intestate succession. Wills were discussed in chapter 28, and gifts will be taken up in the next section.

As a general rule, a transferee receives the rights of the transferor, and a transferee takes no better title than the transferor had. If the transferor of the personal property did not have title to the property, the transferee would not have title, either, even though the transferee believes that his transferor has a good title. Suppose Pastor Jones purchases a new stereo set for a church from parishioner Tithe. Unknown to Pastor Jones, Tithe had stolen the stereo from the Bulldog Music Store. The stereo set still belongs to Bulldog Music, and the church has no title to it. An innocent purchaser from a thief obtains no title to the property purchased, and no subsequent purchaser stands in any better position. Because the thief had no title or ownership, persons who acquired the property from or through the thief have no title or ownership. If the transferor of the property has a voidable title, and he sells property to an innocent purchaser, the transferee may obtain good title to the property. Assume that through fraudulent representations, Fred acquires title to Sam's property. Sam could avoid the transaction with Fred and obtain a return of his property. If Fred sells the property to Ann, and she does not know about his fraudulent representations, Sam cannot disaffirm against Ann. Ann has good title to the property, since she is a good-faith purchaser for value.

Title by gift

There are three elements of a valid gift: intention to make the gift, delivery, and acceptance. From a legal standpoint, delivery is the most significant, because the law requires physical change in possession of the property, with the owner's consent. All elements of a valid gift must be established, however, in the event of a dispute over the ownership of property.

A promise to make a gift is ordinarily not enforceable, because no consideration is present to support the promise; but an executed gift—one accomplished by delivery of the property to the donee—cannot be rescinded except in the case of a gift *causa mortis,* discussed later. The delivery can be actual or constructive or symbolic, if the situation demands. Thus, if the property is in storage, the donor could make a delivery by giving the donee the warehouse receipt. A donor may also accomplish delivery by giving the donee something that is a token representing the donee's dominion and control. A delivery of the keys to an automobile may be a valid symbolic delivery, although a symbolic or constructive delivery will not suffice if actual delivery is reasonably possible.

CASE

P argued that she was the donee of an *inter vivos* gift from the decedent. While the decedent was living, he gave the key to his safety deposit box to P with the clear intention that she be the recipient of its contents, $800,000 in stocks and bonds. The box remained registered in the decedent's name; and even with the key, P did not have access to the lock box, because her name was not on the rental contract with the bank.

ISSUE Was there an effective *inter vivos* gift, the purported donor intending to make a gift; but while making a constructive delivery, he retained dominion over the gift?

DECISION No.

REASONS
1. In order to effectuate an *inter vivos* gift, there must be evidence of an intention to make a gift and a *delivery,* actual or constructive, of a nature sufficient not only to divest the donor of control over the property but also to invest the donee with dominion over the object of the gift. Regardless of how strongly the donor desired or intended that the gift be made, it will fail if there is an ineffective delivery.
2. Delivery here was ineffective because the donor still had access to the contents of the safety box, and the donee, even with the key, did not have access to the contents.

In re Estate of Evans, 356 A.2d 778 (Pa.) 1976.

It was previously noted that gifts *causa mortis* constitute an exception to the general rule on the finality of completed gifts. A gift *causa mortis* is in contemplation of death and refers to the situation in which a person who is, or who believes that he is, facing death makes a gift on the assumption that death is imminent. A person about to embark on a perilous trip or to undergo a serious operation or one who has an apparently incurable and fatal illness might make a gift and deliver the item to the donee on the assumption that he may soon die. If he returns safely or does not die, the donor is allowed to revoke the gift and recover the property from the donee.

Accession

Accession literally means "adding to." In the law of personal property, accession has two basic meanings. First of all, it refers to an owner's right to all that his property produces. The owner of a cow is also the owner of each calf born, and the owner of lumber is the owner of a table made from the lumber by another. *Accession* is also the legal term used to signify the acquisition of title to personal property when it is incorporated into other property or joined with other property.

When accession occurs, who has title is frequently in issue. The general rule is that when the goods of two different owners are united without the willful misconduct of either party, the title to the resulting product goes to the owner of the major portion of the goods. This rule is based on the principle that personal property permanently added to other property and forming a minor portion of the finished product becomes part of the larger unit. Since title can be in only one party, it is in the owner of the major portion. The owner of the minor portion might recover damages if his portion were wrongfully taken from him. The law of accession simply prevents the owner of the minor portion from recovering the property itself.

Suppose that Garrod owns some raw materials, and that Durham inadvertently uses these materials to manufacture a product. The product belongs to Garrod. If Durham also adds some raw materials of his own, the manufactured product belongs to the party who contributed the major portion of the materials. If Durham becomes the owner, Garrod is entitled to recover her damages. If Garrod is the owner, Durham is not entitled to anything, since he used Garrod's materials.

A similar issue arises when a party without authority repairs goods of another. The owner is entitled to the goods as repaired, irrespective of the value of the repair, unless the repairs can be severed without damaging the original goods.

The law of accession distinguishes between the rights of "innocent" and "willful" trespassers, although both are wrongful. An innocent trespasser to personal property is one who acts through mistake or conduct less than intentionally wrongful. A willful trespasser cannot obtain title against the original owner under any circumstances.

If the property that is the subject of accession is sold to a good-faith purchaser, the rights and liabilities of the original owner and the third party are the same as those of the original trespasser. A willful trespasser has no title and can convey none. The owner can recover the property without any liability to the third party. If the third party makes improvements or repairs, he has the right to remove his additions if they can be removed without damaging the original goods. An innocent trespasser can convey this right to remove to a good-faith purchaser.

CASE

An automobile owned by P was stolen. The thief put in a new motor, then sold it to a used-car dealer, who sold it to D. D added a sun visor, seat covers, and a gasoline tank.

ISSUE May P reclaim the automobile and keep the items added?

DECISION P may obtain the automobile, including the motor added by the thief. P may not keep the other items added by D.

REASONS
1. The owner of stolen personal property is not divested of ownership by the theft. He may reclaim from any purchaser, including a good-faith purchaser. The value added by the thief belongs to the owner.
2. Because D was not a willful wrongdoer, the items D placed on the car belong to him if they can be removed without damage to the car.

Farm Bureau Mut. Automobile Ins. Co. v. Moseley, 90 A.2d 485 (Ill.) 1950.

Confusion

Property of such a character that one unit may not be distinguished from another unit and that is usually sold by weight or measure is known as *fungible property*. Grain, hay, logs, wine, oil, and similar property are of this nature. When it belongs to various parties, it may be mixed by intention, accident, mistake, or wrongful misconduct of an owner of some of the goods. Confusion of fungible property belonging to various owners, assuming that no misconduct (confusion by consent, accident, or mistake) is involved, results in an undivided ownership of the total mass. To illustrate: Grain is stored in a public warehouse by many parties. Each owner holds an undivided interest in the total mass, his particular interest being dependent upon the amount stored by him. Should there be a partial destruction of the total mass, the loss would be divided proportionately.

Confusion of goods that results from the wrongful conduct of one of the parties causes the title to the total mass to pass to the innocent party. If the mixture is divisible, an exception exists. The wrongdoer, if he is able to show that the resultant mass is equal in value per unit to that of the innocent party, is able to recover his share. If the new mixture is worth no less per unit than that formerly belonging to the innocent party, the wrongdoer may claim his portion of the new mass by presenting convincing evidence of the amount added by him. If two masses are added together and the wrongdoer can only establish his proportion of one mass, he is only entitled to that proportion of the combined mass.

Abandoned and lost property

Property is said to be abandoned whenever it is discarded by the true owner who, at that time, has no intention of reclaiming it. The property belongs to the first individual again reducing it to possession.

CASE

P was the owner of coal-washing equipment located on D's surface estate. P used the washing operation to clean coal brought from other locations. P considered the real estate "lost land" and did not pay rent to D. P considered the coal valueless; and owing to his physical infirmities, discontinued his coal-washing business. Several years later, D's lessees began extracting coal from the wash settling ponds. P then claimed title to the coal.

ISSUE Did the coal from the wash settling ponds belong to P?

DECISION No.

REASONS

1. Whether personalty (personal property) has been abandoned is determined by consideration of the nature of the particular property, the intent to abandon, and some external act evidencing this intent. Intent is determined from conduct.
2. Though ordinarily there exists a presumption that one does not intend to abandon his property, this presumption is not present where the article claimed to have been abandoned is generally considered valueless.

Milford v. Tenn. River Pulp and Paper Co., 355 So. 2d 687 (Ala.) (1978).

Property is lost whenever, as a result of negligence, accident, or some other cause, it is found at some place other than that chosen by the owner. Title to lost property continues to rest with the true owner; and until he has been ascertained, the finder may keep it. The finder's title is good against everyone except the true owner. The rights of the finder are superior to those of the person in charge of the property upon which the lost article is found unless the finder is a trespasser. Occasionally, state statutes provide for newspaper publicity concerning articles that have been found. If the owner cannot be located, the found property reverts to the state or county if its value exceeds an established minimum.

Property is mislaid or misplaced if its owner has intentionally placed it at a certain spot, but the manner of placement indicates that he has forgotten to pick it up. The presumption is that he will eventually remember where he left it and return for it. The finder must turn it over to the owner of the premises, who may hold it until the owner is located.

Bailments

Possession of personal property is often temporarily surrendered by the owner to another person. The person to whom the goods are delivered may perform some service pertaining to the goods, such as a repair, after which the goods are returned to the owner. Or someone may borrow or rent an article from its owner. Another temporary transfer of possession occurs when the owner causes the goods to be stored in a warehouse.

An agreement whereby possession of personal property is surrendered by the owner with provision for its return at a later time is known as a *bailment.* The owner of the goods is called the *bailor.* The one receiving possession is called the *bailee.*

There are three distinct requirements for a bailment: (1) retention of title by the bailor; (2) possession and temporary control of the property by the bailee; and (3) ultimate possession to revert to the bailor or to someone designated by the bailor. A merchant who sells a certain kind of goods may also lease it. The lease is similar to a sale, so the bailor (lessor) makes the same warranties as does a seller of goods. The provisions of the Code are applicable to such bailments.

Types of bailments

Bailments group naturally into three classes: bailments for the benefit of the bailor; bailments for the benefit of the bailee; and bailments for the mutual benefit of bailor and bailee. Typical of the first group are those cases in which the bailor leaves goods in the safekeeping of the bailee without any provision for paying the bailee for caring for the article. Because the bailee is not to use the goods or to be paid in any manner, the bailment is for the exclusive benefit of the bailor.

A bailment for the benefit of the bailee is best illustrated by a loan of some article by the bailor to the bailee without any compensation to the bailor. A student borrows a professor's automobile for a week-end date. The bailment is one for the sole benefit of the student, the bailee.

The most common type of bailment is the one in which both parties are to benefit. Contracts for repair, carriage, storage, or pledge of property fall within this class. The bailor receives the benefit of some service; the bailee benefits by the receipt of certain agreed compensation. Thus, both parties benefit as a result of the bailment.

To constitute a bailment for mutual benefit, it is not essential that the bailee actually receive compensation in money or tangible property. If the bailment is an incident of the business in which the bailee makes a profit, or it was accepted because of benefits expected to accrue, it is a mutual benefit bailment.

Degree of care required by bailees

Provided that proper care has been exercised by the bailee, any loss or damage to the property bailed falls on the bailor. Each type of bailment requires a different degree of care by the bailee. In a bailment for the benefit of the bailor, the bailee is required to exercise only slight care; in one for the benefit of the bailee, extraordinary care is required. A bailment for the mutual benefit of the parties demands ordinary care on the part of the bailee. *Ordinary care* is defined as care that the average individual usually exercises over his own property.

In addition to the duty to exercise due care, the bailee promises to return the property to the bailor undamaged upon termination of the bailment. This promise can be used to create a prima facie case of negligence. A bailor who proves that property delivered in good condition was returned from the bailee in bad condition establishes a presumption of negligence and is entitled to recover from the bailee unless the presumption is rebutted. If there is no other evidence, the bailor will win the suit. The bailee may rebut this prima facie case by introducing evidence to establish that there was no negligence on its part, but the bailee has the burden of proving that it has used reasonable care and caution after the prima facie case has been established.

The prima facie case of negligence exists only if all elements of a bailment are present. If there is no bailment, there is no prima facie case upon nondelivery or damage to the goods.

CASE

P drove his pickup truck to D's parking lot. Upon entering, P received a ticket, parked his own car, and kept the keys. P's car was stolen. P sued D, contending that the bailment existed and that proof of failure to return the property made out a prima facie case of negligence.

ISSUE Was there a bailment of the truck?

DECISION No.

REASONS 1. In order to constitute a bailment transaction, there must be a contract, express or implied, delivery of the property by the bailor to the bailee, and acceptance of the property by the bailee.

2. The undisputed evidence shows that P chose the place to park his truck, locked the truck, and kept the keys in his possession. No bailment was created or existed. Therefore, there was no prima facie case of negligence when the truck was not returned.

Ragland v. Allright Parking, Inc., 559 S.W. 2d 858 (1977).

The amount of care demanded of a bailee varies with the nature and value of the article bailed. The care found to be sufficient in the case of a carpenter's tool chest would probably not be ample for a diamond ring worth $10,000. A higher standard of protection is required for valuable articles than for those less valuable. Moreover, when damages are assessed against a bailee, they are based on retail replacement value, not the wholesale cost to a bailee.

CASE

P, the owner of an expensive bracelet, took it to D's jewelry store to have it reworked into a pendant. D completed the work, but the jewelry was either lost or stolen before P could reclaim the jewelry.

ISSUE For purposes of determining D's liability, what value criteria should be used—wholesale or retail replacement?

DECISION Retail replacement.

REASONS 1. The general rule is that damages awarded for personal property taken or destroyed are based on the item's market value at the time of the taking or destruction.

2. Ordinarily, market value is defined as the price for which an article is bought and sold and for which there exists a demand in the market place, and the legal definition of the price is retail, not wholesale.

3. If there is no demand for the item, the recovery is based on actual value or—in the case of unique chattels—based on appraisal of value to the owner. The rule is a flexible one that can be modified in the interest of fairness.

Winters v. Charles Anthony, Inc., 586 P.2d 453 (1978).

Disclaimers of liability by bailees

Bailees frequently attempt to disclaim liability for damage to property while it is in their possession. Such a clause in a contract is known as an *exculpatory clause*. Dry cleaners' tickets often bear statements disclaiming liability for damage to property delivered to them for cleaning. An exculpatory clause disclaiming liability for negligence is illegal if the bailee is a quasi-public institution, because such contracts are against public policy. This was discussed in detail in chapter 10.

More and more bailees are being classified as quasi-public businesses because of the inequality of bargaining power between many bailors and their bailees. Not all exculpatory clauses seek to eliminate liability completely; some seek to limit the amount of damages. Contracts limiting the amount of damages are looked upon more favorably than absolute disclaimers are, because it is fair for both parties to know the value of the property and the risk present. In accordance with this theory, the Unifrom Commercial Code provides that the warehouse receipt or storage agreement may limit the amount of liability in case of loss or damage to the covered property, but the agreement cannot disclaim the obligation of reasonable care.

Carriers also attempt to limit their liability. A carrier may not contract away its liability for goods damaged in shipment, but it may limit the liability to a stated amount. A carrier may also, where lower rates are granted, relieve itself from the consequences of causes or conduct over which it has no control.

Because a carrier may limit liability to an agreed valuation, the shipper is limited in his recovery to the value asserted in the bill of lading. The rate charged for transportation will vary with the value of the property shipped. For this reason, the agreed valuation is binding.

Degree of care required by bailors

Property leased by a bailor to a bailee (a mutual benefit bailment) must be reasonably fit for the intended purpose. For this reason, it is the duty of the bailor to notify the bailee of all defects in the property leased, of which the bailor might reasonably have been aware. The bailor is responsible for any damage suffered by the bailee as the result of such defects, unless the notice is given. This rule holds true even though the bailor is not aware of the defect if, by the exercise of reasonable diligence, the defect could have been discovered.

If, on the other hand, an article is merely loaned to a bailee—a bailment for the benefit of the bailee—the bailor's duty is to notify the bailee only of known defects. A bailor who fails to give the required notice of a known defect is liable to any person who might be expected to use the defective article as a result of the bailment. Employees of the bailee and members of the bailee's family may recover from the bailor for injuries received as a consequence of known defects.

Rights and duties of bailees

The bailment agreement governs the rights and duties of the bailee. If the bailee treats the property in a different manner or uses it for some purpose other than that contemplated by the bailment contract, the bailee becomes liable for any loss or damage to the property, even though the damage can in no sense be attributed to the conduct of the bailee. Let us assume that Murray stores a car for the winter in Plante's public garage. Because of a crowded condition, Plante has the car temporarily moved to another garage without Murray's consent. As the result of a tornado, the car is destroyed while at the second location. The loss falls upon Plante, who breached the terms of the bailment contract. In a restricted sense, the bailee is guilty of conversion of the bailor's property during the period in which the contract terms are being violated.

The bailee has no right to deny the title to the bailor unless the bailee has yielded possession to one having a better title than the bailor. The bailee has no right to retain possession of the property merely because he is able to prove that the bailor does not have legal title to the goods. In order to defeat the bailor's right to possession, the bailee must show that the property has been turned over to someone having better title or that he is holding the property under an agreement with the true owner.

Common carriers as bailees

The contract for carriage of goods constitutes a mutual benefit bailment, but the care required of the carrier greatly exceeds that of the ordinary bailee. A common carrier is an absolute insurer of the safe delivery of the goods to their destination. Proof of delivery to a carrier of a shipment in good condition and its arrival at the destination in a damaged condition creates a prima facie case against the carrier. This rule is subject to only five exceptions. Any loss or damage must fall upon the shipper if it results from (1) an act of God, (2) action of an alien enemy, (3) order of public authority, (4) inherent nature of the goods, or (5) misconduct of the shipper. Thus, any loss that results from an accident or the willful misconduct of some third party must be borne by the carrier. A person who wanted to injure a certain railway company set fire to several boxcars loaded with freight. Losses due to damage to the goods fell upon the carrier. On the other hand, if lightning, an act of God, had set fire to the cars, the loss would have fallen upon the shipper. However, the defense of an act of God is narrowly construed to include only events that were not foreseeable.

The shipper must suffer any damage to goods in shipment if damage results from the very nature of the goods, improper crating, or failure to protect the property. Thus, if a dog dies because his crate was poorly ventilated, the shipper is unable to recover from the carrier. Remember, though, that the carrier has the burden of proving that it was free from negligence and that the damage falls within one of the exceptions to the rule establishing the carrier's liability as an insurer of the shipment.

The burden is on the shipper to prove that the goods were in good condition at the time and place of shipment. Although proof that the goods were in good condition when delivered to the carrier and that they were damaged when delivered by the carrier creates a prima facie case of liability, there is no presumption that the goods were in good condition when delivered to the carrier. Actual proof is required.

The liability of the carrier attaches as soon as the goods are delivered. The extreme degree of care required of the carrier may be terminated before the goods are actually delivered to the consignee. Three views in this country determine when the relationship of the carrier ceases. Some states hold that the duties of the carrier end, and those of a warehouseman begin, as soon as the local shipment is unloaded from the car into the freight house. Others hold the carrier to strict liability until the consignee has had a reasonable time in which to inspect and remove the shipment. Still other states hold that the consignee is entitled to notice—and that he has a reasonable time after notice—in which to remove the goods before the liability of the carrier as a carrier is terminated.

Innkeepers as bailees

Issues similar to those involved with common carriers frequently arise in suits against hotel and motel operators. At common law, an innkeeper was an insurer of the safety of the goods of its guests. The law imposed liability as a matter of public policy because the innkeeper and his employees had easy access to the guests' rooms. Exceptions to this general rule relieved the innkeeper from liability for loss caused by an act of God, a public enemy, an act of public authority, the inherent nature of the property, or the fault of the guest.

Most states have enacted statutes pertaining to hotel or motel operators' liability.

These statutes usually provide that if the operator maintains a safe or lockbox for guests to deposit valuable property in, then there is no liability if such property is stolen from the room. Such laws usually cover property of "small compass," which includes money, negotiable instruments, jewelry, and precious stones. The laws further require that notice of the availability of the safe be given with notice of the liability limitation.

CASE

P was a paying guest at the D hotel. He left his $3,685 watch on the nightstand, locked the door, and went out to dinner. When P returned, the watch was gone. It was discovered that the door lock had not been functioning properly, and anyone could readily enter the room. P claimed that keeping the door in such poor condition amounted to "willful and wanton misconduct." D pleaded that a state statute exempted innkeepers from any liability whatsoever for guests who fail to deposit small valuable objects in the hotel's safe deposit box.

ISSUE A state statute protects innkeepers from losses if guests do not keep small valuables in the hotel's safe deposit box. Will it also protect a hotel where the loss arose from "willful and wanton misconduct" as well as negligence?

DECISION Yes.

REASON Where a state statute limits an inn's liability for loss "for any cause whatsoever" unless the guest keeps his valuable possession in the hotel safe deposit box, then it protects against a loss for "willful and wanton misconduct" as well as negligence.

Walls v. Cosmopolitan Hotels, Inc., 435 P.2d 1373 (Wash.App.) 1975.

Some states also have laws that limit the maximum liability of hotel and motel operators to a stated amount, such as $500. Others have changed the liability from that of an insurer to that of a bailee of a mutual benefit bailment (ordinary care as the duty). In all states, the liability of the innkeeper is limited to the value of the property. There is no liability for consequential damages that may flow from the loss of the property.

REVIEW QUESTIONS AND PROBLEMS

1. Alex stole a bicycle belonging to Dave and sold it to Edna, who had no knowledge of the theft. Later, the police located the bicycle in Edna's possession. Who is entitled to the property? Why?
2. While swimming in a pond on Stelter's farm, several boys discovered some money in a watertight jar on the bottom of the pond. Stelter admits it is not his money. Who has the title to the money? Who has the right to possession? Explain.
3. Aunt Bee bought ten lottery tickets on an automobile. She wrote her niece's name on the back of one of the tickets and mailed it to her niece's mother. The niece was not informed. The niece's ticket won the car, but Aunt Bee claimed the car belonged to her. Is she correct? Why?
4. Godfrey purchased a car on the installment plan from Casey. He then purchased tires from Breck, also via installments, to put on the car. Godfrey defaulted on both debts, and the car was repossessed by Casey. Breck then sued Casey for the tires. Casey claims ownership through accession. Should Breck recover? Why?
5. Calhoun had his car serviced regularly at Fred's service station. Sometimes the car was left overnight in Fred's possession. On one occasion when the car was left overnight to be serviced, an employee of Fred's used the car without authorization and demolished it. Calhoun then sued Fred. What was the result? Why?
6. Sally left her mink jacket in the unattended cloakroom at the Ritz Hotel while having lunch. When she returned to the cloakroom, the jacket had been stolen. Sally sued the Ritz for the value of the jacket, contending that a bailment existed. May she recover? Explain.
7. Ronald entered into a bailment agreement to store certain household goods in Billy's warehouse. The warehouse burned, and the goods were destroyed. Ronald sued Billy to recover his loss. Billy cannot establish that the fire was not caused by negligence on his part. Should Ronald recover? Why?
8. Pancho brought his show horse to the Bar H horse farm for breeding purposes, and he paid for this service. While there, the horse broke her leg and had to be destroyed. The horse had been skittish as a result of a prior surgical operation, but no one knows how the injury occurred. Is Bar H liable to Pancho for damages? Why?
9. Core Company shipped by railroad four carloads of apples from Seattle, Washington, to Washington, D.C. The apples arrived spoiled, and Core brought suit, alleging that the negligence of the railroad caused the apples to arrive in improper condition. An employee of Core, who was not present when the apples were inspected or shipped, testified that the apples were in good condition when delivered to the carrier. His testimony was based upon inspection reports of the Department of Agriculture, which were prepared six weeks prior to shipment. Should the railroad be held liable? Why?
10. Pat took a Ski-King's Airways flight from New Orleans to Chicago. The plane passed through turbulence while making an intermediate stop in St. Louis, causing Pat to strike his head against the window trim and break his glasses. The predicted weather conditions included heavy thunderstorms, surface wind gusts of 50 to 70 miles per hour, isolated tornadoes, and moderate to severe turbulence. Ski-King did not inform the passengers of the possibility of serious weather conditions before departing New Orleans. Is Ski-King liable for Pat's injuries? Why?
11. Clay purchased construction equipment from the Bogaty Company. Because delivery would take over a month, the company loaned Clay some used equipment. On demand, Clay returned all of the equipment except one truck, which had been destroyed. May the Bogaty Company recover the value of the truck from Clay? Why?
12. The Delta Company, duly licensed by the ICC as a motor carrier, delivered some wood shipped by Jergen to Haas. The wood was watersoaked, although there was no evidence that this resulted from the Delta Company's negligence or fault. May Jergen recover from Delta? Why?

Real property includes not only land but also fixtures and other things affixed to it. The provisions of the Code are not applicable to contracts involving real property, but they do apply to contracts for the sale of timber, minerals, or other items that the seller will sever from land. This chapter will discuss the various methods of acquiring title to real estate and the different interests in land that may be owned. The next chapter will discuss some of the more common transactions involving it—contracts of sale and leases. Condominiums, a form of ownership rapidly growing in importance, will also be discussed.

30 Real Property

Describing real property

Real property may be described by using (1) the metes and bounds system, (2) the congressional survey system, or (3) the plat system. The metes and bounds system establishes boundary lines by reference to natural or artificial monuments; that is, to fixed points such as roads, streams, fences, and trees. A metes and bounds description starts with a monument, determines the angle of the line and the distance to the next monument, and so forth, until the tract is fully enclosed and described. Because surveyors may not always agree, the law of metes and bounds creates an order of precedence. Courses (angles) control over distances, and it is presumed that lines connect the monuments if the angle is wrong. Some metes and bounds descriptions use only courses and distances starting from a known point.

The term *congressional survey* refers to a system of describing land by using a known base line and principal meridians. The base line runs from east to west, and principal meridians run from north to south. Townships are thus located in relation to these lines. A township may be described as 7 North, Range 3 East of the 3rd Principal Meridian. This township is seven townships north of the base line and three east of the third principal meridian.

The townships are then divided into thirty-six sections, each section being one square mile. (There will be fractional sections, owing to the convergence of the meridians.) With the exception of the fractional sections, each section consists of 640 acres. Parts of the section are described by their locations within it, as Fig. 30•1 illustrates.

A *plat* is a recorded document dividing a tract described by metes and bounds or congressional survey into streets, blocks, and lots. The land may thereafter be described in relation to the recorded plat by simply giving the lot number, block, and subdivision name. Lot 8 in Block 7 of Ben Johnson's Subdivision in the city of Emporia, Kansas, might describe real property located in that municipality.

Methods of Acquisition

Title to real property may be acquired by (1) original entry, called title by occupancy; (2) transfer through a deed from the owner; (3) judicial sale; (4) benefit of the period of the statute of limitations, called adverse possession; (5) will; (6) descent, under intestacy statutes; and (7) accretion, which may happen when a river or a lake creates new land by depositing soil. Transfer by will and by intestacy statute were discussed in chapter 28.

Original entry refers to a title obtained from the sovereign. Except in those portions

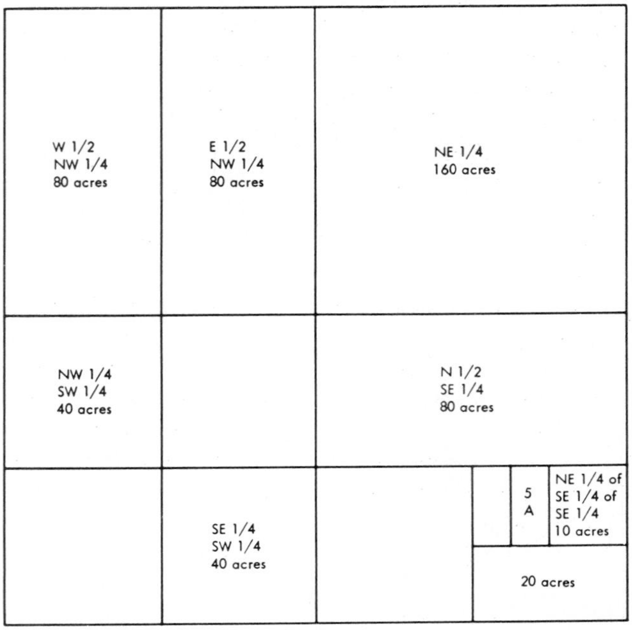

W 1/2
NW 1/4
80 acres

E 1/2
NW 1/4
80 acres

NE 1/4
160 acres

NW 1/4
SW 1/4
40 acres

N 1/2
SE 1/4
80 acres

SE 1/4
SW 1/4
40 acres

5
A

NE 1/4 of
SE 1/4 of
SE 1/4
10 acres

20 acres

Fig. 30•1

of the United States where the original title to the land was derived from grants that were issued by the king of England and other sovereigns who took possession of the land by conquest, title to all the land in the United States was derived from the United States government. Private individuals who occupied land for the period of time prescribed by federal statute and met other conditions established by law acquired title by patent from the federal government.

Types of deeds

The title to real property is most commonly transferred by the owner's executing a document called a deed and delivering it to the transferee. A *deed* is generally a formal instrument under seal that is executed and acknowledged in the presence of a notary public. Many different kinds of deeds are used throughout the country, the statutes of each state providing for the various types. The common types are the warranty deed, the grant deed, the bargain and sale deed, and the quitclaim deed. There are also special types of deeds used when the grantor holds a special legal position at the time of conveyance. Special deeds are used by the executors and administrators of estates, by guardians, and by sheriffs or other court officials executing deeds in their official capacity.

The major distinction among types of deeds relates to the covenants or warranties that the grantor of the deed makes to the grantee. Covenants and warranties are promises or guarantees made by the grantor pertaining to the land and the grantor's bundle of rights with respect to it. A deed may contain several warranties or none at all, depending upon the type of deed and the language used.

Warranty deed

The typical warranty deed that conveys fee simple title includes four common covenants, or warranties that: (1) at the time of making the deed, the grantor has fee simple title and the right and power to convey it (warranty of seizin), (2) the property is free from all encumbrances except those noted in the deed (the warranty against encumbrances), (3) the grantee and his successors will have the quiet and peaceful enjoyment of the property (warranty of quiet enjoyment), and (4) the grantor will defend the title of the grantee if anyone else should claim the property (covenant of further assurances). The warranty of quiet enjoyment and the covenant of further assurances are promises by the grantor to defend the title in legal proceedings if someone else claims it. Such defense includes paying court costs and attorney's fees.

The warranty against encumbrances is the one that is most likely to be breached. All real estate is encumbered at least to the extent of taxes that are a lien. Moreover, unsatisfied judgments against the owners constitute an encumbrance in most states, as do both visible and recorded easements.

CASE

D conveyed certain realty to P by deed, with a covenant against encumbrances. Running across the property was an irrigation ditch that had been in existence so long that it could not legally be removed. P had inspected the property and had seen the ditch but had concluded that it was abandoned.

ISSUE Does a warranty deed with a covenant against encumbrances include a covenant against visible easements such as the ditch?

DECISION Yes.

REASONS 1. An easement is a burden upon the title conveyed. It diminishes the value of the land and constitutes a breach of the covenant against encumbrances in the deed. This breach occurs regardless of whether or not the grantee had knowledge of its existence or that it was visible and notorious.

2. The intention to exclude an encumbrance should be stated in the deed itself as an exception to the warranties. A resort to oral or other extraneous evidence to negate an easement would violate settled principles of law in regard to deeds.

Jones v. Grow Investment and Mortgage Company, 358 P.2d 909 (Utah) 1961.

The person drafting a deed must ascertain which encumbrances actually exist and except them in the deed. A typical deed might provide that the conveyance is "subject to accrued general taxes, visible easements, and easements and restrictions of record." If there is an outstanding mortgage, it would also be included as an exception to the warranty against encumbrances.

Grant deed

In some states—California being one—a deed known as a grant deed is in more common use than is the warranty deed. In a grant deed, the grantor covenants that no interest in the property has been conveyed to another party, that the property has not been encumbered except as noted, and that any title to the property the grantor might receive in the future will be transferred to the grantee. A grantor under a grant deed has liability only as a result of encumbrances or claims that arose while the property was owned by the grantor. A grant deed does not protect the grantee against encumbrances that existed prior to the grantor taking title. As a result, the grant deed is much narrower than the warranty deed in the promises made to the grantee.

Bargain and sale deed

A bargain and sale deed warrants that the grantor has title to the property and the right to convey, but it does not contain any express covenants as to the title's validity. This deed also is sometimes called a warranty deed without covenants. The bargain and sale deed simply states that the grantor "does hereby grant, sell, and convey" some interest in the real property to the grantee. In states that authorize a bargain and sale deed, a grantee who desires the covenants and warranties of a warranty deed must obtain them by contractual agreement. Unless the grantor agrees to make the warranties and covenants, there are none.

Quitclaim deed

A grantor who does not wish to make warranties with respect to the title may execute a quitclaim deed, merely transferring all the "right, title, and interest" of the grantor to the grantee. Whatever title the grantor has, the grantee receives, but the grantor makes no warranties. A quitclaim deed is used when the interest of the grantor is not clear; for example, where a deed will clear a defective title. It is also used to eliminate possible conflicting interests or when, in fact, there may be no interest in the grantor.

The grantee who takes property under a quitclaim deed must understand that he may be receiving nothing at all. A person could give a quitclaim deed to the Brooklyn Bridge to anyone willing to pay for it. The grantee obviously is not given anything at all by such a deed. The grantor simply conveyed all of his interest in the bridge, without assurances that any rights of ownership did, in fact, exist. To transfer all of a person's rights in someone else's property is to transfer nothing at all.

The amount of protection each deed gives to the grantee is the most important distinction to remember. The order in which these types of deeds was discussed is also the order of the amount of protection provided. The warranty deed contains the greatest protection for the grantee. The grant deed protects the grantee from encumbrances placed on the land's title by the grantor but not by others. The bargain and sale deed simply states that the grantor has the right to convey the title involved, but all other covenants and warranties are missing. Finally, the grantor who gives a quitclaim deed does not even promise that he or she has any rights in the land at all.

Execution of Deeds

The statutes of the various states provide the necessary requirements for proper execution of deeds. A deed ordinarily is required to be signed, sealed, acknowledged, and delivered. A deed is not effective until it is delivered to the grantee; that is, placed entirely out of the control of the grantor. This delivery usually occurs by the handing of the instrument to the grantee or his agents. The delivery by the grantor must occur during the lifetime of the grantor. It cannot be delivered by someone else after the grantor's death, even if the grantor has ordered the delivery.

CASE

On June 25, 1958, Lillian W. Cheney signed a deed to certain real estate in which D was named grantee. She placed the deed in a sealed envelope and deposited it in a safety deposit box in her name and P's. Cheney told P that his name was on the safety deposit box and that upon her death, he was to go to the bank, obtain the envelope, and give it to D. At all times prior to her death, Cheney was in possession of a key to the safety deposit box and had sole and complete control over it. P was never given the key to the safety deposit box.

Following Cheney's death, P, after gaining access to the safety deposit box, delivered the deed contained therein to D, the named grantee.

ISSUE Did the acts of P constitute a delivery of the deed that will render it enforceable as a valid conveyance?

DECISION No.

REASONS
1. A deed, to be operative as a transfer of the ownership of land or an interest or estate therein, must be delivered.
2. A valid delivery of a deed requires that it pass beyond the control or domain of the grantor. The requisite relinquishment of control or dominion over the deed may be established, notwithstanding the fact that the deed was in possession of the grantor at her death, by proof of facts that tend to show delivery had been made with the intention to pass title and to explain the grantor's subsequent possession. However, in order for a delivery effectively to transfer title, the grantor must part with possession of the deed or the right to retain it.
3. There was no delivery of the deed by the grantor prior to her death.

Wiggill v. Cheney Cite as 597 P.2d 1351 (Utah) 1979.

When property is purchased on an installment contract—and occasionally in other cases—the deed is placed in the hands of a third party who will deliver it to the grantee upon the happening of some event, usually the final payment by the grantee. Such delivery to a third party is called delivery in *escrow*. In escrow arrangement, control over the deed is entirely out of the hands of the grantor. Only if the conditions are not satisfied is the escrow agent at liberty to return the deed to the grantor.

In order that the owner of real estate may notify all persons of the change in title to the property, the statutes of the various states provide that deeds shall be recorded in the recording office of the county in which the land is located. Failure to record a deed by a new owner makes it possible for the former owner to convey and pass good title to the property to an innocent third party, although the former owner has no right to do so and would be liable to his first grantee in such a case.

Transfer by judicial sale

Title to land may be acquired by a purchaser at a sale conducted by a sheriff or other proper official and made under the jurisdiction of a court having competent authority to order the sale. In order to raise money to pay a judgment secured against an owner, a *judicial sale* of the defendant's property may be necessary. To collect unpaid taxes, land owned by a delinquent taxpayer is sold at a public *tax sale*. The purchaser at a tax sale acquires a tax title. A mortgage foreclosure sale is a proceeding in equity by which a mortgagee obtains, by judicial sale, money to pay the obligation secured by the mortgage. The word *foreclosure* is also applied to the proceedings for enforcing other types of liens, such as mechanics' liens, assessments against realty to pay public improvements, and other statutory liens. The character of title acquired by a purchaser at a judicial sale is determined by state statute.

Title by adverse possession

Title to land may be acquired under a principle known as *adverse possession*. Thus a person who enters into actual possession of land and remains thereon openly and notoriously for the period of time prescribed in the statute of limitations, claiming title thereto in denial of, and adversely to, the superior title of another, will at the end of the statutory period acquire legal title.

CASE

D's land was separated from P's land by a fence. For over 20 years each party farmed the land on his side of the fence. A survey revealed that the fence inaccurately reflected the boundary in that the fence was on a part of P's land. P filed an ejectment suit and sought an injunction to have the fence moved to the correct boundary line as shown on the survey. D claimed title to the fence line by adverse possession.

ISSUE If a fence boundary is inaccurate but is used by the parties for over 20 years, may the landowner whose land boundary was shortchanged eject the other party and obtain an injunction to have the fence removed?

DECISION No.

REASON Where a fence is a boundary between two properties, and parties claim ownership of land up to the fence for the full statutory period without interruption, they will, by adverse possession, gain title to whatever land may have been improperly enclosed within their own fence.

Vetick v. Kula 247 N.W.2d 637 (Neb.) 1976.

The owner's knowledge that his land is occupied adversely is not essential to the claim, but possession must be of a nature that would charge a reasonably diligent legal owner with knowledge of the adverse claim. It has also been held that adverse possession will not run against a municipal corporation or other governmental body.

Color of title is an expression that refers to a title that has a defect but is otherwise good. A mistake in a deed does not convey clear title but does convey color of title. In many states adverse possession by one with color of title and paid real estate taxes will ripen into title in a much shorter period than is required for adverse possession without color of title. A state with a 20-year requirement may require only 10 years if there is color of title and payment of the taxes. This use of adverse possession is very important in clearing defective titles. Errors can be ignored after the statutory period if there is adverse possession, color of title, and payment of taxes.

Title by accretion

Soil added to land by action of water is an *accretion.* If a shore or bank is extended by gradual addition of matter deposited by water, the extension is called an *alluvion.* If water recedes and exposes more land, the increase in the shore or bank is a *reliction.* A sudden deposit of land such as that caused by a flood does not make a change in ownership or boundary lines; but, if the change is slow and gradual by alluvion or reliction, the newly formed land belongs to the owner of the bed of the stream in which the new land was formed. If opposite banks of a private stream belong to different persons, it is a general rule that each owns the bed to the middle of the stream; however, title to lands created by accretion may be acquired by adverse possession. In public waters, such as navigable streams, lakes, and the sea, the title of the bed of water, in the absence of special circumstances, is in the United States. Accretion to the land belongs to the riparian owner; islands created belong to the government.

Covenants and conditions

Quite often the grantor restricts the use of the land conveyed. These restrictions may be contained in the deed, or they may be made applicable to several tracts of land by including them with the plat of a subdivision. Where such restrictions are contained in a plat, they are binding on all subsequent purchasers, and they supplement the applicable zoning laws.

CASE

Ds owned land in a subdivision and proposed to erect two apartment buildings on it. Ps, residents of the subdivision, brought suit to enjoin the construction of the apartment buildings, since the construction would violate the covenants contained in the plat of the subdivision, which restricted buildings to one-story residences. Ds contended that they could construct the apartments because the land had been rezoned for apartment buildings.

ISSUE Will a restrictive covenant be enforced if it is more restrictive than the zoning laws?

DECISION: Yes.

REASONS

1. The covenants control because they require a more restrictive use of the land than is required under the applicable zoning requirements.
2. The zoning ordinance, itself, provides that it shall not interfere with any covenants or agreements between the parties, except where the ordinance imposes a *greater* restriction upon the use of buildings or land.

Lidke v. Martin, 500 P.2d 1184 (Colo. App.) 1972.

The typical restrictions contained in a plat or a deed may provide that the land shall be used exclusively for residential purposes, that the style and cost of the residence must meet certain specifications, and that certain portions shall be dedicated to the public for streets and sewers. These restrictions inserted in the deed are covenants or promises on the part of the grantee to observe them and are said to run with the land. Even though the grantee fails to include them in a subsequent deed made by him, any new owner is nevertheless subject to them. They remain indefinitely as restrictions against the use of the land, although they may not be enforced if conditions change substantially after the inception of the covenants.

Most of these covenants are inserted for the benefit of surrounding property. They may be enforced by surrounding owners, particularly when the owner of a subdivision inserts similar restrictions in each deed or in the plat. The owner of any lot subject to the restrictions is permitted to enforce the restrictions against other lot owners in the same subdivision. Restrictions in a deed, however, are strictly construed against the party seeking to enforce them. Doubts about restrictions are resolved in favor of freedom of the land from servitude, as a matter of public policy.

CASE

Ps owned land restricted against use for any business purpose. They wished to construct an apartment house on the land and asked that the court determine that the deed restriction would not preclude such construction. Ds, other landowners in the neighborhood, objected.

ISSUE Did the restriction prevent the construction of an apartment house on the land?

DECISION No.

REASONS
1. The use of Ps' premises for an apartment house did not violate the deed restriction against the use of those premises for any business purpose. The plaintiffs' apartment building would be used by its occupant for residential purposes.
2. Restrictions in a deed are to be strictly construed against the party seeking to enforce those restrictions, so that any doubt should be "resolved in favor of the freedom of land from servitude."

Walker v. Gross, 290 N.E.2d 543 (Mass.) 1972.

Occasionally, a covenant is inserted for the personal benefit of the grantor and will not run with the land. If a grantee, as part of the consideration, covenants to repair a dam on land owned by the grantor, the covenant will not run with the land and will not place a duty upon a subsequent grantee. The promise neither touches nor concerns the land; it is only a personal covenant for the benefit of the grantor.

It should be emphasized that covenants and conditions that discriminate on the grounds of race, creed, color, or national origin are unconstitutional as a denial of equal protection of the laws. Such covenants were common at one time and many are still incorporated in restrictions that accompany plats. When challenged, they have been held to be unconstitutional; they should today be considered void unless there is a court test case upholding their validity.

Interests in Real Property

Estates in fee simple

A person who owns the entire estate in real property is an *owner in fee simple*. A fee simple title, usually received by the grantee of a warranty deed, is the greatest and most complete interest a person may have in real estate. It is the maximum "bundle of rights."

Life estates

An owner of land may create, either by will or by deed, an interest known as a *life estate*. A life estate may be for the life of the grantee, or it may be created for the duration of the life of some other designated person. It may be created until the happening of an event such as the marriage of the life tenant. A husband may convey property to his wife for life or until she remarries. Unless the instrument that creates the life estate places limitations upon it, the interest can be sold or mortgaged as any other interest in real estate. The buyer or mortgagee must, of course, take into consideration the fact that the life estate may be terminated at any time by the death of the person for whose life it was created.

The life tenant is obligated to use reasonable care to maintain the property in the condition in which it was received, ordinary wear and tear excepted. There is a duty to repair, to pay taxes, and, out of the income received, to pay interest on any mortgage that may have been outstanding at the time the life estate was created. The life tenant has no right to waste the property or to do anything that tends to deplete the value of the property. A life tenant would have no right to drill for oil, mine coal, or cut timber from the land, unless those operations were being conducted at the time the life estate was created. Likewise, a life tenant has no duty to make lasting improvements to the property.

Life estates have many tax-savings features. They are widely used in estate planning to reduce both income and death taxes.

Remainders and reversions

After the termination of a life estate, the remaining estate may be given to someone else, or it may go back to the original owner or to his heirs. If the estate is to be given to someone else upon the termination of a life estate, it is called an *estate in remainder.* If it is to go back to the original owner, it is called a *reversion.* If the original owner of the estate is dead, the property reverts to the heirs of the original owner. A remainder or a reversionary interest may be sold, mortgaged, or otherwise disposed of as if it were any other interest in real property. Upon the death of the life tenant, the remainder or reversion becomes a fee simple interest once more.

Easements

An *easement* is a right granted for the use of real property. The grantor may convey to the grantee a right of way over his land, the right to erect a building that may shut off light or air, the right to lay drain tile under the land, or the right to extend utilities over the land. If these rights of easement are reserved in the deed conveying the property or granted by a separate deed, they pass along with the property to the next grantee and are burdens upon the land. An easement made by separate contract is binding only on the immediate parties to the agreement. If a right to use another's land is given orally, it is not an easement but a *license.* The owner of the land may revoke a license at any time unless it has become irrevocable by conduct constituting estoppel. An easement given by grant cannot be revoked except by deed, as such a right of way is considered a right in real property; nor can it be modified without the consent of the owner of the easement.

CASE

P filed suit against D to cancel or modify private driveway easements. The easements gave D the right to drive across P's land. The easements were granted by P's predecessor in title and were a matter of record. At the time the easements were granted, both the dominant parcel and the servient parcel were used for residential purposes, but the servient parcel is now zoned for commercial uses. P claims a right to terminate or modify because (1) all of the servient lands are now owned by one person, (2) the character of the area has changed, and (3) the easement is causing irreparable damage to the land.

ISSUE Is P entitled to cancel or to modify the easement?

DECISION No.

REASONS

1. An easement consists of two separate estates: the dominant estate—which has the benefit of the easement and to which it is attached—and the servient estate, on which the easement is imposed or rests. If each is owned by different persons, there can be no extinguishment of the easement by merger of estates.
2. The mere fact that the servient estate has changed in character is irrelevant to the question of termination of the easements. The primary restriction placed upon the owner of the dominant estate is that the burden created by the easement upon the servient estate cannot be materially increased, nor may new or additional burdens be imposed.
3. A way once located cannot be changed by either party without the consent of the other. When the right of way has once been exercised in a fixed and definite course, with full acquiescence and consent of both parties, it cannot be changed at the pleasure of either of them.

Edgell v. Divver 402 A.2d 395 (Del. Ch.) 1979.

An owner of land may create an easement for the benefit of another by deed. Usually, a party desiring an easement purchases it from the owner of the servient land. Or a seller of real estate may reserve an easement in his favor when deeding the property to someone else, a situation that will occur when a party sells only part of his land, and the portion retained requires the easement. Assume that farmer Brown sells half of his farm to a neighbor. Since the half sold borders on the only road touching the farm, Farmer Brown will need to reserve an easement for ingress and egress.

Easements may be obtained by adverse possession just as any other interest in land. Such easements are known as easements by prescription. Easements may be obtained also through judicial proceedings in certain cases. Since the law takes the position that an owner of land should be entitled to access to that land, owners of land that would otherwise be landlocked may be entitled to an easement by necessity. Such an easement is, in effect, granted by the owner of the servient land to the owner of the other land by implication. In the previous example of Farmer Brown, if he sold the half that did not touch the road, an easement by implication would be created on the half retained, because the law recognizes the need for access. Government bodies and public utilities may obtain easements by condemnation proceedings without the consent of the owner. Of course, the owner of the land is entitled to just compensation in such cases.

Multiple ownership

In chapter 28, we discussed the ownership of real property by two or more unrelated persons, either as *tenants in common* or as *joint tenants.* The nature of the granting clause in the deed or will by which the title is transferred determines which form of multiple ownership exists. A joint tenancy can be created only by a specific statement that the grantees shall hold title as joint tenants with the right of survivorship, not as tenants in common. Without such a clause, the grantees are tenants in common. Remember that on death, joint tenancy property passes to the surviving joint tenant. Tenancy in common property passes to one's heirs or pursuant to the will of the deceased tenant in common.

If the grantees are related by marriage and the state law so provides, a conveyance to a husband and wife creates a *tenancy by the entireties.* A tenancy by the entirety in states that authorize such common ownership of real estate can exist only between husband and wife. A conveyance of real estate to a husband and wife in these states is automatically a tenancy by the entirety. Neither tenant can unilaterally sever or end the tenancy. It may be terminated only by divorce, a joint transfer to a third party, or a conveyance by one spouse to the other. The inability of either spouse to terminate the tenancy unilaterally is the primary difference between a joint tenancy and a tenancy by the entireties, as the basic characteristic of each is the right of survivorship. In most states that authorize tenancy by the entireties, not only is there a prohibition on one tenant making a voluntary transfer of his or her share, but there are also severe restrictions on the rights of creditors to collect an individual debt from one tenant of the property. Suppose that a husband and wife own their home as tenants by the entireties. A creditor has a judgment for $10,000 against the husband alone. In most states, the creditor could not cause a sale of the house to collect the debt. Of course, if the creditor had a judgment against both husband and wife, he could collect from a judicial sale of the property.

Some states have abolished joint tenancies and tenancies by the entireties. In cases that resolve doubts about which tenancy was created, the law has shown that it favors tenancy in common. The right of survivorship has often been used to defeat the justifiable expectations of creditors and sometimes results in property passing to other than those intended. Hence, there is pressure to abolish this form of ownership in many states.

Several of the southwestern and western states have what is known as *community property,* having inherited it in part from their French and Spanish ancestors. In these states, most property acquired after marriage other than by devise, bequest, or from the proceeds of noncommunity property becomes the joint property of husband and wife. Control of the property is vested primarily in the husband, and he is authorized, in most states, to sell or to mortgage it. The proceeds of the sale or mortgage, in turn, become community property. Upon the death of one of the parties, title to at least half the community property passes to the survivor. In most of the states the disposition of the remainder may be by will or under the rules of descent.

Proving ownership

Ownership of real estate is a matter of public record. Every deed, mortgage, judgment, lien, or other transaction that affects the title to real estate must be made a matter of public record in the county in which the real estate is located. Deeds and other documents are usually recorded in the county recorder's office. The records of the probate court furnish the public documents necessary to prove title by will or descent. Divorce proceedings and other judicial proceedings that affect the title to real estate are also part of the public record.

In order to establish title to real estate, it is necessary to examine all the public records that may affect the title. In a few states, lawyers actually examine all the public records to establish the title to real estate. Because it is extremely difficult for an individual or his attorney to examine all the records, in most states businesses have been formed for the express purpose of furnishing the appropriate records for any given parcel of real estate. These *abstract companies* are usually well-established firms that have maintained tract indexes for many years and keep them current on a daily basis. Upon request, an abstract company prepares an abstract of record that sets forth the history of the parcel in question and all matters that may affect the title. The abstract of title is examined by an attorney, who writes his opinion concerning the title, setting forth any defects in the title as well as encumbrances against it. The abstract of title must be brought up to date each time the property is transferred or proof of title is required, in order that the chain of title might be complete. The opinion on title will be useless unless all court proceedings, such as foreclosures, partitions, transfers by deed, and probate proceedings, are shown. It should be noted that an attorney's opinion on title is just that—an opinion. If the attorney makes a mistake—his opinion states that his client has title to Blackacre, when in fact he does not have title to Blackacre—the client does not have title. His only recourse would be a malpractice suit against the attorney.

Because of limited resources, many lawyers are unable to respond in damages to pay losses caused by their mistakes. Therefore, the abstract of title and attorney's opinion as a means of protecting owners is in many cases not satisfactory. In addition, there may be title defects that do not appear of record and that the attorney does not cover in his title opinion. An illegitimate child may be an unknown heir with an interest in property, as may be a spouse in a secret marriage. To protect owners against such hidden claims and to offset the limited resources of most lawyers, *title insurance* has developed.

Title insurance is, in effect, an opinion of the title company instead of the lawyer. The opinion of the title company is backed up to the extent of the face value of the title insurance policy. If the purported owner loses his property, he collects the insurance just as if it were life insurance and the insured had died. Title insurance can cover matters beyond those in a title opinion. It has the financial backing of the issuing company, which is financially more secure than any law firm. Modern real estate practice uses abstracts and title policies rather than abstracts and title opinions. Title insurance companies usually maintain their own tract records, thus eliminating the cost of bringing the abstract up to date.

Another method used to prove ownership in some localities is known as the *Torrens System,* based on a registered title that can be transferred only upon the official registration records. The original registration of any title usually requires a judicial determination as to the current owner, and then all subsequent transfers merely involve the surrender of the registered title, in much the same way that an automobile title is transferred. The Torrens System is a much simpler system to use after a title has once been registered, but the high cost of obtaining the original registration has prevented the Torrens System from replacing abstracts and title policies as proof of title in most areas.

REVIEW QUESTIONS AND PROBLEMS

1. Define the following terms: life estate, remainder, reversion, adverse possession, easement, joint tenancy, tenancy in common, tenancy by the entireties, and fee simple.
2. List three methods for describing real estate. Illustrate each.
3. Name four types of deeds and distinguish the legal effect of each.
4. What is the purpose of an escrow provision in a real estate transaction?
5. Discuss the advantages of a title policy over an attorney's title opinion.
6. Gail sold a home to Florence and gave a warranty deed. Unknown to both of them, there were valid unrecorded encumbrances against the property. Does Florence have any remedy against Gail? Explain.
7. While selling his home to Ronald, Jimmy discovers that his brother, Billy, may have an interest in the land. Billy, independently wealthy and on good terms with Jimmy, wishes to help Jimmy sell the house. What method can Jimmy use to clear the title? Explain.
8. Alan owned land in a subdivision and planned to construct two apartment buildings on the land. Some residents of the subdivision brought suit for an injunction, contending that the construction would violate the covenants contained in the plat of the subdivision, which restricts buildings to single-family residents. Alan claimed that the covenant was no longer effective, because the land had been rezoned for apartment buildings. Should the restrictive covenant have been enforced? Why?
9. Dick and George owned adjoining property, but ownership of a plot on the boundary of their land was in dispute. Dick had been using the land as a garden for over twenty years. George had a survey made that indicated the plot was his. During the twenty years Dick had worked the land, George had made no claim to ownership. Dick claims ownership by adverse possession. May Dick keep the land? (Assume a twenty-year statute.) Explain.
10. Marguerite sold land to Joe reserving her right of free egress and ingress over the private road. Joe sold the land to Kim, but the deed did not mention that Kim was taking the land subject to the easement contained in the conveyance by Marguerite to Joe. Is the easement effective against Kim? Why?
11. For more than twenty years, Cy took his cattle across land belonging to Cartwright. During this time, Cartwright had always paid the taxes on the property. Is Cy entitled to an easement by prescription? Why?
12. A husband willed certain land to his wife for life, with the remainder to their children. After the husband died, his wife leased the property to a coal company, which strip mined the land. Have the children a good cause of action against the coal company? Why?

31

Real Estate Transactions

Three distinct interests are inherent in land: surface rights, mineral rights, and air rights. Any one of these rights may be bought, sold, or leased without affecting the other two; but unless the instrument transferring property clearly separates the interests, all three are included in a sale or lease.

Real property is subject to a variety of transactions, such as contracts of sale, contracts for a deed, and leases—all governed by the same general principles that apply to other contracts. Some special aspects of the law as it relates to contracts involving real estate were discussed in chapter 7, on offer and acceptance; in chapter 8, on consideration; and in chapter 11, on voidable contracts. There are also special provisions of the statute of frauds relating to real estate contracts. It will be extremely helpful to review these subjects at this time.

The Real Estate Contract of Sale

The offer to purchase

The typical contract for sale of real estate originates with the buyer making an *offer to purchase* from the seller. This offer to purchase is frequently obtained by a real estate broker or an agent. In most states an offer to purchase may be prepared by a real estate broker without the broker's being guilty of unauthorized practice of law. The offer is submitted to the seller for acceptance or rejection. Upon acceptance, this offer is often the only contract between the parties. Or the informal offer and acceptance may be taken to the buyer's or the seller's attorney for preparation of the actual contract. After the seller accepts the offer to purchase, an enforceable contract exists in most states, although it is desirable to have an attorney prepare a formal contract setting forth all aspects of the transaction. Real estate brokers cannot legally prepare such contracts in most states, since the preparation would constitute unauthorized practice of law.

It is important not only that an attorney prepare a contract of sale after the offer and acceptance are complete, but that the other party's attorney review the contract. Each party to a real estate contract needs the advice of legal counsel for several reasons. First of all, the doctrine of caveat emptor has long applied to real estate transactions. Buyers must make sure that the contract gives them all the benefits they have agreed to pay for. If there is to be a warranty that the premises are free of termites, the contract should so provide. Second, the interests of the seller and the interests of the buyer are in conflict and adversary. A seller is best served by a contract requiring delivery of a quitclaim deed, while a buyer's interests are best served by a contract calling for a warranty deed. Because of these conflicts of interest, it is neither wise nor ethical for one attorney to represent both parties to a real estate transaction. Third, several essential provisions are usually omitted from offers to purchase. Among the provisions that may not be found in offers to purchase are those relating to grace periods upon default, the terms of escrow, and forfeiture clauses. These and other provisions are discussed in the following sections.

Terms of the contract and escrows

The typical real estate contract of sale describes the property and sets forth the price, the method of payment, and the date of possession. It also contains provisions concerning the prorating of real estate taxes, the assignment of hazard insurance, the selection of an escrow agent, and whether the proof of title will be made by furnishing an abstract or a title insurance policy. The contract may also contain provisions concerning contingencies such as default by the buyer or destruction of the premises.

An escrow provision is desirable because to be effective, a deed must be delivered during the lifetime of the grantor. Because it is always possible for the grantor to die between the time of executing the contract and the date of delivery of possession and final payment, the deed is executed concurrently with the contract. The deed is then delivered to a third person known as the escrowee or escrow agent, to be delivered to the grantee upon final payment. If the seller grantor dies in the meantime, the transaction can still be consummated without delay.

CASE

H and W had a life estate in a tract of land, and Melford Egan owned the remainder. An agreement between the life tenants and the remainderman provided for a fifty-fifty division of the proceeds of any sale of the property, including a sale to the state in condemnation proceedings. On October 5, 1960, the parties under threat of condemnation executed a contract of sale and deed to the state of Missouri for a sale price of $30,500. The contract and deed were placed in escrow to be held until a check in the amount of the purchase price was received from the state. The check was received November 9, 1960. H and W were killed October 25, 1960, and their estates claim one-half the proceeds. Melford Egan contends that he is entitled to all the proceeds as the remainderman.

ISSUE Was the delivery of the deed to the escrow agent effective to pass title to the state, so that the life tenants were entitled to one-half the proceeds?

DECISION Yes.

REASONS
1. Upon final delivery by a depository of a deed deposited in escrow, the instrument will be treated as relating back to, and taking effect at the time of, the original deposit in escrow. This shall apply even though one of the parties to the deed dies before the second delivery.
2. The relation of vendor and purchaser exists as soon as a contract for the sale and purchase of land is entered into. Equity regards the purchaser as the owner and the vendor as holding the legal title in trust for him. This equitable principle, known as equitable conversion, may be invoked in actions at law, even though the purchaser has not been put in possession.

Donnelly v. Robinson, 406 S.W.2d (Mo.) 1966.

An escrow also prevents a claim of a creditor of the seller from interfering with the rights of the purchasers. The escrow in effect transfers title to the purchaser before the transaction is complete.

Closing the transaction

After the execution of the contract and deed, these documents are placed in escrow until the date for delivery of possession and final payment. During the interim period, the buyer's attorney will seek to verify that the seller has marketable title to the property. This may be done by checking the original records, but it will usually be accomplished by use of either an abstract of title or a title report from a title insurance company.

The *title report* is a letter committing the title company to issue a title policy upon payment of the premium. The preliminary commitment serves as a check of the records to date, to make sure that the title is clear. If the buyer obtains a loan on the premises, the lender will also want its lawyer to examine the title and to prepare the mortgage documents. Many contracts require the seller to furnish to the buyer a survey of the premises. Some contracts require the seller to prepare an affidavit concerning repairs and improvements to the premises within the applicable time period for mechanic's liens. A *mechanic's lien* is an encumbrance on real estate in favor of a contractor, subcontractor, supplier of materials, or laborer. Such persons are given a lien to ensure that they will be paid for their goods or services which have contributed value to the property by means of either a repair or an improvement. When the premises that are being sold have been constructed recently, an affidavit of the building contractor will be obtained, showing what mechanic's liens exist, if any.

At the time of closing the transaction, a closing statement will be prepared showing all sums due the seller and all credits due the buyer. A typical closing statement is shown in Fig. 31•1. Note that in the example a mortgage is being assumed and the buyer is given credit for it. Other credits include title costs, documentary revenue stamps if required by state law, taxes, and special assessments that are liens. The buyer will pay the net amount due to the seller or to the escrow agent for delivery to the seller, and the escrow agent will deliver the deed to the buyer for recording. At the same time, the seller will deliver possession of the premises to the buyer, and the transaction will be completed.

A contract for a deed

One special type of real estate contract is generally referred to as a *contract for a deed.* It is actually a conditional sale of real estate in which the seller retains title to the

CLOSING STATEMENT
LOT 1 OF KENNEDY SUBDIVISION
PARK, GEORGIA

SELLER: MARTHA KENNEDY
BUYER: SALLIE GOULD

Selling price		$75,000.00
Prepaid insurance		250.00
Escrow account for taxes		750.00
Total due seller		$76,000.00
Credits to buyer		
Down payment	$ 5,000.00	
Accrued general taxes	800.00	
Revenue stamps	20.00	
Mortgage principal assumed	54,000.00	
Mortgage interest to date of possession	600.00	
Title search and title policy	250.00	
Total credits to buyer		$60,670.00
Balance due seller		$15,330.00

Additional expenses

1. Buyer to pay to record deed.
2. Seller to pay real estate commission.
3. Both parties to pay own attorney's fees.

Fig. 31·1

property, and the buyer makes payments for an extended period of time. The buyer's right to a deed to the property is conditioned on his making all of the payments. Sometimes called *installment land contracts,* they contain the usual provisions found in other real estate contracts. The purchaser has the risk of loss if the improvements are destroyed during the period of the contract unless there is a state statute to the contrary.

The escrow provision is absolutely essential in contracts for a deed because several years usually intervene between execution of the contract and delivery of the deed. The buyer usually makes payments to the escrow agent, who must at all times be aware of the status of the contract.

Acceleration and forfeiture clauses

Two additional clauses in most installment land contracts are of particular significance. One of them is known as the *acceleration clause;* the other is known as the *forfeiture clause.* The acceleration clause allows the seller to declare the full amount of the contract due and payable in the event the buyer fails to make any of the payments or fails to perform any other of the contract's provisions as agreed. The default or forfeiture clause allows the seller, when the buyer is in default, to terminate the contract and to get the deed back from the escrow agent. The net effect of this clause is to allow the seller to keep all payments and improvements made as liquidated damages for breach of contract and to regain possession of the premises even if leased to a third party.

CASE

P sold real estate to T Corporation by a contract for deed. The contract contained a forfeiture clause in the event of T's failure to make the required payments. T leased the property to D. T defaulted on its contract with P. P declared the contract cancelled and refused to honor the lease agreement between D and T. P sued for possession of the premises.

ISSUE Was P bound by the lease contract between D and T? Is P entitled to possession?

DECISION P is not bound to the lease and is entitled to possession.

REASONS
1. T, by leasing the property to D, could not create any greater interest in D than T possessed, and the lessee took the property subject to all claims of title enforceable against T.
2. To hold that an owner under these circumstances could not regain the possession of his property because of a subsequent lease could lead to ludicrous and perhaps disastrous consequences. A purchaser might lease property to a third party for 99 years at a rental fee far below a fair or reasonable amount. If the purchaser defaulted on his obligation to pay, it would be unjust to force the owner to submit to the lease.

Campus v. Warner, 559 P.2d 1190, (N.M.) 1977.

After a buyer has made substantial payments or has a substantial equity in the land, forfeiture of a contract for a deed might be inequitable. The principles discussed in chapter 6 that apply to liquidated damages and forfeitures are also applicable to these contracts because courts of equity abhor forfeitures. When the buyer's equity is substantial and forfeiture would be inequitable, a court, upon proper application, may prohibit the forfeiture. The court orders the property to be sold and the proceeds distributed to the seller, to the extent necessary to pay off the contract. The balance is paid to the buyer. No general rule can be stated to describe cases in which a forfeiture will be allowed or not. As a part of its equitable jurisdiction, the court will examine all the facts. If the buyer has paid only a small amount, forfeiture usually will be permitted. If the buyer has made only a slight default with regard to the amount and time of payment, or the amount of the unpaid purchase price is much less than the value of the property involved, forfeiture will be denied. Forfeiture clauses are easily waived; but usually, a buyer must be notified if the clause is to be reinstated after he has defaulted without having been required to forfeit.

Housing warranties

Buyers have been allowed to rescind purchases on the ground of fraud or misrepresentation; but historically, warranties were found to exist only when specifically included in the contract. In other words, the seller of housing was not held responsible for the habitability of the structure or the quality of workmanship and materials.

In recent years, most states have changed the law as it relates to the sale of housing. By use of a variety of theories, courts in these states have imposed liability on sellers and builders of housing. Some courts have held that there is an implied warranty against structural defects similar to the implied warranty of fitness in the sale of personal property. They have held that there is no rational basis for differentiating between the sale of a newly constructed house by the builder vendor and the sale of any other manufactured product. These courts usually have not extended the warranty against structural defects to a house built by an individual who decides to sell it. Casual sales are not included, because the warranty arises when the seller is in the business of selling housing.

CASE

P, a home buyer, bought a tract of land from D, a contractor, and hired D to construct a house. The building contract was oral, without any express warranty. Within a year after completion, the sewage system was backed up into P's basement. It could not be repaired for less than $2,000. When sued, D pleaded "caveat emptor" and contended that there is no implied warranty of habitability, or fitness for purpose, in the purchase of a new home.

ISSUE Is there any implied warranty of habitability, or fitness, in the sale of a new home?

DECISION Yes.

REASONS
1. Although at common law there was no implied warranty of quality in the sale of realty, that rule has almost everywhere been reversed by judicial decree. The social mores of contemporary times simply will not allow such a substantial investment to go unprotected.
2. At early common law there might have been a more equal bargaining position between buyer and seller. But today, the buyer must depend upon the seller's competency when he purchases a home.
3. This ruling applies only to sales of new homes.

Tavares v. Horstman, 542 P.2d 1275 (Wyo.) 1975.

Other courts have created an implied warranty that a home is built and constructed in a reasonably workmanlike manner and that it is fit for its intended purpose—habitation. In one case there was no water supply, and the subdivider seller was held liable for breach of this warranty. In another case the air-conditioning system did not work properly, and the seller was held to have breached an implied warranty. In some cases the buyer is entitled to damages. If the breach is so great that the home is unfit for habitation, rescission is the remedy, but the theory of implied warranty does not impose on the builder an obligation to build a perfect house.

Congress is currently considering legislation that would require builders to give buyers of new homes a warranty for a stated period. The warranty would require the builder to repair defects discovered within the period and to replace defective portions of the structure if necessary. Consumer protection is gradually being extended to housing.

Leases

A *lease* is a transfer of possession of real estate from a landlord (lessor) to a tenant (lessee) for a consideration called *rent.* A lease may be oral or written, expressed or simply implied from the facts and circumstances. A lease differs from a mere license, which is a privilege granted by one person to another to use land for some particular purpose. A license is not an interest in the land. A license to the licensee is personal and not assignable.

Duration

A lease may be a tenancy (1) for a stated period, (2) from period to period, (3) at will, or (4) at sufferance. As its name implies, a tenancy for a stated period lasts for the specific time stated in the lease. The statute of frauds requires a written lease if the period exceeds one year. The lease for a stated period terminates without notice at the end of the period. It is not affected by the death of either party during the period. A lease of land for a stated period is not terminated by destruction of the improvements during the period unless the lease so provides. If a lease covers *only* the improvements on land, destruction of them creates impossibility of performance.

A tenancy from period to period may be created by the terms of the lease. A lease may run from January 1, 1981, to December 31, 1982, and from year to year thereafter unless terminated by the parties. Many leases from period to period arise when the tenant, with the consent of the landlord, holds over after the end of a lease for a stated period. When a holdover occurs, the landlord may object and evict the former tenant as a trespasser. Or he may continue to treat the tenant as a tenant; in which case the lease continues from period to period, with the period being identical to that of the original lease, not to exceed one year. The one-year limitation results from the language of the statute of frauds. The amount of rent is identical to that of the original lease.

CASE

P, a hotel, leased space in the lobby to D. The lease was to expire on February 28, 1971. D did not vacate the premises on February 28 but remained in possession and sent a check in payment of the March rent. The check was cashed by P. D contended that by cashing the check, the lease was renewed for another year. Upon D's refusal to vacate the premises, P brought an action to force D to leave, and the lower court found for P.

ISSUE Did the holding over and payment of the rent renew the lease for another year?

DECISION No.

REASON Receiving and cashing the March rent check did not create a holdover year-to-year tenancy. The landlord had the right to treat the tenant as a holdover tenant and to permit the terms of the original lease to continue in effect or to consider D a trespasser. The landlord chose the latter and accordingly, as a trespasser, the defendant was ordered to vacate the premises.

Sheraton-Chicago Corporation v. Lewis, 290 N.E.2d 685 (Ill.) 1972.

Leases from year to year or from month to month can be terminated only upon giving proper notice. The length of the notice is usually prescribed by state statute—usually 30 days for a month-to-month lease, 60 to 90 days for one that is year-to-year. Statutes usually provide the time of the notice, such as on the day the rent is due. Farm leases usually have a special notice period, so that the tenant will have notice before planting the next year's crops.

A tenancy at will, by definition, has no period and can be terminated by either party at any time upon giving the prescribed statutory notice. A few states do not require notice, but if legal action is necessary to obtain possession for the lessor, a time lag will be automatically imposed. A tenancy at sufferance occurs when a tenant holds over without the consent of the landlord. Until the landlord decides to evict him or to allow him to stay, he is a tenant at sufferance.

Rights and duties of lessees

The rights and duties of the parties to the lease are determined by the lease itself and by the statutes of the state in which the property is located. Several rights of lessees are frequently misunderstood. For example, the lessee is entitled to exclusive possession and control of the premises unless the lease provides to the contrary. The landlord has no right to go upon the premises except to collect rent. This means that the owner of an apartment building cannot go into the leased apartments and inspect them unless the lease specifically reserves the right to do so. At the end of the lease, the landlord may retake possession of the premises and inspect for damage. A landlord may also retake possession for purposes of protecting the property, if the tenant abandons the premises.

Unless the lease so provides, a tenant has no duty to make improvements or substantial repairs. A tenant is not obligated to replace a worn-out heating or air conditioning system, but it is his duty to make minor repairs such as replacing a broken window. Because of the difficulty in classifying repairs, the lease should spell out the exact obligations of both parties. If the lease obligates the tenant to make repairs, the obligation includes significant items such as replacing a rotten floor or a defective furnace. The duty to repair usually does not extend to replacing the whole structure if it is destroyed.

An important right in many leases of commercial property is the tenant's right to remove trade fixtures that he has installed during the lease period. Remember the distinction between fixtures and trade fixtures. The former become a part of the real estate and belong to the owner of the land. The latter remain personally and belong to the tenant. The right of removal terminates with the lease, and unremoved trade fixtures become the property of the lessor.

Another important right of the tenant relates to his corresponding duty of payment. The duty to pay rent is subject to setoffs for violations of the provisions of the lease by the landlord. The duty to pay rent is released in the event of an eviction, actual or constructive. Constructive eviction occurs when the premises become untenantable, not because of any fault of the tenant, or when some act of the landlord deprives the tenant of quiet enjoyment of the premises. Assume that Joe College rents a basement apartment on campus. A spring rain floods the apartment and makes it uninhabitable. Joe has been constructively evicted. He may move out, and his duty to pay rent is released. Failure to vacate the premises is a waiver of constructive eviction grounds, however. A tenant who continues in possession despite grounds for constructive eviction must continue to pay rent unless this duty is relieved by statute. Some states and cities in recent years have enacted such laws in an attempt to force landlords to maintain their property in a tenantable condition. These laws allow tenants to withhold rent where the premises are in such disrepair that the health and safety of the tenant is jeopardized. Such laws protect low-income tenants from slum landlords.

Unless prohibited by the lease, a lessee may assign the lease or sublet the premises without the consent of the lessor.

CASE

D Company opened a supermarket as one of the original tenants of a shopping center. Shortly before the conclusion of the ten-year lease, owing to declining sales, D entered into a sublease with T for the store. Subtenant T assumed all of D's obligations under the prime lease. P, the owner of the shopping center, claims that D's sublease to T for use as a commissary was inconsistent with the terms of the prime lease and a breach of the tenant's implied warranty to occupy the premises. There is no clause in the lease concerning the right of the tenant to assign or sublet, but there is a clause that provides that if the tenant voluntarily vacates the premises and they remain vacant for one year, the landlord has the right to cancel the lease and re-enter the business.

ISSUE Did D have the right to sublet to T?

DECISION Yes.

REASONS

1. With regard to subletting and assignment in particular, a lessee may freely transfer the demised premises without the lessor's consent unless there is a covenant in the lease restricting the right of assignment. Also, the general rule is that covenants against subletting are strictly construed against the lessor.
2. Landlord, P, bears a heavy burden in proving that the lease contains an implied limitation on subleasing. Such implied covenants must arise from the terms of the lease itself.
3. The restriction on competition written into this lease is not broad enough to give birth to implied covenants of continuous occupancy and operation of a grocery business and a prohibition against subleasing to a nongrocery without the lessor's permission.

Kroger Co., v. Chemical Securities Co., 526 S.W. 2d 468 (Tenn.) 1975.

In an assignment, the assignee becomes liable to the lessor for the rent (of course, the assignor remains liable also). In a sublease, the subleasee is liable to the lessee, and the lessee is liable to the lessor. An assignment transfers the original leasehold to the assignee. A sublease creates a new leasehold estate. Ordinarily, an assignment is for the balance of the original lease, whereas a sublease is only for part of the term.

If a lease prohibits assignment, it does not necessarily prevent a sublease; if a lease prohibits subleasing, it does not necessarily prevent assignment; if both are to be prohibited, the lease should so provide.

Most leases provide that any assignment or sublease must have the approval of the landlord, but that approval cannot be withheld unreasonably. A landlord's rejection is judged by reasonable commercial standards.

Warranty of habitability

In recent years, courts have been called upon to decide if there is an implied warranty of habitability in a lease of residential property. (This is similar to the issue of warranties on the sale of new housing and is part of the broadened protection given the consuming public.) Some courts have held in all housing leases that there is an implied warranty of habitability. One court held that the fact that a tenant knew of a substantial number of defects when he rented the premises and that rent was accordingly reduced did not remove the tenant from protection of the warranty. The court reasoned that permitting that type of bargaining would be contrary to public policy and the purpose of the doctrine of implied warranty of habitability. In determining the kinds of defects that will be deemed to constitute a breach of warranty of habitability, several factors are considered. Among the common factors are (1) the violation of any applicable housing code or building or sanitary regulations; (2) whether the nature of the deficiency affects a vital facility; (3) the potential or actual effect upon safety and sanitation; and (4) whether the tenant was in any way responsible for the defect. A breach of this warranty may allow a tenant to terminate the lease. It may serve as a defense to a suit for rent and as a means to obtain a rent reduction.

Defects in vital portions of the premises that may affect health are more important than defects in extras such as swimming pools or recreational facilities, which are not likely to render the premises uninhabitable. It should also be kept in mind that not all states recognize that there is an implied warranty of habitability in residential leases and that there is no such warranty in commercial leases.

CASE

P entered into an oral, month-to-month lease of a one-bedroom apartment from D. Tenant P inspected the premises before accepting and occupying them with his family. Numerous defects, confirmed by building inspectors, were not visible to P at the time of his inspection. Electrical wiring was faulty; plumbing burst, resulting in no hot water; structural defects caused bricks of the building to fall. Landlord D received a city notice either to repair or vacate the premises. D gave notice to P to vacate the premises. D did not correct the defects. Subsequently, P stopped paying rent, claiming uninhabitability as an excuse, but did not vacate the premises until several months later. P also sued D for dollar damages.

ISSUE Is P entitled to damages from D because of breach of an implied warranty of habitability?

DECISION Yes.

REASONS

1. In a rental of a dwelling unit, whether for a specified time or at will, there is an implied warranty of habitability by the landlord that the apartment is habitable and fit for living. This means that at the inception of the rental lease there are no latent defects in the facilities that are vital to the use of the premises for residential purposes and that these essential facilities will remain in a condition that makes the property livable.
2. In order to constitute a breach of implied warranty of habitability, the defect must be of a nature that will render the premises unsafe or unsanitary or otherwise unfit for living therein.
3. The nature of the deficiency, its effect on habitability, the length of time for which it persisted, the age of the structure, the amount of the rent, the area in which the premises are located, whether the tenant waived the defects, and whether the defects resulted from malicious, abnormal, or unusual use by the tenant—all are among the factors to be considered in deciding if there has been a breach of the warranty of habitability.

Kamarath v. Bennett, 568 S.W. 2d 658 (Tex.) 1978.

Rights and duties of lessors

A landlord is entitled to possession of the premises upon termination of the tenancy. If the tenancy is lawfully terminated, the right to possession is absolute. The motive of the landlord in termination is usually immaterial. Of course, a landlord may not discriminate in leasing or termination on the basis of race, color, creed, sex, or national origin.

A landlord is entitled to recover from either the tenant or a third party for injuries to the property. In many states and by the express terms of many leases, the landlord has a lien for unpaid rent on the personal property of the tenant physically located on the premises. This lien right is exercised in a statutory proceeding known as *distress for rent.* By following the prescribed procedures, the landlord is able to distrain or physically hold personalty on the premises until the rent is paid. If not paid, the tenant's personal property may be sold pursuant to court order. The proceeds of the sale, after deducting court costs, are applied to the rent.

Tenants sometimes neither keep possession nor pay the rent for the full term of the lease. This is especially true in long-term commercial leases. What are the rights and duties of the parties when the tenant breaches the lease contract by abandoning the premises? Does the landlord have a duty to seek a new tenant? The answer to these questions depends on state law. In some states a landlord need not seek a new tenant, and the full obligation of the tenant remains. In these states, the tenant can look for someone to take over the lease, but the lessor need not. The modern view is that the landlord has a duty to mitigate the tenant's damages. If the landlord fails to attempt to mitigate the damages, the tenants liability is eliminated.

CASE

D, as a tenant, entered into a five-year lease with P, as landlord for premises to be used as a grocery store. When the business failed, D leased the building to a subtenant, who was later adjudicated a bankrupt. P then listed the premises with a broker, but at an annual rent of $33,600, which was $12,600 greater than the rent provided in the original lease with D. P was unable to relet the premises at the higher rental and sued D for accrued rent. D contended that P had failed to mitigate the damages and that this excused him from paying the accrued rent.

ISSUE Is P entitled to the accrued rent?

DECISION No.

REASON A landlord has a duty to mitigate damages that arise out of a tenant's default. Since the new rental figure exceeded the old one by more than 50 percent, the landlord's listing of the premises with a broker did not constitute a good-faith effort to mitigate damages.

MAR-SON, Inc. v. Terwaho Enterprises, 259 N.W. 2d 289 (N.D.) 1977.

It is common practice for a landlord to require that the tenant deposit a stated sum of money, such as one month's rent, as security for the lease. This security deposit covers nonpayment of rent and possible damage to the premises. Many landlords have been reluctant to return these security deposits, contending in most cases that damages were present, requiring repairs. As a result, many tenants have refused to pay the last month's rent, demanding that the security deposit be applied. Such practices by landlords and tenants have created a great deal of animosity and litigation. To alleviate this problem, the legislatures of many states have passed laws governing lease security deposits. Such laws usually require that the landlord pay interest on the deposits and itemize the cost of any repairs that were made from the deposit. They further require the landlord to return the deposit promptly and prohibit the landlord from using it to repair conditions caused by normal wear and tear. In the event a tenant is required to sue the landlord to recover the deposit, the tenant is entitled to collect attorney's fees. Finally, under these statutes, the tenant usually is not allowed to set off the deposit against the last month's rent.

A tenant is estopped from denying his landlord's title and has a duty to redeliver the premises, upon expiration of the lease, in the same condition as received, ordinary wear and tear excepted.

Tenants may not make any material change in the structure without the landlord's permission. They may not move walls, install new ones, or do anything else that constitutes a material change in the premises without the permission of the lessor.

Liability to third persons

Difficult legal questions arise in cases involving the landlord's and tenant's liability for injuries to persons on the premises. As a general rule, a landlord makes no warranty that the premises are safe or suitable for the intended use by the tenant, and third persons are on the premises at their own peril. A landlord owes no greater duty to a tenant's guests than is owed to the tenant. A landlord does have a duty to give notice of latent defects of which he has knowledge, some states add unknown defects of which he *should* have knowledge in the exercise of ordinary care. In recent years, the liability of landlords under this view has expanded, but there still must be a duty that is breached before there is liability.

CASE

P, a tenant's father, was shot and killed in the underground parking garage of an apartment house. There were no known prior incidents of crime in the building. Because of increasing crime in the neighborhood, D, the landlord, was installing additional security measures at the time of the incident. P contended that the landlord had a duty to protect tenants from criminal assaults.

ISSUE Did D violate a duty owed to P?

DECISION No.

REASON The landlord does not have a special duty to protect tenants unless malfeasance or negligence can be shown. Here, the landlord had no prior knowledge of any criminal activities on the premises.

Scott v. Watson, 359 A.2d 548 (Md.) 1976.

Knowing that business invitees of the lessee will be constantly entering the premises to transact business, the owner of business property has an increased responsibility known as the "public use" exception to the general rule. The basis of the exception is that the landlord leases premises on which he knows or should know that there are conditions likely to cause injury to persons, that the purpose for which the premises are leased involve the fact that people will be invited upon the premises as patrons of the tenant, and that the landlord knows or should know that the tenant cannot reasonably be expected to remedy or guard against injury from the defect. Thus a landlord of a business owes a higher duty than does the landlord of essentially private premises. Moreover, landlords of business premises often undertake to care for the common areas. In such cases, they have a duty to inspect, repair, and maintain common areas in a reasonably safe condition.

Many suits against lessors by third persons result from falls on the premises, often associated with ice, snow, or waxed floors. As a general rule, a landlord has no duty to remove ice and snow. The landlord has a duty to use reasonable care; and in the absence of an agreement, most courts hold that this does not require removal of ice and snow. If the landlord does undertake to remove snow and ice, he must do so with ordinary care, taking into account dangerous conditions caused by subsequent thawing and freezing of snow placed near the walkway. This duty to use reasonable care in removing ice and snow has been found to exist by many courts when the lease is a business one. It is part of the "public use" exception previously noted.

Condominiums

A condominium is an individually owned apartment or town house in a multiunit structure such as an apartment building or in a complex. A method of owning and transferring property, it possesses some of the characteristics of a lease and some of a contract of sale. In addition to the individual apartment or townhouse, the owner has an undivided interest in the common areas of the building and land, such as hallways, entrances, yard, and recreation areas. Thus the deed to a condominium covers the housing unit involved and an undivided fractional interest in the common areas. There is usually an organization to operate the common areas, to make repairs, and to make improvements. Each owner of a unit has one vote in the election of a board of governors or directors. The board operates the development subject to approval by the owners. There are limits on the powers of the board as the following case illustrates.

CASE

When P's bought their condominium unit in 1974, the agreement they signed indicated that units could be used by an owner's family, guests, and invitees. One year later, the condominium's board of directors promulgated new rules restricting guest occupancy to an owner's immediate family and only for a limited time. P's sued, claiming that the new rules infringed their right to use their unit as they saw fit. D's board of directors argued that it had authority to promulgate rules reasonably calculated to promote the health and peace of mind of all unit owners.

ISSUE Were the rules limiting occupancy valid?

DECISION No.

REASON The board of directors did not have power to promulgate rules restricting occupancy in this case. It should have amended the declaration and bylaws, subject to approval by association members.

Winter v. Playa del Sol Ass'n., 353 So. 2d 598 (Fla.) 1978.

Taxes are usually prorated on the common areas by using the fractional proportion of the undivided interests. Condominiums are of growing importance in metropolitan and resort areas, and a determination of an owner's rights requires a study of not only the law of real property but also the law of business organizations.

There is a distinction between a *condominium* and a *cooperative* insofar as the ownership of real estate is concerned. A cooperative venture may involve an activity such as a retail store, or it may involve the ownership and operation of a residential development. If a person buys an interest in a cooperative, he is purchasing a share of a not-for-profit corporation. Strictly speaking, the owner of an interest in a cooperative does not own real estate. He owns personal property—his share of the cooperative. The cooperative would pay taxes and upkeep out of the assessments to its members. A condominium contains multiple units for taxing purposes; the cooperative is a single unit. The same may be said for the financing. Each owner of a condominium may mortgage his or her own portion. In a cooperative, if there is financing, there will be only one mortgage. In both the condominium and the cooperative there is a special form of business organization to coordinate the operation of the property.

REVIEW QUESTIONS AND PROBLEMS

1. Give three reasons why both parties to a contract for the sale of real estate should obtain legal advice.
2. What is an *acceleration clause* in a contract for a deed? What is a *forfeiture clause* in a contract for a deed?
3. Compare a real estate contract of sale with a *contract for a deed.*
4. Explain the concept of *equitable conversion.*
5. Eastman purchased Costello's home. The contract of sale did not contain any warranties on the condition of the home. One week after the delivery of possession and final payment, the roof began to leak. Is Costello liable for the cost of repairs? Why?
6. Brownlee, owner of an apartment building, leased an apartment to Reeve, a college student. During Reeve's absence, Brownlee inspected the property to ascertain if Reeve had alcoholic beverages on the premises. When Brownlee confronted Reeve with some empty beer bottles he had taken from the apartment, Reeve sued Brownlee for trespass. Is the landlord guilty? Explain.
7. A hotel leased store space to a toy store for one year ending in February. In September and November, the hotel sent letters to the toy store's owner, informing her that the lease would not be renewed. Nevertheless, when the lease expired, the toy store did not vacate the premises, but the owner mailed a check to the hotel with the notation "March rent" on the reverse side. The check was deposited by the hotel, and the toy store owner claimed that the lease had been renewed for another year. Is she correct? Why?
8. In 1978, Solid Construction Company built and sold a house to Proffitt. Proffitt sold the house to Laser in 1981. After moving into the house, Laser discovered that the basement leaked and that there was a large crack around three of the basement walls. Should Solid Construction be liable to Laser for the cost of repairs, which amounted to $3,500? Why?
9. A landowner and general contractor entered into a contract whereby the contractor agreed to erect a building on the owner's land. Upon completion, the building's roof leaked whenever it rained. The owner brought suit, claiming that the contractor had breached the implied warranty of habitability. Is the owner correct? Why?
10. Lorey agreed to lease a 105-acre tract of land to Termotto for a term of five years. The lease provided, "Lessee will not sublet the premises to any person without the consent of Lessor in writing, thereto first obtained." Subsequently, Termotto subleased the land to Sovia without obtaining the consent of Lorey. Should Lorey be entitled to terminate the lease and collect the amount of the unpaid rent from Termotto? Why?
11. Neill executed a contract for the purchase of a commercial building from Butler. The contract contained a provision stating that if the payments by Neill were more than thirty days overdue, Butler could declare a default and obtain the deed back from the escrowee. After twelve years of the twenty-year contract, Neill fell on hard times and made no payments for almost a year. Would a court allow Butler to default the contract, cancel the deed, and reacquire possession of the property? Explain.

VI

Agency

32 Introduction to Agency

The term *agency* is used to describe the fiduciary relationship that exists when one person acts on behalf, and under the control, of another person. The person who acts for another is called an *agent.* The person for whom he acts, and who controls the agent, is called a *principal.* Traditionally, issues of agency law arise when the agent has attempted to enter into a contract on behalf of his principal; however, the law of agency includes several aspects of the law of torts. Although tort litigation usually uses the terms *master* and *servant,* rather than principal and agent, both relationships are encompassed within the broad legal classification of agency law.

The principles of agency law are essential for the conduct of business transactions. A corporation, as a legal entity, can function only through agents. The law of partnership is, to a large degree, agency principles specially applied to that particular form of business organization. It is not surprising, therefore, that a substantial number of agency issues are involved in litigation. Case law provides us with most of the principles applicable to the law of agency.

Agency issues are usually discussed within a framework of three parties: the principal (P), the agent (A), and the third party (T), with whom A contracts or against whom

A commits a tort while in P's service. The following examples illustrate the problems and issues involved in the law of agency.

T v. P: Third party sues principal for breach of a contract that T entered into with A or for damages because of a tort committed by A.

T v. A: Third party sues agent personally for breach of the contract entered into by the agent or for committing a tort.

P v. T: Principal sues third party for breach of a contract that A entered into with T for P.

A v. T: Agent sues third party for some loss suffered by A, perhaps the loss of a commission due to T's interference with a contract.

P v. A: Principal sues agent for loss caused by A's failure to perform his duties, such as to obey instructions.

A v. P: Agent sues principal for injuries suffered in course of employment, for wrongful discharge, or for sums due for services or advancements.

Terminology

An agent may act on behalf of a designated principal called a *disclosed principal.* If the agent purports to act for himself and keeps his agency a secret, the principal is called an *undisclosed principal.* A third term, *partially disclosed principal,* is used to describe the situation in which the agent acknowledges that he is acting for a principal but does not disclose his identity.

Some persons who perform services for others are known as *independent contractors.* A person may contract for the services of another in a way that gives him full and complete control over the details and manner in which the work will be conducted, or he may simply contract for a certain end result. If the agreement provides merely that the second party is to accomplish a certain result and that he has full control over the manner and methods to be pursued in bringing about the result, he is deemed an independent contractor. The party contracting with an independent contractor and receiving the benefit of his service is usually called a *proprietor.* A proprietor is generally not responsible to third parties for the independent contractor's actions, either in contract or in tort. On the other hand, if the second party places his services at the disposal of the first in such a manner that the action of the second is generally controlled by the former, an agency relation is established.

Some agents are known as *brokers* and others as *factors.* A *broker* is an agent with special, limited authority to procure a customer in order that the owner can effect a sale or exchange of property. A real estate broker has authority to find a buyer for another's real estate, but the real estate remains under the control of the owner. A *factor* is a person who has possession and control of another's personal property, such as goods, and is authorized to sell that property. A factor has a property interest and may sell the property in his own name, whereas a broker may not.

Agents are also classified as *general* or *special* agents. A *general* agent has much broader authority than does a special agent. Some cases define a general agent as one authorized to conduct a series of transactions involving a continuity of service, whereas a *special* agent conducts a single transaction or a series of transactions without continuity of service.

Capacity of parties

It is generally stated that anyone who may act for himself may act through an agent. To this rule there is one well-recognized exception. A minor may enter into a contract and so long as he does not disaffirm, the agreement is binding. However, there is considerable authority to the effect that any appointment of an agent by an infant is void, not merely voidable. Under this view, any agreement entered into by such an agent would be ineffective, and an attempted disaffirmance by the minor would be superfluous. Many recent cases hold, however, that a contract of the agent on behalf of a minor principal is voidable only and is subject to rescission or ratification by the minor, the same as if the minor had personally entered into the contract.

A minor may act as an agent for an adult, and agreements he makes for his principal while acting within his authority are binding on the principal. Although the infant agent has a right to terminate his contract of agency at his will, as long as he continues in the employment, his acts within the scope of the authority conferred upon him become those of his principal.

Formal requirements

As a general rule, no particular formalities are required to create an agency. The appointment may be either written or oral, and the relationship may be expressed or implied.

Two situations do require formalities. First, when the purpose of the agency can be exercised only by the signing of a formal document, the agency must be created in writing. When a formal instrument is used for conferring authority upon the agent, he is said to possess a *power of attorney.* The agent is called an *attorney in fact,* to distinguish him from an *attorney at law,* the term used to describe lawyers. A power of attorney may be general, giving the agent authority to act in all respects as the principal could act; or it may be special, granting to the agent only restricted authority. A power of attorney is customarily executed before a notary public.

Second, the statute of frauds in the majority of the states requires that any agent who is given power to sell or convey any interest in, or concerning, real estate must obtain such power by a written authorization from the principal. In most states, the law does not require a written agreement to contract with a real estate broker. The function of the broker is merely to find a buyer with whom the seller is willing to contract. Normally, a broker has no authority to enter into a binding contract to convey the property. Special statutes in many states require that a "listing agreement" be in writing, or the real estate broker is not entitled to a commission.

Duties of agents

The nature and extent of the duties imposed upon agents and servants are governed largely by the contract of employment. In addition to the duties expressly designated, certain others are implied by the fiduciary nature of the relationship and by the legal effects on the principal of actions or omissions by the agent. The usual implied duties are (1) to be loyal to his principal; (2) to obey all reasonable instructions; (3) not to be negligent; (4) to account for all money or property received for the benefit of the principal; and (5) to inform the principal of all facts that materially affect the subject matter of the agency. The sections that follow will more fully discuss how these implied duties are essential to the employer-employee relationship.

Duty of loyalty

An agent stands in a fiduciary relationship to the principal and thus has a duty of undivided loyalty to the principal. Because of the duty of loyalty, an agent should not undertake a business venture that competes or interferes in any manner with the business of the employer; nor should he make any contract for himself that should have been made for the principal. An agent cannot enter into a contract on behalf of the principal if the agent is also the other party. An agent may deal with himself only if he obtains the permission of the principal. In any case in which the agent obtains the consent of the principal to deal with himself, the agent must disclose fully all facts that materially influence the situation. In such a case, the agent and principal do not deal "at arm's length," and the circumstances demand the utmost good faith on the part of the agent.

Transactions violating the duty of loyalty may always be rescinded by the principal, despite the fact that the agent acted for the best interests of his principal and the contract was as favorable as could be obtained elsewhere. The general rule is applied without favor, in order that every possible motive or incentive for unfaithfulness may be removed.

In addition to the remedy of rescission, a principal is entitled to treat any profit realized by the agent in violation of this duty as belonging to the principal. Such profits include rebates, bonuses, commissions, or divisions of profits received by an agent for dealing with a particular third party. Here again the contracts may have been favorable to the employer, but the result is the same because the agent should not be tempted to abuse the confidence placed in him. The principal may also collect from the agent a sum equal to any damages sustained as the result of the breach of the duty of loyalty.

CASE

P's wanted to buy an apartment house for $80,000 to $90,000. Since they were inexperienced in real estate transactions, they told their agent, Mr. Bunger, an employee of D, a real estate firm, that they were totally dependent upon his advice. Bunger and D did not tell P's that they were also the agents for Johnson, a builder of apartment houses. Nonetheless, D encouraged P's to sign a contract with Johnson to build a new apartment for $120,000. P's sued for damages upon learning of D's "dual agency" status.

ISSUE Is D liable?

DECISION Yes.

REASONS
1. A real estate agent has a fiduciary obligation of the utmost good faith and fidelity toward his principal. The law requires the fiduciary to make full, fair, and timely disclosure to the principal of all facts within his knowledge that are or may be material to the transaction. He must scrupulously avoid representing interests antagonistic to those of the principal.
2. If an agent fails to disclose his dual agency status, he may be obligated to forfeit his commission and may be liable for other damages.

Meerdink v. Krieger, 550 P. 2d 42 (Wash. App.) 1976.

Confidential information

The duty of loyalty demands that information of a confidential character acquired while in the service of the principal shall not be used by the agent to advance his interests in opposition to those of the principal. This confidential information is usually called a *trade secret.* Trade secrets include plans, processes, tools, mechanisms, compounds, and informational data used in business operations. They are known only to the owner of the business and to a limited number of other persons in whom it may be necessary to confide. An employer seeking to prevent the disclosure or use of trade secrets or information must demonstrate that he pursued an active course of conduct designed to inform his employees that such secrets and information were to remain confidential. An issue to be determined in all cases involving trade secrets is whether the information sought to be protected is, in fact and in law, confidential. The result in each case depends on the conduct of the parties and the nature of the information.

An employee who learns of secret processes or formulas or comes into possession of lists of customers may not use this information to the detriment of his employer. Former employees may not use such information in a competing business, regardless of whether the trade secrets were copied or memorized. The fact that a trade secret is spied out does not make it any less a secret, nor does the fact that a product is on the market amount to a divulgence or abandonment of the secrets connected with the product. The employer may obtain an injunction to prevent their use. Such use is a form of unfair competition. The rule relating to trade secrets is applied with equal severity whether the agent acts before or after he severs his connection with the principal.

Knowledge that is important but not a trade secret may be used, although it affects the agent's former employer injuriously. That which by experience has become a part of a former employee's general knowledge cannot and ought not be enjoined from further and different uses. For this reason, there is nothing to hinder a person who has made the acquaintance of his employer's customers from later contacting those whom he can remember. His acquaintanceship is part of his acquired skill. The employer may protect himself by a clause in the employment agreement to the effect that the employee will not compete with the employer or work for a competitor for a limited period of time after his employment is terminated.

Duty to obey instructions

It is the duty of an agent to obey all instructions issued by his principal as long as they refer to duties contemplated by the contract of employment. Burdens not required by the agreement cannot be indiscriminately imposed by the employer, and any material change in an employee's duties may constitute breach of the employment contract.

CASE

P sued D for breach of an alleged employment contract. P had sold D a test-publishing business. D had, in turn, employed P in an executive and supervisory role to head its test book division. Later, D put others in charge of P and relegated him to writing test questions. P refused to take orders from those placed above him in the organization. D discharged P for insubordination.

ISSUE Does a material change in duties constitute a breach of contract sufficient to justify a refusal to perform them?

DECISION Yes.

REASONS
1. If an employee is engaged to fill a particular position, any material changes in his duties or significant reduction in rank constitutes a breach of contract.
2. Acts done by an employee in defense of his contract rights or in assertion of an agreed status or function in an enterprise are not insubordination.
3. Although P could be discharged for nonperformance or misperformance, he could not be reduced to a rank or responsibility beneath that defined by the agreement. Nor could he be put into a state of "deep-freeze" until he was provoked into such gross disobedience of "orders" that a discharge for insubordination would be plausible.

Rudman v. Cowles Communications, Inc., 280 N.E.2d 867 (N.Y.) 1972.

An instruction may not be regarded lightly merely because it departs from the usual procedure and seems fanciful and impractical to the employee. It is not his business to question the procedure outlined by his superior. Any loss that results while he is pursuing any other course makes him absolutely liable to the principal for any resulting loss.

Furthermore, an instruction of the principal does not become improper merely because the motive is bad, unless it is illegal or immoral. The employer may be well aware of the agent's distaste for certain tasks; yet, if those tasks are called for under the employment agreement, it becomes the agent's duty to perform them. Failure to perform often results in proper grounds for discharge.

Closely allied to the duty to follow instructions is the duty to remain within the scope of the authority conferred. Because it often becomes possible for an agent to exceed his authority and still bind his principal, the agent has a duty not to exceed the authority granted. In case the agent does so, the employee or agent becomes responsible for any resulting loss.

Occasionally, circumstances arise that nullify instructions previously given. Because of the new conditions, the old instructions would, if followed, practically destroy the purpose of the agency. Whenever such an emergency arises, it becomes the duty of the agent, provided the principal is not available, to exercise his best judgment in meeting the situation.

Duty not to be negligent

As we shall discuss more fully in chapter 34, the doctrine of *respondeat superior* imposes liability upon a principal or master for the torts of an agent or servant acting within the scope of his employment. The agent or servant is primarily liable, and the principal or master is vicariously or secondarily liable.

It is an implied condition of employment contracts, if not otherwise expressed, that the employee has a duty to act in good faith and to exercise reasonable care and diligence in performing his tasks. Failure to do so is a breach of the employment contract. Therefore, if the employer has liability to third persons because of the employee's acts or negligent omissions, the employer may recover his loss from the employee. This right may be transferred by the doctrine of subrogation to the liability insurance carrier of the employer.

Duty to account

Money or property entrusted to the agent must be accounted for to the principal. Because of this fact, the agent is required to keep proper records showing receipts and expenditures, in order that a complete accounting may be rendered. Any money collected by an agent for his principal should not be mingled with funds of the former. If they are deposited in a bank, they should be kept in a separate account. Otherwise, any loss resulting must be borne by the agent.

An agent who receives money from third parties for the benefit of the principal owes no duty to account to the third parties. The only duty to account is owed to the principal. On the other hand, money paid to an agent who has no authority to collect it, and who does not turn it over to the principal, may be recovered from the agent in an action by the third party.

A different problem is presented when money is paid in error to an agent, as in the overpayment of an account. If the agent has passed the money on to his principal before the mistake is discovered, it is clear that only the principal is liable. Nevertheless, money that is still in the possession of the agent when he is notified of the error should be returned to the third party. The agent does not relieve himself of this burden by subsequently making payment to his principal.

Any payment made in error to an agent and caused by the agent's mistake or misconduct may always be recovered from him, even if he has surrendered it to his principal. Also, any overpayment may be recovered from the agent of an undisclosed principal, because the party dealing with the agent was unaware of the existence of the principal.

Duty to give notice

In the next chapter, we shall see that knowledge acquired by an agent within the scope of his authority binds the principal. Or more succinctly, knowledge of an agent is notice to the principal. The law imposes on the agent the duty to inform his principal of all facts that affect the subject matter of the agency and that are obtained within the scope of the employment. The rule requiring full disclosure of all material facts that might affect the principal is equally applicable to gratuitous and to compensated agents.

This rule extends beyond the duty to inform the principal of conflicting interests of third parties or possible violations of the duty of loyalty in a particular transaction. It imposes upon the agent a duty to give his principal all information that materially affects the interest of the principal. Knowledge of facts that may have greatly advanced the value of property placed with an agent for sale must be communicated before property is sold at a price previously established by the principal.

Duties of Principals

Duty to compensate

The agent is entitled to be compensated for his services in accordance with the terms of his contract of employment. If no definite compensation has been agreed upon, there arises a duty to pay the reasonable value of such services—the customary rate in the community.

Many employment contracts include provisions for paying a percentage of profits to a key employee. If the employment contract does not include a detailed enumeration of the items to be considered in determining net income, it will be computed in accordance with generally accepted accounting principles, taking into consideration past custom and practice in the operation of the employer's business. It is assumed that the methods of determining net income will be consistent and that no substantial changes will be made in the methods of accounting without the mutual agreement of the parties. The employer cannot unilaterally change the accounting methods, nor can the employee require a change in order to effect an increase in his earnings. The right of a real estate broker or agent to a commission is frequently the subject of litigation. In the absence of an express agreement, the real estate broker earns a commission (1) if he finds a buyer who is ready, willing, and able to meet the terms outlined by the seller in the listing agreement or (2) if the owner contracts with the purchaser (whether or not the price is less than the listed price), even though it later develops that the buyer is unable to meet the terms of the contract. The contract is conclusive evidence that the broker found a ready, willing, and able buyer. If a prospective purchaser conditions his obligation to purchase on an approval of credit or approval of a loan, he is not a ready, willing, and able buyer until such approval. If it is not forthcoming, the broker is not entitled to a commission.

The duty to pay a real estate commission is dependent upon which of the three types of listing has been agreed upon. An owner who lists property with several brokers is obligated to pay the first one who finds a satisfactory purchaser, at which time the agency of other brokers is automatically terminated, assuming a simple listing. In a simple listing, the owner is free to sell on his own behalf without a commission. The second type of listing is called an exclusive listing. For an agreed period of time, it gives the broker the exclusive right to find a buyer. In this arrangement, the seller is not free to list the property with other brokers, and a sale through other brokers would be a violation of the contract of listing, although the seller himself is free to find a buyer of his own. With the third type of listing, called an exclusive right to sell, even the seller is not free to find a buyer of his own choosing. If the seller does sell on his own behalf, he is obliged to pay a commission to the broker.

CASE

D entered into an exclusive right-to-sell real estate listing agreement with P, a broker. P advertised D's property, but D found a buyer and sold the property to him. It was undisputed that P was not the "procuring cause" of the sale.

ISSUE Is P entitled to a commission?

DECISION Yes.

REASONS
1. A real estate broker with an "exclusive right-to-sell listing" is entitled to a commission if the broker renders the services required by the contract and if the property is sold during the period of the agreement, regardless of by whom.
2. A broker must be the procuring cause of the sale under a simple listing and under an exclusive agency to sell, but not under an "exclusive agency with the sole right-to-sell" contract.

Wade v. Austin, 524 S.W.2d 79 (Tex.) 1975.

Multiple listing is a newer method of listing property with several brokers simultaneously. These brokers belong to an organization, the members of which share listings and divide the commissions. A typical commission would be split 60 percent to the selling broker, 30 percent to the listing broker, and 10 percent to the organization for operating expenses. These multiple-listing groups give homeowners the advantage of increased exposure to potential buyers. In return for this advantage, most multiple-listing agreements are of the exclusive right-to-sell type.

The right to a real estate commission is subject to statutory limitations in several states. Some require a written contract, and most require a license before a person may engage in this activity.

Duty to compensate sales representatives

Sales representatives who sell merchandise on a commission basis are confronted by problems similar to those of the broker, unless their employment contract is specific in its details. Let us assume that Low Cal Pies, Inc., appoints Albert, on a commission basis, as its exclusive sales representative in a certain territory. A grocery chain in the area involved sends a large order for pies directly to the home office of Low Cal Pies. Is Albert entitled to a commission on the sale? It is generally held that such a salesman is entitled to a commission only on sales solicited and induced by him, unless his contract of employment gives him greater rights.

The sales representative usually earns a commission as soon as an order from a responsible buyer is obtained, unless the contract of employment makes payment contingent upon delivery of the goods or collection of the sale's price. If payment is made dependent upon performance by the purchaser, the employer cannot deny the sales representative's commission by terminating the agency prior to collection of the account. When the buyer ultimately pays for the goods, the seller is obligated to pay the commission.

An agent who receives a weekly or monthly advance against future commissions is not obligated to return the advance if commissions equal thereto are not earned. The advance, in the absence of a specific agreement, is considered by the courts as a minimum salary.

Duty to reimburse and to indemnify

A servant is entitled to indemnity for certain tort losses. They are limited to factual situations in which the servant is not at fault and his liability results from following the instructions of the master. An agent or a servant is justified in presuming that a principal has a lawful right to give his instructions and that performance resulting from his instructions will not injure third parties. When this is not the case, and the agent incurs a liability to some third party because of trespass or conversion, the principal must indemnify the agent against loss. There will ordinarily be no indemnification for losses incurred in negligence actions because the servant's own conduct is involved. The indemnification is usually of the master by the servant in tort situations. If the agent or servant is sued for actions within the course of employment, the agent or servant is entitled to be reimbursed for attorney's fees and court costs incurred if the principal does not furnish them in the first instance.

CASE

P, a newspaper reporter, sued D, his former employer and a California newspaper publisher, seeking to recover the attorney's fees and court costs incurred in the defense of a libel action. P had been sued as the result of an article written by P for D's newspaper. P had won the libel case.

ISSUE Must D indemnify P for his legal expenses?

DECISION Yes.

REASONS
1. In California, an employer is required by statute to defend or indemnify an employee who is sued by a third person for conduct in the course and within the scope of his employment.
2. The obligation of the employer to defend or indemnify the employee is not determined by whether the third person's suit was brought in good faith. If the employee was required to defend the suit solely because of acts that he performed within the scope of his employment, there is a right on indemnity.
3. P is entitled to his court costs and attorney's fees.

Douglas v. Los Angeles *Herald-Examiner,* 123 Cal. Rptr. 683 (1975).

An agent has a general right to reimbursement for money expended on behalf of his principal. It must appear that the money was reasonably spent and that its expenditure was not necessitated by the misconduct or negligence of the agent. It is the duty of the principal to make performance by the agent possible whenever the latter has entered into a contract in his own name for the former's benefit. The undisclosed principal must fully protect his agent by making the funds available to perform the contract as agreed.

Termination of Agency Relationships

Two issues are basic to termination of an agency relationship. First, what acts or facts are sufficient to terminate the authority of the agent insofar as the immediate parties are concerned? Second, what is required to terminate the agent's authority insofar as third parties are concerned? The latter question recognizes that an agent may continue to have the *power* to bind the principal but not the *right* to do so. The methods of termination are usually divided into termination by act of the parties and termination by operation of law. The discussion in the sections that follow is limited to termination of the agency relationship and is not applicable to employment generally.

Termination of the employer-employee relationship will frequently be subject to terms of a collective bargaining agreement. In addition, public policy considerations may deny the employers the right to terminate the employment relationship with impunity. Public policy preventing termination of employment is found in the provisions of the civil rights laws relating to hiring, firing, promoting, and tenure of the employment. Courts in recent years have added other grounds for imposing liability on employers for wrongful discharge, even if the employment relationship is one described as "at will." Liability has been imposed for discharges that resulted from (1) refusing to give perjured testimony, (2) resisting sexual advances, and (3) serving on a jury.

CASE

P, an employee of D, was called for jury duty. D wrote a letter to the court, asking that P be excused. P told the court that she would like to serve. P, after serving three days on a jury, received a notice from D that her employment was terminated. P then sued D in tort for the wrongful termination of her employment.

ISSUE Is an employer liable for discharging an employee if the employer's motive in doing so is socially undesirable?

DECISION Yes.

REASONS

1. Generally, in the absence of a contract or legislation to the contrary, an employer can discharge an employee at any time and for any cause, and an employee can quit at any time for any cause. Such a termination by the employer or the employee is not a breach of contract and ordinarily does not create a tortious cause of action.
2. There are instances, however, in which the employer's reason or motive for discharging the employee harms or interferes with an important interest of the community and therefore justifies compensation to the employee.
3. The jury system and jury duty are high on the scale of American institutions and citizens' obligations. If employers are permitted to discharge employees with impunity for fulfilling these obligations, the system will be adversely affected. The will of the community would be threatened. Therefore the discharge is tortious.

Nees v. Hocks, 536 P.2d 512 (Or.) 1975.

By act of the parties

Termination by act of the parties includes termination by force of their agreement or by the act of one or both of the parties. An example of the former is an agency that is created to continue for a definite period of time. It ceases, by virtue of the terms of the agreement, at the expiration of the stipulated period. If the parties consent to the continuation of the relationship beyond the period, the courts imply the formation of a new contract of employment. The new agreement contains the same terms as the old one and continues for a like period of time, except that no implied contract can run longer than one year because of the statute of frauds.

Another example is an agency created to accomplish a certain purpose, which automatically ends with the completion of the task assigned. In such case third parties are not entitled to notice of the termination. Furthermore, when it is possible for one of several agents to perform the task, such as selling certain real estate, it is held that performance by the first party terminates the authority of the other agents without notice of termination being required.

Many, if not most, agency contracts do not provide for the duration of the agreement. A contract for permanent employment, not supported by any consideration other than the performance of duties and payment of wages, is a contract for an indefinite period and terminable at the will of either party at any time. Some agency agreements purport to be for a definite period but on close examination are actually terminable at will.

CASE

D offered P a contract of employment at $26,400 per year; but before P began working, D canceled the contract. P sued for breach of contract. D denied liability, contending that without a time stipulation, an employment contract is terminable at will. P contended that an annual salary suggested a contract of at least a year's duration.

ISSUE Is an employment contract providing for an annual salary impliedly a contract for at least a year's term?

DECISION No.

REASONS
1. The majority rule is that where the salary is given for a stipulated time, that time is merely for accounting purposes and does not indicate that the parties have agreed to work for that length of time.
2. In the absence of other evidence suggesting that the contract was to last a fixed time, it is terminable at the will of either party.

Singh v. Cities Services Oil Co., 554 P.2d 1367 (OK) 1976.

Any contract may be terminated by mutual agreement; therefore, the agency relationship may be canceled in this manner. Furthermore, as a general rule, either party to the agreement has full *power* to terminate it whenever he desires, although he possesses no *right* to do so. Wrongful termination of the agency by either party subjects him to a suit for damages by the other party. An exercise of the power without the right is a wrongful termination.

Wrongful termination

As a general rule and subject to the exceptions previously noted, an employment that continues at the will of the parties may be rightfully terminated by either party at any time. Termination is not a breach of contract, but tort liability may be incurred if public policy demands it. On the other hand, if the employer wrongfully terminates a contract that was to continue for an agreed period, there is liability for damages for breach of contract. Of course, if the agent is discharged for cause, such as the failure to follow instructions, he may not recover damages from the employer.

The employee whose employment has been wrongfully cut short is entitled to recover compensation for work done before his dismissal and an additional sum for damages. Most states permit him to bring an action either immediately following the breach, in which event he recovers prospective damages, or after the period has expired, in which event he recovers the damages actually sustained. In the latter case, as a general rule, he is compelled to deduct from the compensation called for in the agreement the amount that he has been able to earn during the interim.

Under such circumstances, a wrongfully discharged employee is under a duty to exercise reasonable diligence in finding other work of like character. Idleness is not encouraged by the law. Apparently, this rule does not require him to seek employment in a new locality or to accept work of a different kind or more menial character. The duty is to find work of like kind, provided it is available in the particular locality.

Termination by law

Certain acts are held by law to terminate the agency. Among these are death, insanity, bankruptcy of either of the parties, or destruction of the subject matter of the agency. Bankruptcy has such an effect only in case it affects the subject matter of the agency. It is said of such cases that the agency is immediately terminated and that no notice need be given to either the agent or the third parties. If the principal has not been publicly adjudged insane, it is believed that an agent's contracts are binding on the principal unless the third party is aware of the mental illness, especially where the contract is beneficial to the insane principal's estate.

Agency coupled with an interest

Usually, any agency contract may be terminated at any time by either party. As previously noted, the power to terminate exists even though the right to do so may not. If the power is exercised wrongfully, there is liability. Agency contracts are not specifically enforceable against the principal because of the lack of mutuality in the remedy. Because the principal could not require the agent to work (involuntary servitude), the agent cannot, as a general rule, compel the principal to continue the agency.

To the general rule, however, there is one well-recognized exception known as *an agency coupled with an interest.* The term describes the relationship that exists when the agent has an actual beneficial interest in the property that is the subject matter of the agency. A mortgage that contains a provision naming the mortgagee as agent to sell the property in the event of default creates an agency coupled with an interest in property. An agency coupled with an interest in property cannot be terminated unilaterally by the principal and is not terminated by events (such as death or bankruptcy of the principal) that otherwise terminate agencies by operation of law. The net effect is that an agency coupled with an interest in property cannot be terminated without the consent of the agent.

An agency coupled with an interest in property must be distinguished from *an agency coupled with an obligation,* an agency created as a source of reimbursement to the agent. For example, an agent who is given the right to sell a certain automobile and to apply the proceeds on a claim against the principal is an agency coupled with an obligation. Such an agency is a hybrid between the usual agency and the agency coupled with an interest in property. The agency coupled with an obligation cannot unilaterally be terminated by the principal, but death or bankruptcy of the principal will terminate the agency by operation of law.

Under either type of agency, it should be clear that the interest in the subject matter must be greater than the mere expectation of profits to be realized or in the proceeds to be derived from the sale of the property. The interest must be in the property itself. A real estate broker is not an agent coupled with an interest, even though he expects a commission from the proceeds of the sale. Likewise a principal who has appointed an agent to sell certain goods on commission has the power to terminate the agency at any time, although such conduct might constitute a breach of the agreement.

Notice in event of termination

Termination of the agency, as explained above, may take place by act of the parties or by operation of law. If the parties or either of them by their own action have terminated the agency, it is the duty of the principal to give notice of the termination to all third parties who have learned of the existence of the agency. Without such notice, the agent would still possess apparent authority to act for his principal. Those persons entitled to such notice may be divided into two groups: (1) those who have previously relied upon the agency by dealing with the agent; and (2) those who have never previously dealt with the agent, but who nevertheless have learned of the agency. The principal's duty to the first class can be satisfied only by the third party's actual receipt of notice of the termination.

CASE

P was sued in 1971 for an alleged malpractice occurring in September, 1969. He immediately called his insurance agent. Unknown to P, the agent no longer worked for D, the insuror at the time of the incident. Instead, the agent now worked for his current insuror. The agent notified the current insuror, who mistakenly undertook the defense. When the error was discovered, D was notified but refused the defense because it had not been promptly and timely notified, as the insurance contract required. P retained private counsel, successfully defended the suit, and sued D for reimbursement. P sought to hold D liable on the ground that P had notified the person whom he thought was D's agent. P had no notice that the agency relationship had ended.

ISSUE When an insurance company has canceled its agent's authority without notifying the insured, is the revocation effective against the insured?

DECISION No.

REASONS
1. An insured is entitled to assume that an insurance agent is continuing to act within the scope of the agency until the insured has actual or constructive knowledge to the contrary.
2. Here, the insured promptly notified the agent whom he believed to be the agent of his insuror. Since he did not know and could not have known that the agency relationship had ended, the notice was effective, and the company is liable.

Zukaitis v. Aetna Cas. & Sur. Co., 236 N.W. 2d 819 (Neb.) 1975.

The principal satisfies his duty to the second group by giving public notice, such as newspaper publicity, in the location involved. If any one of the second group, not having seen the newspaper account of the termination, relies upon the continuation of the agency to his detriment, he has no cause of action against the principal. If a member of the first group has not received direct notice from the principal but has learned indirectly of the severance of relation or of facts sufficient to place him on inquiry, he is no longer justified in extending credit to the agent or otherwise dealing with him as a representative of the principal.

Where the agency is terminated by action of law, such as death, insanity, or bankruptcy, no duty to notify third parties is placed upon the principal. Such matters receive publicity through newspapers, official records, and otherwise, and third parties normally become aware of the termination without the necessity for additional notification. If the death of the principal occurs before an agent contracts with a third party, the third party has no cause of action against either the agent or the estate of the principal unless the agent is acting for an undisclosed principal. In the latter case, since the agent makes the contract in his own name, he is liable to the third party. Otherwise, the third party is in as good a position to know of the death of the principal as is the agent.

A special problem exists in regard to notice in cases of special agents as distinguished from general agents. Ordinarily, notice is not required to revoke the authority of a special agent, since the agent possesses no continuing authority, and no one will be in the habit of dealing with him. Only if the principal has directly indicated that the agent has authority in a certain matter or at a certain time will notice be required, to prevent reliance on the principal's conduct by a party dealing with the agent. This is especially true if the agent is acting under a special power of attorney. Actual notice of termination is required in these cases.

REVIEW QUESTIONS AND PROBLEMS

1. What is a power of attorney? Give an illustration of a situation in which it would be used.

2. Pop, the owner of a drive-in grocery store, signed an exclusive-listing agreement with Alice, a licensed real estate broker. After three months, Pop leased the store to Ted and revoked Alice's authority. Does she have any remedy against Pop? Why?

3. Ann, a real estate agent, was authorized by Peter to sell several lots at a specified price. Ann was to receive a 6 percent commission on each lot sold. Before any lots were sold, Peter revoked the authorization. Was Ann's authority irrevocable as a power coupled with an interest? Why?

4. Sam gave two real estate brokers, Andy and Handy, simple listings on his house. Andy found a ready, willing, and able buyer one day, and before Sam could notify Handy, Handy also found a buyer. Is Handy entitled to a commission? Why?

5. Dulcy, appointed to sell merchandise in a certain area for Howard, was to receive a commission of 2 percent on all sales. She received a weekly advance of $750 for ten weeks, but her commissions averaged only $400 a week. Does she owe Howard the $350 difference? Why?

6. Walker listed his house with Ike, a real estate broker, under a contract that gave Ike the exclusive right to sell. During the period of the agreement, Walker sold the house to a friend and refused to pay Ike any commission because Ike did not produce the buyer. Is Ike entitled to a commission? Why?

7. Paul borrowed money from a bank for the construction of a house. Arthur, a bank officer, orally promised to act as agent in the payment of bills incurred in the construction. Arthur paid out money without requiring the construction company to submit releases as required by the mechanic's lien law of Ohio. Liens against the house amounted to $5,500. Paul sued Arthur for failure to exercise due care. What was the result? Why?

8. Amos was sales manager of Plenty, a turkey-packing company. As a member of the management group, Amos was consulted on all phases of the business. He persuaded the company to enter into a contract to purchase 20,000 turkeys, but concealed for some time the fact that he was the seller of the turkeys. Plenty Company did not carry out the contract, and Amos brought suit. Was the contract enforceable? Why?

9. Sandy listed her real property for sale with Rich, a real estate agent. Buford was interested in purchasing land and engaged Rich to represent him. Rich arranged for Sandy to sell her property to Buford and collected a commission from both parties. Neither Sandy nor Buford was aware that Rich was acting as an agent for both of them. Buford now sues to rescind the contract of sale. Should he succeed? Why?

10. Eve, an employee of Pearl Company, had as one of her duties the initiation and negotiation of contracts on behalf of Pearl. Eve was instrumental in securing the awarding of a contract to Adam Construction Company. Shortly thereafter, Eve received $50,000 from Adam. Pearl sues Eve for damages in the amount of $50,000. Should Pearl succeed? Why?

11. State University (S.U.) agreed in writing to employ Brainard as a research assistant at an annual salary of $10,800. Four months later, S.U. discharged Brainard, who brought suit, claiming that the contract of employment was for one year; therefore, she is entitled to compensation for eight months' salary. Is Brainard correct? Why?

12. Dooley, a buyer for Pell's Department Store, was discharged. Bryant had never sold to Dooley but knew that Dooley was Pell's buyer. After Dooley was discharged, an article about his changing jobs was in the newspaper, but Bryant did not read it. If Dooley purchases goods on credit from Bryant, charging them to Pell's, is Pell's liable? Why?

13. Pat worked for Mike on an employment-at-will basis. While at work, Pat sustained an injury to his lower back. When Pat filed a claim for worker's compensation, he was discharged. Pat brought suit for wrongful discharge, but Mike claimed that an "employee at will" can be discharged for any reason. Is Mike correct? Why?

33 Agency and the Law of Contracts

The law of agency is essentially concerned with issues of contractual liability. Because corporations act only through agents, and because partners in a partnership are agents of the partnership, a substantial portion of all contracts entered into by businesses are entered into by agents on behalf of principals. Whenever a contract is entered into by an agent, issues as to the liability of the various parties may arise. Is the agent personally liable on the contract? Is the principal bound? Can the principal enforce the agreement against the third party? This chapter will discuss these issues and others that frequently arise out of contracts entered into by agents on behalf of principals.

The Liability of Agents

Based on the contract

As a general rule, an agent is not personally liable on contracts into which he has entered on behalf of his disclosed principal. The liability is solely that of the principal. To this rule there are three well-recognized exceptions. First, if the agent carelessly executes a written agreement, he may fail to bind his principal and may incur personal liability.

CASE

D, president of a company incorporated under his name, contracted with P, a publishing company, to print four issues of a magazine. P contends that D represented that he personally owned the magazine and that the corporation was not mentioned. D contends that he disclosed his agency and the existence and identity of the corporate principal prior to the agreement. He cites evidence of checks and the company letterhead on which the correspondence between the parties was conducted.

ISSUE Is D personally liable on the contract?

DECISION Yes.

REASONS

1. The defense of agency to avoid a contractual liability is an affirmative defense. The burden of establishing the agency relationship, the corporate existence, and the identity of the principal is upon the one claiming to be an agent.
2. In order to avoid personal liability, an agent must, at the time of contracting, disclose both the capacity in which he acts and the existence and identity of his principal. It is not sufficient that the third person has knowledge of facts and circumstances which would, if reasonably followed by inquiry, disclose the existence and identity of the principal. It is not the duty of third persons to seek out the identity of the principal.
3. Unless the third person knows, or unless the facts are such that a reasonable person would know, of the principal's existence and identity, the agent is acting for an undisclosed principal and is liable in the same manner as if he were the principal.
4. Whether a principal is disclosed, partially disclosed, or undisclosed depends upon the representations of the agent and the knowledge of the third party at the time of the transaction.

Brown v. Owen Litho Serv., Inc., 384 N.E. 2d 1132 (Ind.) 1979.

When an agent signs a simple contract or commercial paper, he should execute it in a way that clearly indicates his representative capacity. If the signature fails to indicate the actual relationship of the parties and fails to identify the party intended to be bound, the agent may be personally liable on the instrument. Many states permit the use of oral evidence to show the intention of the agent and the third party when the signature is ambiguous—the agent is allowed to offer proof that it was not intended that he assume personal responsiblity. The Code contains express provisions on the liability of an agent who signs commercial paper. These were discussed in chapter 20.

Second, the third party may request the agent to be bound personally on the contract. This request may be due to lack of confidence in the financial ability of the principal, because the agent's credit rating is superior to that of the principal, or some personal reason. When the agent voluntarily assumes the burden of performance in his personal capacity, he is liable in the event of nonperformance by his principal.

Third, if the agent does not disclose his agency or name his principal, he binds himself and becomes subject to all liabilities, express and implied, created by the contract and transaction, in the same manner as if he were the principal. If an agent wishes to avoid personal liability, the duty is upon the agent to disclose the agency. There is no duty on the third party to discover the agency.

An agent who purports to be a principal is liable as a principal. The fact that the agent is known to be a commission merchant, auctioneer, or other professional agent is immaterial. He must disclose not only that he is an agent but the identity of his principal if the agent is not to have personal liability. Any agent for an undisclosed or partially disclosed principal assumes personal liability on the contract into which he enters.

Based on breach of warranty

An agent's liability may be implied from the circumstances as well as being the direct result of the contract. Liability in such situations is usually said to be implied and to arise from the breach of an implied warranty. There are two basic warranties that are used to imply liability: the warranty of authority and the warranty that the principal is competent.

As a general rule, an agent impliedly warrants to third parties that he possesses power to effect the contractual relations of his principal. If in any particular transaction the agent fails to possess this power, the agent violates this implied warranty, and he is liable to third parties for the damages resulting from his failure to bind the principal. The agent may or may not be aware of this lack of authority, and he may honestly believe that he possesses the requisite authority. Awareness of lack of authority and honesty is immaterial. If an agent exceeds his authority, he is liable to the third parties for the breach of the warranty of authority.

The agent may escape liability for damages arising from lack of authority by a full disclosure to a third party of all facts relating to the source of the agent's authority. Where all the facts are available, the third party is as capable of judging the limits of the agent's powers as is the agent.

Every agent who deals with third parties warrants that his principal is capable of being bound. Consequently, an agent who acts for a minor or a corporation not yet formed may find himself liable for the nonperformance of his principal. The same rule enables the third party to recover from the agent when his principal is an unincorporated association, such as a club, lodge, or other informal group. An unincorporated association is not a legal entity separate and apart from its members. In most states it cannot sue or be sued in the name it uses, but all members must be joined in a suit involving the unincorporated group. When an agent purports to bind such an organization, a breach of the warranty results because there is no entity capable of being bound. If the third party is fully informed that the principal is an unincorporated organization and he agrees to look entirely to it for performance, the agent is not liable.

The warranty that an agent has a competent principal must be qualified in one respect. An agent is not liable when, unknown to him, his agency has been cut short by the death of the principal. Death of the principal terminates an agency. Because death is usually accompanied by sufficient publicity to reach third parties, the facts are equally available to both parties, and no breach of warranty arises.

Liability of Disclosed Principals

A principal is liable on all contracts properly executed and entered into by an agent possessing actual or apparent authority to enter into the contract, provided that the third party knows that the agent is contracting for the principal. A principal is also liable on unauthorized contracts entered into by a purported agent if the principal, with knowledge of all the facts, ratifies or affirms that he is bound by the contract. Therefore, a principal is not liable upon a contract that he has not actually or apparently authorized and has not ratified.

The burden of proving the requisite authority or ratification is on the party dealing with the agent; the principal does not have the burden of proving lack of authority or lack of ratification. The agent's authority can come only from the principal. The agent, by words or conduct, cannot create his own authority unless the words or conduct are consented to, or ratified by, the principal. One who deals with an agent, knowing that the agent has exceeded his authority, does so at his peril.

Actual authority

A principal may confer actual authority upon the agent or may unintentionally, by want of ordinary care, allow the agent to believe himself to possess it. Actual authority includes express authority and implied authority. The term *express authority* describes authority explicitly given to the agent by the principal. *Implied authority* is used to describe authority that is necessarily incidental to the express authority or that arises because of business custom and usage or prior practices of the parties. Implied authority is sometimes referred to as *incidental authority;* it is required or reasonably necessary in order to carry out the purpose for which the agency was created. Implied authority may be established by deductions or inferences from other facts and circumstances in the case, including prior habits or dealings of a similar nature between the parties.

Implied authority based on custom and usage varies from one locality to another and among different kinds of businesses. To illustrate: Phyllis appoints Andrea as her agent to sell a used automobile for $900. As an incident to her authority to sell, Andrea has authority to enter into a written contract with the purchaser and to sign Phyllis's name to the contract. Whether she has implied or incidental authority to sell on credit instead of cash or to warrant the condition of the car sold depends upon local custom. If it is customary for other agents in this locality to make warranties or sell on credit, this agent and the third party with whom she deals may assume she possesses such authority in the absence of knowledge to the contrary. Custom, in effect, creates a presumption of authority. A marital relationship, however, raises no prescription of agency that a husband is the agent of the wife and vice versa.

Implied authority must be distinguished from *apparent* or *ostensible authority,* which is authority predicated on the theory of estoppel. Apparent or ostensible authority is discussed in the next section.

Implied authority cannot be derived from the words or conduct of the agent. A third person dealing with a known agent may not act negligently in regard to the extent of the agent's authority or blindly trust his statements in such regard but must use reasonable diligence and prudence in ascertaining whether the agent is acting within the scope of his authority. Similarly, if persons who deal with a purported agent desire to hold the principal liable on the contract, they must ascertain not only the fact of the agency but the nature and extent of the agent's authority. Should either the existence of the agency or the nature and extent of the authority be disputed, the burden of proof regarding these matters is upon the third party.

All agents, even presidents of corporations, have limitations on their authority. Authority is not readily implied. Possession of goods by one not engaged in the business of selling such goods does not create the implication of authority to sell. Authority to sell does not necessarily include the authority to extend credit, although custom may create such authority. The officers of a corporation must have actual authority to enter into transactions that are not in the ordinary course of the business of the corporation. For this reason, persons purchasing real estate from a corporation usually require a resolution of the board of directors specifically authorizing the sale.

CASE

P sued D, a farming corporation, for specific performance of a contract for sale of some farmland. The contract had been signed by the president of the corporation. The board of directors had authorized the president to discuss the sale of the land but had not authorized the sale. The contract covered 35 percent of the corporate assets.

ISSUE Is the corporation bound on the contract signed by its president?

DECISION No.

REASONS 1. A president of a corporation is empowered without special authority from the board of directors to transact all acts of ordinary nature that are incident to his office by usage or necessity.

2. A president does not have actual authority to sell 35 percent of a corporation's farmland unless the articles of incorporation give such authority or the board specifically authorized the sale.

3. There is no apparent authority for the president of a farming corporation to sell its land. Such a transaction is not in the usual course of business.

Willsey v. W. C. Porter Farms Company, 522 S.W.2d (Mo.) 1975.

Apparent or ostensible authority

The terms *apparent authority* and *ostensible authority* are synonymous. They describe the authority a principal, intentionally or by want of ordinary care, causes or allows a third person to believe the agent to possess. Liability of the principal for the ostensible agent's acts rests on the doctrine of estoppel. The estoppel is created by some conduct of the principal that leads the third party to believe that a person is his agent or that an actual agent possesses the requisite authority. The third party must know about this conduct and must be injured or damaged by his reliance upon it. The injury or damage may be a change of position, and the facts relied upon must be such that a reasonably prudent person would believe that the authority of the agency existed. Thus, three usual essential elements of an estoppel—conduct, reliance, and injury—are required to create apparent authority.

Theory. The theory of apparent or ostensible authority is that if a principal's words or conduct leads others to believe that he has conferred authority upon an agent, he cannot deny his words or actions to third persons who have relied on them in good faith. The acts may include words, oral or written, or may be limited to conduct that reasonably interpreted by a third person causes that person to believe that the principal consents to have the act done on his behalf by the purported agent. Apparent authority requires more than the mere appearance of authority. The facts must be such that a person exercising ordinary prudence, acting in good faith, and conversant with business practices would be misled. An agent's apparent authority to do an act for a principal must be based on the principal's words or conduct and cannot be based on anything the agent himself has said or done. An agent cannot unilaterally create his own apparent authority.

CASE

D was persuaded by an agent of P Corporation to buy 130 jackets, the sale being based upon the representation that if the jackets did not sell, they could be returned. The jackets were higher priced than items normally carried in D's store. When the jackets did not sell, D attempted to return them. P refused to allow D to do so, contending that the agent had no authority to agree to a sale-or-return contract. When D failed to pay for the jackets, P sued for the purchase price.

ISSUE Is D entitled to return the jackets?

DECISION No

REASONS 1. D, the agent, had no actual or apparent authority to enter into a sale-or-return transaction.

2. Apparent authority of an agent is authority that the principal knowingly permits the agent to assume or that he holds the agent as possessing. The elements that must be present before a third person can hold the principal for the acts of the agent on the theory of apparent authority are (a) conduct of the principal, (b) reliance thereon by the third person, and (c) a change of position by the third person, to his detriment.
3. Apparent authority must come from conduct of the principal, not from the acts of the agent. Here, the principal did nothing to create apparent authority.
4. The mere fact that P authorized its agent to make contracts for the sale of their goods does not mean that he has authority to make any contract, no matter what the terms.

Anglo-American Clothing Corp. v. Marjorie's of Tiburon, Inc., 571 P. 2d 427 (Okla.) 1977.

Apparent authority may be the basis for liability when the purported agent is, in fact, not an agent. It also may be the legal basis for finding that an actual agent possesses authority beyond that actually conferred. In other words, apparent authority may exist in one not an agent or it may expand the authority of an actual agent.

Examples. An agency by estoppel or additional authority by estoppel may arise from the agent's dealings being constantly ratified by the principal, or it may result from a person's acting the part of an agent without any dissent from the purported principal, even though it was the principal's duty to speak. To illustrate: Upon several occasions, an agent indorsed his principal's name to checks and cashed them at a bank. The principal had never given the agent that authority but did not lodge a protest with the bank until the agent appropriated to his own use the proceeds from one of the checks. The principal then attempted to recover from the bank. By approval of the agent's previous unauthorized action, the principal had led the bank to assume reasonably that the agent possessed authority to indorse checks.

Perhaps the most common situation in which apparent authority is found to exist occurs when the actual authority is terminated, but notice of this fact is not given to those entitled to receive it. Cancellation of actual authority does not terminate the apparent authority created by prior transactions.

CASE

P was a former partner in a law firm. The firm had deposited checks in D bank by using a rubber stamp to indorse them. P withdrew from the firm, but he did not notify the bank that use of the stamp was no longer authorized. Using the stamp, the law firm deposited in the D bank a check payable to P. The bank knew that P was no longer a partner. P sued D bank for the amount of the check.

ISSUE Did the law firm have authority to indorse the check for P?

DECISION Yes.

REASONS
1. An indorsement of a check may be made by an agent, and the agent's authority may be actual, implied, or apparent.
2. There was apparent authority for use of the stamp in lieu of a signature. It arose from the former practice of using the stamp and the lack of notice that the authority was canceled.

Keane v. Pan American Bank, 309 So.2d 579 (Fla.App.) 1975.

Ratification by principals

As previously noted, a purported principal may become bound by ratifying an unauthorized contract. Having knowledge of all material matters, he may express or imply adoption or confirmation of a contract entered into on his behalf by someone who had no authority to do so. Ratification is implied by conduct of the principal, which is inconsistent with the intent to repudiate the agent's action. It is similar to ratification by an adult of a contract while a minor. Ratification relates back to, and is the equivalent of, authority at the commencement of the act or time of the contract. It is the affirmance of a contract already made. It cures the defect of lack of authority and creates the relation of principal and agent.

Capacity required. Various conditions must exist before a ratification will be effective in bringing about a contractual relation between the principal and the third party. First, because ratification relates back to the time of the contract, ratification can be effective only when both the principal and the agent were capable of contracting at the time the contract was executed and are still capable at the time of ratification. For this reason, a corporation may not ratify contracts made by its promoters on the corporation's behalf before the corporation was formed. For the corporation to be bound by such agreements, a novation or an assumption of liability by the corporation must occur.

Acting as agent. Second, an agent's act may be ratified only when he holds himself out as acting for the one who is alleged to have approved the unauthorized agreement. In other words, the agent must have professed to act as an agent. A person who professes to act for himself and who makes a contract in his own name does nothing that can be ratified, even though he intends at the time to let another have the benefit of his agreement.

CASE

One of several owners of a parcel of real estate granted an option to X to buy the land. The party granting the option claimed to be the sole owner and did not purport to be the agent of anyone. The other owners refused to go along with the sale. The option consideration had benefited all the owners in that it had been used to pay expenses connected with the land.

ISSUE Is the option binding on all owners? (Has there been a ratification?)

DECISION No.

REASONS
1. The owner granting the option could not have been an agent of the other owners because an agent's authority to bind his principal on a contract to sell real estate must be in writing, according to the statute of frauds.
2. The doctrine of ratification does not apply to an act claimed to have been ratified by a principal unless the original act was done by one who purported to act as an agent for a principal. Here, he claimed to be the sole owner.

Pettit v. Vogt, 495 P.2d 395 (Okla.) 1972.

The above case established that an undisclosed principal may not ratify an unauthorized contract and hold the third party to it. Nor can the undisclosed principal be held liable by the third party on the contract. An undisclosed principal who receives the benefits of a contract, however, is liable in quasi contract for the benefits actually received and retained. To allow him to keep the benefits would be a form of unjust enrichment.

Full knowledge. Third, as a general rule, ratification does not bind the principal unless he acts with full knowledge of all the material facts attending negotiation and execution of the contract. Of course, when there is express ratification and the principal acts without any apparent desire to know or to learn the facts, he may not later defend himself on the ground that he was unaware of all the material facts. When, however, ratification is to be implied from the conduct of the principal, he must act with knowledge of all important details.

The law is almost always concerned with mutuality of obligation. One party should not be bound to a contract if the other party is not also bound. Therefore, the law recognizes that the third party may withdraw from an unauthorized contract entered into by an agent at any time before it is ratified by the principal. If the third party were not allowed to withdraw, the unique situation in which one party is bound and the other is not would exist. Remember, though, that ratification does not require notice to the third party. As soon as conduct constituting ratification has been indulged in by the principal, the third party loses his right to withdraw.

Conduct constituting ratification

Ratification may be either express or implied. Any conduct that definitely indicates an intention on the part of the principal to adopt the transaction will constitute ratification. It may take the form of words of approval to the agent, a promise to perform, or actual performance, such as delivery of the product called for in the agreement. Accepting the benefits of the contract or basing a suit on the validity of an agreement clearly amounts to ratification. Knowing what the agent has done, if the principal makes no objection for an unreasonable time, ratification results by operation of law. Generally, the question of what is an unreasonable time is for the jury.

The issue of whether or not ratification has occurred is also a question to be decided by the jury. Among the facts to be considered by the jury are the relationship of the parties, prior conduct, circumstances pertaining to the transaction, and the action or inaction of the alleged principal upon learning of the contract. Inaction or silence by the principal creates difficulty in determining if ratification has occurred. Failure to speak may mislead the third party, and courts frequently find that a duty to speak exists where silence will mislead. Silence and inaction by the party to be charged as a prinicpal, or failure to dissent and speak up when ordinary human conduct and fair play would normally call for some negative assertion within a reasonable time tends to justify the inference that the principal acquiesced in the course of events and accepted the contract as his own. Acceptance and retention of the fruits of the contract with full knowledge of the material facts of the transaction is probably the most certain evidence of implied ratification. As soon as a principal learns of an unauthorized act by his agent, he should promptly repudiate it if he is to avoid liability on the theory of ratification.

At this point it should be mentioned that an unauthorized act may not be ratified in part and rejected in part. The principal cannot accept the benefits of the contract and refuse to assume its obligations. Because of this rule, a principal, by accepting the benefits of an authorized agreement, ratifies the means used in procuring the agreement, unless within a reasonable time after learning the actual facts he takes steps to return, as far as possible, the benefits he has received. Therefore, if an unauthorized agent commits fraud in procuring a contract, acceptance of the benefits ratifies not only the contract but the fraudulent acts as well, and the principal is liable for the fraud.

Liability of Undisclosed Principals

For various reasons, a principal may desire to hide his identity. To achieve this secrecy, he will direct an agent to enter into all contracts in the agent's own name, leaving the third party either unaware of the existence of the principal (undisclosed principal) or unaware of the principal's *identity* (partially disclosed principal). The law relating to partially disclosed principals is the same as that relating to undisclosed principals, and they are treated together here. Such agreements are always entered into on the strength of the agent's credit, and the agent is liable until the third party elects to hold the principal. The third party, upon learning of the principal's existence or identity, may elect to enforce the contract against the principal rather than against the agent. The undisclosed principal is responsible for all contracts entered into by the agent within the scope of the agent's actual authority, and he may be sued when his existence becomes known. Being unknown, the principal could not have created any apparent authority; consequently, his liability is limited to actual authority—that which is expressly given and that which may be implied as incidental thereto.

Effect of an election on liability

When the existence of the principal or his identity becomes known to the third party, the third party may look to either the agent or the principal for performance. If the third party elects to hold the principal liable, the agent is released. Similarly, if the third party elects to hold the agent liable, the previously undisclosed but now disclosed principal is released. An election to hold one party releases the other from liability.

CASE

P, an electric company, entered into a contract with X Corporation to perform construction work, preparing for a fair. The contract specified that D was the construction consultant for X. D also served as the construction consultant for other companies involved in the fair. As time deadlines became imminent, D orally approved additional work to be done by P for several of the companies.

ISSUE Is D personally liable for the construction work?

DECISION Yes.

REASONS
1. If the other party has no notice that the agent is acting for a principal, the one for whom he acts is an undisclosed principal. Both the agent and the undisclosed principal are liable on such a contract.
2. Such liability, however, is in the alternative; the third party must elect whether to hold the agent or the undisclosed principal liable for the obligation.
3. Because of the time limitation and because D was acting in different capacities (as agent for several disclosed principals and as independent contractor), P was not always aware for which principal the work was ordered, and justifiably so. Therefore, D is personally liable on the contracts unless P elects to hold the principal.

Maxwell's Electric, Inc., v. Hegeman Harris Company of Canada, LTD, 567 P.2d 1149 (Wash. App.) 1977.

It is sometimes difficult to know when an election has occurred. Clearly, conduct by the third party preceding the disclosure of the principal cannot constitute an election. Because of this rule, it has been held that an unsatisfied judgment obtained against the agent before disclosure of the principal will not bar a later action against the principal.

After disclosure, the third party may evidence his election by obtaining a judgment against one of the parties or by making an express declaration of his intention to hold one party and not the other. It has been held that sending a bill to one of the parties does not indicate an election. Most states also hold that the receipt of a negotiable instrument from either principal or agent does not show an election. The mere starting of a suit has been held insufficient to constitute an election; but if the case proceeds to judgment against either the agent or the principal, election has taken place, even though the judgment remains unpaid.

Effect of a settlement on liability

In the preceding section it was stated that the third party, after learning of a previously undisclosed principal's interest in a transaction, might elect to look to the principal rather than to the agent for performance. Suppose that the undisclosed principal supplied the agent with money to purchase the goods, but the agent purchased on credit and appropriated the money. In such a case the principal would be relieved of all responsibility. The same result obtains when the undisclosed principal *settles* with the agent after the contract is made and the goods are received, but before disclosure to the third party. Any bona fide settlement between principal and agent before disclosure releases the principal. A settlement cannot have this effect, however, when it is made after the third party has learned of the existence of the principal, and the principal is aware that his identity is known. The settlement rule is based on equitable principle. It is fair to the third party in that it gives him all the protection he originally bargained for, and it is fair to the principal in that it protects him against a second demand for payment.

Liability of Principals—Special Situations

Many special problems arise in the law of agency as it relates to contractual liability and authority of agents. Some of these problems are founded on the relationship of the parties. A spouse is generally liable for the contracts of the other spouse when the contracts involve family necessities. In most states this liability is statutory. Others involve special factual situations. An existing emergency that necessitates immediate action adds sufficiently to the agent's powers to enable him to meet the situation. If time permits and the principal is available, any proposed remedy for the difficulty must be submitted to the principal for approval. It is only when the principal is not available that the powers of the agent are extended. Furthermore, the agent receives no power greater than that sufficient to solve the difficulty.

Frequently, the liability of the principal is dependent upon whether the agent is, as a matter of fact, a general agent or a special agent. If the agency is general, limitations imposed upon the usual and ordinary powers of the general agent do not prevent the principal from being liable to third parties when the agent acts in violation of such limitations, unless the attention of the third parties has been drawn to them. In other words, the third party, having established that a general agency exists and having determined in a general way the limits of the authority, is not bound to explore for unexpected and unusual restrictions. He is justified in assuming, in the absence of contrary information, that the agent possesses the powers that like agents customarily have. On the other hand, if the proof is only of a special or limited agency, any action in excess of the actual authority would not bind the principal. The authority for a special agent is strictly construed; and if the agent exceeds his authority, the principal is not bound.

To illustrate the foregoing, assume an instruction to a sales agent not to sell to a certain individual or not to sell to him on credit, although credit sales are customary. Such a limitation cannot affect the validity of a contract made with this individual, unless the latter was aware of the limitation at the time the contract was made. The principal, by appointing an agent normally possessed of certain authority, is estopped to set up the limitation as a defense unless the limitation is made known to the third party prior to the making of the contract.

There are other issues directly related to the authority possessed by an agent. A common problem involves whether or not notice to an agent or knowledge possessed by him is imputed to the principal. Some of these questions are covered by statutes. Civil practice statutes contain provisions on service of a summons on an agent. They specify who may be an agent for the service of process and, in effect, provide that notice to such agents constitutes notice to the principal. The general principle relating to notice and to some of the other special issues of authority is discussed in the sections that follow.

Notice to agents

Notice to, or knowledge acquired by, an agent while acting within the scope of his authority binds the principal. This rule is based on the theory that the agent is the principal's other self; therefore, what the agent knows, the principal knows. While *knowledge* possessed by an agent is *notice* to the principal, the principal may not have actual knowledge of the particular fact at all. Knowledge acquired by an agent acting outside the scope of his authority is not effective notice unless the party relying thereon has reasonable ground to believe that the agent is acting within the scope of his authority (similar to apparent authority). An agent who is acquiring property for his principal may have knowledge of certain unrecorded liens against the property. The prinicpal purchases the property subject to those liens. Equal knowledge possessed by another agent who did not represent the principal in the particular transaction, and who did not obtain the knowledge on behalf of his principal, is not imputed to the principal.

A question exists as to whether or not knowledge acquired by an agent before he became an agent can bind the principal. The majority view is that knowledge acquired by an agent before commencement of the relationship of principal and agent is imputable to the principal if the knowledge is present and in the mind of the agent while acting for the principal in the transaction to which the information is material. There is considerable authority to the contrary.

Notice or knowledge received by an agent under circumstances in which the agent would not be presumed to communicate the information to the principal does not bind the principal. This is an exception to the general rule that will be observed when the agent is acting in his own behalf and adversely to the principal or when the agent is under a duty to some third party not to disclose the information. Furthermore, notice to the agent, combined with collusion or fraud between him and the third party that would defeat the purpose of the notice, would not bind the principal.

As a general rule, an agent or person ostensibly in charge of a place of business has apparent authority to accept notices in relation to the business. An employee in charge of the receipt of mail may accept written notifications.

Agent's power to appoint subagents

Agents are usually selected because of their personal qualifications. Owing to these elements of trust and confidence, a general rule has developed that an agent may not delegate his duty to someone else and clothe the latter with authority to bind the principal. An exception has arisen to this rule in cases in which the acts of the agent are purely ministerial or mechanical. An act that requires no discretion and is purely mechanical may be delegated by the agent to a third party. Such a delegation does not make the third party the agent of the principal or give him any action against the principal for compensation unless the agent was impliedly authorized to obtain this assistance. The acts of such a third party become in reality the acts of the agent. They bind the principal if they are within the authority given to the agent. Acts that involve the exercise of skill, discretion, or judgment may not be delegated without permission from the principal.

An agent may, under certain circumstances, have the actual or implied authority to appoint other agents for the principal, in which case they become true employees of the principal and are entitled to be compensated by him. This power on the part of the agent is not often implied; but if the major power conferred cannot be exercised without the aid of other agents, the agent is authorized to hire whatever help is required. Thus, a manager placed in charge of a branch store may be presumed to possess authority to hire the necessary personnel.

Financial powers of agents

An agent who delivers goods sold for cash has the implied authority to collect all payments due at the time of delivery. A salesperson taking orders calling for a down payment has implied authority to accept the down payment. By the very nature of their jobs, salespeople have no implied authority to receive payments on account, and any authority to do so must be expressly given or be implied from custom. Thus, a salesperson in a store has authority to collect payments made at the time of sale but no authority to receive payments on account. If payment to a sales agent who has no authority to collect is not delivered to the principal, it may be collected by the principal either from the agent or from the party who paid the agent.

Possession of a statement of account on the billhead of the principal or in the principal's handwriting does not create implied or apparent authority to collect a debt. Payment to an agent without authority to collect does not discharge the debt.

Authority to collect gives the agent no authority to accept anything other than money in payment. Unless expressly authorized, he is not empowered to accept negotiable notes or property in settlement of an indebtedness. It is customary for an agent to accept checks as conditional payment. Under those circumstances, the debt is not paid unless the check is honored. If the check is not paid, the creditor principal is free to bring suit on the contract that gave rise to the indebtedness or to sue on the check, at his option.

A general agent placed in charge of a business has implied or apparent authority to purchase for cash or on credit. The implied authority is based on the nature of his position and on the fact that the public rightly concludes that a corporation or an individual acting through another person has given him the power and authority that naturally and properly belong to the character in which the agent is held out.

Authority to borrow money is not easily implied. It must be expressly granted or must qualify as incidental authority to the express authority, or the principal will not be bound. The authority to borrow should always be confirmed with the principal.

CASE

D owned a men's clothing store. Her father from time to time did business in D's name. A checking account in P bank had been opened by D, with a power of attorney given to the father "to sign and indorse checks, notes and drafts . . . and transact all business." D's father borrowed money from P bank.

ISSUE Did the power of attorney give the father the power to borrow money?

DECISION No.

REASONS

1. The power of attorney does not expressly authorize the power to borrow money. It will be strictly construed against the party supplying the instrument—the bank.
2. The power to borrow money will be found only if (a) it is directly granted; (b) it is indispensable to the execution of the powers actually granted; or (c) the agent has apparent authority to do so, as by a long course of similar dealing.

Bank of America, Nat. Trust & Sav. Ass'n v. Horowytz, 248 A.2d 446 (N.J.) 1968.

Liability of Third Parties

To principals

A disclosed principal may enforce any contract made by an authorized agent for the former's benefit. This right applies to all contracts in which the principal is the real party in interest, including contracts that are made in the agent's name. Furthermore, if a contract is made for the benefit of a disclosed principal by an agent acting outside the scope of his authority, the principal is still entitled to performance, provided the contract is properly ratified before withdrawal by the third party.

An undisclosed principal is entitled to performance by third parties of all assignable contracts made for his benefit by an authorized agent. It is no defense for the third party to say that he had not entered into a contract with the principal.

If a contract is one that involves the skill or confidence of the agent and is one that would not have been entered into without this skill or confidence, its performance may not be demanded by the undisclosed principal. This rule applies because the contract would not be assignable, since personal rights and duties are not transferable without consent of the other party.

In cases other than those involving commercial paper, the undisclosed principal takes over the contract subject to all defenses that the third party could have established against the agent. If the third party contracts to buy from such an agent and has a right of setoff against the agent, he has this same right of setoff against the undisclosed principal. The third party may also pay the agent prior to discovery of the principal and thus discharge his liability.

To agents

Normally, the agent possesses no right to bring suit on contracts made by him for the benefit of his principal, because he has no interest in the cause of action. The agent who binds himself to the third party, either intentionally or ineptly by a failure properly to express himself, may, however, maintain an action. An agent of an undisclosed principal is liable on the contract and may sue in his own name in the event of nonperformance by the third party. Thus, either the agent or the undisclosed principal might bring suit, but in case of a dispute, the right of the previously undisclosed principal is superior.

Custom has long sanctioned an action by the agent based upon a contract in which he is interested because of anticipated commissions. As a result, a factor may institute an action in his own name to recover for goods sold. He may also recover against a railroad for delay in the shipment of goods sold or to be sold.

Similarly, an agent who has been vested with title to commercial paper may sue the maker of the paper. The same is true of any claim held by the principal that he definitely places with the agent for collection and suit, where necessary. In all cases of this character, the agent retains the proceeds as a trust fund for his principal.

REVIEW QUESTIONS AND PROBLEMS

1. Pat, the owner of a grocery store chain, hires Amy to manage one store. Pat tells Amy to stock the store. Pat also tells Amy: (a) "Be sure to buy soup," (b) "Don't buy soup," (c) nothing about soup. Amy then proceeds to buy forty cases of soup from Tom. In which situations, if any, is Pat liable to Tom? Why?
2. Alex purchased an insurance policy on his own life. He paid the premiums directly to the insurance agent, Hamilton, who appropriated the premiums to his own use. Alex died. May the beneficiaries recover from the insurance company? Explain.
3. For two years, Art had acted as Paul's collection agent. Paul later revoked Art's authority to receive payments from the customers although neither Art nor Paul informed the customers of the termination of authority. Leo, one of Paul's customers, made payment to Art, who failed to turn the payment over to Paul. Is Leo liable to Paul? Why?
4. Aline was authorized by David to purchase bowling alley equipment on credit. She told the seller she was acting as an agent but was not at liberty to disclose her principal's name. The bill remains unpaid, and David is now disclosed. May the seller recover from Aline? Why?
5. Ann worked for Perry's Grocery as purchasing agent for poultry and farm produce. In all transactions with farmers, Ann acted as the principal and purchased on the strength of her own credit. Ann failed to pay for some of the produce purchased. The farmers, having ascertained that Perry's Grocery was the true principal, seek to hold it responsible. May they do so? Suppose Perry's had previously settled with Ann? Explain.
6. Stevens hires Calhoun, an attorney, to sue Brown for a debt. While Stevens is out of town, Calhoun settles the case with Brown, and Calhoun forges Stevens's name to a release. When Stevens returns, he accepts Brown's check. May Stevens claim Calhoun acted without authority and avoid the release? Why?
7. A brother and sister jointly owned land which Carter agreed to buy. The contract was signed by the sister individually and as agent for her brother. The brother had orally agreed to the terms of the contract. Is the brother bound on the contract? Why?
8. Jerry, the managing agent of Pet Shop, Inc., borrowed $3,500 from Turner on the shop's behalf for use in the business. The company had not authorized Jerry to borrow the money, but it did repay $200 of the amount to Turner. Is Turner entitled to collect the balance due from the shop? Why?
9. Rand and Cronin were competitors in business. Rand suspected that Cronin would not sell to him, so he engaged Kahn to purchase asphalt blocks from Cronin. Kahn purchased the blocks, but they were unmerchantable. When sued for breach of warranty by Rand, Cronin defended on the ground that the contract would not have been entered into if the identity of the principal had been known. Can Rand hold Cronin liable on the contract? Why?
10. Barney purchased a new car and called the Friendly Insurance Company's home office to transfer the insurance from his old car to his new one and to obtain collision coverage. He talked to two employees before being switched to Ann, who replied, "O.K., you are covered." Ann had no authority to give additional insurance coverage. Barney had an accident the day after he talked to Ann. Barney sues Friendly for damage to his car. Should he succeed? Why?

34

Agency and the Law of Torts

The fundamental principles of tort liability in the law of agency, which are discussed in this chapter, can be summarized as follows:

1. Agents, servants, and independent contractors are personally liable for their own torts.
2. Agents, servants, and independent contractors are not liable for the torts of their employers.
3. A master is liable under a doctrine known as *respondeat superior* for the torts of his servant if the servant is acting within the scope of his employment.
4. A principal is liable for the torts of an agent who is also a servant in the performance of his duties if the agent is acting within the scope of his employment.
5. A principal, proprietor, employer, or contractee (each of these terms is sometimes used) is not, as a general rule, liable for the torts of an independent contractor.
6. Injured employees may have rights against their employers as well as against third parties who cause their injuries.

In the foregoing list, numbers 3 and 4 actually express the same basic concept. The terms *master* and *servant* are technically more accurate than the terms *principal* and *agent* in describing the parties when tort liability is discussed. Courts nevertheless frequently describe the parties as "principal" and "agent." However, a principal is liable for torts of only those agents who are subject to the kind of control that establishes the master-servant relationship. For the purpose of tort liability, a servant is a person who is employed with or without pay to perform personal services for another in his affairs, and who, in respect to the physical movements in the performance of such service, is subject to the master's right or power of control. A person who renders services for another but retains control over the manner of rendering such services is not a servant but an independent contractor.

The amount of control present will also determine tort liability when other legal relationships exist. The extent of control determines the liability of a franchisor for the torts of a franchisee, because the presence of control creates the agency relationship.

CASE

P, a motel guest, slipped and fell on water draining from an air-conditioning unit. P sued D, the franchisor of the motel system. The motel was owned by a corporation that operated as D's franchisee and licensee. D's name was used in the operation. In addition, D designed the motel, sold the franchisee the equipment, furnishings, and supplies, and trained its employees. D received a license fee plus fifteen cents per room per day from the operator.

ISSUE Is the franchisor liable for the torts of its franchisee?

DECISION No.

REASONS
1. The fact that an agreement is a franchise contract does not insulate the parties from an agency relationship. If a franchise contract "regulates the activities of the franchisee" so that it vests the franchisor with control within the definition of agency, the agency relationship arises even though the parties as a part of the agreement expressly deny it.
2. Whether the power to regulate granted by a franchise contract constitutes control sufficient to establish an agency relationship depends on the nature and the extent of the power defined in the contract.
3. A franchise agreement that permitted the licensee to use the licensor's trade name on a motel, which was intended to achieve a systemwide standardization of business identity, uniformity of commercial service, and optimum public goodwill for benefit of both the contracting parties, and which empowers the licensor to regulate architectural style of buildings and type and style of furnishings and equipment but which gives the licensor no power to control daily maintenance of the premises does not create a principal-agent or master-servant relationship.
4. The regulatory provisions of the franchise contract do not constitute control within the definition of agency.

Murphy v. Holiday Inns, Inc., 219 S.E.2d 874 (Va.) 1975.

Tort liability of agents and servants

Every person who commits a tort is personally liable to the individual whose person or property is injured or damaged by the wrongful act. An agent or officer of a corporation who commits or participates in the commission of a tort, whether or not he acts on behalf of his corporation, is liable to third persons injured. One is not relieved of tort liability by establishing that the tortious act was committed under the direction of someone else or in the course of employment by another. The fact that the employer or principal may be held liable does not in any way relieve the servant or agent from liability. The agent's or servant's liability is joint and several with the liability of the principal. Of course, the converse is not true. An agent, servant, or independent contractor is not liable for the torts of the principal, master, or employer. If Anton commits a tort against Trevor, Trevor can bring action against Anton or against Anton's employer, Pitman. Or Trevor can sue them jointly. Assume that Trevor sues and collects from Pitman, as is typically the case, because the employer's financial standing is usually better than the employee's. Can Pitman, upon paying the judgment, recover his loss from Anton? The answer is yes if the tort arose from Anton's negligence and there was no contributing fault of Pitman. A servant is liable for his own misconduct either to others or to his employer.

Suits by masters against servants for indemnity are not common, for several reasons. First, the servant's financial condition frequently does not warrant suit. Second, the employer knows of the risk of negligence by his employees and covers this risk with insurance. If indemnity were a common occurrence, the ultimate loss would almost always fall on employees or workmen. If this situation developed, it would have an adverse effect on employee morale and would make labor-management relations much more difficult. Therefore, few employers seek to enforce the right to collect losses from employees.

Just as Pitman may have a right to reimbursement or indemnity from Anton, under certain situations Anton may successfully maintain an action for reimbursement or indemnity against Pitman. Such is the case when Anton commits a tort by following Pitman's instructions, not knowing that his conduct is tortious. Pitman may be a retail appliance dealer who instructs Anton to repossess a TV set from Trevor, who had purchased it on an installment contract. Pitman informs Anton that Trevor is in arrears in his payments. Actually, Trevor is current in his payments. A bookkeeping error had been made by Pitman. Following instructions, over Trevor's protests, Anton makes the repossession. Anton has committed a tort, but Pitman must indemnify him and satisfy Trevor's claim against Anton if Trevor elects to collect from Anton.

Tort Liability of Principals and Masters

Respondeat superior

A master is liable to third persons for the torts committed by his servants *within the scope of their employment* and in prosecution of the master's business. This concept, frequently known as *respondeat superior* (let the master respond), imposes vicarious liability on employers as a matter of public policy. Although negligence of the servant is the usual basis of liability, the doctrine of *respondeat superior* is also applicable to intentional torts, such as trepass, assault, libel, and fraud, which are committed by a servant acting within the scope of his employment. It is applicable even though the master did not direct the willful act or assent to it.

This vicarious liability imposed on masters, which makes them pay for wrongs they have not actually committed, is not based on logic and reason but on business and social policy. The theory is that the master is in a better position to pay for the wrong than is the servant. This concept is sometimes referred to as the "deep pocket" theory. The business policy theory is that injuries to persons and property are hazards of doing business, the cost of which the business should bear rather than have the loss borne by the innocent victim of the tort or society as a whole.

The application of the doctrine of *respondeat superior* usually involves the issue of whether the servant was *acting within the scope of his employment* at the time of the commission of the tort. The agent or servant may have detoured from his employment and gone off on a frolic of his own. (The law of frolics and detours is covered in a later section.) In addition, the facts may establish that the control of the master over the servant's employment has ended. If the servant is no longer acting within the scope of his employment on his master's business, but is acting solely on his own behalf, there can obviously be no liability.

CASE

X, an oil-field employee, had a work schedule consisting of 7 days on and 7 days off. On the seventh day of work he traveled 30 miles by boat and then drove his automobile 150 miles to his home. X was paid for oil-field work and for boat travel time, but his pay stopped the moment he disembarked. While homeward bound in his automobile, X struck a car and killed a motorist. Her estate sued D, X's employer, for wrongful death.

ISSUE Is an employer liable for the torts of its employees while the employee is on his way to or from his employment?

DECISION No.

REASONS

1. Employers are liable for the torts of their employees if the employees (servants) commit the torts while exercising functions in which they are employed.
2. The tortious conduct was not so closely connected to the employment that it should be regarded as a risk of harm fairly attributable to the employer's business.
3. The act of going home is purely personal to the employee and is extraneous to the employer's interests.

Boudreaux v. Yancey, 319 So.2d 806 (La.App.) 1975.

As a general rule, the master cannot avoid liability by showing that he has instructed the servant not to do the particular act complained of. When a servant disobeys the instructions of his master, the fact of disobedience alone does not insulate the master from liability. In addition, the master is not released by evidence that the servant was not doing the work his master had instructed him to do, when the servant had misunderstood the instruction. As long as the servant is attempting to further his master's business, the master is liable, because the servant is acting within the scope of his employment.

Expanding vicarious liability

In recent years, the law has been expanding the concept of vicarious liability, even to acts of persons who are not employees. A person engaged in some endeavor gratuitously may still be a "servant" within scope of master-servant doctrine. The two key elements for determination of whether a gratuitous undertaking is a part of master-servant relationship are (1) whether the actor has submitted himself to the directions and to the control of the one for whom the service is done, and (2) whether the primary purpose of the underlying act was to serve another. If so, the "master" is liable for the torts of the unpaid "servant."

Most of the expansion of the application of *respondeat superior* and vicarious liability has been by statute. Liability for automobile accidents has been a major area of expansion. Some states have adopted what is known as the "family car doctrine." Under it, if the car is generally made available for family use, any member of the family is presumed to be an agent of the parent-owner when using the family car for his or her convenience or pleasure. The presumption may be rebutted, however. Other states have gone further and provided that anyone driving a car with the permission of the owner is the owner's agent, and the owner has vicarious liability to persons injured by the driver. The family purpose doctrine may extend to nonfamily members under some circumstances.

CASE

D, the owner of a family purpose automobile, allowed his minor son to drive the car. The son permitted a friend to drive, and a collision occurred, injuring P, who sued D. D contended that there was no liability because there was no master-servant relationship.

ISSUE Was the operator of the automobile an agent of the owner?

DECISION Yes.

REASONS
1. The test of liability of an owner under the "family purpose car doctrine," is whether the car was being operated in the scope of the owner's business. The family purpose car doctrine is but an extension of the principal-agent relationship.
2. A master is responsible for the tortious acts of his servant, done in the master's business, and within the scope of his employment, though the master disapproves, forbids, or is ignorant of a particular act.
3. If a family purpose automobile is being operated for the pleasure of some member of the owner's family, the owner is liable for the acts of the driver, though the driver is a third person.

Dixon v. Phillips, 217 S.E.2d 331 (Ga.) 1975.

Frolics and detours

Respondeat superior requires that the agent or servant be *acting within the scope of his employment* at the time of the commission of the tort. The law imposes liability on the master only when the master's business is being carried on or the wrongful act was authorized or ratified. The master's liability does not arise when the servant steps aside from his employment to commit the tort or does the wrongful act to accomplish some purpose of his own. If the tort is activated by a purpose to serve the master or principal, then he is liable. Otherwise he is not. Although the scope of employment is considerably broader than explicitly authorized acts of the employee, it does not extend to cases in which the servant has stepped aside from his employment to commit a tort that the master neither directed in fact nor could be supposed, from the nature of the servant's employment, to have authorized or expected the servant to do.

Not every deviation from the strict course of duty is a departure that will relieve a master of liability for the acts of a servant. The fact that a servant, while performing his duty to his master, incidentally does something for himself or a third person does not automatically relieve the master from liability for negligence that causes injury to another. To sever the servant from the scope of his employment, the act complained of must be such a divergence from his regular duties that its very character severs the relationship of master and servant.

CASE

P was injured in Nebraska, riding with her mother, when their auto collided with a car driven by Evers. At the time of the accident, Evers was driving to Wyoming to retrieve his clothes and personal belongings, in connection with his job with D, the Union Pacific Railroad. P argued that the railroad should be liable under the doctrine of *respondeat superior* because Evers's trip would incidentally and indirectly benefit his employer.

ISSUE Is D liable for Evers's negligence?

DECISION No.

REASONS 1. It is not enough to establish liability merely to show that the employer has an interest in the employee's activity. *Respondeat superior* is applicable only when the employment relationship can be found to exist at the time of, and with respect to, the conduct giving rise to the injury. Here, Evers's trip was personal and outside the limits of his employment.

2. D exerted no control or authority over Evers at the time of the accident. If an employer were liable merely upon the remote possibility of indirect benefit to him, there would be no limit to the liability that could be imposed upon an employer.

Johnson v. Evers, 238 N.W. 2d 474 (Neb.) 1976.

In the foregoing case, the suit against the railroad was important to the plaintiff because of the defendant's ability to pay. The railroad had significant assets; but in all likelihood, the individual defendant did not.

It is not possible to state a simple test to determine if the tort is committted within the scope of the employment. Factors to be considered include the nature of the employment, the right of control "not only as to the result to be accomplished but also as to the means to be used," the ownership of the instrumentality such as an automobile, whether the instrumentality was furnished by the employer, whether the use was authorized, and the time of the occurrence. Most courts inquire into the intent of the servant and the extent of deviation from expected conduct involved in the tort. The issue is usually one of fact and is left to the jury.

A servant is not acting within the scope of his employment if he is on a "frolic" of his own. The deviation may sometimes be described as a "detour," but when does the detour end and the course of employment resume? Another difficult situation is presented when the servant combines his own business with that of his master. As a general rule, this fact does not relieve the master of liability. The doctrine of *respondeat superior* has been extended to create liability for negligence of strangers while assisting a servant in carrying out the master's business, if the authority to obtain assistance is given or required, as in an emergency.

Intentional or willful torts are not as likely to occur within the scope of the servant's employment as are those predicated upon a negligence theory. If the willful misconduct of the servant has nothing to do with his master's business and is animated entirely by hatred or a feeling of ill will toward the third party, the master is not liable. Nor is the master liable if the employee's act has no reasonable connection with his employment.

CASE

S, an employee of D freight company, was driving a truck-tractor-semitrailer combination. In attempting to pass P, a motorist, S's rig swerved into P's lane, forcing P into another lane and onto another auto. P motioned for S to pull over onto the shoulder of the highway. S again forced P into another lane before they both pulled off the road. S got out of his cab carrying a two-foot-long metal pipe, which he swung at P, grazing the side of P's face, knocking off P's glasses. As P bent over to pick up his glasses, S hit P twice on the side of the head. S was convicted of assault. Prior to this accident, S's record with D had been good. P sued D for personal injuries.

ISSUE Was D liable for S's assault on P?

DECISION No.

REASONS 1. A master is responsible for the servant's acts under the doctrine of *respondeat superior* when the servant acts within the scope of his or her employment and in furtherance of the master's business.

When a servant steps aside from the master's business in order to effect some purpose of his own, the master is not liable.

2. If the assault by the servant is occasioned solely by reason of the servant's ill will, jealousy, hatred, or other ill feelings, independent of the servant's duty, then the master is not liable. To fall within the scope of employment, the assault must be committed by authority of the employer, the authority being either expressly conferred or fairly implied from the nature of the employment or its incidental duties. (A servant may be authorized to maintain discipline, or the character of the employment may create disputes and result in breaches of the peace.)
3. When the servant's intentionally tortious or criminal acts are not performed in furtherance of the master's business, the master will not be held liable as a matter of law, even though the employment situation provided the opportunity for the servant's wrongful acts or the means for carrying them out.
4. S assaulted P because of his anger toward P, not because of any intent to serve the employer.

Kuehn v. White & Inter-City Auto Freight, Inc., 600 P.2d 679, (Wash.) 1979.

Tort suits—procedures

As previously noted, the law of torts in most states, unlike the law of contracts, allows joinder of the master and servant as defendants in one cause of action or permits them to be sued separately. Although the plaintiff is limited to one recovery, the master and servant are jointly and severally liable. The party may collect from either or both in any proportion until the judgment is paid in full. If the servant is sued first and a judgment is obtained that is not satisfied, the suit is not a bar to a subsequent suit against the master, but the amount of the judgment against the servant fixes the maximum limit of potential liability against the master.

If the servant is found to be free of liability, either in a separate suit or as a codefendant with the master, then the suit against the master on the basis of *respondeat superior* will fail. The master's liability is predicated upon the fault of the servant; and if the servant is found to be free of fault, the master has no liability as a matter of law.

Independent contractors

An *independent contractor* has power to control the details of the work he performs for his employer. Because the performance is within his control, he is not a servant, and his only responsibility is to accomplish the result contracted for. To illustrate: Rush contracts to build a boat for Ski-King at a cost of $40,000, according to certain specifications. It is clear that Rush is an independent contractor; the completed boat is the result. Had Ski-King engaged Rush by the day to assist in building the boat under Ski-King's supervision and direction, the master-servant relationship would have resulted. We should keep in mind that an agent with authority to represent his principal contractually will, at the same time, be either a servant or an independent contractor for the purpose of tort liability.

The distinction between servants and independent contractors is important because, as a general rule, the doctrine of *respondeat superior* and the concept of vicarious liability in tort are not applicable to independent contractors. There is no tort liability, as a general rule, because the theories that justify liability on the master for the servant's tort are not present when the person engaged to do the work is not a servant. Nor is any liability imputed to one who controls certain activities of persons not employed by him.

The hallmark of a master-servant relationship is that the master not only controls the result of the work but has the right to direct the manner in which the work shall be accomplished. The distinguishing feature of an independent contractor-contractee relationship is that the person engaged in the work has exclusive control of the manner of performing it, being responsible only for the result, not the means. In ascertaining whether a person is a servant or an independent contractor, the basic inquiry is whether such person is subject to the alleged employer's control or right to control his physical conduct in the performance of services for which he was engaged. Whether the relationship is master-servant or proprietor-independent contractor is usually a question of fact for the jury.

Without changing the relationship from that of owner and independent contractor or the duties arising from that relationship, an employer of an independent contractor may retain a broad, general power of supervision of the work, to ensure satisfactory performance of the contract. He may inspect, *stop the work,* make suggestions or recommendations about details of the work, or *prescribe alterations or deviations.*

The application of the doctrine of *respondeat superior* and the tests for determining if the wrongdoer is an independent contractor are quite difficult to apply to professional and technically skilled personnel. It can be argued that a physician's profession requires such high skill and learning that others, especially laymen, cannot as a matter of law be in control of the physician's activities. That argument, if accepted, would eliminate the liability of hospitals for acts of medical employees.

Notwithstanding the logic of the preceding argument, courts usually hold that *respondeat superior* may be applied to professional persons and that such persons may be servants. Of course, some professional and technical persons are independent contractors. Hospitals and others who render professional service through skilled employees have the same legal responsibilities as everyone else. If the person who commits a tort is an employee acting on the employer's behalf, the employer is liable, even though no one actually "controls" the employee in the performance of his art or skill. These concepts are applicable to doctors, chemists, airline pilots, lawyers, and other highly trained specialists.

Since it is generally understood that one is not liable for the torts of an independent contractor, contracts frequently provide that the relationship is that of independent contractor, not master-servant. Such a provision is not binding on third parties, and the contract cannot be used to protect the contracting parties from the actual relationship as shown by the facts.

Exceptions to independent contractor rule

The rule of insulation from liability in the independent contractor situation is subject to several well-recognized exceptions. The most common of these is related to work inherently dangerous to the public, such as blasting with dynamite. The basis of this exception is that it would be contrary to public policy to allow one engaged in such an activity to avoid his liability by selecting an independent contractor rather than a servant to do the work.

CASE

D employed an independent contractor to spray pesticide on his crops. The spray damaged the P's nearby fishing lake. The trial court held the defendant not liable as a matter of law because the injury was inflicted by an independent contractor. P contends that D is liable because the work was "inherently or intrinsically dangerous."

ISSUE Is crop dusting "inherently dangerous," rendering the employer of an independent contractor liable for injuries to third parties?

DECISION Yes

REASONS 1. Although an employer of an independent contractor is not generally liable for the torts of the independent contractor, when the activity is inherently or intrinsically dangerous, the rule is not applied.

2. This exception to the rule developed so that persons desiring such work to be done could not insulate themselves from potential liability by employing only independent contractors.

3. Crop dusting is inherently or intrinsically dangerous because the poison can be so readily blown to other property, where it can do damage.

Boroughs v. Joiner, 337 So.2d 340 (Ala.) 1976.

Another exception to insulation from vicarious liability applies to illegal work. An employer cannot insulate himself from liability by hiring an independent contractor to perform a task that is illegal. Still another common exception involves employees' duties that are considered to be nondelegable. In discussing the law of contracts, we noted that personal rights and personal duties could not be transferred without consent of the other party. Many statutes impose strict duties on parties such as common carriers and innkeepers. If an attempt is made to delegate these duties to an independent contractor, it is clear that the employer upon whom the duty is imposed has liability for the torts of the independent contractor. Finally, an employer is liable for the torts of an independent contractor if the tort is ratified. If an independent contractor wrongfully repossesses an automobile and the one hiring him refuses to return it on demand, the tort has been ratified, and both parties have liability.

Tort liability is also imposed on the employer who is himself at fault, as he is when he negligently selects the employee. This is true whether the party performing the work is a servant or an independent contractor. Assume that Unisex Hair Salon employs John Bully, a hair stylist with known propensities for violence, including a criminal record for assaults. John assaults a customer after an argument over hair styles. There would be liability even if John were an independent contractor. There would also be liability even though John went beyond the scope of his employment. Liability exists because of the negligence of Unisex in hiring John.

Injuries to Employees

Claims against third parties

Irrespective of other legal relationships, any person injured by the commission of a tort has a cause of action against the wrongdoer. An employee who is injured by the wrongful conduct of the third person may recover from the third person. If the employee has been compensated for his injuries by his employer under the applicable worker's compensation law, the employer is entitled to recover any worker's compensation payments from the sum that the employee recovers from the wrongful third party.

There are three rather unusual tort situations that have a direct relation to the employment contract. First, any third party who maliciously or wrongfully influences a principal to terminate an agent's employment thereby commits a tort. The wrongful third party must compensate the agent for any damages that result from such conduct. Second, any third person who wrongfully interferes with the prospective economic advantage of an agent has liability to the agent for the loss sustained. Third, any person who influences another to breach a contract in which the agent is interested thereby renders himself liable to the agent as well as to the principal. These matters were discussed in chapter 4.

Tort claims against the employer

An employer owes certain nondelegable duties to his employees. These include the duty to (1) warn employees of the hazards of their employment, (2) supervise their activities, (3) furnish a reasonably safe place to work, and (4) furnish reasonably safe instrumentalities with which to work. As part of the obligation to provide a safe place to work, the employer must instruct his employees in the safe use and handling of the products and equipment used in and around the employer's plant or facilities. What is reasonable for the purposes of these rules depends on all the facts and circumstances of each case, including the age and ability of the worker as well as the condition of the premises. It might be negligent to put a minor in charge of a particular instrument without supervision, although it would not be negligent to assign an adult or experienced employee to the same equipment.

At common law, the employer who breached these duties to his employees was liable in tort for injuries received by the employees. The employer was not an insurer of his employee's safety, but liability was based on negligence. In turn, the employee in his tort action was confronted with overcoming three defenses available to the employer, one or more of which frequently barred recovery. The first of these defenses was that the employee was *contributorily negligent.* If the employee was even partially at fault, this defense was successful, even though the majority of the fault was the employer's. Second, if the injury was caused by some other employee, the *fellow-servant* doctrine excused the employer and limited recovery to a suit against the other employee who was at fault. Finally, in many jobs that by their very nature involved some risk of injury, the doctrine of *assumption of risk* would allow the employer to avoid liability.

The common law rules resulted for the most part in imposing on employees the burdens that resulted from accidental injuries, occupational diseases, and even death. Through the legislative process, society has rather uniformly determined that this result is undesirable as a matter of public policy. Statutes known as *worker's compensation* have been enacted in all the states. These laws impose liability without fault (eliminate the common law defenses) on most employers for injuries, occupational diseases, and death of their employees.

Worker's compensation

Worker's compensation laws vary a great deal from state to state in their coverage of industries and employees, the nature of the injuries or diseases that are compensable, and the rates and source of compensation. In spite of these wide variances, certain general observations can be made.

State worker's compensation statutes provide a system of paying for death, illness, or injury that arises out of, and in the course of, the employment. The three defenses the employer had at common law are eliminated. The employers are strictly liable without fault.

Most state statutes exclude certain types of employment from their coverage. Generally, domestic and agricultural employees are not covered. In the majority of states, the statutes are compulsory. In some states, employers may elect to be subject to lawsuits by their employees or their survivors. In such cases, the plaintiff must prove that the death or injury resulted proximately from the negligence of the employer. But the plaintiff is not subject to the common law defenses. In addition, there is no statutory limit to the amount of damages recoverable. Thus, few employers elect to avoid coverage.

The worker's compensation acts give covered employees the right to certain cash payments for their loss of income. A weekly benefit is payable during periods of disability.

In the event of an employee's death, benefits are provided for the spouse and minor children. The amount of such awards is usually subject to a stated maximum and is calculated by using a percentage of the wages of the employee. If the employee suffers permanent partial disability, most states provide compensation for injuries that are scheduled in the statute and those that are nonscheduled. As an example of the former, a worker who loses a hand might be awarded 100 weeks of compensation at $90 per week. Besides scheduling specific compensation for certain specific injuries, most acts also provide compensation for nonscheduled ones, such as back injuries, based upon the earning power the employee lost owing to his injury. In addition to the payments above, all statutes provide for medical benefits and funeral expenses.

In some states, employers have a choice of covering their worker's compensation risk with insurance or being self-insured (i.e., paying all claims directly) if they can demonstrate their capability to do so. In other states, employers pay into a state fund used to compensate workers entitled to benefits. In these states, the amounts of the payments are based on the size of the payroll and the experience of the employer in having claims filed.

Although the right to worker's compensation benefits is given without regard to fault of either the employer or the employee, employers are not always liable. The tests for determining whether an employee is entitled to worker's compensation are simply: (1) Was the injury accidental? and (2) Did the injury arise out of and in the course of the employment? Since worker's compensation laws are remedial in nature, they have been very liberally construed. In recent years, the courts have tended to expand coverage and scope of the employer's liability. It has been held that heart attacks and other common ailments are compensable as "accidental injuries," even though the employee had either a preexisting disease or a physical condition likely to lead to the disease. Likewise, the courts have been more and more liberal in upholding awards that have been challenged on the ground that the injury did not arise out of and in the course of the employment.

The system of separate and varying state worker's compensation laws as they exist today has been subject to much criticism. The laws have been attacked as inadequate because of their restrictive coverage and limited benefits. Not all types of employment or occupational risks are covered. Many states exempt businesses that do not employ a certain minimum number of workers. Criticism has also been leveled at the quality of administration of most worker's compensation programs. The weaknesses in the present laws and the wide variations in worker's compensation acts (as well as case law) from state to state have led to suggestions that worker's compensation be modernized to meet the social needs of today and that it be made uniform from state to state. Some have proposed a Federal Worker's Compensation Act to replace the state ones.

REVIEW QUESTIONS AND PROBLEMS

1. Which party, the master or the servant, has the ultimate liability for torts that are the servant's rather than the master's fault? Explain.
2. Mary, a sales representative for the XYZ company, drove her personal car to a sales convention. XYZ reimbursed Mary for her expenses at the convention. On the way home from the convention, Mary's negligent driving resulted in injury to Nancy. Is XYZ liable to Nancy? Why?
3. *The Daily Bugle* customarily dropped several bundles of newspapers at a certain corner where Mort, a newsboy, picked them up. Mort then folded the newspapers, throwing the bundling wire on the sidewalk. Larry tripped over the wire, injuring himself. Assuming that Mort is an independent contractor, may Larry recover from *The Daily Bugle?* Why?
4. Matt, driving a gasoline truck, negligently ran into and killed Kitty. Matt was driving the truck for his sister, a distributor of Darby oil and gas products. The contract with Darby provided that the truck carry the words "Darby Oil" in certain places, that it be used for delivery of Darby products to designated filling stations, and that the driver, in collecting for deliveries made, sign the receipt in the name of Darby Company. For these services, Matt's sister received a commission. When sued by Kitty's executor for wrongful death, Darby Company claimed that Matt's sister was an independent contractor rather than an agent. What was the result? Explain.
5. Keldene, a doctor, was employed at a regular salary by the QRS shipping lines to serve aboard ship and treat passengers. Keldene treated Barry, a passenger, who died as a result of Keldene's negligence. May Barry's heirs recover from QRS? Explain.
6. Steve was employed by Greta as a trainee photographer. Late one night after photographing a wedding, Steve was returning the camera equipment to the studio (he was not required to return the equipment that night) when his auto collided with Tim's auto, and Tim was killed. Tim's estate sues Greta and Steve. What was the result? Why?
7. A construction company engaged a subcontractor to procure fill dirt. The subcontractor's employee, operating a bulldozer, scraped a high-pressure gas line under the surface of the ground. The gas line exploded, damaging the plaintiff's property. May the plaintiff recover from the construction company? Why?
8. Terry was shopping in Don's store when Larry, an employee, brushed Terry's ankle with a shopping cart. A short time later, while still shopping, Terry told Larry that he should say "Excuse me," and then people would get out of his way. Larry then punched Terry in the face, knocking him to the floor. Terry now sues Don. Should he collect? Why?
9. EZ-Parts employed Borg as a distributor to solicit customers and sell its products. At the time of employment, Borg had committed numerous traffic violations and had been involved in several motor vehicle accidents. While on the way to call on a customer, Borg's car negligently struck another car. Assuming that Borg is an independent contractor, can the passengers of the other car recover from EZ-Parts? Why?
10. Eve was formerly employed at Red Company's store. Following her discharge, she sought other employment. A prospective employer telephoned Red Company's office and asked the reason for Eve's discharge. A secretary said that all the supervisors were out and that all he could do was to pull Eve's personnel file, which he did, and advised the caller that Eve was discharged for cash shortages. The notation was false, and Eve sued Red Company for defamation of character. Should she succeed? Why?

VII

Business Organizations

35

Choosing the Form of Business Organization

Business organizations may operate under a variety of legal forms. The common ones are sole proprietorships, partnerships, limited partnerships, and corporations. There are also some specialized organizations, such as professional service corporations, that are authorized by statute so that doctors, lawyers, dentists, and other professional persons are able to obtain the tax advantages of corporations.

This chapter will examine the various forms of organization and the factors that influence the actual selection of a particular form. The factors involved in this selection are applicable to all businesses, from the smallest to the largest, but the relative influence of the various factors varies greatly, depending on the size of the business. As a practical matter, the very large business must be incorporated, because that is the only method that can bring a large number of owners and investors together for an extended period of time.

The difficulty of deciding which is the best form of organization to select is most often encountered in the closely held business. Taxation is usually the most significant factor. Although a detailed discussion of the tax laws is beyond the scope of this text, some of the general principles of taxation will be presented in order to illustrate the influence taxation brings to bear in choosing between diverse organizational forms.

General partnerships

Partnerships developed logically in the law merchant, and the common law of partnerships has been codified in the Uniform Partnership Act. A partnership is an association of two or more persons to carry on, as co-owners, a business for profit. It is the result of an agreement.

A partnership form of organization has many advantages.

1. Since it is a matter of contract between individuals to which the state is not a party, it is easily formed.
2. Costs of formation are minimal.
3. It is not a taxable entity.
4. Each owner, as a general rule, has an equal voice in management.
5. It may operate in more than one state without being required to comply with many legal formalities.
6. Partnerships are generally subject to less regulation and less governmental supervision than corporations.

The fact that a partnership is not a taxable entity does not mean that partnership income is tax free. A partnership files an information return allocating its income among the partners, and each partner pays income tax on the portion allocated to him.

Several aspects of partnerships may be considered disadvantageous. First, as a personal matter, only a limited number of people may own such a business. Second, a partnership is dissolved any time a member ceases to be a partner either by withdrawal or by death. Although dissolution is the subject matter of Chapter 38, it should be observed here that the perpetual existence of a corporation is often a distinct advantage, compared to easily dissolved partnerships.

Third, the liability of a partner is unlimited, contrasted with the limited liability of a shareholder. The unlimited liability of a partner is applicable both to contract and tort claims. Fourth, since a partner is taxed on his share of the profits of a partnership, whether distributed to him or not, a partner may be required to pay income tax on money that is not received. This burden is an important consideration in a new business that is reinvesting its profits for expansion. A partner in such a business would have to have an independent means of paying the taxes on such income.

Limited partnerships

A *limited* partnership, like other partnerships, comes into existence by virtue of an agreement. Like a corporation, it is authorized by statute, and the liability of one or more, but not all, of the partners is limited to the amount of capital contributed at the time of the creation of the partnership. For liability purposes, a limited partnership is, in effect, a hybrid between the partnership and the corporation.

One or more general partners manage the business and are personally liable for its debts. One or more limited partners also contribute capital and share in profits and losses but take no part in running the business and incur no liability with respect to partnership obligations beyond their contribution to capital. It is from the limited liability of the limited partners that the organization gets it's name.

Limited partnerships are governed in most states by the Uniform Limited Partnership Act provisions. The purpose of this statute is to encourage trade by permitting persons to invest in a business and reap their share of the profits without becoming liable for debts or risking more than the capital contributed. This reduced risk is based on the investor's not being a general partner or participating actively in the conduct of the business.

To create a limited partnership under the Uniform Limited Partnership Act, the parties must sign and swear to a certificate containing, among other matters, the following information: the name of the partnership, the character of the business, its location, the name and place of residence of each member, those who are to be the general and those who are to be the limited partners, the term for which the partnership is to exist, the amount of cash or the agreed value of property to be contributed by each partner, and the share of profit or compensation each limited partner shall receive.

The certificate must be recorded in the county where the partnership has its principal place of business, and a copy must be filed in every community where it conducts business or has a representative office. Most states require notice by newspaper publication. In the event of any change in the facts contained in the certificate as filed—such as a change in the name of the partnership, the capital, or other matters—a new certificate must be filed. If such a certificate is not filed and the partnership continues, the limited partners immediately become liable as general partners.

The statutes of most states require the partnership to conduct its business in a firm name that does not include the name of any of the limited partners or the word *company*. Some states specify that the word *limited* shall be added.

Unless a limited partner participates in management and control of the business, his liability to creditors does not extend beyond his contribution to the business. Participation in management makes the limited partner a general partner with unlimited liability.

In many states, but not all, this unlimited liability cannot be avoided by making the general partner a corporation if the limited partners would be in control of the corporate general partner.

CASE

A limited partnership was formed with a corporation as the general partner. The limited partners were officers and directors of the corporation. P, a creditor of the limited partnership, sought to collect a partnership debt individually from the limited partners. The law provides that a limited partner who takes part in the control of a business is liable as a general partner.

ISSUE Can the personal liability that attaches to a limited partner when he takes part in control of the business be evaded by acting through a corporation?

DECISION No.

REASONS
1. Strict compliance with the limited partnership statute is required if limited partners are to avoid liability as general partners.
2. An exception to the rule that corporate officers are insulated from personal liability arising from their activities or those of a corporation exists where the corporate fiction is used to circumvent a statute.
3. The limited partners effectively controlled the business in their individual capacities. Their personal liability cannot be avoided by the corporate fiction.
4. A limited partner need not hold himself out as a general partner for liability to attach. The liability is statutory, not based on any theory of estoppel.

Delaney v. Fidelity Lease Limited, 526 S.W.2d 543 (Tex.) 1975.

To dissolve a limited partnership voluntarily before the time for termination stated in the certificate, notice of the dissolution must be filed and published. Upon dissolution, the distribution of the assets of the firm is prescribed by statute. As a general rule, the law gives priority to limited partners over general partners after all creditors are paid.

The limited partnership as a tax shelter is of special value in many new businesses, especially real estate ventures such as shopping centers and apartment complexes. It gives the investor limited liability and the operators control of the venture. It allows maximum use of the tax advantages of accelerated depreciation and the investment credit. Accelerated depreciation usually results in a tax loss in early years, which can be immediately deducted by the limited partner. Offsetting this tax loss, usually, is a cash flow that gives a limited partner an income at the same time he has a loss for tax purposes. When such ventures start to show a taxable gain, the limited partnership is often dissolved and a corporation is formed, or the venture is sold.

The obvious disadvantage in a limited partnership is the fact that the limited partner cannot participate in management without a change of status to that of a general partner. Nevertheless, a limited partner does have a right to inspect the books of the business, to receive an accounting, and to engage in activities that are of an advisory nature and do not amount to control of the business.

CASE

Ds were limited partners in a real estate venture. After the business was in financial difficulty, the limited partners had two meetings with the general partners to discuss the problems of the venture. In addition, one limited partner visited the construction site and "obnoxiously" complained of the way the work was being conducted.

ISSUE Do these actions constitute taking part in the control of the business, enough to make the limited partners liable as general partners?

DECISION No.

REASONS

1. It is well established that just because a man is a limited partner in an enterprise, he is not by reason of that status precluded from continuing to have an interest in the affairs of the partnership, from giving advice and suggestions to the general partner or his nominees, and from interesting himself in specific aspects of the business.
2. The casual advice the limited partners may have given in this case can hardly be said to be interference in day-to-day management. Certainly, common sense dictates that in times of severe financial crisis all partners in such an enterprise, limited or general, will become actively interested in any effort to keep the enterprise afloat, and many abnormal problems will arise that are not under any stretch of the imagination mere day-to-day matters of managing the partnership business.
3. It would be unreasonable to hold that a limited partner may not advise with the general partner and may not visit the partnership business, especially in times of severe financial crisis.

Trans-Am Builders, Inc. v. Woods Mill Ltd., 210 S.E.2d 866 (Ga.) 1974.

Revised Uniform Limited Partnership Act

In 1976, the Commissioners on Uniform State Laws issued a revised Uniform Limited Partnership Act. Although this act has not yet been adopted by very many states, it will in all probability become the law in most states in the future. The revised act tends to make a limited partnership more like a corporation.

Under the revised act, the name of the limited partnership must contain the words *limited partnership*. The name may not contain the name of a limited partner unless his name is also the name of a general partner or one that had been used prior to the admission of that limited partner.

A limited partnership under the new law is required to maintain a registered office within the state and an agent to receive notices for it. The law requires that certain records, such as a list of all partners and a copy of the certificate of the limited partnership, be maintained at this office. Copies of the partnership tax returns and copies of all financial statements must be kept for three years.

Under the revised act, the certificate creating the partnership is filed with the state's secretary of state. If it is later amended or canceled, the certificates of amendment and cancellation are also filed in that office.

The revised act makes a substantial change in the liability of a limited partner who participates in control of the business. The liability of a general partner is imposed on a limited partner who participates in the control of the business only if the third party had knowledge of the participation. In addition, the act provides that a limited partner does not participate in the control of the business by (1) being an agent or employee of the business, (2) consulting with or advising a partner with respect to the partnership, (3) acting as surety of the limited partnership, (4) approving or disapproving of an amendment to the certificate, and (5) voting on matters such as dissolution, sale of assets, or a change of name.

The business corporation

The corporation comes into existence when the state issues the corporate charter. A corporation is a legal entity that usually has perpetual existence. The liability of the owners is limited to their investment, unless there is a successful "piercing of the corporate veil." (See Chapter 39 for a further discussion of "piercing the corporate veil.")

A corporation, as a general rule, is a taxable entity paying a tax on its net profits. Dividends paid to stockholders are also taxable, giving rise to the frequently made observation that corporate income is subject to double taxation. The accuracy of this observation will be discussed later.

The advantages of the corporate form of organization may be briefly summarized as follows:

1. It is the only method that will raise substantial capital from a large number of investors.
2. Tax laws have several provisions that are favorable to corporations.
3. Control can be vested in those with a minority of the investment by using techniques such as nonvoting or preferred stock.
4. Ownership may be divided into many separate and unequal shares.
5. Investors have limited liability.
6. The organization can have perpetual existence.
7. Certain laws, such as those relating to usury, are not applicable to corporations.
8. Investors, notwithstanding their status as owners, may also be employees entitled to benefits such as workers' compensation.

Among the frequently cited disadvantages of the corporate form of organization are

1. Cost of forming and maintaining the corporate form with its rather formal procedures.
2. Expenditures such as license fees and franchise taxes that are assessed against corporations but not against partnerships.

3. Double taxation of corporate income and the frequently higher rates.
4. The requirement that it must be qualified to do business in all states where it is conducting intrastate commerce.
5. Subject to more regulation by government at all levels than are other forms.
6. Being required to use an attorney in litigation, whereas a layman can proceed on his own behalf.

CASE

P is incorporated to do business in the state of Maine, where the parties to any legal proceeding must be represented by an attorney authorized to practice law in the state. An exception exists for a person pleading or managing his own cause of action. P filed a lawsuit and was represented in court by its president, who concededly was not authorized to practice law in the state. D moved for dismissal on the ground that P was not properly represented. P contended that it could appear on its own behalf by an agent.

ISSUE May a corporation designate a nonattorney agent to represent it in a legal proceeding?

DECISION No.

REASONS
1. Although an individual may represent himself in court, state law prohibits a corporation from being represented by a nonattorney.
2. A corporation is an artificial entity created by law, and as such it can neither practice law nor appear or act in person. To allow a corporation to be represented by its officer would allow persons not qualified to practice law and unamenable to the general discipline of the court to maintain litigation.

Land Management v. Department of Envir. Prot., 368 A.2d 602 (ME) 1977.

Taxation. The fact that taxation was listed as both an advantage and a disadvantage of the corporate form illustrates the overwhelming importance of the tax factor in choosing this particular form of organization. The corporate tax law provisions that have most encouraged incorporation are those relating to qualified profit-sharing and pension plans. These provisions allow a corporation to deduct from taxable income its payments under qualified plans up to 25 percent of its payroll. These payments are invested, and the earnings are not subject to taxation when earned. No income tax is paid until withdrawals are made either during employment, if permitted, or upon retirement. To illustrate the advantages of such plans, think of A, B, and C as shareholders and employees of the ABC company. The company has five additional employees, and the net income of the company is $150,000. If ABC company pays $20,000 under qualified plans, the income tax reduction is $9,200 (assuming a 46 percent rate). The net cost of the payment to the company is $10,800. The $20,000 is credited to the accounts of the employees by a formula based on wages and years of service. Assume that the amounts credited to A, B, and C total $12,000. This gives them an initial net gain of $1,200 and a tax-free investment. The employees also received substantial benefits and security. A, B, and C, as well as the other employees, will receive their savings upon retirement, at a time when their tax rates will be lower and exemptions increased. Such plans have given impetus to the incorporation of hundreds of thousands of small businesses and professional practices.

Tax laws have other advantages for corporations. (1) Health insurance payments are fully deductible and are not subject to the limitations applicable to individuals. (2) Deferred compensation plans may be adopted. (3) Retained earnings below $100,000 per year are taxed at graduated rates that are frequently lower than the individual tax rates of the shareholders; e.g. the rate on the first $25,000 of taxable income is currently only 17 percent. (4) Income that is needed in the business is not taxed against a person who does not receive it. (5) Accumulated income can be taken out as a capital gain on dissolution. (6) The corporation may provide life insurance for its employees as a deductible expense. (7) Medical expenses in excess of health insurance coverage may be paid on behalf of employees as a deductible expense.

The corporate form is frequently at a disadvantage from a tax standpoint because of the double taxation aspect and because the 46 percent rate often exceeds the individual rate of the owners of the business. Some states impose a higher tax on corporate income than on individual income. There are also many taxes that are imposed on corporations but not on individuals or partnerships.

Avoidance of double taxation. Certain techniques may be used to avoid, in part, the double taxation of corporate income. First of all, reasonable salaries paid to corporate employees may be deducted in computing the taxable income of the business. Thus, in a closely held corporation in which all or most shareholders are officers or employees, this technique can be used to avoid double taxation of much of the corporate income. The Internal Revenue Code disallows a deduction for excessive or unreasonable compensation, and unreasonable payments to shareholder employees are taxable as dividends. Therefore, the determination of the reasonableness of corporate salaries is an ever-present tax problem in the closely held corporation that employs shareholders.

Second, the capital structure of a corporation may include both common stock and interest-bearing loans from shareholders. Envision a company that needs $200,000 to commence business. If $200,000 of stock is purchased, there will be no expense to be deducted. But suppose that $100,000 worth of stock is purchased and $100,000 is loaned to the company at 10 percent interest. In this case, $10,000 of interest each year is deductible as an expense of the company, and thus subject to only one tax as interest income to the owners. Just as in the case of salaries, the Internal Revenue Code contains a counteracting rule relating to corporations that are undercapitalized. If the corporation is undercapitalized, interest payments will be treated as dividends and disallowed as deductible expenses.

The third technique for avoiding double taxation, at least in part, is simply not to pay dividends and to accumulate the earnings. After the earnings have been accumulated, the shareholders can sell their stock or dissolve the corporation. In both situations the difference between the original investment and the amount received is given capital gains treatment. Here again we have tax laws designed to counteract the technique. There is a special income tax imposed on "excessive accumulated earnings" in addition to the normal tax and rules relating to collapsible corporations.

Finally, a special provision in the Internal Revenue Code treats small, closely held business corporations and partnerships similarly for income tax purposes. These corporations, known as Sub-Chapter S corporations, are discussed more fully in the next section.

The Sub-Chapter S corporation

The limited partnership is a hybrid between a corporation and a partnership in the area of liability. A similar hybrid known as a tax-option or Sub-Chapter S corporation exists in the tax area of the law. Such corporations have the advantage of the corporate form without the double taxation of income.

The tax-option corporation is one that elects to be taxed in a manner similar to that of partnerships; that is, to file an information return allocating income among the shareholders for immediate reporting, regardless of dividend distributions, thus avoiding any tax on the corporation.

Sub-Chapter S corporations cannot have more than 10 shareholders to begin with. After it is in existence for 5 years, it may have up to 15 shareholders, each of whom must sign the election to be taxed in the manner similar to a partnership. Corporations with more than 20 percent of their income from rents, interest, dividends, or royalties do not qualify. There are many technical rules of tax law involved in Sub-Chapter S corporations; but as a rule of thumb, this method of taxation has distinct advantages for a business operating at a loss, because the loss is shared and immediately deductible on the returns of the shareholders. It is also advantageous for businesses capable of paying out net profits as earned, thereby avoiding the corporate tax. If net profits must be retained in the business, Sub-Chapter S tax treatment is disadvantageous, because income tax is paid on earnings not received. There is also a danger of double taxation to the individual because undistributed earnings that have been taxed once are taxed again in the event of the death of a shareholder. However, the tax laws relating to pension plans reduce the advantages of such corporations. They have equal status with partnerships and sole proprietorships for pension and profit-sharing plan purposes. This status is discussed more fully in the next section.

The professional service association

Traditionally, professional services, such as those of a doctor, lawyer, or dentist, could be performed only by an individual and could not be performed by a corporation, because the relationship of doctor and patient or attorney and client was considered a highly personal one. The impersonal corporate entity could not render the personal services involved.

The tax advantages of profit-sharing and pension plans previously discussed in connection with corporations are not available to private persons and partnerships to the same extent that they are available to corporations. An individual proprietor or partner is limited to a deduction of 15 percent of income or $7,500, whichever is less, under what is usually referred to as *H.R. 10,* or *Keogh,* pension plan provision. Therefore, professional persons often desire to incorporate or to form a professional association in order to obtain the greater tax advantages of corporate pension and profit-sharing plans. To make this possible, every state has enacted statutes authorizing professional associations. These associations are legal entities similar to corporations, and they are allowed deductions for payments to qualified pension and profit-sharing plans equal to those of business corporations.

The benefits of a professional corporation or association may be seen in the situation of a doctor whose net income is $100,000. If he or she is unincorporated, $7,500 may be paid into a retirement plan. If the practice is incorporated, 10 percent ($10,000) may be paid into a qualified pension plan and 15 percent ($15,000) into a profit-sharing plan. Of this $25,000 total, one half ($12,500) is saved in federal taxes, the income in that bracket would be taxed at 50 percent. Earnings of the $25,000 invested are tax free until retirement. He or she may deduct health insurance premiums, pay additional personal medical expenses as a deductible expense, and provide up to $50,000 of life insurance with tax-free dollars. The cost of these savings is whatever is paid into the plan to cover all employees.

The foregoing illustration may not be typical of all professional persons, but there are obviously great advantages in professional corporations and there are thousands of them.

They can be identified by the letters *S.C.* (Service Corporation), *P.C.* (Professional Corporation), or *Inc.* (Incorporated), or by the word *company* in the name of the professional firm.

Making the decision

A few pages back, under the heading, "The business corporation," we listed advantages of incorporating a business with substantial capital. If the business is to be owned and operated by relatively few people, their choice of the form of organization will be made with those factors in mind—especially taxation, control, liability, perpetual existence, and legal capacity. Legal capacity is the power of the business, in its own name, to sue or be sued, own and dispose of property, and enter into contracts.

In evaluating the impact of taxation, an accountant or attorney will look at the projected profits or losses of the business, the ability to distribute earnings, and the tax brackets of the owners. An estimate of the tax burden under the various forms of organization will be made. The results will be considered along with other factors in making the decision on the form of business organization to be used.

The generalization that partners have unlimited liability and stockholders limited liability must be qualified in the case of a closely held business. A small, closely held corporation with limited assets and capital will find it difficult to obtain credit on the strength of its own credit standing alone; and as a practical matter, the shareholders will usually be required to add their individual liability as security for the debts. If Tom, Dick, and Jane seek a loan at a local bank, the bank will require each one personally to guarantee repayment of the loan. This is not to say that closely held corporations do not have some degree of limited liability. The investors in those types of businesses are protected with limited liability for contractlike obligations that are imposed as a matter of law (such as taxes) and for debts resulting from torts that are committed by company employees while engaged in company business. If the tax aspects dictate that a partnership and limited liability are desired by some investors, the limited partnership will be considered.

Issues of liability are not restricted to the investors in the business or to financial liability. Corporation law has developed several instances in which the directors and officers of the corporation will have liability to shareholders or the corporation for acts or omissions by those directors or officers in their official capacity. These matters will be discussed more fully in Chapter 40.

The significance of the law relating to control will be apparent in the discussions on formation and operation of partnerships and corporations in the chapters that follow. The desire of one or more individuals to control the business is a major factor in selecting the form, and the control issues are second only to taxation in importance.

Table 35-1 summarizes the factors that are considered in choosing a form of organization.

Table 35·1 Comparison of the characteristics of business organizations

	Corporations		Partnerships	
Characteristics	*General*	*Sub-Chapter S*	*General*	*Limited*
Method of creation	Charter issued by state	Same + file agreement with IRS	Created by agreement of the parties	Same + file statutory form in public office
Liability of members	Shareholders have limited liability	Same	Partners have unlimited liability	General partners, unlimited liability; limited partners, limited liability
Duration	May be perpetual	Same	Termination by death, agreement, bankruptcy, or withdrawal of a partner	The term provided in the certificate
Transferability of interest	Generally freely transferable, subject to limits of contracts between shareholders	Same	Not transferable	General partner not transferable; limited partner transferable
Management	Shareholders elect directors, who set policy	Same	All partners in absence of agreement have equal voice	General partners have equal voice; limited partners have no voice
Taxation	Income taxed to corporations; dividends taxed to shareholders	Net income taxed to shareholders whether distributed or not	Not a taxable entity; net income taxed to partners whether distributed or not	Same
Legal entity for purpose of: Suit in firm name Owning property in firm name Bankruptcy Limiting liability	A legal entity in all states, for all purposes	Same	By modern law, an entity for Suit in firm name Owning property in firm name Bankruptcy	Same
Transact business in other states	Must qualify to do business and obtain certificate of authority	Same	No limitation	Copy of certificate must be filed in all counties where doing business
Organization fee, annual license fee, and annual reports	All required	Same	None	None
Modification of amendment of articles	Must obtain state approval	Same	No requirement	Must file changes
Agency	A shareholder is not an agent of the corporation	Same	Each partner is both a principal and an agent of copartners	Limited partners are not principals or agents; general partners are the same as in general partnership

REVIEW QUESTIONS AND PROBLEMS

1. List the advantages and disadvantages of the partnership form of business organization.
2. List the advantages and disadvantages of the corporate form of business organization.
3. List four techniques for avoiding double taxation of corporate income and give an example of each.
4. List characteristics of a limited partnership that are similar to those of a (*a*) general partnership and (*b*) corporation.
5. John Doe and Richard Roe wish to enter the camping equipment manufacturing business. If the following facts exist, which type of business association would be most advantageous in each case? Explain.
   a) Doe is an expert in the field of camping gear production and sale but has no funds. Roe knows nothing about such production but is willing to contribute all necessary capital.
   b) Camping gear production requires large amounts of capital, much more than Doe and Roe can raise personally or together, yet they wish to control the business.
   c) Some phases of production and sale are rather dangerous, and a relatively large number of tort judgments may be anticipated.
   d) Sales will be nationwide.
   e) Doe and Roe are both sixty-five years old. No profits are expected for at least five years, and interruption of the business before that time will make it a total loss.
   f) Several other persons wish to put funds into the business but are unwilling to assume personal liability.
   g) The anticipated earnings over cost, at least for the first few years, will be approximately $70,000. Doe and Roe wish to draw salaries of $25,000 each; they also want a hospitalization and retirement plan, all to be paid from these earnings.
   h) A loss is expected for the first three years, owing to the initial capital outlay and the difficulty, in entering the market.
6. Gold and Silver practiced dentistry together as a partnership. Their individual net income exceeded $100,000, and each invested large sums in real estate and stocks. Should the dentists consider another form of business organization? Explain.
7. Archie and Barry purchased a tavern. They orally agreed that Archie would manage the business at a stipulated salary and receive 50 percent of all profits as his share as a limited partner and that he would not be liable for any losses. Subsequently, the Internal Revenue Service assessed a deficiency in cabaret taxes in the amount of $46,000. Archie contended that the taxes constituted a loss for the business; and since he was a limited partner, he was not liable for such loss. Is Archie correct? Why?
8. A and B formed a limited partnership. Articles of partnership were drawn up establishing that A was a limited partner. Both A and B signed the agreement, but a certificate of limited partnership was not recorded. Eleven years later, the business went into bankruptcy. Should A be held liable as a general partner? Why?
9. Linda and Gladys formed a limited partnership, with Gladys as general partner. The partnership purchased land from Sandy, giving a promissory note on behalf of the partnership to Sandy. The partnership subsequently defaulted on its payments, and Sandy brought suit. If there are insufficient assets in the partnership to cover the balance due on the note, can Sandy hold Gladys personally liable? Why?

36

Formation of Partnerships

A *partnership* is defined as an association of two or more persons to carry on as co-owners of a business for profit. It is the result of an agreement between competent parties to place their money, property, or labor in a business and to divide the profits and losses. Each partner is personally liable for the debts of the partnership.

Express partnership agreements may be either oral or written, but a carefully prepared written agreement is highly preferable to an oral one. The provisions usually contained in articles of partnership will be discussed later in this chapter.

Issues concerning the existence of a partnership may arise between the parties or between the alleged partnership and third parties. The legal issues in these two situations are substantially different. When the issue is between the alleged partners, it is essentially a question of intention. When the issue concerns liability to a third person, the question involves not only intention as to the actual existence of the partnership but issues of estoppel as well.

CASE

P, a seller of goods, sued D, an alleged partner, for the balance due on merchandise shipped to the partnership. When P extended credit, it did not know that D was a partner. The credit was extended to the partnership without the seller's even knowing the names of the partners.

ISSUE Is D liable as a partner?

DECISION Yes.

REASON Persons who join together in a business or venture for a common benefit each contributing property, money, or services to the business or venture having a community of interest in any profits are "partners." A partner is personally liable for the debts of the partnership. The fact that the seller may have sold goods to a partnership in ignorance of the fact that D was a partner does not prevent the seller's recovery for the goods sold.

Johnson v. Plastex Company, 500 So.2d 596 (Okla.) 1972.

Implied partnerships

Between the parties, the intention to create a partnership may be expressed or implied from their conduct. The basic question is whether the parties intend a relationship that includes the essential elements of a partnership, not whether they intend to be partners. In fact, under certain circumstances, a corporation may be held to be a partnership at least between the owners of the business.

CASE

In the latter part of 1974, William Wease (W) and William Koestner (K), began discussing the idea of opening a jewelry store together in a business relationship that would allow a fifty-fifty division of profits, losses, and work. Several possible arrangements were considered, but the men finally agreed on a corporate form with the corporate stock to be evenly divided between themselves. An accountant suggested that a tax advantage for W could be derived if W originally purchased all of the stock issued by the business. The parties agreed that W would initially purchase all of the stock, and K would hold a six-months' option to purchase one-half of the stock. Thus, W became the sole shareholder, buying 10,000 shares of stock for $10,000.

The business commenced operations in January 1975, with W as president and K as vice-president, each working full time and paid $1,200 monthly from the corporation's profits. The expected profits were not realized, and both men were forced to take smaller monthly amounts from the business. The relationship continued through May 1975, with each man receiving a total of $2,600 from the corporation. On May 30, 1975, K terminated his involvement with the business. He had not exercised his option to purchase stock, and at no time was he a shareholder in the corporation. The corporation had a net operating loss of $2,182.98 to date.

K now claims to be an employee entitled to his full salary, and he denies any liability for a share of the loss. W claims that K was in fact a partner without right to a salary but with liability for one-half of the loss.

ISSUE 1. Is it possible for a partnership to exist, notwithstanding the corporate form?

2. Does incorporation of the business change the rights and duties of the partners?

DECISION 1. Yes.

2. No.

REASONS 1. The business's corporate form and the fact that W initially held all of the corporate stock was an attempt by the parties to insulate their personal property from corporate creditors and to achieve tax advantages, rather than a means of defining the legal relationship between them.

2. Some courts have held that parties cannot be partners between themselves and a corporation to the rest of the world. They hold that in such cases the adoption of the corporation eliminates the partnership.
3. The majority rule is that individuals can be partners between themselves but a corporation to the rest of the world so long as the rights of third parties such as creditors are not affected.
4. A corporation can be a mere agency for convenience in carrying out a partnership. For the purposes of determining the rights and liabilities of the parties, it is proper to place the parties in the position they would have occupied had the corporate form not been adopted. Substance, not form, controls the nature of a business relationship.

Koestner v. Wease & Koestner Jewelers, Inc., 381 N.E.2d 11 (Ill. App.) 1978.

If the essential elements of a partnership are present, the mere fact that the parties do not think they are becoming partners is immaterial. If the parties agree upon an arrangement that is a partnership in fact, it is immaterial whether they call it something else or declare that they are not partners. On the other hand, the mere fact that the parties themselves call the relation a partnership will not make it so if they have not, by their contract, agreed upon an arrangement that by the law is a partnership in fact.

The essential attributes of a partnership are a common interest in the business and management and a share in the profits and losses. If there is a sharing of profits, a partnership may be found to exist even though there is no sharing of losses.

The presence of a common interest in property and management is not enough to establish a partnership by implication. Also, an agreement to share the gross returns of a business, sometimes called gross profits, does not of itself prove an intention to form a partnership. The Uniform Partnership Act provides, however, that a share of the real or net profits in a business is *prima facie* evidence that the person who receives it is a partner in the business.

The presumption that a partnership exists by reason of sharing net profits is not conclusive and may be overcome by evidence that the share in the profits is received for some other purpose, such as payment of a debt by installments, wages, rent, annuity to a widow of a deceased partner, interest on a loan, or as payment for good will by installments. Bonuses are frequently paid as a percentage of profit, but they do not make the employees partners. Likewise, many leases provide for rent based on profits.

CASE

D owned grazing land and was looking for someone to pasture cattle on his land. P, a cattle rancher, entered into a grazing contract with D, which provided in part that "net money" from the sale of cattle was to be split evenly between the parties. For many years the operation was a success until, in 1974, P suffered an $89,000 loss. P sued D, contending that the agreement made the parties "partners" and that D was liable for one-half of the loss. D contended that he was not a partner but only a landlord receiving profits as rent.

ISSUE Were the parties partners?

DECISION No.

REASONS 1. As with any contractual relationship, the intent of the parties is controlling. Here, there was no evidence of intent to form a partnership.

2. The agreement was not labeled a partnership contract, nor was a partnership federal income tax

return ever filed. Plaintiff described his payments to defendant on his tax return as "contract feeding."

3. The agreement was a mere contract for grazing cattle.

P & M Cattle Co. v. Holler, 559 P.2d 1019 (Wyo.) 1977.

Partnership by estoppel

Insofar as third persons are concerned, partnership liability, like the apparent authority of an agent, may be predicated upon the legal theory of estoppel. If a person by words spoken or written or by conduct represents himself, or consents to another's representing him as a partner in an existing partnership, that person is not a partner but is liable to any party to whom such representation has been made. If the representation is made in a public manner either personally or with consent of the apparent partner, the apparent partner is liable if credit is extended to the partnership, even if the creditor did not actually know of the representation. This is an exception to the usual estoppel requirement of actual reliance.

CASE

D and X entered into a written agreement with P, whereby D and X were authorized to sell tires, batteries, and accessories to be delivered to them by P. D claims that the agreement was blank when he signed it. X substantiated D's claim and testified that he, X, was the sole owner of the venture engaged as a selling agent for P. D and X made no attempt to pay for any of the merchandise delivered to them. P sued D for the account.

ISSUE Did a partnership exist between D and X, making D liable to P for the merchandise delivered?

DECISION Yes.

REASONS
1. The evidence indicates that a partnership existed between D and X as far as their relationship with P is concerned. One may become a partner of a firm, as to the third persons, without intending to, by words spoken or written or by conduct.
2. Such a partner thereby becomes liable to those who have, on the faith of such words or conduct, given credit to the actual or apparent partnership.
3. D, by signing the service agency agreement and never having his name removed from it, is liable to P for the merchandise delivered to the venture.

Montana Farm Service Co. v. Marquart, 578 P.2d 315 (Mont.) 1978.

The courts are not in accord as to whether a person is under a duty to affirmatively disclaim a reputed partnership where the representation of partnership was not made by or with the consent of the person sought to be charged as a partner. Some court cases hold that if a person is held out as a partner and he knows it, he should be chargeable as a partner unless he takes reasonable steps to give notice that he is not, in fact, a partner. Other cases indicate that there is no duty to deny false representations of partnership where the ostensible partner did not participate in making the misrepresentation.

The Partnership Agreement

The partnership agreement, usually called the *articles of partnership,* will vary from business to business. Among the subjects usually contained in such agreements are the following: the names of the partners and of the partnership, its purpose and duration, the capital contributions of each partner, the method of sharing profits and losses, the effect of advances, the salaries (if any) to be paid the partners, the method of accounting and the fiscal year, the rights and liabilities of the parties upon the death or withdrawal of a partner, and the procedures to be followed upon dissolution.

The Uniform Partnership Act or other partnership statute is a part of the agreement as if it had actually been written into the contract or had been made part of its stipulations. The sections that follow discuss some of the more important provisions of partnership agreement and indicate the effect of the Uniform Act on the agreement.

Profit and loss provision

Unless the agreement is to the contrary, each partner has a right to share equally in the profits of the enterprise, and each partner is under a duty to contribute equally to the losses. Capital contributed to the firm is a liability owing by the firm to the contributing partners. If, on dissolution, there are not sufficient assets to repay each partner his captial, the amount is considered as a loss; and the like any other loss of the partnership, it must be met. For example, a partnership is composed of A, B, and C. A contributed $20,000, B contributed $10,000, and C contributed $4,000. The firm is dissolved, and upon the payment of firm debts only $10,000 of firm assets remain. Because the total contribution to capital was $34,000, the operating loss is $24,000. This loss must be borne equally by A, B, and C, so that the loss for each is $8,000. This means that A is entitled to be reimbursed to the extent of her $20,000 contribution less $8,000, her share of the loss, or net of $12,000. B is entitled to $10,000, less $8,000, or $2,000. Because C has contributed only $4,000, he must now contribute to the firm an additional $4,000, in order that his loss will equal $8,000. The additional $4,000 contributed by C, plus the $10,000 remaining, will now be distributed so that A will receive $12,000 and B $2,000.

Occasionally, articles of copartnership specify the manner in which profits are to be divided, but they neglect to mention possible losses. In such cases the losses are borne in the same proportion that profits are to be shared. In the event that losses occur when one of the partners is insolvent and his share of the loss exceeds the amount owed him for advances and capital, the excess must be shared by the other partners. They share this unusual loss, with respect to one another, in the same ratio that they share profits. Thus, in the above example, if C were insolvent, A and B would each bear an additional $2,000 loss.

In addition to the right to be repaid his contributions, whether by way of capital or advances to the partnership property, the partnership must indemnify every partner in respect of payments made and personal liabilities reasonably incurred by him in the ordinary and proper conduct of its business or for the preservation of its business or property.

Partnership capital provision

Partnership capital consists of the total credits to the capital accounts of the various partners, provided the credits are for permanent investments in the business. Such capital represents the amount that the partnership is obligated to return to the partners at the time of dissolution, and it can be varied only with the consent of all the partners. Undivided profits that are permitted by some of the partners to accumulate in the business do not become part of the capital. They, like temporary advances by firm members, are subject to withdrawal at any time unless the agreement provides to the contrary.

The amount that each partner is to contribute to the firm, as well as the credit he is to receive for assets contributed, is entirely dependent upon the partnership agreement. A person may become a partner without a capital contribution. For example, he may contribute services to balance the capital investment of the other partners. Such a partner, however, has no capital to be returned at the time of liquidation. Only those who receive credit for capital investments—which may include good will, patent rights, and so forth, if agreed upon—are entitled to the return of capital when dissolution occurs.

If the investment is in a form other than money, the property no longer belongs to the contributing partner. He has vested the firm with title, and he has no greater equity in the property than has any other party. At dissolution he recovers only the amount allowed to him for the property invested.

Provisions relating to partnership property

In conducting its business, a partnership may use its own property, the property of the individual partners, or the property of some third person. It frequently becomes important, especially on dissolution and where claims of firm creditors are involved, to ascertain exactly what property constitutes partnership property, in order to ascertain the rights of partners and firm creditors to specific property.

CASE

P and D were equal partners in a real estate business. Prior to dissolution proceedings, D had purchased a piece of property in his own name. He reimbursed himself for the down payment from the partnership checking account. The property was shown on the books of the partnership, and all expenses connected with it were paid for by the partnership.

ISSUE Is the property partnership property, so that each party is entitled to one-half of the profits from its sale?

DECISION Yes.

REASONS
1. An agreement that certain real estate should be part of the firm assets may be implied from the acts and conduct of the partners; the agreement need not be express.
2. Partnership books may be considered to determine the question of partnership property. The manner in which the accounts are kept, whether the purchase money is severally charged to the members of the firm or whether the accounts treat it the same as other firm property may be controlling circumstances in determining such intention.
3. From the record, it appears that the purchase of the real estate was entered on the partnership records prior to the closing of that transaction. Thereafter, abstract fees, taxes, and payments on the purchase money mortgage were paid by the partnership. Profits were reported as partnership income. Therefore, the evidence was adequate to establish that the property was partnership property.

St. Auta v. Stauth, 582 P.2d 116 (Kan.) 1978.

As a general rule, the agreement of the parties will determine what property is properly classified as partnership property. In the absence of an express agreement, what constitutes partnership property is ascertained from the conduct of the parties and from the purpose for, and the way in which, property is used in the pursuit of the business.

The Uniform Partnership Act provides that all property specifically brought into partnership or acquired by it is partnership property. Therefore, unless a contrary intention appears, property acquired with partnership funds is partnership property. In other words, there is a presumption that property acquired with partnership funds is partnership property, but this presumption is rebuttable.

Property acquired by a partner individually is often transferred to the partnership as a part of a partner's contribution to capital. If this property is purchased on credit, the creditor has no claim against the partnership, even though the property can be traced to it. A personal loan made to a partner does not become a partnership debt unless it is expressly assumed by the partnership.

CASE

D corporation loaned money to X to purchase well-drilling equipment. A year later, X and his brother Y formed a partnership for drilling wells and transferred the property to the partnership. Subsequently, the partnership was incorporated into P Company. Six months later, X left P Company, and his stock was taken over by Y. D then employed P Company to repair one of their pumps and perform other services. D did not pay for these services, and P Company brought this action to collect. D sought to offset X's unpaid loan balance against the debt. Y was unaware of X's obligation to D prior to performing these services for D.

ISSUE Did the partnership and subsequent corporation assume an antecedent debt owed by one of the partners for equipment that later transferred to the partnership and then to the corporation?

DECISION No.

REASONS
1. Neither the partnership nor the corporation assumed X's personal obligation to D.
2. A loan made to a partner in his individual capacity before formation of the partnership is not a partnership debt unless it is expressly assumed by the partnership.

Waldrop v. Holland, 588 P.2d 1237 (Wash. App.) 1979.

Because a partnership has the right to acquire, own, and dispose of personal property in the firm name, legal documents affecting the title to partnership personal property may be executed in the firm name by any partner. The Uniform Partnership Act also treats a partnership as a legal entity for the purposes of title to real estate that may be held in the firm name. Title so acquired can be conveyed in the partnership name. Where title to real property is in the partnership name, any partner may convey title to such property by a conveyance executed in the partnership name. To be effective, such a conveyance must be within the terms of the partnership agreement or within the pursuit of the partnership business.

Name provision

Because a partnership is created by the agreement of the parties, they select the name to be used. This right of selection is subject to two limitations by statute in many states. First, a partnership may not use the word *company* or other language that would imply the existence of a corporation. Second, if the name is other than that of the partners, they must comply with an assumed name statute that requires the giving of public notice as to the actual identity of the partners. Failure to comply with this assumed name statute may result in the partnership's being denied access to the courts to sue its debtors, or it may result in criminal actions being brought against those operating under the assumed name.

CASE

A partnership known as Stein Properties brought suit in its firm name against a trustee on a deposit receipt contract. The partnership had not complied with the state's fictitious name statute. The defendant moved to dismiss the suit, contending that the partnership could not sue because of its failure to comply with the state statute.

ISSUE Will the suit be dismissed?

DECISION Yes.

REASONS
1. It is unlawful for a partnership to engage in business under a fictitious name unless the name is registered with the clerk of the court in the county of its principal place of business.
2. The penalty for the failure to comply with this law is that neither the business nor the members may maintain suit in any court of this state as a plaintiff until this law is complied with.
3. "Stein Properties" is a fictitious name because it does not reasonably reveal the names of the partners.
4. Failure to comply with the statute does not prevent the trial court from taking jurisdiction of the cause, but it does act as an inhibition against allowing the plaintiffs to prosecute their complaint until the requirements of the statute are met.

Aronovitz v. Stein Properties, 322 So.2d 74 (Fla.App.) 1975.

The firm name is an asset of the firm, and as such it may also be sold, assigned, or disposed of in any manner upon which the parties agree. At common law, a partnership was not a legal entity that could sue and be sued in the firm name. All actions had to be brought on behalf of, or against, all the partners as individuals. Today, most states by statute have changed the common law and allow partnerships to sue or be sued in the firm name. They may also declare bankruptcy as a firm. To this extent, and to the extent that it can own and dispose of property in the firm name, a partnership is a legal entity. It is not a legal entity to the same extent as a corporation, however.

Provisions relating to good will

Good will, which is usually transferred with the name, is based upon the justifiable expectation of the continued patronage of old customers and the probable patronage of new customers resulting from good reputation, satisfied customers, established location, and past advertising. Good will is usually considered in an evaluation of the assets of the business, and it is capable of being sold and transferred. Upon dissolution caused by the death of one of the partners, it must be accounted for by the surviving partner to the legal representative of the deceased partner, unless otherwise agreed upon in a buy and sell agreement.

When good will and the firm name are sold, an agreement not to compete is usually part of the sales agreement. Such an agreement may be implied but should be a part of the buy and sell provisions.

"Buy and sell" provisions

Either as part of the partnership agreement or by separate contract, the partners should provide for the contingency of death or withdrawal of a partner. This contingency is covered by a *buy and sell agreement,* and it is imperative that the terms of the buy and sell provisions be agreed upon before either party knows whether he is a buyer or a seller. Agreement after the status of the parties becomes known is extremely difficult, if not impossible. If such agreement is lacking, many additional problems will arise upon the death or withdrawal of a partner, and there are many possibilities of litigation and economic loss to all concerned.

A buy and sell agreement avoids these types of problems by providing a method whereby the surviving partner or partners can purchase the interest of the deceased partner, or the remaining partner or partners can purchase the interest of the withdrawing partner. A method of determining the price to be paid for such interest is provided. The time and method of payment are usually stipulated. The buy and sell agreement should specify whether a partner has an option to purchase the interest of a dying or withdrawing partner or whether he has a duty to do so.

It is common for partners to provide for life insurance on each other's lives as a means of funding the buy and sell provisions. In the event of a partner's death, proceeds of the insurance are utilized to purchase the deceased partner's interest. Premiums on such life insurance are not deductible for tax purposes but are usually treated as an expense for accounting purposes. There are a variety of methods for holding title to the insurance. It may be individually owned or business owned. The provisions of the policy should be carefully integrated into the partnership agreement; each partner's estate plan should also properly consider the ramifications of this insurance and of the buy and sell agreement.

REVIEW QUESTIONS AND PROBLEMS

1. List four situations in which a person may receive a percentage of the profits without a presumption being made that he is a partner.
2. List the usual provisions found in partnership agreements.
3. Give reasons for including buy and sell provisions in partnership agreements.
4. Charlotte and Gia, both attorneys, agreed to share office space and other overhead expense, but they did not agree to form a partnership. The sign outside their offices and their common letterhead read "Charlotte Gifford and Gia Hammond, Attorneys at Law." Using this stationery, Charlotte purchased some office equipment from Descor. Gia did not join in the contract in any way. Charlotte did not pay for the equipment. Is Gia liable to Descor? Discuss.
5. Andy and Handy formed a partnership to do kitchen remodeling pursuant to an oral agreement. It was agreed that Andy was to invest $10,000 and manage the business affairs. Handy, who would invest $1,000, was to work as job superintendent and manage the work. Profits were to be split fifty-fifty, but possible losses were not discussed. The business proved unprofitable, and Andy brought action against Handy for one-half of the losses. May he recover? Why?
6. Edison and Thomas formed a partnership. Edison contributed an unpatented invention. He later took out the patent in his own name. Upon dissolution of the partnership, to whom does the patent belong? Why?
7. When one partner died, the other continued the business in her own name; but in accounting for the firm's assets, she refused to make any allowance for good will. May the deceased partner's estate recover an additional sum for the good will of the business? Why?
8. Les and Turner entered into a written agreement whereby Turner was to farm Les's land in exchange for one-third of the crop as rental. The contract also provided that Les was to advance financing and Turner was to furnish the equipment. It was also agreed that after delivery of the one-third of the crops, all net proceeds and losses were to be shared equally. The contract specifically stated that Les and Turner were not partners, but landlord and tenant. Are Les and Turner partners? Why?
9. Two men formed a partnership dealing in real estate. After one died, his widow claimed that the property the two had purchased with the deed listing them as "tenants in common" should not be inventoried in the estate as partnership property. At the trial it was determined that this property had been purchased with partnership funds. Did the property belong to the partnership or to the men individually as joint owners? Why?
10. Richard and Robert Richter formed a partnership under the name "Richter Brothers." The business was operated for years, and the firm name constituted an asset of the partnership. Upon Richard's death a corporation was formed using the name "Richter Brothers Company, Inc." The company advertised that it had been in business for seventy years. A suit was brought by Richard's estate to restrain the corporation from using the name "Richter Brothers" as part of the corporate name. What was the result? Why?

The operation of a partnership is governed by the provisions of the partnership agreement and the applicable statutory law, which in most states is the Uniform Partnership Act. Thus the rights, duties, and powers of partners are both expressed (those in the agreement) and implied (those created by law). Many of the expressed rights, duties, and powers were discussed in the preceding chapter, which covered the typical subjects found in the partnership agreement. Those that are implied will be discussed in this chapter, along with some additional observations

37

Operating the Partnership

about the partnership agreement as it affects operations. Throughout the discussion we should remember that a partner is essentially an agent for the other partners and that the general principles of the law of agency are applicable.

Before examining the rights, duties, and powers of partners, we must understand certain terminology. A *silent partner* in a general partnership is one that does not participate in management. If the silent partner is to have limited liability, the provisions of the Uniform Limited Partnership Act must be complied with. A *secret partner* is unknown to third parties. He may advise management and actually participate in decisions, but his interest is not known to third parties. A *dormant partner* is both secret and silent.

Rights of Partners

Right to participate in management

All partners have equal rights in the management and conduct of the firm business, but they may agree to put one or more partners in control. The right to an equal voice in the management and conduct of the business is not determined by the share that each partner has invested in the business.

Ordinary matters arising in the conduct of a partnership business are decided upon by a majority of the partners. The partnership agreement usually provides for some form of arbitration of deadlocks. Without this provision, disagreement in a partnership of only two people would have to be solved by dissolution.

The majority cannot, however, without the consent of the minority, change the essential nature of the business by altering the partnership agreement or by reducing or increasing the capital of the partners. It cannot embark upon a new business or admit new members to the firm.

Certain acts other than those enumerated above require the unanimous consent of the partners in order to bind the firm; namely, (1) assigning the firm property to a trustee for the benefit of creditors, (2) authorizing a confession of judgment, (3) disposing of the good will of the business, (4) submitting a partnership agreement to arbitration, and (5) doing any act that would make impossible the conduct of the partnership business.

Right to be compensated for services

It is the duty of each partner, in the absence of an agreement to the contrary, to give his entire time, skill, and energy to the pursuit of the partnership affairs. No partner is entitled to payment for services rendered in the conduct of the partnership business unless an agreement to that effect has been expressed or may be implied from the conduct of the partners.

CASE

P sued Ds, his partners, for the reasonable value of services rendered. The parties were partners in the ownership and operation of a fishing vessel. P had perfected a new type of net for catching sharks and contended that he was entitled to compensation for the time and effort expended in constructing the shark nets. P had informed his partners that he was busy getting the nets ready and that it would "be lots of work to fix" them. P did not inform Ds of what the work actually entailed or that he expected any compensation for it.

ISSUE Is P entitled to compensation?

DECISION No.

REASON There was no factual basis for any agreement express or implied to pay compensation. One partner is not entitled to extra compensation from the partnership in the absence of an express or an implied agreement therefor.

Waggen v. Gerde et ux., 36 Wash.2d 563 (1950).

Often, one of the partners does not desire to participate in the management of the business. The partnership agreement in such case usually provides that the active partners receive a salary for their services in addition to their share in the profits. A surviving partner is entitled to reasonable compensation for his services in winding up the partnership affairs, unless he is guilty of misconduct in performing that job.

Right to interest

Contributions to capital are not entitled to draw interest unless they are not repaid when the repayment should be made. The partner's share in the profits constitutes the earnings upon his capital investment. In the absence of an express provision for the payment of interest, it is presumed that interest will be paid only on advances above the amount originally contributed as capital. Advances in excess of the prescribed capital, even though credited to the capital account of the contributing partners, are entitled to draw interest from the date of the advance.

Unwithdrawn profits remaining in the firm are not entitled to draw interest. They are not considered advances or loans merely because they are left with the firm, although custom, usage, and circumstances may show an intention to treat them as loans.

Right to information and to inspection of books

Every partner is entitled to full and complete information concerning the conduct of the business and to inspect the books to secure that information. The partnership agreement usually contains provisions relative to the records that the business will maintain. Each partner is under a duty to give the person responsible for keeping the records whatever information is necessary to carry on the business efficiently and effectively. It is the duty of the person keeping the records to allow each partner access to them, but no partner has a right to remove the records from the agreed-upon location without the consent of the other partners. Each partner is entitled to make copies of the records, provided he does not make his inspection for fraudulent purposes.

Right to an accounting

The partners' proportionate share of the partnership assets or profits, when not determined by a voluntary settlement of the parties, may be ascertained in a suit for an accounting. Such suits are equitable in nature; and in states that still distinguish between suits at law and suits in equity, these actions must be filed in the court of equity.

As a general rule, a partner cannot maintain an *action at law* against other members of the firm on the partnership agreement because until there is an accounting and all partnership affairs are settled, the indebtedness among the firm members is undetermined. This general rule is subject to a few commonsense exceptions.

Because partners ordinarily have equal access to the partnership records, there is usually no need for formal accountings to determine partnership interests. A suit for an accounting is not permitted for settling incidental matters or disputes between the partners. If a dispute is of such grievous nature that the continued existence of the partnership is impossible, a suit for an accounting in equity is allowed.

In all cases, a partner is entitled to an accounting upon the dissolution of the firm. Without a dissolution of the firm, he has a right to a formal accounting in the following situations:

1. There is an agreement for an accounting at a definite date.
2. One partner has withheld profits arising from secret transactions.
3. There has been an execution levied against the interest of one of the partners.
4. One partner does not have access to the books.
5. The partnership is approaching insolvency, and all parties are not available.

Upon an agreement between themselves, the partners may make a complete accounting and settle their claims without resort to a court of equity.

Property rights

A partner is a co-owner with his partners of partnership property. Subject to any agreement among partners, a partner has an equal right among his partners to possess partnership property for partnership purposes. He has no right to possess partnership property for other purposes without the consent of the other partners.

A partner has a right that the property will be used in the pursuit of the partnership business and to pay firm creditors. Since a partner does not own any specific item of the partnership property, he has no right in specific partnership property that is transferable by him. A partner has no right to use the firm property in satisfaction of his personal debts; conversely, his personal creditors cannot make a levy upon specific partnership property.

When a partner dies, his interest in specific partnership property passes to the surviving partner or partners, who have the duty of winding up the affairs of the partnership in accordance with the partnership agreement and the applicable laws. When the winding-up process is complete, the estate of the deceased partner will be paid whatever sum the estate is entitled to, according to law and the partnership agreement. The surviving partner may sell the property, real and personal, of the partnership in connection with winding up the business, in order to obtain the cash to pay the estate of the deceased partner.

A partner's interest *in the firm* consists of his rights to share in the profits that are earned and, after dissolution and liquidation, to the return of his capital and undistributed profits. This assumes, of course, that his capital has not been absorbed or impaired by losses.

A partner may assign his interest, or his right to share, in the profits of the partnership. Such an assignment will not of itself work a dissolution of the firm. The assignee is not entitled to participate in the management of the business. The only right of the assignee is to receive the profits to which the assignor would otherwise have been entitled and, in the event of dissolution, to receive his assignor's interest.

A partner's interest in the partnership cannot be levied upon by his separate creditors and sold at public sale. A judgment creditor of a partner must proceed by obtaining a "charging order" from the court. This order charges the interest of the debtor partner with the unsatisfied amount of the judgment debt. The court will ordinarily appoint a receiver, who will receive the partner's share of the profits and any other money due or to fall due to him in respect of the partnership and apply that money upon the judgment. Likewise, the court may order that the interest charged be sold. Neither the charging order nor the sale of the interest will cause a dissolution of the firm unless the partnership is one that is terminable at will.

If there is more than one judgment creditor seeking a charging order, the first one to seek it is usually paid in full before others are paid anything. There is no pro rata distribution unless the partnership is dissolved.

CASE

X obtained a judgment against D. He sought a charging order against D's interest in a general partnership to collect the judgment. Y also obtained a judgment against D. Y seeks to intervene in X's suit for a charging order, so that he may share in it. X contends that he has a right to full payment before Y is allowed anything.

ISSUE Should the charging order against D pro rate the payments between X and Y?

DECISION No.

REASONS 1. A partner's interest in a partnership is personal property.

2. A charging order is a flexible court-supervised substitute for the more disruptive process of

execution by the sheriff. In the absence of precedent or statute to the contrary, the method of apportioning payment to judgment creditors from a partnership interest is parallel to the method of determining priority among judgment creditors seeking execution on other kinds of personal property. In the ordinary execution process, where more than one judgment has been obtained against a debtor, the one first put in the hands of the sheriff for execution is the first satisfied.

3. Y's argument for a pro rata division is applicable to situations in which there was a final, determinable sum to be divided, as in the dissolution or winding up of a partnership.
4. Where unsecured judgment creditors are concerned, the first to apply to a court of proper jurisdiction for a charging order has priority for the full satisfaction of his judgment from the debtor's partnership interest over subsequent judgment creditors seeking a charging order.

Krauth v. First Continental Dev-Con, Inc., 351 So.2d 1106, (Fla. App.) 1977.

The Duties and Powers of Partners

A partnership is a fiduciary relationship. Each partner owes the duty of undivided loyalty to the other. Therefore, every partner must account to the partnership for any benefit and hold as a trustee for it any profits gained by him without consent of the other partners. This duty also rests upon representatives of deceased partners engaged in the liquidation of the affairs of the partnership.

The partnership relation is a personal one, obligating each partner to exercise good faith and to consider mutual welfare of all the partners in his conduct of the business. If one partner attempts to secure an advantage over the others, he thereby breaches the partnership relation, and he must account for all benefits that he obtains. This includes transactions with partners and with others. It also includes transactions connected with winding up the business.

CASE

P and D were equal partners in a CPA firm. Each had his own clients. The partnership was not harmonious, and the parties dissolved it. In the final accounting between the partners, D "wrote down" several accounts he serviced. He collected $4,610.85 less from these clients than the books showed was owed. D testified that the accounts were adjusted downwards for work in progress because of his desire to retain the clients. P contended that he was entitled to half of the income as shown by the books and that the adjustment was improper.

ISSUE Is D entitled to charge P for half of the adjustment?

DECISION No.

REASONS
1. Since the partnership agreement does not specify the responsibility of partners in collecting partnership debts, this issue must be decided by the general principles of partnership law.
2. Partners have authority to make compromises with partnership debtors, even after dissolution. So D had the power to compromise claims, but in exercising this power he had to follow the fiduciary duty imposed on him as a partner "to act with the utmost candor and good faith."
3. D's motivation to retain the clients falls far short of the duty of good faith imposed on parties.

Oswald v. Leckey, 572 P.2d 1316 (Or.) 1977.

Power to contract

A partner is an agent of the partnership for the purpose of its business, and the general laws of agency are applicable to all partnerships. Each partner has authority to bind the partnership with contractual liability whenever he is apparently carrying on the business of the partnership in the usual way. If it is apparent that he is not carrying on business of the partnership in the usual way, his act does not bind the partnership unless it is authorized by the other partners.

CASE

A, B, and C were partners operating a business that manufactured packing crates and other wood products. The partnership had purchased a tract of timber and was using it for its lumber needs. A, the managing partner, entered into a contract to sell lumber to P and received payment. The lumber was never delivered to P, and A did not account to the partnership for the money received.

ISSUE Is the partnership liable on the contract to sell lumber?

DECISION No.

REASONS 1. A partner is a general agent of the firm but only for the purpose of carrying on the business of the partnership. Any sale by a partner, to be valid, must be in furtherance of the partnership business, within the scope of the business, or of a nature that third persons may reasonably conclude, from all the circumstances, to be embraced within it.

2. Sales made by a partner in a trading firm are not viewed with the same strictness as in nontrading firms such as here involved, because in trading firms, sales are usually within the scope of the business; in nontrading firms, they are exceptional and only incidental to the main business.

3. Here, one of the partners acted in a matter beyond both the real and apparent scope of the business and beyond the real or apparent scope of the agency. The partnership was not in the business of selling lumber.

Bole v. Lyle et al., 287 S.W.2d 931 (Tenn.) 1956.

The rules of agency relating to authority, ratification, and secret limitations on the authority of a partner are applicable to partnerships, but the extent of implied authority is generally greater for partners than for ordinary agents. Each partner has implied power to do all acts necessary for carrying on the business of the partnership. The nature and scope of the business and what is usual in the particular business determine the extent of the implied powers. Among the common implied powers are the following: to compromise, adjust, and settle claims or debts owed by or to the partnership; to sell goods in the regular course of business and to make warranties; to buy property within the scope of the business for cash or upon credit; to buy insurance; to hire employees; to make admissions against interest; to enter into contracts within the scope of the firm; and to receive notices. In a trading partnership, a partner has the implied authority to borrow funds and to pledge the assets of the firm. Some of these implied duties are discussed more fully in the sections that follow.

Power to impose tort liability

A partner has the power to impose tort liability through the doctrine of *respondeat superior.* The law imposes tort liability upon a partnership for all wrongful acts or omissions of any partner acting in the ordinary course of the partnership and for its benefit.

If a partnership has liability because of a tort of a partner, the firm has the right to collect its losses from the partner at fault. In effect, a partnership that is liable in tort to a third person has a right of indemnity against the partner at fault. Likewise, if the injured third party collects directly from the partner at fault, the partner cannot seek contribution from his copartners.

CASE

P, a patient, sued D, a physician, for medical malpractice. D was a partner in a medical partnership. D sought contributions from his partners, contending that his negligence, if any, occurred in the course of the partnership's business.

ISSUE Is D entitled to contributions from his copartners?

DECISION No.

REASONS
1. P could have sued all partners and the partnership. All would have had liability for D's negligence, because the doctrine of *respondeat superior* is applicable to partnerships.
2. If P sues only D, D may not seek contribution, because D's wrong caused the damage. The partners are only constructively negligent, and D's negligence was actual.

Flynn v. Reaves, 218 S.E.2d 661 (Ga.) 1975.

Powers over property

Each partner has implied authority to sell to good-faith purchasers personal property that is held for the purpose of resale and to execute any documents necessary to effect a transfer of title. Of course, if his authority in this connecion has been limited and that is known to the purchaser, the transfer of title will be ineffective or voidable. A partner has no power to sell the fixtures and equipment used in the business unless he has been duly authorized. His acts are not a regular feature of the business, and a prospective purchaser should make certain that the particular partner has been given authority to sell. The power to sell, where it is present, gives also the power to make warranties that normally accompany similar sales.

The right to sell a firm's real property is to be inferred only if the firm is engaged in the real estate business. In other cases there is no right to sell and convey realty unless it has been authorized by a partnership agreement. In most states, a deed by one partner without authority is not binding on the firm, but it does convey the individual interest of the partners executing and delivering the deed. This conveyance, however, is subject to the rights of creditors of the partnership.

Under the Uniform Partnership Act, title to real property may be taken in the firm name as a "tenancy in partnership," and any member of the firm has power to execute a deed thereto by signing the firm name. If that happens, what is the effect of a wrongful transfer of real estate that has been acquired for use in the business and not for resale? The conveyance may be set aside by the other partners, because the purchaser should have known that one partner has no power to sell real estate without the approval of the others. However, if the first purchaser has resold and conveyed the property to an innocent third party the latter takes good title.

If the title to firm property is not held in the firm name but is held in the names of one or more of the partners, a conveyance by those in whose names the title is held passes good title, unless the purchaser knows or should know that title was held for the firm. There is nothing in the record title in such a situation to call the buyer's attention to the fact that the firm has an interest in the property.

The power to mortgage or pledge a firm's property is primarily dependent upon the power to borrow money and bind the firm. A partner with authority to borrow may, as an incident to that power, give the security normally demanded for similar loans. Because no one partner without the consent of the others has the power to commit an act that will destroy or terminate the business, the power to give a mortgage on the entire stock of merchandise and fixtures of a business is usually denied. Such a mortgage would make it possible, upon default, to liquidate the firm's assets and thus destroy its business. Subject to this limitation, the power to borrow carries the power to pledge or mortgage.

Financial powers

To determine the limit of a partner's financial powers, partnerships are divided into two general classes—trading and nontrading partnerships. A *trading partnership* is one that has for its primary purpose the buying and selling of merchandise. In such a trading firm, each partner has an implied power to borrow money and to extend the credit of the firm, in the usual course of business, by signing negotiable paper.

CASE

S and B were partners in the automobile business under the name of Greenwood Sales and Service. B borrowed $6,000 from P and gave a partnership note in return. B borrowed the money to make his initial capital contribution to the partnership.

ISSUE Is the partnership liable on the note?

DECISION Yes.

REASONS 1. Greenwood Sales and Service was a trading or commercial partnership. A partner is an agent of the firm for the purpose of the partnership business and may bind all partners by their acts within the scope of such business. It is of no consequence whether the partner is acting in good faith with his copartners or not, provided the act is within the scope of the partnership's business and professedly for the firm, and third persons are acting in good faith.

2. A partner in a trading partnership has the power to execute negotiable instruments.

Holloway v. Smith et al., 197 Va. 334 (1955).

A *nontrading partnership* is one that does not buy and sell commodities but has for its primary purpose the production of commodities or is organized for the purpose of selling services; for example, professional partnerships in law, medicine, or accounting. In such partnerships, a partner's powers are more limited, and a partner does not have implied power to borrow money or to bind the firm on negotiable paper. If the partner's act is within the scope of partnership business, a member of a nontrading partnership may bind the firm by the exercise of implied authority, just as a partner in a trading partnership may.

Notice and admissions

Each partner has implied authority to receive notice for all other partners concerning matters within the pursuit of the partnership business. Knowledge held by any partner in his mind but not revealed to the other partners is notice to the partnership. Knowledge of one partner is legally knowledge of all partners, providing that the facts became known or were knowledge obtained within the scope of the partnership business. A partner has a duty to communicate known facts to the other partners. Failure to do so is fraud on the partnership by the partner possessing the knowledge.

Admissions or representations pertaining to the conduct of the partnership business and made by a partner may be used as evidence against the partnership.

REVIEW QUESTIONS AND PROBLEMS

1. Define the following terms: *silent partner, secret partner, dormant partner, trading partnership,* and *tenancy in partnership.*
2. When is a partner entitled to be paid interest on funds used by the partnership?
3. List situations in which a partner is entitled to an accounting in a court of equity.
4. Compare the power to bind the firm of a partner in a trading partnership with that of a partner in a nontrading partnership.
5. X, a partner of the XYZ firm, was indebted to B for a personal loan. X defaulted on the loan, and B learned that X had insuffcent personal assets to satisfy the debt. May X's interest in partnership property be levied upon by B? Explain.
6. Two people have been partners for a number of years. Upon the death of one, the other spent considerable time in winding up the partnership affairs. Is the surviving partner legally entitled to compensation for services? Why?
7. A partner in an accountancy firm borrowed $10,000 in the firm name and used the proceeds to pay an individual debt. Is the firm liable for the debt? Why?
8. Lum and Abner were partners in a grocery store. The firm was in need of additional working capital, and Lum advanced $20,000. Is Lum entitled to interest on the advance?
9. Jim and Tim were partners in the used car business. Jim was driving home from the business in a car that was part of the partnership inventory when he negligently injured Pat, who sued the partners individually and the partnership. Jim worked irregular hours, usually returning to the used car lot after going home. Should Jim and the partnership be held liable? Why?
10. Frances, Agatha, and Hilda operated the FAH Health Spa. Frances and Agatha paid themselves high salaries but refused to pay Hilda. They also sold health spa memberships to their families at low rates and would not discuss partnership affairs with Hilda. Does Hilda have a cause of action against Frances and Agatha? Explain.
11. Bedford and Eckhart formed a partnership and built a shopping center. Three years later, Bedford, the managing partner, informed Eckhart that the business was in deep financial trouble and that he had tried to sell the complex but had failed. Bedford said that the best thing to do would be for one to buy the other out, and that their equity in the business was not worth more than $3 million. Eckhart sold his half interest in the partnership to Bedford for $1.5 million. Later he discovered that their equity in the business amounted to over $10 million and that Bedford had received several offers to purchase the business. Eckhart brought suit to rescind the sale, to have the partnership dissolved, and for accounting. Should Eckhart succeed? Why?

Three steps are necessary for complete extinguishment of a partnership: dissolution, winding up, and termination. Dissolution, the legal destruction of the partnership relation, occurs whenever any partner ceases to be a member of the firm or whenever a new partner is admitted. It is the change in the relation of the partners caused by any partner's ceasing to be associated in carrying on—as distinguished from winding up—the business. Dissolution alone does not terminate the partnership but, rather, designates the time when partners cease to carry on business together.

38

Dissolution of Partnerships

Winding up involves the process of reducing the assets to cash, paying off the creditors, and distributing the balance to the partners. *Termination* occurs only when the winding-up process is completed.

Dissolutions will occur without violation of the partnership agreement: (1) at the end of the stipulated term or particular undertaking specified in the agreement; (2) by the express will of any partner when no definite term or particular undertaking is specified; (3) by the agreement of all the partners; or (4) by the expulsion, in good faith, of any partner from the business, in accordance with power conferred by the partnership agreement.

Dissolution by act of the partners

When no definite term of particular undertaking is specified, the express will of any partner may legally, without liability, dissolve the partnership. Dissolution may be accomplished by giving notice to the other parties.

No particular form of notice is required; it will be implied from circumstances inconsistent with the continuation of the partnership. When a partner whose services are essential leaves the community, his departure is an act and notice of dissolution.

Expulsion of a partner is a breach of the partnership agreement unless the agreement confers the power of expulsion upon a majority of the partners. Assume that Able, Baker, and Cain are partners. Able and Baker cannot expel Cain unless that power is specifically granted in the agreement. Without power to expel, partners may seek judicial dissolution if one partner is guilty of violating the partnership agreement. If Cain was not devoting his time to the business, as he was required to do in the partnership agreement, Able and Baker could seek a dissolution on these grounds, although they could not expel Cain.

Dissolution may also occur in violation of the partnership agreement. Although the agreement stipulates the length of time the partnership is to last, dissolution is always possible, because the relationship is essentially a mutual agency not capable of specific performance. Therefore each partner has the *power,* but not the *right,* to revoke the relationship. In the event of wrongful dissolution, the wrongdoer is liable for damages.

Dissolution by operation of law

If during the period of the partnership, events make it impossible or illegal for the partnership to continue, it will be dissolved by operation of law. Such events or conditions are the death or bankruptcy of one of the partners, or a change in the law that makes the continuance of the business illegal.

Since a partnership is a personal relationship existing by reason of contract, the death of one partner dissolves the partnership but does not terminate it. It continues for the purpose of winding up the partnership's affairs. The process of winding up is, in most states, the exclusive obligation and right of the surviving partner or partners. The executor or administrator of the deceased partner has no right to participate in, or interfere with, the winding-up processes, unless, of course, the deceased was the last surviving partner. The only right of the personal representative of a deceased partner is to demand an accounting upon completion of the winding up of the partnership's affairs. As a general rule, the estate of the deceased partner is not bound on contracts entered into by the surviving partners if the contracts are unconnected with the winding up of the affairs of the partnership. This is discussed more fully later in the chapter.

The bankruptcy of a partner will dissolve the partnership because the control of his property passes to the trustee in bankruptcy for the benefit of the creditors. The mere insolvency of a partner will not be sufficient to justify a dissolution. The bankruptcy of the firm itself is a cause for dissolution, as is also a valid assignment of all the firm assets for the benefit of creditors.

Dissolution by court decree

When a partnership by its agreement is to be continued for a term of years, circumstances sometimes make continued existence of the firm impossible and unprofitable. Upon application of one of the partners to a court of equity, the partnership may be dissolved. Under the following circumstances and situations, a court of equity may order dissolution:

1. Total incapacity of a partner to conduct business and to perform the duties required under the contract for partnership.
2. A declaration by judicial process that a partner is insane.
3. Willful and persistent commitment of a breach of the partnership agreement, misappropriation of funds, or commitment of fraudulent acts.
4. An innocent party's application for dissolution because the partnership was entered into as a result of fraud.
5. Gross misconduct and neglect or breach of duty by a partner to such an extent that it is impossible to carry out the purposes of the partnership agreement.

Courts will not interfere and grant a decree of dissolution for mere discourtesy, temporary inconvenience, differences of opinion, or errors in judgment. The misconduct mentioned in the fifth situation must be of such gross nature that the continued operation of the business would be unprofitable.

CASE

P and D were partners in a motel, restaurant, and condominium development. P was responsible for building and selling the condominiums, and D ran the motel and restaurant. After the condominiums were built and sold, a dispute arose between the parties. P charged D with failure to pay taxes and with commingling partnership funds with his own money. D accused P of improper accounting methods on the condominiums. P sued D to dissolve the partnership, contending that the disagreements make continuation impossible.

ISSUE Does this dissension justify termination?

DECISION Yes.

REASONS
1. On application of a partner, a court of equity may order dissolution because circumstances render dissolution just and equitable, or the interests of the partners will be best served by dissolution.
2. Although a court of equity will not order dissolution because of trifling disputes among the partners, dissolution will be granted if dissensions are so serious and persistent that continuance would be impracticable, or if all confidence and cooperation between the parties have been destroyed.

First Western Mortgage Co. v. Hotel Gearhart, Inc., 448 P.2d 450 (Or.) 1971.

Effect of dissolution on powers of partners

Upon dissolution, a partnership is not terminated. The process of winding up, except when the agreement provides for continuation by purchase of former parties' shares, involves liquidation of the partnership assets, so that cash may be available to pay creditors and to make a distribution to the partners. When the agreement provides for continuation and purchase of a deceased partner's interest, the technical dissolution is followed by valuation and payment, and the new firm immediately commences business.

As a general rule, dissolution terminates the actual authority of any partner to act for the partnership except as far as necessary to wind up partnership affairs, to liquidate the assets of the firm in an orderly manner, or to complete transactions begun but not then finished.

CASE

T and E formed a partnership and purchased coal from P. They executed a purchase-money mortgage on the unmined coal, to secure the purchase price. Thereafter, T withdrew from the partnership. T did not inform any of the partnership creditors of his withdrawal. E kept up the payments on the mortgage for some time but then defaulted, and P brought suit against both T and E as partners. Service of process was made on E's private secretary at E's law office. Neither T nor E answered or appeared in the proceedings, and a judgment was entered against the partners. T thereafter petitioned the court to set aside the sheriff's sale on the ground that he hadn't properly been served with process. T claimed that service on the secretary of E did not constitute service upon the partnership, which had already been dissolved.

ISSUE Can service of process be made on an employee of a partnership after the partnership has been dissolved?

DECISION Yes.

REASONS

1. Dissolution of a partnership does not terminate it. The dissolution of a partnership is the change in the relation of the partners caused by any partner's ceasing to be associated in carrying on—as distinguished from winding up—the business. Even after dissolution, a partnership is not terminated but continues to exist until the winding up of partnership affairs is completed. The authority remains to act for the partnership in winding up partnership affairs and completing transactions begun but not yet finished at the time of dissolution.
2. In general, a dissolution operates only with respect to future transactions. As to everything past, the partnership continues until all preexisting matters are terminated. The dissolution does not destroy the authority of a partner to act for his former associates in matters in which they still have a common interest and are under a common liability. There is no reason, therefore, why the statute authorizing a judgment against a partnership by service upon one partner should not be just as effective and applicable during the period subsequent to dissolution, but prior to termination of the partnership, as it is during the period before dissolution.
3. The partnership continues to exist for the purpose of satisfying its obligation to P.

North Star Coal Company v. Eddy, 277 A.2d 154 (Pa.) 1971.

Dissolution of a partnership terminates the actual authority of a partner to bind the partnership except for transactions connected with winding up the business. Insofar as third persons who had dealings with the firm are concerned, apparent authority still exists until notice of termination is given.

This apparent authority means that one partner of a dissolved partnership binds the firm on contracts unconnected with winding up the firm's affairs. When he does so, issues arise as to whether or not the new obligations may be met with partnership funds or whether the contracting partner is entitled to contribution toward payment of the debt or obligation from the other partners.

The resolution of these issues depends upon the cause of the dissolution. If the dissolution is caused by (1) the act of a partner, (2) bankruptcy of the partnership, or (3) the death of a partner, each partner is liable for his share of any liability incurred on behalf of the firm after dissolution, just as if there had been no dissolution, unless the partner incurring the liability had knowledge of the dissolution. In these situations, if knowledge of the dissolution is present, the partner incurring the liability is solely responsible, and he cannot require his fellow partners to share the burden of his unauthorized act. If the dissolution is not caused by the act, bankruptcy, or death of a partner but by some event such as a court decree, no partner has authority to act and therefore has no right to contribution from other partners for liabilities incurred after dissolution.

When dissolution results from the death of a partner, title to partnership property remains in the surviving partner or partners for purposes of winding up and liquidation. Both real and personal property is, through the survivors, thus made available to a firm's creditors. All realty is treated as though it were personal property. It is sold, and the surviving partners finally account, usually in cash, to the personal representative of the deceased partner for the latter's share in the proceeds of liquidation.

Rights of partners after dissolution

Upon dissolution, a withdrawing partner who has not breached the partnership agreement has certain options with regard to his interest in the dissolved partnership. He may require the partnership to be wound up and terminated. The partnership will be liquidated and the assets distributed among the partners. The alternative is to allow the business to continue or accept the fact that it has continued.

If the withdrawing partner allows the business to continue, the value of his interest in the partnership as of the data of dissolution is ascertained. He then has the right to receive, at his option after an accounting, either the value of his interest in the partnership with interest or, in lieu of interest, the profits attributable to the use of his right in the property of the dissolved partnership. The portion of profits to which a withdrawing partner is entitled because of the use of property will almost always be less than his portion prior to dissolution. This is true because a portion of the profit is usually attributable to services of the continuing partners.

CASE

In January, 1972, the parties formed a partnership called Gateway Realty, to sell real estate. D owned the premises upon which the partnership was located. In January, 1973, D told P that the partnership was over. P then established a similar business elsewhere. P was paid her share of the profits up until the time of dissolution. D operated under the name Gateway Realty for a few more months and thereafter under her own name. A Yellow Pages advertisement listed defendant as Gateway Realty until January, 1974. P argued that use of the partnership name was really use of the partnership's assets; therefore, she was entitled to a share of the profits through January, 1974.

ISSUE Does a telephone advertisement listing the name of a dissolved partnership constitute a use of partnership assets rendering the continued user liable to the former partner for her share of the profits?

DECISION No.

REASONS
1. Partnership law requires that upon dissolution, a partner is entitled to have his or her interest ascertained and to be compensated for it or to receive a share of profits attributable to the continued use of the partnership property. By accepting proceeds of sale from the listings at the time of dissolution, P elected the first option.
2. The profit earned by the use of the partnership name for the period after dissolution is entirely too speculative to appraise. Use of the partnership name as an asset is so minimal an asset that there could be no realistic determination of damages.

Hilgendorf v. Denson, 341 So.2d 549 (Fla. App.) 1977.

When dissolution is caused in any way other than breach of the partnership agreement, each partner has a right to insist that all the partnership assets be used first to pay firm debts. After firm obligations are paid, remaining assets are used to return capital contributions and then to provide for a distribution of profits. All the partners except those who have caused a wrongful dissolution of the firm have the right to participate in the winding up of the business. The majority selects the method and procedures to be followed in the liquidation. The assets are turned into cash unless all agree to distribute them in kind.

If a partnership that is to continue for a fixed period is dissolved by the wrongful withdrawal of one partner, the remaining members may continue as partners under the same firm name for the balance of the agreed term of the partnership. They are required to settle with the withdrawing partner for his interest in the partnership and to compensate him, but they are allowed to subtract from the amount due in cash the damages caused by his wrongful withdrawal. In the calculation of his share, the good will of the business is not taken into consideration.

Upon dissolution, it is the duty of the remaining partner or partners to wind up the affairs. If they fail to do so and instead continue the business, they have liability to the withdrawing partner, his assignee, or personal representative for use of partnership assets. The liability may include interest if the value of the former partner's portion of the partnership can be ascertained. It may also include liability for a share of postdissolution profits. This liability arises because the business is continuing to use the assets of all of the former partners.

Just as a partner whose property is used to earn postdissolution profits is entitled to share in those profits, one who continues the partnership business after dissolution and contributes substantial labor and management services is entitled to compensation for that share of the profits attributable to such services. A partner who withdraws from a partnership has no interest in profits that are attributable to labor and management services of continuing partners and which are earned after dissolution and before final accounting. Therefore, in determining profits attributable to use of a withdrawing partner's right in the property of dissolved partnership, a court is entitled to make an equitable allowance for services of partners who continue the partnership business.

It is often difficult to value accurately the interest of a withdrawing or deceased partner when the business continues. The buy and sell provisions will control the method for establishing the value of the interest as of the date of dissolution. If there are no buy and sell provisions and the parties cannot agree, a judicial decision on the value may be required. This decision may sometimes involve which of the parties is to continue the business, as well as the amount to be paid the withdrawing partner, but it cannot be made with mathematical certainty.

CASE

P and D, brother and sister, were partners who had irreconcilable differences. In a suit to dissolve the partnership, a referee was appointed. The referee, in order to dispose of the assets, asked each partner to submit a bid. The brother submitted a bid for $65,000, but the sister did not bid. She now objects to the sale to her brother. The parties had stipulated that one of them could continue the business.

ISSUE On dissolution, is it permissible for the court to order a sale of partnership property to one of the partners for the purpose of continuing the business?

DECISION Yes.

REASONS 1. After dissolution, a partnership continues until liquidated or wound up. Although dissolution is usually followed by liquidation, a withdrawing partner may be paid his partnership contribution and share of profits without liquidation if the parties so agree.

2. The most logical buyers of partnership property are the remaining partners. If the parties agree that one of them may continue the business, the assets may be sold to the partner who is to continue.

Maras v. Stilinovich, 268 N.W. 2d 541 (Minn.) 1978.

Effect of dissolution on third parties

Dissolution of a partnership terminates the authority of the partners to create liability, but it does not discharge any existing liability of any partner. An agreement between the partners themselves that one or more of the partners will assume the partnership liabilities and that a withdrawing partner will not have any liability does not bind the firm's creditors unless they agree to that, also.

When a firm's assets are insufficient to pay its debts, the individual property of partners, including the estate of a deceased partner, is subject to claims of third parties for all debts created while the partnership existed. This liability is subject to the payment of individual debts, however.

Notice on dissolution

After dissolution, two categories of parties are entitled to notice of the dissolution. The first category, the firm's creditors, includes all former creditors. Transactions entered into after dissolution without such notice continue to bind withdrawing partners and the estate of deceased partners. If proper notice is given, former partners are not liable for contracts unconnected with winding up the partnership's affairs. Notice eliminates the apparent authority to bind the former firm and its partners.

CASE

A partnership was in the process of dissolution, with one partner buying out the other. P, who had been doing business with the partnership for some time, was notified of the dissolution. Thereafter, P extended credit to the buying partner. Upon default, P sued the selling partner.

ISSUE Is the selling partner liable on the debt incurred after notice was given?

DECISION No.

REASON A creditor cannot recover if he extends credit to a partner when the creditor knows the partnership is being dissolved. If the creditor does not have notice of dissolution, the partnership's liability to him continues, especially if he has been dealing with the partnership.

Direct Sellers Association v. McBrayer, 492 P.2d 727 (Ariz.) 1972.

Notice of dissolution is required whether the dissolution is caused by an act of the parties or by operation of law, unless a partner becomes bankrupt or the continuation of the business becomes illegal. Therefore, upon death of a partner, the personal representative should give immediate notice of the death and dissolution, in order to avoid further liability.

The second category of parties entitled to notice of dissolution consists of persons who knew about the partnership but who were not creditors. When the dissolution is caused by an act of the parties, the partners will continue to be liable to all such non-creditors unless public notice of dissolution is given. Notice by publication in a newspaper in the community where the business has been transacted is sufficient public notice.

If a partner has not actively engaged in the conduct of the partnership business, creditors have not learned that he was a partner, and have not extended credit to the firm because of their faith in him, there is no duty to give notice to either of the groups mentioned above.

New partners and new firms

A person admitted as a partner into an existing partnership is liable to the extent of his capital contribution for all obligations incurred before his admission, as though he had previously been a partner. The new partner is not personally liable for such obligations, and the creditors of the old firm can look only to the firm's assets and to members of the old firm.

If a business is continued without liquidation of the partnership affairs, creditors of the first, or dissolved, partnership are also creditors of the partnership continuing the business. Likewise, if the partners assign all their interest to a former partner or a third person who continues the business without liquidation of the partnership affairs, creditors of the dissolved partnership are also creditors of the person continuing the business.

Distributions on Dissolution

Solvent partnerships

Upon the dissolution of a solvent partnership and a winding up of its business, an accounting is had to determine its assets and liabilities. Before the partners are entitled to participate in any of the assets, whether or not the firm owes them money, all firm creditors other than partners are entitled to be paid. After firm creditors are paid, the assets of the partnership are distributed among the partners as follows:

1. Each partner who has made advances to the firm or has incurred liability for, or on behalf of, the firm is entitled to be reimbursed.
2. Each partner is then entitled to the return of the capital that he has contributed to the firm.
3. Any balance is distributed as profits in accordance with the partnership agreement.

In many partnerships, one partner contributes capital, the other contributes labor, so the partner contributing labor has nothing to be returned in step number 2. Of course, the original agreement could place a value on such labor; but unless it does, only the partner who contributes cash or other property will be repaid in step number 2.

Insolvent partnerships

When the firm is insolvent and a court of equity is responsible for making the distribution of the assets of the partnership, the assets are distributed in accordance with a rule known as marshaling of assets.

Persons entering into a partnership agreement impliedly agree that the partnership assets shall be used for the payment of the firm debts before the payment of any individual debts of the partners. Consequently, a court of equity, in distributing the firm's assets, will give them to the firm's creditors before awarding them to separate creditors or individual partners. The court will give separate assets of the partners to their private creditors before awarding these assets to the firm's creditors. Neither class of creditors is permitted to use the fund belonging to the other until the claims of the other have been satisfied. The firm's creditors have available two funds out of which to seek payment: assets of the firm and the individual assets of the partners. Individual creditors of the partners have only one fund: the personal assets of the partners. Because of this difference, equity compels the firm's creditors to exhaust the firm's assets before having recourse to the partners' individual assets.

CASE

P and D ran a sawmill and cotton gin business as partners. D had made a loan to the partnership, secured by a deed of trust on partnership property and on the home and farms of P. P seeks to enjoin the foreclosure of the deed of trust until a partnership accounting is had, alleging that partnership assets will discharge all debts.

ISSUE Should such an injunction be issued?

DECISION Yes.

REASONS
1. Generally, when a partnership is dissolved, each partner has the right to have partnership property applied to the discharge of partnership liabilities. The surplus, if any, is then proportionately paid to the partners. The equity of an individual creditor of a partner is subordinate to such right.
2. Only after the partnership assets have been applied may individual assets be reached by creditors. A partner has the right to have partnership property used to pay partnership debts in order to avoid personal liability on the debts.

Casey et al. v. Grantham et al., 239 N.C. 121 (1954).

The doctrine of marshaling of assets does not apply if a partner conceals his existence and permits the other member of the firm to deal with the public as the sole owner of the business. Under these circumstances, the dormant partner's conduct has led the creditors of the active partner to rely upon the firm's assets as the separate property of the active partner; and by reason of his conduct, the dormant partner is estopped from demanding an application of the equity rule that the firm's assets shall be used to pay the firm's creditors first and individual assets used to pay individual creditors. Thus the firm's assets must be shared equally with its creditors and the individual creditors of the active partner. In such a case, because the firm's assets may not be sufficient to pay all its debts when depleted by payments to individual creditors, there may be unpaid firm creditors, and dormant partners will be personally liable. Because the firm's creditors' right to firm property rests upon the partners' right that firm assets be used to pay firm debts, the conduct that estops a dormant partner also denies the creditors such a preference. Furthermore, the creditors who relied upon the assets in the hands of the sole active partner cannot claim a preference when later they learn such assets were partnership assets.

Just as the individual creditors are limited to individual assets, firm creditors are limited to firm assets. Therefore, firm creditors are not entitled to payment out of the individual assets of the partners until the individual creditors have been paid. This rule applies even though the firm creditors may at the same time be individual creditors of a member of the firm. There are two main exceptions to this general rule: (1) The rule for the limit of firm creditors to firm assets applies only where there are firm assets. If no firm assets or no living solvent partner exists, the firm creditors may share equally with the individual creditors in the distribution of the individual estates of the partners. (2) If a partner has fraudulently converted the firm assets to his own use, the firm's creditors will be entitled to share equally with individual creditors in the guilty partner's individual assets.

The doctrine of marshaling of assets is not applicable to tort claims under the Uniform Partnership Act. Partners are individually liable in tort for the acts of the firm, its agent and servants. The liability is joint and several. Thus, the injured party may sue the partners individually or as a partnership. The firm assets need not be first used to collect a judgment, and direct action may be taken against individual assets.

REVIEW QUESTIONS AND PROBLEMS

1. What is the distinction between *dissolution* and *termination* of a partnership?
2. List four situations in which a court may decree dissolution of a partnership.
3. What groups of persons are entitled to notice of dissolution of a partnership? Indicate the type of notice to which each is entitled.
4. Explain the doctrine of marshaling of assets and indicate two situations in which it will not be followed.
5. Anderson, Ernst, and Sells were partners in an accounting firm. Their partnership agreement did not expressly grant the power of a majority to expel any partner. Anderson and Ernst decided that they should carry on the business without Sells, who proved to be lazy and inefficient in producing revenue. How should Anderson and Ernst proceed in removing Sells? Explain.
6. Cheryl paid $5,000 to join an existing partnership. Before she was admitted, an obligation to a supplier had been incurred but not paid. When the debt became long overdue, the supplier sued the partnership and the individual partners. To what extent, if any, is Cheryl liable? Explain.
7. A, B, and C, architects, were in partnership. D, a consulting engineer, did considerable work for the firm in the past and was always paid promptly. A, the senior member of the firm, decided to withdraw from the partnership and retire. The partners executed an indemnity agreement, whereby a new partnership of B and C was formed, and in which the new firm expressly assumed all debts of the old partnership. D was given express notice of A's withdrawal. Without A's services, the firm began to falter and was unable to meet D's bill. A debt in the amount of $5,000 remained from the old partnership, and a new debt of $15,000 was accrued by the new firm. How much may D collect from A? Why?
8. Rose, Morgan, and Carlton are partners under an agreement whereby the firm is to continue in business for ten years. Rose causes a wrongful dissolution of the partnership and demands his interest therein. May he demand that firm assets be liquidated? Is there any asset in which he is not entitled to share? Why?
9. Bush and Baker formed a partnership, but one year later mutually agreed to dissolution. The only notice of dissolution was by publication in a newspaper in the community where their business had been transacted. By agreement, Bush continued to operate the business. O'Neill Company, a previous creditor of the partnership, continued to extend credit to the business. When O'Neill Company was not paid, it brought suit against both Baker and Bush. Should Baker be held liable for the credit extended after dissolution? Why?
10. Cora and Evans owned a newspaper as a partnership. Cora died, and Evans continued to operate the business even though the representative of Cora's estate attempted, unsuccessfully, to sell the newspaper. Three years after Cora's death, Evans began to wind up the business. An accountant performed services of the same type for the newspaper both before and after Cora's death. Should Cora's estate be partially liable for these services? Why?
11. A cosmetics concern operated as a partnership. It bought printing from a local shop that it paid in full. When the partnership became Colette and Monique, Inc., the printer was not informed of the incorporation. Shortly after the change, the printing shop performed additional services for the cosmetics firm but could not collect. Can the printer hold Colette and Monique liable in their individual capacities? Why?

39

Formation of Corporations

Corporations may be classified in a variety of ways: public or private, for profit (business corporations) or not-for-profit. Each state classifies corporations doing business within that state as foreign or domestic, to denote the state where incorporation took place. Moreover, each state has a variety of statutes relating to specialized corporations such as co-operatives, church and religious corporations, and fraternal organizations. In this chapter and those that follow, we are primarily concerned with the private business corporation.

Statutes relating to business corporations vary from state to state, yet they are quite similar. For our discussion, the basic principles of the Model Business Corporation Act will be used as the basic statute. This model act, prepared by the Commissioners on Uniform State Laws, has been wholly adopted by a few states, largely adopted by others. A major influence on the law of corporations throughout the country, its application to any particular issue must nevertheless be checked in each state.

A corporation is an artificial, intangible person or being, created by the law. Incorporating is a method by which individual persons are united into a new legal entity. For this new legal entity, they select a common name and the purposes that it is to accomplish. As a legal entity separate and apart from the persons who had it created, the corporate existence is not affected by the death, incapacity, or bankruptcy of any of the persons involved in its creation or in its operation. Its owners do not have personal liability on its contracts, and it has no liability for the obligations of its shareholders. As a legal entity, a corporation is able to own property and to sue or be sued in its own name in the same manner as a natural person. A corporation is also a person for purposes of both tort and criminal law. As an impersonal entity, it can act only through agents and servants, but the corporation is subject to the doctrine of *respondeat superior* and may be punished for certain criminal acts of its agents or servants.

Although a corporation is considered a person under most statutes, there are a few, such as those allowing the appointment of "suitable persons" as parole officers, in which it is not a "person." A corporation is a person for purpose of the due process clause of the Fifth and Fourteenth Amendments to the United States Constitution. For purposes of the privilege against compulsory self-incrimination, it is not a person.

Procedure for incorporation

The law prescribes the steps to be taken for the creation of the corporation. Most corporate laws provide that a specified number of adult persons, usually not less than three, may file an application for a charter. The application contains the names and addresses of the incorporators, the name of the proposed corporation, the object for which it is to be formed, its proposed duration, the location of its registered office, the name of its registered agent, and information about the stock of the corporation. The information that is supplied about the corporate stock usually includes (1) whether there will be preferred stock or only common stock; (2) the stated or par value of the stock, if any (if the stock has no stated value, then it is called no-par stock); (3) the number of shares of stock that will be authorized; and (4) the number of shares of stock that will actually be issued.

Some states also require the names and addresses of the subscribers to the stock and the amount subscribed and paid in by each. Most applications usually indicate whether the stock is to be paid for in cash or in property.

The application, signed by all the incorporators, is forwarded to a state official, usually the secretary of state. If the application is in order, the official then issues a charter.

CASE

P attempted to file proposed articles of incorporation on behalf of a mortgage company. The proposed articles contained a statement of purpose, which expressed the rates of interest the mortgage company would charge its borrowers. These rates of interest were usurious under state law.

D, the secretary of state, rejected the articles of incorporation because they contained an illegal purpose. P filed suit to force D to issue the charter.

ISSUE Does a secretary of state have the authority to reject articles of incorporation that include an unlawful purpose?

DECISION Yes.

REASONS
1. The Business Corporation Act requires that proposed articles of incorporation conform to certain legal requirements. Articles that fail substantially to conform may be rejected.
2. If articles of the incorporation are for an unlawful corporate purpose, they are not in compliance of the law.

Town and Country Plumbing Co., Inc. v. Delta Real Estate Development, Inc., 357 So.2d 126 (Miss.) 1978.

Upon return of the charter properly signed by the secretary of state, it is filed by the incorporators in the proper recording office. The receipt of the charter and its filing are the operative facts that bring the corporation into existence and give it authority and power to do business.

After the charter has been received and filed, the incorporators and all others who have agreed to purchase stock meet and elect a board of directors. They may also approve the bylaws of the corporation if the applicable law so provides. In most instances, the bylaws are approved by the board, not by the shareholders. The board of directors that has been elected then meets, approves the bylaws, elects the officers, calls for the payment of the subscription price for the stock, and makes whatever decisions are necessary to commence business.

Bylaws

A *bylaw* is a rule for governing and managing the affairs of the corporation. It is binding upon all shareholders but not third parties, unless the third parties have knowledge of it. The bylaws contain provisions establishing the corporate seal and the form of the stock certificate, the number of officers and directors, the method of electing them and removing them from office, as well as the enumeration of their duties. Bylaws specify the time and place of the meetings of the directors and the shareholders. Together with the articles of incorporation and the applicable statute, the bylaws provide rules for operating the corporation. The bylaws are subservient to the articles of incorporation and the statute but are of greater authority than, for instance, a single resolution of the board. Failure to follow the bylaws constitutes a breach of the fiduciary duties of a director or officer.

Disregarding the corporate entity

One of the basic advantages of the corporate form of business organization is the limitation of shareholder liability. Corporations are formed for the express purpose of limiting one's risk to the amount of his investment in the stock. Sometimes suits are brought to hold the shareholders personally liable for an obligation of a corporation or to hold a parent corporation liable for debts of a subsidiary.

Such suits attempt to "pierce the corporate veil." They ask the court to look behind the corporate entity and take action as though no entity separate from the members existed. They may not ask that the corporate entity be disregarded simply because all the stock is owned by the members of a family or by one person or by another corporation.

In certain situations the corporate entity is often disregarded. First, if the use of the corporation is to defraud or to avoid an otherwise valid obligation, the court may handle the problem as though no corporation existed. Let us assume that A and B sold a business and agreed not to compete with the buyer for a given number of years. In violation of the contract, A and B organized a corporation in which they became the principal stockholders and managers; but the buyer may enjoin the corporation from competing with him, and he may do so as effectively as he could have enjoined A and B from establishing a competing business. Second, if the corporate device is used to evade a statute, the corporate entity may be disregarded. If a state law provides that a person may not hold more than one liquor license at a time, this law cannot be circumvented by forming multiple corporations. The attempt to evade the statute would justify "piercing the corporate veil."

The fiction of the corporate entity also may be disregarded when one corporation is organized, controlled, and conducted to make it a mere instrumentality of another corporation. In such circumstances one corporation is said to be the "alter ego" of another. The "alter ego" theory, by which the corporate veil is pierced, may also be used to impose personal liability upon corporate officers and stockholders. If the corporate entity is disregarded by the principals themselves, so that there is such a unity of ownership and interest that separateness of the corporation has ceased to exist, the "alter ego" doctrine will be followed.

Some of the factors considered significant in justifying a disregard of the corporate entity are: (1) undercapitalization of a corporation, (2) failure to observe corporate formalities such as annual meetings, (3) nonpayment of dividends, (4) siphoning of corporate funds by the dominant stockholders, (5) nonfunctioning of other officers or directors, (6) absence of corporate records, (7) use of the corporation as a facade for operations of the dominant stockholders, and (8) use of the corporate entity in promoting injustice or fraud. In other words, the corporate veil will be pierced if the ends of justice require it.

CASE

P obtained a judgment against the X corporation. D was the sole shareholder of X corporation. After the judgment was obtained by P, D caused the corporation to be dissolved. D paid off all the debts of the corporation except P's judgment and kept all the corporate assets. P seeks to collect the judgment from D personally.

ISSUE Does justice require that the corporation and D be treated as identical?

DECISION Yes.

REASONS
1. The doctrine that a corporation is a legal entity existing separate and apart from the persons composing it is a legal theory introduced for purposes of convenience and to subserve the ends of justice. The concept cannot, therefore, be extended to a point beyond its reason and policy; and when invoked in support of an end subversive of this policy, it will be disregarded by the courts. Thus, in an appropriate case and in furtherance of the ends of justice, a corporation and the individual or individuals owning all its stock and assets will be treated as identical.
2. It is basic that a corporation is a distinct and separate entity from the individuals who compose it as stockholders or who manage it as directors or officers. This is not a rule cast in concrete; rather, courts have always looked to substance over form. In a proper case, when the corporate form is being used to evade personal responsibility, courts have disregarded the corporate form and imposed liability on the person controlling the corporation, subverting it to personal use, making it his instrument.
3. Here the corporation was a fictional shield employed by D to avoid personal responsibility. D's actions denigrate the purpose of limited liability, that purpose being to encourage the investment of risk capital.
4. Although each case is decided on its own facts, here the facts require that the parties be treated as identical in order to prevent injustice and inequitable consequences. After the dissolution, there were no assets from which P could collect. The purpose of the dissolution was to avoid the judgment. A corporation dissolved to avoid creditors is no more a separate entity than one formed to defraud them.

Cohen v. Williams, 318 So.2d 279 (Ala.) 1975.

Domestic and foreign corporations

To a state or country, corporations organized under its laws are domestic corporations; those organized under the laws of another state or country are foreign corporations.

Domestic corporations become qualified to do business upon receipt and recording of their charter. Foreign corporations with significant intrastate activities must also "qualify" to do business by obtaining a certificate of authority and by paying the license fees and taxes levied on local businesses. A foreign corporation engaged wholly in *interstate* commerce through a state need not qualify in that state.

Most state statutes require foreign corporations to qualify to do business by filing a copy of their articles of incorporation with the secretary of state. They are also required to appoint an agent upon whom service of process may be served, and to maintain an office in the state. Failure to comply results in a denial of the right of access to the courts.

CASE

P, a construction corporation, filed a suit against D to enforce a construction lien. P was a Tennessee corporation that was not licensed to do business in Mississippi, where the suit was filed, but it had paid Mississippi's contractor's privilege tax. D moved to dismiss the suit, contending that an unlicensed foreign corporation could not file suit in the state courts of Mississippi.

ISSUE Is P entitled to file suit?

DECISION No.

REASONS
1. Foreign corporations transacting intrastate business are required to obtain a Certificate of Authority from the secretary of state. A foreign corporation that fails to do so is not permitted to maintain suits in the courts of the state.
2. Payment of privilege taxes to engage in occupations such as building contracting does not change the requirement of obtaining a Certificate of Authority, because the purpose of the certificate is public convenience and orderly administration of the affairs of the state. The purpose of the licensing law is revenue.

Smith v. Director, Corp. & Securities Bureau, 261 So.2d 228 (Miss.) 1978.

In a real sense, this denial of access to the courts as a plaintiff prevents a corporation from conducting business, because its contracts are not enforceable by suit, and debtors would thus be able to avoid payment to the corporation. To make matters worse for the unqualified corporation, it may still be sued, but it may not use noncompliance as a defense. Transacting business within the state without complying with the statute also subjects the corporation and its officers to statutory penalties, such as fines.

The term *doing business* is not reducible to an exact and certain definition. The Model Business Corporation Act defines the term by saying that a foreign corporation is *doing business* when "some part of its business substantial and continuous in character and not merely casual or occasional" is transacted within a state. A corporation is not *doing business* in a state merely because it is involved in litigation or maintains a bank account or an office within a state for the transfer of its stock. It also states that a foreign corporation is not required to obtain a license to do business by reason of the fact that (1) it is in the mail-order business and receives orders from a state that are accepted and filled by shipment from without the state, and (2) it uses salespeople within a state to obtain orders that are accepted outside the state. If the orders are accepted or filled within the state, or if any sale, repair, or replacement is made from stock physically present within the state in which the order is obtained, a foreign corporation is required to obtain a license.

Powers of Corporations

Application for a charter includes a statement of the powers desired by the corporation. These are usually stated in quite broad language. A corporation has only such powers as are conferred upon it by the state that creates it. The charter, together with the statute under which it is issued, sets forth the express powers of the corporation. All powers reasonably necessary to carry out the expressed powers are implied.

The following general powers are ordinarily granted to the corporation by statute: (1) to have perpetual existence; (2) to sue and be sued; (3) to have a corporate name and corporate seal; (4) to own, use, convey, and deal in both real and personal property; (5) to borrow and lend money other than to officers and directors; (6) to purchase, own, and dispose of securities; (7) to enter into contracts of every kind; (8) to make charitable contributions; (9) to pay pensions and establish pension plans; and (10) all powers necessary or convenient to effect any of the other purposes. Some of these powers will be discussed more fully in the sections that follow.

Power to acquire treasury stock

The power to acquire securities includes the power to acquire treasury stock. Treasury stock is a corporation's own stock, legally issued, fully paid for, and reacquired by gift or purchase but not formally cancelled. A corporation is restricted in its power to purchase treasury stock because the purchase might effect a reduction of its capital, to the detriment of creditors. In most states a corporation is permitted to purchase treasury stock only out of accumulated profits or surplus. This restriction retains stockholders' investment, equivalent to the original capital, as a protective cushion for creditors in case subsequent losses develop.

A corporation may redeem its preferred stock if there is no injury to, or objection by, creditors. Here again, many of the states require the preferred stock to be redeemed out of surplus, or they demand that authority to reduce the capital stock be obtained from the state.

Ultra vires

Any acts of a corporation that are beyond the authority, express or implied, given to it by the state in the charter are said to be *ultra vires* acts—"beyond the authority." If a corporation performs acts or enters into contracts to perform acts that are *ultra vires,* the state creating such a corporation may forfeit its charter for misuse of its corporate authority. The extent of the misuse is controlling in determining whether the state will take away its franchise or merely enjoin the corporation from further *ultra vires* conduct.

Although third parties have no right to object to the *ultra vires* acts of a corporation, a stockholder may bring court action to enjoin a corporation from performing an *ultra vires* contract. If the corporation sustains losses or damages because of the *ultra vires* venture, the corporation may recover from the directors who approved the contracts. When directors exceed corporate powers, they may become personally liable for resulting losses.

At common law, a corporation had no liability on contracts beyond its corporate powers because the corporation has capacity to do only those things expressly authorized within its charter or incidental thereto. Most modern statutes, including the Model Business Corporation Act, provide that all *ultra vires* contracts are enforceable. Neither party to such a contract may use *ultra vires* as a defense. *Ultra vires* conduct on the part of the corporation may be enjoined by the state or any shareholder; but otherwise, contracts previously made are binding, whether they be wholly executory, partially executed, or fully performed.

CASE

D, a religious corporation, leased liquor-dispensing equipment from P. When D defaulted on the lease, P filed suit for the rental. D asserted *ultra vires* as a defense.

ISSUE Is *ultra vires* a defense?

DECISION No.

REASONS
1. Incapacity or lack of power on the part of a corporation does not make a lease invalid, and the defense of *ultra vires* is not available.
2. The Business Corporation Code abolishes the doctrine of *ultra vires* as a means of avoiding a transaction that a corporation later claims is beyond its capacity or power, and it limits the assertion of the defense to three enumerated instances not applicable here.

Free Baptist Church v. Southeastern Bev. Co., Inc., 218 S.E.2d 169 (Ga.) 1975.

Other Aspects of Corporate Formation

Promoters

A *promoter,* as the name implies, promotes the corporation and assists in bringing it into existence. One or more promoters will be involved in making application for the charter, holding the first meeting of shareholders, entering into preincorporation subscription agreements, and engaging in other activities necessary to bring the corporation into existence. Promoters are responsible for compliance with the applicable blue-sky laws (statutes relating to the sale of securities), including the preparation of a prospectus if required.

Many of these activities involve the incurring of contractual obligations or debts. Preparation of the application for a charter usually requires the assistance of a lawyer, and it must be accompanied by the required filing fee. Legal questions about who has liability for these obligations and debts frequently arise. Is the promoter liable? Is the corporation after formation liable? Are both liable?

Certain general principles of contract and agency law prevent simple answers to these questions. First of all, a promoter is not an agent prior to incorporation, because there is no principal. A party who purports to act as an agent for a nonexistent principal is generally liable as a principal. Second, the corporation technically cannot ratify the contracts of promoters because ratification requires capacity to contract both at the time of the contract and at the time of the ratification.

CASE

P sued D to recover a broker's commission. D was a promoter of a corporation to be formed. P knew that D was a promoter and that the corporation was not yet formed. The corporation was subsequently formed, but it failed to pay P the commission.

ISSUE Is the promoter personally liable for the commission?

DECISION Yes.

REASONS
1. As a general rule, the promoter of a corporation is personally liable on the contracts entered into on behalf of the corporation he is organizing.
2. On the other hand, if the contract is on behalf of the corporation, and the person with whom the contract is made agrees to look to the corporation alone for responsibility, the promoter incurs no personal liability. This exception applies when a promoter contracts in the name of a corporation to be formed later, and he does not intend to be liable on it; furthermore, the other party knows that the corporation has not been formed and that the promoter does not intend to be liable.

3. The later formation of a corporation and its adoption of contracts made by its promoters does not release or free the promoters from their liability.

Vodopich v. Collier County Developers, Inc., 319 So.2d 43 (Fla.App.) 1975.

To avoid the difficulties caused by these legal theories, the law has used certain fictions to create an obligation on the part of the corporation and to provide a means to eliminate liability on the part of the promoters. One fiction is that a novation occurs. This theory proceeds on the premise that when the corporation assents to the contract, the third party agrees to discharge the promoter and to look only to the corporation. The discharge of the promoter by the third party is consideration to make binding the corporation's promise to be bound upon the contract. In the absence of a novation, the promoter will continue to be personally liable. Establishing a novation often fails because of a lack of proof of any agreement to release the promoter.

Another theory that is used to determine liability on preincorporation obligations may be described as the *offer and acceptance theory.* Under this theory, a contract made by a promoter for the benefit of the corporation is an offer that may be accepted by the corporation after it comes into existence. Acceptance of the benefits of the contract constitutes a formal ratification of it. If the corporation does not accept the offer, it is not liable. The promoter may or may not be liable, depending on the degree of disclosure.

Corporations have also been held liable on promoters' contracts on theories that may be called the *consideration theory* and the *quasi-contract theory.* After incorporation, directors may promise to pay for expenses and services of promoters. Under the consideration theory, their promise will be binding and supported by sufficient consideration, on the theory of services previously rendered. The quasi-contract theory holds that corporations are liable by implication for the necessary expenses and services incurred by the promoters in bringing them into existence, because such expenses and services accrue or inure to the benefit of the corporation. Finally, it should be noted that some states have abandoned trying to justify corporate liability with a legal theory and have simply provided by statute that corporations are liable for the reasonable expenses incurred by promoters.

The parties frequently do not intend the promoter to be liable on a preincorporation contract. A promoter may avoid personal liability by informing the other party that he does not intend to be liable and that he is acting in the name of, and solely on, the credit of a corporation to be formed. But if the promoter represents that there is an existing corporation when there is none, the promoter is liable. A promoter should make sure that contracts entered into on behalf of the proposed corporation are worded to relieve him of personal liability.

Promoters occupy a fiduciary relationship toward the prospective corporation. Their position does not give them the right to secure any benefit or advantage over the corporation itself or over other shareholders. A promoter cannot purchase property and then sell it to the corporation at an advance, nor has he a right to receive a commission from a third party for the sale of property to the corporation. In general, however, he may sell property acquired by him prior to the time he started promoting the corporation, provided he sells it to an unbiased board of directors after full disclosure of all pertinent facts.

Stock subscriptions

A preincorporation stock subscription is an agreement to purchase stock in a corporation. It is a binding agreement (a subscriber cannot revoke his subscription) created among the subscribers for stock in a corporation to be formed. The subscription is usually drafted in a manner that creates a contract. Some states by statute have provided that a preincorporation subscription constitutes a binding, irrevocable offer to the corporation, by reason of the mutual promises of the parties. The offer is usually limited to a specified period of time, such as six months.

Certain conditions are inherent in the preincorporation subscription contract. The subscriber will not be liable unless: the corporation is completely organized; the full amount of the capital stock is subscribed; and the purpose, articles, and bylaws of the corporation are as originally stated and relied upon by the subscriber. Conditions, express or implied, are often waived by the subscriber if, with knowledge of the nonperformance, he participates in stockholders' meetings, pays part or all of his subscription, or acts as an officer or director of the corporation.

A subscription to stock of a corporation already in existence is a contract between the subscriber and the corporation. Such a contract may come into existence by reason of an offer either made by the corporation and accepted by the subscriber or made by the subscriber and accepted by the corporation. If the corporation opens subscription books and advertises its stock, it is seeking for an offer to be made by the subscriber. The corporation may, however, make a general offer to the public, which may be accepted by the subscriber in accordance with the terms of the general offer.

Corporate name

One of the provisions in the application for a corporate charter is the proposed name of the corporation. In order that persons dealing with a business will know that it is a corporation and that the investors therefore have limited liability, the law requires that the corporate name include one of the following words or end with an abbreviation of them: *corporation, company, incorporated,* or *limited.* A corporate name must not be the same as, or deceptively similar to, the name of any domestic corporation or a foreign corporation authorized to do business in the state to which the application is made.

CASE

P, Legal Aid Services, Inc., brought suit to enjoin D, American Legal Aid, Inc., from using the term "Legal Aid" as a part of its name. The trial court entered judgment in favor of P after finding that the names were deceptively similar and that P was incorporated first.

ISSUE Should D be enjoined from using the words "Legal Aid" in its transactions and name?

DECISION Yes.

REASONS

1. There is not an exact definition or measure of resemblance that will warrant the interference of the court when names are similar. The facts and circumstances must determine each case.
2. A court of equity may grant injunctive relief against a defendant corporation wrongfully using a name similar to a plaintiff corporation's name, particularly where hardship or damage to defendant is not great. Under the Corporation Act, by a comparatively simple process, the defendant may change its name.
3. There was considerable evidence that many people were confused about the two corporations and that many people believed that they were in some way connected.

American Legal Aid, Inc. v. Legal Aid Services, Inc., 503 P.2d (Wyo.) 1972.

Most states have procedures for reserving a corporate name for a limited period. Inquiry is usually made concerning the availability of a name; if it is available, it is reserved while the articles are being prepared. The name may be changed by charter amendment at any time without affecting corporate contracts or title to corporate property in any way.

Corporate buy and sell agreement

The importance of a buy and sell agreement between partners was previously discussed. Frequently, a buy and sell agreement between shareholders in a closely held corporation is also desirable. It is just as important to have a means of getting a shareholder out of a closely held corporation as it is to have a means of getting a partner out of a partnership.

Shareholder buy and sell provisions should be worked out before any shareholder knows whether he is a buyer or a seller. Although withdrawal from active participation will not effect a dissolution, it can have the serious effect of precipitating a lawsuit, or a shareholder may continue to participate in management when he does not desire to do so. Frequently, a withdrawing shareholder will be forced to sell his stock for less than it is worth because a buy and sell agreement was not worked out in advance.

Corporate buy and sell provisions are similar to those in a partnership, except the corporation as an entity is frequently a party to them. Many contracts provide that before a shareholder can sell his stock to an outsider, it must first be offered to the corporation. Some contracts also require that it be offered to other shareholders. Such rights of first refusal are legal.

Corporations may buy life insurance on the life of an officer-shareholder and use the proceeds to buy his stock. Stock redemptions on the death of a shareholder are an integral part of estate planning, and the various alternatives and plans to redeem such stock should be carefully studied at the time the corporation is formed.

The Securities Laws

Government both at federal and state levels is actively involved in the regulation of the sale of securities. Numerous statutes have been enacted not only to protect the investing public but to impose liability on anyone assisting in the sale of securities in violation of the law. These laws are commonly known as blue-sky laws because of their avowed purpose of preventing one person from selling another a patch of blue sky.

The responsibility for administering the federal securities law is vested in an independent regulatory agency, the Securities and Exchange Commission. The SEC exercises vast quasi-legislative and quasi-judicial powers. To prevent fraudulent sales of securities, the agency has adopted rules and regulations relating to financial and other information, which must be included in the documents filed with the commission as well as those given to potential investors. It also regulates the various stock exchanges, utility holding companies, investment trusts, and investment advisers.

Because the objective of the securities laws is to protect innocent persons from investing their money in speculative enterprises over which they have little or no control, the laws are paternalistic in character and are liberally construed to protect the investing public. The securities laws therefore cover not only stocks and bonds but every kind of investment in which one person invests money and looks to others for the success of the venture. Thus the term *security* is broadly defined to include any investment in which a person turns his money or property over to another to manage for profit.

Securities Act of 1933

The Securities Act of 1933 is a disclosure law requiring that securities subject to its provisions be registered and that a prospectus be furnished each investor. The function of the prospectus is to provide the investor with sufficient facts, including financial information about the issuer, to enable the prospective buyer to make an intelligent investment decision.

This law is applicable to transactions in which a security is sold to the general public by the issuer, an underwriter, or a controlling person. A *controlling person* is one who controls or is controlled by the issuer, such as the major stockholder of a corporation. An *underwriter* is anyone who participates in the distribution by selling it for the issuer or by guaranteeing its sale.

The 1933 act is not applicable to transactions by securities dealers after 40 days have elapsed from the effective date of the public offer. If the security is offered by a company with no prior registration statements, this period is 90 days. This exemption allows a dealer to enter into transactions in securities after a minimum period has elapsed. Brokers' transactions executed on any exchange or in the over-the-counter market are exempt if they are unsolicited.

The law covers public sales; private sales are exempt. This exemption for private sales is often difficult to apply. In determining whether or not a sale is being made to the general public, the SEC will examine (1) the number of offerees, (2) their knowledge about the company in which they are investing, (3) the relationship between the offeror and offeree, (4) whether the security comes to rest in the hands of the offeree or is resold, and (5) the amount of advertising involved. At one time, a sale to fewer than 25 persons was not a public sale. Although the SEC does not always follow it, the 25-persons figure is still a good rule of thumb for defining the private sale exemption.

The law also exempts certain securities from the registration and prospectus requirements. Securities such as those of banks, which are regulated by other government agencies, fall into this category. Sales wholly in intrastate commerce as contrasted with interstate commerce are exempt. The intrastate exemption covers securities that are offered and sold only to persons who reside within the state of incorporation; or if the issuer is unincorporated, the purchasers must reside within the state of his residence and place of business. If the sale is to a resident with the intention that it will be resold to a nonresident, the intrastate exemption is lost.

The law also authorizes the SEC to create additional exemptions if it finds that the registration requirement is not necessary in the public interest and is not necessary for the protection of investors by reason of the small amount involved or the limited character of the public offering.

This law does not prevent the sale of low-grade or highly speculative securities. As a disclosure law, it requires only that the negative aspects of the offering be revealed. A prospectus always contains a warning that the securities have not been approved by the commission and that the commission has not passed upon the accuracy of the information contained in the prospectus.

Liability under the 1933 act

The Securities Act of 1933 imposes both civil and criminal liability for violation of its provisions. The criminal liability is for fraud in *any* offer or sale of securities. Fraud in the sale of an exempt security is still a criminal violation if the mail is used or if an instrumentality of interstate commerce has been used.

The civil liability provisions relating to registration statements impose liability on the following persons in favor of purchasers of securities:

1. Every person who signed the registration statement.
2. Every director of the corporation or partner in the partnership issuing the security.
3. Every person who, with his consent, is named in the registration statement as about to become a director or partner.
4. Every accountant, engineer, or appraiser who assists in the preparation of the registration statement or its certification.
5. Every underwriter.

The protection of the 1933 act extends to brokers as well as to purchasers of securities.

CASE

D engaged in a fraudulent "short selling" scheme by placing orders with brokers to sell certain shares of stock, which he believed had peaked in price and which he falsely represented that he owned. The price of the stock rose sharply before the delivery date, so that the defendant was unable to make covering purchases and never delivered the securities. Consequently, the brokers had to buy replacement shares in the open market in order to deliver shares to investor purchasers. While investors were protected from injury, the brokers suffered substantial financial losses. D was convicted of violating Section 17(a) (1) of the Securities Act of 1933 by using a scheme and artifice to defraud in the sale of securities.

ISSUE Does Section 17(a) (1) of the Securities Act of 1933 prohibit frauds against brokers as well as investors?

DECISION Yes.

REASONS
1. Nothing on the face of the statute indicates that it applies solely to frauds directed against investors. The language requires only that the fraud occur "in" an "offer or sale" of securities.
2. Investor protection, while an important part of the securities acts, is not their sole purpose. They are also designed to ensure a high standard of business ethics and to protect honest businesspeople.
3. Frauds against brokers eventually harm investors indirectly by increasing the cost of doing business with brokers, who pass these costs on to consumers. Another possibility was that the brokers might not have been able to borrow the money to make the required purchases.

United States v. Naftalin, 99 S.Ct. 2077 (1979).

Civil liability is imposed if a registration statement (1) contains untrue statements of material facts, (2) omits material facts required by statute or regulation, and (3) omits information that if not given makes the facts stated misleading. This last stipulation describes the factual situation of a statement containing a half-truth that has the net effect of misleading the reader. The test of accuracy and materiality is as of the date the registration statement becomes effective.

A plaintiff purchaser need not prove reliance on the registration statement, but actual knowledge of falsity is a defense. Scienter is not an element of proof; but except for the issuer, reliance on an expert such as an accountant is a defense. The liability here is usually for the difference between the price paid by the investor, not to exceed the original offering price, and the value of the security at the time of the suit.

The law contains a separate provision relating to liability arising in connection with prospectuses and communications. It imposes liability on any person who sells or offers to sell a security without complying with the legal requirements relating to furnishing a proper prospectus. It also imposes liability on anyone who sells a security by use of a prospectus or an oral statement that includes untrue information or omits a material fact necessary to prevent the statements from being misleading.

The statute of limitations both for civil and criminal liability is one year. The statute does not start to run until the discovery of the untrue statement or omission or from the time a discovery would have been made with reasonable diligence. In no event may a suit be brought more than three years after the sale.

The Securities Exchange Act of 1934

The 1934 act, as the title implies, is concerned with securities exchanges and with trading securities after the primary offering stage. The act created the SEC. It regulates various stock exchanges, brokers, and dealers in securities and contains numerous provisions relating to matters such as proxy solicitation and insider transactions.

The Securities Exchange Act prohibits the sale of a security on a national exchange unless a registration is effective for the security. Registration under the 1934 act is somewhat different from registration under the 1933 act. It requires the filing of prescribed forms with the applicable stock exchange and with the SEC. As a general rule, all equity securities that are held by 500 or more owners must be registered if the issuer has more than $1 million in gross assets. This rule picks up issues that are traded over the counter, and it applies to securities that might have qualified under one of the exemptions in the 1933 act.

Issuers of registered securities are required by the 1934 act to file periodic reports with the SEC, as well as to report significant developments to it. The SEC's rules on proxies, applicable to all securities registered under the act, regulate all aspects of proxy solicitation in great detail. The law also prohibits market manipulations and regulates activities such as short sales.

The provisions relating to stockbrokers and dealers prohibit the use of the mails or any instrumentality of interstate commerce to sell securities unless the broker or the dealer is registered. The language is sufficiently broad to cover advertising as well as actual sales. Brokers and dealers are required to keep detailed records and to file annual reports with the SEC.

Some of the most important provisions of the Securities Exchange Act of 1934 are those relating to insider transactions. The insider provisions cover directors and officers of the issuer of the security and every person who owns more than 10 percent of any security. The act requires insiders to file, at the time of the registration or within ten days after becoming an owner, director, officer, or owner of 10 percent of the stock, a statement of the amount of the issues they own. Any change in ownership thereafter must be put on file within ten days after the close of the calendar month in which the change was made. Among those exempt from the insider rules are executors or administrators of estates, who are exempt for twelve months, and odd-lot dealers, who are generally exempt.

The most important aspect of the insider provisions relate to short-swing profits. In order to prevent insiders from profiting from the use of information not available to the general public, the law prevents their making short-swing profits. Thus, if a director, officer, or principal owner realizes profits on the purchase and sale of a security within a six-months' period, the profits inure to and belong to the company. The issuer may sue to collect the profit, or any other shareholder may do so if the issuer does not sue within sixty days of a demand to do so. Technical rules are used to compute the profit liability. These rules ignore the intention of the profit maker, and the existence of insider knowledge is irrelevant. Failure to comply with the rules and the making of a profit within a six-months' period create liability for the profit. The order of purchase and sale is immaterial. The profit is calculated on lowest price in, highest price out, in any six-months' period.

Insider rules are rigidly applied in ordinary sale and purchase transactions. Courts have held that the provisions are not applicable to certain "unorthodox" transactions not within the intent of the law. It has been held that if a purchaser did not own 10 percent of the total stock prior to the purchase, the purchase and later sale within six months was not subject to the law.

Liability under the 1934 act

Liability is imposed under the 1934 Securities Exchange Act for violations in addition to those relating to insider transactions and short-swing profits. Section 18, for example, imposes liability on any person who shall make or cause to be made any false and misleading statements of material fact in any application, report, or document filed under the act. This liability based on fraud is in favor of both purchasers and sellers. Plaintiffs under this section must prove scienter, reliance on the false or misleading statement, and damage. It is a defense that the person sued acted in good faith and without knowledge that the statement was false and misleading. In other words, freedom from fraud is a defense under an action predicated on Section 18. There is no liability for simple negligence under this section.

Most of the litigation under the 1934 act is brought under Section 10b and Rule 10b-5 of the SEC. These provisions are concerned with manipulative and deceptive devices and contrivances. Rule 10b-5 declares that it is unlawful to use the mails or any instrumentality of interstate commerce or any national securities exchange to defraud *any person* in connection with the *purchase or sale* of any security. As a result of judicial interpretation, this section and the rules promulgated under it provide a private remedy for defrauded investors. This remedy may be invoked against "any person" who indulges in fraudulent practices in connection with the purchase or sale of securities. In actual practice, defendants in Section 10b and Rule 10b-5 cases have tended to fall into four general categories: (1) insiders, (2) broker dealers, (3) corporations whose stock is purchased or sold by plaintiffs, and (4) those who "aid and abet" or conspire with a party in one of the first three categories. Accountants are an example of those who may fall into the fourth category. The liability requires proof of fraud, not mere negligence.

CASE

D, an accounting firm, performed periodic audits of F Company's books and prepared the usual reports for the company to file with the SEC. Nay, the president of F, induced P to invest funds in "escrow" accounts over a period of years; but there were no escrow accounts, because Nay converted the money to his own use. P charged that Nay's scheme violated Section 10(b) and Rule 10b-5 of the SEC and that D had "aided and abetted" Nay's violation by its failure to conduct proper audits. Specifically, P alleged that D was negligent when it did not discover Nay's rule that only he could open mail addressed to him or to his attention at F Company. P did not allege fraud on the part of D.

ISSUE Does a private cause of action for damages lie under Section 10(b) and Rule 10b-5 in the absence of any allegation of scienter, intent to deceive, manipulate, or defraud?

DECISION No.

REASONS

1. The language of Section 10(b) indicates that it was intended to proscribe knowing or intentional misconduct.
2. The history of the 1934 act indicates that Section 10(b) was addressed to practices that involve some element of scienter and not to impose liability for negligent conduct.

Ernst & Ernst v. Hochfelder et al., 96 S.Ct. 1375 (1976).

While most causes of action under the 1934 act will be based on misstatements of fact, silence about a material fact may constitute aiding and abetting. Although all persons who have knowledge of improper activities have no general duty to report them, a duty to disclose may arise in the face of a special relationship or set of circumstances, such as an accountant's certifying financial statements.

The concept of fraud under Section 10b encompasses not only untrue statements of material facts but the omission of material facts necessary to prevent other statements from being misleading. In other words, a half-truth that misleads is fraudulent. Finally, a failure to correct a misleading impression left by statements already made or silence when there is a duty to speak gives rise to a violation of Rule 10b-5.

The application of Rule 10b-5 is not limited to securities subject to the act. It applies to all sales of any security. The rule requires that those standing in a fiduciary relationship disclose all material facts before entering into transactions. This means that an officer, a director, or a controlling shareholder has a duty to disclose all material facts. Failure to do so is a violation and, in effect, fraudulent.

The 1934 act provides for criminal penalties for willful violations. Punishment for individuals is a $10,000 fine or imprisonment for two years or both. Failure to file the required reports and documents makes the issuer subject to a $100 forfeiture per day.

REVIEW QUESTIONS AND PROBLEMS

1. What steps are required in forming a corporation? In qualifying it to do business in a foreign state?
2. Give three examples of situations in which courts will "pierce the corporate veil."
3. What is the main limitation on a corporation's acquisition of treasury stock? Explain the reason for this limitation.
4. Who can challenge an *ultra vires* act of a corporation? Under what circumstances? Explain.
5. John, the sole stockholder of a corporation engaged in furnishing equipment for construction sites, has complete control over the business and manages all operations without meetings. All profits flow to John, and the company is undercapitalized. As president of the company, he makes a contract for the purchase of supplies and subsequently fails to pay. Is John personally liable? Why?
6. Donna, a director of a public corporation, participated in a board decision to expand business operations in the near future. Anticipating that the corporation's financial status would improve as a result of this decision, Donna purchased stock from Sam, a shareholder who had no knowledge of the board's action. The market value of the stock rose immediately after the decision was announced. Is Donna liable to Sam for any profits made from this transaction? Why?
7. LST Company was the parent company and BAG Company was a subsidiary. LST Company extended credit to BAG Company. The latter became insolvent, and the other creditors objected to LST's sharing equally in the assets. Is LST entitled to its pro rata share of BAG's assets? Why?
8. Able, Baker, and Charlie were the directors of a company. At the annual stockholders' meeting, Able and Baker, the sole shareholders, voted to amend the bylaws to reduce the number of directors from three to two. They then elected themselves as the two directors. Charlie claimed that this action should be nullified, since neither the state statute nor the articles of incorporation gave the stockholders the power to amend the bylaws. Is Charlie correct? Why?
9. The Glo Corporation sold a variety of products to senior citizens in Florida. Glo was a Delaware corporation with its principal place of business in New York. Not licensed to do business in Florida, it conducted its business through sales personnel that operated out of their own homes. One customer failed to pay his account, and Glo filed suit to collect the debt. What defense is available to the customer? Explain.
10. Describe three theories that may be used to impose liability on a corporation on contracts entered into by its promoters.
11. What are the basic distinctions between the Securities Act of 1933 and the Securities and Exchange Act of 1934?
12. In order to raise additional capital, a corporation sold stock to five carefully selected investors. Is the sale subject to the securities laws? Explain.
13. What is the definition of a security as used in the securities laws?

The preceding chapter was concerned with the legal aspects of forming a corporation. Many of the legal principles that were discussed there are also applicable to the operation of a corporate entity. Many bylaw provisions, for example, are directly concerned with operations. Because some of the subjects dealt with in this chapter, such as stock and the rights of shareholders, have a bearing on formation problems, the preceding chapter and this one should be considered complementary.

40 *Operating the Corporation*

Three distinct groups participate in the management of a corporation. *Shareholders* or *stockholders* (the words are synonymous) comprise the basic governing body. Shareholders exercise their control by electing the *board of directors,* sometimes by approving the bylaws, and by voting on matters such as merger, consolidation, or dissolution. The board of directors is the policy-making group, with responsibility for electing *officers,* who carry out the policies. The duties and powers of the shareholders, the board of directors, and the various officers are regulated by statute, by the bylaws of the corporation, and by corporate resolutions passed by the board of directors.

Shareholders

Fiduciary aspects

The law as it relates to close corporations is somewhat different from the law as it relates to publicly held corporations. Publicly held corporations have many shareholders, none of whom owns a majority of the stock. A *close corporation* is one in which management and ownership are substantially identical, to the extent that it is unrealistic to believe that the judgment of the directors will be independent of that of the shareholders.

The shareholders in a close corporation owe one another substantially the same fiduciary duty in the operation of the enterprise that partners owe to one another. They must discharge their management and shareholder responsibilities in conformity with the strict good-faith standard, and they may not act out of avarice, expediency, or self-interest in derogation of their loyalty to other shareholders and to the corporation.

CASE

P and three other individuals formed the D nursing home many years ago. The four corporate shareholders were also elected directors, and they served as employees of the close corporation. P had a quarrel with one of the other directors after years of successful operations. As a result of the quarrel, the other board members canceled P's salary, refused to reelect him as director, and stopped paying dividends, in an attempt to freeze him out. P sued for damages on the ground that the majority had breached the fiduciary duty owed to him.

ISSUE May the majority shareholder directors of a close corporation take action that has the practical effect of freezing out a minority shareholder?

DECISION No.

REASONS
1. The majority shareholder directors of a close corporation are held to the highest fiduciary standards toward a minority shareholder director.
2. When the effect of a decision is to freeze out the minority, the action is scrutinized to determine whether there is a legitimate business reason for it.
3. Here, the majority could not demonstrate a bona fide reason for canceling D's salary and refusing him a directorship. Consequently, the majority shareholders breached their fiduciary duties and are liable for damages to P.

Wilkes V. Springside Nursing Home, Inc., 353 N.E.2d 657 (Mass.) 1976.

This good-faith standard that shareholders in a close corporation must observe is in contrast to the relationship of the shareholders in a publicly held corporation. As a general rule, there is no fiduciary relationship between shareholders in publicly held corporations. One owner of stock listed on the New York Stock Exchange owes no duty to other owners of the same stock unless, of course, the shareholder is also an insider subject to SEC regulation.

The duty of the majority shareholder or shareholders to the minority shareholders in a close corporation is often involved in litigation. Many cases involve the purchase of stock by a majority shareholder or director from a minority shareholder. Some purchases involve the use of inside information, especially in small, closely held corporations that are not subject to the securities laws. Anyone who sells stock to an insider is aware that the buyer may have inside information, so the law traditionally held that the insider has no fiduciary duty to disclose everything he knows. There is a decided minority to the contrary, however, and many courts find the existence of a fiduciary duty to disclose because of the existence of special facts.

CASE

F was a closely held family corporation. D owned 42 percent, and other members of the family owned 58 percent of the stock. D, who was actively engaged in managing the corporation, negotiated with one other member of the family and acquired an additional 12 percent, giving him majority control. D then notified the other members of the family of his majority ownership and told them "If you would like to sell, let me know."

A few months later at a shareholders meeting, D indicated that he was in ill health and that he would be interested in purchasing the remainder of the stock. D offered every owner $60,000 for their interests. D purchased P's stock at that price. Shortly afterward, D sold the whole corporation at a price equal to $300,000 per shareholder. P sued D, alleging constructive fraud for failure to disclose the pending sale.

ISSUE In North Carolina, does a director of a corporation stand in a fiduciary relationship to a shareholder in the acquisition of the shareholder's stock, so that P is entitled to the $300,000 for the stock?

DECISION Yes.

REASONS
1. There are 3 different views among the various states. The majority view is that a director does not stand in a fiduciary relationship to a shareholder in the acquisition of stock and therefore has no duty to disclose inside information. The minority view is that a director is under a duty to disclose all material information. The third view is that although a director ordinarily owes no fiduciary duty to shareholders when acquiring stock, under special circumstances a fiduciary relationship arises.
2. The special circumstances creating the fiduciary relationship may include the closely held corporation, the familial relationship of the parties, the forthcoming sale of corporate assets, the director's initiation of the sale, and the relative ages and experience in financial affairs of the directors and the shareholder.
3. P in this case establishes each of the foregoing special circumstances; therefore, D breached his fiduciary duties.

Lazenby v. Godwin, 253 S.E. 2d 489 (N.C.) (1979).

Meetings

Action by the shareholders normally binds the corporation only when taken in a regular or properly called special meeting after notice required by the bylaws or statute has been given. It is generally conceded, however—and most states so provide by statute—that action approved informally by *all* shareholders will bind the corporation. If there is less than unanimous approval, informal action is not possible.

Notice. Notice of a special meeting must include a statement concerning matters to be acted upon at the meeting; any action taken on other matters will be ineffective. If unusual action, such as a sale of corporate assets, is to be taken at the regular annual meeting, notice of the meeting must call specific attention to that fact; but otherwise, any business may be transacted at the annual meeting.

Failure to give proper notice of a meeting generally invalidates the action taken at the meeting. A stockholder who has not received notice but attends and participates in a meeting is said to waive the notice by his presence.

Quorum. A quorum of shareholders must be present in person or by proxy (a *proxy* is the authority to vote another's stock) in order to transact business. A *quorum* is usually a majority of the voting shares outstanding, unless some statute or the bylaws provide for a larger or smaller percentage. Affirmative action is approved by majority vote of the shares represented at a meeting, provided a quorum exists. At common law, certain unusual matters such as a merger or sale of all corporate assets required a unanimous vote. Today, statutes usually provide that such actions can be taken by vote of two-thirds or three-fourths of the shareholders. Many of these statutes also provide that the dissenting shareholders have the right to surrender their shares and receive their fair value if they disapprove of the action taken. These matters are discussed in the next chapter.

Purposes. In large, publicly held corporations, the annual meeting of shareholders serves a variety of purposes. Management has usually solicited enough proxies in advance to control any vote that is taken, so the outcome is usually a certainty. Nevertheless, many shareholders attend meetings in order to question management on a variety of issues and to lobby for certain policies. Management uses the annual meeting of shareholders of large corporations as a public relations opportunity, to educate the shareholders on company accomplishments as well as its problems.

Voting

Statutes of the states and the charters issued under their authority prescribe the matters on which shareholders are entitled to vote. Usually, they vote on the election of directors; on major policy issues such as mergers and consolidations and on dissolution; and, in some instances, on a change in the bylaws.

Some state laws allow a corporation to deny some shareholders the vote on certain issues, such as the election of directors. This denial allows a minority of shareholders to obtain control; but since public policy supports the right of an investor to vote, the status of stock as nonvoting must be communicated to the investor, or the stock purchase may be rescinded.

As a general rule, every shareholder is entitled to as many votes as he owns shares of stock. The shareholder whose name appears upon the corporate records is usually designated by the bylaws as the person entitled to vote. Owners of preferred stock, depending on their contract with the corporation, may or may not be entitled to vote.

The statutes of some states provide for cumulative voting in the election of directors. In cumulative voting, a shareholder may cast as many votes for one board candidate as there are board members to be filled, multiplied by the number of his shares of stock, or he may distribute this same number of votes among the candidates as he sees fit. A shareholder owning 100 shares of stock has 300 votes if 3 directors are to be elected. He may cast all 300 for one candidate, or they may be spread among the candidates.

A shareholder is entitled to vote only by virtue of his ownership of the stock, but he may specifically authorize another to vote his stock. Authorization is made by power of attorney and must specifically state that the agent of the shareholder has power to vote his principal's stock. This *voting by proxy* is a personal relationship that the shareholder may revoke before the authority is exercised. Laws pertaining to principal and agent control this relationship.

A shareholder, unlike a director, is permitted to vote on a matter in which he has a personal interest. Although in certain respects he represents the corporate welfare in his voting, in most respects he votes to serve his interest. The majority of shareholders are not permitted to take action, however, that is clearly detrimental to the corporate and minority interest.

Rights of shareholders—in general

A shareholder has the following rights usually created by statute and reiterated in the bylaws: (1) the right to inspect the books and papers of the corporation, (2) the right to attend shareholders' meetings and to vote for directors and on certain other matters such as dissolution or merger, (3) the right to share in the profits when a dividend is declared, (4) the preemptive right, and (5) the right to bring a shareholder's derivative suit. In some states a shareholder has the additional right to cumulative voting, previously discussed.

The right to inspect the books and papers is limited to good-faith inspections for proper and honest purposes at the proper time and the proper place. A *proper purpose* is one that seeks to protect the interest of the corporation as well as the interest of the shareholder seeking the information. The inspection must be made with a justifiable motive, not through idle curiosity or for vexatious purposes. The business hours of the corporation are the reasonable and proper hours in which a stockholder is entitled to inspect the books.

In some states, a shareholder who is refused access to the books and records is entitled to damages as provided by statute. A typical statute provides that a shareholder who is denied the right to inspect books and records is entitled to damages equal to 10 percent of the value of the stock owned.

The right to inspect includes contracts and correspondence as well as books and records. These statutes are given a broad, liberal interpretation. The right extends even to confidential records such as those relating to bank loans.

CASE

P, a bank, brought a declaratory judgment action against three of its shareholders, to determine the bank's obligation to permit shareholders to inspect the bank's books and records. P contended that such inspection would invade the private and confidential relationships between the bank and its customers.

ISSUE Do bank shareholders have the right to inspect the books and records of the bank?

DECISION Yes.

REASONS
1. Generally, inspection rights of shareholders of a bank are the same as those of shareholders of other corporations. The statute is liberally construed.
2. A shareholder's statutory right of inspection can be exercised only at reasonable and proper times so that it does not interfere with the conduct of the business. It must not be exercised because of idle curiosity or for improper or unlawful purposes. In all other respects the statutory right is absolute.
3. The purpose of the statute providing shareholders with a right to inspect a corporation's books and records is to protect small and minority shareholders against the mismanagement and faithlessness of their agents and officers. The inspection right covers books and records, including documents, contracts, and papers, but not secret research or the results of technical investigations.

Bank of Heflin v. Miles, 318 So.2d 697 (Ala.) 1975.

Preemptive right

The original application for a charter specifies the amount of stock the corporation will be authorized to issue and the amount that will be issued without further notice to the state. The amount of authorized stock and the amount of issued stock are used to compute the license fees and franchise taxes due to the state of incorporation. These amounts cannot be increased or exceeded without the authority of the state.

Shareholders may authorize an increase in the authorized capital stock, but such action may not be taken by the directors. An increase in the authorized capital stock is an amendment to the corporate charter, which requires state approval.

The board of directors may authorize the sale of unissued capital stock when the amount previously issued is less than that which is authorized. This authorization does not require an amendment to the charter. All that is required is that the state be informed of the additional issue of the stock, so that the correct taxes may be collected.

When an increase in the capital stock has been properly authorized, the existing shareholders have a prior right over third parties to subscribe to the increased capital stock. This right is called the shareholder's *preemptive right.* It is based upon the shareholder's right to protect and maintain his proportionate control and interest in the corporation.

The preemptive right may be limited or waived by contract and by provisions in the charter or bylaws of the corporation in most states. In many states it is not applicable to treasury stock.

The preemptive right is applicable to new authorizations of stock. It is generally not applicable to new issues of stock previously authorized. If the new issue of an original authorization takes place a long time after the original issue, many states provide that the preemptive right exists. Most states approve the issuance of stock to employees under stock option plans without regard to the preemptive right.

Derivative suits

A shareholder cannot maintain an *action at law* for injuries to the corporation, because the corporation is a legal entity and by law has a right to bring a suit in its own name. Any cause of action based on conduct injurious to the corporation accrues in the first instance to the corporation. Nor can a shareholder bring a suit at law against the directors or other officers of the corporation for negligence, waste, and mismanagement in the conduct of the corporate business. The right to sue for injuries to the corporation rests strictly with the corporation itself, unless modified by statute.

A shareholder may, however, bring a *suit in equity* known as a shareholder's *derivative suit* to enjoin the officers of a corporation from entering into *ultra vires* contracts or from doing anything that would impair the corporate assets. Likewise, the shareholder has a right to bring suit for dollar damages on behalf of the corporation if the officers are acting outside the scope of their authority, are guilty of negligent conduct, or are engaging in fraudulent transactions that are injurious to the corporation itself. The shareholder bringing the derivative suit must have been a shareholder at the time of the action complained of and at the time the suit is filed. Persons are not allowed to acquire stock for the purpose of filing a derivative action.

CASE

On August 2, 1978, P brought a shareholder's derivative action against D, alleging certain financial improprieties by officials of D corporation. The events upon which the derivative action was based had occurred prior to P's becoming a shareholder. D moved to dismiss the case.

ISSUE Is a shareholder entitled to maintain a derivative action complaining of transactions that took place prior to his becoming a shareholder?

DECISION No.

REASONS 1. To maintain a derivative action, a shareholder must have had interest in the defendant corporation at the time of the transaction complained of, unless the mismanagement or its effects continue and are injurious to the shareholder.

2. The law requires that a derivative action be brought by one or more shareholders. A party must also be a shareholder at the time of the occurrence complained of and at the time the suit was filed.

Centrella v. Morris, 597 P.2d 958 (Wyo.) 1979.

Before a shareholder may bring a derivative suit, he must show that he has done everything possible to secure action by the managing officers and directors and that they have refused to act. If the action involves a lawsuit, there must be a demand to sue, or it must be apparent that a demand would be futile under the circumstances. Any judgment received in such an action is paid to the corporation. The shareholder who initiates the action is permitted to recover the expenses involved in the suit.

Mere dissatisfaction with the management of the corporation will not justify a derivative suit. In the law of corporations, it is fundamental that the majority shareholders control the policies and decisions of the corporation. Every shareholder impliedly agrees that he will be bound by the acts and decisions of a majority of the shareholders or by the agents of the corporation they choose. Courts will not undertake to control the business of a corporation, although it may be seen that better decisions might be made and the business might be more successful if other methods were pursued.

The majority of shares of stock are permitted to control the business of a corporation, in their discretion, when not in violation of its charter or some public law or corruptly, oppressively, and fraudulently subversive of the rights and interests of the corporation or of a shareholder. If a majority of disinterested directors acting in good faith and with reasonable business judgment adopt a course of action, it will not be overturned by a derivative suit.

Directors

Qualifications and powers

Directors of a corporation are elected by the shareholders. They ordinarily attend meetings, exercise judgment on propositions brought before the board, vote, and direct management, although they need not be involved actively in the day-to-day operation of the business. A director has no power to issue orders to any officer or employee, nor can he institute policies by himself or command or veto any other action by the board.

It is not essential that directors hold stock in the corporation. Because they are to supervise the business activities, select key employees, and plan for the future development of the enterprise, they are presumably selected for their business ability.

Directors have power to take action necessary or proper to conduct the ordinary business activities of the company. They may not amend the charter, approve a merger, or bring about a consolidation with another corporation without the approval of the shareholders.

Meetings

The bylaws usually provide for the number of directors. Historically, not less than three directors were required; but in recent years, many corporate statutes have authorized two directors—and in some cases, one director. This development is especially prevalent in professional associations or corporations, which frequently have only one shareholder and thus only one director.

Since the board of directors must act as a unit, it is traditional that it assemble at board meetings. The bylaws provide for the method of calling directors' meetings and for the time and the place of the meeting. A record is usually kept of the activities of the board of directors, and the evidence of the exercise of its powers is stated in resolutions kept in the corporate minute book. A majority of the members of the board of directors is necessary to constitute a quorum unless a bylaw provides to the contrary. Special meetings are proper only when all directors are notified or are present at the meetings. Directors may not vote by proxy, having been selected as agents because of their personal qualifications.

Modern statutes make it possible for a board to take informal action (usually by telephone), provided the action is subsequently reduced to writing and signed by all of the directors. This gives a board the flexibility and capability to make decisions without delay. Failure to have unanimous approval of such informal action or to give proper notice is fatal to actions attempted by the board of directors.

Traditionally, a director was forbidden to vote on any matter in which he had a personal interest. Even though his vote was not necessary to carry the proposition considered, many courts would regard any action voidable if it was taken as a result of that vote. Some courts went so far as to hold that if he was present at the meeting, favorable action was not binding. Most courts held that if his presence was required to make a quorum, no transaction in which he was interested could be acted upon. These rather severe rules were developed so that directors would not be tempted to use their position to profit at the expense of the corporation.

Today, many of the traditional rules on director voting and participation have been relaxed somewhat. The trend of the law is to allow interested directors to be present and to be counted as a part of the quorum. Actions taken with interested directors are valid if the participating director's interest is fully and completely disclosed, provided the action is approved by a majority of disinterested directors. The problem of acting in good faith is discussed later in this chapter.

CASE

This is a derivative action brought on behalf of the corporation against certain directors to prevent the payment of a real estate commission. The corporation had seven directors. The real property owned by the corporation had been managed by Strand Management and was later managed by Helmsley-Spear. A contest had developed to decide which management firm was entitled to a commission. One plaintiff was the sole owner of Strand, and three of the defendants were officers of Helmsley. The board of directors held a special meeting on the commission matter, and by a vote of four to two agreed to a resolution to pay the commission to Helmsley. The vote was as follows: two of the three directors who were officers of Helmsley voted for the resolution; two directors who had no interest in either company voted in favor of the resolution; the plaintiff, owner of Strand, voted against the resolution, as did one director who had no interest in either company; one director was absent. The final vote, not counting the votes of the interested directors, was two in favor and one against.

ISSUE Was the resolution properly adopted?

DECISION Yes.

REASONS 1. The resolution was not invalid because of the participation of interested directors, but the interested directors *may* be liable for having participated in a transaction for which they derived an indirect personal benefit.

2. A majority of disinterested directors voted for the resolution.

3. A quorum of disinterested directors is not required.

Rapoport v. Schneider, 278 N.E.2d 642 (N.Y.) 1972.

Compensation

The charter, bylaws, or a resolution by the shareholders usually stipulates payment of directors' fees. If not, service as a director is uncompensated. Directors who are appointed as officers of the corporation should have their salaries fixed at a meeting of the shareholders or in the bylaws. Because directors are not supposed to vote on any matter in which they have a personal interest, director officers of small corporations usually vote on salaries for each other but not their own, and the action to determine salaries should be ratified by the shareholders in order to ensure the validity of the employment contracts.

Liabilities of directors

The directors of a corporation may have personal liability both in tort and in the contract. The principles of the law of agency are applicable; liability is usually to the corporation, although it may extend to shareholders and third parties as well. Officers of corporations may also have personal liability, and the principles herein discussed are applicable to officers as well as to directors.

The liability of corporate officers and directors for tortious conduct is predicated upon basic common law principles. A director who participates in fraudulent conduct by the corporation has personal liability to the third party on the usual common law tort theories, as does any other agent or servant. Moreover, the director need not personally commit fraud. He is liable if he sanctions or approves it.

The liability of corporate directors is most frequently based on a violation of the fiduciary duties owed to the corporation. A director occupies a position of trust and confidence with respect to the corporation and cannot, by reason of his position, directly or indirectly derive any personal benefits that are not enjoyed by the corporation or the shareholders. Several statutes impose liability on directors and officers.

CASE

A Michigan statute requires all corporations to provide funds to meet any worker's compensation claim presented by an employee. A failure to so provide, by insurance or otherwise, renders the officers and directors jointly and severally liable. P was injured during the course of his employment with the corporate defendant and was awarded 215 weeks of compensation. Shortly thereafter, the corporation went bankrupt without paying P's claim. P seeks to hold the directors and officers personally liable.

ISSUE Are the officers and directors of the bankrupt corporation personally liable?

DECISION Yes.

REASONS
1. The state statute allows worker's compensation claimants with unsatisfied awards to hold corporate officers and directors personally liable.
2. The statute reflects the public policy that a corporation should at least have worker's compensation insurance sufficient to meet any claims of an injured employee.

Wyrybkowski v. Cobra Pre-Hung Doors, Inc., 239 N.W.2d 660 (Mich.) 1976.

Officers and directors who have responsibility for federal withholding and social security taxes may be liable to the federal government for failure to collect and transfer these taxes for their employees. Likewise, a director or officer is subject to third-party liability for aiding a corporation in such acts as patent, copyright, or trademark infringements, unfair competition, antitrust violations, violation of the laws relating to discrimination, or violations of the securities laws. They are also personally liable when they issue stock as fully paid when it is not paid in full or when dividends are declared without the requisite retained earnings.

The law requires that a director perform his duties in good faith and in a manner that he reasonably believes to be in the best interests of the corporation. A director is also required to exercise care that an ordinarily prudent person in a like position would use under similar circumstances. These standards of "good faith" and "due care" arise out of the fiduciary relationship existing between the corporation and its directors and the duty of loyalty that exists in such relationships. They are discussed further in the sections that follow.

Good faith

The duty of loyalty or the duty to act in good faith prohibits directors from acting with a conflict of interest. The most common violation of this duty occurs when a director enters into a contract with, or personally deals with, the corporation. A conflict of interest also arises in transactions between the director's corporation and another entity in which he may be a director, employee, investor, or one who is otherwise interested. In all circumstances, the director or officer must fully disclose his conflict of interest to the corporation. If he fails to do so, the contract may be rescinded.

At common law, such a contract was voidable unless it was shown to be approved by a disinterested board and "fair" to the corporation, in that its terms were as favorable as those available from any other person. Under some modern statutes, the transaction is valid if it is approved, with knowledge of the material facts, by a vote of disinterested directors or shareholders or if the director can show it to be "fair."

The good-faith requirement is also lacking when a director or officer takes for himself an opportunity that the corporation should have had. A director must present all possible corporate opportunities to the corporation first. Only after disinterested, informed directors have determined that the corporation should not pursue such opportunities can a director pursue them for his own benefit. If a corporate director acquires property for himself, knowing the corporation desires it, he breaches his fiduciary relation to the corporation, and it may obtain the property.

Three other common conflict-of-interest situations are resolved by the same fiduciary standards set out above. The first involves compensation for officer directors, which was previously discussed. The second conflict arises when the incumbent directors become engaged in a proxy contest to preserve their positions. It is generally recognized that the corporation cannot pay the expense of a proxy fight. Only if a shareholder vote is concerned with a matter of corporate policy can corporate funds be used for proxy fights. Third, a fiduciary duty arises when a director who is also a majority shareholder sells control of the corporation to another. Although the director can and should resign his position upon the sale, he may be liable for placing the corporation in the hands of unscrupulous buyers if, for example, he had warning of the intentions of the buyer to loot the corporation.

Due care

In its simplest terms, the duty of care is synonymous with a duty not to be negligent. The standard may be stated in a variety of ways, but the most common is that a director must exercise the degree of care that an ordinarily prudent man would exercise in managing his own affairs. The standard of care varies with the size and type of the corporation. In large corporations, many duties must be delegated; thus, intimate knowledge of details by the directors is not possible. In corporations invested with a public interest—such as insurance companies, banks, building and loan associations, and public utilities—rigid supervision and specific obligations are imposed upon directors. If a director fails to exercise the requisite degree of care and skill, the corporation will have a right of action against him for resulting losses.

Since many directors are not actively engaged in the day-to-day operation of the business, the law recognizes that they need to rely on others for much of the information used in decision making. In performing his duties, a director is entitled to rely on information, opinions, reports, and statements of others—officers and employees whom the director reasonably believes to be reliable and competent in the matters presented. A director may also rely on legal counsel, public accountants, and other expert professionals. Finally, a director may also rely on committees of the board if they act within the designated authority and he reasonably believes that they merit confidence. A director does not fulfill his duties and does not act in good faith if he has knowledge that would cause the reliance to be unwarranted.

The purpose of the foregoing attitude is to allow directors to use their best business judgment without incurring liability for honest mistakes. Directors must make difficult policy decisions, and they should not have liability if their decisions are based on information that later turns out to be false.

Directors are liable to the corporation for negligence in management. Since no duty runs to third-party creditors, there is no liability to them or to the shareholders. Of course, a shareholder may enforce this liability through a derivative suit.

CASE

P held a corporate note secured by a chattel mortgage and by a mortgage on real property. The note was not paid, so a foreclosure suit was instituted. The foreclosure sale did not bring enough to satisfy the obligation. P brought action against D's, the officers and directors of the corporation, alleging that they had mismanaged the corporate business. The lower court ruled that P, as a creditor, had no standing to sue D's on a theory of negligence.

ISSUE Do creditors of a corporation have a claim against officers and directors for *negligent* mismanagement of its affairs?

DECISION No.

REASONS

1. Directors or officers may be liable to the corporation or shareholders for mismanagement of the business of the corporation or waste of its assets, but they are not liable to its creditors for mere mismanagement or waste of assets constituting a wrong or breach of duty to the corporation.
2. A creditor of a corporation may not maintain a personal action at law against the officers or directors of a corporation who have, by their mismanagement or negligence, committed a wrong against the corporation to the consequent damage of the creditor. The reason given for the rule is the entire lack of privity between the parties.
3. The duty to exercise diligence and care is one owed to the corporation, and it is elementary law

that one person cannot maintain an action against another for a wrong to a third person who is injured only incidentally.

Equitable Life & Casualty Insurance Co. v. Inland Printing Co., 454 P.2d 162 (Utah) 1971.

Indemnification and insurance

In recent years, dissenting shareholders, public-interest groups, and government regulators have caused a dramatic increase in the number of lawsuits filed against directors and officers of publicly held corporations. Many of the lawsuits result from the failure of directors to prevent activities such as bribery of foreign officials and illegal political contributions. Most large corporations carry liability insurance for directors, and their costs for this insurance are soaring because of the increased number of suits.

In order to reimburse directors and officers for the expenses of defending lawsuits if the insurance is nonexistent or inadequate, most states provide by statute for indemnification by the corporation. The Model Business Corporation Act provides that the standard for indemnification is that the director must have "acted in good faith and in a manner he reasonably believed to be in or not opposed to the best interests of the corporation" and if a criminal action, "had no reasonable cause to believe his conduct was unlawful." The indemnification is automatic if the director has been successful in the defense of any action.

Corporate Stock

A certificate of stock is written evidence of the ownership of a certain number of shares of stock of a corporation. It shows upon its face the character of the interest and the method by which it may be transferred. The certificate is the physical evidence that the corporation recognizes a certain person as being a shareholder with rights in the corporation; primarily, the right to share in profits, to participate indirectly in the control of the corporation, and to receive a portion of the assets at time of dissolution. A share of stock is representative of an investment made in the corporation, but it gives the holder no right to share in the active management of the business. The general rules of law applicable to personal property are applicable to stock.

Stock must be distinguished from a *bond.* A bond, unlike stock, is an obligation of the corporation to pay a certain sum of money in the future at a specified rate of interest. It is comparable to a corporation's promissory note. Corporate bonds are often secured by a mortgage on the assets of the corporation; but many corporate bonds, called *debentures,* do not have such security. A bondholder is a creditor of the corporation, whereas a shareholder is an owner of the corporation. A shareholder has a right to receive dividends if they are declared by the board of directors and to participate in the assets of the corporation after all creditors have been paid. A bondholder has no right to vote or to participate in the management and control of a corporation unless, upon insolvency, such rights are given by contract. A shareholder, in the absence of contractual limitations, has a right to participate in management to the extent of electing the directors and voting on matters such as dissolution.

Kinds of stock

Common stock is the simplest type of corporate stock. It entitles the owner to share in the control, profits, and assets of the corporation in proportion to the amount of common stock held. Such a shareholder has no advantage, priority, or preference over any other class of shareholders unless otherwise specified.

Preferred stock has priority over other classes of stock in claiming dividends or assets on dissolution. The most important right given to a preferred shareholder is the right to receive a certain specified dividend, even though the earnings are not sufficient to pay like dividends to common shareholders.

The statutes of most states provide that a corporation may issue stock with *no par value.* The value of no-par stock is determined by its sale price in the open market or by the price set by the directors as a "stated value." Shareholders, creditors of the corporation, and the public are not misled or prejudiced by this type of stock, because there is no holding out that the stock has any particular face value. All persons dealing in no-par stock are put on notice that they should investigate the corporation's assets and its financial condition. Stock with no par value represents its proportionate part of the total assets of the corporation.

A *stock warrant* is a certificate that gives its holder the right to subscribe for and purchase a given number of shares of stock in a corporation at a stated price. It is usually issued in connection with the sale of other shares of stock or of bonds, although the law of some states permits the issuance of stock warrants entirely separate and apart from the sale of other securities. Warrants are transferable. The option to purchase contained in the warrant may or may not be limited as to time or otherwise conditioned. Warrants have value and can readily be sold on the market in the same fashion as other securities.

Watered stock is stock that has been issued as fully paid, when in fact its full par value has not been paid in money, property, or services. The original owner of watered stock has liability for the unpaid portion of its stated value. If Catherine exchanges property worth $200 for 1,000 shares of $1 par value stock, she owes the corporation $800. If the corporation becomes insolvent, a creditor may collect the money.

The liability for watered stock arises because the capital stock of a corporation represents the total par value of all the shares of the corporation (plus the stated value of no-par stock). The public, including corporate creditors, has a right to assume that the capital stock issued has been paid for in full. The corporation in effect represents that assets have been received in payment equal in amount to its issued capital stock. If stock is issued in excess of the actual assets in money value received for it by the corporation, there is watered stock.

Treasury stock is that which has been issued by the corporation for value and returned to the corporation by gift or purchase. It may be sold at any price, including below par, and the proceeds returned to the treasury of the corporation for working capital. It differs from stock originally issued below par in that the purchaser is not liable for the difference between par and the sale price. It may be sold at any price the company sees fit to charge.

Dividends

Although a shareholder has a right to share in dividends when declared, whether or not a dividend is declared is within the discretion of the board of directors. Shareholders are not entitled to the payment of a dividend simply because earned surplus exists. The board of directors may see fit to continue the profits in the business for the purpose of expansion, but it must act reasonably and in good faith. Where fraud or a gross abuse of discretion is shown, and there are profits out of which dividends may be declared, the shareholders may compel the board of directors to declare dividends. Before there is a right to interfere by asking a court to order the payment of dividends, however, it must be clear that the board of directors has illegally, wantonly, and without justification refused to declare a dividend.

When a cash dividend is declared, it becomes a debt of the corporation. It will be paid to the person whose name appears on the corporate stock records as the owner of the share on the record date the dividend is payable. This is known as the *ex-dividend date.* A *cash dividend,* once its declaration has been made public, may not be rescinded. A declaration of dividends is proper so long as it does not impair the capital stock. Any declaration that reduces the net assets of the corporation below the outstanding capital stock is illegal.

Dividends are permissible only after provision has been made for all expenses, including depreciation. In industries with wasting or depleting assets, such as mines and oil wells, it is not necessary to allow for the depletion before declaring dividends.

Directors are personally liable to creditors for dividends improperly declared. In most states, shareholders who receive such dividends may be compelled to return them.

A *stock dividend* is a transfer of retained earnings to capital and is used when the earnings are required for growth of the business. Stock dividends of the issuing company are not taxable income to shareholders. A *stock split* differs from a *stock dividend* in that in the former there is no transfer of surplus to capital but only a reduction in par value and an increase in the number of shares.

Right to transfer stock

The right to transfer freely one's share in the ownership of the business is inherent in corporations. It is one of the features of corporate life that distinguishes it from a partnership. Although shareholders of "close" corporations often attempt by agreement or bylaw to limit the group of potential purchasers, a corporate bylaw that makes shares of stock transferrable only to the corporation or to those approved by the board of directors is unenforceable. It places too severe a restraint upon the alienation of property. Society is best protected when property may be transferred freely, but an agreement or bylaw approved by all shareholders to the effect that no transfer of stock shall be made until it has first been offered to the other shareholders or to the corporation is generally enforced. Notice of the bylaw or agreement should be set forth in the stock certificate because an innocent purchaser without notice of the restriction on alienation receives ownership free from the restriction.

In a close corporation, sometimes the buy and sell agreements between shareholders go even further than a right of first refusal. They may provide for matters such as salary continuation in the event of death or disability and the amount of dividends to be paid in the future. Some agreements even commit the shareholders to vote for certain persons in the election of directors. Such agreements are valid in closely held corporations, providing the duration of the agreement is not so long that it becomes contrary to public policy and providing the agreement does not adversely affect minority interests in the corporation. These agreements are used by the majority owners to ensure the election of the desired board of directors. Corporations are governed by the republican principle that the whole are bound by lawful acts of the majority. It is not against public policy nor is it dishonest for shareholders to contract for the purpose of control.

Transfer of stock and other investment securities

A share of stock is personal property, and the owner has the right to transfer it just as he may transfer any other personal property. A share of stock is generally transferred by an endorsement and the delivery of the certificate of stock and by surrender of the certificate to the stock transfer agent for reissue.

CASE

On June 18, 1973, T executed an assignment of a stock certificate of D Corporation representing 60 shares of 4½ percent preferred stock, and he gave the certificate to P. On February 21, 1976, T told P that the stock certificate had to be exchanged for other stock (6½ percent preferred stock) paying a higher dividend. P gave T the stock certificate, but the 60 shares of 6½ percent preferred stock were never delivered to P, and T refused to return the 4½ percent stock certificate.

P sues the D Corporation, contending that he is entitled to dividends as of June 18, 1973. D contends that P's complaint does not state a cause of action, because there is no allegation that the certificate was ever presented for registration.

ISSUE Is a party entitled to a transfer of shares of stock in the absence of a showing that the certificate was presented to the transfer agent?

DECISION No.

REASONS

1. Article 8 of the Uniform Commerical Code governs transactions in securities that are in registered form.
2. A registrar has a duty to register a transfer of ownership of a security in registered form only upon satisfaction of several conditions including presentation of the security with a request to register transfer.
3. P did not present the certificate; therefore, this condition precedent was not satisfied.

Wanland v. C. E. Thompson Co., 338 N.E. 2d 1012 (Ill. App.) 1978.

A share may be transferred or assigned by a bill of sale or by any other method that will pass title to a *chose in action* (a right to recover money or property from another through judicial procedure) or other intangible property. Whenever a share of stock is sold and a new stock certificate issued, the name of the new owner is entered on the stock records of the corporation. In a small corporation, the secretary of the corporation usually handles all transfers of stock and also the canceling of old certificates and issuing of new. Large corporations, in which there are hundreds and even thousands of transactions, employ transfer agents. The transfer agents transfer stock, cancel old certificates, issue new ones, keep an up-to-date list of the names of shareholders of the corporation, distribute dividends, mail out shareholders' notices, and perform many functions to assist the corporation secretary. Stock exchange rules provide that corporations listing stock for sale must maintain a transfer agency and registry, operated and maintained under exchange regulations. The registrar of stock is an agent of the corporation whose duty is to see that no stock certificates are issued in excess of the authorized capitalization of the corporation.

The volume of transactions in stock sold publicly is so large that many techniques have been developed to reduce the cost and confusion of transfers. In one such technique, title to the stock is held in the house name of a brokerage firm. If the firm has transactions both with buyers and sellers of the same stock, a transfer can be effected by a bookkeeping entry, and new certificates need not be issued. The brokerage firm will solicit proxies and vote the stock in accordance with the instructions of the actual owner. As another means of reducing transfers, many companies are discouraging small shareholders from investing. A company may try to purchase back the stock of every holder of ten shares or less. Such a policy will greatly reduce corporate administrative expenses.

Many people are advocating replacing stock certificates with ''punch cards'' that can be easily transferred by computer. It is anticipated that in the near future, formal stock certificates may disappear from use by large corporations.

Article 8 of the Uniform Commercial Code deals with investment securities. It must be considered along with the blue-sky laws on issues concerning the transfer of stock.

The general approach of Article 8 is that securities are negotiable instruments and that bona fide purchasers have greater rights than they would have ''if the things bought were chattels or simple contracts.'' The particular rules of Article 3 that relate to the establishment of preferred status for commercial paper are applied to securities. Defenses of the issuer are generally not effective against a purchaser for value who has received the securities without being given notice of the particular defense raised.

A bona fide purchaser is one who purchases in good faith and without notice of any adverse claim. He is the equivalent of a holder in due course. A bona fide purchaser takes free of ''adverse claims,'' which include a claim that a transfer was wrongful or that some other person is the owner of, or has an interest in, the security.

REVIEW QUESTIONS AND PROBLEMS

1. What is the principal matter on which shareholders are entitled to vote?
2. Define the following terms: *cumulative voting, preemptive right, derivative suit, stock dividend, watered stock,* and *treasury stock.*
3. Pam is a stockholder in ABAC Corporation. She would like to obtain a list of stockholders before the annual stockholders' meeting, so that she may try to persuade them to vote for a corporate merger that the board of directors opposes. Is Pam entitled to inspect the books and records of the company and prepare a list of stockholders? Why?
4. A corporation board authorized a director, Zoro, to negotiate the purchase of some land. Instead, Zoro secretly bought the land himself and sold it to the corporation at a profit. After learning of the deceit, the corporation failed to act. Do the minority shareholders have any remedy? Explain.
5. On March 1, a company declared a cash dividend of $1.00 per share, payable on June 1 to all stockholders of record on May 1. On April 10, Ann sold 10 shares of her stock to Bob, but the transfer was not recorded on the corporation's books until May 15. To whom will the company pay the dividend? Who is entitled to the dividend? Explain.
6. A creditor sued the directors of a corporation because of alleged negligent mismanagement of corporate business. In defense, the directors contend that the creditor does not have standing to sue. Are the directors correct? Why?
7. Abner owned a majority of the stock of Lum Company, and he ran the corporation by himself. The balance of the stock was owned by Abner's brother and sister, who agreed to sell all their stock to him. At the time of the purchase, Abner was negotiating a sale of the company, but he did not reveal this fact to his brother and sister. The sale of the company resulted in a great profit to Abner. The brother and sister brought suit to recover the difference. Should the brother and sister succeed? Why?
8. All stockholders were present at the annual stockholders' meeting of a corporation whose bylaws required only a majority of shareholders to constitute a quorum. During the meeting, two stockholders who owned a majority of the stock withdrew from the meeting while it was in progress. Following their withdrawal, the remaining stockholders elected five new members to the board of directors. Should the election of the directors be invalidated? Why?
9. Directors of a nonprofit automobile club, which provided automobile service and other benefits to its membership under a franchise from the Automobile Association of America (AAA), purchased the Athens Insurance Agency for themselves. The club already owned the Bogart Insurance Agency, located in a different county, and the Athens Agency operated in a manner indistinguishable from Bogart. Both agencies referred leads to each other. Athens advertised as if it were affiliated with the club and received free advertising space in the club's newsletter. When the membership learned of the acquisition several years later, a shareholder brought suit, contending the directors had breached their fiduciary obligation. Should the directors be held liable? Why?
10. Peter sued the Dallas Company for breach of contract. Peter was a director of Dallas Company, and his presence and vote were necessary to the approval of the contract with him. Dallas Company contends that the contract is not binding. Is the company correct? Explain.

41

Corporate Dissolutions, Mergers, and Consolidations

Corporate existence terminates upon the expiration of the period set forth in the charter or upon the voluntary or involuntary dissolution of the corporation. Voluntary dissolutions may occur when corporations consolidate or merge. In a *consolidation,* corporate existence technically ceases for both corporations when the new corporation is formed. In a *merger,* it ceases for the corporation that is merged into the continuing one. This chapter will discuss these various methods for terminating the corporate existence. Since a corporation is a creation of a statute, it can be dissolved only according to statute. Thus the statute of the state of incorporation is very important.

Most corporate charters provide for perpetual existence. If the charter stipulates that the corporation shall exist for a definite period, it automatically terminates at the expiration of the period, unless application to continue the corporation is made and approved by the authority granting the charter.

Voluntary dissolutions

A corporation that has obtained its charter but has not commenced business may be dissolved by its incorporators. The incorporators file articles of dissolution with the state, and a certificate of dissolution is issued if all fees are paid and the articles are in order.

A corporation that has commenced business may be voluntarily dissolved either by the written consent of *all* its shareholders or by corporate action instituted by its board of directors and approved by the requisite percentage (usually two-thirds) of the shareholders. The board action, usually in the form of a recommendation, directs that the issue be submitted to the shareholders. A meeting of shareholders is called to consider the dissolution issue, and if the vote is in favor of it to the degree required by statute, the officers follow the statutory procedures for dissolution.

These procedures require the corporate officers to file a statement of intent to dissolve. The statement is filed with the state of incorporation, and it includes either the consent of all shareholders or the resolutions instituted by the board of directors. Upon filing the statement of intent to dissolve, the corporation must cease to carry on its business, except for winding up its affairs, even though corporate existence continues until a certificate of dissolution is issued by the state.

The filing of a statement of intent to dissolve is not irrevocable. If the shareholders change their minds before the articles of dissolution are issued, the decision may be revoked by filing a statement of revocation of voluntary dissolution proceedings. When such a statement is filed, the corporation may resume its business.

In winding up its affairs, the corporation must give notice to all creditors of the corporation. Directors become personally liable for any debt of which notice is not given.

CASE

D had been a director of the Parker Laundry Company, a corporation. Personal property taxes levied against the corporation were not paid for the last two years of the corporation's existence. The corporation filed a notice of intent to dissolve with the state but failed to mail a notice of such action to the county taxing authorities. The county brought this action against D personally after the corporation was dissolved.

ISSUE Is the director personally liable?

DECISION Yes.

REASON A director is personally liable for debts of the corporation when the required procedures on dissolution (notice to creditors in this case) are not followed.

People v. Parker, 197 N.E.2d 30 (Ill.) 1964.

In dissolution proceedings, corporate assets are first used to pay debts. After all debts are paid, the remainder is distributed proportionately among the shareholders. If there are insufficient assets to pay all debts, a receiver will be appointed by a court, and the proceedings will be similar to those of involuntary dissolutions, discussed later.

When all funds are distributed, the corporation will prepare duplicate "articles of dissolution" and forward them to the state for approval. When signed by the appropriate state official, usually the secretary of state, one copy is filed with state records, and one copy is returned to the corporation to be kept with the corporate records.

Involuntary Dissolutions

Proceedings commenced by the state

The state, having created the corporation, has the right to institute proceedings to cancel the charter. Suits by a state to cancel or forfeit a charter are known as *quo warranto* proceedings. They are filed by the attorney general, usually at the request of the secretary of state, although they are sometimes filed at the request of a private party.

Quo warranto proceedings may be brought by the attorney general if a corporation (1) did not file its annual report, (2) neglected to pay its franchise tax and license fees, (3) procured its charter by fraud, (4) abused and misused its authority, (5) failed to appoint and maintain a registered agent for the service of notices and process or has not informed the state of the name and address of its registered agent, or (6) ceased to perform its corporate functions for a long period of time. By proper proceedings and without charter forfeiture, the attorney general may also enjoin a corporation from engaging in a business not authorized by its charter. If a corporation is dissolved for any of the foregoing reasons, it may not continue its business. Its officers and directors may wind up the business, but any other contract is null and void.

CASE

P executed a note secured by a mortgage on real estate to D Corporation in payment of home improvements. At the time the documents were executed, D's certificate of incorporation had been revoked for failure to file annual reports. Later, the corporation was reinstated.

P filed suit to have the note and mortgage declared null and void because D was not in fact a corporation at the time they were executed.

ISSUE Did the reinstatement of the corporation retroactively validate the contracts with the corporation?

DECISION No.

REASONS
1. A state statute authorizes dissolution of corporations by proclamation for failure to file annual reports and to pay the fees for them. Upon the issuance of a proclamation, the articles of incorporation are void and all powers are inoperative except for winding up the corporate affairs.
2. The corporation therefore lacked capacity to contract, and the legal instruments were void.
3. The purpose of revocation is obviously to prohibit a corporation from enjoying the privileges of that status when it has failed to perform its resultant responsibilities. Revocation is a disability imposed on a corporation as a penalty. It would deprive the statute of its force and encourage a corporation to default on its taxes, fees, and filing its annual reports if, by subsequent compliance, the corporation could at its convenience completely erase the effects of the penalty. Reinstatement therefore does not operate retroactively.

Accurate Const. Co. v. Washington, 378 A.2d 681 (D.C.) 1977.

Proceedings commenced by shareholders

Involuntary dissolution may be ordered by a court of equity at the request of a shareholder when the directors are deadlocked in the management of corporate affairs or the shareholders are deadlocked and unable to elect a board of directors. Deadlocks require proof that irreparable injury is likely and that the deadlock cannot be broken.

The general rule throughout the country is that a minority shareholder or group of shareholders of a going and solvent corporation cannot, without statutory authority, maintain a suit to have it dissolved. Most states have statutes that authorize courts of equity to liquidate a corporation at the request of a shareholder when it is proved that those in control of the corporation are acting illegally, fraudulently, or oppressively. It is so difficult to define oppressive conduct that each case must be decided on its own facts. In the early law, courts followed the *robber baron theory,* which allowed the majority to do anything, including a squeeze out of minority stockholders, as long as no specific laws were violated and no actual fraud was committed. The robber baron theory was based on the concept that the majority owed no fiduciary duty to minority shareholders.

Modern decisions tend to reject the robber baron theory. Actions intended to squeeze out or freeze out minority shareholders may provide grounds for dissolution or other equitable relief. Minority shareholders have been granted relief when the majority have refused to declare dividends but have paid out all profits to themselves in the form of salaries and bonuses. Relief was also granted in a recent case where the majority shareholders of a corporation that was *not* in need of funds sold additional stock in order to dilute the percentage of control of the minority, who the majority knew were unable financially to exercise their preemptive right.

Today, conduct that is not illegal or fraudulent may be held to be oppressive. Although controlling shareholders in a closely held corporation are not fiduciaries in the strict sense of the word, the general concepts of fiduciary duties are useful in deciding if conduct is oppressive. The law imposes equitable limitations on dominant shareholders. They are under a duty to refrain from using their control to profit for themselves at the expense of the minority. Repeated violations of these duties will serve as a ground for dissolution. Even though it takes substantially less evidence to justify dissolution of a partnership than of a close corporation, the trend is to treat the issues as quite similar. Oppressive conduct may be summarized as conduct that is burdensome, harsh, and wrongful. It is a substantial deviation from fair dealing and a violation of fair play. It is a violation of the fiduciary duty of good faith in those states that recognize such a duty.

All states allow minority shareholders to obtain dissolution when it is established that corporate assets are being wasted or looted or the corporation is unable to carry out its purposes. Some states have by statute broadened the grounds for court-ordered dissolution. These states allow courts to order dissolution when it is reasonably necessary for the protection of the rights or interests of minority shareholders.

CASE

A father and his two sons formed a corporation to conduct a general contracting business. The business had previously been conducted as a partnership, and each shareholder had an equal number of shares in the corporation. Three years later, P, one of the sons, ceased to be employed by the corporation. There had been a dispute, and P had been removed as an officer and director of the corporation. The corporation pays no dividends but invests its profits in real estate. There was no evidence of abuse of authority or persistent unfairness toward P.

P filed suit to dissolve the corporation. California law allows courts to order dissolution where "liquidation is reasonably necessary" for the protection of the rights or interests of any substantial number of shareholders.

ISSUE Will the corporation be dissolved?

DECISION Yes.

REASONS
1. Under the statute, dissolution is not limited to cases of deadlock, persistent mismanagement, or proof of unfairness.
2. Dissolution may be ordered when required to assure fairness to minority shareholders. The law does not authorize dissolution at will. The minority shareholders must convince the court that fairness requires the drastic relief of dissolution.
3. Here, the hostility among the family members was extreme. P received no salary, dividends, or other return on his investment. In all fairness, his investment should be returned.

Stumpf v. C.S. Stumpf & Sons, Inc., 120 Cal. Rptr. 671 (1975).

Even in states with laws similar to the one in the foregoing case, a corporation will not be dissolved by a court for errors of judgment or because the court confronted with a question of policy would decide it differently than would the directors. Dissolutions by decree at the request of a shareholder are rare; but as previously noted, the trend is to give greater protection to the minority shareholders and to reject the robber baron theory.

Proceedings commenced by creditors

A corporation is in the same position as a natural person insofar as its creditors are concerned. A suit may be brought against it; and when a judgment is obtained, an execution may be levied against its property, which may then be sold. Corporate assets may be attached; and if the corporation has no property subject to execution, its assets may be traced by a bill in a court of equity.

The creditors have no right, because they are creditors, to interfere with the management of the business. A creditor who has an unsatisfied judgment against a corporation may bring a bill in equity to set aside conveyances and transfers of corporate property that have been fraudulently transferred for the purpose of delaying and hindering creditors. Creditors may also, under the above circumstances, ask for a receiver to take over the assets of the corporation and to apply them to the payment of debts.

When there is an unsatisfied execution and it is established that the corporation is insolvent, a court may order a dissolution. The same is true if the corporation admits its insolvency. Dissolution in such cases proceeds in the same manner as if instituted by the state or by voluntary proceedings when insolvent. These procedures are discussed in the next section.

Procedure on involuntary dissolution

In liquidating a corporation, courts have the full range of judicial powers at their disposal. They may issue injunctions, appoint receivers, and take whatever steps are necessary to preserve the corporate assets for the protection of creditors and shareholders. The receiver will usually collect the assets, including any amount owed to the corporation for shares. The receiver will then sell the assets, pay the debts and expenses of liquidation, and if any funds are left, divide them proportionately among the shareholders. Courts usually require creditors to prove their claims in court in a manner similar to that in bankruptcy proceedings. When all funds in the hands of a receiver are paid out, the court issues a decree of dissolution that is filed with the secretary of state. Funds due persons who cannot be located are deposited with the state treasurer and held for a specified number of years. If not claimed by the creditor or shareholder within the declared period, the funds belong to the state.

Liability of shareholders on dissolution

As a general rule, shareholders are not liable for the debts of the firm, but a shareholder who has not paid for his stock in full is liable to the receiver or to a creditor for the unpaid balance. Statutes in most states allow creditors to reach assets of the former corporation that are in the hands of shareholders. The assets of a corporation are a fund for the payment of creditors, and the directors must manage this fund for their benefit. The liability of shareholders is often predicated upon the theory that the transfer of corporate assets on dissolution is in fraud of creditors, and a shareholder knowingly receiving such assets ought to have liability.

Claims that existed before dissolution may be enforced after dissolution by statute in most states. For a specified period after dissolution, remedies survive against a corporation, its directors, officers, and shareholders. Suits against the corporation may be prosecuted or defended in the corporate name. The statutory period is not a statute of limitation; it is simply the period during which claims survive. A judgment on such a claim may be collected from property distributed to shareholders on dissolution, or the creditor may proceed directly against the shareholder receiving the property.

CASE

P was injured in a laundromat. The laundromat was incorporated, and D was the sole shareholder. It was insured under a $100,000 liability policy. P obtained a $150,000 judgment against the corporation, on which the insuror paid $100,000. D liquidated the assets of the corporation and as sole shareholder retained the proceeds of the liquidation. P filed suit against D individually for the $50,000 of the judgment not covered by the insurance.

ISSUE May a judgment creditor of a dissolved corporation proceed against the sole shareholder for the value of the liquidated assets of the corporation necessary to satisfy the judgment?

DECISION Yes.

REASONS
1. State law requires that a sufficient amount of a dissolved corporation's assets be retained in order to pay the claims of creditors.
2. The property of the corporation is a fund for the payment of the corporation's debts. The directors and sole shareholder must manage the fund for the interest of the creditors. To the extent they fail to do so, they are personally liable to the extent of the corporate assets in their hands.

United States Fire Ins. Co. v. Morejon, 338 So.2d 223 (Fla. App.) 1976.

Consolidations and Mergers

Definitions

Consolidation is the uniting of two or more corporations, whereby a new corporation is created and the old entities are dissolved. The new corporation takes title to all the property, rights, powers, and privileges of the old corporations, subject to the liabilities and obligations of the old corporations.

In a *merger,* however, one of the corporations continues its existence but absorbs the other corporation, which ceases to have an independent existence. The continuing corporation may expressly or impliedly assume and agree to pay the debts and liabilities of the absorbed corporation, whose creditors become third-party creditor beneficiaries. By statute in most states, the surviving corporation is deemed to have assumed all the liabilities and obligations of the absorbed corporation. In recent years, this has been extended even to product liability claims arising out of sales by the former corporation.

Mergers and acquisitions comprise a major segment of the antitrust laws. This aspect will be discussed more fully in Chapter 44. They also are subject to the securities laws and to regulation by the SEC.

Procedures

The procedures for consolidations and mergers are statutory. Usually, the board of directors gives its approval by resolution that sets forth in detail all facts of the planned merger or consolidation. The plan is submitted to the shareholders for approval. Notice of the meeting typically includes the resolution passed by the directors. If proxies are submitted for the vote, proxy material must disclose all material facts required for an intelligent decision by the shareholders. In most states the shareholders must approve the plan by a two-thirds vote of all shares and two-thirds of each class if more than one class of stock is voting. If the consolidation or merger is approved by the shareholders of both corporations, articles of consolidation or articles of merger will be prepared and filed with the state. If the papers are in order and all fees are paid, a certificate of consolidation or a certificate of merger will be issued.

A shareholder who dissents from a consolidation or merger, and who makes his dissent a matter of record by serving a written demand that the corporation purchase his stock, is entitled to be paid the fair value of his stock on the day preceding the vote on the corporate action. Procedures are established for ascertaining the fair value and for a judicial decision of that issue if necessary. Among the factors to be considered in evaluating a dissenting shareholder's stock are the nature of the corporation, the market demand for the stock, the business of the corporation, its earnings, net assets, general economic conditions, the market prices of comparable companies, the market price and earnings ratio, management and policies, revenues for various contingencies, tax liabilities, and future earnings. A shareholder who dissents from a sale or exchange of all or substantially all the assets or property of the corporation, other than in the usual course of business, has the same right to be paid for his stock. When the statutory procedures are followed, the dissenting shareholder ceases to be a shareholder when notice is given; he then becomes a creditor.

CASE

D was a closely held corporation. The owners of a majority of the stock voted to merge the corporation with another corporation. P, a minority stockholder, dissented. The statute provides that a dissenting shareholder who objects to a merger is entitled to be paid the "fair value" of his shares on the date preceding the vote. P contended that the stock was worth $322 per share, but the corporation took the position that it was worth only $100 per share. The lower court found that the fair value was $230 per share.

ISSUE Was the lower court's determination of the fair value of the stock correct?

DECISION No. (The "fair value" of the stock was $138.65 per share.)

REASONS
1. There are three methods used by the court in determining the fair value of shares of dissenting shareholders: (a) the market value method, (b) the asset value method, and (c) the investment or earnings value method.
2. Although there was no established market for the stock, the average sale price over four years was $69 per share.
3. The fair market value of all assets minus all liabilities gave an asset value of $242.81 per share.
4. The earnings value or investment value method produced a value of zero, because the corporation had lost money for several years.
5. The court assigned weights to each system and computed the value as follows:

	Value ×	Weight =	Result
Asset	$242.81	50%	$121.40
Market	69.00	25	17.25
Earnings	0.00	25	0.00
			$138.65

Brown v. Hedahl's QB&R, Inc., 185 N.W.2d 249 (N.Dak.) 1971.

Tender offers create problems in valuing the stock of dissenting shareholders. Such offers usually include a premium, in order to overcome objections of many shareholders; but dissenting shareholders who refuse a tender offer and insist on a judicial determination of the fair value of shares are not entitled to receive the tender offer premium. A premerger tender offer price does not establish a floor on the amount that the court may fix as the value of shares in an appraisal proceeding, but it does have some evidentiary significance. Corporate stock is appraised on a case-by-case basis with a consideration of all three elements of value: stock market price, investment value, and net asset value. The weight to be given to each factor depends upon circumstances of each case. Fair value cannot be computed according to any precise mathematical formula. If the stock is regularly traded in an exchange, market value may be the dominant factor.

Statutes of the appropriate state may be strictly complied with, yet the courts may block a merger or acquisition. A merger may not be effected for the purpose of freezing out or squeezing out minority shareholders. If a merger has no valid business purpose other than the elimination of minority shareholders, courts will enjoin the merger on consolidation. Even if appraisal is an adequate remedy in the sense that the minority shareholders presumably can receive the investment value of their interest in the merged corporation, the policy favoring corporate flexibility is not furthered by permitting the elimination of minority interests for the benefit of the majority, when no benefit thereby accrues to the corporation. Moreover, the majority shareholders owe the minority shareholders a fiduciary obligation in dealing with corporate assets. This duty includes the protection of corporate interests and restraint from doing anything that would injure the corporation or deprive it of profits or the ability to exercise its powers. Since dissolution may cause these effects, the majority may not dissolve when the only purpose is to get rid of the minority.

REVIEW QUESTIONS AND PROBLEMS

1. What steps are required for a voluntary dissolution?
2. List four grounds on which the state may obtain involuntary dissolution.
3. What are the rights of a shareholder dissenting from a merger or consolidation?
4. Adams, the owner of all the capital stock of the Gazette Corporation, a newspaper business, sold all his shares to Burr and promised to serve as adviser to the newspaper for a period of five years in return for an annual salary of $20,000. After three years, Burr petitioned for dissolution, which was obtained. Does Adams have a right to collect the balance of the salary from the corporation? Explain.
5. Bob and David, father and son, entered into an agreement whereby each was a 50 percent stockholder of a close corporation operating a luncheonette. The agreement provided that in the event of the death of either party, this would constitute an automatic option to the survivor to purchase, at book value, the shares of stock of the deceased. Upon Bob's death, Ann, David's sister and administrator of Bob's estate, refuses to sell for the value shown on the books and creates a deadlock in management. Ann then petitions for dissolution. Should it be granted? Why?
6. The Paper Corporation breached a contract with Yates. A short while later, Paper merged with the Towel Corporation to form the Paper Towel Corporation. Can Yates collect damages from Paper Towel? Explain.
7. David was president of Music, Inc. He owned 53 percent of the common stock. David received a salary of $10,000 per year and bonuses of $7,000 per year. The corporation had a net worth of $100,000 and sales of $245,000. The net profit of the company had been under $2,000 each year, and dividends were either small or nonexistent. Minority shareholders brought suit to compel dissolution of the corporation on the ground of waste, alleging that the waste occurred in the payment of bonuses to David. Should the company be dissolved? Why?
8. Pauline, the past president of a dissolved corporation, brought suit against two shareholders of the corporation to recover the amount of her unpaid salary. The state statute provided that the shareholders are personally liable for unpaid salaries and wages of employees and laborers in an amount equal to the value of the stock owned by them. The stockholders contend that the statute is not applicable to the chief executive officer, who had complete control of the corporation. Should Pauline succeed? Why?
9. ABAC, Inc., owed $35,000 in personal property taxes to the city. The city agreed not to levy on the personal property of the corporation; in turn, ABAC, Inc., agreed to pay the delinquent taxes in installments. The directors then caused the corporation to move personal property outside the jurisdiction of the city and dissolved the corporation while disposing of the assets. The city brought suit to hold the directors personally liable for delinquent taxes. Are the directors liable? Why?
10. TAR Company purchased the assets of BAR Company. Pam was injured while using a defective power press manufactured by BAR Company. Pam brought a product liability suit against TAR Company. TAR contended that it was a corporate stranger to the manufacturer of the press and hence not liable. Should TAR Company be held liable? Why?

American Airlines

VIII

Government and Business

42

The Constitution and Business

The Constitution of the United States not only provides the foundation for our form of government but also contains numerous provisions that have a direct impact upon the legal environment in which business operates. Article I establishes the legislative branch of government, and Section 8 of Article I grants Congress numerous powers, including the power to tax and the power to regulate commerce. Article IV covers the relationship between the states and, in effect, prevents a state from becoming an area of economic isolation. Article VI contains the Supremacy Clause, which makes federal laws supreme over state laws when the two are in conflict. The Supremacy Clause frequently comes into play when states attempt to regulate a business activity that is also regulated by the federal government. Finally, the protections of the Bill of Rights generally apply to business as well as to private individuals. This chapter will discuss some of the more important constitutional concepts as they relate to business.

The Supremacy Clause

Article VI states in part: "This Constitution, and the Laws of the United States which shall be made in Pursuance thereof . . . shall be the supreme Law of the Land . . . ," thereby guaranteeing federal supremacy, even though the states created the federal government.

CASE

Arizona had a statute that suspended licenses of drivers who were unable to satisfy judgments, including bankrupts. P had filed a voluntary petition in bankruptcy and had duly scheduled a judgment debt arising out of a traffic accident. The Court in bankruptcy discharged P. P filed a complaint seeking to retain a driver's license.

ISSUE Under the Supremacy Clause, is the Arizona law invalid, being in conflict with the Bankruptcy Act?

DECISION Yes.

REASONS
1. The two provisions are in direct conflict; therefore, the Arizona Act is constitutionally invalid.
2. The purpose of the Bankruptcy Act is to give debtors new opportunity, unhampered by the pressure and discouragement of preexisting debt.
3. The challenged state statute stands as an obstacle to the accomplishment and execution of the full purposes and objectives of Congress.

Perez v. Campbell, 91 S.Ct. 1704 (1971).

The Contract Clause

Section 10 of Article I of the United States Constitution provides in part that no state shall pass any law impairing the obligation of contracts. This provision has no application to the federal government, which, in fact, frequently enacts laws and adopts regulations that affect existing contracts. The Department of Agriculture from time to time embargoes grain sales to foreign countries, usually as a result of problems in foreign affairs.

The limitation on state action impairing contracts has not been given a literal application. As a result of judicial interpretation, some state laws that affect existing contracts have been approved, especially when the law is passed to deal with a specific emergency situation. On the other hand, this constitutional provision does limit the alternatives available to state government and prevents the enactment of legislation that changes vested contract rights.

CASE

P, an Illinois corporation, maintained an office of 30 employees in Minnesota. P adopted a pension plan in 1963, qualified under Section 401 of the I.R.C., but retained the right to amend the plan or terminate it at any time and for any reason. In 1974, Minnesota enacted the Private Pension Benefits Protection Act. Under it, a private employer of 100 employees or more (at least one of whom was a Minnesota resident), who provided pension benefits under a plan meeting the qualification of Section 401 of the I.R.C., was subject to a "pension funding charge" if he terminated the plan or closed a Minnesota office. Shortly thereafter, P closed its Minnesota office. Several discharged employees then sought to collect a pension funding charge of $185,000 under the act. P brought suit for injunctive and declaratory relief, claiming that the act unconstitutionally impaired its contractual obligations to its employees under its pension plan.

ISSUE Does the Minnesota Private Pension Benefits Protection Act violate the Contract Clause of the United States Constitution?

DECISION Yes.

REASONS
1. The Contract Clause must be understood to impose some limits upon the power of a state to abridge existing contractual relationships, even in the exercise of its otherwise legitimate police power.
2. There was no showing that the severe disruption of contractual expectations was necessary to meet an important social problem.
3. There was a severe, permanent, immediate, and retroactive change in the affected contractual relationships.

Allied Structural Steel Co. v. Spannaus, 98 S.Ct. 2716 (1978).

The taxing power

The taxing power is used by government to raise revenue to defray its expenses. It apportions the cost of government among those who receive its benefits. The taxing power in the broad sense includes all charges and burdens imposed by government upon persons or property for the use and support of government.

Taxes are paid by those able to do so, in order that all persons may share in the general benefits of government. Thus, property can be taxed without an obvious personal benefit to the property owner. The theory supporting taxation is that since governmental functions are a necessity, the government has the right to compel persons and property within its jurisdiction to defray the costs of these functions. The payment of taxes gives no right to a taxpayer. The privilege of enjoying the protection and services of government is not based on taxes paid. As a matter of fact, many examples illustrate that those who receive the most from the government pay the least taxes.

The power of taxation is exercised by the legislative branch of the government. The only limitations on its exercise are found in federal and state constitutions. The fact that a tax may destroy a business or the value of property is no basis for a judicial determination that the tax is unconstitutional. The court must find that the tax violates some specific provision of the Constitution before the tax can be held invalid. The decision as to the wisdom or propriety of the tax is left to the legislature.

The taxing power is used to accomplish many goals other than raising revenue. Taxation is a very important form of regulation. Tax policy is a major ingredient in the efforts of government to regulate the economy. Depreciation allowances have been accelerated from time to time to bolster the economy by making additional cash available for business investment. The gasoline tax has been substantially increased in order to raise the price of gasoline and reduce consumption.

Tax laws are also used by the federal government to equalize competition among different businesses. The gasoline tax is an important part of the equalization of costs between truckers and other forms of transportation. The taxing power has been used to encourage uniform legislation among the states. States were encouraged to adopt unemployment compensation taxes by a federal law that gave a 90 percent credit on the federal tax for taxes paid to states.

The federal taxing power is also used to implement social policies. The federal government pays money to the states to encourage certain activities such as education, road building, and slum clearance. Persons in one part of the country may pay for social improvements in another as a direct result of the exercise of the taxing and spending powers of the federal government. An examination of the implementation policies of the federal government will reveal that many of them are tied directly to taxation.

Few questions are raised today concerning the *validity* of a federally imposed tax. The Sixteenth Amendment to the Constitution and the broad scope of the federal taxing power, which has been approved by the courts, eliminates most such issues. Of course, there is a considerable amount of litigation involving the *interpretation* and *application* of the federal tax laws and regulations. Great deference is given to the position taken by the Commissioner of Internal Revenue in such cases. Courts tend to hold that federal taxing laws are valid unless there is some clear constitutional infirmity.

The Import-Export Clause

Closely connected with the taxing power, the Import-Export Clause prohibits states from taxing imports and prohibits federal and state governments from directly taxing exports. Difficult questions often arise regarding when property ceases to be an import or becomes an export within the protection of this constitutional guarantee.

CASE

D assessed ad valorem property taxes against warehoused tires and tubes imported by P from France and Nova Scotia. P claimed that the assessments were prohibited by the Constitution provision "No state shall, without the Consent of Congress, deny any Imposts or Duties on Imports or Exports, except what may be absolutely necessary for executing its inspection Laws. . . ."

ISSUE Is the nondiscriminatory, ad valorem property tax assessment against imports constitutional?

DECISION Yes.

REASONS

1. States are prohibited from imposing property taxes on imported goods for three reasons: (a) the federal government must speak with one voice; (b) import revenues are major sources of federal revenue; (c) there must be harmony among the states.
2. A nondiscriminatory ad valorem property tax constitutes no danger to those three federal concerns.
3. Taxation is the quid pro quo for benefits conferred by the taxing state.

Michelin Tire Corp. v. Wages, 96 S.Ct. 535 (1976).

The Privileges and Immunities Clause

Section 2 of Article 4 of the U. S. Constitution contains the so-called Privileges and Immunities Clause, providing that "the Citizens of each State shall be entitled to all Privileges and Immunities of Citizens in the several States." Because of similar language in the Fourteenth Amendment, this clause has not often been involved in litigation; nevertheless, it has played a role in assuring equality of treatment for all citizens.

The clause places the citizens of each state upon the same footing as citizens of other states so far as the advantages of citizenship are concerned. It relieves them from the disabilities of alienage in other states: states cannot discriminate against nonresidents. It gives all persons the right of free entry into, and exit from other states. It ensures everyone of the same freedom in the acquisition and enjoyment of property and in the pursuit of happiness. No provision in the Constitution has tended more strongly to constitute the citizens of the United States one people, because it prevents a state from discriminating against citizens of other states in favor of its own.

The Privileges and Immunities Clause does not prevent state citizenship from being used to distinguish among persons. A state may require citizenship for voting, holding office, and paying resident tuition to a state university. Only those privileges and immunities bearing upon the vitality of the nation as a single entity must be granted equally to all citizens—resident and nonresident.

CASE

In 1972, the Alaska legislature passed a local hire act. It required all leases to which the state was a party—such as oil and gas leases—to provide that qualified Alaskan residents of at least one year be employed in preference to nonresidents. P's challenged the act as violative of the Privileges and Immunities Clause.

ISSUE Was the Alaskan Hire statute violative of the Privileges and Immunities Clause?

DECISION Yes.

REASONS

1. The clause bars discrimination against people merely because they are citizens of other states.
2. Discrimination was unreasonable, because the influx of nonresidents was not the cause of Alaska's unemployment problem.

3. Alaska's ownership of the oil and gas is insufficient justification for the discrimination.

Hicklin v. Orbeck, 98 S.Ct. 2982 (1978).

The Commerce Clause

The power of the federal government to regulate business activity is found in the so-called Commerce Clause of the Constitution, which states: "Congress shall have power . . . to regulate Commerce with foreign Nations, and among the several States, and with the Indian Tribes. . . ." This grant of three-pronged power has been broadly interpreted to give the federal government considerable power to regulate business, to prescribe the rules by which commerce is conducted. Among the three regulatory powers—foreign, interstate, and Indian—commerce with the Indian tribes is relatively unimportant, although Congress is responsible for the laws applicable to Indian reservations.

Foreign commerce

The power to regulate foreign commerce is vested exclusively in the federal government and extends to all aspects of foreign trade. State and local governments may not regulate foreign commerce, although they do sometimes attempt directly or indirectly to regulate imports and exports to some degree. Such attempts are unconstitutional. State or local laws regulating or interfering with federal regulation of commerce with foreign nations are invalid as violations of the Commerce and Supremacy clauses.

The right to import includes the right to sell the goods imported. States may not prohibit the sale of imported goods any more than they can prohibit their import. The exclusive federal power over imported goods continues until the goods are mingled with, and become a part of, the general property of the country; so that for all purposes, the imported product is given similar treatment with other property. In most cases, imported goods become a part of internal commerce when the importer or wholesaler disposes of them to retail dealers in local communities. If a state or local law tends to continue to distinguish the goods by their point of origin, the foreign-commerce aspect continues, and the law is invalid. One city required that all retail goods originating behind the Iron Curtain be so labeled. The law was unconstitutional.

Interstate commerce

The key language of the Commerce Clause is the phrase "among the several States." This language has been construed to give Congress power to enact laws covering any business activity in interstate commerce and any intrastate business activity that has a substantial effect—negative or positive—on interstate commerce. The effect of any individual business on interstate commerce need not be substantial if the cumulative effect of all similar businesses is substantial. In recent years this power has been used in a variety of ways. One of the more important pieces of legislation was the public accommodation provisions of the Civil Rights Act of 1964. Activities such as gambling, discrimination in the sale or rental of housing, and loan sharking have been regulated under the Commerce Clause.

CASE

P filed a class action suit charging two real estate trade associations and six named real estate firms with conspiring to fix prices in the purchase and sale of residential real estate. It was alleged that prices were controlled by systematic use of fixed commission rates, widespread fee splitting, and suppression of market information from buyers and sellers. The complaint included allegations that D's activities had an effect on interstate commerce, in that they assisted clients in securing financing and title insurance from sources outside the state.

ISSUE Does the Sherman Act extend to an agreement among real estate brokers in a local market area?

DECISION Yes.

REASONS
1. The activities had a substantial effect on interstate commerce. The power to regulate commerce extends to local activities that affect commerce between the states.
2. In order to establish jurisdiction under the Sherman Act, a plaintiff must show a relationship between the activity involved and some aspect of interstate commerce. The petitioners can satisfy the requirement in this case by demonstrating a substantial effect on interstate commerce generated by defendants' brokerage activity.
3. Financing for many of the transactions was arranged through interstate bank loans made possible by out-of-state investors. Title insurance, required by most lending institutions, was furnished by interstate corporations. An appreciable amount of commerce was therefore involved.

McClain v. Real Estate Board of New Orleans, Inc., 100 S.Ct. 502 (1980).

While the power of Congress to regulate an infinite variety of business activities by use of the Commerce Clause is quite broad, it is subject to some limitations. These limitations are found in other provisions of the Constitution, such as the Sixth Amendment's guarantee of a right to a trial by jury and the Fifth Amendment's Due Process Clause. In addition, the power to regulate commerce cannot be used to destroy state and local governments and thus cannot be used, for example, to regulate the wages of government employees.

The Commerce Clause and the state police power

In granting Congress power over commerce, the Constitution did not expressly exclude the states from exercising authority over commerce. The Supreme Court held that the nature of the commerce power did not by *implication* prohibit state action and that some state power over commerce is compatible with the federal power. Because of the Commerce Clause, nevertheless, state powers over commerce are definitely limited.

State and local governments use their "police power" to enact laws to promote the public health, safety, morals, and general welfare. Of necessity, such laws frequently result in the regulation of business activity. The Commerce Clause and the Supremacy Clause impose several restrictions on the states' use of police power as it affects business.

The first restriction is that state and local governments cannot enact laws on subjects that are considered to be exclusively federal. A state could not pass a law establishing the width of a railroad track or a law concerning air traffic, because those regulations require national uniformity. For this reason, any state law concerning a subject that is exclusively under the federal government's jurisdiction is unconstitutional under the Commerce Clause and Supremacy Clause. This is true even if there is no federal law on the subject.

The second limitation concerns subject matters over which the federal government has taken exclusive jurisdiction by enacting legislation. Federal laws that assert exclusive jurisdiction over a subject are said to preempt the field. Preemption may result from express language or by comprehensive regulation showing an intent by Congress to exercise exclusive dominion over the subject matter. When a federal statute has preempted the field, *any* state or local law pertaining to the same subject matter is unconstitutional, and the state regulation is void.

CASE

P is the owner and operator of an airport, which serves interstate air carriers. D, the city of Burbank, enacted an ordinance prohibiting jet aircraft from taking off between eleven at night and seven in the morning. P sought an injunction against the enforcement of the ordinance. A federal law provides that the United States of America possesses complete and exclusive national sovereignty of air space in the United States, including the authority to regulate the use of such air space.

ISSUE Is the city ordinance constitutional?

DECISION No.

REASONS
1. The pervasive nature of the scheme of federal regulation of aircraft noise leads us to conclude that there is preemption.
2. Federal control is intensive and exclusive. Planes do not wander about in the sky like vagrant clouds. They move only by federal permission, subject to federal inspection, in the hands of federally certified personnel, and under an intricate system of federal commands. The moment an airplane taxes onto a runway it is caught up in an elaborate and detailed system of controls.
3. The interdependence of the factors of safety and efficiency requires a uniform and exclusive system of federal regulation if the congressional objectives underlying the federal law are to be fulfilled.

City of Burbank v. Lockheed Air Terminal, Inc., 93 S.Ct. 1854 (1973).

Not every federal regulatory statute preempts the field. When a federal law does not preempt the field and the subject matter is not exclusively federal, state regulation under the police power is permitted. When a state law is inconsistent or irreconcilably in conflict with a federal statute, it is unconstitutional and void because of the Supremacy Clause that makes federal laws supreme over state laws. Moreover, state laws are unconstitutional under the Commerce Clause if they discriminate against interstate commerce or impose an undue burden on it.

The Commerce Clause does not prohibit the imposition of burdens on interstate commerce—only the imposition of undue burdens. A state law that required train locomotives to have spark arrestors did not impose an undue burden on interstate commerce when the trains traveled frequently through heavy forests. Every regulatory measure is a burden to some degree. If a local law furthers a legitimate public interest, it is valid unless the burden on interstate activities is undue. A state law limiting the lengths of trucks imposed an undue burden on interstate commerce.

We have pointed out that the Commerce Clause prohibits discrimination against interstate commerce in favor of intrastate commerce. On the other hand, state and local governments frequently attempt by legislation to aid local business in its competition with interstate business. The Commerce Clause requires that all taxes and regulations be the same for local businesses as for businesses engaged in interstate commerce. While interstate commerce is required to pay its fair share of all taxes, it must be placed on a plane of equality with local trade or commerce. A state may not place itself in a position of economic isolation from other states.

Every tax is to some extent regulatory. The Commerce Clause also imposes limitations on the taxing power of state and local governments. Although the issues involved are varied and complex, it may be said as a general rule that a state may impose a tax such as an income tax or a property tax on a business engaged in interstate commerce, provided that the tax is *apportioned* by some reasonable formula to local activities within the state and does not discriminate against interstate commerce in favor of intrastate commerce. There must be a connection between the tax and the local enterprise being taxed (*nexus*), or the tax will violate the Commerce Clause. The concepts of nexus and apportionment are used to ensure that interstate commerce pays its fair share for benefits received from the state.

The Bill of Rights and Business

The first ten amendments to the Constitution of the United States, often referred to as the Bill of Rights, have numerous provisions that impact directly on business and economic activity, as well as on all other aspects of our daily lives.

Before examining some of the business implications of the Bill of Rights, we should keep in mind three of their important characteristics. First of all, constitutional rights are not absolutes. They are limited. Mr. Justice Black, dissenting in *Tinker* v. *Des Moines Independent Community School Dist.*, 89 S.Ct. 733 (1969), noted this fact.

> The truth is that a teacher of kindergarten, grammar school, or high school pupils no more carries into a school with him a complete right to freedom of speech and expression than an anti-Catholic or anti-Semitic carries with him a complete freedom of speech and religion into a Catholic church or Jewish synagogue. Nor does a person carry with him into the United States Senate or House, or to the Supreme Court, or any other court, a complete constitutional right to go into those places contrary to their rules and speak his mind on any subject he pleases. It is a myth to say that any person has a constitutional right to say what he pleases, where he pleases, and when he pleases.

The same sense of limitation is applicable to all basic constitutional protections.

Second, the limit of any basic constitutional guarantee depends upon the nature of the competing public policy. In constitutional cases, courts are required to weigh and strike a balance between some goal or policy of society and the constitutional protection involved. They may weigh an ethical standard of a profession and balance it against freedom of speech. That is what they did when they were required to decide if professional persons such as lawyers should be allowed to advertise, notwithstanding codes of professional ethics prohibiting advertising. In such cases, the court weighs the conflicting policies to determine the extent of the constitutional protection.

Finally, constitutional rights vary from time to time. A doctrine known as constitutional relativity means that the Constitution is interpreted in light of current facts and problems. This doctrine is especially applicable to the Bill of Rights, which changes to meet current conditions and emergencies such as war or civil strife.

The First Amendment

The First Amendment gives us five basic freedoms: (1) freedom of religion, (2) freedom of speech, (3) freedom of the press, (4) freedom of assembly, and (5) the right to petition the government for a redress of grievances.

Freedom of religion becomes a business issue when Sunday closing laws are enacted for religious purposes. If the laws are based on economic considerations, they may be valid, providing there are reasonable exceptions for necessary public services. Another example of freedom of religion restricts unions. It has been held that the laws relating to unionization are not applicable to, nor do they protect, parochial school teachers. If the NLRB were to conduct a union certification election for parochial teachers, it would constitute a violation of the doctrine of separation between church and state.

The publishing business is the only organized private business that is given explicit constitutional protection. Freedom of the press as guaranteed by the First Amendment authorizes a private business to make an organized scrutiny of government. Yet, freedom of the press is not absolute. The press is not free to print anything it chooses, without liability. Rather, freedom of the press is usually construed to prohibit prior restraints on publication. If the press publishes that which is improper, mischievous, illegal, or libelous, it has liability for doing so. This liability may be either criminal or civil for damages. Moreover, freedom of the press is not violated when a government agency (FCC) censors obscene words on TV.

Freedom of speech or expression covers verbal and written communications and conduct or actions that are considered symbolic speech. Clearly, it does not extend to obscenity and pornography; the only issue is whether or not the matters are, in fact, obscene or pornographic. The First Amendment not only prohibits prior restraint, it also guards against fear of punishment for the exercise of the right to free speech. Its protection benefits corporations as well as individuals and unions. The right to picket peacefully for lawful reasons is well recognized.

Historically, "commercial speech" was considered unprotected, but that view is no longer accepted, and those conducting businesses frequently assert their rights of free speech. A ban of "for sale" signs in front of residential property is a violation of the amendment, but courts have held that the amendment is not violated when a university bans sales in its residence halls or a state restricts the location of adult theaters to certain areas.

CASE

P's, as consumers of prescription drugs, brought suit against the Virginia State Board of Pharmacy and its individual members, challenging under the First Amendment a Virginia statute which declared that it was unprofessional conduct for a licensed pharmacist to advertise the prices of prescription drugs. D's contended that advertising was not protected by the First Amendment.

ISSUE Is commercial speech protected by the First Amendment?

DECISION Yes.

REASONS

1. Any First Amendment protection enjoyed by advertisers is also enjoyed, and thus may be asserted, by the recipients of such information. "Commercial speech" is not wholly outside the protection of the First and Fourteenth Amendments.
2. The fact that advertisers' interests are purely economic does not disqualify them from protection under the First Amendment.
3. Society has a strong interest in the free flow of commercial information, particularly concerning prescription drugs. Although this interest must be balanced against the state's interest in maintaining a high degree of professionalism among licensed pharmacists, the First Amendment protection is paramount.

Virginia State Board of Pharmacists v. Virginia Cit. Cons. Council, 96 S.Ct. 1817 (1976).

The First Amendment freedoms include the right to assemble and associate and the right to petition the government for a redress of grievances. The purpose of the guarantee of freedom of assembly and association is to prevent guilt by association. It is also designed to ensure privacy in one's association. It has been held that state law may not compel the disclosure of membership lists of a constitutionally valid association. Such a disclosure entails the likelihood of a substantial restraint upon the exercise of the members' rights to freedom of association. The protection extends to the social, legal, and economic benefits of membership in groups; it prevents a state from denying a Communist a license to practice law. In addition to these enumerated protections, the First Amendment has been interpreted to include the right of privacy and the right to knowledge. Freedom of expression includes freedom of inquiry, freedom of thought, and the freedom to teach. Moreover, the right of association surpasses the right to attend a meeting. It includes the right to express an attitude or philosophy by group membership. Thus, the specifics of the Bill of Rights have penumbras or additional implied rights such as the right of privacy.

The Fourth Amendment

The Fourth Amendment protects individuals and corporations from unreasonable searches and seizures. Its primary object is to protect persons from unwarranted intrusions into their individual privacy. While Fourth Amendment issues usually arise in criminal cases, the protection of the Fourth Amendment extends to civil matters as well. Courts have held that building inspectors do not have the right to inspect for building code violations without a warrant if the owner of the premises objects. Reports written for one purpose cannot be used for another without running afoul of the Fourth Amendment. The Securities and Exchange Commission, having obtained confidential reports in the course of its function, could not use those reports to establish a violation of federal law.

The following case is typical of the way the Fourth Amendment protects business in a noncriminal matter. The Occupational Safety and Health Administration (OSHA) has the responsibility to enforce laws requiring that all employees have a safe and healthy place to work.

CASE

P brought suit to obtain injunctive relief to prevent warrantless inspections of its business pursuant to Section 8(a) of OSHA. The act empowered agents of the Secretary of Labor to conduct unannounced searches of the work area of any employment facility for safety hazards and violations of OSHA regulations.

ISSUE Does the Fourth Amendment require a warrant for OSHA inspections?

DECISION Yes.

REASONS

1. The Warrant Clause of the Fourth Amendment protects commercial buildings as well as private homes. The rule that warrantless searches are generally unreasonable applies to business premises as well as homes. The same rules apply in civil and criminal investigations.
2. No serious burden will be imposed by requiring a warrant. Most businesspeople will consent without warrant.
3. Probable cause for a warrant is not required in the criminal law sense; only a showing that reasonable legislative or administrative standards for conducting an inspection are satisfied with respect to a particular establishment.

Marshall v. Barlow's Inc., 98 S.Ct. 1816 (1978).

The Fifth Amendment

The Fifth Amendment, best known for its protection against compulsory self-incrimination, goes much further, to other protections. More specifically, it (1) requires indictment by a grand jury for a capital offense or infamous crime, (2) prohibits double jeopardy, (3) requires just compensation in eminent domain proceedings, and (4) contains a due process clause. Most of these protections are for criminal cases, which are beyond the scope of this text; however, some aspects have special impact for business.

The requirement of just compensation in eminent domain proceedings is very important to many businesses, especially utilities. Public utilities have the power to acquire private property by condemnation, and thus they may be required to pay just compensation. Or the property owned by a business may be taken for public purpose by government bodies. The Fifth Amendment requires just compensation in such cases. This is a question of fact for a jury if the property owner and the condemning governmental unit cannot agree on a fair market value of the property taken.

The Fifth Amendment protects life, liberty, and property from deprivation by the federal government without due process of law. The Fourteenth Amendment contains an identical provision that is applicable to the states. While due process is difficult to define, it basically amounts to "fundamental fairness." Since the interpretations of the due process clauses of the Fifth and Fourteenth Amendments are for all practical purposes identical, the discussion of due process under the Fourteenth Amendment (section after next) will also illustrate due process under the Fifth Amendment.

The protection against compulsory self-incrimination does not apply to corporations. Corporations are citizens for most purposes except this one. Corporate officials do retain their personal privilege against compulsory self-incrimination and cannot be required to testify; but they may be required to deliver all corporate records subpoened for evidentiary purposes, since corporations are not protected by the privilege.

The Seventh Amendment

The Seventh Amendment guarantees the right to a trial by jury in suits at common law in which the amount in controversy exceeds $20. There is no right to a trial by jury in suits in equity or chancery. Likewise, there is no right to a trial by jury when the proceedings such as administrative hearings did not exist at common law but have been created by legislation. The case which follows illustrates this limitation of the rights under the Seventh Amendment.

CASE

The OSHA statute permits the federal government to proceed before an administrative agency to obtain abatement orders and civil penalties. Upon judicial review, the administrative agency's findings of fact, if supported by substantial evidence, are considered conclusive. P's, who were assessed civil penalties, challenged the constitutionality of the act's enforcement procedures under the Seventh Amendment.

ISSUE Do OSHA penalties violate the right to a trial by jury?

DECISION No.

REASONS
1. The Seventh Amendment does not prohibit Congress from assigning the fact-finding function and initial adjudication to an administrative forum with which the jury would be incompatible.
2. Fact finding was never the exclusive province of the jury; whether a jury was used depended on the forum.
3. The Seventh Amendment does not make the jury the exclusive mechanism for fact finding. The right exists only in those cases in which it existed at common law in England.
4. Since this is a new type of proceeding, Congress may decide if the facts are to be forced by a jury.

Atlas Roofing Co. v. OSHA, 97 S.Ct. 1261 (1977).

The Fourteenth Amendment

The Fourteenth Amendment contains three clauses commonly referred to as (1) the privileges and immunities clause, (2) the due process clause, and (3) the equal protection clause. The exact language is as follows:

> No State shall make or enforce any law which shall abridge the privileges or immunities of citizens of the United States; nor shall any State deprive any person of life, liberty or property, without due process of law, nor deny to any person within its jurisdiction the equal protection of the laws.

The language of the original 10 amendments makes them applicable to the federal government, but the Fourteenth Amendment's most significant role has been to make most of the provisions of the Bill of Rights applicable to the states. The courts, by judicial interpretation, have held that the due process clause of the Fourteenth Amendment "incorporates" or "carries over" the Bill of Rights and makes its provisions applicable to the states.

The term *due process of law* is used to describe fundamental principles of liberty and justice. Simply stated, due process means "fundamental fairness and decency." It means that *government* may not act in a manner that is arbitrary, capricious, or unreasonable. The clause does not prevent private individuals or corporations including public utilities from acting in an arbitrary or unreasonable manner.

The issues in due process cases are usually divided into questions of *procedural due process* and *substantive due process.* Substantive due process issues arise when property or other rights are directly affected by governmental action. Procedural due process cases often are concerned with whether proper notice has been given and a proper hearing has been conducted. Such cases frequently involve procedures established by state statute.

Early in this century, many attempts at economic regulation were held to be violations of substantive due process. The judicial attitude toward economic regulation changed in midcentury, and now due process challenges to economic regulation fall on deaf ears. Substantive due process is important in cases involving individual liberties. Today there is a presumption of constitutionality of economic legislation, but legislation that tends to restrict fundamental rights is suspect and subject to more exacting judicial scrutiny under the Fourteenth Amendment. This double standard is often justified because of the crucial importance of these basic freedoms, which must be protected by the judiciary from the "vicissitudes" of political action.

The purpose of the equal protection clause is to prevent "invidious" discrimination. In determining whether or not a statutory classification is "invidious," the courts use two different tests depending on the factual situation. First, the strict judicial scrutiny test is used when a legislative classification interferes with the exercise of a fundamental right or operates to the peculiar disadvantage of a suspect class. A suspect class is one burdened with disabilities or subjected to a history of unequal treatment. Blacks and chicanos have been held to be members of a suspect class. When a suspect class is involved, the state must prove that its statutory classifications are based upon a compelling state interest, or the classifications will be held to constitute a denial of equal protection. Classifications subject to this test are in effect presumed to be unconstitutional, and the state must convince the court that the classification is fair, reasonable, and necessary to accomplish the objective of the legislation.

The second test in equal protection cases is known as the rational basis standard.

Classifications to which the rational basis standard are applied are presumed to be valid. It is only when there is no rational basis for the classification that it is unconstitutional under the equal protection clause. A classification judged by this standard must be rationally related to the state's legitimate objectives. The classification may be imperfect and may not be the best to accomplish the purpose. Yet, it is still constitutional if there is a rational basis for the classification. A state statute that allowed females to purchase alcoholic beverages at 18 while requiring males to be 21 was held to be unconstitutional because the age classification was not substantially related to the achievement of state objectives.

REVIEW QUESTIONS AND PROBLEMS

1. An Arizona statute authorized the Registrar of Contracts to revoke the license of any contractor who filed a petition in voluntary bankruptcy. Hull, a licensee, was declared in voluntary bankruptcy on January 22, 1975, and his contractor's license was revoked on May 16, 1975. He appealed to the courts, contending that the Arizona statute was unconstitutional. What was the result? Why?
2. The state of Arizona, by statute under its police powers, imposed maximum lengths of fourteen cars on passenger trains and seventy cars on freight trains, for the purpose of encouraging railroad safety. No other state imposes such regulations. Is the legislation constitutional? Why?
3. The Department of Agriculture has set up minimum standards of ripeness based on size and weight for the marking of avocados. A California statute was enacted that provided standards of ripeness based on minimum oil content for the distribution and sale of avocados in California. Is the California statute preempted by the federal legislation? Why?
4. The taxing power is used to accomplish goals other than raising revenue. List four such goals.
5. The state of Maryland required nonresident merchants to obtain licenses in order to pursue their trade in the state. No license was required of Maryland residents. A New Jersey resident challenged the constitutionality of the law. Is the law constitutional? Why?
6. A New York State statute entitled "An act prohibiting supersonic transport (SST) planes from landing or taking off in the state" provides: "Notwithstanding the provisions of any law, unless there is an emergency, no commercial supersonic transport plane which is not capable of limiting its noise level to one hundred and eight decibels or less while landing, on the ground, or taking off will be permitted to land or to take off in this state." SSTs are engaged in flights from London and Paris to New York City and Washington, D.C. P files suit to have the state law declared unconstitutional. What will be the result? Why?
7. A Maryland statute prohibits refiners of petroleum products from operating retail service stations within the state. Exxon Corporation challenges the constitutionality of the state statutes. Is the state law constitutional? Why?
8. List four protections of the First Amendment and give an example of each as it relates to business.
9. A city council concerned with block busting passed an ordinance prohibiting the placing of a "for sale" sign in the front yard of any single-family residence within the city. The local board of realtors filed suit challenging the constitutionality of the ordinance. Is the ordinance constitutional? Why?
10. Building inspectors of Metropolis decided on a yearly inspection of all buildings more than 10 years old. When the inspectors arrived at property owned by Slumlord, he refused them admission because they did not have a search warrant. Were the building inspectors entitled to search without the warrants? Why?
11. Government has the power of eminent domain. Under what circumstances may the power be utilized by others?
12. What is the most significant use of the Fourteenth Amendment?

43

Administrative Law

In our complex industrial society, social and economic problems are so numerous that courts and legislative bodies cannot possibly deal with all of them. Legislation must be so general in character that it cannot possibly cover everything the law seeks to control or correct. There must be a method of filling in the gaps in legislation and of adding meat to the bones of legislative policy. There must also be special expertise to solve problems created by advancing technology. To handle these and other situations, our society has turned to the administrative process in government. In doing so, it has created a fourth branch of government: the independent regulatory agencies, bureaus, and commissions that the administrative process relies upon to develop laws and enforce them.

Administrative agencies are necessary in order to lighten the burdens that otherwise must be borne by the executive branch, legislative bodies, and courts. The multitude of administrative agencies performing governmental functions today encompasses almost every aspect of business operation and, indeed, almost every aspect of our daily lives. These agencies provide flexibility in the law and adaptability to changing conditions.

The many local, state, and federal administrative agencies have a far greater, direct, day-to-day, legal impact on business than the impact of the courts and legislative bodies. Administrative agencies create and enforce the greater bulk of the laws that make up the legal environment of business.

Additional reasons for the administrative process

The fourth branch of government exists in part because laws cannot be particularized enough to cover all aspects of a problem. It is probably not possible for Congress to enact an energy program that would cover every issue; therefore, Congress delegates to the Department of Energy the power to make rules and regulations to fill in the gaps and specifics to make the laws workable. In many areas, agencies must develop detailed rules and regulations to carry out legislative policies.

It is also difficult if not impossible for the courts to handle all of the disputes and controversies that arise. Each year, tens of thousands of industrial accidents cause injury or death. If each accident were to result in traditional litigation, the courts simply would not have the time or personnel to handle the multitude of cases. Therefore, we use the administrative process to handle them. Similarly, most cases involving alleged discrimination in employment are decided by use of the administrative process.

Many agencies exist because of the desire for experts to handle difficult problems. The Federal Reserve Board, Nuclear Regulatory Commission, and Pure Food and Drug Administration are examples of agencies with expertise above that of the Congress or the executive branch. Administrative agencies also provide continuity and consistency in the formulation, application, and enforcement of rules and regulations governing business.

Many governmental agencies exist to protect the public and the public interest from some members of the business community. The public interest in clean water and clear air led to the creation of the Environmental Protection Agency. The protection of the investing public was a major force behind the creation of the Securities and Exchange Commission. The manufacture and sale of dangerous products led to the creation of the Consumer Product Safety Commission. It is our practice to turn to a governmental agency for assistance whenever a business or business practice may injure significant numbers of the general public. There is a belief that a legitimate function of many government agencies is to protect the public from harm.

Many agencies such as the Post Office Department were created out of necessity. Welfare programs require government personnel to administer them. The Social Security system cannot function without a federal agency to determine eligibility and to pay the benefits. The mere existence of most government programs automatically causes the creation of a new agency or an expansion of the functions of an existing one.

Today, the legislative and executive branches of government are content to identify problems and to develop policies to solve them. These policies are enacted into law; the responsibility for carrying out the policies and enforcing the laws is delegated to the administrative process. The goals of society are determined by the traditional branches of government, and their achievement is the responsibility of the fourth branch.

Functions

Administrative agencies both at federal and state levels of government tend to perform the six functions of the other three branches of government: (1) legislative or rule making, (2) adjudicating, (3) prosecuting, (4) advising, (5) supervising, and (6) investigating. These functions are not the same degree of concern to all administrative agencies, but all are some concern to each agency. Some agencies are primarily adjudicating bodies, such as the industrial commissions that rule on worker's compensation claims. Others are primarily supervisory, such as the Securities and Exchange Commission (SEC), which oversees the issue and sale of investment securities.

In the legislative function, rules and regulations are made to accomplish the goals of the agency. The rule-making function is based on the authority delegated to the agency by the legislature. This delegation of authority is usually stated in broad, general language. A delegation "to make such rules, regulations, and decisions as the public interest, convenience, and necessity may require" is a typical statement of the authority of an agency.

It is the usual practice for administrative agencies in performing their quasi-legislative functions to hold hearings on proposed rules and regulations. The agency receives testimony on the need for, or desirability of, proposed rules and regulations. Notice of such hearings is usually given to the public, and all interested parties are allowed to present evidence for consideration by the agency.

The adjudicating function means that administrative agencies also decide cases or disputes between private parties after they have conducted hearings. The purpose of the hearing may be to find if a rule of the agency or an applicable statute has been violated. The National Labor Relations Board conducts hearings to determine if an unfair labor practice has been committed. Other quasi-judicial hearings may be held for the purpose of fixing liability, as in a case of worker's compensation, which provides employer liability for employee deaths, sicknesses, and injury arising out of, and in the course of, employment. The quasi-judicial hearings receive detailed evidence and determine the rights and duties of the parties subject to the jurisdiction of the agency. The rules of procedure used in these quasi-judicial hearings are usually more informal in character than court trials, but on the whole they follow the general pattern set by courts.

An agency usually appoints a person to conduct the hearing—an administrative judge, sometimes called a hearing examiner or trial examiner. This person receives the evidence, submits findings of facts, and makes recommendations to the board or commission regarding the disposition to be made in the case. The agency studies the report and issues whatever orders the law in the case appears to demand. The agency may hear objections to the hearing officer's finding, and sometimes it will hear arguments on the issues.

The quasi-judicial function of administrative agencies is the subject of substantial controversy. A frequent complaint is that administrative agencies make a law and investigate to see if it has been violated; they serve as prosecutor, judge, and jury; then they act in the manner of an appellate court in reviewing the decision. Another frequent objection is that the administrative process denies business and others the right to a trial by jury. As noted in the prior chapter, such objections are not constitutionally valid.

Reversing Agency Decisions

How much deference is given to the quasi-legislative and quasi-judicial decisions of administrative agencies? Under what circumstances will a court reverse the decision of an agency? What alternatives are available to a party who is unhappy with either a rule or a decision? What are the powers of courts in reviewing the decision of an administrative agency? The answers to these questions must be clearly understood if one is to appreciate the role of administrative agencies in our system. The principles and issues are somewhat different, depending upon whether the court is reviewing a rule or regulation on one hand or a quasi-judicial decision on the other.

Judicial review of rules and regulations

The rule-making function is essentially legislative in character. Agencies are created, and their powers are derived, from statutes that delegate certain responsibilities or quasi-legislative power to the agency. These statutes usually authorize an administrative agency to "fill in the details" of legislation by making rules and regulations to carry out goals and purposes.

Two basic issues in litigation challenge the validity of a rule or regulation adopted by an administrative agency. First of all, is the delegation valid; second, has the agency exceeded its authority? Delegation of quasi-legislative authority to an administrative agency must be definite, or it will violate due process. Definiteness means that the delegation must be clear enough for reviewing courts to ascertain the extent of the agency's authority, but broad language has been held sufficiently definite to meet this test. The term "unfair methods of competition" has been held to be sufficiently definite to meet the requirements of due process.

The power of administrative agencies to make rules must also be limited. The limited-power concept means that delegation must contain standards by which a court can determine whether the limitations have been exceeded. Just as broad language has been approved as being sufficiently definite for a delegation to be valid under the due process clause, so also have broad standards been approved to meet the limited power test since the 1930s. When an agency is given authority to make rules required for the "public interest, convenience and necessity," there is a valid standard for those rules. The law, recognizing that practical considerations often make definite standards impossible, will hold valid a delegation that includes a criterion as concrete as possible within its field and with the factors involved.

While it is highly unlikely that a court would hold a delegation invalid because of indefiniteness or lack of standards, courts sometimes do find that agencies have exceeded their authority. Delegation of quasi-legislative power usually involves grants of substantial discretion to the board or agency involved. It must be kept in mind that the delegation of discretion is to the agency, not to the courts. Courts cannot interfere with the discretion given to the agency and cannot substitute their judgment for that of the agency simply because they disagree with a rule or regulation. Courts will hold that an agency has exceeded its authority if an analysis of legislative intent confirms the view that the agency has gone beyond that intent.

CASE

The FCC promulgated rules governing cable TV systems that have 3,500 or more subscribers. The systems were required to develop a minimum 20-channel capacity by 1986 and to make available certain channels for access by public, educational, local governmental, and leased access users. Cable operators were deprived of all discretion in such programming, and they were required to allow public users access to the channels without any input by the operators into program content. During the rule-making proceedings, the FCC rejected arguments that they were treating cable TV operators as common carriers.

ISSUE Are these rules within the delegation of authority?

DECISION No. The commission exceeded its authority.

REASONS

1. The access rules have effectively relegated the cable systems to common carrier status, which the law prohibits.
2. Though the court has in the past tended to defer to the commission's judgment regarding the scope of its authority, there are strong indications that agency flexibility was to be sharply delimited in this area.

FCC v. Midwest Video, 99 S.Ct. 1435 (1979).

Judicial review of decisions—procedural aspects

The exercise of quasi-judicial powers by administrative agencies is often criticized because personnel of the agency act as prosecutor, finder of facts, and judge. The law therefore requires that this quasi-judicial power be restricted by procedural safeguards preventing its abuse. In studying this material, keep in mind that the right to a jury trial does not exist in either formal or informal hearings conducted by administrative bodies.

Judicial review of agency adjudications, by its very nature, is quite limited. Since legislatures have delegated authority to agencies because of their expertise and other capabilities, courts usually exercise restraint and give great deference to agency decisions. Courts reviewing administrative interpretations of law do not always decide questions of law for themselves. It is not unusual for a court to accept an administrative interpretation of law as final if it has warrant in the agency's record and rational basis. Administrative agencies are frequently called upon to interpret the statute governing the agency, and the agency's construction is persuasive to courts.

Agencies either develop their own rules of procedure or follow those set forth in administrative procedure acts of the legislature—either way being far less formal than judicial procedure. Administrative agencies usually do not follow the strict rules of evidence used by courts, although they do not ignore all rules of evidence. They cannot deny cross-examination of witnesses, and they must meet judicial standards of fairness, such as giving a fair hearing to all parties. In reviewing the procedures of administrative agencies, courts are not empowered to substitute their judgment or their own procedures for those of the agency. Judicial responsibility is limited to ensuring consistency with statutes and compliance with the demands of the Constitution for a fair hearing.

Standing to sue and exhaustion of remedies are two important procedural aspects of the broad area of judicial review of administrative action. Standing to sue involves two important issues. First, is the action or decision of the agency subject to judicial review? Not all administrative decisions are reviewable. The Federal Administrative Procedure Act provides for judicial review except where "(1) statutes preclude judicial review or (2) agency action is committed to agency discretion by law." Few statutes actually preclude judicial review, and preclusion of judicial review by inference is rare.

The second issue is whether or not the plaintiff in any particular case is able to obtain judicial review. It is generally required that the plaintiff be "an aggrieved party" before he or she has standing to sue or to obtain judicial review. Persons who may suffer economic loss due to agency action have standing to sue. Also, persons who have noneconomic interests, such as First Amendment rights, now have standing to sue.

The doctrine of exhaustion of remedies is based on the proposition that courts should not decide in advance of a hearing that an agency will not conduct it fairly. In general (although there are exceptions), courts refuse to review administrative actions until a complaining party has exhausted all the administrative review procedures available. Otherwise, the administrative system would be denied important opportunities to make a factual record, to exercise its discretion, or to apply its expertise in decision making. Exhaustion gives an agency the opportunity to discover and correct its own errors and thus help to dispense with judicial review.

Exhaustion is most clearly required in cases involving the agency's expertise or specialization, so that exhaustion would not incur unusual expense, or when the administrative remedy is just as likely as the judicial one to provide appropriate relief. If nothing is to be gained from the exhaustion of administrative remedies, and the harm from the continued existence of the administrative ruling is great, the courts have not been reluctant to discard this doctrine. This is especially true when very fundamental constitutional guarantees such as freedom of speech or press are involved or the administrative remedy is likely to be inadequate. When the agency is clearly acting beyond its jurisdiction (because its action is not authorized by statute, or the statute authorizing it is unconstitutional), or when the agency's action would result in irreparable injury (such as great expense) to the petitioner, a court most probably would not insist upon exhaustion.

Judicial review of factual decisions

When a court reviews the findings of fact made by an administrative body, it considers them to be prima facie correct. A court of review examines the evidence by analyzing the record of the agency's proceedings and upholds the agency's findings and conclusions on questions of fact if they are supported by substantial evidence in the record as a whole. In other words, the record must contain material evidence from which a reasonable person might reach the same conclusion as did the agency. If substantial evidence in support of the decision is present, the court will not disturb the agency's findings, even though the court itself might have reached a different conclusion on the basis of the evidence in the record. The determination of credibility of the witnesses who testify in quasi-judicial proceedings is for the agency to determine, not the courts.

Thus it is apparent that on review, courts do not (1) reweigh the evidence, (2) make independent determinations of fact, or (3) substitute their view of the evidence for that of the agency. Courts do determine if there is substantial evidence to support the action taken; but in their examination of the evidence, all that is required is evidence sufficient to convince a reasonable mind to a fair degree of certainty. Thus, substantial evidence is evidence that a reasonable mind might accept as adequate to support the conclusion.

The findings of an administrative body are not set aside unless the record clearly shows that its decision cannot be justified by a fair estimate of (1) the worth and testimony of witnesses or (2) its informed judgment on matters within its special competence, or (3) both. The decision of the agency will be affirmed, even when the court believes it to be erroneous, if a reasonable man could have reached the conclusion stated. Since it is the function of the agency to pass upon the weight to be accorded to the evidence and to make the choice, if necessary, between varying inferences, the possibility of drawing either of two inconsistent inferences from the evidence does not prevent the agency from drawing one of them. Courts, however, do not always agree with the administrative determination, and sometimes they set aside a finding because it is not supported by substantial evidence.

For the courts to exercise their function of limited review, it is necessary for the agency to provide a record of the reasons and basis for its decision. The case that follows discusses the general principles applicable to judicial review of agency decisions.

CASE

P, following his defeat in a union election, filed a complaint with the Secretary of Labor, alleging violations of a federal statute. Federal law requires the Secretary of Labor to investigate the complaint and decide whether to bring a civil action to set aside the election. The Secretary of Labor, upon investigation, decided no such action was warranted. P then filed this action to have the Secretary's opinion declared arbitrary and capricious and asked the court to order D to file suit to set aside the election.

ISSUE Is the decision of the Secretary of Labor subject to judicial review?

DECISION Yes, but the judicial review is not a trial inquiring into the factual issues of the Secretary's conclusions.

REASONS 1. The law contains no provision that explicitly prohibits judicial review.

2. Since the statute relies on the special knowledge and discretion of the Secretary, clearly the reviewing court is not authorized to substitute its judgment for the decision of the Secretary not to bring suit.
3. The Secretary must furnish the court and the complaining witness with copies of a statement of reasons supporting his determinations. If there is any reasonable basis for the decision, the courts will not set it aside.

Dunlop v. Bachowski, 95 S.Ct. 1851 (1975).

Common Criticisms of the Administrative Process

The independent regulatory agencies and the administrative process are subjected to so much criticism, so often accused of being inefficient and ineffective, that political candidates run on platforms committed to deregulation and reform of the regulatory process. Many of the problems associated with the administrative process are directly related to its vastness, a characteristic of all levels of government. There are so many agencies regulating business that it is almost impossible to learn all of the rules applicable to business, let alone comply with them.

Sometimes it is impossible to find the myriad rules and regulations, and frequently they conflict with one another. The regulatory system does not coordinate the efforts of different regulatory bodies even though there is a tremendous overlapping of responsibilities. After the Environmental Protection Agency (EPA) had ordered hoods to be installed on coke ovens, to prevent pollution of the environment, the Occupational Health and Safety Administration (OSHA) ordered them removed because of the danger to workers from pollution in the workplace.

Agencies have been accused of devoting the major part of their efforts to trivial matters. Moreover, agencies have been accused of lack of enforcement and follow-up to ensure compliance with their rules and orders after they have been issued. Many agencies operate without clearly defined goals and priorities.

Regulated businesses are usually forced to create bureaucracies within their own organizations to deal with the regulating agency. Their internal groups tend to be mirror images of the agencies that regulate them. The existence of the Equal Employment Opportunity Commission has caused most large corporations to designate affirmative action employees to assist the company in complying with the laws, rules, and regulations enforced by EEOC. Whenever a bureaucracy exists, firms dealing with it must spend time and money in dealing with the agency.

The major problems of the fourth branch of government may be grouped under the headings (1) personnel, (2) cost, and (3) procedures. Each of these classifications will be discussed in the sections that follow. Not every agency is subject to all of the criticisms and indeed some agencies are probably not subject to any of them. The validity of the criticisms change from time to time and from agency to agency. They are directed at the total system only to illustrate the types of complaints that are made against some agencies. Everyone should recognize that many bureaucrats and commissioners are highly dedicated and competent public servants who work long and hard in the public interest.

Personnel problems

Critics of many agencies usually point to unqualified personnel who operate at low levels of efficiency. Appointments to some positions on boards and commissions often appear to be made as rewards to political friends, rather than on the basis of ability. The Peter Principle that many persons are promoted to their level of incompetency is applicable to many bureaucrats. On the other hand, some people's skills are underemployed, and this also causes job dissatisfaction and reduced efficiency.

The unsatisfactory level of efficiency in some agencies may be attributed to excessive paper work and too many meetings. The bureaucracy is virtually drowning in paper work and choking on meetings. The workday is spent attending committee meetings and arranging others, because the status of many employees is determined by the level of meetings attended, rather than by accomplishments.

Bias and lack of political accountability are two of the more often voiced complaints. Bias is almost always present to some degree, since an agency tends to attract people who believe in its goals. The personnel of EEOC are likely to be biased in favor of equal employment opportunity. They are not likely to be members of the Ku Klux Klan or the Nazi party. Likewise, the personnel of the NLRB are likely to believe in labor unions. Job dissatisfaction would exist at intolerable levels if the people working for an agency did not support the concept of regulation and the general goals of the employing agency or commission.

Lack of political accountability means that voters cannot directly express their dissatisfaction with an agency, its rules, or decisions. About the best they can do is to get the legislature to take steps to affect agency policy. Widespread criticism of the Federal Trade Commission prompted Congress to vote itself power to veto rules adopted by the FTC.

It is often alleged that agencies favor the industries they regulate, rather than the public, as a result of the cozy relationship between the regulator and the regulated. One reason for this rapport is that the regulators are often selected from persons in high executive positions in the industries they regulate. This choice is justified by the argument that they possess the expertise required to understand technical problems of the field. For the same reason, often the key staff members are recruited from the regulated industry. Also, it is not unusual for the reverse to occur. Upon completion of their terms in office, commissioners and their staff members frequently obtain high-paying jobs in the industries they have been regulating. Sweetheart regulation is sometimes a problem.

The cost of regulation

Regulation is a form of taxation because it directly increases the cost of government. More than 3 million people are involved in the regulation of business, at a direct cost of over $6 billion per year. But these direct costs of regulation are only a small fraction of the total cost. Regulation significantly adds to the cost of doing business, and these costs are passed on to the tax-paying, consuming public. Consumers for whose protection many regulations are adopted pay the direct cost of regulation in taxes and the indirect cost in the price of products and services. The total direct and indirect cost of regulation exceeds $100 billion per year, more than 5 percent of GNP. Regulation is clearly one of the causes of inflation at an estimated rate of ¾ to 1 percent per year.

There has been little or no cost-benefit analysis of administrative rules and regulations. Government has tended to assess only the benefits accruing from cleaner environment, safer products, healthier working conditions, and so on, in deciding to embark upon vast new regulatory programs. No one has attempted to balance the costs of the programs against the potential benefits. The public, and especially consumers, have been forced to pay for many things they did not want or did not need, in the sense that the cost far exceeded the benefits.

The financial burden of complying with many regulations is high because it requires new equipment or additional personnel. Perhaps the most disturbing additional cost to the business community is the cost of paperwork—filing applications, returns, reports, and forms. In a recent year, bureaucratic red tape made it necessary to complete and file roughly 2 billion forms at a cost in excess of $20 billion.

Procedural problems

The most often voiced criticism of many agencies is that there is unnecessary delay in rendering decisions. Many agencies are unable to resolve controversies expeditiously, despite the fact that the agencies were created to act faster than courts.

Some agencies have been criticized for weaknesses in their enforcement procedures, which often amount to little more than a slap on the wrist. The FTC and SEC, for example, make widespread use of the consent order. In a consent order, a business agrees or consents not to continue doing an act with which it has been charged. The business does not actually admit a violation; it simply agrees not to do it in the future. While this method reduces the backlog cases, many feel that it is not a proper sanction and does not serve justice.

In preparing rules and regulations, lawyers use legal and technical jargon that laymen (and perhaps even the lawyers) cannot understand. The demand for clear English in the bureaucracy as well as in other areas is growing stronger daily.

Deregulation and regulatory reform

There have been numerous recommendations to deregulate this or that activity or industry, to decrease the number of government programs by reorganizing agencies, and to pare down their functions. There is constant demand for cost-benefit analysis of most agency programs and for a reduction in paperwork. Proponents of deregulation argue that we should replace rigid, unnecessary regulation with the free play of competitive market forces. They believe that competition and the market can allocate resources and achieve efficiency better than government rules and regulations can. Deregulation would reduce the size of the bureaucracy and the direct cost of maintaining it.

Congress recently passed legislation that makes it easier to discharge incompetent federal employees and to reward those whose performance is excellent. Whether or not this new law will be effective is not yet clear, but the possibility of being discharged should stimulate some increase in productivity.

Some critics have proposed that no agency rule or regulation can become effective before the end of a stated period, such as 60 days. During this waiting period, either the House or the Senate or both may pass a resolution preventing the rule from becoming effective. Many object to this concept of congressional "veto" of agency rules because it would encroach upon Congress's time. Moreover, the agencies are supposed to be experts, and this would inject the political process into many technical areas.

Some opponents of the administrative process contend that government ought to contract out to the private sector as many of its functions as possible. They agree that it costs twice as much for government to do something as it does the private sector. Contractors are being used; for example, Blue Cross administrators pay Medicare and Medicaid payments for the government.

The constant demand for the use of cost-benefit analysis to evaluate government regulations itself requires analysis. How do you apply cost-benefit analysis to a rule dealing with human life? How much dollar benefit is to be assigned to a life in measuring it against the cost? Assume that the Department of Transportation rule requiring air bags in all new automobiles adds a cost of $800 to each car. Assume also that it saves 50,000 lives per year. Is the cost worth the benefit? It depends on whether or not you are one of the 50,000. Cost-benefit analysis is not possible for many government rules and regulations. This is not to say that the cost of many agencies cannot be compared with tangible benefits. Cost-benefit analysis applied to some agencies and to some rules and regulations will clearly point toward deregulation, but its use is obviously limited.

It is clear that notwithstanding the many inherent problems, the administrative process and the fourth branch of government are here to stay. The reasons previously given for their creation and existence remain valid. In fact, the trend is toward more regulation and more agencies. Even the business community advocates resort to the administrative process when difficult problems face society. There may be increased public participation in the process, but it is not likely that there will be a reduction in its size or in the scope of activities.

What is needed is not the elimination of regulation but the elimination of bad and excessive regulation. Most agencies exist for valid reasons, and they have proper goals and important roles to play in aiding the legitimate needs of society. They exist because of perceived needs of society. The legitimate goal is a balanced approach—free enterprise with effective regulation to protect the public interest.

Additional matters concerning the administrative process and administrative law will be further illustrated in the next two chapters concerned with antitrust law and labor law and employment.

REVIEW QUESTIONS AND PROBLEMS

1. Give five reasons for the extensive use of administrative agencies in our form of government.
2. List the six functions performed by most administrative agencies.
3. EPA discovered that a chemical company was dumping toxic waste into a local river. The agency conducted a hearing with proper notice to the chemical company and found the company to be in violation of EPA's regulations. A heavy fine was imposed, and the corporation appealed to the court, contending that the hearing had denied it its right to a trial by jury. What was the decision on the appeal? Why?
4. In order to cope with inflation, Congress created an agency to control wages and prices for all businesses engaged in interstate commerce. The agency was to make all rules and regulations necessary in the public interest to keep the rate of inflation at 5 percent or less. Several companies challenged the power of this agency to fix its prices. What was the decision? Explain.
5. Pam owned a tract of real estate across the street from a major shopping center. The lot was at an intersection of a main road leading to the shopping center, and Pam wanted to build a service station on the property. The property was zoned for single-family residences, and she filed a request with the appropriate zoning body, seeking to have the zoning classification changed to commercial. The zoning board denied Pam's request, and she filed suit, contending that the present and best use of the property was for commercial purposes. The zoning board contended that a buffer was needed between the shopping center and the residential area and that the only appropriate buffer was the street. What was the decision? Why?
6. If the oil company to whom Pam intended to lease the property above filed suit to challenge the denial of zoning change, what objection could be raised by the zoning authority? Explain.
7. If the zoning board was only advisory to the city council, what affect would this have on Pam's lawsuit to challenge the board's decision? Explain briefly.
8. List several criticisms of the administrative process.
9. It is often argued that regulation is a cause of inflation. Explain how regulation could be a cause of inflation.
10. Give some examples of techniques that could be used to reduce the high cost of government regulation.

A series of laws commonly referred to as the antitrust laws serve to protect our economic system from monopolies, attempts to monopolize, and activities in restraint of trade. These laws seek to provide a system of workable competition that, in turn, will achieve lower prices, product innovation, and equitable distribution of real income among consumers and the factors of production. Antitrust laws are enforced by the Justice Department and the Federal Trade Commission, but competitors and consumers aid enforcement by instituting private damage suits.

44 The Antitrust Laws

The Sherman Act

In 1890, under its power to regulate interstate commerce, Congress passed the Sherman Antitrust Act, directed essentially at two areas: (1) contracts, combinations, or conspiracies in restraint of trade; and (2) monopoly and attempts to monopolize. The law supplies a means to break up existing monopolies and to prevent others from developing. It is directed at single firms and does not purport to cover shared monopolies or oligopolies.

The law sought to preserve competition by utilization of three basic sanctions. First of all, violation of the act is a federal crime punishable by fine or imprisonment or both.

Second, the Sherman Act authorizes injunctions to prevent and restrain violations or continued violations of its provisions. Failure to obey may be punished by contempt proceedings. Third, a remedy is given to those who have been injured by violation of the act. In a civil action, they may collect treble damages plus court costs and reasonable fees for an attorney. Normally, the objective of money damages is to place the injured party in the position he would have enjoyed, as nearly as this can be done with money, had his rights not been invaded. The treble-damage provision serves not only as a means of punishing the defendant for his wrongful act but also as a means of compensating the plaintiff for his injury.

Today, criminal violations of the Sherman Act are felonies. An individual found guilty may be fined up to $100,000 and imprisoned up to three years. A corporation found guilty may be fined up to $1 million for each offense.

The treble-damage provision is probably the most important today. It may be enforced by the attorneys general of the various states on behalf of the consumers of their state. This provision also allows competitors as well as injured members of the general public to enforce the law if government fails to do so. (For example, H. J. Heinz Company has sued Campbell Soup, alleging predatory market practices designed to eliminate Heinz.) Consumers may collect triple damages from retailers guilty of violating the law. A consumer cannot sue a party that he or she did not deal with directly, however. Triple damage claims are not passed through the channels of distribution. If a manufacturer is guilty of violating the law, only the person who dealt directly with the manufacturer can recover triple damages.

Monopoly and attempts to monopolize

It is a violation of Section 2 of the Sherman Act for a firm to (1) monopolize, (2) attempt to monopolize or (3) conspire to monopolize any part of interstate or foreign commerce. In a case alleging an attempt to monopolize, there must be proof of intent to destroy competition or to achieve monopoly power. Showing that a conspiracy to monopolize existed requires proof of specific intent to monopolize and at least one overt act to accomplish it.

A firm has violated Section 2 if it followed a course of conduct through which it has obtained the power to control price or exclude competition. The mere possession of monopoly power is not a violation. There must be proof that the power has resulted from a deliberate course of conduct or proof of intent to maintain the power by conduct.

Cases involving Section 2 require proof of the power to affect the price of the firm's products in the market. Whether such power exists is determined by an analysis of the reaction of buyers to price changes by the alleged monopolist seller. Related products and geographic markets must be identified, and a study must be made of the degree of concentration within the markets.

Some monopoly cases involve homogenous products; others involve products for which there are numerous substitutes. Aluminum may be considered a product for which it is difficult to find substitutes. If a firm has 90 percent of the virgin aluminum market, a violation would be established. If a firm has 90 percent of the Danish coffee cake market, the decision is less clear, because numerous products compete with Danish coffee cakes. The relevant product is often difficult to define because of differences in products, substitute products, product diversification, and even product clusters.

Courts in monopoly cases examine a variety of factors: the degree of market concentration, barriers to entering the market, structural features such as the market shares of other firms, profit levels, the extent to which prices respond to changes in supply and demand, whether or not a firm discriminates in price among its customers, and the absolute size of the firm. Courts also examine the conduct of the firm. How did it achieve its market share? Was it by internal growth or by acquisition? Does the firm's current conduct tend to injure competition? These and other issues are important aspects in any finding of the existence of monopoly power.

Monopolistic conduct is predatory in that a firm seeks to advance its market share by injuring its actual or potential competitors, not by improved performance. Monopoly power may be used for the purpose of driving out competitors, for keeping them out, or for making them less effective.

Activities in Restraint of Trade

Section 1 of the Sherman Act prohibits contracts (express or implied), combinations, and conspiracies in restraint of trade. For example, discussion of price with one's competitors taken together with conscious parallel pricing establishes a violation.

Activities that may constitute a contract, combination, or conspiracy in restraint of trade are limitless. An agreement by several competitors to buy exclusively from a single supplier may be a violation. A group boycott may be a violation, even though the victim is just one small merchant. Of course, all forms of price fixing or other concentrated action among competitors constitute violations.

Under the Sherman Act, agreements and practices are illegal only if they are unreasonable. In deciding if an agreement or practice is unreasonable, courts divide them into two types or categories. Some are said to be illegal per se. This means that they are conclusively presumed to be unreasonable and thus illegal, so plainly anticompetitive and lacking in any redeeming virtue that it is unnecessary to examine the effects of the activity. If an activity is illegal per se, proof of the activity is proof of a violation and proof that it is in restraint of trade.

The second type or category includes activities that are illegal only if the facts establish that they are unreasonable. An act is unreasonable if it suppresses or destroys competition. An act is reasonable if it promotes competition. In cases under this second category, courts analyze the facts to determine the significance of the activity or restraint on competition.

Price fixing

The most common type of Sherman Act violation is price fixing, which is illegal per se. It is no defense that the prices fixed are fair or reasonable. It also is no defense that price fixing is engaged in by small competitors to allow them to compete with larger competitors. It is just as illegal to fix a low price as it is to fix a high price. Today it is as illegal to fix the price of services as it is to fix the price of goods. Price fixing in the service sector has been engaged in by professional persons as well as by service occupations such as automobile and TV repair workers, barbers, and refuse collectors. For many years it was contended that persons performing services were not engaged in trade or commerce, but the courts today reject such arguments.

CASE

D, a county bar association, developed a schedule of minimum fees to be charged by all lawyers in the county. P got in touch with several lawyers when he was about to buy a home, and all of them quoted the same fee for the legal services to be performed. P sued the bar association, alleging that the use of the minimum-fee schedule was a violation of the Sherman Act. D contended that legal services were not "trade or commerce" and that professional activities were exempt.

ISSUE Is it a violation of the Sherman Act for professional persons to agree on minimum fees to be charged for services?

DECISION Yes.

REASONS
1. The examination of a land title is a service; the exchange of such a service for money is "commerce."
2. It is not disparagement of the practice of law as a profession to acknowledge that it has this business aspect. There is no professional exemption.
3. Section 1 of the Sherman Act on its face shows a carefully studied attempt to bring within the act every person engaged in business whose activities might restrain or monopolize commercial intercourse among the states. In the modern world it cannot be denied that the activity of lawyers plays an important part in commercial intercourse and that anticompetitive activities by lawyers may exert a restraint on commerce.

Goldfarb et ux. v. Virginia State Bar et al., 95 S.Ct. 2004 (1975).

Some professional groups have attempted to avoid the foregoing result through the use of ethical standards. Others have attempted to determine the price of services indirectly by the use of formulas and relative value scales. Some medical organizations have determined that a given medical procedure would be allocated a relative value on a scale of one to ten. Brain surgery might be labeled a nine and a face lift a four. All members of the profession would then use these values in determining professional fees. Such attempts have been uniformly held to be illegal.

Other activities

Many violations of the Sherman Act involve concerted activities among competitors. An exchange of price information has been held to be one of the numerous violations.

CASE

The United States brought a civil antitrust action against D's, who were manufacturers of containers. D's had entered into an agreement that they would exchange price information with regard to specific sales of their product. The evidence showed that by exchanging this information, they kept prices within a fairly narrow range and tended to stabilize them.

ISSUE Was this arrangement to exchange price information a violation of the Sherman Act?

DECISION Yes.

REASONS
1. The result of this reciprocal exchange of prices was to stabilize prices, though at a downward level. Knowledge of a competitor's price usually meant matching that price.
2. Stabilizing prices as well as raising them is within the ban of Section 1 of the Sherman Act. In terms of market operations, stabilization is but one form of manipulation. The inferences are irresistible that the exchange of price information has had an anticompetitive effect in the industry, chilling the vigor of price competition.

United States v. Container Corporation of America, 89 S.Ct. 510 (1969).

Manufacturers frequently license distributors for their products, assigning them an exclusive territory, getting them to agree not to sell in other areas, and sometimes limiting their customers. Manufacturers who seek to control their products after departing with dominion over them through a sale may or may not be in violation of the Sherman Act. Territorial restrictions are not per se violations but may be illegal if they have an unreasonable effect on competition.

Just as manufacturers may desire to improve their channels of distribution by imposing territorial restrictions upon distributors, they may also seek to accomplish the same goal by controlling the ultimate price at which their products are sold to consumers. Retail outlets may be protected from price cutting competition of discount houses by a resale price maintenance agreement that prevents the use of the product as a loss leader. A manufacturer of a brand or trade name product may try to maintain its retail price because of a desire to create an image of high quality, which many consumers often relate to high price. Resale price maintenance schemes are a form of vertical price fixing and as such most run afoul of the Sherman Act.

The Clayton Act

From its adoption, the Sherman Act proved unable to accomplish all its goals. Its language was too broad, and the courts favored big business early in the century. Various amendments designed to make the act more specific have been enacted through the years.

In 1914 Congress enacted the first such amendment, known as the Clayton Act, designed to make the Sherman Act more specific. The Clayton Act declared illegal certain practices that might have an adverse effect on competition but were something less than violations of the Sherman Act. The practices it enumerated were outlawed if they *might* substantially lessen competition or tend to create a monopoly. This effect is sometimes referred to as the prohibited effect of the Clayton Act.

The Clayton Act contained four major provisions. Section 2, later amended by the Robinson-Patman Act, made it unlawful for a seller to discriminate in price among purchasers of commodities when the prohibited effect or tendency might result. Section 3 makes it unlawful for a person engaged in commerce to lease or sell commodities or fix a price with the condition that the lessee or purchaser shall not use or deal in the commodities of a competitor of the lessor or seller when the prohibited effect might result.

Section 7 prohibited the acquisition of all or part of the stock of other corporations if the effect *might* be to lessen competition substantially or to *tend* to create a monopoly. This section has been substantially amended also.

Section 8 of the Clayton Act was aimed at interlocking directorates. It prohibits a person from being a member of the board of directors of two or more corporations at the same time, when one of them has capital, surplus, and undivided profits totaling more than $1 million where elimination of competition by agreement between such corporations would amount to a violation of any of the antitrust laws.

Section 2 price discrimination background

Section 2, as originally adopted, outlawed price discrimination that might substantially lessen competition or tend to create a monopoly in any line of commerce. It was not illegal to discriminate in price because of differences in the grade, quality, or quantity of the commodity sold or to make due allowance for difference in the cost of selling or transportation. This latter provision, which allowed quantity discounts among other things, so weakened Section 2 that it was very difficult, if not impossible, to prevent price discrimination.

In the 1920s and very early 1930s, large-volume retailers and especially chain stores were able to obtain more favorable prices than those available to smaller competitors. Preferential treatment included quantity discounts, brokerage allowances paid to subsidiaries of customers, and promotional allowances. These practices, which were not prohibited by the Clayton Act, led to the enactment in 1936 of the Robinson-Patman amendment, which attempted to eliminate the advantages of large buyers over a small buyer.

To ensure equality of price to all customers of a seller of commodities for resale, where the result of unequal treatment may be substantially to lessen competition or tend to create a monopoly in any line of commerce, the Robinson-Patman Act forbids any person engaged "in commerce" to discriminate in price if the goods involved in such discrimination are "in commerce" and are for resale. The act does not apply to a sale by retailers to consumers. The term *commerce* refers to transactions in interstate commerce, not to intrastate transactions that only *affect* interstate commerce.

Section 2 basic provisions

First of all, the Robinson-Patman amendment made it a crime for a seller to sell at lower prices in one geographical area than elsewhere in the United States in order to eliminate competition or a competitor, or to sell at unreasonably low prices to drive out a competitor. As a result, it is illegal to sell goods below cost for the illegitimate purpose of driving out competition. Not every sale below cost constitutes a violation. Sales for legitimate purposes such as liquidation of excess, obsolete, or perishable merchandise may be legal. It is illegal to charge the low price only where the intention is to drive out a competitor.

Second, it is unlawful for any person to discriminate in price among different purchasers of commodities of like grade and quality if discrimination would substantially lessen competition or tend to create a monopoly in any line of commerce or injure competition with any person. Price discrimination is not illegal per se. An injury to competition may be established by showing injury to a competitor victimized by the discrimination. It is a violation knowingly to receive a benefit of such discrimination or to give such a benefit. The law applies both to buyers and sellers.

The statute recognizes certain exceptions. (1) Price differentials based on differences in the cost of manufacture, sale, or delivery of commodities are permitted (cost justification defense). (2) Sellers may select their own customers in bona fide transactions and not in restraint of trade. (3) Price changes may be made in response to changing conditions such as actual or imminent deterioration of perishable goods, obsolescence of seasonal goods, distress sales under court process, or sales in good faith in discontinuance of business in the goods concerned (changing conditions defense). (4) A seller in good faith may meet the equally low price of a competitor (good-faith meeting of competition defense).

The Robinson-Patman amendment also gave the Federal Trade Commission jurisdiction and authority to eliminate quality discounts. It also outlaws certain hidden or indirect discriminations by sellers in favor of certain buyers. Section 2(c) prohibits an unearned brokerage or commission related to a sale of goods. It is unlawful to pay or receive a commission or discount on sales or purchases except for actual services rendered. Section 2(d) outlaws granting promotional allowances or payments on goods bought for resale unless they are available to all competing customers. A manufacturer who gives a retailer a right to purchase three items for the price of two, as a part of a special promotion, must give the same right to all competitors in the market. Section 2(e) prohibits giving promotional facilities or services on goods bought for resale unless they are available to all competing customers.

Defenses

Several defenses to a charge of price discrimination were previously noted. Two require further comment.

Cost justification defense. If a plaintiff proves differential pricing and injury to competition, a prima facie case of price discrimination is established. Theoretically, a defendant may rebut this prima facie case by proof of cost justification. Practically, the cost defense has proved largely illusory. The complexities of determining what is "cost" results in rare use of the defense. As a practical matter, proof of cost involves direct costs and indirect costs. Indirect costs are based on assumptions, and accountants may make different ones. Disputes occur over the technique to determine actual cost, and proof of it is difficult if not impossible. The status of the defense is such that only the most prosperous and patient business firms can afford pursuit of it.

Good-faith meeting of competition. On the other hand, the good-faith meeting of competition defense is quite important. The act permits a defendant to demonstrate that price discrimination was not unlawful because the lower price, services, or facility was offered in good faith to meet an equally low price, service, or facility of a competitor. "Good faith" is not easily defined. It is a flexible and pragmatic, not a technical or doctrinaire concept. The standard of good faith is simply the standard of the prudent businessperson responding fairly to what he reasonably believes is a situation of competitive necessity. The facts and circumstances in each case govern its interpretation and application.

"Good faith" cannot be established if the purpose of a seller's price discrimination is to eliminate competition. The seller may offer discriminatory prices to customers, whether or not he has done business with them in the past. The timing of the price offers must make it apparent that they are intended to meet an individual competitive situation and are not a part of a general system of competition.

The good faith meeting of competition defense is available to buyers as well as to sellers. A buyer's liability is based on the seller's liability; therefore, if the seller has a defense, so does the buyer.

CASE

P, in an effort to achieve cost savings, entered into an agreement with its long-time supplier, Borden, under which Borden would supply "private label" (as opposed to "brand label") milk to petitioners' stores in the Chicago area. P refused Borden's initial offer and solicited orders from other companies, resulting in a lower offer from one of Borden's competitors. After being informed of this, Borden submitted a new offer, substantially better than its competitor's, and P accepted it. The FTC charged P with violating Section 2(f) of the Robinson-Patman Act by knowingly inducing or receiving illegal price discriminations from Borden.

ISSUE Did P violate Section 2(f) of the Robinson-Patman Act?

DECISION No.

REASONS
1. A buyer who has done no more than accept the lower of two prices competitively offered does not violate Section 2(f), provided the seller has a meeting competition defense and thus could not be liable under Section 2 (b). A buyer cannot be liable if a prima facie case could not be established against a seller or if the seller has an affirmative defense.
2. The meeting competition defense is established when the seller has a good-faith belief that the granting of a lower price would, in fact, meet the equally low price of a competitor.

3. Since good faith rather than certainty is required, the defense is established, even if the seller has unknowingly beat the price of his competition.
4. Borden did act in good faith here because it was in danger of losing a longstanding customer in the Chicago area if it failed to resubmit a bid.

Great Atlantic & Pacific Tea Co. v. F.T.C., 99 S.Ct. 925 (1979).

Section 3 tying arrangements and exclusive dealings

Section 3 of the Clayton Act prohibits arrangements and exclusive dealings that may substantially lessen competition or tend to create a monopoly in any line of commerce. If that should be the effect, anyone engaged in commerce may not lease or sell commodities (patented or unpatented) or fix a price on the condition that the lessee or purchaser should not use or deal in the commodities of a competitor or competitors of the lessor or seller. Section 3 covers tying contracts, reciprocal dealings, and exclusive arrangements.

In a tying contract, a commodity is sold or leased for use only on condition that the buyer or lessee purchase a different product or service from the seller or lessor. Tying arrangements may be violations of Section 1 of the Sherman Act and Section 3 of the Clayton Act. Tying arrangements are illegal without proof of anticompetitive effects. They are treated as unreasonable in and of themselves whenever economic power over the tying product can appreciably restrain free competition for the tied product and affect a "not insubstantial" amount of interstate commerce. The monopolistic power of a patent might be used to tie in a promise to buy an unpatented item. That would be a typical tying contract in violation of Section 3.

In *full-line forcing,* a common form of tying arrangement, the buyer or lessee is compelled to take a complete product line from the seller. If a major oil company requires its service station dealers to purchase a stated amount of regular gasoline and premium priced gasoline in order to obtain no-lead gasoline, Section 3 is violated.

A reciprocal dealing arrangement exists when two parties face each other as both buyer and seller. One party offers to buy the other party's goods, but only if the second party buys other goods from the first party. If one party is both a food wholesaler and a provider of goods used in processing foods, food processors may be faced by a reciprocal requirement. The first party might agree to buy the processors' products only if the processors buy the processing goods from it. One side of the transaction uses its power to force those with whom it deals to make concessions in another market. The law declares such conduct to be illegal because of the extension of market power in one market to another market.

Exclusive dealings do not necessarily involve more than one product and the terms of its sale. An exclusive dealing may be a requirements contract, whereby the buyer agrees to purchase all its business needs of a product supplied by the seller during a certain period of time. The buyer may be a manufacturer who has a reasonably ascertainable need for the raw materials or parts agreed to be supplied, or he may be a retailer who needs goods for resale. An exclusive dealing is present also in a contract whereby a buyer agrees not to purchase an item or items of merchandise from competitors of the seller. Such a contract might take the form of a franchise, in which a dealer agrees to sell only the product manufactured or distributed by the seller—a particular make of automobile, for instance. Such contracts are not illegal per se. They are illegal only if they tend substantially to lessen competition or tend to create a monopoly. Proof that competition is foreclosed in a substantial line of commerce establishes a violation.

CASE

Standard Oil entered into exclusive supply contracts with the operators of 5,937 independent retail service stations in 7 western states. In these contracts the dealers had agreed to purchase from Standard Oil not only all of their requirements for petroleum products but all of their tubes, tires, and batteries. In 1947, the contracts accounted for almost $58 million in gasoline and $8.2 million in other products involved. Standard's 6 leading competitors, who used similar contracts, sold 42.5 percent of the gas in the area in the same year. Standard had 6.7 percent of total sales in the area.

ISSUE Are these TBA (tires, batteries, accessories) contracts illegal?

DECISION Yes.

REASON Proof that competition has been foreclosed in a substantial share of a line of commerce is sufficient to show that an exclusive supply contract may substantially lessen competition. The law does not require a demonstration of economic circumstances once it is shown that the volume of business affected is not insignificant.

Standard Oil of California v. United States, 69 S.Ct. 1051 (1949).

Mergers and Acquisitions

Mergers and acquisitions are usually classified as horizontal, market extension, vertical, or conglomerate. A horizontal merger combines two businesses in the same field or industry, reducing the number of competitors. A market extension merger is an acquisition in which the acquiring company extends its markets. This market extension may be either in new products (product extension) or in new areas (geographical extension).

A vertical merger brings together two companies, one being the customer of the other. Such a combination usually removes the customer from the market as far as other suppliers are concerned. It may remove a source of supply also if the acquiring company is a customer of the acquired one. A conglomerate merger is one in which the businesses involved are neither competitors nor related as customer and supplier in any given line of commerce.

The law of mergers is based primarily upon three statutes—the Sherman Act, the Bank Merger Act, and the Clayton Act. A horizontal merger violates the Sherman Act if it is a combination in unreasonable restraint of trade or if it results in monopolization of a line of commerce or if it is an attempt to monopolize.

A great deal of merger litigation involves banks. Their mergers are subject to the provisions of the Bank Merger Acts of 1960 and 1966 as well as the usual antitrust laws. Bank mergers are illegal unless approved by one of the agencies that regulate banks. If the merger involves a national bank, the approval of the Comptroller of the Currency is required. If the banks are state banks that are members of the Federal Reserve System, the approval of the Federal Reserve Board is necessary. Other mergers of banks insured by the Federal Deposit Insurance Corporation require approval of that agency.

Section 7 of the Clayton Act is the major statute in the merger and acquisition area. It was originally adopted in 1914 and later amended by the Celler-Kefauver amendment in 1950. It is the basis of the discussions in the sections that follow.

Section 7 of the Clayton Act as amended provides essentially that no corporation engaged in commerce shall acquire any of the stock or assets of another such corporation if the effect may be substantially to lessen competition or to tend to create a monopoly in any line of commerce in any section of the country. Violations require only a finding and conclusion that a given acquisition has a reasonable probability of lessening competition or tendency toward monopoly. Section 7 does not deal with certainties, only with probabilities. The goal of the law is to arrest incipient anticompetitive effects and trends toward undue concentration of economic power. In determining whether or not a merger or acquisition is illegal, courts examine both the product market and the geographic market affected.

Clayton Act Section 7

The law has neither adopted nor rejected any particular tests for measuring relevant markets. Both the product market and geographical market of the companies involved are factual issues to be considered by the courts. The more narrowly the product line or geographic area is defined, the greater the impact of a merger or acquisition on competition. Thus, the relevant market frequently determines the probable anticompetitive effects of the merger. A decision that enlarges the line of commerce may be important in establishing that a merger is not anticompetitive.

CASE

The U.S. brought suit under Section 7 of the Clayton Act, challenging a proposed consolidation of the Connecticut National Bank (CNB) with the First New Haven National Bank (FNH), which were, respectively, the fourth and eighth largest commercial banks in Connecticut. The banks operated in adjoining regions of the state. The District Court, in finding for the defendants, held that commercial banking was not a distinct line of commerce and that the relevant geographic market was the whole state of Connecticut.

ISSUE Did the District Court err in its definition of the relevant geographic and product markets?

DECISION Yes. Commercial banking, excluding savings banks operations, constituted the relevant product market and the appropriate "line of commerce" within the meaning of Section 7. The relevant geographic market was the localized area in which each bank was in significant, direct competition with the other.

REASONS

1. Although there is some similarity between the services offered by savings banks and commercial banks, commercial banks provide a distinct cluster of services that savings banks cannot. They do compete in some product markets; but for commercial enterprises, commercial banks offer services that are unique. This is illustrated by the fact that commercial banks in the state had $1.03 billion in outstanding commercial loans, while savings banks accounted for only $26 million in such loans in 1971.
2. The whole state cannot be the relevant geographic market because the two banks are not direct competitors on that basis. Neither bank operates statewide, and its customers as a general rule do not operate on that basis. The majority of commercial bank activities are local; therefore, the market is the area where the effect of the merger on competition will be direct and immediate.

United States v. Connecticut National Bank, 94 S.Ct. 2788 (1974).

For a violation of Section 7, courts must also find that within the market the effect of the merger "may be substantially to lessen competition or to tend to create a monopoly." The degree of market concentration prior to the merger and the relative position of the merged parties are important factors to be considered. If there has been a history of tendency toward concentration in an industry, slight increases in further concentration are prohibited because of the policy of the law to curb such tendencies in their incipiency.

CASE

Von's Grocery, a retail grocery chain doing business in the Los Angeles area, acquired a direct competitor, Shopping Bag Food Store. As a result, Von's became the second largest grocery chain in Los Angeles, with sales of over $172 million annually, which amounted to 7.5 percent of the market. Before the merger, both companies were rapidly growing, aggressive competitors. The Los Angeles market was characterized by an increasing trend toward concentration through acquisitions and a marked decline in the number of single-store owners. The government brought this action, claiming the merger was illegal under Section 7 of the Clayton Act.

ISSUE Is the merger illegal under Section 7 of the Clayton Act?

DECISION Yes.

REASONS

1. A merger between two of the most successful and largest companies in a relevant market may substantially lessen competition, especially where the market is characterized by a long, continuous trend toward fewer and fewer competitors.
2. The primary purpose of antitrust law is to prevent the concentration of economic power in the hands of a few and to preserve competition among a large number of sellers. Congress, under Section 7, therefore sought to preserve competition among many small businesses by arresting a trend toward concentration in its incipiency.

United States v. Von's Grocery Co., 86 S.Ct. 1478 (1966).

A significant concept in the merger field today is the *potential entrant* doctrine. This doctrine finds that the prohibited effect may exist where an acquisition or a merger involves a potential entrant into a market. An acquisition of a competitor by a potential competitor is thus illegal where the effect may be substantially to lessen competition. The potential entrant doctrine has been used to prevent a soap company from acquiring a major bleach company. Since the soap company was a potential entrant into the bleach business, the acquisition was reviewed as anticompetitive. The same doctrine may be used also to stop geographic expansion by mergers and acquisitions. The potential entrant doctrine is applied not only because entry would bring in an additional competitor but also because the mere presence of a potential competitor at the edge of the market has positive effects on those companies actually competing.

Federal Trade Commission Act

Congress enacted a second antitrust law in 1914, creating the Federal Trade Commission as one of the expert, independent regulatory agencies. The Federal Trade Commission was given jurisdiction over cases arising under Sections 2, 3, 7, and 8 of the Clayton Act. Originally, the commission was directed to prevent unfair methods of competition in commerce. A later amendment directed it to make "unfair methods of competition in commerce and unfair or deceptive acts or practices in commerce" unlawful. The commission has to determine what methods, acts, or practices are "unfair" or "deceptive" and thus illegal, because Congress did not define these terms. The term "unfair methods of competition" is a flexible concept, the exact meaning of which evolves on a case-by-case basis. It is capable of application to a variety of unrelated activities, including business conduct in violation of any provision of the antitrust laws. Further, anticompetitive acts or practices that *fall short* of transgressing the Sherman or Clayton Acts may be restrained by the FTC as being "unfair methods of competition."

CASE

The company in question manufactures and sells paint. Its advertisements stated in various ways that for every can of paint purchased, the buyer would get a "free" can of equal quality and quantity. The price paid for the original can of paint was higher than the usual price, thus the second can was not in fact "free."

ISSUE Is this a violation of Section 5 of the FTC Act?

DECISION Yes.

REASONS
1. A business may advertise an article as "free," even though purchase of another article is required, so long as other terms of the offer are clearly stated, the price of the article required to be purchased is not increased, and its quality and quantity are not diminished.
2. In offers of two for the price of one, the sales price for the two must be the advertiser's usual retail price for the single article in the recent, regular course of business, or the ad is deceptive.
3. The seller was marketing twins; and in allocating what is in fact the price of two cans to one can, yet calling one "free," it misrepresented the facts.

FTC v. Mary Carter Paint Co., 382 U.S. 46 (1965).

The major role of the FTC has been in the area of unfair and deceptive business practices; its protection of consumers and debtors runs the whole gamut of purchases from one's birth until death. Great deference is given to the decisions of the commission, which has a wide variety of corrective actions it may require for violations of the law. The FTC sometimes requires that a party guilty of deceptive advertising run a corrective ad admitting the deception. The FTC also has a policy of ad substantiation. Advertisers must be able to prove the truthfulness of their ads. In establishing a violation of the Federal Trade Commission Act, the government is not required to prove that an ad is false.

During the 1960s, the FTC was criticized for its ineffectiveness as a consumer protection agency. The 1970s saw a major change in activities of the agency and in the enforcement of various laws under its jurisdiction. In the 1980s the criticism is the opposite of that in the 1960s. Many people complain that the FTC is too active, that it is placing unconscionable burdens on business, especially on advertising. Businesspeople note that the FTC is trying to create laws that Congress has refused to enact. It has attacked advertising directed at children and has attempted to prevent oil companies from owning pipelines or retail outlets. Because of the many criticisms of the agency, some rules are being reexamined to determine if their impact is beneficial or harmful to the consuming public. Congress has enacted a law allowing it to veto rules of the commission. A disgruntled business community is also challenging the legality of FTC rules, adding to the likelihood that the agency will be a controversial one during most of this decade.

REVIEW QUESTIONS AND PROBLEMS

1. Jack had a home delivery route for the newspaper of Post Company. The contract provided that carriers with exclusive territories were subject to termination if their prices exceeded the suggested maximum. Jack raised the price to his customers, and Post objected. Post hired a company to solicit readers away from this route and hired another carrier to take over part of the route. Jack brought suit, claiming that Post was in violation of the Sherman Act. Is Jack correct? Why?

2. List three defenses to a charge of price discrimination in violation of the Robinson-Patman Amendment.

3. Gulf & Southern Corporation (G&S) is a large conglomerate and is in the toiletry business. For the past two years it has been packaging its brand-name men's cologne "Brut" and selling it to retailers for $4.00 per bottle. It has also been selling the same substance without the name to another company for $3.00 per bottle. There is wide customer recognition of Brut and a willingness to pay more for it. Is G&S violating any law? Explain.

4. The National Collegiate Athletic Association, a voluntary association of 800 colleges and universities located throughout the United States, adopted a bylaw limiting the number of football coaches that a member may employ: one head coach, eight assistant coaches, and two part-time assistant coaches. A university brought suit, contending that this action was unreasonable restraint of trade and in violation of the Sherman Act. Is the bylaw an unreasonable restraint of trade? Why?

5. Gravel Company was the principal supplier of certain raw materials to Baker Company and was also the holder of 23 percent of Baker Company's stock. The Justice Department brought suit, claiming that the acquisition of this stock by Gravel Company violated Section 7 of the Clayton Act. In defense, Gravel Company contended that the Clayton Act was not applicable, since Gravel Company and Baker Company were not in competition with each other. Is Gravel correct? Why?

6. Soft Shoe Company entered into franchise agreements with 650 retail stores. The agreements prohibited the stores from handling any shoes other than Soft Shoe's. Stores that agreed received valuable benefits not available to other customers, including architectural plans, merchandising records, and group insurance. It was determined that the company's activities were not in violation of either the Sherman or Clayton Acts. The FTC brought suit, contending that the franchise agreement constituted an unfair method of competition. Was this action by the FTC proper? Why?

7. The National Society of Professional Engineers adopted an ethical standard that prohibited price bidding for professional engineering work. The rule was adopted to prevent unsafe designs by engineers, unsafe construction, and deceptively low bids. The Department of Justice claimed that the ethical standard violated Section 1 of the Sherman Act. Did the National Society of Professional Engineers violate the Sherman Act? Why?

8. X Railroad Company sold and leased several million acres of land, using deeds that contained "preferential routing clauses." Under these deeds, purchasers and lessees agreed to ship their products on the X Railroad as long as it offered rates and services equal to those of other available carriers. The U.S. government brought suit against X, charging that the "preferential routing clauses" were violations of the Sherman Act. Should the clauses be declared void? Explain.

9. There was a merger between the second largest can producer and third largest glass jar producer. They were in second and sixth places, respectively, in the market embracing glass and metal containers. Glass containers do not generally compete with can containers. Is the merger a violation of Section 7 of the Clayton Act? Why?

10. The Ford Motor Company acquired the assets, including the trade name, of Autolite Company, a manufacturer of spark plugs and automotive parts. At the time of the acquisition, Autolite had 15 percent of the spark plug market. Manufacturers of spark plugs traditionally sell them to auto manufacturers below cost, seeking to make a profit in replacement sales. Ford was the largest purchaser of plugs from independent sources prior to the acquisition, which was made so that Ford could participate in the replacement market. Ford's acquisition of the Autolite spark plug is a violation of the Clayton Act. Why?

11. The Clear-Copy Company manufactured and sold photocopy machines. In order to purchase one of its machines, a buyer had to agree to purchase copy paper only from Clear-Copy. Is this agreement legal? Explain.

45

The Law of Labor and Employment

The goal of this chapter is to understand the major provisions of key laws related to labor-management and employer-employee relations. Some of the laws, such as those governing workers' compensation, are state laws; most are federal—and all are changing. The topics to be discussed—each potentially a complete course—play a major role in our political process, making not only the laws but also the law enforcers subject to change.

Labor law, an important part of any study of the employer-employee relationship, is concerned with all aspects of collective bargaining as well as with the internal operation of labor unions. It is developed not only by statutes and judicial decisions but also by the rules, regulations, and decisions of the National Labor Relations Board and the Department of Labor.

To understand labor law, we must recognize and understand its goals. The primary goal of laws relating to collective bargaining may be simply stated: to create equality of bargaining power between management and labor, so that they will be able to settle their differences on mutually satisfactory terms consistent with the public interest. Some statutory provisions are designed to equalize the bargaining power of management with labor, or vice versa. Other statutory provisions are designed to protect the public interest in the collective bargaining process. The sections that follow will briefly review the various laws that have been enacted to accomplish the goal of equalizing the bargaining power of labor and management.

Labor Laws prior to the Wagner Act

Clayton Act

The Clayton Act of 1914 contained two provisions relating to labor relations. The first attempted to prohibit federal courts from issuing injunctions to prevent strikes and picketing in disputes over terms or conditions of employment. The second provided that the antitrust laws were not applicable to labor unions or their members in carrying out union activities. Prior to the existence of the Clayton Act, the Sherman Antitrust Act was sometimes applied by courts to the activities of those in the labor movement. The Clayton Act provision exempting labor activities followed.

Railway Labor Act

In 1926 Congress enacted the Railway Labor Act to encourage collective bargaining in the railroad industry, so that labor disputes would not interrupt the transportation of goods in interstate commerce. The act was later extended to airlines, and it is now applicable to both forms of transportation. The Railway Labor Act created a National Mediation Board whose duty it is to designate the bargaining representative for any group of employees in the railway or air transport industries. The selection is made by conducting representation elections. The act also outlaws certain unfair labor practices, such as refusing to bargain collectively.

When the parties under the jurisdiction of the National Mediation Board cannot reach a collective bargaining agreement, it is the function of the board to attempt mediation of their differences. If mediation fails, the board encourages voluntary arbitration. If the parties refuse to arbitrate and the dispute is likely to be a substantial interruption of interstate commerce, the board informs the President, who may then appoint a special emergency board. This emergency board investigates the dispute and publishes its findings of fact and recommendations for its resolution. During the period of investigation and for thirty days after the report is made public, neither management nor labor can unilaterally change the condition out of which the dispute arose, such as by striking or discharging workers. The parties have no duty to agree to the special board's recommended solution. Thus, if no new agreement is reached after the thirty-day waiting period, lockouts, strikes, and other actions by the parties are once again legal.

The procedures of the Railway Labor Act sometimes fail to resolve major disputes in transportation, and special action is taken by the President or the Congress. The transportation industry's labor problems have such a potential for irreparable damage to the public that legislative solutions may be required.

The procedures discussed above apply to assisting employers and unions to arrive at a collective bargaining agreement; they do not apply to issues concerning the interpretation of existing contracts. Such issues in transportation must be submitted to compulsory arbitration.

Norris-LaGuardia Act

In 1932 Congress enacted the Norris-LaGuardia Act. Prior to that enactment, management could rather effectively prevent union activity by going to court and obtaining an injunction against a strike or against picketing. The Norris-LaGuardia Act encouraged collective bargaining by limiting the jurisdiction of federal courts in enjoining union activity. Federal courts may not issue an injunction to stop an employee or a union from engaging in lawful union activities such as striking and picketing.

Although Norris-LaGuardia greatly restricts the use of injunctions in labor disputes, it does not prohibit them altogether. The power of state courts to issue injunctions was not affected by Norris-LaGuardia; therefore, a state court may enjoin picketing that violates a no-strike clause of a collective-bargaining agreement. Moreover, an injunction may still be issued by a federal court if an unlawful act is about to be committed that will result in irreparable damage to the party seeking the injunction.

The second major provision of the Norris-LaGuardia Act was to make "yellow dog" contracts (those forbidding union membership) unenforceable. Because of this provision, it is illegal for an employer to have his employees agree that they will not join or form a union.

Norris-LaGuardia attempted to establish a climate in which employees would be free to organize and bargain collectively through a union, without interference or coercion on the part of employers. It did nothing to impose any duty on management to deal with or even recognize unions. As a result, it did little to encourage growth of collective bargaining.

The Wagner Act

In 1935 Congress passed the National Labor Relations Act, commonly called the Wagner Act. Noting that employees individually did not possess bargaining power equal to that of their employers, the Wagner Act stated that its policy was to protect by law the right of employees to organize and bargain collectively in order to encourage the "friendly adjustment of industrial disputes." This policy was to be accomplished by creating for employees equality in their bargaining position with that of employers. In summary, the Wagner Act:

1. Created an administrative agency, the National Labor Relations Board (NLRB), to administer the act. The NLRB was given broad powers.
2. Authorized the NLRB to conduct union certification elections and to certify the union that was to represent a group of workers.
3. Outlawed certain conduct by employers that generally prevented or at least discouraged union activity. These prohibited acts are known as *unfair labor practices.* The NLRB was authorized to enter corrective orders when unfair labor practices had been committed. Unfair labor practices by management will be discussed later in this chapter.

It must be kept in mind that the Wagner Act does not cover all workers. Among those exempt from its coverage are employees of the federal and state governments, political subdivisions of the states, nonprofit hospitals, and persons subject to the Railway Labor Act. Also excluded are independent contractors, agricultural laborers, domestic servants, and those employed by their spouse or a parent.

Taft-Hartley amendment

The Wagner Act provided a climate for rapid union growth. By the end of World War II many people believed that the power and influence of unions was greater than that of management. Although employers had superior bargaining power prior to the Wagner Act, by 1946 many persons felt the pendulum had shifted, and the unions—with their power of nationwide, crippling strikes—had greater bargaining power. It was clear that no one company had equal bargaining power with a union that represented all employees in an industry. Moreover, nationwide strikes were having a substantial adverse effect on an important third party—the public.

In 1947 Congress, attempting once again to equalize the bargaining power of management and labor, passed the Taft-Hartley amendment to the Wagner Act. The amendment contained the following important provisions:

1. Equalized bargaining power by declaring that certain activities are improper. The Wagner Act had been one-sided, recognizing management's unfair treatment of labor but neglecting the other side of the coin. (Unions' unfair labor practices are discussed more fully in subsequent sections.)
2. Established an eighty-day cooling-off period. The President, acting with an emergency board and through the federal courts, may obtain an injunction to stop a strike or lockout that may imperil national safety or health. The injunction is good for eighty days.
3. Created the Federal Mediation and Conciliation Service to assist in settlement of labor disputes. This federal agency is of special importance in strikes that threaten the national economy.
4. Outlawed the *closed* shop, one in which a person must be a union member as a condition of employment. Taft-Hartley did allow a *union* shop, one in which a worker must join the union within thirty days after being employed. Section 14(b) authorized states to enact state right-to-work laws, however, and they may prohibit union shops. Thus Taft-Hartley gave employees some freedom of choice in union membership.
5. Allowed employers to express their opinions. To meet employers' complaints that the Wagner Act violated their right of free speech, Congress added Section 8(c), which provided that expressing any views, arguments, or opinions is not evidence of an unfair labor practice if such expression contains no threat of reprisal or force or promise of benefit. This attempt at free speech is not very effective because of the difficulty of saying things that cannot be construed as either a threat or a promise.

Eighty-day cooling-off period

The eighty-day cooling-off provisions of Taft-Hartley are extremely important. They may be used in any strike under the jurisdiction of the Wagner Act—almost every industry except transportation. The provisions come into play whenever the President is of the opinion that a strike or lockout will, if permitted to occur or to continue, imperil the national health or safety. The President then appoints a board of inquiry to obtain facts about the strike. The board makes a study of the strike and reports back to the President. If the board finds that the national health or safety is indeed affected by the strike, then the President, through the Attorney General, goes to the Federal District Court for an injunction ordering the union to suspend the strike (or company to suspend the lockout) for eighty days. During the eighty-day period, the Federal Mediation Service works with the two parties to try to achieve an agreement. If no agreement is reached during the eighty-day period, the Presidential board holds new hearings and receives the company's final offer. The members of the union are then allowed to vote on this final proposal. If they vote for the new proposal, the dispute is over. If they vote against the proposal, they may again be called out on strike. At this point the strike may continue indefinitely until the disagreement causing it is resolved by collective bargaining—unless Congress passes additional legislation to solve the problem. Experience has shown that most disputes are settled during the eighty-day period. The injunction provided for in the Taft-Hartley Act may not be used for all strikes but is limited to "national emergency" strikes. These must involve national defense or key industries or must have a substantial effect on the economy.

Unfair Labor Practices by Employers

The Wagner Act stated that five practices by employers were unfair to labor:

1. Interference with efforts of employees to form, join, or assist labor organizations or to engage in concerted activities for mutual aid or protection.
2. Domination of a labor organization or contribution of financial or other support to it.
3. Discrimination in hire or tenure of employees because of their union affiliation.
4. Discrimination against employees for filing charges or giving testimony under the act.
5. Refusal to bargain collectively with a duly designated representative of the employees.

Interference with union activity

In order to guarantee the worker's right to organize and bargain collectively, any practice that might discourage union activity is considered unfair. Employers may not threaten to fire employees who attempt to organize, nor may they cut back on benefits if unionization takes place. The act also prohibits conferral of benefits on workers if management is using the benefits to discourage union activity.

Any attempt by management to prevent or discourage employees' activities for the purpose of collective bargaining or other mutual aid or protection may constitute an unfair labor practice.

CASE

Employees sought to distribute a four-part union newsletter in nonworking areas of their plant during nonworking time. The newsletter encouraged employees to write their legislators to oppose a state "right-to-work" statute. It also criticized a presidential veto of an increase in the federal minimum wage and urged employees to register to vote to "defeat our enemies and elect our friends." The company refused to permit the requested distribution of the newsletter. The union then filed an unfair labor practice charge with the NLRB. The board ruled that petitioner's refusal interfered with the employees' exercise of their rights under Section 7 of the National Labor Relations Act.

ISSUE Is the distribution of a newsletter the kind of concerted activity that the Wagner Act protects against employer interference?

DECISION Yes.

REASONS

1. The law provides that "employees shall have the right . . . to engage in . . . concerted activities for the purpose of collective bargaining or other mutual aid or protection. . . ."
2. The "mutual aid or protection" clause extends to channels outside the immediate employer-employee relationship. Thus, it has been held that the clause protects employees from retaliation by their employers when they seek to improve working conditions through resort to administrative and judicial forums, and that employees' appeals to legislators to protect their interests as employees are within the scope of this clause.
3. The state "right-to-work" statute discussion is clearly within the protection of the law because union security is central to the union concept of strength through solidarity.
4. The comments on minimum wage legislation were protected because the board was entitled to note the widely recognized impact that a rise in the minimum wage may have on the level of negotiated wages generally. In the circumstance of this case, the union's call for these employees to back persons who support an increase in the minimum wage, and to oppose those who oppose it, is fairly characterized as concerted activity for the "mutual aid or protection" of petitioner's employees and of employees generally.

Eastex, Inc. v. NLRB, 98 S.Ct. 2505 (1978).

Numerous complaints have been filed against employers contending that certain practices were designed to discourage union activity. The decision on these complaints usually requires a look at the state of mind of the employer at the time of the act in question. A review of past NLRB decisions reveals that the law is liberally interpreted and applied to give maximum effect to the purpose of the act—the encouragement of collective bargaining and the encouragement of union activity.

Although both parties are entitled to freedom of speech during a campaign to organize workers, management especially must be very careful in what it says. It must make sure that its statements do not contain threats of reprisal if a union is voted in, or promises of benefits if the union is rejected. Coercive statements are an unfair labor practice that may result in the election being set aside. For example, a union organizer told the workers that the union would obtain higher wages for the workers. The company responded, "If the union comes in, the wages may go up, but they may also go down." This was a coercive statement because it contained an implied threat and therefore was an unfair labor practice.

A significant penalty for an unfair labor practice is to have an election set aside and a new election ordered. If the climate was such that the activity engaged in was likely to affect a new election, the NLRB, to encourage collective bargaining, has on occasion certified a union that lost the election.

Other unfair labor practices—employers

It is also an unfair labor practice for an employer to dominate a labor organization or contribute financial or other support to it. The law views the relationship of employer and employee in the collective bargaining process to be adversary in character. The union must be independent of the employer. If two unions are seeking to organize workers, the law requires the employer to be neutral. An employer who takes sides is guilty of an unfair labor practice. Under this provision, a company cannot even give the union a place to meet. Company unions are out.

The third unfair labor practice listed in the Wagner Act prohibits discrimination in the hiring or tenure of employees for reason of union affiliation. Under this section, an employer may neither discharge nor refuse to hire an employee either to *encourage* or to *discourage* membership in any labor organization. Nor may he discriminate in regard to any term or condition of employment for such purposes.

CASE

A union went out on strike against an employer. The employer sought to hire replacement workers; and to encourage them to apply, the company gave the new workers "super-seniority." This super-seniority was twenty years' additional seniority insofar as future layoffs were concerned. As a result of this offer, the company hired not only new workers but many former employees who resigned from the union.

ISSUE Is the granting of super-seniority a form of discrimination against the union members and thus an unfair labor practice?

DECISION Yes.

REASONS
1. Super-seniority is a form of discrimination extending far beyond the employer's right to replace striking workers. Here the subjective intent of the employer was to destroy the union and to discourage the worker from further union activity.
2. There was also a desire to penalize union members who were on strike. The stated business purpose was not valid in light of the actual motive of the employer.

NLRB v. Erie Resistor Corp., 373 U.S. 221 (1963).

A fourth unfair labor practice by management is discriminating against employees for filing charges or giving testimony under the Wagner Act. The act protects employees from being discharged or from other reprisals by their employers because the workers have sought to enforce their rights under the law. It protects the NLRB's channels of information by preventing an employer's intimidation of complainants and witnesses.

In cases alleging retaliation for filing charges or giving testimony, the employer will frequently contend that action was taken against the employee for some reason other than his filing charges or giving testimony. Thus, most often these cases boil down to a question of proof of what motivated the employer in pursuing his course of action. If the employer can convince the NLRB that the employee was discharged because of misconduct, low production, personnel cutbacks necessitated by economic conditions, or other legitimate considerations, there is no unfair labor practice.

The Wagner Act as originally passed required employers to bargain collectively with unions. In other words, it was an unfair labor practice for management to refuse to bargain collectively with a duly certified union. The requirement to bargain collectively will be discussed later in this chapter.

Unfair labor practices by unions

The Taft-Hartley amendment to the Wagner Act declared that certain conduct or activities by labor unions were unfair labor practices and thus illegal. The Landrum-Griffin amendment added two more, and now the list includes the following:

1. Restraining or coercing an employee to join a union or restraining or coercing an employer in selecting the company's representatives in bargaining with the union.
2. Causing or attempting to cause the employer to discriminate against an employee who is not a union member, unless there is a legal union-shop agreement in effect. (This outlawed the closed shop, but it allows a union shop unless there is a state right-to-work law.)
3. Refusing to bargain with an employer if the union is the NLRB-designated representative of the employees.
4. Striking, picketing, and engaging in secondary boycotts for illegal purposes.
5. Charging new members excessive or discriminatory initiation fees where there is a union-shop agreement.
6. Causing an employer to pay for work not performed (featherbedding).
7. Picketing to require an employer to recognize or bargain with a union that is not currently certified as representing his employees.
8. Agreeing with an employer to engage in a secondary boycott.

Illustrations of illegal union activity

The first unfair labor practice above includes misconduct by unions directed both toward employees and employers. Most allegations of unfair labor practices filed against unions are brought under this provision.

It is illegal for a union to restrain or coerce employees in the exercise of their right to bargain collectively, just as it is an unfair labor practice by employers to interfere with the same rights. Employees also are guaranteed the right to refrain from union activities unless required by a legal union shop agreement in force between their employer and a labor organization.

Mass picketing, threats of physical violence aimed at employees or their families, and blocking of entrances to plants physically to bar employees from going in have all been held to be union unfair labor practices.

The words *restrain* and *coerce* have the same meanings in reference to union activity and activities by employers. The test is whether the words or conduct by the union are reasonably likely to have deprived the employees of a free choice. The intent is to ensure that the decision of the employees as to whether or not to be represented by a union in bargaining and also the choice of that representative is arrived at freely, without coercion.

CASE

At the request of P, the union, the NLRB conducted a union certification election for D's employees. Prior to the election, "recognition slips" were circulated among the employees. An employee who signed the slip before the election would become a member of the union automatically and would not have to pay an "initiation fee" if the union was voted in. Those who had not signed a recognition slip would have to pay the fee or fine, as it was sometimes called. The union won the election, and the company seeks to set the election aside.

ISSUE Is the waiver of the initiation fee grounds for setting aside the election?

DECISION Yes.

REASONS

1. Whatever his true intentions, an employee who signs a recognition slip prior to an election is indicating to other workers that he supports the union. His outward manifestation of support must often serve as a useful campaign tool in the union's hands to convince other employees to vote for the union, if only because many employees respect their co-workers' views on the unionization issue. By permitting the union to offer to waive an initiation fee for those employees signing a recognition slip prior to the election, the board allows the union to buy endorsements and paint a false portrait of employee support during its election campaign. We do not believe that the policy of fair elections permits endorsements, whether for or against the union, to be bought and sold in this fashion.
2. Any procedure requiring a "fair" election must honor the right of those who oppose a union as well as those who favor it. The act is wholly neutral when it comes to that basic choice. By Section 7 of the act, employees have the right not only to "form, join, or assist" unions but also the right "to refrain from any or all of such activities."

NLRB v. Savair Manufacturing Company, 94 S.Ct. 495 (1973).

One of the unfair labor practices previously listed concerns the union's applying what are called secondary pressures against an employer. Secondary pressures are those whose purpose it is to force an employer to cease using, or dealing in, the products of another. A secondary pressure may take the form of a strike or a boycott or an attempt to encourage a strike or a boycott. It is illegal to strike against an employer for the purpose of forcing him to cease doing business with another employer. Similarly, it is unlawful for a union to boycott an employer because that company uses or deals in the goods of another. *Featherbedding,* another unfair labor practice by unions, occurs when an employer is required to pay for work not performed. It should be understood that "make work" provisions of union contracts are not illegal featherbedding. This provision of Taft-Hartley is not violated as long as some services are performed, even if they are of little or no actual value to the employer.

Organizational picketing to force the recognition of an uncertified union is illegal when:

1. The employer has lawfully recognized another union as the collective bargaining representative of his employees.

2. A valid representation election has been conducted by the NLRB within the past twelve months.
3. Picketing has been conducted for a reasonable time, not in excess of thirty days, without a petition for a representation election being filed with the NLRB.

Such organizational picketing is an unfair labor practice because of the policy of the law to encourage NLRB-conducted elections. The NLRB election procedures are reinforced, and unions that represent only a minority of employees are prevented from continuing a jurisdictional dispute with the union representing the majority of workers.

Hot-cargo contracts are unfair labor practices and illegal insofar as both parties to the contract are concerned. A hot-cargo contract is one in which the parties (employer and union) agree that the employer will not handle, use, sell, or transport products of another business involved in a labor dispute. In other words, the product of the company involved in a labor dispute becomes "hot," and other companies agree with their union that they will not be involved with such products.

The requirement to bargain collectively

As previously noted, it is an unfair labor practice for either the employer or the union to refuse to bargain collectively with each other. The term "to bargain collectively" means to bargain in good faith. Although the parties need not agree with each other's demands, conduct such as the failure to make counterproposals may be evidence of bad faith. Employers and unions must approach the bargaining table with a fair and open mind and sincere purpose to find a basis of agreement. Refusing to meet at reasonable times with representatives of the other party, refusing to reduce agreements to writing, and designating persons with no authority to negotiate as representatives at meetings are examples of conduct that constitute this unfair labor practice.

Another issue is also present in the requirement that the parties bargain collectively. This issue, simply stated, is: about what? Must the employer bargain with the union on all management decisions in which the union or the employees are interested? Are there subjects and issues upon which management is allowed to act unilaterally? The law requires or compels bargaining on issues concerned with wages, hours, and other terms and conditions of employment.

Thus, management decisions affecting labor fall into two categories: those that concern *mandatory* or *compulsory* bargaining issues, and those that involve *voluntary* or *permissive* bargaining issues. Classifications must be made on a case-by-case basis.

CASE

P, the Ford Motor Company, provided its employees with access to vending machines and with an in-plant cafeteria. Both were operated by an independent caterer, but Ford had the right to approve the quality, quantity, and prices of food served. Ford agreed to a price increase requested by the caterer and notified the union of the new prices. The union objected and demanded that Ford bargain with it over the prices. Ford refused to do so; and when a complaint was filed with the NLRB, Ford was found guilty of the unfair labor practice of refusing to bargain.

ISSUE Are in-plant cafeteria food prices a "term or condition of employment," so that they are a compulsory bargaining issue?

DECISION Yes.

REASONS 1. Because the "classification of bargaining subjects as 'terms or conditions of employment' is a matter concerning which the board has special expertise," its judgment as to what is mandatory bargaining subject is entitled to considerable deference.

2. The board's consistent view that in-plant food prices and services are mandatory bargaining subjects is not an unreasonable or unprincipled construction of the statute, and it should be accepted and enforced.
3. The availability of food during working hours and the conditions under which it is to be consumed are matters of deep concern to workers. The terms and conditions under which food is available on the job are plainly germane to the working environment.
4. The establishment of in-plant food prices is not among those "managerial decisions, which lie at the core of entrepreneurial control." The board is in no sense attempting to permit the union to usurp managerial decision making, nor is it seeking to regulate an area from which Congress intended to exclude it.
5. As illustrated by the facts of this case, substantial disputes can arise over the pricing of in-plant supplied food and beverage. National labor policy contemplates that areas of common dispute between employers and employees be funneled into collective bargaining. The assumption is that this is preferable to allowing recurring disputes to fester outside the negotiation process until strikes or other forms of economic warfare occur.

Ford Motor Company v. NLRB, 99 S.Ct. 1842 (1979).

As the Ford case illustrates, courts tend to defer to the special expertise of the NLRB in classifying collective bargaining subjects, especially in the area of "terms or conditions of employment." Among the issues that have been held to be compulsory bargaining issues are merit-pay increases, incentive-pay plans, bonuses, paid vacations and holidays, proposals for effective arbitration and grievance procedures, and no-strike and no-lockout clauses.

Typical of issues that do not involve compulsory bargaining matters are the price of the employer's product, loading and unloading procedures, and other matters that generally qualify as managerial decisions essential to entrepreneurial control.

It should be reemphasized that neither the employer nor the union is required to make concessions to the other concerning a mandatory subject of bargaining. The law demands only that each negotiate such matters in good faith with the other before making a decision and taking unilateral action. If the parties fail to reach an agreement after discussing these problems, each may take steps that are against the wishes and best interests of the other party. The employer may refuse to grant a wage increase requested by the union, and the union is free to strike.

Landrum-Griffin Act

After the enactment of Taft-Hartley, Congress turned its attention to the internal operations of labor unions. Hearings before congressional committees in the 1950s revealed widespread corruption, lack of democratic procedures, and domination of labor unions by elements thought to be undesirable. As a result, Congress in 1959 enacted the Landrum-Griffin Amendment to the Wagner Act.

In order to eliminate internal corruption and to guarantee that the "rank and file" union members had control of their union, Landrum-Griffin contained a "Bill of Rights," protecting the rights of union members:

1. to nominate candidates, to vote in elections, to attend membership meetings, and to have a voice in business transactions, subject to reasonable union rules and regulations.

2. to have free expression in union meetings, business discussions, and conventions subject to reasonable rules and regulations.
3. to vote on an increase of dues or fees.
4. to sue and testify against the union.
5. to receive written, specific charges; to be given a reasonable time for defense; and to be accorded a full and fair hearing before any disciplinary action is taken by the union against them.
6. to be given a copy of the collective bargaining agreement that they work under, upon request.

Landrum-Griffin contains provisions relating to reports that must be filed with the secretary of labor. The purpose of these reports is to reveal practices detrimental to union members. For example, each union must adopt a constitution and bylaws and file them with the secretary of labor. In addition, unions must keep the Department of Labor informed of:

1. the name and address of the union office and the place where records are kept.
2. names and titles of officers.
3. the amount of initiation fees required.
4. the amount of dues charged.
5. a detailed statement of procedures for qualification for office, levying fees, insurance plans, disbursement of funds, audits, selection of officers, removal of officers, determining bargaining demands, fines, approval of contracts, calling strikes, and issuance of work permits.

In addition, yearly financial reports must be filed that indicate

1. assets and liabilities
2. receipts and sources of funds
3. salaries of officers
4. loans to members greater than $250
5. loans to business enterprises
6. other disbursements

A major focus of Landrum-Griffin is on union elections. The law requires that elections be held at minimum regular intervals, to promote democracy. National unions must hold elections at least every five years; locals, every three years; intermediate bodies, every four years. Elections must be by secret ballot of members or of delegates who were chosen by secret ballot of members. Unions may impose reasonable qualifications for union office. The goal of the law is to ensure democratic procedures that will allow the rank and file members to use the ballot box to correct abuses by union officers.

CASE

A union's constitution limited eligibility for local union offices to members who have attended at least one-half of the regular meetings of the local for three years previous to the election (unless prevented by union activities or working hours). The secretary of labor filed suit under the Landrum-Griffin Act to invalidate union elections subject to the Constitution.

ISSUE Is the union constitutional provision on eligibility valid?

DECISION No.

REASONS 1. Landrum-Griffin does not render unions powerless to restrict candidacies for union office. Reasonable restrictions may be imposed.

2. Whether a particular qualification is "reasonable" within the meaning of Section 401(*e*) must therefore be measured in terms of its consistency with the act's command to unions to conduct free and democratic union elections.

3. The antidemocratic effects of the meeting-attendance rule outweigh the interests urged in its support. An attendance requirement that results in the exclusion of 96.5 percent of the members from candidacy for union office hardly seems to be a "reasonable qualification" consistent with the goal of free democratic elections.

Local 3489 United Steelworkers of America v. Usery, 97 S.Ct. 611 (1977).

Regulation of Employment

The law includes numerous statutes regulating employment at both the state and the federal levels. State legislation controls matters such as (1) child labor, (2) hours of work, particularly for minors, (3) minimum wages, (4) unemployment compensation, (5) workers' compensation, (6) safety appliances and conditions of work, (7) factory inspection, (8) wage assignments, (9) employment agencies, and (10) discriminatory practices with regard to hire and tenure of employees. The more significant legislation by the federal government includes statutes dealing with hours and wages, employers' liability for injuries of employees, civil rights, social security, and pensions, as well as the several statutes on labor-management relations previously covered.

This chapter will cover only two very important areas of regulation: workers' compensation and discrimination in employment. These two are the most active areas of litigation and probably impact on more people than do other areas of regulation.

Workers' compensation—general principles

Workers' compensation laws are state statutes designed to protect employees and their families from the risks of accidental injury, death, or disease resulting from their employment. At common law, if an employer acted unreasonably and caused physical injury to an employee, the latter theoretically could sue and recover damages from the employer. However, the common law also gave the employer three defenses: (1) assumption of the risk, (2) contributory negligence, and (3) the fellow-servant doctrine.

Suppose that an employer furnished dangerous machinery not equipped with any safety devices and a worker's arm was mangled when it was caught in one of these machines. Even though the employer was negligent, a worker who was cognizant of the inherent dangers could not recover damages, because she knowingly *assumed the risk* of her injury. If the injury were caused in part by the worker's *contributory negligence,* he or she would lose at common law. And if the injury occurred because of the negligence of another employee, the negligent employee rather than the employer was liable because of the *fellow-servant rule.*

In order to eliminate the defenses, and for other reasons of public policy, all states have enacted workers' compensation statutes. These laws vary a great deal from state to state as to the covered industries and employees, the nature of the injuries or diseases that are compensable, and the rates of compensation. In spite of the wide variances in the laws of the states in this area, certain general observations can be made.

State laws covering workers' compensation provide a system of paying for death, illness, or injury that arises out of and in the course of the employment. The three defenses the employer had at common law are eliminated. The employers are strictly liable without fault. These laws are usually administered exclusively by an administrative agency called the industrial commission or board, which has quasi-judicial powers, formal court action being dispensed with. Of course, the ruling of such boards is subject to review by the courts of the jurisdiction in the same manner as the actions of other administrative agencies.

Most state statutes do not cover certain types of employment, and they may not provide compensation for specified kinds of accidents or diseases. Generally, domestic and agricultural employees are not covered. In the majority of states, the statutes are compulsory; in some states, employers may elect to be subject to lawsuits by employees or their survivors for accidental injuries or death. In such cases, the plaintiff must prove that the death or injury resulted proximately from the negligence of the employer. But the plaintiff is not subject to the common-law defenses, and there is no statutory limit to the amount of damages recoverable if workers' compensation is not elected.

Benefits

The workers' compensation acts give covered employees the right to certain cash payments for their loss of income. In the event of an employee's death, benefits are provided for the spouse and minor children. The amount of such awards is usually subject to a stated maximum and is based upon the wages of the employee and the number of dependents. If the employee suffers disability, most states provide compensation both for injuries that are scheduled in the statute and for those that are nonscheduled. As an example of scheduled injuries, a worker who loses a hand might be awarded 100 weeks of compensation at a specified sum, such as $100 per week. A person who is totally and permanently disabled will receive a pension for life. Compensation for nonscheduled losses include items such as the earning power the employee lost because of his injury: an injured employee receives weekly payments during the period he is unable to work as a result of the injury. In addition to the above payments, all statutes provide payment of all reasonable medical expenses.

As the result of inflation, many states have increased the amounts payable as benefits. In most states, however, the amounts paid are inadequate for a decent standard of living. Even some of the more generous benefits are only about $100 per week for periods of temporary total disability and around $25,000 for death benefits.

In some states, the employers have a choice of covering their risk with insurance or of being self-insured (i.e., paying all claims directly) if they can demonstrate their capability to do so. In other states, employers pay into a state fund used to compensate workers entitled to benefits. In these states, the amounts of the payments are based on the size of the payroll and the experience of the employer in having claims filed.

Proof required for benefits

While the right to workers' compensation is given without regard to fault of either the employer or the employee, employers are not always liable. The tests for determining whether an employee is entitled to workers' compensation are simply: (1) "Was the injury accidental?" and (2) "Did the injury arise out of and in the course of the employment?" Since workers' compensation laws are remedial in nature, they have been very liberally construed. In recent years the courts have tended to expand coverage and the scope of the employer's liability. It has been held that heart attacks as well as other common ailments in which the employee had either a preexisting disease or a physical condition likely to lead to the disease were compensable as "accidental injuries." Likewise, the courts have been more and more liberal in upholding awards that have been challenged on the ground that the injury did not arise out of and in the course of the employment.

CASE

A traveling salesman died as result of suffocation when his head caught between two metal slats of bed headboard in a rooming house where he was staying overnight while on business for his employer. The deceased's blood alcohol content was .19 percent at the time of death. The hearing officer found that his intoxication was not such that he was in a deep alcoholic stupor.

ISSUE Did the salesman's death arise out of and in the course of his employment?

DECISION Yes.

REASON Intoxication is not a sufficient basis to deny benefits unless it is to such an extent that it amounts to an abandonment of employment. The overnight stay was an act necessarily incidental to his work as a traveling employee, and therefore his death arose out of and in the course of employment.

Peterson v. Industrial Commission, 490 P.2d 870 (Ariz.) 1971.

The system of separate and varying workers' compensation laws as they exist today in the states has been subject to much criticism. The laws have been attacked as inadequate because of their restrictive coverage and limited benefits. Not all types of employment or occupational risks are covered. Many states exempt businesses that do not employ a minimum number of workers. Much criticism has also been leveled at the quality of administration of most workers' compensation programs. The weaknesses in the present laws and the wide variations in the workers' compensation acts (as well as case law) from state to state, have led to suggestions that workers' compensation be modernized and reformed to meet the social needs of today and that it be made uniform from state to state. Some have proposed a Federal Workers' Compensation Act which would replace the state ones.

Federal laws

Several feederal statutes pertain to the liability of certain kinds of employers for injuries, diseases, and deaths arising out of the course of employment. Railroad workers are covered by the Federal Employers' Liability Act. This statute does not provide for liability without fault, as in the case of workers' compensation, but it greatly increases the chances of a worker's winning a lawsuit against his or her employer by eliminating or reducing the defenses the latter would have had at common law. While fault of the carrier must be proved for an employee to recover for injuries under the FELA, and a regular lawsuit must be filed in court, the act provides the worker with a distinct advantage over many workers' compensation systems. There is no limit or ceiling to the amount an employee can recover for injuries. The Jones Act gives maritime employees the same rights against their employers as railway workers have against theirs under the FELA.

Other federal statutes require that awards for on-the-job injuries or deaths of certain employees be made in the manner of state laws for workers' compensation: without regard to the fault of the employer. These federal laws provide formulas to use in computing the amounts of the awards for various kinds and degrees of disability, along with upper and lower limits for such awards. One such statute is the Longshoremen's and Harbor Workers' Compensation Act. The coverage of this statute was extended to workers for private employers on United States defense bases by the Defense Bases Act.

OSHA

Because workers' compensation statutes and similar federal laws had not reduced or eliminated accidental injuries, diseases, and deaths connected with employment, in 1970 Congress adopted the Occupational Safety and Health Act (OSHA). Its purpose is to assure safe and healthful working conditions for virtually every employee in the United States. The law requires that employers furnish to each employee a place of employment free from recognized hazards that are causing or are likely to cause death or serious physical harm to the employee. It also requires that the employer comply with occupational safety and health standards promulgated under the act by the Secretary of Labor. In order to accomplish the foregoing, Labor Department investigators conduct unannounced inspections to determine if violations exist. Employers are required to make and preserve certain records relating to accidents and injuries and to conduct periodic inspections to ensure compliance with the standards.

There are civil and criminal penalties for violating OSHA rules and regulations. Most OSHA inspections have resulted in at least some fines. As a result, in the late Seventies, Congress prohibited imposing fines on a business if only ten or less nonserious violations of OSHA standards are cited during a first-time inspection. Today, OSHA is less concerned with safety problems than with health hazards such as chemicals that cause cancer.

Equal Employment Opportunity

Many cities, almost every state, and the federal government have enacted statutes designed to prevent discrimination in hiring, promotion, pay, or layoffs because of race, color, creed, sex, national origin, age, and physical handicaps. These statutes have modified the basic common-law concept that an employer had a free choice in selecting his employees and, in the absence of a contract, a free choice in discharging them. The laws have been enacted as a part of the general philosophy of government that all persons should have equality of opportunity. These statutes frequently contain criminal sanctions and authorize civil suits for damages.

The basic federal law on equal employment opportunity was enacted in 1964. The Civil Rights Act of 1964, as now amended, covers all employers with fifteen or more employees, labor unions with fifteen or more members, labor unions that operate a hiring hall, and employment agencies. The 1972 amendment extended coverage to state and local governments and to educational institutions.

The types of employer action in which discrimination is prohibited include discharge; refusal to hire; compensation; and terms, conditions, or privileges of employment. Additionally, employers are not permitted to segregate or classify employees on any of these bases where the result adversely affects employee status or opportunity.

Equal Opportunity Employment Commission

A federal administrative agency known as the Equal Employment Opportunity Commission has the primary responsibility for enforcing the act. In the course of its investigations, the commission has broad authority to examine and copy evidence, require the production of documentary evidence, hold hearings, and subpoena and examine witnesses under oath.

By a 1972 amendment, the EEOC has the power to file a civil suit in court and to represent a person charging a violation of the act; however, it must first exhaust efforts to conciliate the claim. The remedies available in such an action include reinstatement with back pay for the victim of an illegal discrimination and injunctions against future violations of the law.

The federal law seeks to preserve state and local employment practice laws. Where an alleged violation of federal law, if true, is violative of a state or local law, the commission may not act until sixty days after the proceedings, if any, have been commenced under that law. Similarly, the commission must notify the appropriate officials and defer all action until the local authority has had, in general, at least sixty days to resolve the matter.

Discrimination on the basis of race, color, national origin, and religion

Practices involving recruiting, hiring, and promotion of employees are often charged as being discriminatory on the basis of race, color, or national origin. Though a company's standards or policies for selecting or promoting appear neutral on their face, if they have the effect of discriminating against blacks or other minorities and have no substantial, demonstrable relationship to qualification for the job in question, they are illegal. Under this rule several hiring policies have been found illegal: denying employment to unwed mothers in a locale where the rate of illegitimate births was higher among blacks than among whites; refusing to hire persons because of their poor credit rating; refusing to hire those with an arrest record; and giving priority to relatives of present employees in hiring when there was a very low percentage of minority workers among these employees.

The practice of using personnel tests also has been challenged under this rule. The Civil Rights Act states that it is not unlawful for an employer to hire or promote employees on the basis of the results of professionally developed ability tests, provided they are not designed or used to discriminate illegally. The courts, however, have held that the use of a standardized general intelligence test in selecting and placing personnel is prohibited, being discriminatory on the basis of race. Tests, neutral on their face and even neutral in terms of intent, cannot be maintained if they operate to "freeze" the status quo of prior discriminatory employment practices. If an employment practice cannot be shown to be related to job performance, the practice is prohibited. The Civil Rights Act proscribes not only overt discrimination but also practices that are fair in form but discriminatory in operation. As a result, job tests have been dropped by many companies because of the difficulty of proving that all questions are validly related to job performance.

The law prohibits discrimination also in employment conditions and benefits. EEOC decisions have found practices such as the following to be violations: forbidding the use of Spanish during working and nonworking time without the employer's demonstrating a need to understand all conversations between Spanish-speaking employees; permitting racial insults in the work situation; maintaining all-white or all-black crews for no demonstrable reason; providing better housing for blacks than for whites; and granting higher average Christmas bonuses to whites than to blacks, for reasons that were not persuasive to the commission.

Religious corporations, associations, or societies can discriminate in all their employment practices on the basis of religion, but not on the basis of race, color, sex, or national origin. Other employers cannot discriminate on the basis of religion in employment practices, and they must make reasonable accommodation to the religious needs of their employees if it does not result in undue hardship to the employers.

Sex discrimination

Discrimination based on sex is a major area of equal employment opportunity litigation. A federal law requires that women and men be paid equivalent wages for equivalent work, although executive personnel are exempt from the Equal Pay Act. Many state laws have long protected women from employment in certain occupations (such as those requiring lifting heavy objects) and from working at night or working an excessive number of hours per week or day. Under EEOC guidelines and court decisions, the state laws are unconstitutional and not a defense to a charge of illegal sex discrimination. Other EEOC guidelines forbid (1) employers' classifying jobs as male or female, (2) advertising in help-wanted columns that are designated male or female, unless sex is a bona fide job qualification; and (3) separate male and female seniority lists or lines of progression. For sex to be a valid job qualification, it must be demonstrably relevant to job performance. Very few jobs meet this test.

The EEOC found sex discrimination in typical actions. A radio station refused to hire a woman as a newscaster because "News coming from a woman sounds like gossip." A bank allowed male employees to smoke at their desks in areas of minimal public contact but discouraged females from smoking anywhere except the lounge. A utility firm allowed women to retire at fifty after twenty-five years of service, but men with the same work experience had to wait until they were fifty-five.

Age discrimination

In 1967 Congress passed the Age Discrimination in Employment Act, which protects persons between forty and sixty-five years of age from job discrimination because of age. This law is enforced by the EEOC and will likely have great importance in the years ahead.

A 1978 amendment to the law prohibits mandatory retirement before age 70 of most workers employed by private businesses with over nineteen employees. With the exception of the police and firemen, almost all local and state employees are protected by the act, and most federal employees cannot be forced to retire at *any* age because of their years. "Bona fide executives" and "high policy makers" of private companies who will have pensions of at least $27,000 per year, however, can be forced into early retirement. The statute invalidates retirement plans and labor contracts that call for retirement before age 70, even if they were in force at the time the law became effective in January 1979.

Discrimination on the basis of handicaps

In order to promote and expand employment opportunities for handicapped persons, both in the public and private sectors, Congress enacted the Rehabilitation Act of 1973. This statue requires each department and agency in the executive branch of the federal government to have an approved affirmative action plan for the hiring, placement, and advancement of qualified handicapped people. It also requires every employer with a federal government contract for over $2,500 to take *affirmative action* to hire and advance qualified handicapped persons at all levels, including executive. This affirmative action requirement applies also to job assignments, promotions, training, transfers, accessibility, working conditions, and termination. The federal contracts and subcontracts covered include those for the procurement of personal property and nonpersonal sources.

A handicapped person is anyone who has or has had a physical or mental impairment that substantially limits a major life activity. To be hired, however, that person must be "qualified," or capable of performing a particular job, with reasonable accommodation to his or her handicap. The term *handicapped individual* does not include an alcoholic or drug abuser whose current use of alcohol or drugs prevents him from performing the duties of the job in question or whose current alcohol or drug abuse would constitute a direct threat to the property or safety of others.

Federal contractors covered not only must take affirmative action themselves, but also must include a clause in all their contracts or subcontracts or purchase orders of over $2,500 by which the subcontractor agrees not to discriminate against any qualified handicapped person and also agrees to take affirmative action to hire and advance them. The subcontractor must also agree to post affirmative action notices in conspicuous places around its plant.

Affirmative action programs

The desire to eliminate the adverse effects of past discrimination prompted most governmental bodies and many private employers to adopt policies and practices described as affirmative action programs. These programs usually established goals for hiring and promoting members of minority groups, to be accomplished by active recruitment programs and by giving priority to minorities. Members of minorities were to be given priority when fewer of them were working in a given job category than one would reasonably expect there should be, considering their availability.

Affirmative action programs and similar efforts have led white males to charge reverse discrimination. They argue that it is just as wrong to discriminate in favor of minorities as it is to discriminate against them. In 1980, the Supreme Court held that voluntary affirmative action programs were constitutional and companies that adopted them were not in violation of the law.

REVIEW QUESTIONS AND PROBLEMS

1. What was the purpose of the Norris-LaGuardia Act? Does it prohibit all injunctions in labor disputes?
2. A group of employees of Sweetheart, Inc., seeking to become the exclusive bargaining agent for all employees of Sweetheart, decided to organize. While the election was pending, Sweetheart, Inc., allowed the group to use the company's photocopy machine and in-house mail system for solicitation purposes. A union also seeking to represent the employees filed an unfair labor practice charge to stop these practices. What was the result? Why?
3. Union members employed by the Gable Manufacturing Company were dissatisfied with their salary schedule. Lombard was one of Gable's largest customers. The union threw up a picket line in front of Lombard's store in protest of Lombard's business relationship with Gable. Is this activity legal? Why?
4. A employer, during a strike, tells the strikers that if they are replaced, they will "lose forever their right to reemployment by this company." Is this an unfair labor practice? Explain.
5. Two unions were seeking recognition from the NLRB. The employer wrote a letter to the workers advising them that if he were voting he would vote for union X over union Y. Is this an unfair labor practice? Explain.
6. An employer posted a "no-solicitation rule" that prohibited anyone from soliciting workers on company premises to join a union. The rule also prohibited solicitation at the coffee shop across the street from the plant. Is this an unfair labor practice? Explain.
7. A company fired five employees for "poor workmanship." These five were the leaders in an attempt to unionize the shop. No other employees were fired. Are they entitled to reinstatement? Explain.
8. On the day an election is to be held to determine whether or not employees will organize and become members of a labor union, the company grants all employees a bonus of $100. Is the company guilty of an unfair labor practice?
9. Artie, the owner of a lounge, hired women bartenders, contrary to a state statute that prohibited women from tending bar except when the woman was the holder of a liquor license. The state revoked Artie's liquor license, and he brought suit, claiming that the state statute violated the 1964 Civil Rights Act. In defense, the state contended that a bartender must be physically strong enough to protect himself against inebriated customers and to maintain order in the bar, and that women as a class are unable to do so. Is the state law invalid? Why?
10. Doaks was hired by Zebra Corporation to operate a machine in its factory. Doaks was seriously injured when he was pushed into the machine throught the carelessness of a fellow employee. There was evidence that the two men had been "clowning around" at the time of the incident, even though Doaks knew that the machine was highly dangerous. (a) If Doaks sues his employer for negligently maintaining the machine in a dangerous condition, what would be the result at common law? Why? (Assume Doaks could prove that the machine was negligently maintained.) (b) Would Doaks be entitled to a workers' compensation award from Zebra Corporation for his injury? Explain.
11. Rick is a white male, aged 39, who attends the Baptist church, as has his family for over 100 years. Rick files a claim against his employer, alleging discrimination. The case is *not* based on a theory of reverse discrimination. What portion of the law is asserted in his complaint? (What is the basis for his allegation of discrimination?)
12. The United Mine Workers call a nationwide strike. Thirty days later the issues are unresolved, and several other industries are laying off thousands of workers. Is there any legal remedy available to stop the strike? Explain.
13. What issues between management and labor are compulsory bargaining issues?
14. The Jones Company adopted an affirmative action program. As a result, most promotions went to members of minority groups. A white male, who was denied a promotion, filed suit, alleging that he had been discriminated against because of the affirmative action program. Is he entitled to relief? Why?

Uniform Commercial Code

UNIFORM COMMERCIAL CODE

AN ACT

To be known as the Uniform Commercial Code, Relating to Certain Commercial Transactions in or regarding Personal Property and Contracts and other Documents concerning them, including Sales, Commercial Paper, Bank Deposits and Collections, Letters of Credit, Bulk Transfers, Warehouse Receipts, Bills of Lading, other Documents of Title, Investment Securities, and Secured Transactions, including certain Sales of Accounts, Chattel Paper, and Contract Rights, Providing for Public Notice to Third Parties in Certain Circumstances; Regulating Procedure, Evidence and Damages in Certain Court Actions Involving such Transactions, Contracts or Documents; to Make Uniform the Law with Respect Thereto; and Repealing Inconsistent Legislation.

ARTICLE 1

GENERAL PROVISIONS

PART 1

SHORT TITLE, CONSTRUCTION, APPLICATION AND SUBJECT MATTER OF THE ACT

Section 1-101. Short Title. This act shall be known and may be cited as Uniform Commercial Code.

Section 1-102. Purposes; Rules of Construction; Variation by Agreement.

(1) This Act shall be liberally construed and applied to promote its underlying purposes and policies.

(2) Underlying purposes and policies of this Act are

(a) to simplify, clarify and modernize the law governing commercial transactions;

(b) to permit the continued expansion

of commercial practices through custom, usage and agreement of the parties;

(c) To make uniform the law among the various jurisdictions.

(3) The effect of provisions of this Act may be varied by agreement, except as otherwise provided in this Act and except that the obligations of good faith, diligence, reasonableness and care prescribed by this Act may not be disclaimed by agreement but the parties may by agreement determine the standards by which the performance of such obligations is to be measured if such standards are not manifestly unreasonable.

(4) The presence in certain provisions of this Act of the words "unless otherwise agreed" or words of similar import does not imply that the effect of other provisions may not be varied by agreement under subsection (3).

(5) In this Act unless the context otherwise requires

(a) words in the singular number include the plural, and in the plural include the singular;

(b) words of the masculine gender include the feminine and the neuter, and when the sense so indicates the words of the neuter gender may refer to any gender.

Section 1-103. Supplementary General Principles of Law Applicable. Unless displaced by the particular provisions of this Act, the principles of law and equity, including the law merchant and the law relative to capacity to contract, principal and agent, estoppel, fraud, misrepresentation, duress, coercion, mistake, bankruptcy, or other validating or invalidating cause shall supplement its provisions.

Section 1-104. Construction Against Implicit Repeal. This Act being a general act intended as a unified coverage of its subject matter, no part of it shall be deemed to be impliedly repealed by subsequent legislation if such construction can reasonable be avoided.

Section 1-105. Territorial Application of the Act; Parties' Power to Choose Applicable Law.

(1) Except as provided hereafter in this section, when a transaction bears a reasonable relation to this state and also to another state or nation the parties may agree that the law either of this state or of such other state or nation shall govern their rights and duties. Failing such agreement this Act applies to transactions bearing an appropriate relation to this state.

(2) Where one of the following provisions of this Act specifies the applicable law, that provision governs and a contrary agreement is effective only to the extent permitted by the law (including the conflict of laws rules) so specified:

Rights of creditors against sold goods. Section 2-402.

Applicability of the Article on Bank Deposits and Collections. Section 4-102.

Bulk transfers subject to the Article on Bulk Transers. Section 6-102.

Applicability of the Article on Investment Securities. Section 8-106.

Policy and scope of the Article on Secured Transactions. Sections 9-102 and 9-103.

Section 1-106. Remedies to be Liberally Administered.

(1) The remedies provided by this Act shall be liberally administered to the end that the aggrieved party may be put in as good a position as if the other party had fully performed but neither consequential or special nor penal damages may be had except as specifically provided in this Act or by other rule of law.

(2) Any right or obligation declared by this Act is enforceable by action unless the provision declaring it specifies a different and limited effect.

Section 1-107. Waiver or Renunciation of Claim or Right After Breach. Any claim or right arising out of an alleged breach can be discharged in whole or in part without consideration by a written waiver or renunciation signed and delivered by the aggrieved party.

Section 1-108. Severability. If any provision or clause of this Act or application thereof to any person or circumstances is held invalid, such invalidity shall not affect other provisions or applications of the Act which can be given effect without the invalid provisions or application, and to this end the provisions of this Act are declared to be severable.

GENERAL DEFINITIONS AND PRINCIPLES OF INTERPRETATION

Section 1-201. General Definition. Subject to additional definitions contained in the subsequent Articles of this Act which are applicable to specific Articles or Parts thereof, and unless the context otherwise requires, in this Act:

(1) "Action" in the sense of a judicial proceeding includes recoupment, counterclaim, set-off, suit in equity and any other proceedings in which rights are determined.

(2) "Aggrieved party" means a party entitled to resort to a remedy.

(3) "Agreement" means the bargain of the parties in fact as found in their language or by implication from other circumstances including course of dealing or usage of trade or course of performance as provided in this Act (Sections 1-205 and 2-208). Whether an agreement has legal consequences is determined by the provisions of this Act, if applicable; otherwise by the law of contracts (Section 1-103). (Compare "Contract.")

(4) "Bank" means any person engaged in the business of banking.

(5) "Bearer" means the person in possession of an instrument, document of title, or security payable to bearer or indorsed in blank.

(6) "Bill of lading" means a document evidencing the receipt of goods for shipment issued by a person engaged in the business of transporting or forwarding goods, and includes an airbill. "Airbill" means a document serving for air transportation as a bill of lading does for marine or rail transportation, and includes an air consignment note or air waybill.

(7) "Branch" includes a separately incorporated foreign branch of a bank.

(8) "Burden of establishing" a fact means the burden of persuading the triers of fact that the existence of the fact is more probable than its non-existence.

(9) "Buyer in ordinary course of business" means a person who in good faith and without knowledge that the sale to him is in violation of the ownership rights or security interest of a third party in the goods buys in ordinary course from a person in the business of selling goods of that kind but does not include a pawnbroker. "Buying" may be for cash or by exchange of other property or on secured or unsecured credit and includes receiving goods or documents of title under a pre-existing contract for sale but does not include a transfer in bulk or as security for or in total or partial satisfaction of a money debt.

(10) "Conspicuous": a term or clause is conspicuous when it is so written that a reasonable person against whom it is to operate ought to have noticed it. A printed heading in capitals (as: NON-NEGOTIABLE BILL OF LADING) is conspicuous. Language in the body of a form is "conspicuous" if it is in larger or other contrasting type or color. But in a telegram any stated term is "conspicuous." Whether a term or clause is "conspicuous" or not is for decision by the court.

(11) "Contract" means the total legal obligation which results from the parties' agreement as affected by this Act and any other applicable rules of law. (Compare "Agreement.")

(12) "Creditor" includes a general creditor, a secured creditor, a lien creditor and any representative of creditors, including an assignee for the benefit of creditors, a trustee in bankruptcy, a receiver in equity and an executor or administrator of an insolvent debtor's or assignor's estate.

(13) "Defendant" includes a person in the position of defendant in a cross-action or counterclaim.

(14) "Delivery" with respect to instruments, documents of title, chattel paper or securities means voluntary transfer of possession.

(15) "Document of title" includes bill of lading, dock warrant, dock receipt, warehouse receipt or order for the delivery of goods, and also any other document which

in the regular course of business or financing is treated as adequately evidencing that the person in possession of it is entitled to receive, hold and dispose of the document and the goods it covers. To be a document of title a document must purport to be issued by or addressed to a bailee and purport to cover goods in the bailee's possession which are either identified or are fungible portions of an identified mass.

(16) "Fault" means wrongful act, omission or breach.

(17) "Fungible" with respect to goods or securities means goods or securities of which any unit is, by nature or usage of trade, the equivalent of any other like unit. Goods which are not fungible shall be deemed fungible for the purposes of this Act to the extent that under a particular agreement or document unlike units are treated as equivalents.

(18) "Genuine" means free of forgery or counterfeiting.

(19) "Good faith" means honesty in fact in the conduct or transaction concerned.

(20) "Holder" means a person who is in possession of a document of title or an instrument or an investment security drawn, issued or indorsed to him or to his order or to bearer or in blank.

(21) To "honor" is to pay or to accept and pay, or where a credit so engages to purchase or discount a draft complying with the terms of the credit.

(22) "Insolvency proceedings" includes any assignment for the benefit of creditors or other proceedings intended to liquidate or rehabilitate the estate of the person involved.

(23) A person is "insolvent" who either has ceased to pay his debts in the ordinary course of business or cannot pay his debts as they become due or is insolvent within the meaning of the federal bankruptcy law.

(24) "Money" means a medium of exchange authorized or adopted by a domestic or foreign government as a part of its currency.

(25) A person has "notice" of a fact when

(a) he has actual knowledge of it; or

(b) he has received a notice or notification of it; or

(c) from all the facts and circumstances known to him at the time in question he has reason to know that it exists.

A person "knows" or had "knowledge" of a fact when he has actual knowledge of it. "Discover" or "learn" or a word or phrase of similar import refers to knowledge rather than to reason to know. The time and circumstances under which a notice or notification may cease to be effective are not determined by this Act.

(26) A person "notifies" or "gives" a notice or notification to another by taking such steps as may be reasonably required to inform the other person in ordinary course whether or not such other actually comes to know of it. A person "receives" a notice or notification when

(a) it comes to his attention; or

(b) it is duly delivered at the place of business through which the contract was made or at any other place held out by him as the place for receipt of such communications.

(27) Notice, knowledge or a notice or notification received by an organization is effective for a particular transaction from the time when it is brought to the attention of the individual conducting that transaction, and in any event from the time when it would have been brought to his attention if the organization had exercised due diligence. An organization exercises due diligence if it maintains reasonable routines for communicating significant information to the person conducting the transaction and there is reasonable compliance with the routines. Due diligence does not require an individual acting for the organization to communicate information unless such communication is part of his regular duties or unless he has reason to know of the transaction and that the transaction would be materially affected by the information.

(28) "Organization" includes a corporation, government or governmental subdivision or agency, business trust, estate, trust, partnership or association, two or more persons having a joint or common interest, or any other legal or commercial entity.

(29) "Party," as distinct from "third party," means a person who has engaged in a transaction or made an agreement within this Act.

(30) "Person" includes an individual or an organization (See Section 1-102).

(31) "Presumption" or "presumed" means that the trier of fact must find the existence of the fact presumed unless and until evi-

dence is introduced which would support a finding of its non-existence.

(32) "Purchase" includes taking by sale, discount, negotiation, mortgage, pledge, lien, issue or re-issue, gift or any other voluntary transaction creating an interest in property.

(33) "Purchaser" means a person who takes by purchase.

(34) "Remedy" means any remedial right to which an aggrieved party is entitled with or without resort to a tribunal.

(35) "Representative" includes an agent, an officer of a corporation or association, and a trustee, executor or administrator of an estate, or any other person empowered to act for another.

(36) "Rights" includes remedies.

(37) "Security interest" means an interest in personal property or fixtures which secures payment or performance of an obligation. The retention or reservation of title by a seller or goods notwithstanding shipment or delivery to the buyer (Section 2-401) is limited in effect to a reservation of a "security interest." The term also includes any interest of a buyer of accounts, chattel paper, or contract rights which is subject to Article 9. The special property interest of a buyer of goods on identification or such goods to a contract for sale under Section 2-401 is not a "security interest," but a buyer may also acquire a "security interest" by complying with Article 9. Unless a lease or consignment is intended as security, reservation of title thereunder is not a "security interest" but a consignment is in any event subject to the provisions on consignment sales (Section 2-326). Whether a lease is intended as security is to be determined by the facts of each case; however (a) the inclusion of an option to purchase does not of itself make the lease one intended for security, and (b) an agreement that upon compliance with the terms of the lease the lessee shall become or has the option to become the owner of the property for no additional consideration or for a nominal consideration does make the lease one intended for security.

(38) "Send" in connection with any writing or notice means to deposit in the mail or deliver for transmission by any other usual means of communication with postage or cost of transmission provided for and properly addressed and in the case of an instrument to an address specified thereon or otherwise agreed, or if there be none to any address reasonable under the circumstances. The receipt of any writing or notice within the time at which it would have arrived if properly sent has the effect of a proper sending.

(39) "Signed" includes any symbol executed or adopted by a party with present intention to authenticate a writing.

(40) "Surety" includes guarantor.

(41) "Telegram" includes a message transmitted by radio, teletype, cable, any mechanical method of transmission, or the like.

(42) "Term" means that portion of an agreement which relates to a particular matter.

(43) "Unauthorized" signature or indorsement means one made without actual, implied or apparent authority and includes a forgery.

(44) "Value." Except as otherwise provided with respect to negotiable instruments and bank collections (Sections 3-303, 4-208 and 4-209) a person gives "value" for rights if he acquires them

(a) in return for a binding commitment to extend credit or for the extension of immediately available credit whether or not drawn upon and whether or not a charge-back is provided for in the event of difficulties in collection; or

(b) as security for or in total or partial satisfaction of a pre-existing claim; or

(c) by accepting delivery pursuant to a pre-existing contract for purchase; or

(d) generally, in return for any consideration sufficient to support a simple contract.

(45) "Warehouse receipt" means a receipt issued by a person engaged in the business of storing goods for hire.

(46) "Written" or "writing" includes printing, typewriting or any other intentional reduction to tangible form.

Section 1-202. Prima Facie Evidence by Third Party Documents. A document in due form purporting to be a bill of lading, policy or certificate of insurance, official weigher's or inspector's certificate, consular invoice, or any other document authorized or required by the contract to be issued by a third party shall be prima facie evidence of its own authenticity and genuineness and of the facts stated in the document by the third party.

Section 1-203. Obligation of Good Faith. Every contract or duty within this Act imposes an obligation of good faith in its performance or enforcement.

Section 1-204. Time; Reasonable Time; "Seasonably."

(1) Whenever this Act requires any action to be taken within a reasonable time, any time which is not manifestly unreasonable may be fixed by agreement.

(2) What is a reasonable time for taking any action depends on the nature, purpose and circumstances of such action.

(3) An action is taken "seasonably" when it is taken at or within the time agreed or if no time is agreed at or within a reasonable time.

Section 1-205. Course of Dealing and Usage of Trade.

(1) A course of dealing in a sequence of previous conduct between the parties to a particular transaction which is fairly to be regarded as establishing a common basis of understanding for interpreting their expressions and other conduct.

(2) A usage of trade is any practice or method of dealing having such regularity of observance in a place, vocation or trade as to justify an expectation that it will be observed with respect to the transaction in question. The existence and scope of such a usage are to be proved as facts. If it is established that such a usage is embodied in a written trade code or similar writing the interpretation of the writing is for the court.

(3) A course of dealing between parties and any usage of trade in the vocation or trade in which they are engaged or of which they are or should be aware give particular meaning to and supplement or qualify terms of an agreement.

(4) The express terms of an agreement and an applicable course of dealing or usage of trade shall be construed wherever reasonable as consistent with each other; but wher such construction is unreasonable express terms control both course of dealirg and usage of trade and course of dealing controls usage of trade.

(5) An applicable usage of trade in the place where any part of performance is to occur shall be used in interpreting the agreement as to that part of the performance.

(6) Evidence of a relevant usage of trade offered by one party is not admissible unless and until he has given the other party such notice as the court finds sufficient to prevent unfair surprise to the latter.

Section 1-206. Statute of Frauds for Kinds of Personal Property Not Otherwise Covered.

(1) Except in the cases described in subsection (2) of this section a contract for the sale of personal property is not enforceable by way of action or defense beyond five thousand dollars in amount or value of remedy unless there is some writing which indicates that a contract for sale has been made between the parties at a defined or stated price, reasonably identifies the subject matter, and is signed by the party against whom enforcement is sought or by his authorized agent.

(2) Subsection (1) of this section does not apply to contracts for the sale of goods (Section 2-201) nor of securities (Section 8-319) nor to security agreements (Section 9-203).

Section 1-207. Performance or Acceptance under Reservation of Rights. A party who with explicit reservation of rights performs or promises performance or assents to performance in a manner demanded or offered by the other party does not thereby prejudice the rights reserved. Such words as "without prejudice," "under protect" or the like are sufficient.

Section 1-208. Option to Accelerate at Will. A term providing that one party or his successor in interest may accelerate payment of performance or require collateral or additional collateral "at will" or "when he deems himself insecure" or in words of similar import shall be construed to mean that he shall have power to do so only if he in good faith believes that the prospect of payment or performance is impaired. The burden of establishing lack of good faith is on the party against whom the power has been exercised.

ARTICLE 2

SALES

PART 1

SHORT TITLE, GENERAL CONSTRUCTION AND SUBJECT MATTER

Section 2-101. Short Title. This Article shall be known and may be cited as Uniform Commercial Code—Sales.

Section 2-102. Scope; Certain Security and Other Transactions Excluded from this Article. Unless the context otherwise requires, this Article applies to transactions in goods; it does not apply to any transaction which although in the form of an unconditional contract to sell or present sale is intended to operate only as a security transaction nor does this Article impair or repeal any statute regulating sales to consumers, farmers or other specified classes of buyers.

Section 2-103. Definitions and Index of Definitions.

(1) In this Article unless the context otherwise requires

(a) "Buyer" means a person who buys or contracts to buy goods.

(b) "Good faith" in the case of a merchant means honesty in fact and the observance of reasonable commercial standards of fair dealing in the trade.

(c) "Receipt" of goods means taking physical possession of them.

(d) "Seller" means a person who sells or contracts to sell goods.

(2) Other definitions applying to this Article or to specified parts thereof, and the sections in which they appear are:

"Acceptance." Section 2-606.
"Banker's credit." Section 2-325.
"Between merchants." Section 2-104.
"Cancellation." Section 2-106(4)
"Commercial unit." Section 2-105.
"Confirmed credit." Section 2-325.
"Conforming to contract." Section 2-106.
"Contract for sale." Section 2-106.
"Cover." Section 2-712.
"Entrusting." Section 2-403.
"Financing agency." Section 2-104.
"Future goods." Section 2-105.
"Goods." Section 2-105.
"Identification." Section 2-501.
"Installment contract." Section 2-612.
"Letter of Credit." Section 2-325.
"Lot." Section 2-105.
"Merchant." Section 2-104.
"Overseas." Section 2-323.
"Person on position of seller." Section 2-707.
"Present sale." Section 2-106.
"Sale." Section 2-106.
"Sale on approval." Section 2-326.
"Sale or return." Section 2-326.
"Termination." Section 2-106.

(3) The following definitions in other Articles apply to this Article:

"Check." Section 3-204.
"Consignee." Section 7-102.
"Consignor." Section 7-102.
"Consumer goods." Section 9-109.
"Dishonor." Section 3-507.
"Draft." Section 3-104.

(4) In addition Article 1 contains general definitions and principles of construction and interpretation applicable throughout this Article.

Section 2-104. Definitions: "Merchant"; "Between Merchants"; Financing Agency."

(1) "Merchant" means a person who deals in goods of the kind or otherwise by his occupation holds himself out as having knowledge or skill peculiar to the practices or goods involved in the transaction or to whom such knowledge or skill may be attributed by his employment of an agent or broker or other intermediary who by his occupation holds himself out as having such knowledge or skill.

(2) "Financing agency" means a bank, finance company or other person who in the ordinary course of business makes advances against goods or documents of title or who by arrangement with either the seller or the buyer intervenes in ordinary course to make or collect payment due or claimed under the contract for sale, as by purchasing or paying the seller's draft or making advances against it or by merely taking it for collection whether or not documents of title accompany the draft. "Financing agency" includes also a bank or other person who similarly intervenes between persons who are in the position of seller and buyer in respect to the goods (Section 2-707).

(3) "Between merchants" means in any transaction with respect to which both parties are chargeable with the knowledge or skill of merchants.

Section 2-105. Definitions: Transferability; "Goods"; "Future" Goods; "Lot"; "Commercial Unit."

(1) "Goods" means all things (including specially manufactured goods) which are movable at the time of identification to the contract for sale other than the money in which the price is to be paid, investment securities (Article 8) and things in action. "Goods" also includes the unborn young of animals and growing crops and other identified things attached to realty as described in the section on goods to be severed from realty (Section 2-107).

(2) Goods must be both existing and identified before any interest in them can pass. Goods which are not both existing and identified are "future" goods. A purported present sale of future goods or of any interest therein operates as a contract to sell.

(3) There may be a sale or a part interest in existing identified goods.

(4) An undivided share in an identified bulk of fungible goods is sufficiently identified to be sold although the quantity of the bulk is not determined. Any agreed proportion of such a bulk or any quantity thereof agreed upon by number, weight or other measure may to the extent of the seller's interest in the bulk be sold to the buyer who then becomes an owner in common.

(5) "Lot" means a parcel or a single article which is the subject matter of a separate sale or delivery, whether or not it is usfficient to perform the contract.

(6) "Commercial unit" means such a unit of goods as by commercial usage is a single whole for purposes of sale and division of which materially impairs its character or value on the market or in use. A commercial unit may be a single article (as a machine) or a set of articles (as a suite of furniture or an assortment of sizes) or a quantity (as a bale, gross, or carload) or any other unit treated in use or in the relevant market as a single whole.

Section 2-106. Definitions: "Contract"; "Agreement"; "Contract for Sale"; "Sale"; "Present Sale"; "Conforming" to Contract; "Termination"; "Cancellation."

(1) In this Article unless the context otherwise requires "contract" and "agreement" are limited to those relating to the present or future sale of goods. "Contract for sale" includes both a present sale of goods and a contract to sell goods at a future time. A "sale" consists in the passing of title from the seller to the buyer for a price (Section 2–401). A "present sale" means a sale which is accomplished by the making of the contract.

(2) Goods or conduct including any part of a performance are "conforming" or conform to the contract when they are in accordance with the obligations under the contract.

(3) "Termination" occurs when either party pursuant to a power created by agreement or law puts an end to the contract otherwise than for its breach. On "termination" all obligations which are still executory on both sides are discharged but any right based on prior breach or performance survives.

(4) "Cancellation" occurs when either party puts an end to the contract for breach by the other and its effect is the same as that of "termination" except that the cancelling party also retains any remedy for breach of the whole contract or any unperformed balance.

Section 2-107. Goods to be Severed from Realty: Recording.

(1) A contract for the sale of timber, minerals or the like or a structure or its materials to be removed from realty is a contract for the sale of goods within this Article if they are to be severed by the seller, but until severance a purported present sale thereof which is not effective as

a transfer of an interest in land is effective only as a contract to sell.

(2) A contract for the sale apart from the land of growing crops or other things attached to realty and capable of severance without material harm thereto but not described in subsection (1) is a contract for the sale of goods within this Article whether the subject matter is to be severed by the buyer or by the seller even though it forms part of the realty at the time of contracting, and the parties can by identification effect a present sale before severance.

(3) The provisions of this section are subject to any third party rights provided by the law relating to realty records, and the contract for sale may be executed and recorded as a document transferring an interest in land and shall then constitute notice to third parties of the buyer's rights under the contract for sale.

PART 2

FORM, FORMATION AND READJUSTMENT OF CONTRACT

Section 2-201. Formal Requirements; Statute of Frauds.

(1) Except as otherwise provided in this section a contract for the sale of goods for the price of $500 or more is not enforceable by way of action or defense unless there is some writing sufficient to indicate that a contract for sale has been made between the parties and signed by the party against whom enforcement is sought or by his authorized agent or broker. A writing is not insufficient because it omits or incorrectly states a term agreed upon but the contract is not enforceable under this paragraph beyond the quantity of goods shown in such writing.

(2) Between merchants if within a reasonable time a written confirmation of the contract and sufficient against the sender is received and the party receiving it has reason to know its contents, it satisfies the requirements of subsection (1) against such party unless written notice of objection to its contents is given within ten days after it is received.

(3) A contract which does not satisfy the requirements of subsection (1) but which is valid in other respects is enforceable

(a) if the goods are to be specially manufactured for the buyer and are not suitable for sale to others in the ordinary course of the seller's business and the seller, before notice of repudiation is received and under circumstances which reasonably indicate that the goods are for the buyer, has made either a substantial beginning of their manufacture or commitments for their procurement; or

(b) if the party against whom enforcement is sought admits in his pleading, testimony or otherwise in court that a contract for sale was made, but the contract is not enforceable under this provision beyond the quantity of goods admitted; or

(c) with respect to goods for which payment has been made and accepted or which have been received and accepted (Sec. 2-606).

Section 2-202. Final Written Expression: Parol or Extrinsic Evidence. Terms with respect to which the confirmatory memoranda of the parties agree or which are otherwise set forth in a writing intended by the parties as a final expression of their agreement with respect to such terms as are included therein may not be contradicted by evidence of any prior agreement or of a contemporaneous oral agreement but may be explained or supplemented.

(a) by course of dealing or usage of trade (Section 1-205) or by course of performance (Section 2-208); and

(b) by evidence of consistent additional terms unless the court finds the writing to have been intended also as a complete and exclusive statement of the terms of the agreement.

Section 2-203. Seals Inoperative. The affixing of a seal to a writing evidencing a contract for sale or an offer to buy or sell goods does not constitute the writing a sealed instrument and the law with respect to sealed instruments does not apply to such a contract or offer.

Section 2-204. Formation in General.

(1) A contract for sale of goods may be made in any manner sufficient to show agreement, including conduct by both

parties which recognizes the existence of such a contract.

(2) An agreement sufficient to constitute a contract for sale may be found even though the moment of its making is undetermined.

(3) Even though one or more terms are left open a contract for sale does not fail for indefiniteness if the parties have intended to make a contract and there is a reasonably certain basis for giving an appropriate remedy.

Section 2-205. Firm Offers. An offer by a merchant to buy or sell goods in a signed writing which by its terms gives assurance that it will be held open is not revocable, for lack of consideration, during the time stated or if no time is stated for a reasonable time, but in no event may such period of irrevocability exceed three months; but any such term of assurance on a form supplied by the offeree must be separately signed by the offeror.

Section 2-206. Offer and Acceptance in Formation of Contract.

(1) Unless otherwise unambiguously indicated by the language or circumstances

(a) an offer to make a contract shall be construed as inviting acceptance in any manner and by any medium reasonable in the circumstances;

(b) an order or other offer to buy goods for prompt or current shipment shall be construed as inviting acceptance either by a prompt promise to ship or by the prompt or current shipment of conforming or non-conforming goods, but such a shipment of non-conforming goods does not constitute an acceptance if the seller reasonably notifies the buyer that the shipment is offered only as an accommodation to the buyer.

(2) Where the beginning of a requested performance is a reasonable mode of acceptance an offeror who is not notified of acceptance within a reasonable time may treat the offer as having lapsed before acceptance.

Section 2-207. Additional Terms in Acceptance or Confirmation.

(1) A definite and seasonable expression of acceptance or a written confirmation which is sent within a reasonable time operates as an acceptance even though it states terms additional to or different from those offered or agreed upon, unless acceptance is expressly made conditional on assent to the additional or different terms.

(2) The additional terms are to be construed as proposals for addition to the contract. Between merchants such terms become part of the contract unless:

(a) the offer expressly limits acceptance to the terms of the offer;

(b) they materially alter it; or

(c) notification of objection to them has already been given or is given within a reasonable time after notice of them is received.

(3) Conduct by both parties which recognizes the existence of a contract is sufficient to establish a contract for sale although the writings of the parties do not otherwise establish a contract. In such case the terms of the particular contract consist of those terms on which the writings of the parties agree, together with any supplementary terms incorporated under any other provisions of this Act.

Section 2-208. Course of Performance or Practical Construction.

(1) Where the contract for sale involves repeated occasions for performance by either party with knowledge of the nature of the performance and opportunity for objection to it by the other, any course of performance accepted or acquiesced in without objection shall be relevant to determine the meaning of the agreement.

(2) The express terms of the agreement and any such course of performance, as well as any course of dealing and usage of trade, shall be construed whenever reasonable as consistent with each other; but when such construction is unreasonable, express terms shall control course of performance and course of performance shall control both course of dealing and usage of trade (Section 1-205).

(3) Subject to the provisions of the next section on modification and waiver, such course of performance shall be relevant to show a waiver or modification of any term inconsistent with such course of performance.

Section 2-209. Modification, Rescission and Waiver.

(1) An agreement modifying a contract within this Article needs no consideration to be binding.

(2) A signed agreement which excludes modification or rescission except by a signed writing cannot be otherwise modified or rescinded, but except as between merchants such a requirement on a form supplied by the merchant must be separately signed by the other party.
(3) The requirements of the statute of frauds section of this Article (Section 2-201) must be satisfied if the contract as modified is within its provisions.
(4) Although an attempt at modification or rescission does not satisfy the requirements of subsection (2) or (3) it can operate as a waiver.
(5) A party who has made a waiver affecting an executory portion of the contract may retract the waiver by reasonable notification received by the other party that strict performance will be required of any term waived, unless the retraction would be unjust in view of a material change of position in reliance on the waiver.

Section 2-210. Delegation of Performance; Assignment of Rights.

(1) A party may perform his duty through a delegate unless otherwise agreed or unless the other party has a substantial interest in having his original promisor perform or control the acts required by the contract. No delegation of performance relieves the party delegating of any duty to perform or any liability for breach.
(2) Unless otherwise agreed all rights of either seller or buyer can be assigned except where the assignment would materially change the duty of the other party, or increase materially the burden or risk imposed on him by his contract, or impair materially his chance of obtaining return performance. A right to damages for breach of the whole contract or a right arising out of the assignor's due performance of his entire obligation can be assigned despite agreement otherwise.
(3) Unless the circumstances indicate the contrary a prohibition of assignment of "the contract" is to be construed as barring only the delegation to the assignee of the assignor's performance.
(4) An assignment of "the contract" or of "all my rights under the contract" or an assignment in similar general terms is an assignment of rights and unless the language or the circumstances (as in an assignment for security) indicate the contrary, it is a delegation of performance of the duties of the assignor and its acceptance by the assignee constitutes a promise by him to perform those duties. This promise is enforceable by either the assignor or the other party to the original contract.
(5) The other party may treat any assignment which delegates performance as creating reasonable grounds for insecurity and may without prejudice to his rights against the assignor demand assurances from the assignee (Section 2-609).

PART 3

GENERAL OBLIGATION AND CONSTRUCTION OF CONTRACT

Section 2-301. General Obligations of Parties. The obligation of the seller is to transfer and deliver and that of the buyer is to accept and pay in accordance with the contract.

Section 2-302. Unconscionable Contract or Clause.

(1) If the court as a matter of law finds the contract or any clause of the contract to have been unconscionable at the time it was made the court may refuse to enforce the contract, or it may enforce the remainder of the contract without the unconscionable clause, or it may so limit the application of any unconscionable clause as to avoid any unconscionable result.
(2) When it is claimed or appears to the court that the contract or any clause thereof may be unconscionable the parties shall be afforded a reasonable opportunity to present evidence as to its commercial setting, purpose and effect to aid the court in making the determination.

Section 2-303. Allocation or Division of Risks. Where this Article allocates a risk or a burden as between the parties "unless otherwise agreed," the agreement may not only shift the allocation but may also divide the risk or burden.

Section 2-304. Price Payable in Money, Goods, Realty, or Otherwise.

(1) The price can be made payable in

money or otherwise. If it is payable in whole or in part in goods each party is a seller of the goods which he is to transfer.

(2) Even though all or part of the price is payable in an interest in realty the transfer of the goods and the seller's obligations with reference to them are subject to this Article, but not the transfer of the interest in realty or the transferor's obligations in connection therewith.

Section 2-305. Open Price Term.

(1) The parties if they so intend can conclude a contract for sale even though the price is not settled. In such a case the price is a reasonable price at the time for delivery if

(a) nothing is said as to price; or

(b) the price is left to be agreed by the parties and they fail to agree; or

(c) the price is to be fixed in terms of some agreed market or other standard as set or recorded by a third person or agency and it is not so set or recorded.

(2) A price to be fixed by the seller or by the buyer means a price for him to fix in good faith.

(3) When a price left to be fixed otherwise than by agreement of the parties fails to be fixed through fault of one party the other may at his option treat the contract as cancelled or himself fix a reasonable price.

(4) Where, however, the parties intend not to be bound unless the price be fixed or agreed and it is not fixed or agreed there is no contract. In such a case the buyer must return any goods already received or if unable to do so must pay their reasonable value at the time of delivery and the seller must return any portion of the price paid on account.

Section 2-306. Output, Requirements and Exclusive Dealings.

(1) A term which measures the quantity by the output of the seller or the requirements of the buyer means such actual output or requirements as may occur in good faith, except that no quantity unreasonably disproportionate to any stated estimate or in the absence of a stated estimate to any normal or otherwise comparable prior output or requirements may be tendered or demanded.

(2) A lawful agreement by either the seller or the buyer for exclusive dealing in the kind of goods concerned imposes unless otherwise agreed an obligation by the seller to use best efforts to supply the goods and by the buyer to use best efforts to promote their sale.

Section 2-307. Delivery in Single Lot or Several Lots. Unless otherwise agreed all goods called for by a contract for sale must be tendered in a single delivery and payment is due only on such tender but where the circumstances give either party the right to make or demand delivery in lots the price if it can be apportioned may be demanded for each lot.

Section 2-308. Absence of Specified Place for Delivery. Unless otherwise agreed.

(a) the place for delivery of goods is the seller's place of business or if he has none his residence; but

(b) in a contract for sale of identified goods which to the knowledge of the parties at the time of contracting are in some other place, that place is the place for their delivery; and

(c) documents of title may be delivered through customary banking channels.

Section 2-309. Absence of Specific Time Provisions; Notice of Termination.

(1) The time for shipment or delivery or any other action under a contract if not provided in this Article or agreed upon shall be a reasonable time.

(2) Where the contract provides for successive performances but is indefinite in duration it is valid for a reasonable time but unless otherwise agreed may be terminated at any time by either party.

(3) Termination of a contract by one party except on the happening of an agreed event requires that reasonable notification is invalid if its operation would be unconscionable.

Section 2-310. Open Time for Payment or Running of Credit; Authority to Ship under Reservation. Unless otherwise agreed

(a) payment is due at the time and place at which the buyer is to receive the goods even though the place of shipment is the place of delivery; and

(b) if the seller is authorized to send the goods he may ship them under reservation, and may tender the documents of title, but the buyer may inspect the goods after their arrival before payment is due unless such inspection is inconsistent with the terms of the contract (Section 2-513); and

(c) if delivery is authorized and made by way of documents of title otherwise than by subsection (b) then payment is due at the time and place at which the buyer is to receive the documents regardless of where the goods are to be received; and

(d) where the seller is required or authorized to ship the goods on credit the credit period runs from the time of shipment but post-dating the invoice or delaying its dispatch will correspondingly delay the starting of the credit period.

Section 2-311. Options and Cooperation Respecting Performance.

(1) An agreement for sale which is otherwise sufficiently definite (subsection (3) of Section 2-204) to be a contract is not made invalid by the fact that it leaves particulars of performance to be specified by one of the parties. Any such specification must be made in good faith and within limits set by commercial reasonableness.

(2) Unless otherwise agreed specifications relating to assortment of the goods are at the buyer's option and except as otherwise provided in subsections (1) (c) and (3) of Section 2-319 specifications or arrangements relating to shipment are at the seller's option.

(3) Where such specification would materially affect the other party's performance but is not seasonably made or where one party's cooperation is necessary to the agreed performance of the other but is not seasonably forthcoming, the other party in addition to all other remedies

(a) is excused for any resulting delay in his own performance; and

(b) may also either proceed to perform in any reasonable manner or after the time for a material part of his own performance treat the failure to specify or to cooperate as a breach by failure to deliver or accept the goods.

Section 2-312. Warranty of Title and Against Infringement; Buyer's Obligation Against Infringement.

(1) Subject to subsection (2) there is in a contract for a sale a warranty by the seller that

(a) the title conveyed shall be good, and its transfer rightful; and

(b) the goods shall be delivered free from any security interest or other lien or encumbrance of which the buyer at the time of contracting has no knowledge.

(2) A warranty under subsection (1) will be excluded or modified only by specific language or by circumstances which give the buyer reason to know that the person selling does not claim title in himself or that he is purporting to sell only such right or title as he or a third person may have.

(3) Unless otherwise agreed a seller who is a merchant regularly dealing in goods of the kind warrants that the goods shall be delivered free of the rightful claim of any third person by way of infringement or the like but a buyer who furnishes specifications to the seller must hold the seller harmless against any such claim which arises out of compliance with the specifications.

Section 2-313. Express Warranties by Affirmation, Promise, Description, Sample.

(1) Express warranties by the seller are created as follows:

(a) Any affirmation of fact or promise made by the seller to the buyer which relates to the goods and becomes part of the basis of the bargain creates an express warranty that the goods shall conform to the affirmation or promise.

(b) Any description of the goods which is made part of the basis of the bargain creates an express warranty that the goods shall conform to the description.

(c) Any sample or model which is made part of the basis of the bargain creates an express warranty that the whole of the goods shall conform to the sample or model.

(2) It is not necessary to the creation of an express warranty that the seller use formal words such as "warrant" or "guarantee" or that he have a specific intention to make a warranty, but an affirmation merely of the value of the goods or a statement purporting to be merely the seller's opinion or commendation of the goods does not create a warranty.

Section 2-314. Implied Warranty: Merchantability; Usage of Trade.

(1) Unless excluded or modified (Section

2-316) a warranty that the goods shall be merchantable is implied in a contract for their sale if the seller is a merchant with respect to goods of that kind. Under this section the serving for value of food or drink to be consumed either on the premises or elsewhere is a sale.

(2) Goods to be merchantable must be at least such as

(a) pass without objection in the trade under the contract description; and

(b) in the case of fungible goods, are of fair average quality within the description; and

(c) are fit for the ordinary purposes for which such goods are used; and

(d) run, within the variations permitted by the agreement, of even kind, quality and quantity within each unit and among all units involved; and

(e) are adequately contained, packaged, and labeled as the agreement may require; and

(f) conform to the promises or affirmations of fact made on the container or label if any.

(3) Unless excluded or modified (Section 2-316) other implied warranties may arise from course of dealing or usage of trade.

Section 2-315. Implied Warranty: Fitness for Particular Purpose. Where the seller at the time of contracting has reason to know any particular purpose for which the goods are required and that the buyer is relying on the seller's skill or judgment to select or furnish suitable goods, there is unless excluded or modified under the next section an implied warranty that the goods shall be fit for such purpose.

Section 2-316. Exclusion or Modification of Warranties.

(1) Words or conduct relevant to the creation of an express warranty and words or conduct tending to negate or limit warranty shall be construed wherever reasonable as consistent with each other; but subject to the provisions of this Article on parol or extrinsic evidence (Section 2-202) negation or limitation is inoperative to the extent that such construction is unreasonable.

(2) Subject to subsection (3), to exclude or modify the implied warranty of merchantability or any part of it the language must mention merchantability and in case of a writing must be conspicuous, and to exclude or modify any implied warranty of fitness the exclusion must be by a writing and conspicuous. Language to exclude all implied warranties of fitness is sufficient if it states, for example, that "There are no warranties which extend beyond the description on the face hereof."

(3) Notwithstanding subsection (2)

(a) unless the circumstances indicate otherwise, all implied warranties are excluded by expressions like "as is," "with all faults" or other language which in common understanding calls the buyer's attention to the exclusion of warranties and makes plain that there is no implied warranty; and

(b) when the buyer before entering into the contract has examined the goods or the sample or model as fully as he desired or has refused to examine the goods there is no implied warranty with regard to defects which an examination ought in the circumstances to have revealed to him; and

(c) an implied warranty can also be excluded or modified by course of dealing or course of performance or usage of trade.

(4) Remedies for breach of warranty can be limited in accordance with the provisions of this Article on liquidation or limitation of damages and on contractual modification of remedy (Sections 2-718 and 2-719).

Section 2-317. Cumulation and Conflict of Warranties Express or Implied. Warranties whether express or implied shall be construed as consistent with each other and as cumulative, but if such construction is unreasonable the intention of the parties shall determine which warranty is dominant. In ascertaining that intention the following rules apply:

(a) Exact or technical specifications displace an inconsistent sample or model or general language of description.

(b) A sample from an existing bulk displaces inconsistent general language of description.

(c) Express warranties displace inconsistent implied warranties other than an implied warranty of fitness for a particular purpose.

Section 2-318. Third Party Beneficiaries or Warranties Express or Implied. A seller's warranty whether express or implied extends to any natural person who is in the family or household of his buyer or who is a guest in his home if it is reasonable to expect that such person may use, consume or be affected by the goods and who is injured in person by breach of the warranty. A seller may not exclude or limit the operation of this section.

Section 2-319. F.O.B. and F.A.S. Terms.

(1) Unless otherwise agreed the term F.O.B. (which means "free on board") at a named place, even though used only in connection with the stated price, is a delivery term under which

(a) when the term is F.O.B. the place of shipment, the seller must at that place ship the goods in the manner provided in this article (Section 2-504) and bear the expense and risk of putting them into the possession of the carrier; or

(b) when the term is F.O.B. the place of destination, the seller must at his own expense and risk transport the goods to that place and there tender delivery of them in the manner provided in this Article (Section 2-503);

(c) when under either (a) or (b) the term is also F.O.B. vessel, car or other vehicle, the seller must in addition at his own expense and risk load the goods on board. If the term is F.O.B. vessel the buyer must name the vessel and in an appropriate case the seller must comply with the provisions of this Article on the form of bill of lading (Section 2-323).

(2) Unless otherwise agreed the term F.A.S. vessel (which means "free alongside") at a named port, even though used only in connection with the stated price, is a delivery term under which the seller must

(a) at his own expense and risk deliver the goods alongside the vessel in the manner usual in that port or on a dock designated and provided by the buyer; and

(b) obtain and tender a receipt for the goods in exchange for which the carrier is under a duty to issue a bill of lading.

(3) Unless otherwise agreed in any case falling within subsection (1)(a) or (c) or subsection (2) the buyer must seasonably give any needed instructions for making delivery, including when the term is F.A.S. or F.O.B. the loading berth of the vessel and in an appropriate case its name and sailing date. The seller may treat the failure of needed instructions as a failure of cooperation under this Article (Section 2-311). He may also at his option move the goods in any reasonable manner preparatory to delivery or shipment.

(4) Under the term F.O.B. vessel or F.A.S. unless otherwise agreed the buyer must make payment against tender of the required documents and the seller may not tender nor the buyer demand delivery of the goods in substitution for the documents.

Section 2-320. C.I.F. and C. & F. Terms.

(1) The term C.I.F. means that the price includes in a lump sum the cost of the goods and the insurance and freight to the named destination. The term C. & F. or C.F. means that the price so includes cost and freight to the named destination.

(2) Unless otherwise agreed and even though used only in connection with the stated price and destination, the term C.I.F. destination or its equivalent requires the seller at his own expense and risk to

(a) put the goods into the possession of a carrier at the port for shipment and obtain a negotiable bill or bills of lading covering the entire transportation to the named destination; and

(b) load the goods and obtain a receipt from the carrier (which may be contained in the bill of lading) showing that the freight has been paid or provided for; and

(c) obtain a policy or certificate of insurance, including any war risk insurance, of a kind and on terms then current at the port of shipment in the usual amount, in the currency of the contract, shown to cover the same goods covered by the bill of lading and providing for payment of loss to the order of the buyer or for the account of whom it may concern; but the seller may add to the price the amount of the premium for any such war risk insurance; and

(d) prepare an invoice of the goods and procure any other documents required to effect shipment or to comply with the contract; and

(e) forward and tender with commercial promptness all the documents in due form and with any indorsement necessary to perfect the buyer's rights.

(3) Unless otherwise agreed the term C. & F. or its equivalent has the same effect and imposes upon the seller the same obligations and risks as a C.I.F. term except the obligation as to insurance.

(4) Under the term C.I.F. or C. & F. unless otherwise agreed the buyer must make payment against tender of the required documents and the seller may not tender nor the buyer demand delivery of the goods in substitution for the documents.

Section 2-321. C.I.F. or C. & F.: "Net Landed Weights"; "Payment on Arrival"; Warranty of Condition on Arrival. Under a contract containing a term C.I.F. or C. & F.

(1) Where the price is based on or is to be adjusted according to "net landed weights," "delivered weights," "out turn" quantity or quality or the like, unless otherwise agreed the seller must reasonably estimate the price. The payment due on tender of the documents called for by the contract is the amount so estimated, but after final adjustment of the price a settlement must be made with commercial promptness.

(2) An agreement described in subsection (1) or any warranty of quality or condition of the goods on arrival places upon the seller the risk of ordinary deterioration, shrinkage and the like in transportation but has no effect on the place or time of identification to the contract for sale or delivery or on the passing of the risk of loss.

(3) Unless otherwise agreed where the contract provides for payment on or after arrival of the goods the seller must before payment allow such preliminary inspection as is feasible; but if the goods are lost delivery of the documents and payment are due when the goods should have arrived.

Section 2-322. Delivery "Ex-Ship."

(1) Unless otherwise agreed a term for delivery of goods "ex-ship" (which means from the carrying vessel) or in equivalent language is not restricted to a particular ship and requires delivery from a ship which has reached a place at the named port of destination where goods of the kind are usually discharged.

(2) Under such a term unless otherwise agreed

(a) the seller must discharge all liens arising out of the carriage and furnish the buyer with a direction which puts the carrier under a duty to deliver the goods; and

(b) the risk of loss does not pass to the buyer until the goods leave the ship's tackle or are otherwise properly unloaded.

Section 2-323. Form of Bill of Lading Required in Overseas Shipment; "Overseas."

(1) Where the contract contemplates overseas shipment and contains a term C.I.F. or C. & F. or F. O. B. vessel, the seller unless otherwise agreed must obtain a negotiable bill of lading stating that the goods have been loaded on board or, in the case of a term C.I.F. or C. & F., received for shipment.

(2) Where in a case within subsection (1) a bill of lading has been issued in a set of parts, unless otherwise agreed if the documents are not to be sent from abroad the buyer may demand tender of the full set; otherwise only one part of the bill of lading need be tendered. Even if the agreement expressly requires a full set

(a) due tender of a single part is acceptable within the provisions of this Article on cure of improper delivery (subsection (1) of Section 2-508); and

(b) even though the full set is demanded, if the documents are sent from abroad the person tendering an incomplete set may nevertheless require payment upon furnishing an indemnity which the buyer in good faith deems adequate.

(3) A shipment by water or by air or a contract contemplating such shipment is "overseas" insofar as by usage of trade or agreement it is subject to the commercial, financing or shipping practices characteristic of international deep water commerce.

Section 2-324. "No Arrival, No Sale" Term. Under a term "no arrival, no sale" or terms of like meaning, unless otherwise agreed.

(a) the seller must properly ship conforming goods and if they arrive by any means he must tender them on arrival but he assumes no obligation that the goods will arrive unless he has caused the non-arrival; and

(b) where without fault of the seller the goods are in part lost or have so deteriorated as no longer to conform to the contract or arrive after the contract time, the buyer may proceed as if there had been casualty to identified goods (Section 2-613).

Section 2-325. "Letter of Credit" Term; "Confirmed Credit."

(1) Failure of the buyer seasonably to furnish an agreed letter of credit is a breach of the contract for sale.

(2) The delivery to seller of a proper letter of credit suspends the buyer's obligation to pay. If the letter of credit is dishonored, the seller may on seasonable notification to the buyer require payment directly from him.

(3) Unless otherwise agreed the term "letter of credit" or "banker's credit" in a contract for sale means an irrevocable credit issued by a financing agency of good repute and, where the shipment is overseas, of good international repute. The term "confirmed credit" means that the credit must also carry the direct obligation of such an agency which does business in the seller's financial market.

Section 2-326. Sale on Approval and Sale or Return; Consignment Sales and Rights of Creditors.

(1) Unless otherwise agreed, if delivered goods may be returned to the buyer even though they conform to the contract, the transaction is.

(a) a "sale on approval" if the goods are delivered primarily for use; and

(b) a "sale or return" if the goods are delivered primarily for resale.

(2) Except as provided in subsection (3), goods held on approval are not subject to the claims of the buyer's creditors until acceptance; goods held on sale or return are subject to such claims while in the buyer's possession.

(3) Where goods are delivered to a person for sale and such person maintains a place of business at which he deals in goods of the kind involved, under a name other than the name of the person making delivery, then with respect to claims of creditors of the person conducting the business the goods are deemed to be on sale or return. The provisions of this subsection are applicable even though an agreement purports to reserve title to the person making delivery until payment or resale or uses such words as "on consignment" or "on memorandum." However, this subsection is not applicable if the person making delivery

(a) complies with an applicable law providing for a consignor's interest or the like to be evidenced by a sign, or

(b) establishes that the person conducting the business is generally known by his creditors to be substantially engaged in selling the goods of others, or

(c) complies with the filing provisions of the Article on Secured Transactions (Article 9).

(4) Any "or return" term of a contract for sale is to be treated as a separate contract for sale within the statute of frauds section of this Article (Section 2-201) and as contradicting the sale aspect of the contract within the provisions of this Article on parol or extrinsic evidence (Section 2-202).

Section 2-327. Special Incidents of Sale on Approval and Sale or Return.

(1) Under a sale on approval unless otherwise agreed

(a) although the goods are identified to the contract the risk of loss and the title do not pass to the buyer until acceptance; and

(b) use of the goods consistent with the purpose of trial is not acceptance but failure seasonably to notify the seller of election to return the goods is acceptance, and if the goods conform to the contract acceptance of any part is acceptance of the whole; and

(c) after due notification of election to return, the return is at the seller's risk and expense but a merchant buyer must follow any reasonable instructions.

(2) Under a sale or return unless otherwise agreed

(a) the option to return extends to the whole or any commercial unit of the goods while in substantially their original condition, but must be exercised seasonably; and

(b) the return is at the buyer's risk and expense.

Section 2-328. Sale by Auction.

(1) In a sale by auction if goods are put up in lots each lot is the subject of a separate sale.

(2) A sale by auction is complete when the auctioneer so announces by the fall of the hammer or in other customary manner.

Where a bid is made while the hammer is falling in acceptance of a prior bid the auctioneer may in his discretion reopen the bidding or declare the goods sold under the bid on which the hammer was falling.

(3) Such a sale is with reserve unless the goods are in explicit terms put up without reserve. In an auction with reserve the auctioneer may withdraw the goods at any time until he announces completion of the sale. In an auction without reserve, after the auctioneer calls for bids on an article or lot, that article or lot cannot be withdrawn unless no bid is made within a reasonable time. In either case a bidder may retract his bid until the auctioneer's announcement of completion of the sale, but a bidder's retraction does not revive any previous bid.

(4) If the auctioneer knowingly receives a bid on the seller's behalf or the seller makes or procures such a bid, and notice has not been given that liberty for such bidding is reserved, the buyer may at his option avoid the sale or take the goods at the price of the last good faith bid prior to the completion of the sale. This subsection shall not apply to any bid at a forced sale.

PART 4

TITLE, CREDITORS AND GOOD FAITH PURCHASERS

Section 2-401. Passing of Title; Reservation for Security; Limited Application of this Section. Each provision of this Article with regard to the rights, obligations and remedies of the seller, the buyer, purchasers or other third parties applies irrespective of title to the goods except where the provision refers to such title. Insofar as situations are not covered by the other provisions of this Article and matters concerning title become material the following rules apply:

(1) Title to goods cannot pass under a contract for sale prior to their identification to the contract (Section 2-501), and unless otherwise explicitly agreed the buyer acquires by their identification a special property as limited by this Act. Any retention or reservation by the seller of the title (property) in goods shipped or delivered to the buyer is limited in effect to a reservation of a security interest. Subject to these provisions and to the provisions of the Article on Secured Transactions (Article 9), title to goods passes from the seller to the buyer in any manner and on any conditions explicitly agreed on by the parties.

(2) Unless otherwise explicitly agreed title passes to the buyer at the time and place at which the seller completes his performance with reference to the physical delivery of the goods, despite any reservation of a security interest and even though a document of title is to be delivered at a different time or place; and in particular and despite any reservation of a security interest by the bill of lading

(a) if the contract requires or authorizes the seller to send the goods to the buyer but does not require him to deliver them at destination, title passes to the buyer at the time and place of shipment; but

(b) if the contract requires delivery at destination, title passes on tender there.

(3) Unless otherwise explicitly agreed where delivery is to be made without moving the goods,

(a) if the seller is to deliver a document of title, title passes at the time when and the place where he delivers such documents; or

(b) if the goods are at the time of contracting already identified and no documents are to be delivered, title passes at the time and place of contracting.

(4) A rejection or other refusal by the buyer to receive or retain the goods, whether or not justified, or a justified revocation of acceptance revests title to the goods in the seller. Such revesting occurs by operation of law and is not a "sale."

Section 2-402. Rights of Seller's Creditors Against Sold Goods.

(1) Except as provided in subsections (2) and (3), rights of unsecured creditors of the seller with respect to goods which have been identified to a contract for sale are subject to the buyer's rights to recover the goods under this Article (Sections 2-502 and 2-716).

(2) A creditor of the seller may treat a sale or an identification of goods to a contract

for sale as void if as against him a retention of possession by the seller is fraudulent under any rule of law of the state where the goods are situated, except that retention of possession in good faith and current course of trade by a merchant-seller for a commercially reasonable time after a sale or identification is not fraudulent.

(3) Nothing in this Article shall be deemed to impair the rights of creditors of the seller

(a) under the provisions of the Article on Secured Transactions (Article 9); or

(b) where identification to the contract or delivery is made not in current course of trade but in satisfaction of or as security for a pre-existing claim for money, security or the like and is made under circumstances which under any rule of law of the state where the goods are situated would apart from this Article constitute the transaction a fraudulent transfer or voidable preference.

Section 2-403. Power to Transfer; Good Faith Purchase of Goods; "Entrusting."

(1) A purchaser of goods acquires all title which his transferor had or had power to transfer except that a purchaser of a limited interest acquires rights only to the extent of the interest purchased. A person with voidable title had power to transfer a good title to a good faith purchaser for value. When goods have been delivered under a transaction of purchase the purchaser has such power even though

(a) the transferor was deceived as to the identity of the purchaser, or

(b) the delivery was in exchange for a check which is later dishonored, or

(c) it was agreed that the transaction was to be a "cash sale," or

(d) the delivery was procured through fraud punishable as larcenous under the criminal law.

(2) Any entrusting of possession of goods to a merchant who deals in goods of that kind gives him power to transfer all rights of the entruster to a buyer in ordinary course of business.

(3) "Entrusting" includes any delivery and any acquiescence in retention of possession regardless of any condition expressed between the parties to the delivery or acquiescence and regardless of whether the procurement of the entrusting or the possessor's disposition of the goods have been such as to be larcenous under the criminal law.

(4) The rights of other purchasers of goods and of lien creditors are governed by the Articles on Secured Transactions (Article 9), Bulk Transfers (Article 6) and Documents of Title (Article 7).

PART 5

PERFORMANCE

Section 2-501. Insurable Interest in Goods; Manner of Identification of Goods.

(1) The buyer obtains a special property and an insurable interest in goods by identification of existing goods as goods to which the contract refers even though the goods so identified are non-conforming and he has an opinion to return or reject them. Such identification can be made at any time and in any manner explicitly agreed to by the parties. In the absence of explicit agreement identification occurs

(a) when the contract is made if it is for the sale of goods already existing and identified;

(b) if the contract is for the sale of future goods other than those described in paragraph (c), when goods are shipped, marked or otherwise designated by the seller as goods to which the contract refers;

(c) when the crops are planted or otherwise become growing crops or the young are conceived if the contract is for the sale of unborn young to be born within twelve months after contracting or for the sale of crops to be harvested within twelve months or the next normal harvest season after contracting whichever is longer.

(2) The seller retains an insurable interest in goods so long as title to or any security interest in the goods remains in him and where the identification is by the seller alone he may until default or insolvency or notification to the buyer that the identifica-

tion is final substitute other goods for those identified.

(3) Nothing in this section impairs any insurable interest recognized under any other statute or rule of law.

Section 2-502. Buyer's Right to Goods on Seller's Insolvency.

(1) Subject to subsection (2) and even though the goods have not been shipped a buyer who has paid a part or all of the price of the goods in which he has a special property under the provisions of the immediately preceding section may on making and keeping good a tender of any unpaid portion of their price recover them from the seller if the seller becomes insolvent within ten days after receipt of the first installment on their price.

(2) If the identification creating his special property has been made by the buyer he acquires the right to recover the goods only if they conform to the contract for sale.

Section 2-503. Manner of Seller's Tender of Delivery.

(1) Tender of delivery requires that the seller put and hold conforming goods at the buyer's disposition and give the buyer any notification reasonably necessary to enable him to take delivery. The manner, time and place for tender are determined by the agreement and this Article, and in particular

(a) tender must be at a reasonable hour, and if it is of goods they must be kept available for the period reasonably necessary to enable the buyer to take possession; but

(b) unless otherwise agreed the buyer must furnish facilities reasonably suited to the receipt of the goods.

(2) Where the case is within the next section respecting shipment tender requires that the seller comply with its provisions.

(3) Where the seller is required to deliver at a particular destination tender requires that he comply with subsection (1) and also in any appropriate case tender documents as described in subsections (4) and (5) of this section.

(4) Where goods are in the possession of a bailee and are to be delivered without being moved

(a) tender requires that the seller either tender a negotiable document of title covering such goods or procure acknowledgment by the bailee of the buyer's right to possession of the goods; but

(b) tender to the buyer of a non-negotiable document of title or of a written direction to the bailee to deliver is sufficient tender unless the buyer seasonably objects, and receipt by the bailee of notification of the buyer's rights fixes those rights as against the bailee and all third persons; but risk of loss of the goods and of any failure by the bailee to honor the non-negotiable document of title or to obey the direction remains on the seller until the buyer has had a reasonable time to present the document or direction, and a refusal by the bailee to honor the document or to obey the direction defeats the tender.

(5) Where the contract requires the seller to deliver documents

(a) he must tender all such documents in correct form, except as provided in this Article with respect to bills of lading in a set (subsection (2) of Section 2-323); and

(b) tender through customary banking channels is sufficient and dishonor of a draft accompanying the documents constitutes non-acceptance or rejection.

Section 2-504. Shipment by Seller. Where the seller is required or authorized to send the goods to the buyer and the contract does not require him to deliver them at a particular destination, then unless otherwise agreed he must

(a) put the goods in the possession of such a carrier and make such a contract for their transportation as may be reasonable having regard to the nature of the goods and other circumstances of the case; and

(b) obtain and promptly deliver or tender in due form any document necessary to enable the buyer to obtain possession of the goods or otherwise required by the agreement or by usage of trade; and

Failure to notify the buyer under paragraph (c) or to make a proper contract under paragraph (a) is a ground for rejection only if material delay or loss ensued.

Section 2-505. Seller's Shipment Under Reservation.

(1) Where the seller has identified goods to the contract by or before shipment:

(a) his procurement of a negotiable bill of lading to his own order or otherwise reserves in him a security interest in the goods. His procurement of the bill to the order of a financing agency or of the buyer indicates in addition only the seller's expectation of transferring that interest to the person named.

(b) a non-negotiable bill of lading to himself or his nominee reserves possession of the goods as security but except in a case of conditional delivery (subsection (2) of Section 2-507) a non-negotiable bill of lading naming the buyer as consignee reserves no security interest even though the seller retains possession of the bill of lading.

(2) When shipment by the seller with reservation of a security interest is in violation of the contract for sale it constitutes an improper contract for transportation within the preceding section but impairs neither the rights given to the buyer by shipment and identification of the goods to the contract nor the seller's powers as a holder of a negotiable document.

Section 2-506. Rights of Financing Agency.

(1) A financing agency by paying or purchasing for value a draft which relates to a shipment of goods acquires to the extent of the payment or purchase and in addition to its own rights under the draft and any document of title securing it any rights of the shipper in the goods including the right to stop delivery and the shipper's right to have the draft honored by the buyer.

(2) The right to reimbursement of a financing agency which has in good faith honored or purchased the draft under commitment to or authority from the buyer is not impaired by subsequent discovery of defects with reference to any relevant document which was apparently regular on its face.

Section 2-507. Effect of Seller's Tender; Delivery on Condition.

(1) Tender of delivery is a condition to the buyer's duty to accept the goods and, unless otherwise agreed, to his duty to pay for them. Tender entitles the seller to acceptance of the goods and to payment according to the contract.

(2) Where payment is due and demanded on the delivery to the buyer of goods or documents of title, his right as against the seller to retain or dispose of them is conditional upon his making the payment due.

Section 2-508. Cure by Seller of Improper Tender or Delivery; Replacement.

(1) Where any tender or delivery by the seller is rejected because non-conforming and the time for performance has not yet expired, the seller may seasonably notify the buyer of his intention to cure and may then within the contract time make a conforming delivery.

(2) Where the buyer rejects a non-conforming tender which the seller had reasonable grounds to believe would be acceptable with or without money allowance the seller may if he seasonably notifies the buyer have a further reasonable time to substitute a conforming tender.

Section 2-509. Risk of Loss in the Absence of Breach.

(1) Where the contract requires or authorizes the seller to ship the goods by carrier

(a) if it does not require him to deliver them at a particular destination, the risk of loss passes to the buyer when the goods are duly delivered to the carrier even though the shipment is under reservation (Section 2-505); but

(b) if it does require him to deliver them at a particular destination and the goods are there duly tendered while in the possession of the carrier, the risk of loss passes to the buyer when the goods are there duly so tendered as to enable the buyer to take delivery.

(2) Where the goods are held by a bailee to be delivered without being moved, the risk of loss passes to the buyer

(a) on his receipt of a negotiable document of title covering the goods; or

(b) on acknowledgement by the bailee of the buyer's right to possession of the goods; or

(c) after his receipt of a non-negotiable document of title or other written direction to deliver, as provided in subsection (4) (b) of Section 2-503.

(3) In any case not within subsection (1) or (2), the risk of loss passes to the buyer on his receipt of the goods if the seller is a merchant; otherwise the risk passes to the buyer on tender of delivery.

(4) The provisions of this section are subject to contrary agreement of the parties and to the provisions of this Article on sale on approval (Section 2-327) and on effect of breach on risk of loss (Section 2-510).

Section 2-510. Effect of Breach on Risk of Loss.

(1) Where a tender or delivery of goods so fails to conform to the contract as to give a right of rejection the risk of their loss remains on the seller until cure or acceptance.

(2) Where the buyer rightfully revokes acceptance he may to the extent of any deficiency in his effective insurance coverage treat the risk of loss as having rested on the seller from the beginning.

(3) Where the buyer as to conforming goods already identified to the contract for sale repudiates or is otherwise in breach before risk of their loss has passed to him the seller may to the extent of any deficiency in his effective insurance coverage treat the risk of loss as resting on the buyer for a commercially reasonable time.

Section 2-511. Tender of Payment by Buyer; Payment by Check.

(1) Unless otherwise agreed tender of payment is a condition to the seller's duty to tender and complete any delivery.

(2) Tender of payment is sufficient when made by any means or in any manner current in the ordinary course of business unless the seller demands payment in legal tender and gives any extension of time reasonably necessary to procure it.

(3) Subject to the provisions of this Act on the effect of an instrument on an obligation (Section 3-802), payment by check is conditional and is defeated as between the parties by dishonor of the check on due presentment.

Section 2-512. Payment by Buyer Before Inspection.

(1) Where the contract requires payment before inspection non-conformity of the goods does not excuse the buyer from so making payment unless

(a) the non-conformity appears without inspection; or

(b) despite tender of the required documents the circumstances would justify injunction against honor under the provisions of this Act (Section 5-114).

(2) Payment pursuant to subsection (1) does not constitute an acceptance of goods or impair the buyer's right to inspect or any of his remedies.

Section 2-513. Buyer's Right to Inspection of Goods.

(1) Unless otherwise agreed and subject to subsection (3), where goods are tendered or delivered or identified to the contract for sale, the buyer has a right before payment or acceptance to inspect them at any reasonable place and time and in any reasonable manner. When the seller is required or authorized to send the goods to the buyer, the inspection may be after their arrival.

(2) Expenses of inspection must be borne by the buyer but may be recovered from the seller if the goods do not conform and are rejected.

(3) Unless otherwise agreed and subject to the provisions of this Article on C.I.F. contracts (subsection (3) of Section 2-321), the buyer is not entitled to inspect the goods before payment of the price when the contract provides

(a) for delivery "C.O.D." or on other like terms; or

(b) for payment against documents of title, except where such payment is due only after the goods are to become available for inspection.

(4) A place or method of inspection fixed by the parties is presumed to be exclusive but unless otherwise expressly agreed it does not postpone identification or shift the place for delivery or for passing the risk of loss. If compliance becomes impossible, inspection shall be as provided in this section unless the place or method fixed was clearly intended as an indispensable condition failure of which avoids the contract.

Section 3-514. When Documents Deliverable on Acceptance; When on Payment. Unless otherwise agreed documents against which a draft is drawn are to be delivered to the drawee on acceptance of the draft if it is payable more than three days after presentment; otherwise, only on payment.

Section 2-515. Preserving Evidence of Goods in Dispute. In furtherance of the adjustment of any claim or dispute

(a) either party on reasonable notification to the other and for the purpose of ascertaining the facts and preserving evidence has the right to inspect, test and sample the goods including such of them as may be in the possession or control of the other; and

(b) the parties may agree to a third party inspection or survey to determine the conformity or condition of the goods and may agree that the findings shall be binding upon them in any subsequent litigation or adjustment.

PART 6

BREACH, REPUDIATION AND EXCUSE

Section 2-601. Buyer's Rights on Improper Delivery. Subject to the provisions of this Article on breach in installment contracts (Section 2-612) and unless otherwise agreed under the sections on contractual limitations of remedy (Sections 2-718 and 2-719), if the goods or the tender of delivery fail in any respect to conform to the contract, the buyer may
may

(a) reject the whole; or

(b) accept the whole; or

(c) accept any commercial unit or units and reject the rest.

Section 2-602. Manner and Effect of Rightful Rejection.

(1) Rejection of goods must be within a reasonable time after their delivery or tender. It is ineffective unless the buyer seasonably notifies the seller.

(2) Subject to the provisions of the two following sections on rejected goods (Sections 2-603 and 2-604),

(a) after rejection any exercise of ownership by the buyer with respect to any commercial unit is wrongful as against the seller; and

(b) if the buyer has before rejection taken physical possession of goods in which he does not have a security interest under the provisions of this Article (subsection (3) of Section 2-711), he is under a duty after rejection to hold them with reasonable care at the seller's disposition for a time sufficient to permit the seller to remove them; but

(c) the buyer has no further obligations with regard to goods rightfully rejected.

(3) The seller's rights with respect to goods wrongfully rejected are governed by the provisions of this Article on Seller's remedies in general (Section 2-703).

Section 2-603. Merchant Buyer's Duties as to Rightfully Rejected Goods.

(1) Subject to any security interest in the buyer (subsection (3) of Section 2-711), when the seller has no agent or place of business at the market of rejection a merchant buyer is under a duty after rejection of goods in his possession or control to follow any reasonable instructions received from the seller with respect to the goods and in the absence of such instructions to make reasonable efforts to sell them for the seller's account if they are perishable or threaten to decline in value speedily. Instructions are not reasonable if on demand indemnity for expenses is not forthcoming.

(2) When the buyer sells goods under subsection (1), he is entitled to reimbursement from the seller or out of the proceeds for reasonable expenses of caring for and selling them, and if the expenses include no selling commission then to such commission as is usual in the trade or if there is none to a reasonable sum not exceeding ten per cent on the gross proceeds.

(3) In complying with this section the buyer is held only to good faith and good faith conduct hereunder is neither acceptance nor conversion nor the basis of an action for damages.

Section 2-604. Buyer's Options as to Salvage of Rightfully Rejected Goods. Subject to the provisions of the immediately preceding section on perishables if the seller gives no instructions within a reasonable time after notifcation of rejection the buyer may store the rejected goods for the seller's account or reship them to him or resell them for the seller's account with reimbursement as provided in the preceding section. Such action is not acceptance or conversion.

Section 2-605. Waiver of Buyer's Objections by Failure to Particularize.

(1) The buyer's failure to state in connection with rejection a particular defect which is ascertainable by reasonable inspection precludes him from relying on the unstated defect to justify rejection or to establish breach

(a) where the seller could have cured it if stated seasonably; or

(b) between merchants when the seller has after rejection made a request in writing for a full and final written statement of all defects on which the buyer proposes to rely.

(2) Payment against documents made without reservation of rights precludes recovery of the payment for defects apparent on the fact of the documents.

Section 2-606. What Constitutes Acceptance of Goods.

(1) Acceptance of goods occurs when the buyer

(a) after a reasonable opportunity to inspect the goods signifies to the seller that the goods are conforming or that he will take or retain them in spite of their non-conformity; or

(b) fails to make an effective rejection (subsection (1) of Section 2-602), but such acceptance does not occur until the buyer has had a reasonable opportunity to inspect them; or

(c) does any act inconsistent with the seller's ownership but if such act is wrongful as against the seller it is an acceptance only if ratified by him.

(2) Acceptance of a part of any commercial unit is acceptance of that entire unit.

Section 2-607. Effect of Acceptance; Notice of Breach; Burden of Establishing Breach After Acceptance; Notice of Claim or Litigation to Person Answerable Over.

(1) The buyer must pay at the contract rate for any goods accepted.

(2) Acceptance of goods by the buyer precludes rejection of the goods accepted and if made with knowledge of a non-conformity cannot be revoked because of it unless the acceptance was on the reasonable assumption that the non-conformity would be seasonably cured but acceptance does not of itself impair any other remedy provided by this Article for non-conformity.

(3) Where a tender has been accepted

(a) the buyer must within a reasonable time after he discovers or should have discovered any breach notify the seller of breach or be barred from any remedy; and

(b) if the claim is one for infringement or the like (subsection (3) of Section 2-312) and the buyer is sued as a result of such a breach he must so notify the seller within a reasonable time after he receives notice of the litigation or be barred from any remedy over for liability established by the litigation.

(4) The burden is on the buyer to establish any breach with respect to the goods accepted.

(5) Where the buyer is used for breach of a warranty or other obligation for which his seller is answerable over

(a) he may give his seller written notice of the litigation. If the notice states that the seller may come in and defend and that if the seller does not do so he will be bound in any action against him by his buyer by any determination of fact common to the two litigations, then unless the seller after seasonable receipt of the notice does come in and defend he is so bound.

(b) if the claim is one for infringement or the like (subsection (3) of Section 2-312) the original seller may demand in writing that his buyer turn over to him control of the litigation including settlement or else be barred from any remedy over and if he also agrees to bear all expense and to satisfy any adverse judgment, then unless the buyer after seasonable receipt of the demand does turn over control the buyer is so barred.

(6) The provisions of subsections (3), (4) and (5) apply to any obligation of a buyer to hold the seller harmless against infringement or the like (subsection (3) of Section 2-312).

Section 2-608. Revocation of Acceptance in Whole or in Part.

(1) The buyer may revoke his acceptance of a lot or commercial unit whose non-conformity substantially impairs its value to him if he has accepted it

(a) on the reasonable assumption that

(a) its non-conformity would be cured and it has not been seasonably cured; or

(b) without discovery of such non-conformity if his acceptance was reasonably induced either by the difficulty of discovery before acceptance or by the seller's assurances.

(2) Revocation of acceptance must occur within a reasonable time after the buyer discovers or should have discovered the ground for it and before any substantial change in condition of the goods which is not caused by their own defects. It is not effective until the buyer notifies the seller of it.

(3) A buyer who so revokes has the same rights and duties with regard to the goods involved as if he had rejected them.

Section 2-609. Right to Adequate Assurance of Performance.

(1) A contract for sale imposes an obligation on each party that the other's expectation of receiving due performance will not be impaired. When reasonable grounds for insecurity arise with respect to the performance of either party the other may in writing demand adequate assurance of due performance and until he receives such assurance may if commercially reasonable suspend any performance for which he has not already received the agreed return.

(2) Between merchants the reasonableness of grounds for insecurity and the adequacy of any assurance offered shall be determined according to commercial standards.

(3) Acceptance of any improper delivery or payment does not prejudice the aggrieved party's right to demand adequate assurance of future performance.

(4) After receipt of a justified demand failure to provide within a reasonable time not exceeding thirty days such assurance of due performance as is adequate under the circumstances of the particular case is a repudiation of the contract.

Section 2-610. Anticipatory Repudiation. When either party repudiates the contract with respect to a performance not yet due the loss of which will substantially impair the value of the contract to the other, the aggrieved party may

(a) for a commercially reasonable time await performance by the repudiating party; or

(b) resort to any remedy for breach (Section 2-703 or Section 2-711), even though he has notified the repudiating party that he would await the latter's performance and has urged retraction; and

(c) in either case suspend his own performance or proceed in accordance with the provisions of this Article on the seller's right to identify goods to the contract notwithstanding breach or to salvage unfinished goods (Section 2-704).

Section 2-611. Retraction of Anticipatory Repudiation.

(1) Until the repudiating party's next performance is due he can retract his repudiation unless the aggrieved party has since the repudiation cancelled or materially changed his position or otherwise indicated that he considers the repudiation final.

(2) Retraction may be by any method which clearly indicates to the aggrieved party that the repudiating party intends to perform, but must include any assurance justifiably demanded under the provisions of this Article (Section 2-609).

(3) Retraction reinstates the repudiating party's rights under the contract with due excuse and allowance to the aggrieved party for any delay occasioned by the repudiation.

Section 2-612. "Installment Contract"; Breach.

(1) An "installment contract" is one which requires or authorizes the delivery of goods in separate lots to be separately accepted, even though the contract contains a clause "each delivery is a separate contract" or its equivalent.

(2) The buyer may reject any installment which is non-conforming if the non-conformity substantially impairs the value of that installment and cannot be cured or if the non-conformity is a defect in the required documents; but if the non-conformity does not fall within subsection (3) and the seller gives adequate assurance of its cure the buyer must accept that installment.

(3) Whenever non-conformity or default with respect to one or more installments substantially impairs the value of the whole contract there is a breach of the whole. But

the aggrieved party reinstates the contract if he accepts a non-conforming installment without seasonably notifying of cancellation or if he brings an action with respect only to past installments or demands performance as to future installments.

Section 2-613. Casualty to Identified Goods. Where the contract requires for its performance goods identified when the contract is made, and the goods suffer casualty without fault of either party before the risk of loss passes to the buyer, or in a proper case under a "no arrival, no sale" term (Section 2-324) then

(a) if the loss is total the contract is avoided; and

(b) if the loss is partial or the goods have so deteriorated as no longer to conform to the contract the buyer may nevertheless demand inspection and at his option either treat the contract as avoided or accept the goods with allowance from the contract price for the deterioration or the deficiency in quantity but without further right against the seller.

Section 2-614. Substituted Performance.

(1) Where without fault of either party the agreed berthing, loading, or unloading facilities fail or an agreed type of carrier becomes unavailable or the agreed manner of delivery otherwise becomes commercially impracticable but a commercially reasonable substitute is available, such substitute performance must be tendered and accepted.

(2) If the agreed means or manner of payment fails because of domestic or foreign governmental regulation, the seller may withhold or stop delivery unless the buyer provides a means or manner of payment which is commercially a substantial equivalent. If delivery has already been taken, payment by the means or in the manner provided by the regulation discharges the buyer's obligation unless the regulation is discriminatory, oppressive or predatory.

Section 2-615. Excuse by Failure of Presupposed Conditions. Except so far as a seller may have assumed a greater obligation and subject to the preceding section on substituted performance:

(a) Delay in delivery or non-delivery in whole or in part by a seller who complies with paragraphs (b) and (c) is not a breach of his duty under a contract for sale if performance as agreed has been made impracticable by the occurrence of a contingency and the non-occurrence of which was a basic assumption on which the contract was made or by compliance in good faith with any applicable foreign or domestic governmental regulation or order whether or not it later proves to be invalid.

(b) Where the causes mentioned in paragraph (a) affect only a part of the seller's capacity to perform, he must allocate production and deliveries among his customers but may at his option include regular customers not then under contract as well as his own requirements for further manufacture. He may so allocate in any manner which is fair and reasonable.

(c) The seller must notify the buyer seasonably that there will be delay or non-delivery and, when allocation is required under paragraph (b), of the estimated quota thus made available for the buyer.

Section 2-616. Procedure on Notice Claiming Excuse.

(1) Where the buyer receives notification of a material or indefinite delay or an allocation justified under the preceding section he may by written notification to the seller as to any delivery concerned, and where the prospective deficiency substantially impairs the value of the whole contract under the provisions of this Article relating to breach of installment contracts (Sections 2-612), then also as to the whole,

(a) terminate and thereby discharge any unexecuted portion of the contract; or

(b) modify the contract by agreeing to take his available quota in substitution.

(2) If after receipt of such notification from the seller the buyer fails so to modify the contract within a reasonable time not exceeding thirty days the contract lapses with respect to any deliveries affected.

(3) The provisions of this section may not be negated by agreement except in so far as the seller has assumed a greater obligation under the preceding section.

PART 7

REMEDIES

Section 2-701. Remedies for Breach of Collateral Contracts Not Impaired. Remedies for breach of any obligation or promise collateral or ancillary to a contract for sale are not impaired by the provisions of this Article.

Section 2-702. Seller's Remedies on Discovery of Buyer's Insolvency.

(1) Where the seller discovers the buyer to be insolvent he may refuse delivery except for cash including payment for all goods theretofore delivered under the contract, and stop delivery under this Article (Section 2-705).

(2) Where the seller discovers that the buyer has received goods on credit while insolvent he may reclaim the goods upon demand made within ten days after receipt, but if misrepresentation of solvency has been made to the particular seller in writing within three months before delivery the ten day limitation does not apply. Except as provided in this subsection the seller may not base a right to reclaim goods on the buyer's fraudulent or innocent misrepresentation of solvency or of intent to pay.

(3) The seller's right to reclaim under subsection (2) is subject to the rights of a buyer in ordinary course or other good faith purchaser or lien creditor under this Article (Section 2-403). Successful reclamation of goods excludes all other remedies with respect to them.

Section 2-703. Seller's Remedies in General. Where the buyer wrongfully rejects or revokes acceptance of goods or fails to make a payment due on or before delivery or repudiates with respect to a part or the whole, then with respect to any goods directly affected and, if the breach is of the whole contract (Section 2-612), then also with respect to the whole undelivered balance, the aggrieved seller may

(a) withhold delivery of such goods;

(b) stop delivery by any bailee as hereafter provided (Section 2-705);

(c) proceed under the next section respecting goods still unidentified to the contract;

(d) resell and recover damages as hereafter provided (Section 2-706);

(e) recover damages for non-acceptance (Section 2-708) or in a proper case the price (Section 2-709);

(f) cancel.

Section 2-704. Seller's Right to Identify Goods to the Contract Notwithstanding Breach or to Salvage Unfinished Goods.

(1) An aggrieved seller under the preceding section may

(a) identify to the contract conforming goods not already identified if at the time he learned of the breach they are in his possession or control;

(b) treat as the subject of resale goods which have demonstrably been intended for the particular contract even though those goods are unfinished.

(2) Where the goods are unfinished an aggrieved seller may in the exercise of reasonable commercial judgment for the purposes of avoiding loss and of effective realization either complete the manufacture and wholly identify the goods to the contract or cease manufacture and resell for scrap or salvage value or proceed in any other reasonable manner.

Section 2-705. Seller's Stoppage of Delivery in Transit or Otherwise.

(1) The seller may stop delivery of goods in the possession of a carrier or other bailee when he discovers the buyer to be insolvent (Section 2-702) and may stop delivery of carload, truckload, planeload or larger shipments of express or freight when the buyer repudiates or fails to make a payment due before delivery or if for any other reason the seller has a right to withhold or reclaim the goods.

(2) As against such buyer the seller may stop delivery until

(a) receipt of the goods by the buyer; or

(b) acknowledgement to the buyer by any bailee of the goods except a carrier that the bailee holds the goods for the buyer; or

(c) such acknowledgement to the buyer by a carrier by reshipment or as warehouseman; or

(d) negotiation to the buyer of any negotiable document of title covering the goods.

(3) (a) To stop delivery the seller must so notify as to enable the bailee by reasonable diligence to prevent delivery of the goods.

(b) After such notification the bailee must hold and deliver the goods according to the directions of the seller but the seller is liable to the bailee for any ensuing charges or damages.

(c) If a negotiable document of title has been issued for goods the bailee is not obliged to obey a notification to stop until surrender of the document.

(d) A carrier who has issued a non-negotiable bill of lading is not obliged to obey a notification to stop received from a person other than the consignor.

Section 2-706. Seller's Resale Including Contract for Resale.

(1) Under the conditions stated in Section 2-703 on seller's remedies, the seller may resell the goods concerned or the undelivered balance thereof. Where the resale is made in good faith and in a commercially reasonable manner the seller may recover the difference between the resale price and the contract price together with any incidental damages allowed under the provisions of this Article (Section 2-710), but less expenses saved in consequence of the buyer's breach.

(2) Except as otherwise provided in subsection (3) or unless otherwise agreed resale may be at public or private sale including sale by way of one or more contracts to sell or of identification to any existing contract of the seller. Sale may be as a unit or in parcels and at any time and place and on any terms but every aspect of the sale including the method, manner, time, place and terms must be commercially reasonable. The resale must be reasonably identified as referring to the broken contract, but it is not necessary that the goods be in existence or that any or all of them have been identified to the contract before the breach.

(3) Where the resale is at private sale the seller must give the buyer reasonable notification of his intention to resell.

(4) Where the resale is at public sale

(a) only identified goods can be sold except where there is a recognized market for a public sale of futures in goods of the kind; and

(b) it must be made at a usual place or market for public sale if one is reasonably available and except in the case of goods which are perishable or threaten to decline in value speedily the seller must give the buyer reasonable notice of the time and place of the resale; and

(c) if the goods are not to be within the view of those attending the sale the notification of sale must state the place where the goods are located and provide for their reasonable inspection by prospective bidders; and

(d) the seller may buy.

(5) A purchaser who buys in good faith at a resale takes the goods free of any rights of the original buyer even though the seller fails to comply with one or more of the requirements of this section.

(6) The seller is not accountable to the buyer for any profit made on any resale. A person in the position of a seller (Section 2-707) or a buyer who has rightfully rejected or justifiably revoked acceptance must account for any excess over the amount of his security interest, as hereinafter defined (subsection (3) of Section 2-711).

Section 2-707. "Person in the Position of a Seller."

(1) A "person in the position of a seller" includes as against a principal an agent who has paid or become responsible for the price of goods on behalf of his principal or anyone who otherwise holds a security interest or other right in goods similar to that of the seller.

(2) A person in the position of a seller may as provided in this Article withhold or stop delivery (Section 2-705) and resell (Section 2-706) and recover incidental damages (Section 2-710).

Section 2-708. Seller's Damages for Non-Acceptance or Repudiation.

(1) Subject to subsection (2) and to the provisions of this Article with respect to

proof of market price (Section 2-723), the measure of damages for non-acceptance or repudiation by the buyer is the difference between the market price at the time and place for tender and the unpaid contract price together with any incidental damages provided in this Article (Section 2-710), but less expenses saved in consequence of the buyer's breach.

(2) If the measure of damages provided in subsection (1) is inadequate to put the seller in as good a position as performance would have done then the measure of damages is the profit (including reasonable overhead) which the seller would have made from full performance by the buyer, together with any incidental damages provided in this Article (Section 2-710), due allowance for costs reasonably incurred and due credit for payments or proceeds of resale.

Section 2-709. Action for the Price.

(1) When the buyer fails to pay the price as it becomes due the seller may recover, together with any incidental damages under the next section, the price

(a) of goods accepted or of conforming goods lost or damaged within a commercially reasonable time after risk of their loss has passed to the buyer; and

(b) of goods identified to the contract if the seller is unable after reasonable effort to resell them at a reasonable price or the circumstances reasonably indicate that such effort will be unavailing.

(2) Where the seller sued for the price he must hold for the buyer any goods which have been identified to the contract and are still in his control except that if resale becomes possible he may resell them at any time prior to the collection of the judgment. The net proceeds of any such resale must be credited to the buyer and payment of the judgment entitles him to any goods not resold.

(3) After the buyer has wrongfully rejected or revoked acceptance of the goods or has failed to make a payment due or has repudiated (Section 2-610), a seller who is held not entitled to the price under this section shall nevertheless be awarded damages for non-acceptance under the preceding section.

Section 2-710. Seller's Incidental Damages. Incidental damages to an aggrieved seller include any commercially reasonable charges, expenses or commissions incurred in stopping delivery, in the transportation, care and custody of goods after the buyer's breach, in connection with return or resale of the goods or otherwise resulting from the breach.

Section 2-711. Buyer's Remedies in General; Buyer's Security Interest in Rejected Goods.

(1) Where the seller fails to make delivery then with respect to any goods involved, and with respect to the whole if the breach goes to the whole contract (Section 2-612), the buyer may cancel and whether or not he has done so may in addition to recovering so much of the price as has been paid

(a) "cover" and have damages under the next section as to all the goods affected whether or not they have been identified to the contract; or

(b) recover damages for non-delivery as provided in this Article (Section 2-713).

(2) Where the seller fails to deliver or repudiates the buyer may also

(a) if the goods have been identified recover them as provided in this Article (Section 2-502); or

(b) in a proper case obtain specific performance or replevy the goods as provided in this Article (Section 2-716).

(3) On rightful rejection or justifiable revocation of acceptance a buyer has a security interest in goods in his possession or control for any payments made on their price and any expenses reasonably incurred in their inspection, receipt, transporation, care and custody and may hold such goods and resell them in like manner as an aggrieved seller (Section 2-706)).

Section 2-712. "Cover"; Buyer's Procurement of Substitute Goods.

(1) After a breach within the preceding section the buyer may "cover" by making in good faith and without unreasonable delay any reasonable purchase of or contract to purchase goods in substitution for those due from the seller.

(2) The buyer may recover from the seller as damages the difference between the cost of cover and the contract price together with any incidental or consequential damages as hereinafter defined (Section 2-715), but less expenses saved in consequence of the seller's breach.

(3) Failure of the buyer to effect cover

within this section does not bar him from any other remedy.

Section 2-713. Buyer's Damages for Non-Delivery or Repudiation.

(1) Subject to the provisions of this Article with respect to proof of market price (Section 2-723), the measure of damages for non-delivery or repudiation by the seller is the difference between the market price at the time when the buyer learned of the breach and the contract price together with any incidental and consequential damages provided in this Article (Section 2-715), but less expenses saved in consequence of the seller's breach.

(2) Market price is to be determined as of the place for tender or, in cases of rejection after arrival or revocation of acceptance, as of the place of arrival.

Section 2-714. Buyer's Damages for Breach in Regard to Accepted Goods.

(1) Where the buyer has accepted goods and given notification (subsection (3) of Section 2-607) he may recover as damages for any non-conformity of tender the loss resulting in the ordinary course of events from the seller's breach as determined in any manner which is reasonable.

(2) The measure of damages for breach of warranty is the difference at the time and place of acceptance between the value of the goods accepted and the value they would have had if they had been as warranted, unless special circumstances show proximate damages of a different amount.

(3) In a proper case any incidental and consequential damages under the next section may also be recovered.

Section 2-715. Buyer's Incidental and Consequential Damages.

(1) Incidental damages resulting from the seller's breach include expenses reasonably incurred in inspection, receipt, transportation and care and custody of goods rightfully rejected, any commercially reasonable charges, expenses or commissions in connection with effecting cover and any other reasonable expense incident to the delay or other breach.

(2) Consequential damages resulting from the seller's breach include

(a) any loss resulting from general or particular requirements and needs of which the seller at the time of contracting had reason to know and which could not reasonably be prevented by cover or otherwise; and

(b) injury to person or property proximately resulting from any breach of warranty.

Section 2-716. Buyer's Right to Specific Performance or Replevin.

(1) Specific performance may be decreed where the goods are unique or in other proper circumstances.

(2) The decree for specific performance may include such terms and conditions as to payment of the price, damages, or other relief as the court may deem just.

(3) The buyer has a right of replevin for goods identified to the contract if after reasonable effort he is unable to effect cover for such goods or the circumstances reasonably indicate that such effort will be unavailing or if the goods have been shipped under reservation and satisfaction of the security interest in them has been made or tendered.

Section 2-717. Deduction of Damages from the Price. The buyer on notifying the seller of his intention to do so may deduct all or any part of the damages resulting from any breach of the contract from any part of the price still due under the same contract.

Section 2-718. Liquidation or Limitation of Damages; Deposits.

(1) Damages for breach by either party may be liquidated in the agreement but only at an amount which is reasonable in the light of the anticipated or actual harm caused by the breach, the difficulties of proof of loss, and the inconvenience or non-feasibility of otherwise obtaining an adequate remedy. A term fixing unreasonably large liquidated damages is void as a penalty.

(2) Where the seller justifiably withholds delivery of goods because of the buyer's breach, the buyer is entitled to restitution of any amount by which the sum of his payments exceeds

(a) the amount to which the seller is entitled by virtue of terms liquidating the seller's damages in accordance with subsection (1), or

(b) in the absence of such terms, twenty per cent of the value of the total performance for which the buyer is obligated under the contract or $500, whichever is smaller.

(3) The buyer's right to restitution under subsection (2) is subject to offset to the extent that the seller establishes

(a) a right to recover damages under the provisions of this Article other than subsection (1), and

(b) the amount or value of any benefits received by the buyer directly or indirectly by reason of the contract.

(4) Where a seller has received payment in goods their reasonable value or the proceeds of their resale shall be treated as payments for the purposes of subsection (2); but if the seller has notice of the buyer's breach before reselling goods received in part performance, his resale is subject to the conditions laid down in this Article on resale by an aggrieved seller (Section 2-706).

Section 2-719. Contractual Modification or Limitation of Remedy.

(1) Subject to the provisions of subsections (2) and (3) of this section and of the preceding section on liquidation and limitation of damages,

(a) the agreement may provide for remedies in addition to or in substitution for those provided in this Article and may limit or alter the measure of damages recoverable under this Article, as by limiting the buyer's remedies to return of the goods and repayment of the price or to repair and replacement of nonconforming goods or parts; and

(b) resort to a remedy as provided is optional unless the remedy is expressly agreed to be exclusive, in which case it is the sole remedy.

(2) Where circumstances cause an exclusive or limited remedy to fail of its essential purpose, remedy may be had as provided in this Act.

(3) Consequential damages may be limited or excluded unless the limitation or exclusion is unconscionable. Limitation of consequential damages for injury to the person in the case of consumer goods is prima facie unconscionable but limitation of damages where the loss is commercial is not.

Section 2-720. Effect of "Cancellation" or "Rescission" on Claims for Antecedent Breach.
Unless the contrary intention clearly appears, expressions of "cancellation" or "rescission" of the contract or the like shall not be construed as a renunciation or discharge of any claim in damages for an antecedent breach.

Section 2-712. Remedies for Fraud.
Remedies for material misrepresentation or fraud include all remedies available under this Article for non-fraudulent breach. Neither rescission or a claim for rescission of the contract for sale nor rejection or return of the goods shall bar or be deemed inconsistent with a claim for damages or other remedy.

Section 2-722. Who can sue Third Parties for Injury to Goods. Where a third party so deals with goods which have been identified to a contract for sale as to cause actionable injury to a party to that contract

(a) a right of action against the third party is in either party to the contract for sale who has title to or a security interest or a special property or an insurable interest in the goods; and if the goods have been destroyed or converted a right of action is also in the party who either bore the risk of loss under the contract for sale or has since the injury assumed that risk as against the other;

(b) if at the time of the injury the party plaintiff did not bear the risk of loss as against the other party to the contract for sale and there is no arrangement between them for disposition of the recovery, his suit or settlement is, subject to his own interest, as a fiduciary for the other party to the contract;

(c) either party may with the consent of the other sue for the benefit of whom it may concern.

Section 2-723. Proof or Market Price: Time and Place.

(1) If an action based on anticipatory repudiation comes to trial before the time for performance with respect to some or all of the goods, any damages based on market price (Section 2-708 or Section 2-713) shall be determined according to the price of such goods prevailing at the time when the aggrieved party learned of the repudiation.

(2) If evidence of a price prevailing at the times or places described in this Article is not readily available the price prevailing within any reasonable time before or after the time described or at any other place which in commercial judgment or under

usage of trade would serve as a reasonable substitute for the one described may be used, making any proper allowance for the cost of transporting the goods to or from such other place.

(3) Evidence of a relevant price prevailing at a time or place other than the one described in this Article offered by one party is not admissible unless and until he has given the other party such notice as the court finds sufficient to prevent unfair surprise.

Section 2-724. Admissibility of Market Quotations. Whenever the prevailing price or value of any goods regularly bought and sold in any established commodity market is in issue, reports in official publications or trade journals or in newspapers or periodicals of general circulation published as the reports of such market shall be admissible in evidence. The circumstances of the preparation of such a report may be shown to affect its weight but not its admissibility.

Section 2-725. Statute of Limitations in Contracts for Sale.

(1) An action for breach of any contract for sale must be commenced within four years after the cause of action has accrued. By the original agreement the parties may reduce the period of limitation to not less than one year but may not extend it.

(2) A cause of action accrues when the breach occurs, regardless of the aggrieved party's lack of knowledge of the breach. A breach of warranty occurs when tender of delivery is made, except that where a warranty explicitly extends to future performance of the goods and discovery of the breach must await the time of such performance the cause of action accrues when the breach is or should have been discovered.

(3) Where an action commenced within the time limited by subsection (1) is so terminated as to leave available a remedy by another action from the same breach such other action may be commenced after the expiration of the time limited and within six months after the termination of the first action unless the termination resulted from voluntary discontinuance or from dismissal for failure or neglect to prosecute.

(4) This section does not alter the law on tolling of the statute of limitations nor does it apply to causes of action which have accrued before this Act becomes effective.

ARTICLE 3

COMMERCIAL PAPER

PART 1

SHORT TITLE, FORM AND INTERPRETATION

Section 3-101. Short Title. This article shall be known and may be cited as Uniform Commercial Code—Commercial Paper.

Section 3-102. Definitions and Index of Definitions.

(1) In this Article unless the context otherwise requires

(a) "Issue" means the first delivery of an instrument to a holder or a remitter.

(b) An "order" is a direction to pay and must be more than an authorization or request. It must identify the person to pay with reasonable certainty. It may be addressed to one or more such persons jointly or in the alternative but not in succession.

(c) A "promise" is an undertaking to pay and must be more than an acknowledgment of an obligation.

(d) "Secondary party" means a drawer or endorser.

(e) "Instrument" means a negotiable instrument.

(2) Other definitions applying to this Article and the sections in which they appear are:

"Acceptance." Section 3-410.
"Accommodation party." Section 3-415.
"Alteration." Section 3-407.
"Certificate of deposit." Section 3-104.
"Certification." Section 3-411.
"Check." Section 3-104.
"Definite time." Section 3-109.
"Dishonor." Section 3-507.
"Draft." Section 3-104.
"Holder in due course." Section 3-302.
"Negotiation." Section 3-202.
"Note." Section 3-104.

"Notice of dishonor." Section 3-508.
"On demand." Section 3-108.
"Presentment." Section 3-504.
"Protest." Section 3-509.
"Restrictive Indorsement." Section 3-205.
"Signature." Section 3-401.

(3) The following definitions in other Articles apply to this Article:

"Account." Section 4-104.
"Banking Day." Section 4-104.
"Clearing house." Section 4-104.
"Collecting bank." Section 4-105.
"Customer." Section 4-104.
"Depositary Bank." Section 4-105.
"Documentary Draft." Section 4-104.
"Intermediary Bank." Section 4-105.
"Item." Section 4-104.
"Midnight deadline." Section 4-104.
"Payor bank." Section 4-105.

(4) In addition Article 1 contains general definitions and principles of construction and interpretation applicable throughout this Article.

Section 3-103. Limitations on Scope of Article.

(1) This Article does not apply to money, documents of title or investment securities.

(2) The provisions of this Article are subject to the provisions of the Article on Bank Deposits and Collections (Article 4) and Secured Transactions (Article 9).

Section 3-104. Form of Negotiable Instruments: "Draft"; "Check"; "Certificate of Deposit"; "Note."

(1) Any writing to be a negotiable instrument within this Article must

(a) be signed by the maker or drawer; and

(b) contain an unconditional promise or order to pay a sum certain in money and no other promise, order, obligation or power given by the maker or drawer except as authorized by this Article; and

(c) be payable on demand or at a definite time; and

(d) be payable to order or to bearer.

(2) A writing which complies with the requirements of this section is

(a) a "draft" ("bill of exchange") if it is an order;

(b) a "check" if it is a draft drawn on a bank and payable on demand;

(c) a "certificate of deposit" if it is an acknowledgment by a bank of receipt of money with an engagement to repay it;

(d) a "note" if it is a promise other than a certificate of deposit.

(3) As used in other Articles of this Act, and as the context may require, the terms "draft," "check," "certificate of deposit" and "note" may refer to instruments which are not negotiable within this Article as well as to instruments which are so negotiable.

Section 3-105. When Promise or Order Unconditional.

(1) A promise or order otherwise unconditional is not made conditional by the fact that the instrument

(a) is subject to implied or constructive conditions; or

(b) states its consideration, whether performed or promised, or the transaction which gave rise to the instrument, or that the promise or order is made or the instrument matures in accordance with or "as per" such transaction; or

(c) refers to or states that it arises out of a separate agreement or refers to a separate agreement for rights as to prepayment or acceleration; or

(d) states that it is drawn under a letter of credit; or

(e) states that it is secured, whether by mortgage, reservation of title or otherwise; or

(f) indicates a particular account to be debited or any other fund or source from which reimbursement is expected; or

(g) is limited to payment out of a particular fund or the proceeds of a particular source, if the instrument is issued by a government or governmental agency or unit; or

(h) is limited to payment out of the entire assets of a partnership, unincorporated association, trust or estate by or on behalf of which the instrument is issued.

(2) A promise or order is not unconditional if the instrument

(a) states that it is subject to or governed by any other agreement; or

(b) states that it is to be paid only out of a particular fund or source except as provided in this section.

Section 3-106. Sum Certain.

(1) The sum payable is a sum certain even though it is to be paid

(a) with stated interest or by stated installments; or
(b) with stated different rates of interest before and after default or a specified date; or
(c) with a stated discount or addition if paid before or after the date fixed for payment; or
(d) with exchange or less exchange, whether at a fixed rate or at the current rate; or
(e) with costs of collection or an attorney's fee or both upon default.

(2) Nothing in this section shall validate any term which is otherwise illegal.

Section 3-107. Money.

(1) An instrument is payable in money if the medium of exchange in which it is payable is money at the time the instrument is made. An instrument payable in "currency" or "current funds" is payable in money.

(2) A promise or order to pay a sum stated in a foreign currency is for a sum certain in money and, unless a different medium of payment is specified in the instrument, may be satisfied by payment of that number of dollars which the stated foreign currency will purchase at the buying sight rate for that currency on the day on which the instrument is payable or, if payable on demand, on the day of demand. If such an instrument specifies a foreign currency as the medium of payment the instrument is payable in that currency.

Section 3-108. Payable on Demand.
Instruments payable on demand include those payable at sight or on presentation and those in which no time for payment is stated.

Section 3-109. Definite Time.

(1) An instrument is payable at a definite time if by its terms it is payable
(a) on or before a stated date or at a fixed period after a stated date; or
(b) at a fixed period after sight; or
(c) at a definite time subject to any acceleration; or
(d) at a definite time subject to extension at the option of the holder, or to extension to a further definite time at the option of the maker or acceptor or automatically upon or after a specified act or event.

(2) An instrument which by its terms is otherwise payable only upon an act or event uncertain as to time of occurrence is not payable at a definite time even though the act or event has occurred.

Section 3-110. Payable to Order.

(1) An instrument is payable to order when by its terms it is payable to the order or assigns of any person therein specified with reasonable certainty, or to him or his order, or when it is conspicuously designated on its face as "exchange" or the like and names a payee. It may be payable to the order of
(a) the maker or drawer; or
(b) the drawee; or
(c) a payee who is not maker, drawer or drawee; or
(d) two or more payees together or in the alternative; or
(e) an estate, trust or fund, in which case it is payable to the order of the representative of each estate, trust or fund or his successors; or
(f) an office, or an officer by his title as such in which case it is payable to the principal but the incumbent of the office or his successors may act as if he or they were the holder; or
(g) a partnership or unincorporated association, in which case it is payable to the partnership or association and may be indorsed or transferred by any person thereto authorized.

(2) An instrument not payable to order is not made so payable by such words as "payable upon return of this instrument properly indorsed."

(3) an instrument made payable both to order and to bearer is payable to order unless the bearer words are handwritten or typewritten.

Section 3-111. Payable to Bearer. An instrument is payable to bearer when by its terms it is payable to
(a) bearer or the order of bearer; or
(b) a specified person or bearer; or
(c) "cash" or the order of "cash," or any other indication which does not purport to designate a specific payee.

Section 3-112. Terms and Omissions Not Affecting Negotiability.

(1) The negotiability of an instrument is not affected by
(a) the omission of a statement of any

consideration or of the place where the instrument is drawn or payable; or

(b) a statement that collateral has been given to secure obligations either on the instrument or otherwise of an obligor on the instrument or that in case of default on those obligations the holder may realize on or dispose of the collateral; or

(c) a promise or power to maintain or protect collateral or to give additional collateral; or

(d) a term authorizing a confession of judgment on the instrument if it is not paid when due; or

(e) a term purporting to waive the benefit of any law intended for the advantage or protection of any obligor; or

(f) a term in a draft providing that the payee by indorsing or cashing it acknowledges full satisfaction of an obligation of the drawer; or

(g) a statement in a draft drawn in a set of parts (Section 3-801) to the effect that the order is effective only if no other part has been honored.

(2) Nothing in this section shall validate any term which is otherwise illegal.

Section 3-113. Seal. An instrument otherwise negotiable is within this Article even though it is under a seal.

Section 3-114. Date, Antedating, Postdating.

(1) The negotiability of an instrument is not affected by the fact that it is undated, antedated or postdated.

(2) Where an instrument is antedated or postdated the time when it is payable is determined by the stated date if the instrument is payable on demand or at a fixed period after date.

(3) Where the instrument or any signature thereon is dated, the date is presumed to be correct.

Section 3-115. Incomplete Instruments.

(1) When a paper whose contents at the time of signing show that it is intended to become an instrument is signed while still incomplete in any necessary respect it cannot be enforced until completed.

(2) If the completion is unauthorized the rules as to material alteration apply (Section 3-407), even though the paper was not delivered by the maker or drawer; but the burden of establishing that any completion is unauthorized is on the party so asserting.

Section 3-116. Instruments Payable to Two or More Persons. An instrument payable to the order of two or more persons

(a) if in the alternative is payable to any one of them and may be negotiated, discharged or enforced by any of them who has possession of it;

(b) if not in the alternative is payable to all of them and may be negotiated, discharged or enforced only by all of them.

Section 3-117. Instruments Payable with Words of Description. An instrument made payable to a named person with the addition of words describing him

(a) as agent or officer of a specified person is payable to his principal but the agent or officer may act as if he were the holder;

(b) as any other fiduciary for a specified person or purpose is payable to the payee and may be negotiated, discharged or enforced by him;

(c) in any other manner is payable to the payee unconditionally and the additional words are without effect on subsequent parties.

Section 3-118. Ambiguous Terms and Rules of Construction. The following rules apply to every instrument:

(a) Where there is doubt whether the instrument is a draft or a note the holder may treat it as either. A draft drawn on the drawer is effective as a note.

(b) Handwritten terms control typewritten and printed terms, and typewritten control printed.

(c) Words control figures except that if the words are ambiguous figures control.

(d) Unless otherwise specified a provision for interest means interest at the judgment rate at the place of payment from the date of the instrument, or if it is undated from the date of issue.

(e) Unless the instrument otherwise specifies two or more persons who sign as maker, acceptor or drawer or indorser and as a part of the same transaction are jointly and severally liable even though the instrument contains such words as "I promise to pay."

(f) Unless otherwise specified consent to extension authorizes a single extension for not longer than the original period. A consent to extension, expressed in the instrument, is binding on secondary parties and accommodation makers. A holder may not exercise his option to extend an instrument over the objection of a maker or acceptor or other party who in accordance with Section 3-604 tenders full payment when the instrument is due.

Section 3-119. Other Writings Affecting Instrument.

(1) As between the obligor and his immediate obligee or any transferee the terms of an instrument may be modified or affected by any other written agreement executed as a part of the same transaction, except that a holder in due course is not affected by any limitation of his rights arising out of the separate written agreement if he had no notice of the limitation when he took the instrument.

(2) A separate agreement does not affect the negotiability of an instrument.

Section 3-120. Instruments "Payable Through" Bank. An instrument which states that it is "payable through" a bank or the like designates that bank as a collecting bank to make presentment but does not of itself authorize the bank to pay the instrument.

Section 3-121. Instruments Payable at Bank.

NOTE: *If this Act is introduced in the Congress of the United States this section should be omitted.*

(States to select either alternative)

Alternative A—

A note or acceptance which states that it is payable at a bank is the equivalent of a draft drawn on the bank payable when it falls due out of any funds of the maker or acceptor in current account or otherwise available for such payment.

Alternative B—

A note or acceptance which states that it is payable at a bank is not of itself an order or authorization to the bank to pay it.

Section 3-122. Accrual of Cause of Action.

(1) A cause of action against a maker or an acceptor accrues

(a) in the case of a time instrument on the day after maturity;

(b) in the case of a demand instrument upon its date or, if no date is stated, on the date of issue.

(2) A cause of action against the obligor of a demand or time certificate of deposit accrues upon demand, but demand on a time certificate may not be made until on or after the date of maturity.

(3) A cause of action against a drawer of a draft or an indorser of any instrument accrues upon demand following dishonor of the instrument. Notice of dishonor is a demand.

(4) Unless an instrument provides otherwise, interest runs at the rate provided by law for a judgment

(a) in the case of a maker, acceptor or other primary obligor of a demand instrument, from the date of demand;

(b) in all other cases from the date of accrual of the cause of action.

PART 2

TRANSFER AND NEGOTIATION

Section 3-201. Transfer: Right to Indorsement.

(1) Transfer of an instrument vests in the transferee such rights as the transferor has therein, except that a transferee who has himself been a party to any fraud or illegality affecting the instrument or who as a prior holder had notice of a defense or claim against it cannot improve his position by taking from a later holder a due course.

(2) A transfer of a security interest in an instrument vests the foregoing rights in the transferee to the extent of the interest transferred.

(3) Unless otherwise agreed any transfer for value of an instrument not then payable to bearer gives the transferee the specifically enforceable right to have the unqualified indorsement of the transferor. Negotiation takes effect only when the indorsement is made and until that time there is no presumption that the transferee is the owner.

Section 3-202. Negotiation.

(1) Negotiation is the transfer of an instrument in such form that the transferee becomes a holder. If the instrument is payable to order it is negotiated by delivery

with any necessary indorsement; if payable to bearer it is negotiated by delivery.

(2) An indorsement must be writted by or on behalf of the holder and on the instrument or on a paper so firmly affixed thereto as to become a part thereof.

(3) An indorsement is effective for negotiation only when it conveys the entire instrument or any unpaid residue. If it purports to be of less it operates only as a partial assignment.

(4) Words of assignment, condition, waiver, guaranty, limitation or disclaimer of liability and the like accompanying an indorsement do not affect its character as an indorsement.

Section 3-203. Wrong or Misspelled Name. Where an instrument is made payable to a person under a misspelled name or one other than his own he may indorse in that name or his own or both; but signature in both names may be required by a person paying or giving value for the instrument.

Section 3-204. Special Indorsement; Blank Indorsement.

(1) A special indorsement specifies the person to whom or to whose order it makes the instrument payable. Any instrument specially indorsed becomes payable to the order of the special indorsee and may be further negotiated only by his indorsement.

(2) An indorsement in blank specifies no particular indorsee and may consist of a mere signature. An instrument payable to order and indorsed in blank becomes payable to bearer and may be negotiated by delivery alone until specially indorsed.

(3) The holder may convert a blank indorsement into a special indorsement by writing over the signature of the indorser in blank any contract consistent with the character of the indorsement.

Section 3-205. Restrictive Indorsements. An indorsement is restrictive which either

(a) is conditional; or

(b) purports to prohibit further transfer of the instrument; or

(c) includes the words "for collection," "for deposit," "pay any bank" or like terms signifying a purpose of deposit or collection; or

(d) otherwise states that it is for the benefit or use of the indorser or of another person.

Section 3-206. Effect of Restrictive Indorsement.

(1) No restrictive indorsement prevents further transfer or negotiation of the instrument.

(2) An intermediary bank, or a payor bank which is not the depositary bank, is neither given notice nor otherwise affected by a restrictive indorsement of any person except the bank's immediate transferor or the person presenting for payment.

(3) Except for an intermediary bank, any transferee under an indorsement which is conditional or includes the words "for collection," "for deposit," "pay any bank," or like terms (subparagraphs (a) and (c) of Section 3-205) must pay or apply any value given by him for or on the security of the instrument consistently with the indorsement and to the extent that he does so he becomes a holder for value. In addition such transferee is a holder in due course if he otherwise complies with the requirements of Section 3-302 on what constitutes a holder in due course.

(4) The first taker under an indorsement for the benefit of the indorser of another person (subparagraph (d) of Section 3-205) must pay or apply any value given by him for or on the security of the instrument consistently with the indorsement and to the extent that he does so he becomes a holder for value. In addition such taker is a holder in due course if he otherwise complies with the requirements of Section 3-302 on what constitutes a holder in due course. A later holder for value is neither given notice nor otherwise affected by such restrictive indorsement unless he has knowledge that a fiduciary or other person has negotiated the instrument in any transaction for his own benefit or otherwise in breach of duty (subsection (2) of Section 3-304).

Section 3-207. Negotiation Effective Although it may be Rescinded.

(1) Negotiation is effective to transfer the instrument although the negotiation is

(a) made by an infant, a corporation exceeding its power, or any other person without capacity; or

(b) obtained by fraud, duress or mistake of any kind; or

(c) part of an illegal transaction; or

(d) made in breach of duty.

(2) Except as against a subsequent holder

in due course such negotiation is in an appropriate case subject to rescission, the declaration of a constructive trust or any other remedy permitted by law.

Section 3-208. Reacquisition. Where an instrument is returned to or reacquired by a prior party he may cancel any indorsement which is not necessary to his title and reissue or further negotiate the instrument, but any intervening party is discharged as against the reacquiring party and subsequent holders not in due course and if his indorsement has been cancelled is discharged as against subsequent holders in due course as well.

PART 3

RIGHTS OF A HOLDER

Section 3-301. Rights of a Holder.
The holder of an instrument whether or not he is the owner may transfer or negotiate it and, except as otherwise provided in Section 3-603 on payment or satisfaction, discharge it or enforce payment in his own name.

Section 3-302. Holder in Due Course.

(1) A holder in due course is a holder who takes the instrument

(a) for value; and

(b) in good faith; and

(c) without notice that it is overdue or has been dishonored or of any defense against or claim to it on the part of any person.

(2) A payee may be a holder in due course.

(3) A holder does not become a holder in due course of an instrument:

(a) by purchase of it at judicial sale or by taking it under legal process; or

(b) by acquiring it in taking over an estate; or

(c) by purchasing it as part of a bulk transaction not in regular course of business of the transferor.

(4) A purchaser of a limited interest can be a holder in due course only to the extent of the interest purchased.

Section 3-303. Taking for Value. A holder takes the instrument for value

(a) to the extent that the agreed consideration has been performed or that he acquires a security interest in or a lien on the instrument otherwise than by legal process; or

(b) when he takes the instrument in payment of or as security for an antecedent claim against any person whether or not the claim is due; or

(c) when he gives a negotiable instrument for it or makes an irrevocable commitment to a third person.

Section 3-304. Notice to Purchaser.

(1) The purchaser has notice of a claim or defense if

(a) the instrument is so incomplete, bears such visible evidence of forgery or alteration, or is otherwise so irregular as to call into question its validity, terms or ownership or to create an ambiguity as the party to pay; or

(b) the purchaser has notice that the obligation of any party is voidable in whole or in part, or that all parties have been discharged.

(2) The purchaser has notice of a claim against the instrument when he has knowledge that a fiduciary has negotiated the instrument in payment of or as security for his own debt or in any transaction for his own benefit or otherwise in breach of duty.

(3) The purchaser has notice that an instrument is overdue if he has reason to know

(a) that any part of the principal amount is overdue or that there is an uncured default in payment of another instrument of the same series; or

(b) that acceleration of the instrument has been made; or

(c) that he is taking a demand instrument after demand has been made or more than a reasonable length of time after its issue. A reasonable time for a check drawn and payable within the states and territories of the United States and the District of Columbia is presumed to be thirty days.

(4) Knowledge of the following facts does

not of itself give the purchaser notice of a defense of claim

(a) that the instrument is antedated or postdated;

(b) that it was issued or negotiated in return for an executory promise or accompanied by a separate agreement, unless the purchaser has notice that a defense or claim has arisen from the terms thereof;

(c) that any party has signed for accommodation;

(d) that an incomplete instrument has been completed, unless the purchaser has notice of any improper completion;

(e) that any person negotiating the instrument is or was a fiduciary;

(f) that there has been default in payment of interest on the instrument or in payment of any other instrument, except one of the same series.

(5) The filing or recording of a document does not of itself constitute notice within the provisions of this Article to a person who would otherwise be a holder in due course.

(6) To be effective notice must be received at such time and in such manner as to give a reasonable opportunity to act on it.

Section 3-305. Rights of a Holder in Due Course. To the extent that a holder is a holder in due course he takes the instrument free from

(1) all claims to it on the part of any person; and

(2) all defenses of any party to the instrument with whom the holder has not dealt except

(a) infancy, to the extent that it is a defense to a simple contract; and

(b) such other incapacity, or duress, or illegality of the transaction, as renders the obligation of the party a nullity; and

(c) such misrepresentation as has induced the party to sign the instrument with neither knowledge nor reasonable opportunity to obtain knowledge of its character or its essential terms; and

(d) discharge in insolvency proceedings; and

(e) any other discharge of which the holder has notice when he takes the instrument.

Section 3-306. Rights of One Not Holder in Due Course. Unless he has the rights of a holder in due course any person takes the instrument subject to

(a) all valid claims to it on the part of any person; and

(b) all defenses of any party which would be available in an action on a simple contract; and

(c) the defenses of want or failure of consideration, non-performance of any condition precedent, non-delivery, or delivery for a special purpose (Section 3-408); and

(d) the defense that he or a person through whom he holds the instrument acquired it by theft, or that payment or satisfaction to such holder would be inconsistent with the terms of a restrictive indorsement. The claim of any third person to the instrument is not otherwise available as a defense to any party liable thereon unless the third person himself defends the action for such party.

Section 3-307. Burden of Establishing Signatures, Defenses and Due Course.

(1) Unless specifically denied in the pleadings each signature on an instrument is admitted. When the effectiveness of a signature is put in issue

(a) the burden of establishing it is on the party claiming under the signature; but

(b) the signature is presumed to be genuine or authorized except where the action is to enforce the obligation of a purported signer who has died or become incompetent before proof is required.

(2) When signatures are admitted or established, production of the instrument entitles a holder to recover on it unless the defendant establishes a defense.

(3) After it is shown that a defense exists a person claiming the rights of a holder in due course has the burden of establishing that he or some person under whom he claims is in all respects a holder in due course.

PART 4

LIABILITY OF PARTIES

Section 3-401. Signature.

(1) No person is liable on an instrument unless his signature appears thereon.

(2) A signature is made by use of any name, including any trade or assumed name, upon an instrument, or by any word or mark used in lieu of a written signature.

Section 3-402. Signature in Ambiguous Capacity. Unless the instrument clearly indicates that a signature is made in some other capacity it is an indorsement.

Section 3-403. Signature of Authorized Representative.

(1) A signature may be made by an agent or other representative, and his authority to make it may be established as in other cases of representation. No particular form of appointment is necessary to establish such authority.

(2) An authorized representative who signs his own name to an instrument

(a) is personally obligated if the instrument neither names the person represented nor shows that the representative signed in a representative capacity;

(b) except as otherwise established between the immediate parties, is personally obligated if the instrument names the person represented but does not show that the representative signed in a representative capacity, or if the instrument does not name the person represented but does show that the representative signed in a representative capacity.

(3) Except as otherwise established the name of an organization preceded or followed by the name and office of an authorized individual is a signature made in a representative capacity.

Section 3-404. Unauthorized Signatures.

(1) Any unauthorized signature is wholly inoperative as that of the person whose name is signed unless he ratifies it or is precluded from denying it; but it operates as the signature of the unauthorized signer in favor of any person who in good faith pays the instrument or takes it for value.

(2) Any unauthorized signature may be ratified for all purposes of this Article. Such ratification does not of itself affect any rights of the person ratifying against the actual signer.

Section 3-405. Impostors; Signature in Name of Payee.

(1) An indorsement by any person in the name of a named payee is effective if

(a) an impostor by use of the mails or otherwise has induced the maker or drawer to issue the instrument to him or his confederate in the name of the payee; or

(b) a person signing as or on behalf of a maker or drawer intends the payee to have no interest in the instrument; or

(c) an agent or employee of the maker or drawer has supplied him with the name of the payee intending the latter to have no such interest.

(2) Nothing in this section shall affect the criminal or civil liability of the person so indorsing.

Section 3-406. Negligence Contributing to Alteration or Unauthorized Signature. Any person who by his negligence substantially contributes to a material alteration of the instrument or to the making of an unauthorized signature is precluded from asserting the alteration or lack of authority against a holder in due course or against a drawee or other payor who pays the instrument in good faith and in accordance with the reasonable commercial standards of the drawee's or payor's business.

Section 3-407. Alteration.

(1) Any alteration of an instrument is material which changes the contract of any party thereto in any respect, including any such change in

(a) the number or relations of the parties; or

(b) an incomplete instrument, by completing it otherwise than as authorized; or

(c) the writing as signed, by adding to it or by removing any part of it.

(2) As against any person other than a subsequent holder in due course

(a) alteration by the holder which is both fraudulent and material discharges any party whose contract is thereby

changed unless that party assents or is precluded from asserting the defense;
(b) no other alteration discharges any party and the instrument may be enforced according to its original tenor, or as to incomplete instruments according to the authority given.
(3) A subsequent holder in due course may in all cases enforce the instrument according to its original tenor, and when an incomplete instrument has been completed, he may enforce it as completed.

Section 3-408. Consideration. Want or failure of consideration is a defense as against any person not having the rights of a holder in due course (Section 3-305), except that no consideration is necessary for an instrument or obligation thereon given in payment of or as security for an antecedent obligation of any kind. Nothing in this section shall be taken to displace any statute outside this Act under which a promise is enforceable notwithstanding lack or failure of consideration. Partial failure of consideration is a defense pro tanto whether or not the failure is in an ascertained or liquidated amount.

Section 3-409. Draft Not an Assignment.

(1) A check or other draft does not of itself operate as an assignment of any funds in the hands of the drawee available for its payment, and the drawee is not liable on the instrument until he accepts it.
(2) Nothing in this section shall affect any liability in contract, tort or otherwise arising from any letter of credit or other obligation or representation which is not an acceptance.

Section 3-410. Definition and Operation of Acceptance.

(1) Acceptance is the drawee's signed engagement to honor the draft as presented. It must be written on the draft, and may consist of his signature alone. It becomes operative when completed by delivery or notification.
(2) A draft may be accepted although it has not been signed by the drawer or is otherwise incomplete or is overdue or has been dishonored.
(3) Where the draft is payable at a fixed period after sight and the acceptor fails to date his acceptance the holder may complete it by supplying a date in good faith.

Section 3-411. Certificate of a Check.

(1) Certification of a check is acceptance. Where a holder procures certification the drawer and all prior indorsers are discharged.
(2) Unless otherwise agreed a bank has no obligation to certify a check.
(3) A bank may certify a check before returning it for lack of proper indorsement. If it does so the drawer is discharged.

Section 3-412. Acceptance Varying Draft.

(1) Where the drawee's proffered acceptance in any manner varies the draft as presented the holder may refuse the acceptance and treat the draft as dishonored in which case the drawee is entitled to have his acceptance cancelled.
(2) The terms of the draft are not varied by an acceptance to pay at any particular bank or place in the United States, unless the acceptance states that the draft is to be paid only at such bank or place.
(3) Where the holder assents to an acceptance varying the terms of the draft each drawer and indorser who does not affirmatively assent is discharged.

Section 3-413. Contract of Maker, Drawer and Acceptor.

(1) The maker or acceptor engages that he will pay the instrument according to its tenor at the time of his engagement or as completed pursuant to Section 3-115 on incomplete instruments.
(2) The drawer engages that upon dishonor of the draft and any necessary notice of dishonor or protest he will pay the amount of the draft to the holder or to any indorser who takes it up. The drawer may disclaim this liability by drawing without recourse.
(3) By making, drawing or accepting the party admits as against all subsequent parties including the drawee the existence of the payee and his then capacity to indorse.

Section 3-414. Contract of Indorser; Order of Liability.

(1) Unless the indorsement otherwise specifies (as by such words as "without recourse") every indorser engages that upon dishonor and any necessary notice of dishonor and protest he will pay the instrument according to its tenor at the time of his indorsement to the holder or to any subsequent indorser who takes it up, even though the indorser who takes it up was not obligated to do so.
(2) Unless they otherwise agree indorsers

are liable to one another in the order in which they indorse, which is presumed to be the order in which their signatures appear on the instrument.

Section 3-415. Contract of Accommodation Party.

(1) An accommodation party is one who signs the instrument in any capacity for the purpose of lending his name to another party to it.

(2) When the instrument has been taken for value before it is due the accommodation party is liable in the capacity in which he has signed even though the taker knows of the accommodation.

(3) As against a holder in due course and without notice of the accommodation oral proof of the accommodation is not admissible to give the accommodation party the benefit of discharges dependent on his character as such. In other cases the accommodation character may be shown by oral proof.

(4) An indorsement which shows that it is not in the chain of title is notice of its accommodation character.

(5) An accommodation party is not liable to the party accommodated, and if he pays the instrument has a right of recourse on the instrument against such party.

Section 3-416. Contract of Guarantor.

(1) "Payment guaranteed" or equivalent words added to a signature means that the signer engages that if the instrument is not paid when due he will pay it according to its tenor without resort by the holder to any other party.

(2) "Collection guaranteed" or equivalent words added to a signature mean that the signer engages that if the instrument is not paid when due he will pay it according to its tenor, but only after the holder has reduced his claim against the maker or acceptor to judgment and execution has been returned unsatisfied, or after the maker or acceptor has become insolvent or it is otherwise apparent that it is useless to proceed against him.

(3) Words of guaranty which do not otherwise specify guarantee payment.

(4) No words of guaranty added to the signature of a sole maker or acceptor affect his liability on the instrument. Such words added to the signature of one of two or more makers or acceptors create a presumption that the signature is for the accommodation of the others.

(5) When words of guaranty are used presentment, notice of dishonor and protest are not necessary to charge the user.

(6) Any guaranty written on the instrument is enforcible notwithstanding any statute of frauds.

Section 3-417. Warranties on Presentment and Transfer.

(1) Any person who obtains payment or acceptance and any prior transferor warrants to a person who in good faith pays or accepts that

(a) he has a good title to the instrument or is authorized to obtain payment or acceptance on behalf of one who has a good title; and

(b) he has no knowledge that the signature of the maker or drawer is unauthorized, except that this warranty is not given by a holder in due course acting in good faith

(i) to a maker with respect to the maker's own signature; or

(ii) to a drawer with respect to the drawer's own signature, whether or not the drawer is also the drawee; or

(iii) to an acceptor of a draft if the holder in due course took the draft after the acceptance or obtained the acceptance without knowledge that the drawer's signature was unauthorized; and

(c) the instrument has not been materially altered, except that this warranty is not given by a holder in due course acting in good faith

(i) to the maker of a note; or

(ii) to the drawer of a draft whether or not the drawer is also the drawee; or

(iii) to the acceptor of a draft with respect to alteration made prior to the acceptance, even though the acceptance provided "payable as originally drawn" or equivalent terms; or

(iv) to the acceptor of a draft with respect to an alteration made after the acceptance.

(2) Any person who transfers an instrument and receives consideration warrants to

his transferee and if the transfer is by indorsement to any subsequent holder who takes the instrument in good faith that

(a) he has a good title to the instrument or is authorized to obtain payment or acceptance on behalf of one who has a good title and the transfer is otherwise rightful; and

(b) all signatures are genuine or authorized; and

(c) the instrument has not been materially altered; and

(d) no defense of any party is good against him; and

(e) he has no knowledge of any insolvency proceeding instituted with respect to the maker or acceptor or the drawer of an unaccepted instrument.

(3) By transferring "without recourse" the transferor limits the obligation stated in subsection (2) (d) to a warranty that he has no knowledge of such a defense.

(4) A selling agent or broker who does not disclose the fact that he is acting only as such gives the warranties provided in this section, but if he makes such disclosure warrants only his good faith and authority.

Section 3-418. Finality of Payment or Acceptance. Except for recovery of bank payments as provided in the Article on Bank Deposits and Collections (Article 4) and except for liability for breach of warranty on presentment under the preceding section, payment or acceptance of any instrument is final in favor of a holder in due course, or a person who has in good faith changed his position in reliance on the payment.

Section 3-419. Conversion of Instrument; Innocent Representative.

(1) An instrument is converted when

(a) a drawee to whom it is delivered for acceptance refuses to return it on demand; or

(b) any person to whom it is delivered for payment refuses on demand either to pay or to return it; or

(c) it is paid on a forged indorsement.

(2) In an action against a drawee under subsection (1) the measure of the drawee's liability is the face amount of the instrument. In any other action under subsection (1) the measure of liability is presumed to be the face amount of the instrument.

(3) Subject to the provisions of this Act concerning restrictive indorsements a representative, including a depositary or collecting bank, who has in good faith and in accordance with the reasonable commercial standards applicable to the business of such representative dealt with an instrument or its proceeds on behalf of one who was not the true owner is not liable in conversion or otherwise to the true owner beyond the amount of any proceeds remaining in his hands.

(4) An intermediary bank or payor bank which is not a depositary bank is not liable in conversion solely by reason of the fact that proceeds of an item indorsed restrictively (Sections 3-205 and 3-206) are not paid or applied consistently with the restrictive indorsement of an indorser other than its immediate transferor.

PART 5

PRESENTMENT, NOTICE OF DISHONOR AND PROTEST

Section 3-501. When Presentment, Notice of Dishonor, and Protest Necessary or Permissible.

(1) Unless excused (Section 3-511) presentment is necessary to charge secondary parties as follows:

(a) presentment for acceptance is necessary to charge the drawer and indorsers of a draft where the draft so provides, or is payable elsewhere than at the residence or place of business of the drawee, or its date of payment depends upon such presentment. The holder may at his option present for acceptance any other draft payable at a stated date;

(b) presentment for payment is necessary to charge any indorser;

(c) in the case of any drawer, the acceptor of a draft payable at a bank or the maker of a note payable at a bank, presentment for payment is necessary, but failure to make presentment discharges such drawer, acceptor or maker only as stated in Section 3-502(1) (b).

(2) Unless excused (Section 3-511)

(a) notice of any dishonor is necessary to charge any indorser;

(b) in the case of any drawer, the acceptor of a draft payable at a bank or the maker of a note payable at a bank, notice of any dishonor is necessary, but failure to give such notice discharges such drawer, acceptor or maker only as stated in Section 3-502(1) (b).

(3) Unless excused (Section 3-511) protest of any dishonor is necessary to charge the drawer and indorsers of any draft which on its face appears to be drawn or payable outside of the states and territories of the United States and the District of Columbia. The holder may at his option make protest of any dishonor of any other instrument and in the case of a foreign draft may on insolvency of the acceptor before maturity make protest for a better security.

(4) Notwithstanding any provision of this section, neither presentment nor notice of dishonor nor protest is necessary to charge an indorser who has indorsed an instrument after maturity.

Section 3-502. Unexcused Delay; Discharge.

(1) Where without excuse any necessary presentment or notice of dishonor is delayed beyond the time when it is due

(a) any indorser is discharged; and

(b) any drawer or the acceptor of a draft payable at a bank or the maker of a note payable at a bank who because the drawee or payor bank becomes insolvent during the delay is deprived of funds maintained with the drawee or payor bank to cover the instrument may discharge his liability by written assignment to the holder of his rights against the drawee or payor bank in respect of such funds, but such drawer, acceptor or maker is not otherwise discharged.

(2) Where without excuse a necessary protest is delayed beyond the time when it is due any drawer or indorser is discharged.

Section 3-503. Time of Presentment.

(1) Unless a different time is expressed in the instrument the time for any presentment is determined as follows:

(a) where an instrument is payable at or a fixed period after a stated date any presentment for acceptance must be made on or before the date it is payable;

(b) where an instrument is payable after sight it must either be presented for acceptance or negotiated within a reasonable time after date or issue whichever is later;

(c) where an instrument shows the date on which it is payable presentment for payment is due on that date;

(d) where an instrument is accelerated presentment for payment is due within a reasonable time after the acceleration;

(e) with respect to the liability of any secondary party presentment for acceptance or payment of any other instrument is due within a reasonable time after such party becomes liable thereon.

(2) A reasonable time for presentment is determined by the nature of the instrument, any usage of banking or trade and the facts of the particular case. In the case of an uncertified check which is drawn and payable within the United States and which is not a draft drawn by a bank the following are presumed to be reasonable periods within which to present for payment or to initiate bank collection:

(a) with respect to the liability of the drawer, thirty days after date or issue which ever is later and

(b) with respect to the liability of an indorser, seven days after his indorsement.

(3) Where any presentment is due on a day which is not a full business day for either the person making presentment or the party to pay or accept, presentment is due on the next following day which is a full business day for both parties.

(4) Presentment to be sufficient must be made at a reasonable hour, and if at a bank during its banking day.

Section 3-504. How Presentment Made.

(1) Presentment is a demand for acceptance or payment made upon the maker, acceptor, drawee or other payor by or on behalf of the holder.

(2) Presentment may be made

(a) by mail, in which even the time of presentment is determined by the time or receipt of the mail; or

(b) through a clearing house; or

(c) at the place of acceptance or payment specified in the instrument or if there be none at the place of business or residence of the party to accept or pay. If neither the party to accept or pay nor anyone authorized to act for him is present or accessible at such place presentment is excused.

(3) It may be made

(a) to any one of two or more makers, acceptors, drawees or other payors; or

(b) to any person who has authority to make or refuse the acceptance or payment.

(4) A draft accepted or a note made payable at a bank in the United States must be presented at such bank.

(5) In the cases described in Section 4-210 presentment may be made in the manner and with the result stated in that section.

Section 3-505. Rights of Party to Whom Presentment is Made.

(1) The party to whom presentment is made may without dishonor require

(a) exhibition of the instrument; and

(b) reasonable identification of the person making presentment and evidence of his authority to make it if made for another; and

(c) that the instrument be produced for acceptance or payment at a place specified in it, or if there be none at any place reasonable in the circumstances; and

(d) a signed receipt on the instrument for any partial or full payment and its surrender upon full payment.

(2) Failure to comply with any such requirement invalidates the presentment but the person presenting has a reasonable time in which to comply and the time for acceptance or payment runs from the time of compliance.

Section 3-506. Time Allowed for Acceptance or Payment.

(1) Acceptance may be deferred without dishonor until the close of the next business day following presentment. The holder may also in good faith effort to obtain acceptance and without either dishonor of the instrument or discharge of secondary parties allow postponement of acceptance for an additional business day.

(2) Except as a longer time is allowed in the case of documentary drafts drawn under a letter of credit, and unless an earlier time is agreed to by the party to pay, payment of an instrument may be deferred without dishonor pending reasonable examination to determine whether it is properly payable, but payment must be made in any event before the close of business on the day of presentment.

Section 3-507. Dishonor; Holder's Right of Recourse; Term Allowing Representment.

(1) An instrument is dishonored when

(a) a necessary or optional presentment is duly made and due acceptance or payment is refused or cannot be obtained within the prescribed time or in case of bank collections the instrument is seasonably returned by the midnight deadline (Section 4-301); or

(b) presentment is excused and the instrument is not duly accepted or paid.

(2) Subject to any necessary notice of dishonor and protest, the holder has upon dishonor an immediate right of recourse against the drawers and indorsers.

(3) Return of an instrument for lack of proper indorsement is not dishonor.

(4) A term in a draft or an indorsement thereof allowing a stated time for representment in the event of any dishonor of the draft by nonacceptance if a time draft or by nonpayment if a sight draft gives the holder as against any secondary party bound by the term an option to waive the dishonor without affecting the liability of the secondary party and he may present again up to the end of the stated time.

Section 3-508. Notice of Dishonor.

(1) Notice of dishonor may be given to any person who may be liable on the instrument by or on behalf of the holder or any party who has himself received notice, or any other party who can be compelled to pay the instrument. In addition an agent or bank in whose hands the instrument is dishonored may give notice to his principal or customer or to another agent or bank from which the instrument was received.

(2) Any necessary notice must be given by a bank before its midnight deadline and by any other person before midnight of the third business day after dishonor or receipt of notice of dishonor.

(3) Notice may be given in any reasonable manner. It may be oral or written and in

any terms which identify the instrument and state that it has been dishonored. A misdescription which does not mislead the party notified does not vitiate the notice. Sending the instrument bearing a stamp, ticket or writing stating that acceptance or payment has been refused or sending a notice of debit with respect to the instrument is sufficient.

(4) Written notice is given when sent although it is not received.

(5) Notice to one partner is notice to each although the firm has been dissolved.

(6) When any party is in insolvency proceedings instituted after the issue of the instrument notice may be given either to the party or to the representative of his estate.

(7) When any party is dead or incompetent notice may be sent to his last known address or given to his personal representative.

(8) Notice operates for the benefit of all parties who have rights on the instrument against the party notified.

Section 3-509. Protest; Noting for Protest.

(1) A protest is a certificate of dishonor made under the hand and seal of a United States consul or vice consul or a notary public or other person authorized to certify dishonor by the law of the place where dishonor occurs. It may be made upon information satisfactory to such person.

(2) The protest must identify the instrument and certify either that due presentment has been made or the reason why it is excused and that the instrument has been dishonored by a nonacceptance or nonpayment.

(3) The protest may also certify that notice of dishonor has been given to all parties or to specified parties.

(4) Subject to subsection (5) any necessary protest is due by the time that notice of dishonor is due.

(5) If, before protest is due, an instrument has been noted for protest by the officer to make protest, the protest may be made at any time thereafter as of the date of the noting.

Section 3-510. Evidence of Dishonor and Notice of Dishonor. The following are admissible as evidence and create a presumption of dishonor and of any notice or dishonor therein shown:

(a) a document regular in form as provided in the preceding section which purports to be a protest;

(b) the purported stamp or writing of the drawee, payor bank or presenting bank on the instrument or accompanying it stating that acceptance or payment has been refused for reasons consistent with dishonor;

(c) any book or record of the drawee, payor bank, or any collecting bank kept in the usual course of business which shows dishonor, even though there is no evidence of who made the entry.

Section 3-511. Waived or Excused Presentment, Protest or Notice of Dishonor or Delay Therein.

(1) Delay in presentment, protest or notice of dishonor is excused when the party is without notice that it is due or when the delay is caused by circumstances beyond his control and he exercises reasonable diligence after the cause of the delay ceases to operate.

(2) Presentment or notice or protest as the case may be is entirely excused when

(a) the party to be charged has waived it expressly or by implication either before or after it is due; or

(b) such party has himself dishonored the instrument or has countermanded payment or otherwise has no reason to expect or right to require that the instrument be accepted or paid; or

(c) by reasonable diligence the presentment or protest cannot be made or the notice given.

(3) Presentment is also entirely excused when

(a) the maker, acceptor or drawee of any instrument except a documentary draft is dead or in insolvency proceedings instituted after the issue of the instrument; or

(b) acceptance or payment is refused but not for want of proper presentment.

(4) Where a draft has been dishonored by nonacceptance a later presentment for payment and any notice of dishonor and protest for nonpayment are excused unless in the meantime the instrument has been accepted.

(5) A waiver of protest is also a waiver of presentment and of notice of dishonor even though protest is not required.

(6) Where a waiver of presentment or

notice or protest is embodied in the instrument itself it is binding upon all parties; but where it is written above the signature of an indorser it binds him only.

PART 6

DISCHARGE

Section 3-601. Discharge of Parties.

(1) The extent of the discharge of any party from liability on an instrument is governed by the section on

(a) payment or satisfaction (Section 3-603; or

(b) tender of payment (Section 3-604); or

(c) cancellation or renunciation (Section 3-605); or

(d) impairment of right of recourse or of collateral (Section 3-606); or

(e) reacquisition of the instrument by a prior party (Section 3-208); or

(f) fraudulent and material alteration (Section 3-407); or

(g) certification of a check (Section 3-411); or

(h) acceptance varying a draft (Section 3-412); or

(i) unexcused delay in presentment or notice of dishonor or protest (Section 3-502).

(2) Any party is also discharged from his liability on an instrument to another party by any other act or agreement with such party which would discharge his simple contract for the payment of money.

(3) The liability of all parties is discharged when any party who has himself no right of action or recourse on the instrument

(a) reacquires the instrument in his own right; or

(b) is discharged under any provision of this Article, except as otherwise provided with respect to discharge for impairment of recourse or of collateral (Section 3-606).

Section 3-602. Effect of Discharge Against Holder in Due Course. No discharge of any party provided by this Article is effective against a subsequent holder in due course unless he has notice thereof when he takes the instrument.

Section 3-603. Payment or Satisfaction.

(1) The liability of any party is discharged to the extent of his payment or satisfaction to the holder even though it is made with knowledge of a claim of another person to the instrument unless prior to such payment or satisfaction the person making the claim either supplies indemnity deemed adequate by the party seeking the discharge or enjoins payment or satisfaction by order of a court of competent jurisdiction in an action in which the adverse claimant and the holder are parties. This subsection does not, however, result in the discharge of the liability

(a) of a party who in bad faith pays or satisfies a holder who acquired the instrument, by theft or who (unless having the rights of a holder in due course) holds through one who so acquired it; or

(b) of a party (other than an intermediary bank or a payor bank which is not a depositary bank) who pays or satisfies the holder of an instrument which has been restrictively indorsed in a manner not consistent with the terms of such restrictive indorsement.

(2) Payment or satisfaction may be made with the consent of the holder by any person including a stranger to the instrument. Surrender of the instrument to such a person gives him the rights of a transferee (Section 3-201).

Section 3-604. Tender of Payment.

(1) Any party making tender of full payment to a holder when or after it is due is discharged to the extent of all subsequent liability for interest, costs and attorney's fees.

(2) The holder's refusal of such tender wholly discharges any party who has a right or recourse against the party making the tender.

(3) Where the maker or acceptor of an instrument payable otherwise than on demand is able and ready to pay at every place of payment specified in the instrument when it is due, it is equivalent to tender.

Section 3-605. Cancellation and Renunciation.

(1) The holder of an instrument may even without consideration discharge any party

(a) in any manner apparent on the face of the instrument or the indorsement, as by intentionally cancelling the instrument or the party's signature by destruction or mutilation, or by striking out the party's signature; or

(b) by renouncing his rights by a writing signed and delivered or by surrender of the instrument to the party to be discharged.

(2) Neither cancellation nor renunciation without surrender of the instrument affects the title thereto.

Section 3-606. Impairment of Recourse or of Collateral.

(1) The holder discharges any party to the instrument to the extent that without such party's consent the holder

(a) without express reservation of rights releases or agrees not to sue any person against whom the party has to the knowledge of the holder a right of recourse or agrees to suspend the right to enforce against such person the instrument or collateral or otherwise discharges such person, except that failure or delay in effecting any required presentment, protest or notice of dishonor with respect to any such person does not discharge any party as to whom presentment, protest or notice of dishonor is effective or unnecessary; or

(b) unjustifiably impairs any collateral for the instrument given by or on behalf of the party or any person against whom he has a right of recourse.

(2) By express reservation of rights against a party with a right of recourse the holder preserves

(a) all his rights against such party as of the time when the instrument was originally due; and

(b) the right of the party to pay the instrument as of that time; and

(c) all rights of such party to recourse against others.

PART 7

ADVICE OF INTERNATIONAL SIGHT DRAFT

Section 3-701. Letter of Advice of International Sight Draft.

(1) A "letter of advice" is a drawer's communication to the drawee that a described draft has been drawn.

(2) Unless otherwise agreed when a bank receives from another bank a letter of advice of an international sight draft the drawee bank may immediately debit the drawer's account and stop the running of interest pro tanto. Such a debit and any resulting credit to any account covering outstanding drafts leaves in the drawer full power to stop payment or otherwise dispose of the amount and creates no trust or interest in favor of the holder.

(3) Unless otherwise agreed and except where a draft is drawn under a credit issued by the drawee, the drawee of an international sight draft owes the drawer no duty to pay an unadvised draft but if it does so and the draft is genuine, may appropriately debit the drawer's account.

PART 8

MISCELLANEOUS

Section 3-801. Drafts in a Set.

(1) Where a draft is drawn in a set of parts, each of which is numbered and expressed to be an order only if no other part has been honored, the whole of the parts constitutes one draft but a taker of any part may become a holder in due course of the draft.

(2) Any person who negotiates, indorses or accepts a single part of a draft drawn in a set thereby becomes liable to any holder in due course of that part as if it were the whole set, but as between different holders in due course to whom different parts have been negotiated the holder whose title first accrues has all rights to the draft and its proceeds.

(3) As against the drawee the first presented part of a draft drawn in a set is the part entitled to payment, or if a time draft to acceptance and payment. Acceptance of any subsequently presented part renders the drawee liable thereon under subsection (2). With respect both to a holder and to the drawer payment of a subsequently presented part of a draft payable at sight has the same effect as payment of a check notwithstanding an effective stop order (Section 4-407).

(4) Except as otherwise provided in this section, where any part of a draft in a set is discharged by payment or otherwise the whole draft is discharged.

Section 3-802. Effect of Instrument on Obligation for Which it is Given.

(1) Unless otherwise agreed where an instrument is taken for an underlying obligation

(a) the obligation is pro tanto discharged if a bank is drawer, maker or acceptor of the instrument and there is no recourse on the instrument against the underlying obligor; and

(b) in any other case the obligation is suspended pro tanto until the instrument is due or if it is payable on demand until its presentment. If the instrument is dishonored action may be maintained on either the instrument or the obligation; discharge of the underlying obligor on the instrument also discharges him on the obligation.

(2) The taking in good faith of a check which is not postdated does not of itself so extend the time on the original obligation as to discharge a surety.

Section 3-803. Notice to Third Party.
Where a defendant is sued for breach of an obligation for which a third person is answerable over under this Article he may give the third person written notice of the litigation, and the person notified may then give similar notice to any other person who is answerable over to him under this Article. If the notice states that the person notified may come in and defend and that if the person notified does not do so he will in any action against him by the person giving the notice be bound by any determination of fact common to the two litigations, then unless after seasonable receipt of the notice the person notified does come in and defend he is so bound.

Section 3-804. Lost, Destroyed or Stolen Instruments. The owner of an instrument which is lost, whether by destruction, theft or otherwise, may maintain an action in his own name and recover from any party liable thereon upon due proof of his ownership, the facts which prevent his production of the instrument and its terms. The court may require security indemnifying the defendant against loss by reason of further claims on the instrument.

Section 3-805. Instruments Not Payable to Order or to Bearer. This Article applies to any instrument whose terms do not preclude transfer and which is otherwise negotiable within this Article but which is not payable to order to bearer, except that there can be no holder in due course of such an instrument.

ARTICLE 4

BANK DEPOSITS AND COLLECTIONS

PART 1

GENERAL PROVISIONS AND DEFINITIONS

Section 4-101. Short Title. This Article shall be known and may be cited as Uniform Commercial Code—Bank Deposits and Collections.

Section 4-102. Applicability.

(1) To the extent that items within this Article are also within the scope of Articles 3 and 8, they are subject to the provisions of those Articles. In the event of conflict the provisions of this Article govern those of Article 3 but the provisions of Article 8 govern those of this Article.

(2) The liability of a bank for action or non-action with respect to any item handled by it for purposes of presentment, payment or collection is governed by the law of the place where the bank is located. In the case of action or non-action by or at a branch or separate office of a bank, its liability is gov-

erned by the law of the place where the branch or separate office is located.

Section 4-103. Variation by Agreement; Measure of Damages; Certain Action Constituting Ordinary Care.

(1) The effect of the provisions of this Article may be varied by agreement except that no agreement can disclaim a bank's responsibility for its own lack of good faith or failure to exercise ordinary care or can limit the measure of damages for such lack or failure; but the parties may by agreement determine the standards by which such responsibility is to be measured if such standards are not manifestly unreasonable.

(2) Federal Reserve regulations and operating letters, clearing house rules, and the like, have the effect of agreements under subsection (1), whether or not specifically assented to by all parties interested in items handled.

(3) Action or non-action approved by this Article or pursuant to Federal Reserve regulations or operating letters constitutes the exercise of ordinary care and, in the absence of special instructions, action or non-action consistent with clearing house rules and the like or with a general banking usage not disapproved by this Article, prima facie constitutes the exercise of ordinary care.

(4) The specification or approval of certain procedures by this Article does not constitute disapproval of other procedures which may be reasonable under the circumstances.

(5) The measure of damages for failure to exercise ordinary care in handling an item is the amount of the item reduced by an amount which could not have been realized by the use of ordinary care, and where there is bad faith it includes other damages, if any, suffered by the party as a proximate consequence.

Section 4-104. Definitions and Index of Definitions.

(1) In this Article unless the context otherwise requires

(a) "Account" means any account with a bank and includes a checking, time, interest or savings account;

(b) "Afternoon" means the period of a day between noon and midnight;

(c) "Banking day" means that part of any day on which a bank is open to the public for carrying on substantially all of its banking functions;

(d) "Clearing house" means any association of banks or other payors regularly clearing items;

(e) "Customer" means any person having an account with a bank or for whom a bank has agreed to collect items and includes a bank carrying an account with another bank;

(f) "Documentary draft" means any negotiable or non-negotiable draft with accompanying documents, securities or other papers to be delivered against honor of the draft;

(g) "Item" means any instrument for the payment of money even though it is not negotiable but does not include money;

(h) "Midnight deadline" with respect to a bank is midnight on its next banking day following the banking day on which it receives the relevant item or notice or from which the time for taking action commences to run, whichever is later;

(i) "Properly payable" includes the availability of funds for payment at the time of decision to pay or dishonor;

(j) "Settle" means to pay in cash, by clearing house settlement, in a charge or credit or by remittance, or otherwise as instructed. A settlement may be either provisional or final;

(k) "Suspends payments" with respect to a bank means that it has been closed by order of the supervisory authorities, that a public officer has been appointed to take it over or that it ceases or refuses to make payments in the ordinary course of business.

(2) Other definitions applying to this Article and the sections in which they appear are:

"Collecting bank." Section 4-105.
"Depositary bank." Section 4-105.
"Intermediary bank." Section 4-105.
"Payor bank." Section 4-105.
"Presenting bank." Section 4-105.
"Remitting bank." Section 4-105.

(3) The following definitions in other Articles apply to this Article:

"Acceptance." Section 3-410.
"Certificate of deposit." Section 3-104.
"Certification." Section 3-411.
"Check." Section 3-104.
"Draft." Section 3-104.
"Holder in due course." Section 3-302.

"Notice of dishonor." Section 3-508.
"Presentment." Section 3-504.
"Protest." Section 3-509.
"Secondary party." Section 3-102.

(4) In addition Article 1 contains general definitions and principles of construction and interpretation applicable throughout this Article.

Section 4-105. "Depositary Bank"; "Intermediary Bank"; "Collecting Bank"; "Payor Bank"; "Presenting Bank"; "Remitting Bank." In this Article unless the context otherwise requires:

(a) "Depositary bank" means the first bank to which an item is transferred for collection even though it is also the payor bank;

(b) "Payor bank" means a bank by which an item is payable as drawn or accepted;

(c) "Intermediary bank" means any bank to which an item is transferred in course of collection except the depositary or payor bank;

(d) "Collecting bank" means any bank handling the item for collection except the payor bank;

(e) "Presenting bank" means any bank presenting an item except a payor bank;

(f) "Remitting bank" means any payor or intermediary bank remitting for an item.

Section 4-106. Separate Office of a Bank. A branch or separate office of a bank [maintaining its own deposit ledgers] is a separate bank for the purpose of computing the time within which and determining the place at or to which action may be taken or notices or orders shall be given under this Article and under Article 3.

NOTE: *The words in Brackets are optional.*

Section 4-107. Time of Receipt of Items.

(1) For the purpose of allowing time to process items, prove balances and make the necessary entries on its books to determine its position for the day, a bank may fix an afternoon hour of two P.M. or later as a cut-off hour for the handling of money and items and the making of entries on its books.

(2) Any item or deposit of money received on any day after a cut-off hour so fixed or after the close of the banking day may be treated as being received at the opening of the next banking day.

Section 4-108. Delays.

(1) Unless otherwise instructed, a collecting bank in a good faith effort to secure payment may, in the case of specific items and with or without the approval of any person involved, waive, modify or extend time limits imposed or permitted by this Act for a period not in excess of an additional banking day without discharge of secondary parties and without liability to its transferor or any prior party.

(2) Delay by a collecting bank or payor bank beyond time limits prescribed or permitted by this Act or by instructions is excused if caused by interruption of communication facilities, suspension of payments by another bank, war, emergency conditions or other circumstances beyond the control of the bank provided it exercises such diligence as the circumstances require.

Section 4-109. Process of Posting. The "process of posting" means the usual procedure followed by a payor bank in determining to pay an item and in recording the payment including one or more of the following or other steps as determined by the bank:

(a) verification of any signature;

(b) ascertaining that sufficient funds are are available;

(c) affixing a "paid" or other stamp;

(d) entering a charge or entry to a customer's account;

(e) correcting or reversing an entry or erroneous action with respect to the item.

PART 2

COLLECTION OF ITEMS: DEPOSITARY AND COLLECTING BANKS

Section 4-201. Presumption and Duration of Agency Status of Collecting Banks and Provisional Status of Credits; Applicability of Article; Item Indorsed "Pay any Bank."

(1) Unless a contrary intent clearly appears and prior to the time that a settlement given by a collecting bank for an item is or becomes final (subsection (3) of Section 4-211 and Sections 4-212 and 4-213) the bank is an agent or sub-agent of the owner of the item and any settlement given for the item is provisional. This provision applies regardless of the form of indorsement or lack of indorsement and even though credit given for the item is subject to immediate withdrawal as of right or is in fact withdrawn; but the continuance of ownership of an item by its owner and any rights of the owner to proceeds of the item are subject to rights of a collecting bank such as those resulting from outstanding advances on the item and valid rights of setoff. When an item is handled by banks for purposes of presentment, payment and collection, the relevant provisions of this Article apply even though action of parties clearly establishes that a particular bank has purchased the item and is the owner of it.

(2) After an item has been indorsed with the words "pay any bank" or the like, only a bank may acquire the rights of a holder

(a) until the item has been returned to the customer initiating collection; or

(b) until the item has been specially indorsed by a bank to a person who is not a bank.

Section 4-202. Responsibility for Collection; when Action Seasonable.

(1) A collecting bank must use ordinary care in

(a) presenting an item or sending it for presentment; and

(b) sending notice of dishonor or non-payment or returning an item other than a documentary draft to the bank's transferor [or directly to the depositary bank under subsection (2) of Section 4-212] (*see note to Section 4-212*) after learning that the item has not been paid or accepted, as the case may be; and

(c) settling for an item when the bank receives final settlement; and

(d) making or providing for any necessary protest; and

(e) notifying its transferor of any loss or delay in transit within a reasonable time after discovery thereof.

(2) A collecting bank taking proper action before its midnight deadline following receipt of an item, notice or payment acts seasonably; taking proper action within a reasonably longer time may be seasonable but the bank has the burden of so establishing.

(3) Subject to subsection (1) (a), a bank is not liable for the insolvency, neglect, misconduct, mistake or default of another bank or person or for loss or destruction of an item in transit or in the possession of others.

Section 4-203. Effect of Instructions. Subject to the provisions of Article 3 concerning conversion of instruments (Section 3-429) and the provisions of both Article 3 and this Article concerning rectrictive indorsements only a collecting bank's transferor can give instructions which affect the bank or constitute notice to it and a collecting bank is not liable to prior parties for any action taken pursuant to such instructions or in accordance with any agreement with its transferor.

Section 4-204. Methods of Sending and Presenting; Sending Direct to Payor Bank.

(1) A collecting bank must send items by reasonably prompt method taking into consideration any relevant instructions, the nature of the item, the number of such items on hand, and the cost of collection involved and the method generally used by it or others to present such items.

(2) A collecting bank may send

(a) any item direct to the payor bank;

(b) any item to any non-bank payor if authorized by its transferor; and

(c) any item other than documentary drafts to any non-bank payor, if authorized by Federal Reserve regulation or operating letter. clearing house rule or the like.

(3) Presenting may be made by a present-

ing bank at a place where the payor bank has requested that presentment be made.

Section 4-205. Supplying Missing Indorsement; No Notice from Prior Indorsement.

(1) A depositary bank which has taken an item for collection may supply any indorsement of the customer which is necessary to title unless the item contains the words "payee's indorsement required" or the like. In the absence of such a requirement a statement placed on the item by the depositary bank to the effect that the item was deposited by a customer or credited to his account is effective as the customer's indorsement.

(2) An intermediary bank, or payor bank which is not a depositary bank, is neither given notice nor otherwise affected by a restrictive indorsement of any person except the bank's immediate transferor.

Section 4-206. Transfer Between Banks. Any agreed method which identifies the transferor bank is sufficient for the item's further transfer to another bank.

Section 4-207. Warranties or Customer and Collecting Bank on Transfer or Presentment of Items; Time for Claims.

(1) Each customer or collecting bank who obtains payment or acceptance of an item and each prior customer and collecting bank warrants to the payor bank or other payor who in good faith pays or accepts the item that

(a) he has a good title to the item or is authorized to obtain payment of acceptance on behalf of one who has a good title and the transfer is otherwise rightful; and

(b) he has no knowledge that the signature of the maker or drawer is unauthorized, except that this warranty is not given by any customer or collecting bank that is a holder in due course and acts in good faith

(i) to a maker with respect to the maker's own signature; or

(ii) to a drawer with respect to the drawer's own signature, whether or not the drawer is also the drawee; or

(iii) to an acceptor of an item if the holder in due course took the item after the acceptance or obtained the acceptance without knowledge that the drawer's signature was unauthorized; and

(c) the time has not been materially altered, except that this warranty is not given by any customer or collecting bank that is a holder in due course and acts in good faith

(i) to the maker of a note; or

(ii) to the drawer of a draft whether or not the drawer is also the drawee; or

(iii) to the acceptor of an item with respect to an alteration made prior to the acceptance if the holder in due course took the item after the acceptance provided "payable as originally drawn" or equivalent terms; or

(iv) to the acceptor of an item with respect to an alteration made after the acceptance.

(2) Each customer and collecting bank who transfers an item and receives a settlement or other consideration for it warrants to his transferee and to any subsequent collecting bank who takes the item in good faith that

authorized to obtain payment or acceptance on behalf of one who has a good title and the transfer is otherwise rightful; and

(b) all signatures are genuine or authorized; and

(c) the item has not been materially altered; and

(d) no defense of any party is good against him; and

(e) he has no knowledge of any insolvency proceeding instituted with respect to the maker or acceptor or the drawer of an unaccepted item.

In addition each customer and collecting bank so transferring an item and receiving a settlement or other consideration engages that upon dishonor and any necessary notice of dishonor and protest he will take up the item.

(3) The warranties and the engagement to honor set forth in the two preceding subsections arise notwithstanding the absence of indorsement or words of guaranty or warranty in the transfer or presentment and a collecting bank remains liable for their breach despite remittance to its transferor. Damages for breach of such warranties or engagement to honor shall not exceed the consideration received by the customer or collecting bank responsible plus finance

charges and expenses related to the item, if any.

(4) Unless a claim for breach of warranty under this section is made within a reasonable time after the person claiming learns of the breach, the person liable is discharged to the extent of any loss caused by the delay in making claim.

Section 4-208. Security Interest of Collecting Bank in Items, Accompanying Documents and Proceeds.

(1) A bank has a security interest in an item and any accompanying documents or the proceeds of either

(a) in case of an item deposited in an account to the extent to which credit given for the item has been withdrawn or applied;

(b) in case of an item for which it has given credit available for withdrawal as of right, to the extent of the credit given whether or not the credit is drawn upon and whether or not there is a right of charge-back; or

(c) if it makes an advance on or against the item.

(2) When credit which has been given for several items received at one time or pursuant to a single agreement is withdrawn or applied in part the security interest remains upon all the items, any accompanying documents or the proceeds of either. For the purpose of this section, credits first given are first withdrawn.

(3) Receipt by a collecting bank of a final settlement for an item is a realization on its security interest in the item, accompanying documents and proceeds. To the extent and so long as the bank does not receive final settlement for the item or give up possession of the item or accompanying documents for purposes other than collection, the security interest continues and is subject to the provisions of Article 9 except that

(a) no security agreement is necessary to make the security interest enforceable (subsection (1) (b) of Section 9-203); and

(b) no filing is required to perfect the security interest; and

(c) the security interest has priority over conflicting perfected security interests in the item, accompanying documents or proceeds.

Section 4-209. When Bank Gives Value for Purposes of Holder in Due Course. For purposes of determining its status as a holder in due course, the bank has given value to the extent that it has a security interest in an item provided that the bank otherwise complies with the requirements of Section 3-302 on what constitutes a holder in due course.

Section 4-210. Presentment by Notice of Item Not Payable by, through or at a Bank; Liability of Secondary Parties.

(1) Unless otherwise instructed, a collecting bank may present an item not payable by, through or at a bank by sending to the party to accept or pay a written notice that the bank holds the item for acceptance or payment. The notice must be sent in time to be received on or before the day when presentment is due and the bank must meet any requirement of the party to accept or pay under Section 3-505 by the close of the bank's next banking day after it knows of the requirement.

(2) Where presentment is made by notice and neither honor nor request for compliance with a requirement under Section 3-505 is received by the close of business on the day after maturity or in the case of demand items by the close of business on the third banking day after notice was sent, the presenting bank may treat the item as dishonored and charge any secondary party by sending him notice of the facts.

Section 4-211. Media or Remittance; Provisional and Final Settlement in Remittance Cases.

(1) A collecting bank may take in settlement of an item

(a) a check of the remitting bank or of another bank on any bank except the remitting bank; or

(b) a cashier's check or similar primary obligation of a remitting bank which is a member of or clears through a member of the same clearing house or group as the collecting bank; or

(c) appropriate authority to charge an account of the remitting bank or of another bank with the collecting bank; or

(d) if the item is drawn upon or payable by a person other than a bank, a cashier's check, certified check or other bank check or obligation.

(2) If before its midnight deadline the collecting bank properly dishonors a remittance check or authorization to charge on itself or presents or forwards for collection a remittance instrument of or on another bank which is of a kind approved by subsection (1) or has not been authorized by it, the collecting bank is not liable to prior parties in the event of the dishonor of such check, instrument or authorization.

(3) A settlement for an item by means of a remittance instrument or authorization to charge is or becomes a final settlement as to both the person making and the person receiving the settlement

(a) if the remittance instrument or authorization to charge is of a kind approved by subsection (1) or has not been authorized by the person receiving the settlement and in either case the person receiving the settlement acts seasonably before its midnight deadline in presenting, forwarding for collection or paying the instrument or authorization is finally paid by the payor by which it is payable;

(b) if the person receiving the settlement has authorized remittance by a non-bank check or obligation or by a cashier's check or similar primary obligation of or a check upon the payor or other remitting bank which is not of a kind approved by subsection (1) (b),—at the time of the receipt of such remittance check or obligation; or

(c) if in case not covered by sub-paragraphs (a) or (b) the person receiving the settlement fails to seasonably present, forward for collection, pay or return a remittance instrument of authorization to it to charge before its midnight deadline,—at such midnight deadline.

Section 4-212. Right of Charge-Back or Refund.

(1) If a collecting bank has made provisional settlement with its customer for an item and itself fails by reason of dishonor, suspension of payments by a bank or otherwise to receive a settlement for the item which is or becomes final, the bank may revoke the settlement given by it, charge back the amount of any credit given for the item to its customer whether or not it is able to return the items if by its midnight deadline or within a longer reasonable time after it learns the facts it returns the item or sends notification of the facts. These rights to revoke, charge-back and obtain refund terminate if and when a settlement for the item received by the bank is or becomes final (subsection (3) of Section 4-211 and subsections (2) and (3) of Section 4-213).

[(2) Within the time and manner prescribed by this section and Section 4-301, an intermediary or payor bank, as the case may be, may return an unpaid item directly to the depositary bank and may send for collection a draft on the depositary bank and obtain reimbursement. In such case, if the depositary bank has received provisional settlement for the item, it must reimburse the bank drawing the draft and any provisional credits for the item between banks shall become and remain final.]

NOTE: *Direct returns is recognized as an innovation that is not yet established bank practice, and therefore, Paragraph 2 has been bracketed. Some lawyers have doubted whether it should be included in legislation or left to development by agreement.*

(3) A depositary bank which is also the payor may charge-back the amount of an item to its customer's account or obtain refund in accordance with the section governing return of an item received by a payor bank for credit on its books (Section 4-301).

(4) The right to charge-back is not affected by

(a) prior use of the credit given for the item; or

(b) failure by any bank to exercise ordinary care with respect to the item but any bank so failing remains liable.

(5) A failure to charge-back or claim refund does not affect other rights of the bank against the customer or any other party.

(6) If credit is given in dollars as the equivalent of the value of an item payable in a foreign currency the dollar amount of any charge-back or refund shall be calculated on the basis of the buying site rate for the foreign currency prevailing on the day when the person entitled to the charge-back or refund learns that it will not receive payment in ordinary course.

Section 4-213. Final Payment of Item by Payor Bank; When Provisional Debits and Credits become Final; When Certain Credits become Available for Withdrawal.

(1) An item is finally paid by a payor bank when the bank has done any of the following whichever happens first:

(a) paid the item in cash; or

(b) settled for the item without reserving a right to revoke the settlement and without having such right under statute, clearing house rule or agreement; or

(c) completed the process of posting the item to the indicated account of the drawer, maker or other person to be charged therewith; or

(d) made a provisional settlement for the item and failed to revoke the settlement in the time and manner permitted by statute, clearing house rule or agreement.

Upon a final payment under subparagraphs (b), (c) or (d) the payor bank shall be accountable for the amount of the item.

(2) If provisional settlement for an item between the presenting and payor banks is made through a clearing house or by debits or credits in an account between them, then to the extent that provisional debits or credits for the item are entered in accounts between the presenting and payor banks or between the presenting and successive prior collecting banks seratim, they become final upon final payment of the item by the payor bank.

(3) If a collecting bank receives a settlement for an item which is or becomes final (subsection (3) of Section 4-211, subsection (2) of Section 4-213) the bank is accountable to its customer for the amount of the item and any provisional credit given for the item in an account with its customer becomes final.

(4) Subject to any right of the bank to apply the credit to an obligation of the customer, credit given by a bank for an item in an account with its customer becomes available for withdrawal as of right

(a) in any case where the bank has received a provisional settlement for the item,—when such settlement becomes final and the bank has had a reasonable time to learn that the settlement is final;

(b) in any case where the bank is both a depositary bank and a payor bank and the item is finally paid,—at the opening of the bank's second banking day following receipt of the item.

(5) A deposit of money in a bank is final when made but, subject to any right of the bank to apply the deposit to an obligation of the customer, the deposit becomes available for withdrawal as of right at the opening of the bank's next banking day following receipt of the deposit.

Section 4-214. Insolvency and Preference.

(1) Any item in or coming into the possession of a payor or collecting bank which suspends payment and which item is not finally paid shall be returned by the receiver, trustee or agent in charge of the closed bank to the presenting bank or the closed bank's customer.

(2) If a payor bank finally pays an item and suspends payments without making a settlement for the item with its customer or the presenting bank which settlement is or becomes final, the owner of the item has a preferred claim against the payor bank.

(3) If a payor bank gives or a collecting bank gives or receives a provisional settlement for an item and thereafter suspends payments, the suspension does not prevent or interfere with the settlement becoming final if such finality occurs automatically upon the lapse of certain time or the happening of certain events (subsection (3) of Section 4-211, subsections (1)(d), (2) and (3) of Section 4-213).

(4) If a collecting bank receives from subsequent parties settlement for an item which settlement is or becomes final and suspends payments without making a settlement for the item with its customer which is or becomes final, the owner of the item has a preferred claim against such collecting bank.

PART 3

COLLECTION OF ITEMS: PAYOR BANKS

Section 4-301. Deferred Posting; Recovery of Payment by Return of Items; Time of Dishonor.

(1) Where an authorized settlement for a demand item (other than a documentary draft) received by a payor bank otherwise than for immediate payment over the counter has been made before midnight of the banking day of receipt the payor bank may revoke the settlement and recover any payment if before it has made final payment (subsection (1) of Section 4-213) and before its midnight deadline it

(a) returns the item; or

(b) sends written notice of dishonor or nonpayment if the item is held for protest or is otherwise unavailable for return.

(2) If a demand item is received by a payor bank for credit on its books it may return such item or send notice of dishonor and may revoke any credit given or recover the amount thereof withdrawn by its customer, if it acts within the time limit and in the manner specified in the preceding subsection.

(3) Unless previous notice of dishonor has been sent an item is dishonored at the time when for purposes of dishonor it is returned or notice sent in accordance with this section.

(4) An item is returned:

(a) as to an item received through a clearing house, when it is delivered to the presenting or last collecting bank or to the clearing house or is sent or delivered in accordance with its rules; or

(b) in all other cases, when it is sent or delivered to the bank's customer or transferor or pursuant to his instructions.

Section 4-302. Payor Bank's Responsibility for Late Return of Item. In the absence of a valid defense such as breach of a presentment warranty (subsection (1) of Section 4-207), settlement effected or the like, of an item is presented on and received by a payor bank the bank is accountable for the amount of

(a) a demand item other than a documentary draft whether properly payable or not if the bank, in any case where it is not also the depositary bank, retains the item beyond midnight of the banking day of receipt without settling for it or, regardless of whether it is also the depositary bank, does not pay or return the item or send notice of dishonor until after its midnight deadline; or

(b) any other properly payable item unless within the time allowed for acceptance or payment of that item the bank either accepts or pays the item or returns it and accompanying documents.

Section 4-303. When Items Subject to Notice, Stop-Order, Legal Process or Setoff; Order in which Items may be Charged or Certified.

(1) Any knowledge, notice or stop-order received by, legal process served upon or setoff exercised by a payor bank, whether or not effective under other rules of law to terminate, suspend or modify the bank's right or duty to pay an item or to charge its customer's account for the item, comes too late to so terminate, suspend or modify such right or duty if the knowledge, notice, stop-order or legal process is received or served and a reasonable time for the bank to act thereon expires or the setoff is exercised after the bank has done any of the following:

(a) accepted or certified the item;

(b) paid the item in cash;

(c) settled for the item without reserving the right to revoke the settlement and without having such right under statute, clearing house rule or agreement;

(d) completed the process of posting the item to the indicated account of the drawer, maker or other person to be charged therewith or otherwise has evidenced by examination of such indicated account and by action its decision to pay the item; or

(e) become accountable for the amount of the item under subsection (1) (d) of Section 4-213 and Section 4-302 dealing with the payor bank's responsibility for late return of items.

(2) Subject to the provisions of subsection (1) items may be accepted, paid, certified or charged to the indicated account of its customer in any order convenient to the bank.

PART 4

RELATIONSHIP BETWEEN PAYOR BANK AND ITS CUSTOMER

Section 4-401. When Bank May Charge Customer's Account.

(1) As against its customer, a bank may charge against his account any item which is otherwise properly payable from that account even though the charge creates an overdraft.

(2) A bank which in good faith makes payment to a holder may charge the indicated account of its customer according to

(a) the original tenor of his altered item; or

(b) the tenor of his completed item, even though the bank knows the item has been completed unless the bank has notice that the completion was improper.

Section 4-402. Bank's Liability to Customer for Wrongful Dishonor. A payor bank is liable to its customer for damages proximately caused by the wrongful dishonor of an item. When the dishonor occurs through mistake liability is limited to actual damages proved. If so proximately caused and proved damages may include damages for an arrest or prosecution of the customer or other consequential damages. Whether any consequential damages are proximately caused by the wrongful dishonor is a question of fact to be determined in each case.

Section 4-403. Customer's Right to Stop Payment; Burden of Proof of Loss.

(1) A customer may by order to his bank stop payment of any item payable for his account but the order must be received at such time and in such manner as to afford the bank a reasonable opportunity to act on it prior to any action by the bank with respect to the item described in Section 4-303.

(2) An oral order is binding upon the bank only for fourteen calendar days unless confirmed in writing within that period. A written order is effective for only six months unless renewed in writing.

(3) The burden of establishing the fact and amount of loss resulting from the payment of an item contrary to a binding stop payment order is on the customer.

Section 4-404. Bank not Obligated to Pay Check more than Six Months old. A bank is under no obligation to a customer having a checking account to pay a check, other than a certified check, which is presented more than six months after its date, but it may charge its customer's account for a payment made thereafter in good faith.

Section 4-405. Death or Incompetence of Customer.

(1) A payor or collecting bank's authority to accept, pay or collect an item or to account for proceeds of its collection if otherwise effective is not rendered ineffective by incompetence of a customer of either bank existing at the time the item is issued or its collection is undertaken if the bank does not know of an adjudication of incompetence. Neither death nor incompetence of a customer revokes such authority to accept, pay, collect or account until the bank knows of the fact of death or of an adjudication of incompetence and has reasonable opportunity to act on it.

(2) Even with knowledge a bank may for ten days after the date of death pay or certify checks drawn on or prior to that date unless ordered to stop payment by a person claiming an interest in the account.

Section 4-406. Customer's Duty to Discover and Report Unauthorized Signature or Alteration.

(1) When a bank sends to its customer a statement of account accompanied by items paid in good faith in support of the debit entries or holds the statement and items

pursuant to a request or instructions of its customer or otherwise in a reasonable manner makes the statement and items available to the customer, the customer must exercise reasonable care and promptness to examine the statement and items to discover his unauthorized signature or any alteration on an item and must notify the bank promptly after discovery thereof.

(2) If the bank establishes that the customer failed with respect to an item to comply with the duties imposed on the customer by subsection (1) the customer is precluded from asserting against the bank

(a) his unauthorized signature or any alteration on the item of the bank also establishes that it suffered a loss by reason of such failure; and

(b) an unauthorized signature or alteration by the same wrongdoer on any other item paid in good faith by the bank after the first item and statement was available to the customer for a reasonable period not exceeding fourteen calendar days and before the bank receives notification from the customer of any such unauthorized signature or alteration.

(3) The preclusion under subsection (2) does not apply if the customer establishes lack of ordinary care on the part of the bank in paying the item(s).

(4) Without regard to care or lack of care of either the customer or the bank a customer who does not within one year from the time the statement and items are made available to the customer (subsection (1)) discover and report his unauthorized signature or any alteration on the fact or back of the item or does not within three years from that time discover and report any unauthorized indorsement is precluded from asserting against the bank such unauthorized signature or indorsement or such alteration.

(5) If under this section a payor bank has a valid defense against a claim of a customer upon or resulting from payment of an item and waives or fails upon request to assert the defense the bank may not assert against any collecting bank or other prior party presenting or transferring the item a claim based upon the unauthorized signature or alteration giving rise to the customer's claim.

Section 4-407. Payor Bank's Right to Subrogation on Improper Payment. If a payor bank has paid an item over the stop payment order of the drawer or maker, or otherwise under circumstances giving a basis for objection by the drawer or maker, to present unjust enrichment and only to the extent necessary to prevent loss to the bank by reason of its payment of the item, the payor bank shall be subrogated to the rights

(a) of any holder in due course on the item against the drawer or maker; and

(b) of the payee or any other holder of the item against the drawer or maker either on the item or under the transaction out of which the item arose; and

(c) of the drawer or maker against the payee or any other holder of the item with respect to the transaction out of which the item arose.

PART 5

COLLECTION OF DOCUMENTARY DRAFTS

Section 4-501. Handling of Documentary Drafts; Duty to Send for Presentment and to Notify Customer of Dishonor. A bank which takes a documentary draft for collection must present or send the draft and accompanying documents for presentment and upon learning that the draft has not been paid or accepted in due course must seasonably notify its customer of such fact even though it may have discounted or bought the draft or extended credit available for withdrawal as if right.

Section 4-502. Presentment of "On Arrival" Drafts. When a draft or the relevant instructions require presentment "on arrival," "when goods arrive" or the like, the collecting bank need not present until in its judgment a reasonable time for arrival of the goods has expired. Refusal to pay or accept because the goods have not arrived is not dishonor; the bank must notify its transferor of such refusal but need not present the draft again until it is instructed to do so or learns of the arrival of the goods.

Section 4-503. Responsibility of Presenting Bank for Documents and Goods; Report or Reasons for Dishonor; Referee in Case of Need. Unless otherwise instructed and except as provided in Article 5 a bank presenting a documentary draft

(a) must deliver the documents to the drawee on acceptance of the draft if it is payable more than three days after presentment; otherwise, only on payment; and

(b) upon dishonor, either in the case of presentment for acceptance or presentment for payment, may seek and follow instructions from any referee in case of need designated in the draft or if the presenting bank does not choose to utilize his services it must use diligence and good faith to ascertain the reason for dishonor, must notify its transferor of the dishonor and of the results of its effort to ascertain the reasons therefor and must request instructions.

But the presenting bank is under no obligation with respect to goods represented by the documents except to follow any reasonable instructions seasonably received; it has a right to reimbursement for any expense incurred in following instructions and to prepayment of or indemnity for such expenses.

Section 4-504. Privilege of Presenting Bank to Deal with Goods, Security Interest for Expenses.

(1) A presenting bank which, following the dishonor of a documentary draft, has seasonably requested instructions but does not receive them within a reasonable time may store, sell, or otherwise deal with the goods in any reasonable manner.

(2) For its reasonable expenses incurred by action under subsection (1) the presenting bank has a lien upon the goods or their proceeds, which may be foreclosed in the same manner as an unpaid seller's lien.

ARTICLE 5

LETTERS OF CREDIT

Section 5-101. Short Title. This Article shall be known and may be cited as Uniform Commercial Code—Letters of Credit.

Section 5-102. Scope.

(1) This Article applies

(a) to a credit issued by a bank if the credit requires a documentary draft or a documentary demand for payment; and

(b) to a credit issued by a person other than a bank if the credit requires that the draft or demand for payment be accompanied by a document of title; and

(c) to a credit issued by a bank or other person if the credit is not within subparagraphs (a) or (b) but conspicuously states that it is a letter of credit or is conspicuously so entitled.

(2) Unless the engagement meets the requirements of subsection (1), this Article does not apply to engagements to make advances or to honor drafts or demands for payment, to authorities to pay or purchase, to guarantees or to general agreements.

(3) This Article deals with some but not all of the rules and concepts of letters of credit as such rules or concepts have developed prior to this act or may hereafter develop. The fact that this Article states a rule does not by itself require, imply or negate application of the same or a converse rule to a situation not provided for or to a person not specified by this Article.

Section 5-103. Definitions.

(1) In this Article unless the context otherwise requires

(a) "credit" or "letter of credit" means an engagement by a bank or other person made at the request of a customer and of a kind within the scope of this Article (Section 5-201) that the issuer will honor drafts or other demands for payment upon compliance with the conditions specified in the credit. A credit may be either revocable or irrevocable. The engagement may be either an agreement to honor or a statement that the bank or other person is authorized to honor.

(b) a "documentary draft" or a "documentary demand for payment" is one honor of which is conditioned upon the presentation of a document or documents. "Document" means any paper including document of title, security, invoice, certificate, notice of default and the like.

(c) an "issuer" is a bank or other person issuing a credit.

(d) a "beneficiary" of a credit is a person who is entitled under its terms to draw or demand payment.

(e) an "advising bank" is a bank which gives notification of the issuance of a credit by another bank.

(f) a "confirming bank" is a bank which engages either that it will itself honor a credit already issued by another bank or that such a credit will be honored by the issuer or a third bank.

(g) a "customer" is a buyer or other person who causes an issuer to issue a credit. The term also includes a bank which procures issuance or confirmation on behalf of that bank's customer.

(2) Other definitions applying to this Article and the sections in which they appear are:

"Notation of Credit." Section 5-108.
"Presenter." Section 5-112(3).

(3) Definitions in other Articles applying to this Article and the sections in which they appear are:

"Accept" or "Acceptance." Section 3-410.
"Contract for sale." Section 2-106.
"Draft." Section 3-104.
"Holder in due course." Section 3-302.
"Midnight deadline." Section 4-104.
"Security." Section 8-102.

(4) In addition, Article 1 contains general definitions and principles of construction and interpretation applicable throughout this Article.

Section 5-104. Formal Requirements; Signing.

(1) Except as otherwise required in subsection (1) (c) of Section 5-102 on scope, no particular form of phrasing is required for a credit. A credit must be in writing and signed by the issuer and a confirmation must be in writing and signed by the confirming bank. A modification of the terms of a credit or confirmation must be signed by the issuer or confirming bank.

(2) A telegram may be a sufficient signed writing if it identifies its sender by an authorized authentication. The authentication may be in code and the authorized naming of the issuer in an advice of credit is a sufficient signing.

Section 5-106. Time and Effect of Establishment of Credit.

(1) Unless otherwise agreed a credit is established

(a) as regards the customer as soon as a letter of credit is sent to him or the letter of credit or an authorized written advice of its issuance is sent to the beneficiary; and

(b) as regards the beneficiary when he receives a letter of credit or an authorized written advice of its issuance.

(2) Unless otherwise agreed once an irrevocable credit is established as regards the customer it can be modified or revoked only with the consent of the customer and once it is established as regards the beneficiary it can be modified or revoked only with his consent.

(3) Unless otherwise agreed after a revocable credit is established it may be modified or revoked by the issuer without notice to or consent from the customer or beneficiary.

(4) Notwithstanding any modification or revocation of a revocable credit any person authorized to honor or negotiate under the terms of the original credit is entitled to reimbursement for or honor of any draft or demand for payment duly honored or negotiated before receipt of notice of the modification or revocation and the issuer in turn is entitled to reimbursement from its customer.

Section 5-107. Advice of Credit; Confirmation: Error in Statement of Terms.

(1) Unless otherwise specified an advising bank by advising a credit issued by another bank does not assume any obligation to honor drafts drawn or demands for payment made under the credit but it does assume obligation for the accuracy of its own statement.

(2) A confirming bank by confirming a credit becomes directly obligated on the credit to the extent of its confirmation as though it were its issuer and acquires the rights of an issuer.

(3) Even though an advising bank incor-

rectly advises the terms of a credit it has been authorized to advise the credit is established as against the issuer to the extent of its original terms.

(4) Unless otherwise specified the customer bears as against the issuer all risks of transmission and reasonable translation or interpretation of any message relating to a credit.

Section 5-108. "Notation Credit"; Exhaustion of Credit.

(1) A credit which specifies that any person purchasing or paying drafts drawn or demands for payment made under it must note the amount of the draft or demand on the letter or advice of credit is a "notation credit."

(2) Under a notation credit

(a) a person paying the beneficiary or purchasing a draft or demand for payment from him acquires a right to honor only if the appropriate notation is made and by transferring or forwarding for honor the documents under the credit such a person warrants to the issuer that the notation has been made; and

(b) unless the credit or a signed statement that an appropriate notation has been made accompanies the draft or demand for payment the issuer may delay honor until evidence of notation has been procured which is satisfactory to it but its obligation and that of its customer continue for a reasonable time not exceeding thirty days to obtain such evidence.

(3) If the credit is not a notation credit

(a) the issuer may honor complying drafts or demands for payment presented to it in the order in which they are presented and is discharged pro tanto by honor of any such draft or demand;

(b) as between competing good faith purchasers of complying drafts or demands the person first purchasing has priority over a subsequent purchaser even though the later purchased draft or demand has been first honored.

Section 5-109. Issuer's Obligation to its Customer.

(1) An issuer's obligation to its customer includes good faith and observance of any general banking usage but unless otherwise agreed does not include liability or responsibility

(a) for performance of the underlying contract for sale or other transaction between the customer and the beneficiary; or

(b) for any act or omission of any person other than itself or its own branch or for loss or destruction of a draft, demand or document in transit or in the possession of others; or

(c) based on knowledge or lack of knowledge or any usage of any particular trade.

(2) An issuer must examine documents with care so as to ascertain that on their face they appear to comply with the terms of the credit but unless otherwise agreed assumes no liability or responsibility for the genuineness, falsification or effect of any document which appears on such examination to be regular on its face.

(3) A non-bank issuer is not bound by any banking usage of which it has no knowledge.

Section 5-110. Availability of Credit in Portions; Presenter's Reservation of Lien or Claim.

(1) Unless otherwise specified a credit may be used in portions in the discretion of the beneficiary.

(2) Unless otherwise specified a person by presenting a documentary draft or demand for payment under a credit relinquishes upon its honor all claims to the documents and a person by transferring such draft or demand or causing such presentment authorizes such relinquishment. An explicit reservation of claim makes the draft or demand non-complying.

Section 5-111. Warranties on Transfer and Presentment.

(1) Unless otherwise agreed the beneficiary by transferring or presenting a documentary draft or demand for payment warrants to all interested parties that the necessary conditions of the credit have been complied with. This is in addition to any warranties arising under Articles 3, 4, 7 and 8.

(2) Unless otherwise agreed a negotiating, advising, confirming, collecting or issuing bank presenting or transferring a draft or demand for payment under a credit warrants only the matters warranted by a collecting bank under Article 4 and any such bank transferring a document warrants only the matters warranted by an intermediary under Articles 7 and 8.

Section 5-112. Time Allowed for Honor or Rejection; Withholding Honor or Rejection by Consent; Presenter."

(1) A bank to which a documentary draft or demand for payment is presented under a credit may without dishonor of the draft, demand or credit

(a) defer honor until the close of the third banking day following receipt of the documents; and

(b) further defer honor if the presenter has expressly or impliedly consented thereto.

Failure to honor within the time here specified constitutes dishonor of the draft or demand and of the credit [except as otherwise provided in subsection (4) of Section 5-114 on conditional payment].

NOTE: *The bracketed language in the last sentence of subsection (1) should be included only if the optional provisions of Section 5-114(4) and (5) are included.*

(2) Upon dishonor the bank may unless otherwise instructed fulfill its duty to return the draft or demand and the documents by holding them at the disposal of the presenter and sending him an advice to that effect.

(3) "Presenter" means any person presenting a draft or demand for payment for honor under a credit even though that person is a confirming bank or other correspondent which is acting under an issuer's authorization.

Section 5-113. Indemnities.

(1) A bank seeking to obtain (whether for itself or another) honor, negotiation or reimbursement under a credit may give an indemnity to induce such honor, negotiation or reimbursement.

(2) An indemnity agreement inducing honor, negotiation or reimbursement

(a) unless otherwise explicitly agreed applies to defects in the documents but not in the goods; and

(b) unless a longer time is explicitly agreed expires at the end of ten business days following receipt of the documents by the ultimate customer unless notice of objection is sent before such expiration date. The ultimate customer may send notice of objection to the person from whom he received the documents and any bank receiving such notice is under a duty to send notice to its transferor before its midnight deadline.

Section 5-114. Issuer's Duty and Privilege to Honor; Right to Reimbursement.

(1) An issuer must honor a draft or demand for payment which complies with the terms of the relevant credit regardless of whether the goods or documents conform to the underlying contract for sale or other contract between the customer and the beneficiary. The issuer is not excused from honor of such a draft or demand by reason of an additional general term that all documents must be satisfactory to the issuer, but an issuer may require that specified documents must be satisfactory to it.

(2) Unless otherwise agreed when documents appear on their face to comply with the terms of a credit but a required document does not in fact conform to the warranties made on negotiation or transfer of a document of title (Section 7-507) or of a security (Section 8-306) or is forged or fraudulent or there is fraud in the transaction

(a) the issuer must honor the draft or demand for payment if honor is demanded by a negotiating bank or other holder of the draft or demand which has taken the draft or demand under the credit and under circumstances which would make it a holder in due course (Section 3-302) and in an appropriate case would make it a person to whom a document of title has been duly negotiated (Section 7-502) or a bona fide purchaser of a security (Section 8-302); and

(b) in all other cases as against its customer, an issuer acting in good faith may honor the draft or demand for payment despite notification from the customer of fraud, forgery or other defect not apparent on the face of the documents but a court of appropriate jurisdiction may enjoin such honor.

(3) Unless otherwise agreed an issuer which has duly honored a draft or demand for payment is entitled to immediate reimbursement of any payment made under the credit and to be put in effectively available funds not later than the day before maturity of any acceptance made under the credit.

[(4) When a credit provides for payment by the issuer on receipt of notice that the required documents are in the possession of a correspondent or other agent of the issuer

(a) any payment made on receipt of such notice is conditional; and

(b) the issuer may reject documents which do not comply with the credit if it does so within three banking days following its receipt of the documents; and

(c) in the event of such rejection, the issuer is entitled by charge back or otherwise to return of the payment made.]

[(5) In the case covered by subsection (4) failure to reject documents within the time specified in sub-paragraph (b) constitutes acceptance of the documents and makes the payment final in favor of the beneficiary.]

NOTE: *Subsections (4) and (5) are bracketed as optional. If they are included the bracketed language in the last sentence of Section 5-112(1) should also be included.*

Section 5-115. Remedy for Improper Dishonor or Anticipatory Repudiation.

(1) When an issuer wrongfully dishonors a draft or demand for payment under a credit the person entitled to honor has with respect to any documents the rights of a person in the position of a seller (Section 2-707) and may recover from the issuer the face amount of the draft or demand together with incidental damages under Section 2-710 on seller's incidental damages and interest but less any amount realized by resale or other use or disposition of the subject matter of the transaction. In the event no resale or other utilization is made the documents, goods or other subject matter involved in the transaction must be turned over to the issuer on payment of judgment.

(2) When an issuer wrongfully cancels or otherwise repudiates a credit before presentment of a draft or demand for payment drawn under it the beneficiary has the rights of a seller after anticipatory repudiation by the buyer under Section 2-610 if he learns of the repudiation in time reasonably to avoid procurement of the required documents. Otherwise the beneficiary has an immediate right of action for wrongful dishonor.

Section 5-116. Transfer and Assignment.

(1) The right to draw under a credit can be transferred or assigned only when the credit is expressly designated as transferable or assignable.

(2) Even though the credit specifically states that it is nontransferable or nonassignable the beneficiary may before performance of the conditions of the credit assign his right to proceeds. Such an assignment is an assignment of a contract right under Article 9 on Secured Transactions and is governed by that Article except that

(a) the assignment is ineffective until the letter of credit or advice of credit is delivered to the assignee which delivery constitutes perfection of the security interest under Article 9; and

(b) the issuer may honor drafts or demands for payment drawn under the credit until it receives a notification of the assignment signed by the beneficiary which reasonably identifies the credit involved in the assignment and contains a request to pay the assignee; and

(c) after what reasonably appears to be such a notification has been received the issuer may without dishonor refuse to accept or pay even to a person otherwise entitled to honor until the letter of credit or advice of credit is exhibited to the issuer.

(3) Except where the beneficiary has effectively assigned his right to draw or his right to proceeds, nothing in this section limits his right to transfer or negotiate drafts or demands drawn under the credit.

Section 5-117. Insolvency of Bank Holding Funds for Documentary Credit.

(1) Where an issuer or an advising or confirming bank or a bank which has for a customer procured issuance of a credit by another bank becomes insolvent before final payment under the credit and the credit is one to which this Article is made applicable by paragraphs (a) or (b) of Section 5-102(1) on scope, the receipt or allocation of funds or collateral to secure or meet obligations under the credit shall have the following results:

(a) to the extent of any funds or collateral turned over after or before the insolvency as indemnity against or specifically for the purpose of payment of drafts or demand for payment drawn under the designated credit, the drafts or demands are entitled to payment in preference over depositors or other general creditors of the issuer or bank; and

(b) on expiration of the credit or surrender of the beneficiary's rights under it unused any person who has given such funds or collateral is similarly entitled to return thereof; and

(c) a change to a general or current account with a bank if specifically consented to for the purpose of indemnity against or payment of drafts or demands for payment drawn under the designated credit falls under the same rules as if the funds had been drawn out in cash and then turned over with specific instructions.

(2) After honor or reimbursement under this section the customer or other person for whose account the insolvent bank has acted is entitled to receive the documents involved.

ARTICLE 6

BULK TRANSFERS

Section 6-101. Short Title. This Article shall be known and may be cited as Uniform Commercial Code—Bulk Transfers.

Section 6-102. "Bulk Transfers"; Transfers of Equipment; Enterprises Subject to this Article; Bulk Transfers Subject to this Article.

(1) A "bulk transfer" is any transfer in bulk and not in the ordinary course of the transferor's business of a major part of the materials, supplies, merchandise or other inventory (Section 9-109) of an enterprise subject to this Article.

(2) A transfer of a substantial part of the equipment (Section 9-109) of such an enterprise is a bulk transfer if it is made in connection with a bulk transfer of inventory, but not otherwise.

(3) The enterprises subject to this Article are all those whose principal business is the sale of merchandise from stock, including those who manufacture what they sell.

(4) Except as limited by the following section all bulk transfers of goods located within this state are subject to this Article.

Section 6-103. Transfers Excepted from this Article. The following transfers are not subject to this Article:

(1) Those made to give security for the performance of an obligation;

(2) General assignments for the benefit of all the creditors of the transferor, and subsequent transfers by the assignee thereunder;

(3) Transfers in settlement or realization of a lien or other security interest;

(4) Sales by executors, administrators, receivers, trustees in bankruptcy, or any public officer under judicial process;

(5) Sales made in the course of judicial or administrative proceedings for the dissolution or reorganization of a corporation and of which notice is sent to the creditors of the corporation to order of the court or administrative agency;

(6) Transfers to a person maintaining a known place of business in this State who becomes bound to pay the debts of the transferor in full and gives public notice of that fact, and who is solvent after becoming so bound;

(7) A transfer to a new business enterprise organized to take over and continue the business, if public notice of the transaction is given and the new enterprise assumes the debts of the transferor and he receives nothing from the transaction except an interest in the new enterprise junior to the claims of creditors;

(8) Transfers of property which is exempt from execution.

Public notice under subsection (6) or subsection (7) may be given by publishing once a week for two consecutive weeks in a newspaper of general circulation where the transferor had its principal place of business in this state an advertisement including the names and addresses of the transferor and transferee and the effective date of the transfer.

Section 6-104. Schedule of Property, List of Creditors.

(1) Except as provided with respect to auction sales (Section 6-108), a bulk transfer subject to this Article is ineffective against any creditor of the transferor unless:

(a) The transferee requires the transferor to furnish a list of his existing creditors prepared as stated in this section; and

(b) The parties prepare a schedule of the property transferred sufficient to identify it; and

(c) The transferee preserves the list and schedule for six months next following the transfer and permits inspection of either or both and copying therefrom at all reasonable hours by any creditor of the transferor, or files the list and schedule in (a public office to be here identified).

(2) The list of creditors must be signed and sworn to or affirmed by the transferot or his agent. It must contain the names and business addresses of all creditors of the transferor, with the amounts when known, and also the names of all persons who are known to the transferor to assert claims against him even though such claims are disputed. If the transferor is the obligor of an outstanding issue of bonds, debentures or the like as to which there is an indenture trustee, the list of creditors need include only the name and address of the indenture trustee and the aggregate outstanding principal amount of the issue.

(3) Responsibility for the completeness and accuracy of the list of creditors rests on the transferor, and the transfer is not rendered ineffective by errors or omissions therein unless the transferee is shown to have had knowledge.

Section 6-105. Notice to Creditors. In addition to the requirements of the preceding section, any bulk transfer subject to this Article except one made by auction sale (Section 6-108) is ineffective against any creditor of the transferor unless at least ten days before he takes possession of the goods or pays for them, whichever happens first, the transferee gives notice of the transfer in the manner and to the persons hereafter provided (Section 6-107).

Section 6-106. Application of the Proceeds. In addition to the requirements of the two preceding sections:

(1) Upon every bulk transfer subject to this Article for which new consideration becomes payable except those made by sale at auction it is the duty of the transferee to assure that such consideration is applied so far as necessary to pay those debts of the transferor which are either shown on the list furnished by the transferor (Section 6-104) or filed in writing in the place stated in the notice (Section 6-107) within thirty days after the mailing of such notice. This duty of the transferee runs to all the holders of such debts, and may be enforced by any of them for the benefit of all.

(2) If any of said debts are in dispute the necessary sum may be withheld from distribution until the dispute is settled or adjudicated.

(3) If the consideration payable is not enough to pay all of the said debts in full distribution shall be made pro rata]

NOTE: *This section is bracketed to indicate division of opinion as to whether or not it is a wise provision, and to suggest that this is a point on which state enactments may differ without serious damage to the principle of uniformity.*

In any State where this section is omitted, the following parts of sections also bracketed in the text, should also be omitted, namely:

Section 6-107(2)(e).
6-108(3)(c).
6-109(2).

In any State where this section is enacted, these other provisions should be also.

Optional Subsection (4) [(4) The transferee may within ten days after he takes possession of the goods pay the consideration into the (specify court) in the county where the transferor had its principal place of business in this state and thereafter may discharge his duty under this section by giving notice by registered or certified mail to all the persons to whom the duty runs that the consideration has been paid into that court and that they should file their claims there. On motion of any interested party, the court may order the distribution of the consideration to the persons entitled to it.]

NOTE: *Optional subsection (4) is recommended for those states which do not have a general statute providing for payment of money into court.*

Section 6-107. The Notice.

(1) The notice to creditors (Section 6-105) shall state:

(a) that a bulk transfer is about to be made; and

(b) the names and business addresses of the transferor and transferee, and all other business names and addresses used by the transferor within three years last past so far as known to the transferee; and

(c) whether or not all the debts of the transferor are to be paid in full as they fall due as a result of the transaction, and if so, the address to which creditors should send their bills.

(2) If the debts of the transferor are not to be paid in full as they fall due or if the transferee is in doubt on that point then the notice shall state further:

(a) the location and general description of the property to be transferred and the estimated total of the transferor's debts;

(b) the address where the schedule of property and list of creditors (Section 6-104) may be inspected;

(c) whether the transfer is to pay existing debts and if so the amount of such debts and to whom owing;

(d) whether the transfer is for new consideration and if so the amount of such consideration and the time and place of payment; [and]

[(e) if for new consideration the time and place where creditors of the transferor are to file their claims.]

(3) The notice in any case shall be delivered personally or sent by registered mail to all the persons shown on the list of creditors furnished by the transferor (Section 6-104) and to all other persons who are known to the transferee to hold or assert claims against the transferor.

NOTE: *The words in brackets are optional.*

Section 6-108. Auction Sales; "Auctioneer."

(1) A bulk transfer is subject to this Article even though it is by sale at auction, but only in the manner and with the results stated in this section.

(2) The transferor shall furnish a list of his creditors and assist in the preparation of a schedule of the property to be sold, both prepared as before stated (Section 6-104).

(3) The person or persons other than the transferor who direct, control or are responsible for the auction are collectively called the "auctioneer." The auctioneer shall:

(a) receive and retain the list of creditors and prepare and retain the schedule of property for the period stated in this Article (Section 6-104);

(b) give notice of the auction personally or by registered or certified mail at least ten days before it occurs to all persons shown on the list of creditors and to all other persons who are known to him to hold or assert claims against the transferor; [and]

[(c) assure that the net proceeds of the auction are applied as provided in this Article (Section 6-106).]

(4) Failure of the auctioneer to perform any of these duties does not affect the validity of the sale or the title of the purchasers, but if the auctioneer knows that the auction constitutes a bulk transfer such failure renders the auctioneer liable to the creditors of the transferor as a class for the sums owing to them from the transferor up to but not exceeding the net proceeds of the auction. If the auctioneer consists of several persons their liability is joint and several.

NOTE: *The words in brackets are optional.*

Section 6-109. What Creditors Protected; Credit for Payment to Particular Creditors.

(1) The creditors of the transferor mentioned in this Article are those holding claims based on transactions or events occurring before the bulk transfer, but creditors who become such after notice to creditors is given (Sections 6-105 and 6-107) are not entitled to notice.

[(2) Against the aggregate obligation imposed by the provisions of this Article concerning the application of the proceeds (Section 6-106 and subsection (3) (c) of 6-108) the transferee or auctioneer is entitled to credit for sums paid to particular creditors of the transferor, not exceeding the sums believed in good faith at the time of the payment to be properly payable to such creditors.]

Section 6-110. Subsequent Transfers. When the title of a transferee to property is subject to a defect by reason of his noncompliance with the requirements of this Article, then:

(1) a purchaser of any of such property from such transferee who pays no value or who takes with notice of such non-compliance takes subject to such defect, but

(2) a purchaser for value in good faith and

without such notice takes free of such defect.

Section 6-111. Limitation of Actions and Levies. No action under this Article shall be brought nor levy made more than six months after the date on which the transferee took possession of the goods unless the transfer has been concealed. If the transfer has been concealed, actions may be brought or levies made within six months after its discovery.

NOTE TO ARTICLE 6: *Section 6-106 is bracketed to indicate division of opinion as to whether or not it is a wise provision, and to suggest that this is a point on which State enactments may differ without serious damage to the principle of uniformity.*

In any State where Section 6-106 is not enacted, the following parts of sections, also bracketed in the text, should also be omitted, namely:

Sec. 6-107(2)(e)
6-109(3)(c)
6-109(2).

In any State where Section 6-106 is enacted, these other provisions should be also.

ARTICLE 7

WAREHOUSE RECEIPTS, BILLS OF LADING AND OTHER DOCUMENTS OF TITLE

PART 1

GENERAL

Section 7-101. Short Title. This Article shall be known and may be cited as Uniform Commercial Code—Documents of Title.

Section 7-102. Definitions and Index of Definitions.

(1) In this Article, unless the context otherwise requires:

(a) "Bailee" means the person who by a warehouse receipt, bill of lading or other document of title acknowledges possession of goods and contracts to deliver them.

(b) "Consignee" means the person named in a bill to whom or to whose order the bill promises delivery.

(c) "Consignor" means the person named in a bill as the person from whom the goods have been received for shipment.

(d) "Delivery order" means a written order to deliver goods directed to a warehouseman, carrier or other person who in the ordinary course of business issues warehouse receipts of bills of lading.

(e) "Document" means document of title as defined in the general definitions in Article 1 (Section 1-201).

(f) "Goods" means all things which are treated as movable for the purposes of a contract of storage or transportation.

(g) "Issuer" means a bailee who issues a document except that in relation to an unaccepted delivery order it means the person who orders the possessor of goods to deliver. Issuer includes any person for whom an agent or employee purports to act in issuing a document if the agent or employee has real or apparent authority to issue documents, notwithstanding that the issuer received no goods or that the goods were misdescribed or that in any other respect the agent or employee violated his instructions.

(h) "Warehouseman" is a person engaged in the business of storing goods for hire.

(2) Other definitions applying to this Article or to specified Parts thereof, and the sections in which they appear are:

"Duly negotiate." Section 7-501.
"Person entitled under the document." Section 7-403(4).

(3) Definitions in other Articles applying to this Article and the sections in which they appear are:

"Contract for sale." Section 2-106.
"Overseas." Section 2-323.
"Receipt" of goods. Section 2-103.

(4) In addition Article 2 contains general

definitions and principles of construction and interpretation applicable throughout this Article.

Section 7-103. Relation of Article to Treaty, Statute, Tariff, Classification or Regulation. To the extent that any treaty or statute of the United States, regulatory statute of this State or tariff, classification or regulation filed or issued pursuent thereto is applicable, the provisions of this Article are subject thereto.

Section 7-104. Negotiable and Non-Negotiable Warehouse Receipt, Bill of Lading or Other Document of Title.

(1) A warehouse receipt, bill of lading or other document of title is negotiable

(a) if by its terms the goods are to be delivered to bearer or to the order of a named person; or

(b) where recognized in overseas trade, if it runs to a named person or assigns.

(2) Any other document is non-negotiable. A bill of lading in which it is stated that the goods are consigned to a named person is not made negotiable by a provision that the goods are to be delivered only against a written order signed by the same or another named person.

Section 7-105. Construction Against Negative Implication. The omission from either Part 2 or Part 3 of this Article of a provision corresponding to a provision made in the other Part does not imply that a corresponding rule of law is not applicable.

PART 2

WAREHOUSE RECEIPTS: SPECIAL PROVISIONS

Section 7-201. Who may issue a Warehouse Receipt; Storage under Government Bond.

(1) A warehouse receipt may be issued by any warehouseman.

(2) Where goods including distilled spirits and agricultural commodities are stored under a statute requiring a bond against a withdrawal or a license for the issuance of receipts in the nature of warehouse receipts, a receipt for the goods has like effect as a warehouse receipt even though issued by a person who is the owner of the goods and is not a warehouseman.

Section 7-202. Form of Warehouse Receipt; Essential Terms; Optional Terms.

(1) A warehouse receipt need not be in any particular form.

(2) Unless a warehouse receipt embodies within its written or printed terms each of the following, the warehouseman is liable for damages caused by the omission to a person injured thereby:

(a) the location of the warehouse where the goods are stored;

(b) the date of issue of the receipt;

(c) the consecutive number of the receipt;

(d) a statement whether the goods received will be delivered to the bearer, to a specified person, or to a specified person or his order;

(e) the rate of storage and handling charges, except that where goods are stored under a field warehousing arrangement a statement of that fact is sufficient on a non-negotiable receipt;

(f) a description of the goods or of the packages containing them;

(g) the signature of the warehouseman, which may be made by his authorized agent;

(h) if the receipt is issued for goods of which the warehouseman is owner, either solely or jointly or in common with others, the fact of such ownership; and

(i) a statement of the amount of advances made and of liabilities incurred for which the warehouseman claims a lien or security interest (Section 7-209). If the precise amount of such advances made or of such liabilities incurred is, at the time of the issue of the receipt, unknown to the warehouseman or to his agent who issues it, a statement of the fact that advances have been made or liabilities incurred and the purpose thereof is sufficient.

(3) A warehouseman may insert in his receipt any other terms which are not contrary to the provisions of this Act and do not impair his obligation of delivery (Sec-

tion 7-403) or his duty to care (Section 7-204). Any contrary provisions shall be ineffective.

Section 7-203. Liability for Non-Receipt or Misdescription. A party to or purchaser for value in good faith of a document of title other than a bill of lading relying in either case upon the description therein of the goods may recover from the issuer damages caused by the non-receipt or misdescription of the goods, except to the extent that the document conspicuously indicates that the issuer does not know whether any part or all of the goods in fact were received or conform to the description, as where the description is in terms of marks or labels or kind, quantity or condition, or the receipt or description is qualified by "contents, condition and quality unknown," "said to contain" or the like, if such indication be true, or the party or purchaser otherwise has notice.

Section 7-204. Duty of Care: Contractual Limitation of Warehouseman's Liability.

(1) A warehouseman is liable for damages for loss of or injury to the goods caused by his failure to exercise such care in regard to them as a reasonably careful man would exercise under like circumstances but unless otherwise agreed he is not liable for damages which could not have been avoided by the exercise of such care.

(2) Damages may be limited by a term in the warehouse receipt or storage agreement limiting the amount of liability in case of loss or damage, and setting forth a specific liability per article or item, or value per unit of weight, beyond which the warehouseman shall not be liable; provided, however, that such liability may on written request of the bailor at the time of signing such storage agreement or within a reasonable time after receipt of the warehouse receipt be increased on part or all of the goods thereunder, in which event increased rates may be charged based on such increased valuation, but that no such increase shall be permitted contrary to a lawful limitation of liability contained in the warehouseman's tariff, if any. No such limitation is effective with respect to the warehouseman's liability for conversion to his own use.

(3) Reasonable provisions as to the time and manner of presenting claims and instituting actions based on the bailment may be included in the warehouse receipt or tariff.

(4) This section does not impair or repeal . .

NOTE: *Insert in subsection (4) a reference to any statute which imposes a higher responsibility upon the warehouseman or invalidates contractual limitations which would be permissible under this Article.*

Section 7-205. Title Under Warehouse Receipt Defeated in Certain Cases. A buyer in the ordinary course of business of fungible goods sold and delivered by a warehouseman who is also in the business of buying and selling such goods takes free of any claim under a warehouse receipt even though it has been duly negotiated.

Section 7-206. Termination of Storage at Warehouseman's Option.

(1) A warehouseman may on notifying the person on whose account the goods are held and any other person known to claim an interest in the goods require payment of any charges and removal of the goods from the warehouse at the termination of the period of storage fixed by the document, or, if no period is fixed, within a stated period not less than thirty days after the notification. If the goods are not removed before the date specified in the notification, the warehouseman may sell them in accordance with the provisions of the section on enforcement of a warehouseman's lien (Section 7-210).

(2) If a warehouseman in good faith believes that the goods are about to deteriorate or decline in value to less than the amount of his lien within the time prescribed in subsection (1) for notification, advertisement and sale, the warehouseman may specify in the notification any reasonable shorter time for removal of the goods and in case the goods are not removed, may sell them at public sale held not less than one week after a single advertisement or posting.

(3) If as a result of a quality or condition of the goods of which the warehouseman had no choice at the time of deposit the goods are a hazard to other property or to the warehouse or to persons, the warehouseman may sell the goods at public or private

sale without advertisement on reasonable notification to all persons known to claim an interest in the goods. If the warehouse man after a reasonable effort is unable to sell the goods he may dispose of them in any lawful manner and shall incur no liability by reason of such disposition.

(4) The warehouseman must deliver the goods to any person entitled to them under this Article upon due demand made at any time prior to the sale or other disposition under this section.

(5) The warehouseman may satisfy his lien from the proceeds of any sale or disposition under this section but must hold the balance for delivery on the demand of any person to whom he would have been bound to deliver the goods.

Section 7-207. Goods Must be Kept Separate; Fungible Goods.

(1) Unless the warehouse receipt otherwise provides, a warehouseman must keep separate the goods covered by each receipt so as to permit at all times identification and delivery of those goods except that different lots of fungible goods may be commingled.

(2) Fungible goods so commingled are owned in common by the persons entitled thereto and the warehouseman is severally liable to each owner for that owner's share. Where because of overissue a mass of fungible goods is insufficient to meet all the receipts which the warehouseman has issued against it, the persons entitled include all holders to whom overissued receipts have been duly negotiated.

Section 7-208. Altered Warehouse Receipts. Where a blank in a negotiable warehouse receipt has been filled in without authority, a purchaser for value and without notice of the want of authority may treat the insertion as authorized. Any other unauthorized alteration leaves any receipt enforceable against the issuer according to its original tenor.

Section 7-209. Lien of Warehouseman.

(1) A warehouseman has a lien against the bailor on the goods covered by a warehouse receipt or on the proceeds thereof in his possession for charges for storage or transportation (including demurrage and terminal charges), insurance, labor, or charges present or future in relation to the goods, and for expenses necessary for preservation of the goods or reasonably incurred in their sale pursuant to law. If the person on whose account the goods are held is liable for like charges or expenses in relation to other goods whenever deposited and it is stated in the receipt that a lien is claimed for charges and expenses in relation to other goods, the warehouseman also has a lien against him for such charges and expenses whether or not the other goods have been delivered by the warehouseman. But against a person to whom a negotiable warehouse receipt is duly negotiated a warehouseman's lien is limited to charges in an amount or at a rate specified on the receipt or if no charges are so specified then to a reasonable charge for storage of the goods covered by the receipt subsequent to the date of the receipt.

(2) The warehouseman may also reserve a security interest against the bailor for a maximum amount specified on the receipt for charges other than those specified in subsection (1), such as for money advanced and interest. Such a security interest is governed by the Article on Secured Transactions (Article 9).

(3) A warehouseman's lien for charges and expenses under subsection (1) or a security interest under subsection (2) is also effective against any person who so entrusted the bailor with possession of the goods that a pledge of them by him to a good faith purchaser for value would have been valid but is not effective against a person as to whom the document confers no right in the goods covered by it under Section 7-503.

(4) A warehouseman loses his lien on any goods which he voluntarily delivers or which he unjustifiably refuses to deliver.

Section 7-210. Enforcement of Warehouseman's Lien.

(1) Except as provided in subsection (2), a warehouseman's lien may be enforced by public or private sale of the goods in block or in parcels, at any time or place and on any terms which are commercially reasonable, after notifying all persons known to claim an interest in the goods. Such notification must include a statement of the amount due, the nature of the proposed sale and the

time and place of any public sale. The fact that a better price could have been obtained by a sale at a different time or in a different method from that selected by the warehouseman is not of itself sufficient to establish that the sale was not made in a commercially reasonable manner. If the warehouseman either sells the goods in the usual manner in any recognized market therefore, or if he sells at the price current in such market at the time of his sale, or if he has otherwise sold in conformity with commercially reasonable practices among dealers in the type of goods sold, he has sold in a commercially reasonable manner. A sale of more goods than apparently necessary to be offered to insure satisfaction of the obligation is not commercially reasonable except in cases covered by the preceding sentence.

(2) A warehouseman's lien on goods other than goods stored by a merchant in the course of his business may be enforced only as follows:

(a) All persons known to claim an interest in the goods must be notified.

(b) The notification must be delivered in person or sent by registered or certified letter to the last known address of any person to be notified.

(c) The notification must include an itemized statement of the claim, a description of the goods subject to the lien, a demand for payment within a specified time not less than ten days after receipt of the notification, and a conspicuous statement that unless the claim is paid within that time the goods will be advertised for sale and sold by auction at a specified time and place.

(d) The sale must conform to the terms of the notification.

(e) The sale must be held at the nearest suitable place to that where the goods are held or stored.

(f) After the expiration of the time given in the notification, an advertisement of the sale must be published once a week for two weeks consecutively in a newspaper of general circulation where the sale is to be held. The advertisement must include a description of the goods, the name of the person on whose account they are being held, and the time and place of the sale. The sale must take place at least fifteen days after the first publication. If there is no newspaper of general circulation where the sale is to be held, the advertisement must be posted at least ten days before the sale in not less than six conspicuous places in the neighborhood of the proposed sale.

(3) Before any sale pursuant to this section any person claiming a right in the goods may pay the amount necessary to satisfy the lien and the reasonable expenses incurred under this section. In that event the goods must not be sold, but must be retained by the warehouseman subject to the terms of the receipt and this Article.

(4) The warehouseman may buy at any public sale pursuant to this section.

(5) A purchaser in good faith of goods sold to enforce a warehouseman's lien takes the goods free of any rights of persons against whom the lien was valid, despite noncompliance by the warehouseman with the requirements of this section.

(6) The warehouseman may satisfy his lien from the proceeds of any sale pursuant to this section but must hold the balance, if any, for delivery on demand to any person to whom he would have been bound to deliver the goods.

(7) The rights provided by this section shall be in addition to all other rights allowed by law to a creditor against his debtor.

(8) Where a lien is on goods stored by a merchant in the course of his business the lien may be enforced in accordance with either subsection (1) or (2).

(9) The warehouseman is liable for damages caused by failure to comply with the requirements for sale under this section and in case of willful violation is liable for conversion.

BILLS OF LADING: SPECIAL PROVISIONS

Section 7-301. Liability for Non-receipt or Misdescription; "Said to Contain"; "Shipper's Load and Count"; Improper Handling.

(1) A consignee of a non-negotiable bill who has given value in good faith or a holder to whom a negotiable bill has been duly negotiated relying in either case upon the description therein of the goods, or upon the date therein shown, may recover from the issuer damages caused by the misdating of the bill or the nonreceipt or misdescription of the goods, except to the extent that the document indicates that the issuer does not know whether any part or all of the goods in fact were received or conform to the description, as where the description is in terms of marks or labels or kind, quantity, or condition of the receipt or description is qualified by "contents or condition of contents of packages unknown," "said to contain," "shipper's weight, load and count" or the like, if such indication be true.

(2) When goods are loaded by an issuer who is a common carrier, the issuer must count the packages of goods if package freight and ascertain the kind and quantity if bulk freight. In such cases "shipper's weight, load and count" or other words indicating that the description was made by the shipper are ineffective except as to freight concealed by packages.

(3) When bulk freight is loaded by a shipper who makes available to the issuer adequate facilities for weighing such freight, an issuer who is a common carrier must ascertain the kind and quantity within a reasonable time after receiving the written request of the shipper to do so. In such cases "shipper's weight" or other words of like purport are ineffective.

(4) The issuer may by inserting in the bill the words "shipper's weight, load and count" or other words of like purport indicate that the goods were loaded by the shipper; and if such statement be true the issuer shall not be liable for damages caused by the improper loading. But their omission does not imply liability for such damages.

(5) The shipper shall be deemed to have guaranteed to the issuer the accuracy at the time of shipment of the description, marks, labels, number, kind, quantity, condition and weight, as furnished by him; and the shipper shall indemnify the issuer against damage caused by inaccuracies in such particulars. The right of the issuer to such indemnity shall in no way limit his responsibility and liability under the contract of carriage to any person other than the shipper.

Section 7-302. Through Bills of Lading and Similar Documents.

(1) The issuer of a through bill of lading or other document embodying an undertaking to be performed in part by persons acting as its agents or by connecting carriers is liable to anyone entitled to recover on the document for any breach by such other persons or by a connecting carrier of its obligation under the document but to the extent that the bill covers an undertaking to be performed overseas or in territory not contiguous to the continental United States or an undertaking including matters other than transportation this liability may be varied by agreement of the parties.

(2) Where goods covered by a through bill of lading or other document embodying an undertaking to be performed in part by persons other than the issuer are received by any such person, he is subject with respect to his own performance while the goods are in his possession to the obligation of the issuer. His obligation is discharged by delivery of the goods to another such person pursuant to the document, and does not

include liability for breach by any other such persons or by the issuer.

(3) The issuer of such through bill of lading or other document shall be entitled to recover from the connecting carrier or such other person in possession of the goods when the breach of the obligation under the document occurred, the amount it may be required to pay to anyone entitled to recover on the document therefor, as may be evidenced by any receipt, judgment, or transcript thereof, and the amount of any expense reasonably incurred by it in defending any action brought by anyone entitled to recover on the document therefor.

Section 7-303. Diversion; Reconsignment; Change of Instructions.

(1) Unless the bill of lading otherwise provides, the carrier may deliver the goods to a person or destination other than that stated in the bill or may otherwise dispose of the goods on instructions from

(a) the holder of a negotiable bill; or

(b) the consignor on a non-negotiable bill notwithstanding contrary instructions from the consignee; or

(c) the consignee on a non-negotiable bill in the absence of contrary instructions from the consignor, if the goods have arrived at the billed destination or if the consignee is in possession of the bill; or

(d) the consignee on a non-negotiable bill if he is entitled as against the consignor to dispose of them.

(2) Unless such instructions are noted on a negotiable bill of lading, a person to whom the bill is duly negotiated can hold the bailee according to the original terms.

Section 7-304. Bills of Lading in a Set.

(1) Except where customary in overseas transportation, a bill of lading must not be issued in a set of parts. The issuer is liable for damages caused by violation of this subsection.

(2) Where a bill of lading is lawfully drawn in a set of parts, each of which is numbered and expressed to be valid only if the goods have not been delivered against any other part, the whole of the parts constitute one bill.

(3) Where a bill of lading is lawfully issued in a set of parts and different parts are negotiated to different persons, the title of the holder to whom the first due negotiation is made prevails as to both the document and the goods even though any later holder may have received the goods from the carrier in good faith and discharged the carrier's obligation by surrender of his part.

(4) Any person who negotiates or transfers a single part of a bill of lading drawn in a set is liable to holders of that part as if it were the whole set.

(5) The bailee is obliged to deliver in accordance with Part 4 of this Article against the first presented part of a bill of lading lawfully drawn in a set. Such delivery discharges the bailee's obligation on the whole bill.

Section 7-305. Destination Bills.

(1) Instead of issuing a bill of lading to the consignor at the place of shipment a carrier may at the request of the consignor procure the bill to be issued at destination or at any other place designated in the request.

(2) Upon request of anyone entitled as against the carrier to control the goods while in transit and on surrender of any outstanding bill of lading or other receipt covering such goods, the issuer may procure a substitute bill to be issued at any place designated in the request.

Section 7-306. Altered Bills of Lading. An unauthorized alteration or filling of a blank in a bill of lading leaves the bill enforceable according to its original tenor.

Section 7-307. Lien of Carrier.

(1) A carrier has a lien on the goods covered by a bill of lading for charges subsequent to the date of its receipt of the goods for storage or transportation (including demurrage and terminal charges) and for expenses incurred in their sale pursuant to law. But against a purchaser for value of a negotiable bill of lading a carrier's lien is limited to charges stated in the bill or the applicable tariffs, or if no charges are stated then to a reasonable charge.

(2) A lien for charges and expenses under subsection (1) on goods which the carrier was required by law to receive for transportation is effective against the consignor or any person entitled to the goods unless the carrier had notice that the consignor lacked authority to subject the goods to

such charges and expenses. Any other lien under subsection (1) is effective against the consignor and any person who permitted the bailor to have control or possession of the goods unless the carrier had notice that the bailor lacked such authority.

(3) A carrier loses his lien on any goods which he voluntarily delivers or which he unjustifiably refuses to deliver.

Section 7-308. Enforcement of Carrier's Lien.

(1) A carrier's lien may be enforced by public or private sale of the goods, in bloc or in parcels, at any time or place and on any terms which are commercially reasonable, after notifying all persons known to claim an interest in the goods. Such notification must include a statement of the amount due, the nature of the proposed sale and the time and place of any public sale. The fact that a better price could have been obtained by a sale at a different time or in a different method from that selected by the carrier is not of itself sufficient to establish that the sale was not made in a commercially reasonable manner. If the carrier either sells the goods in the usual manner in any recognized market therefor or if he sells at the price current in such market at the time of his sale or if he has otherwise sold in conformity with commercially reasonable practices among dealers in the type of goods sold he has sold in a commercially reasonable manner. A sale of more goods than apparently necessary to be offered to ensure satisfaction of the obligation is not commercially reasonable except in cases covered by the preceding sentence.

(2) Before any sale pursuant to this section any person claiming a right in the goods may pay the amount necessary to satisfy the lien and the reasonable expenses incurred under this section. In that event the goods must not be sold, but must be retained by the carrier subject to the terms of the bill and this Article.

(3) The carrier may buy at any public sale pursuant to this section.

(4) A purchaser in good faith of goods sold to enforce a carrier's lien takes the goods free of any rights of persons against whom the lien was valid, despite non-compliance by the carrier with the requirements of this section.

(5) The carrier may satisfy his lien from the proceeds of any sale pursuant to this section but must hold the balance, if any, for delivery on demand to any person to whom he would have been bound to deliver the goods.

(6) The rights provided by this section shall be in addition to all other rights allowed by law to a creditor against his debtor.

(7) A carrier's lien may be enforced in accordance with either subsection (1) or the procedure set forth in subsection (2) of Section 7-210.

(8) The carrier is liable for damages caused by failure to comply with the requirements for sale under this section and in case of willful violation is liable for conversion.

Section 7-309. Duty of Care; Contractual Limitation of Carrier's Liability.

(1) A carrier who issues a bill of lading whether negotiable or non-negotiable must exercise the degree of care in relation to the goods which a reasonably careful man would exercise under like circumstances. This subsection does not repeal or change any law or rule of law which imposes liability upon a common carrier for damages not caused by its negligence.

(2) Damages may be limited by a provision that the carrier's liability shall not exceed a value stated in the document if the carrier's rates are dependent upon value and the consignor by the carrier's tariff is afforded an opportunity to declare a higher value or a value as lawfully provided in the tariff, or where no tariff is filed he is otherwise advised of such opportunity; but no such limitation is effective with respect to the carrier's liability for conversion to its own use.

(3) Reasonable provisions as to the time and manner of presenting claims and instituting actions based on the shipment may be included in a bill of lading or tariff.

PART 4

WAREHOUSE RECEIPTS AND BILLS OF LADING: GENERAL OBLIGATIONS

Section 7-401. Irregularities in Issue of Receipt or Bill or Conduct of Issue. The obligations imposed by this Article on an issuer apply to a document of title regardless of the fact that

(a) the document may not comply with the requirements of this Article or of any other law or regulation regarding its issue, form or content; or

(b) the issuer may have violated laws regulating the conduct of his business; or

(c) The goods covered by the document were owned by the bailee at the time the document was issued; or

(d) the person issuing the document does not come within the definition of warehouseman if it purports to be a warehouse receipt.

Section 7-402. Duplicate Receipt or Bill; Overissue. Neither a duplicate nor any other document of title purporting to cover goods already represented by an outstanding document of the same issuer confers any right in the goods, except as provided in the case of bills in a set, overissue of documents for fungible goods and substitutes for lost, stolen or destroyed documents. But the issuer is liable for damages caused by his overissue or failure to identify a duplicate document as such by conspicuous notation on its face.

Section 403. Obligation of Warehouseman or Carrier to Deliver; Excuse.

(1) The bailee must deliver the goods to a person entitled under the document who complies with subsection (2) and (3), unless and to the extent that the bailee establishes any of the following:

(a) delivery of the goods to a person whose receipt was rightful as against the claimant;

(b) damage to or delay, loss or destruction of the goods for which the bailee is not liable [,but the burden of establishing negligence in such cases is on the person entitled under the document];

NOTE: *The brakets in (1) (b) indicate that State enactments may differ on this point without serious damage to the principle of uniformity.*

(c) previous sale or other disposition of the goods in lawful enforcement of a lien or on warehouseman's lawful termination of storage;

(d) the exercise by a seller of his right to stop delivery pursuant to the provisions of the Article on Sales (Section 2-705);

(e) a diversion, reconsignment or other disposition pursuant to the provisions of this Article (Section 7-303) or tariff regulating such right;

(f) release, satisfaction or any other fact affording a personal defense against the claimant;

(g) any other lawful excuse.

(2) A person claiming goods covered by a document of title must satisfy the bailee's lien where the bailee so requests or where the bailee is prohibited by law from delivering the goods until the charges are paid.

(3) Unless the person claiming is one against whom the document confers no right under Sec. 7-503 (1), he must surrender for cancellation or notation of partial deliveries any outstanding negotiable document covering the goods, and the bailee must cancel the document or conspicuously note the partial delivery thereon or be liable to any person to whom the document is duly negotiated.

(4) "Person entitled under the document" means holder in the case of a negotiable document, or the person to whom delivery is to be made by the terms of or pursuant to written instructions under a non-negotiable document.

Section 7-404. No Liability for Good Faith Delivery Pursuant to Receipt or Bill. A bailee who in good faith including observance of reasonable commercial standards has received goods and delivered or otherwise disposed of them according to the terms of the document of title or pursuant to this Article is not liable therefor. This rule applies even though the person from whom he received the goods had no authority to procure the document or to dispose of the goods and even though the person to whom he delivered the goods had no authority to receive them.

WAREHOUSE RECEIPTS AND BILLS OF LADING: NEGOTIATION AND TRANSFER

Section 7-501. Form of Negotiation and Requirements of "Due Negotiation."

(1) A negotiable document of title running to the order of a named person is negotiated by his indorsement and delivery. After his indorsement in blank or to bearer any person can negotiate it by delivery alone.

(2)(a) A negotiable document of title is also negotiated by delivery alone when by its original terms it runs to bearer.

(b) When a document running to the order of a named person is delivered to him the effect is the same as if the document had been negotiated.

(3) Negotiation of a negotiable document of title after it has been indorsed to a specified person requires indorsement by the special indorsee as well as delivery.

(4) A negotiable document of title is "duly negotiated" when it is negotiated in the manner stated in this section to a holder who purchases it in good faith without notice of any defense against or claim to it on the part of any person and for value, unless it is established that the negotiation is not in the regular course of business or financing or involves receiving the document in settlement or payment of a money obligation.

(5) Indorsement of a non-negotiable document neither makes it negotiable nor adds to the transferee's rights.

(6) The naming in a negotiable bill of a person to be notified of the arrival of the goods does not limit the negotiability of the bill nor constitute notice to a purchaser thereof of any interest of such person in the goods.

Section 7-502. Rights Acquired by Due Negotiation.

(1) Subject to the following section and to the provisions of Section 7-205 on fungible goods, a holder to whom a negotiable document of title has been duly negotiated acquires thereby:

(a) title to the document;

(b) title to the goods;

(c) all rights accruing under the law of agency or estoppel, including rights to goods delivered to the bailee after the document was issued; and

(d) the direct obligation of the issuer to hold or deliver the goods according to the terms of the document free of any defense or claim by him except those arising under the terms of the document or under this Article. In the case of a delivery order the bailee's obligation accrued only upon acceptance and the obligation acquired by the holder is that the issuer and any indorser will procure the acceptance of the bailee.

(2) Subject to the following section, title and rights so acquired are not defeated by any stoppage of the goods represented by the document or by surrender of such goods by the bailee, and are not impaired even though the negotiation or any prior negotiation constituted a breach of duty or even though any person has been deprived of possession of the document by misrepresentation, fraud, accident, mistake, duress, loss, theft or conversion, or even though a previous sale or other transfer of the goods has been made to a third person.

Section 7-503. Documents of Title to Goods Defeated in Certain Cases.

(1) A document of title confers no right in goods against a person who before issuance of the document had a legal interest or a perfected security interest in them and who neither

(a) delivered or entrusted them or any document of title covering them to the bailor or his nominee with actual or apparent authority to ship, store or sell or with power to obtain delivery under this Article (Section 7-403) or with power of disposition under this Act (Sections 2-403 and 9-307) or other statute or rule of law; nor

(b) acquiesced in the procurement by the bailor or his nominee of any document of title.

(2) Title to goods based upon an unaccepted delivery order is subject to the rights of anyone to whom a negotiable warehouse receipt or bill of lading covering the goods has been duly negotiated. Such a title may be defeated under the next section to the same extent as the rights of the issuer or a transferee from the issuer.

(3) Title to goods based upon a bill of lading issued to a freight forwarder is subject to the rights of anyone to whom a bill issued by the freight forwarder is duly negotiated; but delivery by the carrier in accordance with Part 4 of this Article pursuant to its own bill of lading discharges the carrier's obligation to deliver.

Section 7-504. Rights Acquired in the Absence of Due Negotiation; Effect of Diversion; Seller's Stoppage of Delivery.

(1) A transferee of a document, whether negotiable or non-negotiable, to whom the document has been delivered but not duly negotiated, acquires the title and rights which his transferor had or had actual authority to convey.

(2) In the case of a non-negotiable document, until but not after the bailee receives notification of the transfer, the rights of the transferee may be defeated

(a) by those creditors of the transferor who could treat the sale as void under Section 2-402; or

(b) by a buyer from the transferor in ordinary course of business if the bailee has delivered the goods to the buyer or received notification of his rights; or

(c) as against the bailee by good faith dealings of the bailee with the transferor.

(3) A diversion or other change of shipping instructions by the consignor in a non-negotiable bill of lading which causes the bailee not to deliver to the consignee defeats the consignee's title to the goods if they have been delivered to a buyer in ordinary course of business and in any event defeats the consignee's rights against the bailee.

(4) Delivery pursuant to a non-negotiable document may be stopped by a seller under Section 2-705, and subject to the requirement of due notification there provided. A bailee honoring the seller's instructions is entitled to be indemnified by the seller against any resulting loss or expense.

Section 7-505. Indorser Not a Guarantor for Other Parties. The indorsement of a document of title issued by a bailee does not make the indorser liable for any default by the bailee or by previous indorsers.

Section 7-506. Delivery Without Indorsement: Right to Compel Indorsement. The transferee of a negotiable document of title has a specifically enforceable right to have his transferor supply any necessary indorsement but the transfer becomes a negotiation only as of the time the indorsement is supplied.

Section 7-507. Warranties on Negotiation or Transfer of Receipt or Bill. Where a person negotiates or transfers a document of title for value otherwise than as a mere intermediary under the next following section, then unless otherwise agreed he warrants to his immediate purchaser only in addition to any warranty made in selling the goods

(a) that the document is genuine; and

(b) that he has no knowledge of any fact which would impair its validity or worth; and

(c) that his negotiation or transfer is rightful and fully effective with respect to the title to the document and the goods it represents.

Section 7-508. Warranties of Collecting Bank as to Documents. A collecting bank or other intermediary known to be entrusted with documents on behalf of another or with collection of a draft or other claim against delivery of documents warrants by such delivery of the documents only its own good faith and authority. This rule applies even though the intermediary has purchased or made advances against the claim or draft to be collected.

Section 7-509. Receipt or Bill: When Adequate Compliance with Commercial Contract. The question whether a document is adequate to fulfill the obligations of a contract for sale or the conditions of a credit is governed by the Articles on Sales (Article 2) and on Letters of Credit (Article 5).

PART 6

WAREHOUSE RECEIPTS AND BILLS OF LADING: MISCELLANEOUS PROVISIONS

Section 7-601. Lost and Missing Documents.

(1) If a document has been lost, stolen or destroyed, a court may order delivery of the goods or issuance of a substitute document and the bailee may without liability to any person comply with such order. If the document was negotiable the claimant must post security approved by the court to indemnify any person who may suffer loss as a result of non-surrender of the document. If the

document was not negotiable, such security may be required at the discretion of the court. The court may also in its discretion order payment of the bailee's reasonable costs and counsel fees.

(2) A bailee who without court order delivers goods to a person claiming under a missing negotiable document is liable to any person injured thereby, and if the delivery is not in good faith becomes liable for conversion. Delivery in good faith is not conversion if made in accordance with a filed classification or tariff or, where no classification or tariff is filed, if the claimant posts security with the bailee in an amount at least double the value of the goods at the time of posting to indemnify any person injured by the delivery who files a notice of claim within one year after the delivery.

Section 7-602. Attachment of Goods Covered by a Negotiable Document. Except where the document was originally issued upon delivery of the goods by a person who had no power to dispose of them, no lien attaches by virtue of any judicial process to goods in the possession of a bailee for which a negotiable document of title is outstanding unless the document be first surrendered to the bailee or its negotiation enjoined, and the bailee shall not be compelled to deliver the goods pursuant to process until the document is surrendered to him or impounded by the court. One who purchases the document for value without notice of the process or injunction takes free of the lien imposed by judicial process.

Section 7-603. Conflicting Claims; Interpleader. If more than one person claims title or possession of the goods, the bailee is excused from delivery until he has had a reasonable time to ascertain the validity of the adverse claims or to bring an action to compel all claimants to interplead and may compel such interpleader, either in defending an action for non-delivery of the goods, or by original action, whichever is appropriate.

ARTICLE 8

INVESTMENT SECURITIES

PART 1

SHORT TITLE AND GENERAL MATTERS

Section 8-101. Short Title. This Article shall be known and may be cited as Uniform Commercial Code—Investment Securities.

Section 8-102. Definitions and Index of Definitions.

(1) In this Article unless the context otherwise requires

(a) A "security" is an instrument which

(i) is issued in bearer or registered form; and

(ii) is of a type commonly dealt in upon securities exchanges or markets or commonly recognized in any area in which it is issued or dealt in as a medium for investment; and

(iii) is either one of a class or series or by its terms is divisible into a class or series of instruments; and

(iv) evidences a share, participation or other interest in property or in an enterprise or evidences an obligation of the issuer.

(b) A writing which is a security is governed by this Article and not by Uniform Commercial Code-Commercial Paper even though it also meets the requirements of that Article. This Article does not apply to money.

(c) A security is in "registered form" when it specifies a person entitled to the security or to the rights it evidences and when its transfer may be registered upon books maintained for that purpose by or on behalf of an issuer or the security so states.

(d) A security is in "bearer form" when it runs to bearer according to its terms and not by reason of any indorsement.

(2) A "subsequent purchaser" is a person who takes other than by original issue.

(3) A "clearing corporation" is a corporation all of the capital stock of which is held by or for a national security exchange or association registered under a statute of the United States such as the Securities Exchange Act of 1934.

(4) A "custodian bank" is any bank or trust company which is supervised and examined by state or federal authority having supervision over banks and which is acting as custodian for a clearing corporation.

(5) Other definitions applying to this Article or to specified Parts thereof and the sections in which they appear are:

"Adverse claim." Section 8-301.
"Bona fide purchaser." Section 8-302.
"Broker." Section 8-303.
"Guarantee of the signature." Section 8-402.
"Intermediary bank." Section 4-105.
"Issuer." Section 8-201.
"Overissue." Section 8-104.

(6) In addition Article 1 contains general definitions and principles of construction and interpretation applicable throughout this Article.

Section 8-103. Issuer's Lien. A lien upon a security in favor of an issuer thereof is valid against a purchaser only if the right of the issuer to such lien is noted conspicuously on the security.

Section 8-104. Effect of Overissue; "Overissue."

(1) The provisions of this Article which validate a security or compel its issue or reissue do not apply to the extent that validation, issue or reissue would result in overissue; but

(a) if an identical secuirty which does not constitute an overissue is reasonably available for purchase, the person entitled to issue or validation may compel the issuer to purchase and deliver such a security to him against surrender of the security, if any, which he holds; or

(b) if a security is not so available for purchase, the person entitled to issue or validation may recover from the issuer the price he or the last purchaser for value paid for it with interest from the date of his demand.

(2) "Overissue" means the issue of securities in excess of the amount which the issuer has corporate power to issue.

Section 8-105. Securities Negotiable; Presumptions.

(1) Securities governed by this Article are negotiable instruments.

(2) In any action on a security

(a) unless specifically denied in the pleadings, each signature on the security or in a necessary indorsement is admitted;

(b) when the effectiveness of a signature is put in issue the burden of establishing it is on the party claiming under the signature but the signature is presumed to be genuine or authorized;

(c) when signatures are admitted or established production of the instrument entitles a holder to recover on it unless the defendant establishes a defense or a defect going to the validity of the security; and

(d) after it is shown that a defense or defect exists the plaintiff has the burden of establishing that he or some person under whom he claims is a person against whom the defense or defect is ineffective (Section 8-202).

Section 8-106. Applicability. The validity of a security and the rights and duties of the issuer with respect to registration of transfer are governed by the law (including the conflict of laws rules) or the jurisdiction of organization or the issuer.

Section 8-107. Securities Deliverable; Action for Price.

(1) Unless otherwise agreed and subject to any applicable law or regulation respecting short sales, a person obligated to deliver securities may deliver any security of the specified issue in bearer form or registered in the name of the transferee or indorsed to him or in blank.

(2) When the buyer fails to pay the price as it comes due under a contract of sale the seller may recover the price

(a) of securities accepted by the buyer; and

(b) of other securities if efforts at their resale would be unduly burdensome or if there is no readily available market for their resale.

ISSUE–ISSUER

Section 8-201. "Issuer."

(1) With respect to obligations on or defenses to a security "issuer" includes a person who

(a) places or authorizes the placing of his name on a security (otherwise than as authenticating trustee, registrar, transfer agent or the like) to evidence that it represents a share, participation or other interest in his property or in an enterprise or to evidence his duty to perform an obligation evidenced by the security; or

(b) directly or indirectly creates fractional interests in his rights or property which fractional interests are evidenced by securities; or

(c) becomes responsible for or in place of any other person described as an issuer in this section.

(2) With respect to obligations on or defenses to a security a guarantor is an issuer to the extent of his guaranty whether or not his obligation is noted on the security.

(3) With respect to registration of transfer (Part 4 of this Article) "issuer" means a person on whose behalf transfer books are maintained.

Section 8-202. Issuer's Responsibility and Defenses; Notice of Defect or Defense.

(1) Even against a purchaser for value and without notice, the terms of a security include those stated on the security and those made part of the security by reference to another instrument, indenture or document or to a constitution, statute, ordinance, rule, regulation, order or the like to the extent that the terms so referred to do not conflict with the stated terms. Such a reference does not of itself charge a purchaser for value with notice of a defect going to the validity of the security even though the security expressly states that a person accepting it admits such notice.

(2) (a) A security other than one issued by a government or governmental agency or unit even though issued with a defect going to its validity is valid in the hands of a purchaser for value and without notice of the particular defect unless the defect involves a violation of constitutional provisions in which case the security is valid in the hands of a subsequent purchaser for value and without notice of the defect.

(b) The rule of subparagraph (a) applies to an issuer which is a government or governmental agency or unit only if either there has been substantial compliance with the legal requirements governing the issue or the issuer has received a substantial consideration for the issue as a whole or for the particular security and a stated purpose of the issue is one for which the issuer has power to borrow money or issue the security.

(3) Except as otherwise provided in the case of certain unauthorized signatures on issue (Section 8-205), lack of genuineness of a security is a complete defense even against a purchaser for value and without notice.

(4) All other defenses of the issuer including nondelivery and conditional delivery of the security are ineffective against a purchaser for value who has taken without notice of the particular defense.

(5) Nothing in this section shall be construed to affect the right of a party to a "when, as and if issued" or a "when distributed" contract to cancel the contract in the event of a material change in the character of the security which is the subject of the contract or in the plan or arrangement pursuant to which such security is to be issued or distributed.

Section 8-203. Staleness as Notice of Defects or Defenses.

(1) After an act or event which creates a right to immediate performance of the principal obligation evidenced by the security or which sets a date on or after which the security is to be presented or sur-

rendered for redemption or exchange, a purchaser is charged with notice of any defect in its issue or defense of the issuer

(a) if the act or event is one requiring the payment of money or the delivery of securities or both on presentation or surrender of the security and such funds or securities are available on the date set for payment or exchange and he takes the security more than one year after that date; and

(b) if the act or event is not covered by paragraph (a) and he takes the security more than two years after the date set for surrender or presentation or the date on which such performance became due.

(2) A call which has been revoked is not within subsection (1).

Section 8-204. Effect of Issuer's Restrictions on Transfer. Unless noted conspicuously on the security a restriction on transfer imposed by the issuer even though otherwise lawful is ineffective except against a person with actual knowledge of it.

Section 8-205. Effect of Unauthorized Signature on Issue. An unauthorized signature placed on a security prior to or in the course of issue is ineffective except that the signature is effective in favor of a purchaser for value and without notice of the lack of authority if the signing has been done by

(a) an authenticating trustee, registrar, transfer agent or other person entrusted by the issuer with the signing of the security or of similar securities or their immediate preparation for signing; or

(b) an employee of the issuer or of any of the foregoing entrusted with responsible handling of the security.

Section 8-206. Completion or Alteration of Instrument.

(1) Where a security contains the signatures necessary to its issue or transfer but is incomplete in any other respect

(a) any person may complete it by filling in the blanks as authorized; and

(b) even though the blanks are incorrectly filled in, the security as completed is enforceable by a purchaser who took it for value and without notice of such incorrectness.

(2) A complete security which has been improperly altered even though fraudulently remains enforceable but only according to its original terms.

Section 8-207. Rights of Issuer with Respect to Registered Owners.

(1) Prior to due presentment for registration of transfer of a security in registered form the issuer or indenture trustee may treat the registered owner as the person exclusively entitled to vote, to receive notifications and otherwise to exercise all the rights and powers of an owner.

(2) Nothing in this Article shall be construed to affect the liability of the registered owner of a security for calls, assessments or the like.

Section 8-208. Effect of Signature of Authenticating Trustee, Registrar or Transfer Agent.

(1) A person placing his signature upon a security as authenticating trustee, registrar, transfer agent or the like warrants to a purchaser for value without notice of the particular defect that

(a) the security is genuine; and

(b) his own participation in the issue of the security is within his capacity and within the scope of the authorization received by him from the issuer; and

(c) he has reasonable grounds to believe that the security is in the form and within the amount the issuer is authorized to issue.

(2) Unless otherwise agreed, a person by so placing his signature does not assume responsibility for the validity of the security in other respects.

PART 3

PURCHASE

Section 8-301. Rights Acquired by Purchaser; "Adverse Claim"; Title Acquired by Bona Fide Purchaser.

(1) Upon delivery of a security the purchaser acquires the rights in the security which his transferor had or had actual authority to convey except that a purchaser who has himself been a party to any fraud or illegality affecting the security or who as a prior holder had notice of an adverse claim cannot improve his position by taking from a later bona fide purchaser. "Adverse claim"

includes a claim that a transfer was or would be wrongful or that a particular adverse person is the owner of or has an interest in the security.

(2) A bona fide purchaser in addition to acquiring the rights of a purchaser also acquires the security free of any adverse claim.

(3) A purchaser of a limited interest acquires rights only to the extent of the interest purchased.

Section 8-302. "Bona Fide Purchaser." A "bona fide purchaser" is a purchaser for value in good faith and without notice of any adverse claim who takes delivery of a security in bearer form or of one in registered form issued to him or indorsed to him or in blank.

Section 8-303. "Broker." "Broker" means a person engaged for all or part of his time in the business of buying and selling securities, who in the transaction concerned acts for, or buys a security from or sells a security to a customer. Nothing in this Article determines the capacity in which a person acts for purposes of any other statute or rule to which such person is subject.

Section 8-304. Notice to Purchaser of Adverse Claims.

(1) A purchaser (including a broker for the seller or buyer but excluding an intermediary bank) of a security is charged with notice of adverse claims if

(a) the security whether in bearer or registered form has been indorsed "for collection" or "for surrender" or for some other purpose not involving transfer; or

(b) the security is in bearer form and has on it an unambiguous statement that it is the property of a person other than the transferor. The mere writing of a name on a security is not such a statement.

(2) The fact that the purchaser (including a broker for the seller or buyer) has notice that the security is held for a third person or is registered in the name of or indorsed by a fiduciary does not create a duty of inquiry into the rightfulness of the transfer or constitute notice of adverse claims. If, however, the purchaser (excluding an intermediary bank) has knowledge that the proceeds are being used or that the transaction is for the individual benefit of the fiduciary or otherwise in breach of duty, the purchaser is charged with notice of adverse claims.

Section 8-305. Staleness as Notice of Adverse Claims. An act or event which creates a right to immediate performance of the principal obligation evidenced by the security or which sets a date on or after which the security is to be presented or surrendered for redemption or exchange does not of itself constitute any notice of adverse claims except in the case of a purchase

(a) after one year from any date set for such presentment or surrender for redemption or exchange; or

(b) after six months from any date set for payment of money against presentation or surrender of the security if funds are available for payment on that date.

Section 8-306. Warranties on Presentment and Transfer.

(1) A person who presents a security for registration on transfer or for payment or exchange warrants to the issuer that he is entitled to the registration, payment or exchange. But a purchaser for value without notice of adverse claims who receives a new, reissued or registered security on registration of transfer warrants only that he has no knowledge of any unauthorized signature (Section 8-311) in a necessary indorsement.

(2) A person by transferring a security to a purchaser for value warrants only that

(a) his transfer is effective and rightful; and

(b) the security is genuine and has not been materially altered; and

(c) he knows no fact which might impair the validity of the security.

(3) Where a security is delivered by an intermediary known to be entrusted with delivery of the security on behalf of another or with collection of a draft or other claim against such delivery, the intermediary by such delivery warrants only his own good faith and authority even though he has purchased or made advances against the claim to be collected against the delivery.

(4) A pledgee or other holder for security who redelivers the security received, or after payment and on order of the debtor delivers that security to a third person makes only the warranties of an intermediary under subsection (3).

(5) A broker gives to his customer and to

the issuer and a purchaser the warranties provided in this section and has the rights and privileges of a purchaser under this section. The warranties of and in favor of the broker acting as an agent are in addition to applicable warranties given by and in favor of his customer.

Section 8-307. Effect of Delivery Without Indorsement; Right to Compel Indorsement. Where a security in registered form has been delivered to a purchaser without a necessary indorsement he may become a bona fide purchaser only as of the time the indorsement is supplied, but against the transferor the transfer is complete upon delivery and the purchaser has a specifically enforceable right to have any necessary indorsement supplied.

Section 8-308. Indorsement, How Made; Special Indorsement; Indorser Not a Guarantor; Partial Assignment.

(1) An indorsement of a security in registered form is made when an appropriate person signs on it or on a separate document an assignment or transfer of the security or a power to assign or transfer it or when the signature of such person is written without more upon the back of the security.

(2) An indorsement may be in blank or special. An indorsement in blank includes an indorsement to bearer. A special indorsement specifies the person to whom the security is to be transferred, or who has power to transfer it. A holder may convert a blank indorsement into a special indorsement.

(3) "An appropriate person" in subsection (1) means

(a) the person specified by the security or by special indorsement to be entitled to the security; or

(b) where the person so specified is described as a fiduciary but is no longer serving in the described capacity,—either that person or his successor; or

(c) where the security or indorsement so specifies more than one person as fiduciaries and one or more are no longer serving in the described capacity,—the remaining fiduciary or fiducaries, whether or not a successor has been appointed or qualified; or

(d) where the person so specified is an individual and is without capacity to act by virtue of death, incompetence, infancy or otherwise,—his executor, administrator, guardian or like fiduciary; or

(e) where the security or indorsement so specifies more than one person as tenants by the entirety or with right of survivorship and by reason of death all cannot sign,—the survivor or survivors; or

(f) a person having power to sign under applicable law or controlling instrument; or

(g) to the extent that any of the foregoing persons may act through an agent,—his authorized agent.

(4) Unless otherwise agreed the indorser by his indorsement assumes no obligation that the security will be honored by the issuer.

(5) An indorsement purporting to be only a part of a security representing units intended by the issuer to be separately transferable is effective to the extent of the indorsement.

(6) Whether the person signing is appropriate is determined as of the date of signing and an indorsement by such a person does not become unauthorized for the purposes of this Article by virtue of any subsequent change of circumstances.

(7) Failure of a fiduciary to comply with a controlling instrument or with the law of the state having jurisdiction of the fiduciary relationship, including any law requiring the fiduciary to obtain court approval of the transfer, does not render his indorsement unauthorized for the purposes of this Article.

Section 8-309. Effect of Indorsement Without Delivery. An indorsement of a security whether special or in blank does not constitute a transfer until delivery of the security on which it appears or if the indorsement is on a separate document until delivery of both the document and the security.

Section 8-310. Indorsement of Security in Bearer Form. An indorsement of a security in bearer form may give notice of adverse claims (Section 8-304) but does not otherwise affect any right to registration the holder may possess.

Section 8-311. Effect of Unauthorized Indorsement. Unless the owner has ratified an unauthorizeindorsement or is otherwise precluded from asserting its ineffectiveness

(a) he may assert its ineffectiveness against the issuer or any purchaser other than a purchaser for value and without notice of adverse claims who has in good faith received a new, reissued or re-registered security on registration of transfer; and

(b) an issuer who registers the transfer of a security upon the unauthorized indorsement is subject to liability for improper registration (Section 8-404).

Section 8-312. Effect of Guaranteeing Signature or Indorsement.

(1) Any person guaranteeing a signature of an indorser of a security warrants that at the time of signing

(a) the signature was genuine; and

(b) the signer was an appropriate person to indorse (Section 8-308); and

(c) the signer had legal capacity to sign.

But the guarantor does not otherwise warrant the rightfulness of the particular transfer.

(2) Any person may guarantee an indorsement of a security and by so doing warrants not only the signature (subsection 1) but also the rightfulness of the particular transfer in all respects, but no issuer may require a guarantee of indorsement as a condition to registration of transfer.

(3) The foregoing warranties are made to any person taking or dealing with the security in reliance on the guarantee and the guarantor is liable to such person for any loss resulting from breach of the warranties.

Section 8-313. When Delivery to the Purchaser Occurs; Purchaser's Broker as Holder.

(1) Delivery to a purchaser occurs when

(a) he or a person designated by him acquires possession of a security; or

(b) his broker acquires possession of a security specially indorsed to or issued in the name of the purchaser; or

(c) his broker sends him confirmation of the purchase and also by book entry or otherwise identifies a specific security in the broker's possession as belonging to the purchaser; or

(d) with respect to an identified security to be delivered while still in the possession of a third person when that person acknowledges that he holds for the purchaser; or

(e) appropriate entries on the books of a clearing corporation are made under Section 8-320.

(2) The purchaser is the owner of a security held for him by his broker, but is not the holder except as specified in subparagraphs (b), (c) and (e) of subsection (1). Where a security is part of a fungible bulk the purchaser is the owner of a proportionate property interest in the fungible bulk.

(3) Notice of an adverse claim received by the broker or by the purchaser after the broker takes delivery as a holder for value is not effective either as to the broker or as to the purchaser. However, as between the broker and the purchaser the pruchaser may demand delivery of an equivalent security as to which no notice of an adverse claim has been received.

Section 8-314. Duty to Deliver, When Completed.

(1) Unless otherwise agreed where a sale of a security is made on an exchange or otherwise through brokers

(a) the selling customer fulfills his duty to deliver when he places such a security in the possession of the selling broker or of a person designated by the broker or if requested causes an acknowledgement to be made to the selling broker that it is held for him; and

(b) the selling broker including a correspondent broker acting for a selling customer fulfills his duty to deliver by placing the security or a like security in the possession of the buying broker or a person designated by him or by effecting clearance of the sale in accordance with the rules of the exchange on which the transaction took place.

(2) Except as otherwise provided in this section and unless otherwise agreed, a transferor's duty to deliver a security under a contract of purchase is not fulfilled until he places the security in form to be negotiated by the purchaser in the possession of the purchaser or of a person designated by him or at the purchaser's request causes an acknowledgment to be made to the purchaser that it is held for him. Unless made on an exchange a sale to a broker purchasing for his own account is within this subsection and not within subsection (1).

Section 8-315. Action Against Purchaser Based Upon Wrongful Transfer.

(1) Any person against whom the transfer of a security is wrongful for any reason,

including his incapacity, may against anyone except a bona fide purchaser reclaim possession of the security or obtain possession of any new security evidencing all or part of the same rights or have damages.

(2) If the transfer is wrongful because of an unauthorized indorsement, the owner may also reclaim or obtain possession of the security or new security even from a bona fide purchaser if the ineffectiveness of the purported indorsement can be asserted against him under the provisions of this Article on unauthorized indorsements (Section 8-311).

(3) The right to obtain or reclaim possession of a security may be specifically enforced and its transfer enjoined and the security impounded pending the litigation.

Section 8-316. Purchaser's Right to Requisites for Registration of Transfer on Books. Unless otherwise agreed the transferor must on due demand supply his purchaser with any proof of his authority to transfer or with any other requisite which may be necessary to obtain registration of the transfer of the security but if the transfer is not for value a transferor need not do so unless the purchaser furnishes the necessary expenses. Failure to comply with a demand made within a reasonable time gives the purchaser the right to reject or rescind the transfer.

Section 8-317. Attachment or Levy Upon Security.

(1) No attachment or levy upon a security or any share or other interest evidenced thereby which is outstanding shall be valid until the security is actually seized by the officer making the attachment or levy but a security which has been surrendered to the issuer may be attached or levied upon at the source.

(2) A creditor whose debtor is the owner of a security shall be entitled to such aid from courts of appropriate jurisdiction, by injunction or otherwise, in reaching such security or in satisfying the claim by means thereof as is allowed at law or in equity in regard to property which cannot readily be attached or levied upon by ordinary legal process.

Section 8-318. No Conversion by Good Faith Delivery. An agent or bailee who in good faith (including observance of reasonable commercial standards if he is in the business of buying, selling or otherwise dealing with securities) has received securities and sold, pledged or delivered them according to the instructions of his principal is not liable for conversion or for participation in breach of fiduciary duty although the principal had no right to dispose of them.

Section 8-319. Statute of Frauds. A contract for the sale of securities is not enforceable by way of action or defense unless

(a) there is some writing signed by the party against whom enforcement is sought or by his authorized agent or broker sufficient to indicate that a contract has been made for sale of a stated quantity of described securities at a defined or stated price; or

(b) delivery of the security has been accepted or payment has been made but the contract is enforceable under this provision only to the extent of such delivery or payment; or

(c) within a reasonable time a writing in confirmation of the sale or purchase and sufficient against the sender under paragraph (a) has been received by the party against whom enforcement is sought and he has failed to send written objection to its contents within ten days after its receipt; or

(d) the party against whom enforcement is sought admits in his pleading, testimony or otherwise in court that a contract was made for the sale of a stated quantity of described securities at a defined or stated price.

Section 8-320. Transfer or Pledge Within a Central Depository System.

(1) If a security

(a) is in the custody of a clearing corporation or of a custodian bank or a nominee of either subject to the instructions of the clearing corporation; and

(b) is in bearer form or indorsed in blank by an appropriate person or registered in the name of the clearing corporation or custodian bank or a nominee of either; and

(c) is shown on the account of a transferor or pledgor on the books of the clearing corporation;

then, in addition to other methods, a transfer or pledge of the security or any interest therein may be effected by the making of appropriate entries on the books of the clearing corporation reducing the account of the transferor or pledgor and increasing the account of the transferee or pledgee by the amount of the obligation or the number of shares or rights transferred or pledged.

(2) Under this section entries may be with respect to like securities or interests therein as a part of a fungible bulk and may refer merely to a quantity of a particular security without reference to the name of the registered owner, certificate or bond number or the like, and, in appropriate cases, may be on a net basis taking into account other transfers or pledges of the same security.

(3) A transfer or pledge under this section has the effect of a delivery of a security in bearer form or duly indorsed in blank (Section 8-301) representing the amount of the obligation or the number of shares or rights transferred or pledged. If a pledge or the creation of a security interest is intended, the making of entries has the effect of a taking of delivery by the pledgee or a secured party (Sections 9-304 and 9-305). A transferee or pledgee under this section is a holder.

(4) A transfer or pledge under this section does not constitute a registration of transfer under Part 4 of this Article.

(5) That entries made on the books of the clearing corporation as provided in subsection (1) are not appropriate does not affect the validity or effect of the entries nor the liabilities or obligations of the clearing corporation to any person adversely affected thereby.

PART 4

REGISTRATION

Section 8-401. Duty of Issuer to Register Transfer.

(1) Where a security in registered form is presented to the issuer with a request to register transfer, the issuer is under a duty to register the transfer as requested if

(a) the security is indorsed by the appropriate person or persons (Section 8-308); and

(b) reasonable assurance is given that those indorsements are genuine and effective (Section 8-402); and

(c) the issuer has no duty to inquire into adverse claims or has discharged any such duty (Section 8-403); and

(d) any applicable law relating to the collection of taxes has been complied with; and

(e) the transfer is in fact rightful or is to a bona fide purchaser.

(2) Where an issuer is under a duty to register a transfer of a security the issuer is also liable to the person presenting it for registration or his principal for loss resulting from any unreasonable delay in registration or from failure or refusal to register the transfer.

Section 8-402. Assurance that Indorsements are Effective.

(1) The issuer may require the following assurance that each necessary indorsement (Section 8-308) is genuine and effective

(a) in all cases, a guarantee of the signature (subsection (1) of Section 8-312) of the person indorsing; and

(b) where the indorsement is by an agent, appropriate assurance of authority to sign;

(c) where the indorsement is by a fiduciary, appropriate evidence of appointment or incumbency;

(d) where there is more than one fiduciary, reasonable assurance that all who are required to sign have done so;

(e) where the indorsement is by a person not covered by any of the foregoing, assurance appropriate to the case corresponding as nearly as may be to the foregoing.

(2) A "guarantee of the signature" in subsection (1) means a guarantee signed by or on behalf of a person reasonably believed by the issuer to be responsible. The issuer may adopt standards with respect to responsibility provided such standards are not manifestly unreasonable.

(3) "Appropriate evidence of appointment or incumbency" in subsection (1) means

(a) in the case of a fiduciary appointed or qualified by a court, a certificate issued by or under the direction or supervision of that court or an officer thereof and dated within sixty days before the date of presentation for transfer; or

(b) in any other case, a copy of a document showing the appointment or a certificate issued by or on behalf of a person reasonably believed by the issuer to be responsible or, in the absence of such a document or certificate, other evidence reasonably deemed by the issuer to be appropriate. The issuer may adopt standards with respect to such evidence provided such standards are not manifestly unreasonable. The issuer is not charged with notice of the contents of any document obtained pursuant to this paragraph (b) except to the extent that the contents relate directly to the appointment or incumbency.

(4) The issuer may elect to require a reasonable assurance beyond that specified in this section but if it does so and for a purpose other than that specified in subsection (3) (b) both requires and obtains a copy of a will, trust, indenture, articles of co-partnership, by-laws or other controlling instrument it is charged with notice of all matters contained therein affecting the transfer.

Section 8-403. Limited Duty of Inquiry.

(1) An issuer to whom a security is presented for registration is under a duty to inquire into adverse claims if

(a) a written notification of an adverse claim is received at a time and in a manner which affords the issuer a reasonable opportunity to act on it prior to the issuance of a new, reissued or re-registered security and the notification identifies the claimant, the registered owner and the issue of which the security is a part and provides an address for communications directed to the claimant; or

(b) the issuer is charged with notice of an adverse claim from a controlling instrument which it has elected to require under subsection (4) of Section 8-402.

(2) The issuer may discharge any duty of inquiry by any reasonable means, including notifying an adverse claimant by registered or certified mail at the address furnished by him or if there be no such address at his residence or regular place of business that the security has been presented for registration of transfer by a named person, and that the transfer will be registered unless within thirty days from the date of mailing the notification, either

(a) an appropriate restraining order, injunction or other process issues from a court of competent jurisdiction; or

(b) an indemnity bond sufficient in the issuer's judgment to protect the issuer and any transfer agent, registrar or other agent of the issuer involved, from any loss which it or they may suffer by complying with the adverse claim is filed with the issuer.

(3) Unless an issuer is charged with notice of an adverse claim from a controlling instrument which it has elected to require under subsection (4) of Section 8-402 or receives notification of an adverse claim under subsection (1) of this section, where a security presented for registration is indorsed by the appropriate person or persons the issuer is under no duty to inquire into adverse claims. In particular

(a) an issuer registering a security in the name of a person who is a fiduciary or who is described as a fiduciary is not bound to inquire into the existence, extent, or correct description of the fiduciary relationship and thereafter the issuer may assume without inquiry that the newly registered owner continues to be the fiduciary until the issuer receives written notice that the fiduciary is no longer acting as such with respect to the particular security;

(b) an issuer registering transfer on an indorsement by a fiduciary is not bound to inquire whether the transfer is made in compliance with a controlling instrument or with the law of the state having jurisdiction of the fiduciary relationship, including any law requiring the fiduciary to obtain court approval of the transfer; and

(c) the issuer is not charged with notice of the contents of any court record or file or other recorded or unrecorded documents even though the document is in its possession and even though the transfer is made on the indorsement of a fiduciary to the fiduciary himself or to his nominee.

Section 8-404. Liability and Non-Liability for Registration.

(1) Except as otherwise provided in any law relating to the collection of taxes, the issuer is not liable to the owner or any other person suffering loss as a result of the registration of a transfer of a security if

(a) there were on or with the security the necessary indorsements (Section 8-308); and

(b) the issuer had no duty to inquire into adverse claims or has discharged any such duty (Section 8-403).

(2) Where an issuer has registered a transfer of a security to a person not entitled to it the issuer on demand must deliver a like security to the true owner unless

(a) the registration was pursuant to subsection (1); or

(b) the owner is precluded from asserting any claim for registering the transfer under subsection (1) of the following section; or

(c) such delivery would result in overissue, in which case the issuer's liability is governed by Section 8-104.

Section 8-405. Lost, Destroyed and Stolen Securities.

(1) Where a security has been lost, apparently destroyed or wrongfully taken and the owner fails to notify the issuer of that fact within a reasonable time after he has notice of it and the issuer registerers a transfer of the security before receiving such a notification, the owner is precluded from asserting against the issuer any claim for registering the transfer under the preceding section or any claim to a new security under this section.

(2) Where the owner of a security claims that the security has been lost, destroyed or wrongfully taken, the issuer must issue a new security in place of the original security if the owner

(a) so requests before the issuer has notice that the security has been acquired by a bona fide purchaser; and

(b) files with the issuer a sufficient indemnity bond; and

(c) satisfies any other reasonable requirements imposed by the issuer.

(3) If, after the issue of the new security, a bona fide purchaser of the original security presents it for registration of transfer, the issuer must register the transfer unless registration would result in overissue, in which event the issuer's liability is governed by Section 8-104. In addition to any rights on the indemnity bond, the issuer may recover the new security from the person to whom it was issued or any person taking under him except a bona fide purchaser.

Section 8-406. Duty of Authenticating Trustee, Transfer Agent or Registrar.

(1) Where a person acts as authenticating trustee, transfer agent, registrar, or other agent for an issuer in the registration of transfers of its securities or in the issue of new securities or in the cancellation of surrendered securities

(a) he is under a duty to the issuer to exercise good faith and due diligence in performing his functions; and

(b) he has with regard to the particular functions he performs the same obligation to the holder or owner of the security and has the same rights and privileges as the issuer has in regard to those functions.

(2) Notice to an authenticating trustee, transfer agent, registrar or other such agent is notice to the issuer with respect to the functions performed by the agent.

REVISED ARTICLE 9

SECURED TRANSACTIONS; SALES OF ACCOUNTS AND CHATTEL PAPER

PART 1

SHORT TITLE, APPLICABILITY AND DEFINITIONS

Section 9-101. Short Title. This Article shall be known and may be cited as Uniform Commercial Code—Secured Transactions.

Section 9-102. Policy and Subject Matter of Article.

(1) Except as otherwise provided in Section 9-104 on excluded transactions, this Article applies

(a) to any transaction (regardless of its form) which is intended to create a security interest in personal property or fixtures including goods, documents, instruments, general intangibles, chattel paper or accounts; and also

(b) to any sale of accounts or chattel paper.

(2) This Article applies to security interests created by contract including pledge, assignment, chattel mortgage, chattel trust, trust deed, factor's lien, equipment trust, conditional sale, trust receipt, other lien or title retention contract and lease or consignment intended as security. This Article does not apply to statutory liens except as provided in Section 9-310.

(3) The application of this Article to a security interest in a secured obligation is not affected by the fact that the obligation is itself secured by a transaction or interest to which this Article does not apply.

Section 9-103. Perfection of Security Interests in Multiple State Transactions.

(1) Documents, instruments and ordinary goods.

(a) This subsection applies to documents and instruments and to goods other than those covered by a certificate of title described in subsection (2), mobile goods described in subsection (3), and minerals described in subsection (5).

(b) Except as otherwise provided in this subsection, perfection and the effect of perfection or non-perfection of a security interest in collateral are governed by the law of the jurisdiction where the collateral is when the last event occurs on which is based the assertion that the security interest is perfected or unperfected.

(c) If the parties to a transaction creating a purchase money security interest in goods in one jurisdiction understand at the time that the security interest attaches that the goods will be kept in another jurisdiction, then the law of the other jurisdiction governs the perfection and the effect of perfection or non-perfection of the security interest from the time it attaches until thirty days after the debtor receives possession of the goods and thereafter if the goods are taken to the other jurisdiction before the end of the thirty-day period.

(d) When collateral is brought into and kept in this state while subject to a security interest perfected under the law of the jurisdiction from which the collateral was removed, the security interest remains perfected, but if action is required by Part 3 of this Article to perfect the security interest,

(i) if the action is not taken before the expiration of the period of perfection in the other jurisdiction or the end of four months after the collateral is brought into this state, whichever period first expires, the security interest becomes unperfected at the end of that period and is thereafter deemed to have been unperfected as against a person who became a purchaser after removal;

(ii) if the action is taken before the expiration of the period specified in subparagraph (i), the security interest continues perfected thereafter;

(iii) for the purpose of a priority over a buyer of consumer goods (subsection (2) of Section 9-307), the period of the effectiveness of a filing in the jurisdiction from which the collateral is removed is governed by the rules with respect to perfection in subparagraphs (i) and (ii).

(2) Certificate of title.

(a) This subsection applies to goods covered by a certificate of title issued under a statute of this state or of another jurisdiction under the law of which indication of a security interest on the certificate is required as a condition of perfection.

(b) Except as otherwise provided in this subsection, perfection and the effect of perfection or non-perfection of the security interest are governed by the law (including the conflict of laws rules) of the jurisdiction issuing the certificate until four months after the goods are removed from that jurisdiction and thereafter until the goods are registered in another jurisdiction, but in any event not beyond surrender of the certificate. After the expiration of that period, the goods are not covered by the certificate of title within the meaning of this section.

(c) Except with respect to the rights of a buyer described in the next paragraph, a security interest, perfected in another jurisdiction otherwise than by notation on a certificate of title, in goods brought into this state and thereafter covered by a certificate of title issued by this state is subject to the rules stated in paragraph (d) of subsection (1).

(d) If goods are brought into this state while a security interest therein is perfected in any manner under the law of the jurisdiction from which the goods are removed and a certificate of title is issued by this state and the certificate does not show that the goods are subject to the security interest or that they may be subject to security interests not shown on the certificate, the security interest is subordinate to the rights of a buyer of the goods who is not in the business of selling goods of that kind to the extent that he gives value and receives delivery of the goods after issuance of the certificate and without knowledge of the security interest.

(3) Accounts, general intangibles and mobile goods.

(a) This subsection applies to accounts (other than an account described in subsection (5) on minerals) and general intangibles and to goods which are mobile and which are of a type normally used in more than one jurisdiction, such as motor vehicles, trailers, rolling stock, airplanes, shipping containers, road building and construction machinery and commercial harvesting machinery and the like, if the goods are equipment or are inventory leased or held for lease by the debtor to others, and are not covered by a certificate of title described in subsection (2).

(b) The law (including the conflict of laws rules) of the jurisdiction in which the debtor is located governs the perfection or non-perfection of the security interest.

(c) If, however, the debtor is located in a jurisdiction which is not a part of the United States, and which does not provide for perfection of the security interest by filing or recording in that jurisdiction, the law of the jurisdiction in the United States in which the debtor has its major executive office in the United States governs the perfection and the effect of perfection or non-perfection of the security interest through filing. In the alternative, if the debtor is located in a jurisdiction which is not a part of the United States or Canada and the collateral is accounts or general intangibles for money due or to become due, the security interest may be perfected by notification to the account debtor. As used in this paragraph, "United States" includes its territories and possessions and the Commonwealth of Puerto Rico.

(d) A debtor shall be deemed located at his place of business if he has one, at his chief executive office if he has more than one place of business, otherwise at his residence. If, however, the debtor is a foreign air carrier under the Federal Aviation Act of 1958, as amended, it shall be deemed located at the designated office of the agent upon whom service of process may be made on behalf of the foreign air carrier.

(e) A security interest perfected under the law of the jurisdiction of the location of the debtor is perfected until the expiration of four months after a change of the debtor's location to another jurisdiction, or until perfection would have ceased by the law of the first jurisdiction, whichever period first expires. Unless perfected in the new jurisdiction before the end of that period, it becomes unperfected thereafter and is deemed to have been unperfected as against a person who became a purchaser after the change.

(4) Chattel paper.

The rules stated for goods in subsection (1) apply to a possessory security interest in chattel paper. The rules stated for accounts in subsection (3) apply to a non-possessory security interest in chattel paper, but the security interest may not be perfected by notification to the account debtor.

(5) Minerals.

Perfection and the effect of perfection or non-perfection of a security interest which is created by a debtor who has an interest in minerals or the like (including oil and gas) before extraction and which attaches thereto as extracted, or which attaches to an account resulting from the sale thereof at the wellhead or minehead are governed by the law (including the conflict or laws rules) of the jurisdiction wherein the wellhead or minehead is located.

Section 9-104. Transactions Excluded From Article. This Article does not apply

(a) to a security interest subject to any statute of the United States to the extent that such statute governs the rights of parties to and third parties affected by transactions in particular types of property; or

(b) to a landlord's lien; or

(c) to a lien given by statute or other rule of law for services or materials except as provided in Section 9-310 on priority of such liens; or

(d) to a transfer of a claim for wages, salary or other compensation of an employee; or

(e) to a transfer by a government or governmental subdivision or agency; or

(f) to a sale of accounts or chattel paper as part of a sale of the business out of which they arose, or an assignment of accounts or chattel paper which is for the purpose of collection only, or a transfer of a right to payment under a contract to an assignee who is also to do the performance under the contract or a transfer of a single account to an assignee in whole or partial satisfaction of a preexisting indebtedness; or

(g) to a transfer of an interest in or claim in or under any policy of insurance, except as provided with respect to proceeds (Section 9-306) and priorities in proceeds (Section 9-312); or

(h) to a right represented by a judgment (other than a judgment taken on a right to payment which was collateral); or

(i) to any right of set-off; or

(j) except to the extent that provision is made for fixtures in Section 9-313, to the creation or transfer of an interest in or lien on real estate, including a lease or rents thereunder; or

(k) to a transfer in whole or in part of any claim arising out of tort; or

(l) to a transfer of an interest in any deposit account (subsection (1) or Section 9-105), except as provided with respect to proceeds (Section 9-306) and priorities in proceeds (Section 9-312).

Section 9-105. Definitions and Index of Definitions.

(1) In this Article unless the context otherwise requires:

(a) "Account debtor" means the person who is obligated on an account, chattel paper or general intangible;

(b) "Chattel paper" means a writing or writings which evidence both a monetary obligation and a security interest in or a lease of specific goods, but a charter or other contract involving the use or hire of a vessel is not chattel paper. When a transaction is evidenced both by such a security agreement or a lease and by an instrument or a series of instruments, the group of writings taken together constitutes chattel paper;

(c) "Collateral" means the property subject to a security interest, and includes accounts and chattel paper which have been sold;

(d) "Debtor" means the person who owes payment or other performance of the obligation secured, whether or not he owns or has rights in the collateral, and includes the seller of accounts or chattel paper. Where the debtor and the owner of the collateral are not the same person, the term "debtor" means the owner of the collateral in any provision of the Article dealing with the collateral, the obligor in any provision dealing with the obligation, and may include both where the context so requires;

(e) "Deposit account" means a demand, time, savings, passbook or like account maintained with a bank, savings and loan association, credit union or like organization, other than an account evidenced by a certificate of deposit;

(f) "Document" means the document of title as defined in the general definitions of Article 1 (Section 1-201), and a receipt of the kind described in subsection (2) of Section 7-201;

(g) "Encumbrance" includes real estate

mortgages and other liens on real estate and all other rights in real estate that are not ownership interests;

(h) "Goods" includes all things which are movable at the time the security interest attaches or which are fixtures (Section 9-313), but does not include money, documents, instruments, accounts, chattel paper, general intangibles, or minerals or the like (including oil and gas) before extraction. "Goods" also includes standing timber which is to be cut and removed under a conveyance or contract for sale, the unborn young of animals, and growing crops;

(i) "Instrument" means a negotiable instrument (defined in Section 3-104), or a security (defined in Section 8-102) or any other writing which evidences a right to the payment of money and is not itself a security agreement or lease and is of a type which is in ordinary course of business transferred by delivery with any necessary indorsement or assignment;

(j) "Mortgage" means a consensual interest created by a real estate mortgage, a trust deed on real estate, or the like;

(k) An advance is made "pursuant to commitment" if the secured party has bound himself to make it, whether or not a subsequent event of default or other event not within his control has relieved or may relieve him from his obligation;

(l) "Security agreement" means an agreement which creates or provides for a security interest;

(m) "Secured party" means a lender, seller or other person in whose favor there is a security interest, including a person to whom accounts or chattel paper have been sold. When the holders of obligations issued under an indenture of trust, equipment trust agreement or the like are represented by a trustee or other person, the representative is the secured party;

(n) "Transmitting utility" means any person primarily engaged in the railroad, street railway or trolley bus business, the electric or electronics communications transmission business, the transmission of goods by pipeline, or the transmission or the production and transmission of electricity, steam, gas or water, or the provision of sewer service.

(2) Other definitions applying to this Article and the sections in which they appear are:

"Account". Section 9-106.
"Attach". Section 9-203.
"Construction mortgage". Section 9-313(1).
"Consumer goods". Section 9-109(1).
"Equipment". Section 9-109(2).
"Farm products". Section 9-109(3).
"Fixture". Section 9-313(1).
"Fixture filing". Section 9-313(1).
"General intangibles". Section 9-106.
"Inventory". Section 9-109(4).
"Lien creditor". Section 9-301(3).
"Proceeds". Section 9-306(1).
"Purchase money security interest". Section 9-107.
"United States". Section 9-103.

(3) The following definitions in other Articles apply to this Article:

"Check". Section 3-104.
"Contract for sale". Section 2-106.
"Holder in due course". Section 3-302.
"Note". Section 3-104.
"Sale". Section 2-106.

(4) In addition Article 1 contains general definitions and principles of construction and interpretation applicable throughout this Article.

Section 9-106. Definitions: "Account"; "General Intangibles." "Account means any right to payment for goods sold or leased or for services rendered which is not evidenced by an instrument or chattel paper, whether or not it has been earned by performance. "General intangibles" means any personal property (including things in action) other than goods, accounts, chattel paper, documents, instruments, and money. All rights to payment earned or unearned under a charter or other contract involving the use or hire of a vessel and all rights incident to the charter or contract are accounts.

Section 9-107. Definitions: "Purchase Money Security Interest." A security interest is a "purchase money security interest" to the extent that it is

(a) taken or retained by the seller of the collateral to secure all or part of its price; or

(b) taken by a person who by making advances or incurring an obligation gives value to enable the debtor to acquire rights in or the use of collateral if such value is in fact so used.

Section 9-108. When After-Acquired Collateral Not Security for Antecedent Debt. Where a secured party makes an advance, incurs an obligation, releases a perfected security interest, or otherwise gives new value which is to be secured in whole or in part by after-acquired property his security interest in the after-acquired collateral shall be deemed to be taken for new value and not as security for an antecedent debt if the debtor acquired his rights in such collateral either in the ordinary course of his business or under a contract of purchase made pursuant to the security agreement within a reasonable time after new value is given.

Section 9-109. Classification of Goods; "Consumer Goods"; "Equipment"; "Farm Products"; "Inventory." Goods are

(1) "consumer goods" if they are used or bought for use primarily for personal, family or household purposes;

(2) "equipment" if they are used or bought for use primarily in business (including farming or a profession) or by a debtor who is a non-profit organization or a governmental subdivision or agency or if the goods are not included in the definitions of inventory, farm products or consumer goods;

(3) "farm products" if they are crops or livestock or supplies used or produced in farming operations or if they are products or crops or livestock in their unmanufactured states (such as ginned cotton, wool-clip, maple syrup, milk and eggs), and if they are in the possession of a debtor engaged in raising, fattening, grazing or other farming operations. If goods are farm products they are neither equipment nor inventory;

(4) "inventory" if they are held by a person who holds them for sale or lease or to be furnished under contracts of service or if he has so furnished them, or if they are raw materials, work in process or materials used or consumed in a business. Inventory of a person is not to be classified as his equipment.

Section 9-110. Sufficiency of Description. For the purposes of this Article any description of personal property or real estate is sufficient whether or not it is specific if it reasonably identifies what is described.

Section 9-111. Applicability of Bulk Transfer Laws. The creation of a security interest is not a bulk transfer under Article 6 (see Section 6-103).

Section 9-112. Where Collateral is Not Owned by Debtor. Unless otherwise agreed, when a secured party knows that collateral is owned by a person who is not the debtor, the owner of the collateral is entitled to receive from the secured party any surplus under Section 9-502(2) or under Section 9-504(1), and is not liable for the debt or for any deficiency after resale, and he has the same right as the debtor

(a) to receive statements under Section 9-208;

(b) to receive notice of and to object to a secured party's proposal to retain the collateral in satisfaction of the indebtedness under Section 9-505;

(c) to redeem the collateral under Section 9-506;

(d) to obtain injunctive or other relief under Section 9-507(1); and

(e) to recover losses caused to him under Section 9-208(2).

Section 9-113. Security Interests Arising Under Article on Sales. A security interest arising solely under the Article on Sales (Article 2) is subject to the provisions of this Article except that to the extent that and so long as the debtor does not have or does not lawfully obtain possession of the goods

(a) no security agreement is necessary to make the security interest enforceable; and

(b) no filing is required to perfect the security interest; and

(c) the rights of the secured party on default by the debtor are governed by the Article on Sales (Article 2).

Section 9-114. Consignment.

(1) A person who delivers goods under a consignment which is not a security interest and who would be required to file under this Article by paragraph (3) (c) of Section 2-326 has priority over a secured party who is or becomes a creditor of the consignee and who would have a perfected security interest in the goods if they were the property of the consignee, and also has priority with respect to identifiable cash proceeds received on or before delivery of the goods to a buyer, if

(a) the consignor complies with the filing provision of the Article on Sales with respect to consignments (paragraph (3) (c) of Section 2-326) before the consignee receives possession of the goods;

and
(b) the consignor gives notification in writing to the holder of the security interest if the holder has filed a financing statement covering the same types of goods before the date of the filing made by the consignor; and
(c) the holder of the security interest receives the notification within five years before the consignee receives possession of the goods; and
(d) the notification states that the consignor expects to deliver goods on consignment to the consignee, describing the goods by item or type.

(2) In the case of a consignment which is not a security interest and in which the requirements of the preceding subsection have not been met, a person who delivers goods to another is subordinate to a person who would have a perfected security interest in the goods if they were the property of the debtor.

PART 2

VALIDITY OF SECURITY AGREEMENT AND RIGHTS OF PARTIES THERETO

Section 9-201. General Validity of Security Agreement. Except as otherwise provided by this Act a security agreement is effective according to its terms between the parties, against purchasers of the collateral and against creditors. Nothing in this Article validates any charge or practice illegal under any statute or regulation thereunder governing usury, small loans, retail installment sales, or the like, or extends the application of any such statute or regulation to any transaction not otherwise subject thereto.

Section 9-202. Title to Collateral Immaterial. Each provision of this Article with regard to rights, obligations and remedies applies whether title to collateral is in the secured party or in the debtor.

Section 9-203. Attachment and Enforceability of Security Interest; Proceeds; Formal Requisites.

(1) Subject to the provisions of Section 4-208 on the security interest of a collecting bank and Section 9-113 on a security interest arising under the Article on Sales, a security interest is not enforceable against the debtor or third parties with respect to the collateral and does not attach unless
(a) the collateral is in the possession of the secured party pursuant to agreement, or the debtor has signed a security agreement which contains a description of the collateral and in addition, when the security interest covers crops growing or to be grown or timber to be cut, a description of the land concerned; and
(b) value has been given; and
(c) the debtor has rights in the collateral.

(2) A security interest attaches when it becomes enforceable against the debtor with respect to the collateral. Attachment occurs as soon as all of the events specified in subsection (1) have taken place unless explicit agreement postpones the time of attaching.

(3) Unless otherwise agreed a security agreement gives the secured party the rights to proceeds provided by Section 9-306.

(4) A transaction, although subject to this Article, is also subject to ....*, and in the case of conflict between the provisions of this Article and any such statute, the provisions of such statute control. Failure to comply with any applicable statute has only the effect which is specified therein.

Section 9-204. After-Acquired Property; Future Advances.

(1) Except as provided in subsection (2), a security agreement may provide that any or all obligations covered by the security agreement are to be secured by after-acquired collateral.

(2) No security interest attaches under an after-acquired property clause to consumer goods other than accessions (Section 9-314) when given as additional security unless the debtor acquires rights in them within ten days after the secured party gives value.

(3) Obligations covered by a security agreement may include future advances or other value whether or not the advances or value are given pursuant to commitment (subsection (1) of Section 9-105).

Section 9-205. Use or Disposition of Collateral Without Accounting Permissible. A security interest is not invalid or fraudulent against creditors by reason of liberty in the debtor to use, commingle or dispose of all or part of the collateral (including returned or repossessed goods) or to collect or compromise accounts or chattel paper, or to accept the return of goods or make repossessions, or to use, commingle or dispose of proceeds, or by reason of the failure of the secured party to require the debtor to account for proceeds or replace collateral. This section does not relax the requirements of possession where perfection of a security interest depends upon possession of the collateral by the secured party or by a bailee.

Section 9-206. Agreement Not to Assert Defenses Against Assignee; Modification of Sales Warranties Where Security Agreement Exists.

(1) Subject to any statute or decision which establishes a different rule for buyers or lessees of consumer goods an agreement by a buyer or lessee that he will not assert against an assignee any claim or defense which he may have against the seller or lessor is enforceable by an assignee who takes his assignment for value, in good faith and without notice of a claim or defense, except as to defenses of a type which may be asserted against a holder in due course of a negotiable instrument under the Article on Commercial Paper (Article 3). A buyer who as part of one transaction signs both a negotiable instrument and a security agreement makes such an agreement.

(2) When a seller retains a purchase money security interest in goods the Article on Sales (Article 2) governs the sale and any disclaimer, limitation or modification of the seller's warranties.

Section 9-207. Rights and Duties When Collateral Is In Secured Party's Possession.

(1) A secured party must use reasonable care in the custody and preservation of collateral in his possession. In the case of an instrument or chattel paper reasonable care includes taking necessary steps to preserve rights against prior parties unless otherwise agreed.

(2) Unless otherwise agreed, when collateral is in the secured party's possession

(a) reasonable expenses (including the cost of any insurance and payment of taxes or other charges) incurred in the custody, preservation, use or operation of the collateral are chargeable to the debtor and are secured by the collateral;

(b) the risk of accidental loss or damage is on the debtor to the extent of any deficiency in any effective insurance coverage;

(c) the secured party may hold as additional security any increase or profits (except money) received from the collateral, but money so received, unless remitted to the debtor, shall be applied in reduction of the secured obligation;

(d) the secured party must keep the collateral identifiable but fungible collateral may be commingled;

(e) the secured party may repledge the collateral upon terms which do not impair the debtor's right to redeem it.

(3) A secured party is liable for any loss caused by his failure to meet any obligation imposed by the preceding subsections but does not lose his security interest.

(4) A secured party may use or operate the collateral for the purpose of preserving the collateral or its value or pursuant to the order of a court of appropriate jurisdiction or, except in the case of consumer goods, in the manner and to the extent provided in the security agreement.

Section 9-208. Request for Statement of Account or List of Collateral.

(1) A debtor may sign a statement indicating what he believes to be the aggregate amount of unpaid indebtedness as of a specified date and may send it to the secured party with a request that the statement be approved or corrected and returned to the debtor. When the security agreement or any other record kept by the secured party identifies the collateral a debtor may similarly request the secured party to approve or correct a list of the collateral.

(2) The secured party must comply with such a request within two weeks after receipt by sending a written correction or approval. If the secured party claims a security interest in all of a particular type of collateral owned by the debtor he may indicate that fact in his reply and need not approve or correct an itemized list of such collateral. If the secured party without reasonable excuse fails to comply he is liable for any loss caused to the debtor thereby; and if the debtor has properly included in his request a good faith statement of the obligation or a list of the collateral or both the secured party may claim a security in-

terest only as shown in the statement against persons misled by his failure to comply. If he no longer has an interest in the obligation or collateral at the time the request is received he must disclose the name and address of any successor in interest known to him and he is liable for any loss caused to the debtor as a result of failure to disclose. A successor in interest is not subject to this section until a request is received by him.

(3) A debtor is entitled to such a statement once every six months without charge. The secured party may require payment of a charge not exceeding $10 for each additional statement furnished.

PART 3

RIGHTS OF THIRD PARTIES; PERFECTED AND UNPERFECTED SECURITY INTERESTS; RULES OF PRIORITY

Section 9-301. Persons Who Take Priority Over Unperfected Security Interests; Rights of "Lien Creditor."

(1) Except as otherwise provided in subsection (2), an unperfected security interest is subordinate to the rights of

(a) persons entitled to priority under Section 9-312;

(b) a person who becomes a lien creditor before the security interest is perfected;

(c) in the case of goods, instruments, documents, and chattel paper, a person who is not a secured party and who is a transferee in bulk or other buyer not in ordinary course of business or is a buyer of farm products in ordinary course of business, to the extent that he gives value and receives delivery of the collateral without knowledge of the security interest and before it is perfected;

(d) in the case of accounts and general intangibles, a person who is not a secured party and who is a transferee to the extent that he gives value without knowledge of the security interest and before it is perfected.

(2) If the secured party files with respect to a purchase money security interest before or within ten days after the debtor receives possession of the collateral, he takes priority over the rights of a transferee in bulk or of a lien creditor which arise between the time the security interest attaches and the time of filing.

(3) A "lien creditor" means a creditor who has acquired a lien on the property involved by attachment, levy or the like and includes an assignee for benefit of creditors from the time of assignment, and a trustee in bankruptcy from the date of filing of the petition or a receiver in equity from the time of appointment.

(4) A person who becomes a lien creditor while a security interest is perfected takes subject to the security interest only to the extent that it secures advances made before he becomes a lien creditor or within 45 days thereafter or made without knowledge of the lien pursuant to a commitment entered into without knowledge of the lien.

Section 9-302. When Filing is Required to Perfect Security Interest; Security Interests to Which Filing Provisions of This Article Do Not Apply.

(1) A financing statement must be filed to perfect all security interests except the following:

(a) a security interest in collateral in possession of the secured party under Section 9-305;

(b) a security interest temporarily perfected in instruments or documents without delivery under Section 9-304 or in proceeds for a 10 day period under Section 9-306;

(c) a security interest created by an assignment of a beneficial interest in a trust or a decedent's estate;

(d) a purchase money security interest in consumer goods; but filing is required for a motor vehicle required to be registered; and fixture filing is required for priority over conflicting interests in fixtures to the extent provided in Section 9-313;

(e) an assignment of accounts which does not alone or in conjunction with other assignments to the same assignee transfer a significant part of the outstanding accounts of the assignor;

(f) a security interest of a collecting bank

(Section 4-208) or arising under the Article on Sales (see Section 9-113) or covered in subsection (3) of this section;

(g) an assignment for the benefit of all the creditors of the transferor, and subsequent transfers by the assignee thereunder.

(2) If a secured party assigns a perfected security interest, no filing under this Article is required in order to continue the perfected status of the security interest against creditors of and transferees from the original debtor.

(3) The filing of a financing statement otherwise required by this Article is not necessary or effective to perfect a security interest in property subject to

(a) a statute or treaty of the United States which provides for a national or international registration or a national or international certificate of title or which specifies a place of filing different from that specified in this Article for filing of the security interest; or

(b) the following statutes of this state; [list any certificate of title statute covering automobiles, trailers, mobile homes, boats, farm tractors, or the like, and any central filing statute*.]; but during any period in which collateral is inventory held for sale by a person who is in the business of selling goods of that kind, the filing provisions of this Article (Part 4) apply to a security interest in that collateral created by him as debtor; or

(c) a certificate of title statute of another jurisdiction under the law of which indication of a security interest on the certificate is required as a condition of perfection (subsection (2) of Section 9-103).

(4) Compliance with a statute or treaty described in subsection (3) is equivalent to the filing of a financing statement under this Article, and a security interest in property subject to the statute or treaty can be perfected only by compliance therewith except as provided in Section 9-103 on multiple state transactions. Duration and renewal of perfection of a security interest perfected by compliance with the statute or treaty are governed by the provisions of the statute or treaty; in other respects the security interest is subject to this Article.

Section 9-303. When Security Interest Is Perfected; Continuity of Perfection.

(1) A security interest is perfected when it has attached and when all of the applicable steps required for perfection have been taken. Such steps are specified in Sections 9-302, 9-304, 9-305 and 9-306. If such steps are taken before the security interest attaches, it is perfected at the time when it attaches.

(2) If a security interest is originally perfected in any way permitted under this Article and is subsequently perfected in some other way under this Article, without an intermediate period when it was unperfected, the security interest shall be deemed to be perfected continuously for the purposes of this Article.

Section 9-304. Perfection of Security Interest in Instruments, Documents, and Goods Covered by Documents; Perfection by Permissive Filing; Temporary Perfection Without Filing or Transfer of Possession.

(1) A security interest in chattel paper or negotiable documents may be perfected by filing. A security interest in money or instruments (other than instruments which constitute part of chattel paper) can be perfected only by the secured party's taking possession, except as provided in subsections (4) and (5) of this section and subsections (2) and (3) of Section 9-306 on proceeds.

(2) During the period that goods are in the possession of the issuer of a negotiable document therefor, a security interest in the goods is perfected by perfecting a security interest in the document, and any security interest in the goods otherwise perfected during such period is subject thereto.

(3) A security interest in goods in the possession of a bailee other than one who has issued a negotiable document therefor is perfected by issuance of a document in the name of the secured party or by the bailee's receipt of notification of the secured party's interest or by filing as to the goods.

(4) A security interest in instruments or negotiable documents is perfected without filing or the taking of possession for a period of 21 days from the time it attaches to the extent that it arises for new value given under a written security agreement.

(5) A security interest remains perfected for

a period of 21 days without filing where a secured party having a perfected security interest in an instrument, a negotiable document or goods in possession of a bailee other than one who has issued a negotiable document therefor

(a) makes available to the debtor the goods or documents representing the goods for the purpose of ultimate sale or exchange or for the purpose of loading, unloading, storing, shipping, transshipping, manufacturing, processing or otherwise dealing with them in a manner preliminary to their sale or exchange, but priority between conflicting security interests in the goods is subject to subsection (3) of Section 9-312; or

(b) delivers the instrument to the debtor for the purpose of ultimate sale or exchange or of presentation, collection, renewal or registration of transfer.

(6) After the 21 day period in subsections (4) and (5) perfection depends upon compliance with applicable provisions of this Article.

Section 9-305. When Possession by Secured Party Perfects Security Interest Without Filing. A security interest in letters of credit and advices of credit (subsection (2) (a) of Section 5-116), goods, instruments, money, negotiable documents or chattel paper may be perfected by the secured party's taking possession of the collateral. If such collateral other than goods covered by a negotiable document is held by a bailee, the secured party is deemed to have possession from the time the bailee receives notification of the secured party's interest. A security interest is perfected by possession from the time possession is taken without relation back and continues only so long as possession is retained, unless otherwise specified in this Article. The security interest may be otherwise perfected as provided in this Article before or after the period of possession by the secured party.

Section 9-306. "Proceeds"; Secured Party's Rights on Disposition of Collateral.

(1) "Proceeds" includes whatever is received upon the sale, exchange, collection or other disposition of collateral or proceeds. Insurance payable by reason of loss or damage to the collateral is proceeds, except to the extent that it is payable to a person other than a party to the security agreement. Money, checks, deposit accounts, and the like are "cash proceeds". All other proceeds are "non-cash proceeds".

(2) Except where this Article otherwise provides, a security interest continues in collateral notwithstanding sale, exchange or other disposition thereof unless the disposition was authorized by the secured party in the security agreement or otherwise, and also continues in any identifiable proceeds including collections received by the debtor.

(3) The security interest in proceeds in a continuously perfected security interest if the interest in the original collateral was perfected but it ceases to be a perfected security interest and becomes unperfected ten days after receipt of the proceeds by the debtor unless

(a) a filed financing statement covers the original collateral and the proceeds are collateral in which a security interest may be perfected by filing in the office or offices where the financing statement has been filed and, if the proceeds are acquired with cash proceeds, the description of collateral in the financing statement indicates the types of property constituting the proceeds; or

(b) a filed financing statement covers the original collateral and the proceeds are identifiable cash proceeds; or

(c) the security interest in the proceeds is perfected before the expiration of the ten day period.

Except as provided in this section, a security interest in proceeds can be perfected only by the methods or under the circumstances permitted in this Article for original collateral of the same type.

(4) In the event of insolvency proceedings instituted by or against a debtor, a secured party with a perfected security interest in proceeds has a perfected security interest only in the following proceeds:

(a) in identifiable non-cash proceeds and in separate deposit accounts containing only proceeds;

(b) in identifiable cash proceeds in the form of money which is neither commingled with other money nor deposited in a deposit account prior to the insolvency proceedings;

(c) in identifiable cash proceeds in the form of checks and the like which are not deposited in a deposit account prior to the insolvency proceedings; and

(d) in all cash and deposit accounts of the debtor in which proceeds have been commingled with other funds, but the perfected security interest under this paragraph (d) is

(i) subject to any right to set-off; and

(ii) limited to an amount not greater than the amount of any cash proceeds received by the debtor within ten days before the institution of the insolvency proceedings less the sum of (I) the payments to the secured party on account of cash proceeds received by the debtor during such period and (II) the cash proceeds received by the debtor during such period to which the secured party is entitled under paragraphs (a) through (c) of this subsection (4).

(5) If a sale of goods results in an account or chattel paper which is transferred by the seller to a secured party, and if the goods are returned to or are repossessed by the seller or the secured party, the following rules determine priorities:

(a) If the goods were collateral at the time of sale, for an indebtedness of the seller which is still unpaid, the original security interest attaches again to the goods and continues as a perfected security interest if it was perfected at the time when the goods were sold. If the security interest was originally perfected by a filing which is still effective, nothing further is required to continue the perfected status; in any other case, the secured party must take possession of the returned or repossessed goods or must file.

(b) An unpaid transferee of the chattel paper has a security interest in the goods against the transferor. Such security interest is prior to a security interest asserted under paragraph (a) to the extent that the transferee of the chattel paper was entitled to priority under Section 9-308.

(c) An unpaid transferee to the account has a security interest in the goods against the transferor. Such security interest is subordinate to a security interest asserted under paragraph (a).

(d) A security interest of an unpaid transferee asserted under paragraph (b) or (c) must be perfected for protection against creditors of the transferor and purchasers of the returned or repossessed goods.

Section 9-307. Protection of Buyers of Goods.

(1) A buyer in ordinary course of business (subsection (9) of Section 1-201) other than a person buying farm products from a person engaged in farming operations takes free of a security interest created by his seller even though the security interest is perfected and even though the buyer knows of its existence.

(2) In the case of consumer goods, a buyer takes free of a security interest even though perfected if he buys without knowledge of the security interest, for value and for his own personal, family or household purposes unless prior to the purchase the secured party has filed a financing statement covering such goods.

(3) A buyer other than a buyer in ordinary course of business (subsection (1) of this section) takes free of a security interest to the extent that it secures future advances made after the secured party acquires knowledge of the purchase, or more than 45 days after the purchase, whichever first occurs, unless made pursuant to a commitment entered into without knowledge of the purchase and before the expiration of the 45 day period.

Section 9-308. Purchase of Chattel Paper and Instruments. A purchaser of chattel paper or an instrument who gives new value and takes possession of it in the ordinary course of his business has priority over a security interest in the chattel paper or instrument

(a) which is perfected under Section 9-304 (permissive filing and temporary perfection) or under Section 9-306 (perfection as to proceeds) if he acts without knowledge that the specific paper or instrument is subject to a security interest; or

(b) which is claimed merely as proceeds of inventory subject to a security interest (Section 9-306) even though he knows that the specific paper or instrument is subject to the security interest.

Section 9-309. Protection of Purchasers of Instruments and Documents. Nothing in this Article limits the rights of a holder in due course of a negotiable instrument (Section 3-302) or a holder to whom a negotiable document of title has been duly negotiated (Section 7-501) or a bona fide purchaser of a security (Section 8-301) and such holders or purchasers take priority over an earlier security interest even though perfected. Filing under this Article does not constitute notice of the security interest to such holders or purchasers.

Section 9-310. Priority of Certain Liens Arising by Operation of Law. When a person in the ordinary course of his business furnishes services or materials with respect to goods subject to a security interest, a lien upon goods in the possession of such person given by statute or rule of law for such materials or services takes priority over a perfected security interest unless the lien is statutory and the statute expressly provides otherwise.

Section 9-311. Alienability of Debtor's Rights: Judicial Process. The debtor's rights in collateral may be voluntarily or involuntarily transferred (by way of sale, creation of a security interest, attachment, levy, garnishment or other judicial process) notwithstanding a provision in the security agreement prohibiting any transfer or making the transfer constitute a default.

Section 9-312. Priorities Among Conflicting Security Interests in the Same Collateral.

(1) The rules of priority stated in other sections of this Part and in the following sections shall govern when applicable: Section 4-208 with respect to the security interests of collecting banks in items being collected, accompanying documents and proceeds; Section 9-103 on security interests related to other jurisdictions; Section 9-114 on consignments.

(2) A perfected security interest in crops for new value given to enable the debtor to produce the crops during the production season and given not more than three months before the crops become growing crops by planting or otherwise takes priority over an earlier perfected security interest to the extent that such earlier interest secured obligations due more than six months before the crops become growing crops by planting or otherwise, even though the person giving new value has knowledge of the earlier security interest.

(3) A perfected purchase money security interest in inventory has priority over a conflicting security interest in the same inventory and also has priority in identifiable cash proceeds received on or before the delivery of the inventory to a buyer if

(a) the purchase money security interest is perfected at the time the debtor receives possession of the inventory; and

(b) the purchase money secured party gives notification in writing to the holder of the conflicting security interest if the holder had filed a financing statement covering the same types of inventory (i) before the date of the filing made by the purchase money secured party, or (ii) before the beginning of the 21 day period where the purchase money security interest is temporarily perfected without filing or possession (subsection (5) of Section 9-304); and

(c) the holder of the conflicting security interest receives the notification within five years before the debtor receives possession of the inventory; and

(d) the notification states that the person giving the notice has or expects to acquire a purchase money security interest in inventory of the debtor, describing such inventory by item or type.

(4) A purchase money security interest in collateral other than inventory has priority over a conflicting security interest in the same collateral or its proceeds if the purchase money security interest is perfected at the time the debtor receives possession of the collateral or within ten days thereafter.

(5) In all cases not governed by other rules stated in this section (including cases of purchase money security interests which do not qualify for the special priorities set forth in subsections (3) and (4) of this section), priority between conflicting security interests in the same collateral shall be determined according to the following rules:

(a) Conflicting security interests rank according to priority in time of filing or perfection. Priority dates from the time a filing is first made covering the collateral or the time the security interest is first perfected, whichever is earlier, provided that there is no period thereafter when there is neither filing nor perfection.

(b) So long as conflicting security interests are unperfected, the first to attach has priority.

(6) For the purposes of subsection (5) a date of filing or perfection as to collateral is also a date of filing or perfection as to proceeds.

(7) If future advances are made while a security interest is perfected by filing or the taking of possession, the security interest has the same priority for the purposes of subsection (5) with respect to the future advances as it does with respect to the first advance. If a commitment is made before or while the security interest is so perfected, the security interest has the same priority with respect to advances made pursuant thereto. In other cases a perfected security interest has priority from the date the advance is made.

Section 9-313. Priority of Security Interests in Fixtures.

(1) In this section and in the provisions of Part 4 of this Article referring to fixture filing, unless the context otherwise requires

(a) goods are "fixtures" when they become so related to particular real estate that an interest in them arises under real estate law

(b) a "fixture filing" is the filing in the office where a mortgage on the real estate would be filed or recorded of a financing statement covering goods which are or are to become fixtures and conforming to the requirements of subsection (5) of Section 9-402

(c) a mortgage is a "construction mortgage" to the extent that it secures an obligation incurred for the construction of an improvement on land including the acquisition cost of the land, if the recorded writing so indicates.

(2) A security interest under this Article may be created in goods which are fixtures or may continue in goods which become fixtures, but no security interest exists under this Article in ordinary building materials incorporated into an improvement on land.

(3) This Article does not prevent creation of an encumbrance upon fixtures pursuant to real estate law.

(4) A perfected security interest in fixtures has priority over the conflicting interest of an encumbrancer or owner of the real estate where

(a) the security interest is a purchase money security interest, the interest of the encumbrancer or owner arises before the goods become fixtures, the security interest is perfected by a fixture filing before the goods become fixtures or within ten days thereafter, and the debtor has an interest of record in the real estate or is in possession of the real estate; or

(b) the security interest is perfected by a fixture filing before the interest of the encumbrancer or owner is of record, the security interest has priority over any conflicting interest of a predecessor in title of the encumbrancer or owner, and the debtor has an interest of record in the real estate or is in possession of the real estate; or

(c) the fixtures are readily removable factory or office machines or readily removable replacements of domestic appliances which are consumer goods, and before the goods become fixtures the security interest is perfected by any method permitted by this Article; or

(d) the conflicting interest is a lien on the real estate obtained by legal or equitable proceedings after the security interest was perfected by any method permitted by this Article.

(5) A security interest in fixtures, whether or not perfected, has priority over the conflicting interest of an encumbrancer or owner of the real estate where

(a) the encumbrancer or owner has consented in writing to the security interest or has disclaimed an interest in the goods as fixtures; or

(b) the debtor has a right to remove the goods as against the encumbrancer or owner. If the debtor's right terminates, the priority of the security interest continues for a reasonable time.

(6) Notwithstanding paragraph (a) of subsection (4) but otherwise subject to subsections (4) and (5), a security interest in fixtures is subordinate to a construction

mortgage recorded before the goods become fixtures if the goods become fixtures before the completion of the construction. To the extent that it is given to refinance a construction mortgage, a mortgage has this priority to the same extent as the construction mortgage.

(7) In cases not within the preceding subsections, a security interest in fixtures is subordinate to the conflicting interest of an encumbrancer or owner of the related real estate who is not the debtor.

(8) When the secured party has priority over all owners and encumbrancers of the real estate, he may, on default, subject to the provisions of Part 5, remove his collateral from the real estate but he must reimburse any encumbrancer or owner of the real estate who is not the debtor and who has not otherwise agreed for the cost of repair of any physical injury, but not for any diminution in value of the real estate caused by the absence of the goods removed or by any necessity of replacing them. A person entitled to reimbursement may refuse permission to remove until the secured party gives adequate security for the performance of this obligation.

Section 9-314. Accessions.

(1) A security interest in goods which attaches before they are installed in or affixed to other goods takes priority as to the goods installed or affixed (called in this section "accessions") over the claims of all persons to the whole except as stated in subsection (3) and subject to Section 9-315(1).

(2) A security interest which attaches to goods after they become part of a whole is valid against all persons subsequently acquiring interests in the whole except as stated in subsection (3) but is invalid against any person with an interest in the whole at the time the security interest attaches to the goods who has not in writing consented to the security interest or disclaimed an interest in the goods as part of the whole.

(3) The security interests described in subsections (1) and (2) do not take priority over

(a) a subsequent purchaser for value of any interest in the whole; or

(b) a creditor with a lien on the whole subsequently obtained by judicial proceedings; or

(c) a creditor with a prior perfected security interest in the whole to the extent that he makes subsequent advances

if the subsequent purchase is made, the lien by judicial proceedings obtained or the subsequent advance under the prior perfected security interest is made or contracted for without knowledge of the security interest and before it is perfected. A purchaser of the whole at a foreclosure sale other than the holder of a perfected security interest purchasing at his own foreclosure sale is a subsequent purchaser within this section.

(4) When under subsections (1) or (2) and (3) a secured party has an interest in accessions which has priority over the claims of all persons who have interests in the whole, he may on default subject to the provisions of Part 5 remove his collateral from the whole but he must reimburse any encumbrancer or owner of the whole who is not the debtor and who has not otherwise agreed for the cost of repair of any physical injury but not for any diminution in value of the whole caused by the absence of the goods removed or by any necessity for replacing them. A person entitled to reimbursement may refuse permission to remove until the secured party gives adequate security for the performance of this obligation.

Section 9-315. Priority When Goods Are Commingled or Processed.

(1) If a security interest in goods was perfected and subsequently the goods or a part thereof have become part of a product or mass, the security interest continues in the product or mass if

(a) the goods are so manufactured, processed, assembled or commingled that their identity is lost in the product or mass; or

(b) a financing statement covering the original goods also covers the product into which the goods have been manufactured, processed or assembled.

In a case to which paragraph (b) applies, no separate security interest in that part of the original goods which has been manufactured, processed or assembled into the product may be claimed under Section 9-314.

(2) When under subsection (1) more than

one security interest attaches to the product or mass, they rank equally according to the ratio that the cost of the goods to which each interest originally attached bears to the cost of the total product or mass.

Section 9-316. Priority Subject to Subordination. Nothing in this Article prevents subordination by agreement by any person entitled to priority.

Section 9-317. Secured Party Not Obligated on Contract of Debtor. The mere existence of a security interest or authority given to the debtor to dispose of or use collateral does not impose contract or tort liability upon the secured party for the debtor's acts or omissions.

Section 9-318. Defenses Against Assignee; Modification of Contract After Notification of Assignment; Term Prohibiting Assignment Ineffective; Identification and Proof of Assignment.

(1) Unless an account debtor has made an enforceable agreement not to assert defenses or claims arising out of a sale as provided in Section 9-206 the rights of an assignee are subject to

(a) all the terms of the contract between the account debtor and assignor and any defense or claim arising therefrom; and

(b) any other defense or claim of the account debtor against the assignor which accrues before the account debtor receives notification of the assignment.

(2) So far as the right to payment or a part thereof under an assigned contract has not been fully earned by performance, and notwithstanding notification of the assignment, any modification of or substitution for the contract made in good faith and in accordance with reasonable commercial standards is effective against an assignee unless the account debtor has otherwise agreed but the assignee acquires corresponding rights under the modified or substituted contract. The assignment may provide that such modification or substitution is a breach by the assignor.

(3) The account debtor is authorized to pay the assignor until the account debtor receives notification that the amount due or to become due has been assigned and that payment is to be made to the assignee. A notification which does not reasonably identify the rights assigned is ineffective. If requested by the account debtor, the assignee must seasonably furnish reasonable proof that the assignment has been made and unless he does so the account debtor may pay the assignor.

(4) A term in any contract between an account debtor and an assignor is ineffective if it prohibits assignment of an account or prohibits creation of a security interest in a general intangible for money due or to become due or requires the account debtor's consent to such assignment or security interest.

PART 4

FILING

Section 9-401. Place of Filing; Erroneous Filing; Removal of Collateral.

First Alternative Subsection (1)

(1) The proper place to file in order to perfect a security interest is as follows:

(a) when the collateral is timber to be cut or is minerals or the like (including oil and gas) or accounts subject to subsection (5) of Section 9-103, or when the financing statement is filed as a fixture filing (Section 9-313) and the collateral is goods which are or are to become fixtures, then in the office where a mortgage on the real estate would be filed or recorded;

(b) in all other cases, in the office of the [Secretary of State].

Second Alternative Subsection (1)

(1) The proper place to file in order to perfect a security interest is as follows:

(a) when the collateral is equipment used in farming operations, or farm products, or accounts or general intangibles arising from or relating to the sale of farm products by a farmer, or consumer goods, then in the office of the .... in the county of the debtor's residence or if the debtor is not a resident in this state then in the office of the .... in the county where the goods are kept, and in addition when the collateral is crops growing or to be grown in the office of the .... in the county where the land is located;

(b) when the collateral is timber to be cut or is minerals or the like (including oil and gas) or accounts subject to subsection (5) of Section 9-103, or when the financing statement is filed as a fixture filing (Section 9-313) and the collateral is goods which are or are to become fixtures, then in the office where a mortgage on the real estate would be filed or recorded;

(c) in all other cases, in the office of the [Secretary of State].

Third Alternative Subsection (1)

(1) The proper place to file in order to perfect a security interest is as follows:

(a) when the collateral is equipment used in farming operations, or farm products, or accounts or general intangibles arising from or relating to the sale of farm products by a farmer, or consumer goods, then in the office of the .... in the county of the debtor's residence or if the debtor is not a resident of this state then in the office of the .... in the county where the goods are kept, and in addition when the collateral is crops growing or to be grown in the office of the .... in the county where the land is located;

(b) when the collateral is timber to be cut or is minerals or the like (including oil and gas) or accounts subject to subsection (5) of Section 9-103, or when the financing statement is filed as a fixture filing (Section 9-313) and the collateral is goods which are or are to become fixtures, then in the office where a mortgage on the real estate would be filed or recorded;

(c) in all other cases, in the office of the [Secretary of State] and in addition, if the debtor has a place of business in only one county of this state, also in the office of .... of such county, or, if the debtor has no place of business in this state, but resides in the state, also in the office of .... of the county in which he resides.

NOTE: *One of the three alternatives should be selected as subsection (1).*

(2) A filing which is made in good faith in an improper place or not in all of the places required by this section is nevertheless effective with regard to any collateral as to which the filing complied with the requirements of this Article and is also effective with regard to collateral covered by the financing statement against any person who has knowledge of the contents of such financing statement.

(3) A filing which is made in the proper place in this state continues effective even though the debtor's residence or place of business or the location of the collateral or its use, whichever controlled the original filing, is thereafter changed.

Alternative Subsection (3)

[(3) A filing which is made in the proper county continues effective for four months after a change to another county of the debtor's residence or place of business or the location of the collateral, whichever controlled the original filing. It becomes ineffective thereafter unless a copy of the financing statement signed by the secured party is filed in the new county within said period. The security interest may also be perfected in the new county after the expiration of the four-month period; in such case perfection dates from the time of perfection in the new county. A change in the use of the collateral does not impair the effectiveness of the original filing.]

(4) The rules stated in Section 9-103 determine whether filing is necessary in this state.

(5) Notwithstanding the preceding subsections, and subject to subsection (3) of Section 9-302, the proper place to file in order to perfect a security interest in collateral, including fixtures, of a transmitting utility is the office of the [Secretary of State]. This filing constitutes a fixture filing (Section 9-313) as to the collateral described

therein which is or is to become fixtures.

(6) For the purposes of this section, the residence of an organization is its place of business if it has one or its chief executive office if it has more than one place of business.

Section 9-402. Formal Requisites of Financing Statement; Amendments; Mortgage as Financing Statement.

(1) A financing statement is sufficient if it gives the names of the debtor and the secured party, is signed by the debtor, gives an address of the secured party from which information concerning the security interest may be obtained, gives a mailing address of the debtor and contains a statement indicating the types, or describing the items, of collateral. A financing statement may be filed before the security agreement is made or a security interest otherwise attaches. When the financing statement covers crops growing or to be grown, the statement must also contain a description of the real estate concerned. When the financing statement covers timber to be cut or covers minerals, or the like, (including oil and gas) or accounts subject to subsection (5) of Section 9-103, or when the financial statement is filed as a fixture filing (Section 9-313) and the collateral is goods which are or are to become fixtures, the statement must also comply with subsection (5). A copy of the security agreement is sufficient as a financing statement if it contains the above information and is signed by the debtor. A carbon, photographic or other reproduction of a security agreement or a financing statement is sufficient as a financing statement if the security agreement so provides or if the original has been filed in this state.

(2) A financing statement which otherwise complies with subsection (1) is sufficient when it is signed by the secured party instead of the debtor if it is filed to perfect a security interest in

(a) collateral already subject to a security interest in another jurisdiction when it is brought into this state, or when the debtor's location is changed to this state. Such a financing statement must state that the collateral was brought into this state or that the debtor's location was changed to this state under such circumstances; or

(b) proceeds under Section 9-306 if the security interest in the original collateral was perfected. Such a financing statement must describe the original collateral; or

(c) collateral as to which the filing has lapsed; or

(d) collateral acquired after a change of name, identity or corporate structure of the debtor (subsection (7)).

(3) A form substantially as follows is sufficient to comply with subsection (1):

Name of debtor (or assignor) . . . .
Address . . . .
Name of secured party (or assignee) . . . .
Address . . . .

1. This financing statement covers the following types (or items) of property:
   (Describe) . . . .
2. (If collateral is crops) The above crops are growing or are to be grown on:
   (Describe Real Estate) . . . .
3. (If applicable) The above goods are to become fixtures on*
   (Describe Real Estate) . . . .
   and this financing statement is to be filed [for record] in the real estate records. (If the debtor does not have an interest of record) The name of a record owner is . . . .
4. (If products of collateral are claimed) Products of the collateral are also covered. Signature of Debtor (or Assignor). . . . .
   Signature of Secured Party (or Assignee). . . . .
   (use whichever is applicable)

(4) A financing statement may be amended by filing a writing signed by both the debtor and the secured party. An amendment does not extend the period of effectiveness of a financing statement. If any amendment adds collateral, it is effective as to the added collateral only from the filing date of the amendment. In this Article, unless the context otherwise requires, the term "financial statement" means the original financing statement and any amendments.

(5) A financing statement covering timber

*Where appropriate substitute either "The above timber is standing on . . . ." or "The above minerals or the like (including oil and gas) or accounts will be financed at the wellhead or minehead of the well or mine located on . . . ."

to be cut or covering minerals or the like (including oil and gas) or accounts subject to subsection (5) of Section 9-103, or a financing statement filed as a fixture filing (Section 9-313) where the debtor is not a transmitting utility, must show that it covers this type of collateral, must recite that it is to be filed [for record] in the real estate records, and the financing statement must contain a description of the real estate [sufficient if it were contained in a mortgage of the real estate to give constructive notice of the mortgage under the law of this state]. If the debtor does not have an interest of record in the real estate, the financing statement must show the name of a record owner.

(6) A mortgage is effective as a financing statement filed as a fixture filing from the date of its recording if

(a) the goods are described in the mortgage by item or type; and

(b) the goods are or are to become fixtures related to the real estate described in the mortgage; and

(c) the mortgage complies with the requirements for a financing statement in this section other than a recital that it is to be filed in the real estate records; and

(d) the mortgage is duly recorded.

No fee with reference to the financing statement is required other than the regular recording and satisfaction fees with respect to the mortgage.

(7) A financing statement sufficiently shows the name of the debtor if it gives the individual, partnership or corporate name of the debtor, whether or not it adds other trade names or names of partners. Where the debtor so changes his name or in the case of an organization its name, identity or corporate structure that a filed financing statement becomes seriously misleading, the filing is not effective to perfect a security interest in collateral acquired by the debtor more than four months after the change, unless a new appropriate financing statement is filed before the expiration of that time. A filed financing statement remains effective with respect to collateral transferred by the debtor even though the secured party knows of or consents to the transfer.

(8) A financing statement substantially complying with the requirements of this section is effective even though it contains minor errors which are not seriously misleading.

Section 9-403. What Constitutes Filing; Duration of Filing; Effect of Lapsed Filing; Duties of Filing Officer.

(1) Presentation for filing of a financing statement and tender of the filing fee or acceptance of the statement by the filing officer constitutes filing under this Article.

(2) Except as provided in subsection (6) a filed financing statement is effective for a period of five years from the date of filing. The effectiveness of a filed financing statement lapses on the expiration of the five year period unless a continuation statement is filed prior to the lapse. If a security interest perfected by filing exists at the time insolvency proceedings are commenced by or against the debtor, the security interest remains perfected until termination of the insolvency proceedings and thereafter for a period of sixty days or until the expiration of the five year period, whichever occurs later. Upon lapse the security interest becomes unperfected, unless it is perfected without filing. If the security interest becomes unperfected upon lapse, it is deemed to have been unperfected as against a person who became a purchaser or lien creditor before lapse.

(3) A continuation statement may be filed by the secured party within six months prior to the expiration of the five year period specified in subsection (2). Any such continuation statement must be signed by the secured party, identify the original statement by file number and state that the original statement is still effective. A continuation statement signed by a person other than the secured party of record must be accompanied by a separate written statement of assignment signed by the secured party of record and complying with subsection (2) of Section 9-405, including payment of the required fee. Upon timely filing of the continuation statement, the effectiveness of the original statement is continued for five years after the last date to which the filing was effective whereupon it lapses in the same manner as provided in subsection (2) unless another continuation statement is filed prior to such lapse. Succeeding continuation statements may be filed in the same

manner to continue the effectiveness of the original statement. Unless a statute on disposition of public records provides otherwise, the filing officer may remove a lapsed statement from the files and destroy it immediately if he has retained a microfilm or other photographic record, or in other cases after one year after the lapse. The filing officer shall so arrange matters by physical annexation of financing statements to continuation statements or other related filings, or by other means, that if he physically destroys the financing statements of a period more than five years past, those which have been continued by a continuation statement or which are still effective under subsection (6) shall be retained.

(4) Except as provided in subsection (7) a filing officer shall mark each statement with a file number and with the date and hour of filing and shall hold the statement or a microfilm or other photographic copy thereof for public inspection. In addition the filing officer shall index the statement according to the name of the debtor and shall note in the index the file number and the address of the debtor given in the statement.

(5) The uniform fee for filing and indexing and for stamping a copy furnished by the secured party to show the date and place of filing for an original financing statement or for a continuation statement shall be $ . . . . if the statement is in the standard form prescribed by the [Secretary of State] and otherwise shall be $. . . . . , plus in each case, if the financing statement is subject to subsection (5) of Section 9-402, $. . . . . The uniform fee for each name more than one required to be indexed shall be $. . . . . The secured party may at his option show a trade name for any person and an extra uniform indexing fee of $. . . . . shall be paid with respect thereto.

(6) If the debtor is a transmitting utility (subsection (5) of Section 9-401) and a filed financing statement so states, it is effective until a termination statement is filed. A real estate mortgage which is effective as a fixture filing under subsection (6) of Section 9-402 remains effective as a fixture filing until the mortgage is released or satisfied of record or its effectiveness otherwise terminates as to the real estate.

(7) When a financing statement covers timber to be cut or covers minerals or the like (including oil and gas) or accounts subject to subsection (5) of Section 9-103, or is filed as a fixture filing, [it shall be filed for record and] the filing officer shall index it under the names of the debtor and any owner of record shown on the financing statement in the same fashion as if they were the mortgagors in a mortgage of the real estate described, and, to the extent that the law of this state provides for indexing of mortgages under the name of the mortgagee, under the name of the secured party as if he were the mortgagee thereunder, or where indexing is by description in the same fashion as if the financing statement were a mortgage of the real estate described.

Section 9-404. Termination Statement.

(1) If a financing statement covering consumer goods is filed on or after . . . . , then within one month or within ten days following written demand by the debtor after there is no outstanding secured obligation and no commitment to make advances, incur obligations or otherwise give value, the secured party must file with each filing officer with whom the financing statement was filed, a termination statement to the effect that he no longer claims a security interest under the financing statement, which shall be identified by file number. In other cases whenever there is no outstanding secured obligation and no commitment to make advances, incur obligations or otherwise give value, the secured party must on written demand by the debtor send the debtor, for each filing officer with whom the financing statement was filed, a termination statement to the effect that he no longer claims a security interest under the financing statement, which shall be identified by file number. A termination statement signed by a person other than the secured party of record must be accompanied by a separate written statement of assignment signed by the secured party of record and complying with subsection (2) of Section 9-405, including payment of the required fee. If the affected secured party fails to file such a termination statement within ten days after proper demand therefor, he shall be liable to the debtor for one hundred dollars, and in

addition for any loss caused to the debtor by such failure.

(2) On presentation to the filing officer of such a termination statement he must note it in the index. If he has received the termination statement in duplicate, he shall return one copy of the termination statement to the secured party stamped to show the time of receipt thereof. If the filing officer has a microfilm or other photographic record of the financing statement, and of any related continuation statement, statement of assignment and statement of release, he may remove the originals from the files at any time after receipt of the termination statement, or if he has no such record, he may remove them from the files at any time after one year after receipt of the termination statement.

(3) If the termination statement is in the standard form prescribed by the [Secretary of State], the uniform fee for filing and indexing the termination statement shall be $. . . . . and otherwise shall be $. . . . . , plus in each case an additional fee of $. . . . . for each name more than one against which the termination statement is required to be indexed.

Section 9-405. Assignment of Security Interest; Duties of Filing Officer; Fees.

(1) A financing statement may disclose an assignment of a security interest in the collateral described in the financing statement by indication in the financing statement of the name and address of the assignee or by an assignment itself or a copy thereof on the face or back of the statement. On presentation to the filing officer of such a financing statement the filing officer shall mark the same as provided in Section 9-403(4). The uniform fee for filing, indexing and furnishing filing data for a financing statement so indicating an assignment shall be $. . . . . if the statement is in the standard form prescribed by the [Secretary of State] and otherwise shall be $. . . . . , plus in each case an additional fee of $. . . . . for each name more than one against which the financing statement is required to be indexed.

(2) A secured party may assign of record all or part of his rights under a financing statement by the filing in the place where the original financing statement was filed of a separate written statement of assignment signed by the secured party of record and setting forth the name of the secured party of record and the debtor, the file number and the date of filing of the financing statement and the name and address of the assignee and containing a description of the collateral assigned. A copy of the assignment is sufficient as a separate statement if it complies with the preceding sentence. On presentation to the filing officer of such a separate statement, the filing officer shall mark such separate statement with the date and hour of the filing. He shall note the assignment on the index of the financing statement, or in the case of a fixture filing, or a filing covering timber to be cut, or covering minerals or the like (including oil and gas) or accounts subject to subsection (5) of Section 9-103, he shall index the assignment under the name of the assignor as grantor and, to the extent that the law of this state provides for indexing the assignment of a mortgage under the name of the assignee, he shall index the assignment of the financing statement under the name of the assignee. The uniform fee for filing, indexing and furnishing filing data about such a separate statement of assignment shall be $. . . . . if the statement is in the standard form prescribed by the [Secretary of State] and otherwise shall be $. . . . . , plus in each case an additional fee of $. . . . . for each name more than one against which the statement of assignment is required to be indexed. Notwithstanding the provisions of this subsection, an assignment of record of a security interest in a fixture contained in a mortgage effective as a fixture filing (subsection (6) of Section 9-402) may be made only by an assignment of the mortgage in the manner provided by the law of the state other than this Act.

(3) After the disclosure of filing of an assignment under this section, the assignee is the secured party of record.

Section 9-406. Release of Collateral; Duties of Filing Officer; Fees. A secured party of record may by his signed statement release all or a part of any collateral described in a filed financing statement. The statement of release is sufficient if it contains a description of the collateral being released, the name and address of the debtor, the name and address of the secured party, and the file number of the financing statement. A statement of release signed by a person other than the secured party of record must be accompanied by a separate written statement of assignment signed by the secured party of record and complying with subsection (2) of Section 9-405, including payment of the required fee. Upon presentation of such a statement of release to the filing officer he shall mark the statement with the hour and date of filing and shall note the same upon the margin of the index of the filing of the financing statement. The uniform fee for filing and noting such a statement of release shall be $. . . . . if the statement is in the standard form prescribed by the [Secretary of State] and otherwise shall be $. . . . . , plus in each case an additional fee of $. . . . . for each name more than one against which the statement of release is required to be indexed.

[Section 9-407. Information From Filing Officer].

[(1) If the person filing any financing statement, termination statement, statement of assignment, or statement of release, furnishes the filing officer a copy thereof, the filing officer shall upon request note upon the copy the file number and date and hour of the filing of the original and deliver or send the copy to such person.]

[(2) Upon request of any person, the filing officer shall issue his certificate showing whether there is on file on the date and hour stated therein, any presently effective financing statement naming a particular debtor and any statement of assignment thereof and if there is, giving the date and hour of filing of each such statement and the names and addresses of each secured party therein. The uniform fee for such a certificate shall be $. . . . . if the request for the certificate is in the standard form prescribed by the [Secretary of State] and otherwise shall be $. . . . . Upon request the filing officer shall furnish a copy of any filed financing statement or statement of assignment for a uniform fee of $. . . . . per page.]

Section 9-408. Financing Statements Covering Consigned or Leased Goods. A consignor or lessor of goods may file a financing statement using the terms "consignor," "consignee," "lessor," "lessee" or the like instead of the terms specified in Section 9-402. The provisions of this Part shall apply as appropriate to such a financing statement but its filing shall not of itself be a factor in determining whether or not the consignment or lease is intended as security (Section 1-201(37)). However, if it is determined for other reasons that the consignment or lease is so intended, a security interest of the consignor or lessor which attaches to the consigned or leased goods is perfected by such filing.

Added in 1972.

PART 5

DEFAULT

Section 9-501. Default; Procedure When Security Agreement Covers Both Real and Personal Property.

(1) When a debtor is in default under a security agreement, a secured party has the rights and remedies provided in this Part and except as limited by subsection (3) those provided in the security agreement. He may reduce his claim to judgment, foreclose or otherwise enforce the security interest by any available judicial procedure. If the collateral is documents the secured party may proceed either as to the documents or as to the goods covered thereby. A secured party in possession has the rights, remedies and duties provided in Section 9-207. The rights and remedies referred to in this subsection are cumulative.

(2) After default, the debtor has the rights and remedies provided in this Part, those provided in the security agreement and those provided in Section 9-207.

(3) To the extent that they give rights to the debtor and impose duties on the secured party, the rules stated in the subsections referred to below may not be waived or varied except as provided with respect to compulsory disposition of collateral (subsection (3) of Section 9-504 and Section 9-505) and with respect to redemption of collateral

(Section 9-506) but the parties may by agreement determine the standards by which the fulfillment of these rights and duties is to be measured if such standards are not manifestly unreasonable:

(a) subsection (2) of Section 9-502 and subsection (2) of Section 9-504 insofar as they require accounting for surplus proceeds of collateral;

(b) subsection (3) of Section 9-504 and subsection (1) of Section 9-505 which deal with disposition of collateral;

(c) subsection (2) of Section 9-505 which deals with acceptance of collateral as discharge of obligation;

(d) Section 9-506 which deals with redemption of collateral; and

(e) subsection (1) of Section 9-507 which deals with the secured party's liability for failure to comply with this Part.

(4) If the security agreement covers both real and personal property, the secured party may proceed under this Part as to the personal property or he may proceed as to both the real and the personal property in accordance with his rights and remedies in respect of the real property in which case the provisions of this Part do not apply.

(5) When a secured party has reduced his claim to judgment the lien of any levy which may be made upon his collateral by virtue of any execution based upon the judgment shall relate back to the date of the perfection of the security interest in such collateral. A judicial sale, pursuant to such execution, is a foreclosure of the security interest by judicial procedure within the meaning of this section, and the secured party may purchase at the sale and thereafter hold the collateral free of any other requirements of this Article.

Section 9-502. Collection Rights of Secured Party.

(1) When so agreed and in any event on default the secured party is entitled to notify an account debtor or the obligor on an instrument to make payment to him whether or not the assignor was theretofore making collections on the collateral, and also to take control of any proceeds to which he is entitled under Section 9-306.

(2) A secured party who by agreement is entitled to charge back uncollected collateral or otherwise to full or limited recourse against the debtor and who undertakes to collect from the account debtors or obligors must proceed in a commercially reasonable manner and may deduct his reasonable expenses of realization from the collections. If the security agreement secures an indebtedness, the secured party must account to the debtor for any surplus, and unless otherwise agreed, the debtor is liable for any deficiency. But, if the underlying transaction was a sale of accounts or chattel paper, the debtor is entitled to any surplus or is liable for any deficiency only if the security agreement so provides.

Section 9-503. Secured Party's Right to Take Possession After Default. Unless otherwise agreed a secured party has on default the right to take possession of the collateral. In taking possession a secured party may proceed without judicial process if this can be done without breach of the peace or may proceed by action. If the security agreement so provides the secured party may require the debtor to assemble the collateral and make it available to the secured party at a place to be designated by the secured party which is reasonably convenient to both parties. Without removal a secured party may render equipment unusable, and may dispose of collateral on the debtor's premises under Section 9-504.

Section 9-504. Secured Party's Right to Dispose of Collateral After Default; Effect of Disposition.

(1) A secured party after default may sell, lease or otherwise dispose of any or all of the collateral in its then condition or following any commercially reasonable preparation or processing. Any sale of goods is subject to the Article on Sales (Article 2). The proceeds of disposition shall be applied in the order following to

(a) the reasonable expenses of retaking, holding, preparing for sale or lease, selling, leasing and the like and, to the extent provided for in the agreement and not prohibited by law, the reasonable attorneys' fees and legal expenses incurred by the secured party;

(b) the satisfaction of indebtedness secured by the security interest under which the disposition is made;

(c) the satisfaction of indebtedness secured by any subordinate security interest in the collateral if written notification of demand therefor is received before distribution of the proceeds is completed. If requested by the secured party, the holder of a subordinate security interest must seasonably furnish reasonable proof of his interest, and unless he does so, the secured party need not comply with his demand.

(2) If the security interest secured an indebtedness, the secured party must account to the debtor for any surplus, and, unless otherwise agreed, the debtor is liable for any deficiency. But if the underlying transaction was a sale of accounts or chattel paper, the debtor is entitled to any surplus or is liable for any deficiency only if the security agreement so provides.

(3) Disposition of the collateral may be by public or private proceedings and may be made by way of one or more contracts. Sale or other disposition may be as a unit or in parcels and at any time and place and on any terms but every aspect of the disposition including the method, manner, time, place and terms must be commercially reasonable. Unless collateral is perishable or threatens to decline speedily in value or is of a type customarily sold on a recognized market, reasonable notification of the time and place of any public sale or reasonable notification of the time after which any private sale or other intended disposition is to be made shall be sent by the secured party to the debtor, if he has not signed after default a statement renouncing or modifying his right to notification of sale. In the case of consumer goods no other notification need be sent. In other cases notification shall be sent to any other secured party from whom the secured party has received (before sending his notification to the debtor or before the debtor's renunciation of his rights) written notice of a claim of an interest in the collateral. The secured party may buy at any public sale and if the collateral is of a type customarily sold in a recognized market or is of a type which is the subject of widely distributed standard price quotations he may buy at private sale.

(4) When collateral is disposed of by a secured party after default, the disposition transfers to a purchaser for value all of the debtor's rights therein, discharges the security interest under which it is made and any security interest or lien subordinate or lien subordinate thereto. The purchaser takes free of all such rights and interests even though the secured party fails to comply with the requirements of this Part or of any judicial proceedings.

(a) in the case of a public sale, if the purchaser has no knowledge of any defects in the sale and if he does not buy in collusion with the secured party, other bidders or the person conducting the sale; or

(b) in any other case, if the purchaser acts in good faith.

(5) A person who is liable to a secured party under a guaranty, indorsement, repurchase agreement or the like and who receives a transfer of collateral from the secured party or is subrogated to his rights has thereafter the rights and duties of the secured party. Such a transfer of collateral is not a sale or disposition of the collateral under this Article.

Section 9-505. Compulsory Disposition of Collateral; Acceptance of the Collateral as Discharge of Obligation.

(1) If the debtor has paid sixty per cent of the cash price in the case of a purchase money security interest in consumer goods, and has not signed after default at statement renouncing or modifying his rights under this Part a secured party who has taken possession of collateral must dispose of it under Section 9-504 and if he fails to do so within ninety days after he takes possession the debtor at his option may recover in conversion or under Section 9-507(1) on secured party's liability.

(2) In any other case involving consumer goods or any other collateral a secured party in possession may, after default, propose to retain the collateral in satisfaction of the obligation. Written notice of such proposal shall be sent to the debtor if he has not signed after default a statement renouncing or modifying his rights under this subsec-

tion. In the case of consumer goods no other notice need be given. In other cases notice shall be sent to any other secured party from whom the secured party has received (before sending his notice to the debtor or before the debtor's renunciation of his rights) written notice of a claim of an interest in the collateral. If the secured party receives objection in writing from a person entitled to receive notification within twenty-one days after the notice was sent, the secured party must dispose of the collateral under Section 9-504. In the absence of such written objection the secured party may retain the collateral in satisfaction of the debtor's obligation.

Section 9-506. Debtor's Right to Redeem Collateral. At any time before the secured party has disposed of collateral or entered into a contract for its disposition under Section 9-504 or before the obligation has been discharged under Section 9-505(2) the debtor or any other secured party may unless otherwise agreed in writing after default redeem the collateral by tendering fulfillment of all obligations secured by the collateral as well as the expenses reasonably incurred by the secured party in retaking, holding and preparing the collateral for disposition, in arranging for the sale, and to the extent provided in the agreement and not prohibited by law, his reasonable attorneys' fees and legal expenses.

Section 9-507. Secured Party's Liability for Failure to Comply With This Part.

(1) If it is established that the secured party is not proceeding in accordance with the provisions of this Part disposition may be ordered or restrained on appropriate terms and conditions. If the disposition has occurred the debtor or any person entitled to notification or whose security interest has been made known to the secured party prior to the disposition has a right to recover from the secured party any loss caused by a failure to comply with the provisions of this Part. If the collateral is consumer goods, the debtor has a right to recover in any event an amount not less than the credit service charge plus ten per cent of the principal amount of the debt or the time price differential plus ten per cent of the cash price.

(2) The fact that a better price could have been obtained by a sale at a different time or in a different method from that selected by the secured party is not of itself sufficient to establish that the sale was not made in a commercially reasonable manner. If the secured party either sells the collateral in the usual manner in any recognized market therefor or if he sells at the price current in such market at the time of his sale or if he has otherwise sold in conformity with reasonable commercial practices among dealers in the type of property sold he has sold in a commercially reasonable manner. The principles stated in the two preceding sentences with respect to sales also apply as may be appropriate to other types of disposition. A disposition which has been approved in any judicial proceeding or by any bona fide creditors' committee or representative of creditors shall conclusively be deemed to be commercially reasonable, but this sentence does not indicate that any such approval must be obtained in any case nor does it indicate that any disposition not so approved is not commercially reasonable.

ARTICLE 10

EFFECTIVE DATE AND REPEALER

Section 10-101. Effective Date. This Act shall become effective at midnight on December 31st following its enactment. It applies to transactions entered into and events occurring after that date.

Section 10-102. Specific Repealer; Provision for Transition.

(1) The following acts and all other acts and parts of acts inconsistent herewith are hereby repealed:

(Here should follow the acts to be specifically repealed including the following:
Uniform Negotiable Instruments Act
Uniform Warehouse Receipts Act
Uniform Sales Act
Uniform Bills of Lading Act
Uniform Stock Transfer Act
Uniform Trust Receipts Act
Also any acts regulating:
Bank collections

Bulk sales
Chattel mortgages
Conditional sales
Factor's lien acts
Farm storage of grain and similar acts
Assignment of accounts receivable)

(2) Transactions validly entered into before the effective date specified in Section 10-101 and the rights, duties and interests flowing from them remain valid thereafter and may be terminated, completed, consummated or enforced as required or permitted by any statute or other law amended or repealed by this Act as though such repeal or amendment had not occurred.

NOTE: *Subsection (1) should be separately prepared for each state. The foregoing is a list of statutes to be checked.*

Section 10-103. General Repealer.

Except as provided in the following section, all acts and parts of acts inconsistent with this Act are hereby repealed.

Section 10-104. Laws Not Repealed.

(1) The Article on Documents of Title (Article 7) does not repeal or modify any laws prescribing the form or contents of regulating bailees' businesses in respects not specifically dealt with herein; but the fact that such laws are violated does not affect the status of a document of title which otherwise complies with the definition of a document of title (Section 1-201).

[(2) This Act does not repeal . . . .*, cited as the Uniform Act for the Simplification of Fiduciary Security Transfers, and if in any respect there is any inconsistency between that Act and the Article of this Act on investment securities (Article 8) the provisions of the former Act shall control.]

NOTE: *At * in subsection (2) insert the statutory reference to the Uniform Act for the Simplification of Fiduciary Security Transfers if such Act has previously been enacted. If it has not been enacted, omit subsection (2).*

Glossary

Abandonment Applies to many situations. Abandonment of property is giving up dominion and control over it, with intention to relinquish all claims to it. Losing property is an involuntary act; abandonment is voluntary. When used with duty, the word *abandonment* is synonymous with *repudiation.*

Abatement of a nuisance An action to end any act detrimental to the public; e.g., suit to enjoin a plant from permitting the escape of noxious vapors.

Acceptance* Under Article 3—Commercial Paper, this is the drawee's signed engagement to honor a draft as presented. It must be written on the draft and may consist of drawee's signature alone. It becomes operative when completed by delivery or notification.

Accord and satisfaction An agreement between two persons—one of whom has a right of action against the other—that the latter should do or give, and the former accept, something in satisfaction of the right of action—something different from, and usually less than, what might legally be enforced.

Account* Any right to payment for goods sold or leased or for services rendered but not evidenced by an instrument or chattel paper. Under Article 4—Bank Deposits and Collections, *account* is any account with a bank and includes a checking, time, interest, or savings account.

Account debtor The person who is obligated on an account, chattel paper, contract right, or general intangible.

Accretion Gradual, imperceptible accumulation of land by natural causes, usually next to a stream or river.

Action ex contractu An action at law to recover damages for the breach of a duty arising out of contract. There are two types of causes of action: those arising out of contract, ex contractu, and those arising out of tort, ex delicto.

Action ex delicto An action at law to recover damages for the breach of a duty existing by reason of a general law. An action to recover damages for an injury caused by the negligent use of an automobile is an ex delicto action. Tort or wrong is the basis of the action. *See* Action ex contractu.

Adjudicate The exercise of judicial power by hearing, trying, and determining the claims of litigants before the court.

Administrative law The branch of public law dealing with the operation of the various agency boards and commissions of government.

Administrator A person to whom letters of administration have been issued by a probate court, giving such person authority to administer, manage, and close the estate of a deceased person.

Adverse possession Acquisition of legal title to another's land by being in continuous possession during a period prescribed in the statute. Possession must be actual, visible, known to the world, and with intent to claim title as owner, against the rights of the true owner. Claimant usually must pay taxes and liens lawfully charged against the property. Cutting timber or grass from time to time on the land of another is not the kind of adverse possession that will confer title.

Advising bank* A bank that gives notification of the issuance of a credit by another bank.

Affidavit A voluntary statement of facts formally reduced to writing, sworn to, or affirmed before, some officer authorized to administer oaths. The officer is usually a notary public.

Affirmative action program Active recruitment and advancement of minority workers.

Affirmative defense A matter that constitutes opposition to the allegations of a complaint, which are assumed to be true.

A fortiori Latin words meaning "by a stronger reason." Often used in judicial opinions to say that since specific proven facts lead to a certain conclusion, there are for this reason other facts that logically follow and strengthen the argument for the conclusion.

Agency coupled with an interest When an agent has possession or control over the property of his principal and has a right of action against interference by third parties, an agency with an interest has been created. An agent who advances freight for goods sent him by his principal has an interest in the goods.

Agent A person authorized to act for another (principal). The term may apply to a person in the service of another; but in the strict sense, an agent is one who stands in place of his principal. A works for B as a gardener and is thus a servant, but he may be an agent. If A sells goods for B, he becomes more than a servant. He acts in the place of B.

Agreement* The bargain of the parties in fact as found in their language or by implication from other circum-

*Terms followed by an asterisk are defined in the Uniform Commercial Code and have significance in connection with Code materials. They are often given a particular meaning in relation to the Code, and their definitions do not necessarily conform with meanings outside the framework of the Code.

stances, including course of dealing or usage of trade or course of performance as provided in the Uniform Commercial Code.

Amicus curiae A friend of the court who participates in litigation, usually on appeal, though not a party to the lawsuit.

Annuity A sum of money paid yearly to a person during his lifetime. The sum arises out of a contract by which the recipient or another had previously deposited sums in whole or in part with the grantor—the grantor to return a designated portion of the principal and interest in periodic payments when the beneficiary attains a designated age.

Appellant The party who takes an appeal from one court or jurisdiction to another.

Appellee The party in a cause against whom an appeal is taken.

A priori A generalization resting on presuppositions, not upon proven facts.

Arbitration The submission for determination of disputed matter to private, unofficial persons selected in a manner provided by law or agreement.

Architect's certificate A formal statement signed by an architect that a contractor has performed under his contract and is entitled to be paid. The construction contract provides when and how such certificates shall be issued.

Artisan's lien One who has expended labor upon, or added to, another's property is entitled to possession of the property as security until reimbursed for the value of labor or material. A repairs B's watch. A may keep the watch in his possession until B pays for the repairs.

Assignee An assign or assignee is one to whom an assignment has been made.

Assignment The transfer by one person to another of a right that usually arises out of a contract. Such rights are called *choses in action.* A sells and assigns to C his contract right to purchase B's house. A is an assignor. C is an assignee. The transfer is an assignment.

Assignment* A transfer of the "contract" or of "all my rights under the contract" or an assignment in similar general terms is an assignment of rights. Unless the language or the circumstances (as in an assignment for security) indicate the contrary, it is a delegation of performance of the duties of the assignor, and its acceptance by the assignee constitutes a promise by him to perform those duties. This promise is enforceable by either the assignor or the other party to the original contract.

Assignment for the benefit of creditors A, a debtor, has many creditors. An assignment of his property to X, a third party, with directions to make distribution of his property to his creditors, is called an assignment for the benefit of creditors. *See* Composition of creditors.

Assignor One who makes an assignment.

Assumption of the risk Negligence doctrine that bars the recovery of damages by an injured party on the ground that such party acted with actual or constructive knowledge of the hazard causing the injury.

Attachment A legal proceeding accompanying an action in court by which a plaintiff may acquire a lien on a defendant's property as a security for the payment of any judgment that the plaintiff may recover. It is provisional and independent of the court action and is usually provided for by statute. A sues B. Before judgment, A attaches B's automobile, in order to make sure of the payment of any judgment that A may secure.

Attorney at law A person to whom the state grants a license to practice law.

Attorney in fact A person acting for another under a grant of special power created by an instrument in writing. B, in writing, grants special power to A to execute and deliver for B a conveyance of B's land to X.

Bad faith "Actual intent" to mislead or deceive another. It does not mean misleading by an honest, inadvertent, or careless misstatement.

Bail (verb) To set at liberty an arrested or imprisoned person after that person or at least two others have given security to the state that the accused will appear at the proper time and place for trial.

Bailee A person into whose possession personal property is delivered.

Bailee* The person who, by a warehouse receipt, bill of lading, or other document of title, acknowledges possession of goods and contracts to deliver it.

Bailment Delivery of personal property to another for a special purpose. Delivery is made under a contract, either expressed or implied, that upon the completion of the special purpose, the property shall be redelivered to the bailor or placed at his disposal. A loans B his truck. A places his watch with B for repair. A places his furniture in B's warehouse. A places his securities in B Bank's safety deposit vault. In each case, A is a bailor and B is a bailee.

Bailor One who delivers personal property into the possession of another.

Banking day* Under Article 4—Bank Deposits and Collections, this is the part of any day on which a bank is open to the public for carrying on substantially all of its banking functions.

Bearer* The person in possession of an instrument, document of title, or security payable to bearer or indorsed in blank.

Bearer form* A security is in bearer form when it runs to bearer according to its terms and not by reason of any indorsement.

Beneficiary A person (not a promisee) for whose benefit a trust, an insurance policy, a will, or a contract promise is made.

Beneficiary* A person who is entitled under a letter of credit to draw or demand payment.

Bequest In a will, a gift of personal property.

Bid An offering of money in exchange for property placed for sale. At an ordinary auction sale, a bid is an offer to purchase. It may be withdrawn before acceptance is indicated by the fall of the hammer.

Bilateral contract One containing mutual promises, with each party being both a promisor and a promisee.

Bill of lading* A document evidencing the receipt of goods for shipment, issued by a person engaged in the business of transporting or forwarding goods. Includes an airbill, a document that serves air transportation as a bill of lading serves marine or rail transportation. It includes an air consignment note or air waybill.

Bill of particulars In legal practice, a written statement that one party to a lawsuit gives to another, describing in detail the elements upon which the claim of the first party is based.

Bill of sale Written evidence that the title to personal property has been transferred from one person to another. It must contain words of transfer and be more than a receipt.

Blue-sky laws Popular name for acts providing for the regulation and supervision of investment securities.

Bona fide purchaser* A purchaser of a security for value, in good faith, and without notice of any adverse claim, who takes delivery of a security in bearer form or in registered form issued to him or indorsed to him or in blank.

Bond A promise under seal to pay money. The term generally designates the promise made by a corporation, either public or private, to pay money to bearer. E.g., U.S. government bonds or Illinois Central Railroad bonds. Also, an obligation by which one person promises to answer for the debt or default of another—a surety bond.

Broker A person employed to make contracts with third persons on behalf of his principal. The contracts involve trade, commerce, buying and selling for a fee (called brokerage or commission).

Broker* A person engaged full or part time in the business of buying and selling securities, who in the transaction concerned acts for, or buys a security from, or sells a security to, a customer.

Bulk transfer* Transfer made outside the ordinary course of the transferor's business but involving a major part of the materials, supplies, merchandise, or other inventory of an enterprise subject to Article 6.

Buyer* A person who buys or contracts to buy goods.

Buyer in ordinary course of business* A person who, in good faith and without knowledge that the sale to him is in violation of the ownership rights or security interest of a third party in the goods, buys in ordinary course from a person in the business of selling goods of that kind. Does not include a pawnbroker. "Buying" may be for cash or by exchange of other property or on secured or unsecured credit. Includes receiving goods or documents of title under a preexisting contract for sale but does not include a transfer in bulk or as security for, or in total or partial satisfaction of, a money debt.

Bylaws Rules for government of a corporation or other organization. Adopted by members or the board of directors, these rules must not be contrary to the law of the land. They affect the rights and duties of the members of the corporation or organization, only, not third persons.

Call An assessment upon a subscriber for partial or full payment on shares of unpaid stock of a corporation. Also, the power of a corporation to make an assessment, notice of an assessment, or the time when the assessment is to be paid.

Cancellation* Either party puts an end to the contract because of breach by the other. Its effect is the same as that of "termination," except that the canceling party also retains any remedy for breach of the whole contract or any unperformed balance.

Capital The net assets of an individual enterprise, partnership, joint stock company, corporation, or business institution, including not only the original investment but also all gains and profits realized from the continued conduct of the business.

Carrier A natural person or a corporation who receives goods under a contract to transport for a consideration from one place to another. A railroad, truckline, busline, airline.

Cashier's check A bill of exchange drawn by the cashier of a bank, for the bank, upon the bank. After the check is delivered or issued to the payee or holder, the drawer bank cannot put a "stop order" against itself. By delivery of the check, the drawer bank has accepted and thus becomes the primary obligor.

Cause of action When one's legal rights have been invaded either by a breach of a contract or by a breach of a legal duty toward one's person or property, a cause of action has been created.

Caveat Literally, "let him beware." It is used generally to mean a warning.

Caveat emptor An old idea at common law—"let the buyer beware." When a vendor sells goods without an express warranty as to their quality and capacity for a particular use and purpose, the buyer must take the risk of loss due to all defects in the goods.

Caveat venditor "Let the seller beware." Unless the seller, by express language, disclaims any responsibility, he shall be liable to the buyer if the goods delivered are different in kind, quality, use, and purpose from those described in the contract of sale.

Cease and desist order An administrative agency order directing a party to refrain from doing a specified act.

Certiorari An order issuing out of an appellate court to a lower court, at the request of an appellant, directing that the record of a case pending in the lower court be transmitted to the upper court for review.

Cestui que trust A person who is the real or beneficial owner of property held in trust. The trustee holds the legal title to the property for the benefit of the cestui que trust.

Chancery Court of equity.

Charter Referring to a private corporation, *charter* includes the contract between the created corporation and the state, the act creating the corporation, and the articles of association granted to the corporation by authority of the legislative act. Referring to municipal corporations, *charter* does not mean a contract between the legislature and the city created. A city charter is a delegation of powers by a state legislature to the governing body of the city. The term includes the creative act, the powers enumerated, and the organization authorized.

Chattel A very broad term derived from the word *cattle*. Includes every kind of property that is not real property. Movable properties, such as horses, automobiles, choses in action, stock certificates, bills of lading, and all "good wares, and merchandise" are chattels personal. Chattels real concern real property such as a lease for years, in which case the lessee owns a chattel real.

Chattel paper* A writing or writings that evidence both a monetary obligation and a security interest in, or a lease of, specific goods. When a transaction is evidenced both by such a security agreement or a lease and by an instrument or a series of instruments, the group of writings taken together constitutes chattel paper.

Chose in action The "right" one person has to recover

money or property from another by a judicial proceeding. The right arises out of contract, claims for money, debts, and rights against property. Notes, drafts, stock certificates, bills of lading, warehouse receipts, and insurance policies are illustrations of choses in action. They are called tangible choses. Book accounts, simple debts, and obligations not evidenced by formal writing are called intangible choses. Choses in action are transferred by assignment.

Circumstantial evidence If, from certain facts and circumstances, according to the experience of mankind, an ordinary, intelligent person may infer that other connected facts and circumstances must necessarily exist, the latter facts and circumstances are considered proven by circumstantial evidence. Proof of fact A from which fact B may be inferred is proof of fact B by circumstantial evidence.

Civil action A proceeding in a law court or a suit in equity by one person against another for the enforcement or protection of a private right or the prevention of a wrong. It includes actions on contract, ex delicto, and all suits in equity. Civil action is in contradistinction to criminal action, in which the state prosecutes a person for breach of a duty.

Civil law The area of law dealing with rights and duties of private parties as individual entities. To be distinguished from criminal law. Sometimes the phrase refers to the European system of codified law.

Clearinghouse* Under Article 4—Bank Deposits and Collections, clearinghouse is any association of banks or other payors regularly clearing items.

Cloud on title Some evidence of record that shows a third person has some prima facie interest in another's property.

Code A collection or compilation of the statutes passed by the legislative body of a state. Often annotated with citations of cases decided by the state supreme courts. These decisions construe the statutes. Examples: Oregon Compiled Laws Annotated, United States Code Annotated.

Codicil An addition to, or a change in, an executed last will and testament. It is a part of the original will and must be executed with the same formality as the original will.

Coinsurer A term in a fire insurance policy that requires the insured to bear a certain portion of the loss when he fails to carry complete coverage. For example, unless the insured carries insurance that totals 80 percent of the value of the property, the insurer shall be liable for only that portion of the loss that the total insurance carried bears to 80 percent of the value of the property.

Collateral With reference to debts or other obligations, *collateral* means security placed with a creditor to assure the performance of the obligator. If the obligator performs, the collateral is returned by the creditor. A owes B $1,000. To secure the payment, A places with B a $500 certificate of stock in X company. The $500 certificate is called collateral security.

Collateral* The property subject to a security interest. Includes accounts, contract rights, and chattel paper that have been sold.

Collecting bank* Under Article 4—Bank Deposits and Collections, any bank handling the item for collection except the payor bank.

Collective bargaining The process of good-faith negotiation between employer's and employees' representatives, concerning issues of mutual interest.

Commerce clause Article I, Section 8, Clause 3 of the Constitution of the United States, granting Congress the authority to regulate commerce with foreign nations and among the states.

Commercial unit* A unit of goods that, by commercial usage, is a single whole for purposes of sale. Its division would materially impair its character or value on the market or in use. A commercial unit may be a single article (as a machine) or a set of articles (as a suite of furniture or an assortment of sizes) or a quantity (as a bale, gross, or carload) or any other unit treated in use or in the relevant market as a single whole.

Commission The sum of money, interest, brokerage, compensation, or allowance given to a factor or broker for carrying on the business of his principal.

Commission merchant An agent or factor employed to sell "goods, wares, and merchandise" consigned or delivered to him by his principal.

Common carrier One who is engaged in the business of transporting personal property from one place to another for compensation. Such person is bound to carry for all who tender their goods and the price for transportation. A common carrier operates as a public utility and is subject to state and federal regulations.

Common law That body of law deriving from judicial decisions, as opposed to legislatively enacted statutes and administrative regulations.

Community property All property acquired after marriage by husband and wife, other than separate property acquired by devise, bequest, or from the proceeds of noncommunity property. Community property is a concept of property ownership by husband and wife inherited from the civil law. The husband and wife are somewhat like partners in their ownership of property acquired during marriage.

Complaint The first paper a plaintiff files in a court in a lawsuit. It is called a pleading. It is a statement of the facts upon which the plaintiff rests his cause of action.

Composition of creditors An agreement among creditors and their debtors by which the creditors will take a lesser amount in complete satisfaction of the total debt. A owes B and C $500 each. A agrees to pay B and C $250 each in complete satisfaction of the $500 due each. B and C agree to take $250 in satisfaction.

Compromise An agreement between two or more persons, usually opposing parties in a lawsuit, to settle the matters of the controversy without further resort to hostile litigation. An adjustment of issues in dispute by mutual concessions before resorting to a lawsuit.

Condemnation proceedings An action or proceeding in court authorized by legislation (federal or state) for the purpose of taking private property for public use. It is the exercise by the judiciary of the sovereign power of eminent domain.

Condition A clause in a contract, either expressed or implied, that has the effect of investing or divesting the legal rights and duties of the parties to the contract. In a deed, a condition is a qualification or restriction providing for the happening or nonhappening of events that, on occurrence, will destroy, commence, or enlarge an estate. "A grants Blackacre to B, so long as said land shall be used for church purposes." If it ceases to be used for church purposes, the title to Blackacre will revert to the grantor.

Condition precedent A clause in a contract providing that immediate rights and duties shall vest only upon the happening of some event. Securing an architect's certificate by a contractor before the contractor is entitled to payment is a condition precedent. A condition is not a promise; hence, its breach will not give rise to a cause of action for damages. A breach of a condition is the basis for a defense. If the contractor sues the owner without securing the architect's certificate, the owner has a defense.

Conditions concurrent Conditions concurrent are mutually dependent and must be performed at the same time by the parties to the contract. Payment of money and delivery of goods in a cash sale are conditions concurrent. Failure to perform by one party permits a cause of action upon tender by the other party. If S refuses to deliver goods in a cash sale, B, upon tender but not delivery of the money, places S in default and thus may sue S. B does not part with his money without getting the goods. If S sued B, B would have a defense.

Condition subsequent A clause in a contract providing for the happening of an event that divests legal rights and duties. A clause in a fire insurance policy providing that the policy shall be null and void if combustible material is stored within 10 feet of the building is a condition subsequent. If a fire occurs and combustible material was within 10 feet of the building, the insurance company is excused from its duty to pay for the loss.

Confirming bank A bank that engages either that it will itself honor a credit already issued by another bank or that such a credit will be honored by the issuer or a third bank.

Conforming* Goods or conduct, including any part of a performance, are "conforming" or conform to the contract when they are in accordance with the obligations under contract.

Conglomerate merger Merging of companies that have neither the relationship of competitors nor that of supplier and customer.

Consideration An essential element in the creation of contract obligation. A detriment to the promisee and a benefit to the promisor. One promise is consideration for another promise. They create a bilateral contract. An act is consideration for a promise. This creates a unilateral contract. Performance of the act asked for by the promisee is a legal detriment to the promisee and a benefit to the promisor.

Consignee A person to whom a shipper usually directs a carrier to deliver goods; generally the buyer of goods and called a consignee on a bill of lading.

Consignee* The person named in a bill to whom or to whose order the bill promises delivery.

Consignment The delivery, sending, or transferring of property, "goods, wares, and merchandise" into the possession of another, usually for the purpose of sale. Consignment may be a bailment or an agency for sale.

Consignor The shipper who delivers freight to a carrier for shipment and who directs the bill of lading to be executed by the carrier. May be the consignor-consignee if the bill of lading is made to his own order.

Consignor* The person named in a bill as the person from whom the goods have been received for shipment.

Conspicuous* A term or clause is conspicuous when it is written so that a reasonable person against whom it is to operate ought to have noticed it. A printed heading in capitals (as NONNEGOTIABLE BILL OF LADING) is conspicuous. Language in the body of a form is "conspicuous" if it is in larger or other contrasting type or color. But in a telegram, any stated term is "conspicuous." Whether a term or clause is "conspicuous" or not is for decision by the court.

Conspiracy A combination or agreement between two or more persons for the commission of a criminal act.

Constructive delivery Although physical delivery of personal property has not occurred, the conduct of the parties may imply that possession and title has passed between them. S sells large and bulky goods to B. Title and possession may pass by the act and conduct of the parties.

Consumer goods* Goods that are used or bought for use primarily for personal, family, or household purposes.

Contingent fee An arrangement whereby an attorney is compensated for services in a lawsuit according to an agreed percentage of the amount of money recovered.

Contract* The total obligation that results from the parties' agreement as affected by the Code and any other applicable rules of law.

Contract right* Under a contract, any right to payment not yet earned by performance and not evidenced by an instrument or chattel paper.

Contributory negligence In a negligence suit, failure of the plaintiff to use reasonable care.

Conversion* Under Article 3—Commercial Paper, an instrument is converted when a drawee to whom it is delivered for acceptance refuses to return it on demand; or any person to whom it is delivered for payment refuses on demand either to pay or to return it; or it is paid on a forged indorsement.

Conveyance A formal written instrument, usually called a deed, by which the title or other interests in land (real property) are transferred from one person to another. The word expresses also the fact that the title to real property has been transferred from one person to another.

Corporation A collection of individuals created by statute as a legal person, vested with powers and capacity to contract, own, control, convey property, and transact business within the limits of the powers granted.

Corporation de facto If persons have attempted in good faith to organize a corporation under a valid law (statute) and have failed in some minor particular but have thereafter exercised corporate powers, they are a corporation de facto. Failure to notarize incorporators' signatures on applications for charter is an illustration of noncompliance with statutory requirements.

Corporation de jure A corporation that has been formed by complying with the mandatory requirements of the law authorizing such a corporation.

Corporeal Physical; perceptible by the senses. Automobiles, grain, fruit, and horses are corporeal and tangible and are called chattels. *Corporeal* is used in contradistinction to *incorporeal* or *intangible.* A chose in action (such as a check) is corporeal and tangible, or a chose in action may be a simple debt, incorporeal and intangible.

Costs In litigation, an allowance authorized by statute to a party for expenses incurred in prosecuting or defending a lawsuit. The word *costs,* unless specifically designated by statute or contract, does not include attorney's fees.

Counterclaims By cross-action, the defendant claims that he is entitled to recover from the plaintiff. Claim must arise out of the same transaction set forth in the plaintiff's complaint and be connected with the same subject matter. S sues B for the purchase price. B counterclaims that the goods were defective and that he thereby suffered damages.

Course of dealing A sequence of previous conduct between the parties to a particular transaction. The conduct is fairly to be regarded as establishing a common basis of understanding for interpreting their expressions and other conduct.

Covenant A promise in writing under seal. It is often used as a substitute for the word *contract.* There are convenants (promises) in deeds, leases, mortgages, and other instruments under seal. The word is used sometimes to name promises in unsealed instruments such as insurance policies.

Cover* After a breach by a seller, the buyer may "cover" by making in good faith and without unreasonable delay any reasonable purchase of, or contract to purchase, goods in substitution for those due from the seller.

Credit* ("Letter of credit.") An engagement by a bank or other person made at the request of a customer and of a kind within the scope of Article 5—Letters of Credit, that the issuer will honor drafts or other demands for payment upon compliance with the conditions specified in the credit. A credit may be either revocable or irrevocable. The engagement may be either an agreement to honor or a statement that the bank or other person is authorized to honor.

Creditor* Includes a general creditor, a secured creditor, a lien creditor, and any representative of creditors, including an assignee for the benefit of creditors, a trustee in bankruptcy, a receiver in equity, and an executor or administrator of an insolvent debtor's or assignor's estate.

Creditor beneficiary One who, for a consideration, promises to discharge another's duty to a third party. A owes C $100. B, for a consideration, promises A to pay A's debt to C. B is a creditor beneficiary.

Cumulative voting In voting for directors, a stockholder may cast as many votes as he has shares of stock multiplied by the number to be elected. His votes may be all for one candidate or distributed among as many candidates as there are offices to be filled.

Custodian bank* A bank or trust company that acts as custodian for a clearing corporation. It must be supervised and examined by the appropriate state or federal authority.

Custody (personal property) The words *custody* and *possession* are not synonymous. *Custody* means in charge of, to keep and care for under the direction of the true owner, without any interest therein adverse to the true owner. A servant is in custody of his master's goods. *See* Possession.

Customer* Under Article 4—Bank Deposits and Collections, a customer is any person having an account with a bank or for whom a bank has agreed to collect items. It includes a bank carrying an account with another bank. As used in Letters of Credit, a customer is a buyer or other person who causes an issuer to issue a credit. The term also includes a bank that procures insurance or confirmation on behalf of that bank's customer.

Damages A sum of money the court imposes upon a defendant as compensation for the plaintiff because the defendant has injured the plaintiff by breach of a legal duty.

d.b.a. "Doing business as." A person who conducts his business under an assumed name is designated "John Doe d.b.a. Excelsior Co."

Debenture A corporate obligation sold as an investment. Similar to a corporate bond but not secured by a trust deed. It is not like corporate stock.

Debtor* The person who owes payment or other performance of the obligation secured, whether or not he owns, or has rights in, the collateral. Includes the seller of accounts, contract rights, or chattel paper. When the debtor and the owner of the collateral are not the same person, *debtor* means the owner of the collateral in any provision of the Article dealing with the obligation and may include both if the context so requires.

Deceit Conduct in a business transaction by which one person, through fraudulent representations, misleads another who has a right to rely on such representations as the truth or who, by reason of an unequal station in life, has no means of detecting such fraud.

Declaratory judgment A determination by a court on a question of law, the court simply declaring the rights of the parties but not ordering anything to be done.

Decree The judgment of the chancellor (judge) in a suit in equity. Like a judgment at law, it is the determination of the rights between the parties and is in the form of an order that requires the decree to be carried out. An order that a contract be specifically enforced is an example of a decree.

Deed A written instrument in a special form, signed, sealed, delivered, and used to pass the legal title of real property from one person to another. (*See* Conveyance.) In order that the public may know about the title to real property, deeds are recorded in the Deed Record office of the county where the land is situated.

Deed of trust An instrument by which title to real property is conveyed to a trustee to hold as security for the holder of notes or bonds. It is like a mortgage, except the security title is held by a person other than the mortgagee creditor. Most corporate bonds are secured by a deed of trust.

De facto Arising out of, or founded upon, fact, although merely apparent or colorable. A de facto officer is one who assumes to be an officer under some color of right, acts as an officer, but in point of law is not a real officer. *See* Corporation de facto.

Defendant A person who has been sued in a court of law; the person who answers the plaintiff's complaint. The word is applied to the defending party in civil actions. In criminal actions, the defending party is referred to as the accused.

Deficiency judgment If, upon the foreclosure of a mortgage, the mortgaged property does not sell for an amount sufficient to pay the mortgage indebtedness, the difference is called a deficiency and is chargeable to the mortgagor or to any person who has purchased the property and assumed and agreed to pay the mortgage. M borrows $10,000 from B and as security gives a mortgage on Blackacre. At maturity, M does not pay the debt. B forecloses, and at public sale Blackacre sells for $8,000. There is a deficiency of $2,000, chargeable against M. If M had sold Blackacre to C and C had assumed and agreed to pay the mortgage, he would also be liable for the deficiency.

Defraud To deprive one of some right by deceitful means. To cheat; to withhold wrongfully that which belongs to another. Conveying one's property for the purpose of avoiding payment of debts is a transfer to "hinder, delay, or defraud creditors."

Del credere agency When an agent, factor, or broker guarantees to his principal the payment of a debt due from a buyer of goods, that agent, factor, or broker is operating under a del credere commission or agency.

Delivery A voluntary transfer of the possession of property; actual or constructive, from one person to another, with the intention that title vests in the transferee. In the law of sales, delivery contemplates the absolute giving up of control and dominion over the property by the vendor, and the assumption of the same by the vendee.

Delivery* With respect to instruments, documents of title, chattel paper, or securities, delivery means voluntary transfer of possession.

Delivery order* A written order to deliver goods directed to a warehouseman, carrier, or other person who, in the ordinary course of business, issues warehouse receipts or bills of lading.

Demand A request by a party entitled, under a claim of right, to the performance of a particular act. In order to bind an indorser on a negotiable instrument, the holder must first make a demand on the primary party, who must dishonor the instrument. Demand notes mean "due when demanded." The word *demand* is also used to mean a claim or legal obligation.

Demurrage Demurrage is a sum provided for in a contract of shipment, to be paid for the delay or detention of vessels or railroad cars beyond the time agreed upon for loading or unloading.

Demurrer A common-law procedural method by which the defendant admits all the facts alleged in the plaintiff's complaint but denies that such facts state a cause of action. It raises a question of law on the facts, which must be decided by the court.

Dependent covenants (promises) In contracts, covenants are either concurrent or mutual, dependent or independent. Dependent covenants mean the performance of one promise must occur before the performance of the other promise. In a cash sale, the buyer must pay the money before the seller is under a duty to deliver the goods.

Depositary bank* Under Article 4—Bank Deposits and Collections, this means the first bank to which an item is transferred for collection, even though it is also the payor bank.

Descent The transfer of the title of property to the heirs upon the death of the ancestor; heredity succession. If a person dies without making a will, his property will "descend" according to the Statute of Descent of the state wherein the property is located.

Detriment Legal detriment that is sufficient consideration constitutes change of position or acts of forbearance by a promisee at the request of a promisor. *See* Consideration.

Devise A gift, usually of real property, by a last will and testament.

Devisee The person who receives title to real property by will.

Dictum The written opinion of a judge, expressing an idea, argument, or rule that is not essential for the determination of the issues. It lacks the force of a decision in a judgment.

Directed verdict If it is apparent to reasonable men and the court that the plaintiff, by his evidence, has not made out his case, the court may instruct the jury to bring in a verdict for the defendant. If, however, different inferences may be drawn from the evidence by reasonable men, then the court cannot direct a verdict.

Discharge The word has many meanings. An employee, upon being released from employment, is discharged. A guardian or trustee, upon termination of his trust, is discharged by the court. A debtor released from his debts is discharged in bankruptcy. A person who is released from any legal obligation is discharged.

Discovery practice The disclosure by one party of facts, titles, documents, and other things in his knowledge or possession and necessary to the party seeking the discovery as a part of a cause of action pending.

Dishonor A negotiable instrument is dishonored when it is presented for acceptance or payment but acceptance or payment is refused or cannot be obtained.

Distress for rent The taking of personal property of a tenant in payment of rent on real estate.

Divestiture The antitrust remedy that forces a company to get rid of assets acquired through illegal mergers or monopolistic practices.

Dividend A stockholder's pro rata share in the profits of a corporation. Dividends are declared by the board of directors of a corporation. They are paid in cash, script, property, and stock.

Docket A book containing a brief summary of all acts done in court in the conduct of each case.

Documentary draft* Under Article 4—Bank Deposits and Collections, this means any negotiable or nonnegotiable draft with accompanying documents, securities, or other papers to be delivered against honor of the draft. Also called a "documentary demand for payment" (Article 5—Letters of Credit). Honoring is conditioned upon the presentation of a document or documents. "Document" means any paper, including document of title, security, invoice, certificate, notice of default, and the like.

Document of title* Includes bill of lading, dock warrant, dock receipt, warehouse receipt, or order for the delivery of goods, and any other document that in the regular course of business or financing is treated as adequately evidencing that the person in possession of it is entitled to receive, hold, and dispose of the document and the goods it covers. To be a document of title, a document must purport to be issued by, or addressed to, a bailee and purport to cover goods in the bailee's possession that are either identified or are fungible portions of an identified mass.

Domicile The place a person intends as his fixed and permanent home and establishment and to which, if he is absent, he intends to return. A person can have but one domicile. The old one continues until the acquisition of a new one. One can have more than one residence at a time, but only one domicile. The word is not synonymous with *residence*.

Dominion Applied to the delivery of property by one person to another, *dominion* means all control over the possession and ownership of the property being separated from the transferor or donor and endowed upon the transferee or donee. *See* Gift.

Donee Recipient of a gift.

Donee beneficiary If a promisee is under no duty to a third party, but for a consideration secures a promise from a promisor for the purpose of making a gift to a third party, then the third party is a donee beneficiary. A, promisee for a premium paid, secures a promise from the insurance company, the promisor, to pay A's wife $10,000 upon A's death. A's wife is a donee beneficiary.

Donor One that gives, donates, or presents.

Dormant partner A partner who is not known to third persons but is entitled to share in the profits and is subject to the losses. Since credit is not extended upon the strength of the dormant partner's name, he may withdraw without notice and not be subject to debts contracted after his withdrawal.

Double jeopardy A constitutional doctrine that prohibits an individual from being prosecuted twice in the same tribunal for the same criminal offense.

Due process Fundamental fairness. Applied to judicial proceedings, it includes adequate notice of a hearing and an opportunity to appear and defend in an orderly tribunal.

Duress (of person) A threat of bodily injury, criminal prosecution, or imprisonment of a contracting party or his near relative to such extent that the threatened party is unable to exercise free will at the time of entering into or discharging a legal obligation.

Duress (of property) Seizing by force or withholding goods by one not entitled, and such person's demanding something as a condition for the release of the goods.

Duty (in law) A legal obligation imposed by general law or voluntarily imposed by the creation of a binding promise. For every legal duty there is a corresponding legal right. By general law, A is under a legal duty not to injure B's person or property. B has a right that A not injure his person or property. X may voluntarily create a duty in himself to Y by a promise to sell Y a horse for $100. If Y accepts, X is under a legal duty to perform his promise. *See* Right.

Earnest money A term used to describe money that one contracting party gives to another at the time of entering into the contract in order to "bind the bargain" and which will be forfeited by the donor if he fails to carry out the contract. Generally, in real estate contracts such money is used as part payment of the purchase price.

Easement An easement is an interest in land—a right that one person has to some profit, benefit, or use in or over the land of another. Such right is created by a deed, or it may be acquired by prescription (the continued use of another's land for a statutory period).

Ejectment An action to recover the possession of real property. It is now generally defined by statute and is a statutory action. *See* Forcible entry and detainer.

Ejusdem generis "Of the same class." General words taking their meaning from specific words which precede the general words. General words have the same meaning as specific words mentioned.

Embezzlement The fraudulent appropriation by one person, acting in a fiduciary capacity, of the money or property of another. *See* Conversion.

Eminent domain The right that resides in the United States, state, county, city, school, or other public body to take private property for public use upon payment of just compensation.

Enjoin To require performance or abstention from some act through issuance of an injunction.

Entity "In being" or "existing." The artificial person created when a corporation is organized is "in being" or "existing" for legal purposes, thus an entity. It is separate from the stockholders. The estate of a deceased person while in administration is an entity. A partnership for many legal purposes is an entity.

Equal protection A principle of the Fifth and Fourteenth Amendments to the Constitution, ensuring that individuals under like circumstances shall be accorded the same benefits and burdens under the law of the sovereign.

Equipment* Goods that are used or bought for use primarily in business (including farming or a profession) or by a debtor who is a nonprofit organization or a governmental subdivision or agency; or goods not included in the definitions of inventory, farm products, or consumer goods.

Equitable action In Anglo-American law, there have developed two types of courts and procedures for the administration of justice: law courts and equity courts. Law courts give as a remedy money damages only, whereas equity courts give the plaintiff what he bargains for. A suit for specific performance of a contract is an equitable action. In many states these two courts are now merged.

Equitable conversion An equitable principle that, for certain purposes, permits real property to be converted into personalty. Thus, real property owned by a partnership is, for the purpose of the partnership, personal property because to ascertain a partner's interest, the real property must be reduced to cash. This is an application of the equitable maxim, "Equity considers that done which ought to be done."

Equitable mortgage A written agreement to make certain property security for a debt, and upon the faith of which the parties have acted in making advances, loans, and thus creating a debt. Example: an improperly executed mortgage, one without seal where a seal is required. An absolute deed made to the mortgagee and intended for security only is an equitable mortgage.

Equity Because the law courts in early English law did not always give an adequate remedy, an aggrieved party sought redress from the king. Since this appeal was to the king's conscience, he referred the case to his spiritual adviser, the chancellor. The chancellor decided the case according to rules of fairness, honesty, right, and natural justice. From this there developed the rules in equity. The laws of trust, divorce, rescission of contracts for fraud, injunction, and specific performance are enforced in courts of equity.

Equity of redemption The right a mortgagor has to redeem or get back his property after it has been forfeited for nonpayment of the debt it secured. By statute, within a certain time before final foreclosure decree, a mortgagor has the privilege of redeeming his property by paying the amount of the debt, interest, and costs.

Escrow An agreement under which a grantor, promisor, or obligor places the instrument upon which he is bound with a third person called escrow holder, until the performance of a condition or the happening of an event stated in the agreement permits the escrow holder to make delivery or performance to the grantee, promisee, or obligee. A (grantor) places a deed to C (grantee) accompanied by the contract of conveyance with B bank, conditioned upon B bank delivering the deed to C (grantee) when C pays all moneys due under contract. The contract and deed have been placed in "escrow."

Estate All the property of a living, deceased, bankrupt, or insane person. Also applied to the property of a ward. In the law of taxation, wills, and inheritance, *estate* has a broad meaning. Historically, the word was limited to an interest in land: i.e., estate in fee simple, estate for years, estate for life, and so forth.

Estoppel When one ought to speak the truth but does not, and by one's acts, representations, or silence intentionally or through negligence induces another to believe certain facts exist, and the other person acts to his detriment on the belief that such facts are true, the first person is estopped to deny the truth of the facts. B, knowingly having kept and used defective goods delivered by S under a contract of sale, is estopped to deny the goods are defective. X holds out Y as his agent. X is estopped to deny that Y is his agent. Persons are estopped to deny the legal effect of written instruments such as deeds, contracts, bills and notes, court records, and judgments. A man's own acts speak louder than his words.

Et al. "And other persons." Used in pleadings and cases to indicate that persons other than those specifically named are parties to a lawsuit.

Eviction An action to expel a tenant from the estate of the landlord. Interfering with the tenant's right of possession or enjoyment amounts to an eviction. Eviction may be actual or constructive. Premises made uninhabitable because the landlord maintains a nuisance is constructive eviction.

Evidence In law, *evidence* has two meanings. (1) Testimony of witnesses and facts presented to the court and jury by way of writings and exhibits, which impress the minds of the court and jury, to the extent that an allegation has been proven. *Testimony* and *evidence* are not synonymous. Testimony is a broader word and includes all the witness says. *Proof* is distinguished from *evidence,* in that proof is the legal consequence of evidence. (2) The rules of law, called the law of evidence, that deter what evidence shall be introduced at a trial and what shall not; also, what importance shall be placed upon the evidence.

Ex contractu *See* Action ex contractu.

Exculpatory clause A provision in a contract whereby one of the parties attempts to relieve itself of liability for breach of a legal duty.

Exclusive dealing contract A contract under which a buyer agrees to purchase a certain product exclusively from the seller or in which the seller agrees to sell all his product production to the buyer.

Ex delicto *See* Action ex delicto.

Executed Applied to contracts or other written instruments, *executed* means signed, sealed, and delivered. Effective legal obligations have thus been created. The term is also used to mean that the performances of a contract have been completed. The contract is then at an end. All is done that is to be done.

Execution Execution of a judgment is the process by which the court, through the sheriff, enforces the payment of the judgment received by the successful party. The sheriff, by a "writ," levies upon the unsuccessful party's property and sells it to pay the judgment creditor.

Executor (of an estate) The person whom the testator (the one who makes the will) names or appoints to administer his estate upon his death and to dispose of it according to his intention. The terms *executor* and *administrator* are not synonyms. A person who makes a will appoints an executor to administer his estate. A court appoints an administrator to administer the estate of a person who dies without having made a will. *See* Intestate.

Executory (contract) Until the performance required in a contract is completed, it is said to be executory as to that part not executed. *See* Executed.

Exemplary damages A sum assessed by the jury in a tort action (over and above the compensatory damages) as punishment, in order to make an example of the wrongdoer and to deter like conduct by others. Injuries caused by willful, malicious, wanton, and reckless conduct will subject the wrongdoers to exemplary damages.

Exemption The condition of a person who is free or excused from a duty imposed by some rule of law, statutory or otherwise.

Express warranty When a seller makes some positive representation concerning the nature, quality, character, use, and purpose of goods, which induces the buyer to buy, and the seller intends the buyer to rely thereon, the seller has made an express warranty.

Factor An agent for the sale of merchandise. He may hold possession of the goods in his own name or in the name of his principal. He is authorized to sell and to receive payment for the goods. *See* Agent.

Factor's lien A factor's right to keep goods consigned to him if he may reimburse himself for advances previously made to the consignor.

Farm products* Crops or livestock or supplies used or produced in farming operations; products of crops or livestock in their unmanufactured states (such as ginned cotton, wool-clip, maple syrup, milk, and eggs); and goods in the possession of a debtor engaged in raising, fattening, grazing, or other farming operations. If goods are farm products, they are neither equipment nor inventory.

Featherbedding In labor relations, a demand for the payment of wages for a service not actually rendered.

Fee simple estate The total interest a person may have in land. Such an estate is not qualified by any other interest, and it passes upon the death of the owners to the heirs, free from any conditions.

Fellow servant doctrine Precludes an injured employee from recovering damages from his employer when the injury resulted from the negligent act of another employee.

Felony All criminal offenses that are punishable by death or imprisonment in a penitentiary.

Fiduciary In general, a person is a fiduciary when he occupies a position of trust or confidence in relation to another person or his property. Trustees, guardians, and executors occupy fiduciary positions.

Financing agency* A bank, finance company, or person who, in the ordinary course of business, makes advances against goods or documents of title; or who, by arrangement with either the seller or the buyer, intervenes in ordinary course to make or collect payment due or claimed under the contract for sale, as by purchasing or paying the seller's draft or making advances against it or by merely taking it for collection, whether or not documents of title accompany the draft. "Financing agency" includes a bank or person who similarly intervenes between persons who are in the position of seller and buyer in respect to the goods.

Fine A sum of money collected by a court from a person guilty of some criminal offense. The amount may be fixed by statute or left to the discretion of the court.

Firm offer* An offer by a merchant to buy or sell goods in a signed writing that, by its terms, gives assurance it will be held open.

Forbearance Giving up the right to enforce what one honestly believes to be a valid claim, in return for a promise. It is sufficient "consideration" to make a promise binding.

Forcible entry and detainer A remedy given to a landowner to evict persons unlawfully in possession of his land. A landlord may use such remedy to evict a tenant in default.

Forfeiture Money or property taken as compensation and punishment for injury or damage to the person or property of another or to the state. One may forfeit interest earnings for charging a usurious rate.

Forgery False writing or alteration of an instrument with the fraudulent intent of deceiving and injuring another. Writing another's name upon a check, without his consent, to secure money.

Franchise A right conferred or granted by a legislative body. It is a contract right and cannot be revoked without cause. A franchise is more than a license. A license is only a privilege and may be revoked. A corporation exists by virtue of a "franchise." A corporation secures a franchise from the city council to operate a waterworks within the city. *See* License.

Franchise tax A tax on the right of a corporation to do business under its corporate name.

Fraud An intentional misrepresentation of the truth for the purpose of deceiving another person. The elements of fraud are (1) intentionally false representation of fact, not opinion, (2) intent that the deceived person act thereon, (3) knowledge that such statements would naturally deceive, and (4) that the deceived person acted to his injury.

Fraudulent conveyance A conveyance of property by a debtor for the intent and purpose of defrauding his creditors. It is of no effect, and such property may be reached by the creditors through appropriate legal proceedings.

Freehold An estate in fee or for life. A freeholder is usually a person who has a property right in the title to real estate amounting to an estate of inheritance (in fee), or one who has title for life or an indeterminate period.

Full-line forcing An arrangement in which a manufacturer refuses to supply any portion of the product line unless the retailer agrees to accept the entire line.

Fungible* Goods and securities of which any unit is, by nature or usage of trade, the equivalent of any other like unit.

Fungible goods Fungible goods are those "of which any unit is from its nature of mercantile usage treated as the equivalent of any other unit." Grain, wine, and similar items are examples.

Future goods* Goods that are not both existing and identified.

Futures Contracts for the sale and delivery of commodities in the future, made with the intention that no commodity be delivered or received immediately.

Garnishee A person upon whom a garnishment is served. He is a debtor of a defendant and has money or property that the plaintiff is trying to reach in order to satisfy a debt due from the defendant. Also used as a verb: "to garnishee wages or property."

Garnishment A proceeding by which a plaintiff seeks to reach the credits of the defendant that are in the hands of a third party, the garnishee. A garnishment is distinguished from an attachment in that by an attachment, an officer of the court takes actual possession of property by virtue of his writ. In a garnishment, the property or money is left with the garnishee until final adjudication.

General agent An agent authorized to do all the acts connected with carrying on a particular trade, business, or profession.

General intangibles* Any personal property (including things in action) other than goods, accounts, contract rights, chattel paper, documents, and instruments.

Gift A gift is made when a donor delivers the subject matter of the gift into the donee's hands or places in the donee the means of obtaining possession of the subject matter, accompanied by such acts that show clearly the donor's intentions to divest himself of all dominion and control over the property.

Gift causa mortis A gift made in anticipation of death. The donor must have been in sickness and have died as expected, otherwise no effective gift has been made. If the donor survives, the gift is revocable.

Gift inter vivos An effective gift made during the life of the donor. By a gift inter vivos, property vests immediately in the donee at the time of delivery, whereas a gift causa mortis is made in contemplation of death and is effective only upon the donor's death.

Good faith* Honesty in fact in the conduct or transaction concerned. Referring to a merchant, good faith means honesty in fact and the observance of reasonable commercial standards of fair dealing in the trade.

Goods* All things that are movable at the time of identification to the contract for sale, including specially manufactured goods but not money in which the price is to be paid, investment securities, and things in action. Includes unborn young animals, growing crops, and other identified things attached to realty as described in the section on goods to be severed from realty.

Grant A term used in deeds for the transfer of the title to real property. The words *convey, transfer,* and *grant,* as operative words in a deed to pass title, are equivalent. The words *grant, bargain,* and *sell* in a deed, in absence of statute, mean the grantor promises he has good title to transfer free from incumbrances and warrants it to be such.

Grantee A person to whom a grant is made; one named in a deed to receive title.

Grantor A person who makes a grant. The grantor executes the deed by which he divests himself of title.

Gross negligence The lack of even slight or ordinary care.

Guarantor One who by contract undertakes "to answer for the debt, default, and miscarriage of another." In general, a guarantor undertakes to pay if the principal debtor does not; a surety, on the other hand, joins in the contract of the principal and becomes an original party with the principal.

Guardian A person appointed by the court to look after the property rights and person of minors, the insane, and other incompetents or legally incapacitated persons.

Guardian ad litem A special guardian appointed for the sole purpose of carrying on litigation and preserving the interests of a ward. He exercises no control or power over property.

Habeas corpus A writ issued to a sheriff, warden, or other official having allegedly unlawful custody of a person, directing the official to bring the person before a court, in order to determine the legality of the imprisonment.

Hearsay evidence Evidence that is learned from someone else. It does not derive its value from the credit of the witness testifying but rests upon the veracity of another person. It is not good evidence, because there is no opportunity to cross-examine the person who is the source of the testimony.

Hedging contract A contract of purchase or sale of an equal amount of commodities in the future, by which brokers, dealers, or manufacturers protect themselves against the fluctuations of the market. It is a type of insurance against changing prices. A grain dealer, to protect himself, may contract to sell for future delivery the same amount of grain he has purchased in the present market.

Heirs Persons upon whom the statute of descent casts the title to real property upon the death of the ancestor. Consult Statute of Descent for the appropriate state. *See* Descent.

Holder* A person who is in possession of a document of title or an instrument or an investment security drawn, issued, or indorsed to him or to his order or to bearer or in blank.

Holder in due course One who has acquired possession of a negotiable instrument through proper negotiation for value, in good faith, and without notice of any defenses to it. Such a holder is not subject to personal defenses that would otherwise defeat the obligation embodied in the instrument.

Holding company A corporation organized for the purpose of owning and holding the stock of other corporations. Shareholders of underlying corporations receive in exchange for their stock, upon an agreed value, the shares in the holding corporation.

Homestead A parcel of land upon which a family dwells or resides, and which to them is home. The statute of the state or federal governments should be consulted to determine the meaning of the term as applied to debtor's exemptions, federal land grants, and so forth.

Honor* To pay or to accept and pay or, where a creditor so engages, to purchase or discount a draft complying with the terms of the instrument.

Horizontal merger Merger of corporations that were competitors prior to the merger.

Hot-cargo contract An agreement between employer and union, whereby an employer agrees to refrain from handling, using, selling, transporting, or otherwise dealing in the products of another employer or agrees to cease doing business with some other person.

Illegal Contrary to public policy and the fundamental principles of law. Illegal conduct includes not only violations of criminal statutes but also the creation of agreements that are prohibited by statute and the common law.

Illusory That which has a false appearance. If that which appears to be a promise is not a promise, it is said to be illusory. "I promise to buy your lunch if I decide to." This equivocal statement would not justify reliance, so it is not a promise.

Immunity Freedom from the legal duties and penalties imposed upon others. The "privileges and immunities" clause of the United States Constitution means no state can deny to the citizens of another state the same rights granted to its own citizens. This does not apply to office holding. *See* Exemption.

Implied The finding of a legal right or duty by inference from facts or circumstances. *See* Warranty.

Implied-in-fact contract A legally enforceable agreement inferred from the circumstances and conduct of the parties.

Imputed negligence Negligence that is not directly attributable to the person himself but is the negligence of a person who is in privity with him and with whose fault he is chargeable.

Incidental beneficiary If the performance of a promise would indirectly benefit a person not a party to a contract, such person is an incidental beneficiary. A promises B, for a consideration, to plant a valuable nut orchard on B's land. Such improvement would increase the value of the adjacent land. C, the owner of the adjacent land, is an incidental beneficiary. He has no remedy if A breaches his promise with B.

Incumbrance A burden on either the title to land or thing or upon the land or thing itself. A mortgage or other lien is an incumbrance upon the title. A right-of-way over the land is an incumbrance upon the land and affects its physical condition.

Indemnify Literally, "to save harmless." Thus, one person agrees to protect another against loss.

Indenture A deed executed by both parties, as distinguished from a deed poll that is executed only by the grantor.

Independent contractor The following elements are essential to establish the relation of independent contractor, in contradistinction to principal and agent. An independent contractor must (1) exercise his independent judgment on the means used to accomplish the result; (2) be free from control or orders from any other person; (3) be responsible only under his contract for the result obtained.

Indictment A finding by a grand jury that it has reason to believe the accused is guilty as charged. It informs the accused of the offense with which he is charged, so that he may prepare its defense. It is a pleading in a criminal action.

Indorsement Writing one's name upon paper for the purpose of transferring the title. When a payee of a negotiable instrument writes his name on the back of the instrument, his writing is an indorsement.

Infringement Infringement of a patent on a machine is the manufacturing of a machine that produces the same result by the same means and operation as the patented machine. Infringement of a trademark consists in reproduction of a registered trademark and its use upon goods in order to mislead the public to believe that the goods are the genuine, original product.

Inherit The word is used in contradistinction to acquiring property by will. *See* Descent.

Inheritance An estate that descends to heirs. *See* Descent.

Injunction A writ of judicial process issued by a court of equity, by which a party is required to do a particular thing or to refrain from doing a particular thing.

In personam A legal proceeding, the judgment of which binds the defeated party to a personal liability.

In rem A legal proceeding, the judgment of which binds, affects, or determines the status of property.

Insolvent* Refers to a person who either has ceased to pay his debts in the ordinary course of business or cannot pay his debts as they become due or is insolvent within the meaning of the federal bankruptcy law.

Installment contract* One which requires or authorizes the delivery of goods in separate lots to be separately accepted, even though the contract contains a clause "each delivery is a separate contract" or its equivalent.

Instrument* A negotiable instrument or a security or any other writing that evidences a right to the payment of money and is not itself a security agreement or lease and is of a type that is in ordinary course of business transferred by delivery with any necessary indorsement or assignment.

Insurable interest A person has an insurable interest in a person or property if he will be directly and financially affected by the death of the person or the loss of the property.

Insurance By an insurance contract, one party, for an agreed premium, binds himself to another, called the insured, to pay the insured a sum of money conditioned upon the loss of life or property of the insured.

Intangible property Something which represents value but has no intrinsic value of its own, such as a note or bond.

Intent A state of mind that exists prior to, or contemporaneous with, an act. A purpose or design to do or forbear to do an act. It cannot be directly proven but is inferred from known facts.

Interlocutory decree A decree of a court of equity that does not settle the complete issue but settles only some intervening part, awaiting a final decree.

Intermediary bank* Under Article 4—Bank Deposits and Collections, it is any bank—except the depositary or payor bank—to which an item is transferred in course of collection.

Interpleader A procedure whereby a person who has an obligation, e.g., to pay money, but does not know which of two or more claimants are entitled to performance, can bring a suit that requires the contesting parties to litigate between themselves.

Interrogatory A written question from one party to another in a lawsuit; a type of discovery procedure.

Intestate The intestate laws are the laws of descent or distribution of the estate of a deceased person. A person who has not made a will dies intestate.

Inventory* Goods that a person holds for sale or lease or to be—or which have been—furnished under contracts of service, or goods that are raw materials, work in process, or materials used or consumed in a business. Inventory of a person is not to be classified as his equipment.

Irreparable damage or injury *Irreparable* does not mean injury beyond the possibility of repair, but it does mean that it is so constant and frequent in occurrence that no fair or reasonable redress can be had in a court of law. Thus, the plaintiff must seek a remedy in equity by way of an injunction.

Issue* Under Article 3—Commercial Paper, *issue* means the first delivery of an instrument to a holder or a remitter.

Issuer* A bailee who issues a document; but in relation to an unaccepted delivery order, the issuer is the person who orders the possessor of goods to deliver. Issuer includes any person for whom an agent or employee purports to act in issuing a document if the agent or employee has real or apparent authority to issue documents, notwithstanding that the issuer received no goods or that the goods were misdescribed or that in any other respect the agent or employee violated the issuer's instructions.

Item* Under Article 4—Bank Deposits and Collections, *item* means any instrument for the payment of money, even though it is not negotiable, but does not include money.

Jeopardy A person is in jeopardy when he is regularly charged with a crime before a court properly organized and competent to try him. If acquitted, he cannot be tried again for the same offense.

Joint and several Two or more persons have an obligation that binds them individually as well as jointly. The obligation can be enforced either by joint action against all of them or by separate actions against one or more.

Joint ownership The interest that two or more parties have in property. *See* Joint tenants.

Joint tenants Two or more persons to whom land is deeded in such manner that they have "one and the same interest, accruing by one and the same conveyance, commencing at one and the same time, and held by one and the same undivided possession." Upon the death of one joint tenant, his property passes to the survivor or survivors.

Joint tortfeasors When two persons commit an injury with a common intent, they are joint tortfeasors.

Judgment (in law) The decision, pronouncement, or sentence rendered by a court upon an issue in which it has jurisdiction.

Judgment in personam A judgment against a person, directing the defendant to do or not to do something. *See* In personam.

Judgment in rem A judgment against a thing, as distinguished from a judgment against a person. *See* In rem.

Judicial restraint A judicial philosophy. Those following it believe that the power of judicial review should be exercised with great restraint.

Judicial review The power of courts to declare laws and executive actions unconstitutional.

Judicial sale A sale authorized by a court that has jurisdiction to grant such authority. Such sales are conducted by an officer of the court.

Jurisdiction The authority to try causes and determine cases. Conferred upon a court by the Constitution.

Jury A group of persons, usually twelve, sworn to declare the facts of a case as they are proved from the evidence presented to them and, upon instructions from the court, to find a verdict in the cause before them.

Laches A term used in equity to name conduct that neglects to assert one's rights or to do what, by the law, a person should have done. Failure on the part of one to assert a right will give an equitable defense to another party.

Latent defect A defect in materials not discernible by examination. Used in contradistinction to patent defect, which is discernible.

Lease A contract by which one person divests himself of possession of lands or chattels and grants such possession to another for a period of time. The relationship in which land is involved is called landlord and tenant.

Leasehold The land held by a tenant under a lease.

Legacy Personal property disposed of by a will. Sometimes the term is synonymous with *bequest*. The word *devise* is used in connection with real property distributed by will. *See* Bequest; Devise.

Legatee A person to whom a legacy is given by will.

Liability In its broadest legal sense, *liability* means any obligation one may be under by reason of some rule of law. It includes debt, duty, and responsibility.

Libel Malicious publication of a defamation of a person by printing, writing, signs, or pictures, for the purposes of injuring the reputation and good name of such person. "The exposing of a person to public hatred, contempt, or ridicule."

License (governmental regulation) A license is a privilege granted by a state or city upon the payment of a fee. It confers authority upon the licensee to do some act or series of acts, which otherwise would be illegal. A license is not a contract and may be revoked for cause. It is a method of governmental regulation exercised under the police power.

License (privilege) A mere personal privilege given by the owner to another to do designated acts upon the land of the owner. It is revocable at will and creates no estate in the land. The licensee is not in possession. "It is a mere excuse for what otherwise would be a trespass."

Lien The right of one person, usually a creditor, to keep possession of, or control, the property of another for the purpose of satisfying a debt. There are many kinds of liens: judgment lien, attorney's lien, innkeeper's lien, logger's lien, vendor's lien. Consult statute of state for type of lien. *See* Judgment.

Lien creditor* A creditor who has acquired a lien on property involved by attachment, levy, or the like. Includes an assignee for benefit of creditors from the time of assignment and a trustee in bankruptcy from the date of the filing of the petition or a receiver in equity from the time of appointment. Unless all the creditors represented had knowledge of the security interest, such a representative of creditors is a lien creditor without knowledge even though he personally has knowledge of the security interest.

Limitation of actions Statutes of limitations exist for the purpose of bringing to an end old claims. Because witnesses die, memory fails, papers are lost, and the evidence becomes inadequate, stale claims are barred. Such statutes are called statutes of repose. Within a certain period of time, action on claims must be brought; otherwise, they are barred. The period varies from 6 months to 20 years.

Limited partnership A partnership in which one or more individuals are general partners and one or more individuals are limited partners. The limited partners contribute assets to the partnership without taking part in the conduct of the business. They are liable for the debts of the partnership only to the extent of their contributions.

Liquidated A claim is liquidated when it has been made fixed and certain by the parties concerned.

Liquidated damages A fixed sum agreed upon between the parties to a contract, to be paid as ascertained damages by the party who breaches the contract. If the sum is excessive, the courts will declare it to be a penalty and unenforceable.

Liquidation The process of winding up the affairs of a corporation or firm for the purpose of paying its debts and disposing of its assets. May be done voluntarily or under the orders of a court.

Lis pendens "Pending the suit nothing should be changed." The court, having control of the property involved in the suit, issues notice *lis pendens,* that persons dealing with the defendant regarding the subject matter of the suit do so subject to final determination of the action.

Lot* A parcel or a single article that is the subject matter of a separate sale or delivery, whether or not it is sufficient to perform the contract.

Magistrate A public officer, usually a judge, "who has power to issue a warrant for the arrest of a person charged with a public offense." The word has wide application and includes justices of the peace, notaries public, recorders, and other public officers who have power to issue executive orders.

Malice Describes a wrongful act done intentionally without excuse. It does not necessarily mean ill will, but it indicates a state of mind that is reckless concerning the law and the rights of others. *Malice* is distinguished from *negligence*. With *malice* there is always a purpose to injure, whereas such is not true of the word *negligence*.

Malicious prosecution The prosecution of another at law with malice and without probable cause to believe that such legal action will be successful.

Mandamus A writ issued by a court of law, in the name of the state. Writs of mandamus are directed to inferior courts, officers, corporations, or persons, commanding them to do particular things that appertain to their offices or duties.

Mandatory injunction An injunctive order issued by a court of equity that compels affirmative action by the defendant.

Marketable title A title of such character that no apprehension as to its validity would occur to the mind of a reasonable and intelligent person. The title to goods is not marketable if it is in litigation, subject to incumbrances, in doubt as to a third party's right, or subject to lien.

Marshaling assets A principle in equity for a fair distribution of a debtor's assets among his creditors. For example, a creditor of A, by reason of prior right, has two funds, *X* and *Y*, belonging to A, out of which he may satisfy his debt. But another creditor of A also has a right to *X* fund. The first creditor will be compelled to exhaust *Y* fund before he will be permitted to participate in *X* fund.

Master in chancery An officer appointed by the court to assist the court of equity in taking testimony, computing interest, auditing accounts, estimating damages, ascertaining liens, and doing other tasks incidental to a suit, as the court requires. The power of a master is merely advisory, and his tasks are largely fact finding.

Maxim A proposition of law that because of its universal approval needs no proof or argument; the mere statement of which gives it authority. Example: "A principal is bound by the acts of his agent when the agent is acting within the scope of his authority."

Mechanic's lien Created by statute to assist suppliers and laborers in collecting their accounts and wages. Its purpose is to subject the land of an owner to a lien for material and labor expended in the construction of buildings and other improvements.

Merchant A person who deals in goods of the kind involved in a transaction; or one who otherwise, by his occupation, holds himself out as having knowledge or skill peculiar to the practices or goods involved; or one to whom such knowledge or skill may be attributed because he employs an agent or broker or other intermediary who, by his occupation, holds himself out as having such knowledge or skill.

Merger Two corporations are merged when one corporation continues in existence and the other loses its identity by its absorption into the first. *Merger* must be distinguished from *consolidation*. In consolidation, both corporations are dissolved, and a new one is created, the new one taking over the assets of the dissolved corporations.

Metes and bounds The description of the boundaries of real property.

Midnight deadline* Under Article 4—Bank Deposits and Collections, this is midnight on the next banking day following the banking day on which a bank receives the relevant item or notice, or from which the time for taking action commences to run, whichever is later.

Ministerial duty A prescribed duty that requires little judgment or discretion. A sheriff performs ministerial duties.

Minutes The record of a court or the written transactions of the members or board of directors of a corporation. Under the certificate of the clerk of a court or the secretary of a corporation, the minutes are the official evidence of court or corporate action.

Misdemeanor A criminal offense, less than a felony, that is not punishable by death or imprisonment. Consult the local statute.

Misrepresentation The affirmative statement or affirmation of a fact that is not true; the term does not include concealment of true facts or nondisclosure or the mere expression of opinion.

Mistake of fact The unconscious ignorance or forgetfulness of the existence or nonexistence of a fact, past or present, which is material and important to the creation of a legal obligation.

Mistake of law An erroneous conclusion of the legal effect of known facts.

Mitigation of damages A plaintiff is entitled to recover damages caused by the defendant's breach, but the plaintiff is also under a duty to avoid increasing or enhancing such damages. This duty is called a duty to mitigate damages. If a seller fails to deliver the proper goods on time, the buyer, where possible, must buy other goods, thus mitigating damages.

Monopoly Exclusive control of the supply and price of a commodity. May be acquired by a franchise or patent from the government; or the ownership of the source of a commodity or the control of its distribution.

Mortgage A conveyance or transfer of an interest in property for the purpose of creating a security for a debt. The mortgage becomes void upon payment of the debt, although the recording of a release is necessary to clear the title of the mortgaged property.

Mutual assent In every contract, each party must agree to the same thing. Each must know what the other intends; they must mutually assent or be in agreement.

Mutual mistake A situation in which parties to a contract reach a bargain on the basis of an incorrect assumption common to each party.

Mutuality The binding of both parties in every contract. Each party to the contract must be bound to the other party to do something by virtue of the legal duty created.

Negligence Failure to do that which an ordinary, reasonable, prudent man would do, or the doing of some act that an ordinary, prudent man would not do. Reference must always be made to the situation, the circumstances, and the knowledge of the parties.

Negotiation* Under Article 3—Commercial Paper, this is the transfer of an instrument in such form that the transferee becomes a holder. If the instrument is payable to order, it is negotiated by delivery with any necessary indorsement; if payable to bearer, it is negotiated by delivery.

Net assets Property or effects of a firm, corporation, institution, or estate, remaining after all its obligations have been paid.

Nexus Connection, tie, or link used in the law of taxation to establish a connection between a tax and the activity or person being taxed.

NLRB National Labor Relations Board.

No-fault laws Laws barring tort actions by injured persons against third-party tortfeasors and requiring injured persons to obtain recovery from their own insurers.

Nolo contendere A plea by an accused in a criminal action. It does not admit guilt of the offense charged but does equal a plea of guilty for purpose of sentencing.

Nominal damages A small sum assessed as sufficient to

award the case and cover the costs when no actual damages have been proven.

Nonsuit A judgment given against the plaintiff when he is unable to prove his case or fails to proceed with the trial after the case is at issue.

Noscitur a sociis The meaning of a word is or may be known from the accompanying words.

Notary A public officer authorized to administer oaths by way of affidavits and depositions. Attests deeds and other formal papers, in order that they may be used as evidence and be qualified for recording.

Notice* A person has "notice" of a fact when (a) he has actual knowledge of it; or (b) he has received a notice or notification of it; or (c) from all the facts and circumstances known to him at the time in question, he has reason to know that it exists. A person "knows" or has "knowledge" of a fact when he has actual knowledge of it. "Discover" or "learn" or a word or phrase of similar import refers to knowledge rather than to reason to know.

Novation The substitution of one obligation for another. When debtor A is substituted for debtor B, and by agreement with the creditor C, debtor B is discharged, a novation has occurred.

Nudum pactum A naked promise—one for which no consideration has been given.

Nuisance Generally, any continuous or continued conduct that causes annoyance, inconvenience, and damage to person or property. *Nuisance* usually applies to unreasonable, wrongful use of property, causing material discomfort, hurt, and damage to the person or property of another. Example: fumes from a factory.

Obligee A creditor or promisee.

Obligor A debtor or promisor.

Oligopoly Control of a commodity or service in a given market by a small number of companies or suppliers.

Option A right secured by a contract to accept or reject an offer to purchase property at a fixed price within a fixed time. It is an irrevocable offer sometimes called a "paid-for offer."

Order* Under Article 3—Commercial Paper, *order* is a direction to pay and must be more than an authorization or request. It must, with reasonable certainty, identify the person to pay. It may be addressed to one or more such persons jointly or in the alternative but not in succession.

Ordinance Generally speaking, the legislative act of a municipality. A city council is a legislative body, and it passes ordinances that are the laws of the city.

Ordinary care Care that a prudent man would take under the circumstances of the particular case.

Par value "Face value." The par value of stocks and bonds on the date of issuance is the principal. At a later date, the par value is the principal plus interest.

Pari delicto The fault or blame is shared equally.

Pari materia "Related to the same matter or subject." Statutes and covenants concerning the same subject matter are in pari materia and as a general rule, for the purpose of ascertaining their meaning, are construed together.

Parol evidence Legal proof based on oral statements; with regard to a document, any evidence extrinsic to the document itself.

Partition Court proceedings brought by an interested party's request that the court divide real property among respective owners as their interests appear. If the property cannot be divided in kind, then it is to be sold and the money divided as each interest appears.

Party* A person who has engaged in a transaction or made an agreement within the Uniform Commercial Code.

Patent ambiguity An obvious uncertainty in a written instrument.

Payor bank* Under Article 4—Bank Deposits and Collections, a bank by which an item is payable as drawn or accepted.

Penal bond A bond given by an accused, or by another person in his behalf, for the payment of money if the accused fails to appear in court on a certain day.

Pendente lite "Pending during the progress of a suit at law."

Per curiam A decision by the full court without indicating the author of the decision.

Peremptory challenge An objection raised by a party to a lawsuit who rejects a person serving as a juror. No reason need be given.

Perjury False swearing upon an oath properly administered in some judicial proceedings.

Per se "By itself." Thus, a contract clause may be inherently unconscionable—unconscionable per se.

Personal property The rights, powers, and privileges a person has in movable things, such as chattels and choses in action. Personal property is used in contradistinction to real property.

Personal representative The administrator or executor of a deceased person or the guardian of a child or the conservator of an incompetent.

Personal service The sheriff personally delivers a service of process to the defendant.

Plaintiff In an action at law, the complaining party or the one who commences the action. The person who seeks a remedy in court.

Plea An allegation or answer in a court proceeding.

Pleading Process by which the parties in a lawsuit arrive at an issue.

Pledge Personal property, as security for a debt or other obligation, deposited or placed with a person called a pledgee. The pledgee has the implied power to sell the property if the debt is not paid. If the debt is paid, the right to possession returns to the pledgor.

Polling jury Calling the name of each juror to inquire what his verdict is before it is made a matter of record.

Possession The method recognized by law and used by one's self or by another to hold, detain, or control either personal or real property, thereby excluding others from holding, detaining, or controlling such property.

Power of attorney An instrument authorizing another to act as one's agent or attorney in fact.

Precedent A previously decided case that can serve as an authority to help decide a present controversy. Use of such case is called the doctrine of *stare decisis,* which means to adhere to decided cases and settled principles. Literally, "to stand as decided."

Preference The term is used most generally in bankruptcy law. If a bankrupt pays some creditors a greater percentage of the debts than he pays other creditors in the same class, and if the payments are made within 4 months prior to his filing a bankruptcy petition, those payments constitute illegal and voidable preference. An intention to prefer such creditors must be shown.

Preferred stock Stock that entitles the holder to dividends from earnings before the owners of common stock can receive a dividend.

Preponderance Preponderance of the evidence means that evidence, in the judgment of the jurors, is entitled to the greatest weight, appears to be more credible, has greater force, and overcomes not only the opposing presumptions but also the opposing evidence.

Presenting bank* Under Article 4—Bank Deposits and Collections, this is any bank presenting an item except a payor bank.

Presentment* Under Article 3—Commercial Paper, presentment is a demand for acceptance or payment made upon the maker, acceptor, drawee, or other payor by, or on behalf of, the holder.

Presumption (presumed)* The trier of fact must find the existence of the fact presumed unless and until evidence is introduced that would support a finding of its nonexistence.

Prima facie Literally, "at first view." Thus, that which first appears seems to be true. A prima facie case is one that stands until contrary evidence is produced.

Privilege A legal idea or concept of lesser significance than a right. An invitee has only a privilege to walk on another's land, because such privilege may be revoked at will; whereas a person who has an easement to go on another's land has a right created by a grant, which is an interest in land and cannot be revoked at will. To be exempt from jury service is a privilege.

Privity Mutual and successive relationship to the same interest. Offeror and offeree, assignor and assignee, grantor and grantee are in privity. Privity of estate means that one takes title from another. In contract law, privity denotes parties in mutual legal relationship to each other by virtue of being promisees and promisors. At early common law, third-party beneficiaries and assignees were said to be not in "privity."

Probate court Handles the settlement of estates.

Proceeds* Whatever is received when collateral or proceeds are sold, exchanged, collected or otherwise disposed of. Includes the account arising when the right to payment is earned under a contract right. Money, checks, and the like are "cash proceeds." All other proceeds are "noncash proceeds."

Process In a court proceeding, before or during the progress of the trial, an instrument issued by the court in the name of the state and under the seal of the court, directing an officer of the court to do, act, or cause some act to be done incidental to the trial.

Product extension merger A merger that extends the products of the acquiring company into a similar or related product but one which is not directly in competition with existing products.

Promise* Under Article 3—Commercial Paper, it is an undertaking to pay, and it must be more than an acknowledgment of an obligation.

Property All rights, powers, privileges, and immunities that one has concerning tangibles and intangibles. The term includes everything of value subject to ownership.

Proximate cause The cause that sets other causes in operation. The responsible cause of an injury.

Proxy Authority to act for another, used by absent stockholders or members of legislative bodies to have their votes cast by others.

Punitive damages Damages by way of punishment. Allowed for an injury caused by a wrong that is willful and malicious.

Purchase* Includes taking by sale, discount, negotiation, mortgage, pledge, lien, issue or re-issue, gift, or any other voluntary transaction creating an interest in property.

Purchase-money security interest* A security interest that is taken or retained by the seller of the collateral to secure all or part of its price; or taken by a person who, by making advances or incurring an obligation, gives value to enable the debtor to acquire rights in, or the use of, collateral if such value is in fact so used.

Quasi contract A situation in which there arises a legal duty that does not rest upon a promise but does involve the payment of money. In order to do justice by a legal fiction, the court enforces the duty as if a promise in fact exists. Thus, if A gives B money by mistake, A can compel B to return the money by an action in quasi contract.

Quasi-judicial Administrative actions involving factual determinations and the discretionary application of rules and regulations.

Quid pro quo The exchange of one thing of value for another.

Quiet title A suit brought by the owner of real property for the purpose of bringing into court any person who claims an adverse interest in the property, requiring him either to establish his claim or be barred from asserting it thereafter. It may be said that the purpose is to remove "clouds" from the title.

Quitclaim A deed that releases a right or interest in land but does not include any covenants of warranty. The grantor transfers only that which he has.

Quo warranto A proceeding in court by which a governmental body tests or inquires into the authority or legality of the claim of any person to a public office, franchise, or privilege.

Ratification The confirmation of one's own previous act or act of another: e.g., a principal may ratify the previous unauthorized act of his agent. B's agent, without authority, buys goods. B, by keeping the goods and receiving the benefits of the agent's act, ratifies the agency.

Ratio decidendi Logical basis of judicial decision.

Real property Land with all its buildings, appurtenances, equitable and legal interests therein. In contradistinction to personal property, which refers to movables or chattels.

Reasonable care The care that prudent persons would exercise under the same circumstances.

Receiver An officer of the court appointed on behalf of all parties to the litigation to take possession of, hold, and control the property involved in the suit, for the benefit of the party who will be determined to be entitled thereto.

Recoupment "A cutting back." A right to deduct from the plaintiff's claim any payment or loss that the defendant has suffered by reason of the plaintiff's wrongful act.

Redemption To buy back. A debtor buys back or redeems his mortgaged property when he pays the debt.

Referee A person to whom a cause pending in a court is referred by the court, to take testimony, hear the parties, and report thereon to the court.

Registered form* A security is in registered form when it specifies a person entitled to the security or to the rights it evidences and when its transfer may be registered upon books maintained for that purpose by, or on behalf of, an issuer, as security states.

Reinsurance In a contract of reinsurance, one insurance company agrees to indemnify another insurance company in whole or in part against risks that the first company has assumed. The original contract of insurance and the reinsurance contract are distinct contracts. There is no privity between the original insured and the reinsurer.

Release The voluntary relinquishing of a right, lien, or any other obligation. A release need not be under seal, nor does it necessarily require consideration. The words *release, remise,* and *discharge* are often used together to mean the same thing.

Remand To send back a case from the appellate court to the lower court, in order that the lower court may comply with the instructions of the appellate court. Also to return a prisoner to jail.

Remedy The word is used to signify the judicial means or court procedures by which legal and equitable rights are enforced.

Remitting bank* Under Article 4—Bank Deposits and Collections, any payor or intermediary bank remitting for an item.

Replevin A remedy given by statute for the recovery of the possession of a chattel. Only the right to possession can be tried in such action.

Res "Thing."

Res adjudicata A controversy once having been decided or adjudged upon its merits is forever settled so far as the particular parties involved are concerned. Such a doctrine avoids vexatious lawsuits.

Rescind To cancel or annul a contract and return the parties to their original positions.

Rescission An apparently valid act may conceal a defect that will make it null and void if any of the parties demand that it be rescinded.

Respondeat superior "The master is liable for the acts of his agent."

Respondent One who answers another's bill or pleading, particularly in an equity case. Quite similar, in many instances, to a defendant in a law case.

Responsible bidder In the phrase "lowest responsible bidder," *responsible,* as used by most statutes concerning public works, means that such bidder has the requisite skill, judgment, and integrity necessary to perform the contract involved and has the financial resources and ability to carry the task to completion.

Restraining order Issued by a court of equity in aid of a suit, to hold matters in abeyance until parties may be heard. A temporary injunction.

Restraint of trade Monopolies, combinations, and contracts that impede free competition.

Right The phrase "legal right" is a correlative of the phrase "legal duty." One has a legal right if, upon the breach of the correlative legal duty, he can secure a remedy in a court of law.

Right of action Synonymous with *cause of action:* a right to enforce a claim in a court.

Right-to-work law A state statute that outlaws a union shop contract; one by which an employer agrees to require membership in the union sometime after an employee has been hired, as a condition of continued employment.

Riparian A person is a riparian owner if his land is situated beside a stream of water, either flowing over or along the border of the land.

Satisfaction In legal phraseology, the release and discharge of a legal obligation. Satisfaction may be partial or full performance of the obligation. The word is used with *accord,* a promise to give a substituted performance for a contract obligation; *satisfaction* means the acceptance by the obligee of such performance.

Scienter Knowledge by a defrauding party of the falsity of a representation. In a tort action of deceit, knowledge that a representation is false must be proved.

Seal A seal shows that an instrument was executed in a formal manner. At early common law, sealing legal documents was of great legal significance. A promise under seal was binding by virtue of the seal. Today under most statutes, any stamp, wafer, mark, scroll, or impression made, adopted, and affixed, is adequate. The printed word *seal* or the letters *L.S.* (*locus sigilli,* "the place of the seal") are sufficient.

Seasonably* An action is taken "seasonably" when it is taken at, or within, the time agreed; or if no time is agreed, at or within a reasonable time.

Secondary boycott Conspiracy or combination to cause the customers or suppliers of an employer to cease doing business with that employer.

Secondary party* Under Article 3—Commercial Paper, a drawer or indorser.

Secured party* A lender, seller, or other person in whose favor there is a security interest, including a person to whom accounts, contract rights, or chattel paper have been sold. When the holders of obligations issued under an indenture of trust, equipment trust agreement, or the like are represented by a trustee or other person, the representative is the secured party.

Security May be bonds, stocks, and other property that a debtor places with a creditor, who may sell them if the debt is not paid. The plural, *securities,* is used broadly to mean tangible choses in action, such as promissory notes, bonds, stocks, and other vendible obligations.

Security* An instrument issued in bearer form or registered form; commonly dealt in on securities exchanges or markets or commonly recognized in any area in which it is issued or dealt in as a medium for investment; one of a class or series of instruments; evidences a share, a participation or other interest in property or in an enterprise or evidences an obligation of the issuer.

Security agreement* Creates or provides for a security interest.

Security interest* An interest in personal property or fixtures that secures payment or performance of an obligation.

Sell To negotiate or make arrangement for a sale. A sale is an executed contract, a result of the process of selling.

Separation of powers The doctrine that the legislative, executive, and judicial branches of government function independently of one another and that each branch serves as a check on the others.

Servant A person employed by another and subject to the direction and control of the employer in performance of his duties.

Setoff A matter of defense, called a cross-complaint, used by the defendant for the purpose of making a demand on the plaintiff. It arises out of contract but is independent and unconnected with the cause of action set out in the complaint. *See* Counterclaims and Recoupment.

Settle* Under Article 4—Bank Deposits and Collections, *settle* means to pay in cash, by clearinghouse settlement, in a charge or credit or by remittance or otherwise as instructed. A settlement may be either provisional or final.

Severable contract A contract in which the performance is divisible. Two or more parts may be set over against each other. Items and prices may be apportioned to each other without relation to the full performance of all of its parts.

Share of stock A proportional part of the rights in the management and assets of a corporation. It is a chose in action. The certificate is the evidence of the share.

Situs "Place, situation." The place where a thing is located. The situs of personal property is the domicile of the owner. The situs of land is the state or county where it is located.

Slander An oral utterance that tends to injure the reputation of another. *See* Libel.

Special appearance The appearance in court of a person through his attorney for a limited purpose only. A court does not get jurisdiction over a person by special appearance.

Special verdict The jury finds the facts only, leaving it to the court to apply the law and draw the conclusion as to the proper disposition of the case.

Specific performance A remedy in personam in equity that compels performance of a contract to be substantial enough to do justice among the parties. A person who fails to obey a writ for specific performance may be put in jail by the equity judge for contempt of court. The remedy applies to contracts involving real property. In the absence of unique goods or peculiar circumstances, damages generally are an adequate remedy for breach of contracts involving personal property.

Standing to sue The doctrine that requires the plaintiff in a lawsuit to have a sufficient legal interest in the subject matter of the case.

Stare decisis "Stand by the decision." The law should adhere to decided cases. *See* Precedent.

Statute A law passed by the legislative body of a state.

Status quo The conditions or state of affairs at a given time.

Stock dividend New shares of its own stock issued as a dividend by a corporation to its shareholders, in order to transfer retained earnings to capital stock.

Stockholders Persons whose names appear on the books of a corporation as owners of shares of stock and who are entitled to participate in the management and control of the corporation.

Stock split A readjustment of the financial plan of a corporation, whereby each existing share of stock is split into new shares, usually with a lowering of par value.

Stock warrant A certificate that gives the holder the right to subscribe for and purchase, at a stated price, a given number of shares of stock in a corporation.

Stoppage in transitu Upon learning of the insolvency of a buyer of goods, the seller has the right to stop the goods in transit and hold them as security for the purchase price. The right is an extension of the unpaid seller's lien.

Strict liability The doctrine under which a party may be required to respond in tort damages, without regard to that party's use of due care.

Subordinate In the case of a mortgage or other security interest, the mortgagee may agree to make his mortgage inferior to another mortgage or interest.

Subpoena A process issued out of a court requiring the attendance of a witness at a trial.

Subrogation The substitution of one person in another's place, whether as a creditor or as the possessor of any lawful right, so that the substituted person may succeed to the rights, remedies, or proceeds of the claim. It rests in equity on the theory that a party who is compelled to pay a debt for which another is liable should be vested with all the rights the creditor has against the debtor. For example: an insurance company pays Y for damage to Y's car, caused by Z's negligent act. The insurance company will be subrogated to Y's cause of action against Z.

Subsequent purchaser* A person who takes a security other than by original issue.

Substantial performance The complete performance of all the essential elements of a contract. The only permissible omissions or derivations are those that are trivial, inadvertent, and inconsequential. Such performance will not justify repudiation. Compensation for defects may be substituted for actual performance.

Substantive law Law that regulates and controls the rights and duties of all persons in society. In contradistinction to the term *adjective law,* which means the rules of court procedure or remedial law, which prescribe the methods by which substantive law is enforced.

Succession The transfer by operation of law of all rights and obligations of a deceased person to those who are entitled to them.

Summary judgment A judicial determination that no genuine factual dispute exists and that one party to the lawsuit is entitled to judgment as a matter of law.

Summons A writ issued by a court to the sheriff, directing him to notify the defendant that the plaintiff claims to have a cause of action against the defendant and that he is required to answer. If the defendant does not answer, judgment will be taken by default.

Supremacy Clause Article VI, U.S. Constitution, which states that the Constitution, laws, and treaties of the United States shall be the "supreme law of the land" and shall take precedence over conflicting state laws.

Suspends payments* Under Article 4—Bank Deposits and Collections, with respect to a bank this means that it has been closed by order of the supervisory authorities, that a public officer has been appointed to take it over, or that it ceases or refuses to make payments in the ordinary course of business.

Tangible Describes property that is physical in character and capable of being moved. A debt is intangible, but a promissory note evidencing such debt is tangible. *See* Chattel, Chose in action.

Tenancy The interest in property that a tenant acquired from a landlord by a lease. It may be at will or for a term. It is an interest in land.

Tenancy by the entireties Property acquired by husband and wife whereby upon the death of one, the survivor takes the whole property. The tenancy exists in only a few states. The husband and wife are both vested with the whole estate, so that the survivor takes no new title upon death of the other but remains in possession of the whole as originally granted. For the legal effect of such estate, the state statute should be consulted. *See* Joint tenants.

Tenant The person to whom a lease is made. A lessee.

Tender To offer and produce money in satisfaction of a debt or obligation and express to the creditor a willingness to pay.

Tender of delivery* The seller must put and hold conforming goods at the buyer's disposition and give the buyer any notification reasonably necessary to enable him to take delivery.

Testamentary capacity A person is said to have testamentary capacity when he understands the nature of his business and the value of his property, knows those persons who are natural objects of his bounty, and comprehends the manner in which he has provided for the distribution of his property.

Testator A male who has died leaving a will. A female is a testatrix.

Testimony Statements made by a witness under oath or affirmation in a legal proceeding.

Title This word has limited or broad meaning. When a person has the exclusive rights, powers, privileges, and immunities to property, real and personal, tangible and intangible, against all other persons, he may be said to have the complete title thereto. The aggregate of legal relations concerning property is the title. The term is used to describe the means by which a person exercises control and dominion over property. A trustee has a limited title. *See* Possession.

Tort "Twisted" or "wrong." A wrongful act committed by one person against another person or his property. It is the breach of a legal duty imposed by law other than by contract. X assaults Y, thus committing a tort. *See* Duty, Right.

Tortfeasor One who commits a tort.

Trade fixtures Personal property placed upon, or annexed to, land leased by a tenant for the purpose of carrying on a trade or business during the term of the lease. Such property is generally to be removed at the end of the term, providing removal will not destroy or injure the premises. Trade fixtures include showcases, shelving, racks, machinery, and the like.

Trademark No complete definition can be given for a trademark. Generally it is any sign, symbol, mark, word, or arrangement of words in the form of a label adopted and used by a manufacturer or distributor to designate his particular goods, and which no other person has the legal right to use. Originally, the design or trademark indicated origin, but today it is used more as an advertising mechanism.

Transfer In its broadest sense, the word means the act by which an owner sets over or delivers his right, title, and interest in property to another person. A "bill of sale" to personal property is evidence of a transfer.

Treason The offense of attempting by overt acts to overthrow the government of the state to which the offender owes allegiance; or of betraying the state into the hands of a foreign power.

Treasury stock Stock of a corporation that has been issued by the corporation for value but is later returned to the corporation by way of gift or purchase or otherwise. It may be returned to the trustees of a corporation for the purpose of sale.

Treble damages An award of damages allowable under some statutes equal to three times the amount found by the jury to be a single recovery.

Trespass An injury to the person, property, or rights of another person committed by actual force and violence or under such circumstances that the law will infer that the injury was caused by force or violence.

Trust A relationship between persons by which one holds property for the use and benefit of another. The relationship is called fiduciary. Such rights are enforced in a court of equity. The person trusted is called a trustee. The person for whose benefit the property is held is called a beneficiary or "cestui que trust."

Trustee (generally) A person who is entrusted with the management and control of another's property and estate. A person occupying a fiduciary position. An executor, an administrator, a guardian.

Trustee in bankruptcy An agent of the court authorized to liquidate the assets of the bankrupt, protect them, and bring them to the court for final distribution for the benefit of the bankrupt and all the creditors.

Truth in lending A federal law that requires disclosure of total finance charges and the annual percentage rate for credit in order that borrowers may be able to shop for credit.

Tying contract Ties the sales of one piece of property (real or personal) to the sale or lease of another item of property.

Ultra vires "Beyond power." The acts of a corporation are ultra vires when they are beyond the power or capacity of the corporations as granted by the state in its charter.

Unauthorized* Refers to a signature or indorsement made without actual, implied, or apparent authority. Includes a forgery.

Unconscionable In the law of contracts, provisions that are oppressive, overreaching, or shocking to the conscience.

Unfair competition The imitation, by design, of the goods of another, for the purpose of palming them off on the public, misleading it, and inducing it to buy goods made by the imitator. Includes misrepresentation and deceit; thus, such conduct is fraudulent not only to competitors but to the public.

Unilateral contract A promise for an act or an act for a promise, a single enforceable promise. C promises B $10 if B will mow C's lawn. B mows the lawn. C's promise, now binding, is a unilateral contract. *See* Bilateral contract.

Usage of trade* Any practice or method of dealing so regularly observed in a place, vocation, or trade that observance may justly be expected in the transaction in question. The existence and scope of such usage are to be proved as facts. If it is established that such a usage is embodied in a written trade code or similar writing, the interpretation of the writing is for the court.

Usurious A contract is usurious if made for a loan of money at a rate of interest in excess of that permitted by statute.

Utter "Put out" or "pass off." To utter a check is to offer it to another in payment of a debt. To "utter a forged writing" means to put such writing in circulation, knowing of the falsity of the instrument, with the intent to injure another.

Value* Except as otherwise provided with respect to negotiable instruments and bank collections, a person gives "value" for rights if he acquires them (a) in return for a binding commitment to extend credit or for the extension of immediately available credit, whether or not drawn upon and whether or not a chargeback is provided for in the event of difficulties in collection; or (b) as security for, or in, total or partial satisfaction of a preexisting claim; or (c) by accepting delivery pursuant to a preexisting contract for purchase; or (d) generally, in return for any consideration sufficient to support a simple contract.

Vendee A purchaser of property. Generally, the purchaser of real property. A *buyer* is usually a purchaser of chattels.

Vendor The seller of property, usually real property. The word *seller* is used with personal property.

Vendor's lien An unpaid seller's right to hold possession of property until he has recovered the purchase price.

Venire To come into court, a writ used to summon potential jurors.

Venue The geographical area over which a court presides. Venue designates the county in which the action is tried. Change of venue means to move to another county.

Verdict The decision of a jury, reported to the court, on matters properly submitted to the jury for consideration.

Vertical merger A merger of corporations, one corporation being the supplier of the other.

Void Has no legal effect. A contract that is void is a nullity and confers no rights or duties.

Voidable That which is valid until one party, who has the power of avoidance, exercises such power. An infant has the power of avoidance of his contract. A defrauded party has the power to avoid his contract. Such contract is voidable.

Voir dire Preliminary examination of a prospective juror.

Voting trust Two or more persons owning stock with voting powers divorce those voting rights from ownership but retain to all intents and purposes the ownership in themselves and transfer the voting rights to trustees in whom voting rights of all depositors in the trust are pooled.

Wager A relationship between persons by which they agree that a certain sum of money or thing owned by one of them will be paid or delivered to the other upon the happening of an uncertain event, which event is not within the control of the parties and rests upon chance.

Waive (verb) To "waive" at law is to relinquish or give up intentionally a known right or to do an act that is inconsistent with the claiming of a known right

Waiver (noun) The intentional relinquishment or giving up of a known right. It may be done by express words or conduct that involves any acts inconsistent with an intention to claim the right. Such conduct creates an estoppel on the part of the claimant. *See* Estoppel.

Warehouseman* A person engaged in the business of storing goods for hire.

Warehouse receipt* Issued by a person engaged in the business of storing goods for hire.

Warehouse receipt An instrument showing that the signer has in his possession certain described goods for storage. It obligates the signer, the warehouseman, to deliver the goods to a specified person or to his order or bearer upon the return of the instrument. Consult Uniform Warehouse Receipts Act.

Warrant (noun) An order in writing in the name of the state, signed by a magistrate, directed to an officer, commanding him to arrest a person; (verb) to guarantee, to answer for, to assure that a state of facts exists.

Warranty An undertaking, either expressed or implied, that a certain fact regarding the subject matter of a contract is presently true or will be true. The word has particular application in the law of sales of chattels. It relates to title and quality. *Warranty* should be distinguished from *guaranty,* which means a contract or promise by one person to answer for the performance of another.

Warranty of merchantability A promise implied in a sale of goods by merchants: that the goods are reasonably fit for the general purpose for which they are sold.

Waste Damage to the real property, so that its value as security is impaired.

Watered stock Corporate stock issued by a corporation for property at an overvaluation, or stock issued for which the corporation receives nothing in payment.

Will (testament) The formal instrument by which a person makes disposition of his property, to take effect upon his death.

Working capital The amount of cash necessary for the convenient and safe transaction of present business.

Workers' compensation A plan for compensating employees for occupational disease, accidental injury, and death suffered in connection with employment.

Writ An instrument in writing, under seal in the name of the state, issued out of a court of justice at the commencement of, or during, a legal proceeding; directed to an officer of the court, commanding him to do some act or requiring some person to do or refrain from doing some act pertinent or relative to the cause being tried.

Writ of certiorari A discretionary proceeding by which an appellate court may review the ruling of an inferior tribunal.

Writ of habeas corpus A court order to one holding custody of another, to produce that individual before the court for the purpose of determining whether such custody is proper.

Yellow-dog contract A worker agrees not to join a union and to be discharged if he breaches the contract.

Zoning ordinance Passed by a city council by virtue of police power. Regulates and prescribes the kind of buildings, residences, or businesses that shall be built and used in different parts of a city.

Index

Index

C

D

E

J

K

L

M

N

O

P

Q

R

S

T

U

V

W

Y

Z